New York City

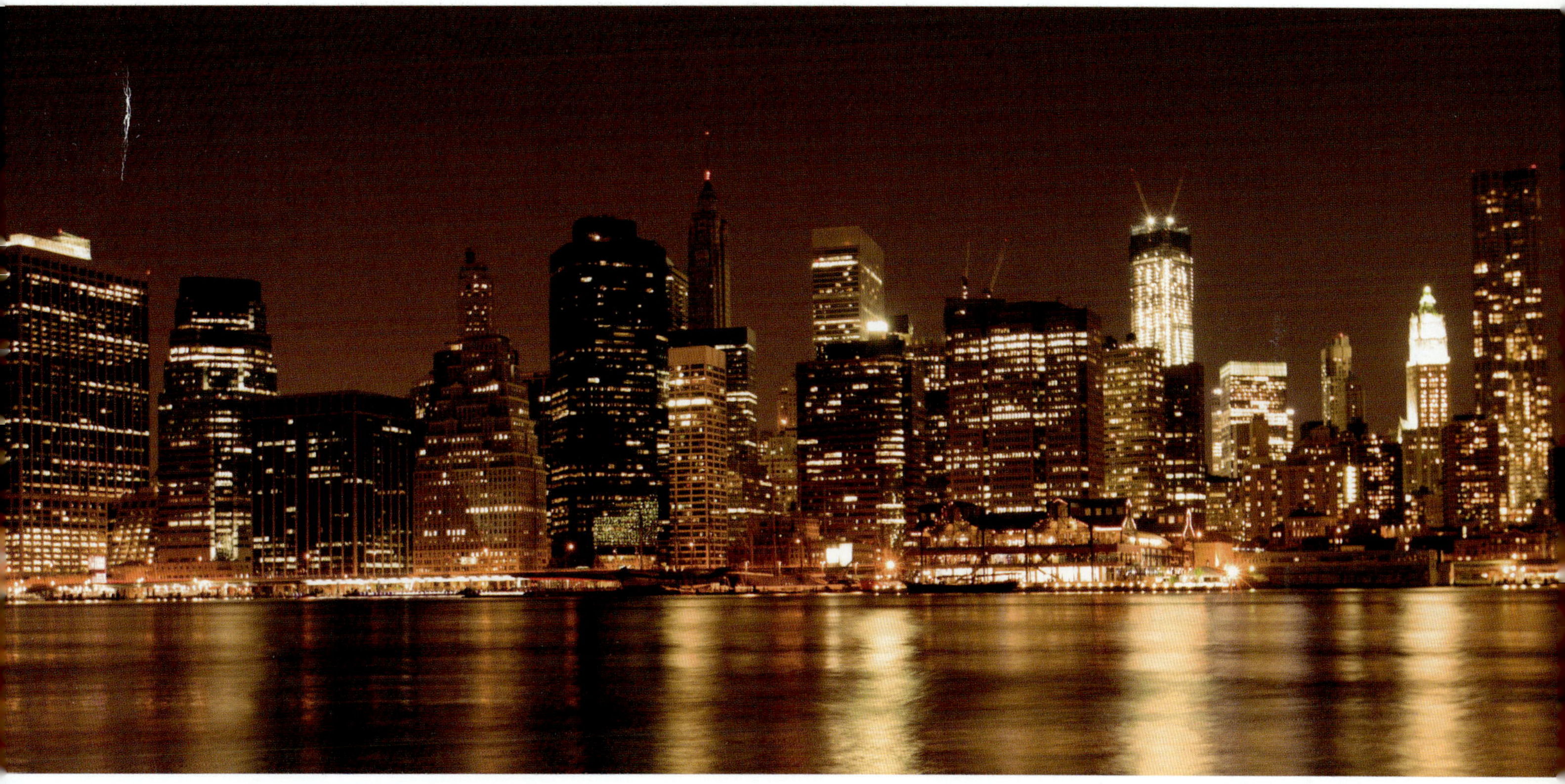

A PHOTOGRAPHIC PORTRAIT II

PHOTOGRAPHY BY STUART MONK
NARRATIVE BY BETHANY KANDEL

TWIN LIGHTS PUBLISHERS | ROCKPORT, MASSACHUSETTS

First published in the United States of America by:

Twin Lights Publishers, Inc.
51 Broadway
Rockport, Massachusetts 01966
Telephone: (978) 546-7398
http://www.twinlightspub.com

ISBN: 978-1-934907-21-4

10 9 8 7 6 5 4 3 2 1

(*opposite*)
Brooklyn Bridge

(*frontispiece*)
Lower Manhattan

(*jacket front*)
Statue of Liberty

(*jacket back*)
Unisphere

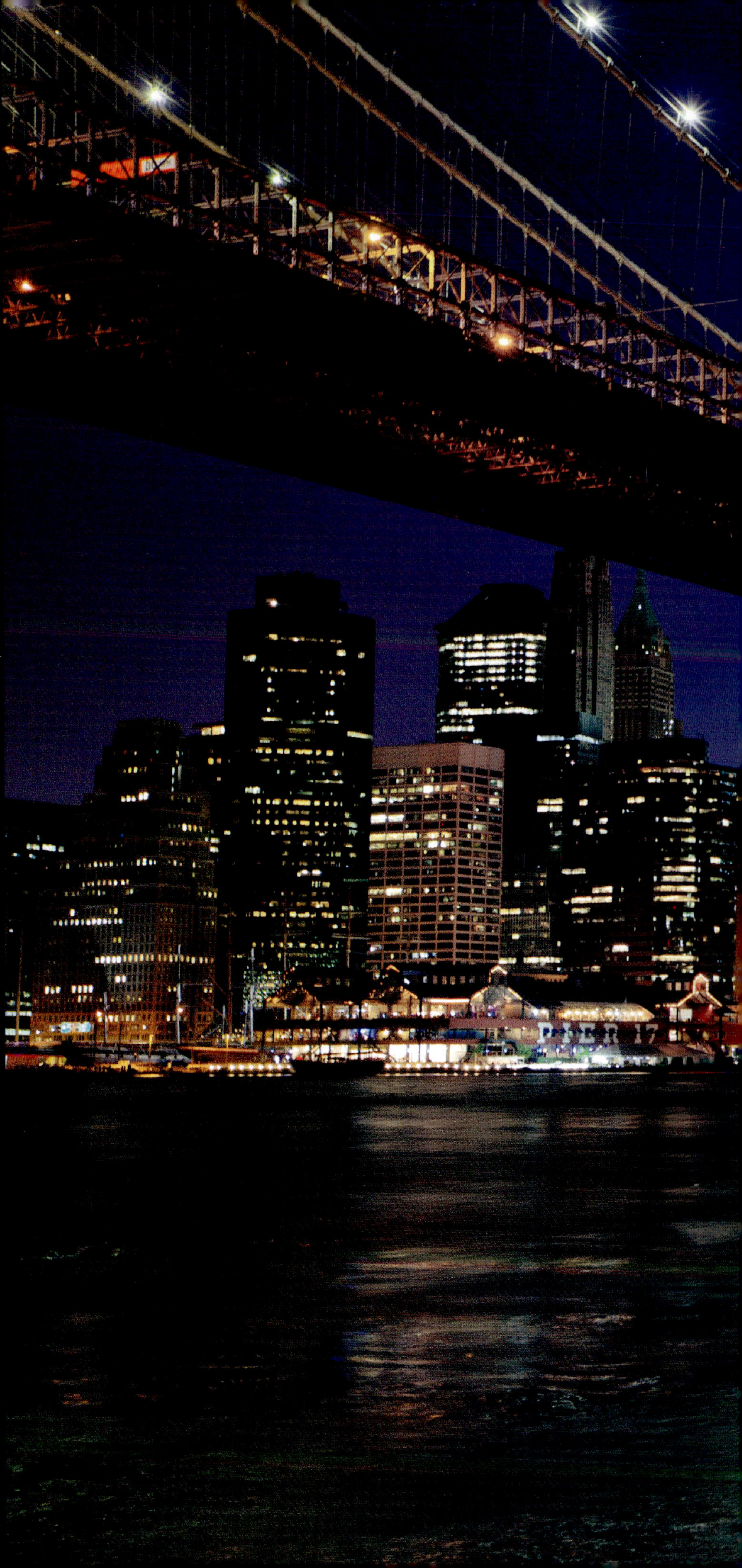

Book design by:
SYP Design & Production, Inc.
www.sypdesign.com

Printed in China

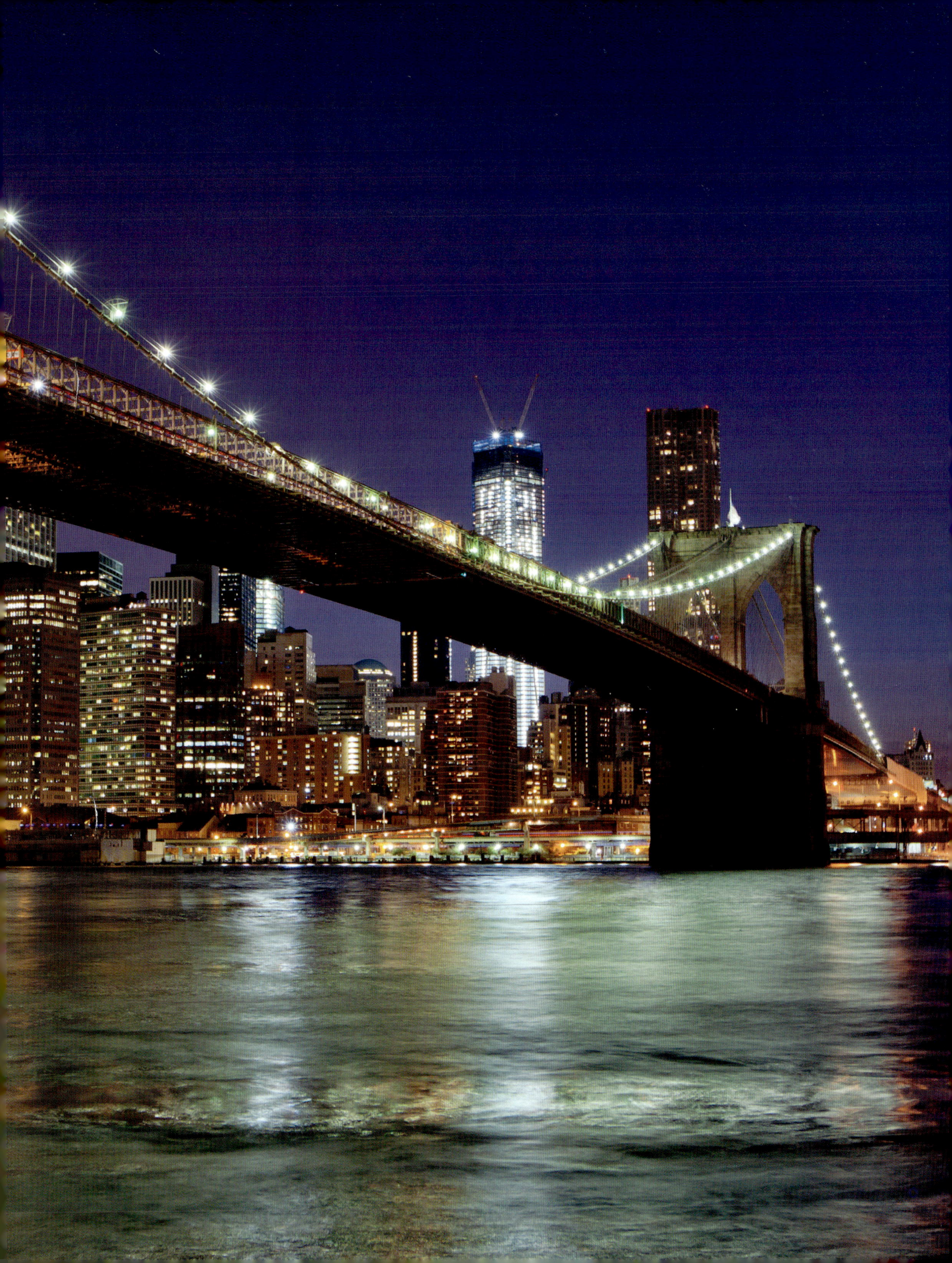

INTRODUCTION

"The City That Never Sleeps." "The Big Apple." New York has many nicknames to describe its excitement, vitality, style, and joie de vivre. It is a thriving metropolis with round-the-clock, non-stop action-packed adventure.

From its first sighting by Italian explorer Giovanni da Verrazano in 1524, all of Europe coveted the New York harbor. First settled by the Dutch, they soon lost it to the English, and eventually New York became the first capital of our new nation when George Washington was sworn in at Federal Hall on Wall Street as the country's first president in 1789.

Since then the city has become a major port, center of commerce, and a cultural, shopping, and entertainment mecca other cities try to emulate.

New York has it all, from giant statues, of Liberty no less, to enormous spans connecting the boroughs; amazing sports teams and history on every corner. Look up at the soaring skyscrapers and head down into the subways. There is much to do uptown in Central Park, downtown at the South Street Seaport, and all around the town. With more than 8 million residents from everywhere around the globe, there's an ethnic flair that makes the city a gigantic melting pot reflecting its immigrant story. Each of the five boroughs has its own distinctive flavor, while neighborhoods and even individual streets have personalities all their own. There's a reason our T-shirts proclaim: I Love New York!

The city is rich with culture, including Museum Mile with its world-class institutions like the Metropolitan Museum of Art and the Guggenheim, and hundreds of galleries scattered about Chelsea, SoHo, and the Lower East Side. There is classical music, opera, and jazz at Lincoln Center and Carnegie Hall, and the Great White Way highlights the best of Broadway theatre. New York is the home of Wall Street and more Fortune 500 companies than any other city around the globe. It is a city of big dreams.

New York's streets pulsate with a 24/7 energy that attracts more than 45 million visitors each year. Whether it is your first visit or your hundredth, there is too much to do in a day, a week, or even a month, so you have to keep coming back. Or take a tour through our pages to get a taste of all that is here. Photographer Stuart Monk brings the bright lights and vibrancy of the big city to life with his evocative photography, creating a visual love letter to the greatest city in the world. After all, if you can make it here, you can make it anywhere!

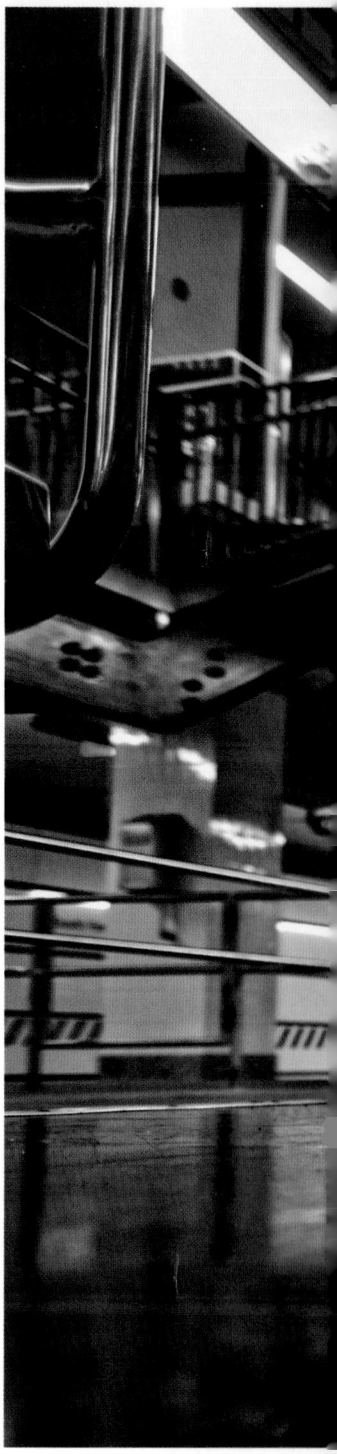

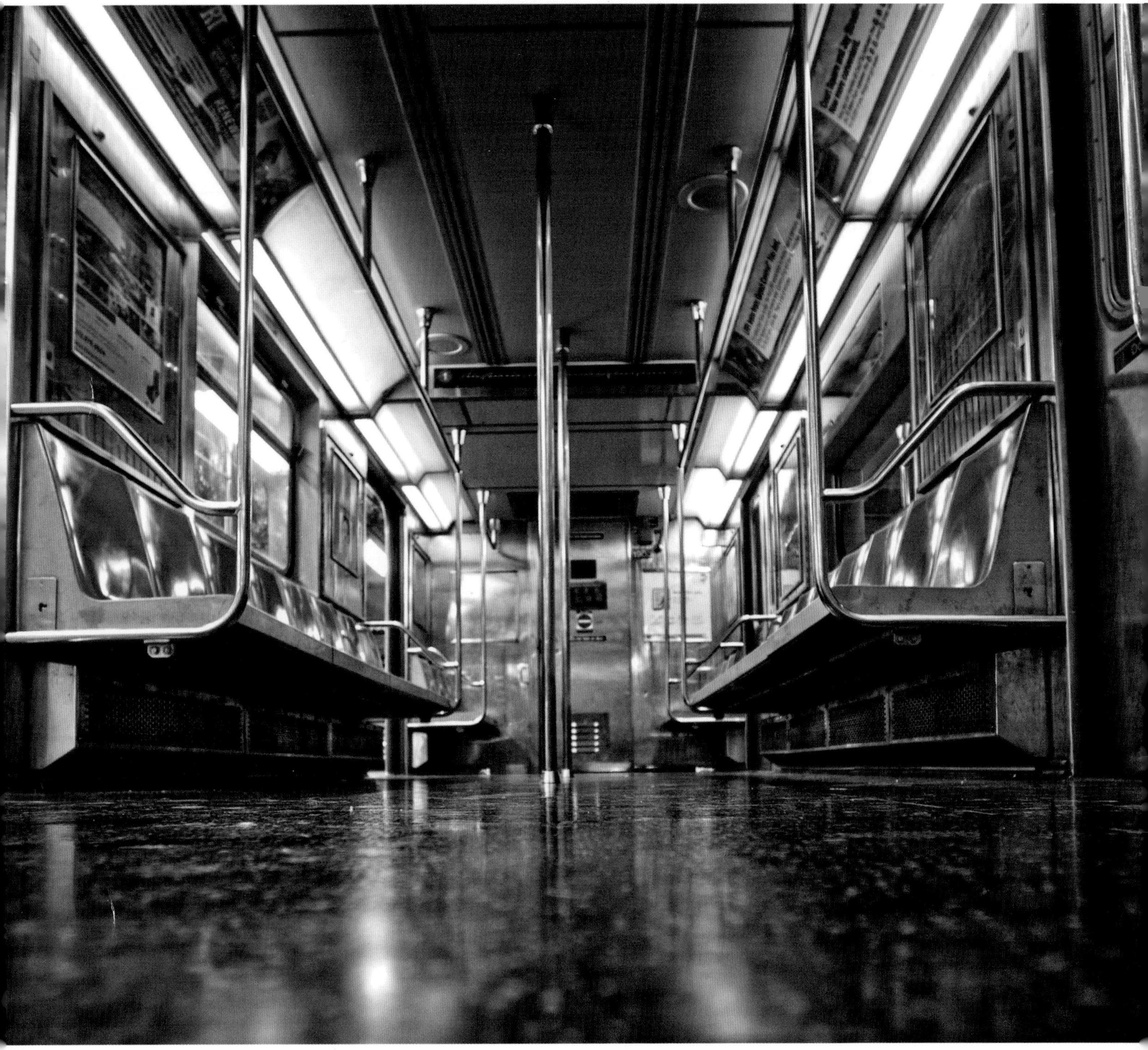

New York City Subways

First opened in 1904, the subways are still the fastest way to get around town. With more than 840 miles of track, not only can you travel from borough to borough on a single fare, you can also enjoy underground musicians, sponsored by "Music Under New York."

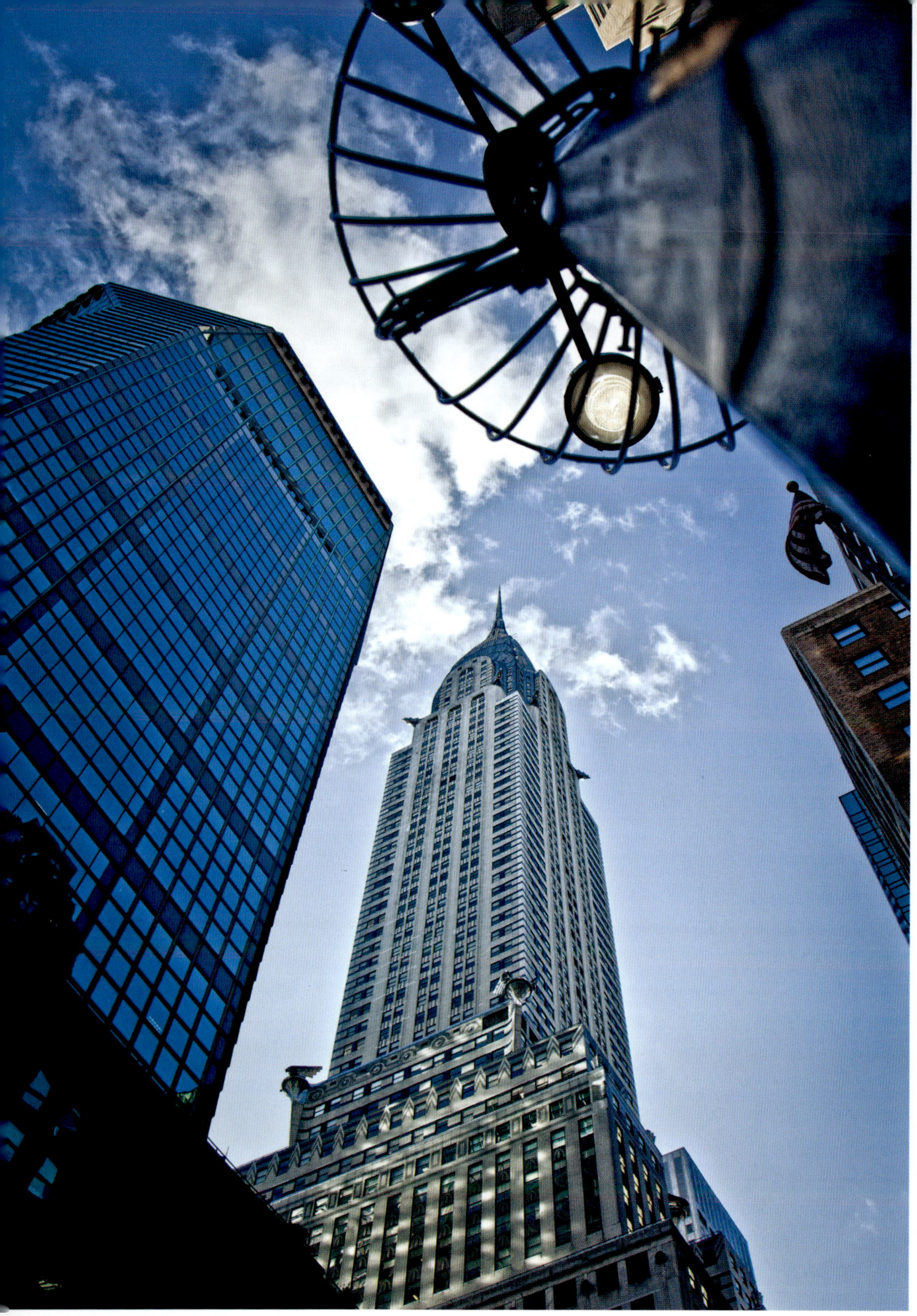

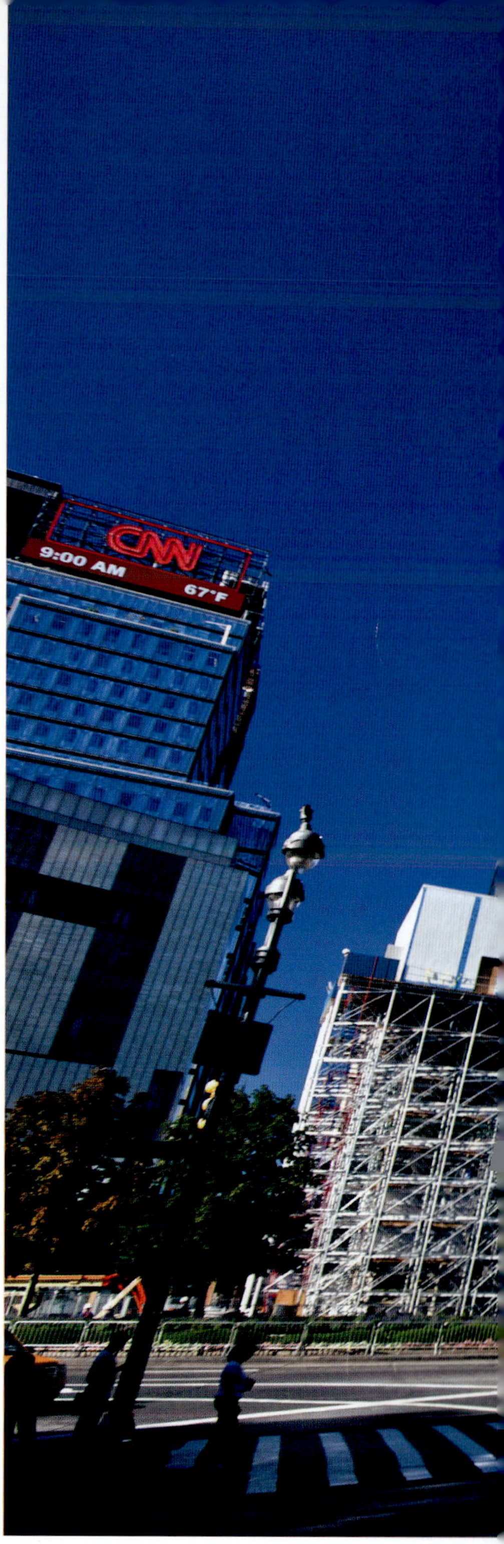

Chrysler Building

Upon completion in 1930, this iconic skyscraper on East 42nd Street was the tallest building in the world until it was surpassed 11 months later by the Empire State Building. Today, its Art Deco details, marbled lobby, and illuminated helmet-like crown make it one of the city's jewels.

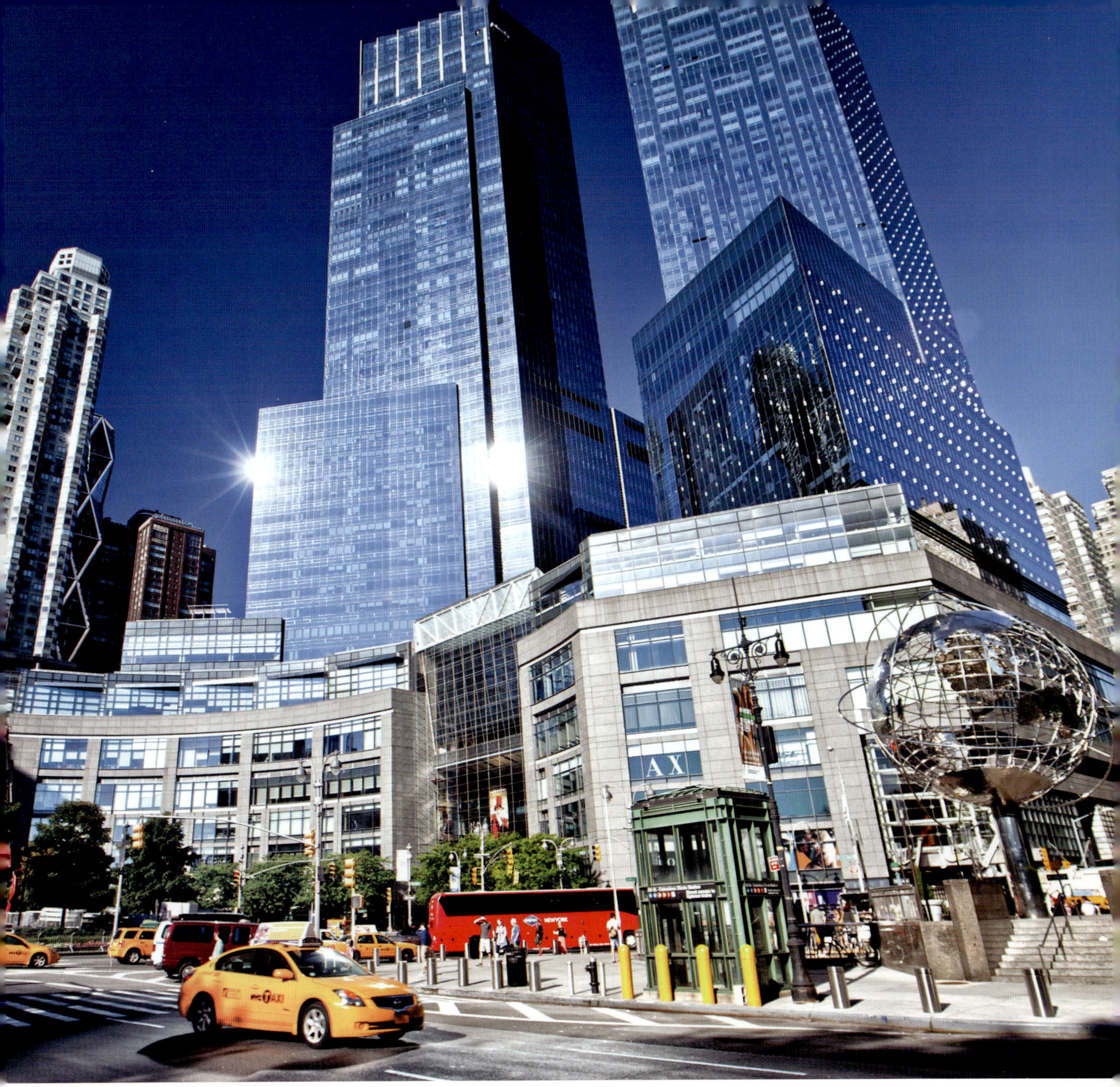

Time Warner Center

The intersection of 59th Street, Broadway, Eighth Avenue, and Central Park South is anchored by this upscale indoor shopping mall with high-end shops, restaurants, condominiums, and a luxury hotel. Based here are Jazz at Lincoln Center and the CNN studios. Across the street is the Trump Hotel with its steel globe.

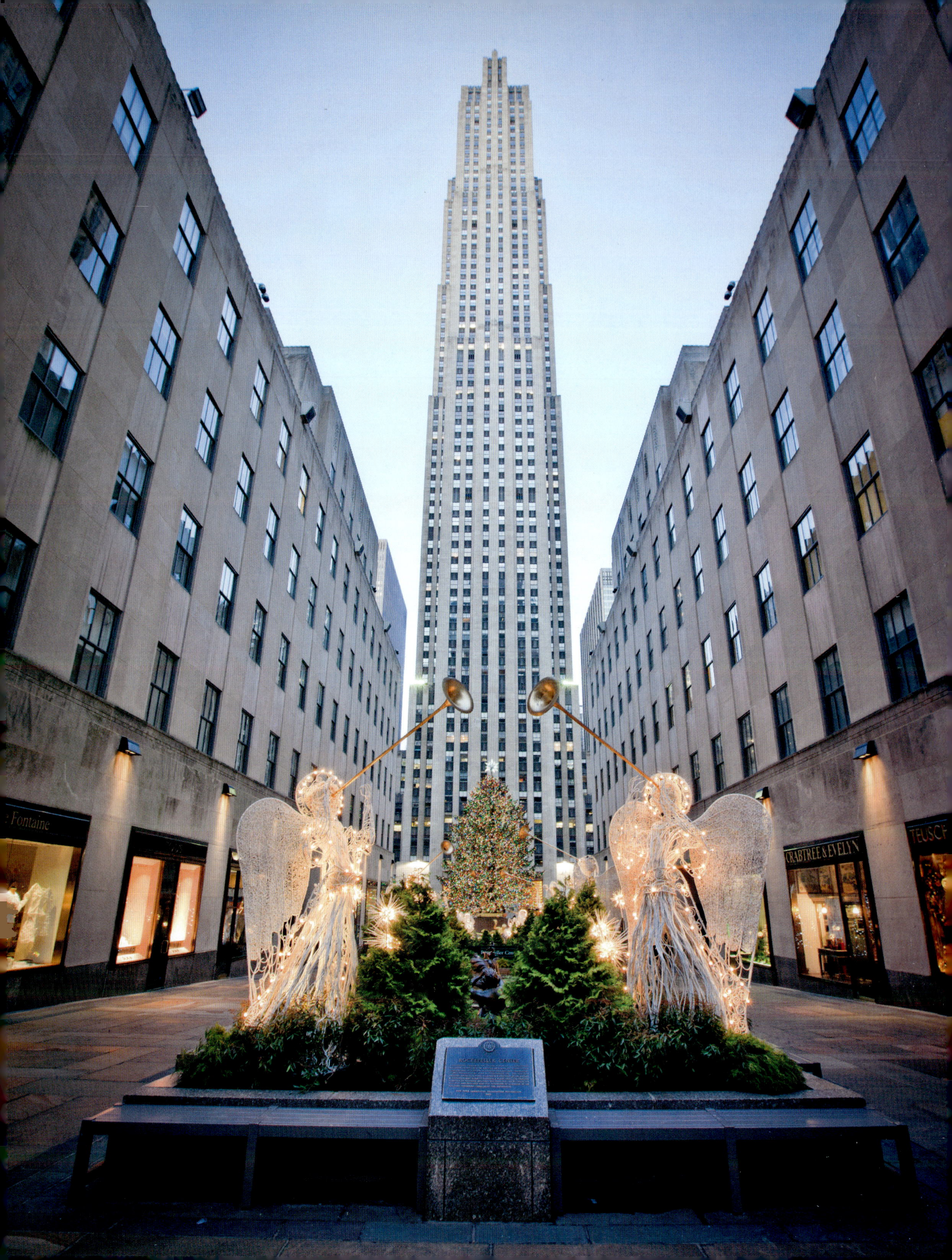
CRABTREE & EVELYN

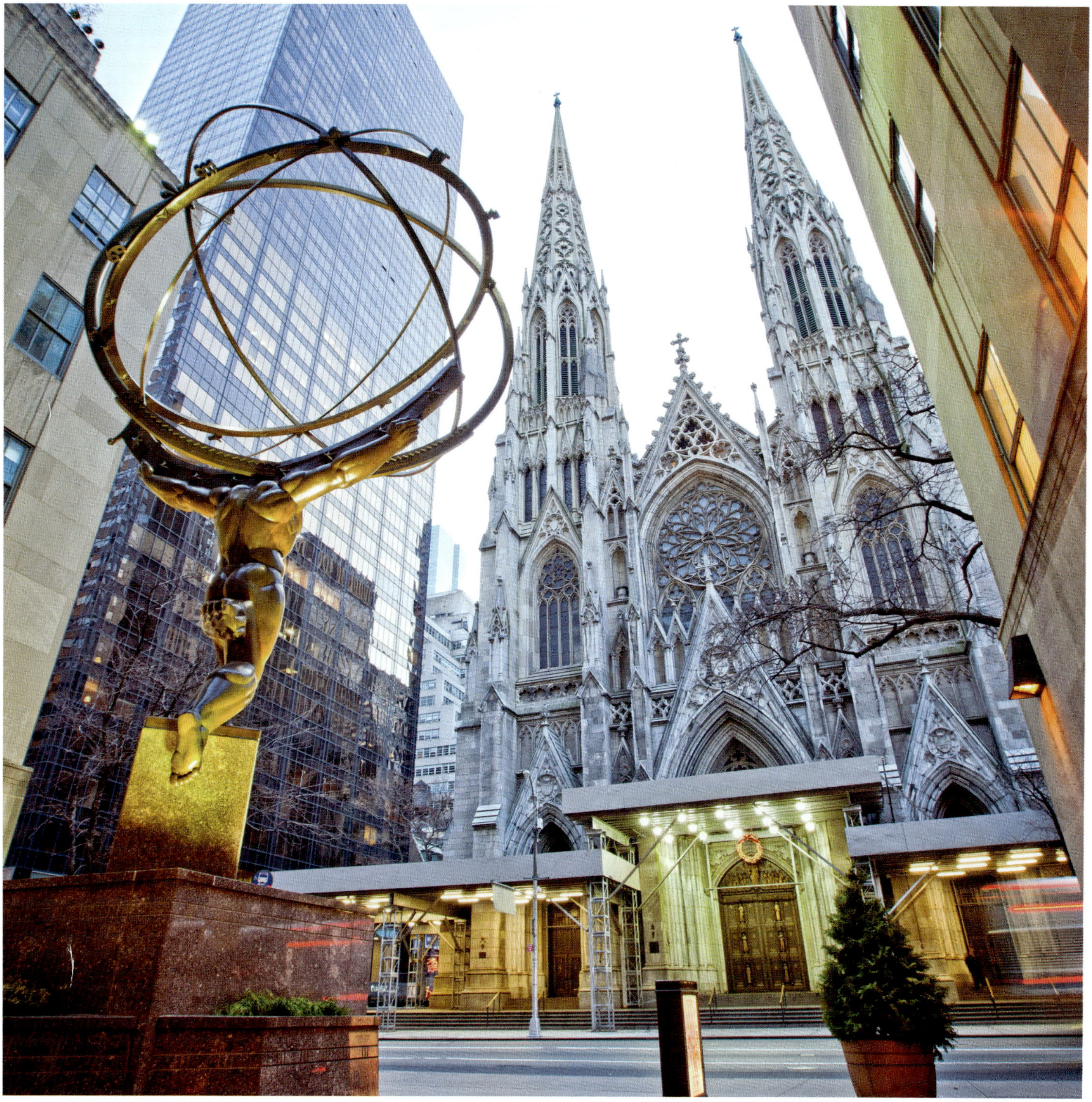

Rockefeller Center *(opposite)*

This multi-block complex of Art Deco office buildings and shops centers on the General Electric Building, commonly known as "30 Rock," headquarters of NBC studios. Visitors head to the plaza early mornings to become part of the *Today Show* audience and during the holidays for the annual Christmas tree lighting.

Atlas Statue *(above)*

Atlas carries the weight of the heavens on his bronze shoulders at the entrance to Rockefeller Center's International Building across from St. Patrick's Cathedral, the largest Catholic cathedral in the United States. The marble and stone sanctuary provides an escape from Midtown for quiet contemplation or a mid-day mass.

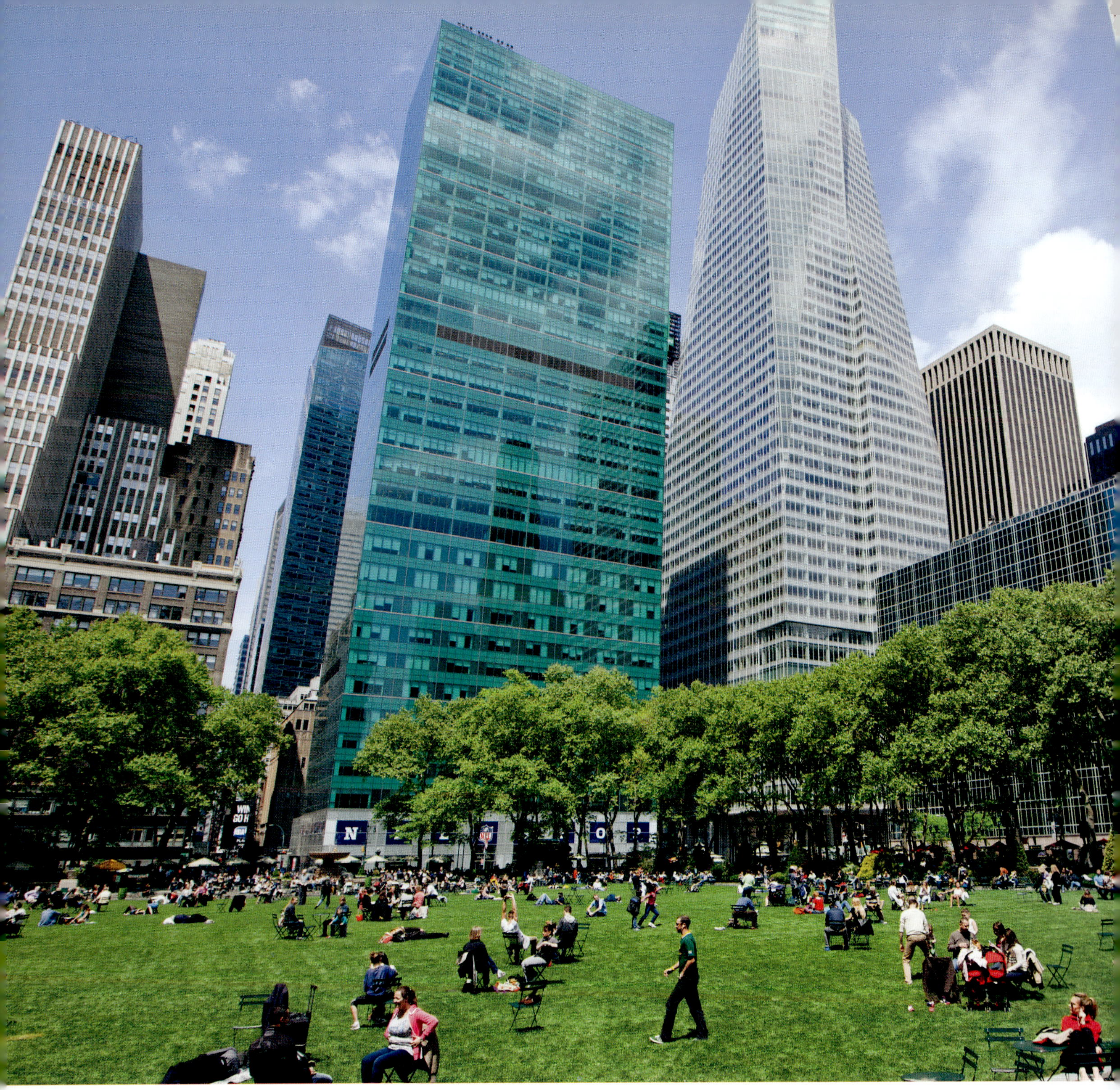

Bryant Park

The 9.6 -acre lawn behind the main public library is perfect for picnicking, and the site of outdoor movies, concerts, craft fairs, a carousel, and ice-skating rink. This "Town Square of Midtown" fills with office workers and visitors during the day and has become a popular entertainment venue.

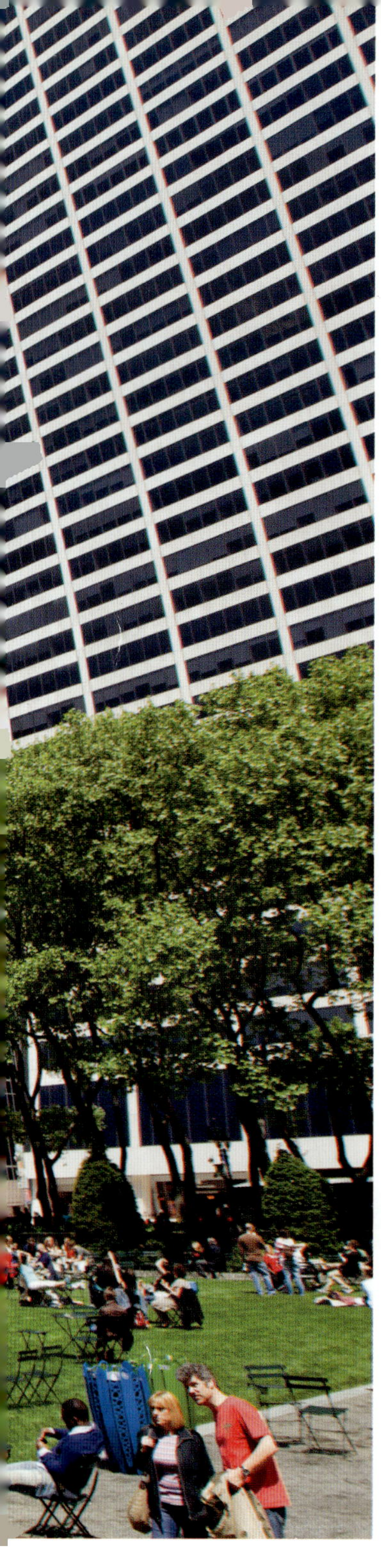

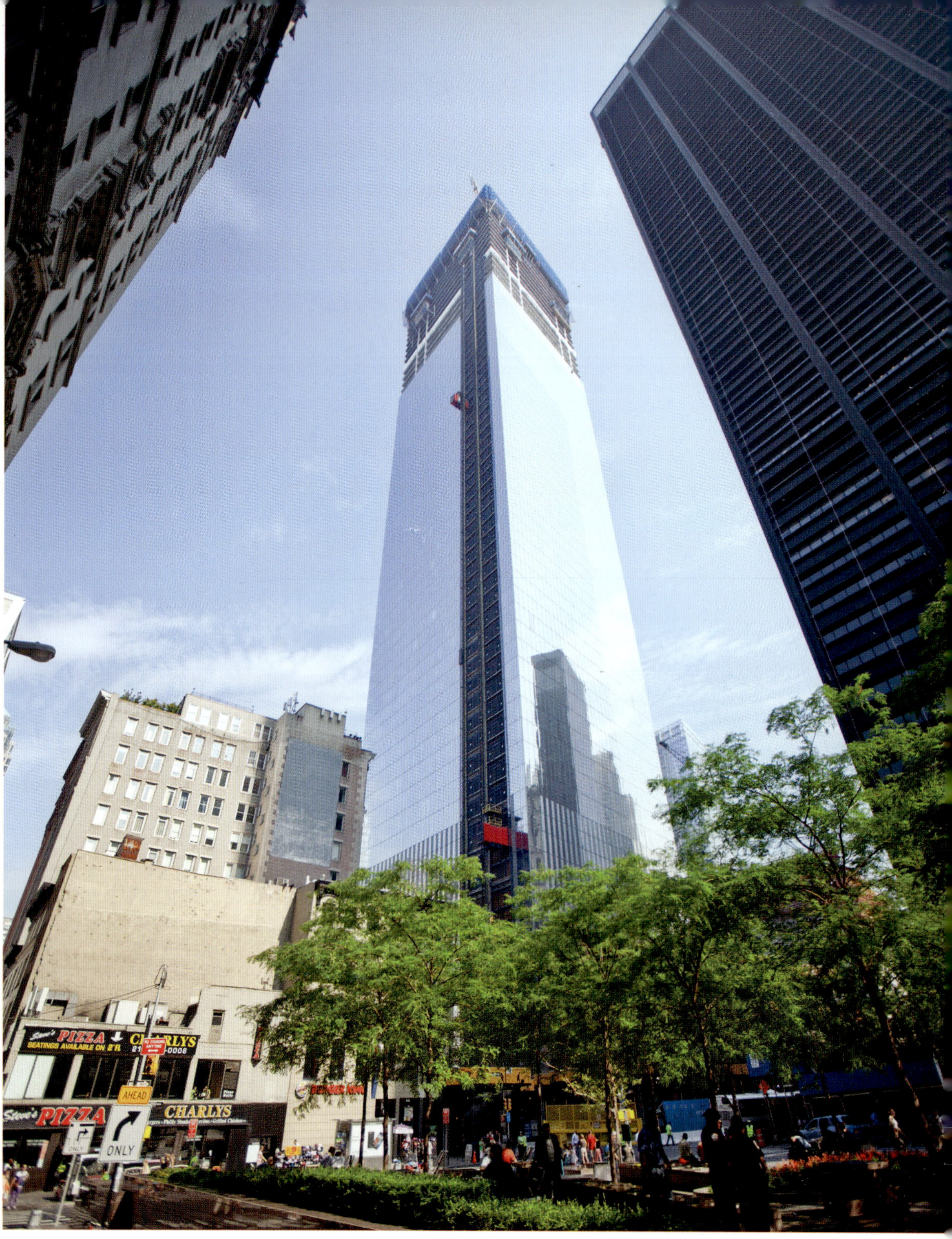

Freedom Tower

More than a decade after the destruction of the Twin Towers on September 11, 2001, One World Trade Center, also known as the Freedom Tower, rises proudly as a symbol that New York stands strong and resilient to terrorism. At 104 floors, it will be the third tallest building in the world.

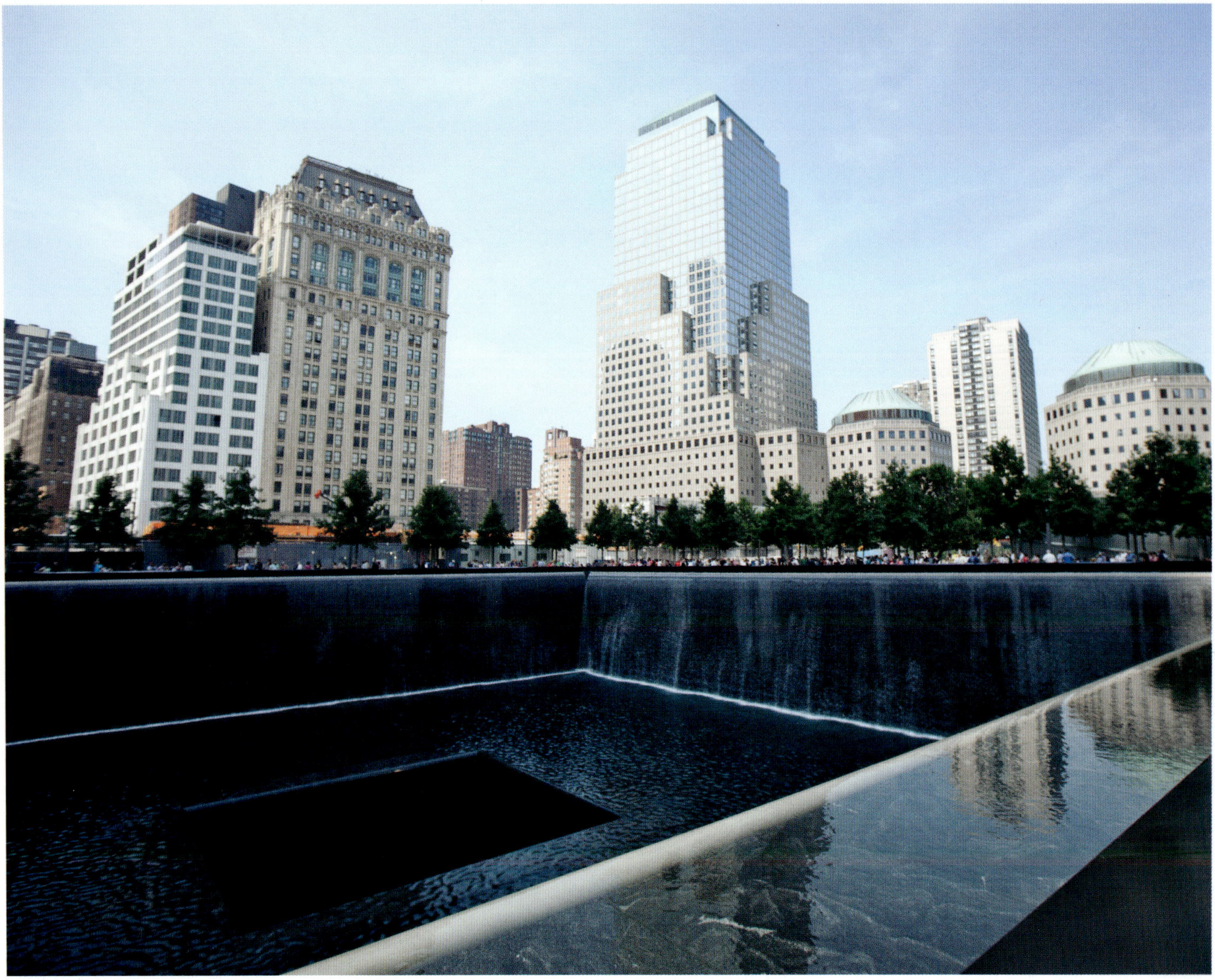

National September 11 Memorial

(above and opposite)

The National September 11 Memorial, located at the site of the former World Trade Center, is a national tribute of remembrance and honor to the men, women, and children killed in the terror attacks. Visitors can wander through a forest of trees and watch water cascading into two square reflecting pools set within the footprints of the original Twin Towers. The name of every person who died in the terrorist attacks of both 1993 and 2001 are inscribed on bronze panels edging the memorial pools, serving as a tribute to the past and a place of hope for the future.

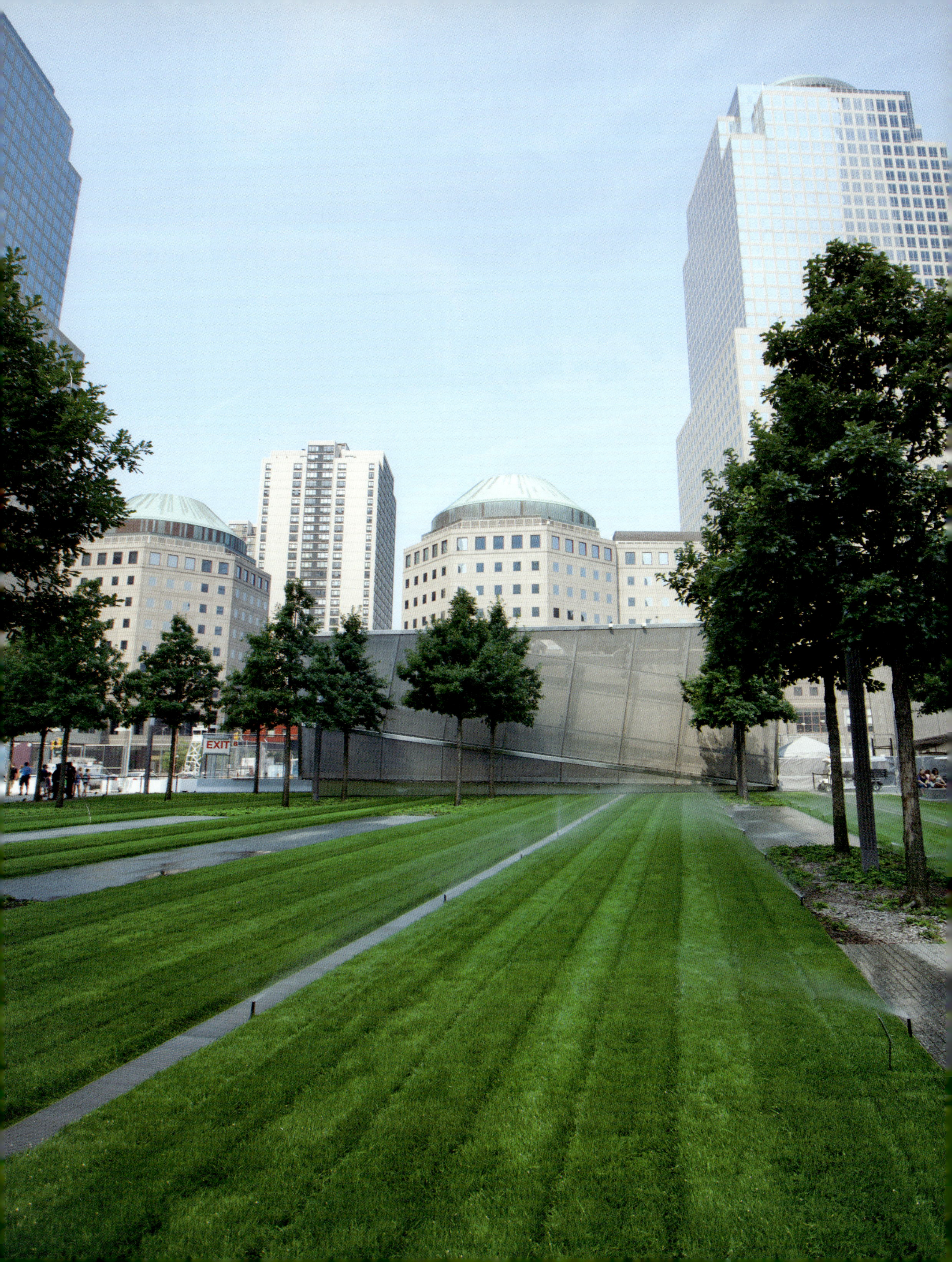
EXIT

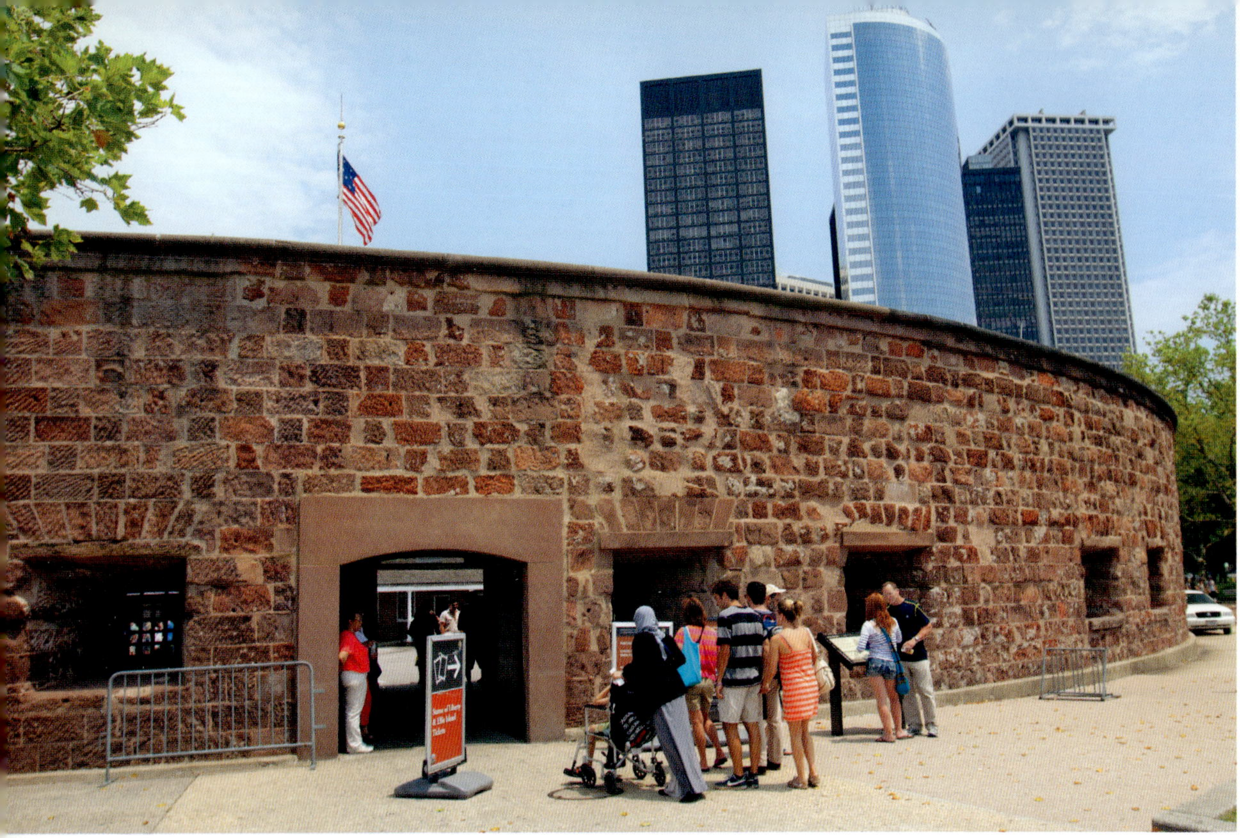

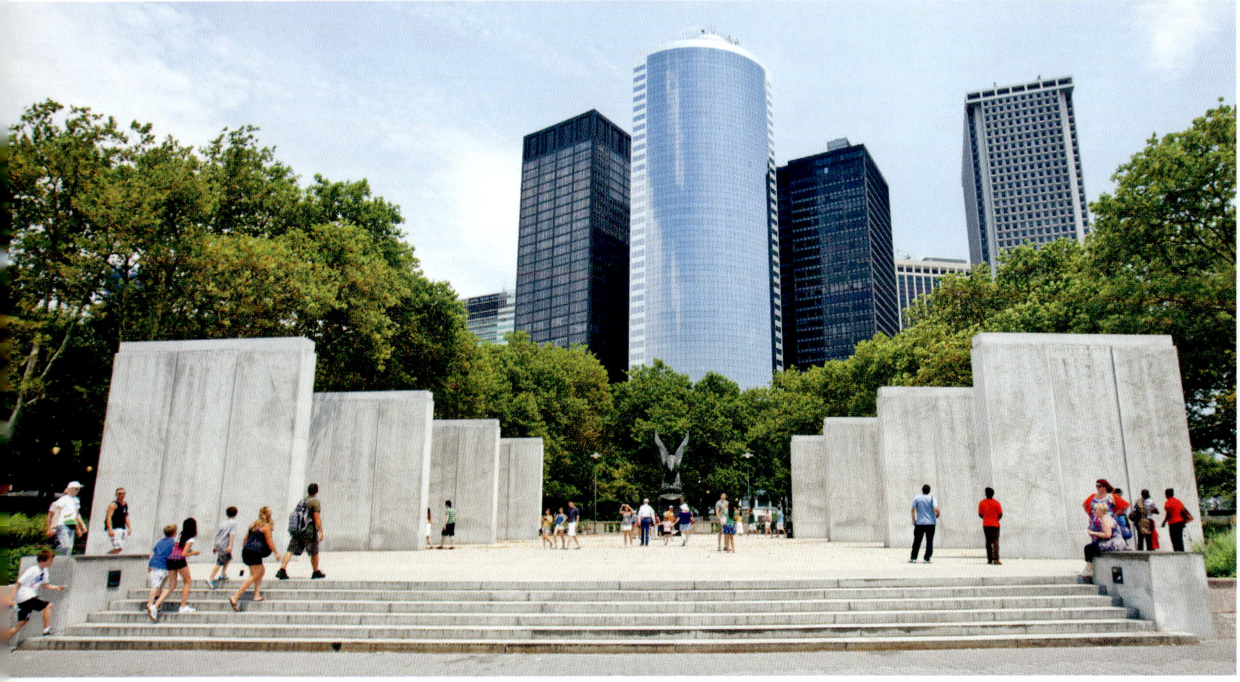

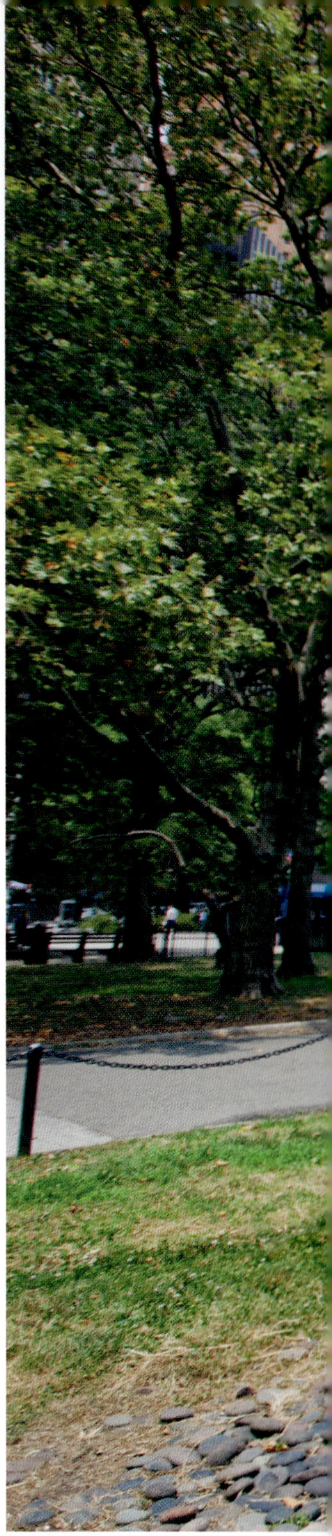

Castle Clinton *(top)*

Built to defend New York Harbor before the War of 1812, this circular fort was a strategic military presence at the southern tip of Manhattan. It has since been an aquarium, performance center, and immigration station. Today, it houses museum exhibits and ticket sales for Statue of Liberty-Ellis Island ferries.

WWII Memorial Battery Park *(bottom)*

Facing the Statue of Liberty are eight 19-foot-tall pylons inscribed with the names of 4,600 American service men and women who lost their lives or went missing during World War II. At the center is a bronze eagle sitting on a wave, holding a wreath, as a symbol of mourning at sea.

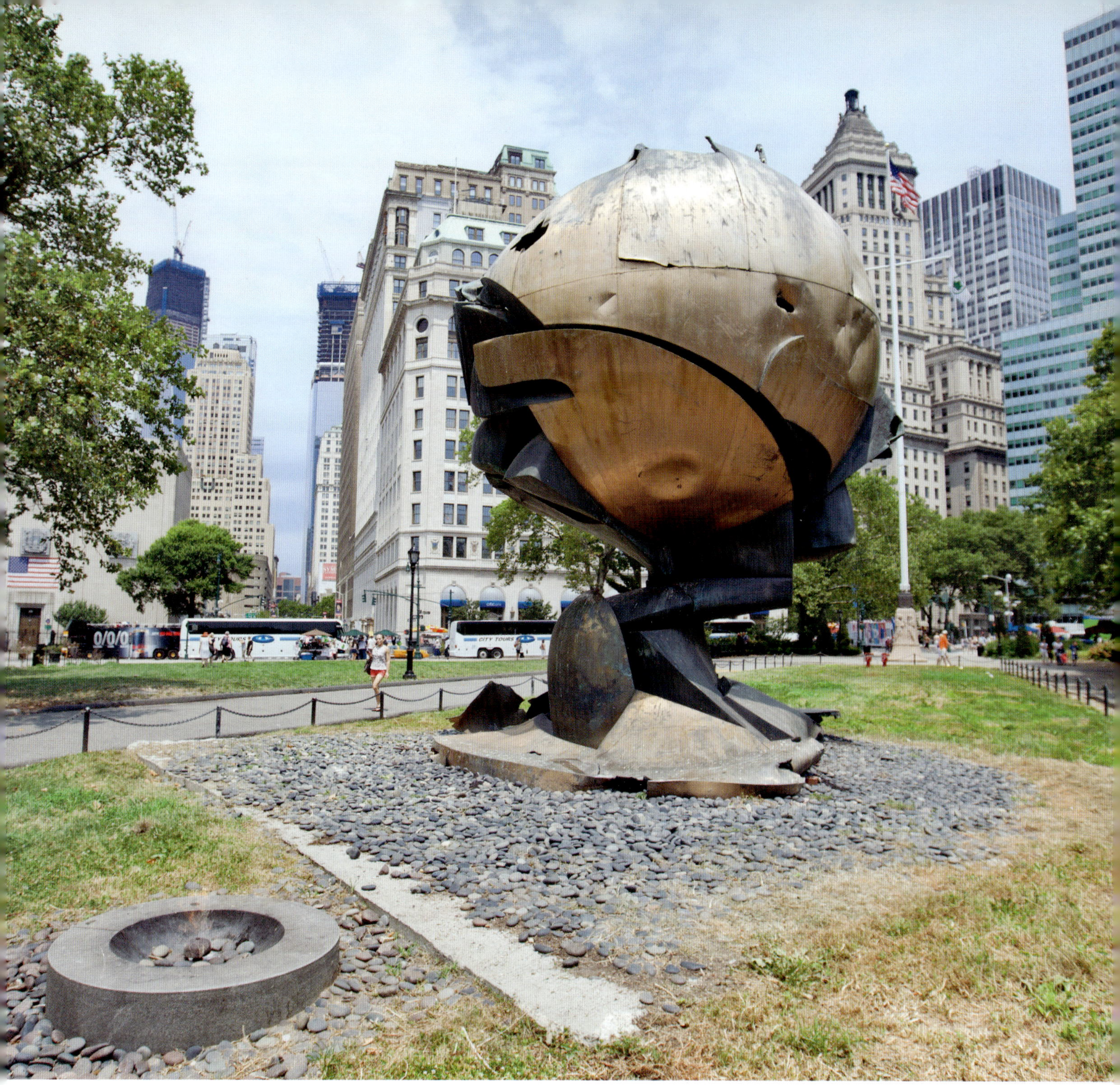

The Sphere

Conceived as a symbol of world peace, this 25-foot-tall bronze statue once stood on the plaza between the two World Trade Center towers. Recovered in the rubble after the 9/11 attacks, it's now located in Battery Park with an eternal flame as a memorial to honor the September 11th victims.

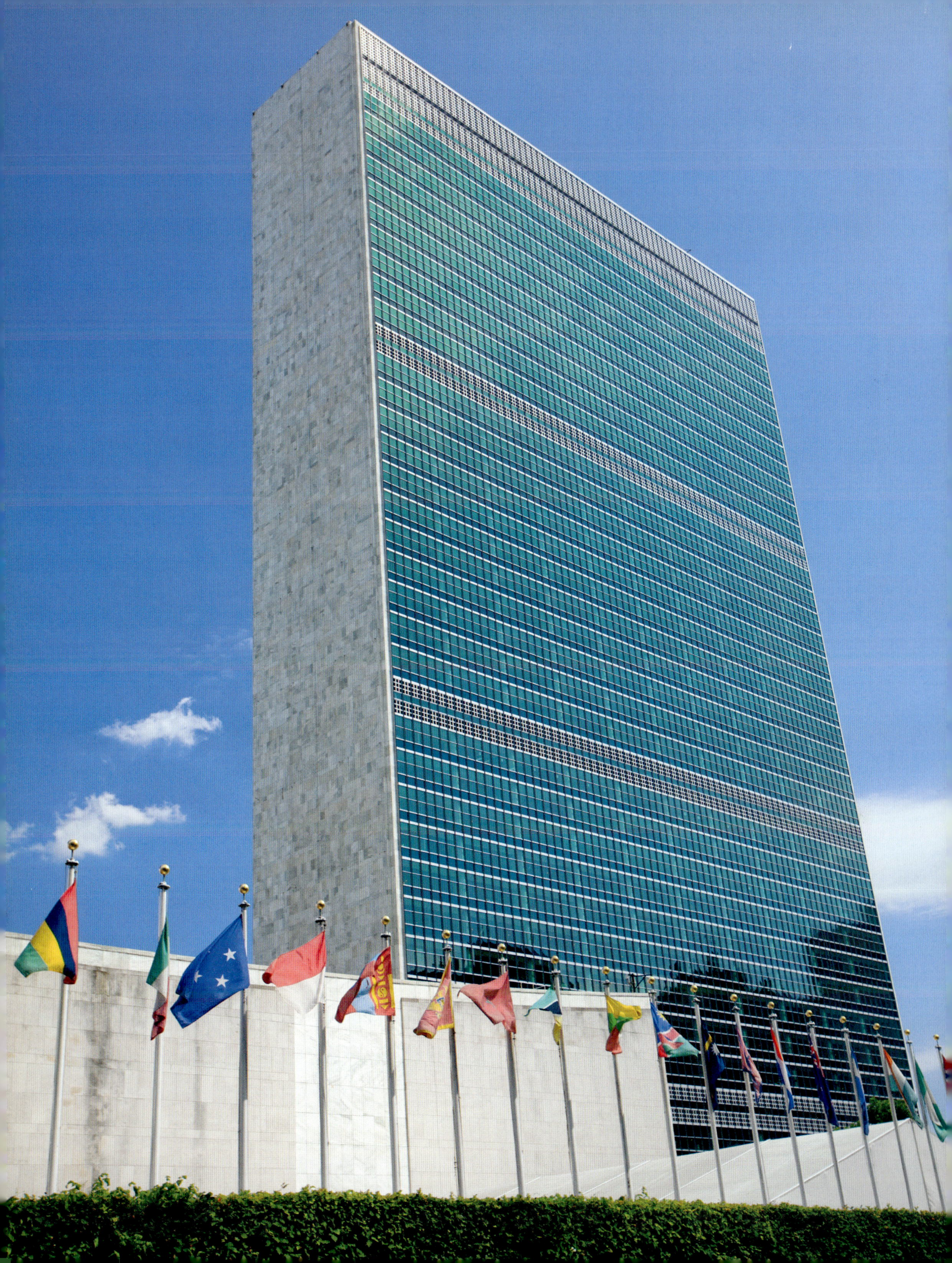

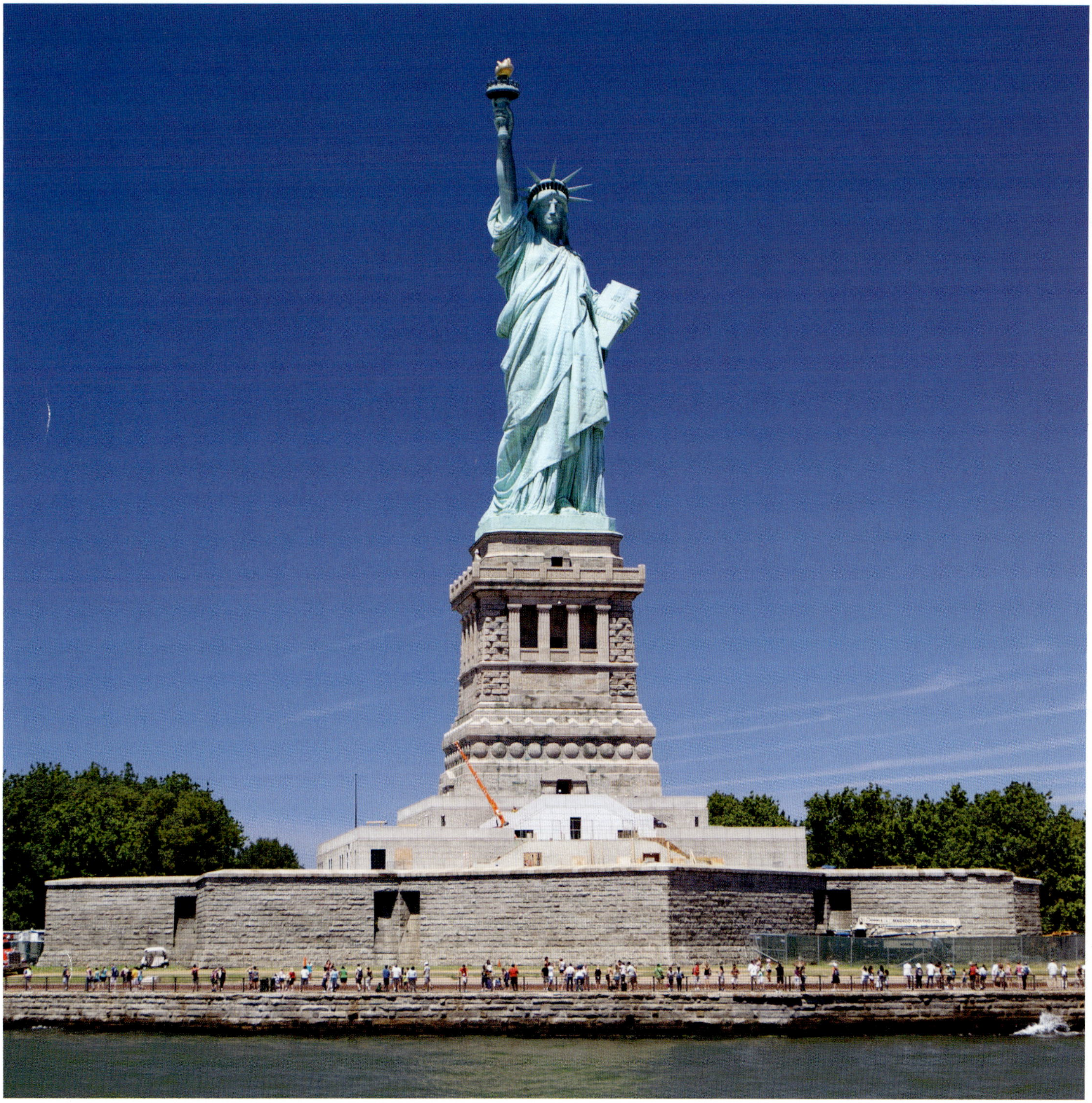

United Nations *(opposite)*

Founded in 1945, the UN is an international organization whose aim is to promote global peace, security, and economic development. Outside the multi-building headquarters fly flags of all 193 member nations in alphabetical order. Daily tours show visitors the various council chambers and General Assembly hall.

Statue of Liberty *(above)*

Designed by artist Frederic-Auguste Bartholdi, the Statue of Liberty, officially known as *Liberty Enlightening the World*, has been welcoming visitors to New York since it was given by France as a gift of friendship in 1886. It has become an international icon of freedom and liberty and recognized worldwide as a symbol of democracy.

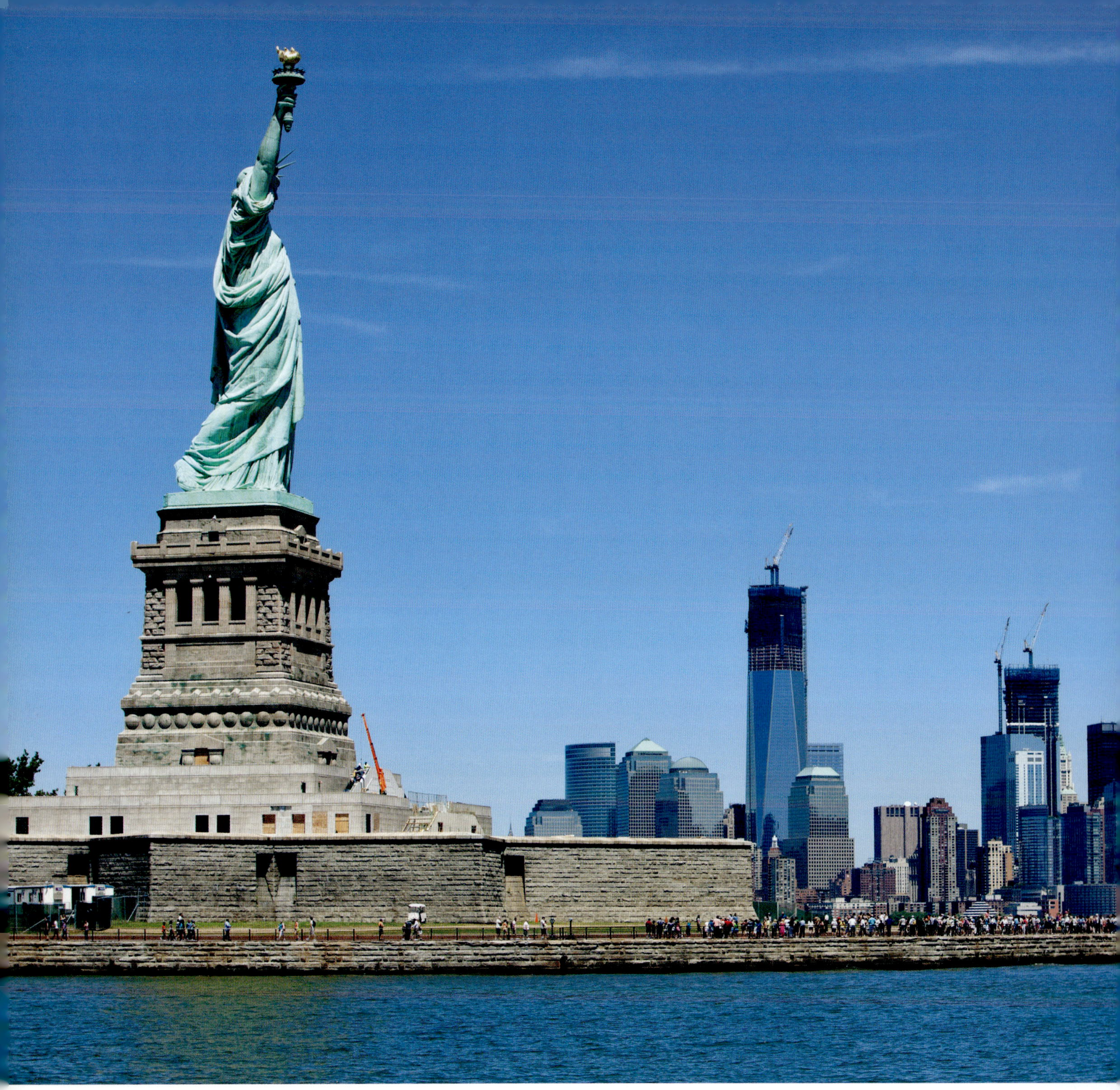

Statue of Liberty Museum

Beginning with the arrival of the Dutch to New York's shores, the Statue of Liberty Museum chronicles the history of immigration to the New World. It includes artifacts from the statue itself, including the original torch which was recreated and restored for the centennial on July 4, 1986.

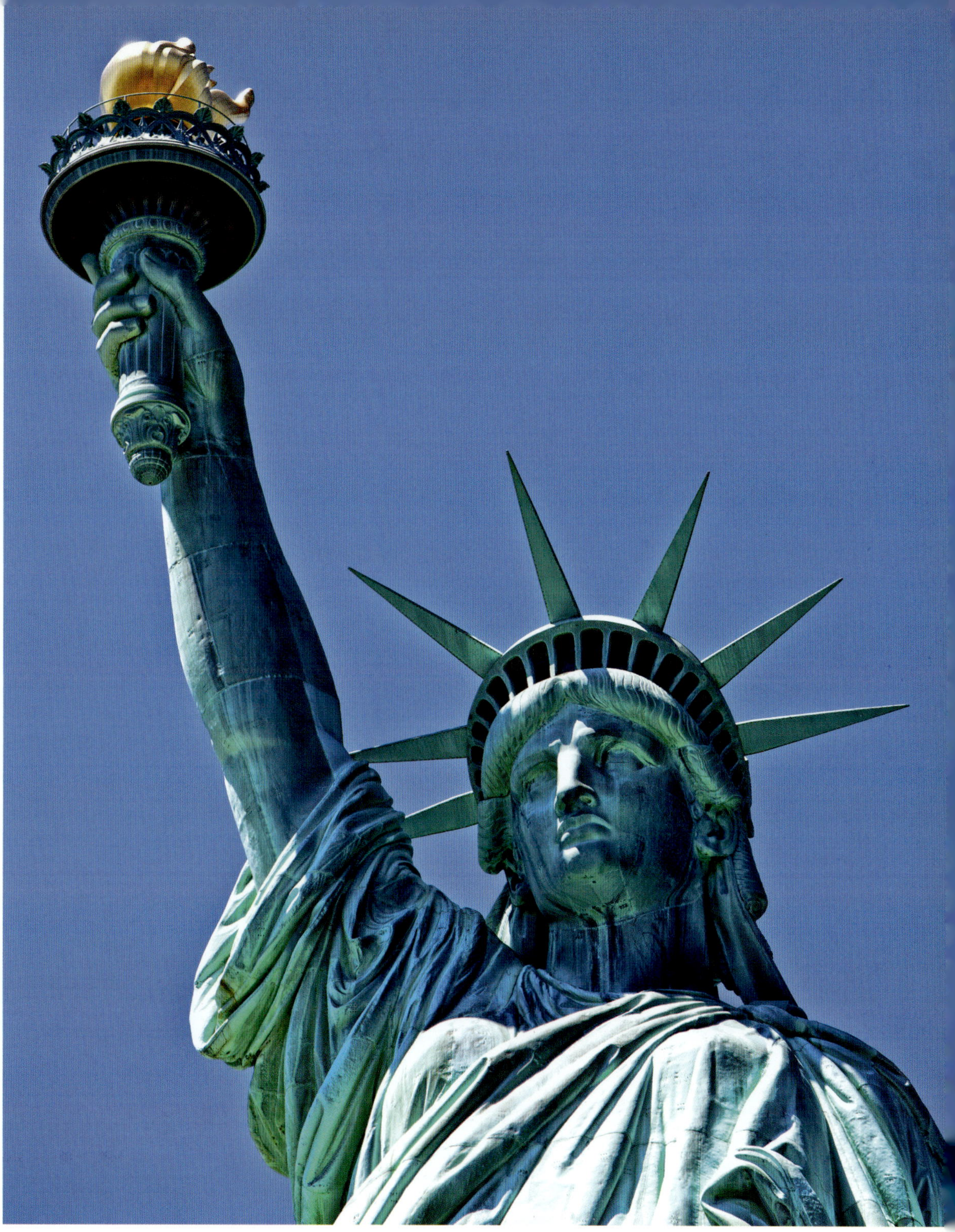

Up Close

Visitors to Liberty Island can take an elevator to the top of the pedestal beneath Lady Liberty's enormous feet for an up-close view. Those with reserved tickets can climb the 393 spiral stairs, or the equivalent of 22 floors, to her crown for panoramic views of the city and harbor.

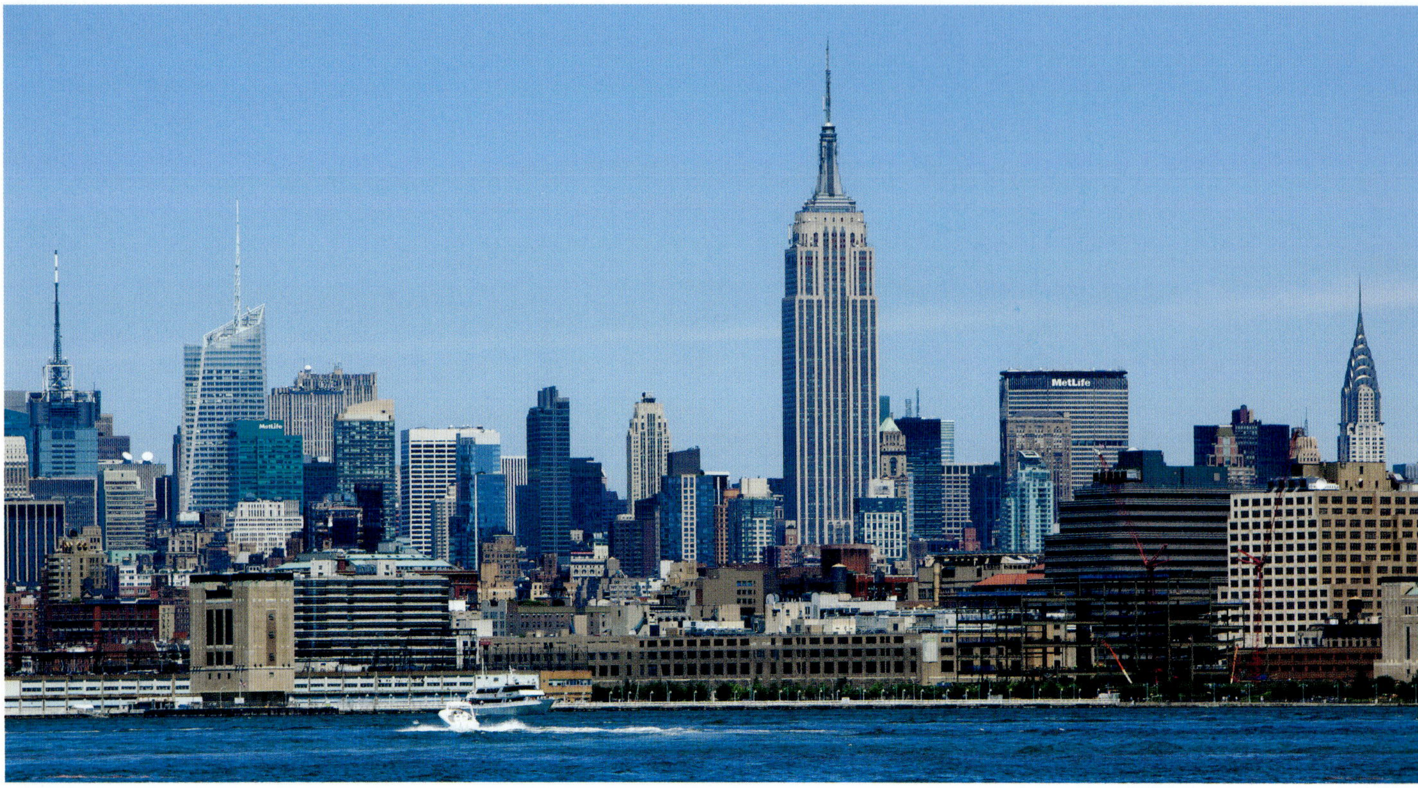

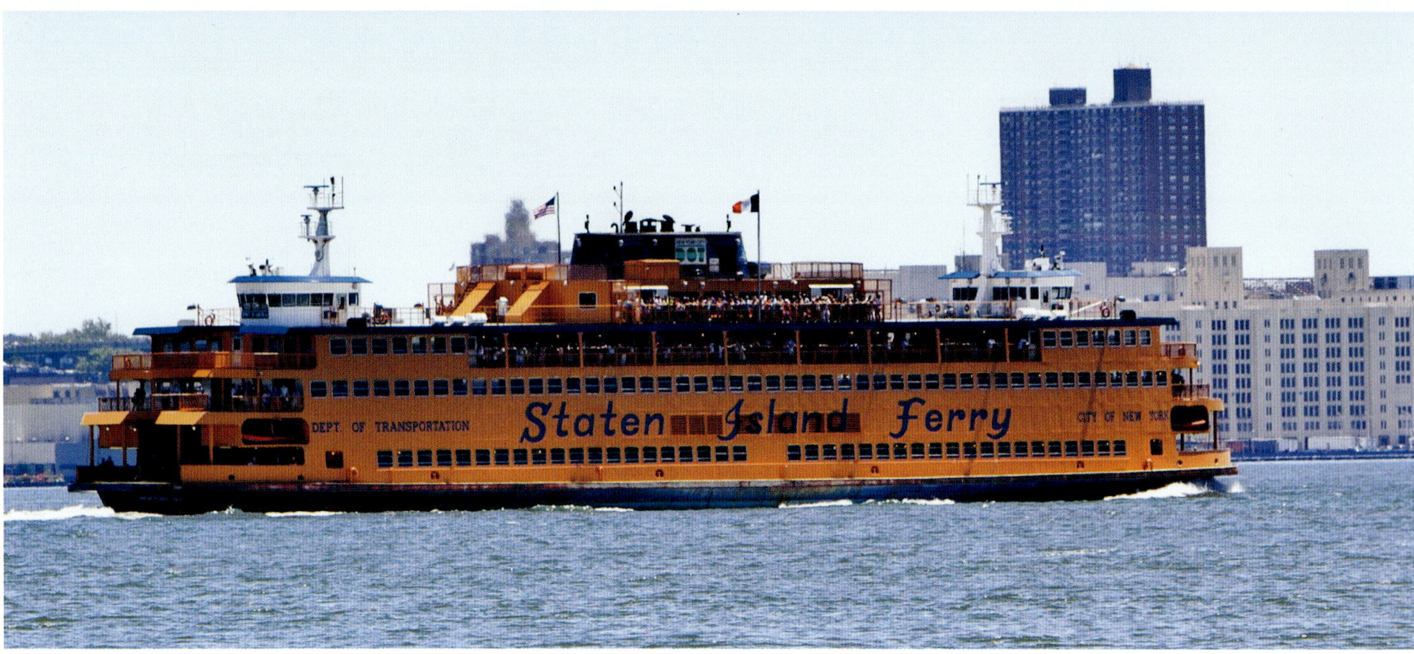

Midtown Manhattan *(top)*

The heart of Manhattan lies in Midtown, which runs from about 34th to 59th streets and encompasses some of the city's most famous skyscrapers, including the Empire State and Chrysler buildings, and some of the world's most exclusive stores, including Bergdorf Goodman, Saks Fifth Avenue, and Tiffany & Co.

Staten Island Ferry *(bottom)*

A free ride on the Staten Island Ferry offers sweeping vistas of New York Harbor, the downtown skyline, and the Statue of Liberty. The ferry operates 24/7 to transport Staten Island residents back and forth to Manhattan and typically carries 60,000 passengers a day.

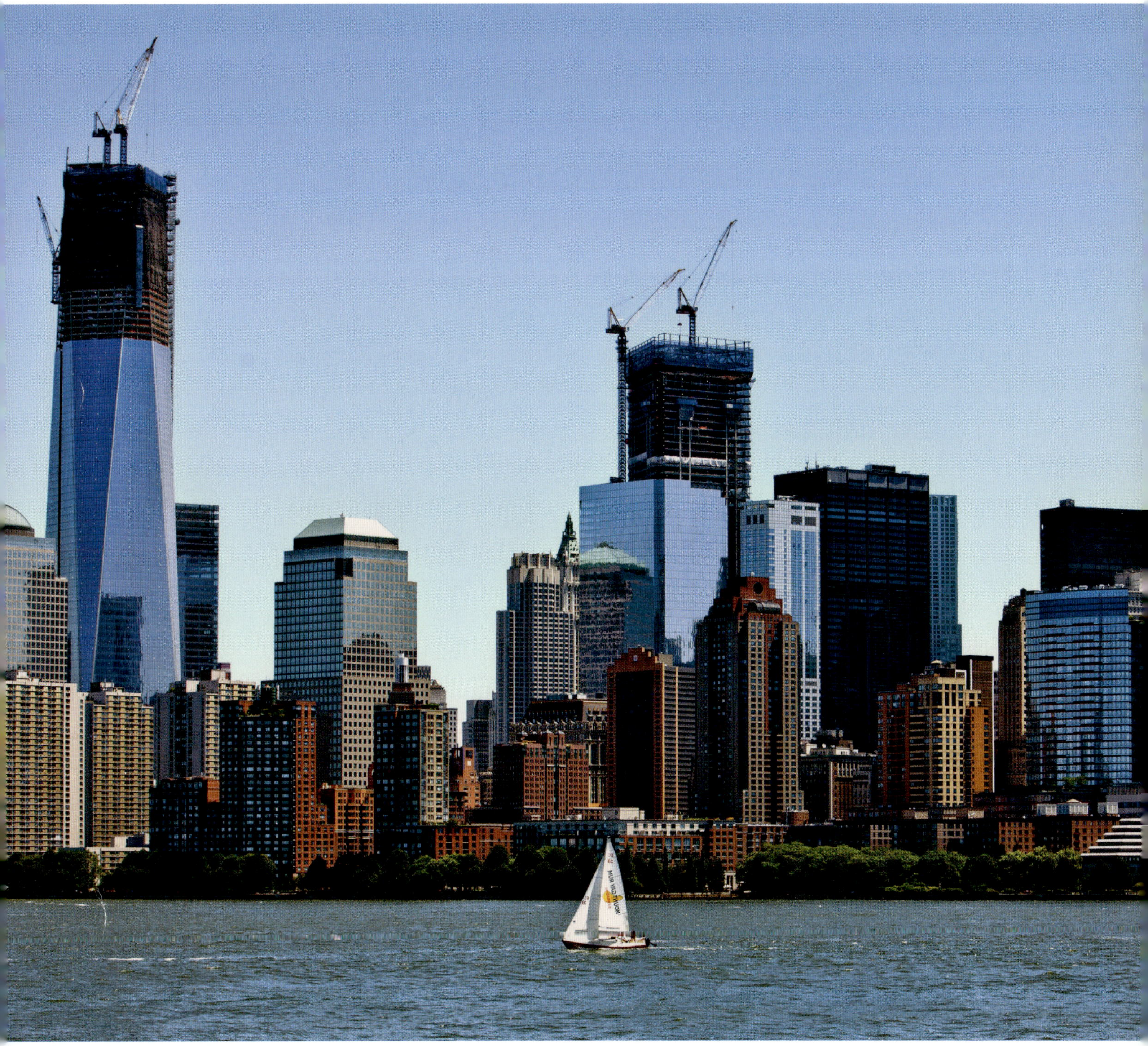

Lower Manhattan

On a crystal clear day the tip of Manhattan gleams as a shiny steel and glass skyline. But look closely and you'll catch glimpses into New York's past as the ornate spires of some of the city's first office buildings still stand proudly amidst their boxy modern neighbors.

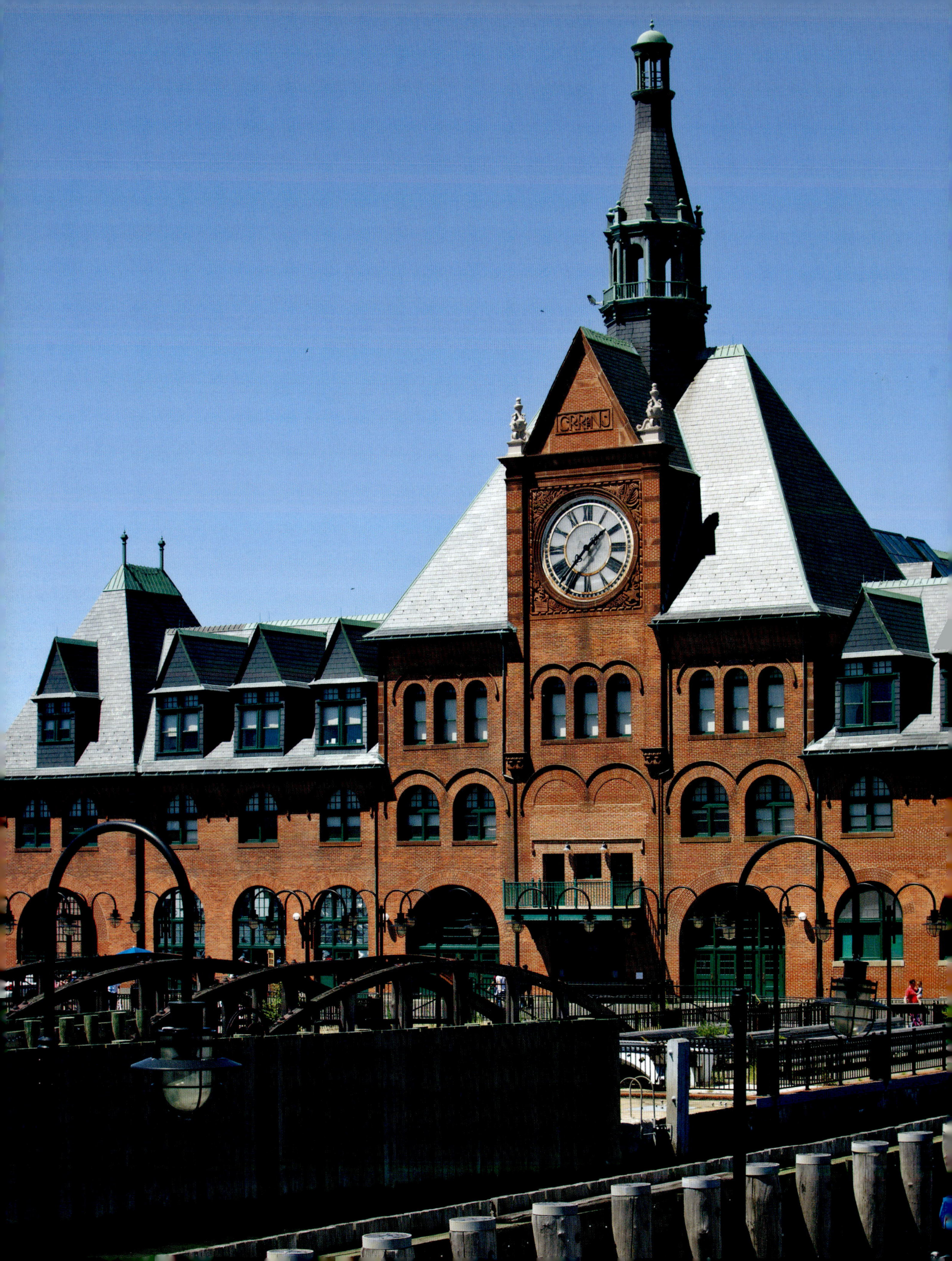

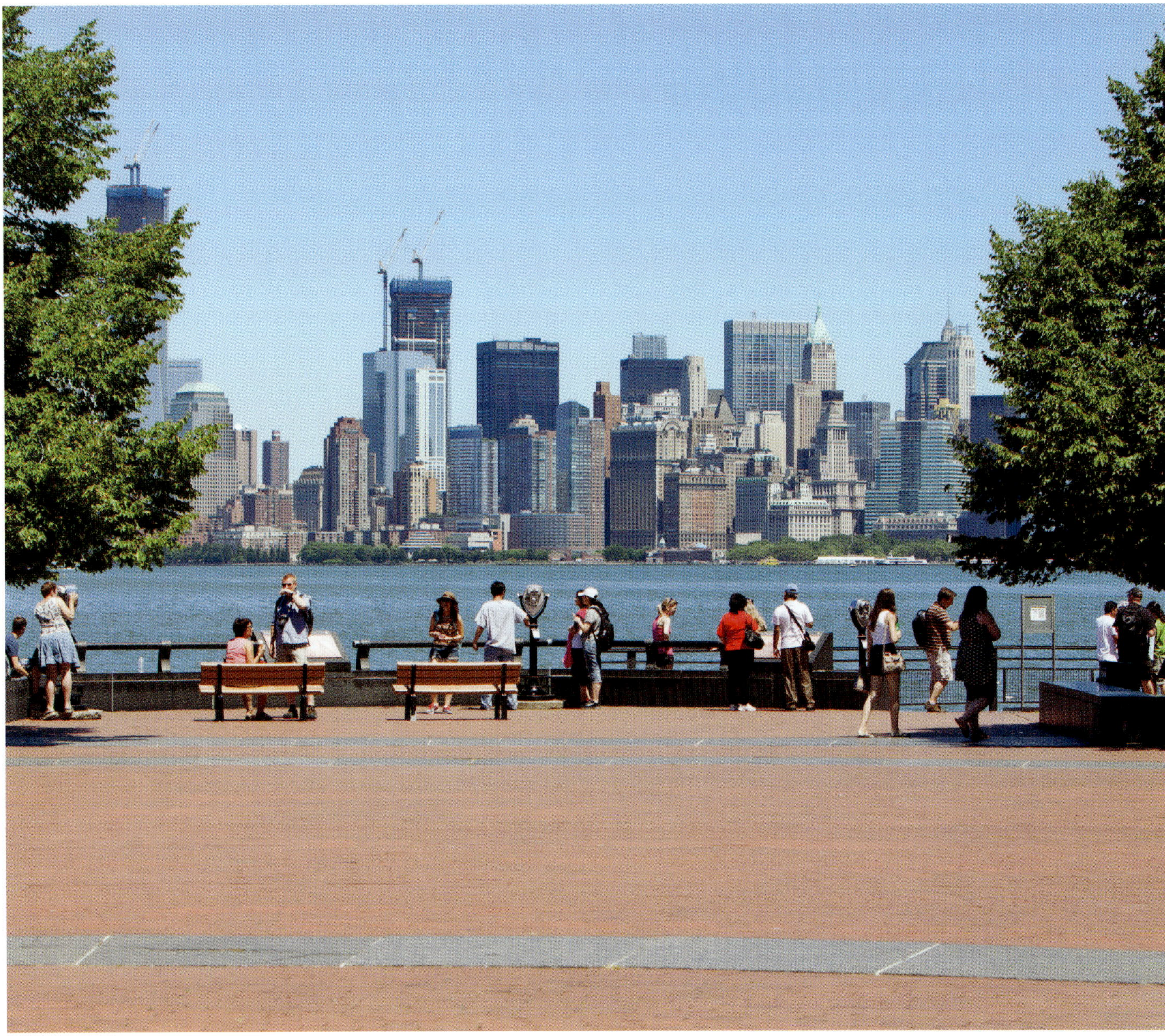

Liberty Island State Park *(opposite)*

Liberty State Park in New Jersey was once a major waterfront industrial area on New York Harbor, with an extensive freight and passenger transportation network. Many immigrants who arrived at Ellis Island started their new lives in this country via the Central Railroad Terminal here.

View from Liberty Island *(above)*

Visitors to Liberty Island are treated to great views of downtown Manhattan and the skyline at the tip of the island. Although the iconic Twin Towers are sorely missing, the new, shiny Freedom Tower rises as an anchor to the city.

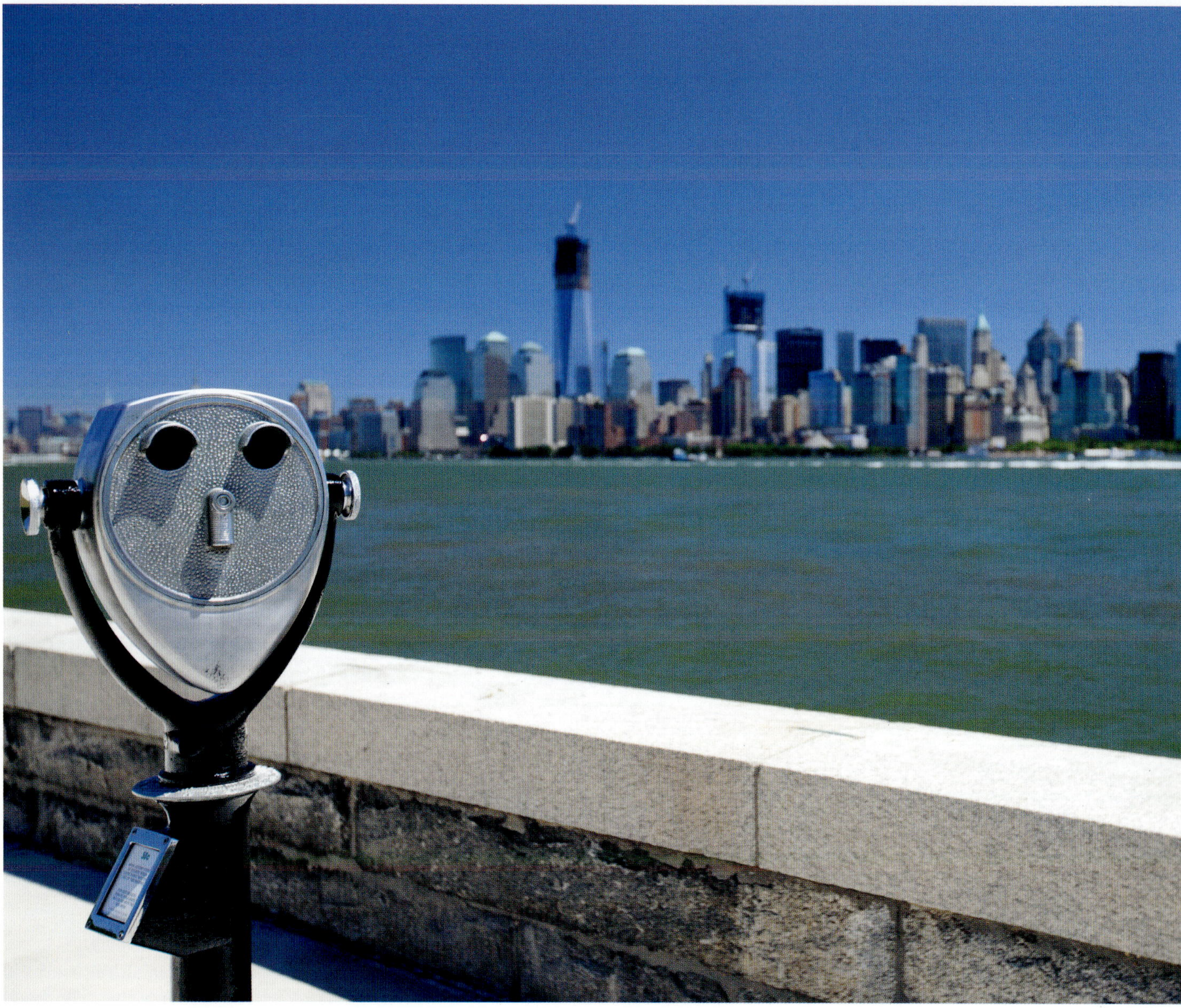

View from Ellis Island

The point of entry for more than 12 million immigrants who entered New York Harbor by steamship between 1892 and 1954, Ellis Island is a moving tribute to those who made the journey across the seas to America. Today, you still arrive here by boat, albeit the ferry from Battery Park or New Jersey.

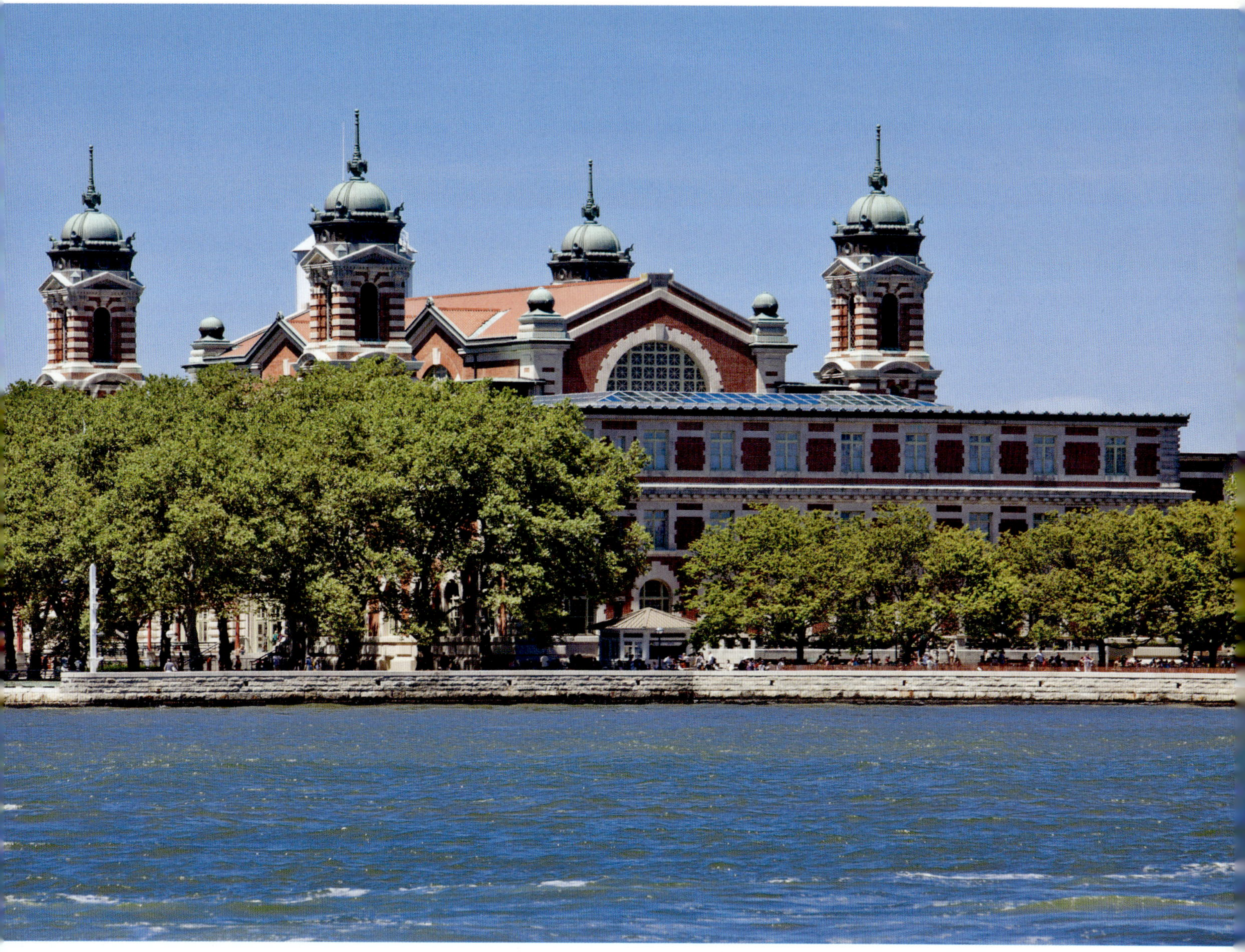

Ellis Island Immigration Museum

Once in disrepair, Ellis Island underwent a major $160 million restoration in 1984 and reopened to the public in 1990 as the Ellis Island Immigration Museum. Today, it receives almost 2 million visitors annually, many of whom can trace their family history in America back to Ellis Island.

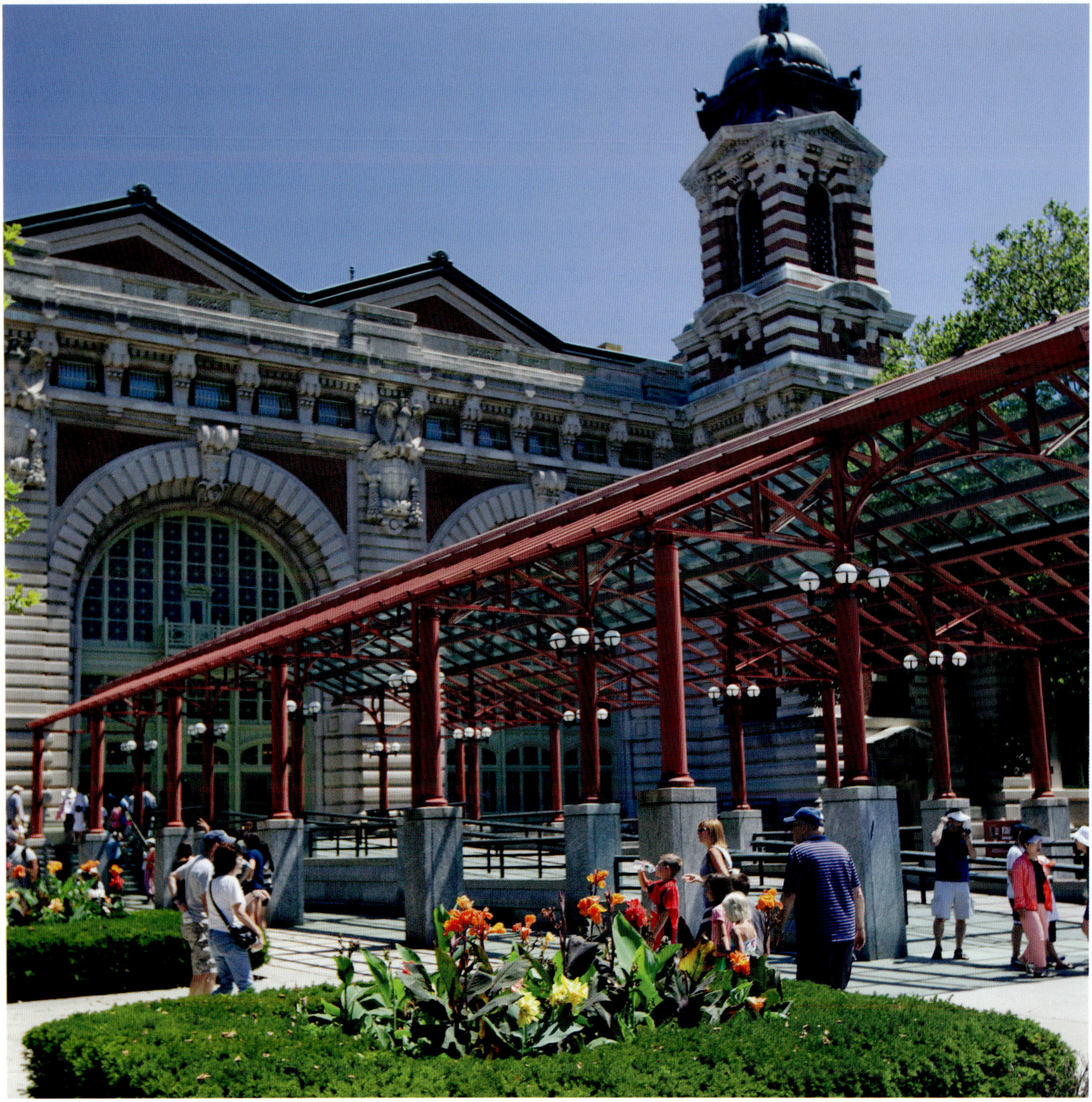

Welcome to Ellis Island

When Ellis Island officially opened on January 1, 1892, the first passenger processed through the immigration station was Annie Moore from County Cork, Ireland. It was her 15th birthday. She is immortalized by a statue that represents the millions who came here in pursuit of the American dream.

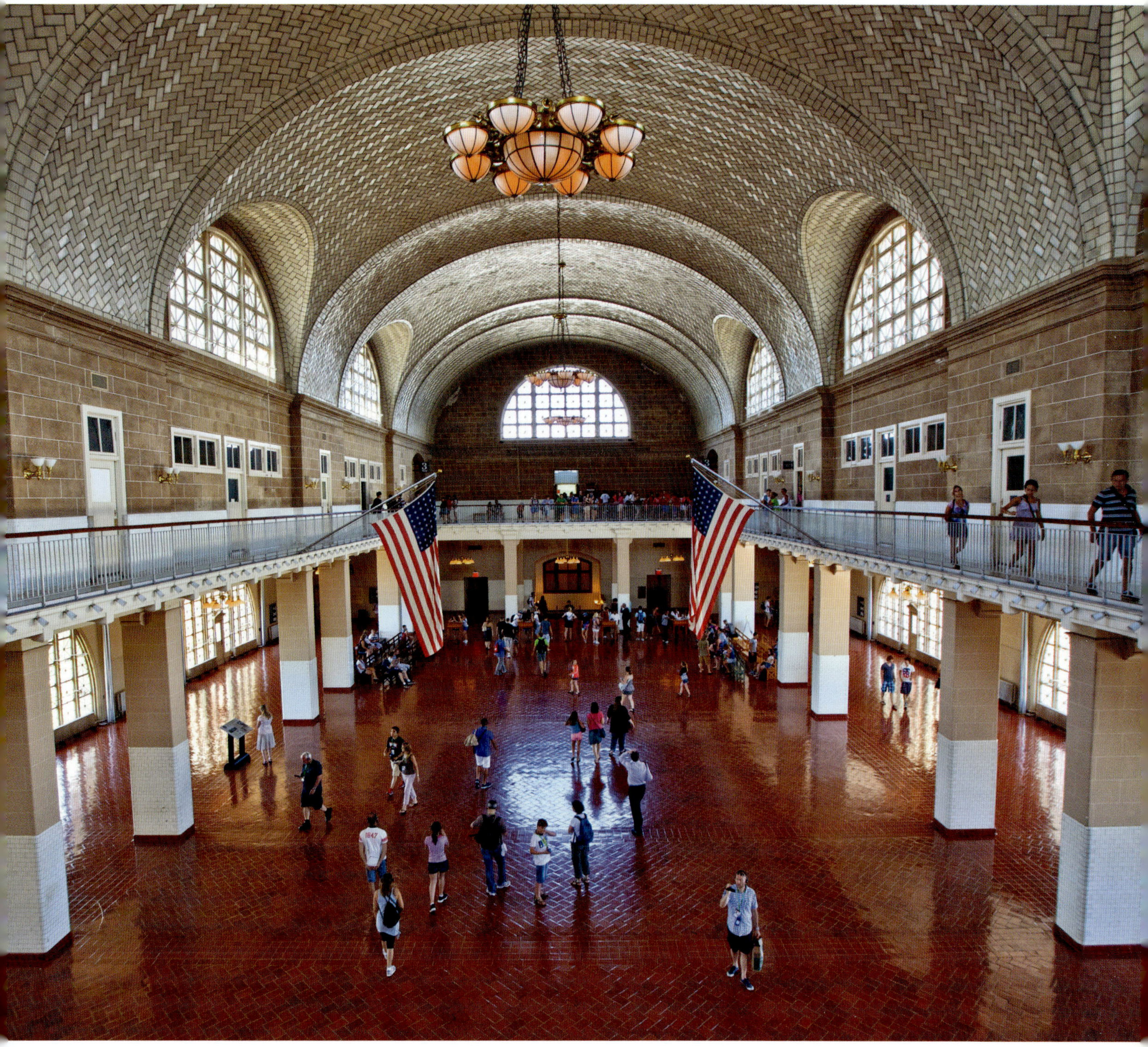

Great Hall at Ellis Island

Known as the "Island of Hope, Island of Tears," many of the immigrants hoping to settle in the U.S. were inspected and sent back home because of health or legal issues. Inspections took place in the Registry Room or Great Hall. Those who passed were free to begin their new lives in America.

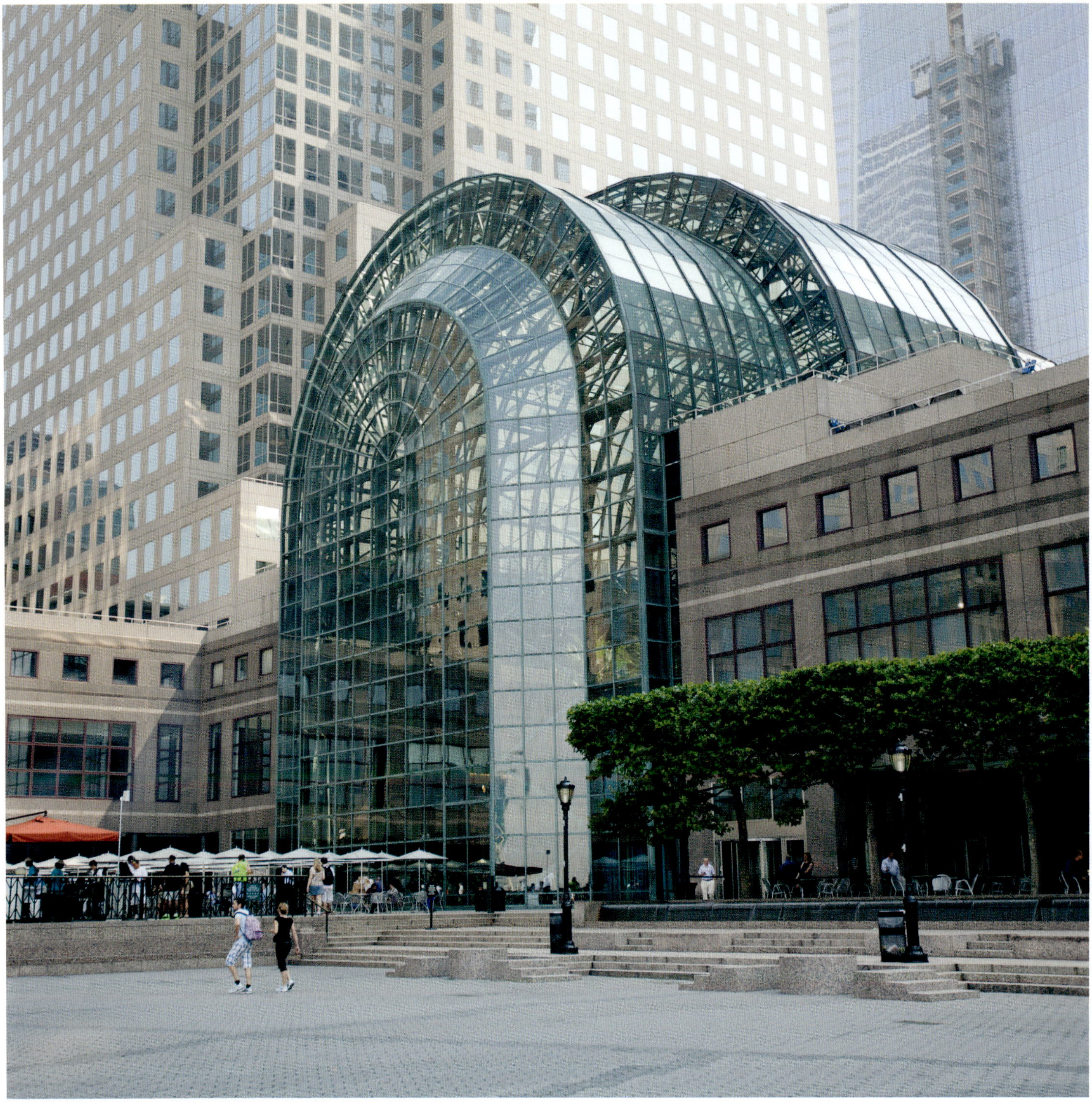

World Financial Center *(above)*

The upper floors of the World Financial Center are home to international corporations, including American Express. At street level, there is an upscale marketplace with retailers, restaurants, and specialty stores which surround the Winter Garden Atrium.

Winter Garden Atrium *(opposite)*

This soaring, 10-story, glass-vaulted pavilion casts natural sunlight onto sixteen 40-foot-tall palm trees. Located in the World Financial Center, these iconic trees welcome visitors to a quiet reprieve from the bustling city. The center also hosts a series of free concerts, film-screenings, and art exhibitions.

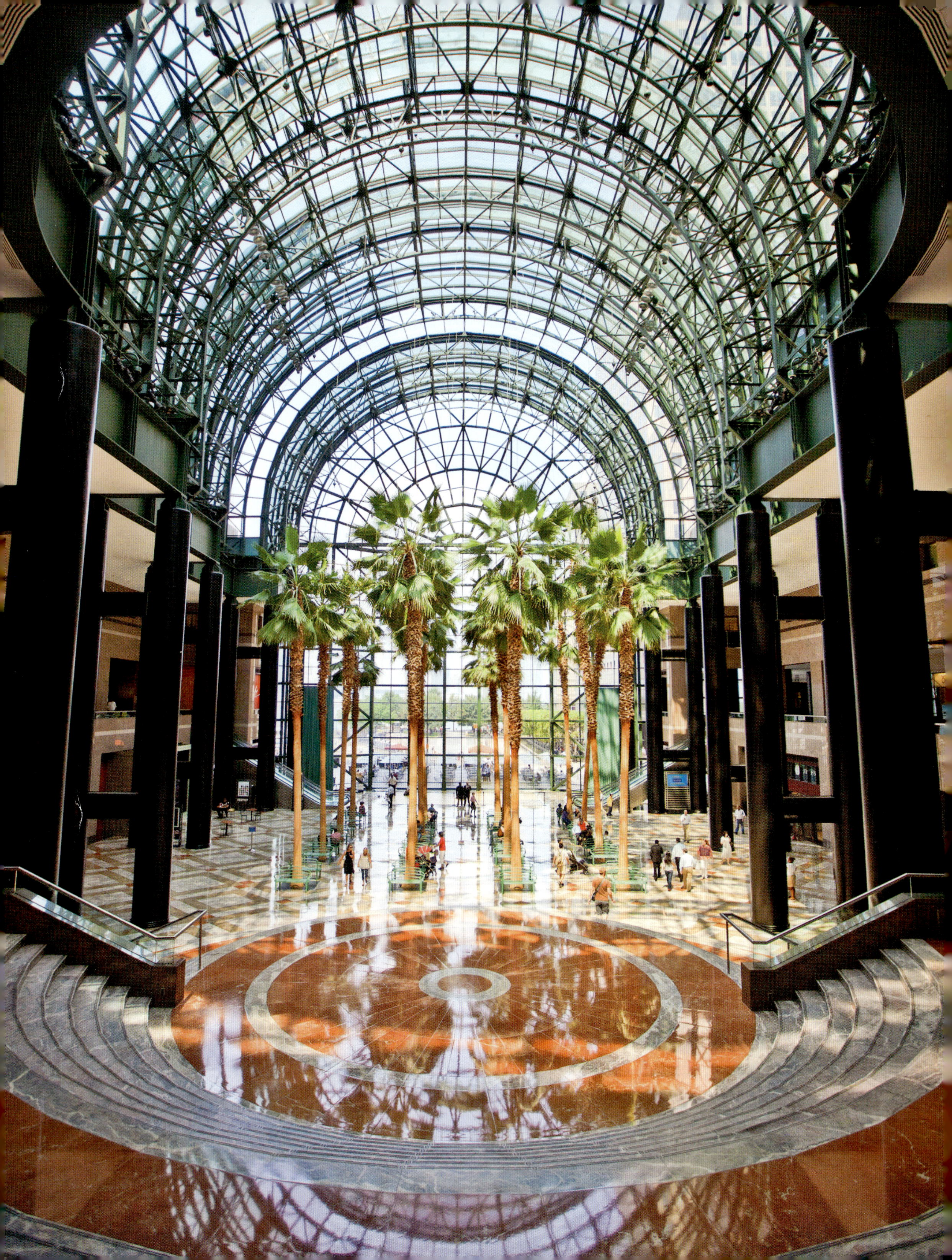

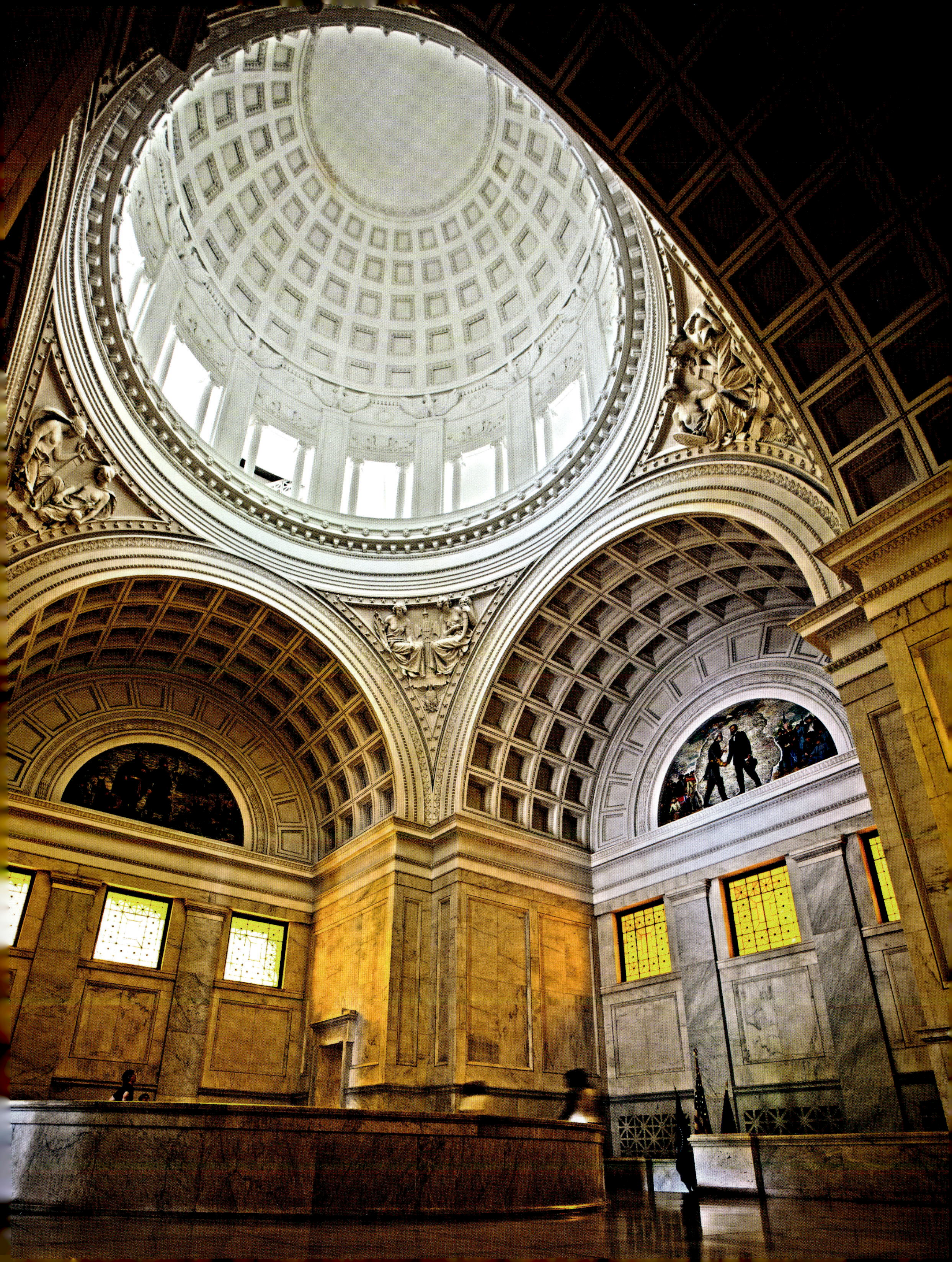

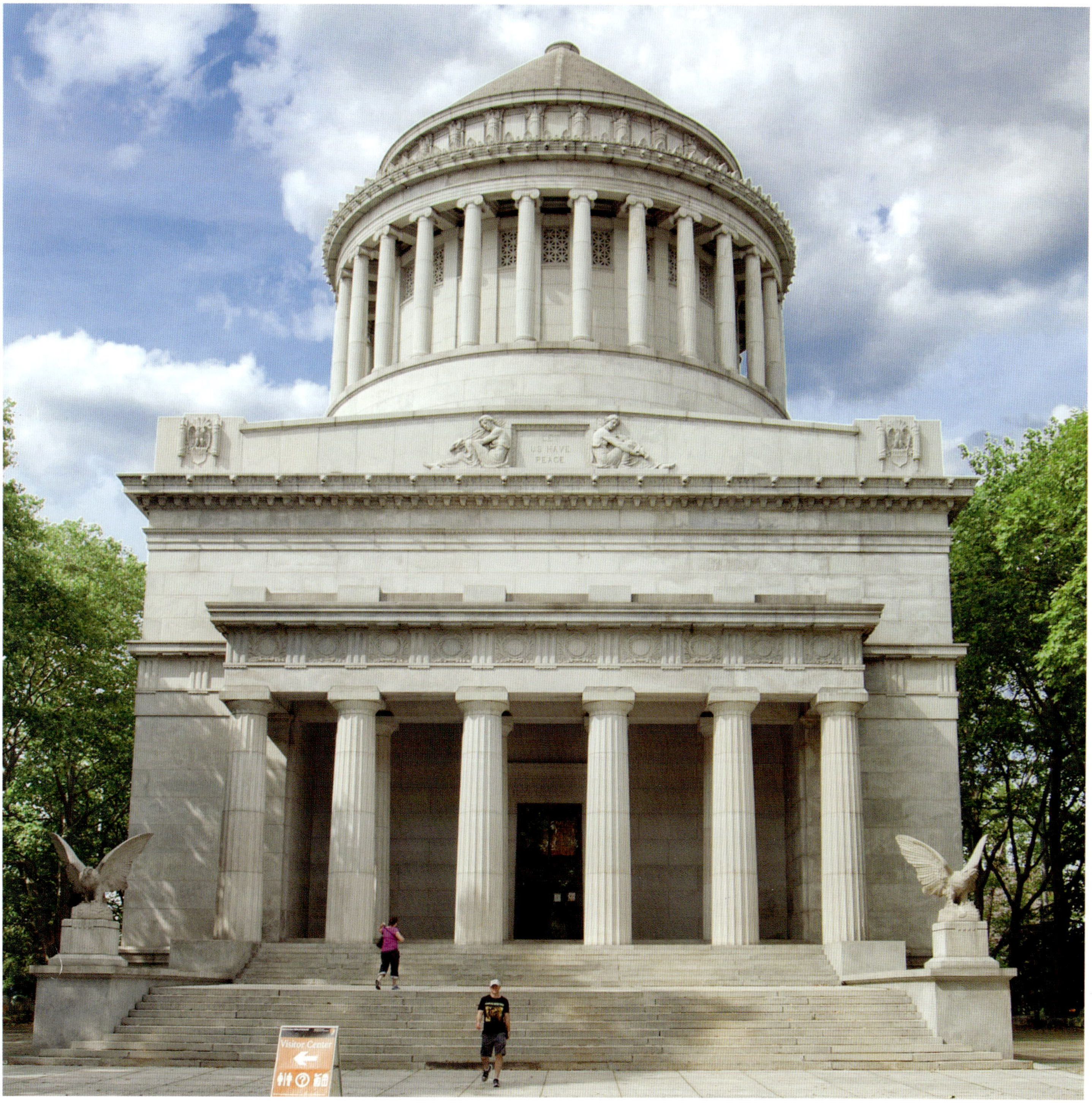

Inside Grant's Tomb *(opposite)*

The interior of the final resting place of Civil War General and U.S. President Ulysses S. Grant is largely made of Italian Carrara marble and decorated with mosaic murals depicting scenes from Grant's greatest triumphs, including Robert E. Lee's surrender at Appomattox. Look up and see the dramatic coffered dome.

Grant's Tomb *(above)*

The joke is that most New Yorkers don't know who is buried in Grant's Tomb. But it's actually Ulysses S. Grant and his wife Julia. Grant is the only president buried in the city where he spent much of his last years, and his tomb is one of the largest mausoleums in the Western Hemisphere.

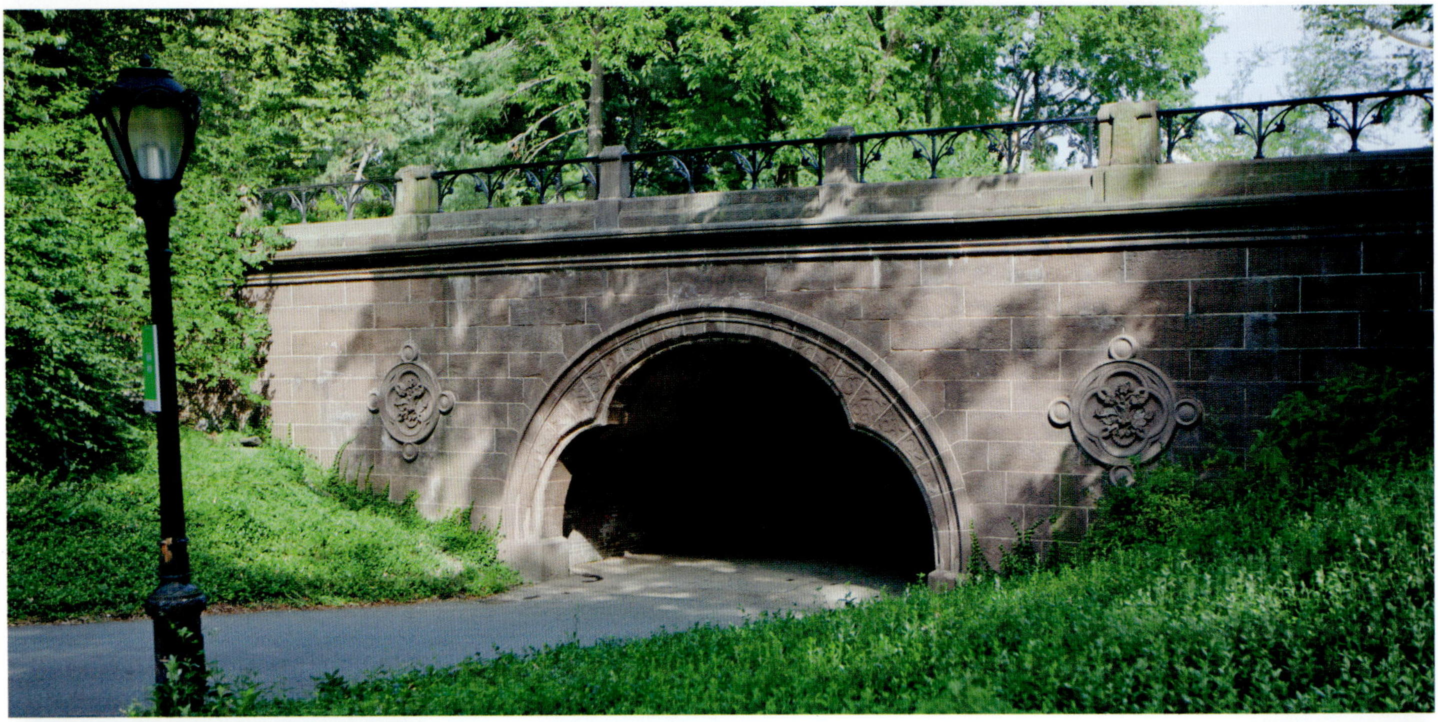

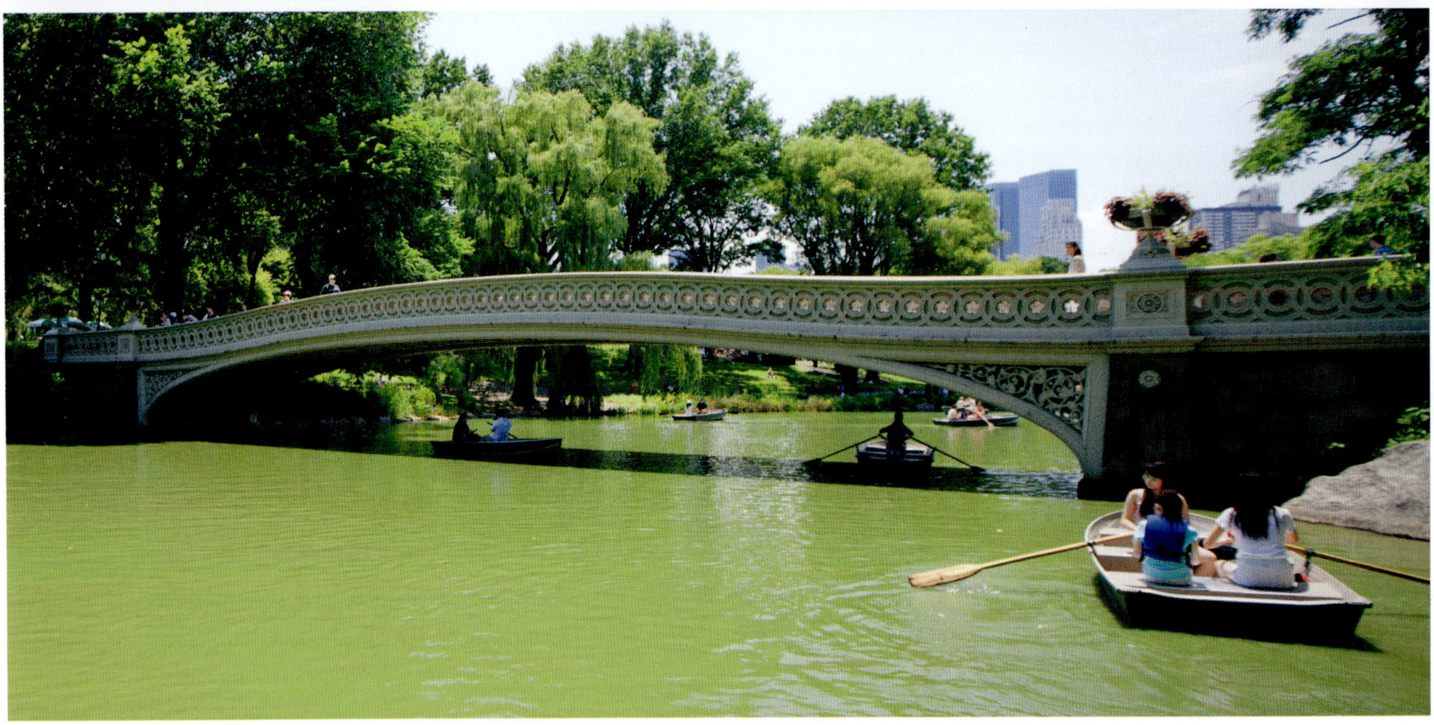

Central Park Tunnel *(top)*

Much like the city itself, Central Park is full of bridges and tunnels that draw visitors to meander over its 843 acres of lawns, woodlands, and water. The tunnels also provide great acoustics and are a favorite spot for the many musicians who play there.

Bow Bridge *(bottom)*

This original cast-iron bridge offers expansive views of Central Park and is a romantic setting for wedding photos. It was designed as a "bow," gracefully tying together two sections of the lake and providing a pathway from the Ramble woodland to the flowering landscape of Cherry Hill.

Bethesda Fountain *(opposite)*

One of the more formal elements in the naturalistic Central Park landscape, Bethesda Terrace Fountain is a popular gathering spot where you'll often find musicians, mimes, and exercisers. The neoclassical bronze *Angel of the Water* sculpture was designed by Emma Stebbins, the first woman to receive a public art commission from the city.

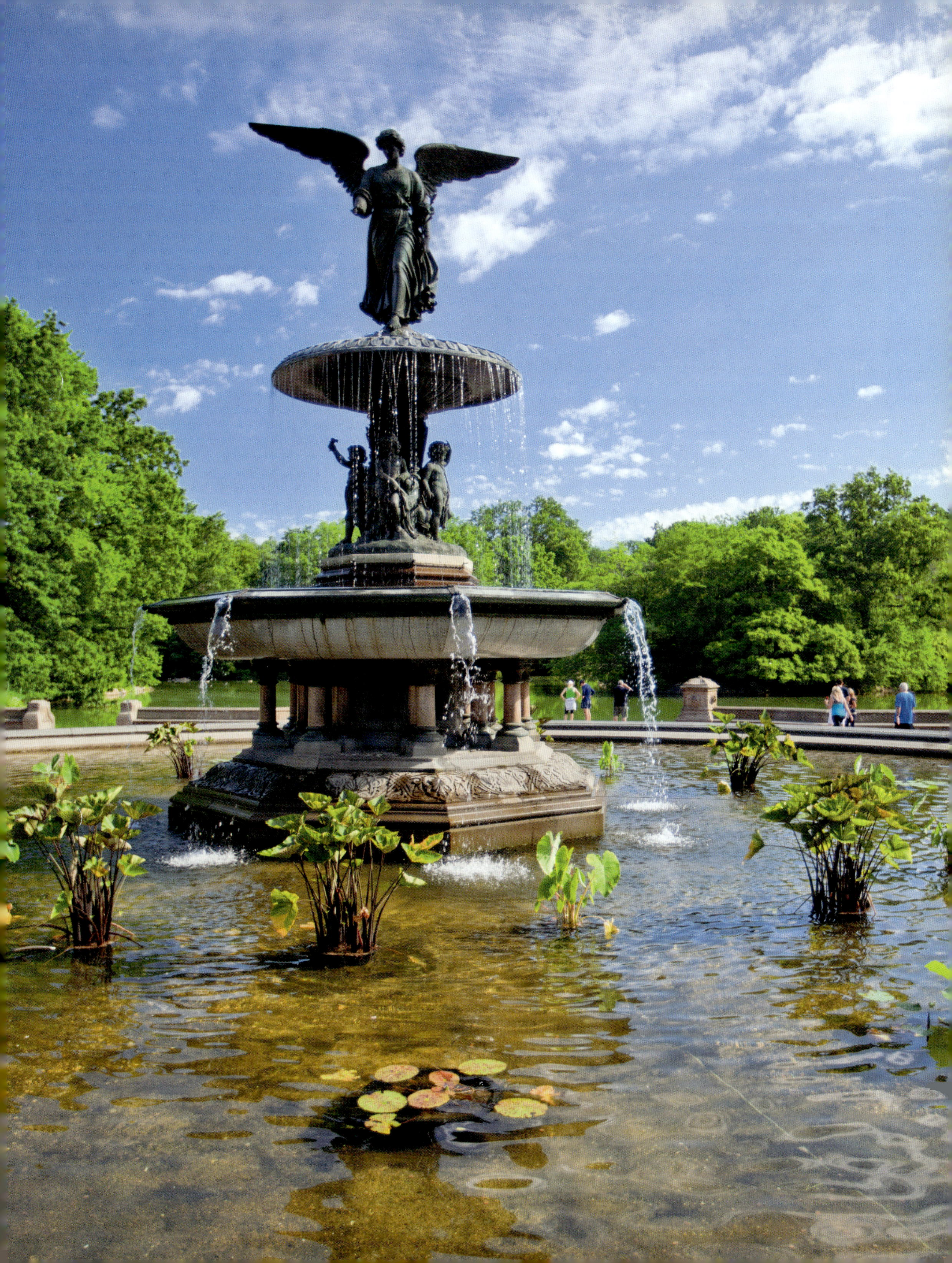

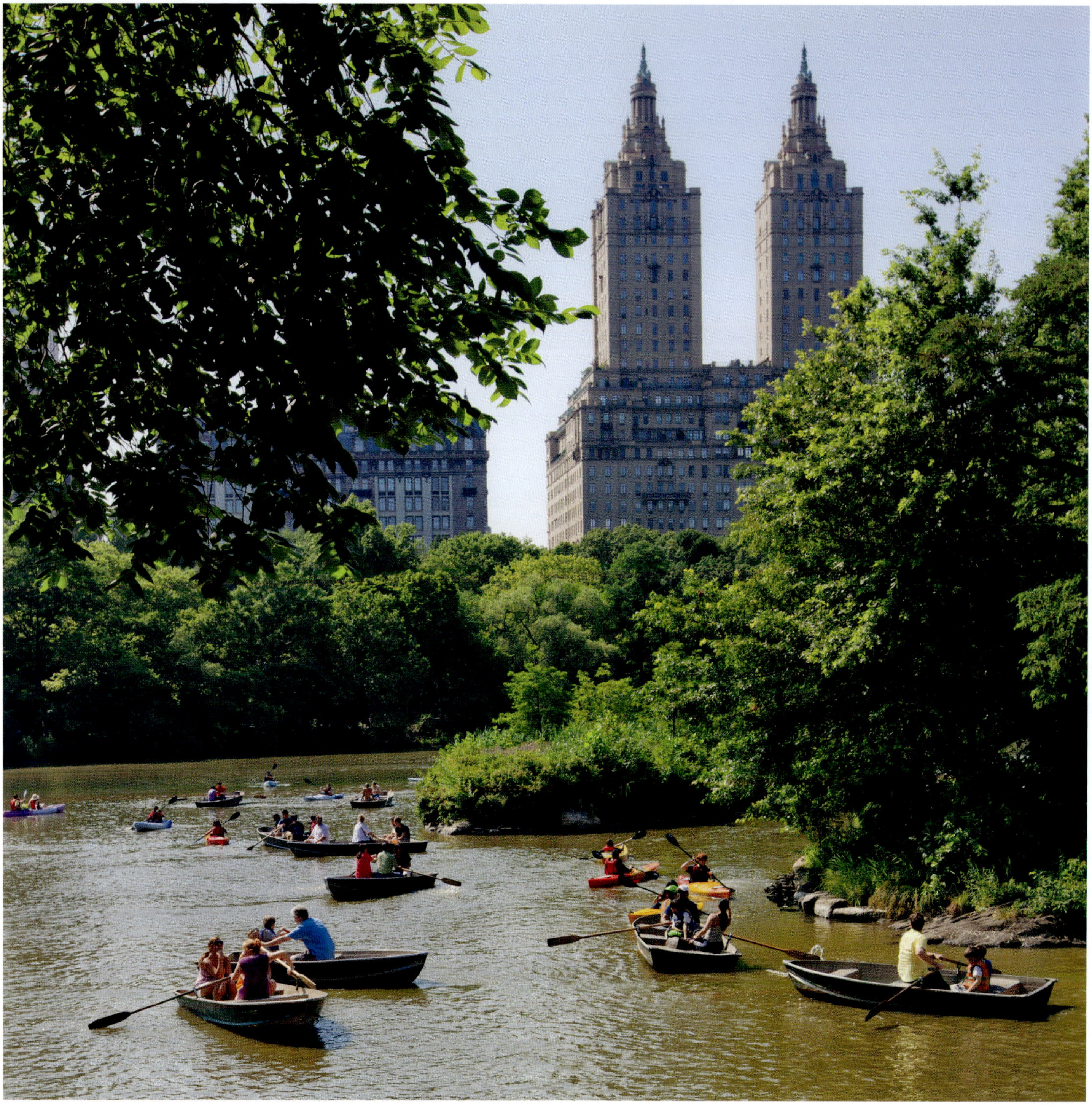

The Lake *(above)*

Float along in a Central Park rowboat and you can almost imagine you are in the country, unless you see the towers of luxury apartment buildings like the San Remo in the distance. The 18-acre lake is the second largest man-made body of water in Manhattan, after the uptown reservoir.

Strawberry Fields *(opposite)*

Central Park's Strawberry Fields has become a peaceful place to pay respect to the late, great Beatle John Lennon. You'll often find musicians playing his tunes and piles of flowers atop the mosaic inscribed with the word "Imagine," Lennon's famous song.

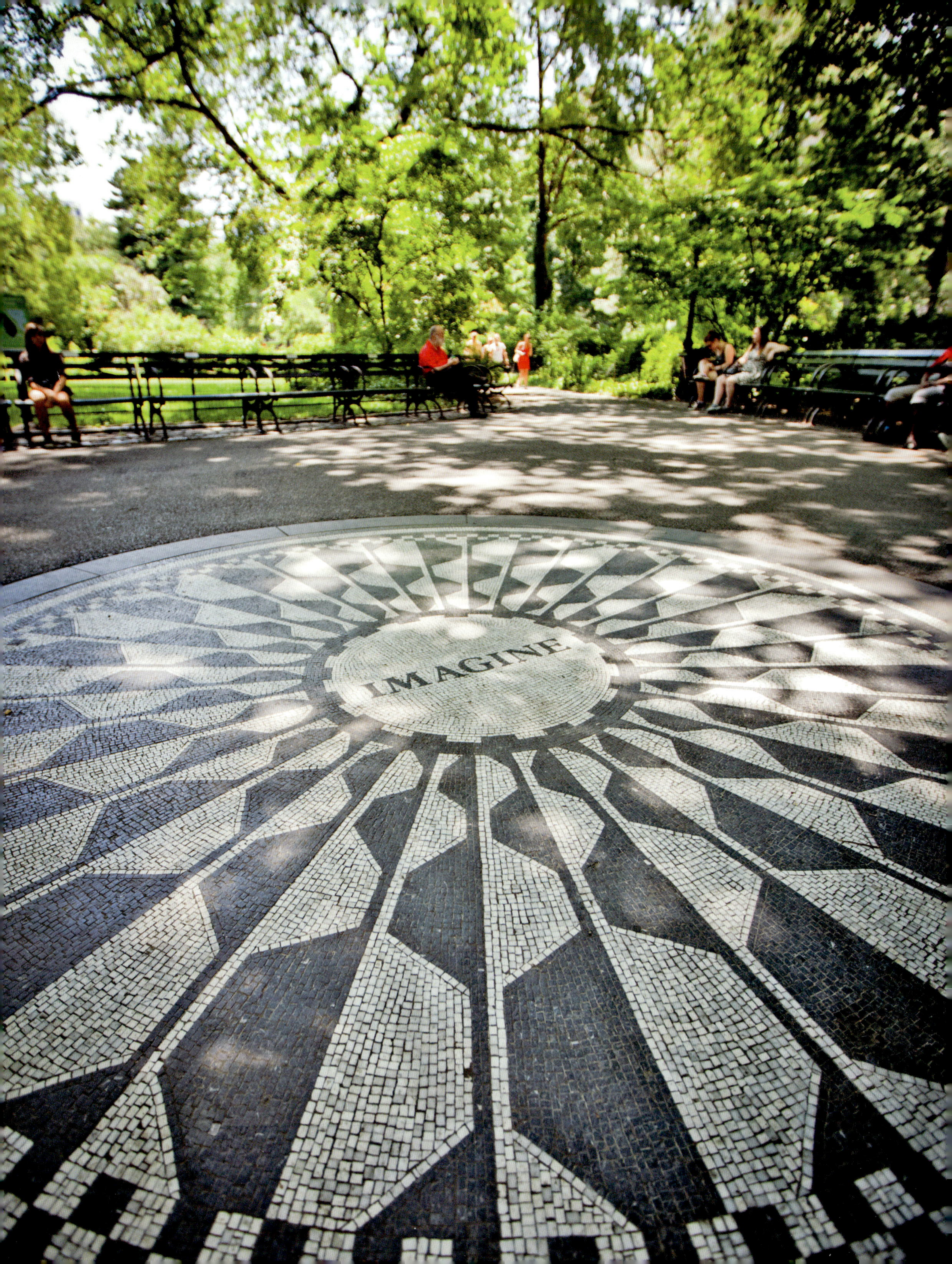
IMAGINE

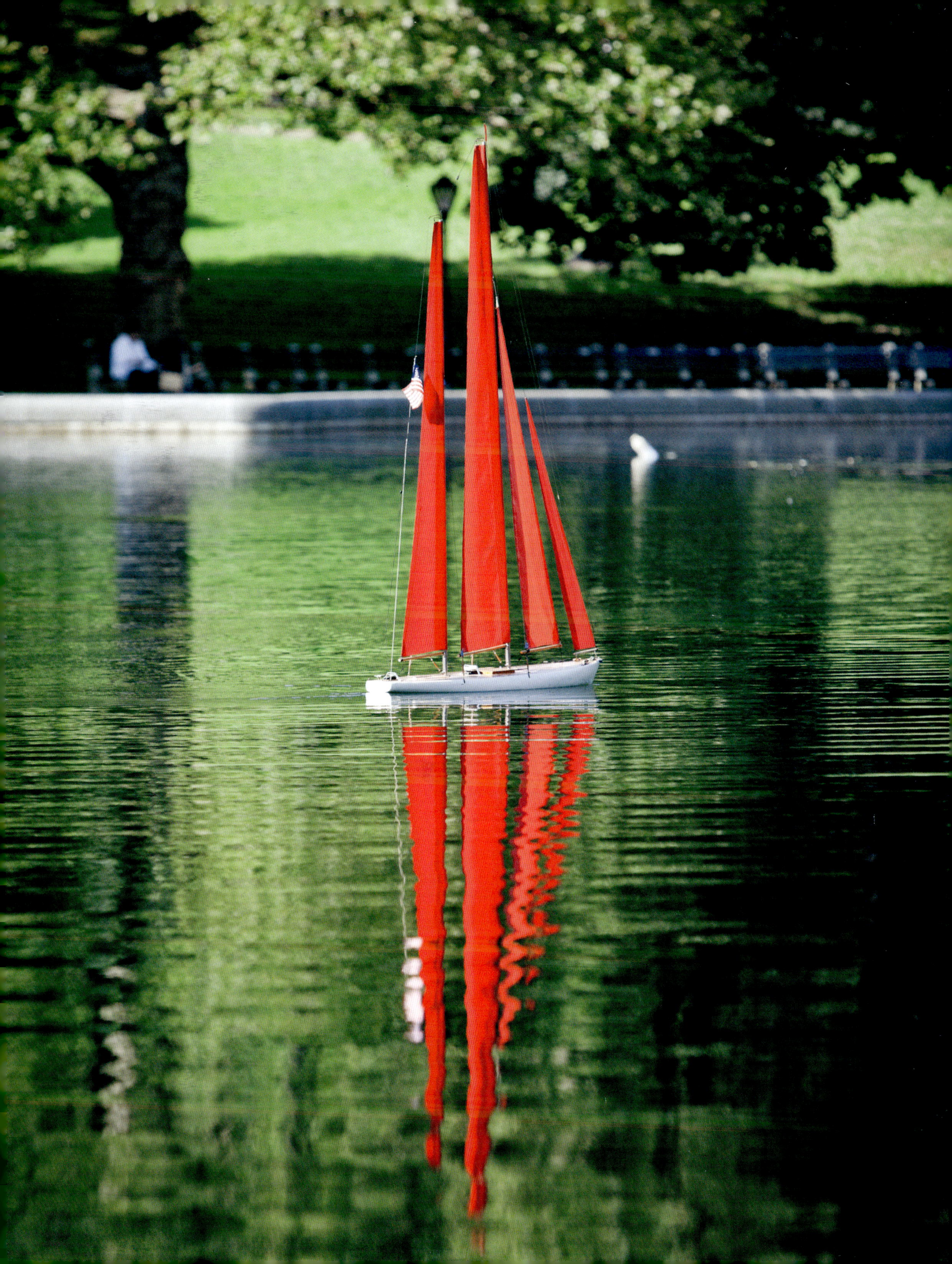

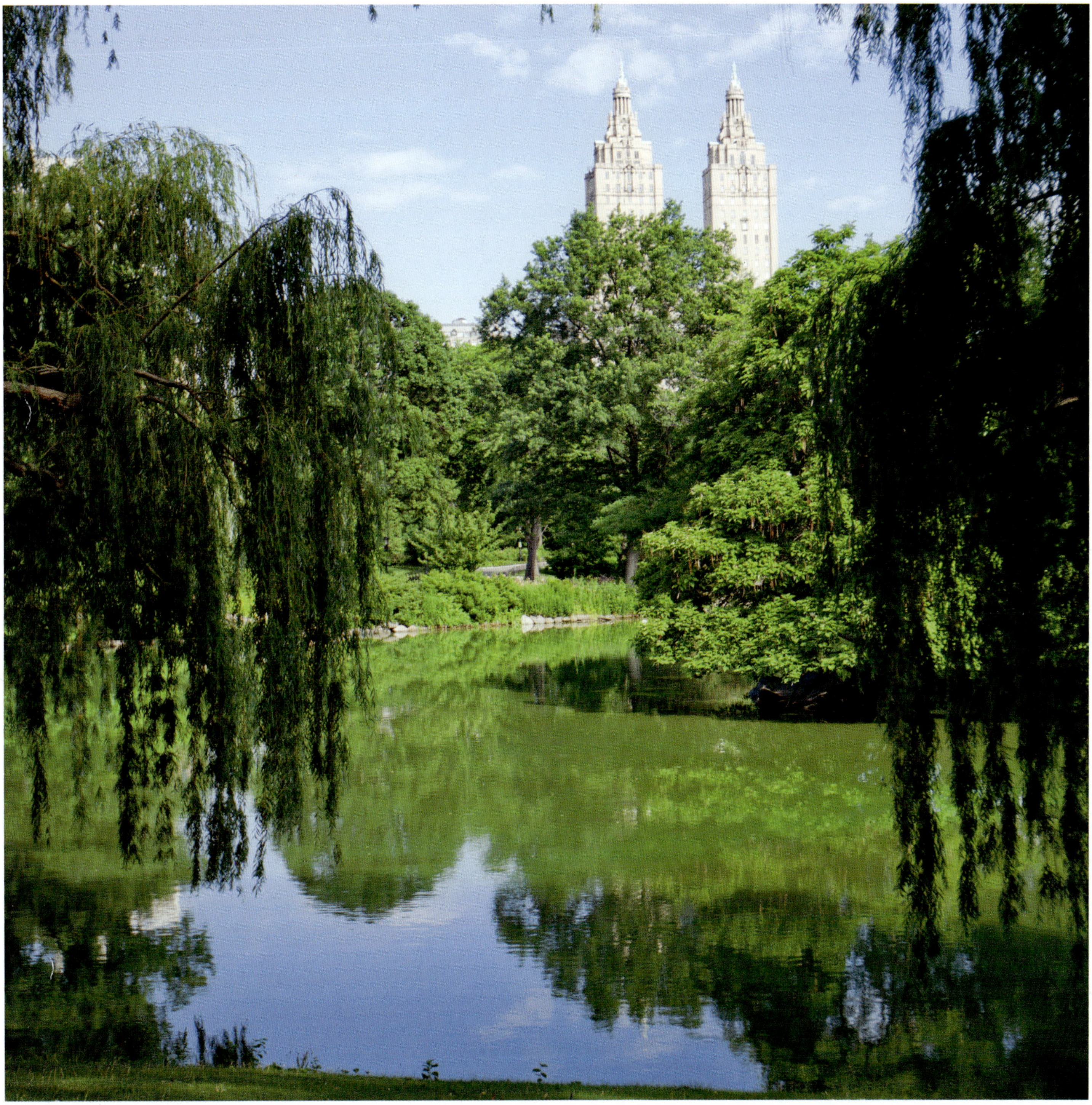

Conservatory Water *(opposite)*

Inspired by boat ponds in Parisian parks, the Conservatory Water stars in the well-known E.B. White children's classic, *Stuart Little*, in which a little mouse captains a boat across the pond. Today, kids can be captains of their own sailboats as they race wind-powered and motorized models here.

Central Park *(above)*

For a respite from busy city life, New Yorkers head to the park to exchange views of concrete for greenery. The 843-acre oasis designed by Frederick Law Olmsted and Calvert Vaux opened in 1857 as America's first major urban public space, and it still serves as Manhattan's backyard.

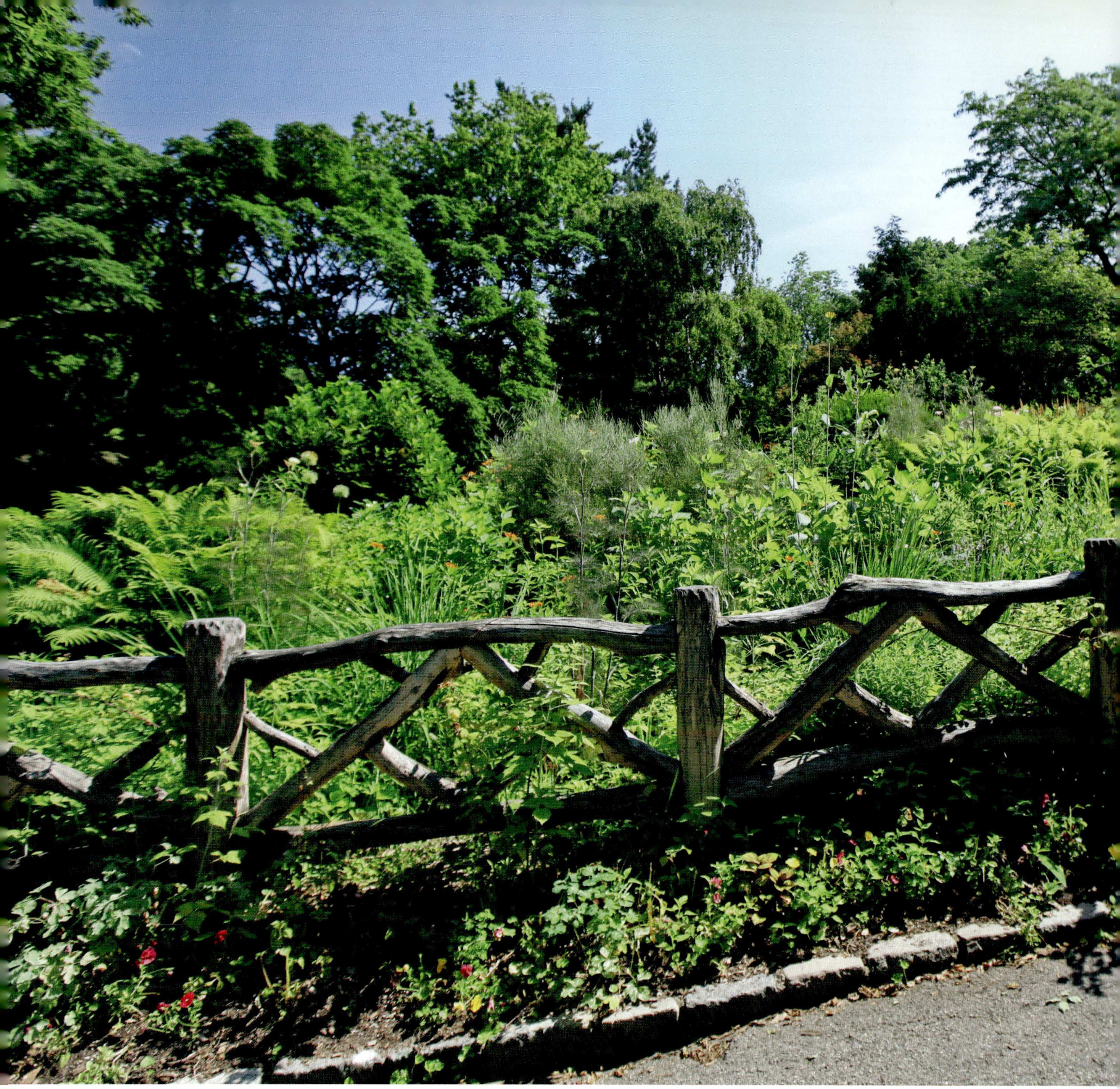

Shakespeare Garden

One of the park's hidden gems is a charming four-acre section planted with flowers and plants mentioned in the English playwright's work, like the rosemary and pansies from Hamlet. Look closely for bronze plaques identifying the various species, along with corresponding quotations from the Bard's plays.

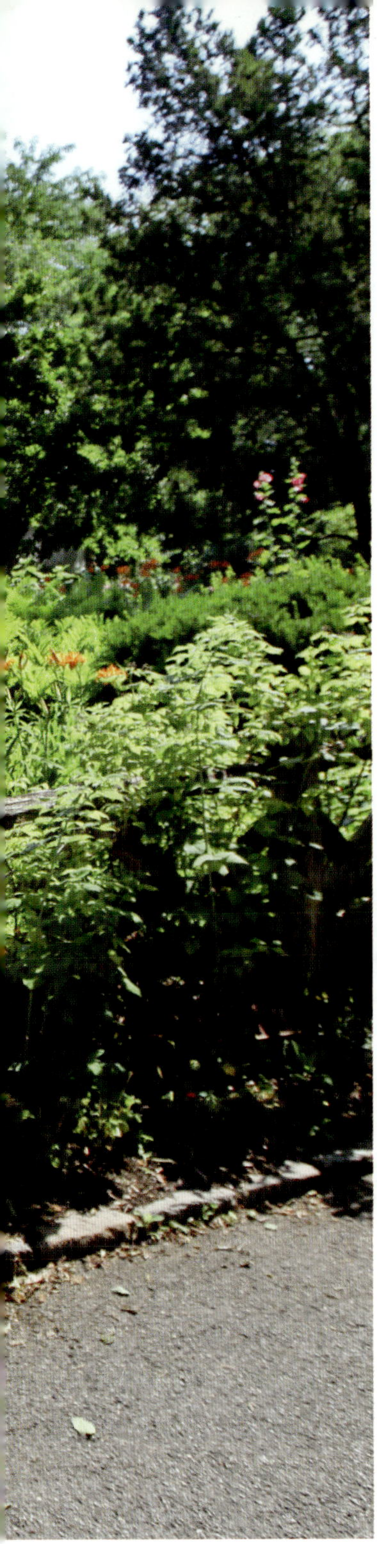

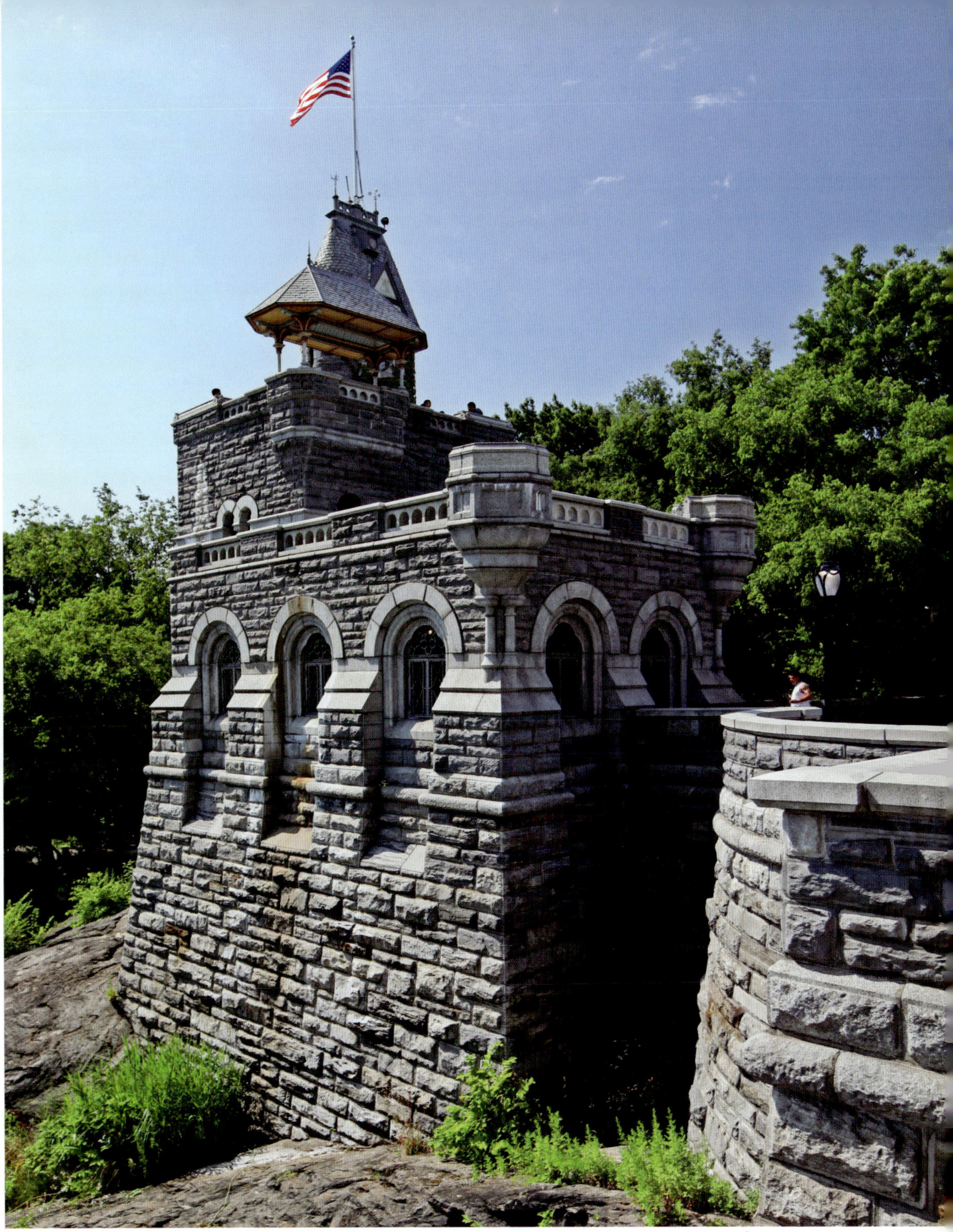

Belvedere Castle

Climb this stone castle for some of the best views of Central Park, the adjacent Delacorte Theater, and the city beyond. Unknown to most, it's also where the National Weather Service records daily temperatures and takes measurements to determine the city's rain and snowfall amounts.

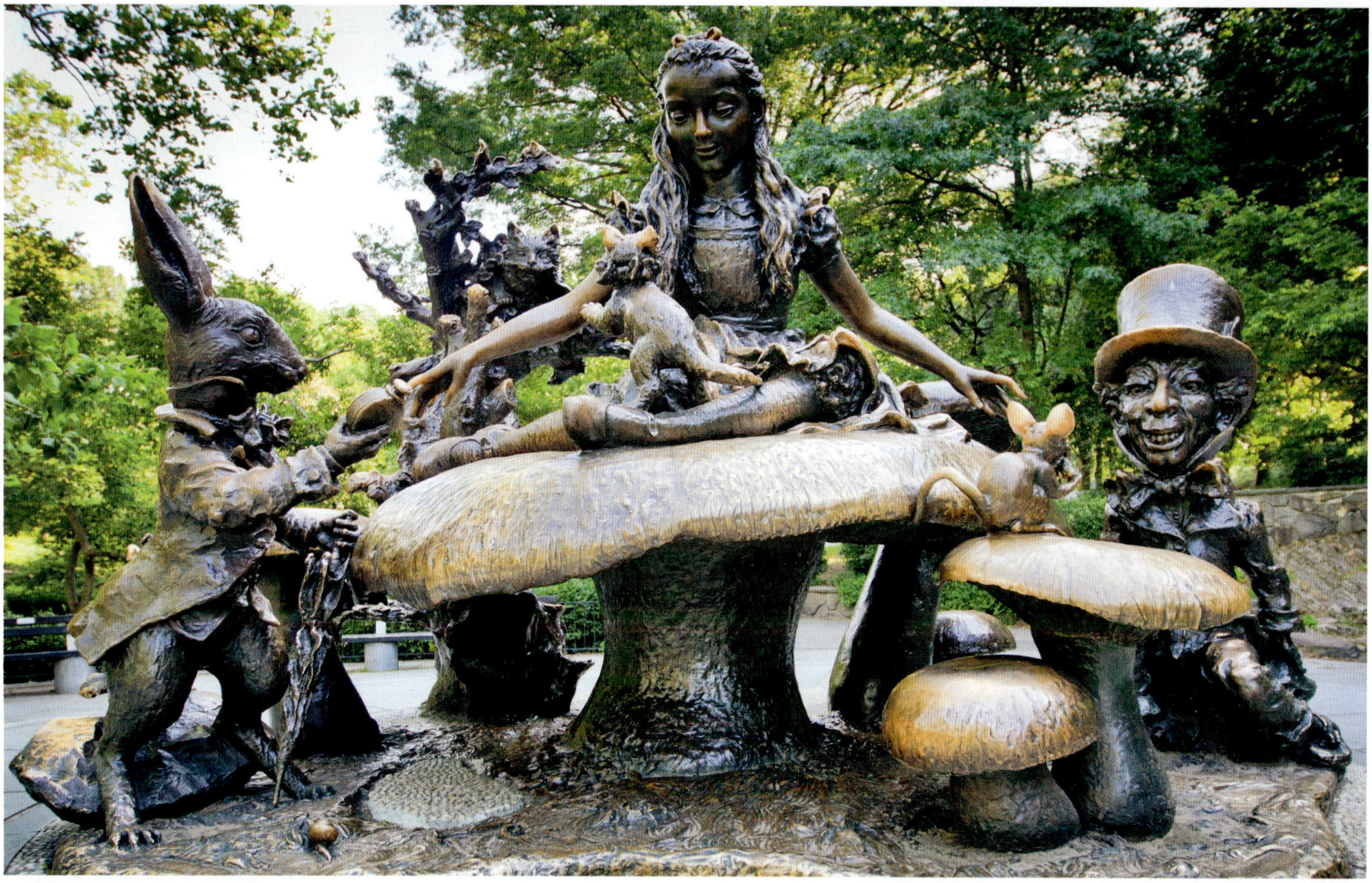

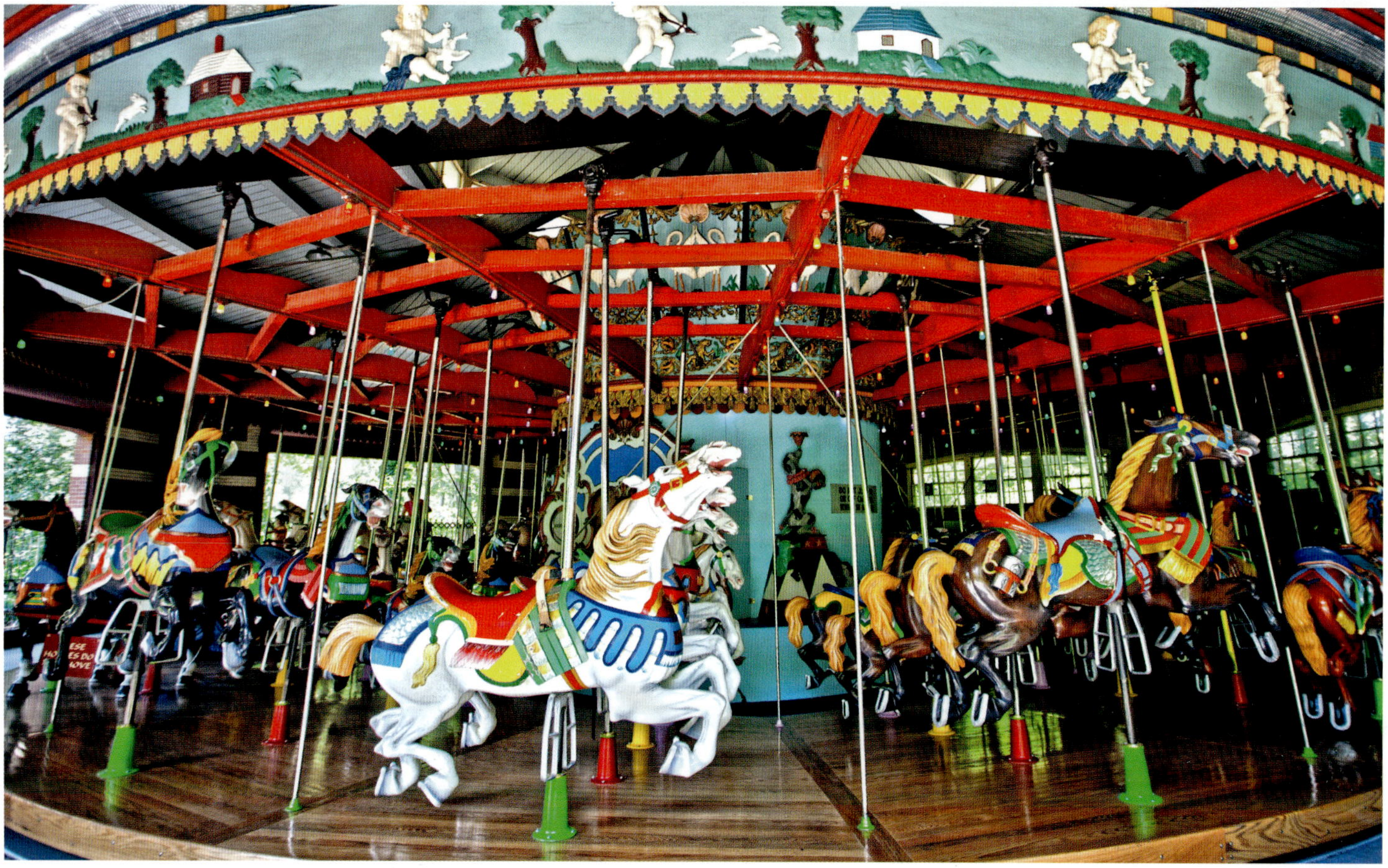

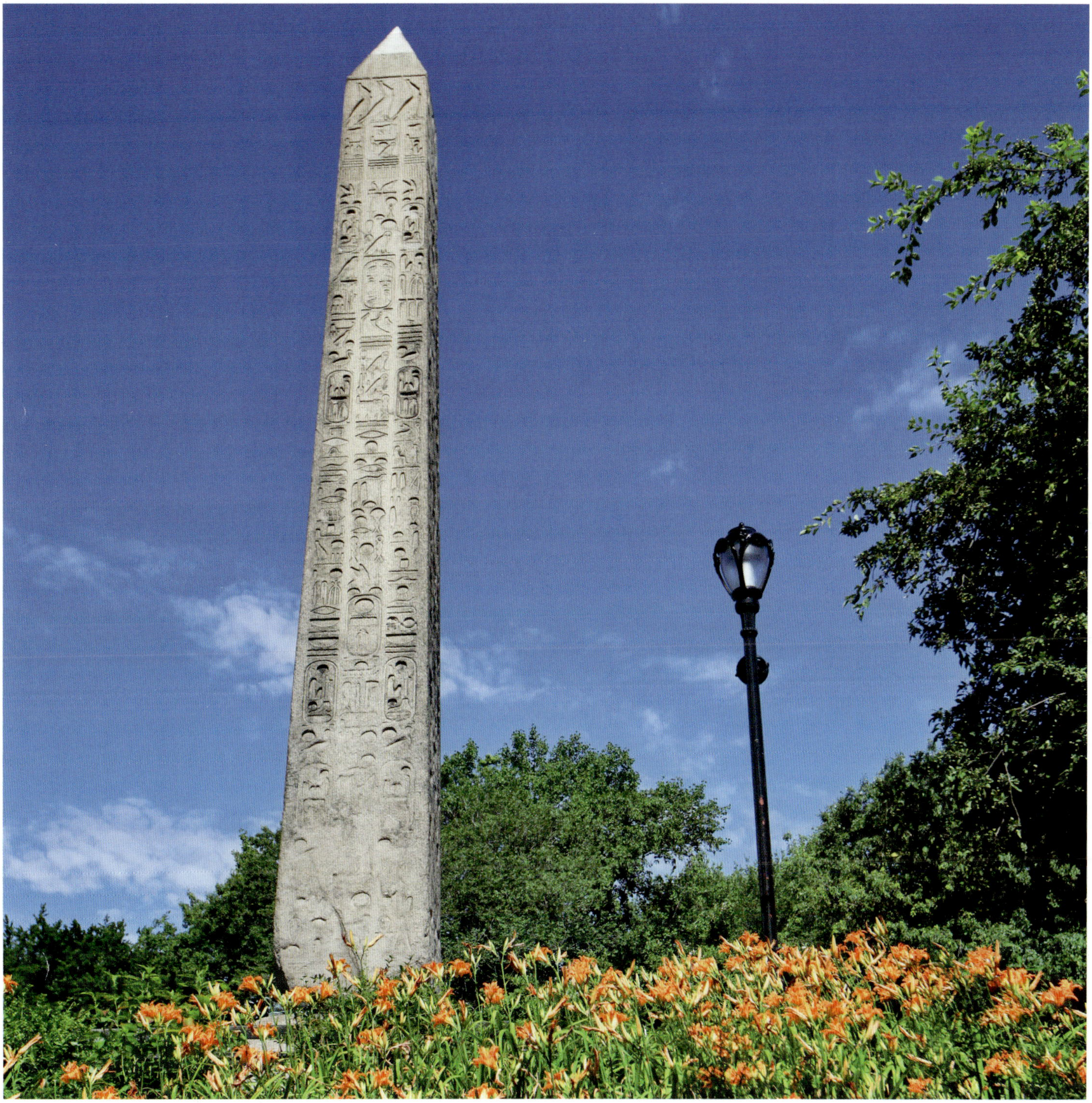

Alice in Wonderland *(opposite, top)*

Lewis Carroll's classic story *Alice in Wonderland* is immortalized in this 11-foot-tall bronze statue in Central Park. Children love to climb, touch, and crawl all over Alice and her storybook friends as they slide down her toadstool seat, grab the White Rabbit's ears, and search for the Dormouse.

Carousel *(opposite, bottom)*

A classic New York gem, the Central Park Carousel has been giving rides to kids of all ages since 1871, though no longer powered by a horse and a mule as it once was. The current carousel was crafted in 1908 and features 57 hand-carved horses and two decorative chariots.

Cleopatra's Needle *(above)*

Nicknamed "Cleopatra's Needle," the granite obelisk is part of a pair dating back to 1450 BC and commissioned by an Egyptian pharaoh in celebration of his 30-year-reign. Egypt gave it to New York in 1881. Getting the 71-foot-tall, 244-ton obelisk to Central Park from the Hudson River was a feat that took 112 days.

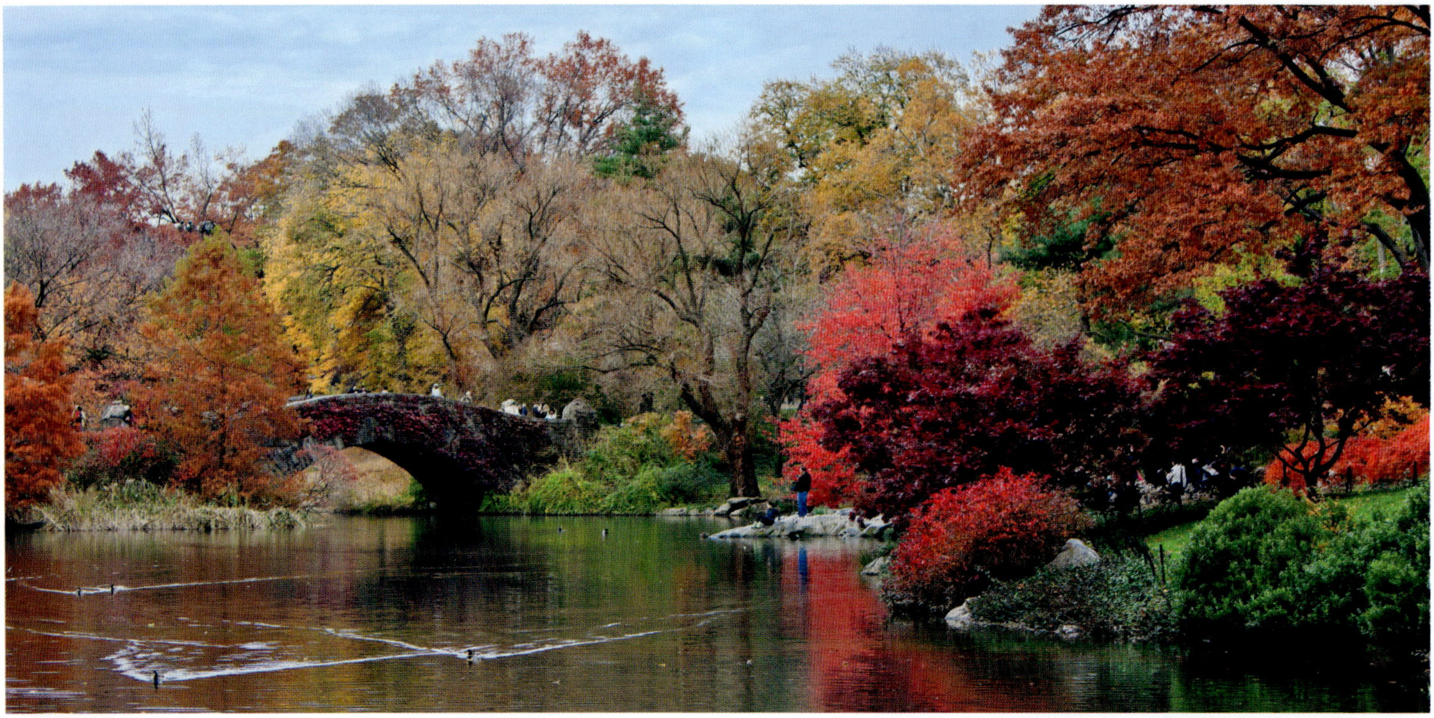

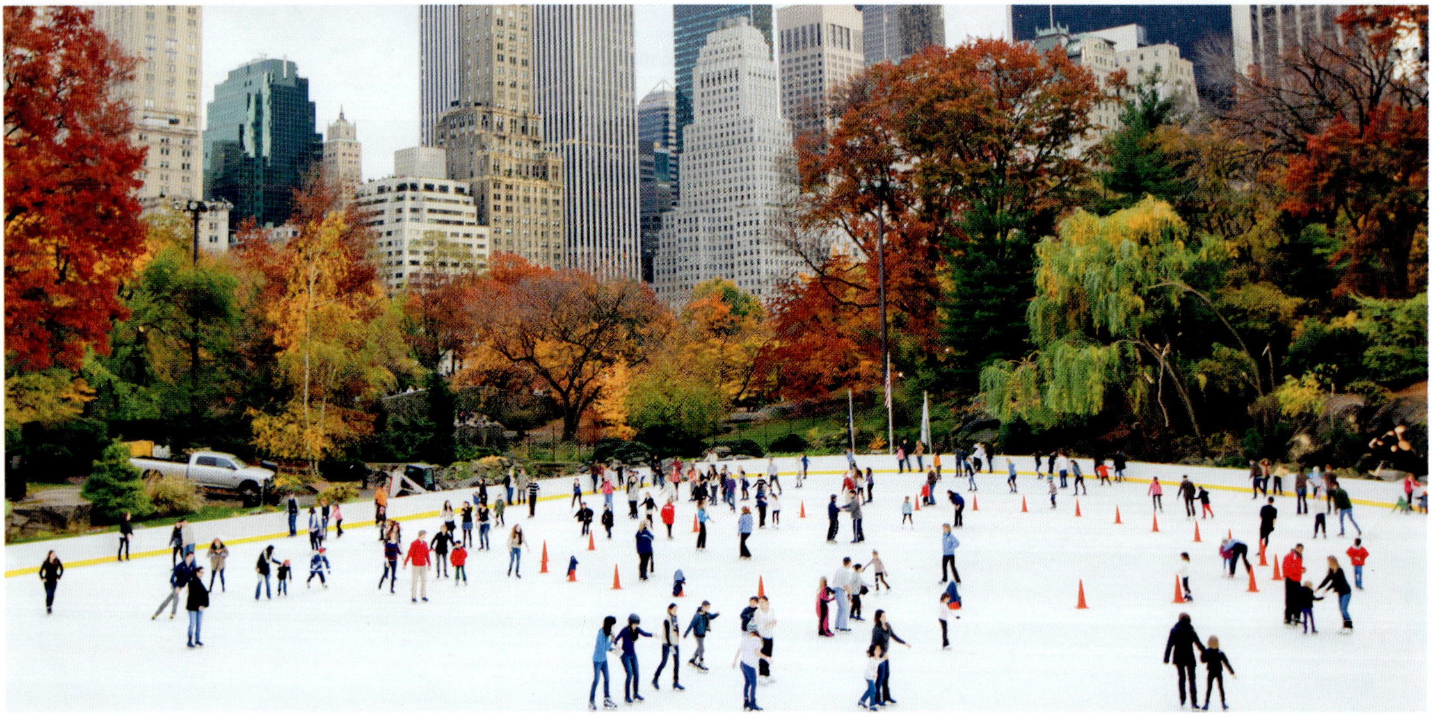

Fall Colors *(top)*

When autumn arrives, Central Park is one of the best spots in Manhattan to see the seasons change and the fall foliage awash in color. Millions of locals and visitors flock here to bike, stroll, or watch the finish of the New York City Marathon each November.

Wollman Rink *(bottom)*

Situated in the heart of Central Park, Wollman Rink is the ideal place to learn to skate and enjoy New York's winter. Breathing in the crisp cold air with the city skyline in the background is a fun and memorable way to spend an afternoon.

Washington Square Park *(opposite)*

This park is a showcase for Greenwich Village musicians and artists, a playground for local children, a battleground for chess enthusiasts, and a study spot for NYU students. Modeled after the Arc de Triomphe in Paris, the arch was erected in 1889 to celebrate the centennial of George Washington's inauguration as president.

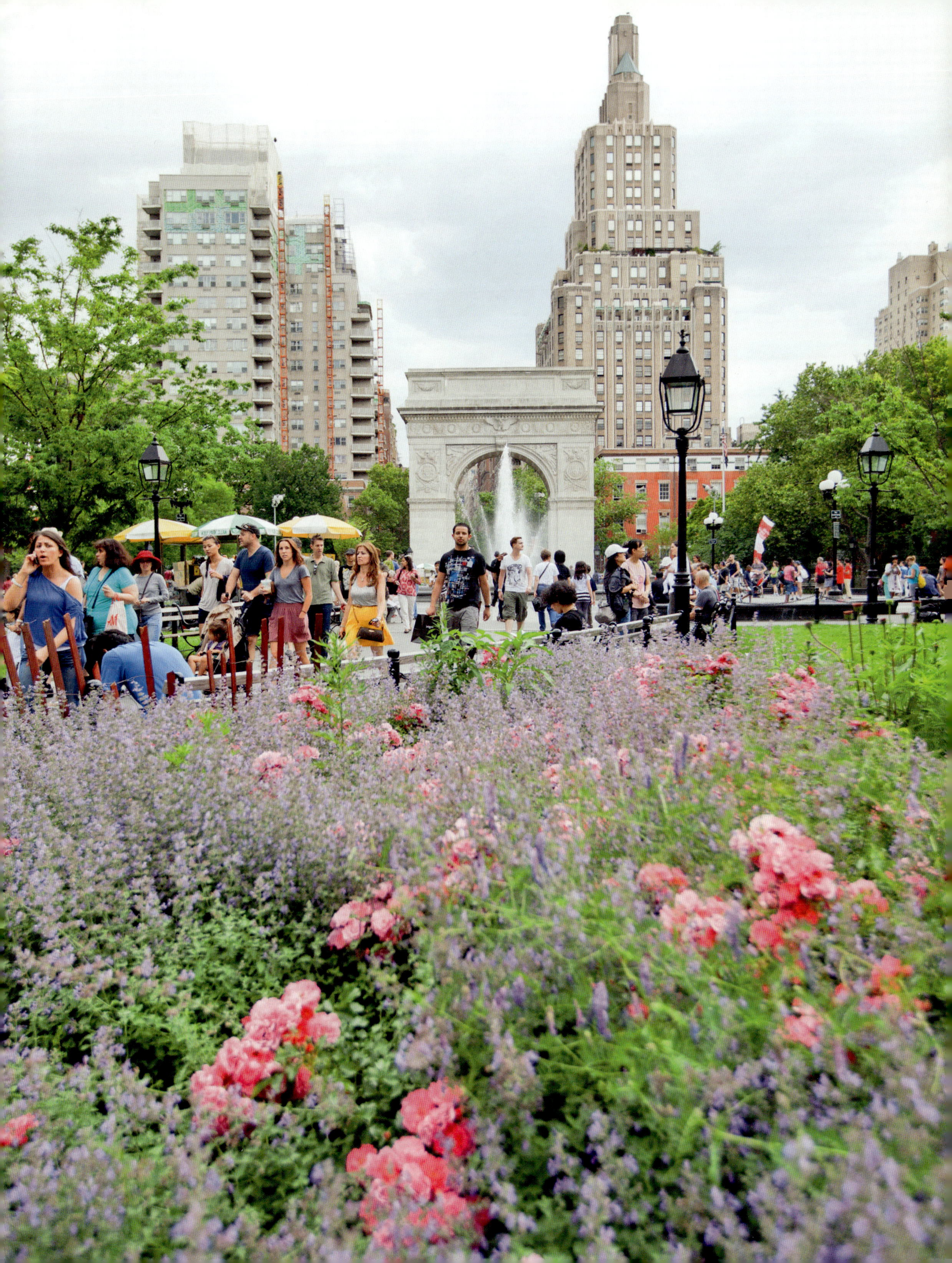

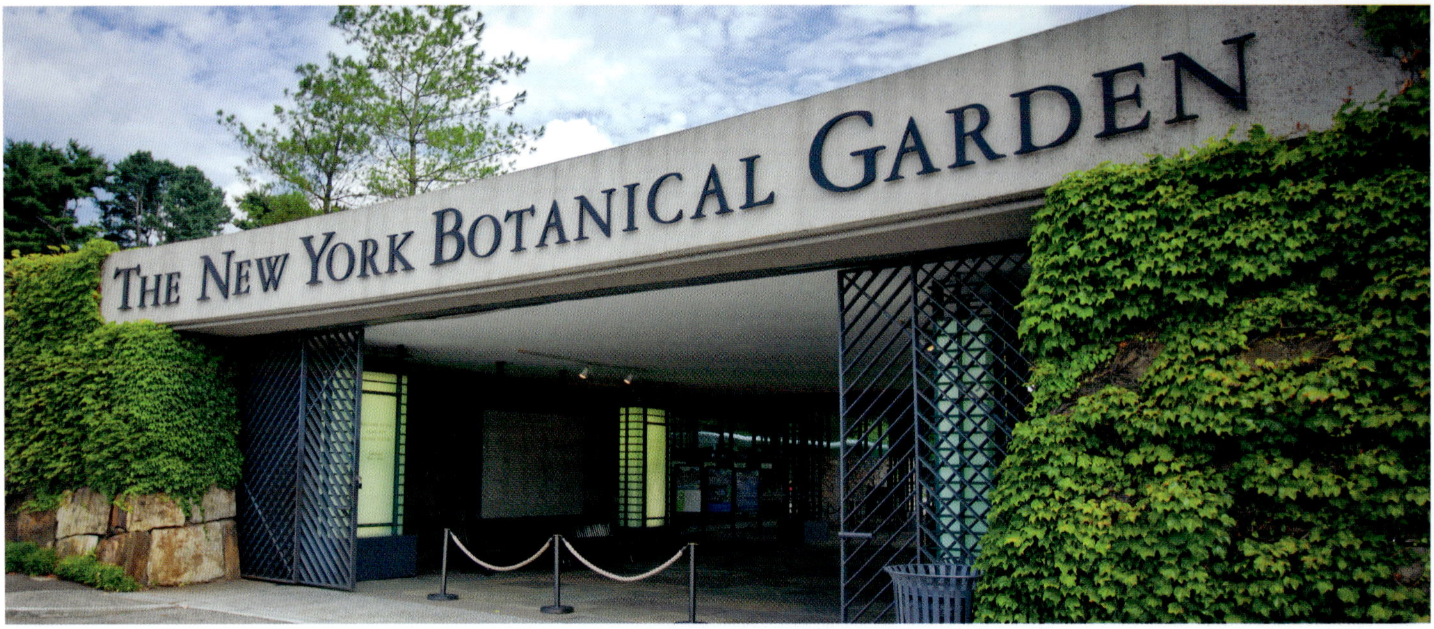

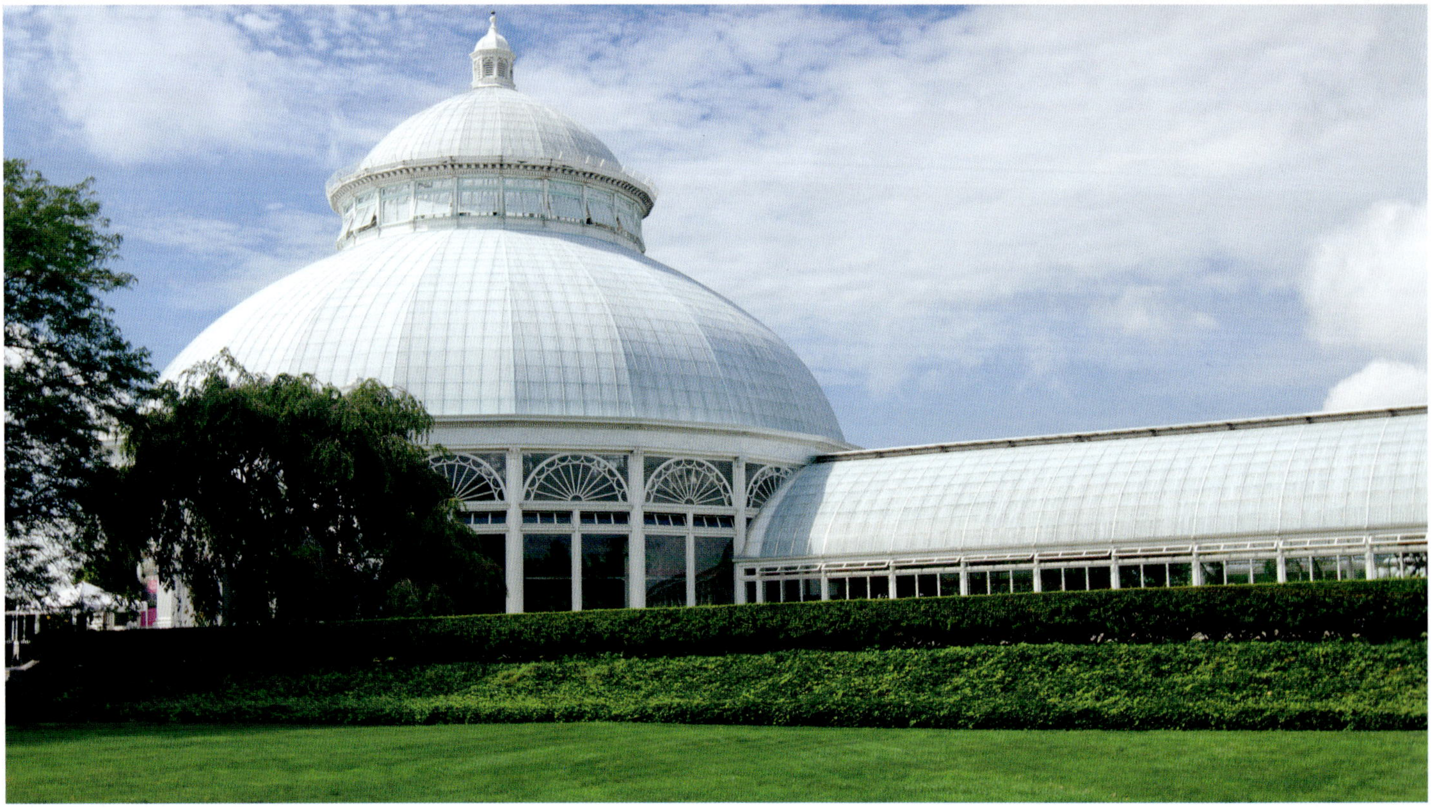

New York Botanical Garden *(top)*

Across 250 acres in the Bronx with 50 garden and plant collections, the Botanical Garden contains a waterfall, wetlands, and a remnant of the original forest, which once covered all of New York City more than three centuries ago. Open year-round, there's something to see in every season.

Enid A. Haupt Conservatory *(bottom)*

A Victorian-style glasshouse, the Enid A. Haupt Conservatory features a tropical rainforest, a cactus-filled desert, and a changing landscape of flowers and foliage. Its annual Holiday Train Show features model trains whizzing through gardens and past replicas of city landmarks made of plant parts including nuts, bark, and leaves.

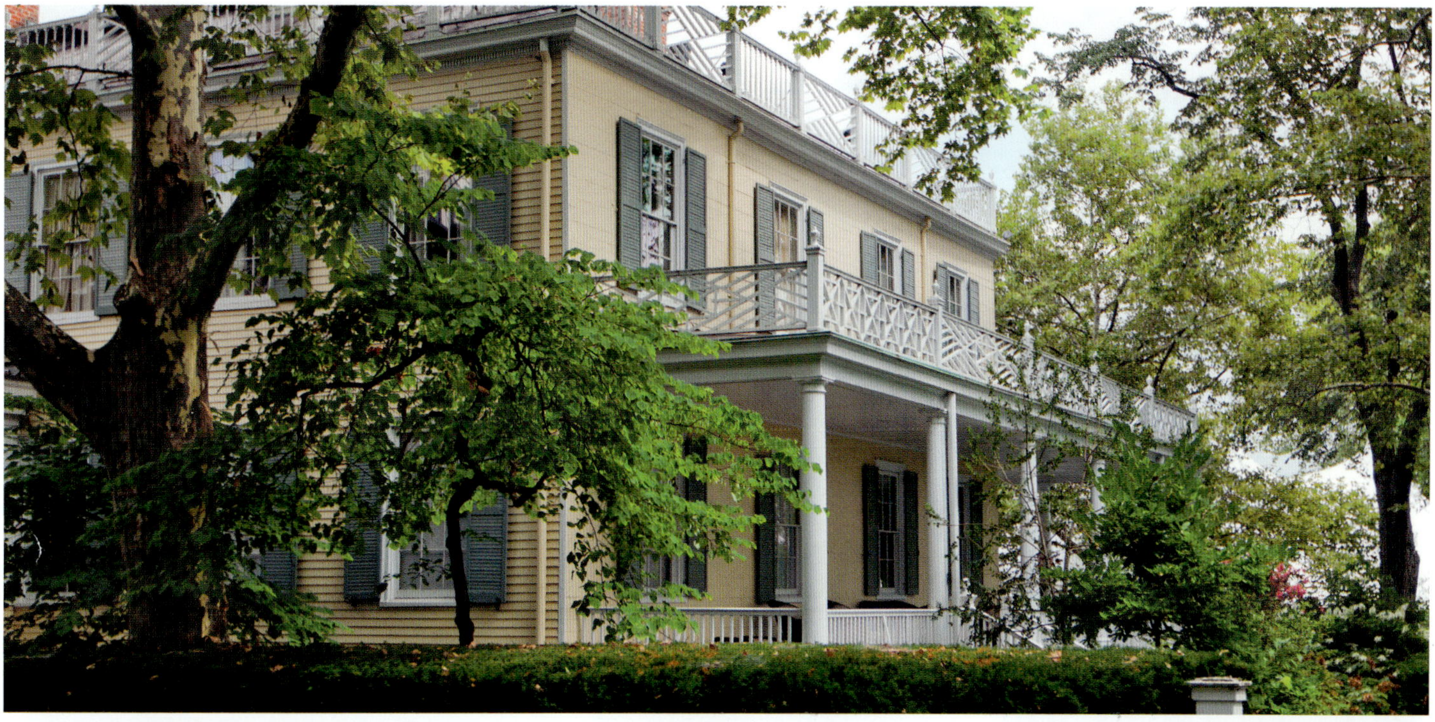

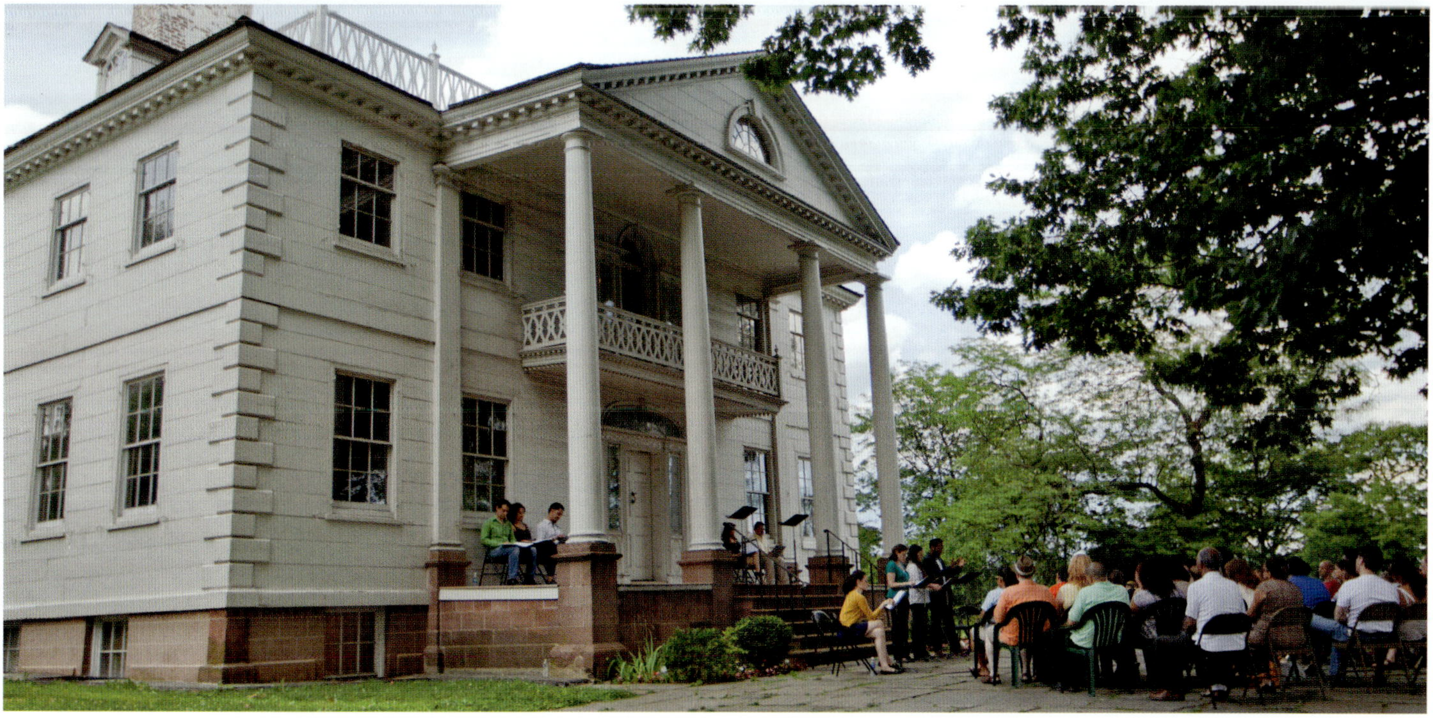

Gracie Mansion *(top)*

This beautiful Federal-style home that overlooks the East River was built by wealthy merchant Archibald Gracie in 1799 and is one of the oldest wood structures in Manhattan. Today, it is owned by the city and is the official residence of the mayor of the City of New York. One hour tours are offered most Wednesdays.

Morris-Jumel Mansion *(bottom)*

Built in 1765 as a country home for a British army colonel and his American wife, this hilltop mansion in Harlem Heights was strategically important during the American Revolution when it served as George Washington's headquarters. Manhattan's oldest house is now a museum.

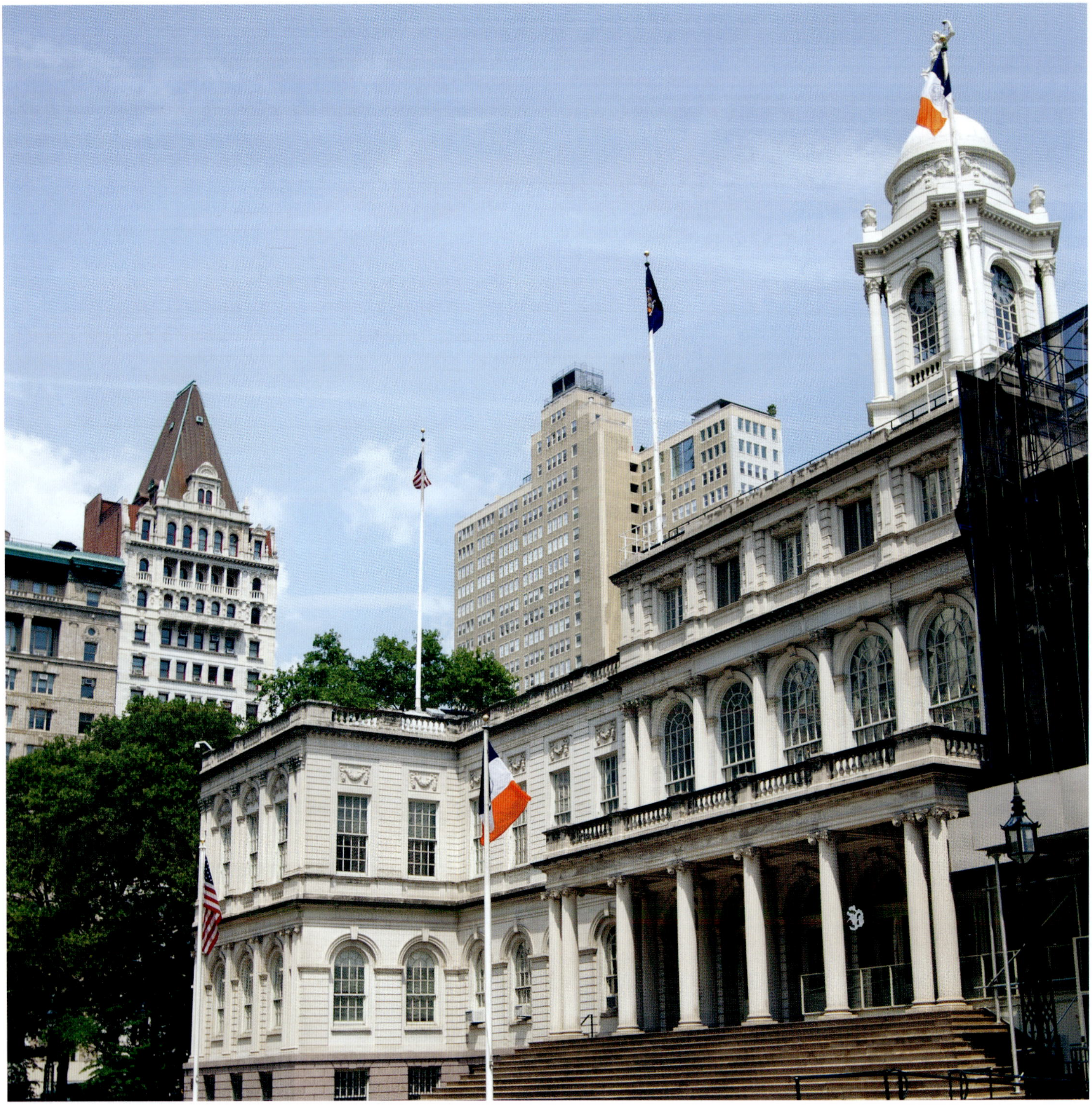

New York City Hall

The seat of New York City government since 1812, this French Renaissance-style building houses the mayor's offices and City Council chambers. Tours are offered of the American-Georgian interior with its sweeping grand marble stairway and coffered dome, which was added in a 1912 restoration.

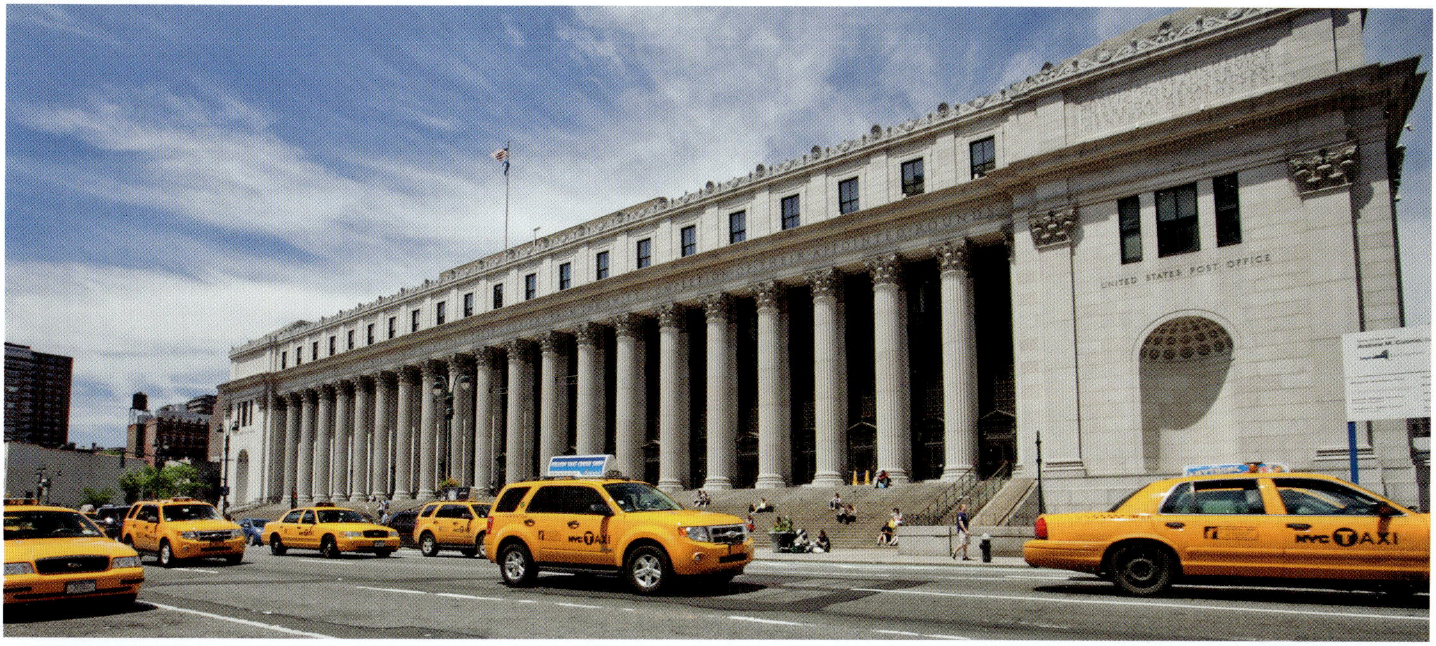

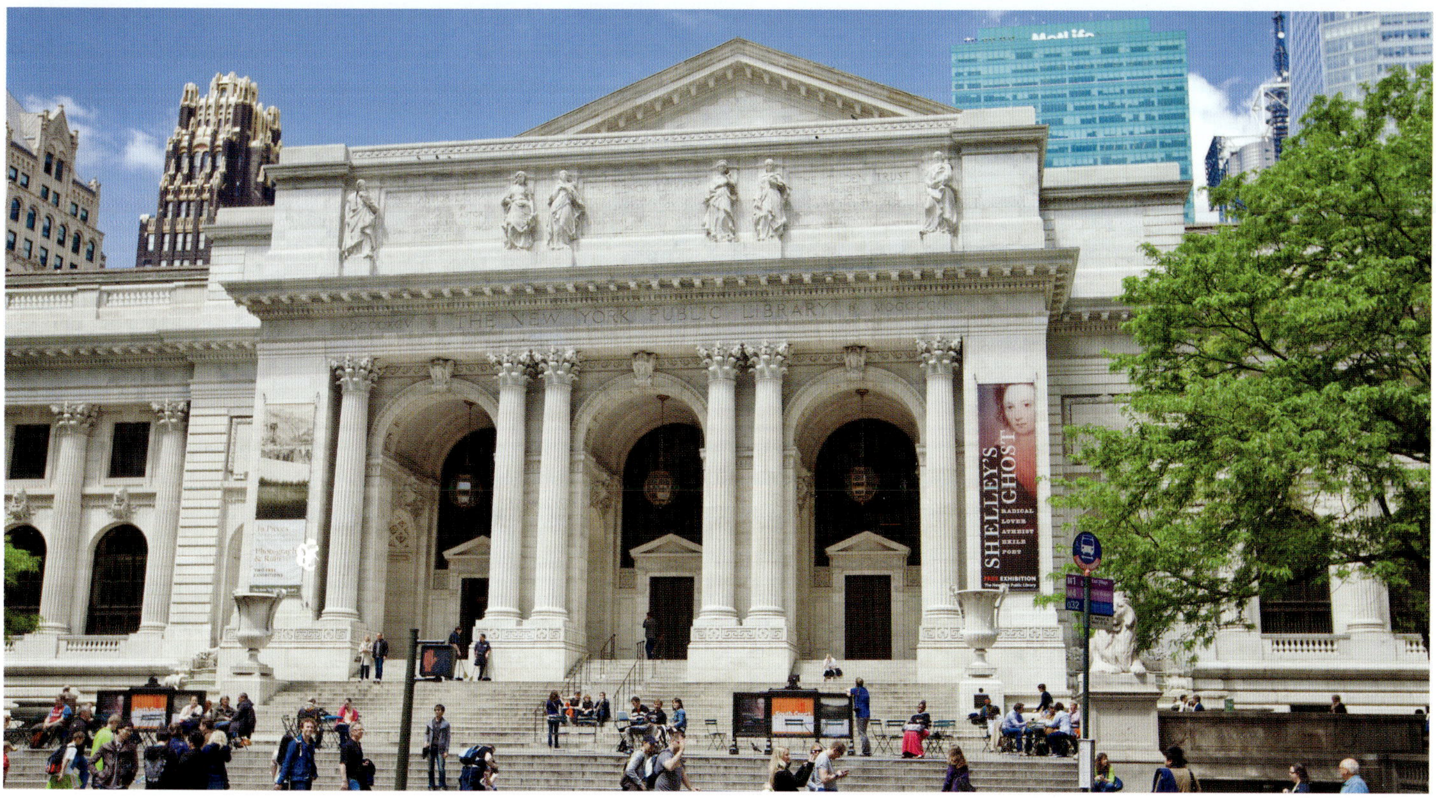

Post Office Building *(top)*

Located on 8th Avenue and spanning two city blocks, the James A. Farley Building, named after the nation's 53rd Postmaster General, was completed in 1913 and designated a New York City Landmark in 1966. This majestic Beaux-Arts style building showcases 33 sweeping steps which lead up to 20 Corinthian colonnades.

Public Library *(bottom)*

The main branch of the city's public library system sits on what was once the Croton Reservoir. A leading reference center with miles of underground shelf space for its vast collection, the Beaux-Arts building is flanked by two marble lion statues nicknamed "Patience" and "Fortitude" by former Mayor Fiorello LaGuardia.

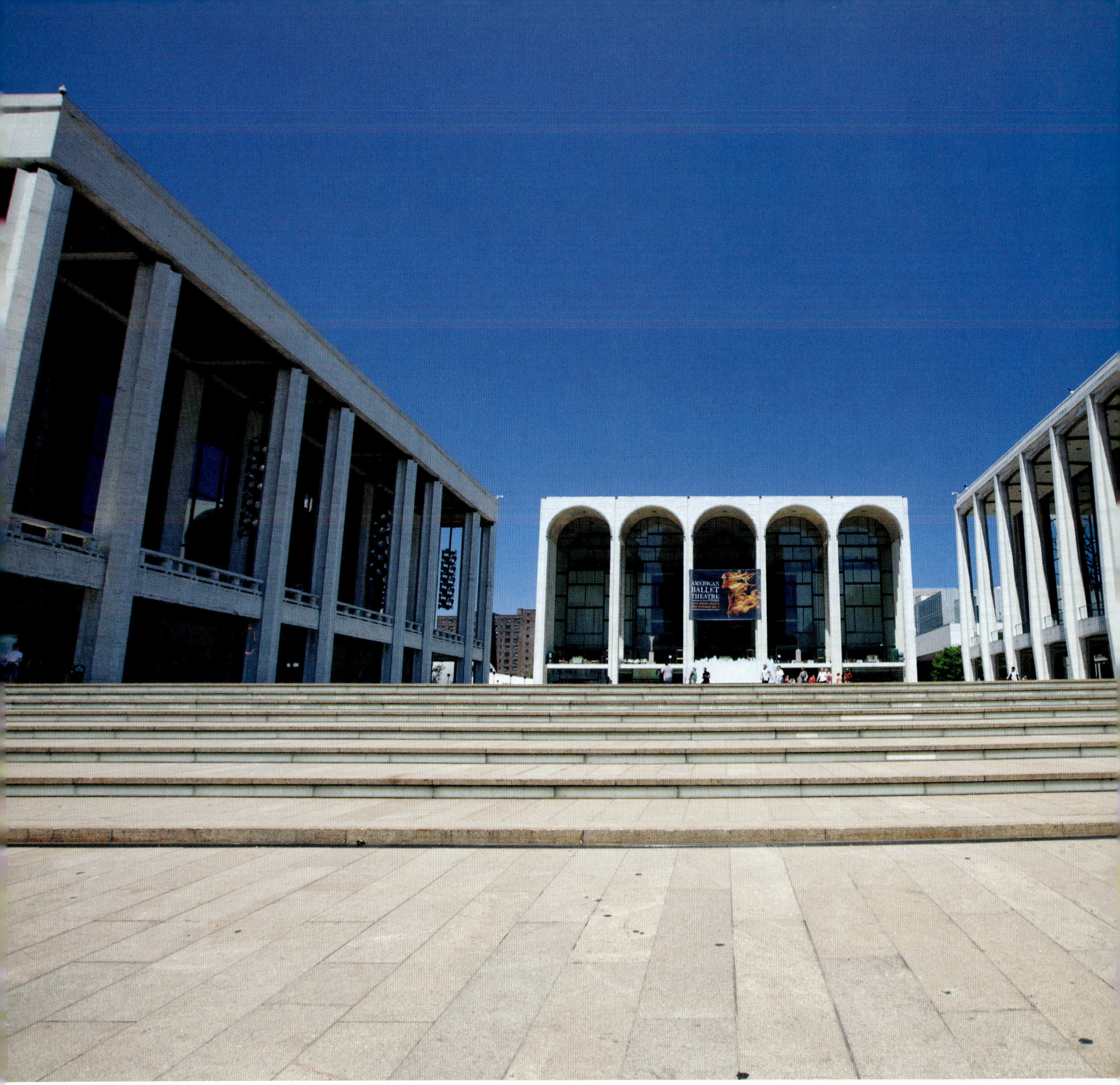

Lincoln Center Plaza

Home to the Metropolitan Opera, the New York City Ballet and the New York Philharmonic Orchestra, Lincoln Center is a performing arts mecca on the Upper West Side. The plaza becomes an outdoor extension each summer with Lincoln Center Out of Doors, a series of free music and dance performances.

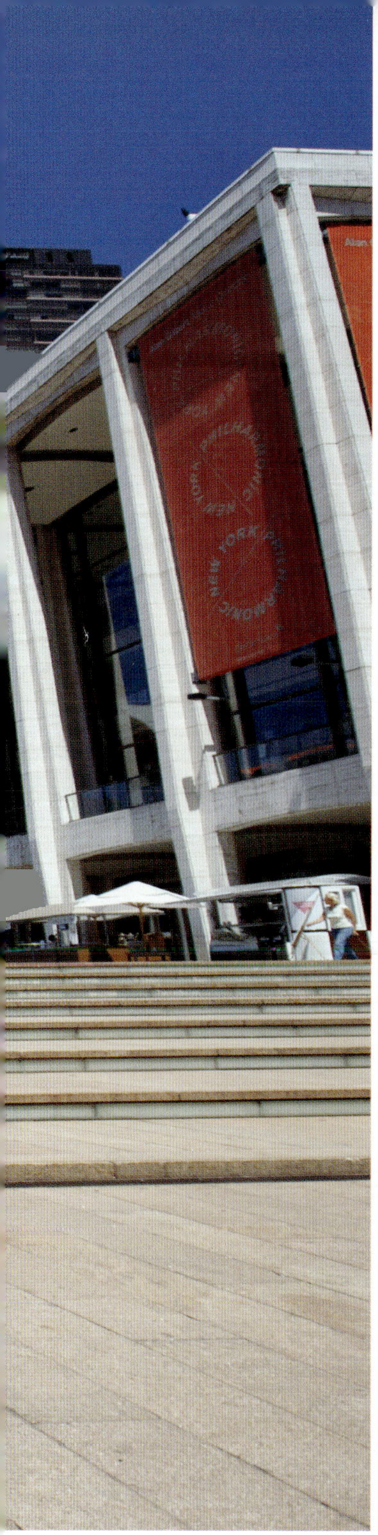

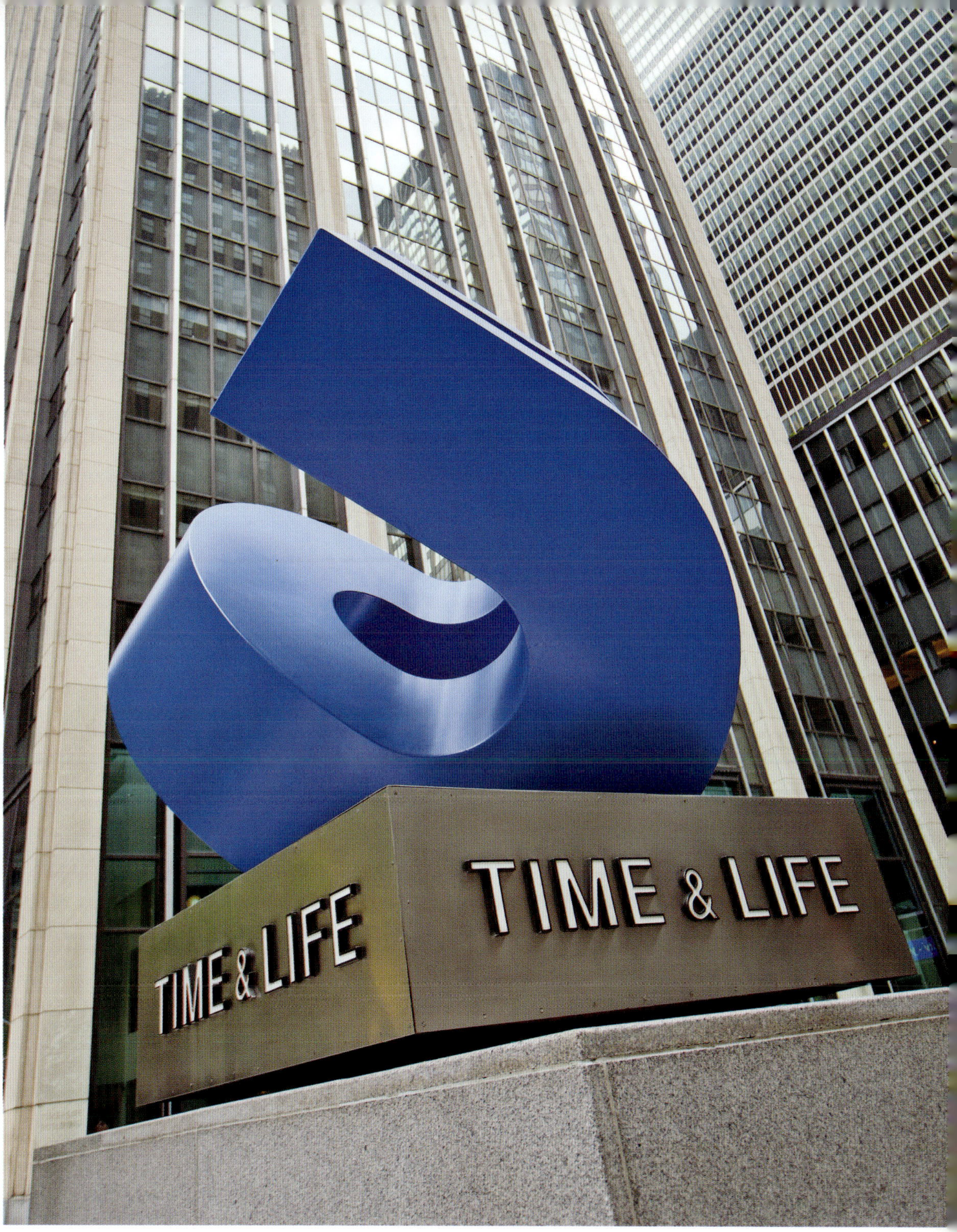

Time-Life Building

Time Inc., publisher of *Time*, *Sports Illustrated*, and *People*, has been housed in this modernism limestone building since 1959. Located in Rockefeller Center, *Curved Cube* by sculptor William Crovello has been a presence outside the Time-Life Building since it was installed in 1972.

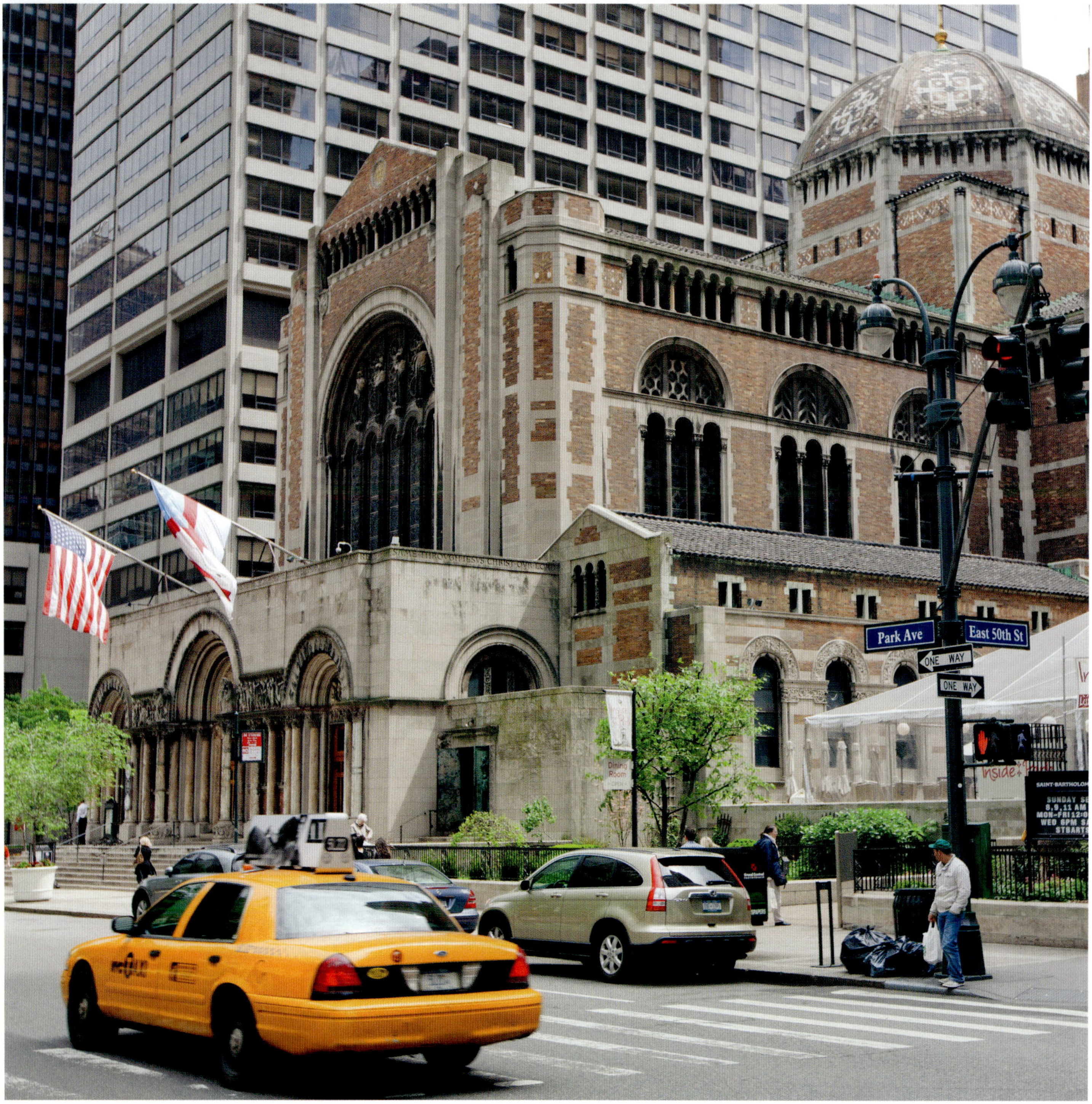

St. Bartholomew's Church

Known as "St. Bart's," this landmark Episcopal church on Park Avenue has daily services, concerts, a soup kitchen, and an outdoor café. Built in 1917 with salmon and cream colored bricks, Byzantine style, it features breathtaking stained-glass windows and a tile-pattern dome.

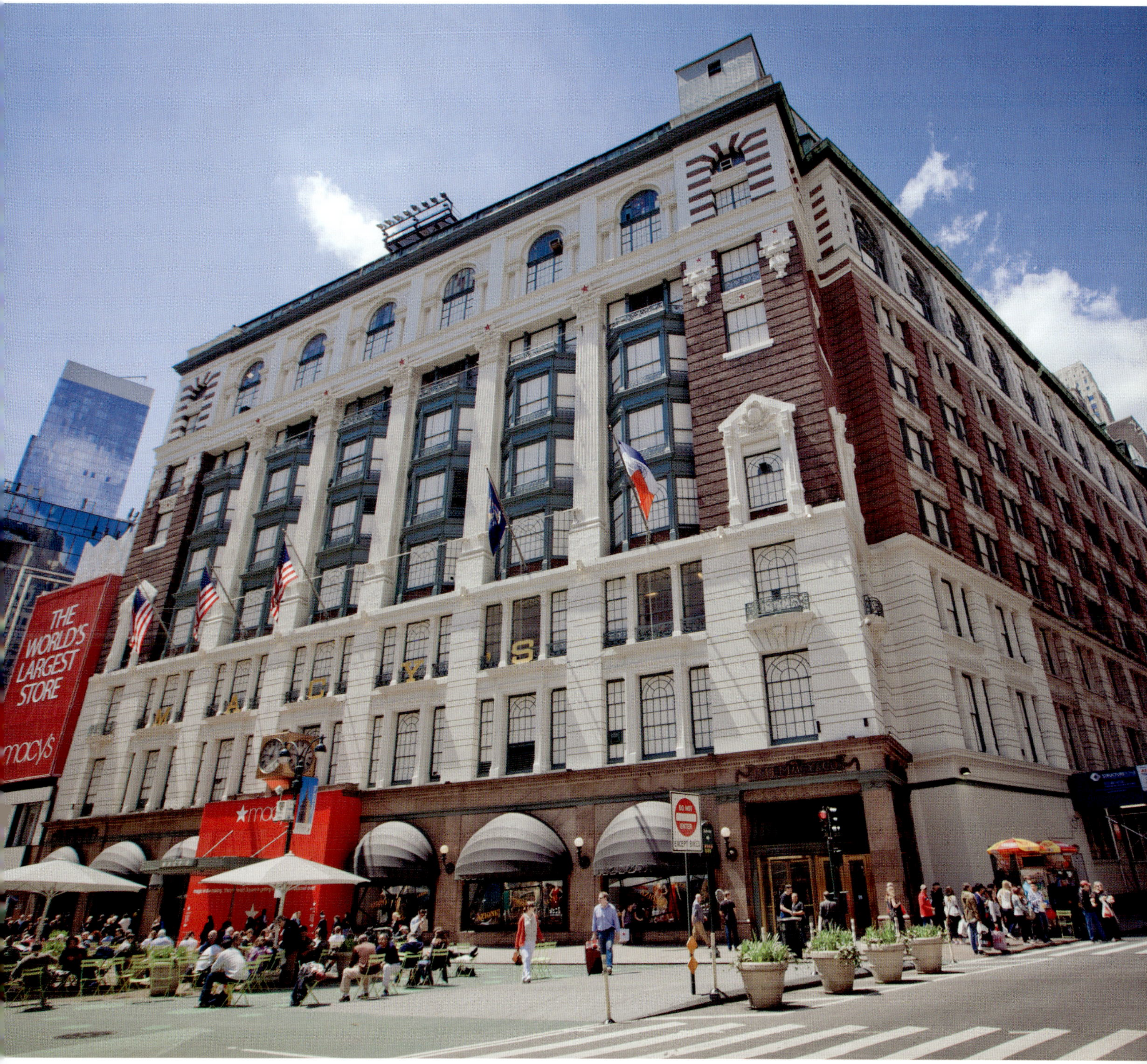

Macy's

Billed as the "world's largest" department store, Macy's flagship Herald Square location takes up an entire city block. Sponsor of the annual Macy's Thanksgiving Day Parade, Fourth of July fireworks, and famed Christmas windows, the retail behemoth recently unveiled "the world's largest shoe floor" with over 300,000 pairs on sale.

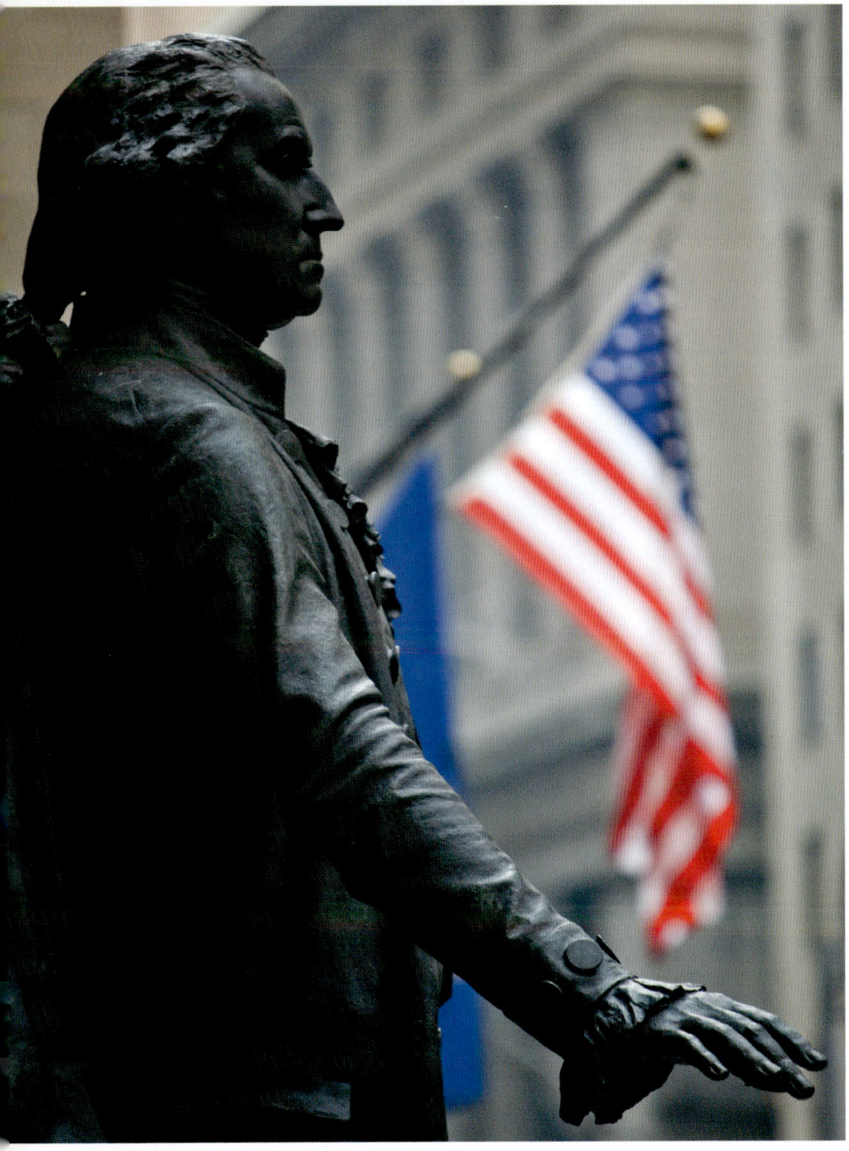

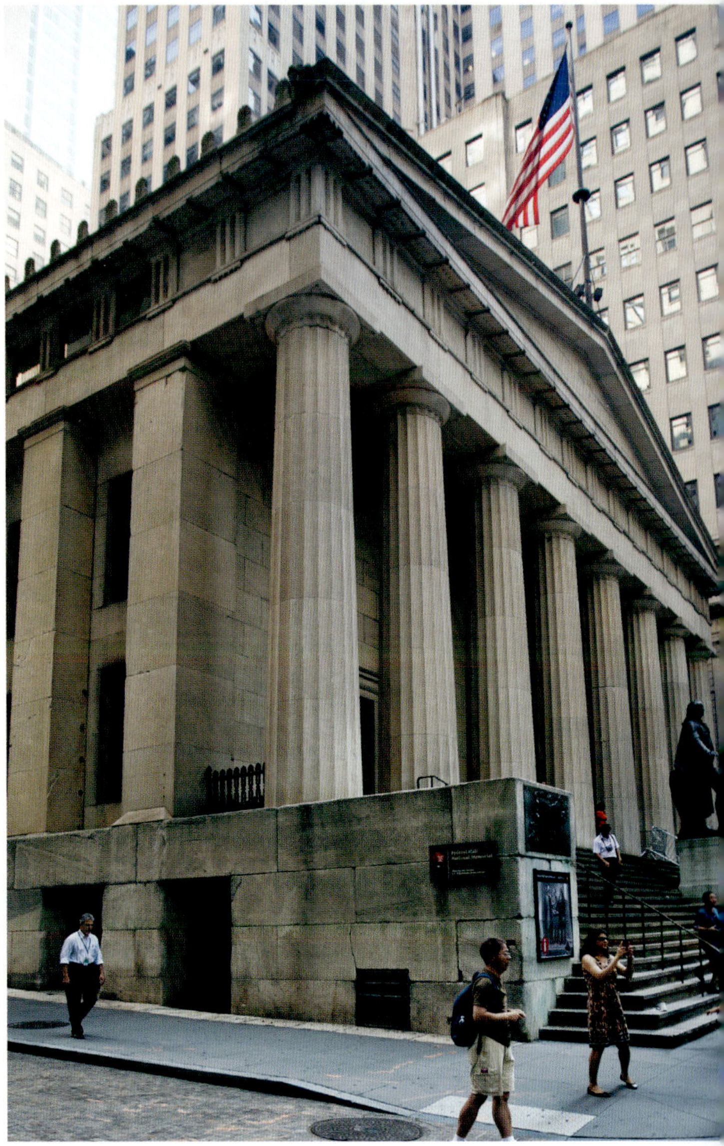

Federal Building *(left and right)*

An example of Greek Revival architecture, the Federal Hall National Memorial is where Revolutionary War General George Washington became the nation's first president, commemorated by the statue outside. The first Congress, Supreme Court, and Executive Branch offices were all located here when New York was the country's capital.

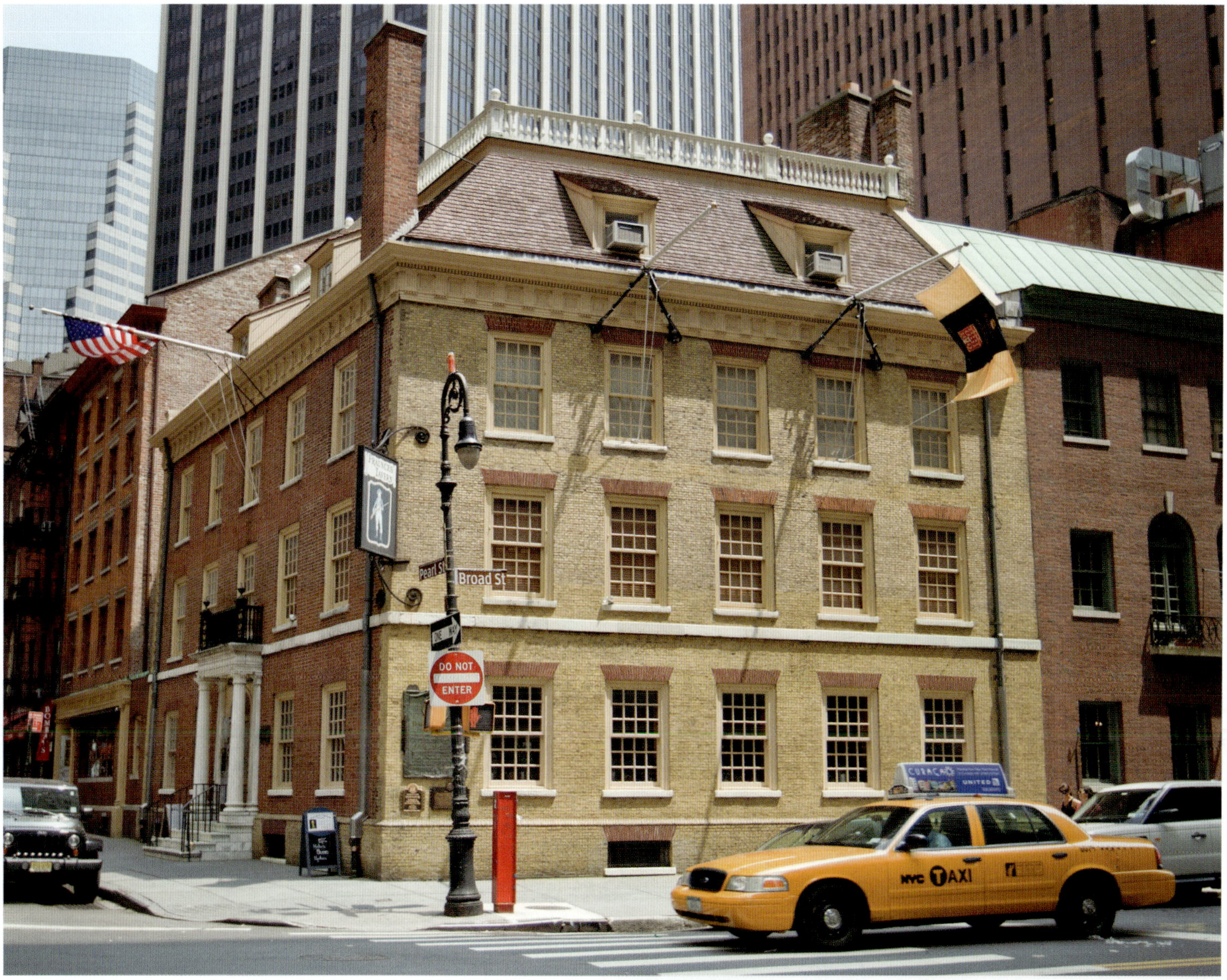

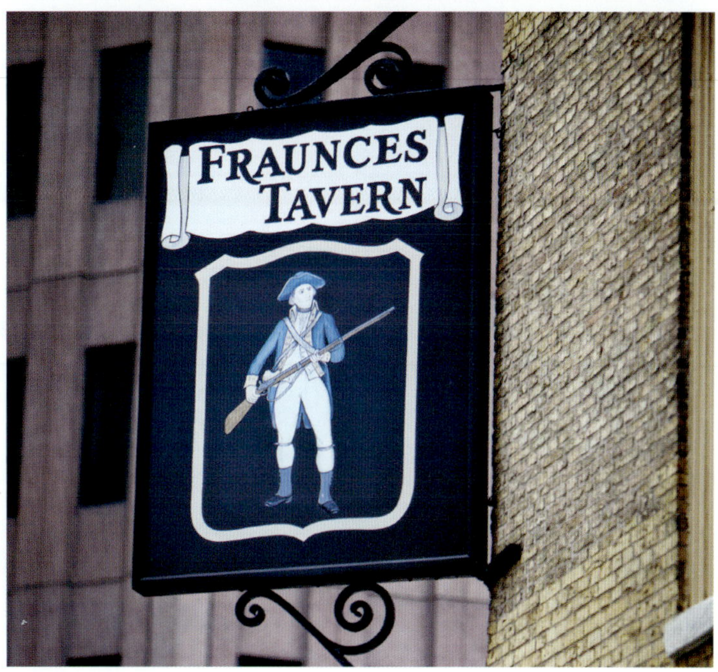

Fraunces Tavern *(above and right)*

A former meeting hall and inn, Fraunces Tavern is the site of George Washington's farewell to his officers in 1783. The building later housed the Departments of War, Treasury, and Foreign Affairs. Now a bar and museum, it contains such relics as a lock of Washington's hair and one of his false teeth.

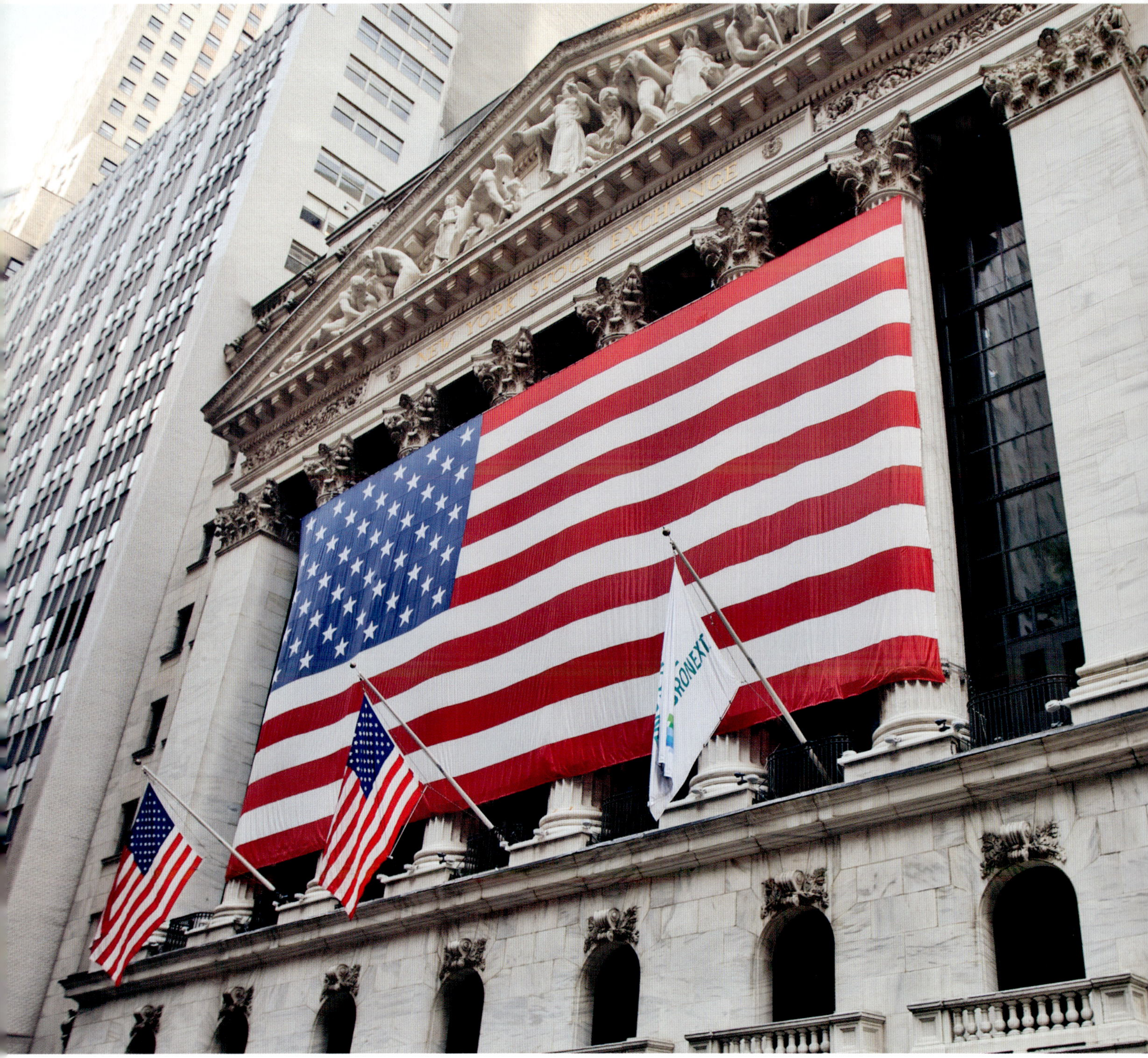

NYSE *(above)*

The New York Stock Exchange, or the "Big Board," is the world's largest stock exchange. Completed in 1903 and located on Wall Street, the Exchange Building was designed by architect George B. Post and considered a masterpiece. Built to resemble a Greek temple, six Corinthian columns rise to a beautiful series of sculptures.

Charging Bull *(opposite)*

The iconic statue in the financial district at the southern tip of Manhattan has become the symbol of Wall Street. A popular photo op, the 11-foot-tall bronze bovine was created by Arturo Di Modica and gifted to the city as a symbol of the "strength and power of the American people."

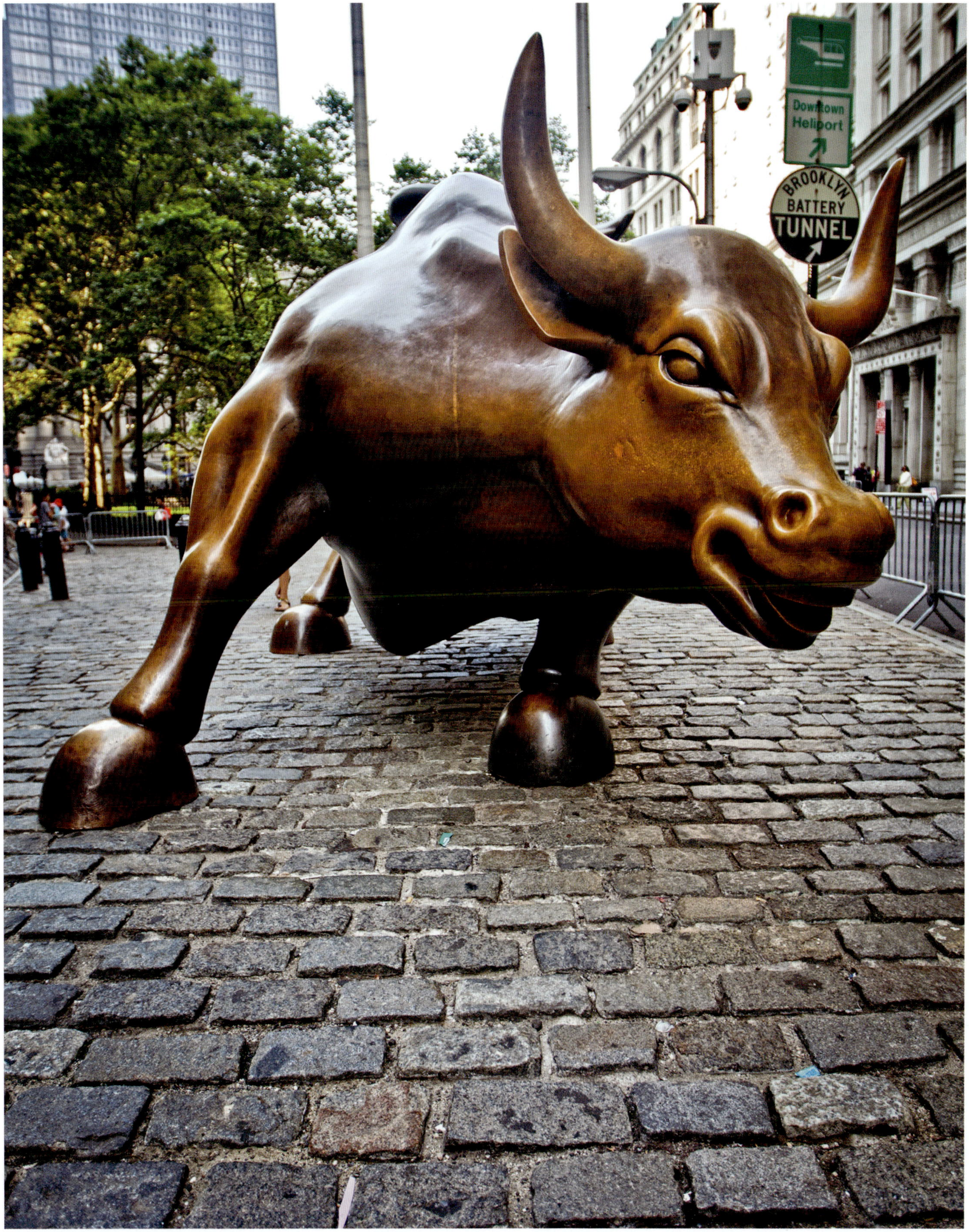
Downtown
Heliport
BROOKLYN
BATTERY
TUNNEL

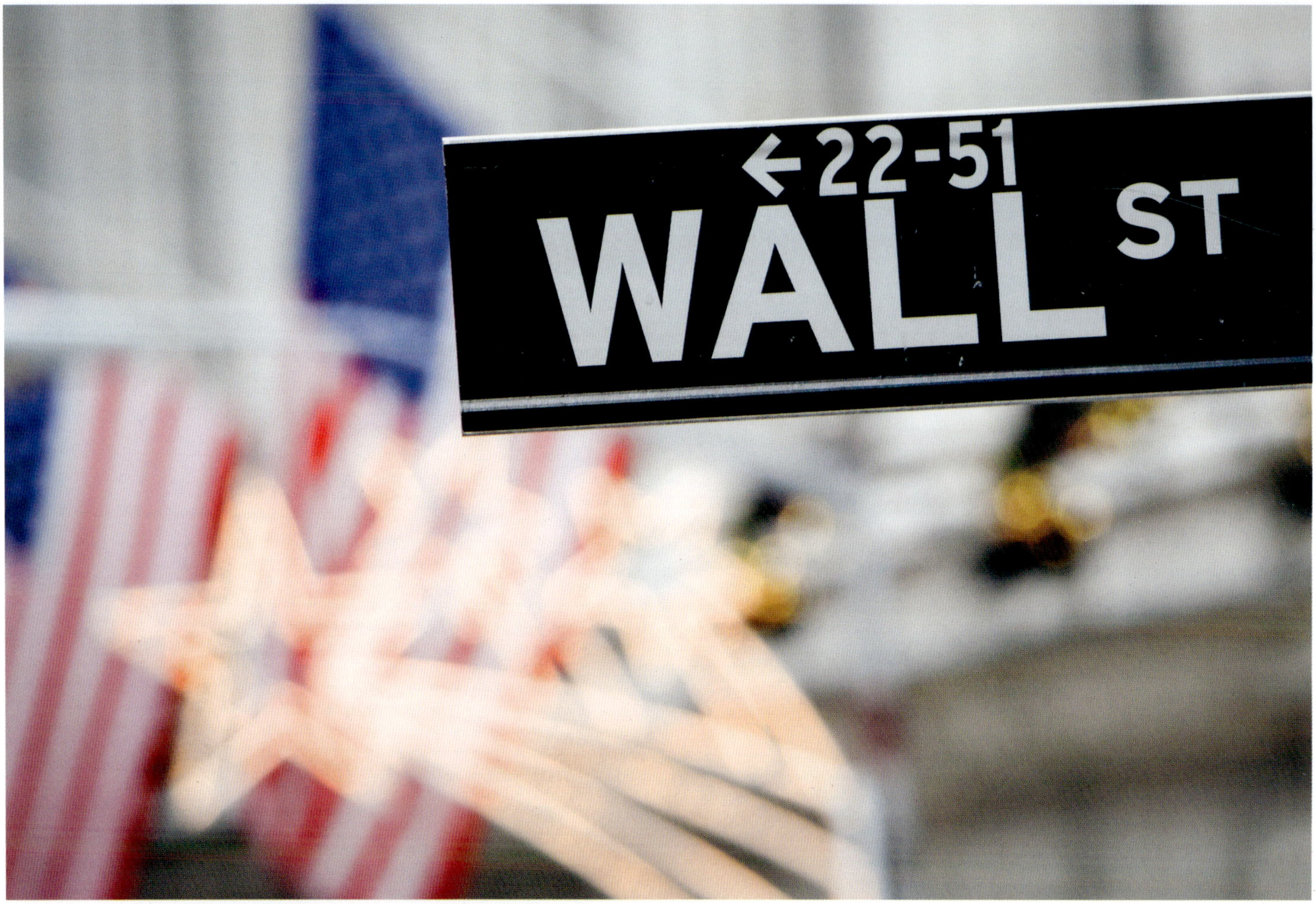

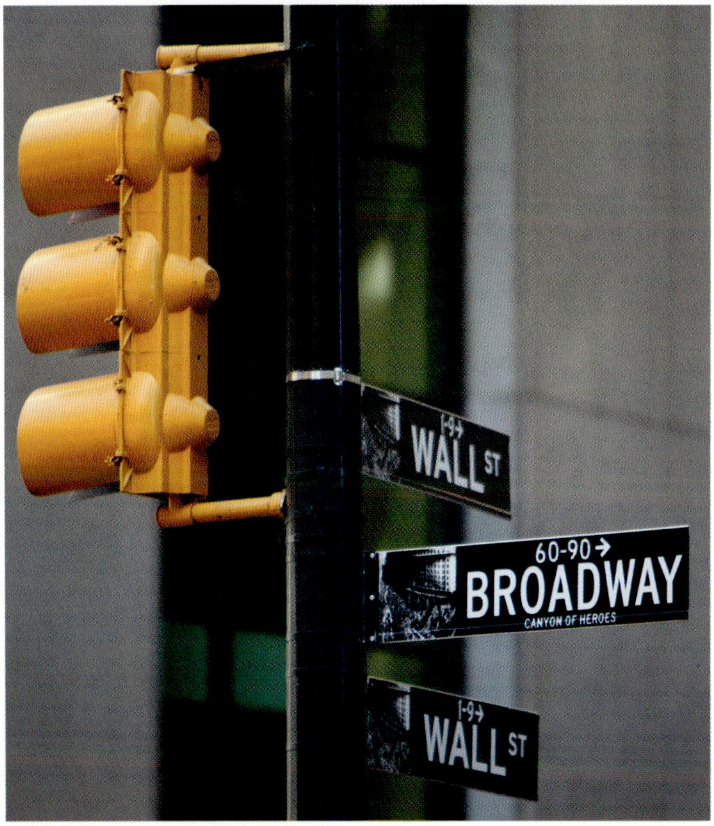

Wall Street *(above and left)*

Synonymous with money and high finance, Wall Street was once the site of an actual wall built to protect against possible attacks by Native Americans and the British. Today, it remains a global financial engine and home of the New York Stock Exchange and the Museum of American Finance.

Mounted Patrol *(opposite)*

New York City's Mounted Unit originated in 1871 and is one of the most recognized in the nation. Visitors are often drawn to these "10- foot-tall cops" for photo opportunities, making these officers wonderful ambassadors to the city. Romantics may have a nostalgic attachment to them, but these units have proven invaluable because of their visibility.

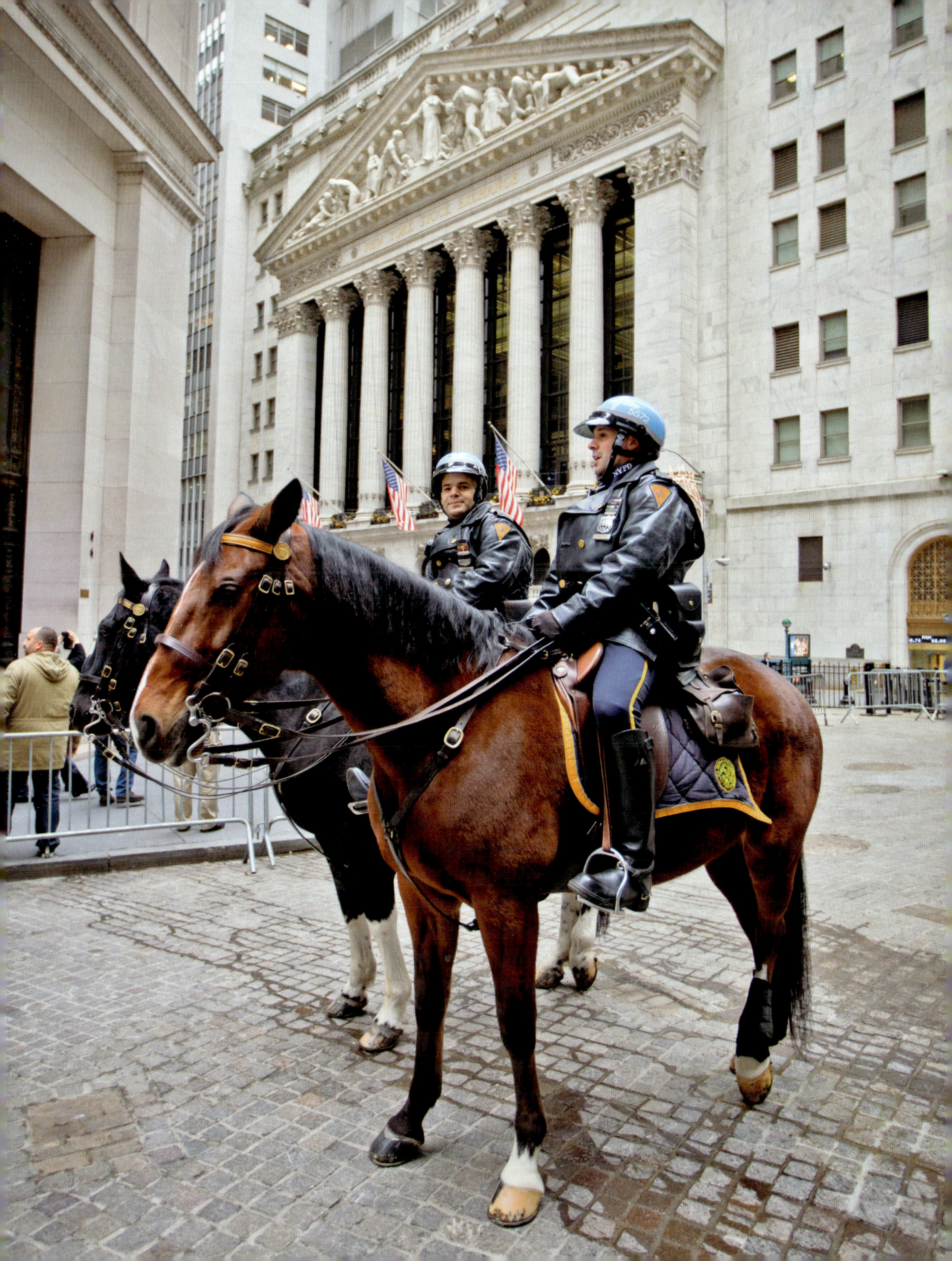
NEW YORK STOCK EXCHANGE
5572
NYPD

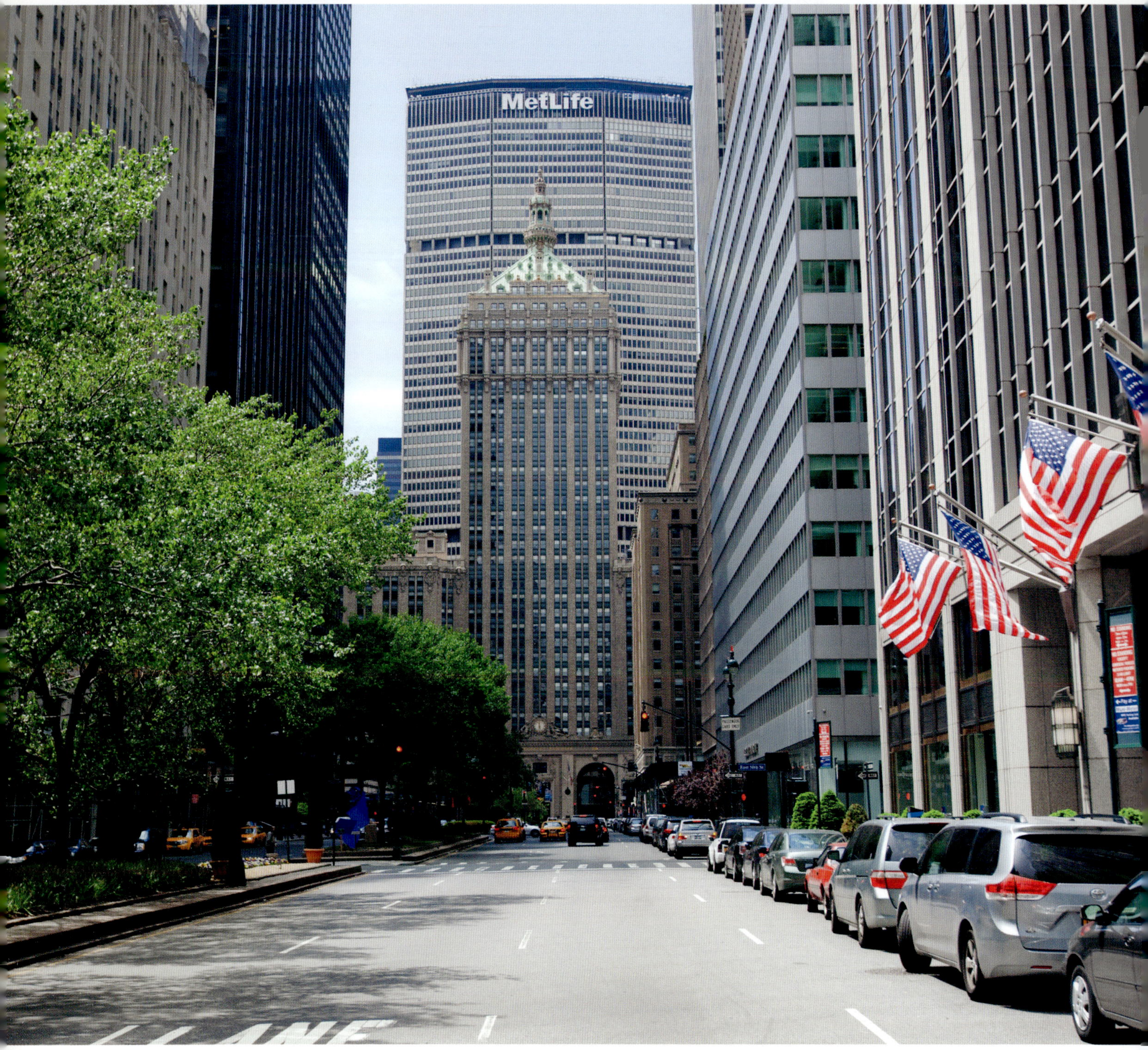

Park Avenue *(above)*

Look Uptown along the wide boulevard that is Park Avenue and you'll see rows of elegant apartment buildings that are home to the city's power brokers. Look Downtown and you'll see some of the modern skyscrapers that are headquarters of the world's largest corporations where they work.

Waldorf Astoria Hotel *(opposite, top)*

A symbol of old-world elegance, the legendary Art Deco luxury Park Avenue hotel has housed many of the world's most famous celebrities and world leaders. It once had its own private elevator and underground railway platform for President Franklin D. Roosevelt and other VIPs to slip away unnoticed.

FAO Schwarz *(opposite, bottom)*

Here on Fifth Avenue is a wonderland filled with life-sized stuffed animals, a candy store, and more toys, puzzles, books, and Barbies than any child could imagine. Maybe that's why some parents tell their children it's a museum, not a toy store. Don't miss the gigantic floor piano that stared in Tom Hanks' film *Big*.

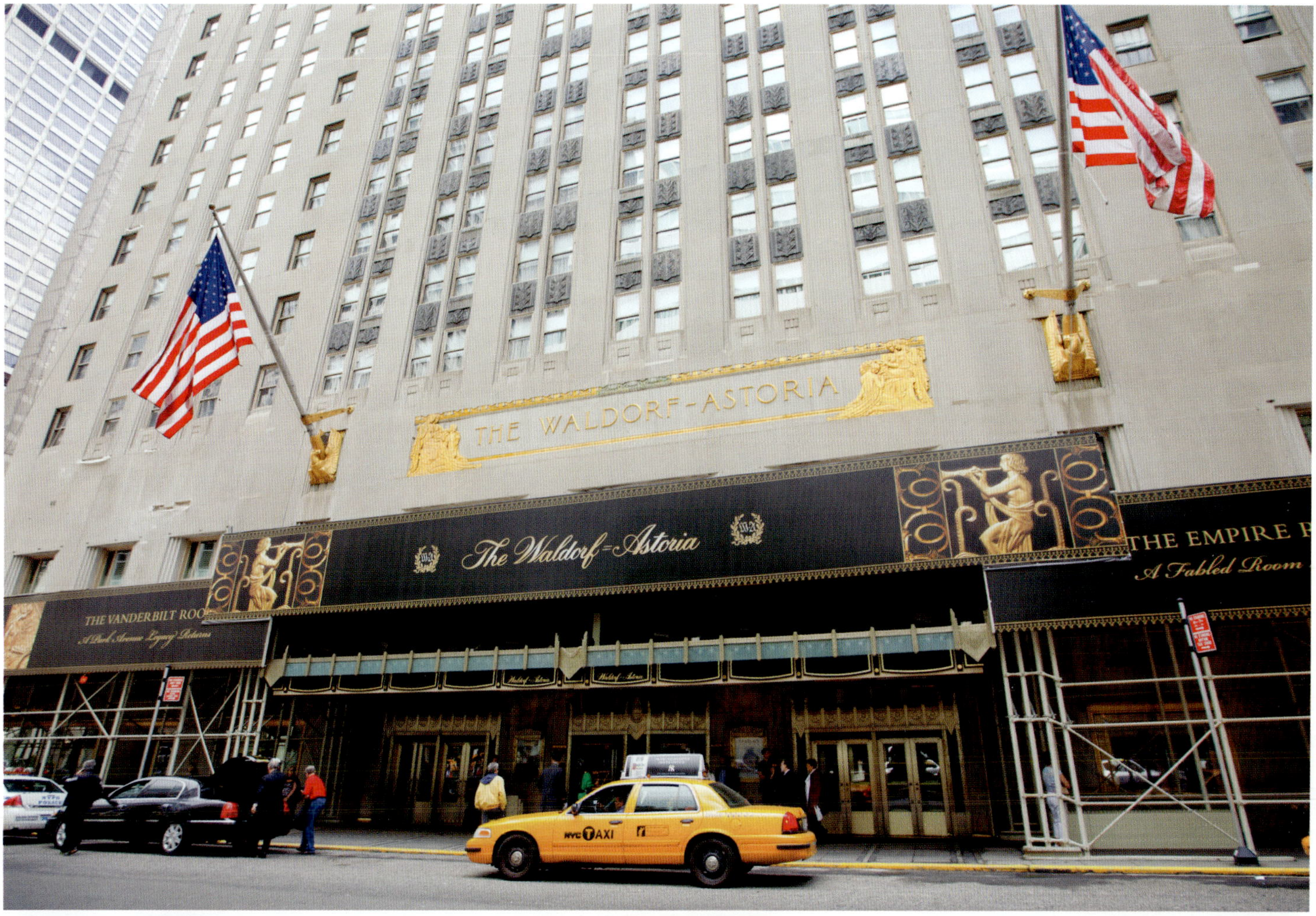
THE WALDORF-ASTORIA
The Waldorf=Astoria
THE VANDERBILT ROO
THE EMPIRE R
A Fabled Room
NYC TAXI

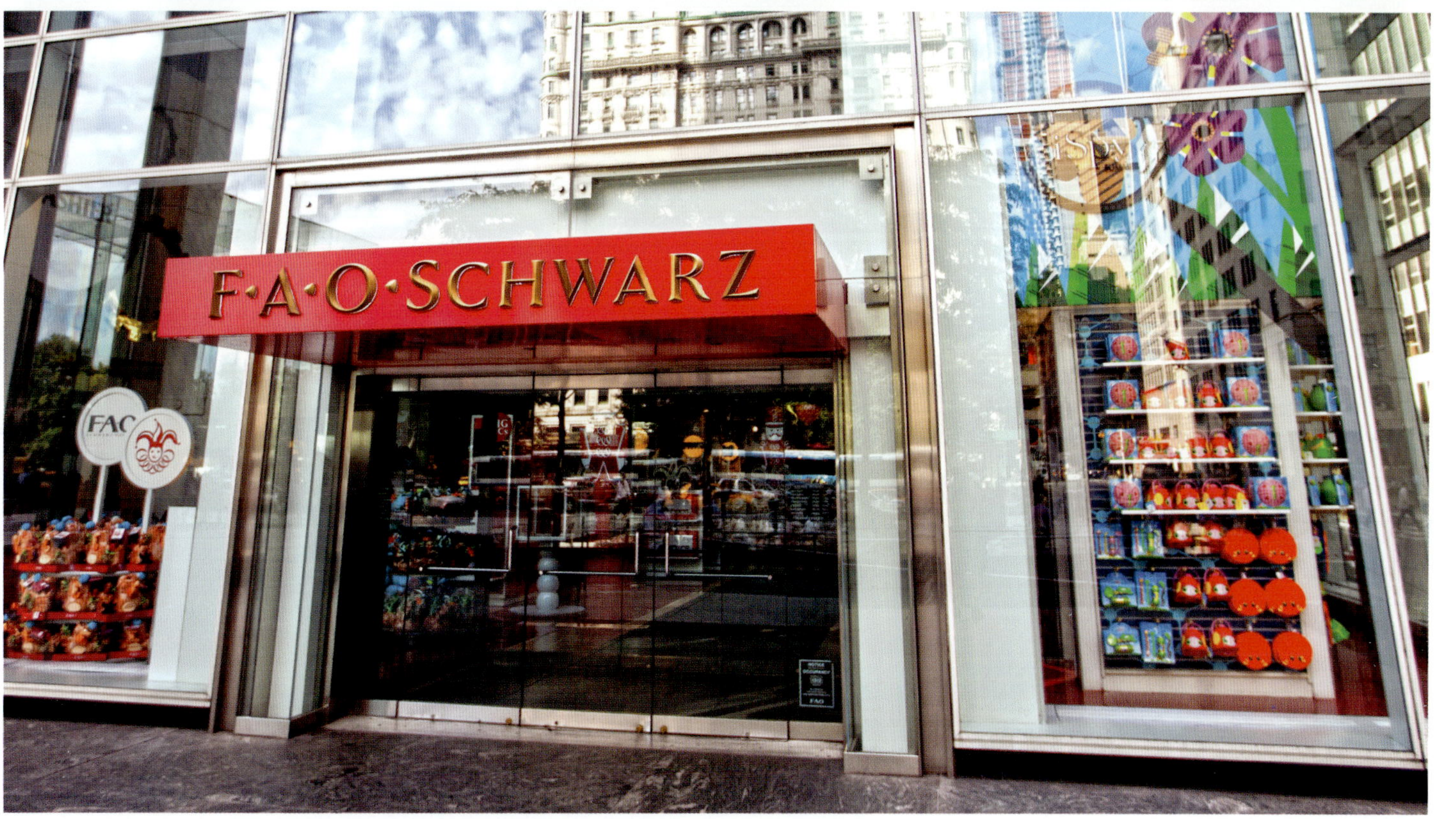
F·A·O·SCHWARZ

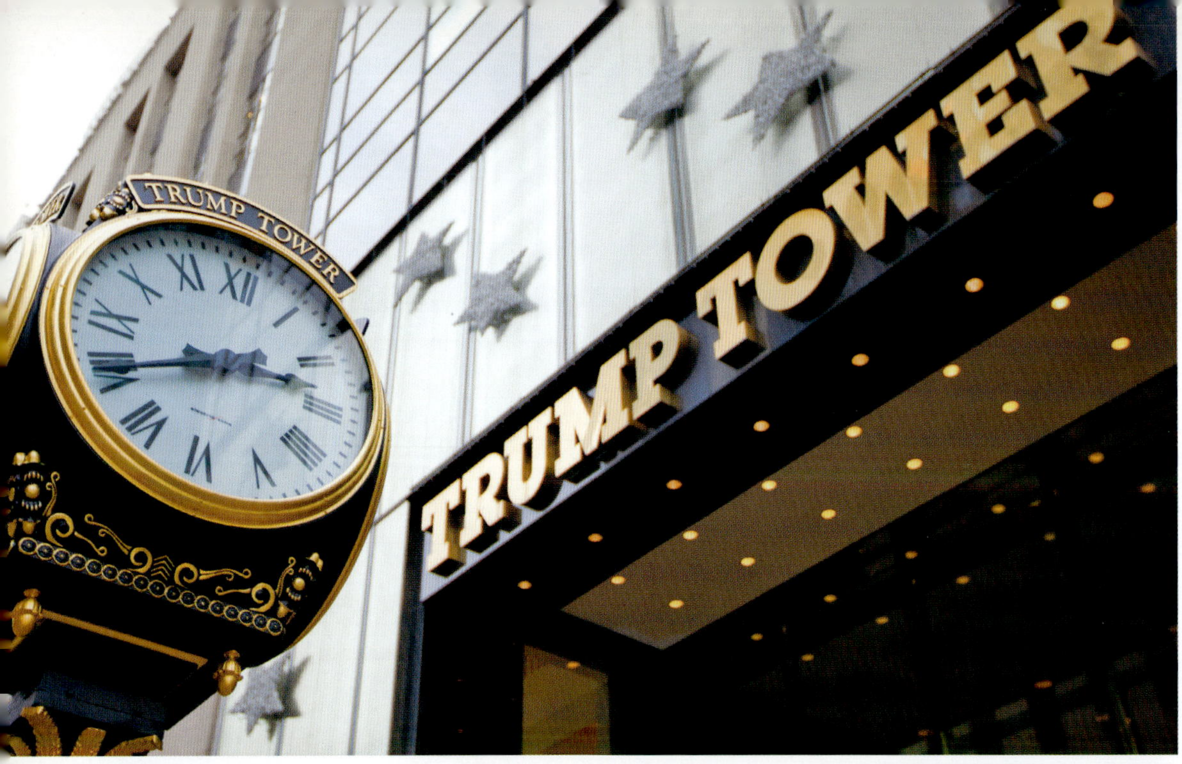

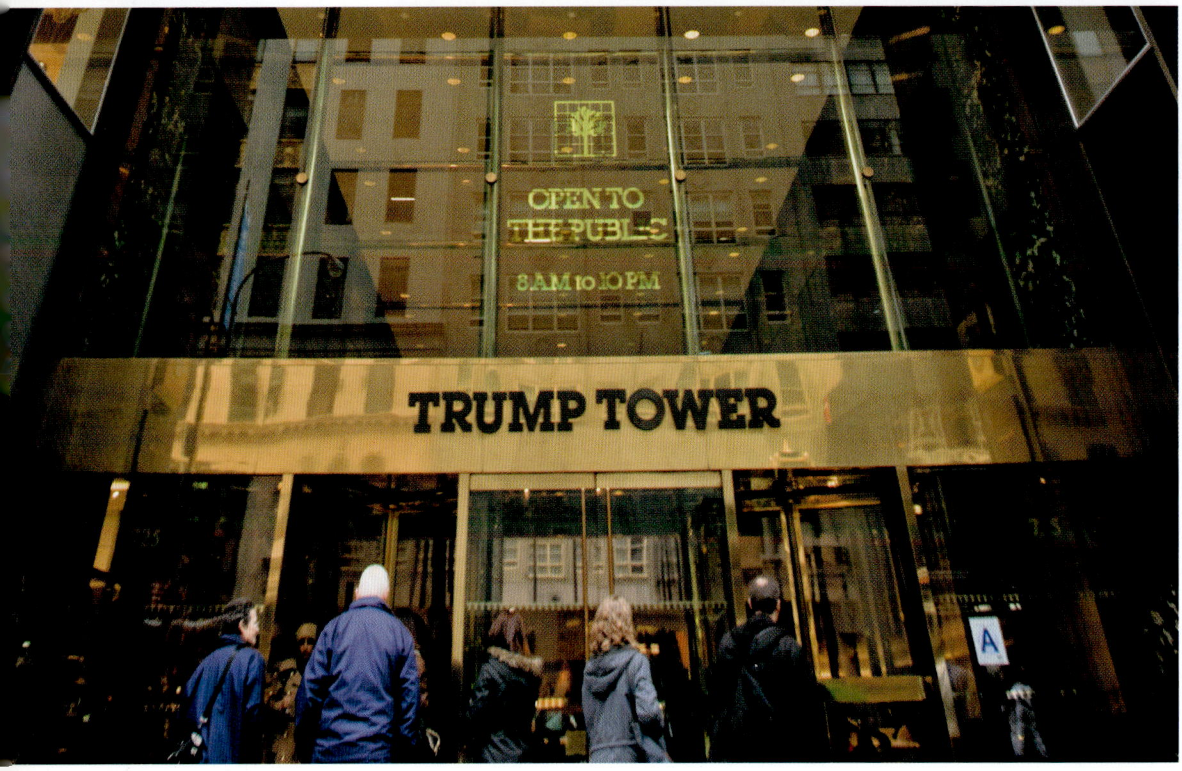

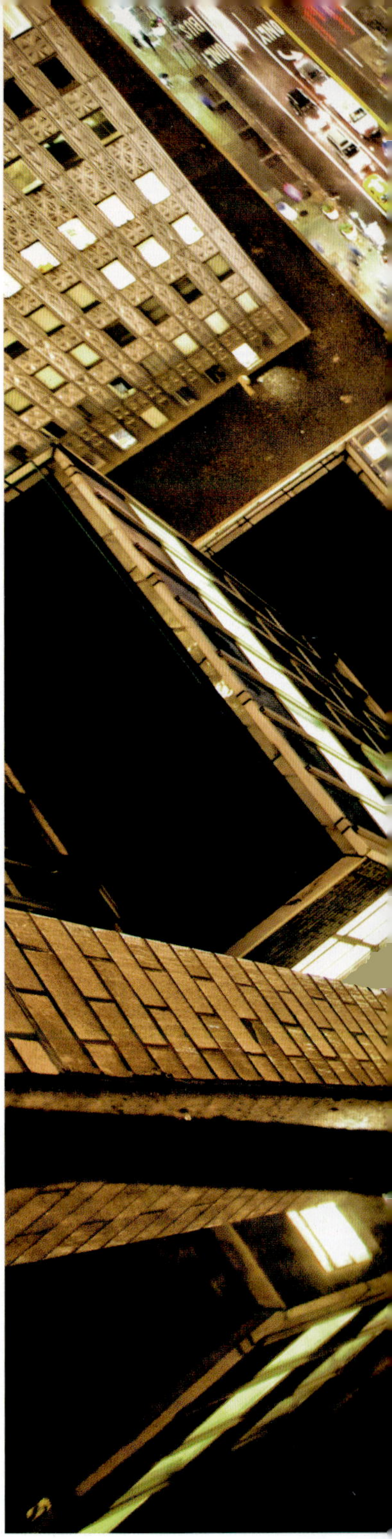

Trump Tower and Clock *(top)*

While real estate developer Donald Trump is no wallflower, he became a household name with the airing of his NBC show *The Apprentice* starring this Fifth Avenue glass tower with his name emblazoned across the front in massive gold lettering.

Trump Tower *(bottom)*

Trump Tower is a 58-story luxury condominium next door to Tiffany & Co. It features a lavish, six-story-high atrium with a cascading waterfall and pink marble walls. Many famous residents live there with soaring views of Central Park, including "The Donald" himself, who calls the penthouse home.

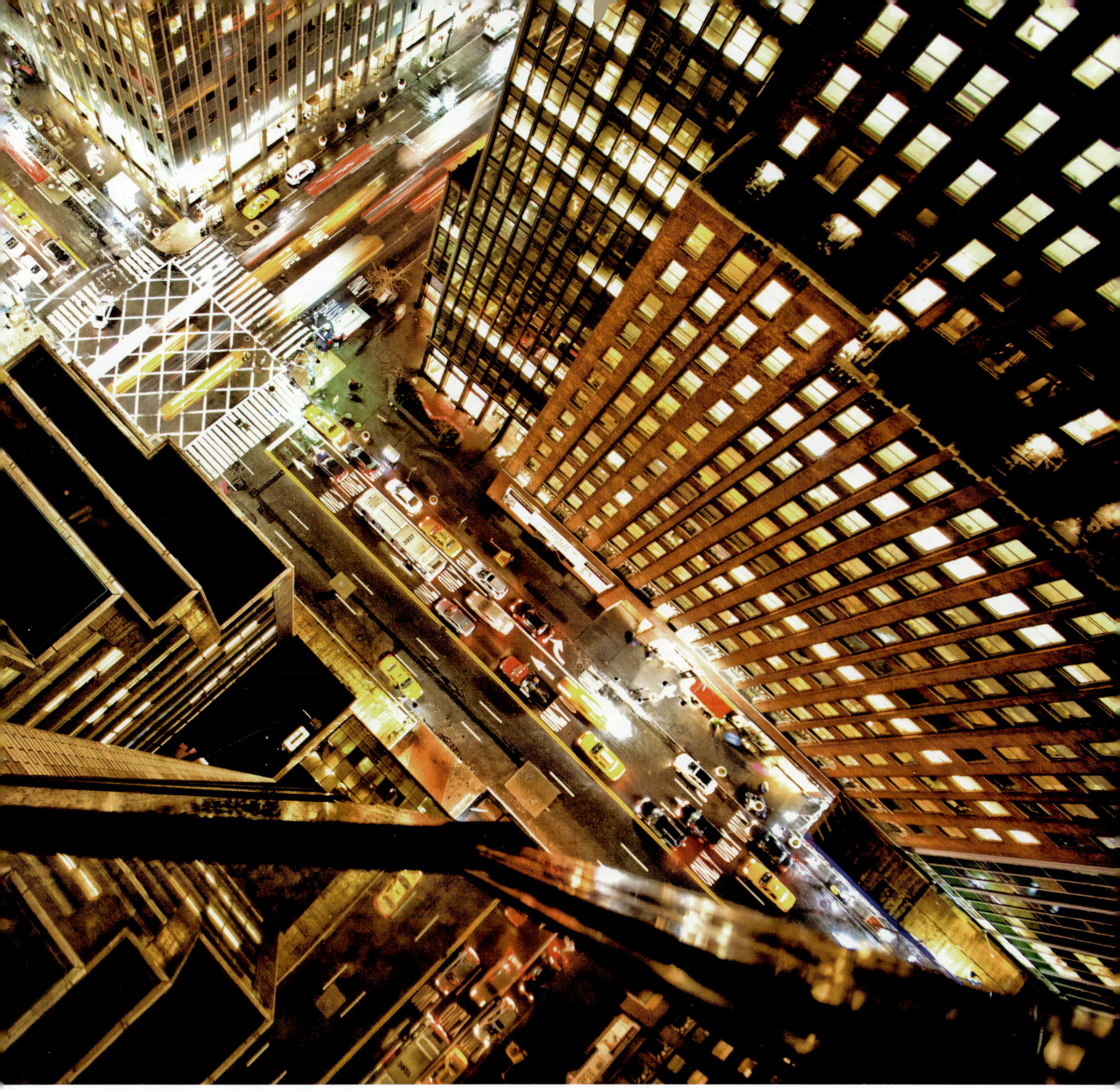

Midtown Streets

Look out any Midtown office building and you'll see a sea of traffic as taxis, cars, buses, pedestrians, and bicyclists vie for a piece of the crowded streets below. Look up at the massive skyscrapers standing shoulder-to-shoulder and you'll see a wall of glass that seems to stretch to the sky.

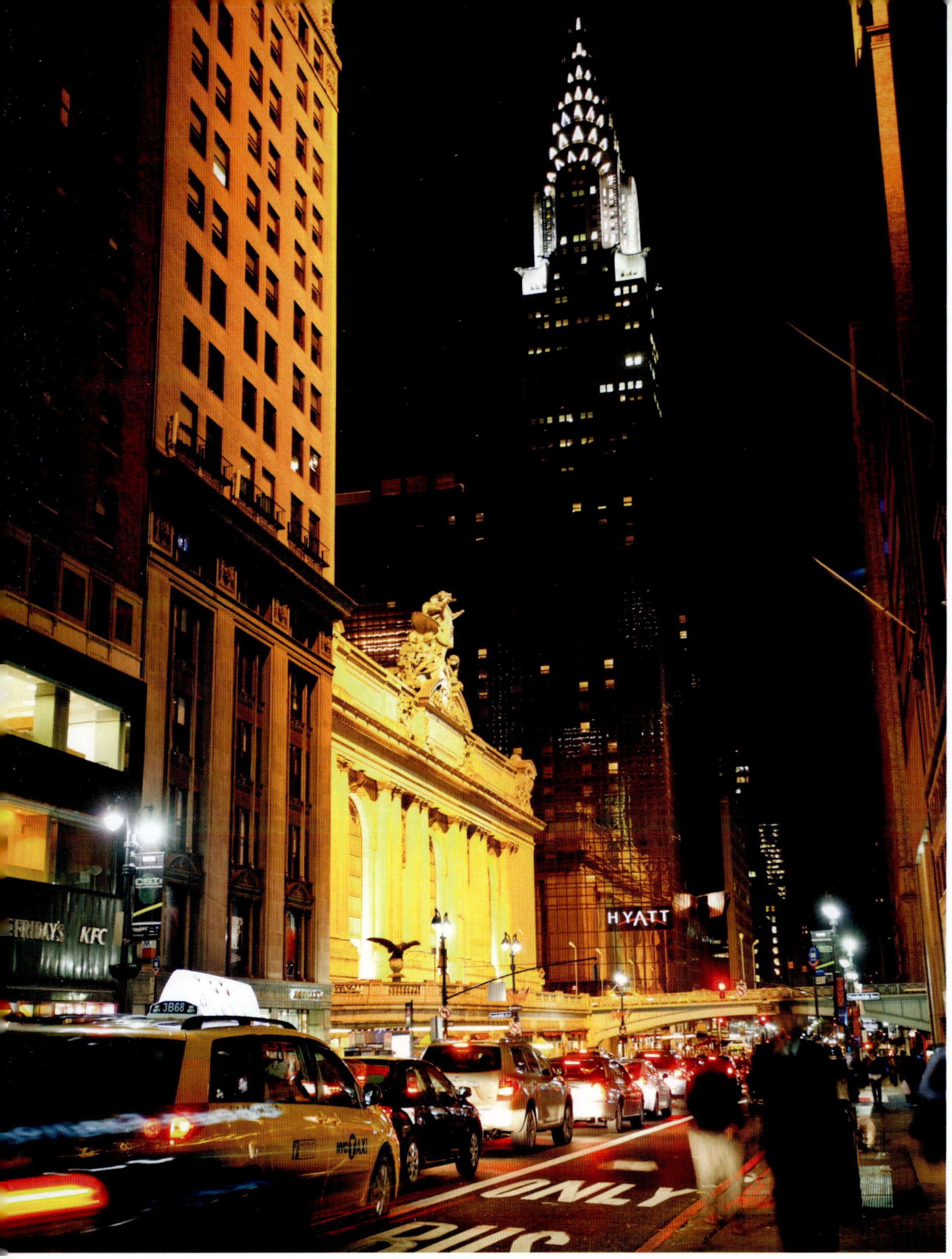

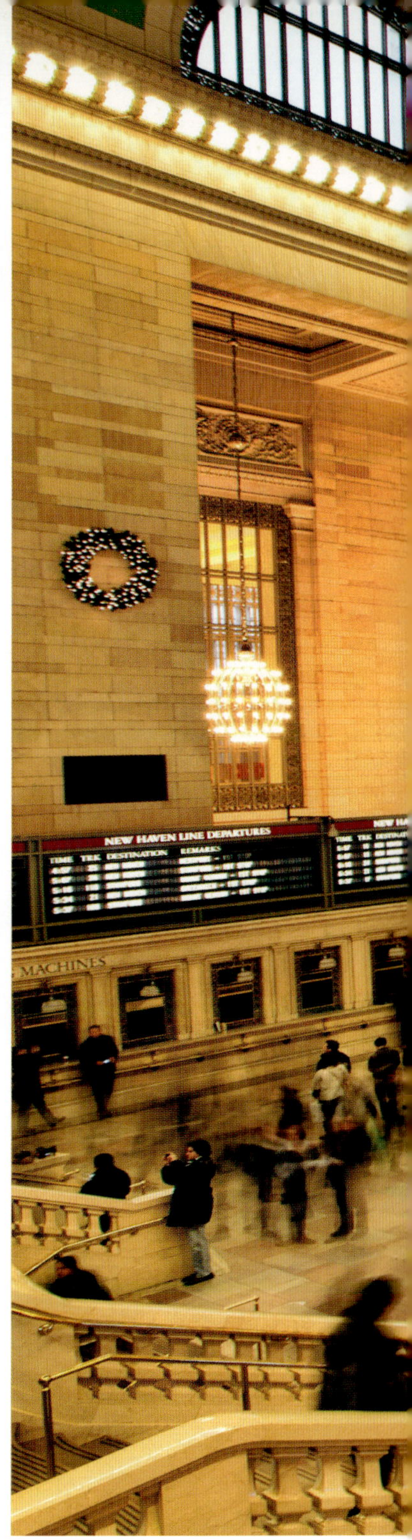

42nd Street and Grand Central

In 1975, this Beaux-Arts building was threatened with demolition until activists, including Jacqueline Kennedy Onassis, fought to save it and had it restored to its former glory. Now Grand Central is not only a transportation hub, but a shopping and eating destination with food stalls, restaurants, and a new Apple store.

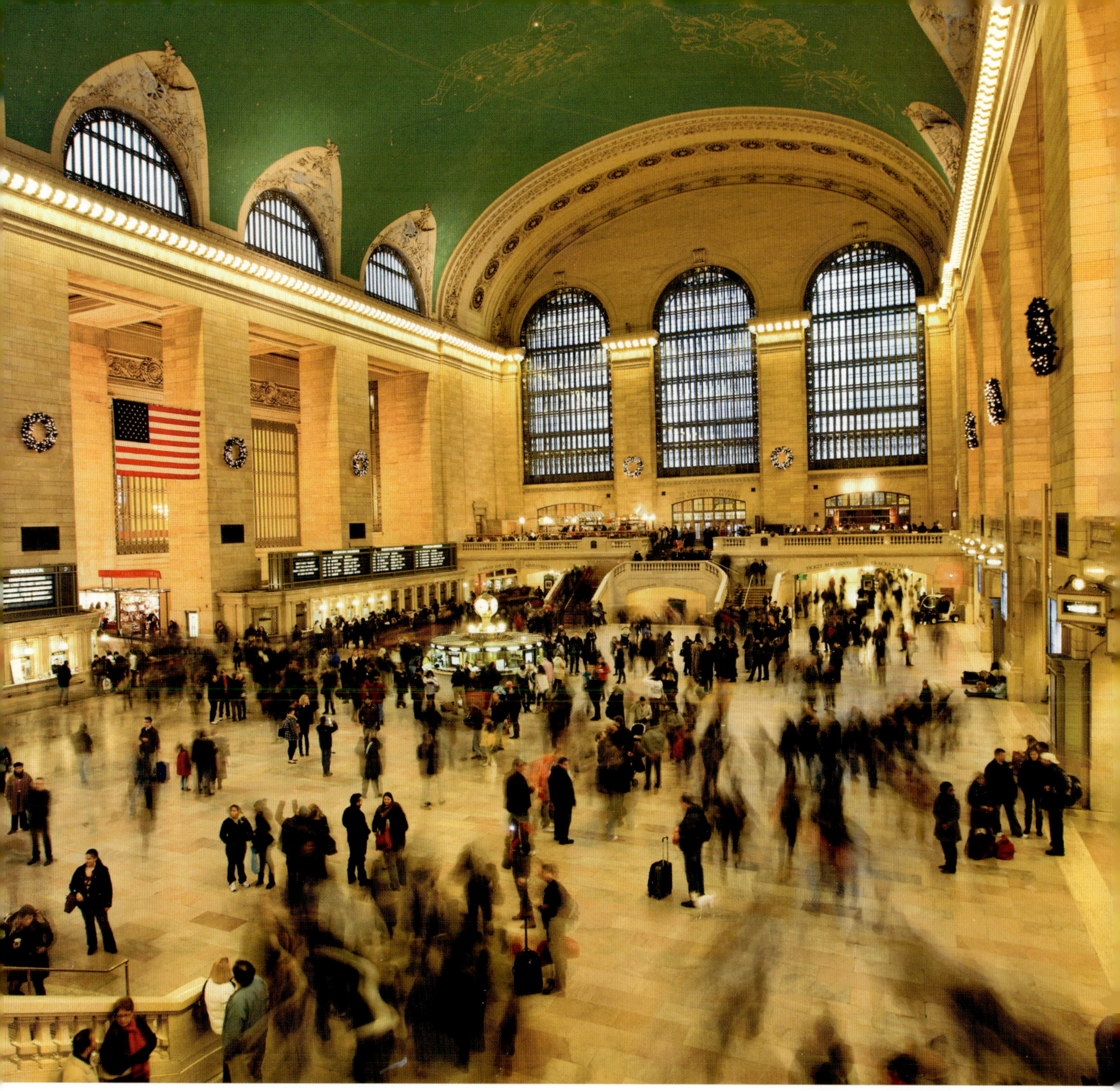

Concourse at Grand Central

Visit this railroad terminal at rush hour and you'll understand how the cliché, "busy as Grand Central" came about. Each weekday almost three-quarters of a million people pass through one of the city's greatest public spaces on their way to points north; to get their shoes shined, or to buy lunch.

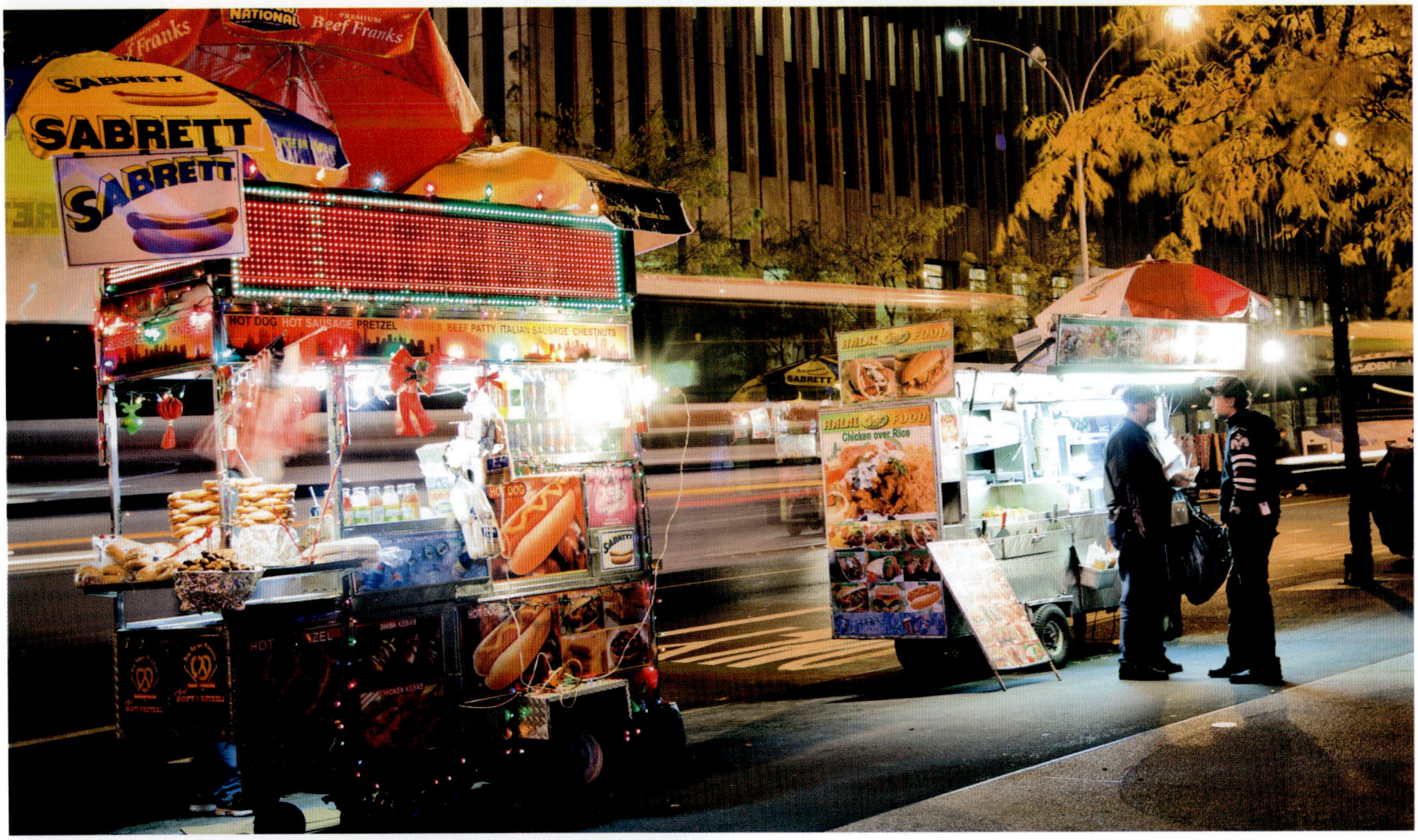

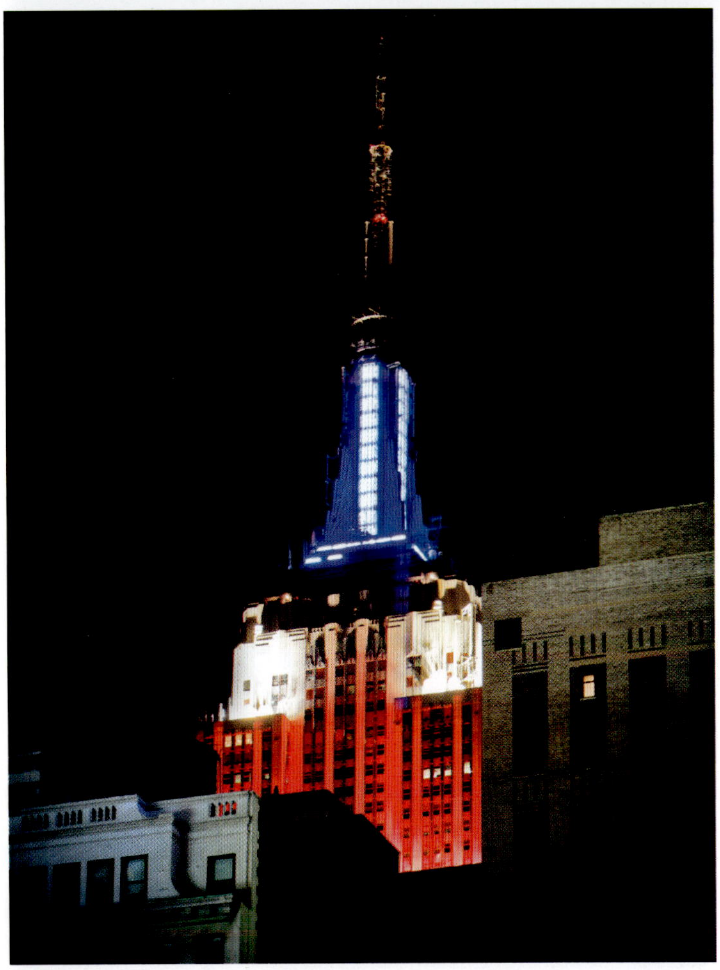

Street Vendor *(above)*

You could eat your way around the world at New York's food carts, which offer more than the traditional peanuts and hotdogs. The expansive fare includes such delicacies as Indian curry, lamb kebobs, Mexican tacos, Japanese dumplings, and vegan seitan burgers, plus lots of cupcakes, donuts, and custom-made ice cream sandwiches.

Empire State Building *(left)*

When the Empire State Building opened in 1931 it was the tallest building in the world. Since then, millions have flocked to the 86th and 102nd floor observatories to get a 360-degree view of the city. Check the lights nightly when the color changes to match the season, holiday, or special events.

Radio City Music Hall *(opposite)*

The Art Deco theatre that opened in 1932 has been home to the Grammys, Tonys, MTV Music Awards, and the Daytime Emmys. But its most famous show is the annual Christmas Spectacular featuring the world-famous Rockettes, a troupe of long-legged dancers whose signature synchronized high kicks have made them legend.

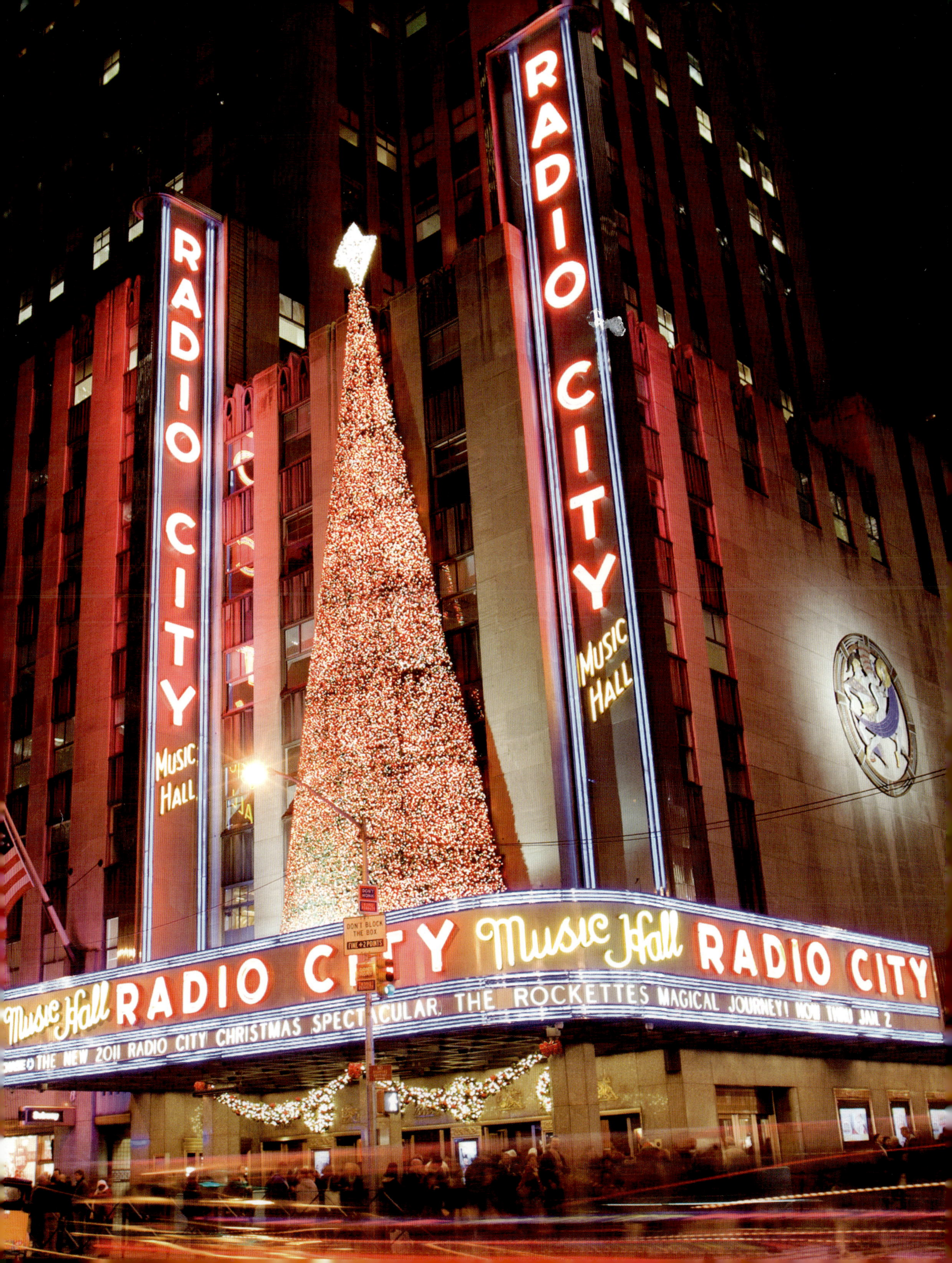
RADIO CITY
MUSIC HALL
RADIO CITY
MUSIC HALL
Music Hall RADIO CITY Music Hall RADIO CITY
RADIO CITY CHRISTMAS SPECTACULAR THE ROCKETTES MAGICAL JOURNEY! NOW THRU JAN 2
THE NEW 2011 RADIO CITY
DON'T BLOCK THE BOX
FINE+2 POINTS

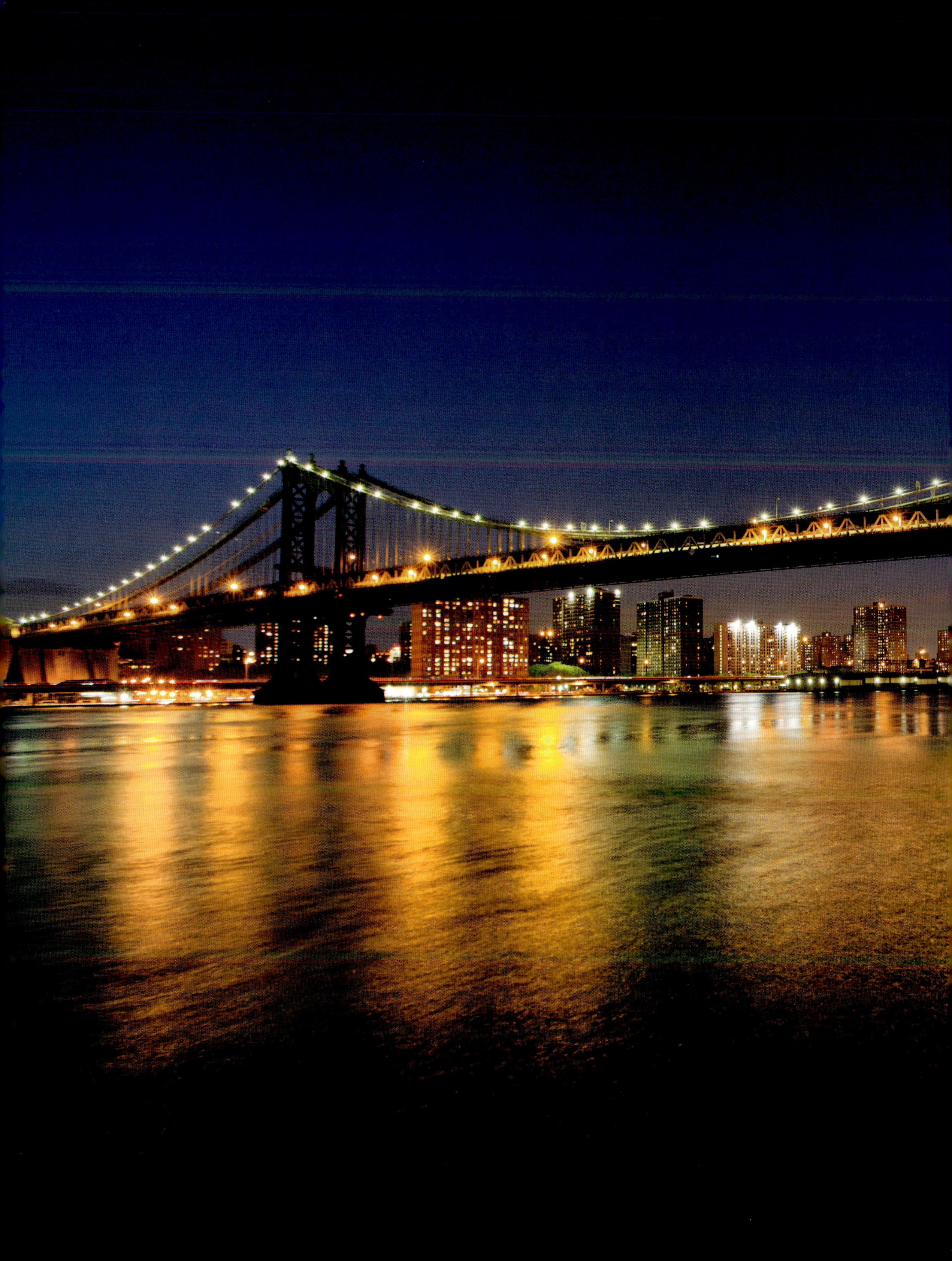

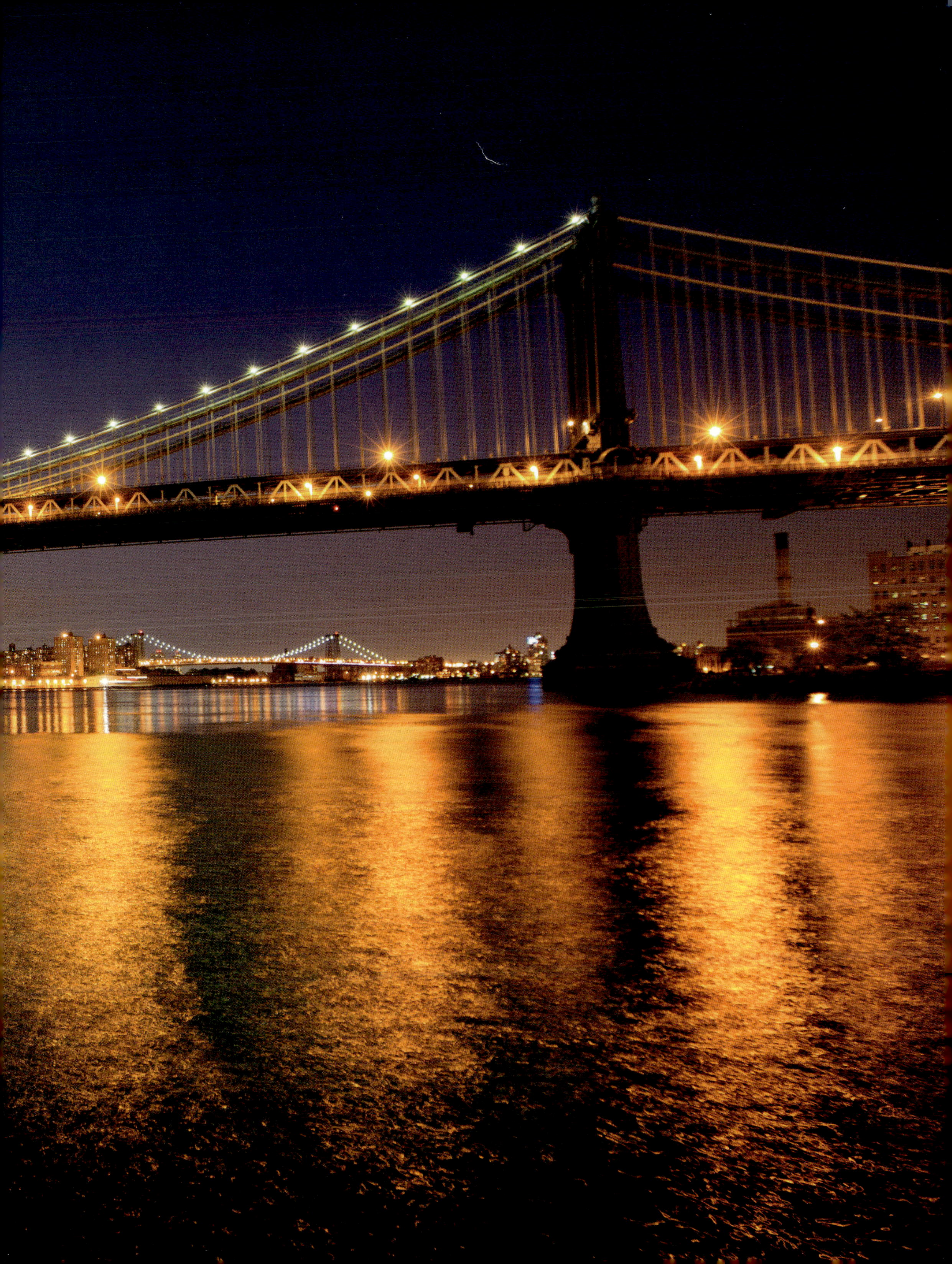

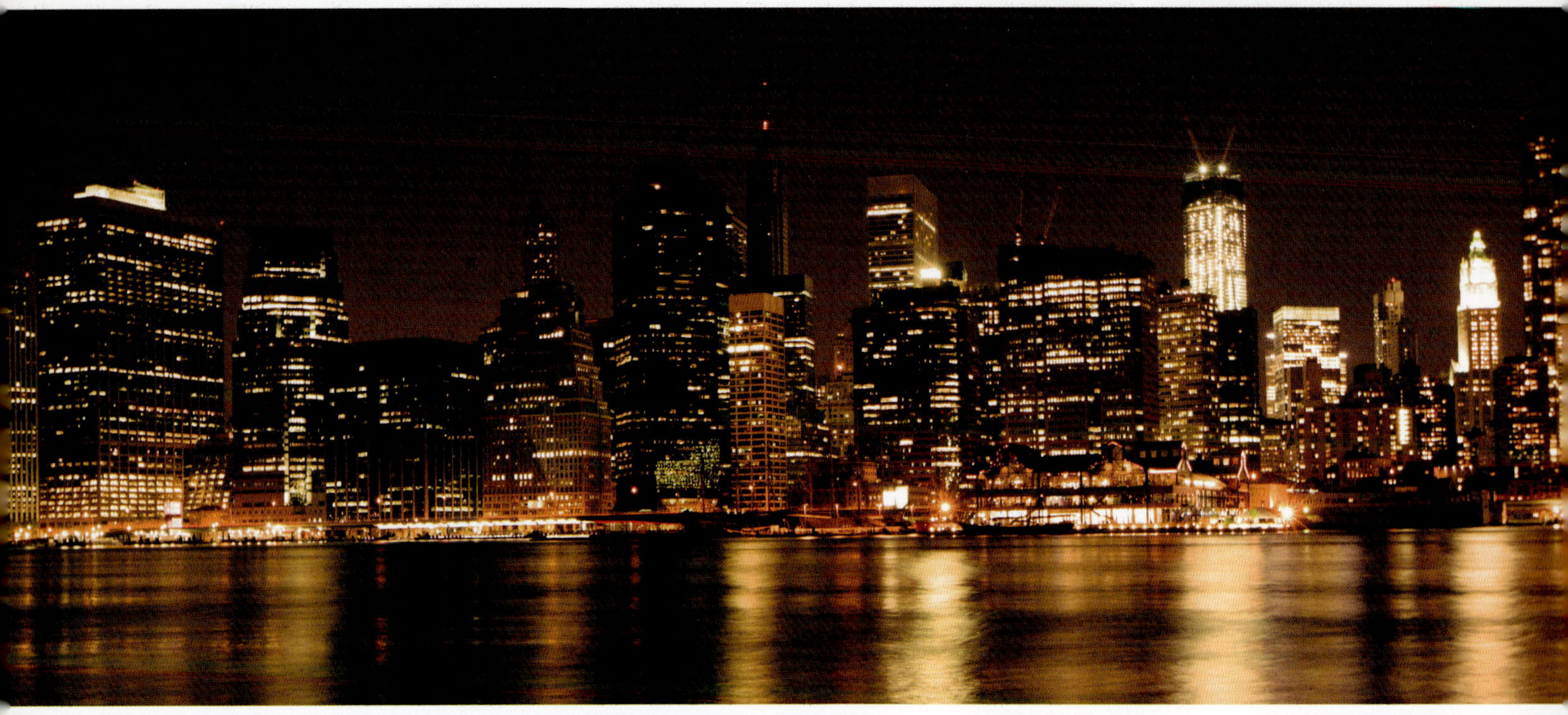

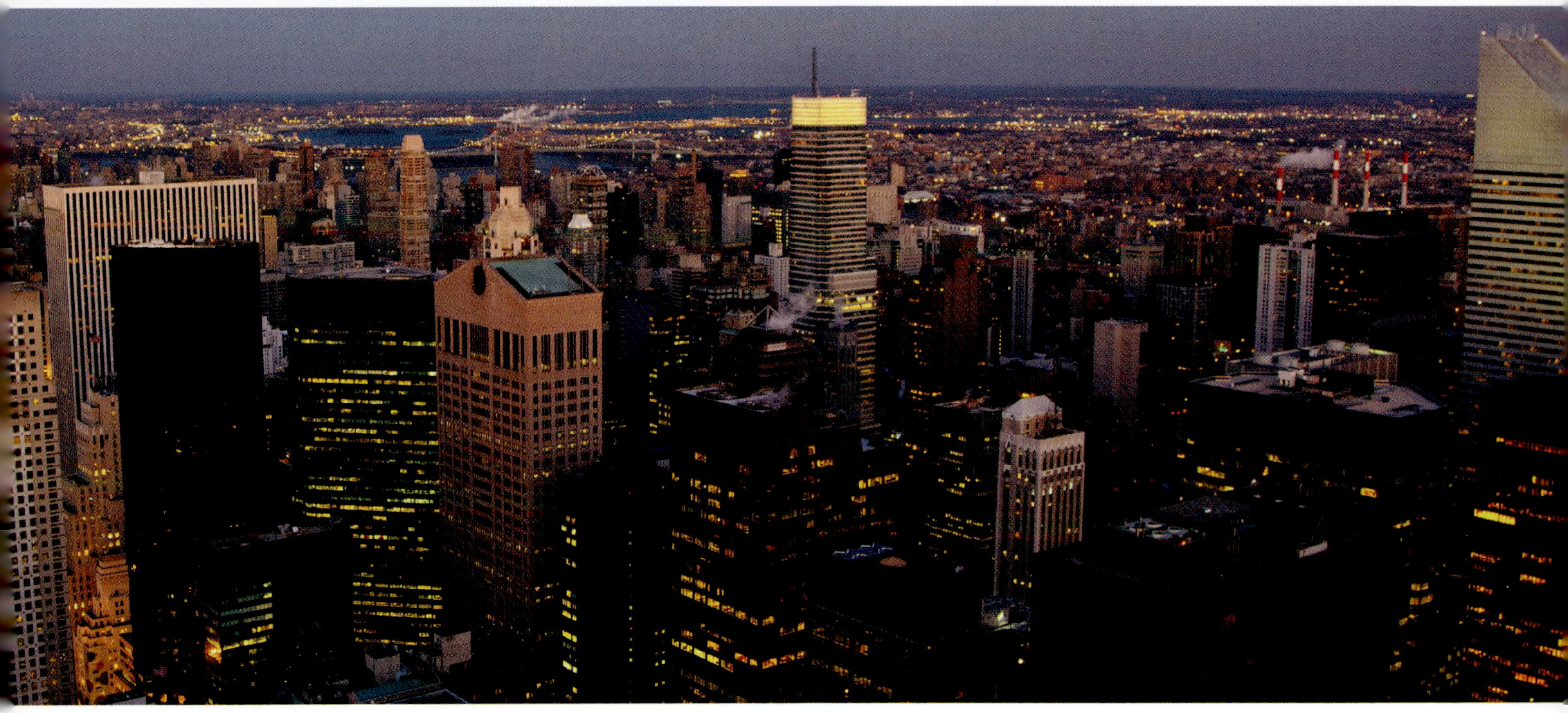

Manhattan Bridge *(pages 66 – 67)*

Bright lights, big city. As the sky darkens, the city's bridges and buildings illuminate as millions of lights switch on, twinkling like the stars above. The skyline looks magical. It's a romantic backdrop for a city full of promises and welcoming all to explore its many wonders.

Lower Manhattan *(top)*

Lower Manhattan's architecture is among the city's most distinctive, with some of its oldest and most historic structures preserving the past, and its newest pointing to the future. Notable buildings include the Empire State Building, the Chrysler Building, and the Freedom Tower.

Midtown Manhattan *(bottom)*

One of the busiest commercial districts in the U.S., Midtown condenses residents, tourists, and business people into prime real estate. Important buildings include the Citigroup Center with its distinctive angled top, the post-modernist Sony Building, and the "Lipstick Building" with its layered oval contour and red stripes.

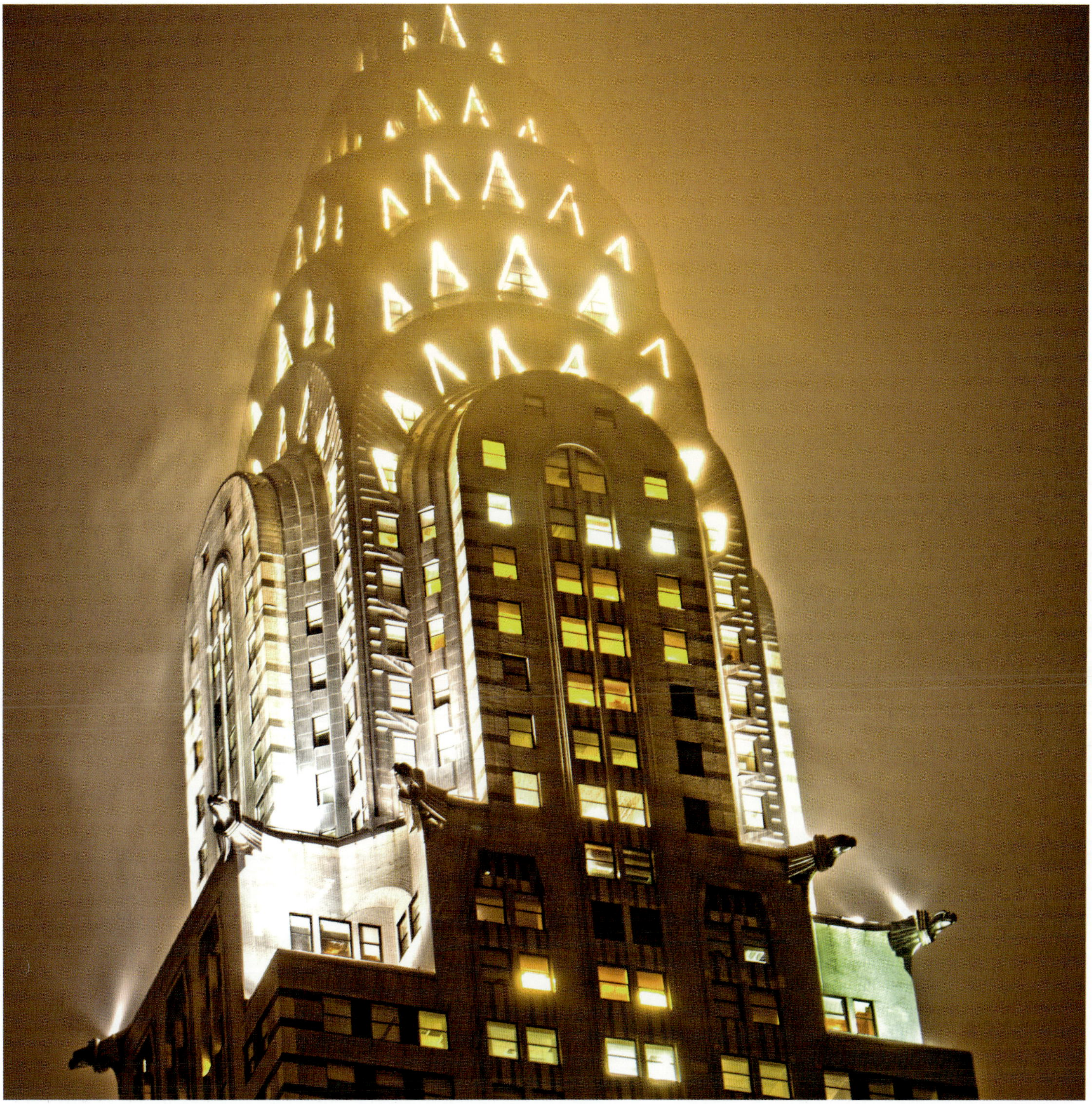

Chrysler Building

Built for car manufacturer Walter P. Chrysler, the landmarked Chrysler building gives many nods to the industry. Its gargoyle eagles depict car ornaments and the crescent-shaped stainless steel spire with its stylized sunburst motif resembles a radiator grille, while winged radiator caps decorate lower setbacks.

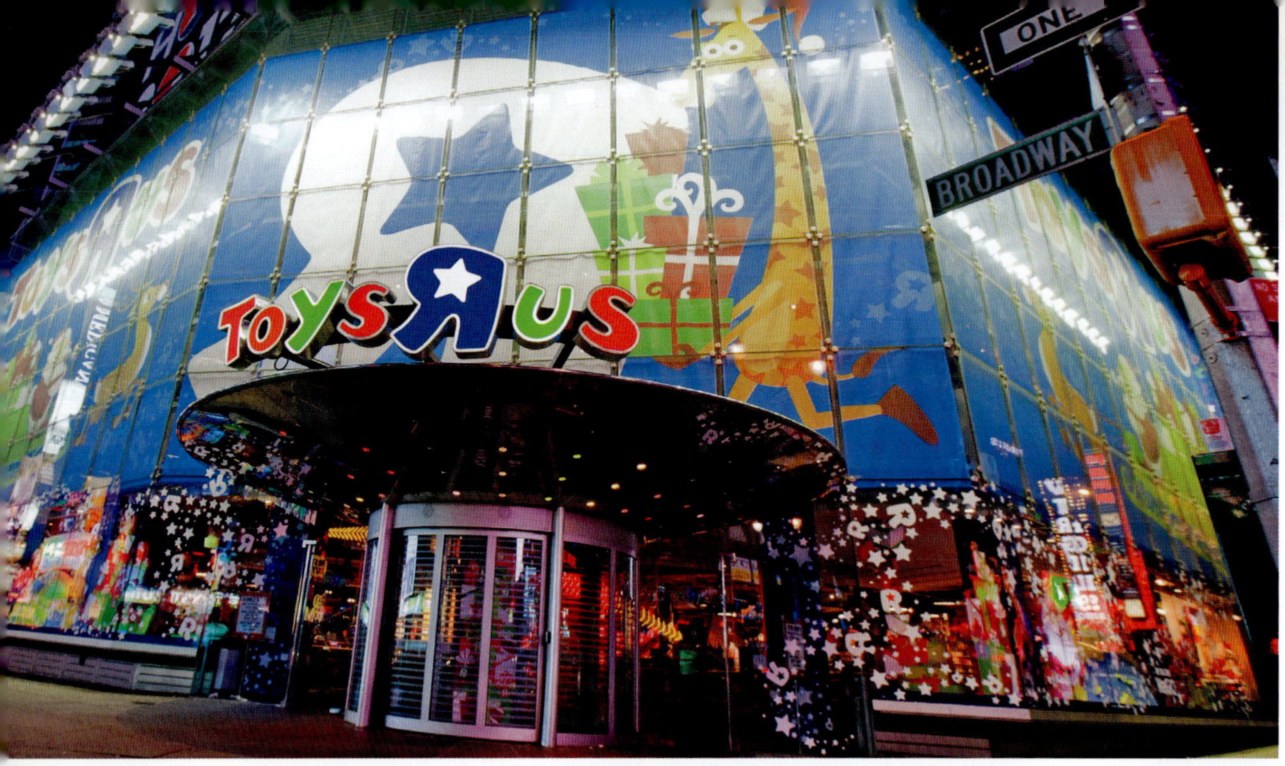

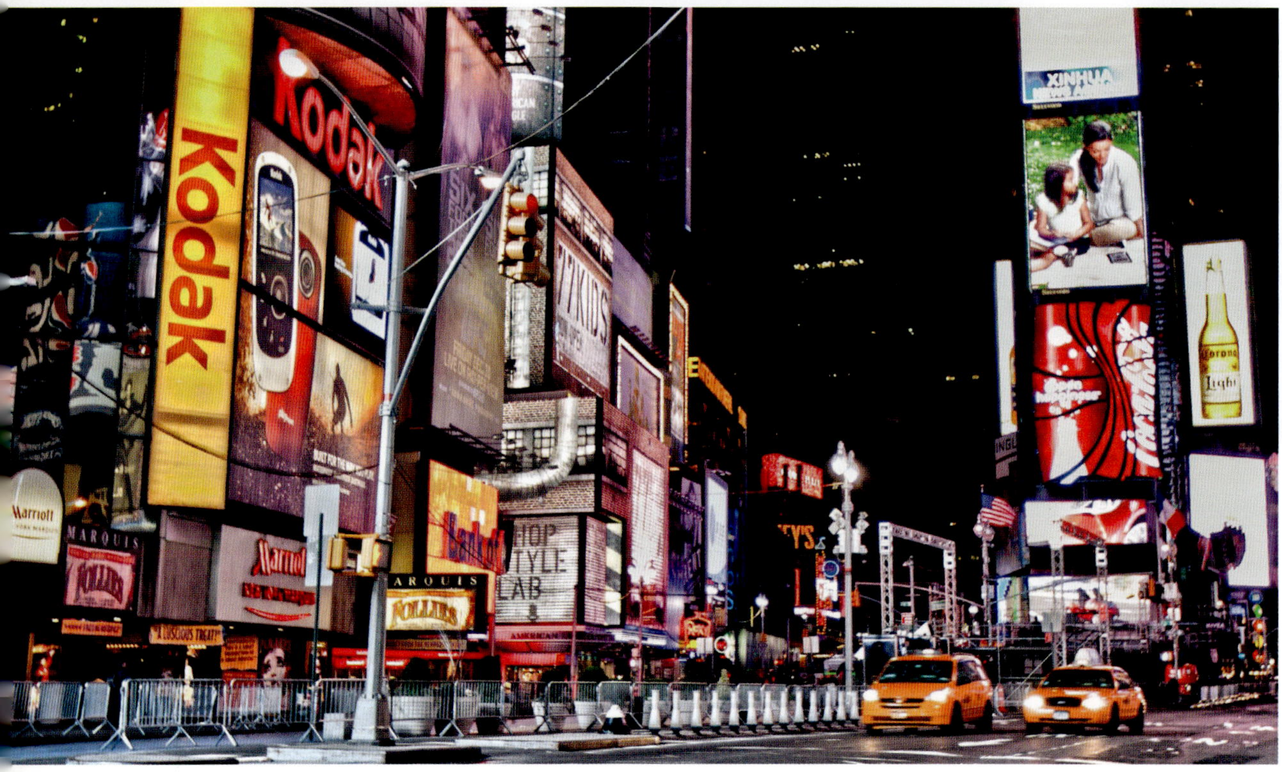

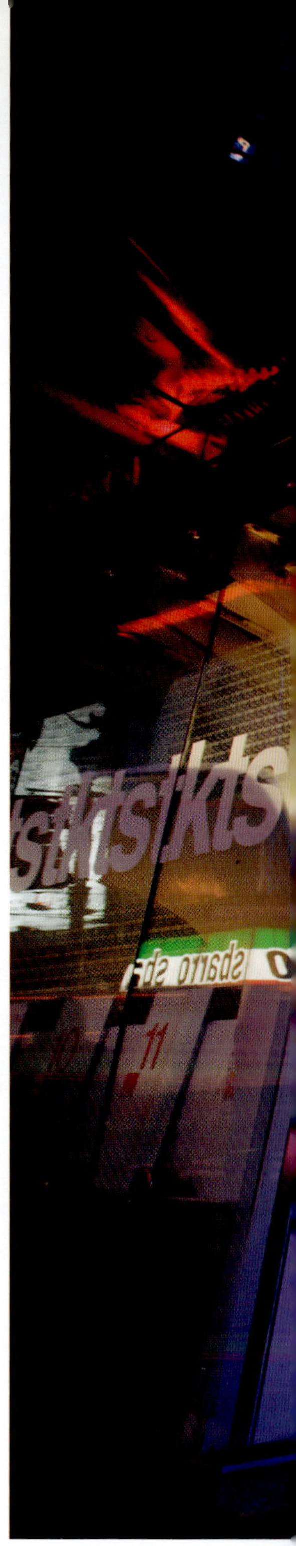

Toys "R" Us *(top)*

Complete with a full-sized indoor Ferris wheel and a life-sized Barbie house, the 110,000-square-foot toy store in the heart of Times Square is a perfect kid-friendly diversion in a typical tourist trek around town. Play with interactive displays, marvel at a giant animatronic T-Rex, and get your picture taken with a cartoon character.

Times Square *(bottom)*

Times Square is truly the crossroads of the world with a frenzy of activity day and night as tourists and locals pack its theatres, restaurants, and shops. Tune in on New Year's Eve when a million people gather to see the famed Waterford Crystal ball drop, ringing in the New Year.

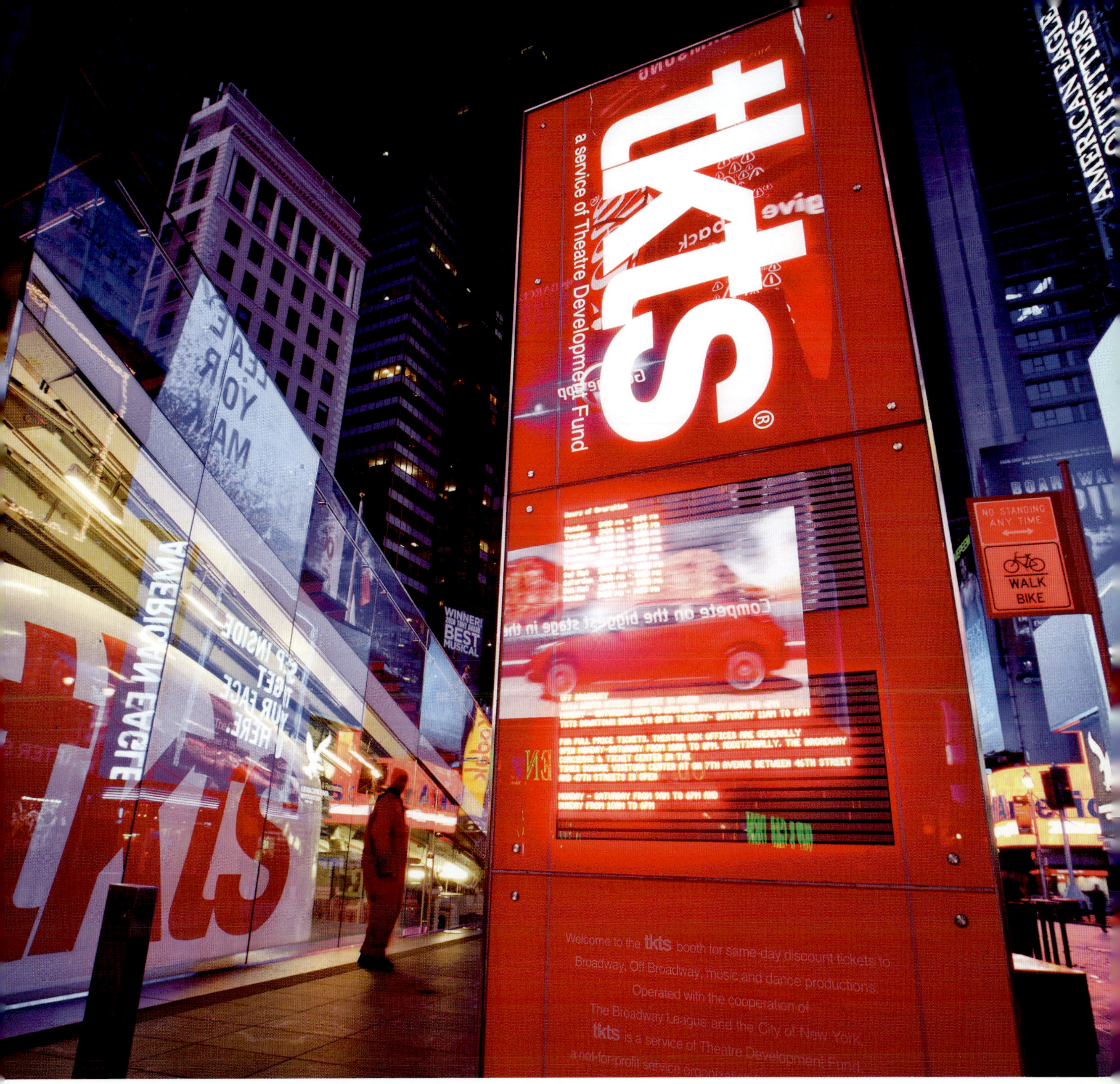

TKTS

Lines start early in the day at the TKTS booth at the north end of Times Square for half-price theatre tickets to both matinee and evening performances. The new booth, completed in 2008, features red bleacher-like stairs covering the roof which serve as a prime spot for New York's favorite sport, people watching.

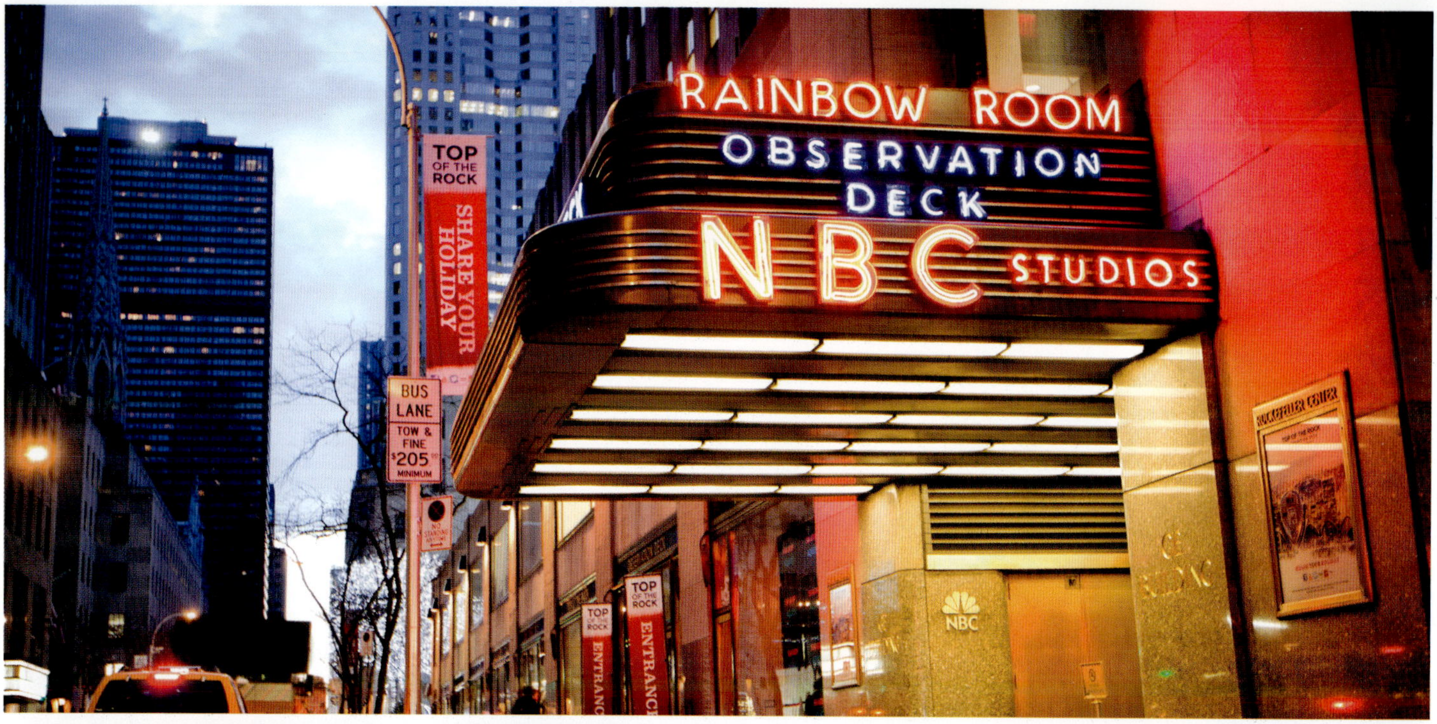

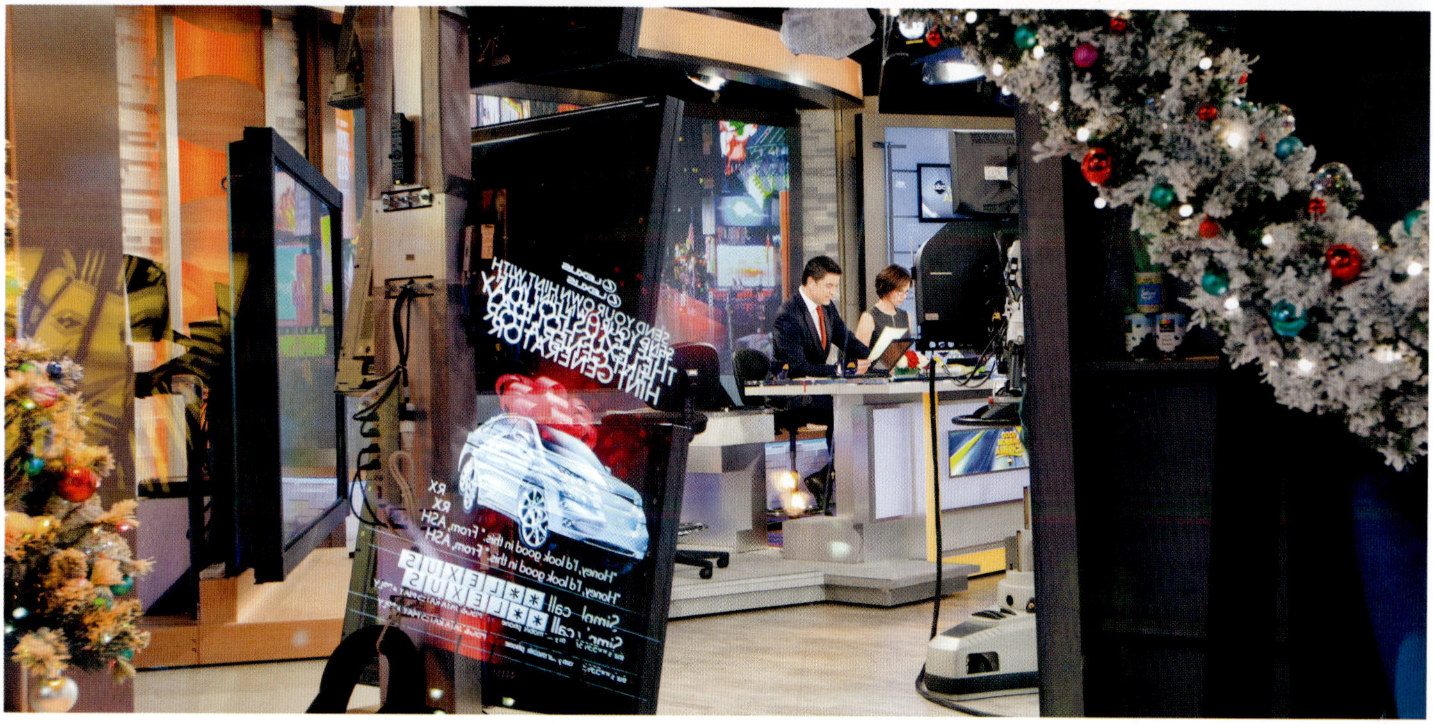

NBC Studios *(top)*

Come for a studio tour of the Art Deco 30 Rock, NBC headquarters and home to the *Today Show* and *Saturday Night Live*. On Fridays you'll often see diehard fans lining up to spend the night on the street in the hopes of scoring stand-by tickets to live tapings of the comedy show.

Good Morning America *(bottom)*

Stop by the GMA studio in Times Square and you may end up on TV as part of the outside audience often shown on screen. Remember, the crowd arrives at the crack of dawn, especially if a celebrity or popular band is expected.

Hershey's *(opposite)*

Got a hankering for a piece of chocolate? Hershey's will satisfy every time at this candy store/tourist attraction. Here in Times Square you can personalize your own Hershey's Kisses, see your name in lights on Broadway on the scrolling marquee, and shop for everything Hershey's in an interactive world of sweet commercialism.

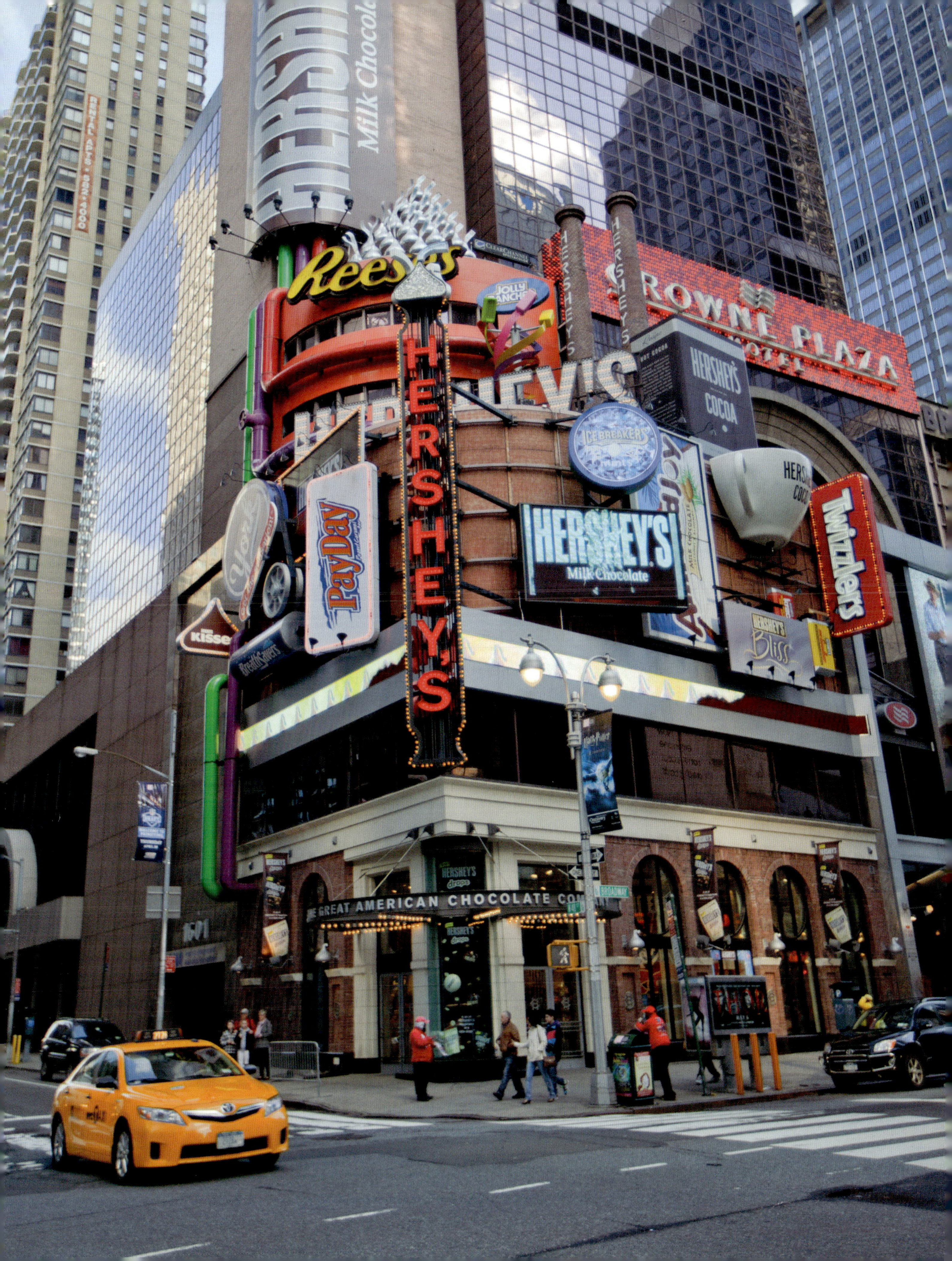
HERSHEY'S
Milk Chocolate
Reese's
HERSHEY'S
CROWNE PLAZA
HOTEL
HERSHEY'S
COCOA
ICE BREAKERS
HERSHEY'S
Milk Chocolate
PayDay
Twizzlers
HERSHEY'S
Bliss
Kisses
GREAT AMERICAN CHOCOLATE CO
BROADWAY
1501

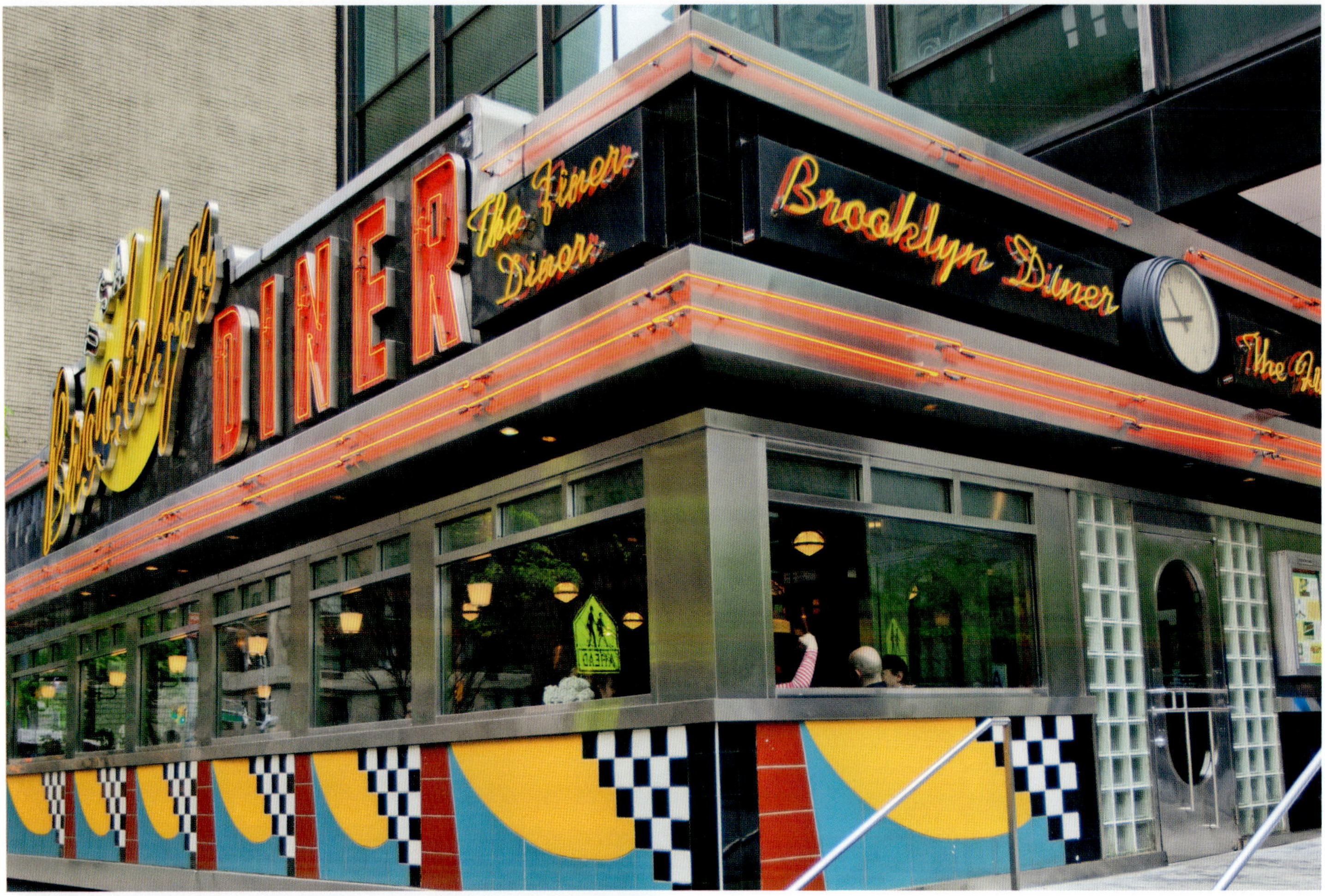

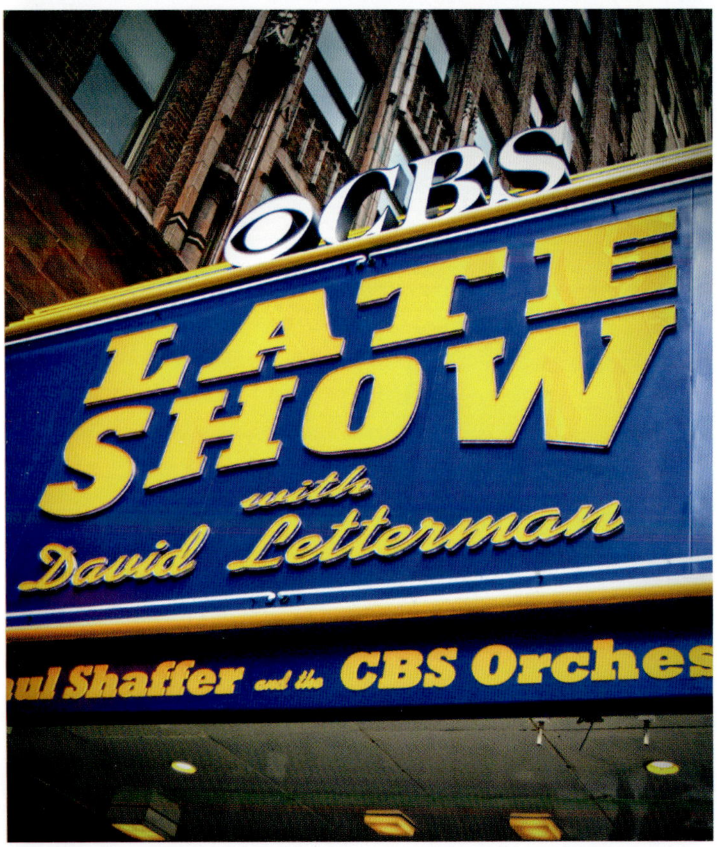

Brooklyn Diner *(top)*

At this traditional Brooklyn diner on 57th Street, the menu is filled with classic favorites, including "piled-high" corned beef and pastrami sandwiches, chicken soup, and noodle kugel. Be sure to try their famous Brooklyn Diner Egg Cream.

Late Show *(left)*

New York is headquarters for many TV and talk shows including *The Late Show with David Letterman*. Request advance audience tickets or show up early at the Ed Sullivan Theater for stand-by. Who knows what celebrity guest you might spot.

Theatre District *(opposite)*

Known as "The Great White Way" for the brilliant bright lights, the Times Square Theatre District includes approximately 36 theatres crammed into a thin strip of Manhattan showing world-famous productions nightly.

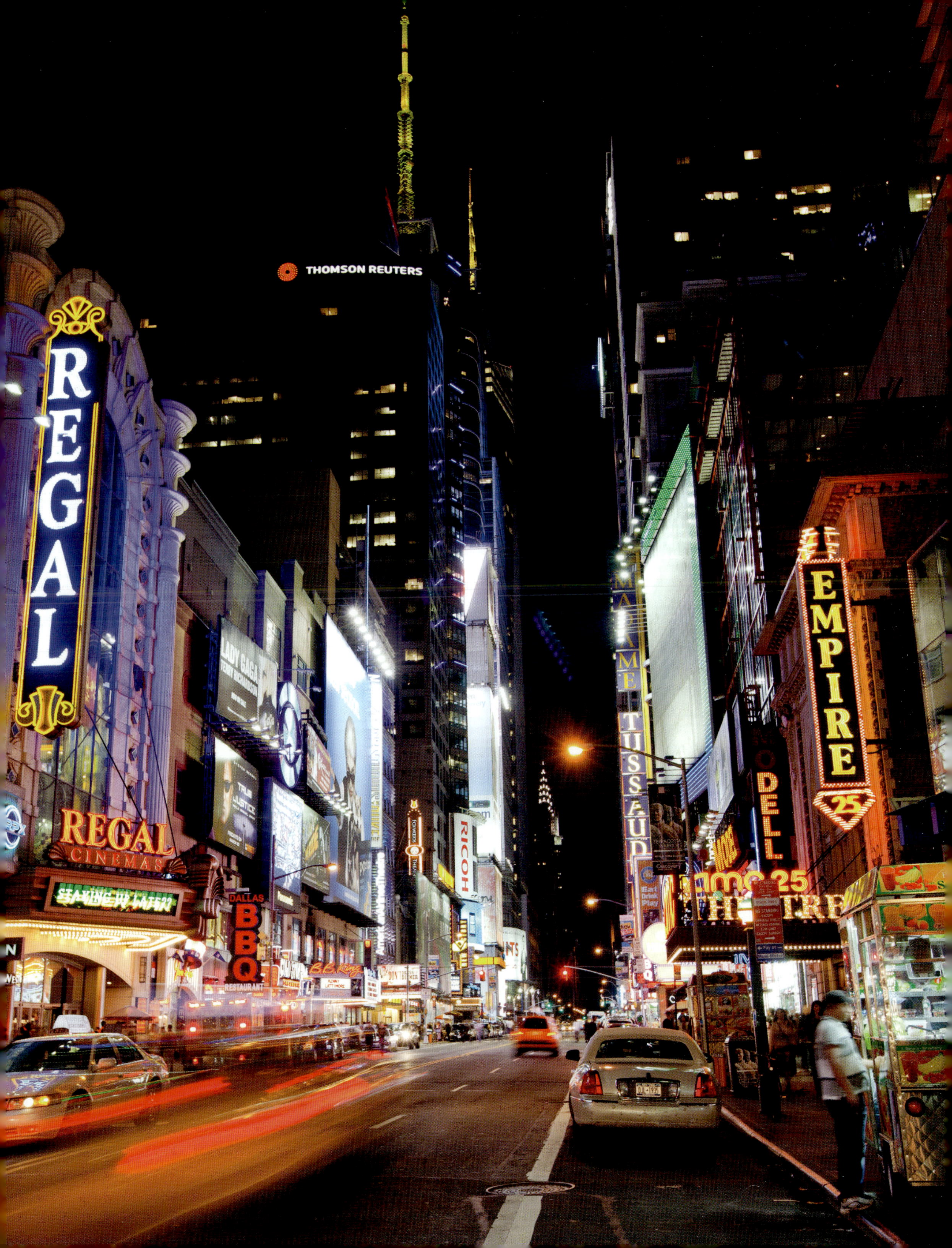
THOMSON REUTERS
REGAL
REGAL
CINEMAS
DALLAS
BBQ
RESTAURANT
RICOH
EMPIRE
25
THEATRE

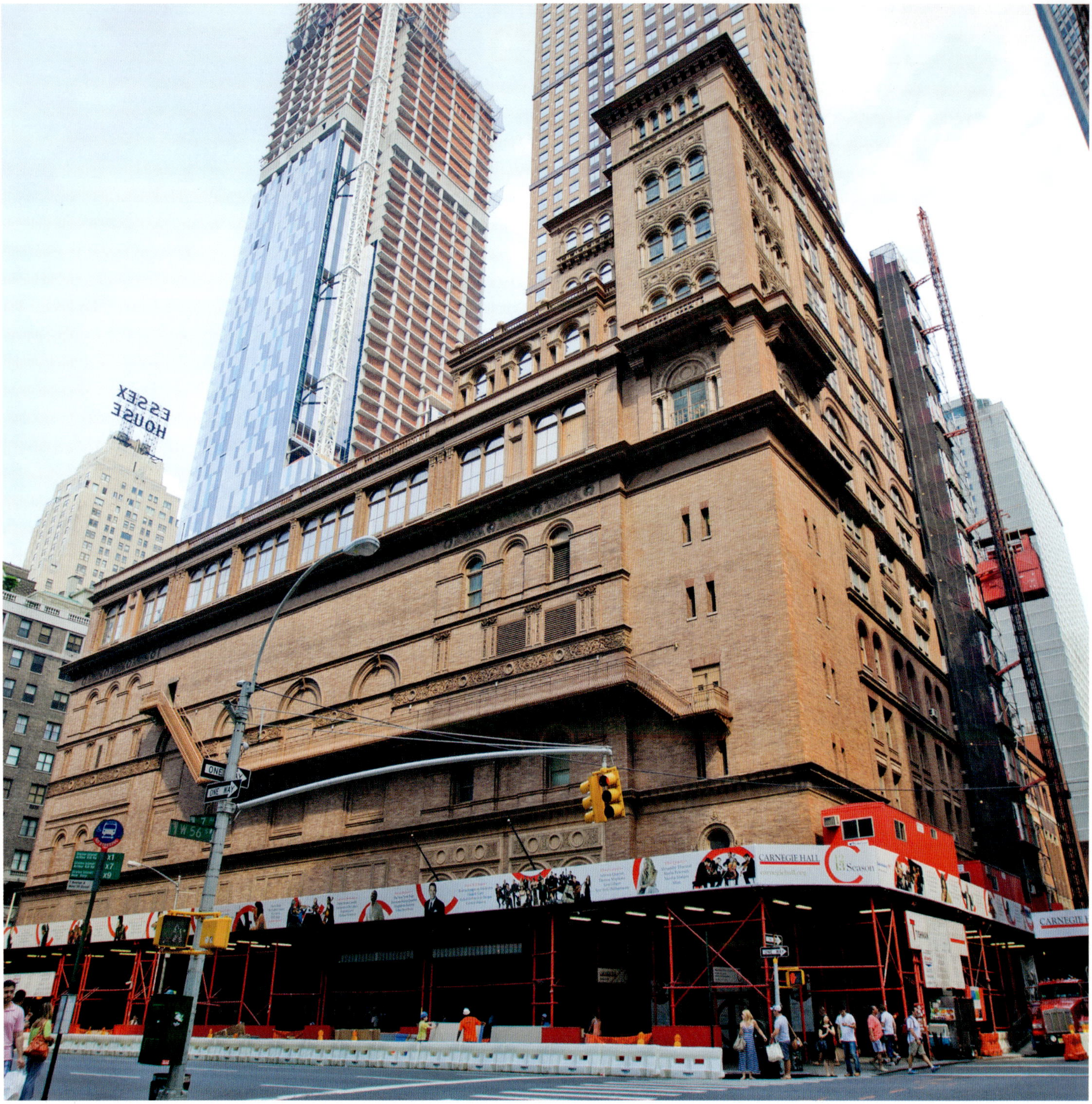

Carnegie Hall *(above)*

How do you get to Carnegie Hall? Practice! You can also buy tickets to concerts ranging from the National Youth Orchestra to the Chicago Symphony and leading classical and popular musicians from around the world. Check out the Rose Museum to see artifacts and memorabilia of the building's history.

Apollo Theater *(opposite)*

Originally a burlesque theater in Harlem, the Apollo later became the country's showcase of African-American entertainment. It helped launch the careers of some great entertainers, including Sammy Davis, Jr., James Brown, and Josephine Baker. It continues to feature both major performers and local amateur talent.

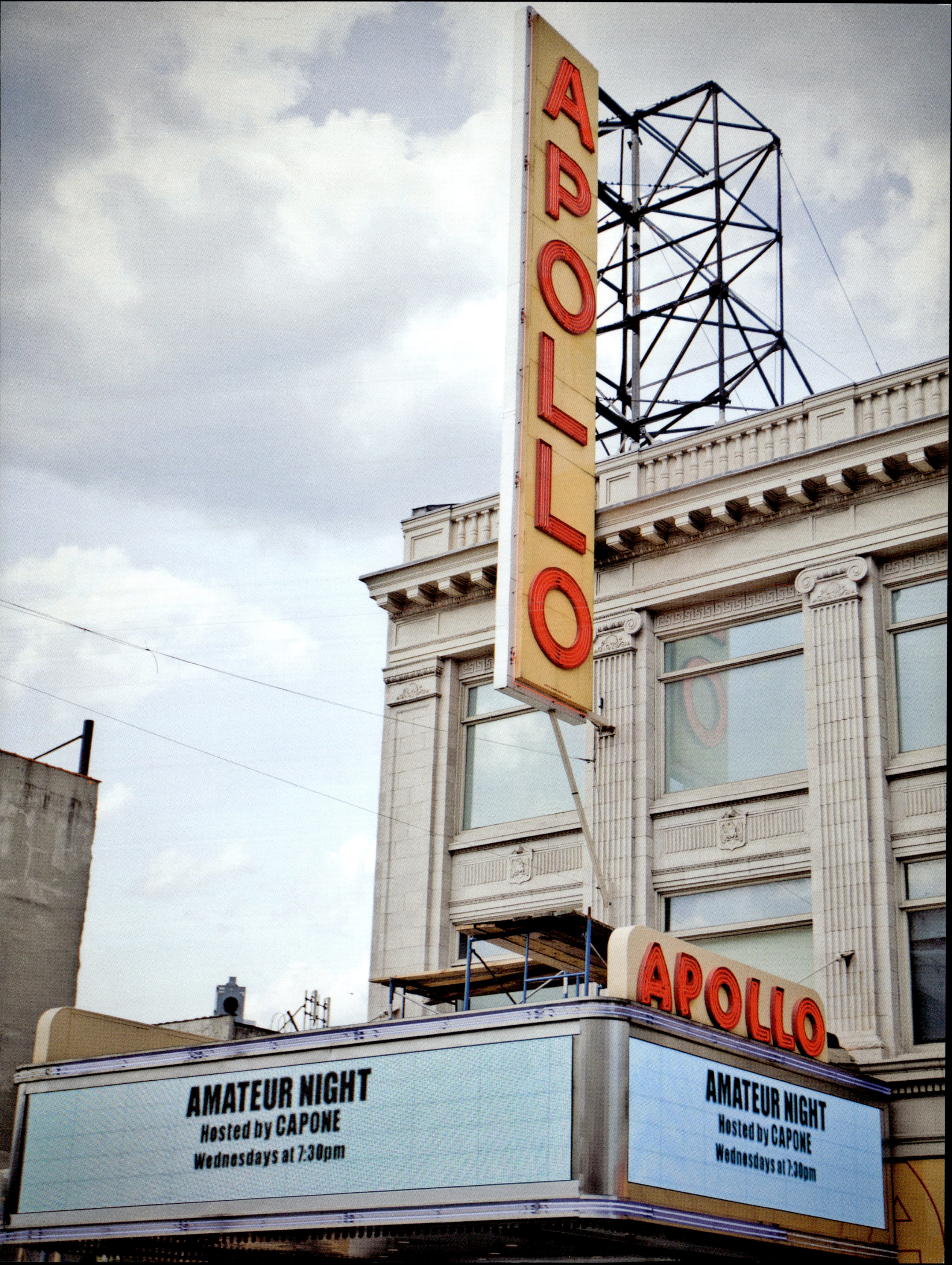
APOLLO
APOLLO
AMATEUR NIGHT
Hosted by CAPONE
Wednesdays at 7:30pm
AMATEUR NIGHT
Hosted by CAPONE
Wednesdays at 7:30pm

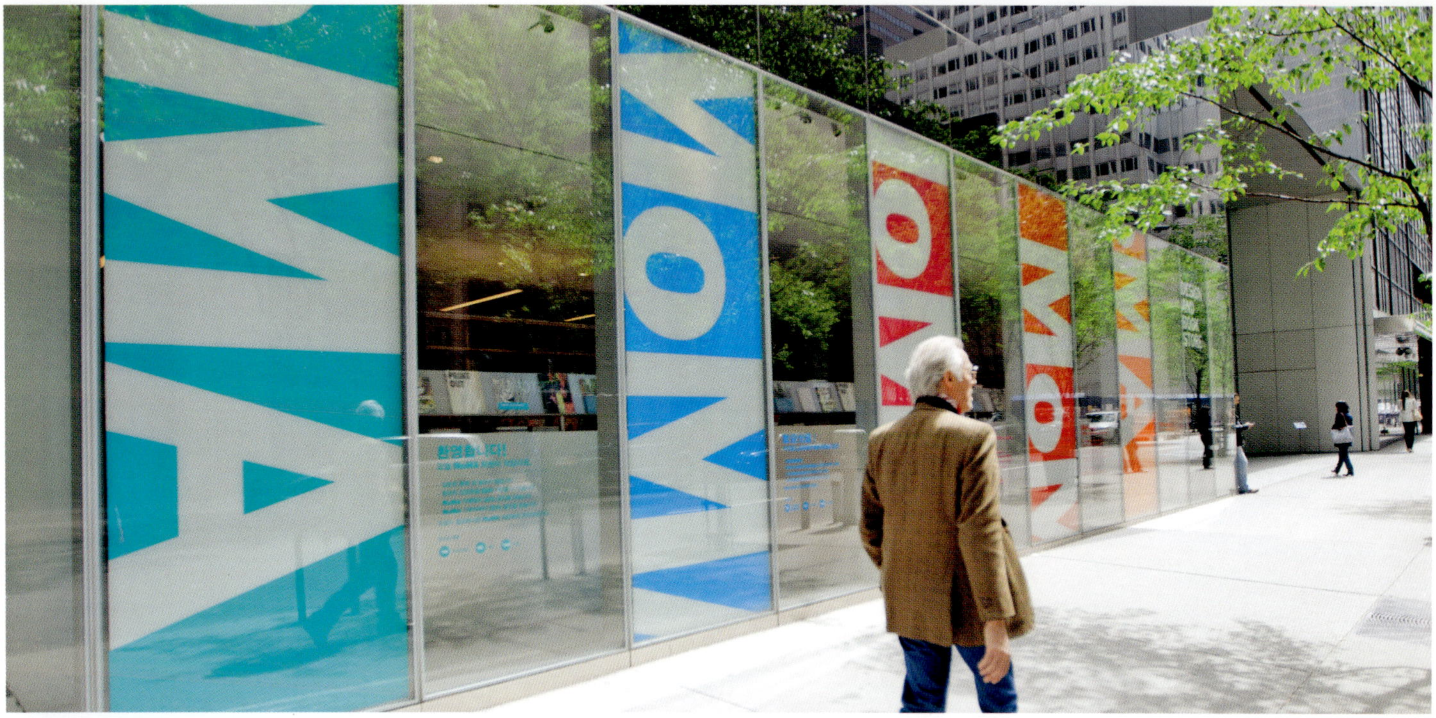

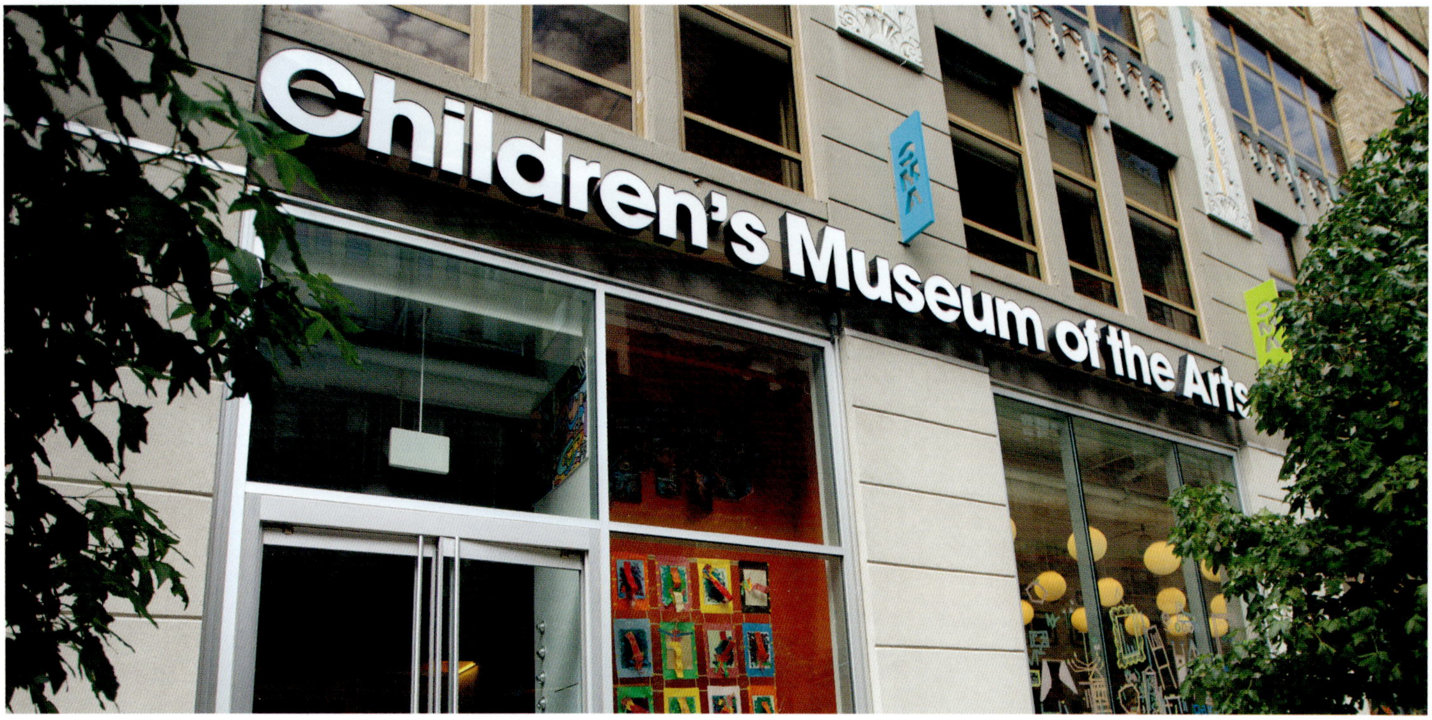

MOMA *(top)*

The Museum of Modern Art has one of the world's best collections of modern and contemporary art, including the works of Pablo Picasso, Henri Matisse, Jackson Pollock, and Jasper Johns. One room is devoted to *Water Lilies*, Claude Monet's nearly 42-foot-long triptych masterpiece. It's also known for its sculpture garden.

Children's Museum of the Arts *(bottom)*

At this SoHo museum it's OK for young artists to touch anything and everything and get their hands really dirty. There's a media lab for film-making, sound booth for music production, clay bar for sculpting, and fine art studio for painting. And don't forget the ball pond for jumping in.

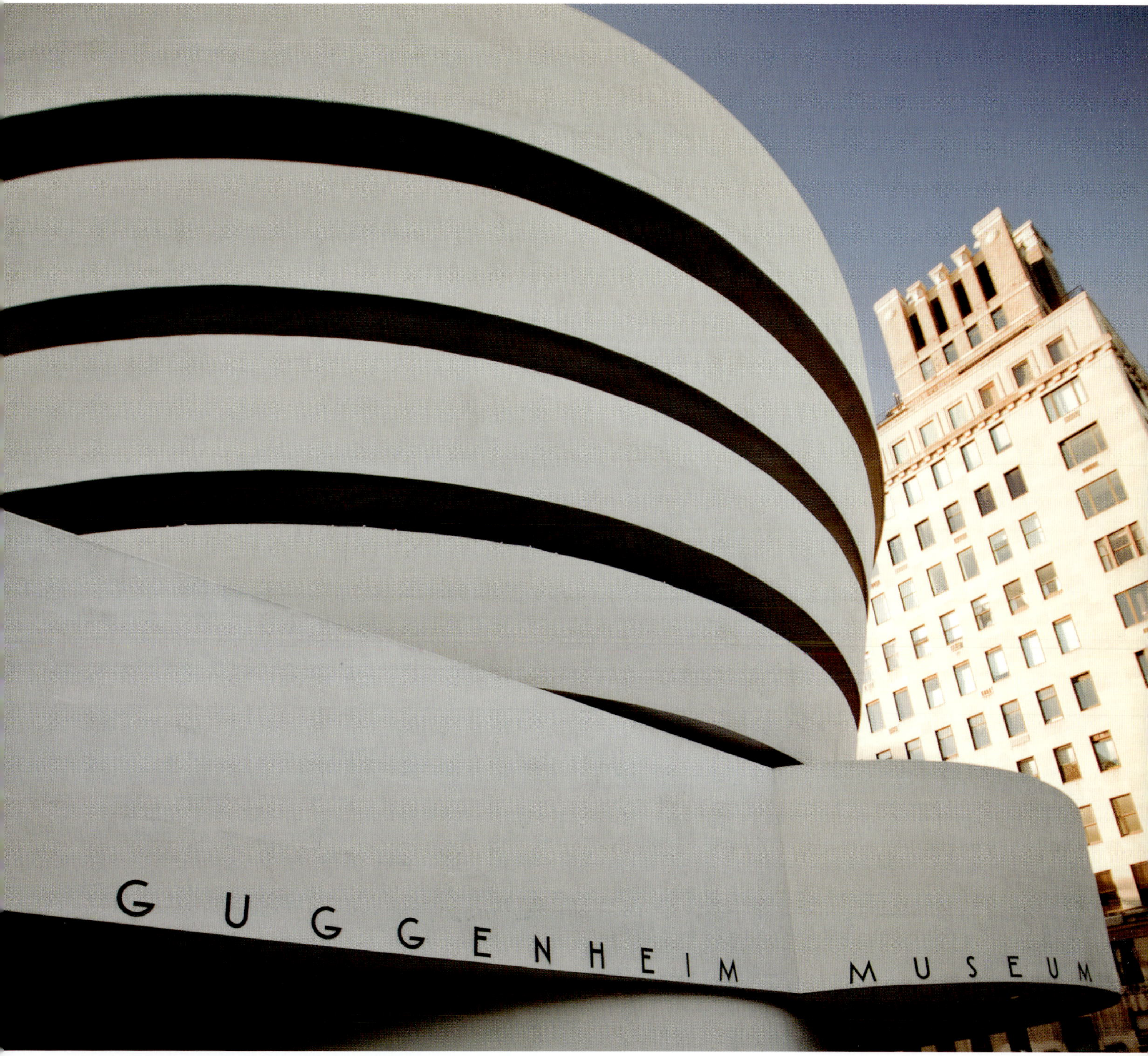

Guggenheim Museum

Although the Solomon R. Guggenheim Museum on Fifth Avenue houses a world famous collection of modern art, it's the building itself that is the greatest masterpiece. Designed by architect Frank Lloyd Wright in 1959, the unique spiral ramping gallery is among the 20th century's most important architectural landmarks.

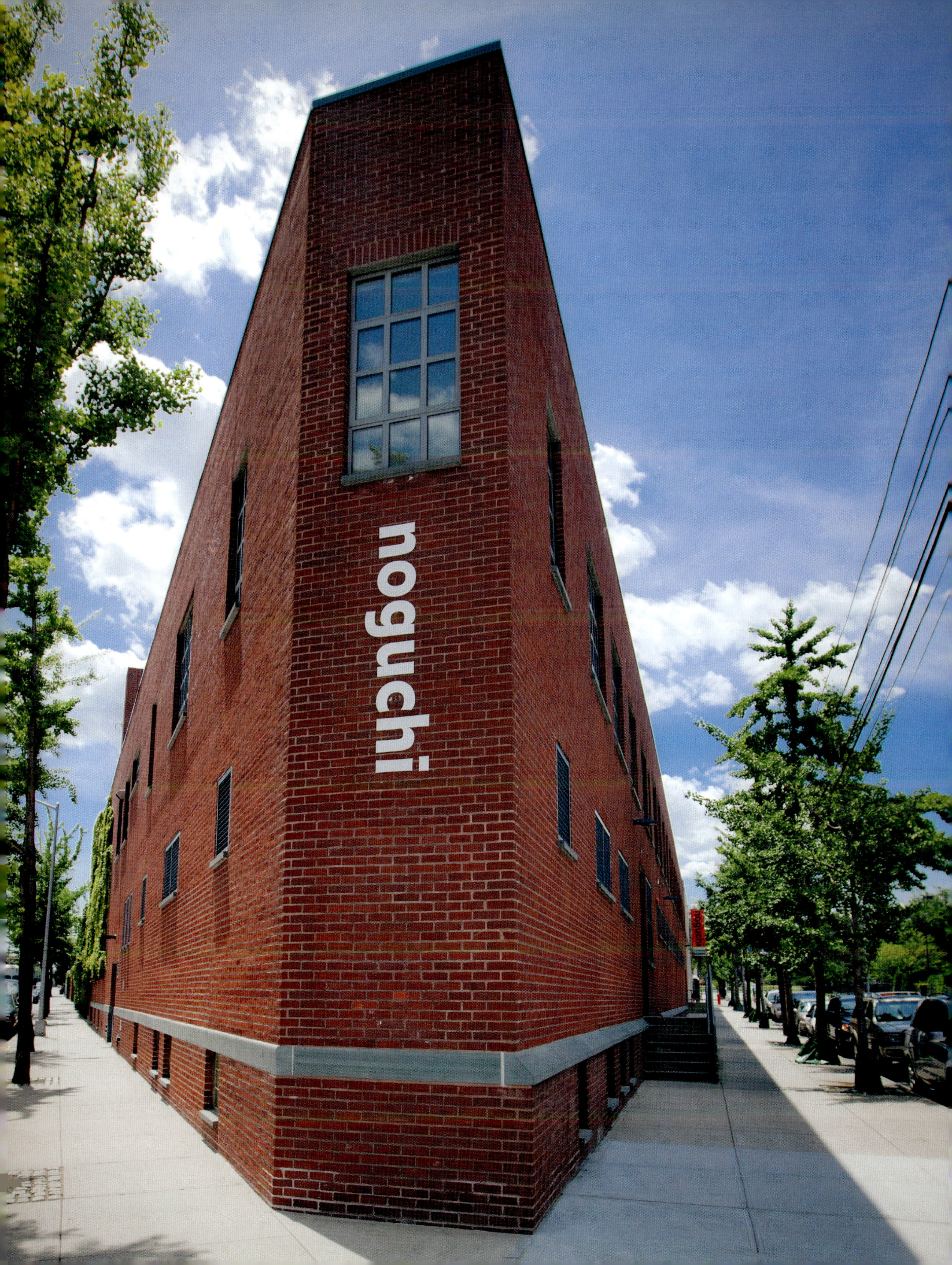
noguchi

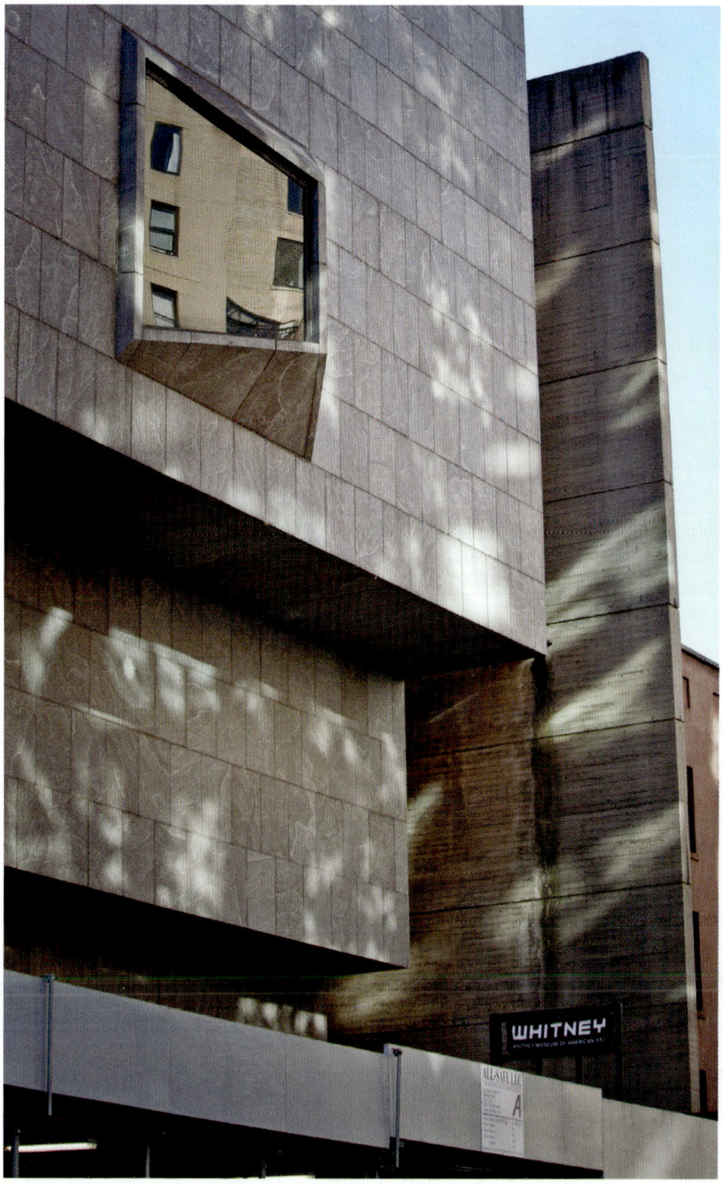

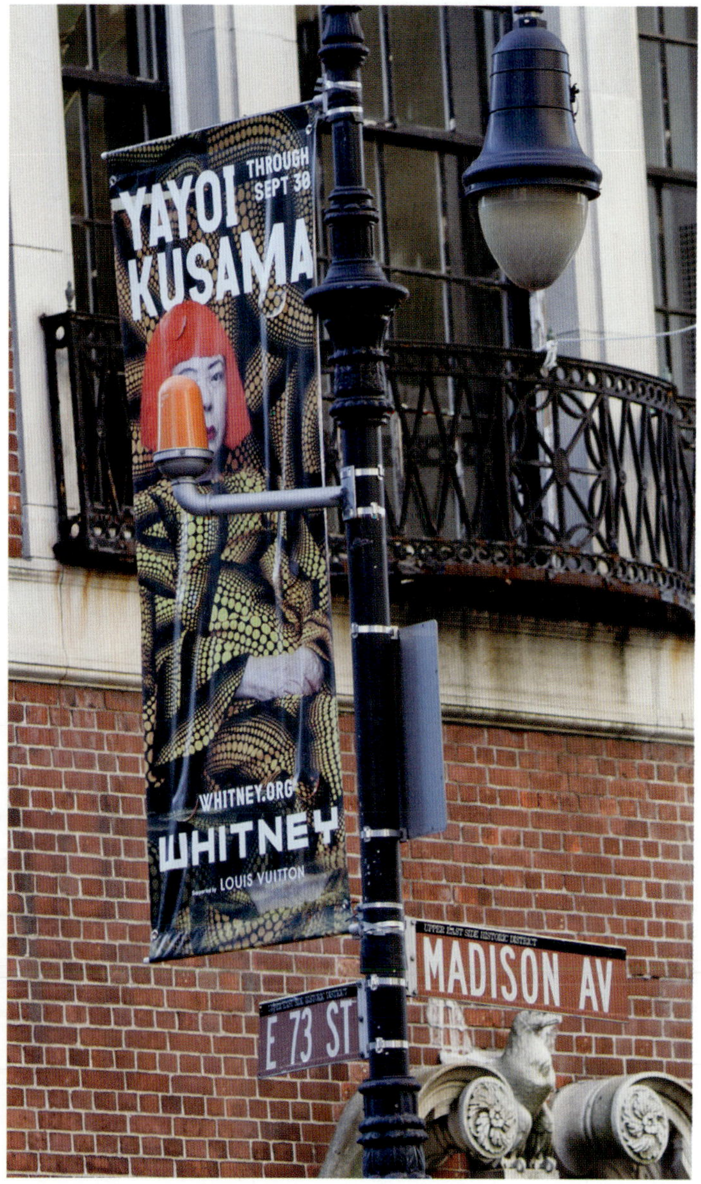

Noguchi Museum *(opposite)*

Designed and built by Japanese-American sculptor, Isamu Noguchi to house his work, this Long Island City museum is off the radar of many visitors but well worth a visit to Queens. A two-story museum and sculpture garden displays Noguchi's sculptures, architectural models, and furniture designs.

Whitney Museum *(left and right)*

Devoted to 20th-and 21st-century art of the United States, the Whitney focuses on exhibiting works by living artists. The museum is known for its oft-controversial and provocative Biennial shows of new trends in American art. The modern inverted staircase facade sets a striking presence on Madison Avenue.

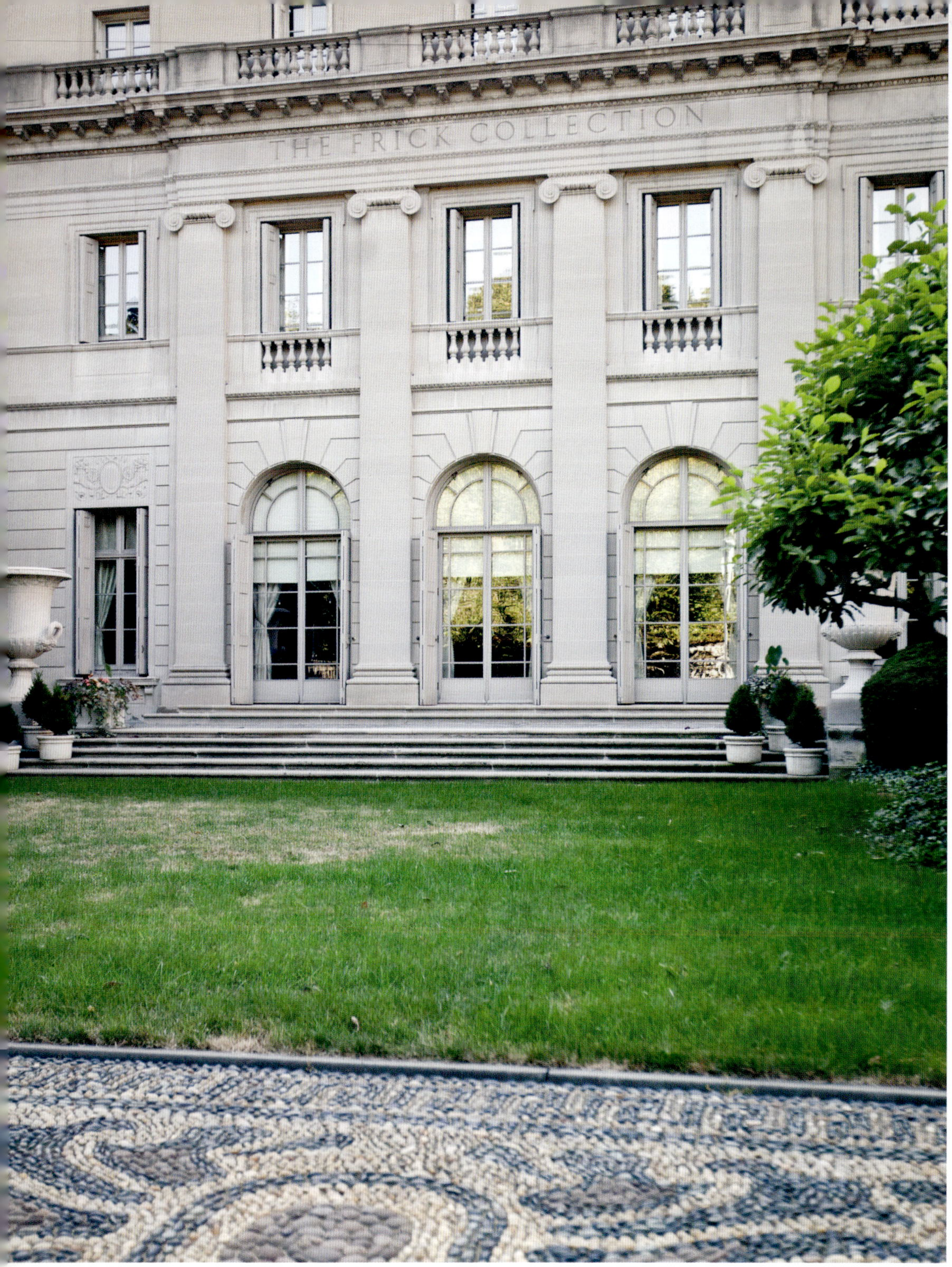

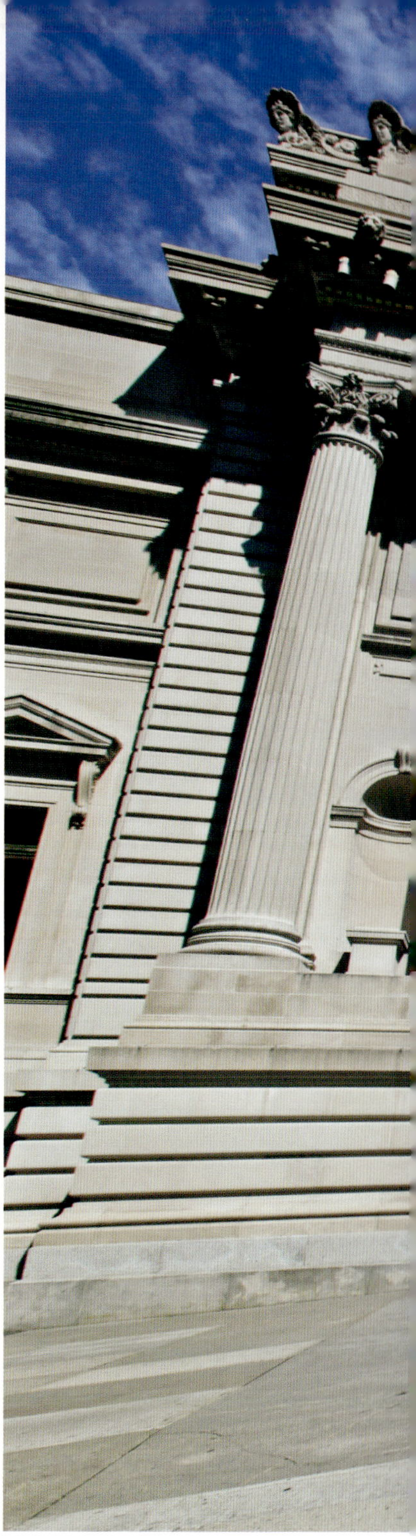

The Frick Collection

Housed in what was once one of Fifth Avenue's most opulent mansions with private gardens and an interior courtyard, this small museum holds a high quality collection of fine furniture and old master paintings, including those of Rembrandt, Hans Holbein, Velazquez, El Greco, and Turner.

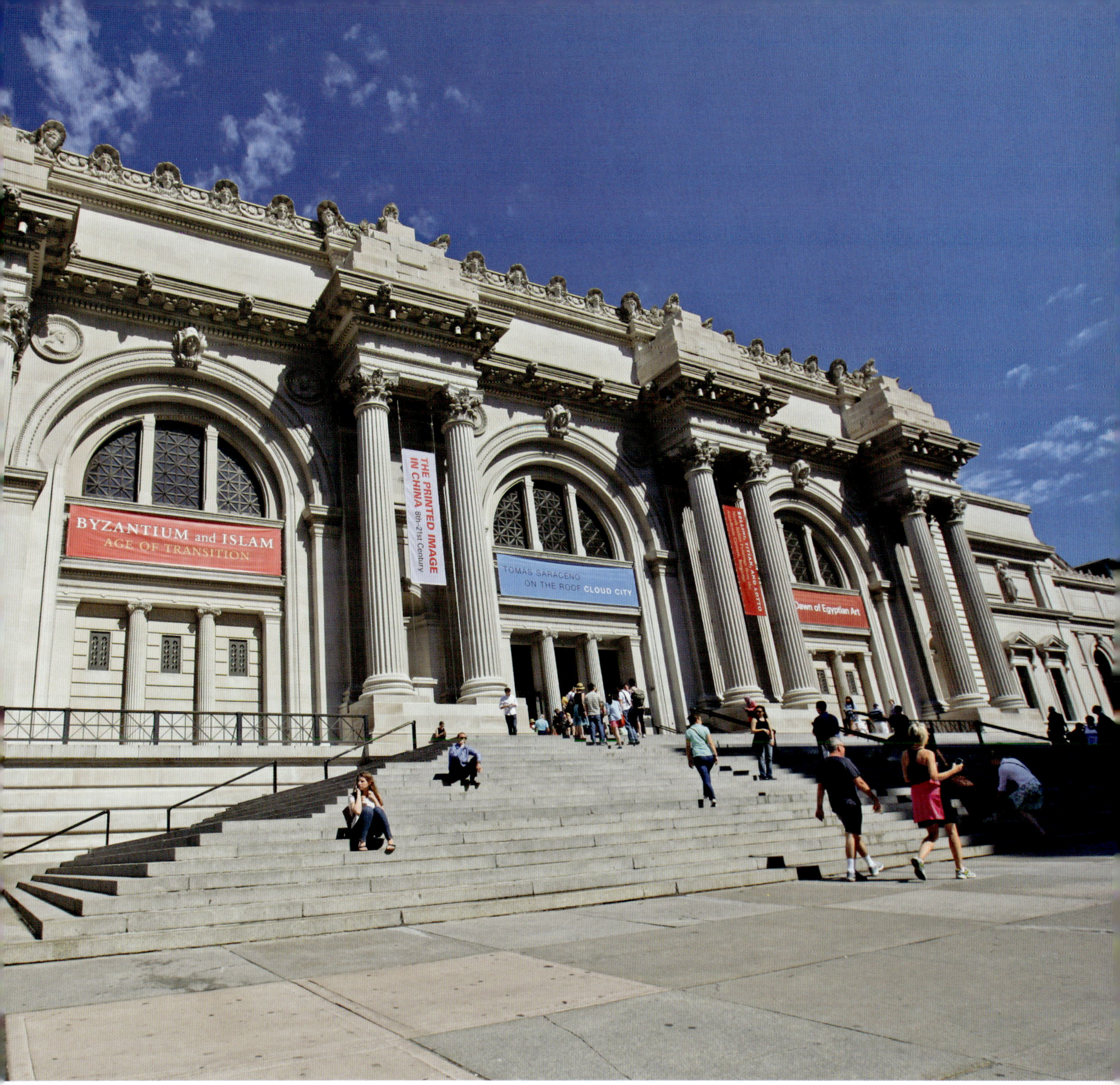

Metropolitan Museum of Art

The Met's collections are so vast that it's impossible to see them all. The museum's two-million-square-foot building houses over two million objects including the largest collection of Egyptian art outside of Cairo, ancient arms and armor, Islamic art, photography, modern and contemporary art, plus world-famous paintings.

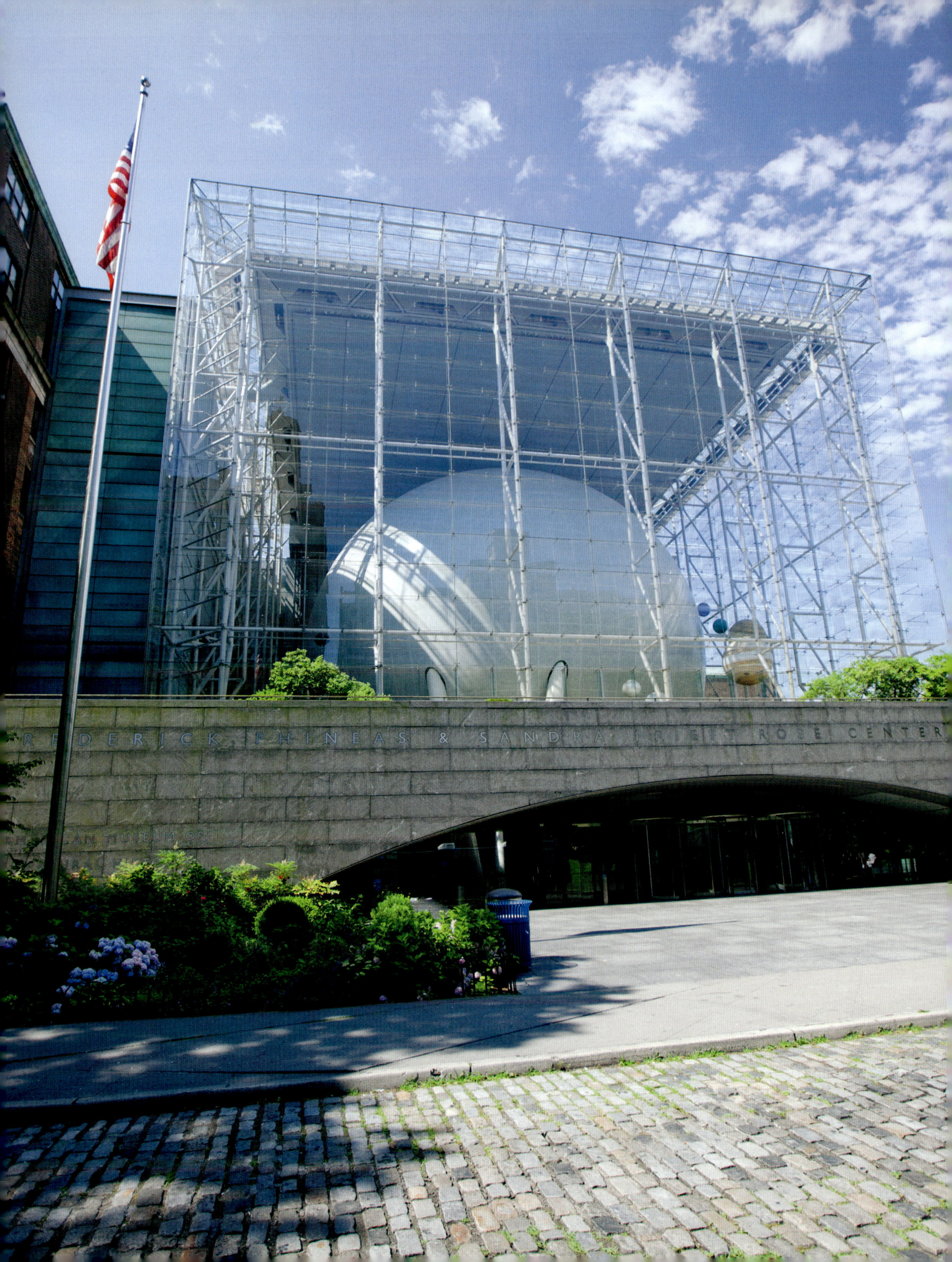

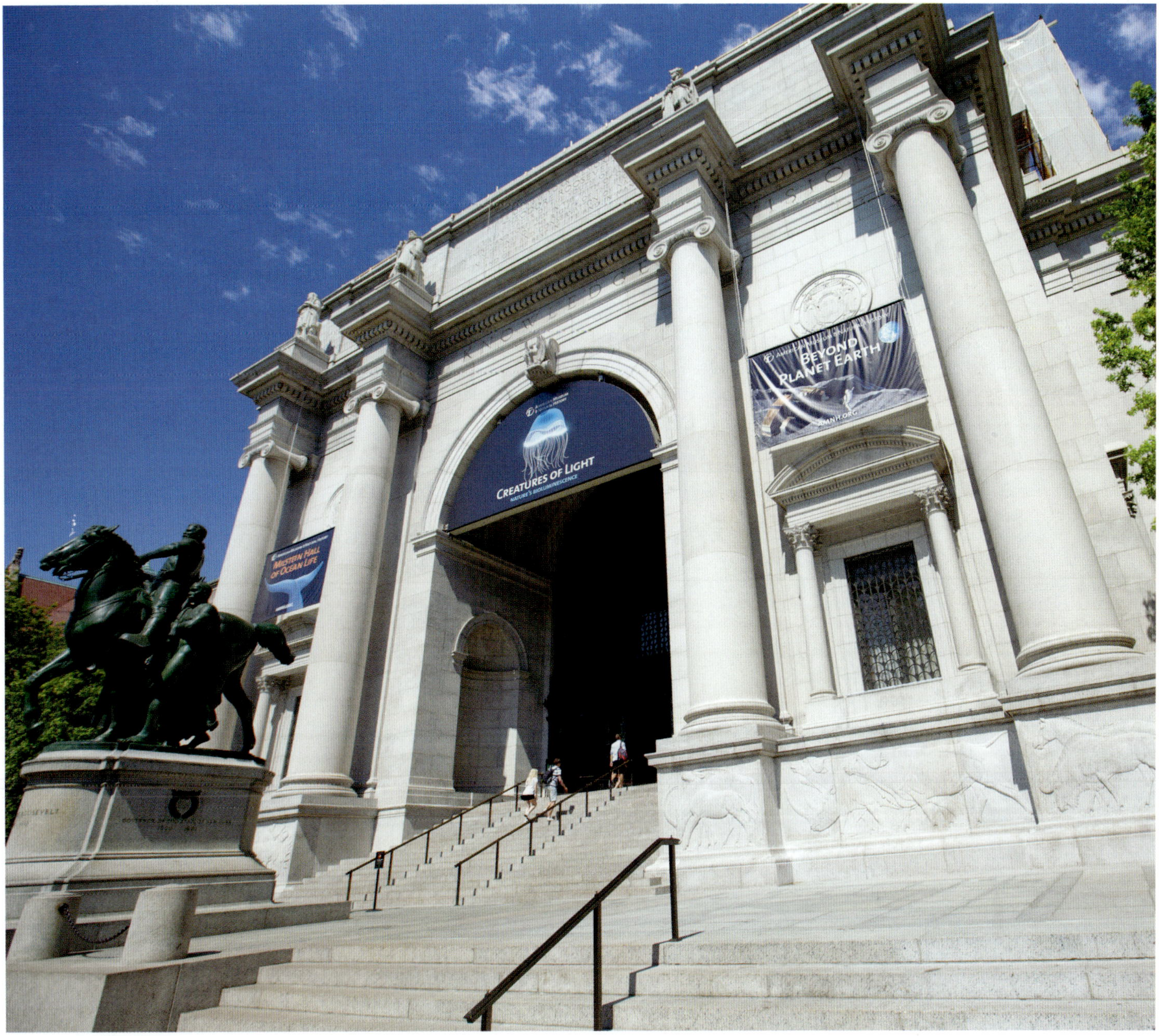

Hayden Planetarium *(opposite)*

Those who are fascinated by planets, stars, galaxies, and constellations should head to the Hayden Planetarium, which is part of the Rose Center for Earth and Space at the American Museum of Natural History. Here the universe unfolds in 3-D laser light shows, lectures, videos, and real moon rocks, tracing life from the Big Bang.

Museum of Natural History *(above)*

This museum has one of the world's largest collection of dinosaur fossils and built-to-scale Tyrannosaurus Rex and Apatosaurus skeletons. Check out the 94-foot-long blue whale suspended from the ceiling in the Hall of Ocean Life, the glistening gems in the Hall of Minerals, and habitat dioramas of life-size gorillas and bison.

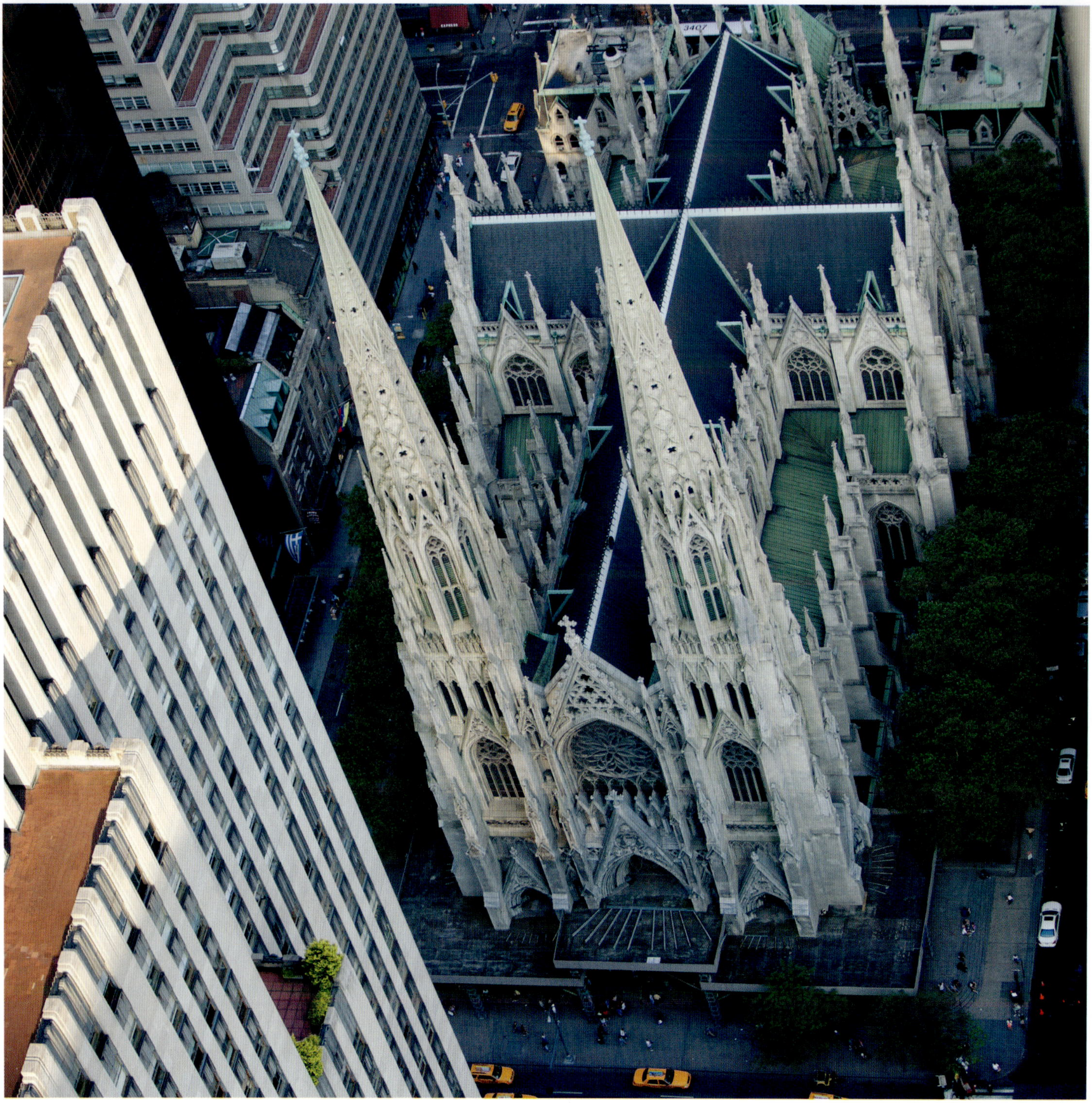

St. Patrick's Cathedral *(above)*

When first proposed in the 1880s, this Gothic church at 50th Street and Fifth Avenue was considered too far outside the city limits, but now it's in the heart of it. St. Patrick's is the center of Catholic life in this country and visited by over 3 million people annually.

George Washington Bridge *(opposite)*

Spanning the Hudson River, this bridge connects Manhattan to New Jersey. In its shadow sits the lighthouse immortalized by the classic children's book, *The Little Red Lighthouse and the Great Gray Bridge*, about the 40-foot-tall structure that once helped ships through a treacherous stretch of river before the bridge's bright lights took over.

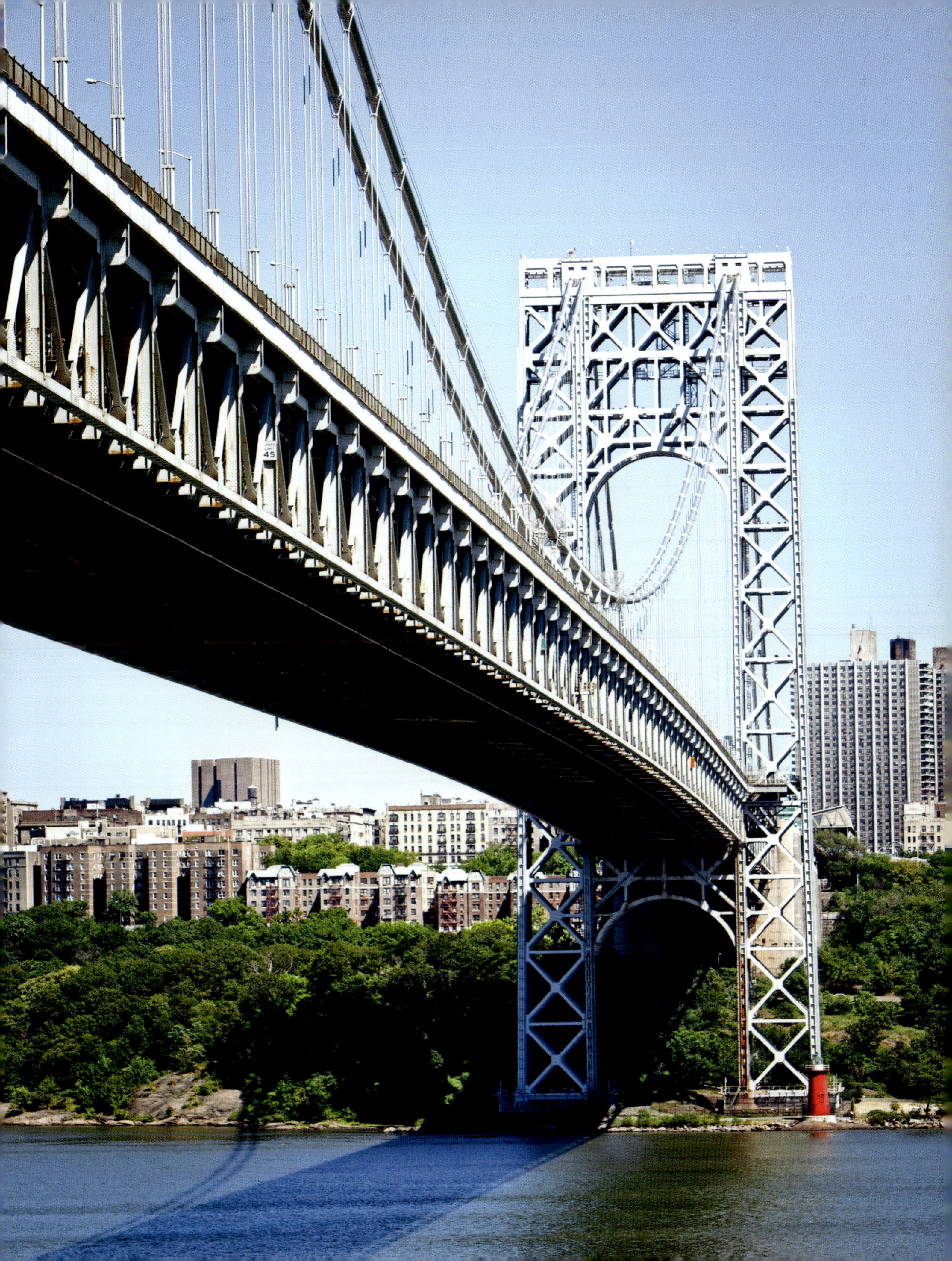

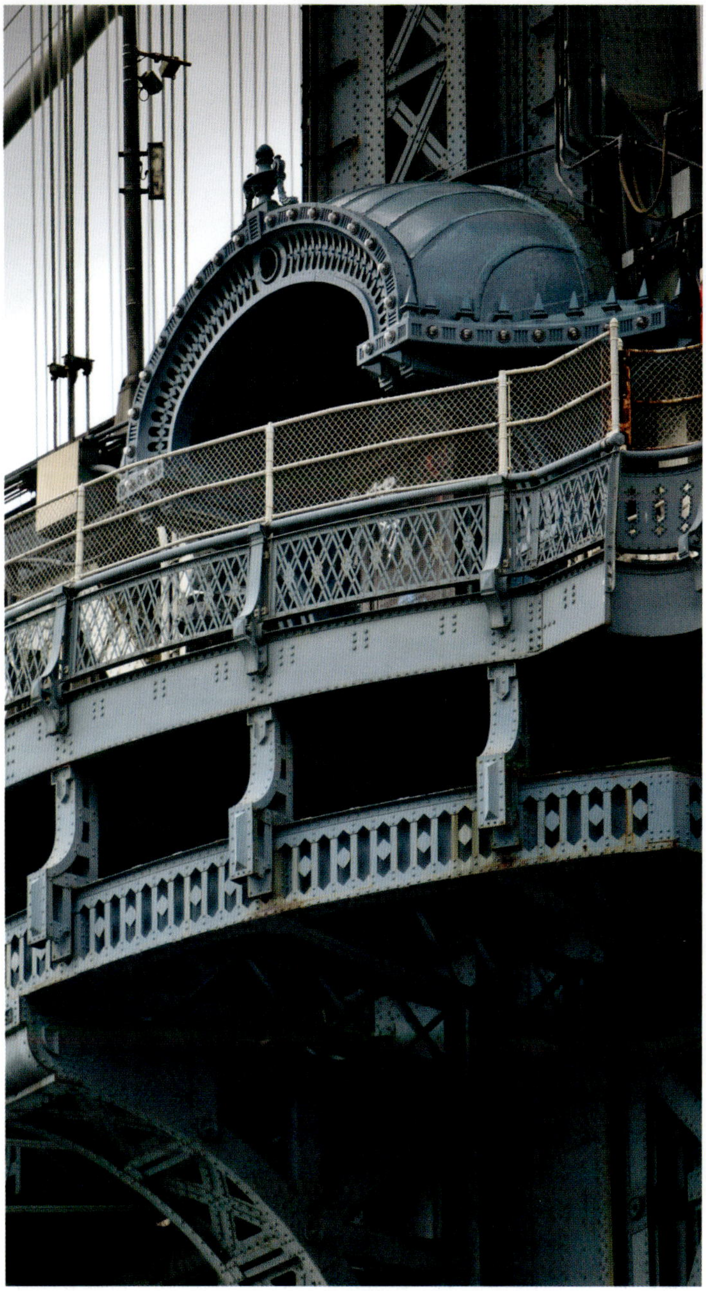

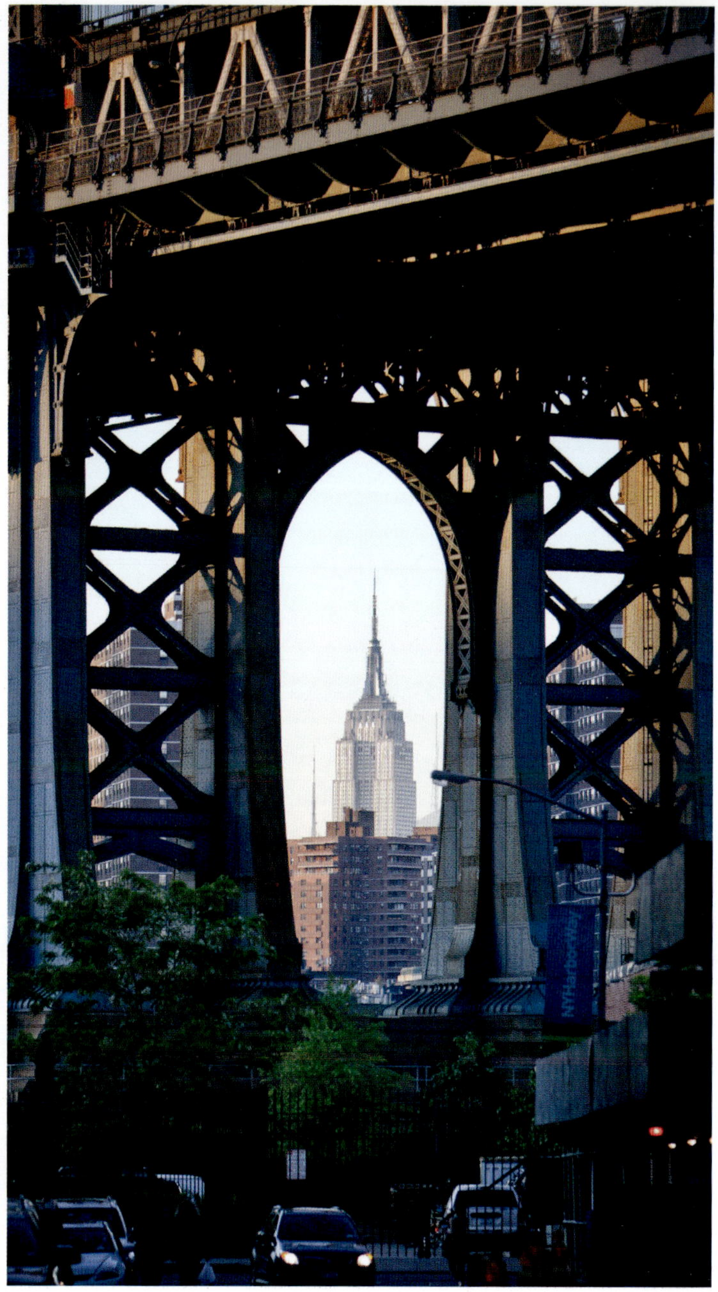

Architectural Detail *(left)*

Sometimes unfavorably compared to its more famous sister, the Brooklyn Bridge, the Manhattan Bridge has in fact been lauded for its combination of function and design. The two-level steel suspension bridge connecting Lower Manhattan with Brooklyn has a European appearance due to its ornate architectural embellishments.

DUMBO *(right)*

Tucked under the Brooklyn side of the Manhattan Bridge is DUMBO (Down Under the Manhattan Bridge Overpass), an area of warehouses and factories converted into galleries, boutiques, theaters, and pricey loft apartments with great views of Manhattan. It's become a hub for technology start-ups and creative entrepreneurs.

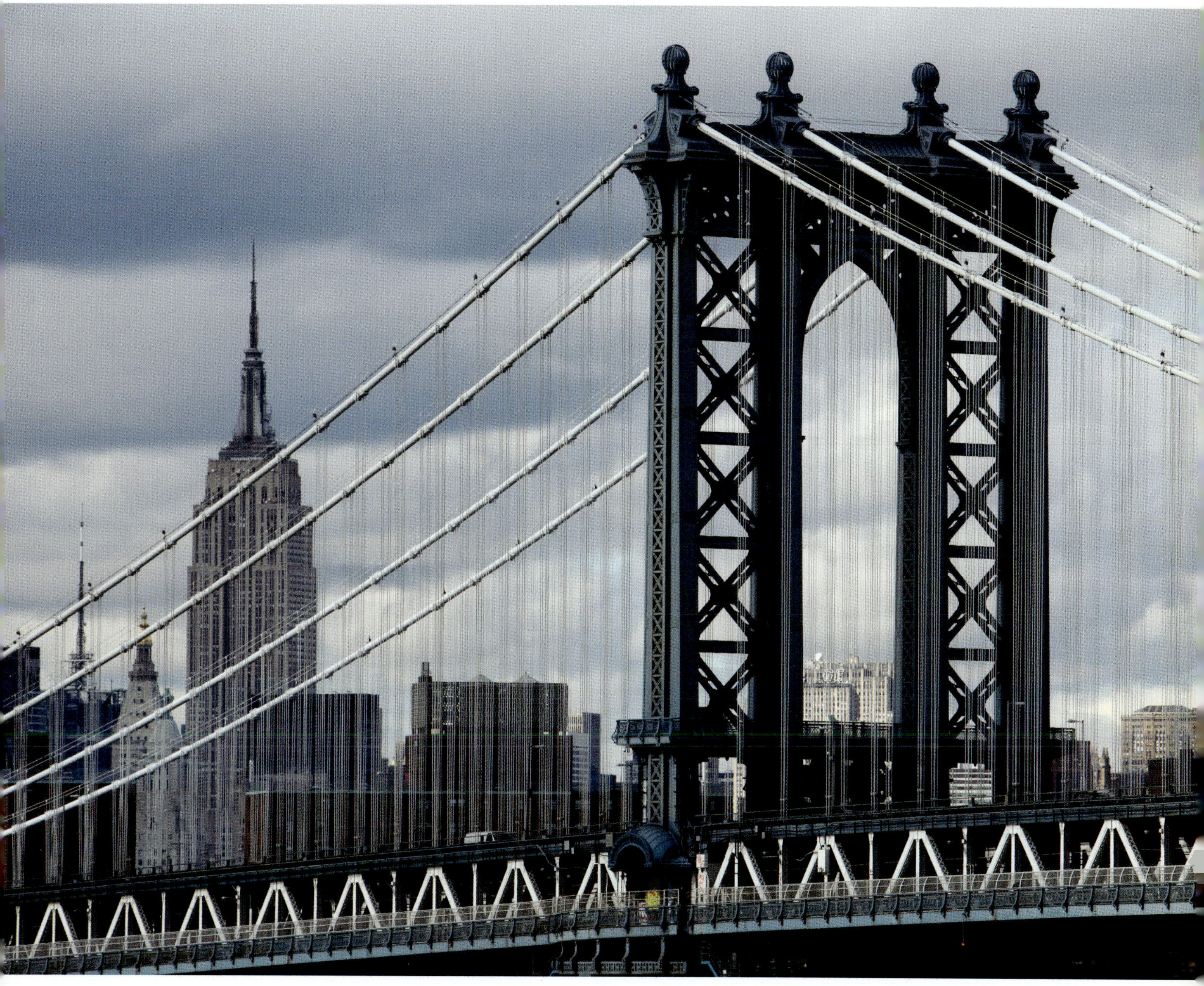

Manhattan Bridge

Walk, ride, or drive over the Manhattan Bridge from Brooklyn and you'll get spectacular vistas of both the Brooklyn and Williamsburg bridges, and New York Harbor, plus a bird's eye view of both Downtown and the Midtown skyline complete with the Empire State and Chrysler buildings.

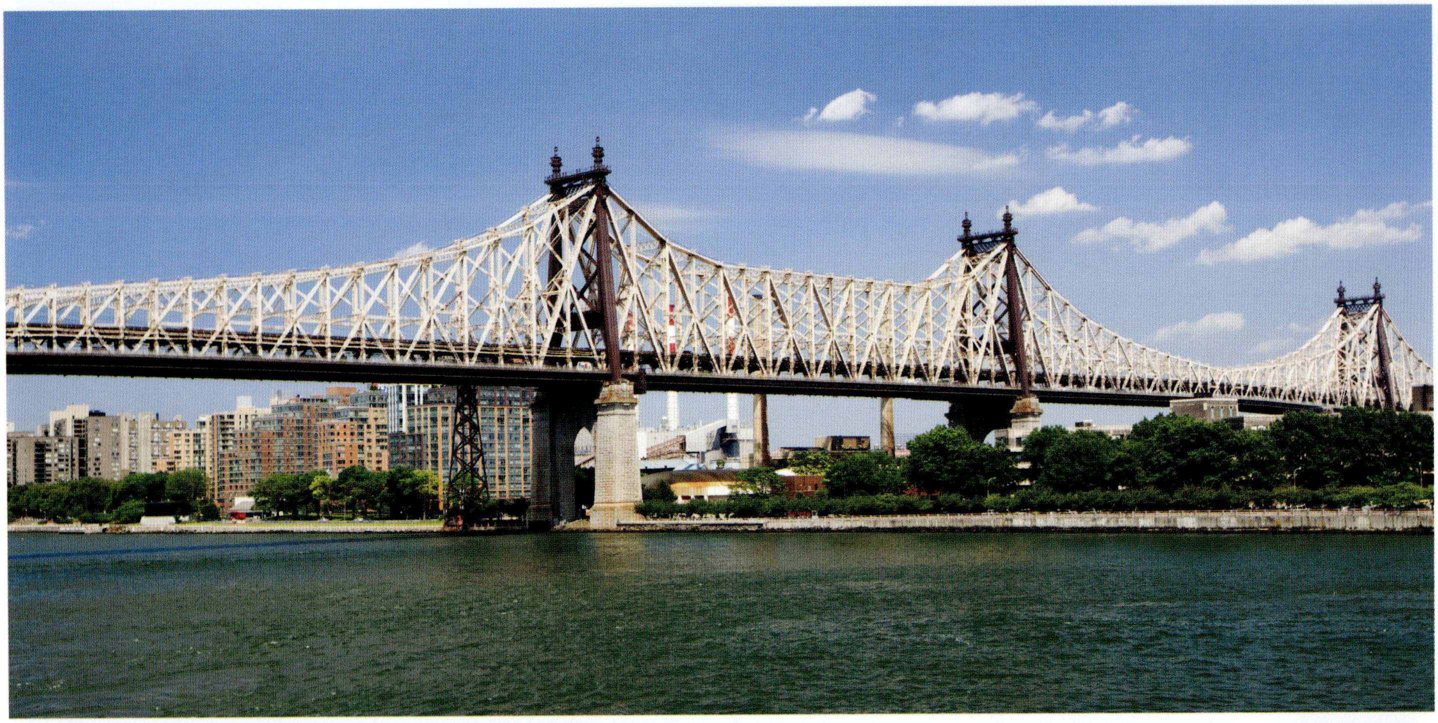

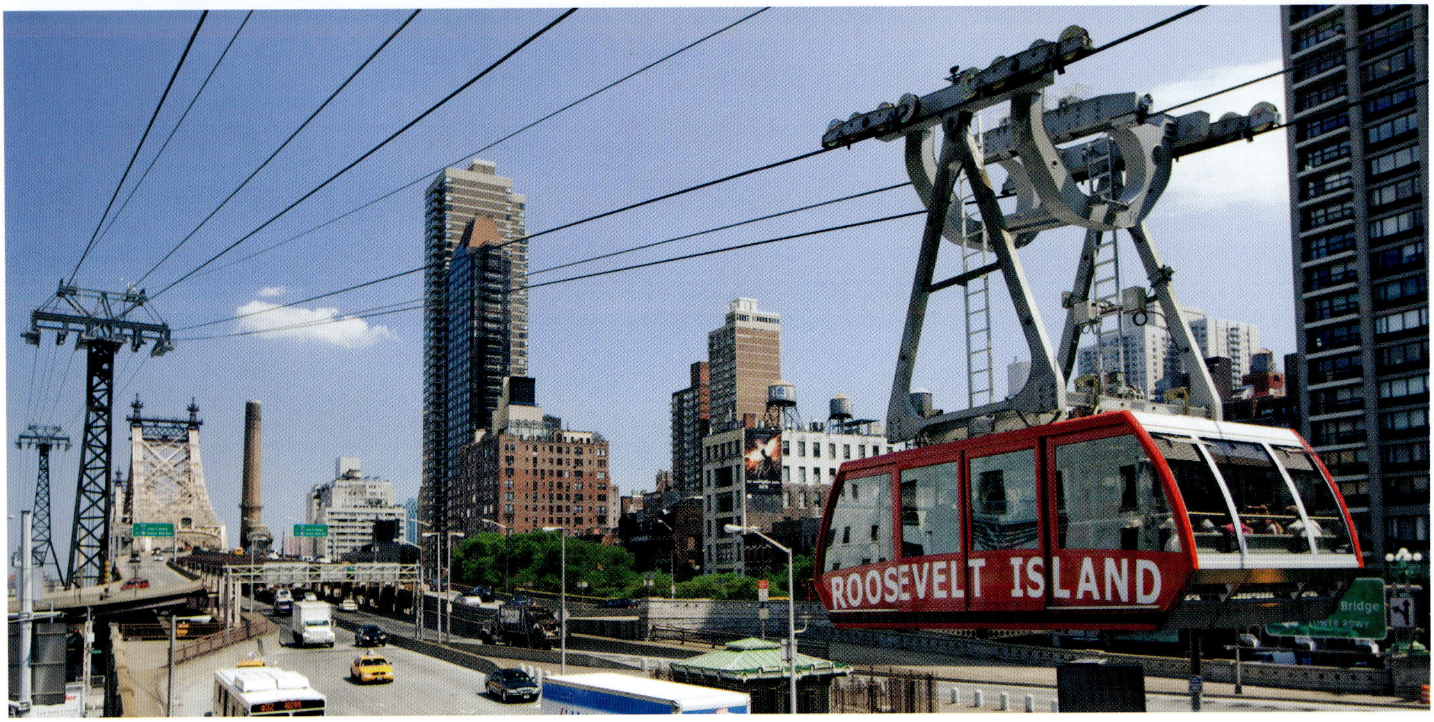

Queensboro Bridge *(top)*

Renamed the Ed Koch Queeensboro Bridge for the city's former mayor, this cantilever crossing over the East River is known to locals simply as the 59th Street Bridge. It connects Long Island City in Queens with Midtown Manhattan, passing over Roosevelt Island.

Roosevelt Island Tram *(bottom)*

For residents of Roosevelt Island the tram is one of their main forms of transportation into Manhattan; for the rest of us, it's like an amusement park ride over the East River with great aerial views of the East Side. The fare is just one swipe on a Metrocard.

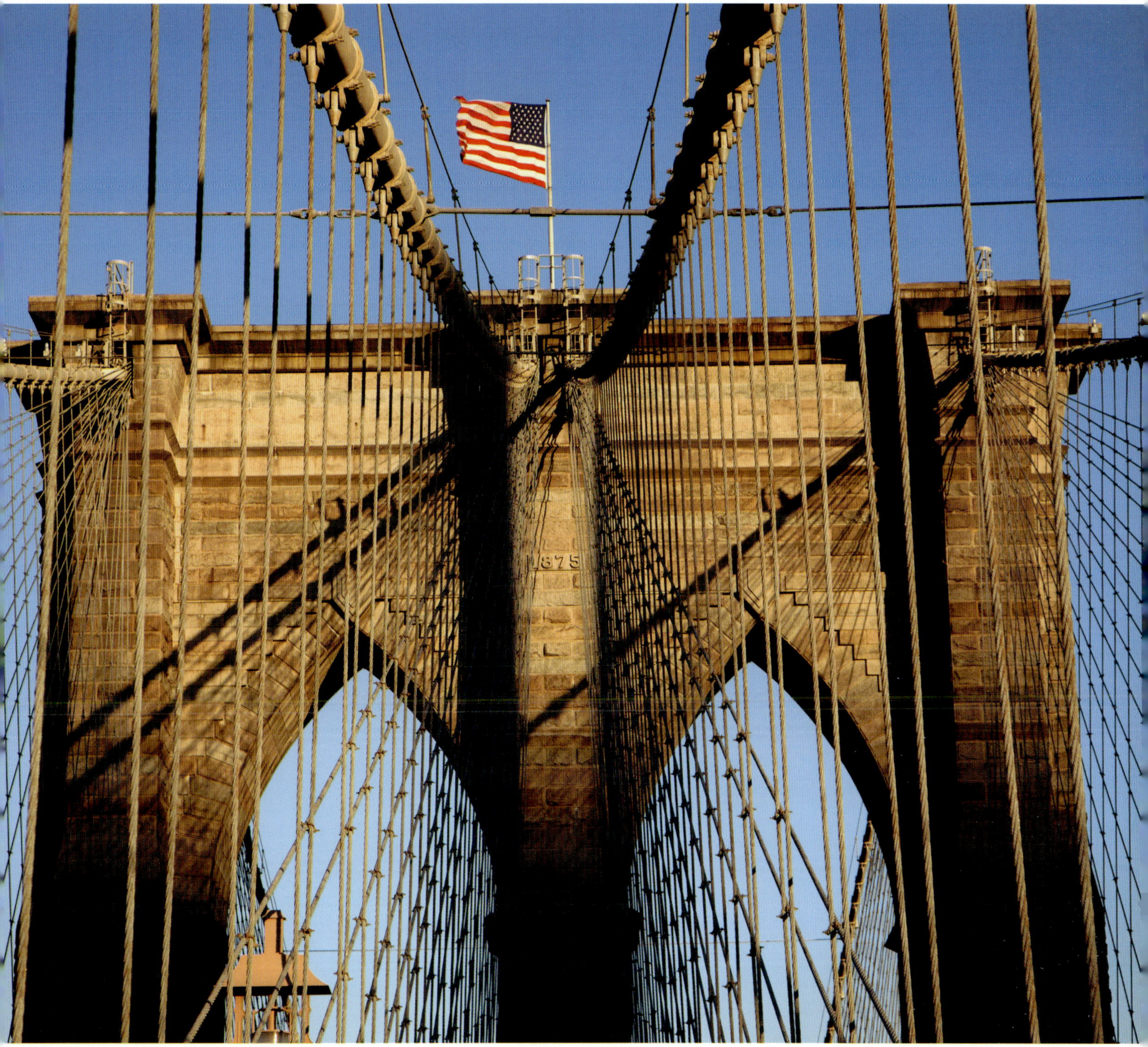

Brooklyn Bridge

One of the oldest, and once the world's longest suspension bridge, the Brooklyn Bridge has spanned the East River, connecting Lower Manhattan with Brooklyn since 1883. Its Gothic arches and graceful lines have made it an iconic part of the New York skyline. It was designated a National Historic Landmark in 1964.

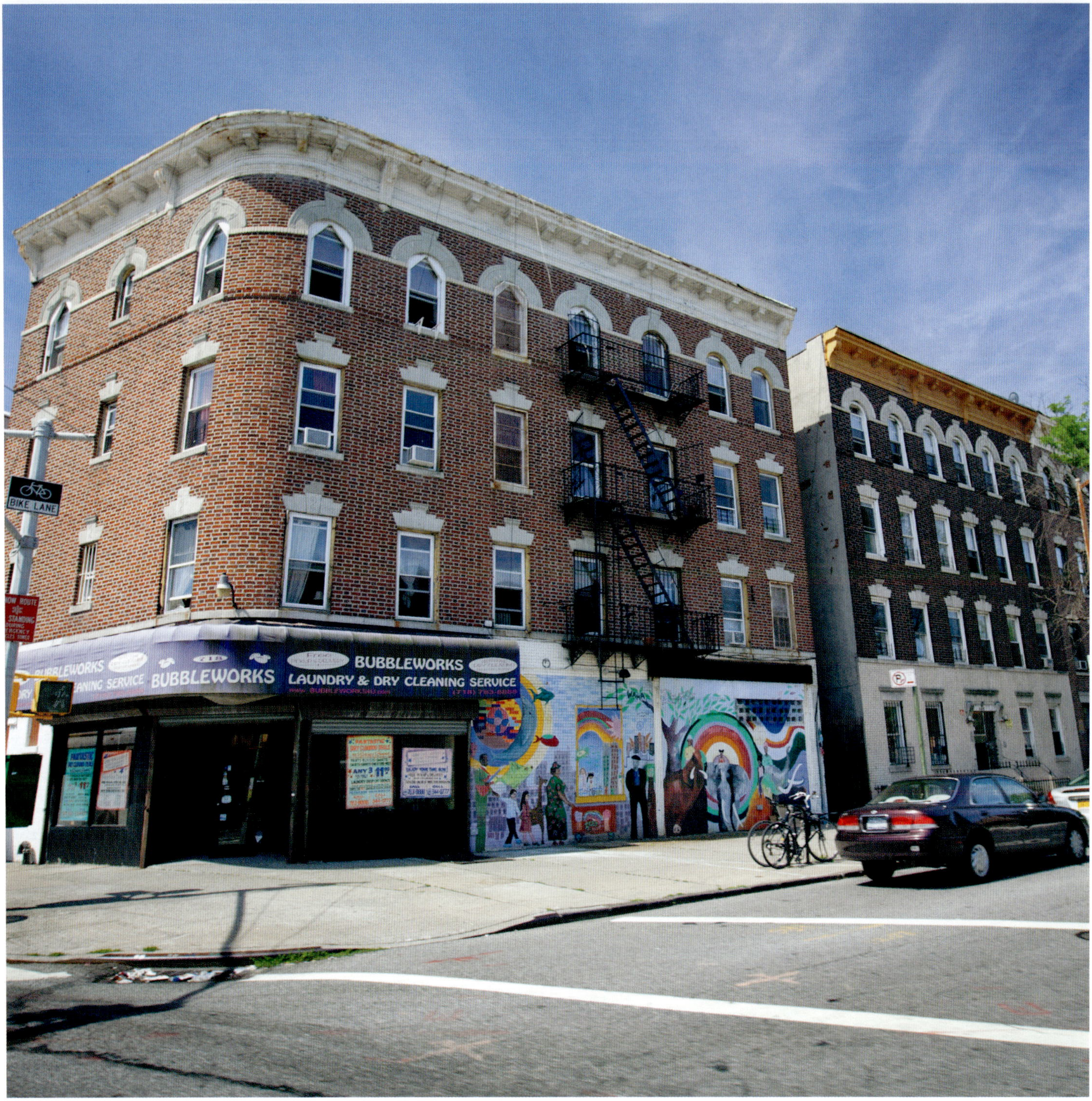

Brooklyn

If Brooklyn was a separate city, as it once was, it would be the fourth most populous one in America. Situated across the East River from Manhattan, Brooklyn has world-class theatre and museums, hipster neighborhoods, and the new Frank Gehry-designed Barclays Center indoor arena that hosts the NBA Brooklyn Nets.

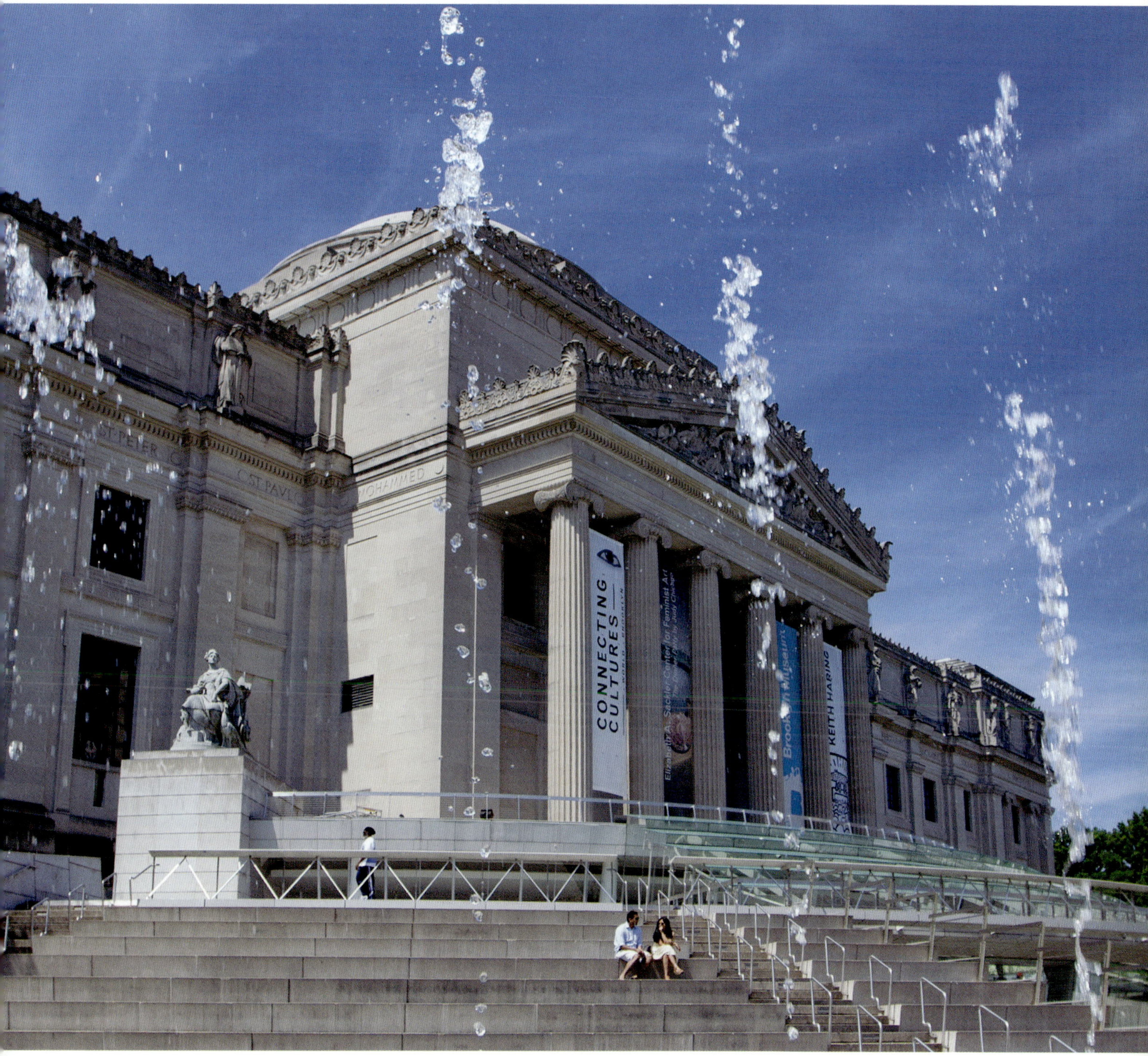

Brooklyn Museum

This massive, five-story museum holds the city's second largest art collection, with about 1.5 million pieces. It's as known for its 18th-century portraits as for major exhibitions of such modern artists as Basquiat and Haring. Created by WET Design, the front plaza includes a fountain with "dancing" water jets that are irresistible to kids.

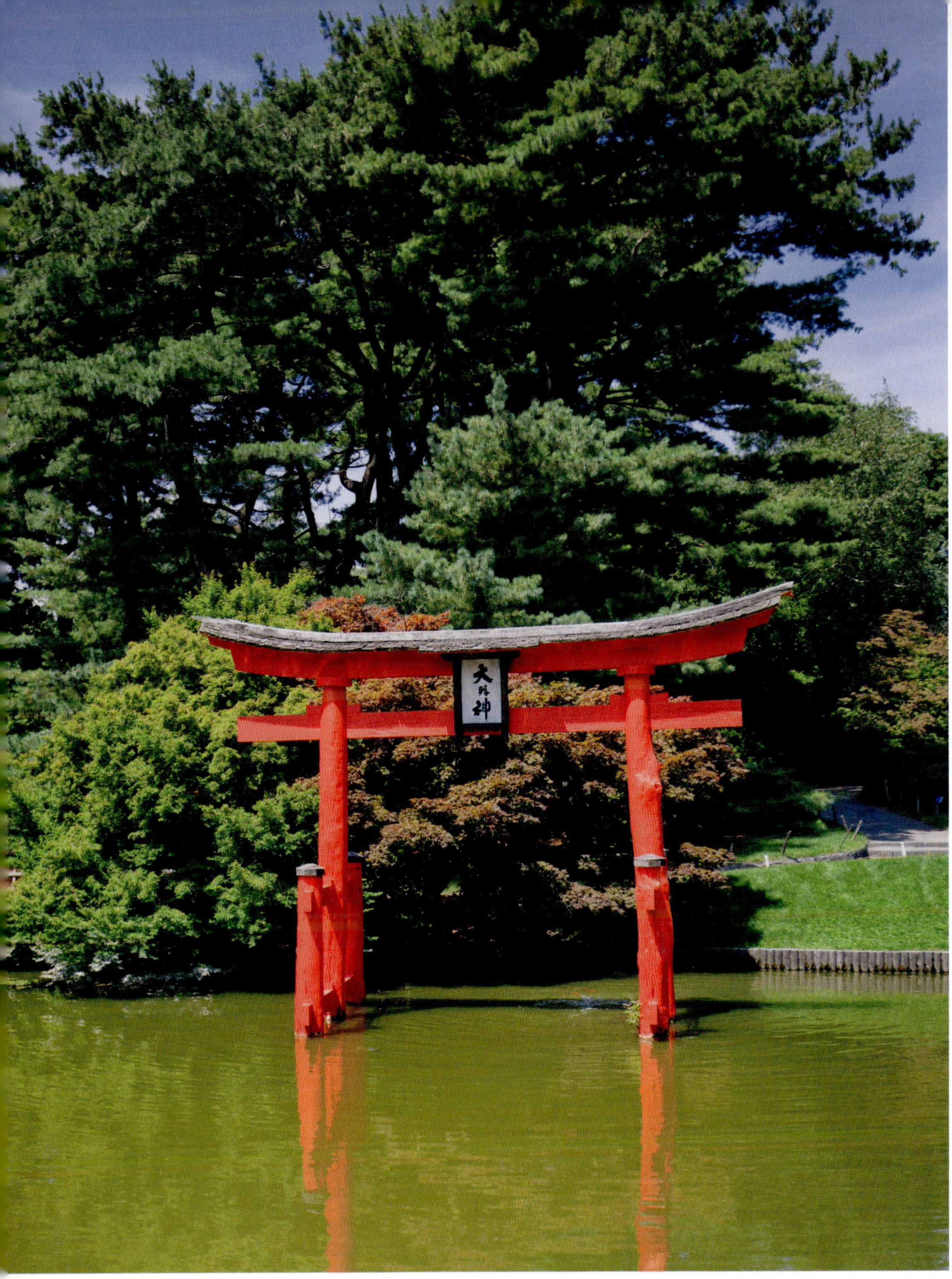

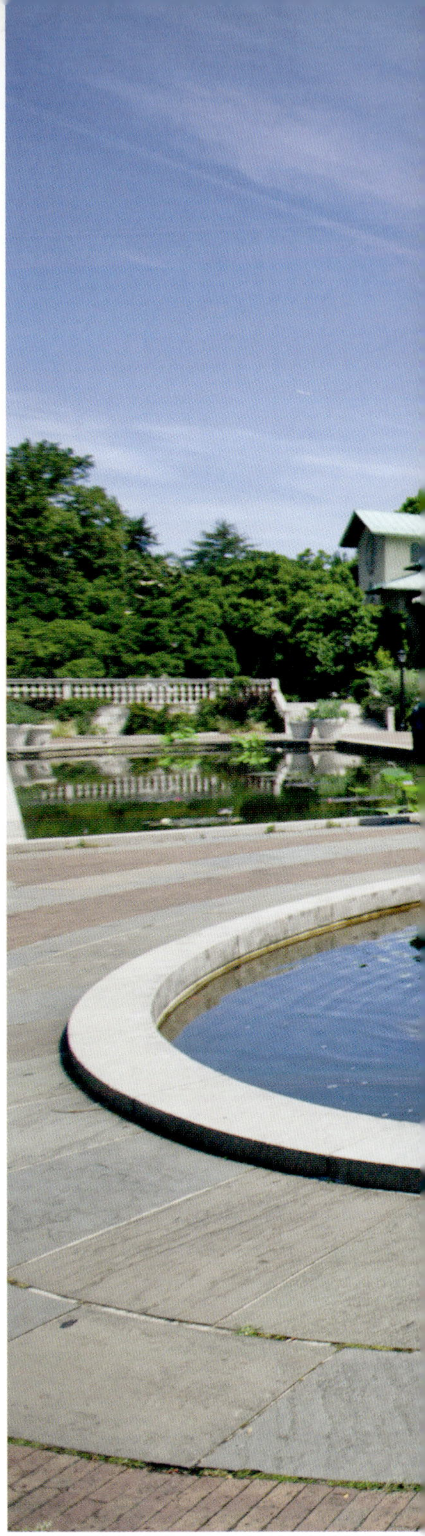

Japanese Hill-and-Pond Garden

A central feature of the Brooklyn Botanic Garden idyll is its Japanese Garden, complete with a torii and Shinto shrine. Each spring when more than 200 cherry trees are abloom, the garden hosts the annual Sakura Matsuri Festival featuring traditional and contemporary Japanese culture, music, and arts.

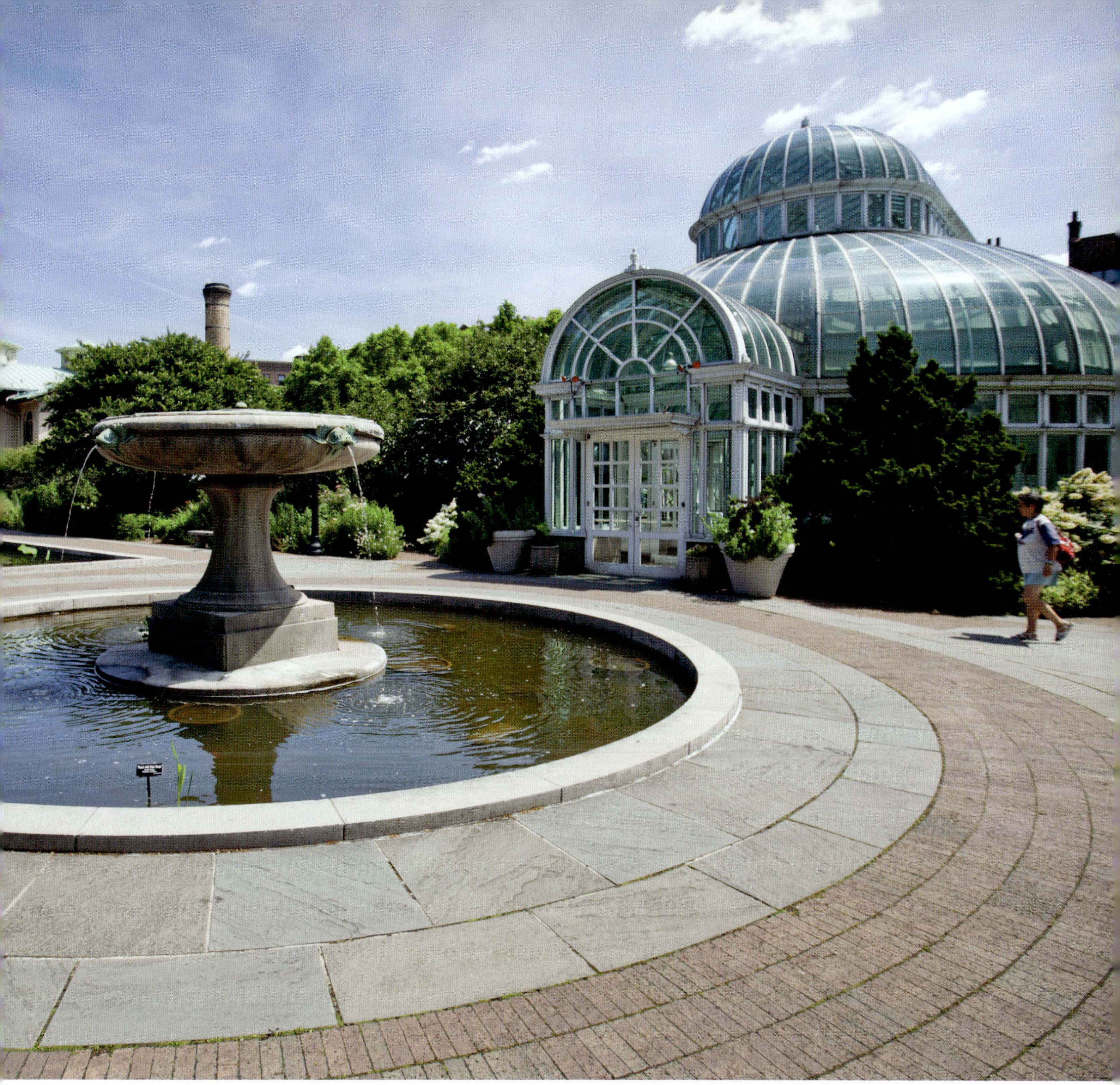

Brooklyn Botanic Garden

Ever blossoming, the Brooklyn Botanic Garden is 52 acres of woods, herb gardens, flower beds, and the Cranford Rose Garden with 1,200 varieties in every shape, size, and hue imaginable. Inside the glass-domed conservatory is a Bonsai Museum. Located near the Palm House are the Lily Pool Terrace and Jenkins Fountain.

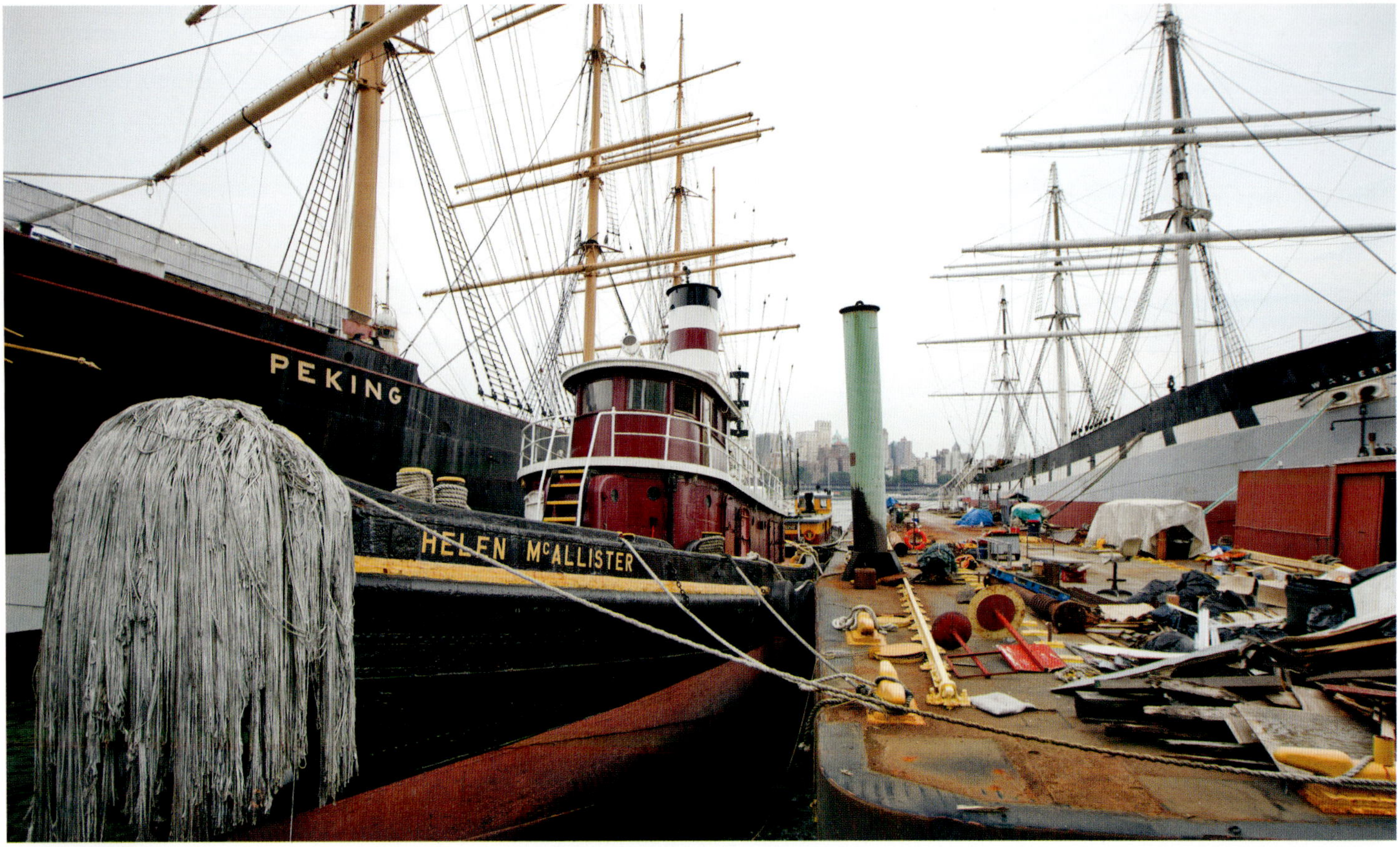

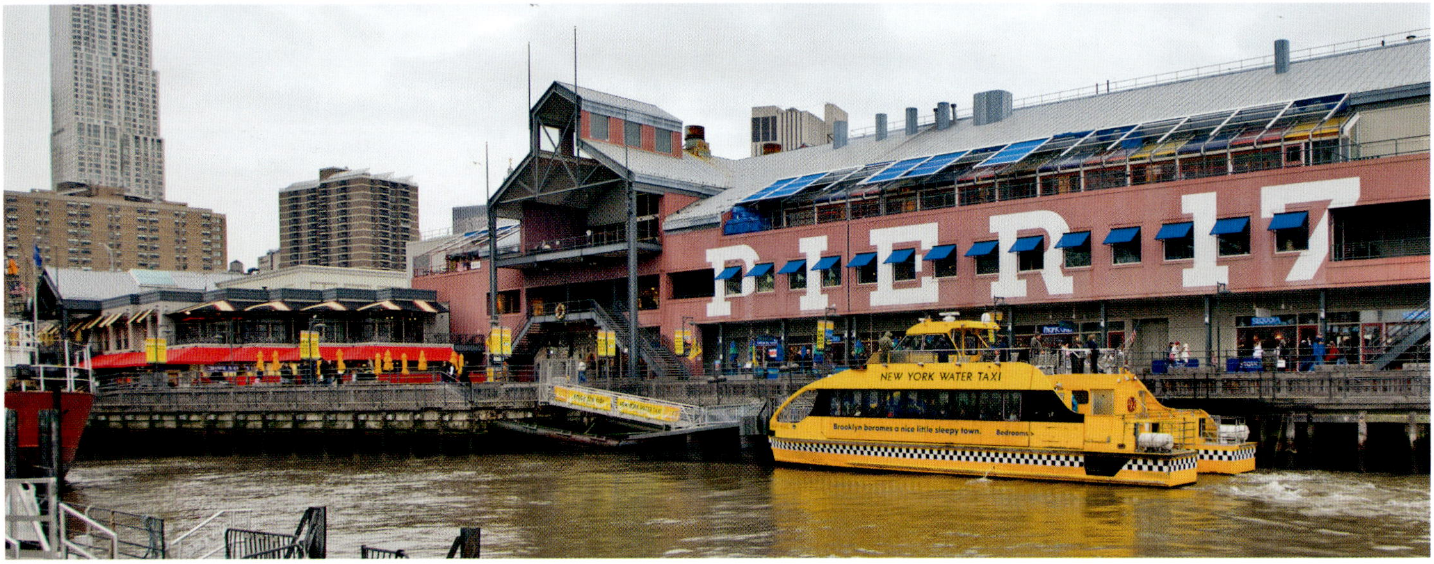

South Street Seaport *(top)*

Wander the cobblestone streets of what was once the city's original port. Today, this historic area adjacent to the financial district is a living museum of restored early 19th century commercial buildings and renovated ships, some of which take the public out for a sail on the East River.

Pier 17 *(bottom)*

In 1985, the city's original Fulton Fish Market was turned into a shopping, eating, entertainment emporium, and downtown destination. Here you can also catch the distinctive black and yellow checkered Water Taxi for a hop-on-hop-off ride around town.

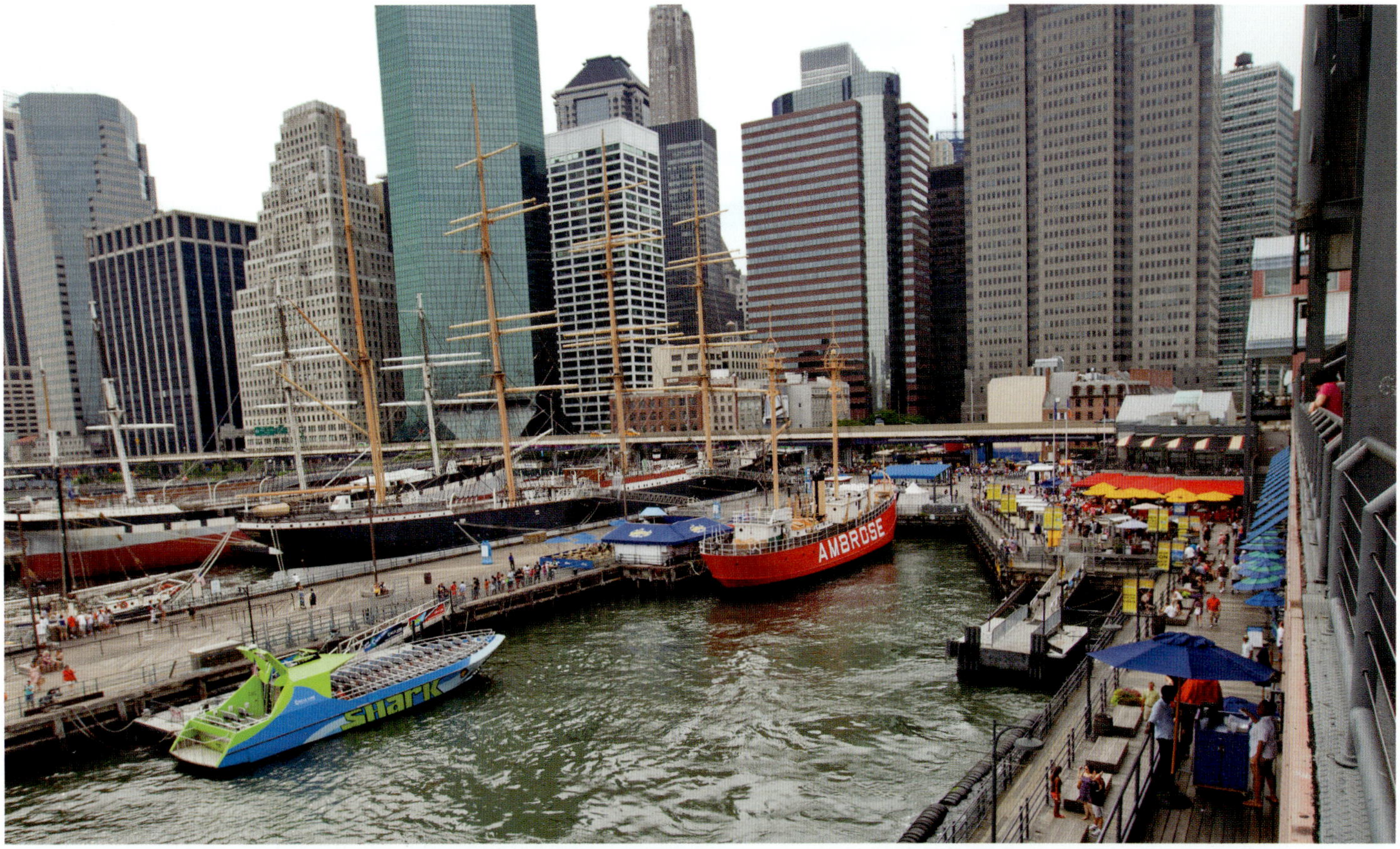

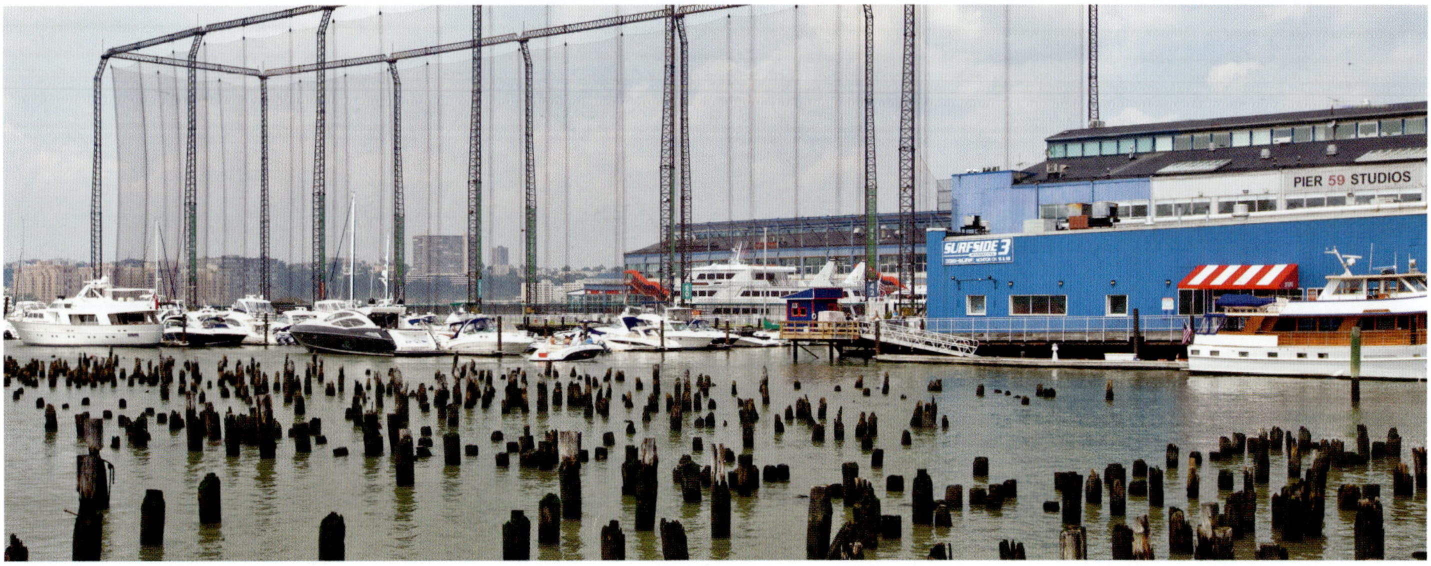

Water Tours *(top)*

There are lots of ways to see New York City's towering skyline from the water. Visit the historical displays and preserved cabins aboard the newly restored 1907 historic lightship *Ambrose* at the South Street Seaport, or head for the seas aboard the *Shark*, a speedboat ride that captures the energy and excitement of the city.

Chelsea Piers *(bottom)*

Where else can you go ice skating, hit golf balls, climb a wall, play indoor soccer, and refresh at a day spa? Why at Chelsea Piers, of course! This series of once underused piers along the Hudson River has been transformed into a 30-acre sports and entertainment complex revitalizing the waterfront.

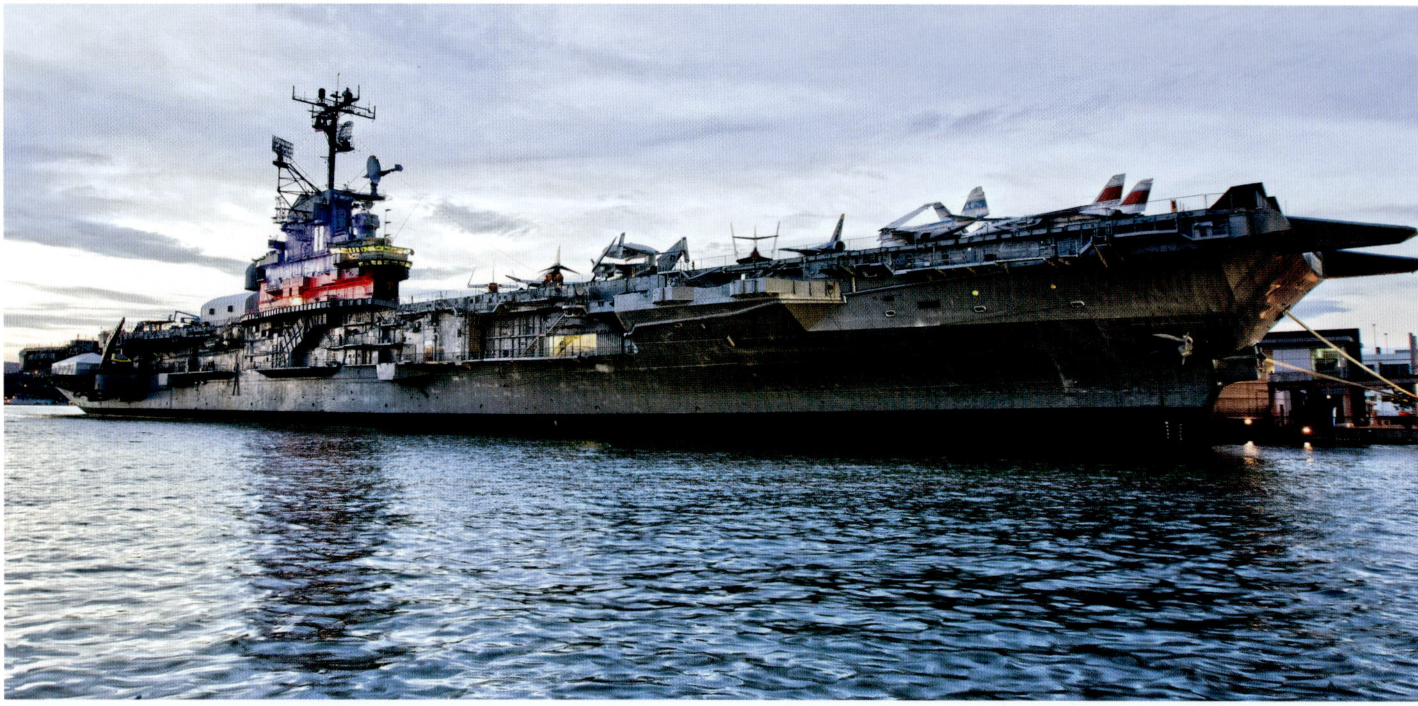

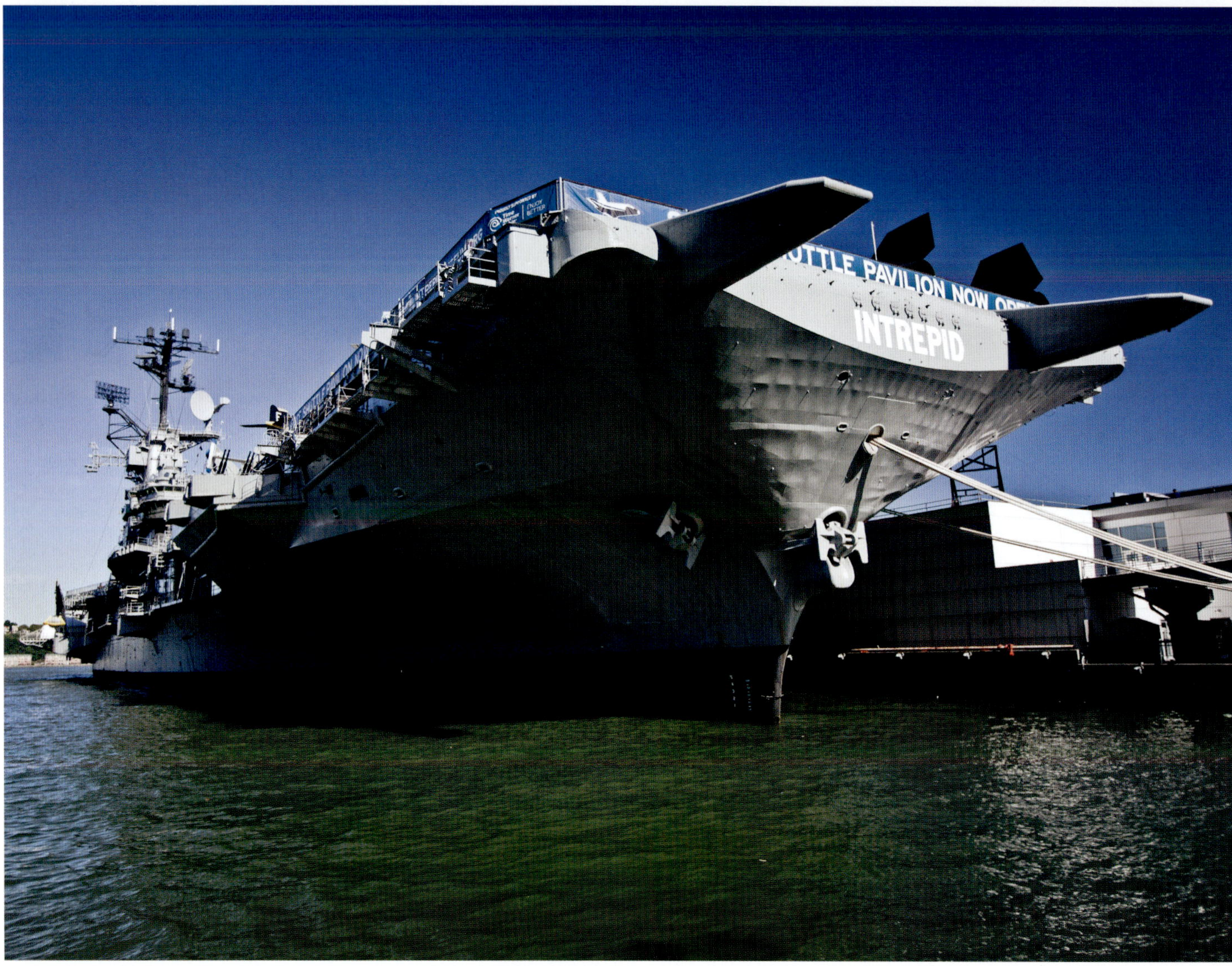
INTREPID

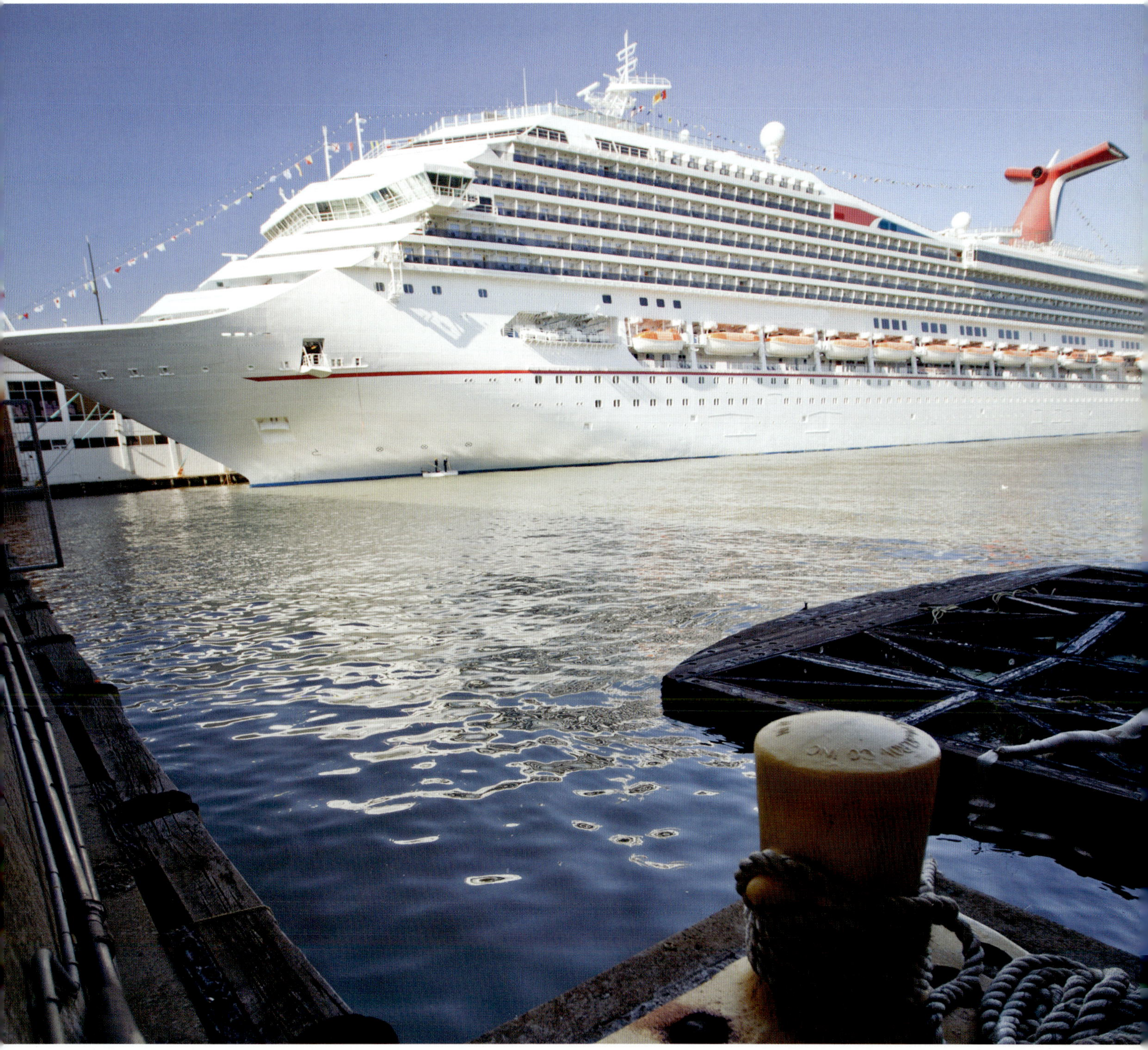

Intrepid *(opposite, top and bottom)*

The Sea, Air & Space Museum on the Hudson River is centered on the *Intrepid*, an aircraft carrier that proudly served in World War II and Vietnam. Examine original artifacts, view historic videos, and climb its numerous decks to explore every nook and cranny for a real hands-on, interactive experience.

Cruise Ship Docks *(opposite)*

If you want to hit the high seas you can start right here on the Hudson River, where some of the world's largest cruise ships dock. Or just ride your bike over to the waterfront piers to gawk at these floating cities and wave goodbye as they take off to foreign lands.

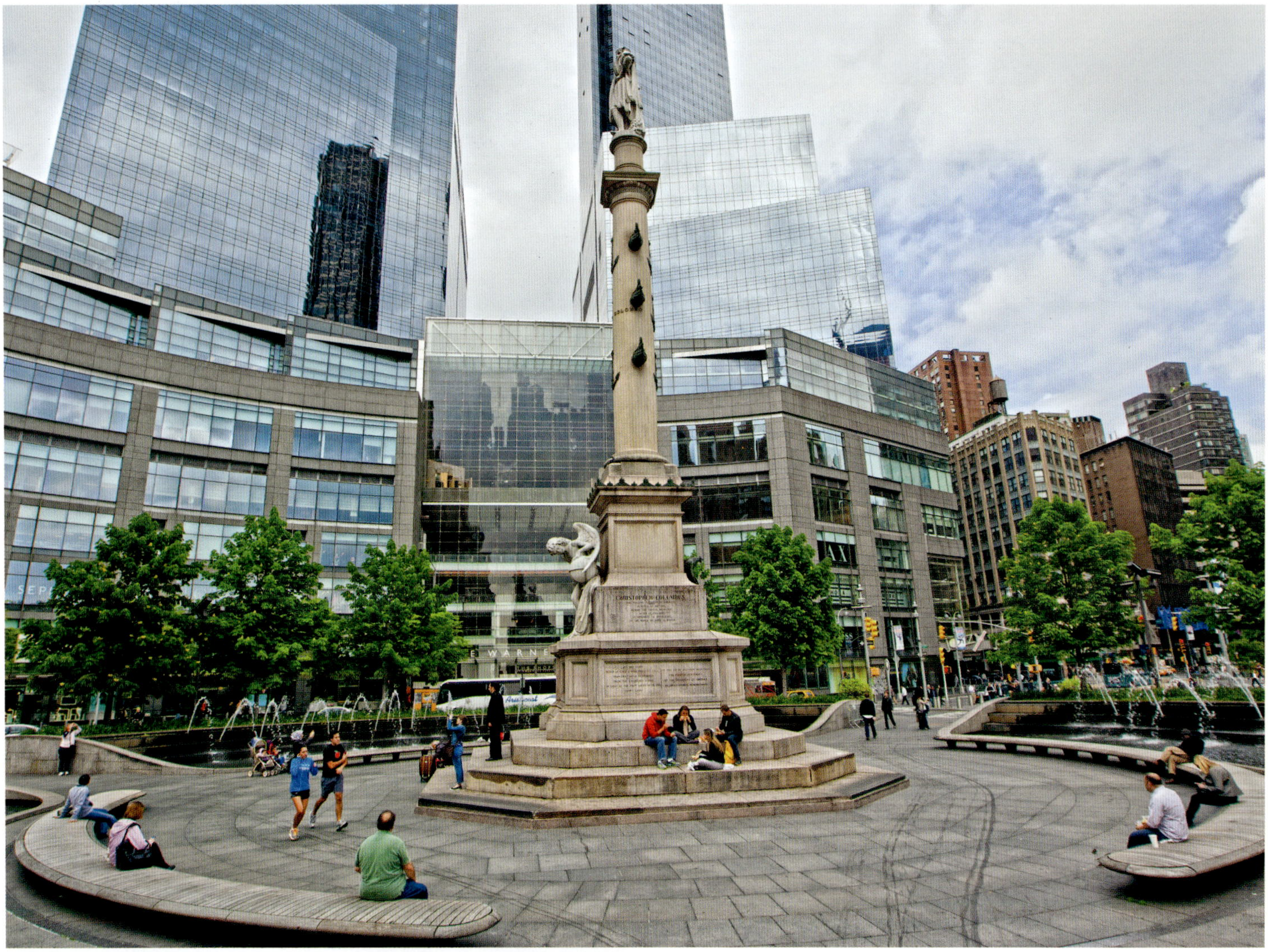

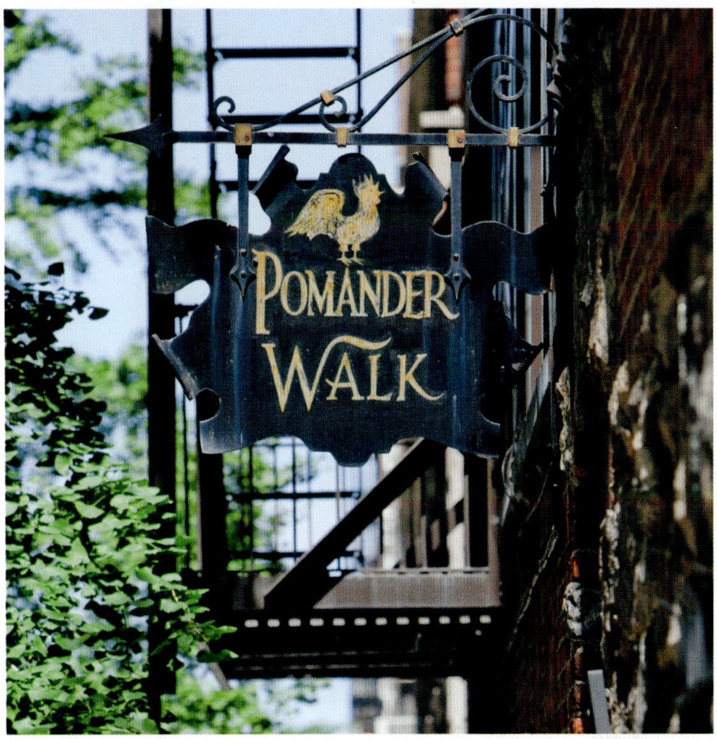

Columbus Circle *(above)*

A larger-than-life statue of Christopher Columbus rises more than 75 feet atop a granite column in a traffic circle near the Museum of Art and Design, Time Warner Center, and Trump International Hotel and Tower. Commemorating the 400th anniversary of Columbus' landing in America, it is the point from which all distances from New York City are measured.

Pomander Walk *(left and opposite)*

This little-known residential enclave is the closest thing to an English Country Lane on the Upper West Side. Now a co-op, residents of the 16 diminutive attached Tudor-style houses live behind locked wrought-iron gates in a tranquil urban oasis that hasn't changed since it was built in 1921.

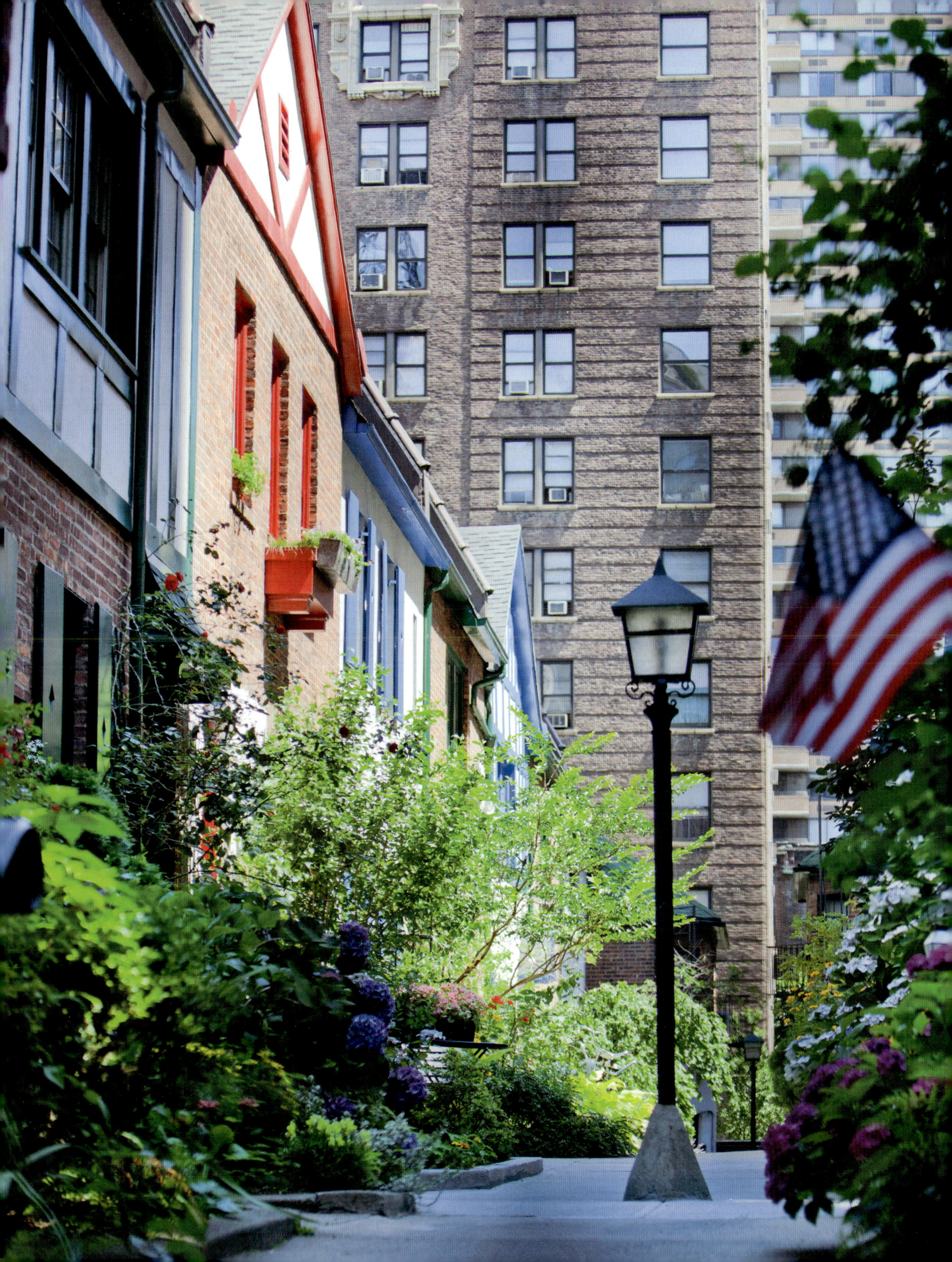

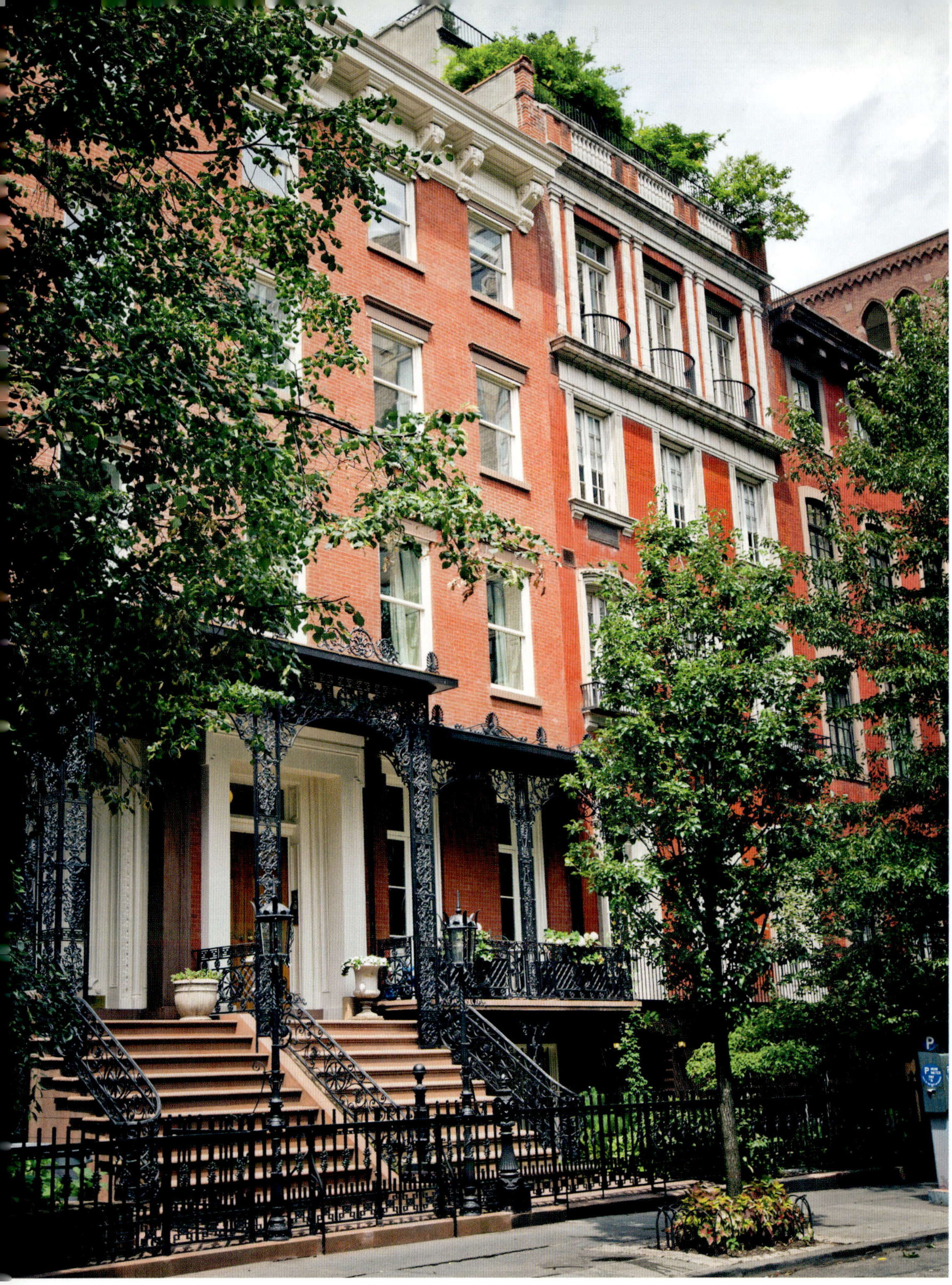

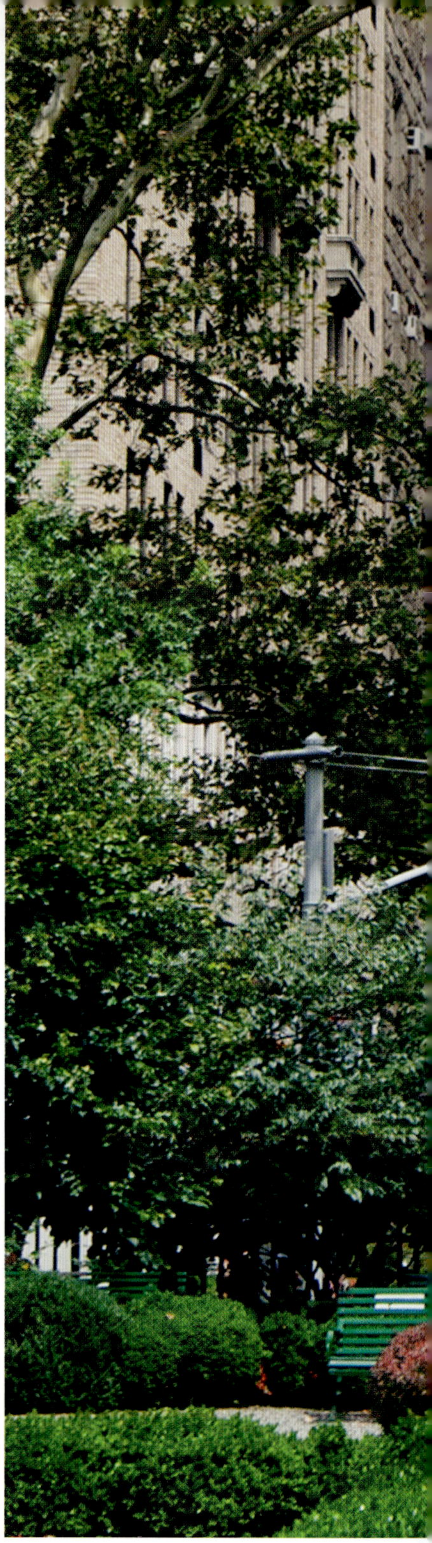

Gramercy Park

Gramercy Park is a fashionable, tranquil neighborhood located in the East 20s where time has stood still. Many of the elegant townhouses that surround its central park are historic landmarks that date back to the 1840s and 50s. Since then, some have been remodeled and converted into apartments and private clubs.

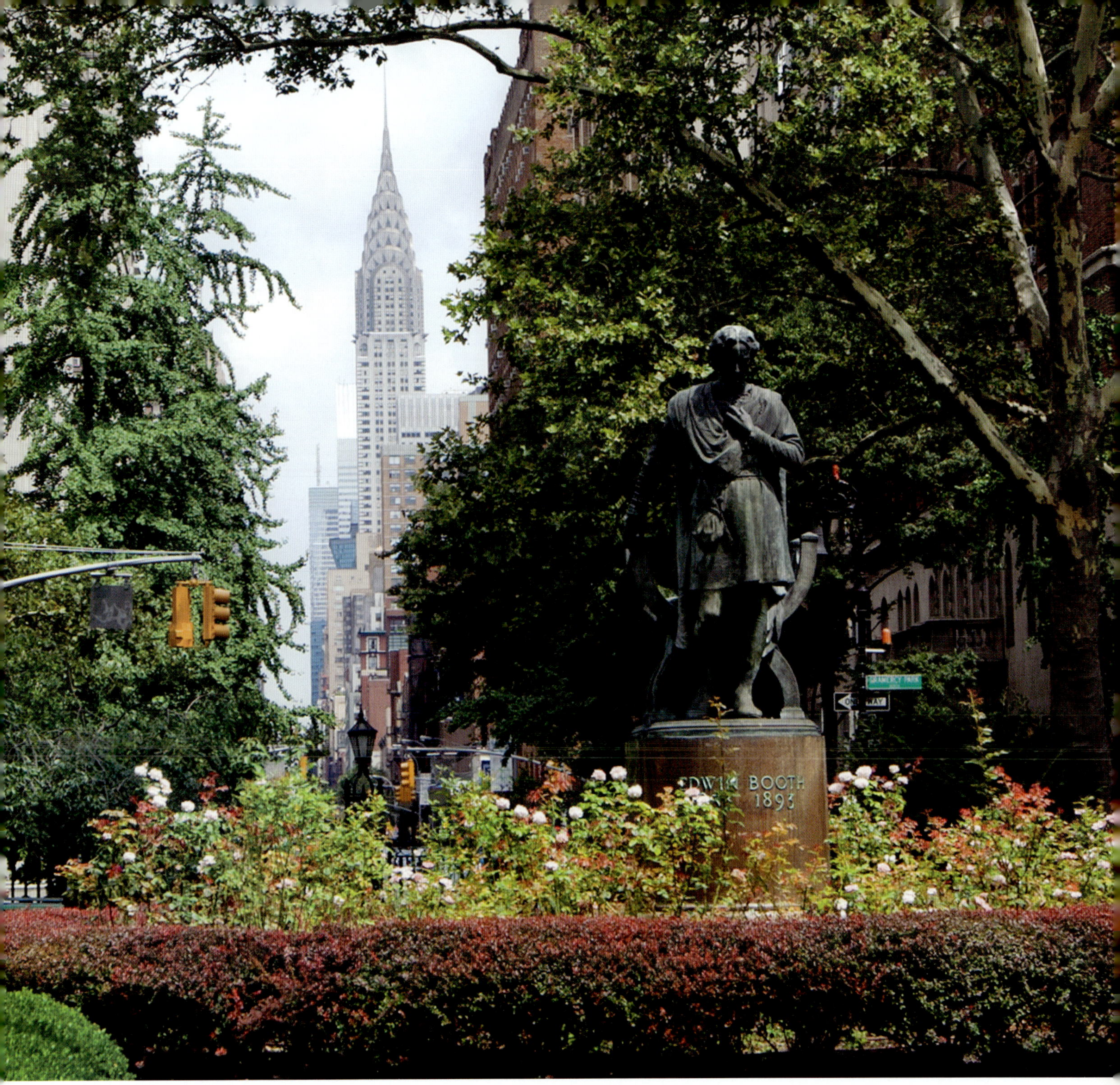

Gramercy's Private Park

Residents lucky enough to live along Gramercy Park get a prized key to the city's only private park. Its most famous resident was Shakespearean actor Edwin Booth, brother of John Wilkes, who assassinated Abraham Lincoln. Well known for his role as Hamlet and for founding the Players Club, this memorial was unveiled in 1918.

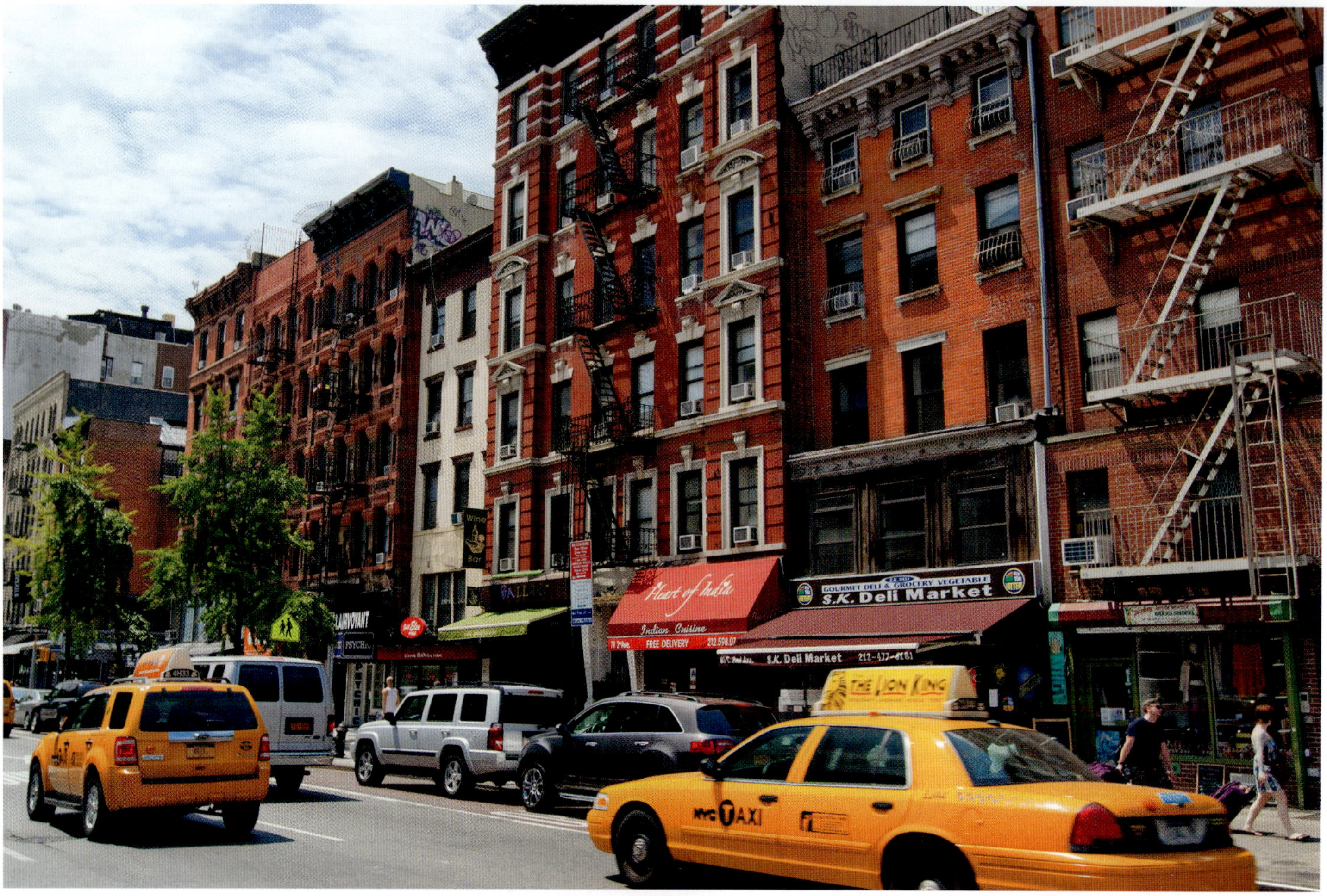

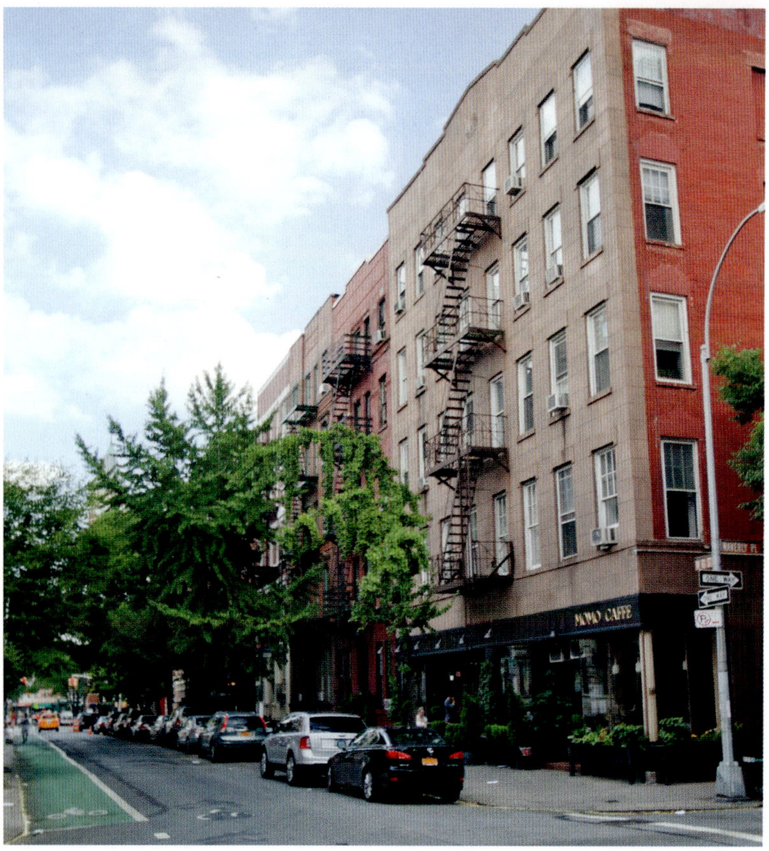

East Village *(above)*

The ethnically diverse East Village has culinary treats that span the world reflecting its immigrants both past and present. Feast on Sicilian pizza, Mexican tacos, Chinese dumplings, Vietnamese *bánh mì* sandwiches, or Indian curry.

Greenwich Village *(left)*

With its narrow tree-lined streets completely off Manhattan's grid, "The Village" was once a bohemian artist's haven. Today, it's an eclectic mix of small shops, restaurants, theaters, and is still a center for New York and America's social movements.

Jefferson Market Library *(opposite)*

At the heart of Greenwich Village stands the Victorian Gothic Jefferson Market Library with its prominent four-sided clock tower and variegated roof slates. Built in 1877 as a courthouse, today this architectural gem is the village's library and a National Historic Landmark.

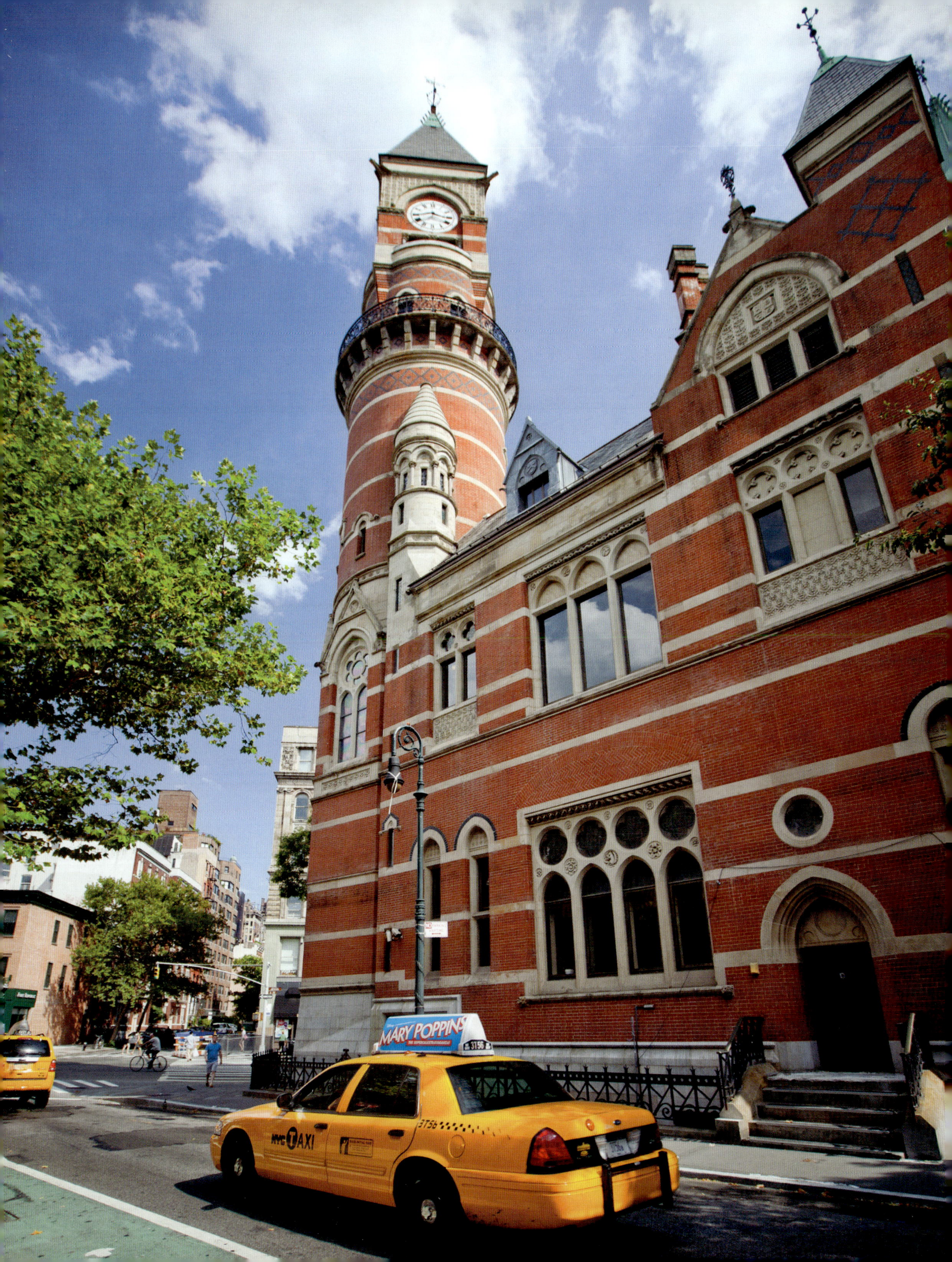
MARY POPPINS
3156
NYC TAXI

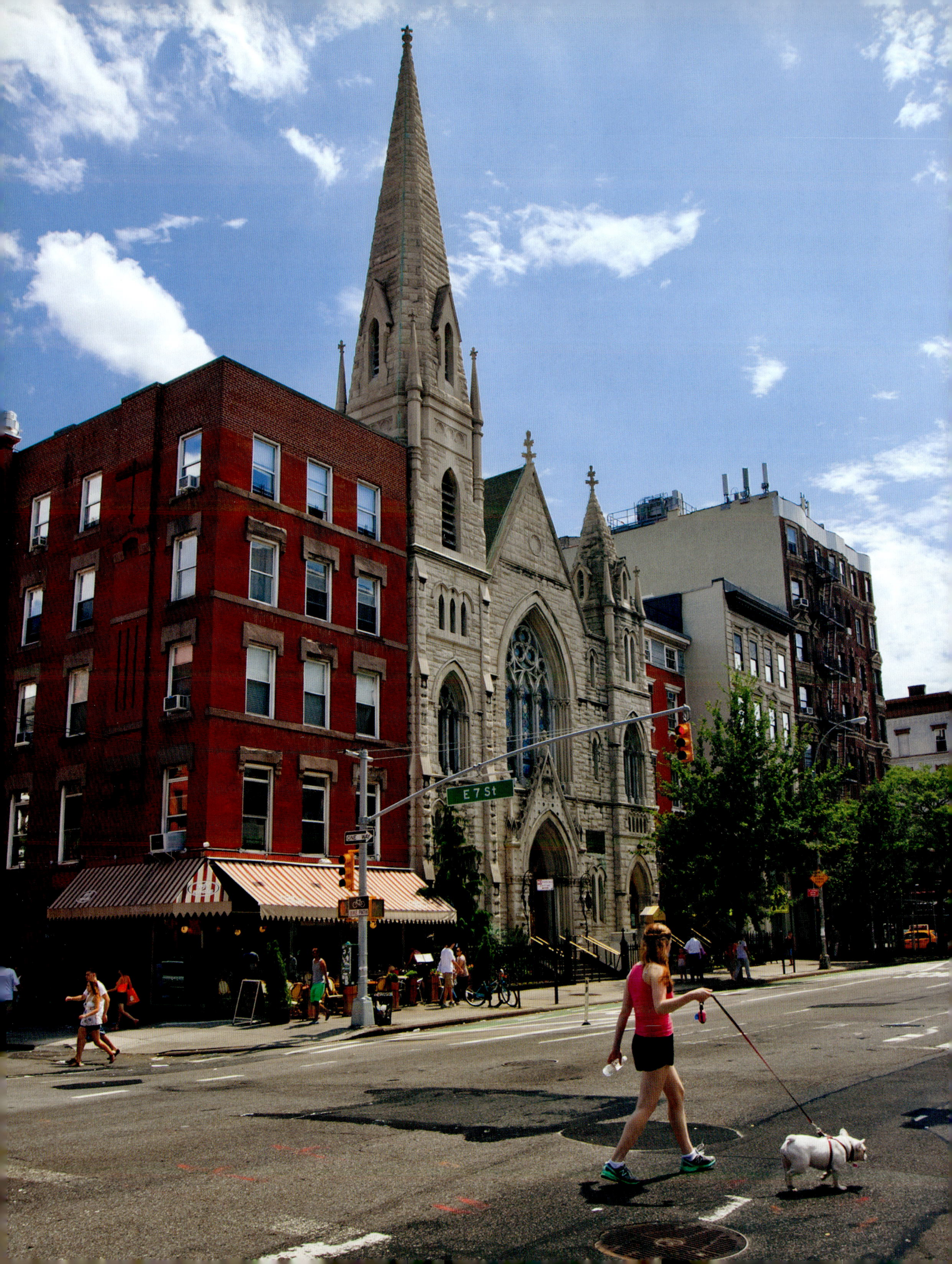
E 7 St

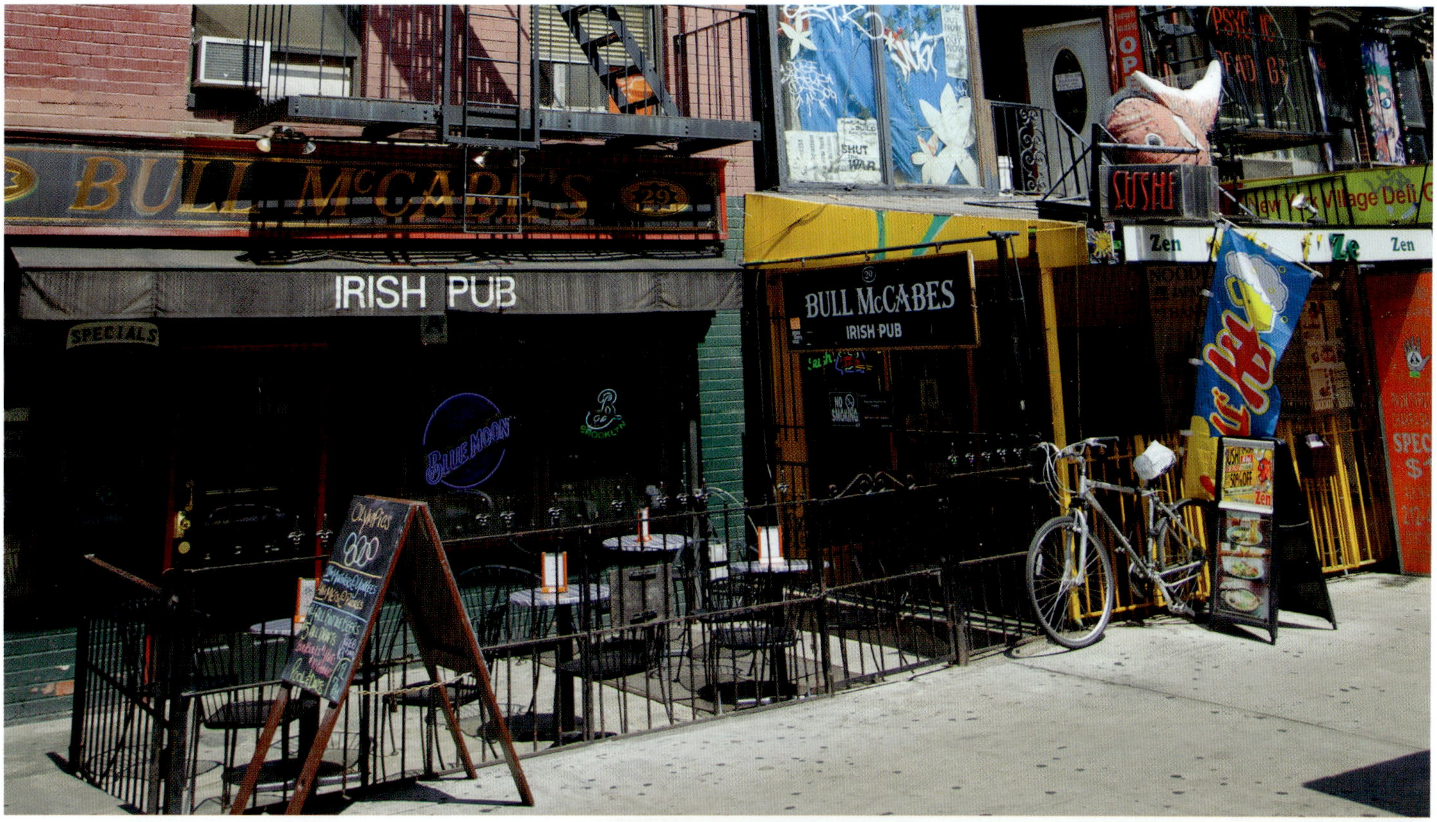

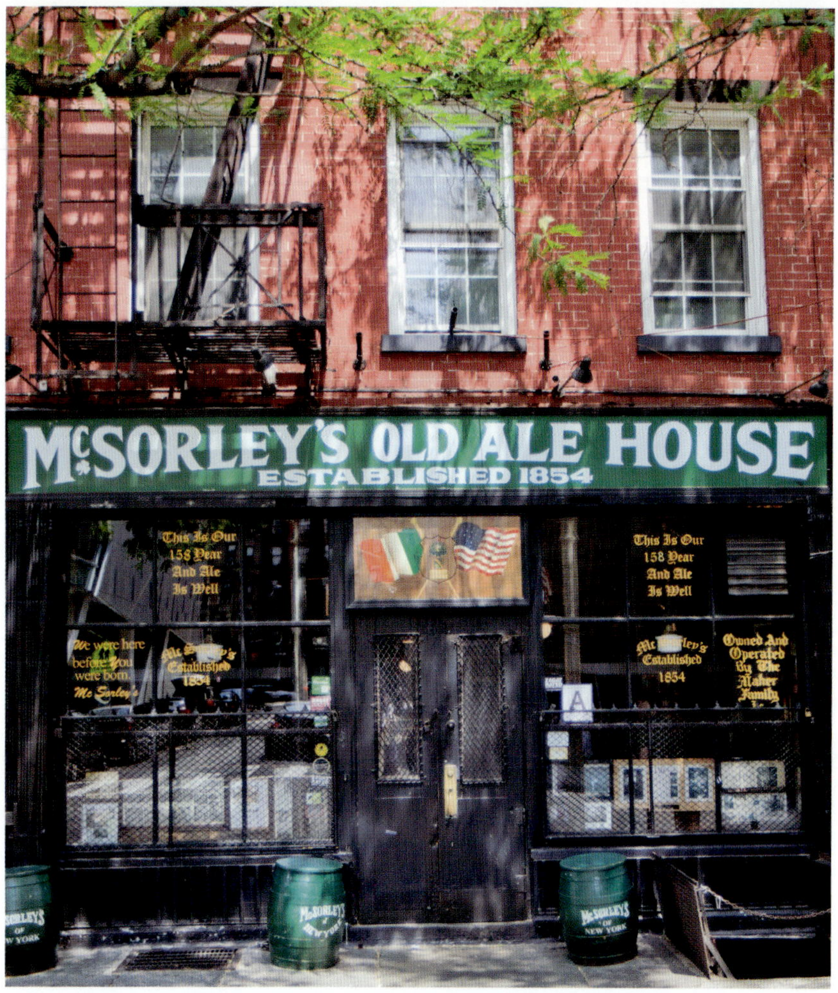

East Village Pub *(above)*

Whether you're into punk rock or the immigrant story, you can find a walking tour to explore the history and lore of this diverse city neighborhood. And when you're done you can hit one of the local Irish pubs, like Bull McCabe's, that stand as a time capsule of days of yore.

McSorley's Old Ale House *(right)*

One of New York's oldest bars, McSorley's has been serving cold brews on the same East 7th Street spot since 1854 and boasts that everyone from Abe Lincoln to John Lennon has passed through its swinging doors. Woody Guthrie supposedly inspired the union movement from a table there, but women weren't allowed until 1970.

East Village *(opposite)*

Gentrification has hit this once gritty neighborhood that attracted artists, musicians, and writers for its cheap housing. It retains a vibrant nightlife and artistic sensibility, but is now home to many middle-class families. The Middle Collegiate Church, built in 1892, represents the neighborhood's historic past and diverse, multicultural community.

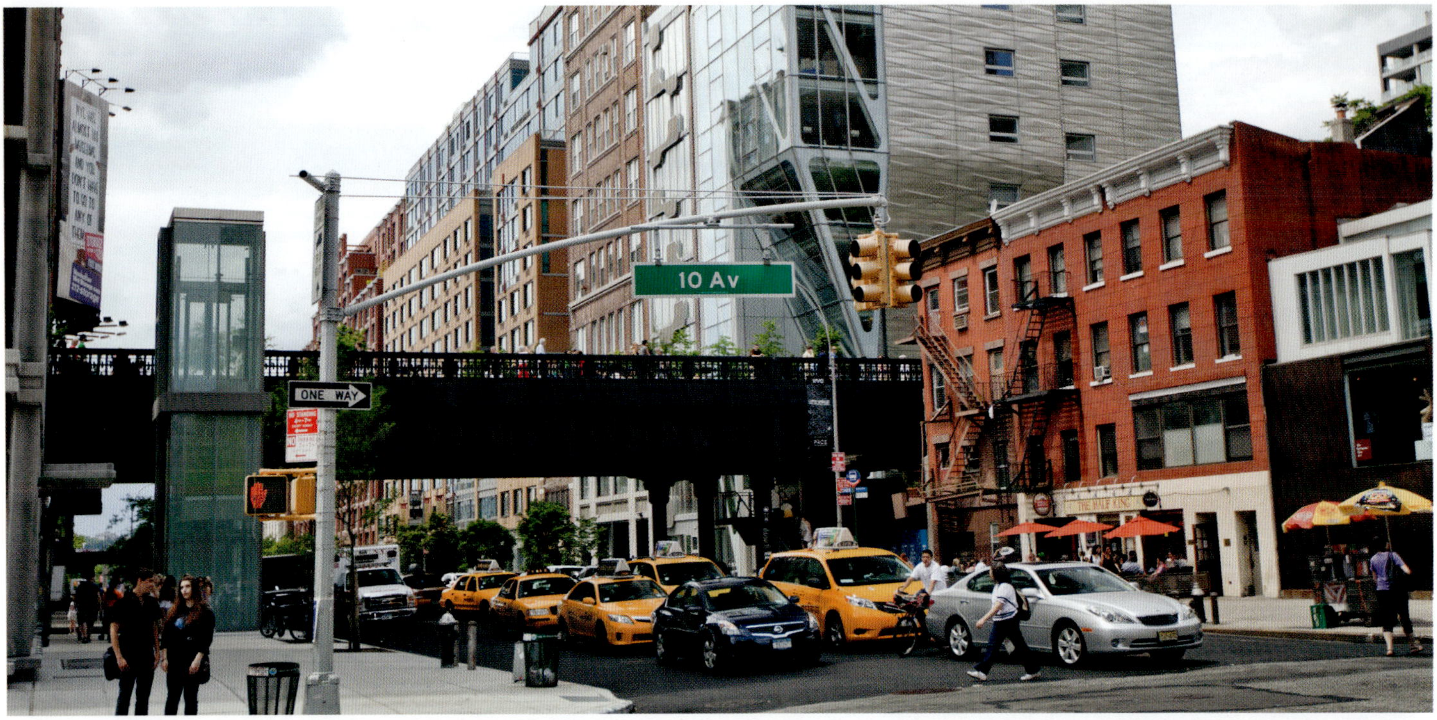

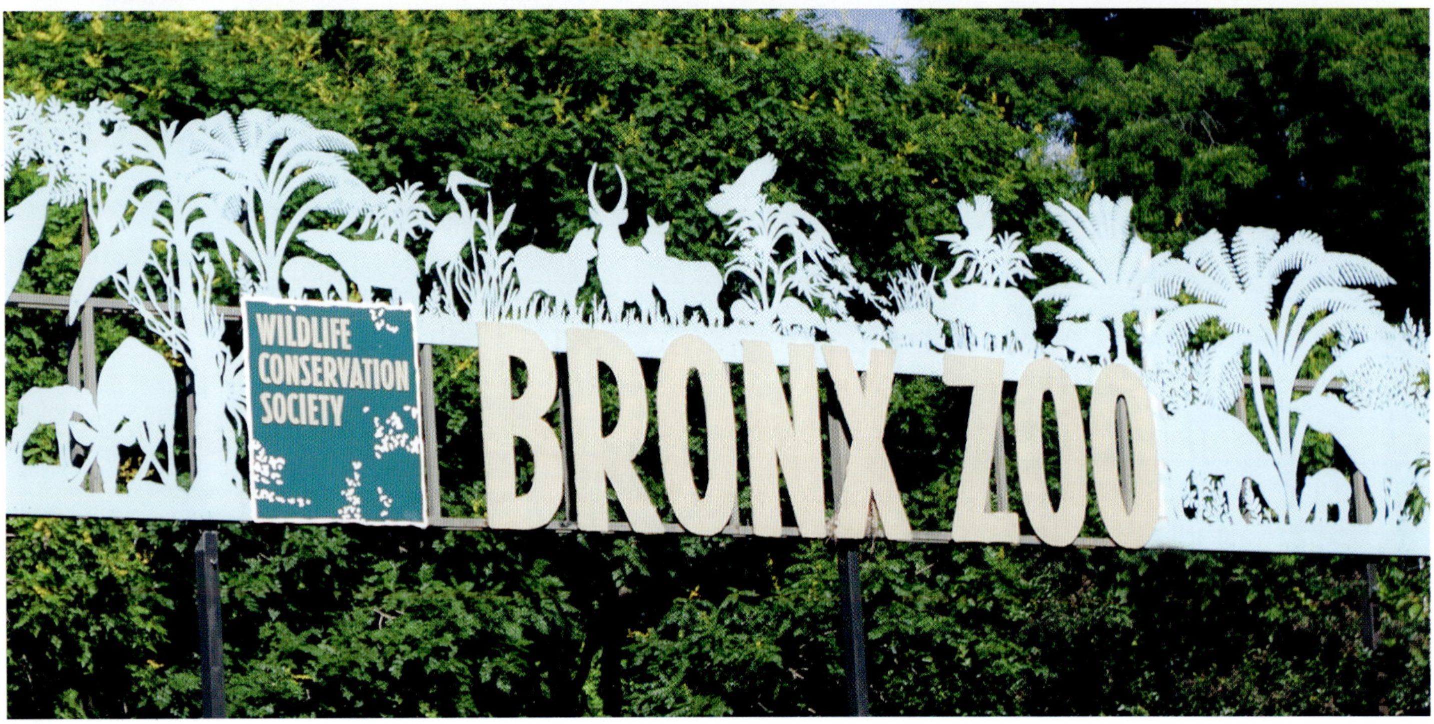

High Line *(top and opposite)*

The city's hottest new downtown attraction is its park in the sky, 30 feet above the streets. This former freight railway was saved from demolition and transformed into an urban greenway for nature tours, architecture exploration, star-gazing, and simply strolling with great views of the Hudson River.

Bronx Zoo *(bottom)*

Opened in 1899, the Bronx Zoo sits on 265 acres of hardwood forest. It is the largest urban zoo in the country and home to more than 6,000 animals representing more than 600 species, including gelada baboons, which are the largest troop of western lowland gorillas in the U.S.

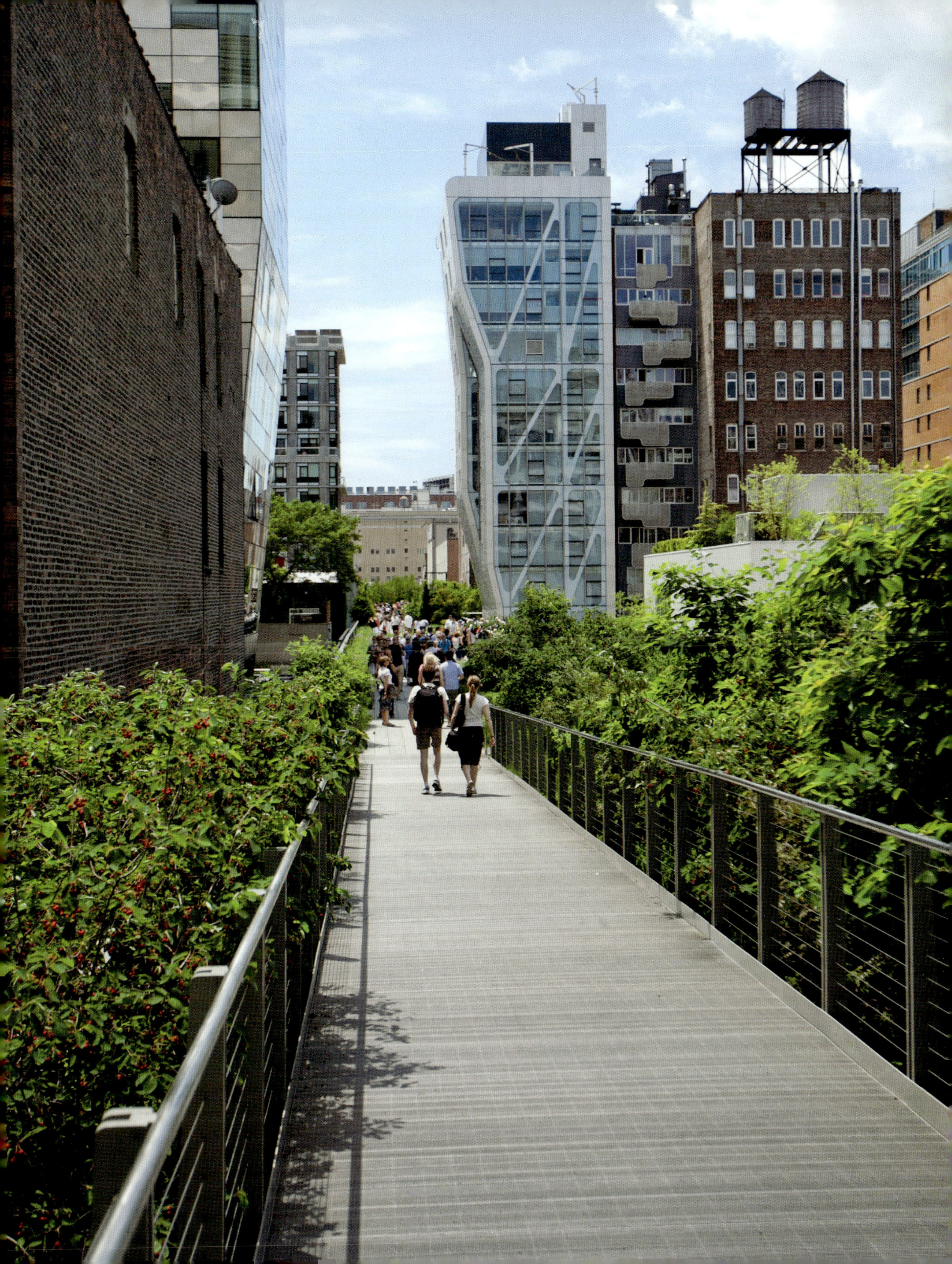

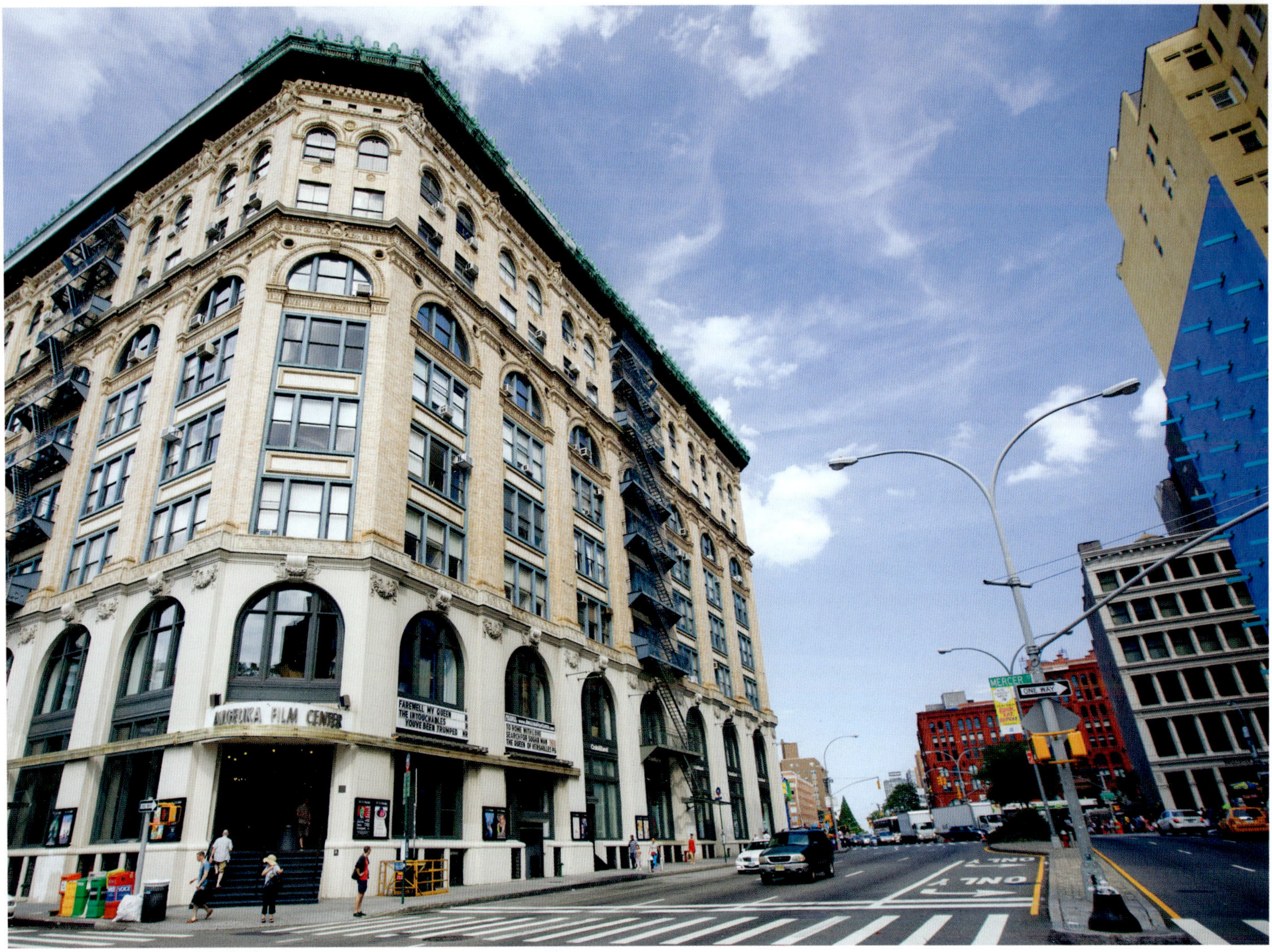

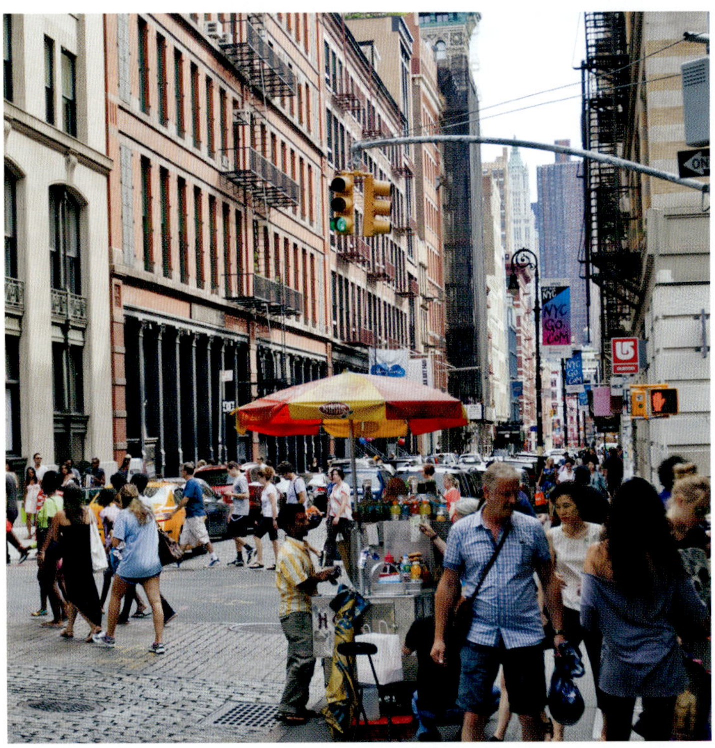

SoHo *(above and left)*

One of the city's distinctive shopping areas, SoHo stands for "South of Houston" Street. Along its cobblestone streets are galleries, fine restaurants, trendy boutiques, and jewelry and art dealers selling right on the sidewalks. Many of its buildings are included in the SoHo-Cast Iron Historic District for their architectural elements.

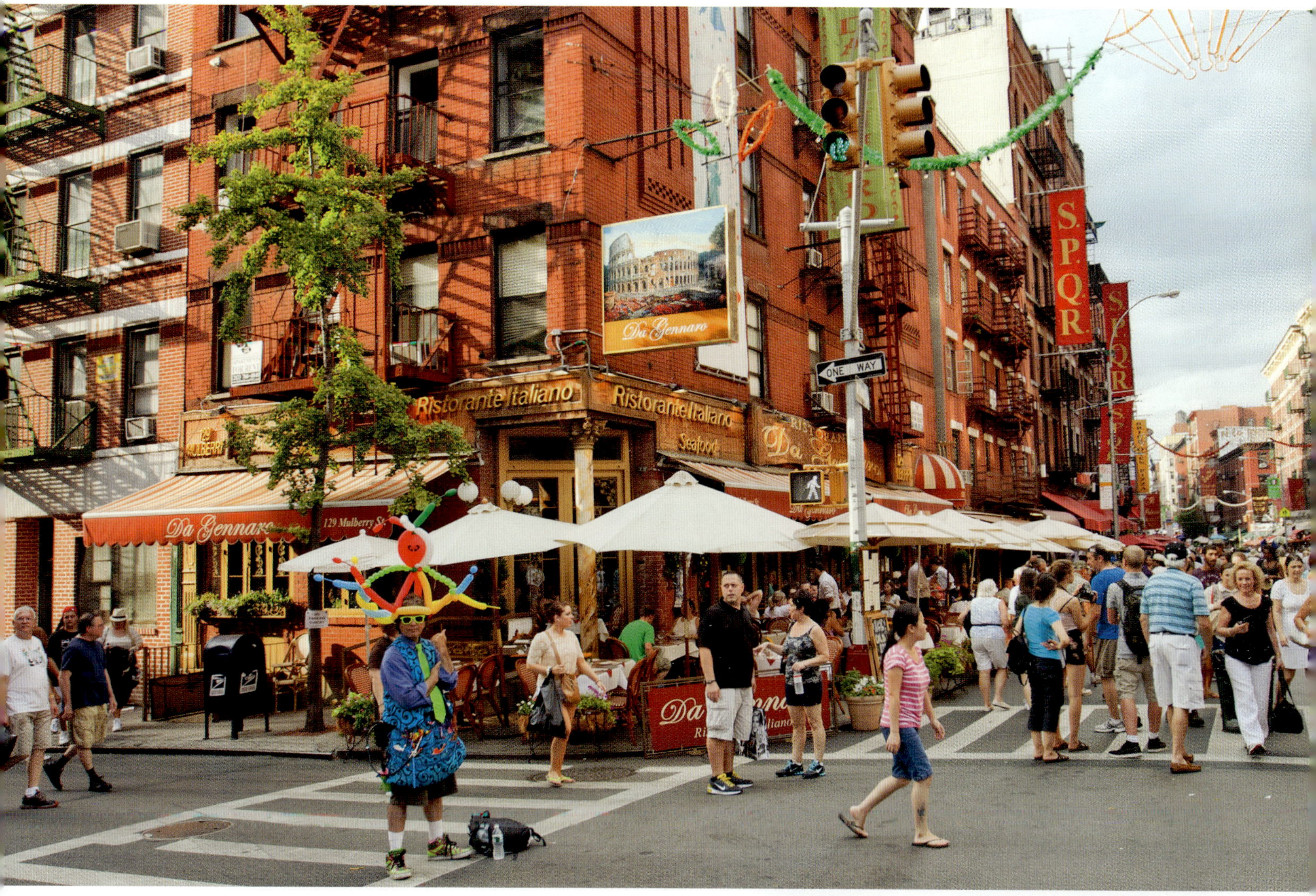

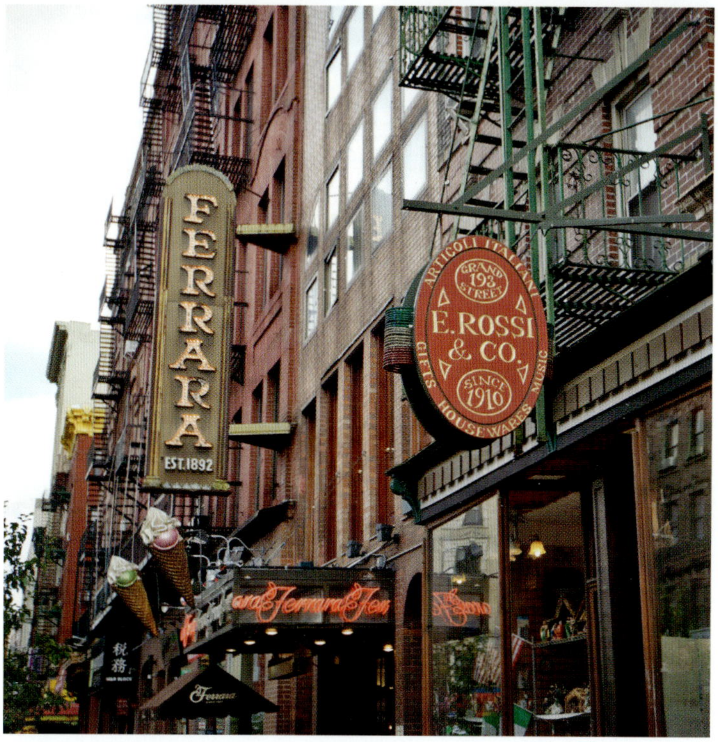

Little Italy *(above and right)*

You can usually smell Little Italy before you get there, as its dozens of restaurants cook up batches of Italian delicacies daily in the neighborhood bordering Chinatown. The streets come alive with hungry crowds each September for one of the city's largest street fairs, the annual San Gennaro Festival celebrating Italian culture and food.

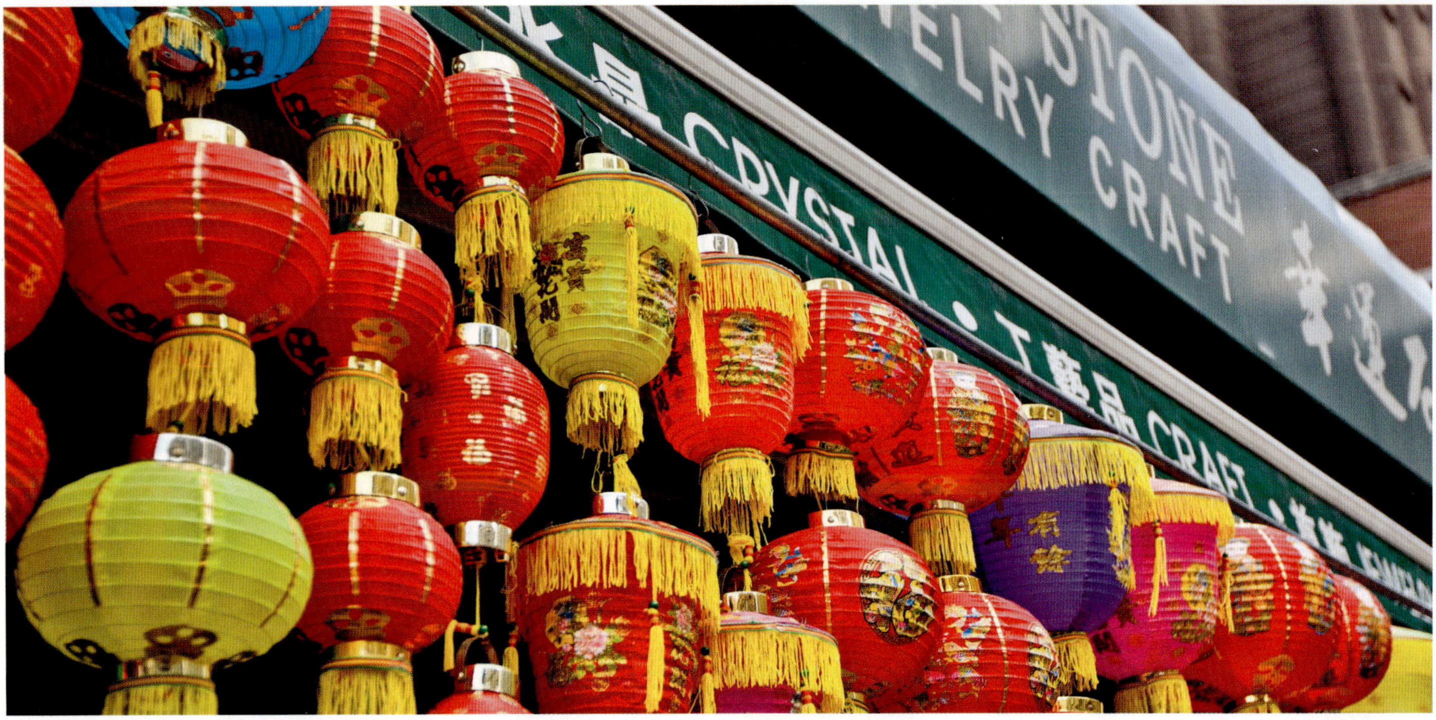

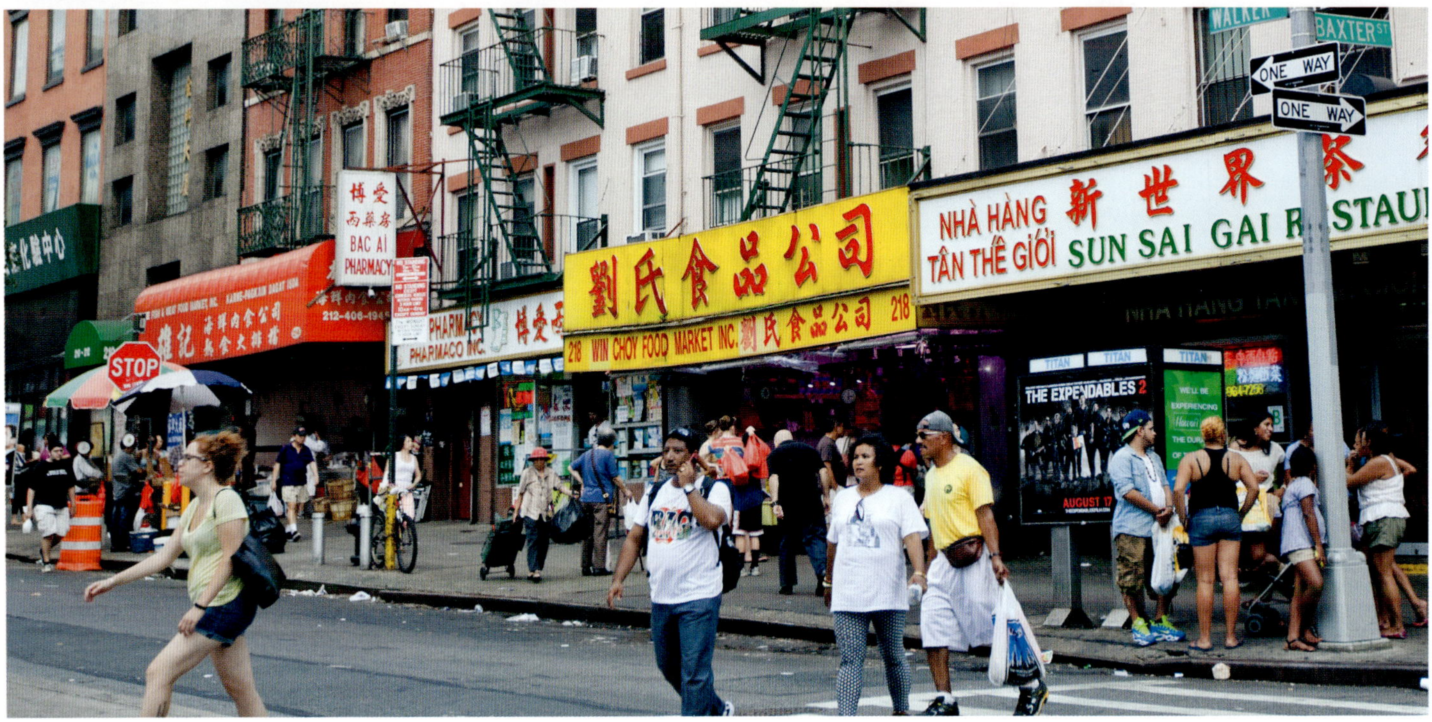

Chinatown Lanterns *(top)*

No Chinese New Year would be complete without a visit to Chinatown for this cultural festival rich in tradition, complete with drumming, dancing, feasting, firecrackers, and dragon parades winding through narrow streets. The Lantern Festival officially ends the two-week celebration on the night of the first full moon.

Chinatown *(bottom)*

Manhattan's Chinatown is one of the largest enclaves of Chinese people in the Western hemisphere. Visitors are treated to a vast array of food from China's various regions and introduced to many items that they may never have seen before, including exotic herbs, dried fish, and vegetables like lotus root and bamboo shoots.

Koreatown *(opposite)*

Manhattan's Korean business district centers around "Korea Way," one city block from the Empire State Building. On 32nd Street between Fifth Avenue and Broadway you can find a little slice of Korea in the heart of the city with stores, restaurants, and nightclubs featuring both traditional and regional Korean cuisine.

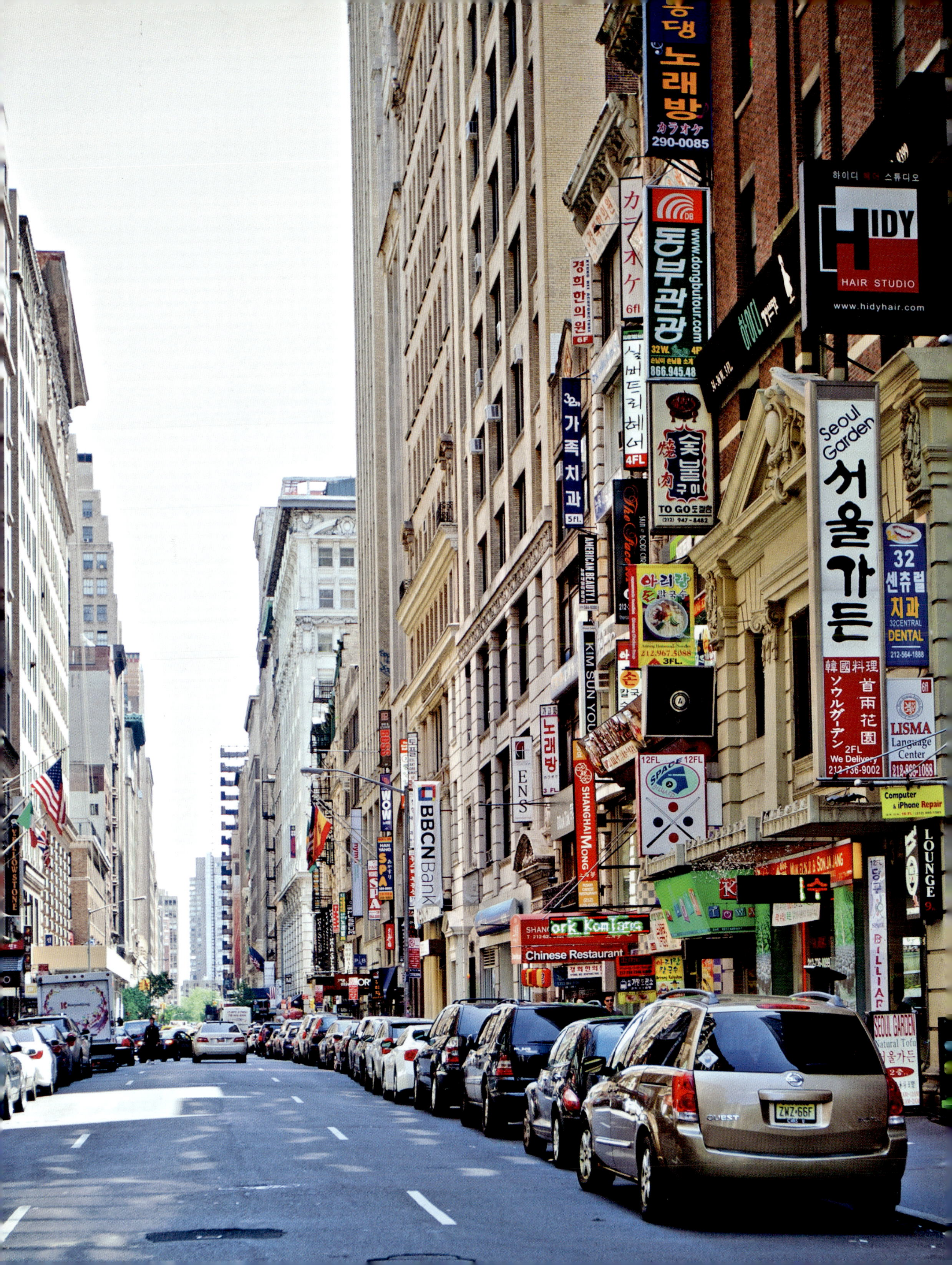

노래방
カラオケ
290-0085
HIDY
HAIR STUDIO
www.hidyhair.com
동부관광
www.dongbutour.com
866.945.48
カラオケ
6fl
경희한의원
6F
실버트리헤어
4FL
숯불구이
TO GO
가족치과
5Fl.
Seoul Garden
서울가든
韓國料理
ソウルガーデン
首爾花園
2FL
We Delivery
212-736-9002
32
센츄럴
치과
32CENTRAL
DENTAL
212-564-1888
LISMA
Language
Center
Computer
& iPhone Repair
LOUNGE
AMERICAN BEAUTY
아리랑
칼국수
212.967.5088
3FL.
KIM SUN YOU
노래방
ENS
SHANGHAI MONG
BBCN Bank
SPA
Chinese Restaurant
SEOUL GARDEN
Natural Tofu

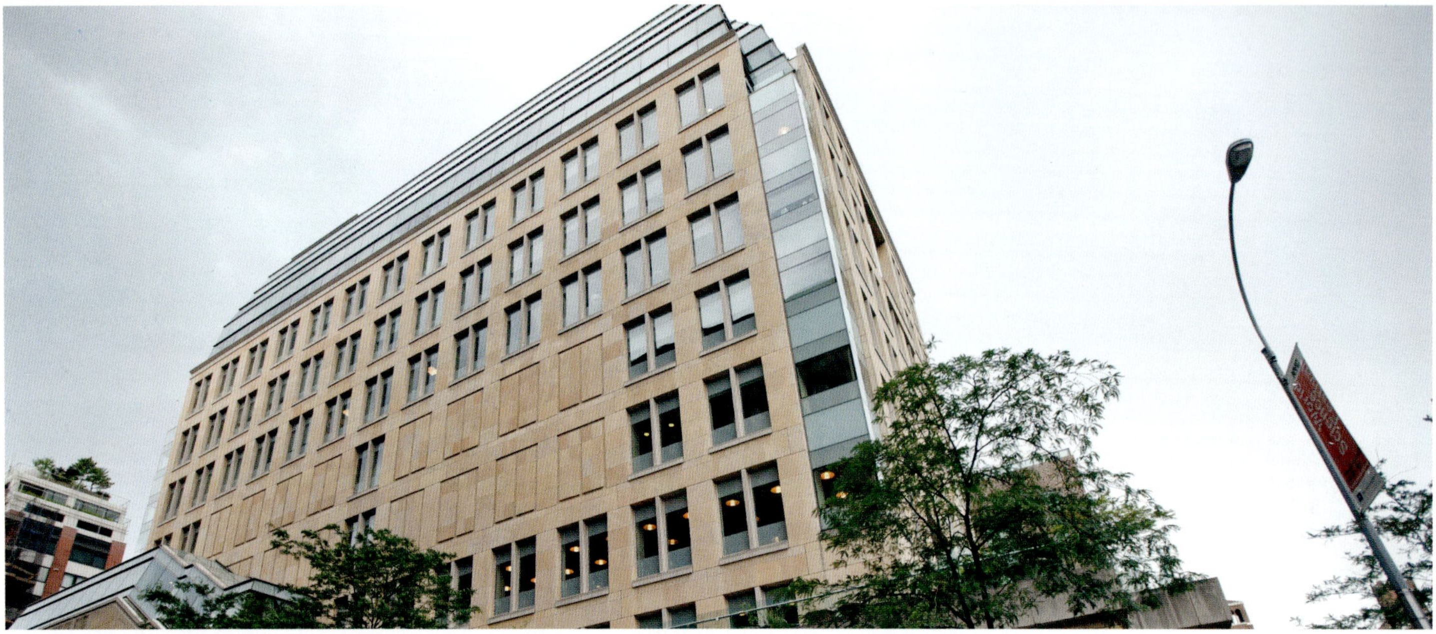

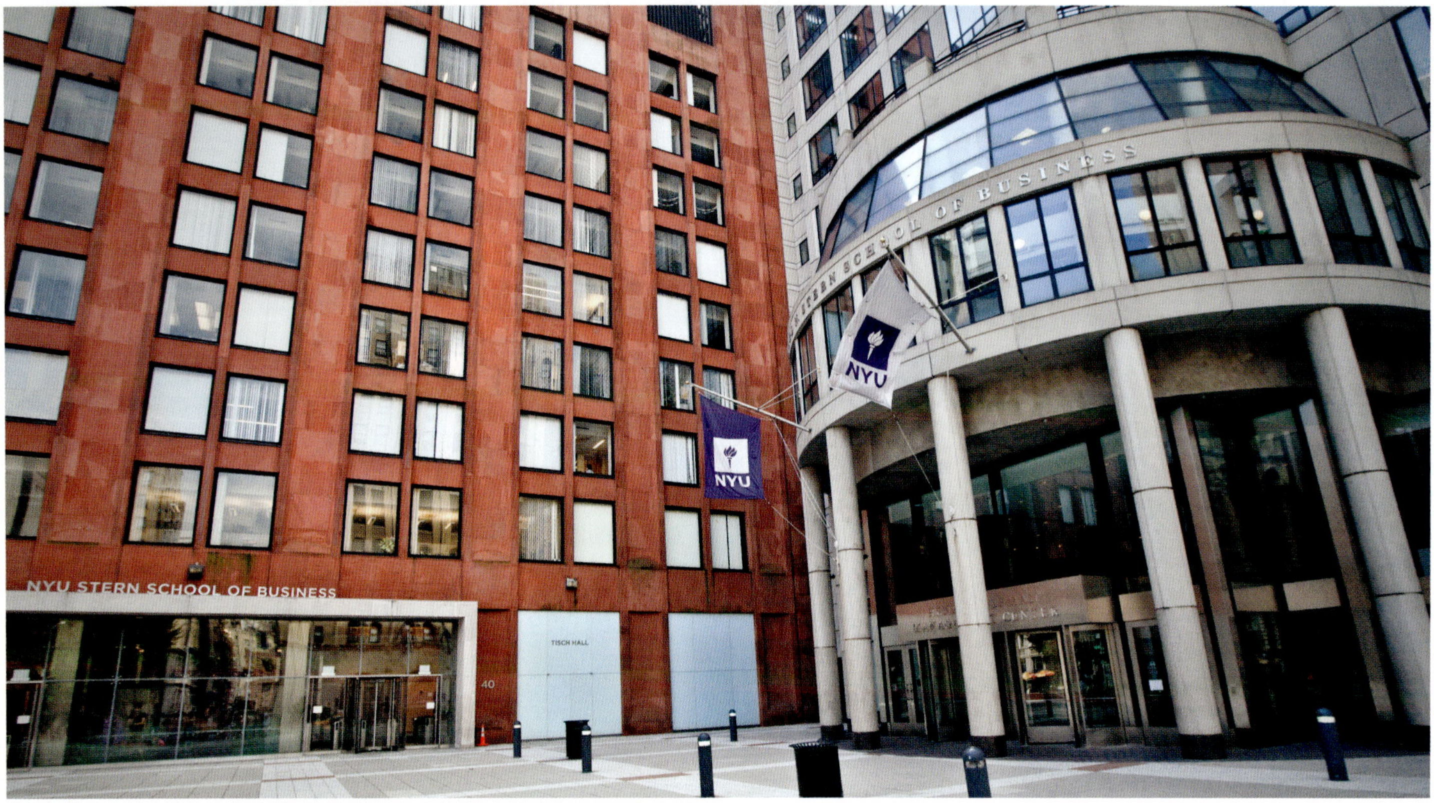

New York University *(top)*

Founded in 1831, NYU is one of the largest private universities in the U.S. From a student body of 158 during its first semester, enrollment has grown to 40,000 students attending its 18 schools and colleges at five major centers in the city and around the world.

NYU Stern *(bottom)*

New York University's business school was founded in 1900 to provide business training to the city's immigrants. Today, this highly selective school is ranked within the top ten business schools in the world. Located in Greenwich Village, its three buildings recently underwent an 84,500 square foot renovation.

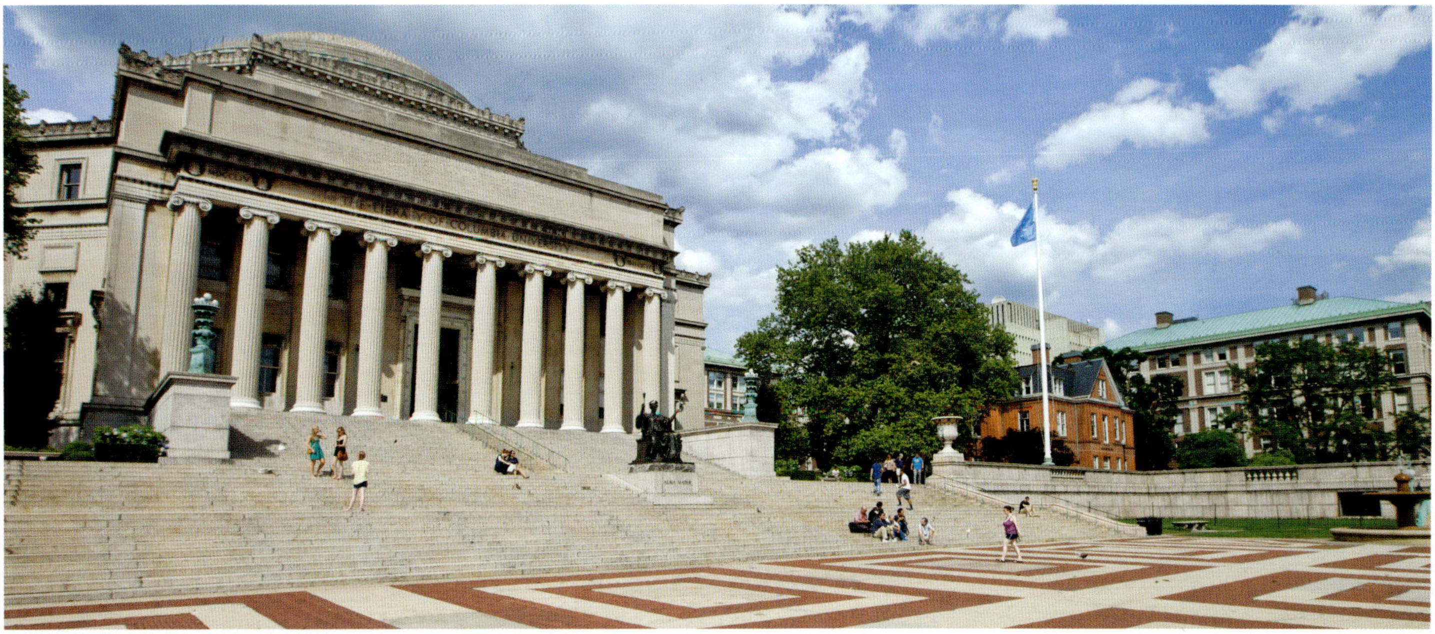

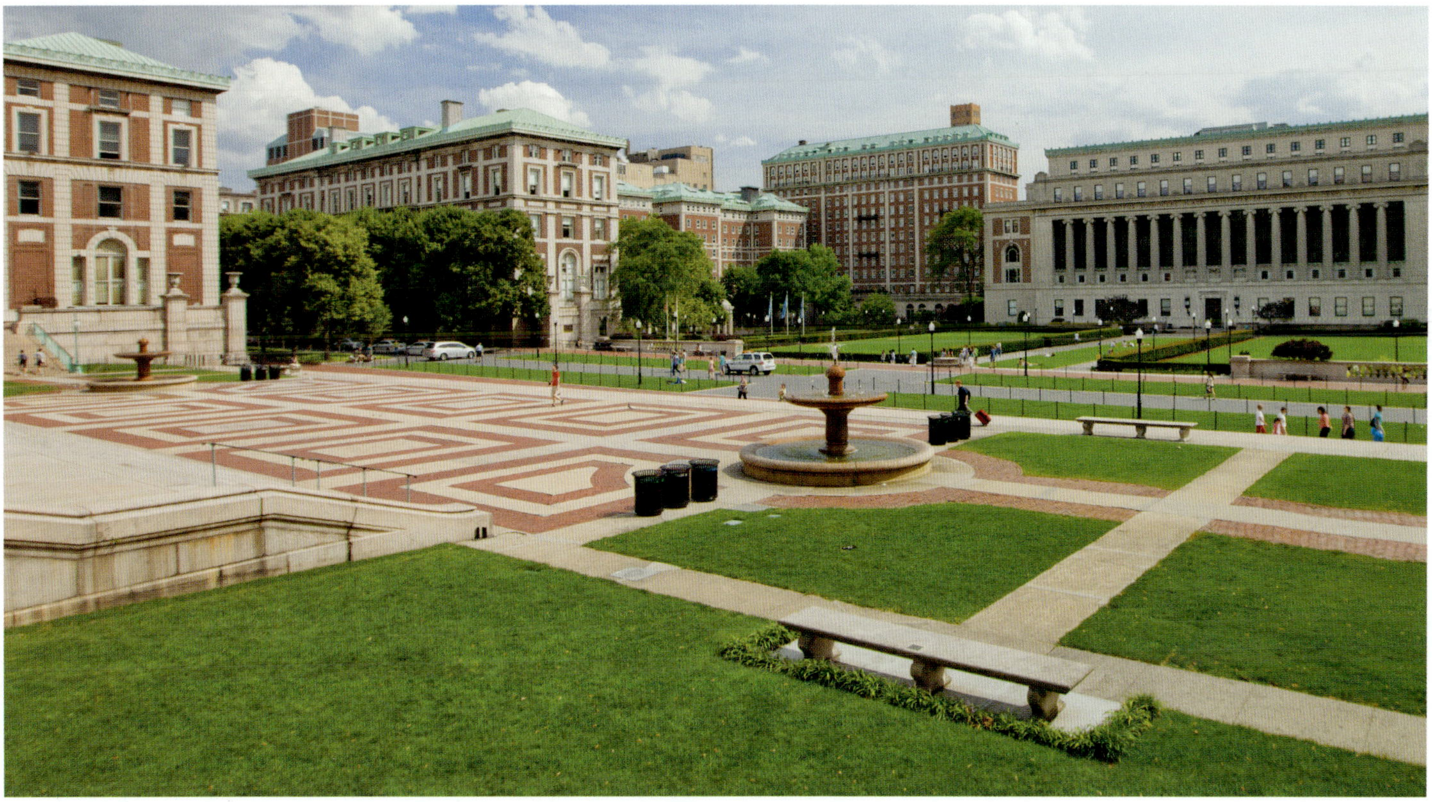

Columbia University *(top and bottom)*

This private Ivy League university is the oldest institution of higher learning in the state of New York. It was founded in 1754 as King's College by royal charter of George II of England and renamed Columbia College after the Revolutionary War, a name that embodied the nation's patriotic fervor.

In 1897, the university moved from downtown to its current Morningside Heights campus, designed as an urban academic village with stately Italian Renaissance buildings. Today, more than 28,000 students attend the school, many of whom gather daily on the broad flight of steps from Low Library to the plaza below.

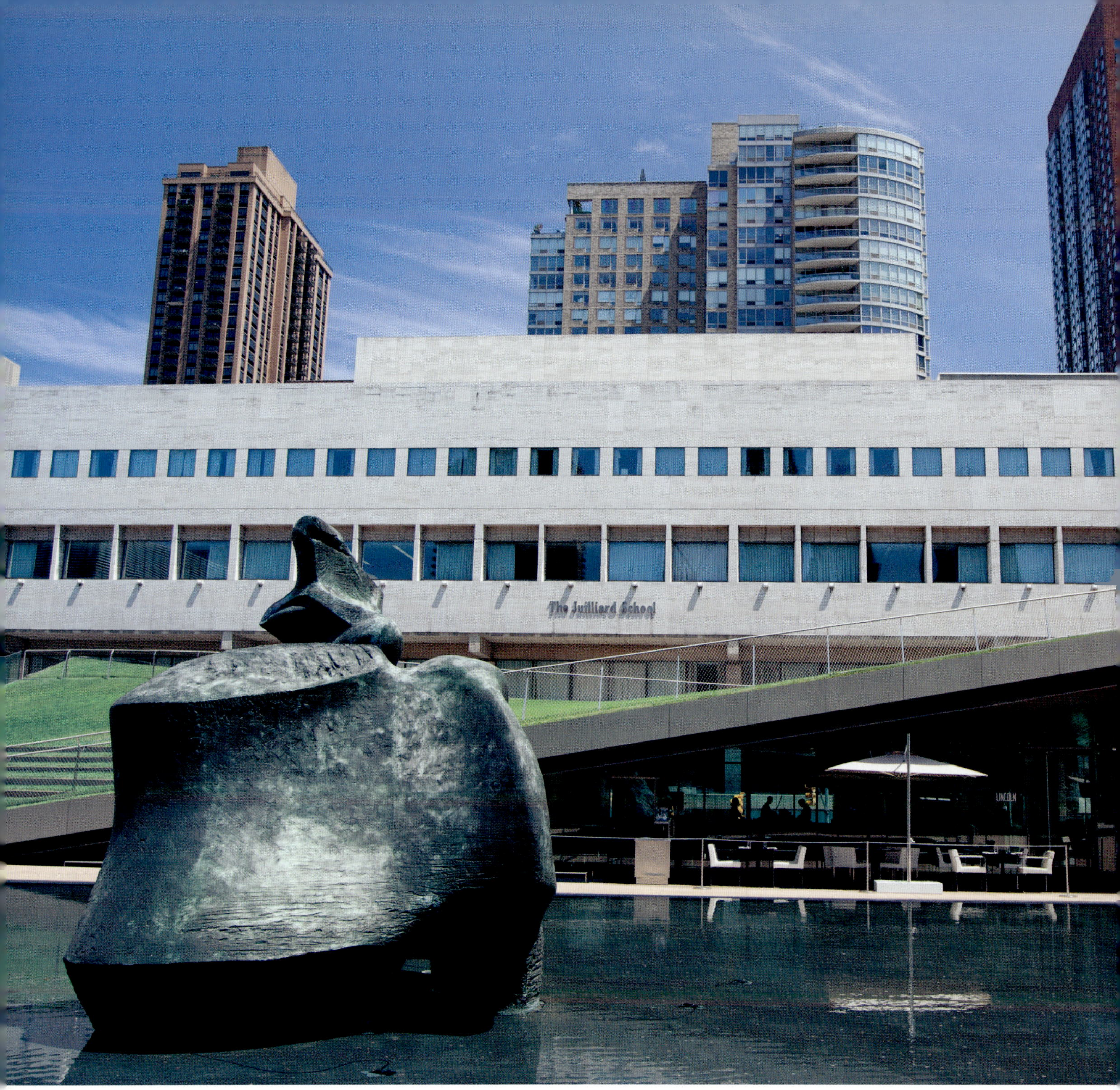

Julliard

Students who want to dance, sing, or perform, head to Julliard in Lincoln Center for the Performing Arts. The conservatory has been training the crème de la crème of the arts world since 1905, with famous graduates like Patti LuPone, Bebe Neuwirth, Mandy Patinkin, Barry Manilow, Miles Davis, and Yo-Yo Ma.

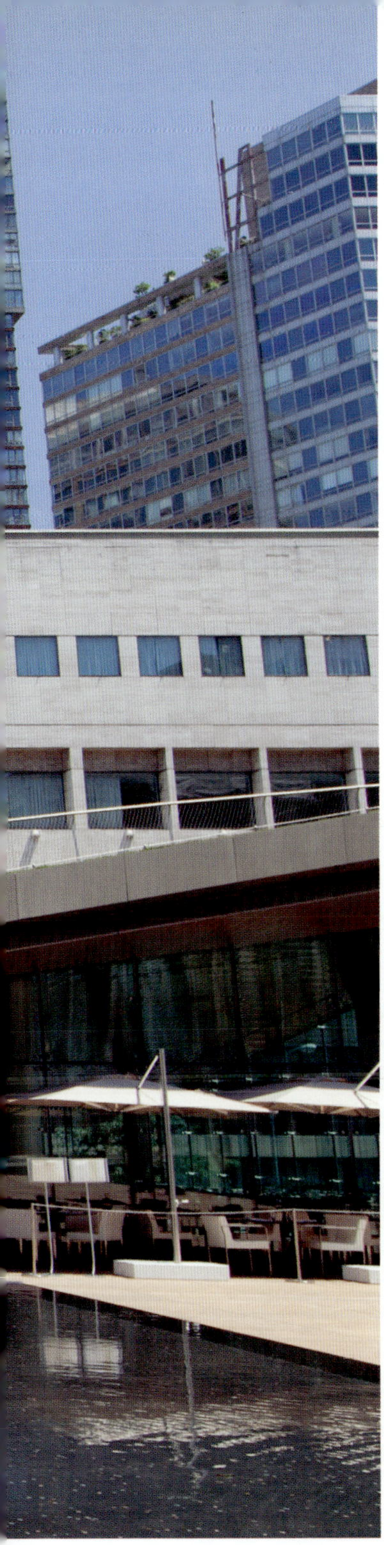

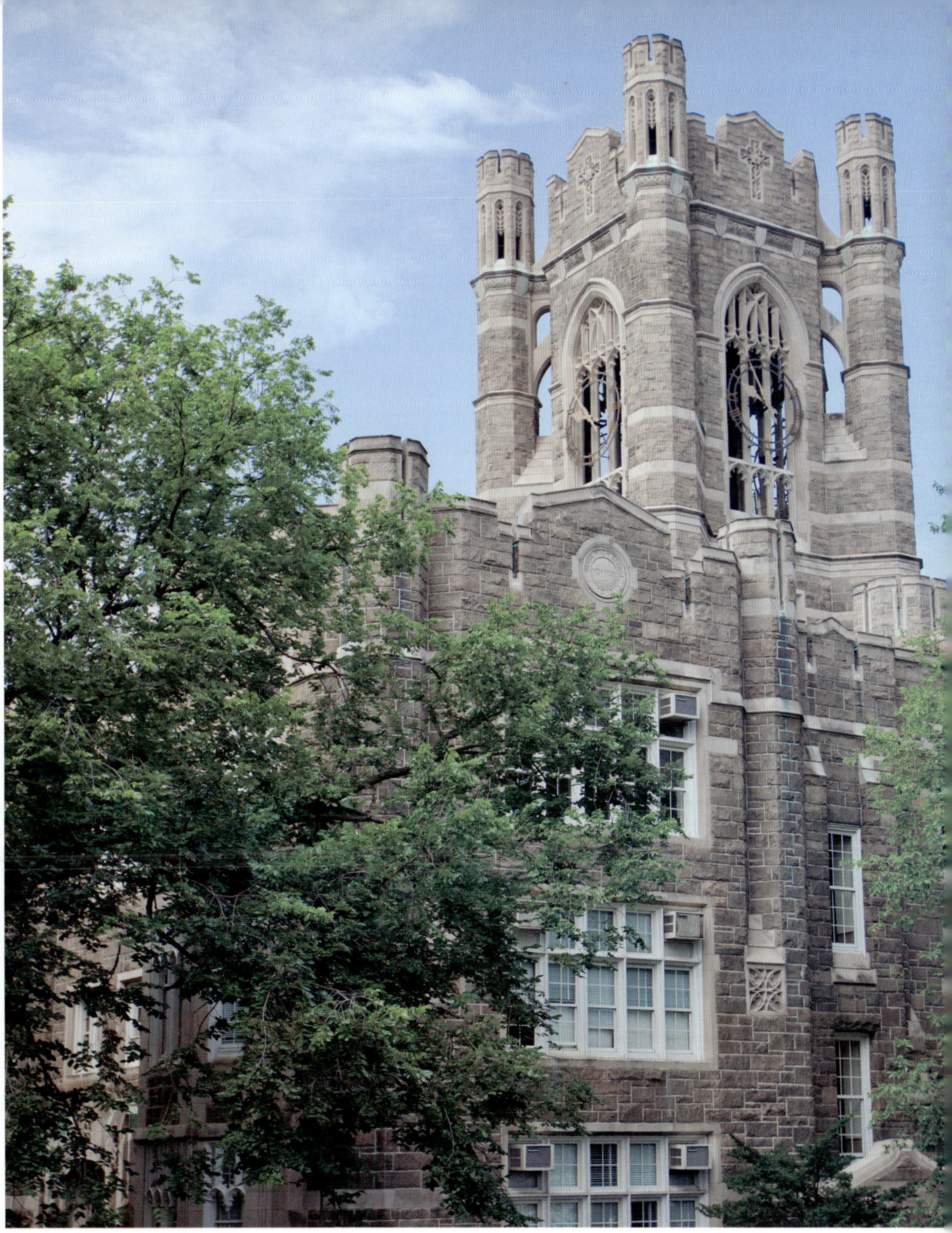

Fordham University

With three campuses in the Bronx, Westchester, and adjacent to Lincoln Center in Manhattan, Fordham University enrolls more than 15,000 student in 10 schools. Founded in 1841 as St. John's College by the Roman Catholic Diocese of New York, Fordham has since become an independent institution "in the Jesuit tradition."

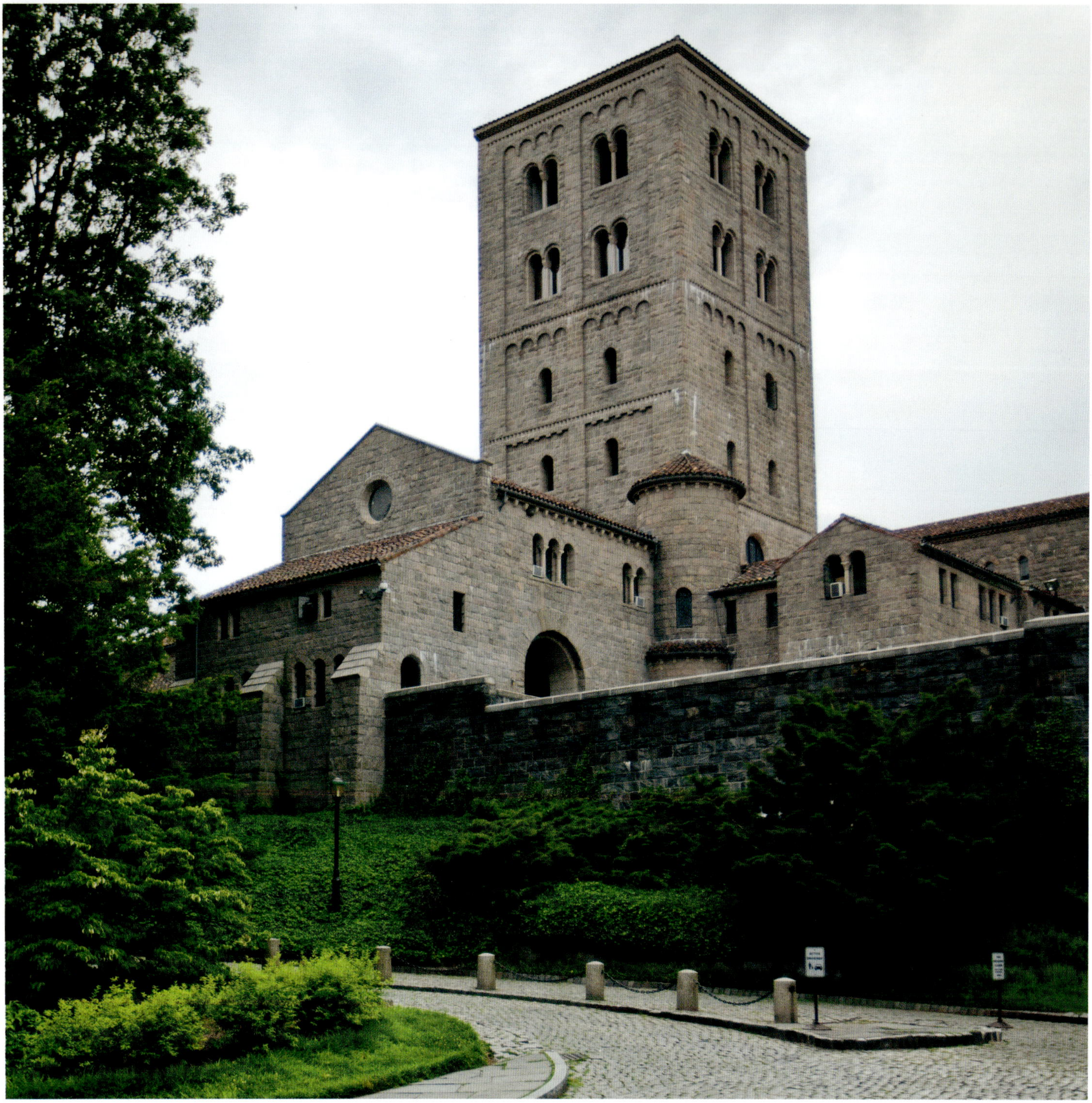

The Cloisters *(above)*

A visit to this museum on the northern tip of Manhattan takes you to a medieval world of wonder with beautiful gardens overlooking the Hudson River. Inside the building that incorporates parts from five French cloistered abbeys, is a treasure trove of illuminated manuscripts, stained glass, and the renowned *Unicorn Tapestries.*

Riverside Church *(opposite)*

This two-block-wide Upper West Side interdenominational church, inspired by the cathedral in Chartres, France, is famous for its elaborate Gothic architecture and its history of social justice and progressive causes. Its tower contains a 74-bell carillon, including the 20-ton Bourdon bell, the largest tuned bell in the world.

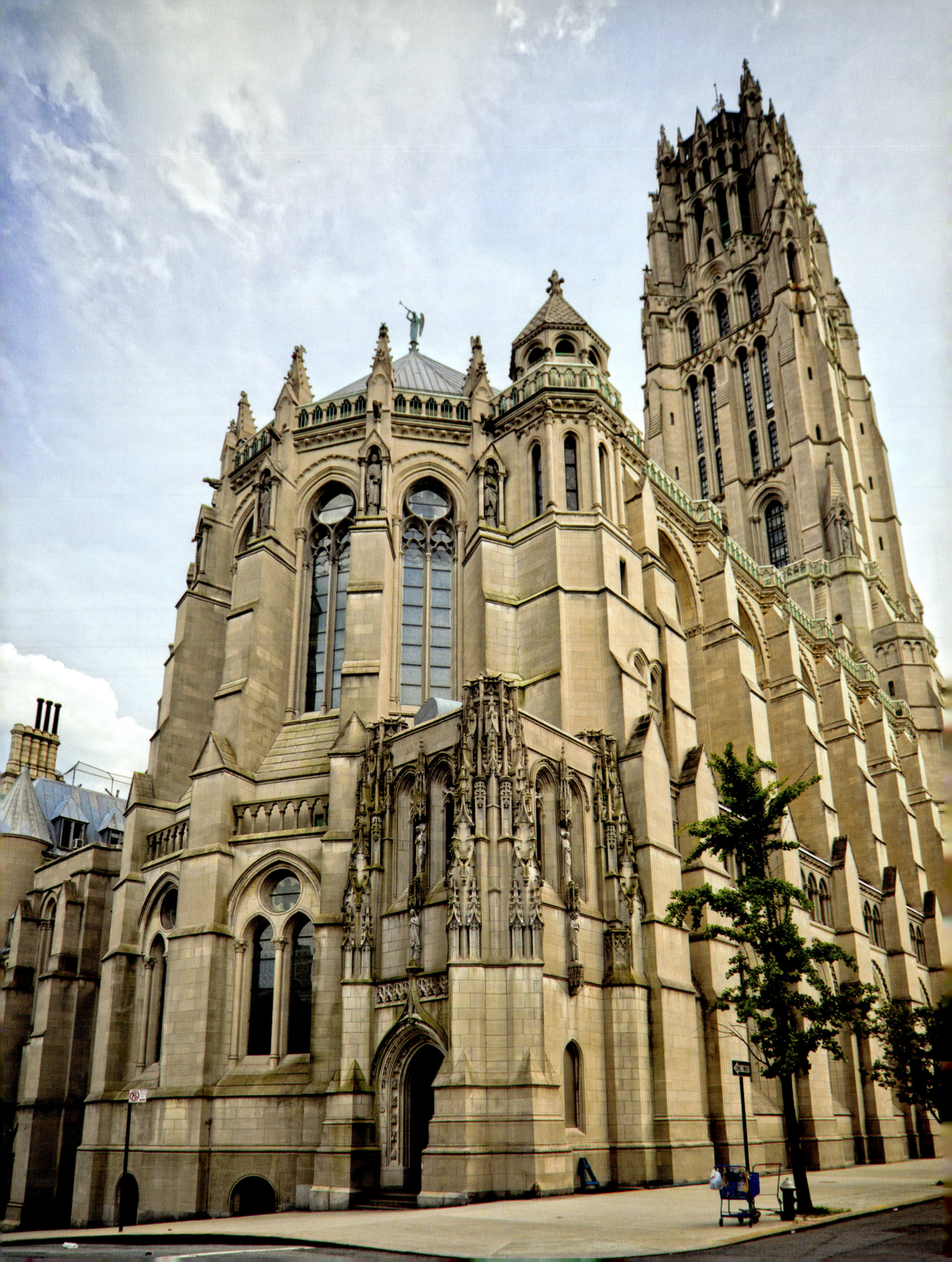

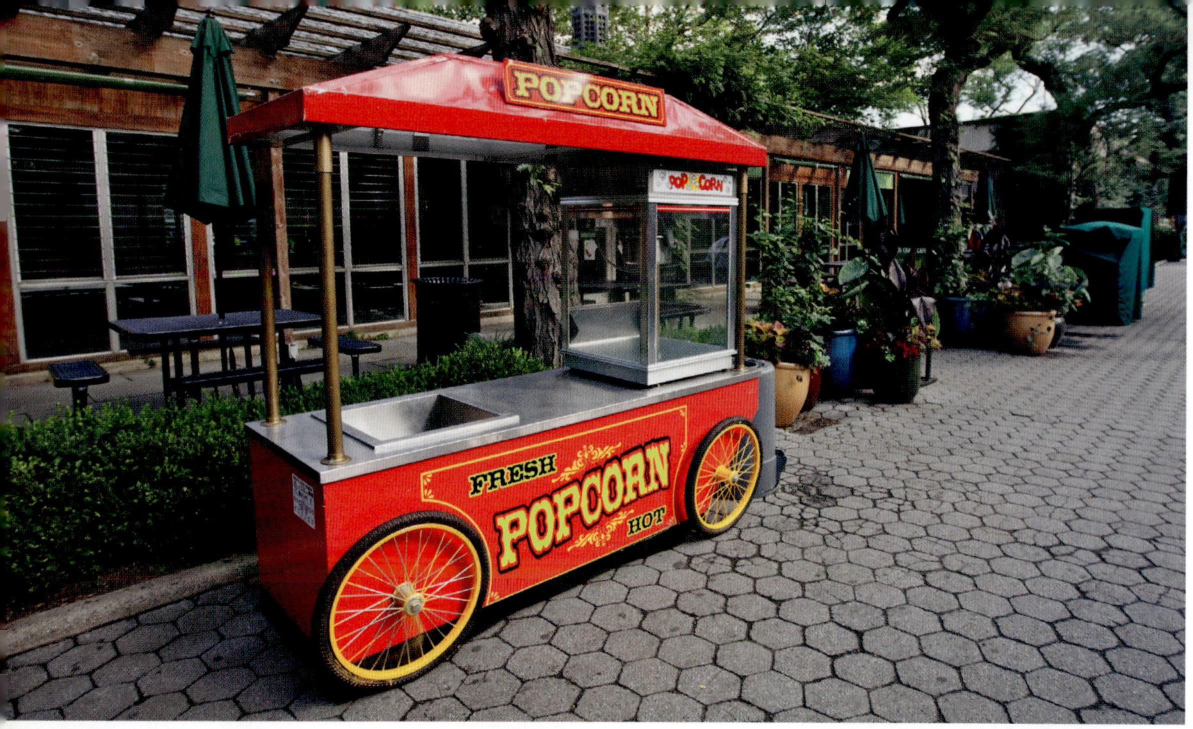

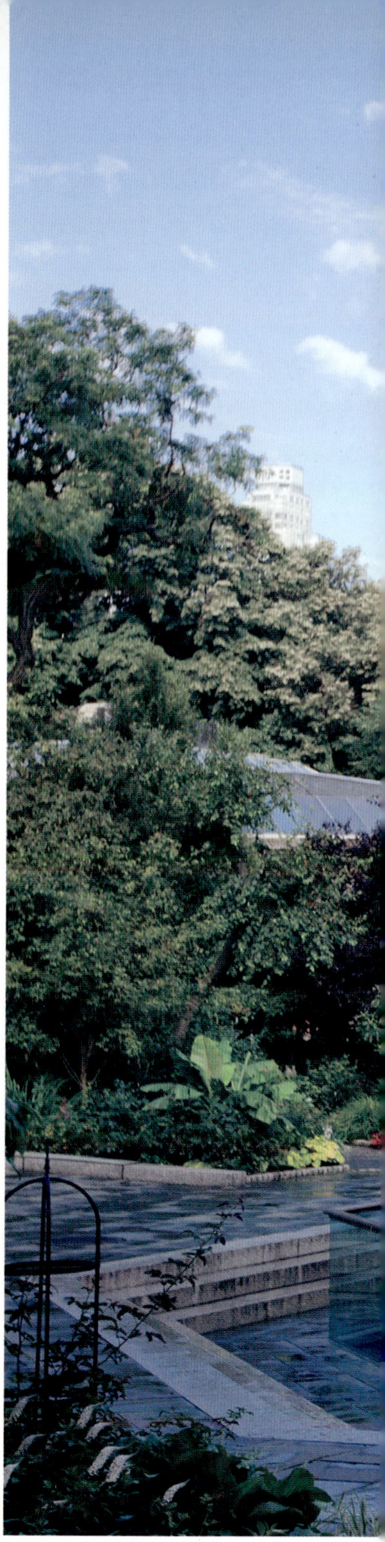

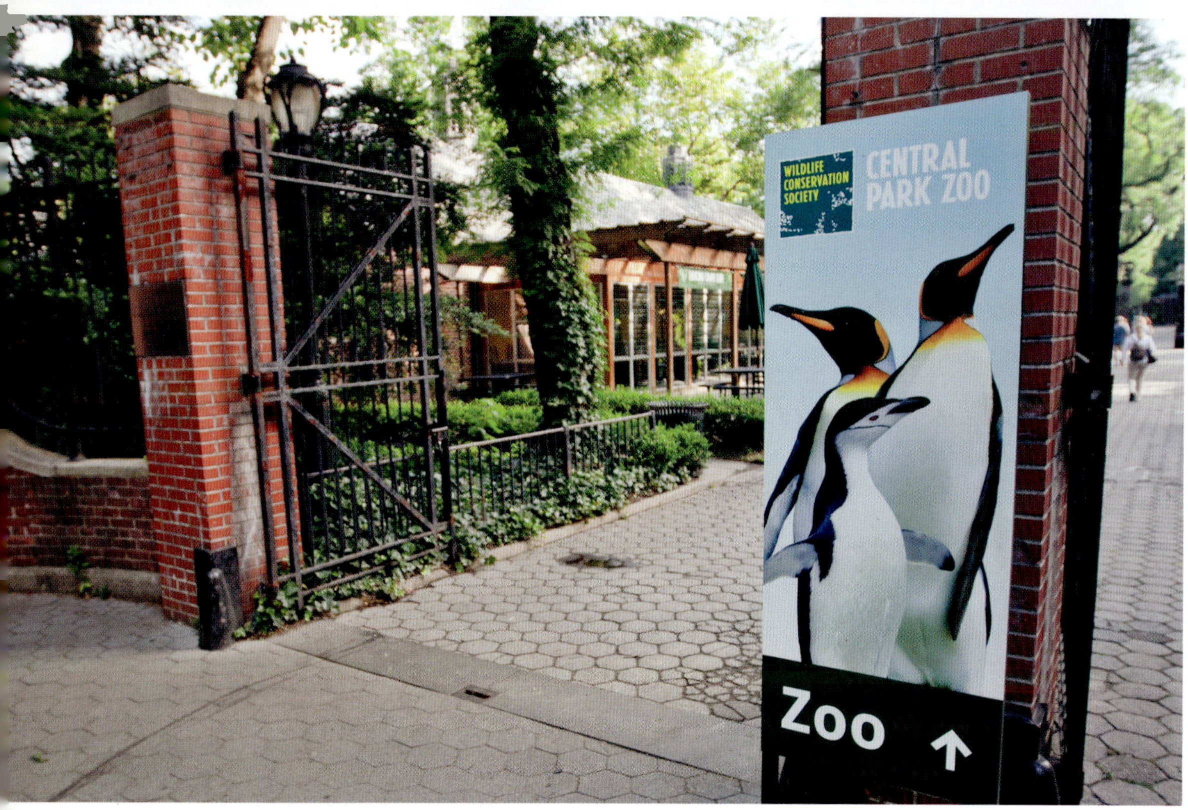

Central Park Zoo *(top and bottom)*

Just steps off Fifth Avenue is Central Park's Zoo, with more than 130 species from tropical, temperate, and polar zones around the world. Visitors can see giant polar bears, red pandas, monkeys, puffins, penguins, and endangered snow leopards. Young children love to visit the animals here and then head to the nearby Tisch Children's Zoo, where they can touch, feel, and feed rabbits, sheep, pigs, and goats in a safe and educational environment. Open 365 days a year, this small zoo was founded in 1864 and is the second oldest zoo in the United States.

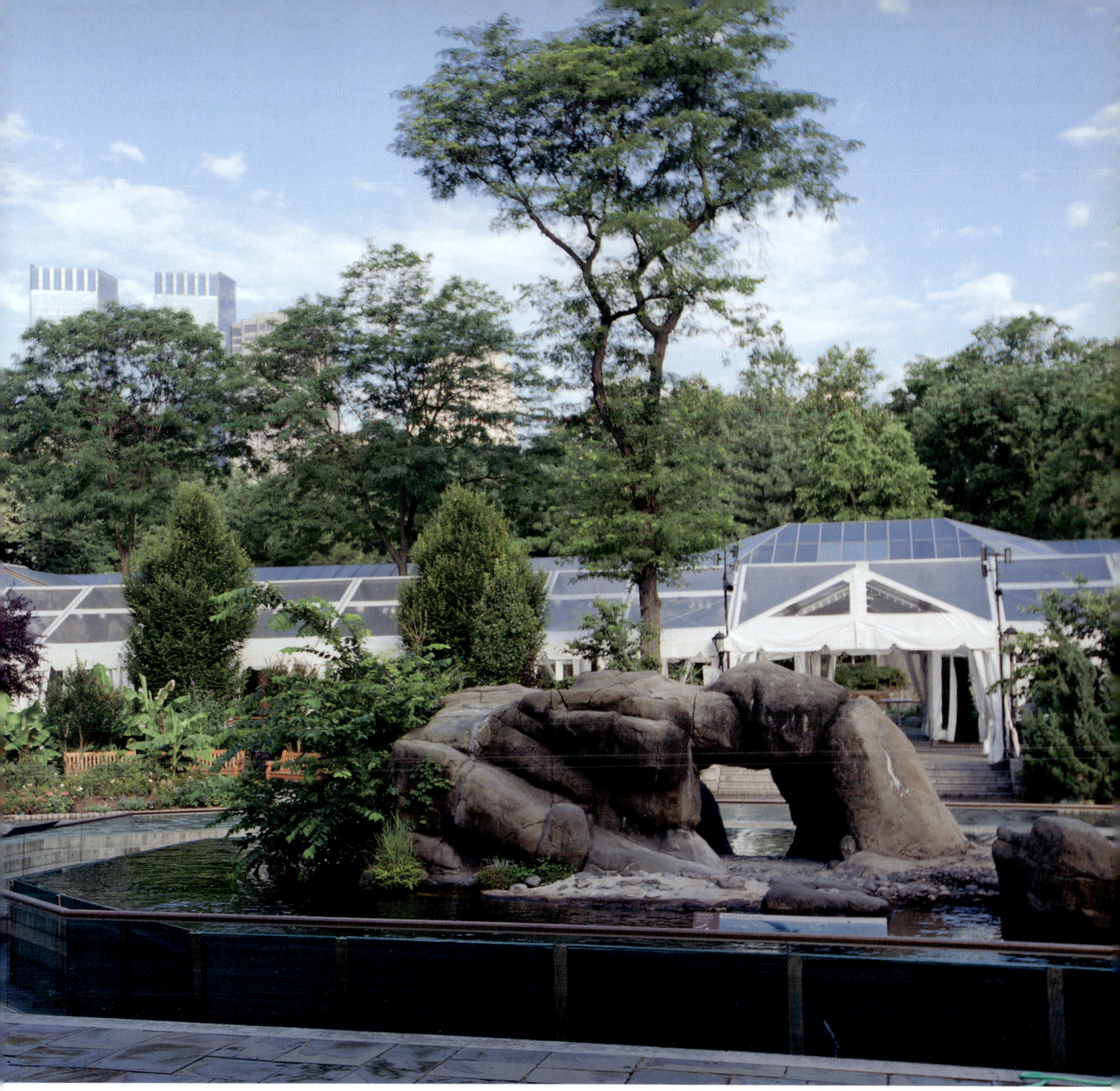

Sea Lion Pool

The highlight of any visit to the Central Park Zoo is the show that the four California sea lions put on three times a day at feeding time. Watch them dive, jump, twist, and shout as they each consume 15-20 pounds of fish and marine life each day.

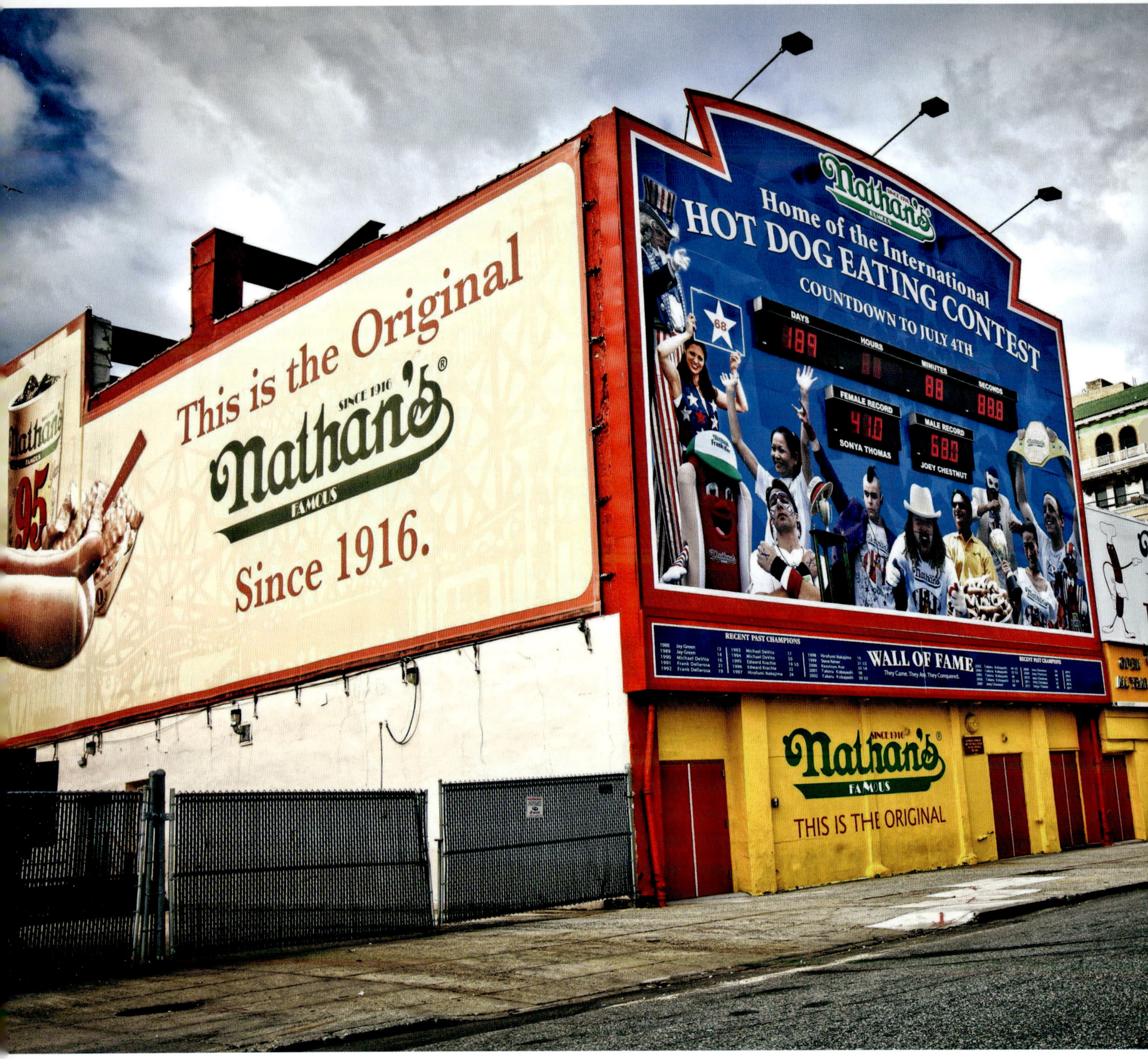

Nathan's Famous

Perhaps the most famous Coney Island landmark is Nathan's Famous, founded in 1916. The small hotdog stand has grown into a fast food empire but the original is still at the corner of Surf and Stillwell avenues in Brooklyn. It draws fans from around the world, particularly on July 4th for its annual hot dog eating contest.

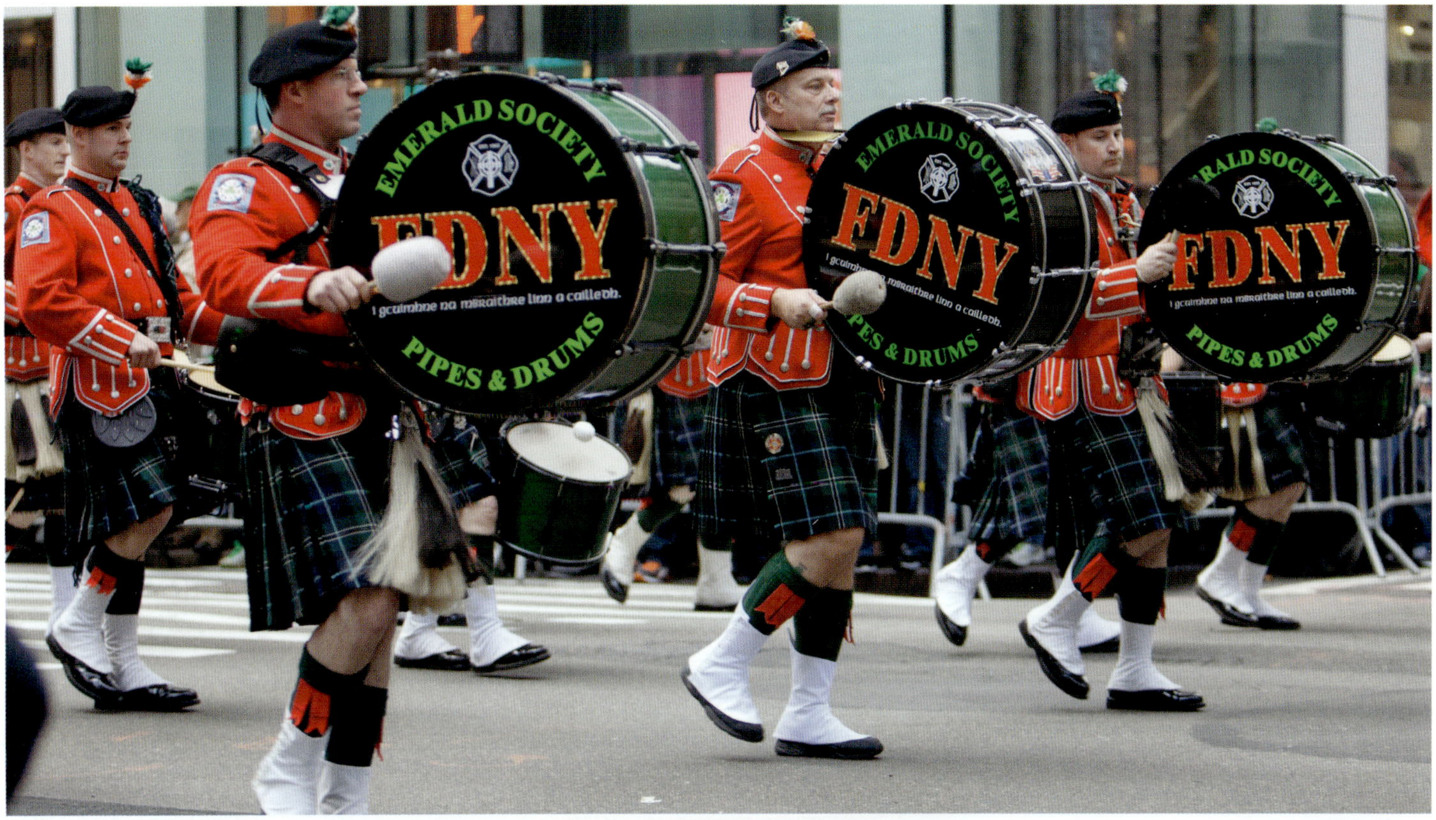

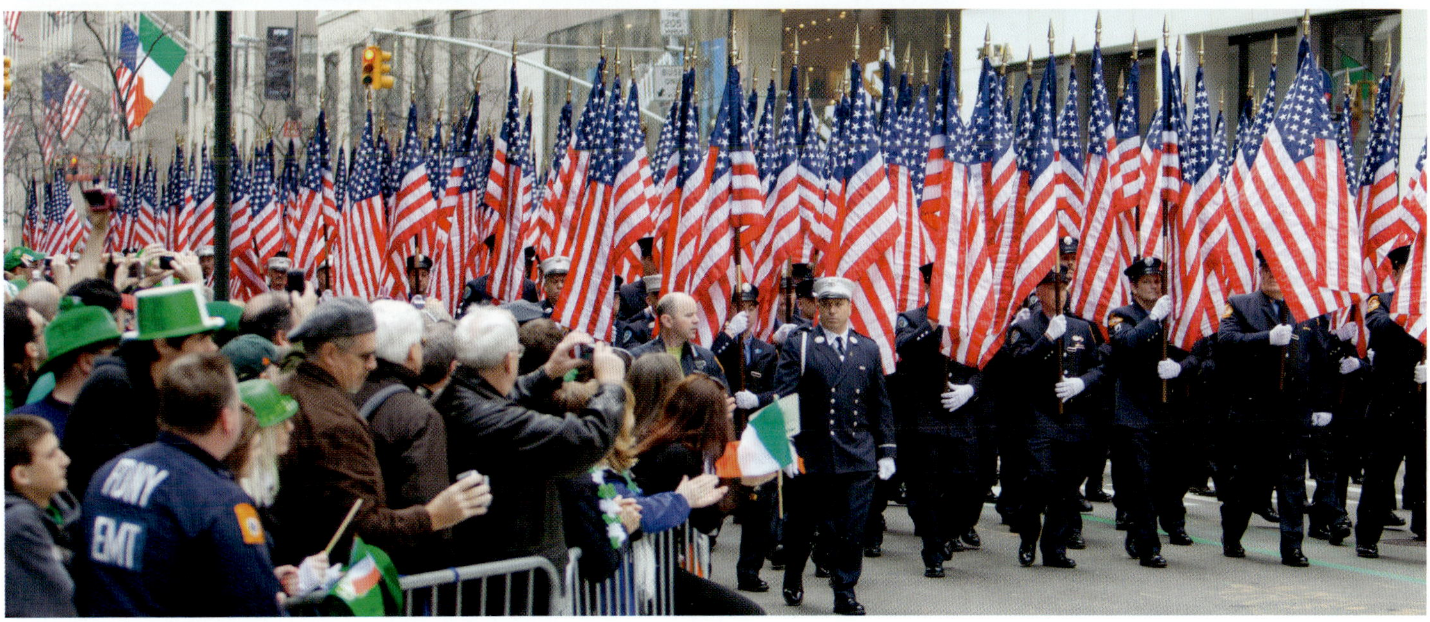

St. Patrick's Day Parade *(top)*

New York City turns green on St. Patrick's Day as the annual parade marches up Fifth Avenue and past St. Patrick's Cathedral in a show of Irish pride each March. First held in 1766 by Irish military men serving in the American colonies, it's become one of the city's most popular parades.

Marching with Pride *(bottom)*

Marching in the St. Patrick's Day Parade each year are Irish step dancers, school bands, dozens of Irish county societies and clans, firefighters, and police as thousands of New Yorkers without a trace of Irish in their blood come out to cheer on the more than 150,000 marchers.

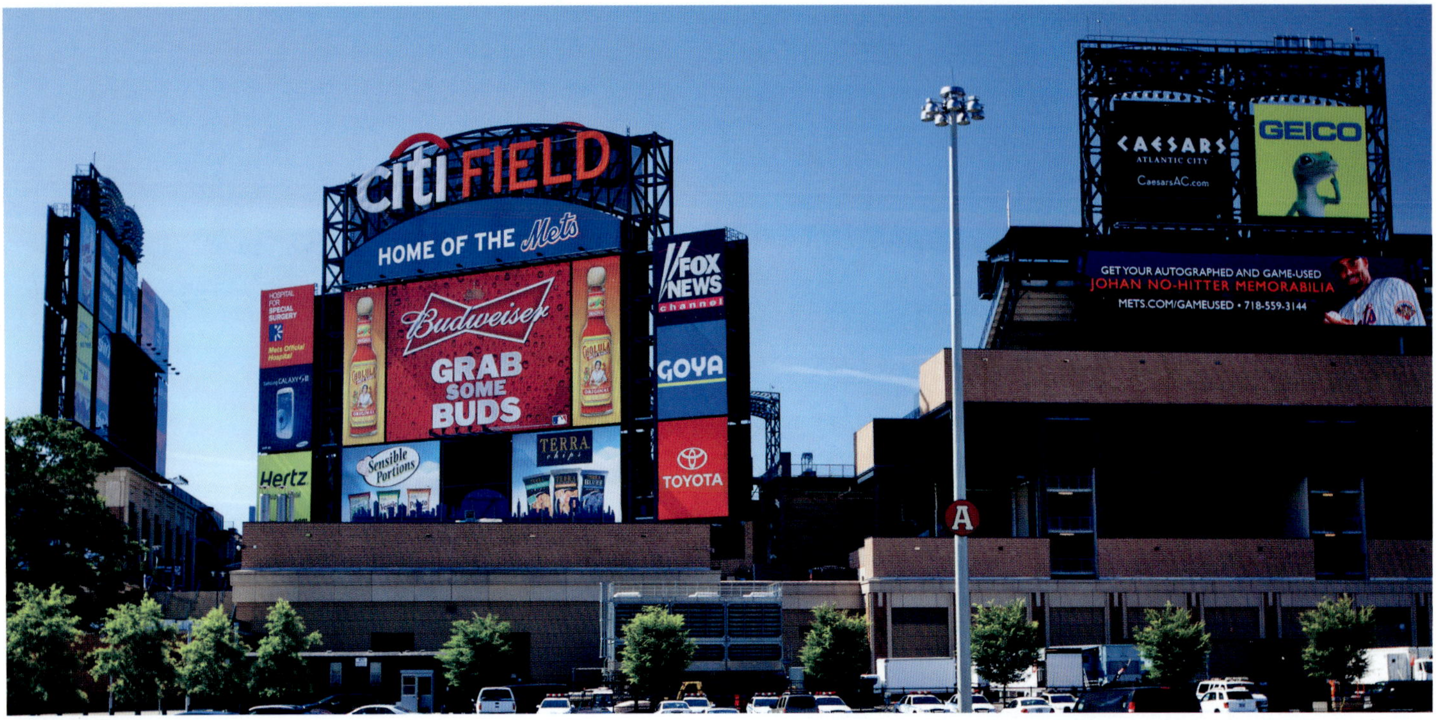

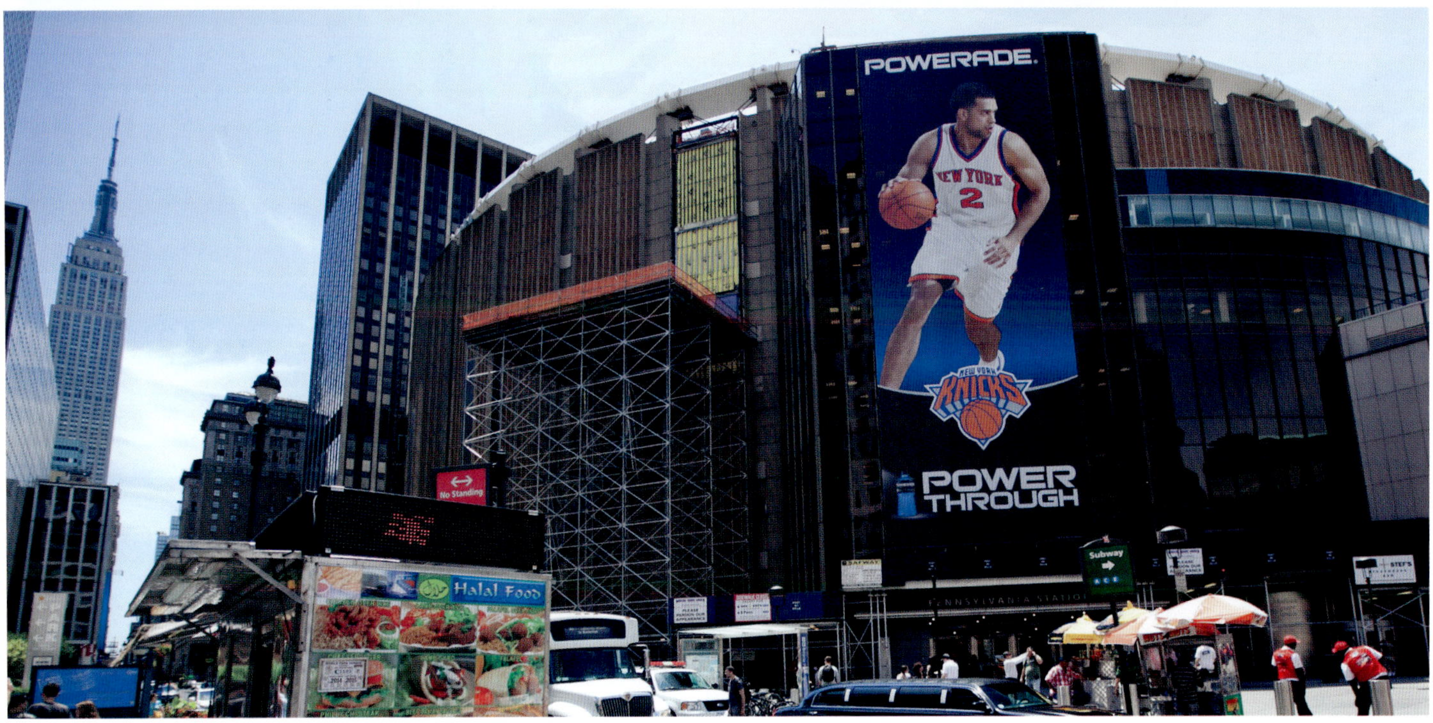

Citi Field Stadium *(top)*

Major League Baseball's New York Mets got a new home in 2009 when they moved into Citi Field, built as a replacement to the adjacent Shea Stadium. With its red brick and limestone façade and arched entrances, the exterior evokes memories of Ebbets Field, the beloved former home of the Brooklyn Dodgers.

Madison Square Garden *(bottom)*

The world's most famous indoor arena, Madison Square Garden is home to the New York Knicks and Liberty basketball teams and the New York Rangers ice hockey team. It also hosts college basketball, track and field events, and concerts by leading performers.

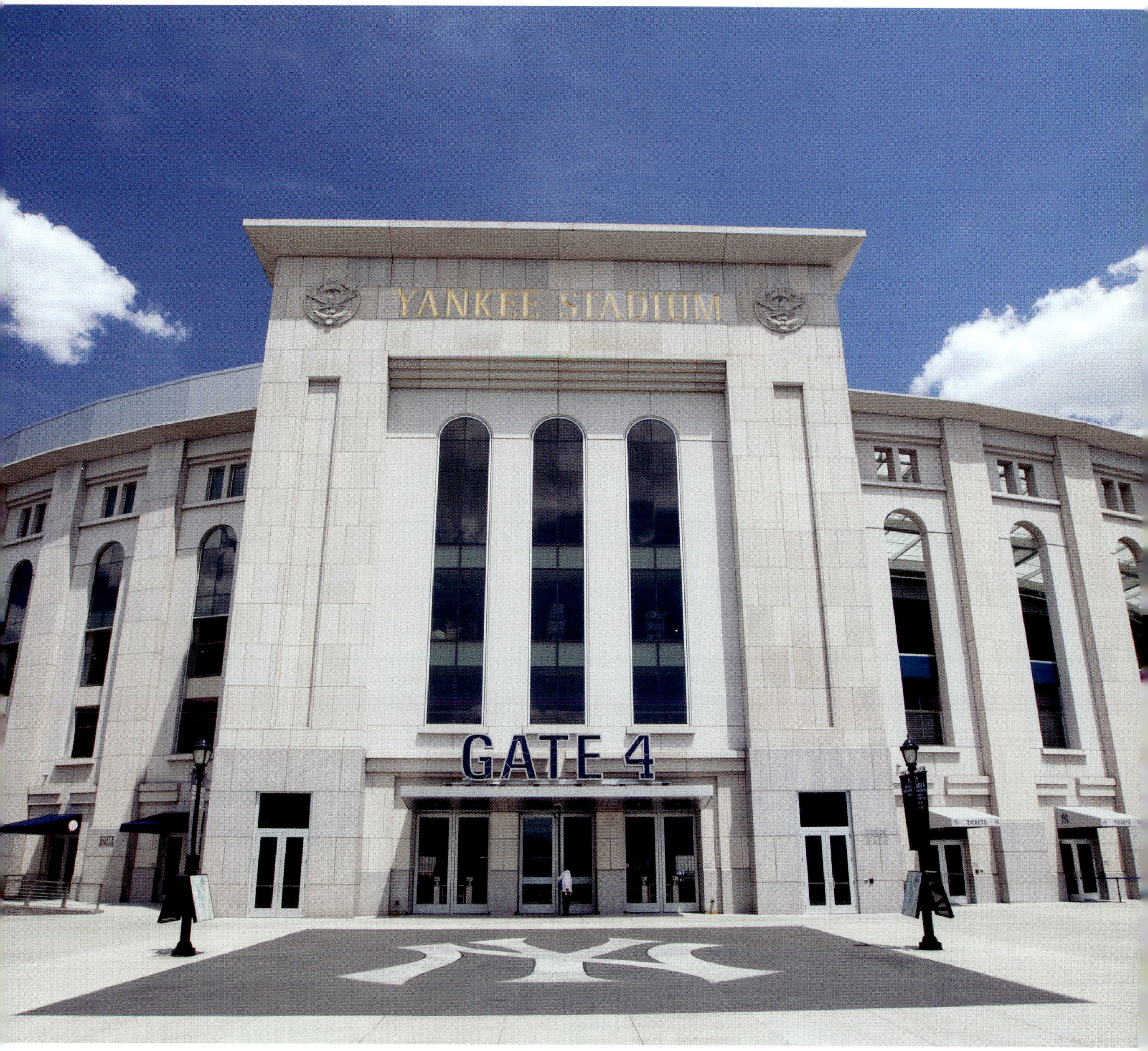

Yankee Stadium

The World Series Champion New York Yankees moved into their new Bronx stadium in 2009. Many design elements of the previous "House that Ruth Built" were incorporated into the new stadium, which at a cost of $1.5 billion is the most expensive baseball stadium ever built.

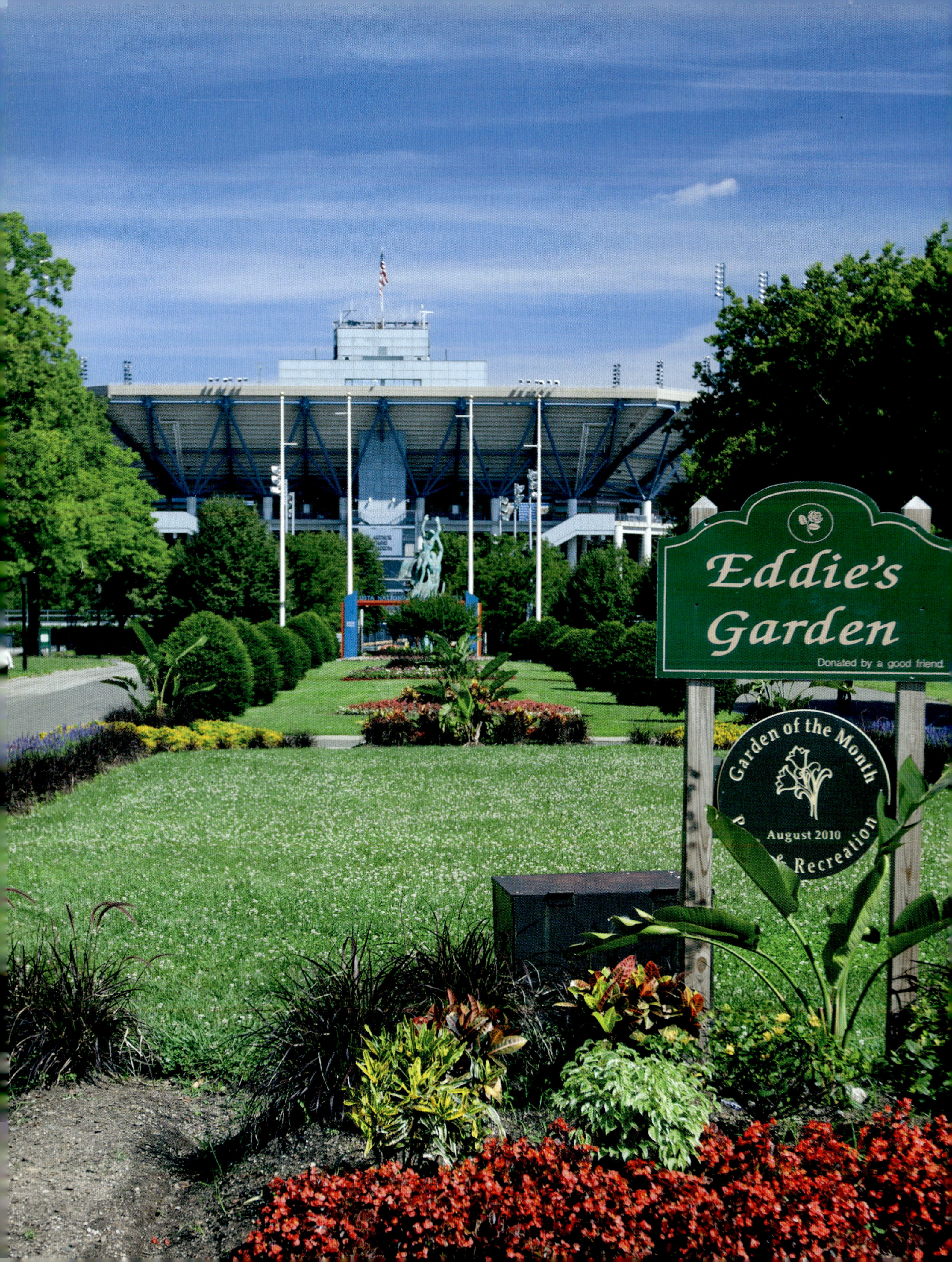
Eddie's Garden
Donated by a good friend.
Garden of the Month
August 2010
& Recreation

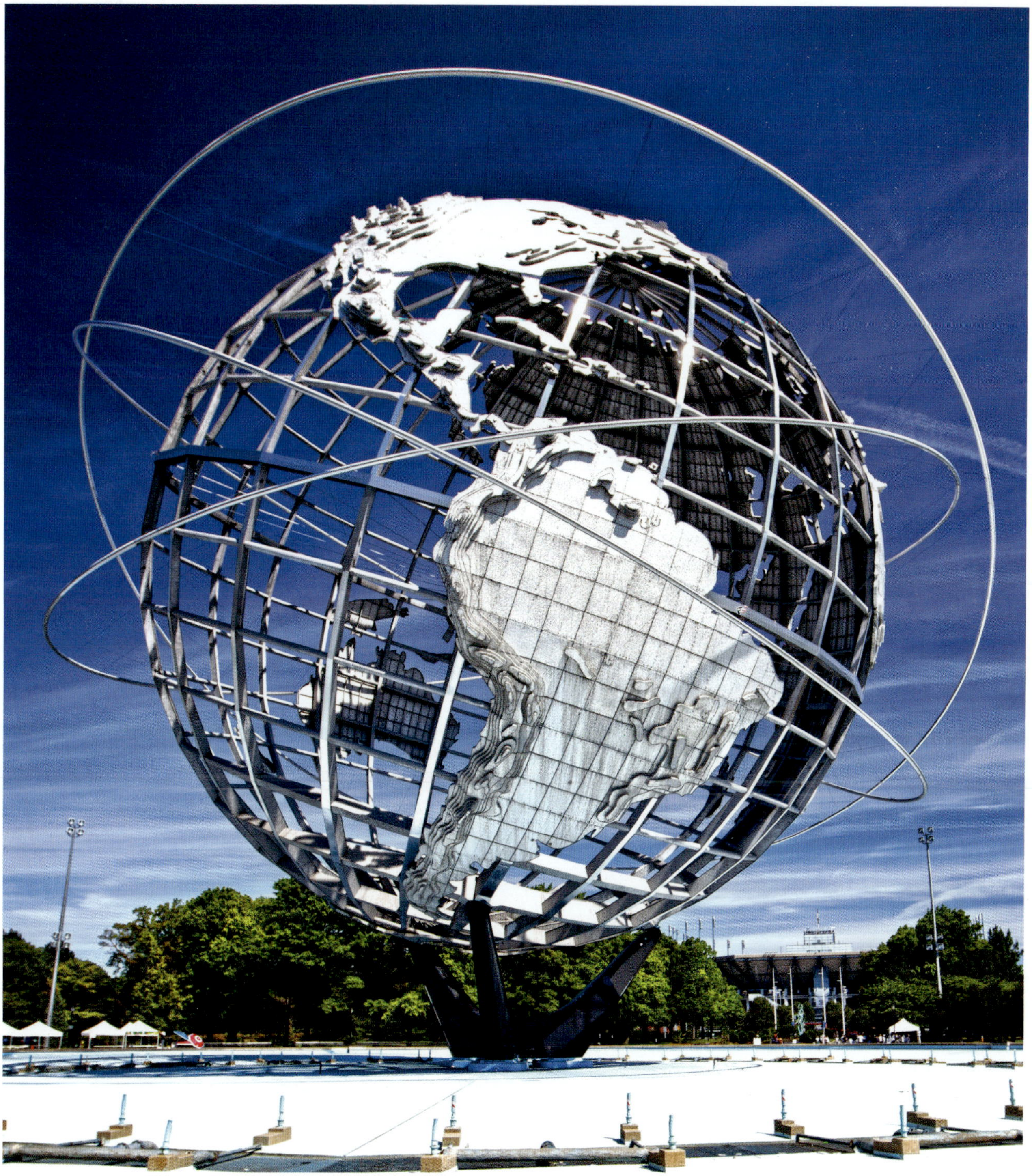

Arthur Ashe Tennis Stadium *(opposite)*

Arthur Ashe Stadium is part of the USTA Billie Jean King National Tennis Center located in Queens, and where the prestigious U.S. Open tournament is played each summer. It is named for Arthur Ashe Jr., the legendary tennis champion who won the inaugural U.S. Open in 1968.

Unisphere *(above)*

This 12-story stainless steel globe in Flushing Meadows, Queens, is a remnant of the World's Fair of 1964. One of the borough's most recognizable symbols, the Unisphere was commissioned to celebrate the fair's theme, "Peace Through Understanding." Designated a city landmark, it stands as the centerpiece of a public park.

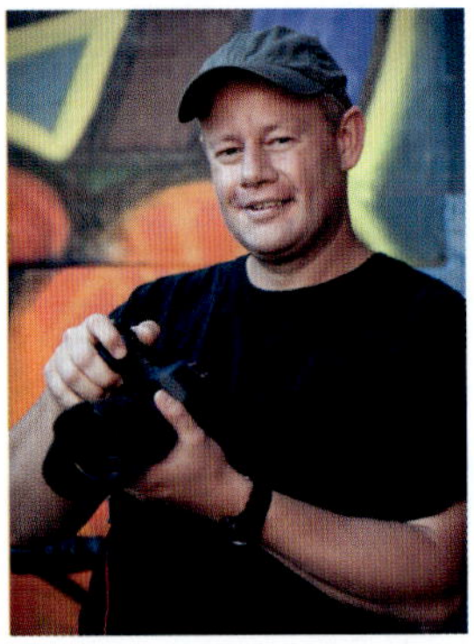

Stuart Monk

With his detail-oriented eye, Stuart Monk captures all facets and wonders of New York City, from its historic buildings and bridges to its sparkling skyline and diverse neighborhoods. Originally from England, Stuart now lives in Connecticut with his wife and three sons. He spends as much time as possible photographing the city he has become passionate about. He works for a leading stock photography agency based in New York and sells his own photography through a number of major agencies. His work has appeared in numerous publications worldwide. Stuart is also a freelance photographer creating commercial images and selling fine art imagery. Prints of images in this book are available from his website at www.stuartmonk.zenfolio.com.

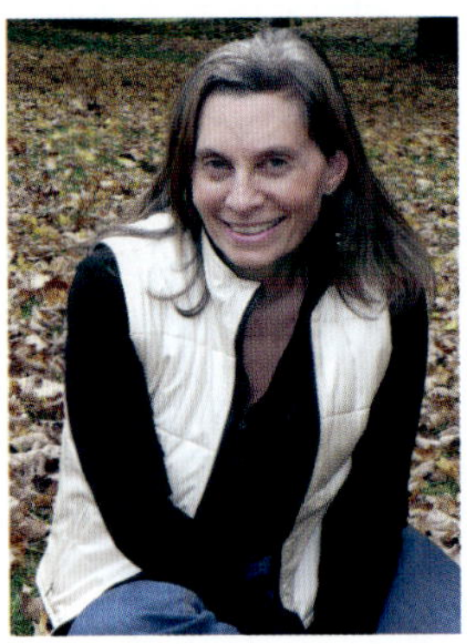

Bethany Kandel

New York City is not only in Bethany Kandel's heart, but in her blood. She is a born and bred New Yorker, as are her parents and two sons. (Her husband was born upstate, but has called Manhattan home for more than 30 years.) Bethany has lived on the same Manhattan block – in three different buildings – for 47 years. A prolific health, travel, and lifestyle writer, Bethany has been a New York-based reporter for *USA Today, New York Daily News*, and the *Associated Press.* Her freelance articles have appeared in *The New York Times, PARADE, Woman's Day*, msnbc.com and numerous other national publications and major websites. She is the author of a parenting resource book, *The Expert Parent* (Pocket Books). Visit www.bethanykandel.wordpress.com to learn more about her.

THE COMPLETE BOOK OF HOUSEPLANTS

THE COMPLETE BOOK OF HOUSEPLANTS

CLIVE INNES

WHSMITH
EXCLUSIVE
· BOOKS ·

Produced exclusively for WH Smith Ltd by
Marshall Cavendish Books Limited,
58 Old Compton Street,
London W1V 5PA

ISBN 1 85435 198 2

Typeset by Litho Link Limited, Welshpool, Powys
Printed and bound in Hong Kong

CONTENTS

INTRODUCTION

This book is for everyone who owns a houseplant. You may have one beside you at work; you might want to start a collection, but wonder if your home is large enough or light enough, and not have much idea of where to begin; or you could be the proud owner of a houseful of thriving specimens, acquired over many years and lovingly cared for. Whether you're a seasoned collector or a 'newcomer', *The Complete Book of Houseplants* offers a wealth of sound advice and information for those who want to know more about their plants.

And it really is a 'complete' book, because it looks at keeping houseplants from every angle. As living, 'breathing' organisms, they require food, light and warmth. Neglect will result in untimely death – the right care can keep a plant strong and healthy long after many would have consigned it to the dustbin. In the *Living With Plants* section, you can find out exactly how to nurture your plants to give them the ideal conditions in which to flourish.

Plants are also capable of producing offspring, of course, and the various methods are dealt with in *Perfect Propagation,* to ensure you obtain sturdy new plants every time. You can get quite a sense of achievement when you grow a new young plant from an old one – not to mention an inexpensive and novel source of gifts for your friends!

And then there is the decorative value of houseplants. It is safe to say that there is no more economic, versatile and attractive way to bring a room to life than the thoughtful addition of some flowers and foliage. Whether you want to add subtle touches of colour, create a striking focal point, or live in a riotous mass of greenery, in *Display & Design* you'll be able to discover the plants and the know-how to achieve your desired effect. You can either buy plants the size you want them to be to fit straight into your scheme, or have the pleasure of buying them young or starting them from seeds or cuttings and watching them grow over the years to become well-established members of your household. Flowering plants need not be thrown away once they have died down – some can be transferred to the garden, where they will continue to flower year after year.

Something Different covers some of the more unusual plants and methods of growing, in case you prefer to go for a more out-of-the ordinary effect with your collection. It will hopefully spur you on to think of all kinds of new ideas, for the possibilities with houseplants are virtually limitless.

Finally, the main section of the book is an *A-Z of Plants,* which forms a comprehensive encyclopedia in itself. Its clear format and uniformity of style means you can look up any aspect of plant care in seconds. For advice on your existing houseplants, or suggestions for new ones, you will find it an invaluable companion.

If you have never thought of yourself as having 'green fingers' before – now's the time to prove otherwise! *The Complete Book of Houseplants* will give you all the know-how you need to create and maintain your houseplant collection with the minimum of effort and the maximum of enjoyment.

DISPLAY AND DESIGN

Plants are one of the easiest and best ways to make any room in the house look eyecatching and 'alive'. You don't need to spend a fortune, or have any special flair for design – just experiment with the plants you already have, perhaps buy a few more to create a particular effect – and you'll be surprised and delighted at the results you can achieve.

Does your living room lack direct light? There are plently of wonderful houseplants you can use to fill the darker corners, where they will actually flourish out of the sun. Is your bathroom uninviting? Turn it into an exotic oasis with a mass of ferns and palms. Could your kitchen do with a little greenery? There are plants to suit every spare space you can think of.

With a little time and a lot of fun, you can make your houseplants a vibrant feature of your interior decoration – and they'll grow all the better for it!

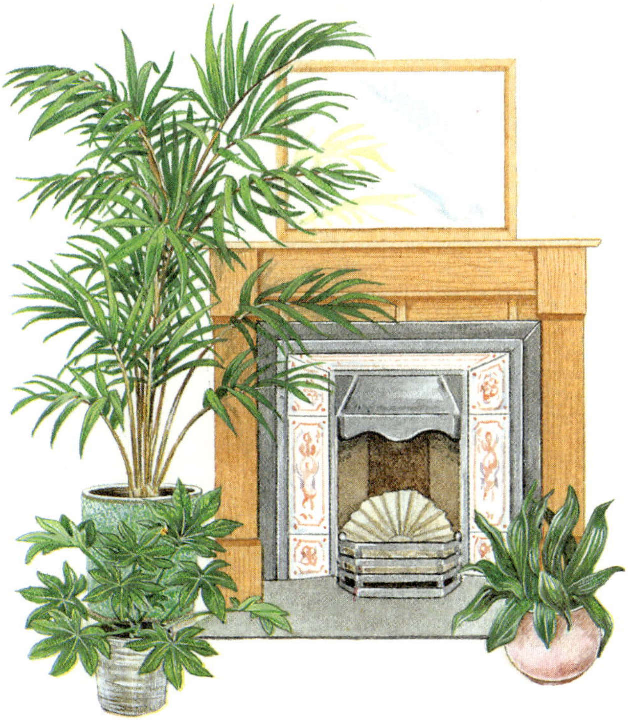

How to display your houseplants

There can't be many homes without a few houseplants dotted about, and you will probably already have a fairly wide selection. But are you doing them justice and displaying them to their greatest effect? It's true that even a solitary African Violet on a coffee table will make a room look better, but why not go further and use plants to change the whole image of your home?

Use foliage plants and flowers as an important part of your interior design, and transform a bare bathroom into a lush jungle or a drab kitchen into a leafy bower. Anything's possible, and you don't need a magic wand or lots of money.

Taking stock of your rooms

Once you realise just how versatile your houseplants can be, you'll be itching to use them in many different ways. There are absolutely no strict rules to follow, though there are a few guidelines that will help to guarantee success.

It makes good sense to choose plants that will be happy in the normal conditions of your home. Find out which plants will flourish in your particular surroundings — there's no point in trying to nurture a sub-tropical

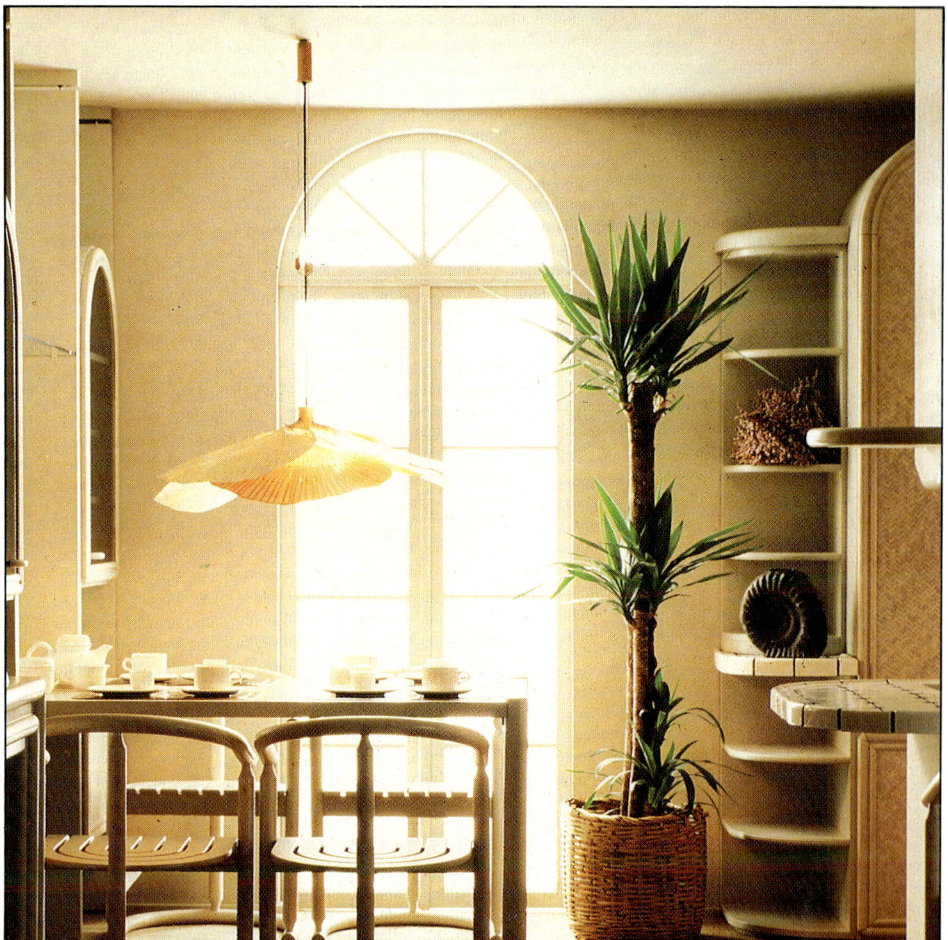

This striking spiky yucca emphasises the height of the elegant French windows and makes a dramatic focal point. A number of smaller plants would fail to give as much impact to the design of the room.

DISPLAY TIP

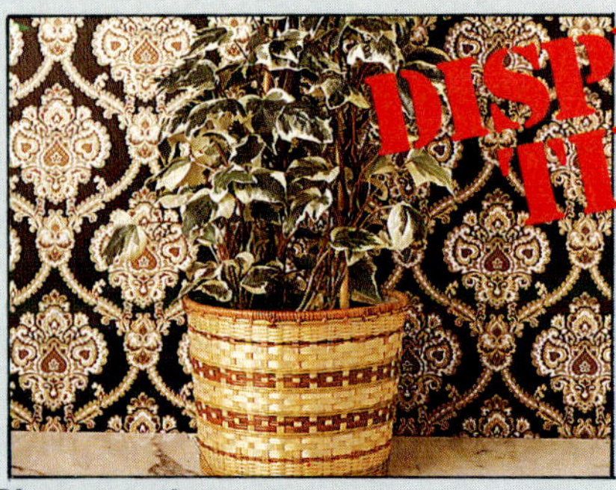

Plants against a pattern
The shape and effect of this Ivy and Dieffenbachia are lost against such a heavily patterned background. Instead, use a plant like an Aspidistra or Rubber Plant with well-defined leaves.

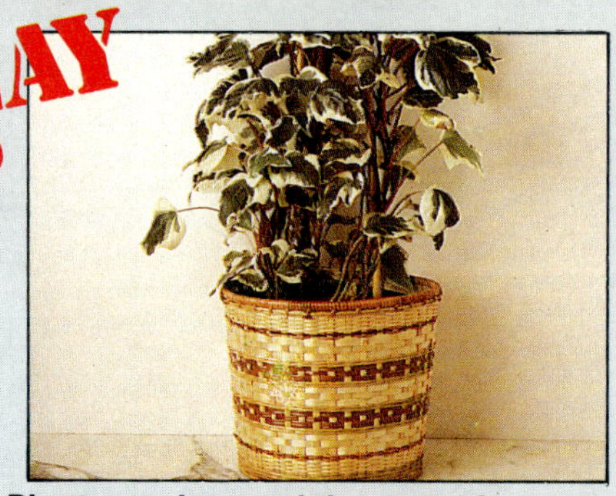

Plants against a plain ground
The plain background makes all the difference to the colours and impact of the arrangement. Any plant stands out well and looks good against a pale, plain, unfussy background.

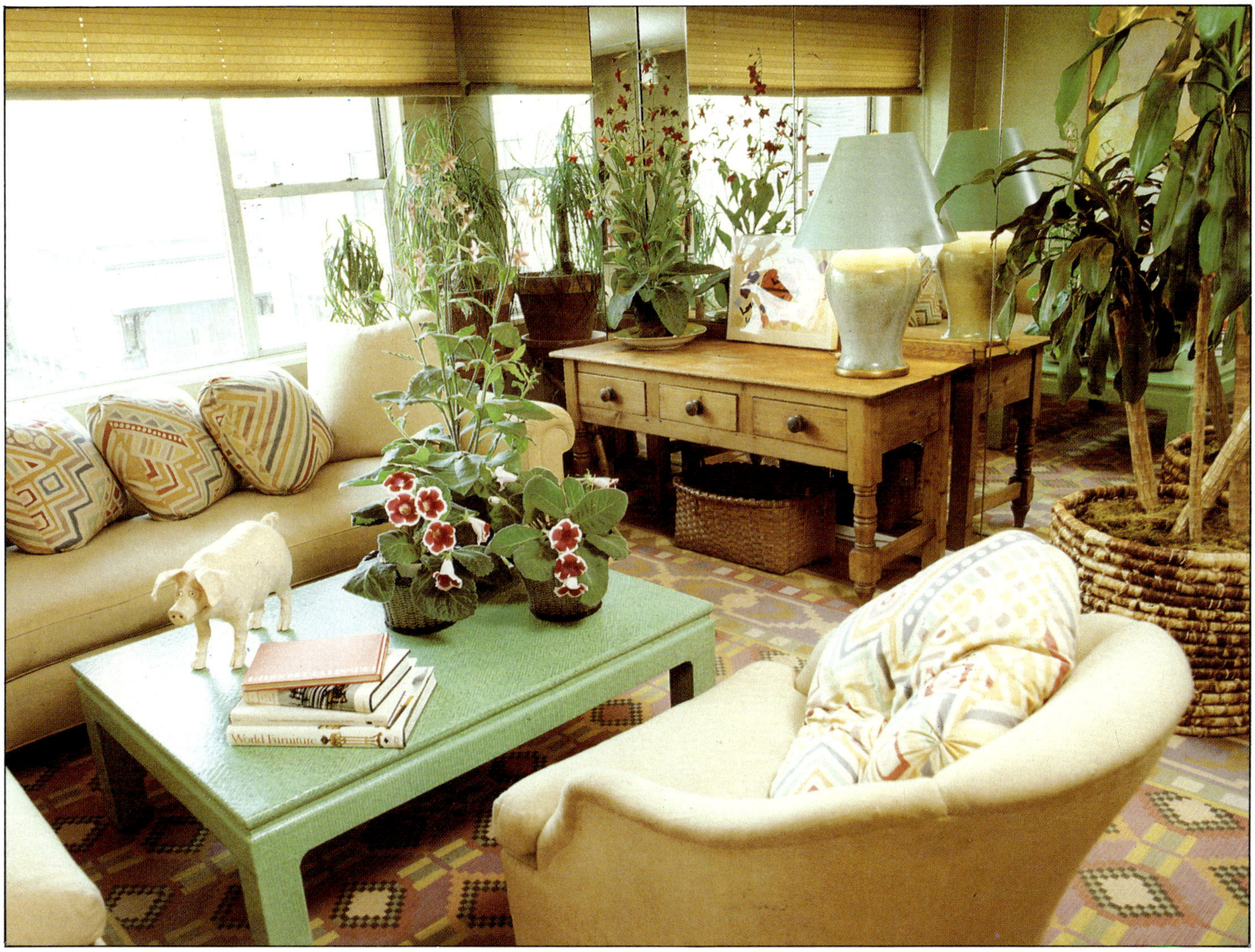

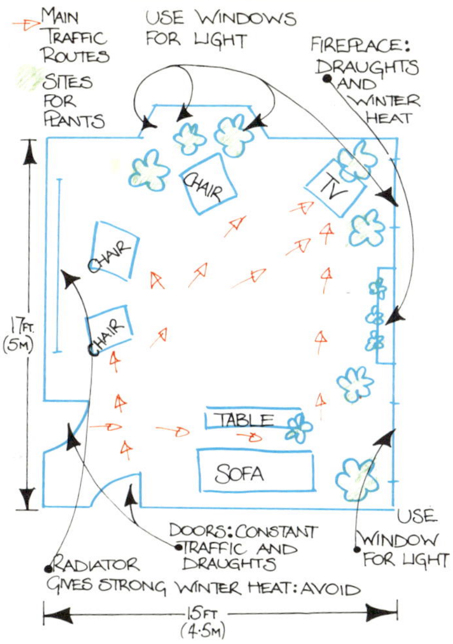

Draw a sketch of your room to tell you where there's scope for houseplants. Put in doors, windows, furniture, heating and traffic ways to show possibilities.

The clever use of mirrors gives a room the illusion of more space and makes the plants look bigger and better. On the table sit a couple of Gloxinias and a Nicotiana. A Beaucarnea enjoys the window and a Dracaena lives cn the right.

orchid which needs hot-house temperatures if you've got a cold flat.

It's worth doing a quick sketch of each room, just to map out where the light comes from — windows, skylights, doors which are left permanently open — and don't forget that there's furniture to fit in too!

Measure the distances as well, so there's no guesswork when it comes to investing in large plants, as you'll be sure that there's enough room for them. A good tip is to draw arrows to show the well-worn traffic routes and avoid such mistakes as putting the most delicately arranged group of plants slap in the middle of the children's bee-line from the front door to the kitchen.

Now think about your four walls and the height of the ceiling — their scale and proportion are important, for practical as well as design reasons. A gorgeous collection of small houseplants would get lost in a large open-plan room, while a splendid weeping fig in the cloakroom would mean there's no room for you or anything else!

If you are lucky enough to have high-ceilinged rooms you have twice the canvas to work with — you can use plants to fill the otherwise empty upper part of the room, by cascading down to meet those growing upward from floor level. As a general rule of thumb, the bigger the room, the larger the plants it can accommodate and vice versa, and the better the effect if the plants and room are all in proportion.

Design for effect

Next look at your colour scheme — too often it's something many of us forget to consider. Houseplants can look good against plain white or soft pastel colour walls — the colours that reflect light. But if you do have a dark, heavily patterned wallpaper, avoid putting plants with brilliantly coloured leaves against it — they'll just cancel each other out. Try instead the calmer effect of simple plain green foliage plants which will stand out against a detailed background without competing with it.

Still at the planning stage, try to think of plants being used in conjunction with other features, particularly your furniture. There's a whole world of possibilities — why not twine ivy or Kangaroo Vine (*Cissus*) around bannisters, or create a living green frame for a favourite picture you can't afford to have framed professionally.

Best of all, try to use mirrors in at least one display. Using reflected light and images is one of the magical ways to add an entirely new visual dimension to a room, and like an illusionist you can produce something from nothing — a double size sitting room, a seemingly flower-filled alcove, twice the sunlight — try it and see.

A point to remember although not exactly a guideline: do experiment, as the unexpected effect can often be the most dramatic. The final choice of plants and their arrangement is up to your personal taste, and the joy of houseplants, unlike garden flowers, is that you can change your mind and move them around until you arrive at something you love. Once you start thinking, you'll get ideas at every turn, and soon everywhere you look will inspire you — magazine features, shop displays, other people's windows . . .

Good companions

Grouping plants together is the most effective and immediately dramatic way of displaying your houseplants. Plants love each other's company and really do thrive in a group — they create their own mini environment with the higher group humidity, and watering is made easier too!

Of course some plants merit solitary confinement to show off the beauty of their form. Large specimens such as Howea palms and mature castor oil plants *(Ricinus communis)* are sufficiently imposing standing alone.

If you decide to plan a group, the possibilities are endless, and the only

Grouping houseplants

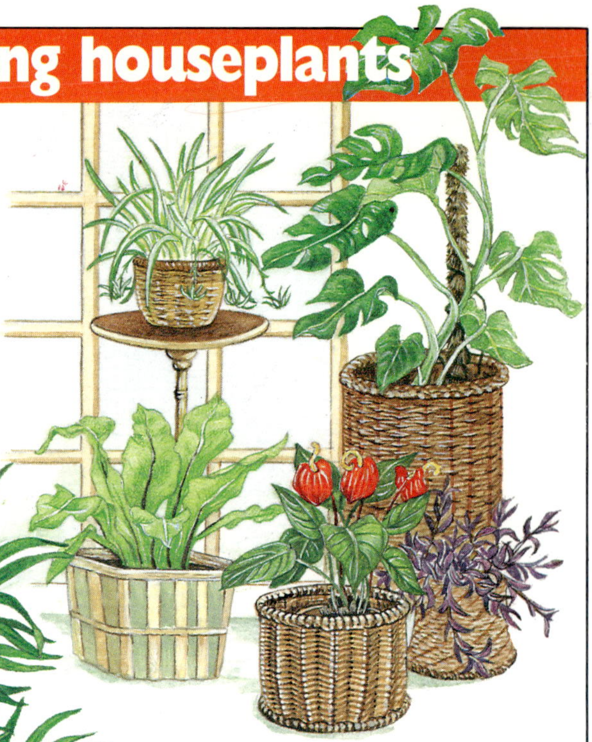

Informal plant group
Provide unity by growing your plants in the same type of container. Baskets are effective as you can get them in a good range of sizes and interesting shapes and their natural colours blend well with the green leaves of the plants.

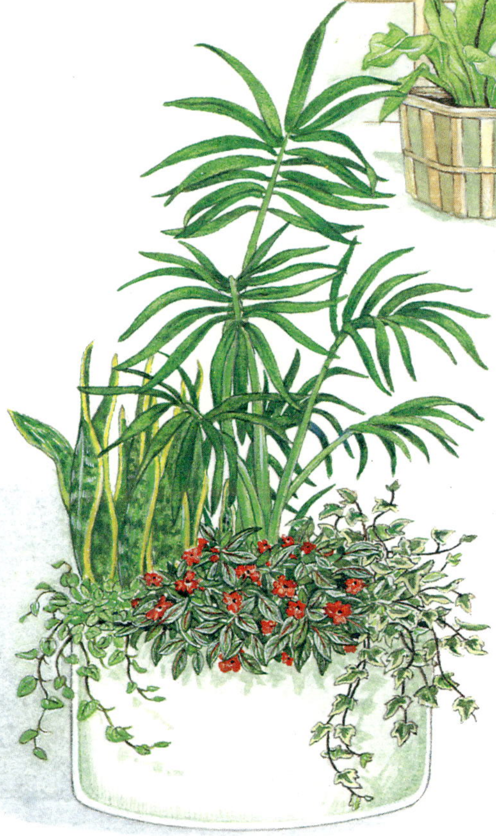

Group in a large container
Fill the main pot with peat and plunge the plants still in their individual pots into the peat; then you can change them around whenever you want. Set a stately Mother-in-Law's Tongue against a small leaved ficus and a tall arching palm to get a geometric contrast of leaf shapes; and use just one flowering plant such as a Busy Lizzie to provide a vivid splash of colour in the centre.

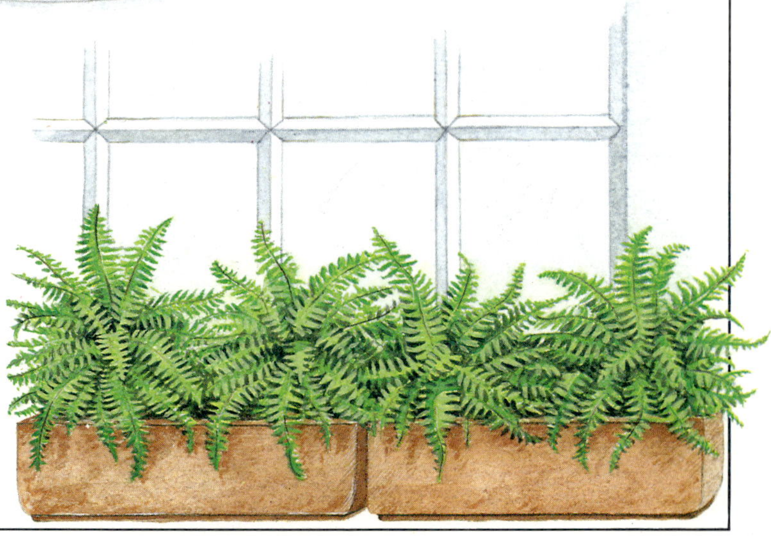

A formal group
Grow a row of the same plant in the same type of container to create a formal grouping. You can do this with lots of different plants - palms, crotons, ivies, geraniums or, as here, Sword Ferns.

To fix glass shelves securely, run a double row of metal struts either side of your window, and fix the shelves with special glass shelving clips. The best ones have smooth jaws into which the glass slides. The height of the different shelves can be adjusted to fit the size of your plants.

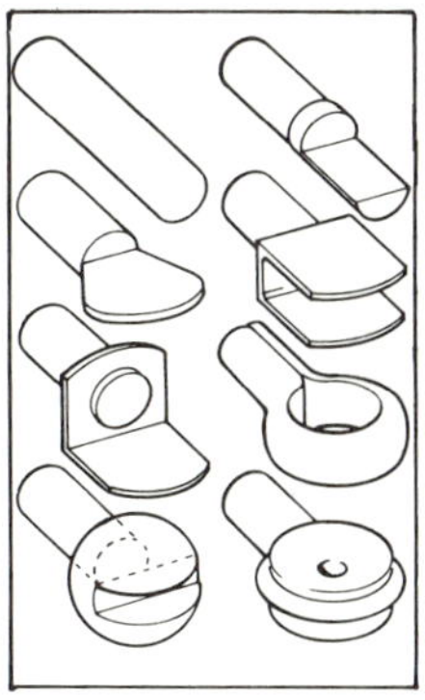

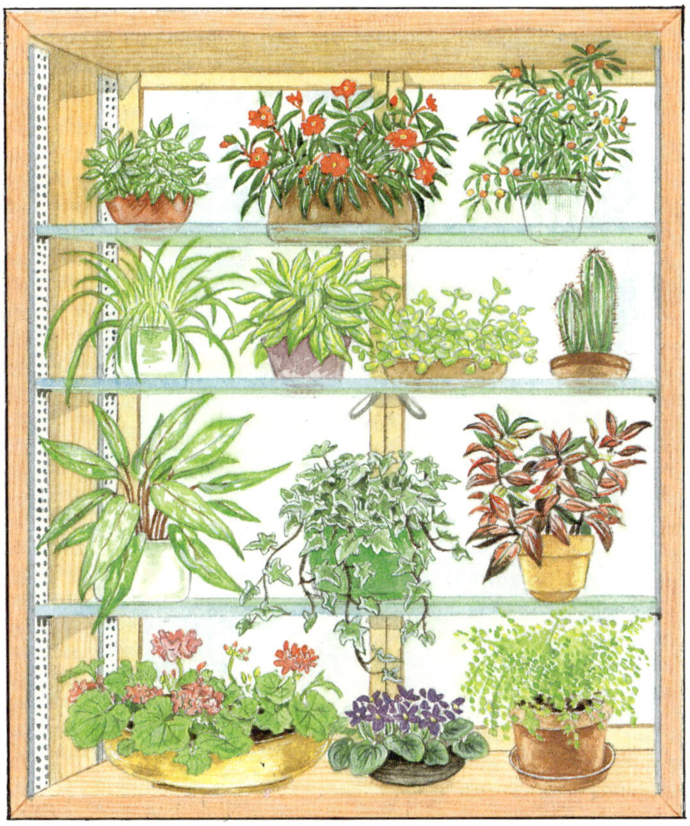

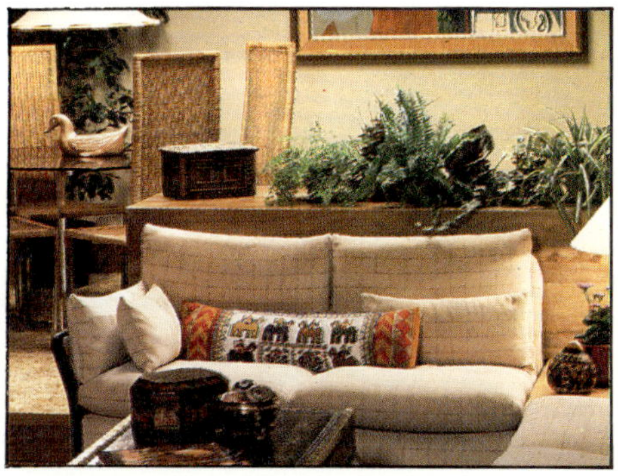

A permanent room divider can be emphasised by a plant trough: fill it with plants which like artificial light, such as ferns, ivies and peperomias.

thing to ensure is that all the plants have the same likes and dislikes — don't put a thirsty, humidity-loving Philodendron next to a cactus that loves to be parched.

A group can be just that — any number of plants standing together; there's no limitation. They can be free-standing, shoulder to shoulder, or sharing the same container. This last method is probably one of the best ways and all you need is a container large enough to take all the plants. Fill the container with peat and plunge your chosen plants (still in their individual pots) into the peat. Keep standing back to check the balance of your display as you go, then when you've finished, water the whole lot well. For best results, the plant pots should be clay rather than plastic, as clay is porous and allows the moisture from the damp peat to get through to the plant.

How to balance a display

This is the chance to use all those design talents you know you have. Look at florists' displays and other people's successful groupings and notice how it seems instinctive and natural to balance shapes — tall and narrow with low and bushy; to contrast textures with something like a feathery fern against the arching leaves of a Spider Plant and to use colour and variegated leaves together, such as a delicately speckled Dumb Cane with a dark green Sweetheart Vine.

When designing a display don't forget those houseplants with bright coloured foliage, as they add a touch of real flamboyance. Only include one variety in any group and don't let it overpower the others: the plants should complement each other, like jewels in a lovely setting.

Containers

What you display your plants in can be as important as the plants themselves, though this doesn't mean the container need be an expensive one. Almost anything will do — but try for one which enhances the effect you're aiming at, rather than detracting from it. A large specimen plant or tree that you want to use as a focal point for a room will do a handsome Victorian jardinière proud, while a waterfall of trailing plants will hide the prettiest pot in no time.

If you like the unusual, and haven't much money, rummage in junk shops and rubbish skips — it's amazing what you can find; and instead of ripping out that old iron fire grate, why not give it a lick of paint and fill it with a froth of ferns? But one word of caution — many glazed china pots will let water seep through and leave nasty white water rings on your furniture or stains on your carpet. So either paint the inside of the pot with polyurethane varnish or put an old plate underneath to catch all the drips and you won't have any accidents!

Some more display ideas

Learning to display your houseplants to better effect can have a practical as well as a visually pleasing result, and you'll find too that designing with plants is about the cheapest way of decorating. Here are some unusual ideas:

- Create a curtain effect using plants; hang pots at different levels from secure hooks in the ceiling and choose plants that climb, arch or trail. They act as a privacy screen as well so you can manage without net curtains.
- Have you ever thought of dividing a large room with a screen or trellis of plants? You can group several large varieties together, or build a proper plant trough.
- Do you want to disguise an ugly view? One of the prettiest ways of hiding the fact that you're just 3 feet away from the house next door, or overlooking a row of dustbins, is to use plants instead of a roller blind. Put glass shelves up at a window — make sure they're secure — and fill every inch with plants. The glass shelves don't blot out any light and the plants let the sun through in a lovely dappled way.

Once your enthusiasm has been fired, the sky (or the ceiling) is the limit. The pleasure in having achieved the effect you want is amazing, so sit back and enjoy it — you deserve to.

Choosing your plants

The secret of success with houseplants is to choose plants which will easily settle down and flourish in the particular environment of your home. We'll help you to sort out exactly what your problems and limitations are so that you can grow the healthiest and happiest possible houseplants

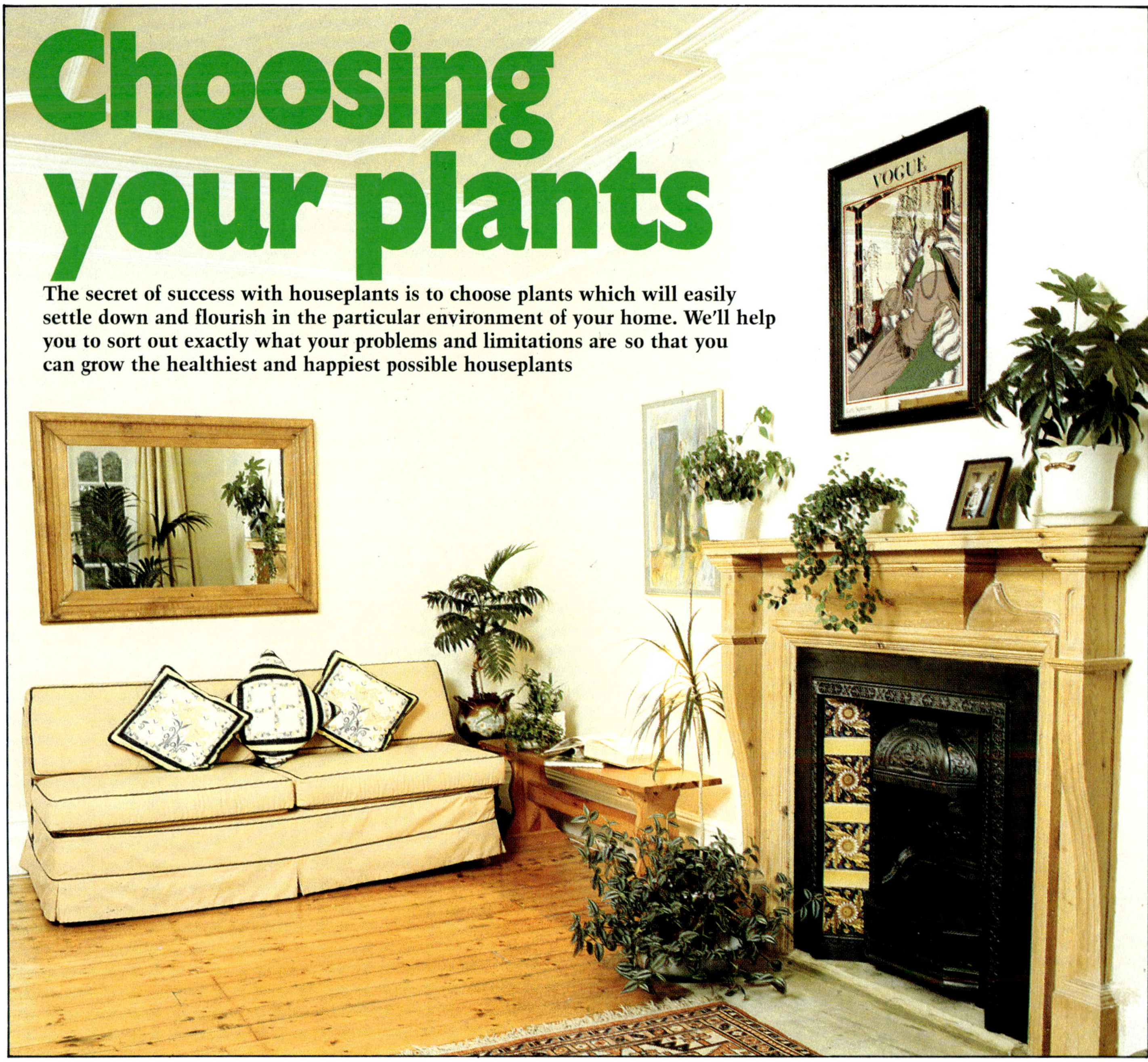

Cool white walls, natural pine and green leaves create a calming atmosphere to sit and relax in.

There are so many different kinds of flowering and foliage plants sold as houseplants that the choice can seem overwhelming. Choosing which ones to buy is a process of elimination of the varying factors you can provide, like the amount of light and heat, weighed against the plants you actually want to grow in your house.

There's no point in choosing plants which need extreme conditions you can't achieve — or can only just manage at a pinch. You will do better with your houseplants if you grow ones which are happy with the existing conditions in your home, rather than struggle with tricky plants which are only hanging on to life by the skin of their leaves.

Narrow the field down by taking a long, cool, assessment of your house; light and heat are the two main controlling factors. Your range is wider if you have good, bright light but there are lots of plants which grow well in light shade and some which even prefer gloom.

Desert cacti, for example, thrive in good, bright light, but this would be fatal for African Violets which need direct sunlight for only part of the day or their leaves turn yellow and they stop growing. Ferns are happiest in subdued light and high humidity — most just shrivel up and die if they sit in the sun. Before you buy a plant, read its label to see which plants need plenty of light and which prefer shade.

Then decide which plants you like — shapes and colours have varying appeal to different people. After this, let your home conditions decide which range of plants you can grow, as they all have their own special requirements.

Never be afraid to ask what a particular plant is, especially if it is growing in the sort of conditions you can provide. Houseplant enthusiasts are always happy to talk about their plants and are often very generous with cuttings as well.

Most people can keep tropical species in summer without problems, but trouble starts in winter if plants don't get high enough temperatures. Try not to fall in love with a plant which needs a high temperature if you can't give it a warm room to live in. Buy instead plants that prefer a cooler winter. Fluctuating heat and cold can be harmful and, while the temperature range may not be dangerous, just the fact that the central heating goes on and off can be damaging.

Draughts are another danger which cause houseplants to drop leaves and flowers. Seal all windows well and don't create a through-draught by leaving doors open.

What kind of plants?

Some people treat their houseplants like children, looking after them every day, touching and talking to them; if this sounds like you, get plants which respond well to constant, daily care. Have a look at our room plan for ideas. Flowering plants always want more tending than foliage plants, as they need their dead flowers removed. They also need attentive watering to prevent the flowers and buds shrivelling, which will happen if they've been forgotten for a few days. You'll find that your plants change with the seasons as they come into and out of flower, so there will always be something different to enjoy.

Not all plants need such a close eye kept on them, and if you want beautiful plants without effort, choose plants which don't need much attention. These are, generally speaking, evergreen foliage plants which have tougher constitutions and so are more tolerant of neglect. The famous Aspidistra is the toughest houseplant of the lot, and will put up with a wide range of conditions — though that's not to say that it won't grow much better if you treat it well!

Solving problems

Although most houseplants hail from the tropics, they object to temperatures much higher than 75° F (24° C) because normally they get very high humidity, and our air is too dry, which leads to shrivelled, dry, falling leaves. The answer is to stand your pots on saucers of wet pebbles and spray the plants frequently with warm water or install humidifiers to freshen the air.

Other problems occur if you keep plants near fumes from anthracite coal fires, oil heaters, coke stoves and fresh paint. If this is unavoidable, choose leathery-leaved Swiss Cheese Plants, Rubber Plants and Jade Plants, all of which are literally too thick-skinned to suffer at all.

It inevitably happens that despite all this good advice, you'll buy or be given a houseplant which is not suitable for your home. Do the best you can for it; find out what it needs and get as close to the conditions as possible.

If the plant needs lots more light than you can give it, move it to the lightest spot in your home, and buy some fluorescent tubes or special growing bulbs. If it needs warmer winter temperatures, put it in the warmest possible spot; if it's small enough, protect it inside a propagator or glass fish tank, or even warm a room especially for it. If your problem plant needs a cold winter and you live in a warm house, find the coolest spot, well away from all heat sources, and mist spray it frequently. The best solution is to give the plant to someone who can look after it properly; but, by using emergency measures, you might be able to keep your plant going until spring when you can revive it.

Dangerous plants

There are a few plants you should avoid or stand on top of a high shelf, if you have children at the 'everything's-worth-tasting' stage. The Dieffenbachia,(**1**), is not nick-named the Dumb Cane for nothing. The sap contains a poison which swells the glands in the throat. Prickly cacti,(**2**), too, are better not grown if there are small, prying fingers around — similarly, plants like Citrus and Asparagus Ferns which hide vicious spines among their pretty foliage. Beware of any plant with berries: the ones on Winter Cherry ,(**3**),look like sweets, but are actually poisonous.

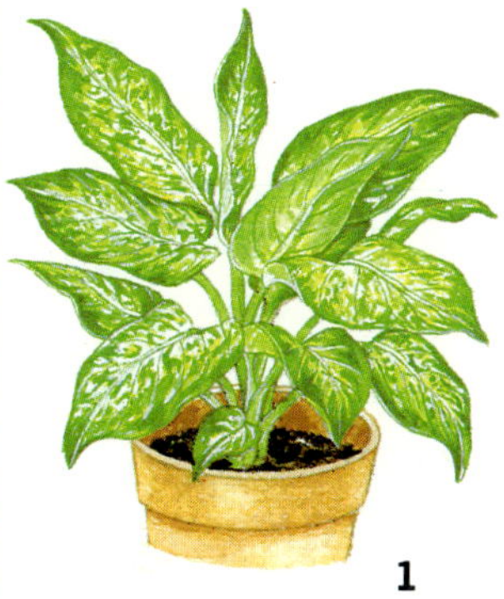

1

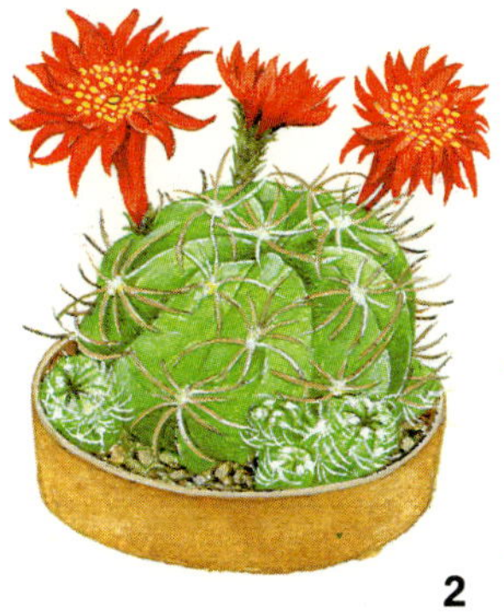

2

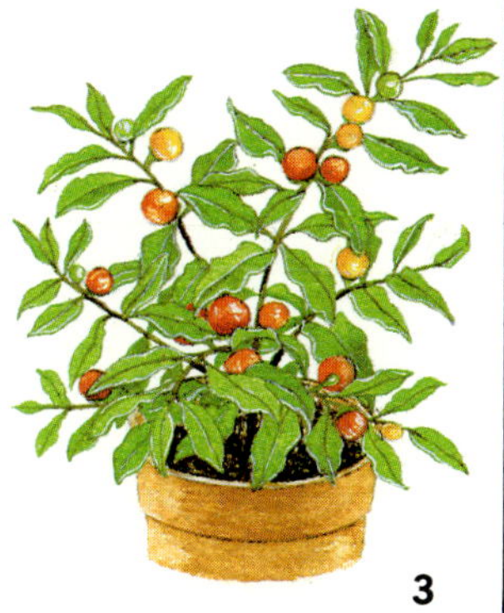

3

Beginner's houseplants

Some plants thrive on neglect, so here are some you don't need to feel too guilty about if you forget them for a while.

Aspidistra – **Aspidistra elatior**
Asparagus fern – **Aspargus plumosus, Asparagus sprengari**
Urn Plant – **Aechmea fasciata**
Spider plant – **Chlorophytum comosum**
Coleus – **Coleus**
Dragon Tree – **Dracaena marginata**
Castor Oil Plant – **Ricinus**
Baby's Tears – **Helxine**
Swiss Cheese Plant – **Monstera deliciosa**
Sweetheart Plant – **Philodendron scadens**
Swedish Ivy – **Plectranthus oertendahlii**
Grape Ivy – **Rhoicissus rhomboidea**
Mother-in-Law's Tongue – **Sansevieria**
Mother of Thousands – **Saxifraga sarmentosa**
Succulents – **Aeonium. Aloe, Crassula**
Cacti – **Mammillaria, Rebutia, Echinopsis**
Wandering Jew – **Tradescantia**

Easy care plants

All these plants need the absolute minimum of attention. Just remember to water and feed them regularly and they'll be fine.

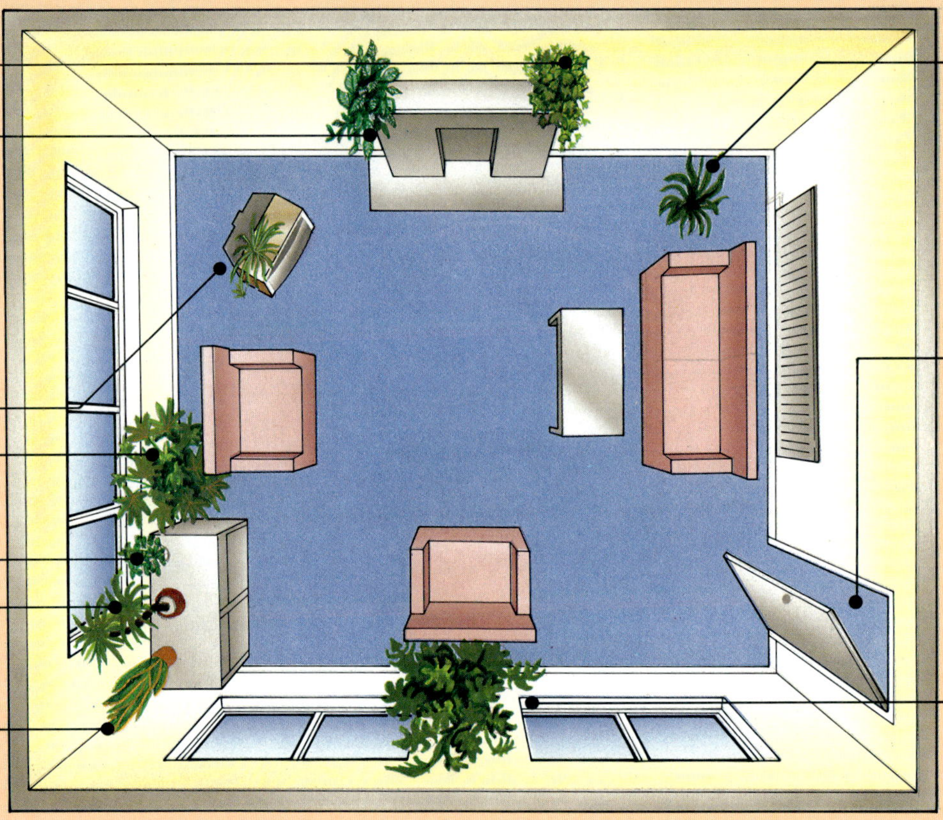

Constant care plants

Most of these plants change with the seasons as their flowers come and go — so there's always something new to enjoy.

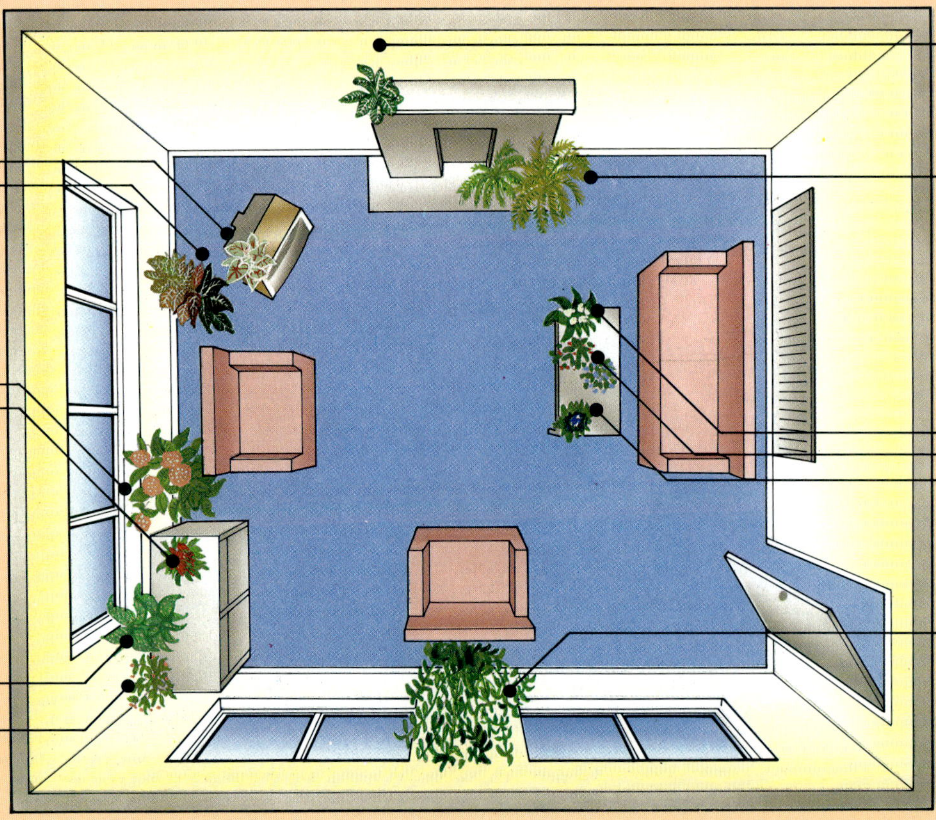

Fabulous flowers

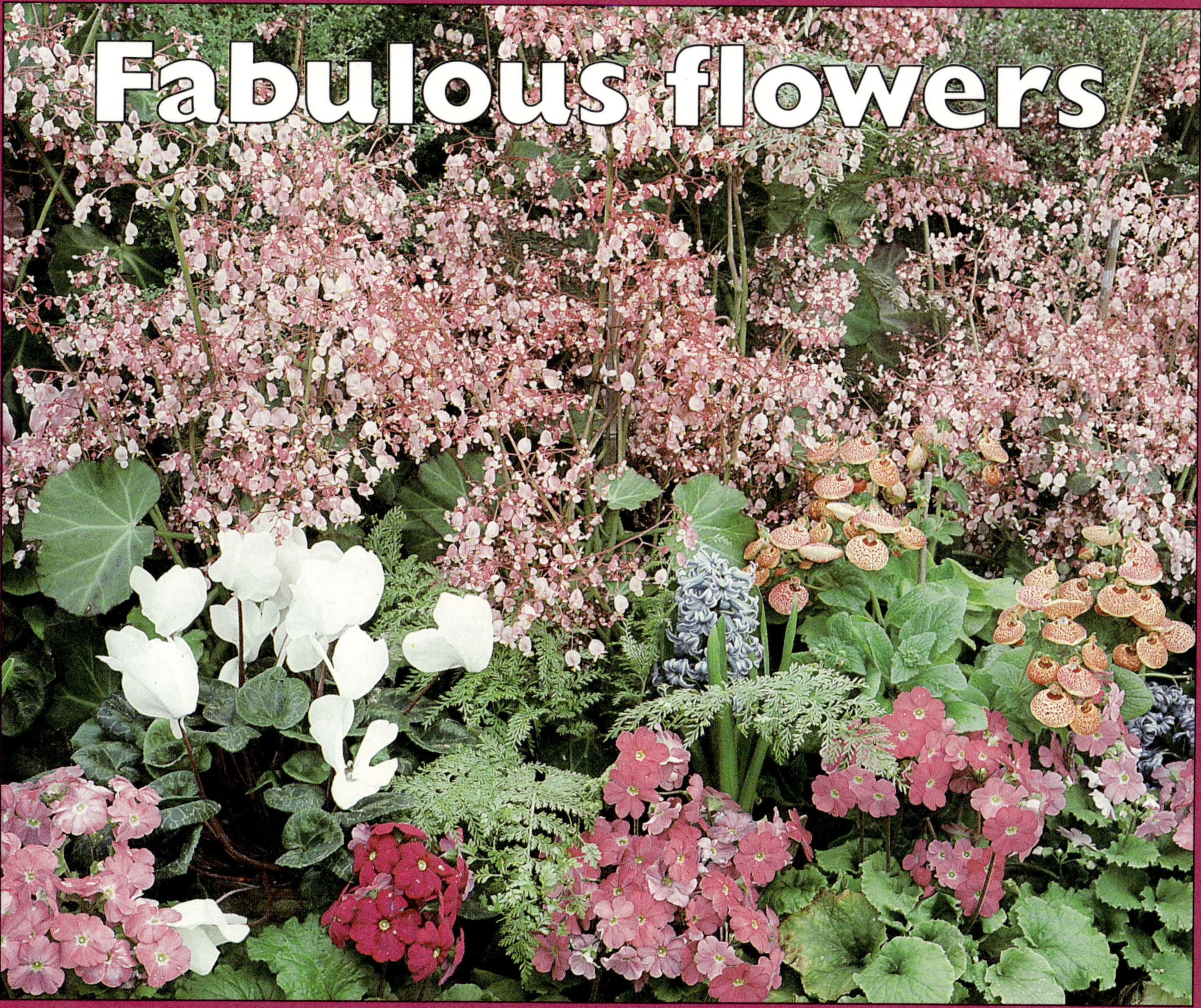

Houseplants that flower — whether in a riot of bright colours or in muted, pastel shades — will give permanent pleasure to any plant lover. They brighten up any room, and count among the most popular and appreciated of presents, both in springtime and in the depths of winter, at Christmas. But a healthy, well-grown flowering plant can often be expensive to buy, so you should know what to look out for to avoid disappointment.

At some time or another, almost everyone must have had the experience of buying a flowering plant and getting it home, only to see it start dying almost immediately. Flowers fall off, buds refuse to open, leaves wilt — and your new acquisition, far from giving you the pleasure you anticipated, is simply a dead loss. But if you check over a plant carefully in the shop before you buy it, you should be able to avoid this sort of disappointment in the future.

When and where to buy

The best time to buy flowering plants is always when they are in bloom and at their most active period of growth. For winter-flowering plants — such as Cyclamen, Azalea and Camellia — this could well be around Christmas time. But when you're not buying such a seasonal plant, it makes sense always to buy in spring or summer. Plants will then be stronger than at any other time of the year, and so better able to withstand the shock of being transported first from a nursery to a retailer, and then from the shop to your home.

It's always very important to get your plant from a reliable stockist. The shop where you buy should be well-maintained, and the retailer and the staff should be knowledgeable and helpful, as well as attentive to the needs of the plants. You are more likely to meet such expertise in a specialist garden centre than in, say, a department store. If you care about your plants — and certainly if you're going to spend a lot of money — you should consider making the extra effort of going to a good garden or plant centre rather than simply buying from the nearest or most convenient

A range of shades, *above,* makes a splash of colour, from the tall pink Begonias to the pink and purple Primulas at the front, complemented by the white and blue of a Cyclamen and a Hyacinth.

What to

It makes sense to buy more than one flowering plant at a time, and to have a colour key in mind. You'll achieve a more decorative effect if you set out to match or contrast flower shades — and don't forget to take into consideration the dominant colours of the room you intend to put them in. Flowers form a definite part of the interior decor of your home, just as wallpaper or furnishing fabrics do — the only difference is that it's easier to change your mind with flowers, and much less expensive to experiment!

Your choice will be affected by what your local shops and garden centres have on offer. Luckily, many of the most popular plants appear in a range of colours — this chart does not attempt to cover all of them, but lists ten of the best in each colour.

Key

E: Evergreen shrub
D: Deciduous shrub
A: Annual
P: Perennial

WHITE

African Violet P
Year round

Bleeding Heart Vine E
(***Clerodendrum thomsonae***)
Spring-autumn, large white bracts with small red blossoms

Camellia E
Winter-spring

Cape Primrose E
(***Streptocarpus hybridus***)
Spring-autumn

Cyclamen P
Winter-spring

Gardenia E
Summer, fragrant

Hydrangea D or E
Summer

Jasmine D or E
Winter-spring, fragrant

Stephanotis E
Spring-autumn, fragrant

Wax plant (miniature) E
(***Hoya bella***)
Summer, fragrant

BLUE

African Violet P
Year round

Bush Violet A
(***Browallia speciosa***)
Winter or summer

Campanula P
Summer-autumn

Cape Primrose E
(***Streptocarpus hybridus***)
Spring-autumn

Cineraria P
Winter-spring

Hydrangea D or E
Summer

Pansy P
Summer-winter

Plumbago E
Spring-autumn

Primula D or E
Winter-spring

Yesterday, Today and Tomorrow E
(***Brunfelsia calycina***)
Spring-summer, fragrant

PURPLE

African Violet P
Year round

Bush Violet A
(***Browallia speciosa***)
Winter or summer

Cape Primrose E
(***Streptocarpus hybridus***)
Spring-autumn

Cineraria P
Winter-spring

Cyclamen P
Winter-spring

Fuchsia D
Summer-autumn

Pansy P
Summer-winter

Pelargonium D or E
Summer

Primula D or E
Winter-spring

Yesterday, Today and Tomorrow E
(***Brunfelsia calycina***)
Spring-summer, fragrant

shop. If you want something a bit unusual, it pays to look at the advertisements in gardening magazines to find specialist nurseries near you: they are bound to have a greater choice than a shop that caters only for casual trade.

The plants in the shop should be on display without any plastic wrappers. Adequately watered and fed, they should be in good positions — neither too shady nor too sunny, and not in any draught from doors or windows. The shop should feel comfortably warm — any severe drop in temperature at night can do a lot of harm. A stockist who seems conscientious is much more likely to provide you with a healthy plant than one who seems ignorant or slapdash.

Points to look out for

- **Do** check the plant for firm and plentiful buds. If the buds are droopy the plant may have been in a draught.
- **Do** check the leaves. They should be firm and glossy. Pick the pot right up, and turn the plant over carefully so that you can see the undersides. This is where any pests will lurk: whitefly, red spider mite, mealy bug. Any blisters or brown areas on the leaves may be a sign of bacterial infection or fungus, while rings or mottling may well be the result of a virus.
- **Do** inspect the flowers carefully. Always choose a plant that has flowers in bloom as well as buds — you can't be sure exactly how the flowers will turn out unless you've actually seen them! Also, if flowers have already come out, you will know the plant is growing vigorously and will be likely to survive the journey home. A plant in bud only may be upset enough by a change in conditions for the buds never to open once you've got the plant home.

Keep an eye out for any flowers that are wilting or withered — this could mean that the plant has not been properly fed.

- **Don't** forget to give the stems a quick look over as well. If they're at all white and powdery it may be a sign of mildew, caused by overwatering.
- **Don't** choose a plant that's already covered with fully opened flowers. It's already past its best, and may be near the end of its life.
- **Don't** buy a plant if the compost in the pot has shrunk away from the sides. This almost certainly means that at some stage the plant has been allowed to dry out, and its subsequent growth may well be affected.
- **Don't** buy a plant that is wilting or that shows any sign of disease.

Asking for advice

Never be afraid of asking for advice. A good retailer should be able to advise you on the best plants to buy if you describe the conditions of your room. Say where you're thinking of placing the plant, and what sort of temperature and light it can expect.

A general rule is that flowering plants demand quite a good light to produce blooms. Many of them — including the popular Azalea, Camellia and Cyclamen — also prefer a rather cool, airy atmosphere to a hot, dry one.

choose

RED

Azalea D or E
Winter-spring

Begonia P
Summer-autumn

Buzy Lizzie A or P
Year round

Camellia E
Winter-spring

Chrysanthemum A or P
Year round

Cineraria P
Winter-spring

Fuchsia D
Summer-autumn

Gloxinia P
(***Sinningia speciosa***)
Spring-autumn

Hibiscus D or E
Summer

Pelargonium D or E
Summer

PINK

Azalea D or E
Winter-spring

Begonia P
Summer-autumn

Buzy Lizzie A or P
Year round

Camellia E
Winter-spring

Cineraria P
Winter-spring

Cyclamen P
Winter-spring

Gloxinia P
(***Sinningia speciosa***)
Spring-autumn

Hibiscus D or E
Summer

Oleander E
Summer, fragrant

Pelargonium D or E
Summer

ORANGE

Calceolaria A or P
Spring

Clivia E
Spring-summer

Cytisus D or E
Winter-spring, fragrant

Firecracker Flower E
(***Crossandra undulifolia***)
Spring-summer

Glory Lily P
(***Gloriosa rothschildiana***)
Summer

Goldfish Plant P
(***Columnea gloriosa***)
Spring

Kohleria E
Summer

Lipstick Vine E
(***Aeschynanthus lobbianus***)
Spring-summer

Marigold A
(***Calendula officinalis***)
Summer

Primula P
Winter-spring

YELLOW

Allamanda E
Summer

Cape Cowslip P
(***Lachenalia aloides***)
Winter-spring

Chrysanthemum A or P
Year round

Freesia P
Spring

Hibiscus D or E
Summer

Jasmine D or E
Winter-spring

Kohleria P
Summer

Pansy P
(Viola hybrids)
Summer-winter

Primula P
Winter-spring

Zebra Plant E
(***Aphelandra squarrosa***)
Spring-summer

Getting it home

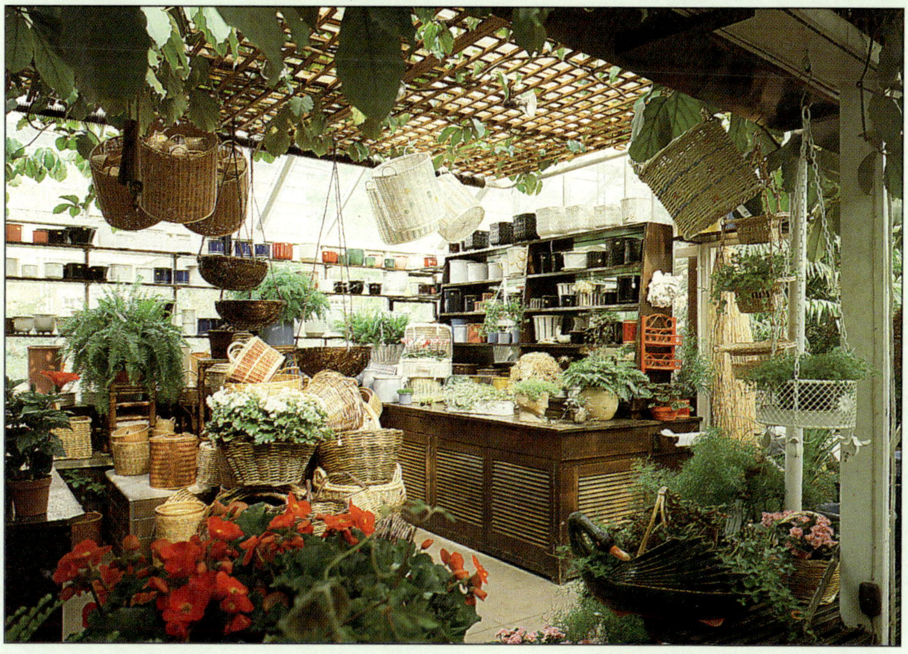

Many plants, such as African Violets, have leaves and stems that are very brittle and easily damaged. Take care not to crush them when carrying them home; if you have a long journey, it's wise to ask the shop to pack the plant in a cardboard box padded out with newspaper. A good retailer should not mind doing this for you.

If you have to buy plants during very cold weather, then make sure they are very well wrapped and protected from icy winds; screwed-up newspaper between the plant and its wrapping will help to insulate the plant.

You may want to transport a very tall plant — like a palm — in an ordinary car. The best way is to get someone to hold it virtually on its side, but if you're on your own wedge the pot at an angle — don't rest it with the stem taking all the strain.

Finally, when you get home, if you have trouble getting the plant out of its bag, cut it out rather than drag coverings over the foliage, which might damage it.

Houseplants for the sitting room

Making a focal point of your fireplace

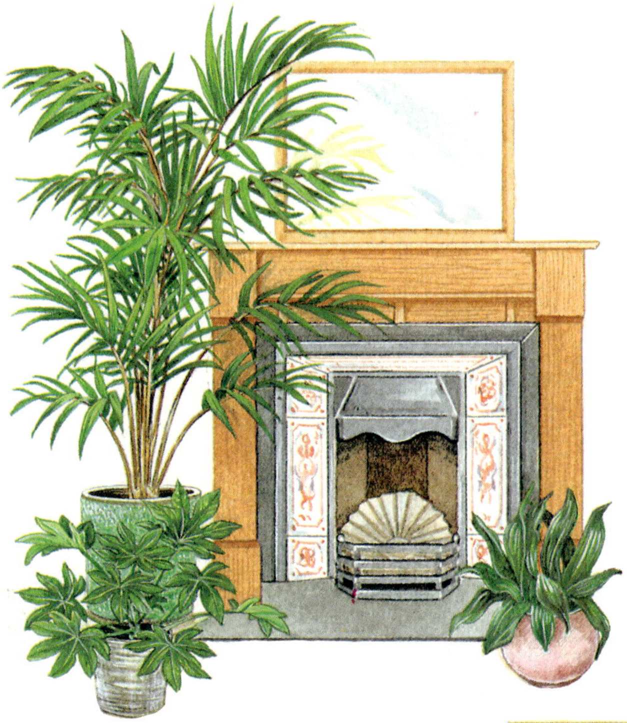

A fireplace is the main feature of most sitting rooms, which makes it an ideal position for displaying houseplants. If your budget can stretch to a really large plant you can create an arrangement such as the display on the *left*. Use a tall plant such as an elegant, arching Palm to emphasise the height and shape of the fireplace. Then, at a lower level, balance the design with an Aspidistra and a Castor Oil Plant. None of these plants need a great deal of light so they should grow well in such a situation, provided they are well looked after.

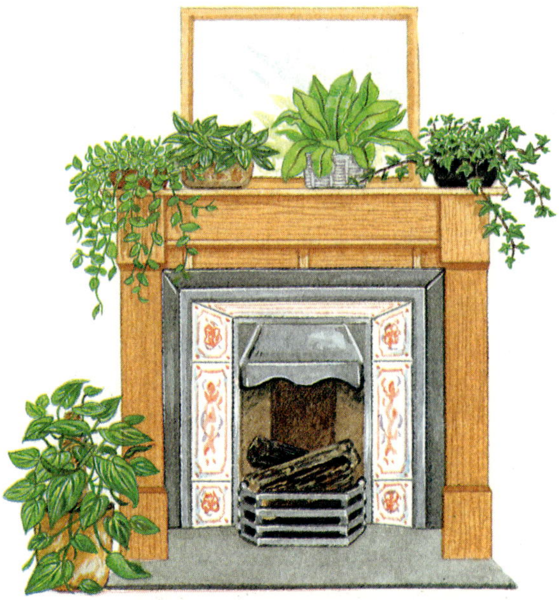

A more 'cottagey' style of displaying plants around a fireplace is to grow them in a row along the top of the mantelpiece, *right*. You can soften the effect, as we have here, by trailing an Ivy and a Tradescantia over the side edges and sitting a Scindapsus on the hearth stone.

The sitting room is the easiest place in the house to choose plants for as it's light and airy and free of draughts, as well as being comfortably warm in winter. It is a happy coincidence that the same conditions that keep us cosy when we are relaxing are also near-perfect for a wide range of indoor plants.

If you've ever visited the Netherlands the chances are that you have come away thinking what wonderful houseplants they have. Every window is crammed full of plants — so are their living rooms. But, although they look sensational, Dutch houseplants are actually no better than ours. The trick lies in the way they are displayed.

Given a bit of design sense even the most ordinary collection of pot plants can be completely transformed into a stunning arrangement. Don't worry if you aren't particularly artistic; if you have ever decorated a room by teaming wallpaper, soft furnishings and carpet, or chosen an outfit with accessories to match — you're already half way there.

A good focal point

The focal point of a sitting room is usually the fireplace. This is an ideal place to arrange plants, whether in such a way as to hide an ugly fireplace or to emphasise its beauty.

If you block off the shaft to stop draughts whistling down the chimney you can grow all sorts of plants there. Only grow shade-loving houseplants as

Plants give a room a casual atmosphere as well as being a decorative feature in their own right. A sitting room is absolutely perfect for both plants and people as it is designed to be welcoming, warm and comfortable. The plain green leaves of the Ivy, *opposite*, have been allowed to trail downwards and trained to fill an otherwise blank wall. In the corner a Palm curves in a relaxed fashion over the table.

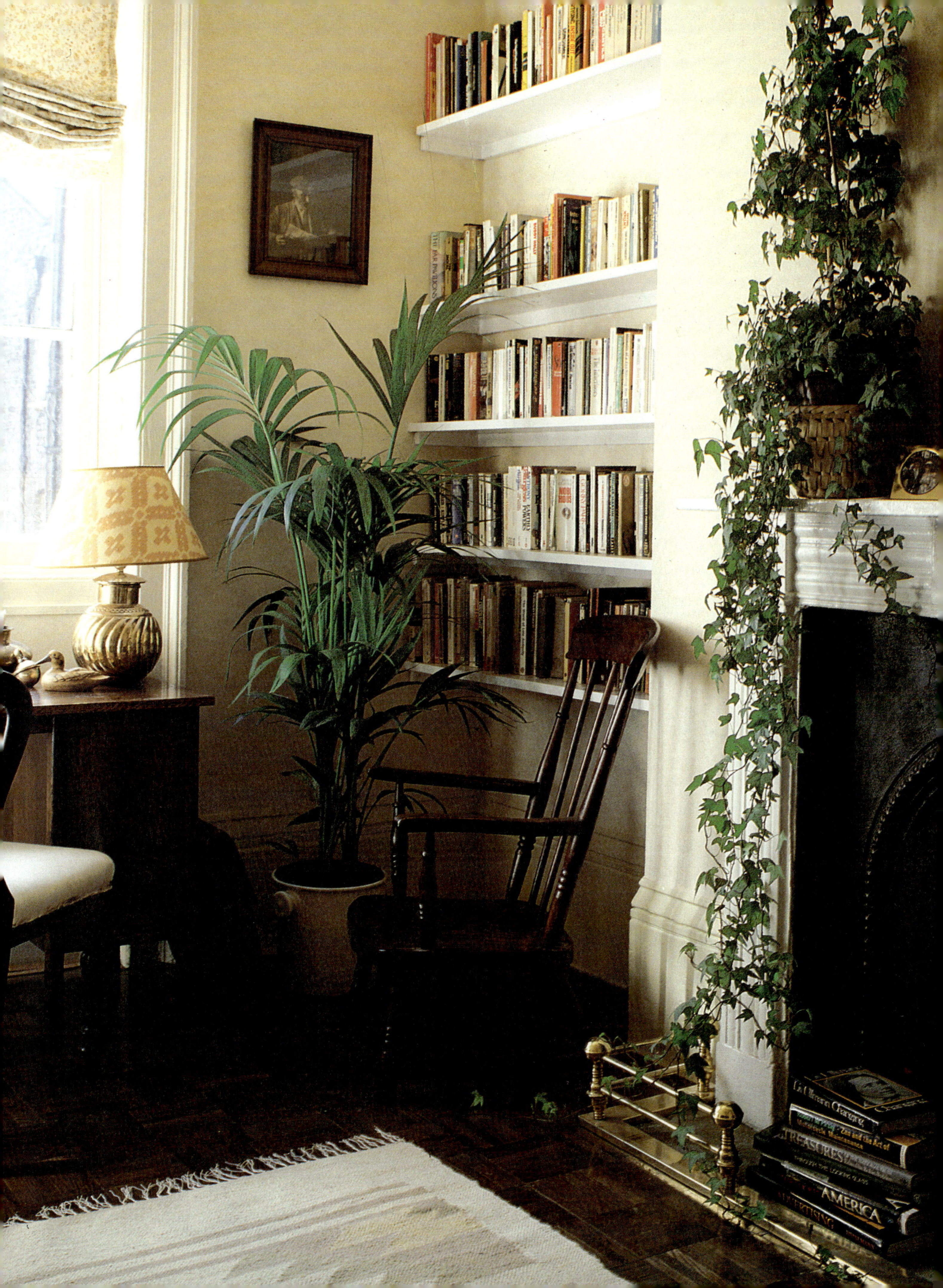
TREASURES
AMERICA

Points to ponder

● **Dry air.** Central heating makes the air very dry. Most plants other than the real sun lovers such as Bougainvillea and Pony Tail Plant, Cacti and many Succulents, grow best in moist air. Some plants, such as Ferns and African Violets, cannot survive without moisture as this keeps their leaves fresh. These plants must be grown standing in trays of damp gravel to maintain the humidity in a dry heated room.

● **Cold nights.** Tropical houseplants need constant warmth, which they are unlikely to keep when you turn your heating off at night. Unless the temperature stays above 55°F (13°C), you would do better to grow plants which will tolerate lower temperatures. There's a good list to choose from: Aspidistra, Ivy, Hexline, Cyclamen, Azalea, Hydrangea, spring flowering bulbs, Euonymus, Eucalyptus, Cineraria, Aucuba, Grape Ivy, Hoya, Passion Flower, Geranium, Plumbago, Cape Heather, Primula and Schizanthus.

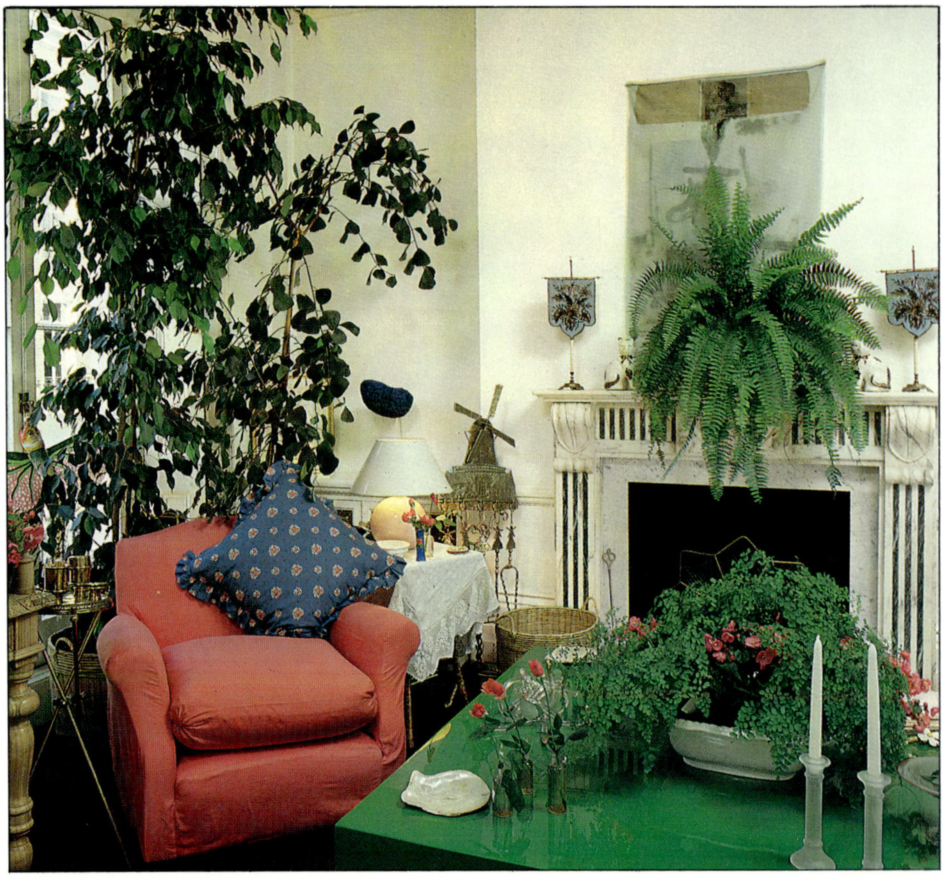

The jungle atmosphere created by the huge Weeping Fig is echoed by the luxuriant Boston Fern on the fireplace and delicate Maidenhair Ferns and flowering Begonias.

Points to watch when placing your houseplant

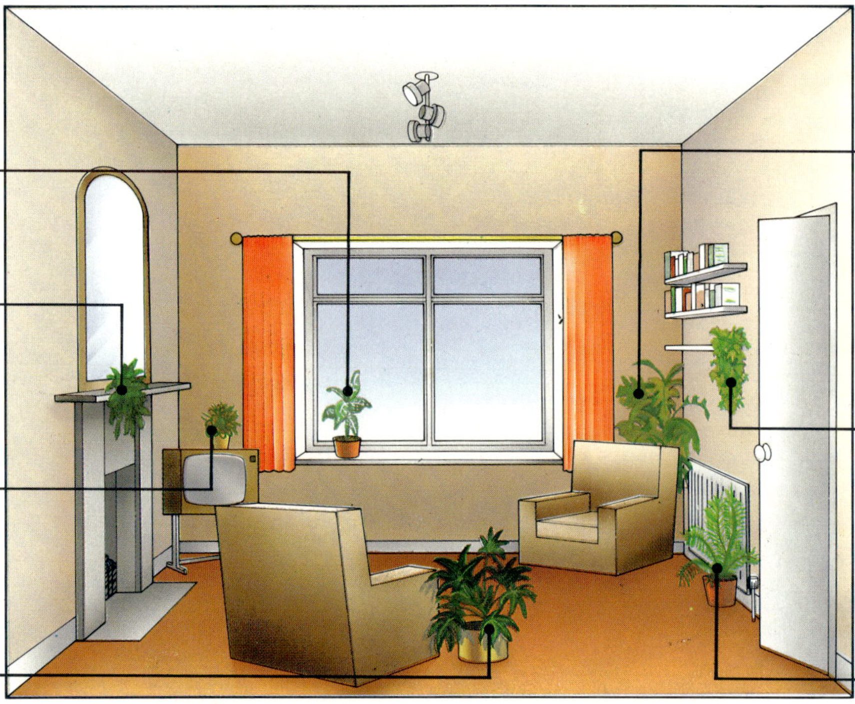

the fireplace tends to be well away from the window so there is not much natural light for the plants to use. Don't choose variegated plants as they won't get enough light to keep their patterns. The arrangement can be as permanent as you want, although if you have a working fire in winter make sure that the leaves are not in danger of being scorched, or move your plants away altogether to safety.

Displaying your plants

In a large room large plants look most effective as they echo the scale of the room. Plants used on their own for their design and foliage impact are called 'specimen' plants; choose those with evergreen leaves as they will look good all year round.

The Swiss Cheese Plant and Weeping Fig are popular choices but there are lots of other plants to consider: large-leaved Philodendrons, Cyperus plants including the Papyrus, all sorts of Palm trees, Boston and Ladder Ferns and the unusual Stag's Horn Fern. Try a Norfolk Island Pine, a Castor Oil Plant, a Fiddle Leaf Fig or even a Eucalyptus.

Large specimen plants are expensive, but given time you can grow your own — starting with a good young plant from a garden centre or chain store.

Plants that don't really merit being displayed on their own can be made to look unusually striking if you group them together well. Try growing trailing plants like Ivy or the Sweetheart Vine up a moss-covered pole and then let it trail down from the top. Alternatively, grow a climber like a Black-Eyed Susan with a Kangaroo Vine up a framework of bamboos or branches of contorted willows or even some bare branches collected from the garden.

Experiment with ways of linking plants visually by standing them close together on a polished slice of wood or in a tray of moss or pebbles. Where possible hide the pot if it is not ornamental.

A collection of small plants can be displayed in a group to make the most of the mass effect of the foliage. Such a close arrangement is good for the plants as well, because this way they can create their own mini environment of moist air. For the best results, group together foliage and flowering plants, choosing a selection of tall and spreading kinds with colours which harmonise and shapes that contrast.

Windowsill plants

For a windowsill display to look really good, the plants need to be healthy and for this they must be given an environment that suits them. Depending on whether your windowsill faces north, south, east or west, choose your plants from the information below to make up a healthy and happy display.

North facing windowsill

Grow plants here which actually dislike the sun.

Ivies, Aspidistra, Aucuba, all sorts of Ferns, Streptocarpus, Scindapsus, Grape Ivy, Sweetheart Vine, Peperomia, Maranta, Hibiscus, Palms, Creeping Fig, Cyperus, Kaffir Lily, Cissus, Spider Plant, Bird's Nest Fern, Castor Oil Plant.

South facing windowsill

This position is for sun-loving plants only.

Geraniums (Pelargoniums), lots of Cacti, most succulents such as Sanseveria, Living Stones (Lithops), Aloe, Agave, Crassula. Other plants include Celosia, Oleander, Black-Eyed Susan and Coleus.

East and West facing windowsill

Here you can grow most flowering pot plants and variegated foliage plants without fear of them burning in the strong sun.

Capsicum, Cyclamen, Fuchsia, Calceolaria, Cineraria, Celosia, Busy Lizzies, Pot Chrysanthemum, Aphelandra, Shrimp Plant, Italian Bellflower, Hibiscus, Hoya, Begonia, Azalea, Hippeastrum, Poinsettia, Primula, Winter Cherry, Christmas Cactus, Dracaena, Cordyline, Dieffenbachia, Polka Dot Plant, Pilea, Tradescantia, and also Orchids and carnivorous plants like the Venus Fly Trap and Pitcher Plant.

Windowsills at night

When you draw the curtains at night leaving your plants behind on the windowsill you are trapping them in a pocket of cold air. This is less important in summer than winter when plants run the risk of frost damage. It is much safer to move your plants inside the room at night where they can be protected by curtains.

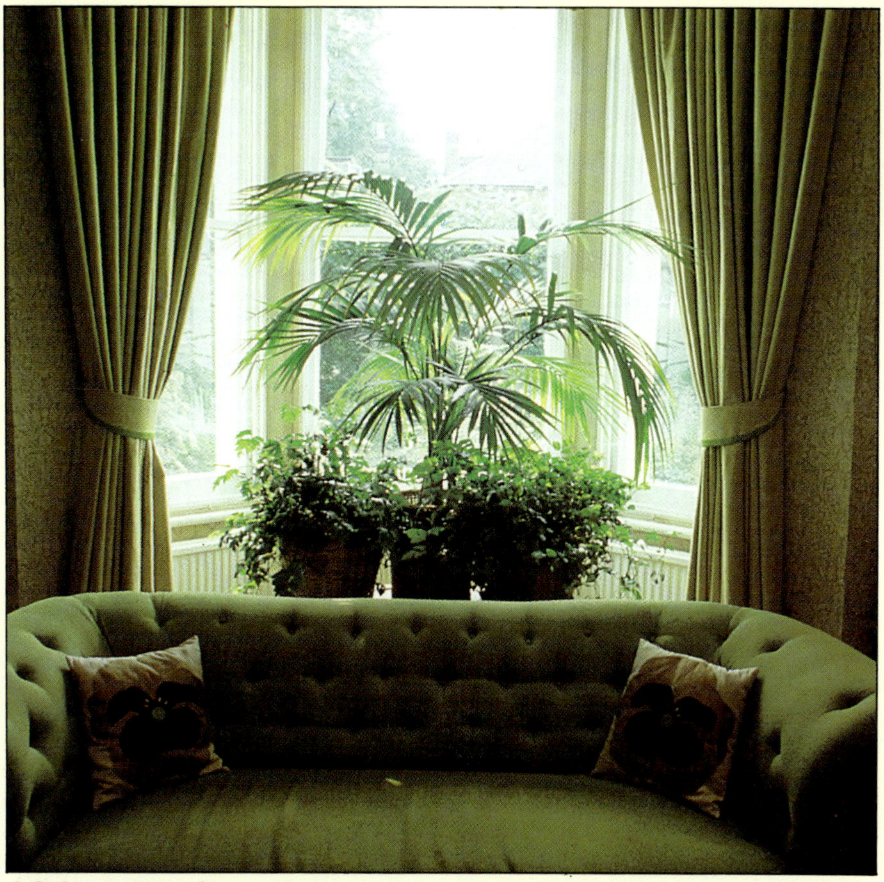

A Palm and two Cissus vines are ideal companions for a north-facing window.

Plants in the bathroom

The trouble with a bathroom is that it is so changeable — one minute it's nice and warm and steamy and an absolute paradise for tropical, jungle-type plants and the next it can be cold, damp and gloomy and be perfect for almost nothing except mushrooms! But this doesn't mean you can't grow plants; we'll tell you how to adapt to such extremes.

A basic problem in many bathrooms is a lack of natural light. Because the view from a bathroom window is not considered important, an awful lot of bathrooms face north or overlook a brick wall, so that only a tiny trickle of light can find its way in. And this is if you're lucky — some bathrooms don't have any windows at all.

The other thing sadly lacking in most bathrooms is space. Plants have to jostle for elbow-room between bottles of aftershave and perfume and tins of talc — it's enough to give a Sensitive Plant a nervous breakdown or a Weeping Fig a fit of the vapours!

But do not despair. There are lots of plants that can make themselves very much at home in such circumstances. The secret lies in providing extra heat and light and adding that touch of design that lets pot plants work their own miracles.

Heat

Minimum temperature 40°F (4°C)

- Asparagus Fern
- Aspidistra
- Azalea
- Baby's Tears ▼
- Castor Oil Plant
- Cyclamen
- Fatshedera
- Grape Ivy
- Ivy
- Mother-of-Thousands
- Primula ▼
- Sago Palm
- Silk Oak
- Spider Plant

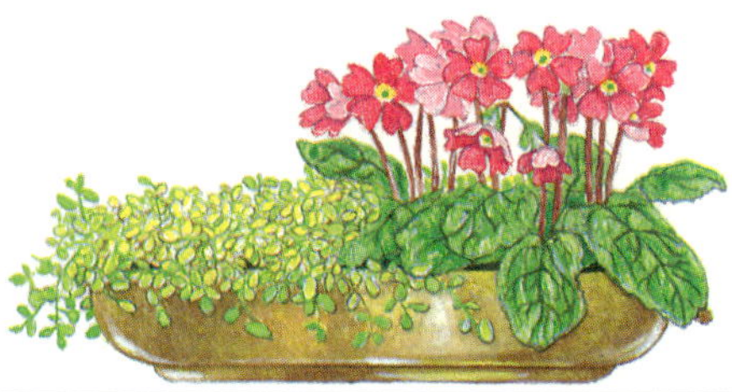

Minimum temperature 50°F (10°)

- Air Plants
- Bromeliads
- Calceolaria
- Cape Primrose
- Cineraria ▼
- Cyperus
- Ferns
- Figs
- Hot Water Plant ▼
- Palms
- Philodendrons
- Polka Dot Plant

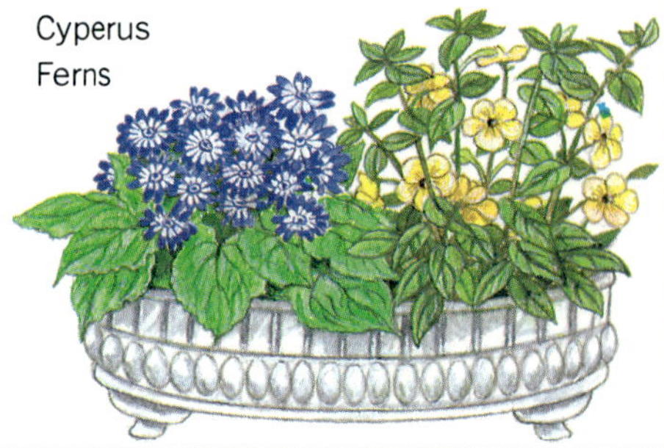

Light

Low light plants

- Baby's Tears
- Castor Oil Plant ▶
- Fatshedera
- Ivy
- Kentia Palm
- Parlour Palm

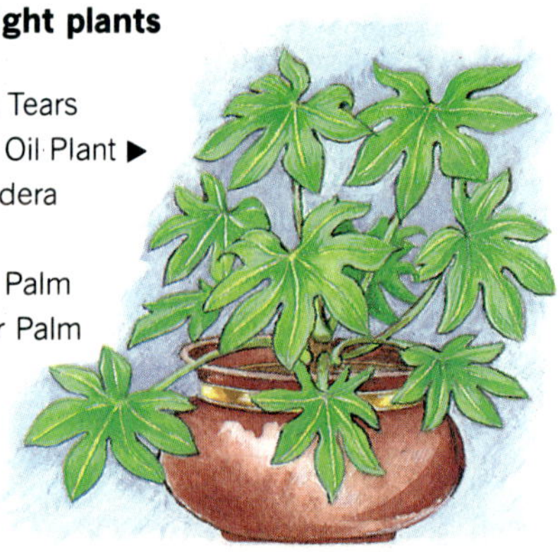

Good not strong light

- African Violet
- Air Plants
- Azalea
- Bromeliads
- Cape Primrose
- Cyclamen ▶
- Ferns
- Figs
- Fittonia
- Philodendron

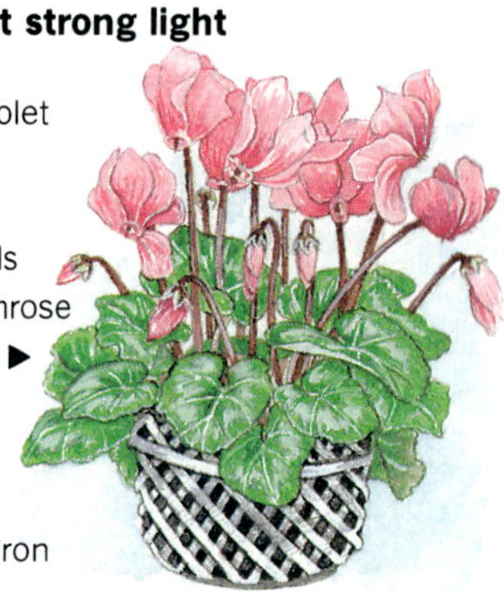

Heat and light

Start by assessing the amount of light your bathroom receives and how cold it is likely to get. If you aren't sure about the temperature, use an ordinary minimum-maximum thermometer — you can buy one at most garden centres and department stores — and use it to see how much your temperature differs every day.

You can safely assume that humidity will be high, as there is usually a lot of moisture in a bathroom. The light level is more difficult to assess but if there is enough natural light for you to read by, then there is enough to grow low-light tolerant plants. If you have good light then you can happily grow most foliage plants; but to grow flowering plants successfully you need to have a lot of light — though of course you can always move them into your bathroom for a temporary splash of colour.

Even if you have no windows in your bathroom you can still grow some plants under artificial light. Choose plants suited to this way of growing, such as African Violets and all sorts of pretty Ferns. Fix a small wall cabinet with fluorescent tubes, or find a place for a hanging basket lit from above by a special plant light, and you can make an attractive display of plants.

To work out what plants will grow where, check how much light and heat your bathroom gets. You can then make your selection of plants from those listed in the Heat and Light boxes above.

How to find space

Even in the tiniest bathroom there's bound to be a corner of space somewhere. Windowsills are great places for houseplants. Don't worry about frosted glass — it looks as if it cuts out light but it only diffuses the light. This is absolutely perfect for growing a wide range of foliage plants without burning their leaves in the sun.

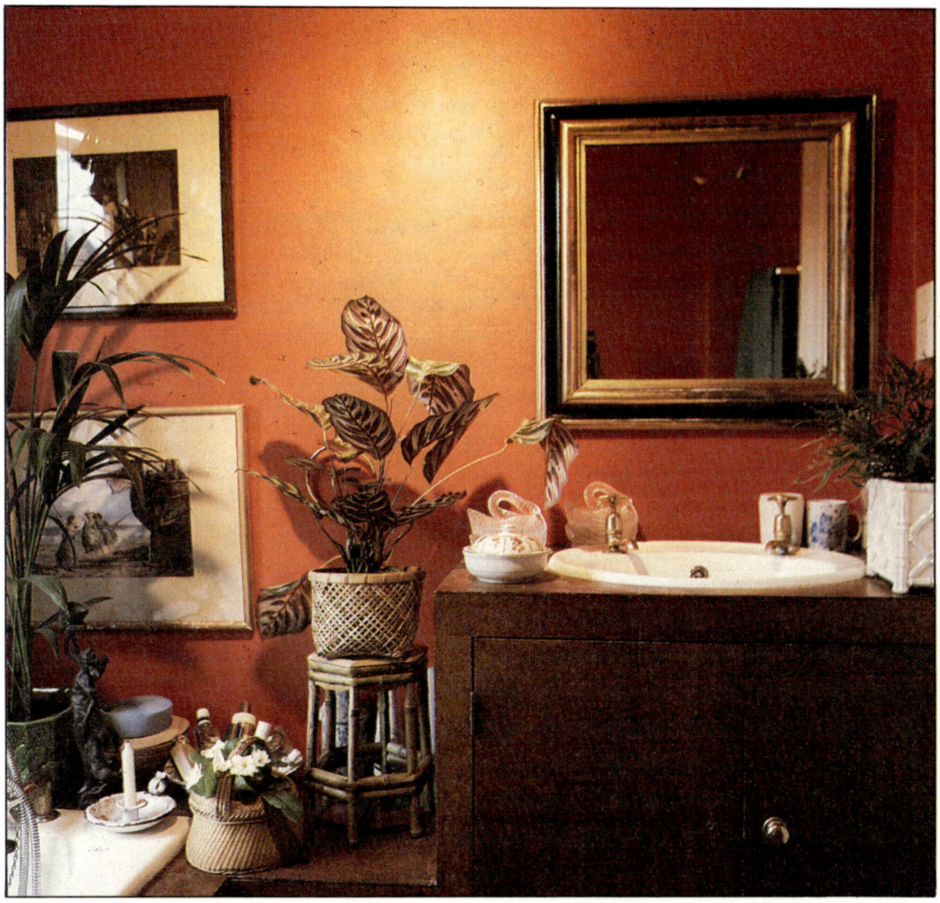

A variety of heights, leaves and flowers makes for an attractive display.

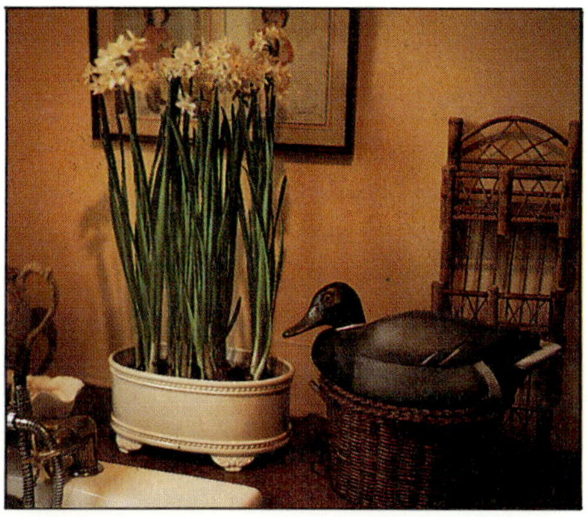

Narcissus bulbs are specially prepared to flower inside in late winter and early spring.

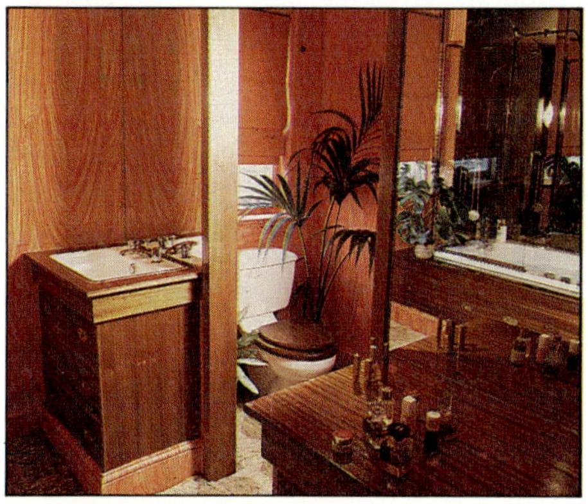

A dramatic plant — or two — can give a plain bathroom character.

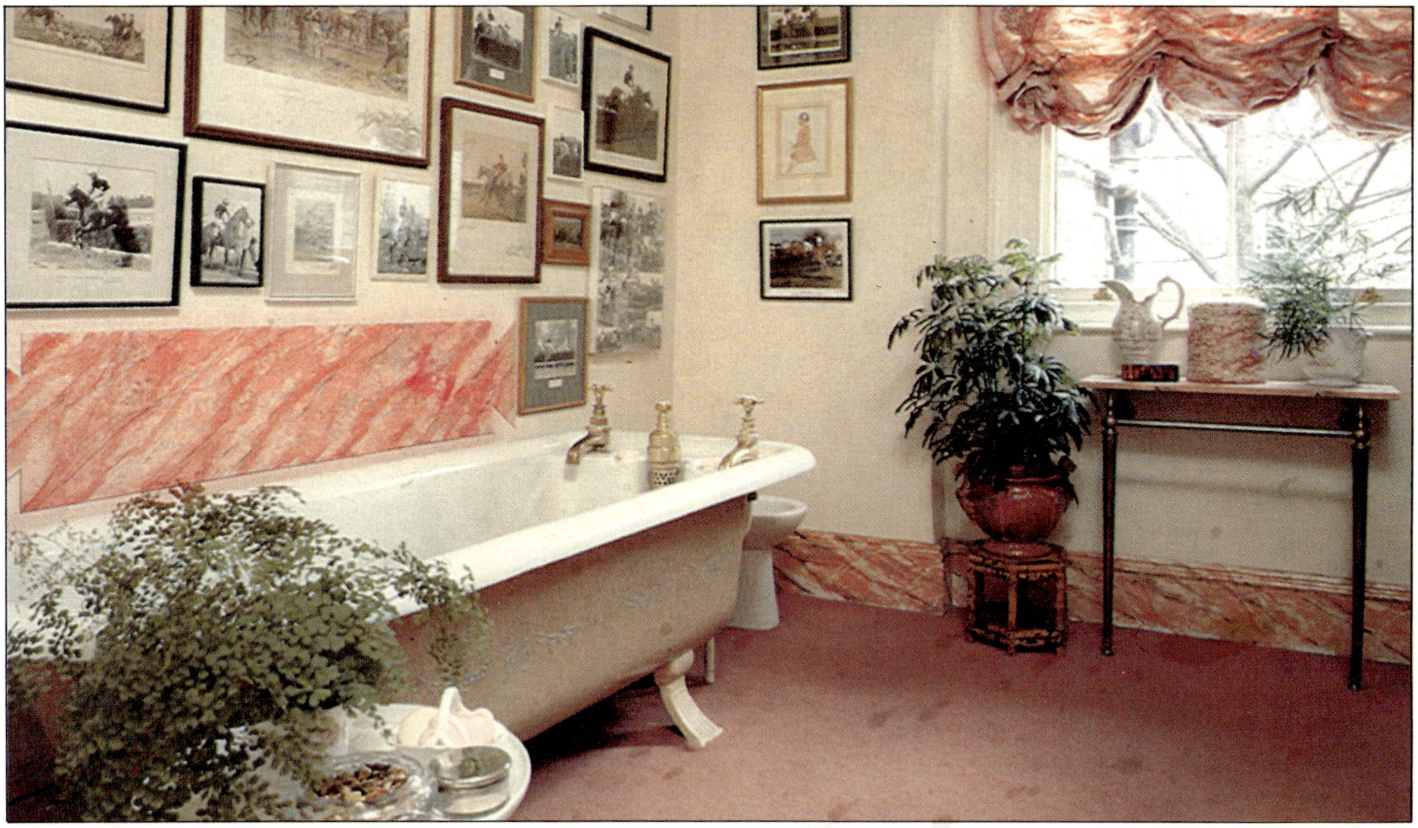

The fresh green foliage of a Maidenhair Fern, a Pteris and an Umbrella Plant have been used to enhance a light, airy bathroom.

Solitary Plants

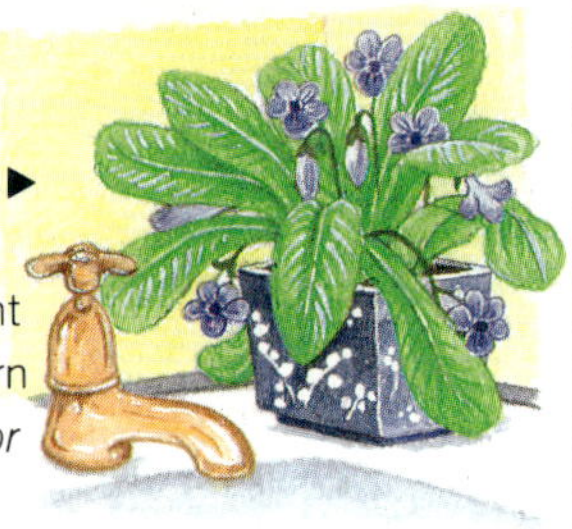

African Violet
Begonia rex
Cape Primrose ▶
Club Moss
Hot Water Plant
Maidenhair Fern
Maranta tricolor
Primula

Solitary plants

As for other flat surfaces, if you have a cupboard or sink surround, banish all those bottles of potions to under the basin and leave some extra plant standing room. Also have a look at the corners of your bath; they may be just about big enough to stand a plant on. If you do, though, it's essential to pick a plant that will look good on its own, shapewise. Nor must the plant be the least bit top-heavy either, or there's a good chance that it will overbalance and end up joining you in the bath! So choose low, spreading plants or roughly pyramidal kinds. In limited space, choosing the plant with the right shape is half the battle.

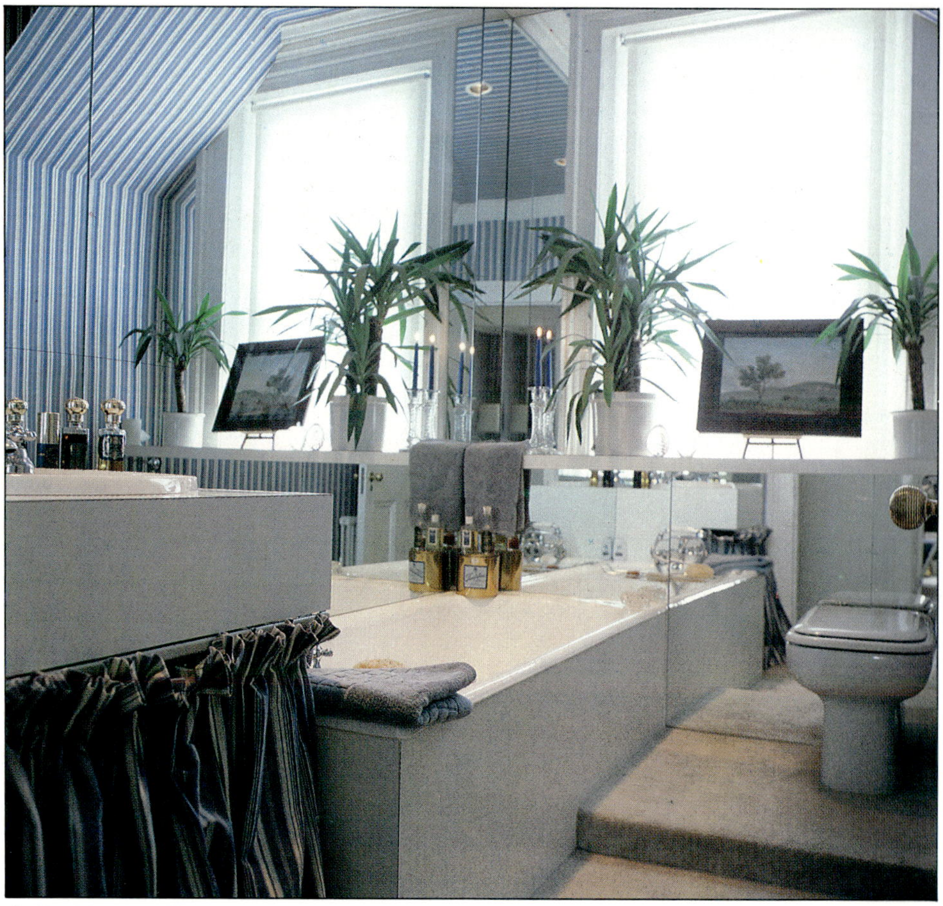

Spiky Yucca silhouettes make this room simple yet striking.

Dramatic Plants

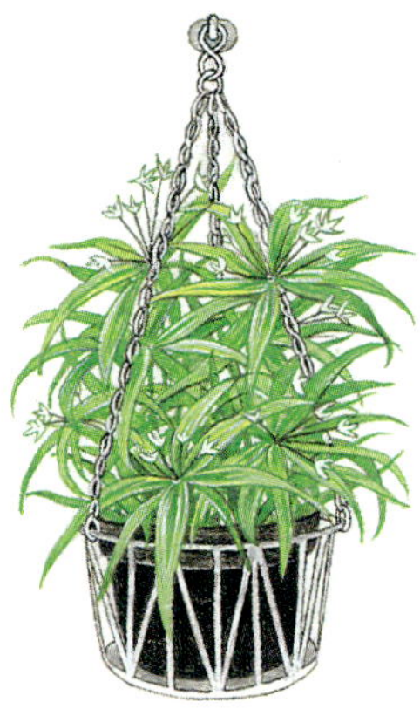

Air Plants
Aspidistra
Bromeliads
Coconut Palm
Cyperus ▶
Grape Ivy
Kentia Palm
Parlour Palm
Sago Palm
Silk Oak
Spathiphyllum
Weeping Fig

Dramatic plants

If space is a bit more generous, you might also find room for a single dramatic specimen plant.

If there isn't room for an enormous one, create the impression of size by standing a medium size pendulous plant on a pedestal. Or hang it from the ceiling. If the plant is reflected in a mirror, it will look even bigger.

Trailing Plants

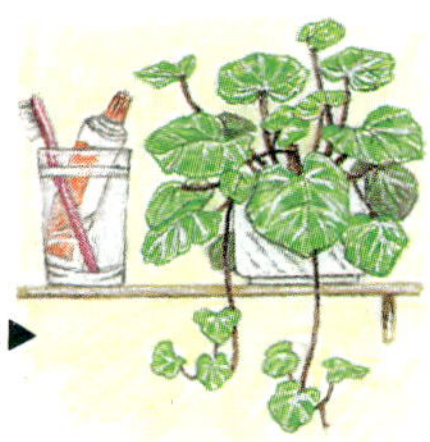

Asparagus Fern
Boston Fern
Creeping Fig
Ivy
Mother-of-Thousands ▶
Spider Plant

Trailing plants

There's usually some wall space in the bathroom where you can hang a shelf or two. Instead of cluttering these up with bath salts and empty shells, seize the golden opportunity the shelves offer to grow trailing plants in pretty containers. You can also make an unusual and decorative feature from seashells filled with Air Plants.

Design secrets

The final trick is the designer touch — how to 'make' the room with your plants. In a small space, using a little to achieve a lot is an essential skill; all you need are just two or three really good plants of the right size, colour and shape.

- In a small space lots of different colours give a cluttered and bitty effect, so base your bathroom colour scheme on a single colour, with darker and lighter tones of that colour, and the greens of your plants as a contrast. When choosing flowering plants, you can create a restful effect if you can find flowers that tone in with the rest of your colour scheme.
- You don't have to rely on a single plant to provide an interesting shape; several similar or contrasting plants grouped together can be very effective. Remember that a group of plants should have plenty of room to make them stand out from their surroundings. The space around your plant arrangement is almost as important as the plants themselves.
- A plain, uncluttered background allows plants to stand out well from their surroundings. Unpatterned tiles, whether white or coloured, are one of the best backgrounds for bathroom plants. Cork tiles are great for a touch of luxury, and combine beautifully with

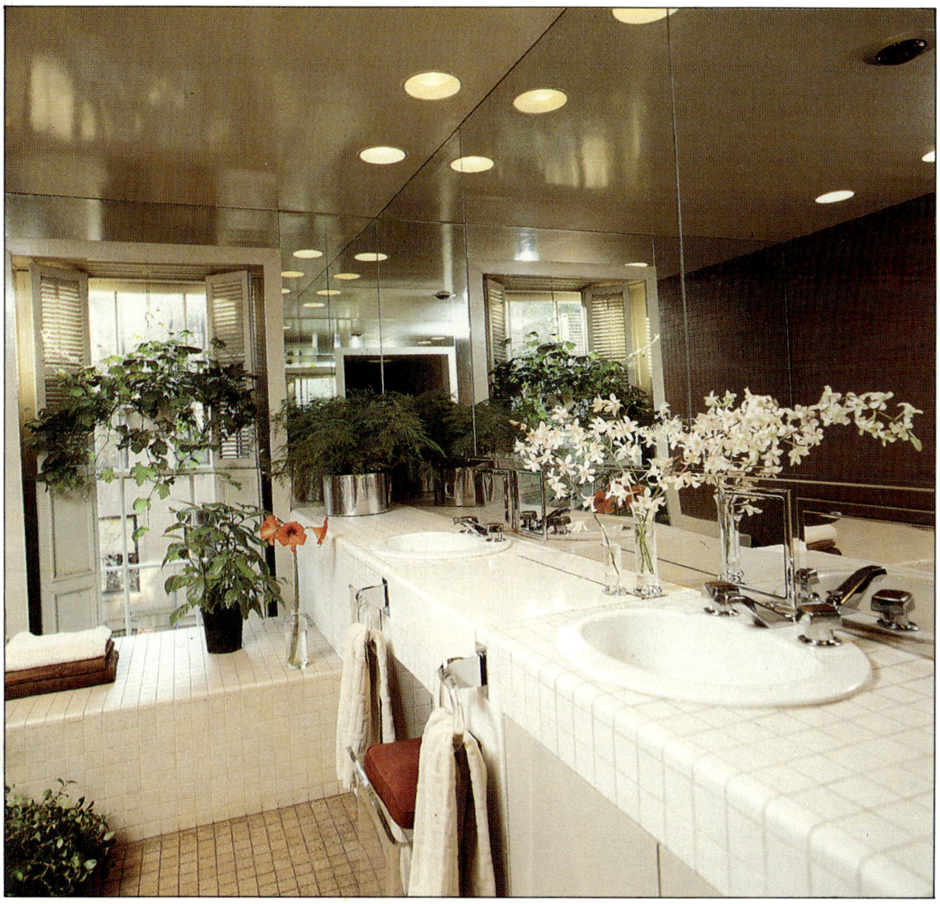
This bathroom would look discouragingly stark without its collection of plants.

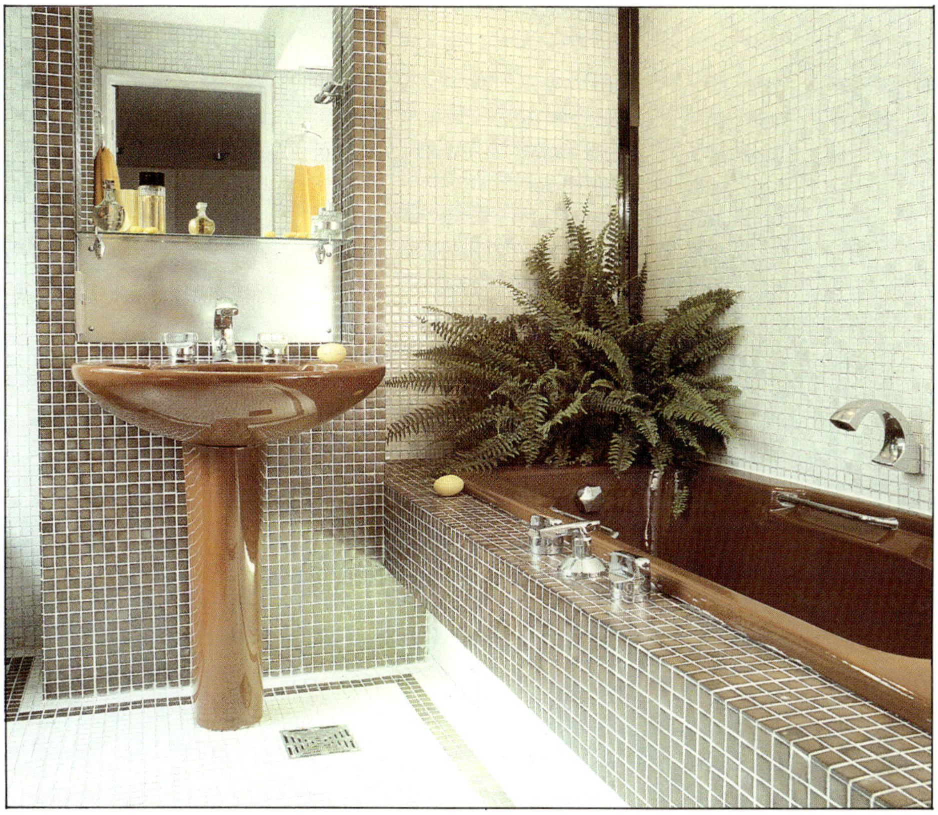
Brighten an empty corner with a luxuriant Ladder Fern.

large-leaved plants to create the atmosphere of a jungle.

Mirrors are another terrific background too. Not only do they create an illusion of space, they also help to make a bathroom lighter and brighter, and you'll get lots of lovely reflections.

Containers and accessories are the finishing touch for beautiful plants. For a restful effect, choose containers in colours and materials that harmonise well with the rest of your decorative scheme. Baskets and pastel coloured porcelain blend in quietly; or you can make your containers stand out in bright contrast by choosing loud, brilliant colours. If you do this, team them with the colour of your towels or some other highlight in the room.

Creating the display

For best results arrange your larger foliage plants first — then add the smaller plants with coloured leaves and flowers. You can draw attention to particular areas with something really eyecatching.

Air Plants offer plenty of exciting possibilities as they are small and don't have roots — so they can grow without pots. You can mount them on cork tiles in sea shells, or attach them to chunks of semi-precious stone. Grow a collection of them on a piece of driftwood, or make mobiles by dangling Air Plants from lumps of cork or small pieces of wood.

If you're a real plant enthusiast and don't have to share a bathroom with small children, why not allow yourself the luxury of transforming your bathroom into a tropical jungle? For this effect, ignore all the advice about using a little to achieve a lot — go over the top! It's easily done by filling every nook and cranny with vegetation.

Choose good size plants with large leaves like the Swiss Cheese Plant, Philodendrons, Palms, and large Ferns, in as many shades of green as you can find. Use these plants to form the basis of the display, overlapping plants with contrasting leaf shapes; then add highlights in the shape of brightly coloured plants such as Fittonia, *Begonia rex*, African Violet, Maranta or the exotic flowering Spathiphyllum. Gnarled branches draped with Spanish Moss and hung with Air Plants make a very dramatic centrepiece — if you have the room. Then, if you have trouble finding the bath, you can be sure you've got the effect just right!

Plants for kitchens

Because the kitchen is the heart of the home it's only sensible to make it look nice by 'furnishing' it with plants. The idea is to make your kitchen really comfortable, rather than regarding it as just somewhere to work.

The kitchen is the place where all the cooking is done, as well as a hundred and one other things. If you count up all the time you spend in the kitchen you'll probably find that it's more than you spend in any other room except the bedroom — where you're mostly asleep!

A lot of thought goes into planning a kitchen and the permanent equipment, but it takes more than expensive units and the latest equipment to make an ideal kitchen. It's the finishing touches that count, and this is where plants can make all the difference. No matter what style of kitchen you've got, whether it's stripped pine, antique finish, ultra modern or classic, plants will help to make it a welcoming place and the heart of your home.

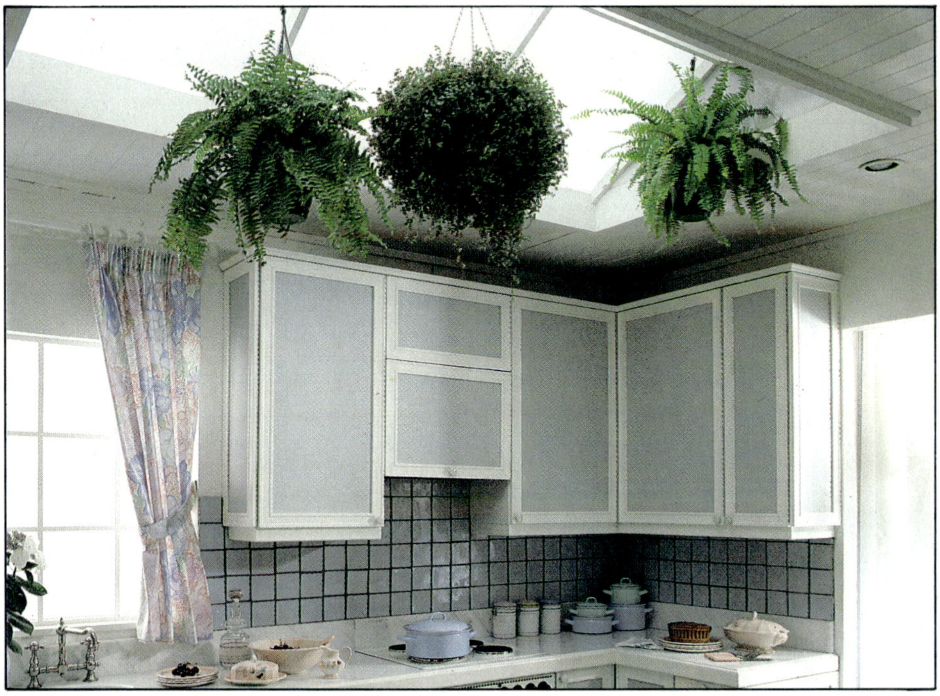

Grow plants in hanging baskets if you have a skylight but no spare worktop space.

Practical planning

As the kitchen is essentially a functional place, it is a more challenging environment for your plants than any other room in the house. You have to position your plants quite carefully; you don't want to steam your Philodendron along with the potatoes or blast your African Violets with cold air every time you open the freezer. And as there is always a good deal of coming and going in the kitchen there's the constant risk of plants being knocked over and landing among the breakfast marmalade and toast!

Because of the special nature of the kitchen you'll find that no matter how careful you are there'll inevitably be a few disasters. Even if the plants don't get knocked over and broken, they are likely to show signs of strain by developing dead patches on their leaves or brown crease lines where they've been bent. You'll have to be prepared to replace casualties as necessary.

The biggest problem in kitchens without doubt is lack of space. There's never enough work-top room at the best of times, and plants really don't mix successfully with hot toasters and coffee makers.

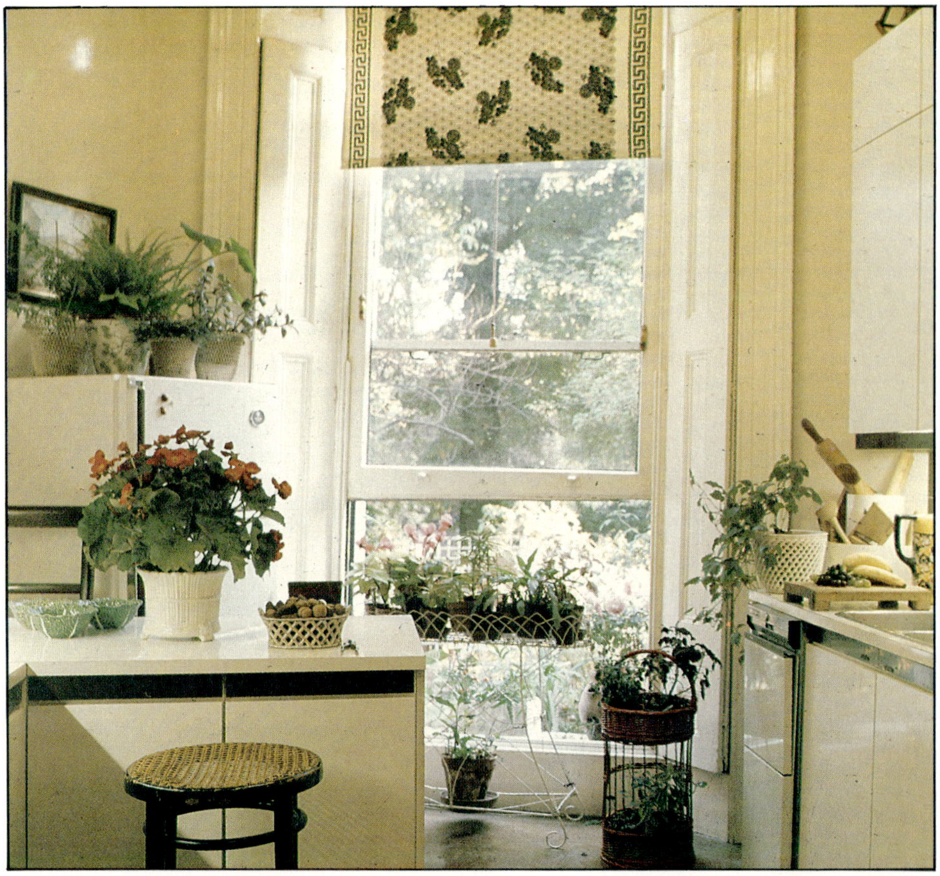

Create an informal kitchen by growing a variety of plants in different kinds of pots.

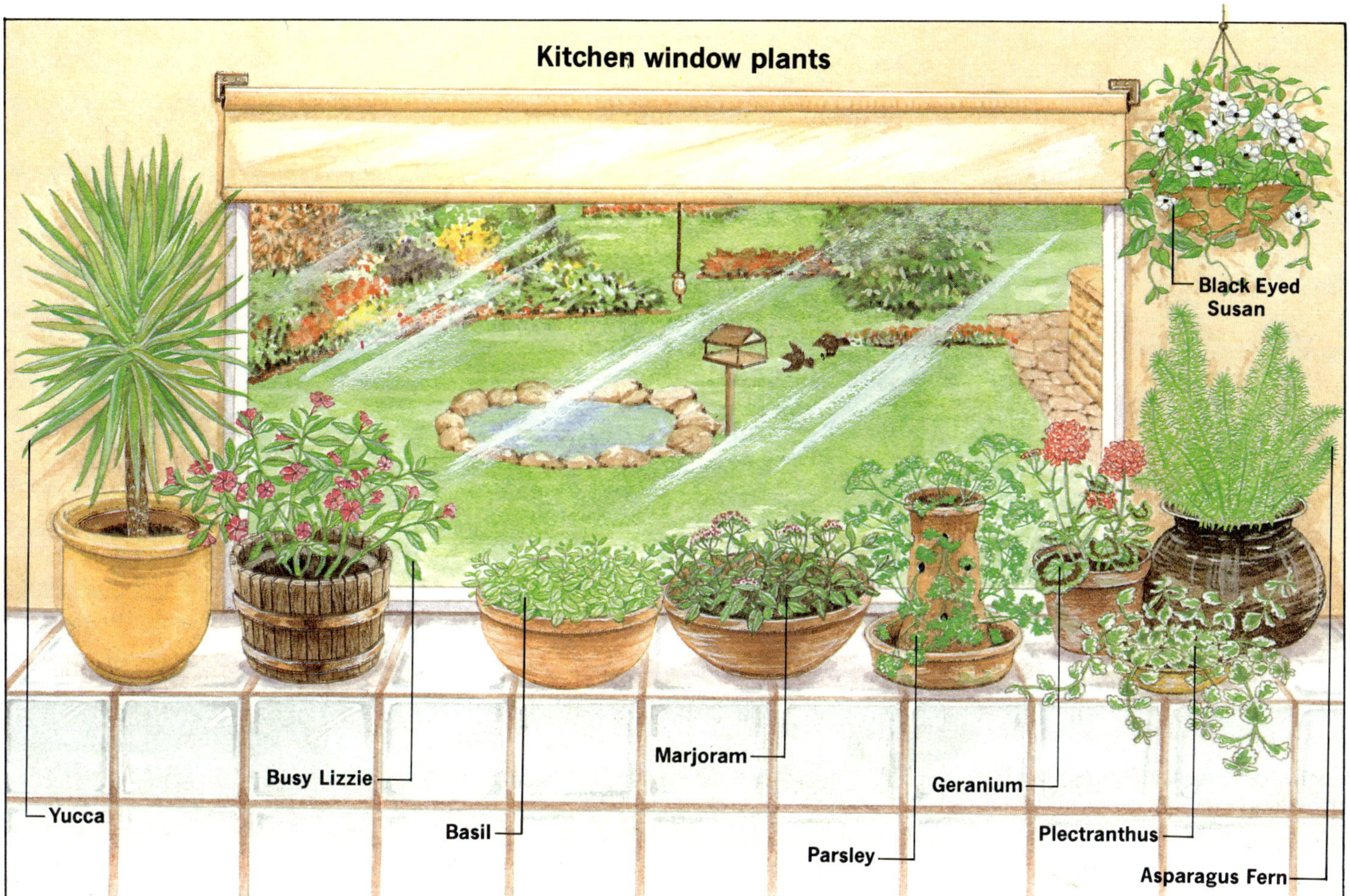

A windowsill is an obvious place to stand pot plants. In many kitchens the sink is in front of a window, and here it's particularly important to have an attractive arrangement simply because you'll be spending quite a bit of time looking at it while you're doing the washing up.

If you have a nice view from your window you won't want to hide it; choose smaller plants so that they don't shut out the scene outside. A row of identical plants, such as African Violets, in a long trough looks perfect here and won't distract from the view. By keeping to one kind of plant, rather than a mixture, you'll get a sophisticated uncluttered look.

There's no need to stick with the same plants all the time — ring the changes. Since your windowsill is the ideal spot for flowering plants, take the opportunity to alternate between winter and summer flowering annuals. Or how about a row of potted herbs? You can snip them for cooking, and replace them with new plants when they are used up.

If you don't have a particularly nice view from your window, you could consider blanking it out entirely with a curtain of trailing plants. By growing plants in hanging containers you can find room for many more. To fill up the window, dangle several plants at different heights.

Kitchen window plants

Summer annuals: Busy Lizzie, Geraniums, Hot Water Plants, Polka Dot Plant, giant double flowered Petunias (these grow far better indoors than they do outside).

Winter annuals: Persian Violets, Cineraria, flowering Azalea (not strictly speaking an annual),Pot Chrysanthemums, Hyacinths (short-lived in the kitchen).

Herbs: any of the small ones — Parsley, Marjoram, Chervil and Basil. Sow new potfuls to replace plants as they are used for cooking.

Trailing plants for windows: Black Eyed Susan, Lipstick Plant, Ceropegia woodii, Creeping Fig.

Lack of light is another common kitchen failing, particularly in older houses and flats. Small windows, blinds and overhanging trees can all cut down the amount of light that enters the room. But this does not have to be a problem: you can choose shade-loving plants for the main part of the room and put flowering plants on the windowsills where the light is strongest.

On the plus side, a kitchen is usually warm enough to keep most plants happy, thanks to the central-heating boiler and the oven. And activities such as washing up and cooking guarantee comfortably high humidity.

Shapes and sizes

When choosing plants for limited spaces it is especially important to take the shape of the plant into account. Avoid rambling, sprawling plants. Choose instead compact, rounded or long narrow plants, or opt for striking sculpted shapes. All of these contrast well with boxy kitchen cupboards, and make the maximum impact in the minimum of space.

Size is another factor to consider. While it is certainly cheaper to buy

Plants for shady shelves
Ivy, all sorts of trailing Asparagus Ferns, Maidenhair Fern, Fittonia, Miniature Bulrush.

Plants for work tops
Boston Fern, Weeping Fig, Mother-in-Law's Tongue, Schefflera, Foxtail Fern and Begonias.

small plants (and lots of fun to watch them grow) it's worth spending rather more to get plants the size you need if you want instant results decor-wise. One or two large plants can look far more striking in a restricted space, and take up less room, than lots of small plants — but it depends entirely on the effect you want to create.

Using colour

The most effective scheme in a room already filled with bits and pieces is to go for plain green foliage plants. These are very restful on the eye and will also blend well with all the various colours of the containers and equipment in your kitchen. If you want your kitchen filled with flowers you'll find it best to stick to a single colour scheme; warm peaches and pinks, for instance, work wonders at brightening up a dark kitchen and highlighting interesting corners.

One of the most difficult kitchen colours to work with — as far as plants are concerned — is plain white; in theory anything goes with white, but in practice it can make rather a harsh background. Not only does it seem to drain flowers of their colour, but it can also look boring with green. The answer with such a kitchen is to use coloured foliage plants to add warmth and interest to the scheme.

Where to put plants

An effective way of using plants at and above eye level is to stand them on shelves or dressers. Make sure that they are shade tolerant plants, and as long as you don't forget to water them, they'll grow beautifully.

You can make a special feature out of a cork notice board pinned to the wall and covered with Air Plants. These are small plants in a range of strange shapes rather like starfish; because they don't have roots, they can be mounted on bark (which you can get at a garden centre) and pinned to the board. To water them you just give them a light mist spray every day.

If you have the space, work tops are the place for large plants. Here again, you'll probaby need to choose plants that thrive in shade, such as most Ferns and some foliage plants. Alternatively, a small group of plants with colourful or attractively patterned leaves, or in pretty containers, look very attractive. It's wise to avoid flowering plants, or you may end up with unwelcome additions to your cooking!

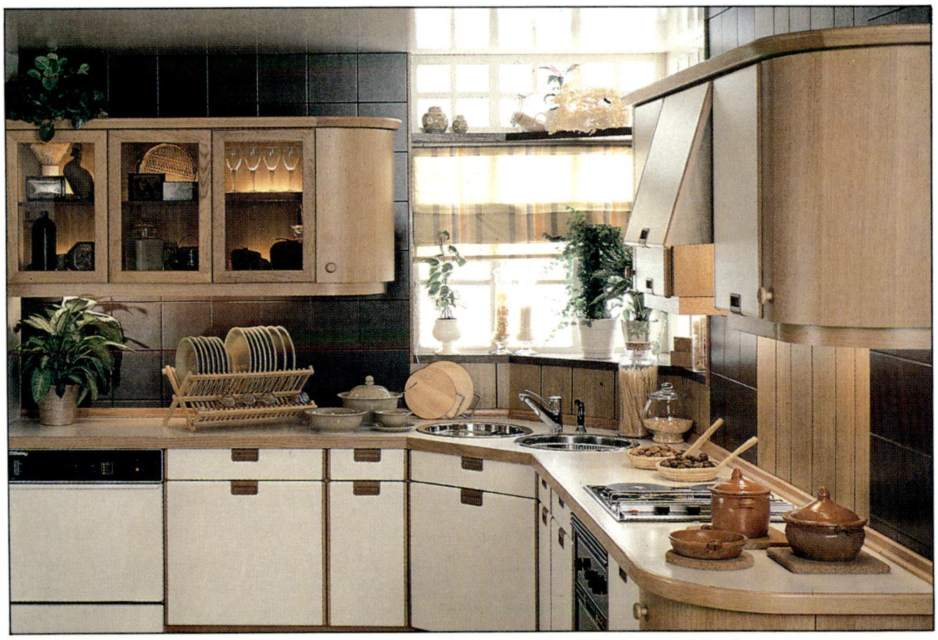

Use all the kitchen surfaces — worktops, shelves and windowsills for your plants.

Ideas for kitchen plant containers

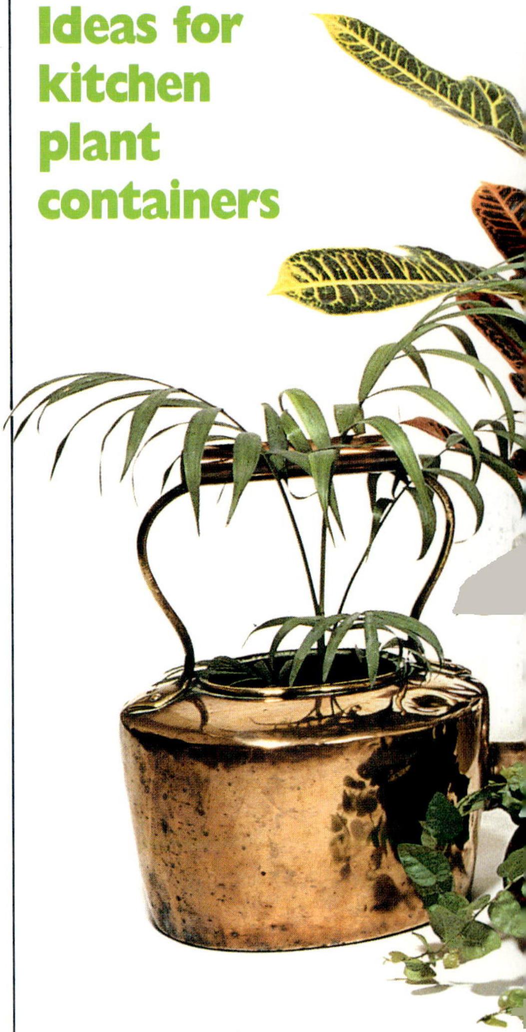

The containers you put your plant pots in are almost as important — in design terms — as the plants themselves, so try and make the most of the opportunity your kitchen offers to get away from the type of container you use around the rest of the house. Containers that look good in 'farmhouse' or natural wood kitchens include brass, copper and rustic pottery. Or, instead of standing the pots in containers, why not just show off plain clay or terracotta pots on matching drip trays. If terracotta doesn't go with your decor, you can use brightly coloured plastics — green, yellow, white or pillar box red.

Another idea is to use old equipment such as saucepans and kettles as containers. Or you can liven up a collection of plates, interesting tins or teapots by placing your plants among them.

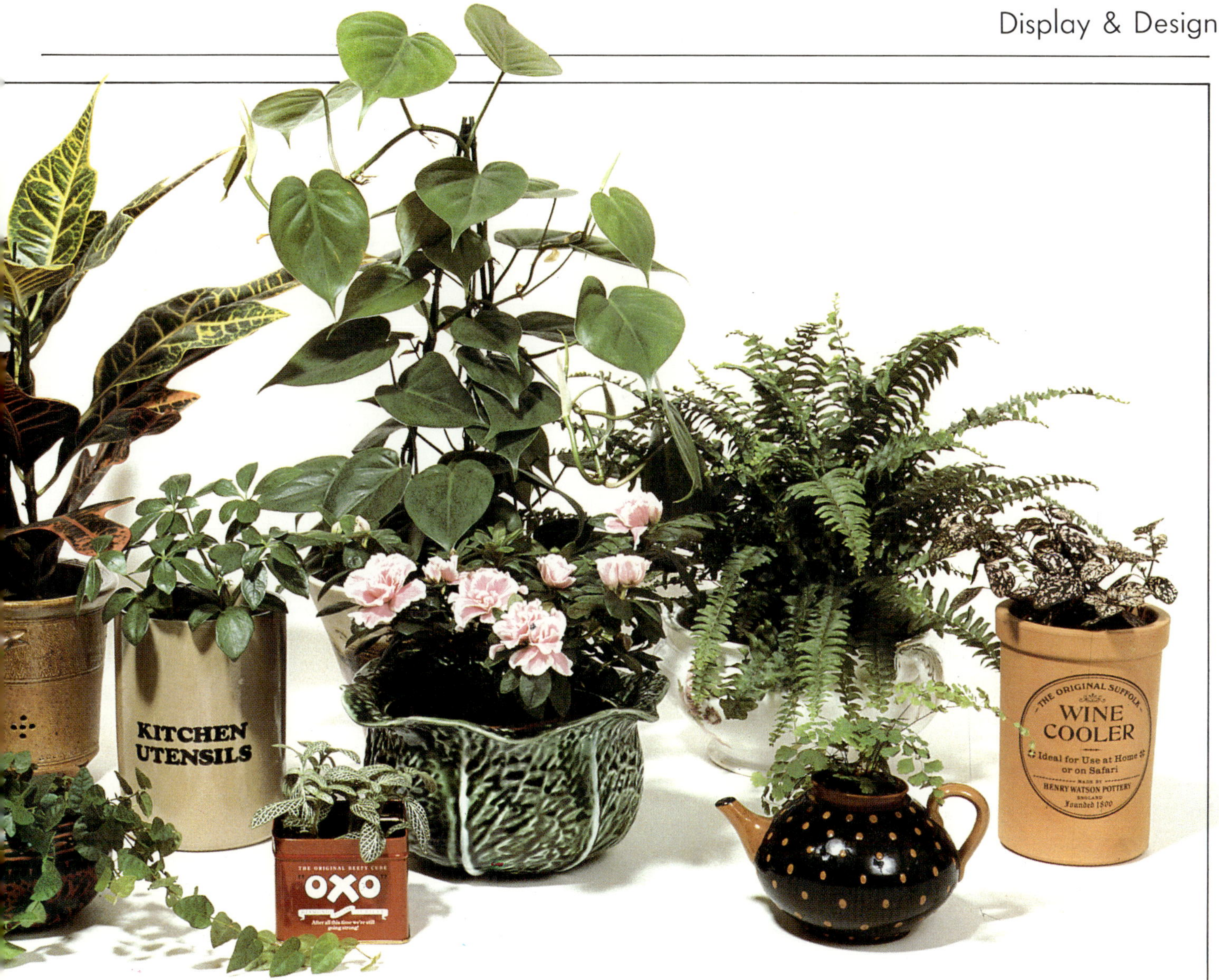

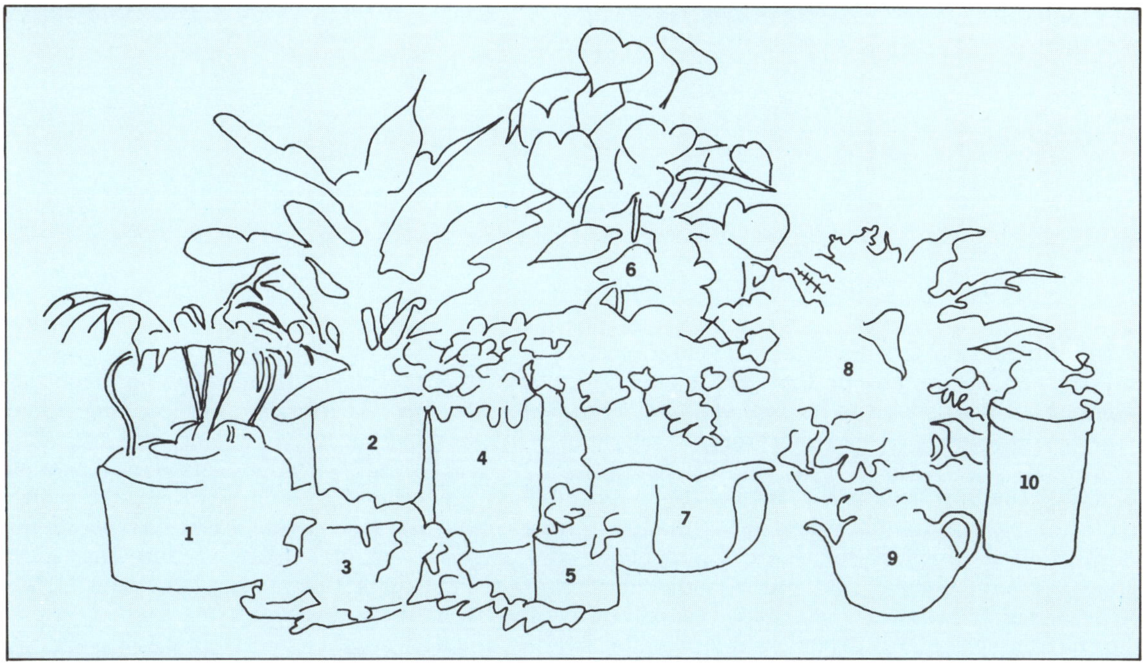

1 Shiny copper kettle with a small and elegant Parlour Palm.

2 Solid stoneware pot looks terrific holding a Croton.

3 A Creeping Fig and a jazzy painted gourd.

4 Heavy kitchen pot with a young Umbrella Plant.

5 A cheerful Oxo tin goes well with a tiny Snakeskin Plant.

6 A large ceramic bowl is useful for a tall Sweetheart Vine.

7 They could be made for each other — a cabbage pot and Azalea.

8 Even a potty comes into its own with a leafy Sword Fern!

9 Put your old teapot to work holding a Maidenhair Fern.

10 This Polka Dot Plant cheers up the sober wine cooler.

Plants for hallways

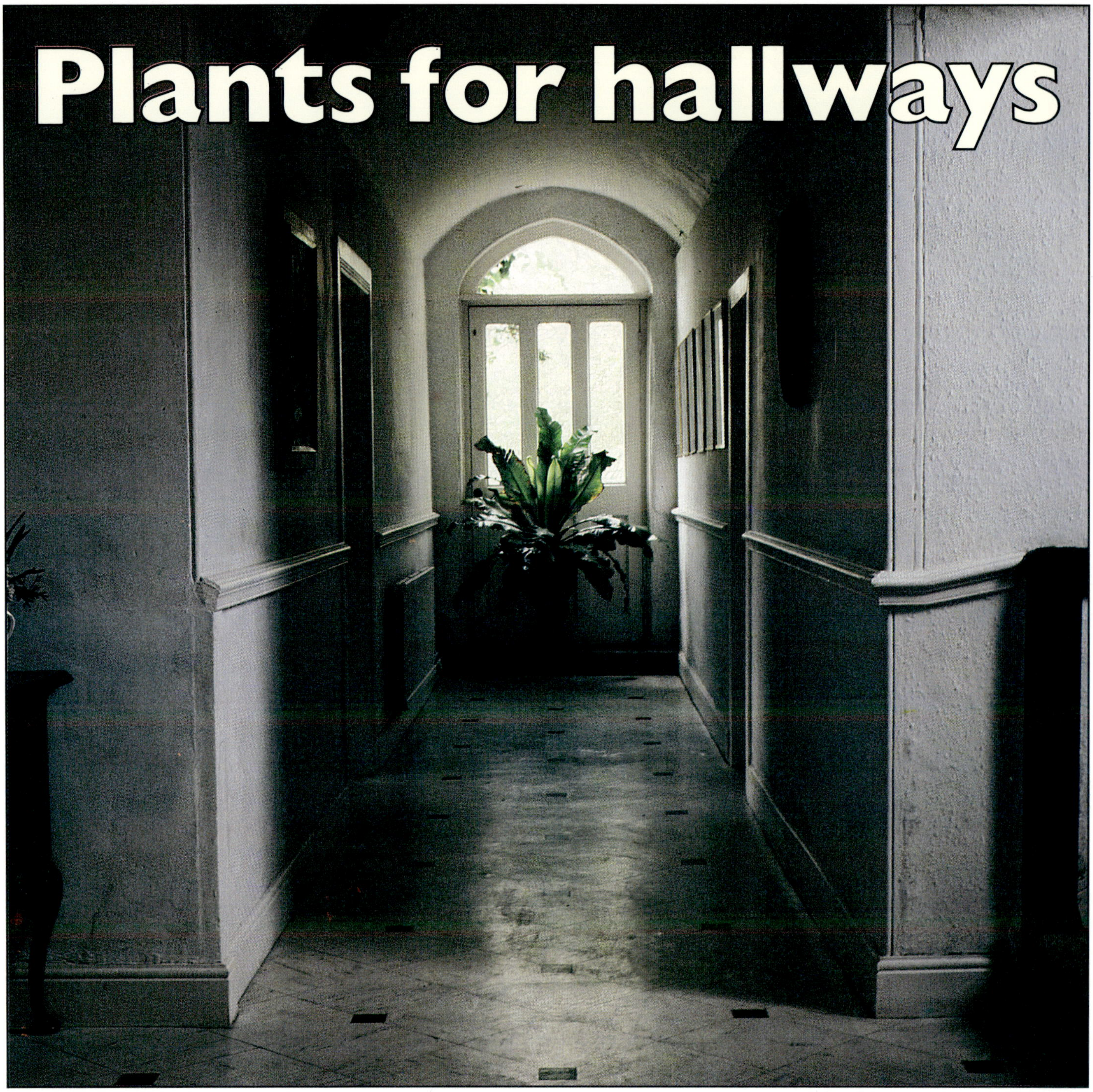

Your hall provides the first impression a visitor receives as he comes through your front door, and it is often one that will endure. An eyecatching and decorative arrangement of your favourite houseplants — or even one single, but well chosen plant — can do much to create a welcoming atmosphere in those first few seconds.

Even the smallest hall can benefit from the homely, brightening touch that houseplants can bring. Warm colour-schemes, tasteful furnishings and a well-planned interior are all helpful and, on the practical side, plenty of cupboard space for coats and shoes will cut down the clutter. But, for the finishing touches, there's nothing like living greenery for making people feel instantly 'at home'. Good quality plants, thoughtfully displayed, can transform even the smallest and dullest space into something worthy of a second look.

Unfortunately, from the plant's point of view, a hall is just about the most inhospitable room in the house. Often dark, chilly and draughty, halls aren't the place for the same sort of plants that you would grow in your living-room. But the plants don't have to be boring because they are tough; there are very many interesting plants you can grow.

An Aspidistra, *above*, catches the light in front of an unused door.

Making a hallway display

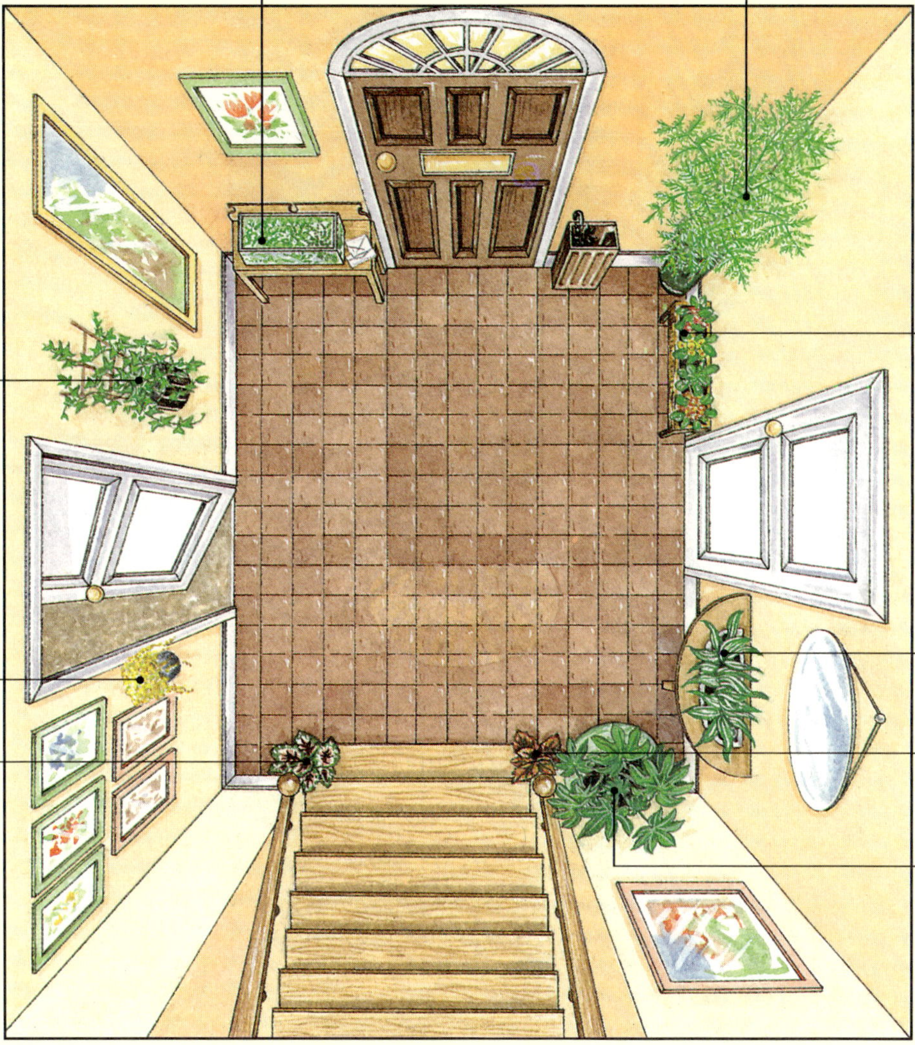

In the top right corner of the hallway, *above*, a *Grevillea* makes the most of the sheltered space, set off by the pretty colours of the Primulas on a low trestle next to it. Variegated Aspidistras and a Figleaf Palm grow on side tables — both species are able to endure a wide range of conditions. *Begonia rex* is a good choice to adorn the bottom of the stairs, since it doesn't grow too tall. The pale green *Helxine* will be happy next to the door, being extremely adaptable, while the Ivy is an excellent choice for an unheated room. In the terrarium are more delicate plants, protected by the glass from draughts and knocks.

And, if you are prepared to hunt them out, there are some very special new plants around that are perfect for halls. What's more, you'll have something that very few people will ever have come across before!

Assessing the setting

The first step is to take stock of the conditions you can offer houseplants in your hall. You may, for instance, have an open stairwell, where you can make a feature of climbing plants, or plants of various heights. A beautiful cascading effect can be created, if you have an open landing gallery, by growing trailing plants along its edge and letting them hang down into the hallway.

However, it's the amount of light available that is probably the most important factor, though usually it's a case of little, or none at all. Even the best of halls are generally quite a bit darker than living-rooms. What natural light there is probably comes from glass panels in the front door. But, unpromising though it sounds, this will generally be enough to grow plants that are dedicated shade lovers. To qualify as a good candidate for hallways, plants will need to be tough enough to tolerate draughts, and won't mind the occasional knock.

Among the suitable kinds of plant, you can choose from traditional species and exciting newcomers, so there's bound to be something you fancy.

Success with shade

Some halls have no natural light at all, yet even here it is possible to grow successful plants, as long as you think of them as temporary visitors and not permanent decorations. Just select any of the plants from those mentioned, but move them back to a lighter position every few days. Alternatively, you could stick to annual flowering plants that like it cool, such as *Cineraria (right)* or *Primula.*

Some outdoor plants, such as the Christmas Rose (*Helleborus niger*) and *Polyanthus*, are often grown in pots and sold in flower by garden centres. These can be brought inside to provide a spot of colour when and where it's needed, and the cool of the hall is the best place for a temporary home. Once you've enjoyed the flowers, just plant them out in the garden as usual for next year. Bulbs are another good bet: Christmas

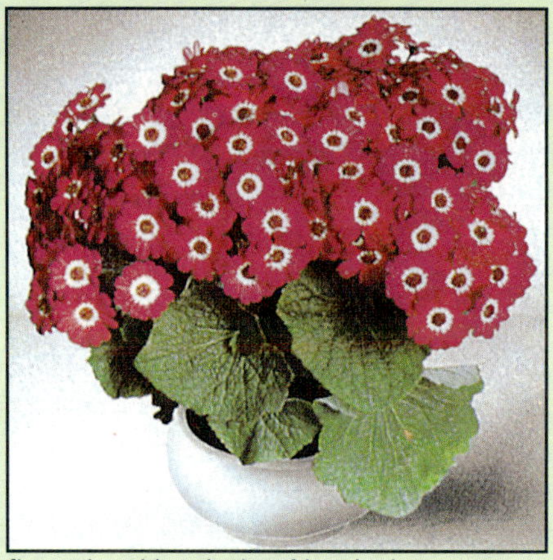

flowering Hyacinths, Narcissi or even exotic Lilies will last quite well in the cool of a hall, even if there isn't much light. You can still plant the bulbs outside once the flowers are finished.

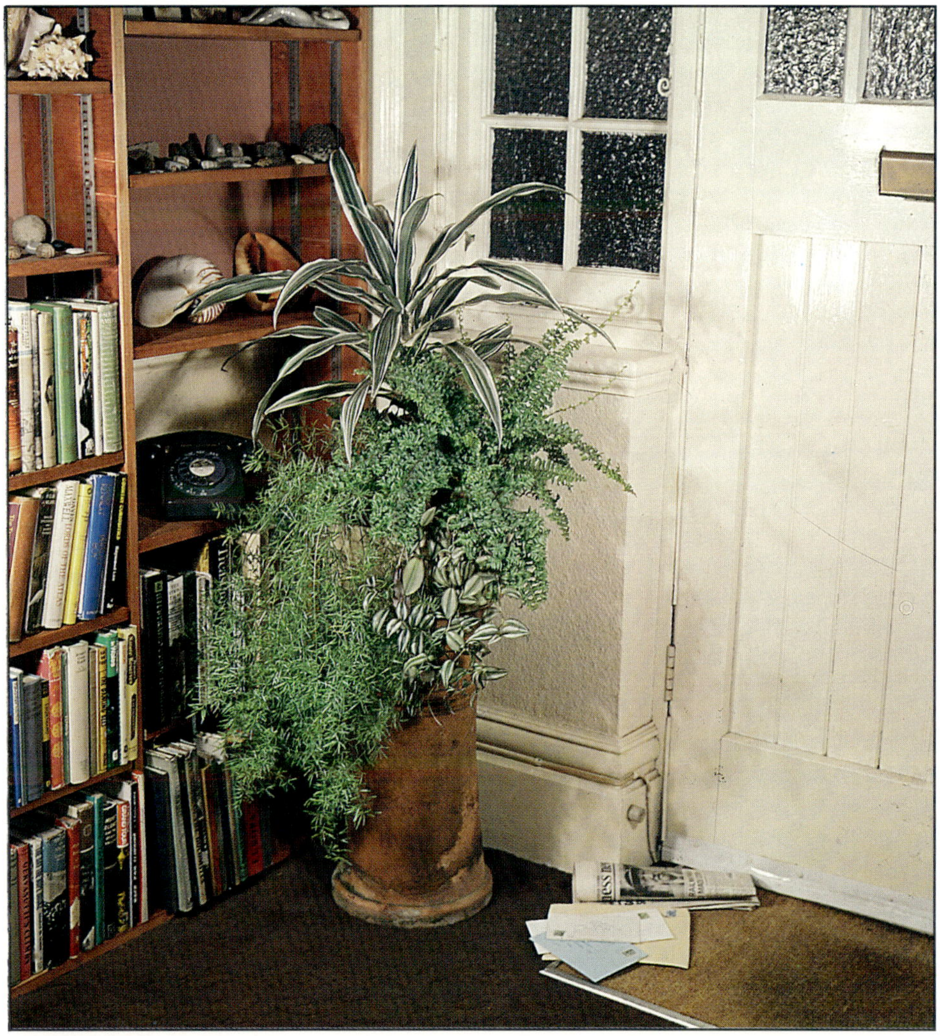

A sheltered spot with good light is home for an Asparagus Fern, a Tradescantia (*Zebrina pendula*), a *Nephrolepsis exaltata* and a stripy *Dracaena deremensis.*

Starting with old favourites, at the top of the indestructibility ratings and perfect for larger hallways comes the original Cast-Iron Plant, the Aspidistra, now enjoying a new surge in popularity. Aspidistras exist in both plain green and cream-and-green variegated versions. While most people think of the Aspidistra as a non-flowering plant, it does in fact have flowers — if you know where to look for them. Instead of growing on stems, Aspidistra flowers grow pressed close to the compost, for the very good reason that in the wild they are pollinated by slugs. Look out for them in summer: they are dull mauve and about 1in (2.5cm) across.

Then there is the Figleaf Palm *(Fatsia Japonica)*. This has large leaves — 6-12 in (15-30 cm) across, depending on the size of your plant — and grows into a short, shrubby specimen that's almost as robust as the Aspidistra. Both plants look good as large display 'specimens' standing on the floor in ornamental pot holders. Or you can raise them up by supporting the pot in the neck of a large ceramic vase.

Classic foliage plants

Ivy is another rugged individual that's perfect for halls. It is available in a wide range of variegations, in silver, gold and lime green. One of the prettiest is 'Goldheart', a variety with glossy green leaves, each with a splash of gold in the centre. You will also find plain green frilly leaves, arrow-shaped leaves and all sorts of other forms, too. Ivy looks good grown in troughs, where the stems can trail down: but, for a change, why not train it up to make a 'tree'. Simply plant three Ivies in a 10in (25cm) pot, and wire the trailing stems vertically up a moss-covered pole, letting the ends cascade down when they reach the top.

For a nice mossy green creeping plant to fill a hanging basket, choose *Helxine,* otherwise called Mind-Your-Own-Business; a good place to hang this would be at a small window or behind a glass panel alongside the front door. *Grevillea* — the Silk Oak — is a foliage plant very similar to a fern, but it can survive much lower temperatures than the more delicate Maidenhair Fern. To see it at its best, plant three of them in a 5in (13cm) pot — one on its own looks a little sparse. Or you could make up a mixed bowl: plant *Grevillea, Helxine* and a variegated plant such as Japanese Sedge, which has short, pointed, grass-like leaves in green and gold stripes, or *Euonymus* — a small, evergreen shrubby plant, variegated in green and gold or silver. This makes a perfect 'feature' for a low telephone table.

Alternatively, in a warmer hall where the temperature stays above 50°F (10°C), you could grow Club Moss (*Sellaginella*), or miniature ferns like Button Fern (*Pellaea rotundifolia*) in a terrarium. The glass walls will keep the humidity in and the draughts out, so you'll be able to grow a couple of plants that would otherwise be unhappy there.

Something new

For something that bit different and definitely much more colourful, look out for the newest strain of houseplants — a range of plants that grow naturally out of doors in mild climates, like New Zealand. A few of them are easily mistaken for tropical foliage plants, but need half the heat. Most will be quite happy if you shut down the heating when you're away — and you won't find many tropical plants surviving that treatment!

For a start, there's *Pseudopanax sabre,* which looks very much like an Aralia with long, narrow, bronze-coloured leaves. This makes a short, elegant, shrubby plant that could be placed on the floor or on a table where it will create an impact as a 'specimen' plant from your collection. Gold Splash, another *Pseudopanax,* looks just like a *Heptapleurum* or *Schleffera,* but has most attractive gold splashes on its foliage, as the name suggests. Very similar in shape and size is *Pseudopanax purpurea,* but instead of being variegated, its leaves are bronze-purple.

Entirely different is *Libertia peregrinans,* with bright red and gold grassy stems 6-8in (15-20cm) high. It looks delightful grown in a planter along with contrasting green foliage plants like *Helxine.* Or how about a small, chunky specimen for a pot of its own — *Astelia* 'Silver Spear,' a little like an Agave with spiky leaves coming from a short, central stem. The *Astelia* can be beautifully highlighted by growing it in a rough, hand-painted pot.

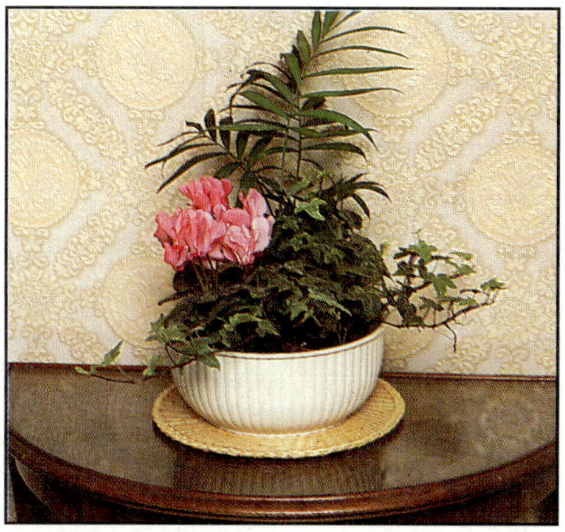

The pink of a Cyclamen contrasts with an Ivy and a Parlour Palm.

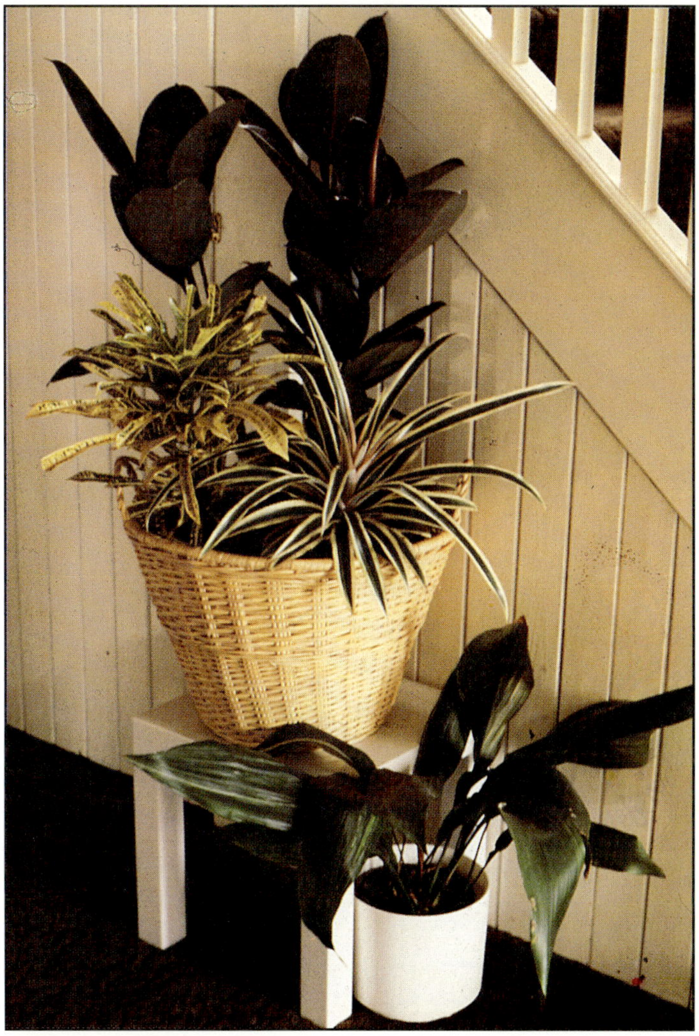

Different levels for a Cast Iron Plant, an *Ananas bracteatus striatus*, a Croton and a *Ficus elastica* 'Black Prince'.

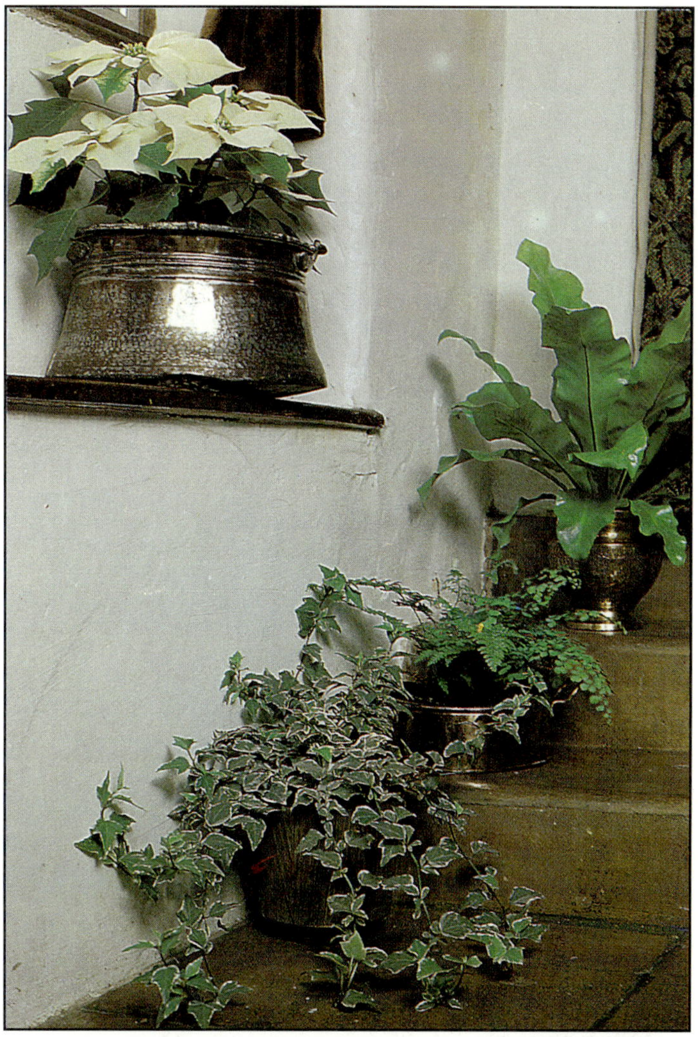

Low-growing plants: an *Asplenium nidus*, a Maidenhair Fern, a *Davallia* and an Ivy contrast with a white-bracted Poinsettia.

Plants for hot dry rooms

Warm, dry air may be just what the doctor ordered for humans — but it doesn't suit many plants very well! And if you're particularly sensitive to the cold, you're likely to have the heating in your home much higher than most houseplants will happily tolerate.

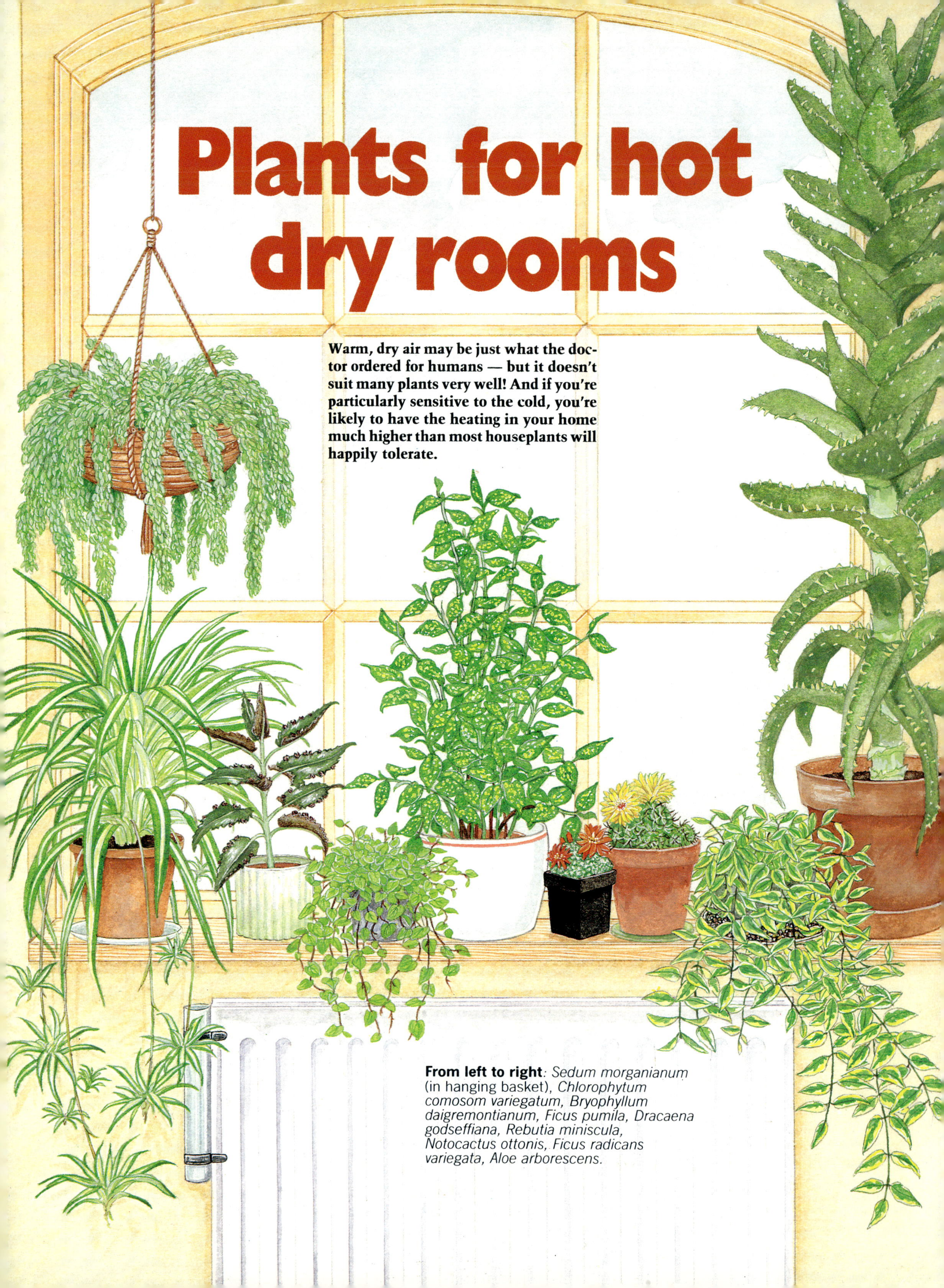

From left to right: *Sedum morganianum* (in hanging basket), *Chlorophytum comosom variegatum, Bryophyllum daigremontianum, Ficus pumila, Dracaena godseffiana, Rebutia miniscula, Notocactus ottonis, Ficus radicans variegata, Aloe arborescens.*

So to have happy and healthy plants, you must choose those that naturally enjoy such conditions, and make sure that you regularly give them any extra care or watering that they need. Under natural conditions, warm or hot, dry air occurs principally in desert regions, where it favours the growth of cacti and succulents or leathery-leaved plants that transpire slowly and are able to withstand considerable fluctuations in temperature and humidity. Thin-leaved exotics from the tropics, on the other hand, which thrive only in a humid environment, cannot tolerate such dehydrating conditions. Our selection of candidates for hot, dry rooms has therefore been determined by their natural habitat and their ability to withstand the loss of moisture from their leaves.

Desert cacti

For the warmest, dryest rooms, the first choice has to be desert cacti. Shaped by nature into moisture-conserving stems with spines rather than leaves, most desert cacti are baked by fierce daytime temperatures in the wild and then severely chilled at night, before receiving a cold douche of morning dew.

There are many species and varieties which we can buy, all of which are ideal for warm dry rooms. They are especially appealing grouped together in a dish garden which shows off their different bizarre forms to advantage. 'Growing cacti' page 142, and 'Designing a cactus garden' page 145, will give you many ideas on which cacti to choose and how to display them.

To get the best out of your cacti, keep them in the sunniest spot available — a south-facing window is ideal — and cool them down every morning with a misting of cold water, which simulates the dew in their natural habitat. They also enjoy a breath of fresh air, but take care to guard against chilling draughts. Most cacti will flower only on new growth, which calls for summer care and winter neglect — so they need very litttle or no water between mid October and late March — just the time when an overheated room is at its dryest.

Forest cacti

Let us turn next to the forest cacti, which grow in their natural home as epiphytes, attached to trees in woodland and jungles. These include the Rat's Tail Cactus (*Aporocactus flagelliformis*), Christmas Cactus (*Schlumbergera*) and Easter Cactus (*Rhipsalidopsis gaertneri*).

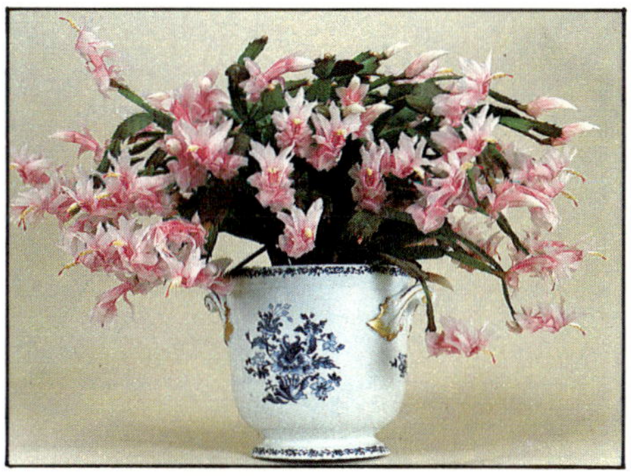

Schlumbergera x buckleyi will add a cool pink note to a hot, dry room.

Their natural habitat is the forest regions of tropical America and, not surprisingly, most of them need altogether moister conditions than the desert cacti. Happily these can be provided by misting them daily — or at least as often as possible — with tepid water, to simulate the steam which rises among them in their native tropical jungle habitat. They prefer a position in diffused rather than bright, hot sunlight so a north- or east-facing windowsill is best. For further details on Forest cacti see pages 143 and 144.

Succulents

This is another group of plants that thrive where thinner-leaved species would turn brown and shed their 'mantle'. There are many attractive forms. The Saucer Plant (*Aeonium tabuliforme*) is a remarkable miracle of nature. Its stems are topped with tightly packed little 'saucers' — hence its common name — which are neatly and symmetrically arranged. Its close relation, *A. arborum atropurpureum*, is tree-like, with stems terminating in sprays of handsome purple, shiny leaves.

The fleshy leaved Aloes are numerous. Impressive, with sharply saw-edged leaves, the Tree Aloe (*A. arborescens*) grows into a fairly sizeable plant. The Partridge Breasted Aloe (*A. variegata*) is much smaller, growing to about 1ft (0.3m). Its sword-shaped leaves, which are patterned with transverse light and dark green bands, form a stiff and arresting rosette. In summer, it sends up a spike of pinkish red, tubular flowers. The Hedgehog Aloe (*A. humilis*) also has upward-pointing, spiky leaves that curve gently inwards to resemble a clutching hand.

We come next to the Crassula family, its most famous member being the Jade Plant (*Crassula argentea*). Mature plants take on the appearance of old, stunted corky barked trees. The leaves, which are deep green, spoon-shaped and very thick, are remarkably resilient to neglect, and happily suffer the driest soils.

The Good Luck Plant (*Bryophyllum daigremontianum*) is a great favourite with children and has a party trick that never fails to amuse: it reproduces itself by forming tiny embryo plants in serried rows along the edges of its leaves. These grow to about ¼in (6mm) across, produce a wisp of roots, and then fall to the ground where they root in the compost on which they alight. The tubular-leaved *B. tubiflorum* is equally appealing; this forms its plantlets at the tips of its leaves.

Rosette-shaped Echeverias are hardy or half-hardy, and some are used as summer bedding plants. The Mexican Snowball (*Echeveria harmsii*) is especially attractive.

Other succulents that can be grown successfully in hot, dry places are the

Increasing humidity

Cacti and succulents need little regular care apart from feeding and occasional repotting, but the other houseplants mentioned on these pages will thank you for introducing a little moisture into the atmosphere. Here are a few ways in which you can do this.

- Fit humidifiers to the radiators.
- Sit pots on a tray of gravel or coarse perlite and keep it wet all the time. Make sure, however, that the base of the pot is not actually standing in a pool of water.
- Put a small plant pot into a larger one and surround it with peat or perlite that you keep damp. You can also group several plants together in a single large pot in the same way.
- Use self-watering containers or other devices so that the plant always has enough moisture to draw on.
- Put a layer of leca — special absorbent clay granules — on the top of the soil and keep it dampened.
- Keep a mist sprayer handy to spray the plants — steamy heat is just what tropical plants enjoy.

Sedums. Burro's Tail (*Sedum morganianum*), for example, is most unusual. Its cascading stems are composed of intricately overlapping, fleshy, waxy leaves that form a beautifully 'sculpted' rope, some 1in (2.5cm) in diameter. This is most successful in a hanging basket.

Another exciting succulent is the Candle Plant (*Kleinia articulata*), which has curious cigar-shaped stems strung together to make a strange little bush topped with fleshy, grey-green, ivy-like leaves. It is easily propagated by sectioning the stems into individual 'cigars' and rooting them in gritty compost.

Thick-leaved houseplants

There are several undemanding leathery-leaved houseplants that will happily withstand the excessively dry air of a centrally heated sunroom or living room, though they will all thank you for introducing a little humidity into the atmosphere — see suggestions below.

All the following will return care with a lavish display of exotic foliage.

The aptly named Cast Iron Plant (Aspidistra) and its pretty cream-striped variety can both withstand long periods of dryness. You can, on the other hand, kill them all quickly by keeping their 'feet' in water for any length of time, so it's better to err on the side of under- rather than overwatering.

The Spider Plant (*Chlorophytum comosom variegatum*) is incredibly long-suffering. Its leaf tips may turn brown in excessively hot air, but its general constitution will remain unaffected either by heat or by fluctuating temperatures. It is particularly effective displayed on a pillar, where its arching stems will cascade in a series of 'waterfalls', each tipped with young plants from which further wiry stems emerge and develop new plants.

A shrubby Dracaena, like the Gold Dust Dracaena (*D. godseffiana*) with gold-spotted green leaves, comes into its own in warm, dry conditions. There it will really thrive, producing a handsome rounded bush, much admired by visitors. Another member of the genus, the Dragon Tree (*D.draco*), is equally undemanding and thrusts forth its shuttlecock rosette of sword-shaped leaves to enhance any decor.

The Australian Eucalyptus can also be successfully grown indoors and is tolerant of warm, dry conditions. Blue Gum (*E. globulus*), which is highly valued for its distinctive, rich blue-green, triangular leaves, is best encouraged to form a shapely plant by nipping out the growing tips regularly during the spring and summer.

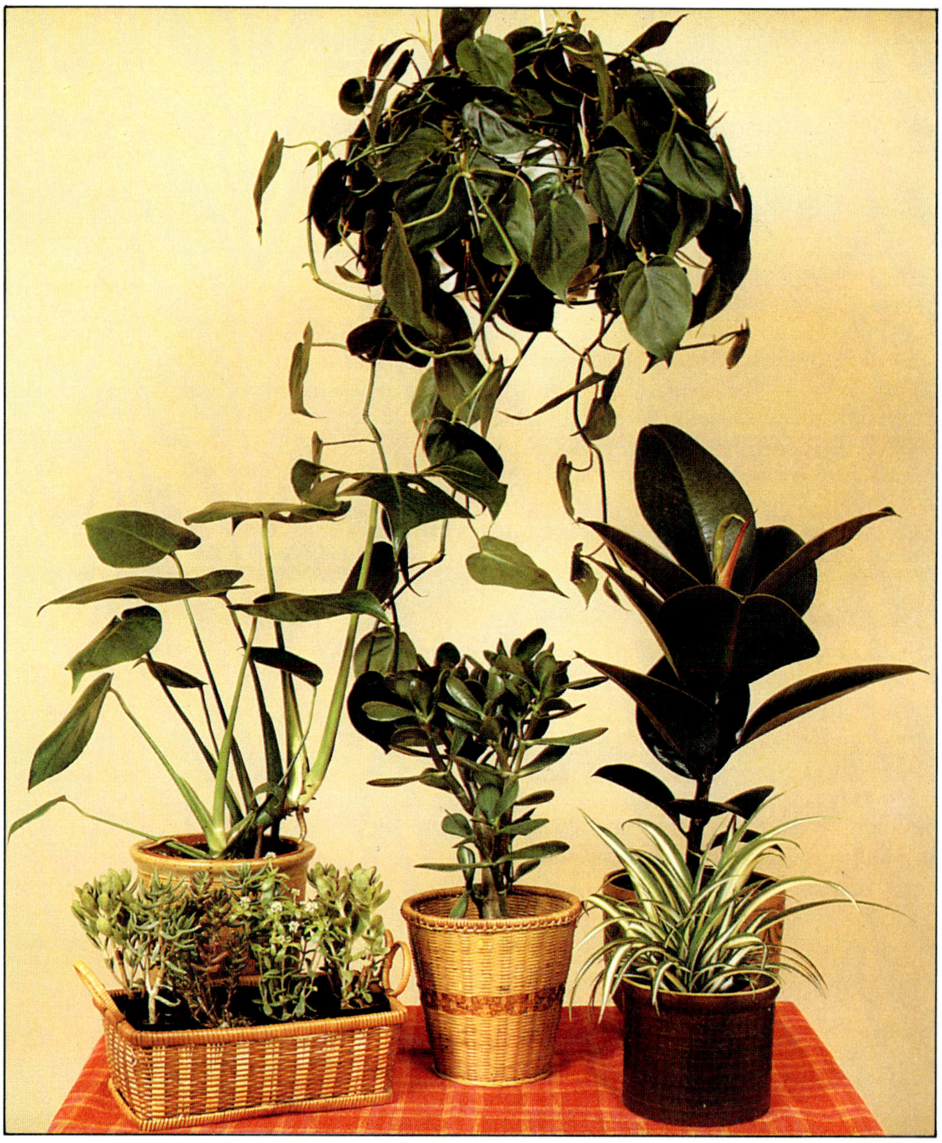

No need to limit yourself to cacti — many plants will thrive in dry conditions. Among these are: Philodendron (in hanging basket); *from left to right, back row,* Monstera, Crassula, *Ficus elastica*; *front row,* various Sedums and a Spider Plant (Chlorophytum).

The Ficus or Ornamental Fig family has for many years been used to decorate draughty reception areas as well as stuffy, very dry, ill-lit rooms. It excels in both capacities and has gained a reputation for its ability to endure many hardships. The common upright Rubber Plant (*Ficus elastica decora*), which is much prized for its large, glossy leaves, also has some creamy variegated forms. *F. e. doescheri* is a particularly splendid example. The Weeping Fig (*F. benjamina*) has long been popular as an indoor tree because of its slender, elegant branches. A very different plant, with its huge wavy-edged leaves, is the Fiddle Leaf Fig (*F. lyrata*), which is magnificent as the eye-catching centrepiece for a generous-sized room.

Figs can also be grown in hanging baskets. Two contenders for this treatment are the Trailing Fig (*F. radicans variegata*), with creamy yellow-rimmed leaves, and its smaller relation, the Creeping Fig (*F. pumila*), a determined tumbler or sprawler.

Finally, there are three other stalwarts which seem to thrive on virtual neglect. These are the Swiss Cheese Plant (*Monstera deliciosa*), Sweetheart Plant (*Philodendron scandens*), and Mother-in-law's Tongue (Sansevieria) of which the gold-edged (*S. trifasciata laurentii*) is the most spectacular.

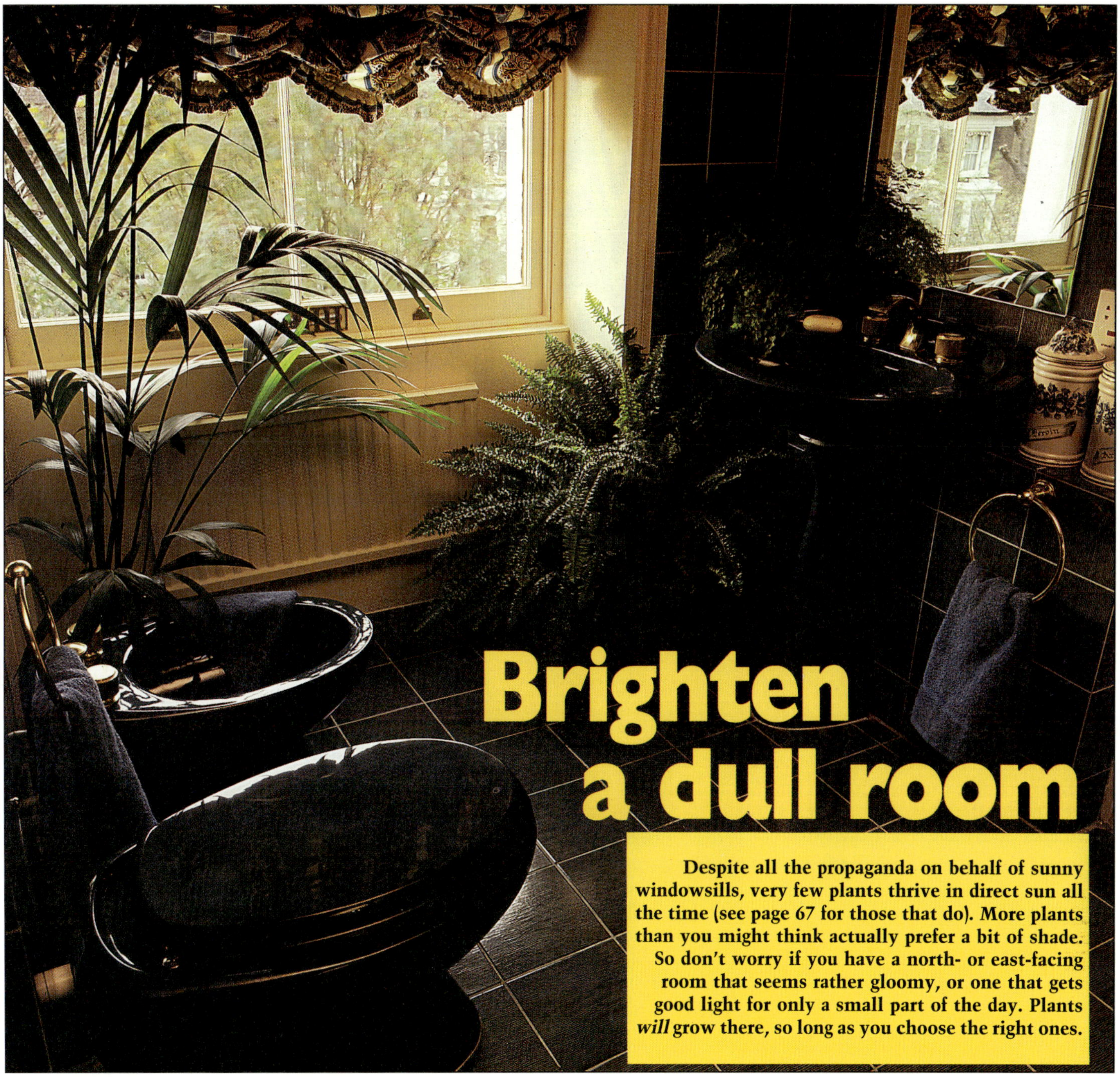

Brighten a dull room

Despite all the propaganda on behalf of sunny windowsills, very few plants thrive in direct sun all the time (see page 67 for those that do). More plants than you might think actually prefer a bit of shade. So don't worry if you have a north- or east-facing room that seems rather gloomy, or one that gets good light for only a small part of the day. Plants *will* grow there, so long as you choose the right ones.

Most palms and ferns prefer the shade — they are thriving in this rather gloomy bathroom.

The first thing to be aware of is that not all shade-loving plants like the same amount of shade. Start by thinking of a tropical forest, the natural home of many of the plants that we now grow as houseplants. Not many of these grow in bright sunshine — most are found in the shade cast by other, taller plants. There's a progression from the top down, with each layer of plant life growing in deeper shade than the one above. By the time you reach the forest floor, it's really too dark for anything apart from the odd fern to survive.

Much the same thing happens indoors, too — the room gets darker the further away from the window you go. Imagine your room divided into a series of 'zones', each one getting a different amount of light. To get the best from your plants, you should carefully grade them according to the amount of light each one needs, and grow them in the correct zone.

Good indirect light

Most plants in fact do very well in bright light without direct sunlight, provided they get the right amount of warmth and water. Windowsills that get no, or very little, direct sun are a good place for plants that flower, and you can choose from some fairly exotic kinds.

Gesneriads are one of the few groups of flowering plants that will thrive out of sunlight. They include the popular African Violet, as well as less well known kinds such as Streptocarpus,

Achimenes and Columnea, which have beautiful, delicate flowers in a range of pinks, violets and reds. Then there are Episcia, with unusual dark, variegated foliage, and Aeschynanthus, a long-stemmed trailing plant with strikingly decorative orange flowers, which is perfect for a hanging basket. You should be able to find all of these in a good specialist garden centre or nursery.

All these Gesneriads require much the same conditions as the African Violet — good light, but protected from direct sun, constant warmth and moisture, and a humid, draught-free environment. They should be stood in a bowl of damp gravel so that they get adequate moisture. They dislike lime, so it's best to boil and cool their water, which helps to reduce the amount of lime in it. Feed them once a fortnight in spring and summer when they're growing — this is enough for them because they don't grow very fast. Don't feed them at all in the winter, but keep the gravel just damp. If you keep these plants on a windowsill all the time, but not in direct sun, they will flower even in the winter.

Orchids are becoming fashionable as houseplants, and there are at least a dozen kinds that you can grow in the home. Slipper Orchids (Paphiopedilum) are low-light orchids — they must never be given direct sun and are best kept away from the window. Their bright colours are perfect for shade.

Orchids take a bit of getting used to if you have never grown them before — they have special needs, including unusual compost, and can be rather tricky. We tell you all about how to grow them on pages 147-151.

Tropical plants include some unusual and very exciting plants from the family *Araceae*. Caladium, for example, has beautiful heart-shaped paper-thin leaves, ranging in colour from white to very deep red. It needs to be kept warm and humid, and moderately well-lit, but away from direct sun.

Alocasia, also from the same family, is another ornamental foliage plant with huge deeply-lobed leaves. It needs warm humid conditions and good but indirect light — light shade is ideal. You could also try the Tree Philodendron (*Philodendron bipinnatifidum*), which has very large, glossy green, deeply indented leaves, or the even more shade-tolerant Sweetheart Plant (*P.scandens*).

For a really dramatic splash of colour, you could grow the Flamingo Flower (*Anthurium scherzerianum*) — its huge, scarlet blooms appear from February to July. Needing average warmth, the Flamingo Flower should be protected from the summer sun, and kept in bright light in winter. The Peace Lily *(Spathiphyllum wallisii)* has similarly shaped flowers, but in white — it needs warmth, semi-shade in summer, and bright light in winter.

Bromeliads are a huge family of exotic jungle plants. Some of them, the 'terrestrial' ones, live near the forest floor in their natural habitat, so they're very suitable as houseplants in shady rooms. All of them are, in any case, very slow-growing, so a week or two in shade will do them no harm.

Commonly called Urn Plants, Bromeliads belong to the same family as the pineapple: they grow a rosette of pineapple-like leaves with their own reservoir of water in the middle. Some grow tall and upright, others wide and flat. They should be topped up regularly with water, preferably rainwater or boiled and cooled tapwater. They like warm conditions and high humidity.

Temporary visitors

Varieties which would not actually *grow* very happily in deep shade may be perfectly suited to such conditions for a short while, when they are near the end of their lives. Some annuals die after flowering in any case, so you needn't feel guilty about them; use them to liven up a shady room when they're in flower. Good choices would be Calceolaria, Cineraria, Cockscomb, Exacum, Prince of Wales Feather and Schizanthus.

Some perennials are often thrown away after flowering because they are not very appealing for the rest of the year; try Ornamental Capsicum, *right*, Pot Chrysanthemum, Primula and Miniature Rose. Bulbs will live happily in a shady room while they are in flower; you can put them in the garden when the flowers are over, and they'll survive another year; try Hyacinths, Lily of the Valley and Pot Lillies.

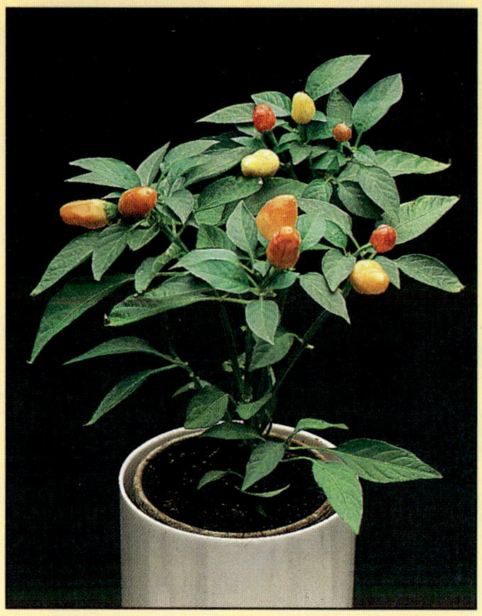

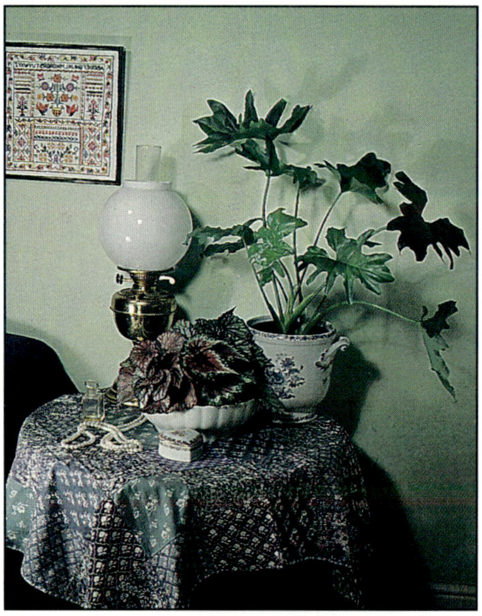

The Tree Philodendron and Begonias make the most of limited light conditions.

Permanent shade

You might think that no plant could grow in dull light all the time, but palms and ferns both do — and there's an enormous number of these to choose from.

Palms come in all shapes and sizes, and a variety of leaf shapes — fans, plumes, diamonds and fishtails. Coconut Palms, Date Palms and Parlour Palms have leaves that grow from the top of short stems, while Kentia Palms have reed-like stems that grow in a cluster. All of these love shade and, as a rule of thumb, if it's light enough to read by, it's light enough to grow them.

Palms can be expensive to buy, but they're worth it. They make marvellous centrepieces for groups, and dramatic specimen plants if placed on their own, with their tall, upright, branching growth and their glossy green leaves.

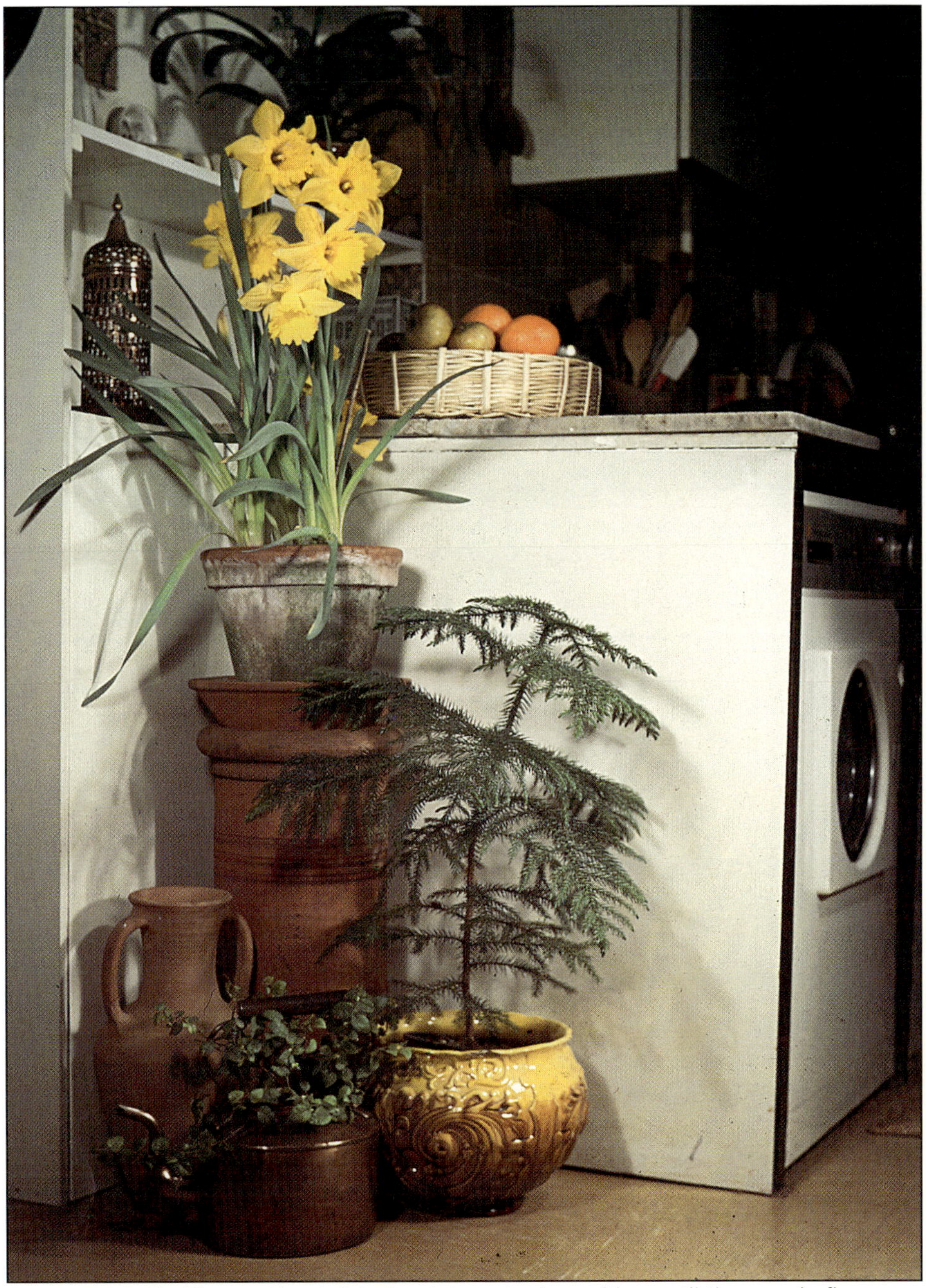

Don't put daffodils, or other tall bulbs, into a shady position until they are in flower — otherwise they grow too tall and flop over.

Some of them grow very tall, which makes them perfect for adding interest to the corners of a room. The Parlour Palm (*Neanthe bella*) and the Kentia Palm (*Howea forsteriana*) are both very easy to look after, requiring cool winters, and summers with average warmth. The Sago Palm (*Cycas revoluta*) is an interesting one, with tall fronds growing out of a ball-like base.

Palms need a moist atmosphere, so it's a good idea to spray them with tepid water every day in summer. This will also help to keep the dust down — if you let dust lie on palms it will literally choke the leaves and kill the plant. Standing them outdoors in a light summer shower is an ideal way to clean them up, or you can wipe them occasionally with a soft, damp cloth. Never be tempted to use a proprietary leaf shiner on palms since it damages their leaves.

Ferns will grow, in the wild, in the shade of most plants, making them very suitable as houseplants. Yet very few members of this large group of plants are commonly found in shops. Specialists will have a much more interesting selection, including frilly ferns, trailing ferns, golden, silver and even pinkish-coloured ferns. They all need average warmth and watering, and indirect light.

Specially interesting and unusual ferns to look out for include the Mother Spleenwort (*Asplenium bulbiferum*) with feathery green fronds and offsets along the edges of the older leaves which gradually weigh down the fronds. The Button Fern (*Pellaea rotundifolia*) is a pretty miniature with neat rows of shiny round leaflets, while the Bird's Nest Fern (*Asplenium nidus*) has broad leaves that uncurl from a central boss. The Feather Fern (*Nephrolepsis* 'Fluffy Ruffles') and the Boston Fern (*N.bostoniensis*) have broad leaves with frilly edges, while Rabbit's Foot Fern (*Davallia canariensis*) has tiny leaflets on tall fronds, and enlarged, fleshy stems (called rhizomes) which give it its strange appearance — and its name.

Creeping Mosses (Selaginellas) used to be great favourites, and it is high time that they became popular again. They are low, creeping or mound-shaped plants which come in all sorts of different colours as well as green —bronze and gold are particularly attractive. The Peacock Fern (*Selaginella uncinata*) and Creeping Moss (*S.martensii*) should both be easy to find in shops. Grow them in shallow, well-drained pots well away from the window. Use boiled, cooled water and keep the compost moist at all times — spraying the leaves helps too. They need average warmth and should do very well in a shady room that gets no direct light.

Finally for a really dramatic effect in a high-ceilinged room, you could grow the aptly named Tree Fern (*Cyathea dealbata*). It comes from New Zealand, and can grow up to 10ft (3m) high!

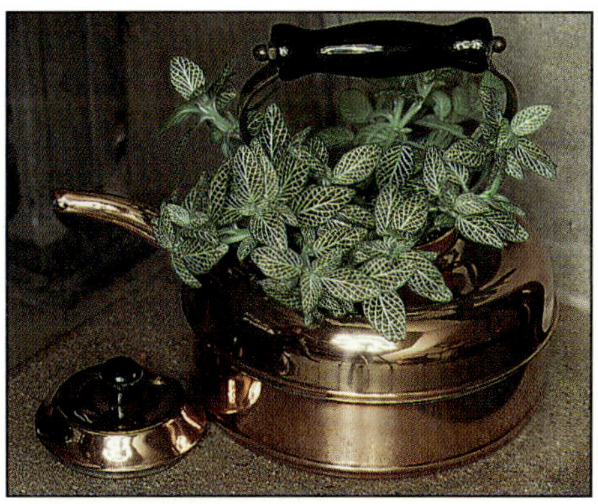

Fittonias brighten up a shady spot.

Creating a formal display

If you've ever admired the stupendous displays at a flower show and wondered enviously whether you could do the same sort of thing at home, the answer is, quite definitely, yes!

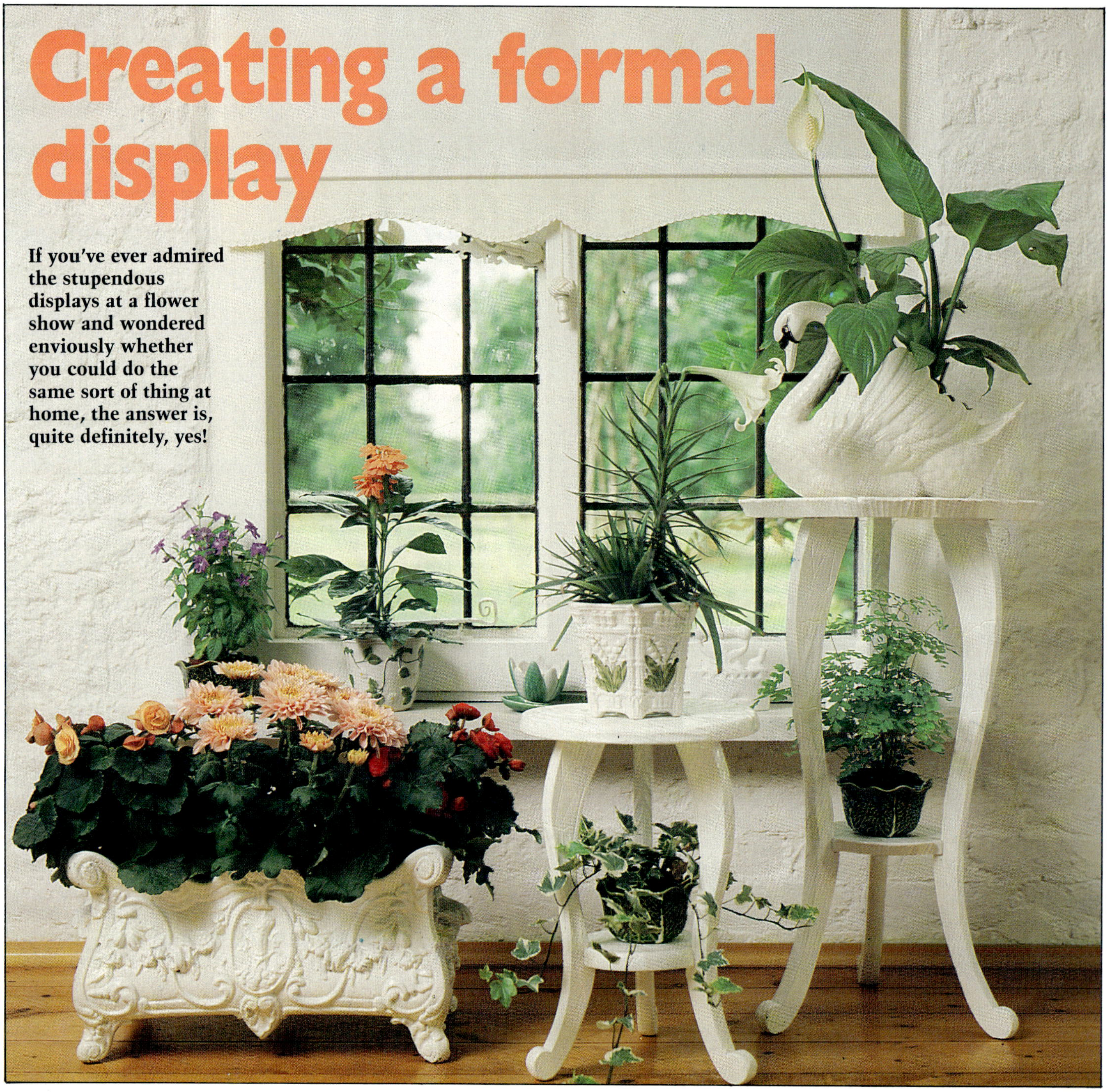

It goes without saying that not everyone has the space to stage a full-sized show exhibit indoors — and certainly not on a permanent basis. But for special occasions there's nothing to beat a large formal display of plants in the entrance hall, sitting or dining room to make your party that bit more special and your guests feel thoroughly welcome.

And on a smaller scale, formal displays translate beautifully into part of your everyday decor. Why settle for a few plants dotted about the place when you could combine them to make something far more eye-catching?

At major flower shows, of course, the displays are usually created by professional flower designers who, to be really successful, need to be part flower arranger, part interior decorator, and part landscape architect. But there's no reason why a do-it-yourself enthusiast, given a little practice, shouldn't achieve equally stunning results at home.

If you were to commission a professional flower designer to create a display in your home, there's one thing he or she would need, above all else, before even thinking about plants or containers — a brief. And even when you're doing the job yourself, it's surprising how much it helps to formalise things in your own mind before you actually start to create your display.

This eyecatching permanent display, *above*, owes as much to the painted furniture and fine collection of containers as it does to the selection of healthy, well-tended plants.

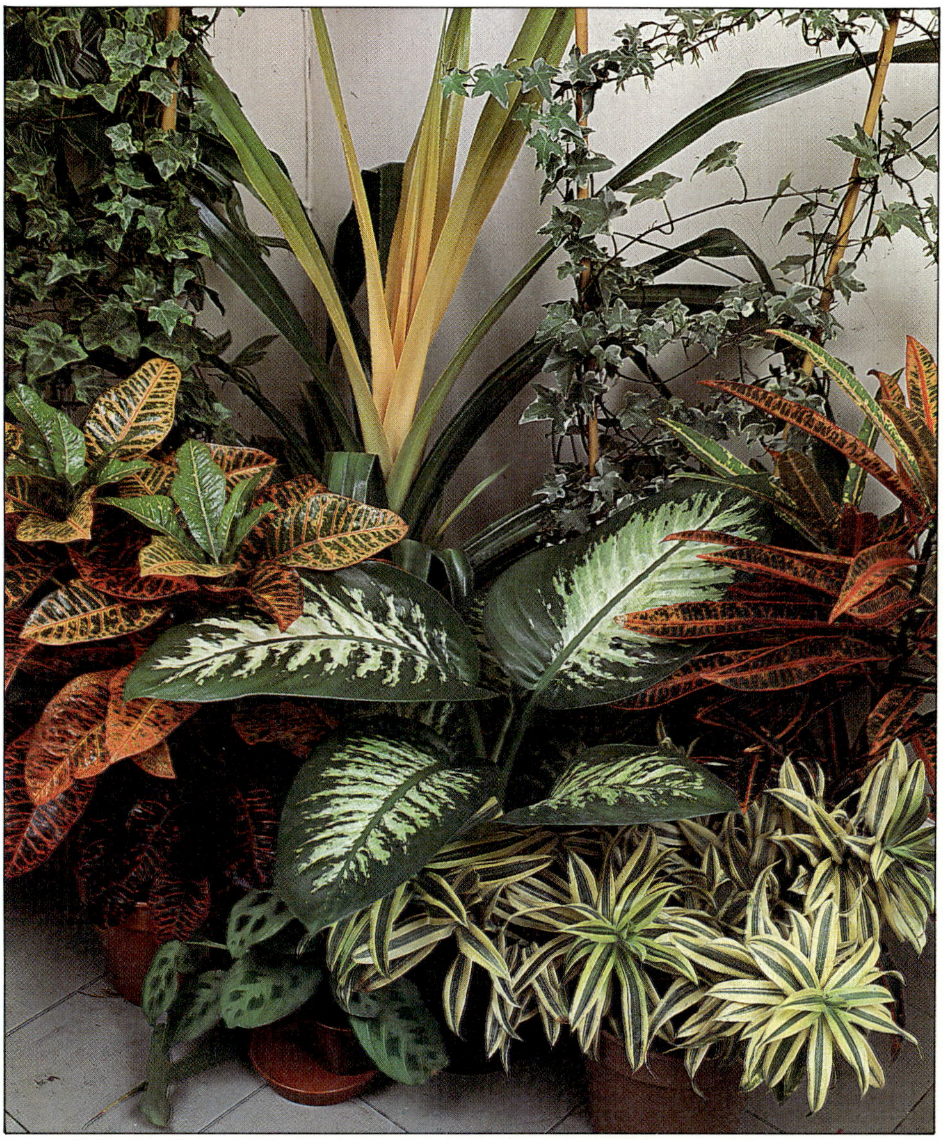

A careful selection of foliage plants: the tall sword-shaped leaves of Dracaena are set off by the rounded leaves of Croton and Dieffenbachia; in the front are Maranta and rosettes of Pineapple. The background is filled in with Hedera.

So ask yourself the same questions as the professional would ask you. For example, are you after something extravagant for a special occasion, or something rather more down-to-earth that will become part of your permanent room decor? What are the background colours to the display — walls, carpets, curtains and furniture — and are they plain or patterned? What plants, containers and accessories have you already got? And how much are you prepared to spend?

The next thing your professional would do is to look around the house, trying to spot places that lend themselves particularly well to plant decoration — such as fireplaces, alcoves, table tops and deep windowsills. He'd also be on the look-out for places that would benefit from plants to give them a 'lift' — uninteresting corners, open room dividers, large unfurnished open spaces, or even under the stairs. Don't think that lack of daylight means you can't put plants there: you just need to rig up some special plant lights.

Then, with the basics taken care of, it's time to start getting on with the job.

Choosing plants

There are two quite different considerations to be taken into account when you are choosing your plants. The first is an entirely practical consideration — are the conditions suitable? This is particularly important if you want your display to last. Look especially at the temperature, humidity and amount of light in the room, and take note of any draughty areas. Then, if you aren't sure which plants like what, check them out in our A-Z. Temporary displays allow you a bit more leeway when it comes to light, because most plants will tolerate a darker-than-usual spot just for a day or two, provided you return them to a brighter position afterwards. But do avoid keeping plants in too low a temperature in winter or too much sun in summer, even for only a few days — unless it's such an important occasion that you're prepared to risk losing some of your plants.

Once you've arrived at a shortlist of plants that fit the conditions you have to offer them, the other consideration is the decorative one. Are they the right colour, shape and size for the type of display you have in mind, and what will they contribute to your finished design? This is the point where your design really starts to take shape.

Designing your display

Plants come in all shapes, sizes, textures and colours, so how do you decide which will 'go' together? This is no more difficult that choosing clothes that coordinate, or curtains, carpets and soft furnishings to complement each other. The easiest way is to spend an afternoon in a plant shop, trying out different combinations of plants together until you end up with something that you like.

But if you want to be sure of getting good results every time — and without spending too long — it pays to know a little about composition. Start by splitting up the problem into its various component parts as listed below.

- **Colour.** This is the first consideration. Most people think of plants as predominantly green, but even foliage plants can be variegated and some, such as Croton (Codiaeum), have very brightly coloured leaves in shades of red, gold or purple.

When it comes to flowers, there is an almost unlimited choice of colours available. Depending on the sort of plants you choose, you'll usually see your flowers set against a background of green leaves but some plants — such as Cineraria (*Senecio cruentus*), Prince of Wales' Feather (*Celosia plumosa*) and Cockscomb (*Celosia cristata*) — are so covered with flowers that you can't see any green at all by the time they have been grouped together in a display. You can choose plants with mixed, bright

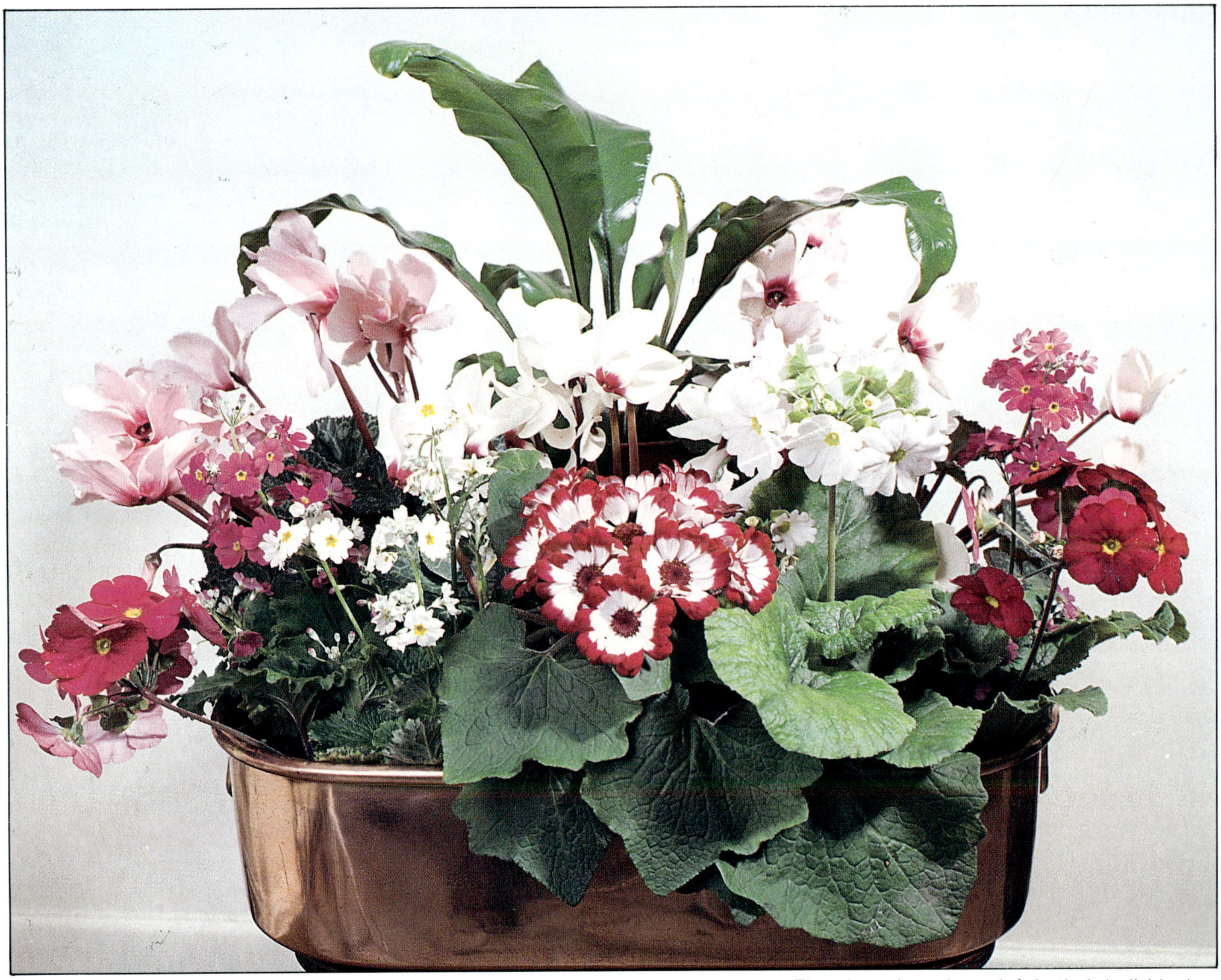

Cyclamen, Cineraria, Primulas and Bird's Nest Fern make up this fine spring display. The plants have been left in their individual pots to make replacement easy and the Bird's Nest Fern (*centre back*) has been raised to dominate the arrangement.

colours for a really cheerful display, or you may prefer something a little more sophisticated — say, several plants in different shades of one single colour, or perhaps two contrasting colours.

If you want to get technical about this, you might find a flower arranger's colour wheel useful. This will help you to decide which colours tone well together, and which make the most effective contrasts.

Another aspect of choosing colour for displays is the idea of using certain colours to suggest certain seasons or occasions. Use yellow for spring, for example, bronze for autumn, crimson for Christmas, and white for Easter, weddings, christenings and winter.

But while you are thinking of colour, don't think only of the plants — the background they'll be seen against is an equally important factor. And, since you can't usually do much about the colour of the background, it's a case of choosing plants to suit it rather than the other way round. The trick lies in making your display stand out by choosing a contrasting colour to the background — if it's too similar a colour, the plants will simply merge into it and 'disappear'.

Thus if the background is very dark, you'll need to choose flowers with really luminous colours — bright red, white or yellow, for example — which will show up well against it. Most flowers stand out well against a pastel background, but you can go one step further and choose plants that pick out a minor colour from your furnishings to give a well co- ordinated colour scheme.

The best backgrounds are relatively plain and unfussy, because plants don't stand out against violent floral wallpapers, though of course you can always create an artificial background by draping a piece of fabric, such as velvet, say, behind your display, as is often done at flower shows.

● **Shape and texture.** These are two more design elements which are both likely to figure strongly in plant arrangements. Just imagine how uninteresting a display would look if all plants had rounded leaves, or they all grew short and dumpy. But fortunately, plants come in an enormous range of different shapes, so make the most of them. Contrast tall pointed leaves with a mass of small shiny leaves or large round felty ones; upright plants with trailing or climbing ones; and spiky blooms with large flat flower heads.

But quite apart from the shape of plants and their individual flowers and leaves, you also need to think about the overall shape of the display. Formal displays need to have a very definite shape, or they will end up looking somehow not quite right. The basic display shapes, all of which are easily achieved, include flame, round, oval and hedge.

You also need to consider the space round the display, and the relationship between the two. This is particularly important in an enclosed space like an alcove or fireplace, where you have to decide whether to fill the space entirely with your display so that it looks as if it is bursting out of it, or leave a margin around the edge of the display to emphasise its shape.

● **Size.** It's no good putting a tiny little miniature garden into something the size of the Chelsea Flower Show and expecting it to be noticed — you've got to do something big in a big area. So always make your display an appropriate size for the room it's in.

Don't worry if you can't afford large enough plants for the purpose you have in mind. You can create the semblance of a large display by using quite small plants raised up on a table, or banked up in tiers, or simply by including a few standard plants — standard Fuchsias, for example, are easily available.

But basically, any display requires plants of several different sizes to enable you to fill in your shape, from bottom to top, with no empty spaces. The trick here is very simple: put the tallest plants to the back and the shortest to the front; or, if it's a display which you can walk round, then the tallest to the centre and the shortest round the edges.

● **Containers.** These are a much overlooked part of display technique, when in fact they are every bit as much a part of the design as the plants you put in them. A formal display looks best if you use a large, single container to hold all the plants which gives a sense of unity.

All sorts of containers can be used but, as a general rule, the simpler the better. Plain white china, for example, or very shiny good quality plastic, timber, bamboo or wicker are all ideal. They can be any shape you like — urns, troughs, baskets or whatever you fancy.

It is important to choose a container of the right size for the display. As a rough guide, use the 'two-and-a-half times' rule: for a tall, upright display, for example, measure the height of the container and add to this its width across the top; the display should be about two-and-a-half times as tall as this total measurement. And conversely, if your display is a long low one, the container needs to be about two-and-a-half times as long as the display is high.

If the price of really large containers puts you off, you can achieve the same effect much less expensively by simply giving an edging to your display. This can be done using a row of cascading plants round the edge which hides the pots and saucers, or a border of bark, cork, stones, or whatever else you can find which looks attractive.

Putting it all together

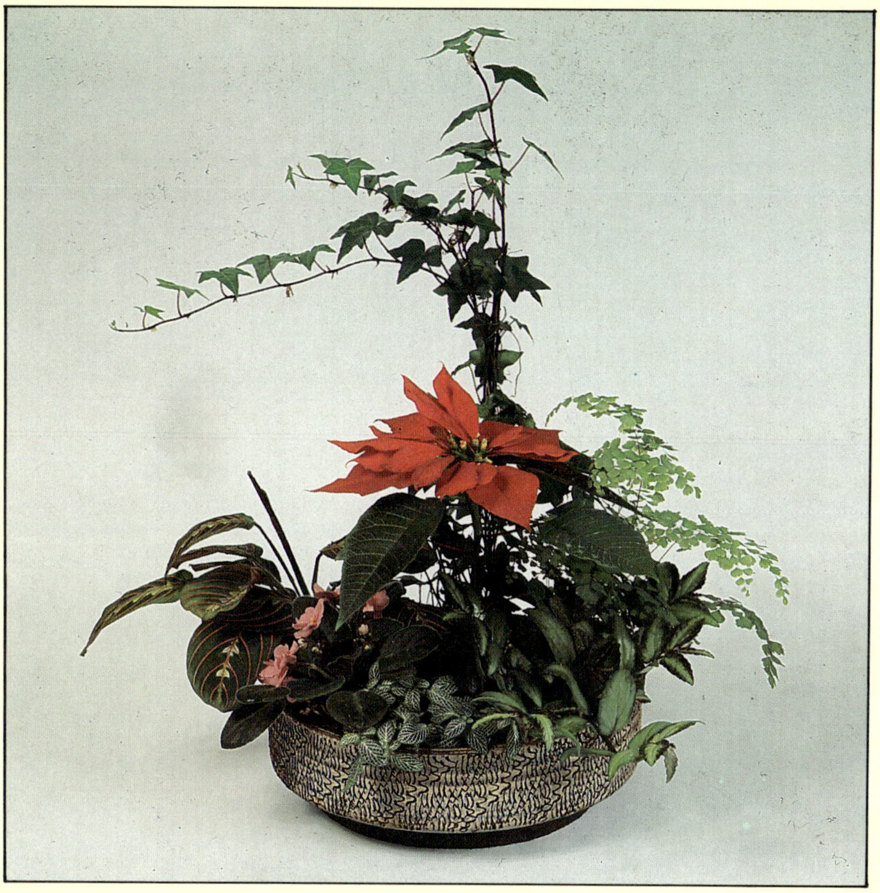

Planning a display takes a bit of theory and a lot of good ideas, plus the plants and containers to make the arrangement work.

Temporary displays are the easiest to stage manage as plants can be left to fend for themselves for a few days without the need to make too much provision for watering or replacing plants as they outgrow their space.

But permanent displays are a different story. With these, you have to make allowances for upkeep and maintenance as well. One useful tip here is to fill your container with peat and plunge your plants into it, pot and all. This way it's very easy to lift out a flowering plant when it is over, and switch it for another. Anything that grows too big or gets untidy can be treated in the same way. Plunging your plants, ready-potted, into peat is also a good idea because it keeps the air round them moist and makes it very easy to keep them correctly watered by simply keeping the peat damp. You can even feed the whole display in one go by pushing a few fertiliser spikes into the peat.

And, for the final finishing touch, you could plant Mind Your Own Business, a creeping mossy looking plant, directly into the peat. It does for formal displays what moss does for hanging baskets — dotting the i's and crossing the t's. Or choose some other low growing, spreading plants to cover the soil such as the Fittonia and the trailing Pellionia which have been used in the arrangement above.

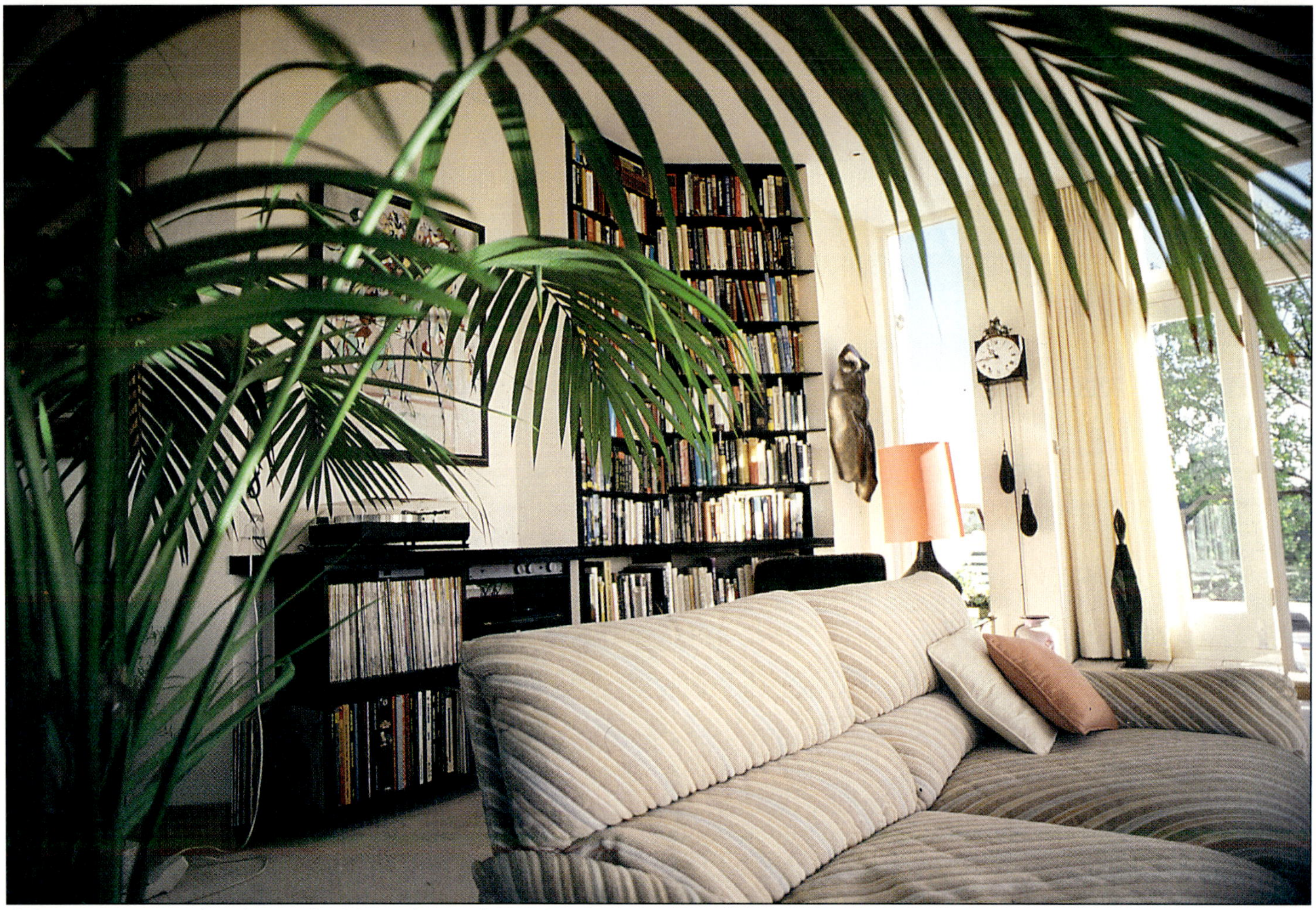

A large room needs a large plant to make any impact.

Displaying plants in a large room

Have you noticed how you can hardly pass a hotel lobby, office reception area or foyer that isn't inundated with masses of plants? They've become part of the essential decorations — just like wall-to-wall carpet and pictures on the walls — and they're not there just to make the place look nice. Part of their intention is to create a relaxed atmosphere, so that people feel welcome, comfortable, and want to come back again — very much the same sort of feelings that you want to create in your own home. The plants you choose can be as important, or otherwise, as you like to the decor, depending on how many you use.

Plants can provide the finishing touches in a room to set off your other decorations, or they can be your main decorative theme, around which everything else revolves. You can even create a major display, using plants along with other 'props', as a dramatic centrepiece to a room.

However 'green' you want to go, there is one basic principle underlying the use of plants to decorate any large room — and that is scale. In other words, the plants *must* be appropriate for the size of room they're in, or they'll just get 'lost'. So it's no good trying to use lots of small plants dotted indiscriminately around the room. Large rooms call for grand features — be they plants or anything else — that create an immediate impact on entering the room.

Specimen plants

Large single specimen plants, or groups of three or five identical plants (for some

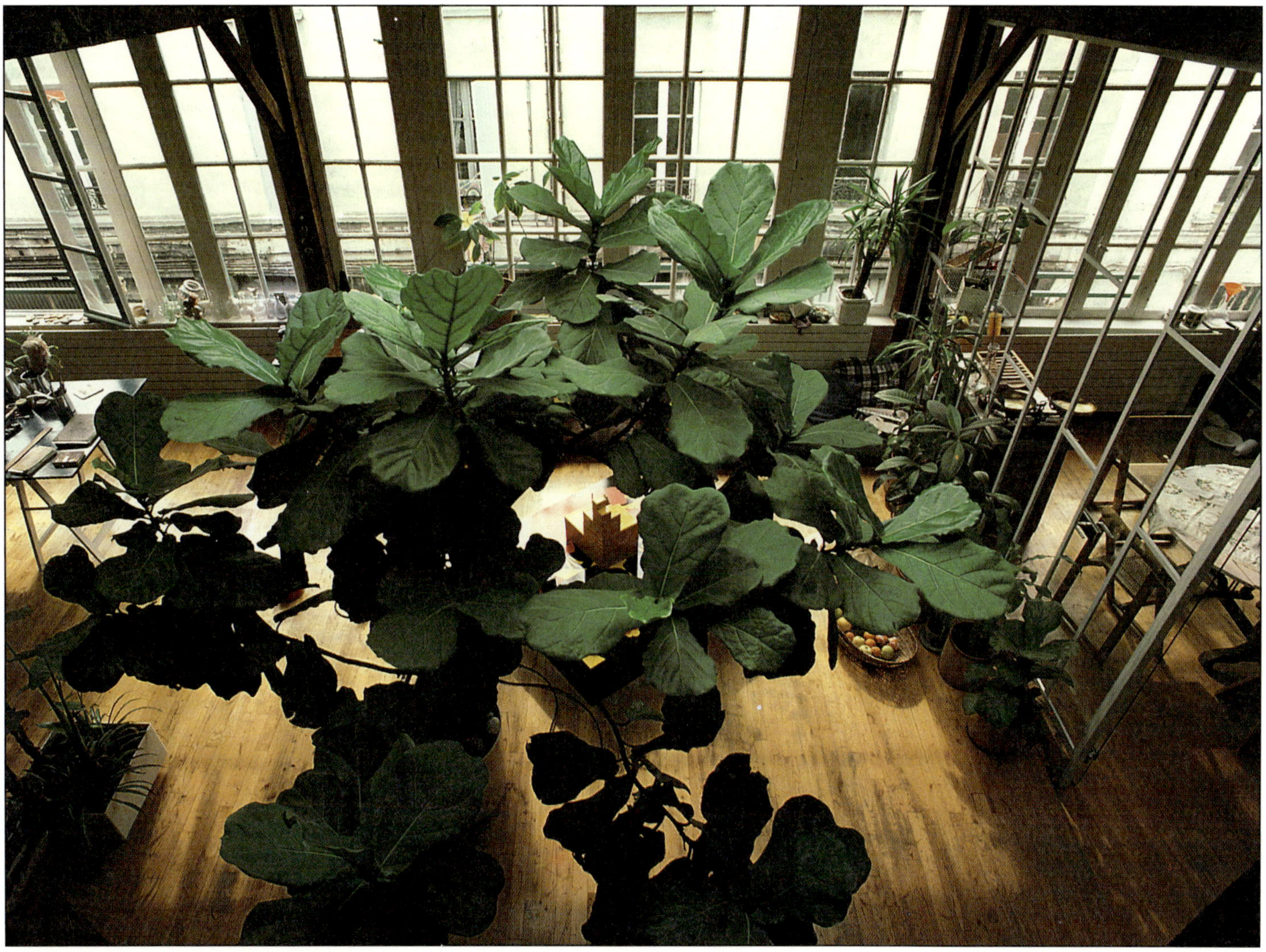

If you have the room, a Fiddle-leaf Fig is a fine choice for an indoor tree.

Single specimens

Cast Iron Plant (Aspidistra)
Boston Fern *(Nephrolepis exaltata bostonienis)*, grown on a pedestal
Large cacti, such as Opuntia
Castor Oil Plant *(Ricinus communis)*
Coconut, Date and **Parlour Palms**
Fiddle-leaf Fig *(Ficus lyrata)*
Norfolk Island Pine (Araucia excelsa)
Large-leaved Philodendrons, such as Tree Philodendron *(P. bipinnatifidum) P.* 'Red Emerald' and *P.* 'Burgundy'
Large succulents, such as Agave
Swiss Cheese Plant *(Monstera deliciosa)*
Weeping fig *(Ficus benjamina)*

reason any group of plants always seems to look best if it is made up of an odd number), are extremely effective as long as you choose plants with suitably dramatic qualities. So go for plants with architectural shapes, or large, striking leaves such as those suggested.

Foliage plants are more suitable than flowering plants for use as specimens because they provide a year-round display. And if you opt for a group, create a feeling of unity by standing all the pots in a large basket or other container that harmonises well with the plants.

Plant groups

Arrange a combination of both foliage and flowering plants, grouped together in rather the same way as you would do a flower arrangement. Use the foliage plants to create the basic shape of the arrangement, and use the flowers as highlights.

Be sure to choose plants that harmonise well together. If you are buying new plants specially for your arrangement, it's a good idea to try out several different combinations together in the shop before you buy.

If inspiration fails you, try the following rule of thumb guide, which works well using a variety of plants.

Aim to include:

- A large, upright, plain green plant with small leaves as a background, such as Grape Ivy, Heptapleurum, curly-leaved Ivy, or Weeping Fig.
- A flattish, spreading plant, such as African Violet, Creeping Moss (Selaginella), Episcia, variegated Ivy, *Maranta tricolor*, and Mind Your Own Business (Helxine).
- One or three quite differently shaped plants, such as Cape Primrose (Streptocarpus), Euonymus, Goose Foot Plant (Syngonium), Maidenhair Fern (Adiantum), Scindapsus, and *Philodendron scandens.*
- Then, to pull the whole arrangement together, place them all in the same container, perhaps standing the

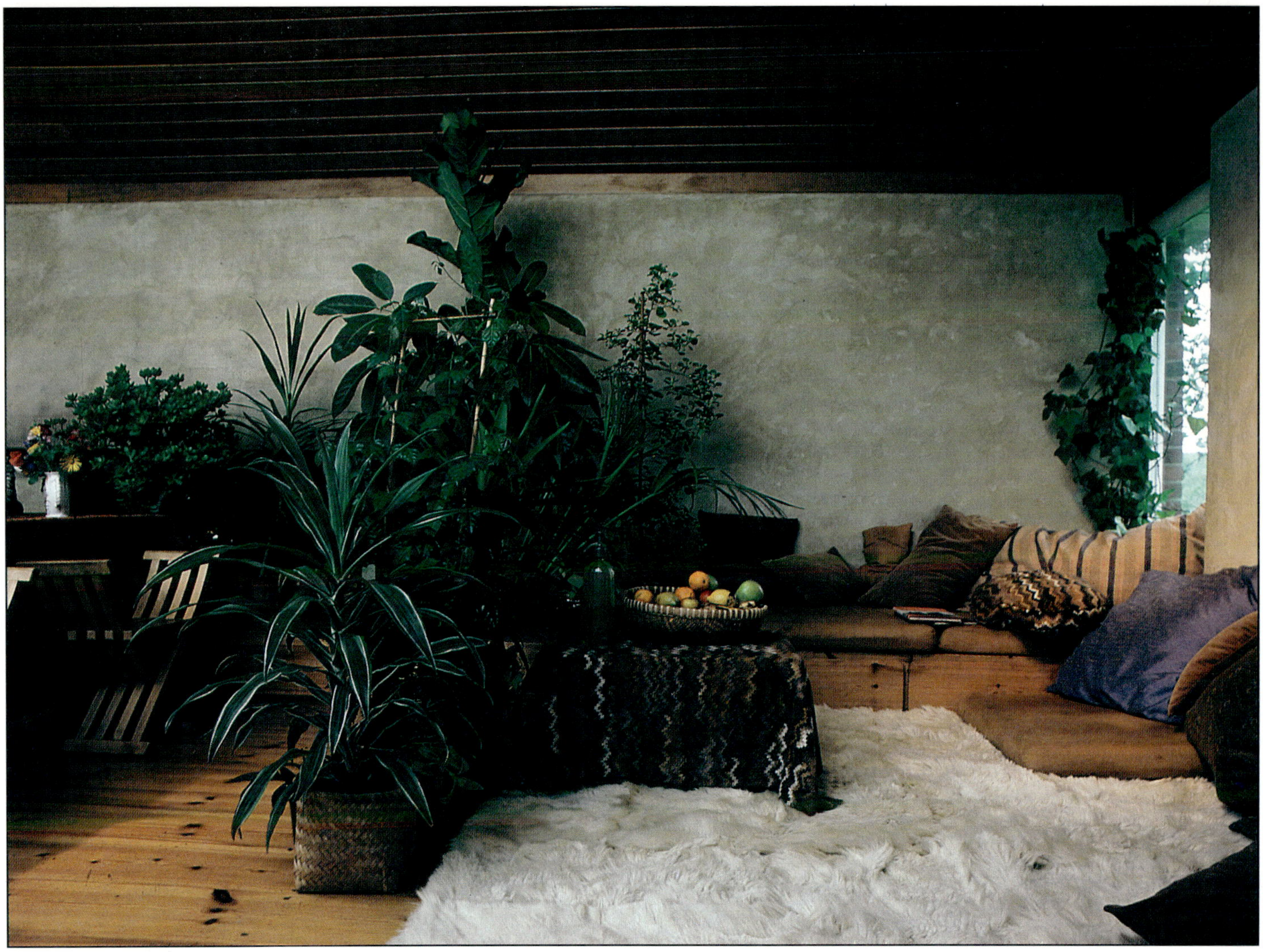

Here, a group of upright plants acts as a screen to divide up a large area.

individual pots in peat or on dampened gravel in order to maintain a humid environment. Stand the container on the floor if the plants are tall, or raise it up slightly if it needs extra height.

A focal point

Taking the group theme one step further, what about using plants along with other 'props' to make a special feature that will provide your room with a focal point? This is particularly useful in a room that doesn't have a fireplace, which is often a natural focal point. It is also a very helpful way of filling a large empty space in a big room that is somewhat short of furniture — as is so often the case if you've recently moved from a smaller house. Here are a few suggestions for special plant features.

Plant cases. Glass cases make a special feature of a collection of tropical plants. Incorporate chunks of driftwood draped with Spanish Moss (*Tillandsia usneoides*) and interplanted with creeping Helxine or perhaps strewn with pebbles to link the different plants together.

Cases like this are an ideal way of growing tropical plants, as the conditions inside can be tailor-made to suit the choosiest of plants. They can be heated independently of the rest of the room, using soil-warming cables; and lit artificially, using special plant lights which allow you to grow plants that natural light would never permit.

The extra humidity that tropical plants need is easy to maintain behind glass. Plant cases like this are sometimes built to quite large dimensions in the USA, and may even take over one wall of a room. On a less ambitious scale, a case can be purpose-built into an alcove, or simply a large fish tank.

Plants for grouping

Angel's Wing (Caladium)
Anthurium
Croton (Codiaeum)
Dracaena
Eucalyptus
Goose Foot Plant (Syngonium), trained up a moss pole
Grape Ivy (*Cissus rhombifolia*), trained up a fan-shaped framework of canes
Parasol Plant (Heptapleurum)
Umbrella Plant (Cyperus)
Umbrella Tree (Schefflera)
Yucca

Air plant trees. These make fascinating features, for which you'll need a well shaped, stripped or bleached and washed twiggy branch to act as your framework. You can either find one of these yourself, or obtain a ready-prepared one from a specialist air plant nursery.

To keep the branch upright, mount it on to a flat board, which can be disguised by standing a chunk of driftwood on it or by covering it with moss, pebbles or bark chippings. Then position a collection of air plants artistically among the branches.

As they don't have roots, they are easily positioned simply by sitting them in place. Group two or three plants of the same variety together rather than dotting several individual ones around the branch.

Plant plaques. Another slightly out-of-the-ordinary feature is to make a wall plaque. Choose a large piece of rough bark and wire a group of three or five Staghorn Ferns (Platycerium) into the centre. Water them by spraying daily.

Still life. This is a more traditional idea. Here a group of plants are turned into something just that bit special by the addition of appropriately sized ornaments — figurines, statues, abstract pieces, or maybe even a lamp. This works very well on a table top or sideboard or, using large plants and ornaments, on the floor in a corner of a room.

Lighting

This can make all the difference to the way plants look in a large room. Use ordinary domestic spotlights to pick out plants from their background, and try playing light from different directions on to your plants to see the difference it makes.

To bring out their colours, light plants from slightly in front — either from above or at ground level. Side lighting can also sometimes give interesting results. Or, for a more artistic effect, choose special uplighters or downlighters which dramatically highlight the shape of architectural leaves and stems — ideal for illuminating your specimen plants.

And, if you want to make a plant feature when natural light would seem to prevent it, just substitute special plant light bulbs in conventional spotlight fittings. Plants need lighting for 12 hours a day and you can plug these lights into an automatic timer, just to be absolutely certain.

Backgrounds

As with any plants, the choice of background is important. And in a large room, working with large plants, you can achieve very dramatic results if you are prepared to experiment a little.

Instead of always going for a 'safe' background, why not strike out and contrast a dramatic specimen plant in an alcove against a brilliant red backdrop? Try using a large mirror to exaggerate the foliar feel in a group of plants. Or create a screen of foliage using deep green plants as the background for a striking display of flowering plants such as Hibiscus and Anthurium, or for a collection of strongly marked, decorative foliage plants such as Caladium and Calathea.

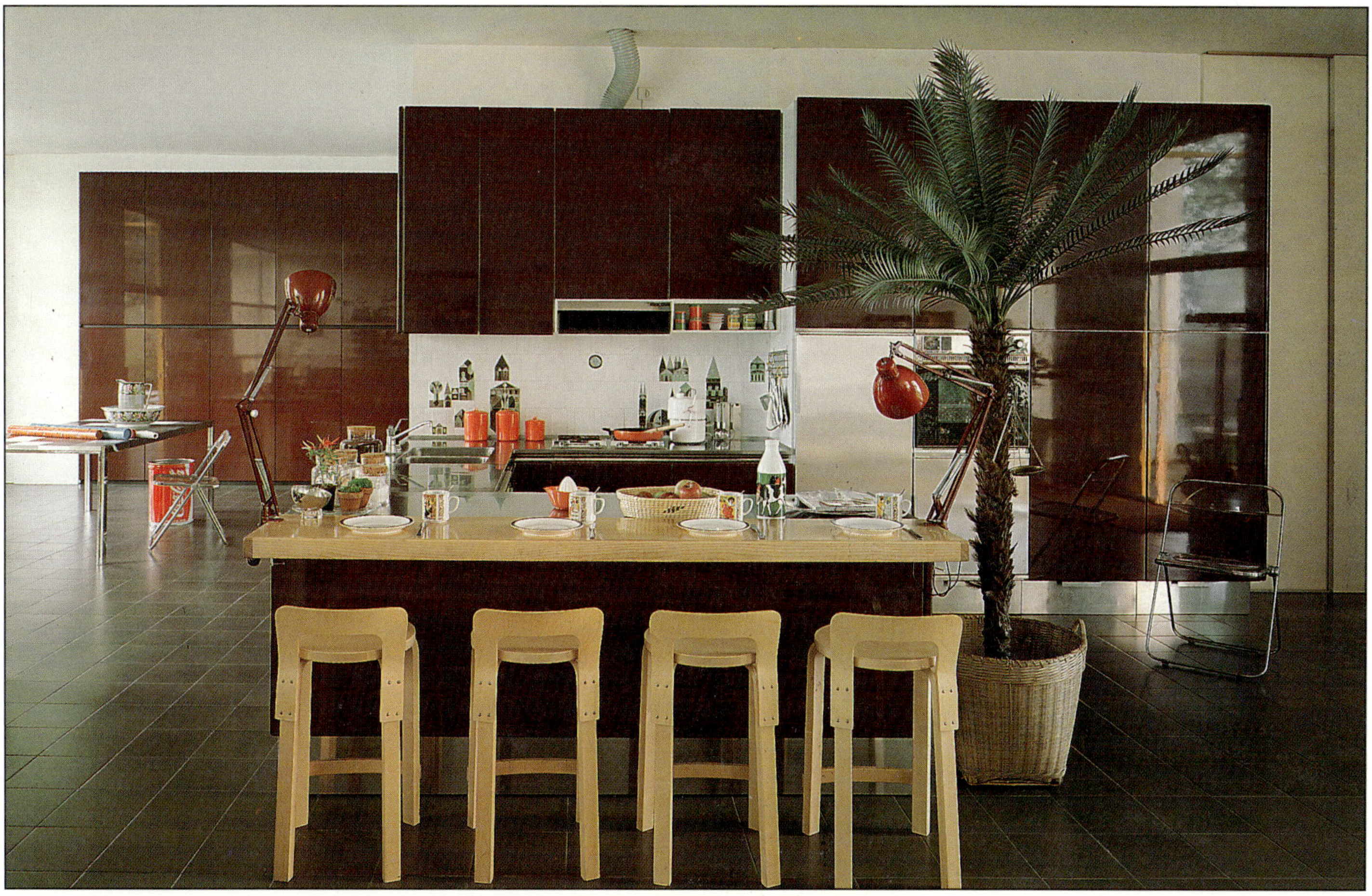

For a dramatic specimen plant a palm is hard to beat.

Small is beautiful

Small rooms may be the natural outcome of having a small home, or they may be secondary rooms in a bigger house — a study or a breakfast room, for example. But just because a room is small doesn't mean it can't be special. You can often create a warm, friendly atmosphere in a small room more easily than in a large one — and the right plants can play an important part. Small areas call for a different approach to plants: you'll want to create points of interest — little 'cameos' — instead of filling up space. A bit of thought and planning will enable you to lift a small room right out of the ordinary.

When space is short, there isn't room to display plants in the same way as you would to make an effect in a bigger room — in groups, for example. There may well only be room for a single plant in any given space, so make the most of a limited resource. But even if you have several places suitable for plants in a small room, you shouldn't necessarily fill them all — if you overdo it, you might end up with a room that looks like a Victorian parlour, so cluttered that it's impossible to see anything properly.

The best rule is to choose plants that have something special to offer in themselves — they may be unusual or exceptionally interesting to look at, or a rare variety, which will excite comment and admiration. But a pleasing effect doesn't depend only on the plants, it also derives from how they're arranged and what containers they're in. If you create fascinating little cameos in unexpected places, visitors will always want to take a second look.

Creating a style

Because you have less space to work in, it's specially important to go for a coherent style in a small room — when decorations and furniture co-ordinate it, it can have the effect of making the room look more spacious. Usually, your style will, to some extent, be determined by the type of home you have: traditional or modern, old or new. Your plants should reflect the style of decor you have chosen in terms of furniture, fittings and soft furnishings.

Some plants do more for particular styles of decoration than others.

- In modern rooms, Bromeliads — such as 'air plants' (Tillandsia) and Cryptanthus — cacti, succulents and any spiky leaved plant can look stunning.

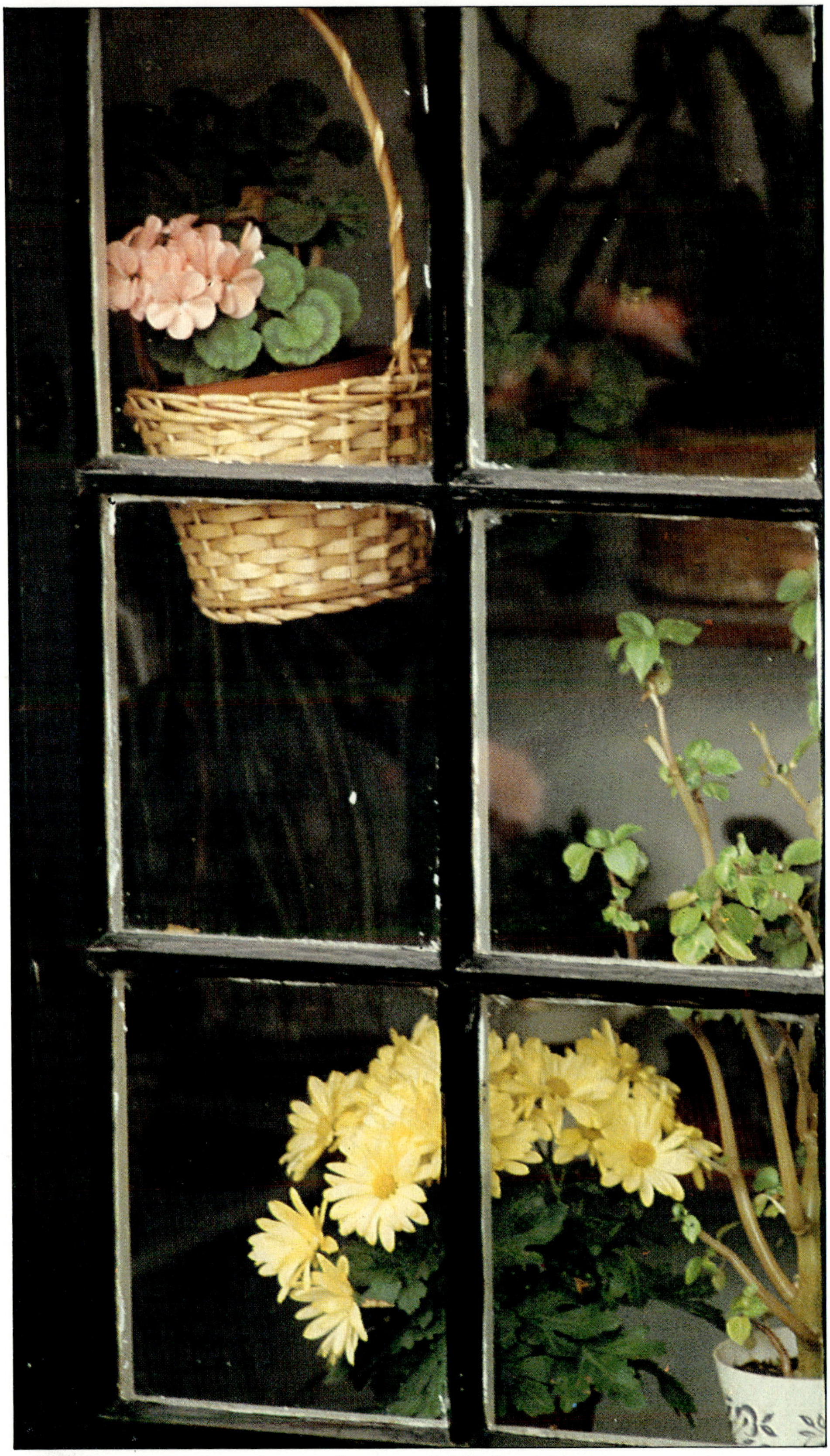

Place your plants where they won't encroach into the room space.

Shapes and styles

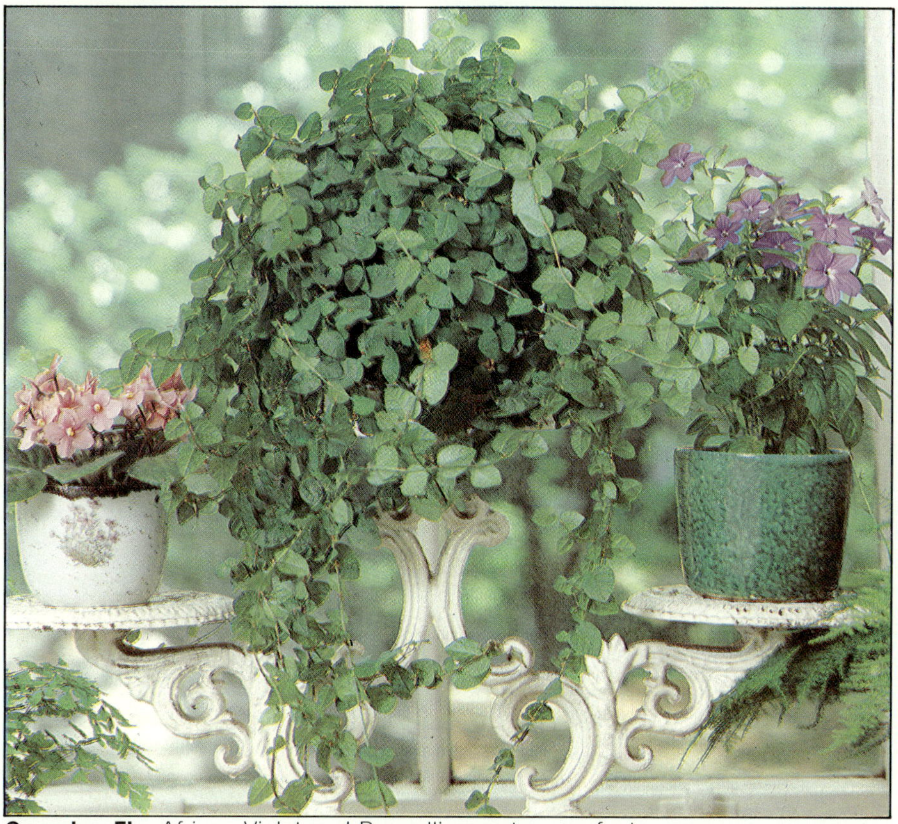

Creeping Fig, African Violet and Browallia create a perfect cameo.

ROSETTE SHAPES

African Violets (Saintpaulia)
New double-flowered varieties, and those with variegated leaves, are eye-catching
Air Plants (Tillandsia)
Epiphytic Bromeliads with arching leaves
Earth Star (Cryptanthus)
Low-growing, spiky plants with variegated leaves

Episcia hybrids
Oval, puckered leaves with silver, white and pink variations
Fittonia argyroneura
Vivid green oval leaves with silvery veins
Fittonia verschaffeltii
Long, dark green leaves with pink veins
Variegated Aspidistra
Tall, upright green leaves with white or cream stripes

ROUND SHAPES

Friendship Plant *(Pilea involucrata)*
Fleshy, quilted, almost circular leaves, dark green with purple undersides
Peperomia caperata
Slow-growing and compact, with green leaves marked with darker green
Watermelon Peperomia *(Peperomia argyreia)*
Similar to *P.caperata* with leaves striped with white

ORNAMENTAL LEAVES

Begonia boweri
Emerald green leaves with black edging
Begonia rex
Heart-shaped leaves with stunning red, pink and green variegations

FERNS

Button Fern *(Pellaea rotundifolia)*
Tall, arching fronds with tiny, dark green leaves
Sensitive Plant *(Mimosa pudica)*
Feathery dark green leaves which close up temporarily when touched

GRASSES

Acorus gramineus variegatus
Dense clump of slender, white-striped leaves
Japanese Sedge (*Carex morrowii variegata)*
Clusters of tall, slender yellowish-green leaves
Miniature Bulrush *(Scirpus cernuus)*
Graceful, thread-like bright green trailer

MOSSY PLANTS

Artillery Plant *(Pilea microphylla)*
Fine green leaves in feathery sprays
Mind Your Own Business *(Helxine soleirolii)*
Low-growing with masses of tiny leaves
Selaginella martensii
Glistening, fleshy green leaves on low, arching stems

TRAILERS AND CREEPERS

Bead Plant *(Nertera depressa)*
Matted stems with green leaves and shiny, bright orange berries
Creeping Fig *(Ficus pumila)*
Heart-shaped, small, thin green leaves
Miniature Ivies
Pointed leaves with white, cream and golden variations

CACTI AND SUCCULENTS

Astrophytums
Globe-shaped, deeply segmented stems with cup-like flowers
Jatropha podagrica
Swollen brown stems crowned by bright red flowers
Living Stones (Lithops)
Pebble-like plants with stunning flowers
Moonstones *(Pachyphytum oviferum)*
Rosette-like clusters of leaves which are shaped like eggs
Pony Tail Palm *(Beaucarnea recurvata* or ***Nolina recurvata)***
A 'false palm' with shaggy, grey-green leaves
String of Beads Plant *(Senecio rowleyanus)*
Tiny green globules on trailing stems

FLOWERING PLANTS

Achimenes
Heart-shaped, velvety leaves with red, purple, blue or white flowers
Cape Cowslip *(Lachenalia aloides)*
Pale yellow, bell-like winter flowers
Exacum
Lavender flowers with golden centres; treat as an annual
French Marigold *(Tagetes patula)*
Annual with red, orange or yellow flowers
Lily of the Valley *(Convallaria majalis)*
Annual with dainty white and very fragrant flowers
Miniature Cyclamen
Variegated leaves and white or pink flowers; treat as an annual
Miniature Pelargonium
Striking flowers in a range of colours and sometimes scented leaves
Petunias
Annuals available in a wide range of colours, single and double blooms, some with frilly petals

With their assertive, dramatic shapes they really function like living sculptures, and are favourites of interior designers for just this reason.

- For colourful, chintzy rooms you could choose country cottage favourites — such as miniature Pelargoniums, Achimenes, Lily of the Valley, Helxine, Pilea and miniature ivies. Go for colours that will enhance your existing colour scheme.
- Traditional rooms, reminiscent of the Victorian style, would favour African Violets, Peperomias, miniature Cyclamen, Begonias and ferns.

These are only rough guidelines, of course — a good many plants will fit in with any style, and you can always aim for the unexpected.

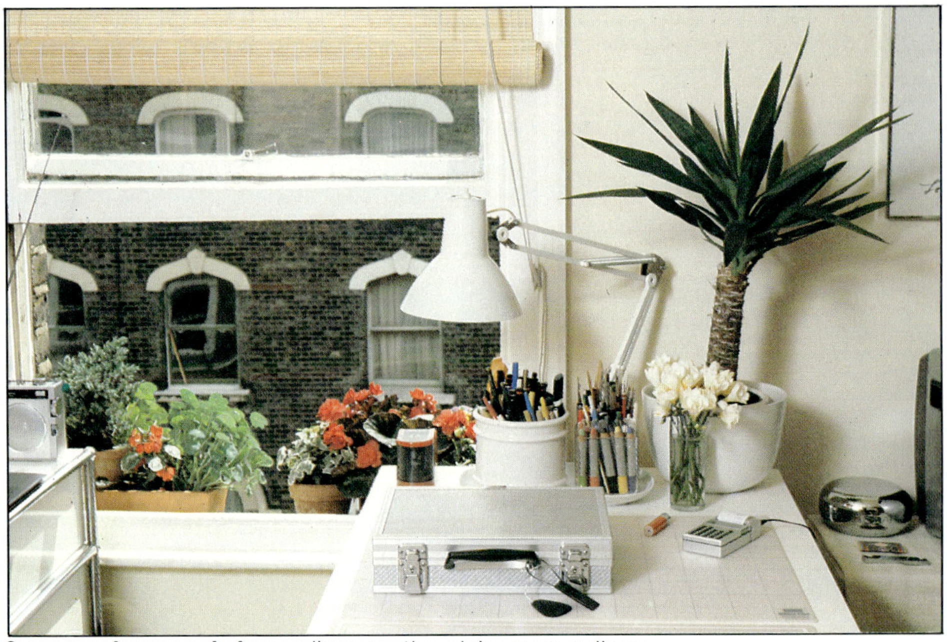

Strong colours and shapes liven up the plain surroundings.

Matching plant to place

In small rooms particularly, it pays to avoid the obvious. A solitary plant in the middle of a windowsill or coffee table entirely lacks the element of surprise. If you think of plants as ornaments, it should help you to find the most interesting places for them. Tuck them away in little nooks and crannies — a gap in a bookshelf, a corner of a hearth, hanging down from a beam or among a group of ornaments. In a bathroom, plants can trail down from the edge of a bath or from a shelf.

Of course, it goes without saying that plants should only be put in positions where they'll thrive and be happy. If available light is low, go for ferns or the mossy Selaginella, which will be happy almost anywhere out of direct sunlight. Other plants will need good indirect light most of the time, while some — such as cacti and Pelargoniums — need sun at least some of the time.

Remember, you can get away with keeping plants in poorly lit places if you only leave them there for a short time, and you can also grow plants under special plant lights. Flowering annuals will always brighten up a dull place, and they'll die after flowering in any case.

Plant containers

If you're aiming for a striking effect, containers are a good place to start. Try to avoid conventional ones, and choose objects that are not usually associated with plants — copper kettles, brass scuttles, ice buckets or old stone jars. The mellow golden colour of brass makes a very good contrast with predominantly green plants, such as ferns.

By using pots and jars that aren't designed for plants you can often create an individual style without great expense — these items can often be picked up quite cheaply in junk shops because no one can think of a practical use for them! Even quite mundane objects can be transformed with a carefully chosen plant — a goldfish bowl, for example, or a modern storage jar.

Small and special

The chart (p.49), listing plants under their major characteristics, will give you some ideas on what to choose. The unusual requirements of small rooms may mean you should go to a specialist garden centre or nursery to get what you want; specialist nurseries also advertise in gardening magazines. And you can always try growing an unusual plant that you fancy from seed.

Plants to look out for include those with interesting shapes or textures, unusual flowers, leaf textures or colourful patterns, or those that particularly suit a space or container that you have in mind.

Any grouping of plants in a small room will probably need to be small itself — miniature gardens, terrariums or bowls of water plants are ideal.

Ringing the changes

One of the biggest problems with a small room is that once you have arranged it, it can be very difficult to change. With bigger rooms you can create a fresh look from time to time by moving the furniture around; in a small room, things probably only work well in one position. So to make a change it is the smaller items that you must rearrange or replace: lamps, cushions, ornaments — and plants.

Don't expect to keep the same plants circulating for ever, or you'll soon get bored. Small plants are the cheapest to buy, so you can afford to replace your stock regularly. Try out new combinations of plant and container, and hoard interesting containers for a possible change of scene. And if you choose a plant that outgrows its welcome, don't leave it to spoil your scheme — move it to a bigger room, or donate it to friends with more baronial premises!

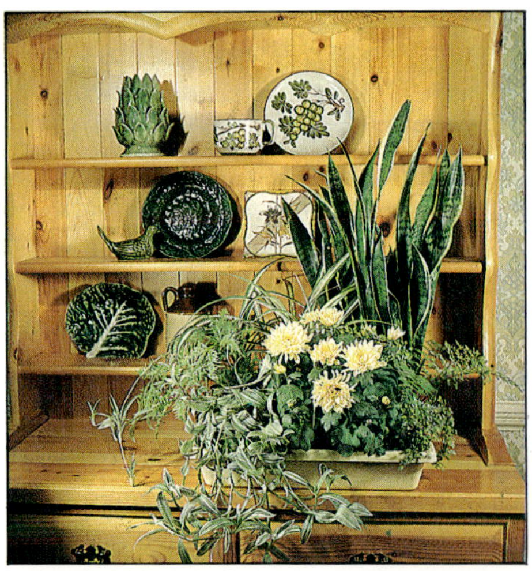

A careful blend of shape and colour.

Lighting-up time

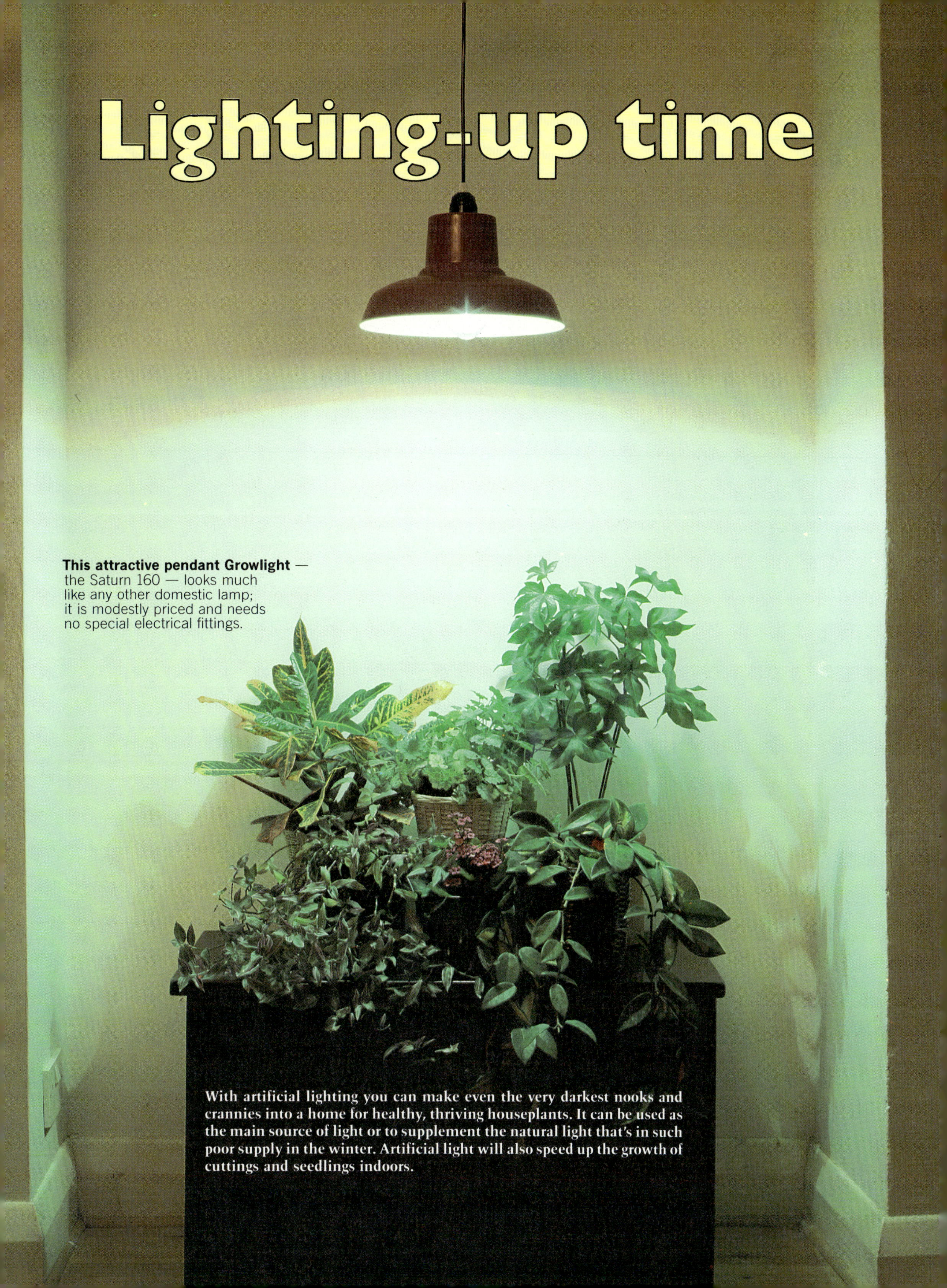

This attractive pendant Growlight — the Saturn 160 — looks much like any other domestic lamp; it is modestly priced and needs no special electrical fittings.

With artificial lighting you can make even the very darkest nooks and crannies into a home for healthy, thriving houseplants. It can be used as the main source of light or to supplement the natural light that's in such poor supply in the winter. Artificial light will also speed up the growth of cuttings and seedlings indoors.

What to choose

What you choose to buy in the way of equipment depends on whether you want simply to supplement natural daylight or to do without it altogether. And that can depend on how much money you're prepared to spend — from just a few pounds to over £100.

Some bulbs will fit conventional bayonet or screw cap light fittings. But the more powerful systems need lamps with special fittings.

LIGHTS FOR CONVENTIONAL FITTINGS

The two types mentioned below are both widely available and fairly cheap to buy. And they're not too bright for the home. Though you can use them with existing light fittings, there are several that are purpose-built fittings with reflectors, which disperse the light more efficiently over a wider area.

These lamps aren't able to light as large an area as the more sophisticated discharge lights in the same wattage (see below). And you'll need to place the plants quite close to the lights, while still taking care that they don't get scorched — the lamps give out quite a lot of heat. Nor can they take the place of natural daylight entirely.

Filtered incandescent lamps are just ordinary filament lamps with an internal coating which filters out the harmful warm red rays. Unfortunately, they also filter out some of the other non-harmful light, at the same time. However, as long as you buy them in a suitable voltage (no more than 100 watt if you want to use them in an ordinary light fitting), they're certainly a relatively cheap and easy way to give plants a boost.

A 75 watt bulb, set 1ft (30cm) above the plant, will light an area up to 2sq ft.

Mercury blended lamps, known as MBTF/R, are one up on the filtered incandescent lamps. They give a better balanced light, with less heat, but they are twice or three times the price of the incandescent lamps, on average.

SPECIAL LIGHTING UNITS

Fluorescent lights (or low-pressure mercury discharge lamps) are hard to beat, and are the best type of artificial lighting for indoor plants. They're efficient, give a good spread and are widely available. They also produce much more useful light and less heat. What's more, the fittings they need are much cheaper than for the other sorts of mercury discharge lamp.

Tubes come in a choice of 'colours', determined by the coating on the inside of the glass. Some let through too little warm red light, but too much of the light at the other end of the spectrum. But there are several suitable 'daylight' fluorescent tubes which are suitable for growing plants, such as 'Warm White', ' Northlite' or 'Cool White', which give a relatively well-balanced combination, although the Warm White can make plants look too red.

It's best to buy tubes on adjustable stands, so that they can be raised or lowered according to the plants you're growing. You can also buy plant containers — display cases, tiers or troughs — that incorporate fluorescent tubes.

As a general rule, it's unwise to use less than two tubes. With one tube, only 25-30 per cent of the light provided is usefully employed; with two, the percentage is increased to 40 per cent.

The tubes come in a choice of lengths, with wattage varying according to the length. In effect, though, they all give out more or less the same amount of light per 12in (30cm).

Two tubes, placed parallel to each other about 4-6in (10-15cm) apart and suspended about 2ft (60cm) above the plants, will suit a single row of foliage plants. By putting in more tubes, you can increase the distance from the plants; four tubes would mean you could hang them up to 4½ft (1.35m) above the plants. Or, alternatively, it could mean increasing the depth of the area you want to light, and including another row, or two, of plants.

Flowering plants, and others that like higher light intensity, need to be nearer the lights — a distance of 6-12in (15-30cm) instead of 1-2ft (0.3-0.6m).

High pressure mercury and metal halide lamps are two other types of mercury discharge bulbs. Both systems are much more expensive to buy, initially, but have cheaper running costs and last longer than other types. Because they aren't so common, you may find it difficult to buy replacement bulbs.

Their great advantage is that they can be used as a sole source of light for plants. Most are really more suitable for large-scale and commercial use, but you can find lower wattage versions, some with reflectors, which are suitable for houseplants in the home.

These mercury discharge lamps produce a bright beam of light, which does tend to be a bit bright in the home. The metal halide types are marginally more efficient and give plants a slightly better colour.

For the ordinary high pressure lamps, choose a 125 watt bulb, with a reflector. For the metal halide, an 80 watt lamp is adequate. Suspend them about 3ft (0.9m) above the plants, and they will light an area with a diameter of about 18in (45cm).

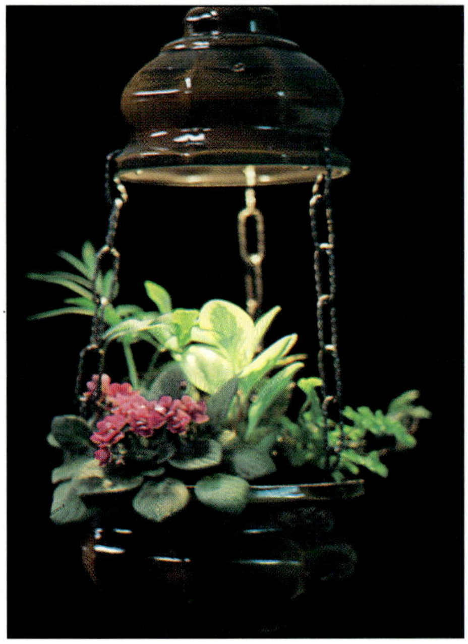

Fittings that combine lamps and plant containers can provide charming displays. These are best used with shallow rooting plants that enjoy additional light in the evenings — African Violet is an ideal candidate. But you'll need to keep an eye on the compost which will tend to dry out rapidly.

A well-placed lamp or spotlight can highlight the colour and shape of an attractive plant — but unless you know what you're about, you could do it harm. With the right equipment, you can give your plants a beneficial boost, and cultivate plants you wouldn't otherwise be able to. An indoor herb garden, to keep you supplied summer and winter alike, is one good idea.

What's in light

To imitate natural daylight and the good effects of sunlight, an artificial light has to produce the right balance of different light rays. Get the balance wrong, and plants will become stunted and deformed or weak and leggy.

Natural daylight is made up of a wide spectrum of coloured rays ranging from violet through indigo, blue, green, yellow, orange to red; mixed together, they come out as 'white' light.

Unfortunately, the easiest and most convenient artificial light source is the ordinary light bulb (known as an incandescent or filament bulb) which won't do. It gives off too many rays from the 'warm' red end of the spectrum and too much heat. If placed too close (it doesn't have to be touching, even), it will scorch the leaves and rupture the plant cells.

Even spot lights, including the newer type which runs on a lower voltage, aren't much help. To do the job, you need special lamps.

Supplementary lighting

There are few spots where absolutely no natural daylight can penetrate, and most people will want artificial lighting to supplement rather than to replace the natural light.

In winter, for instance, plants may only get 8 hours of light. But if you can reproduce the 12 hours of light many of them would find in their natural habitats (the tropics or sub-tropics), they'll go on growing all year round. Remember, though, that they'll need to be kept warm and fed all year as well! And, of course, not all plants can be treated like this — many do need a winter rest.

There are other benefits, too. Artificial lighting can give winter-flowering plants — like orchids — the vital extra hours of light they need to come into flower. And it will also let you grow light-loving plants in the murkier depths of a room.

Flowering plants usually need about 13-14 hours of light daily, foliage plants 9-10 hours. To calculate how much extra light to give each plant, take away the number of good daylight hours it actually receives from the total amount it should receive. Use this as a starting point, and make any adjustments as the plant requires.

Artificial light only

If you've got a dim, dark hall, which is otherwise inhospitable, a small lighting system — a bowl full of plants lit with a single light — can bring it to life.

In theory, you can grow absolutely any plant under artificial lighting — there need be no difference in the quality of the light needed. But you would have to give them just as long an exposure, and just as good a light, as they would experience normally. So plants requiring long hours of bright, direct sunlight might be an impractical proposition as you'd have to be prepared to spend an awful lot of money on the necessary lighting equipment. Cacti and other succulents, Joseph's Coat (Crotons), Zebra Plants (Aphelandra), Cyclamens, Busy Lizzies (Impatiens) and Azaleas, for instance, would be out.

But there are plenty of less demanding plants to choose from — Marantas, Calatheas, Philodendrons, some bromeliads (Cryptanthus and Vriesea), African Violets (Saintpaulias), Creeping Figs (Ficus pumila), members of the palm family and ferns. The green of the ferns looks particularly good, and their feathery fronds throw interesting patterns of light and shade.

Creating a fluorescent growing unit

A fluorescent light fitting may well look out of place suspended from the ceiling in some rooms. But tubes can be tucked neatly and almost invisibly beneath a shelf, especially if you fix a lip along the edge of the shelf. A white shiny surface, or some aluminium foil, can make a good reflecting surface, increasing light levels by 10 per cent.

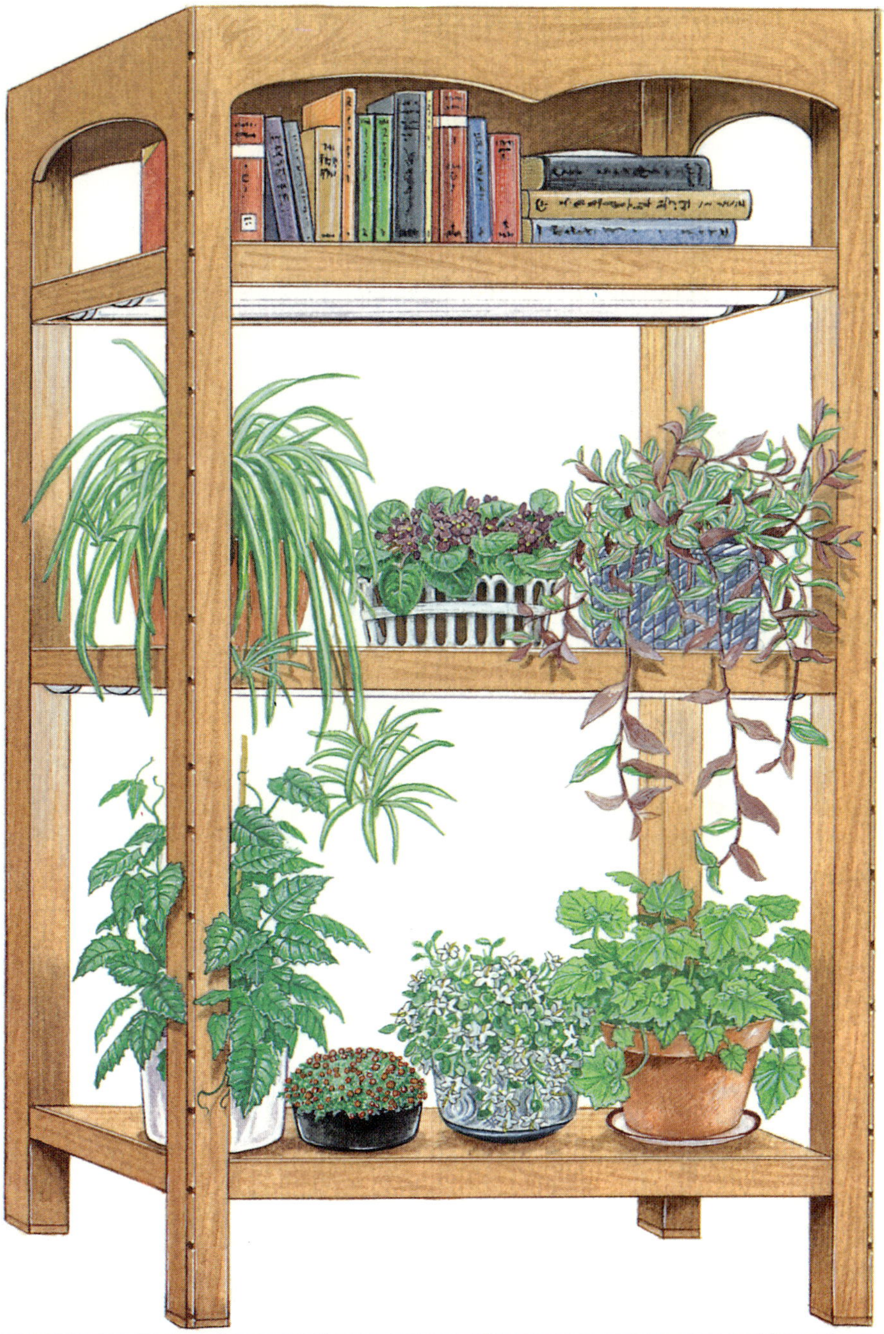

Time clocks

Timing devices will relieve you of the chore of switching the lights on and off again each day — and time clocks don't forget, either. To use them, your light will have to be wired to a plug rather than to the lighting circuit.

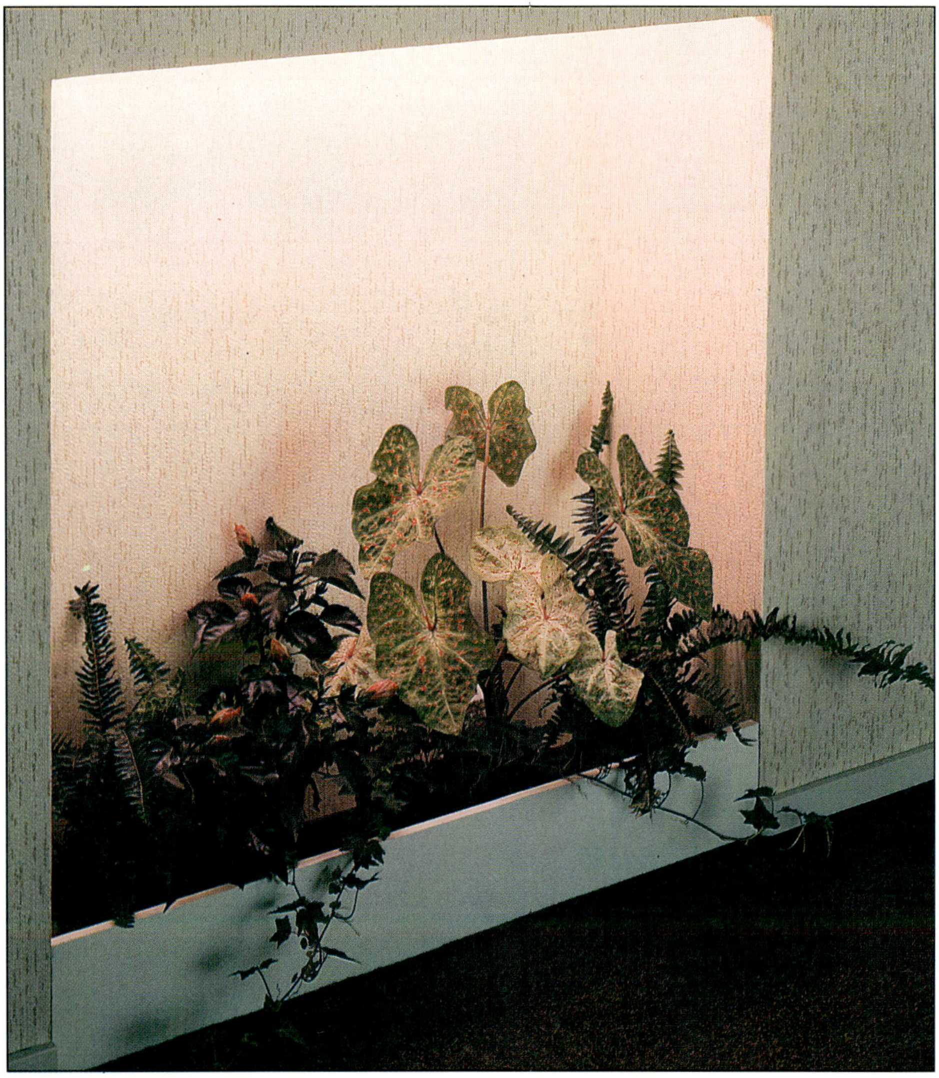

A lighted display of Ivy, Hibiscus, Caladium and Fern in a disused fireplace provides a good focal point for a room.

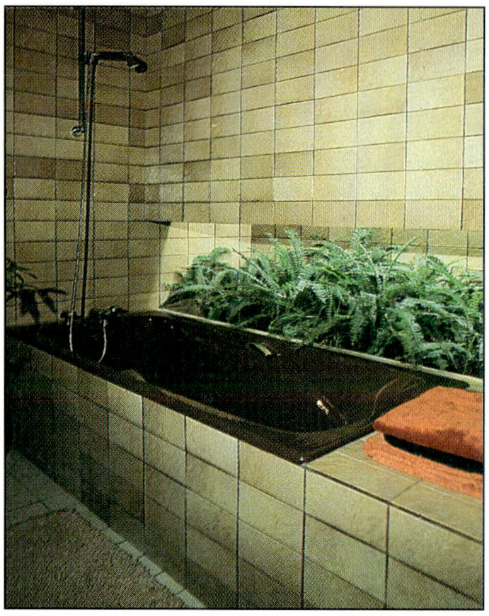

While many plants thrive in the humid conditions of a bathroom, if you want them to be illuminated you should have the lighting installed by a qualified electrician — and be sure to position the light switch outside the bathroom.

They are particularly handy for the flowering plants that will bloom only in response to a certain number of hours of alternate light and darkness (see individual plant guides for details). Poinsettias are a case in point, and show you just how sensitive a plant can be to barely discernible changes of light. Poinsettias are 'short day responsive' plants, which means they aren't 'triggered' to flower until the days are short enough. If a plant doesn't get just the right amount of light — and no more — it won't produce its wonderful bracts in time for Christmas.

Reflectors

Many of the lights and fittings mentioned come complete with 'reflectors' which direct the light more efficiently. Some bulbs have part of their inside surface silvered, others have silvered shades to do the job.

A herb garden

You can have fresh herbs throughout the year — where you want them, and whenever you want them.

Mount a parallel pair of 2ft (60cm), 40 watt fluorescent tubes (Warm White or Cool White) — under a kitchen cupboard which has first been painted white to give extra reflection. Position the lighting tubes not more than 2ft (60cm) above the pots, and if you can organise a reflector, as well, above the tubes you will be making even more effective use of the light.

For the best results, you should aim to give plants between 14 and 16 hours of artificial light a day, but if you have a bright sunny kitchen, you can cut this down to just six or eight hours in summer, switching lights on in the late afternoon, when natural light is beginning to fade.

Monitoring your plants

If you notice that the plants are not doing very well, try adjusting their distance from the light. If they aren't close enough to the light, plants will be tall and spindly, new leaves will be smaller and mature leaves will turn yellow or fall. And variegated plants will produce all-green leaves.

Plants can become distressed if placed too close; foliage becomes scorched, growth is stunted and leaf colour fades.

Don't be in a hurry to blame the lighting for all ills, however. Do check that humidity, watering and other factors are all in order.

What to consider

Whatever system you choose, artificial lighting is going to cost money. You will have to estimate the costs not only of the equipment, the fittings and any timing devices, but also the cost of the electricity they use. You may also need to get a qualified electrician to fix it up for you, unless you're more than a layman.

Don't forget that there'll be a lot of water usage in this environment — in the form of condensation, as well as in mist sprayers, etc — and water and electricity don't mix! So take care when fitting any lights and always follow the manufacturer's instructions. And take their advice, too, on positioning your plants to best advantage.

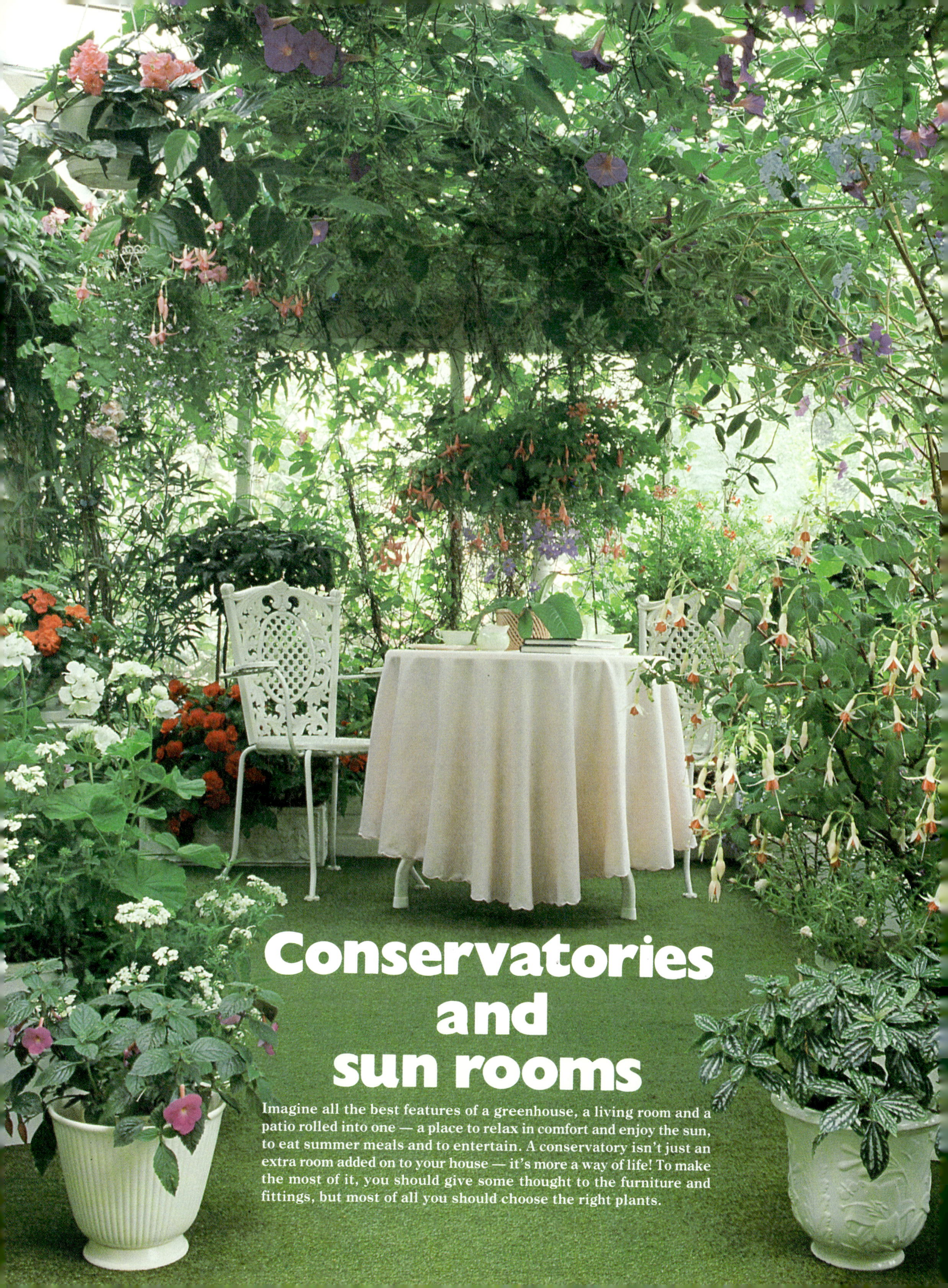

Conservatories and sun rooms

Imagine all the best features of a greenhouse, a living room and a patio rolled into one — a place to relax in comfort and enjoy the sun, to eat summer meals and to entertain. A conservatory isn't just an extra room added on to your house — it's more a way of life! To make the most of it, you should give some thought to the furniture and fittings, but most of all you should choose the right plants.

When it comes to conservatories or sun rooms, don't just settle for more of the same kinds of plants you already have on your windowsills or tables — go for those that are tailor-made for conservatory life. These are the large, flamboyant or fast-growing plants, too big for the greenhouse, and too sun-loving for indoors. They include small trees and shrubs, climbers and wall plants, bulbs — and even water plants! The choice is yours.

Planning for effect

When you're enthusiastic about plants, it can be all too easy to buy anything that takes your fancy, and end up with a miscellaneous collection that has no real coherence or style. This may not matter much with occasional plants in a sitting room, but your conservatory should be the one room where the plants come first, and other things, such as furniture and ornaments, are designed around them.

Be firm from the start: decide what you want and reject anything that

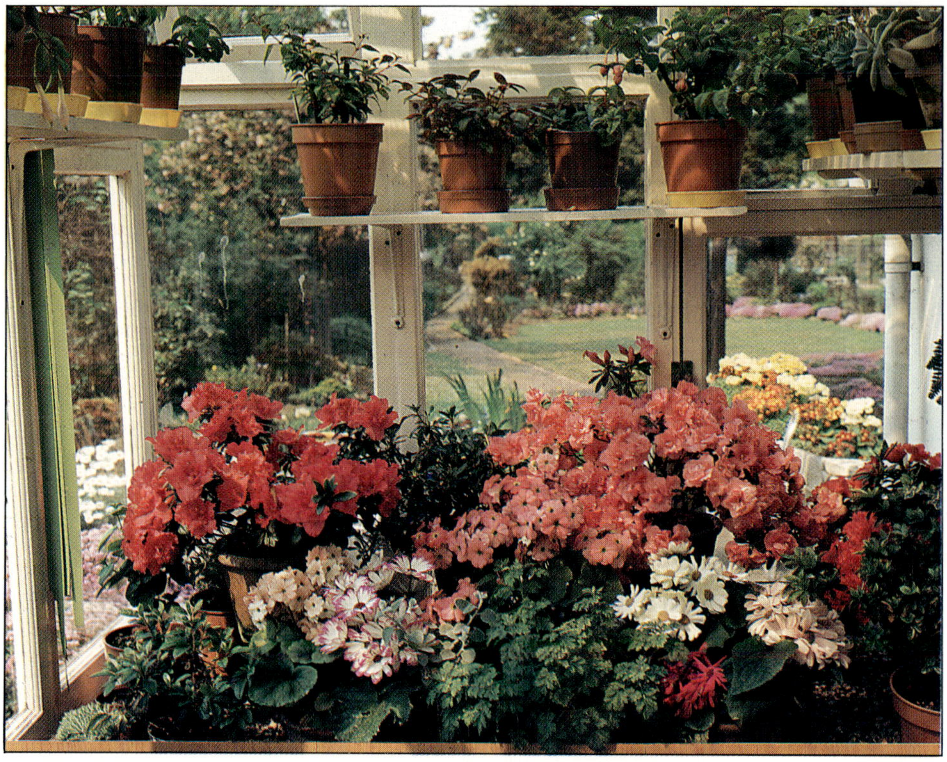

A garden view is framed by Primulas, Cinerarias and Azaleas.

Plants for

CONSERVATORIES HEATED TO 40-45°F (5-7°C)

Abutilon
Trees or shrubs with large orange or red bell-shaped flowers often carried right through the winter.

Acacia *(Acacia mimosaceae)*
Small evergreen tree or shrub with yellow flowers. Try also *A.baileyana purpurea* with purple foliage and *A.dunnii* with silvery blue leaves.

Arum Lily *(Zantedeschia aethiopica)*
Bulb with white flowers in early spring.

Banana (Musa)
Fast-growing tree and a real conversation piece. Try the dwarf *Musa velutina* if you want to have fruit, although it will not be edible.

Bougainvillea
Climber available in various colours, including the well-known purple.

Camellia
Flowering shrub. Grow greenhouse *C.reticulata* varieties for their beautiful blooms.

Castor Oil Plant *(Ricinus communis)*
Shrub with large, palm-shaped leaves. 'Gibsonii' and 'Impala' have red or bronze foliage and may also produce spiky red fruit.

Citrus
Orange, lemon, kumquat and lime all have glossy leaves, fragrant flowers and should produce ripe, full-sized fruit in a heated conservatory.

Clivia
Bulb with large clusters of orange flowers on thick stems.

Cordyline *(Dracaena)*
Small shrub that will grow to an imposing height in a conservatory.

Eucalyptus
Try the unusual, lemon-scented *Eucalyptus citriodora* or, for flowers, the dwarfs *E.forrestiana* and *E.ficifolia.*

Floating Water Hyacinth *(Eichhornia crassipes)*
Aquatic plant with orchid-like flowers.

Ginger Lily (Hedychium)
Tassel-like flowers produced at the ends of tall canes.

Glory Lily (Gloriosa)
Bulb with large red or yellow flowers on long, climbing stems.

House Lime *(Sparmannia africana)*
An unusual shrub with enormous, heart-shaped, lime green leaves.

Lobster Claw *(Clianthus puniceus)*
Climber with large flowers, red or turquoise, shaped like claws.

Oleander *(Nerium oleander)*
Sweet-scented flowering shrub; grow from seed or cuttings.

Passion Flower (Passiflora)
Vigorous climbing plants producing exotic flowers as well as fruit. *P.edulis* and *P.quadrangularis* are the most reliable for fruit; *P.coccinea* has brilliant red flowers.

Plumbago
Unusual climber with striking, blue flowers; easily grown from seed.

Sago Palm (Cycas)
Victorian favourite with unusual fronds growing from a short stump.

Stephanotis
Sweetly scented, slow-growing plant; raise from seeds or cuttings.

Trumpet Flower (Datura)
Exotic, trumpet-shaped flowers in white, purple, yellow or pink.

Water Lily (Nymphaea)
Aquatic plants with large, beautiful flowers. Try the tropical varieties.

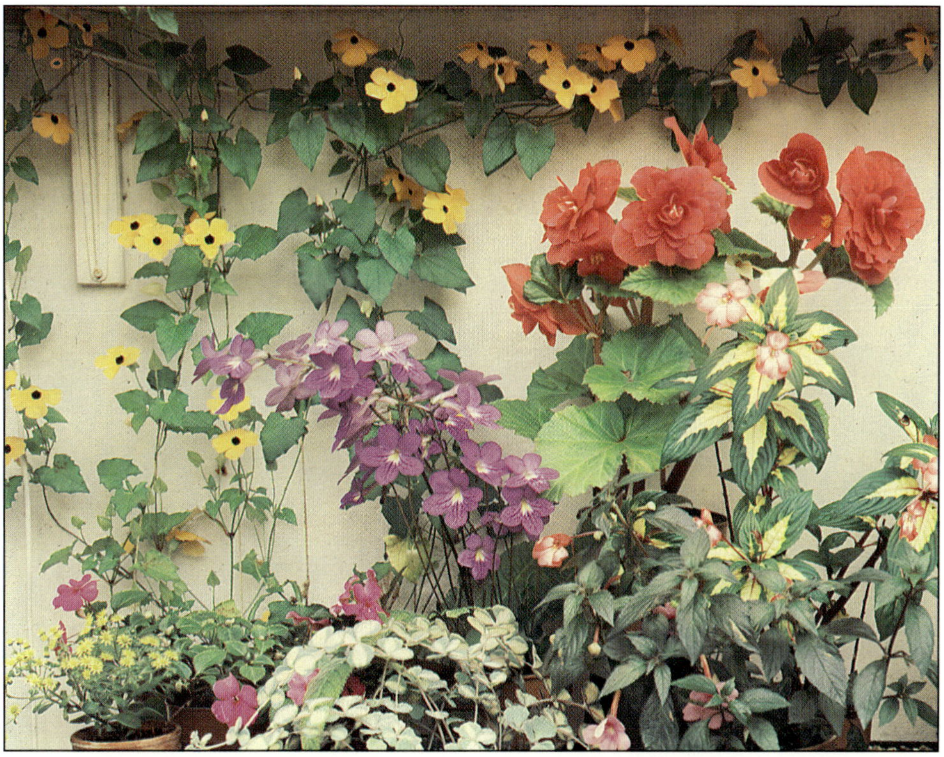

A stunning arrangement of flowering plants brightens up a plain wall.

conservatories

UNHEATED CONSERVATORIES

Arum Lily *(Zantedeschia aethiopica)*
The white variety of bulb needs less warmth than the coloured ones.

Black-eyed Susan (*Thunbergia alata*)
Fast-growing annual climber with brilliant orange, black-centred flowers. It is not hardy, so avoid sowing seeds until April or May, when the frosts have finished.

Camellia
Grow outdoor varieties of the shrub in tubs and bring them inside for early spring flowers.

Eucalyptus
Small trees. *Eucalyptus perriniana* and *E.gunnii* both have beautiful, bluish leaves.

Fig (Ficus)
Fascinating to grow, with luscious fruit in late summer. Choose indoor varieties for the best flavour, such as 'White Marseilles' or 'Negro Largo'. Can also be grown in a heated conservatory.

Grape Vine (Vitis)
Easiest grown in a bed and trained up on roof supports. Mainly ornamental, yet may yield edible fruit. Can also be grown in a heated conservatory.

Guernsey Lily (Nerine)
Enormous flower heads in pink or red. Bring indoors during exceptionally cold winter spells.

Hibiscus
Try the large-flowered annuals grown from seed, such as 'Dixie Bell' and 'Southern Belle'.

Kiwi Fruit (*Actinidia chinensis*)
Fast-growing climber; to get it to fruit you will need both a male and a female plant.

Mind Your Own Business (Helxine)
Creeping foliage plant, very useful among taller plants to make ground cover or as a fill-in.

Nile Lily (Agapanthus)
Bulb with stately stems of blue or white flowers.

Pineapple Flower (Eucomis)
Beautiful plant with a flower shaped like a pineapple at the end of a stalk. Bring indoors during exceptionally cold winter spells.

Yucca
Sword-shaped leaves that grow in rosettes; will reach 6ft (1.8m) in a conservatory.

doesn't fit into your scheme. Take into account both the style and the size of your conservatory. If you have an old-fashioned, Victorian-style one, you could arrange it in the authentic fashion, with plants in beds, tiled floors and cast-iron furniture. If the ceiling is high you can go in for tall plants, such as citrus trees or large palms. If you have a much more modern room, with a cleaner, less cluttered look, you could go for a few well-chosen specimen plants to create a sculptural effect.

A flexible approach

You'll probably find that the traditional, Victorian style of laying down permanent beds will be too restricting unless you have a very large conservatory. It's more useful with a smaller conservatory or sun room to stick to plants in individual pots and tubs, so that you can move them around easily. This option also has a practical side to it: if any of your plants become affected by disease, it's much easier to move them out to treat them, reducing the risk of infection being passed to the other plants.

Climbing plants are a boon in a conservatory. You can train them up wire netting or a trellis attached to a wall, and they will eventually hide the brickwork completely.

Making a focal point

Most rooms have a particular feature that draws the eye and provides a starting point for the decor — in living rooms, for example, it's often a fireplace. It's a good idea to aim to create a kind of focal point in your conservatory, too.

You can do this very successfully by designing a particularly attractive group of plants for a corner of the room, or you could be more adventurous and use trailing plants to frame a view into the garden. An even more exciting, and rewarding feature would be a small water garden — provided you have enough space to incorporate one safely.

If you don't have enough room for a pool, but like the idea of some water in the conservatory, you can always fill a large glass tank or a half-barrel with water and just float a single tropical Water Lily (Nymphaea) or a clump of Floating Water Hyacinth (*Eichhornia crassipes*) in it.

Keeping it warm

When a conservatory takes a certain amount of heat from the house and has

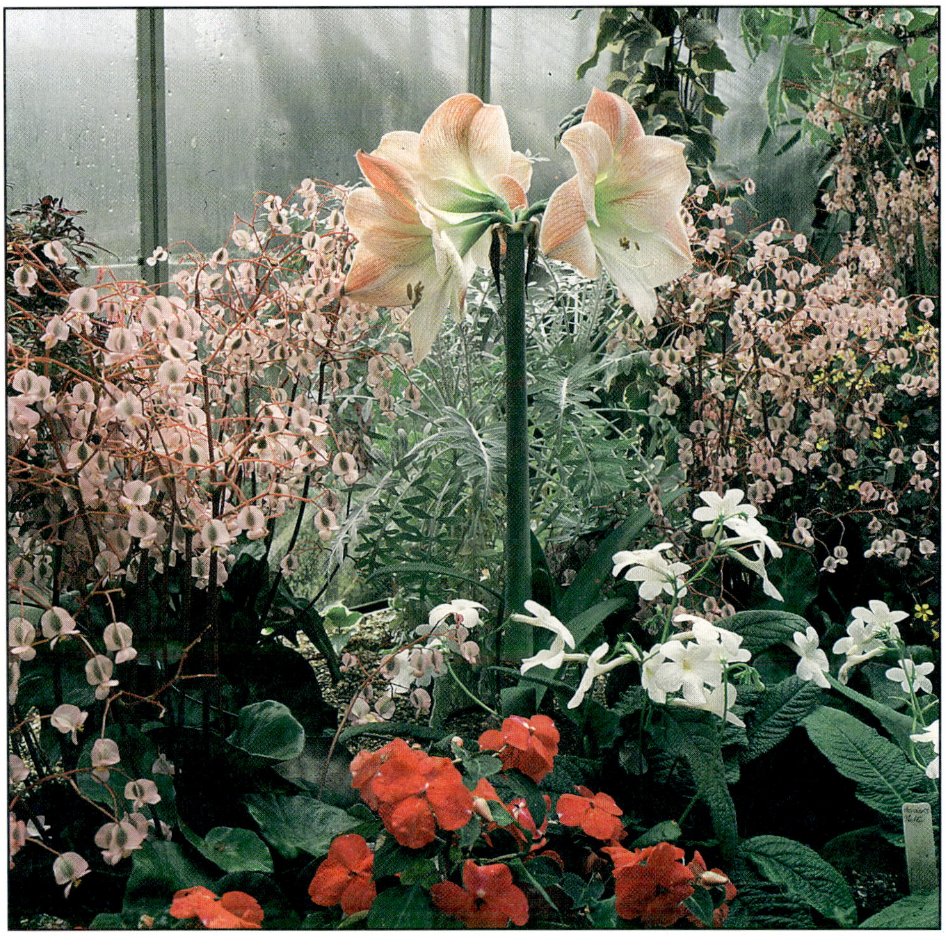

An Amaryllis stands out among Begonias, Streptocarpus and a scarlet Busy Lizzie.

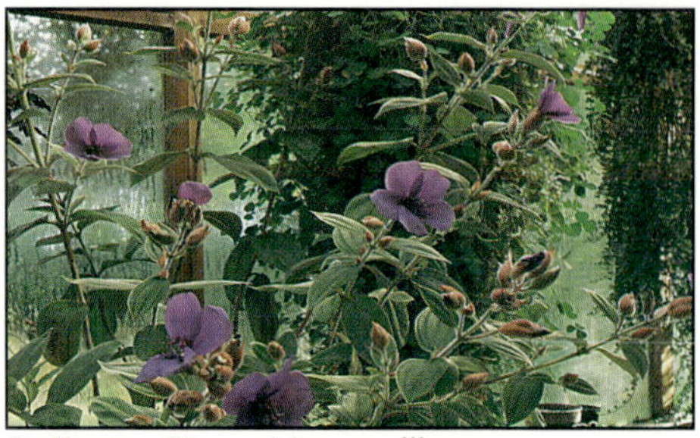

Delicate *Tibouchina urvilleana.*

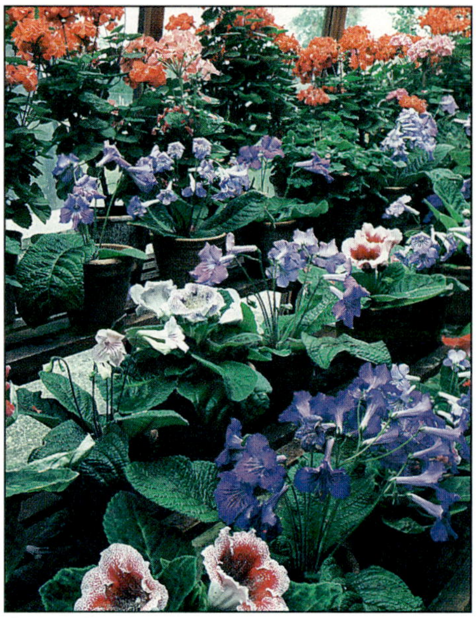

Colourful Gloxinia and Streptocarpus.

windows that catch the sun, it will be quite warm enough for most of the year without your help. In winter, however, it will get too cold unless you take precautions. You should provide a heater that is capable of keeping the room at a temperature of 40-45°F (5-7°C) at nights. One or two electric heaters controlled by a thermostat will be the most convenient and the most economical, since they operate automatically depending on the air temperature.

Keeping it cool

Even more of a problem than the cold in winter may be the heat in summer! If your conservatory is a real sun trap, it may simply get too hot, causing plants to flag. And too much direct sun can scorch plants, especially if they get too dry. The two things you must provide are ventilation and shade.

As with heating, ventilation that operates automatically is by far the easiest, and doesn't need to be expensive. You can get gadgets that work by using tubes of paraffin wax: when the sun has heated them to a certain temperature, the wax expands, pushing open the ventilator. When the temperature cools down a little, the wax contracts again and the ventilator closes.

Shading may also be necessary, especially if your conservatory is south-facing. A special liquid is available for greenhouse roofs which you paint on to the glass. It doesn't look very attractive, however, and will remain until you wash it off — not ideal for changeable summer weather. A much better bet is to use blinds. Most domestic blinds will work very well in a conservatory. Venetian blinds stand up well to intense heat and light, and they're easy to clean, but if you prefer roller blinds, choose a plasticised fabric that will not fade in the bright light. You can buy these — and wooden, slatted blinds that you attach to the outside — from greenhouse suppliers, or direct from the manufacturers.

Watering

It's very handy to have a tap in or near the conservatory, since watering can be a long job in summer if you have a lot of plants. You can douse permanent beds easily with a watering can or hosepipe, but remember that plants in pots dry out more quickly and will therefore need watering more often.

A tiled floor is a must if you want to splash water about to increase the humidity — if possible it should slope a little towards a drain so that water will run off quickly and not remain to make the floor dangerously slippery. You can always brighten up the floor with rugs when you've finished watering.

Where to get your plants

Many of the commoner conservatory plants can easily be obtained from good garden centres. More unusual ones are often available from specialists who advertise in gardening magazines.

Of course, you can always grow your own from seed — indeed, if you want something really out of the way, you'll have to! You may have to wait two or three years before you have a really well established specimen, but the effort will be well worth it when you have a beautiful plant to enjoy and to share with others in the years to come.

LIVING WITH PLANTS

It's all too easy to think your houseplants will go on looking lush and attractive with little or no effort on your part. This, however, is not the case – even the hardiest plant requires regular care and attention. A few minutes set aside every day to check up on the requirements of your plants will keep them in excellent condition.

You don't need to be an expert to give your plants the right environment in which to thrive. The right soil, the correct amounts of light, water and fertilizer, the best kind of container and range of temperature, and an awareness of what to do to your plant and when to do it – with this knowledge you should be assured of healthy specimens. Of course, the odd pest or disease may creep in, but these usually respond to early treatment – and, naturally, it pays to make a few special arrangements if you're going away for any length of time to make sure your good work is kept up in your absence!

Learning to live with your plants is not difficult – and you'll certainly be able to see the benefits as your plants continue to flourish year after year.

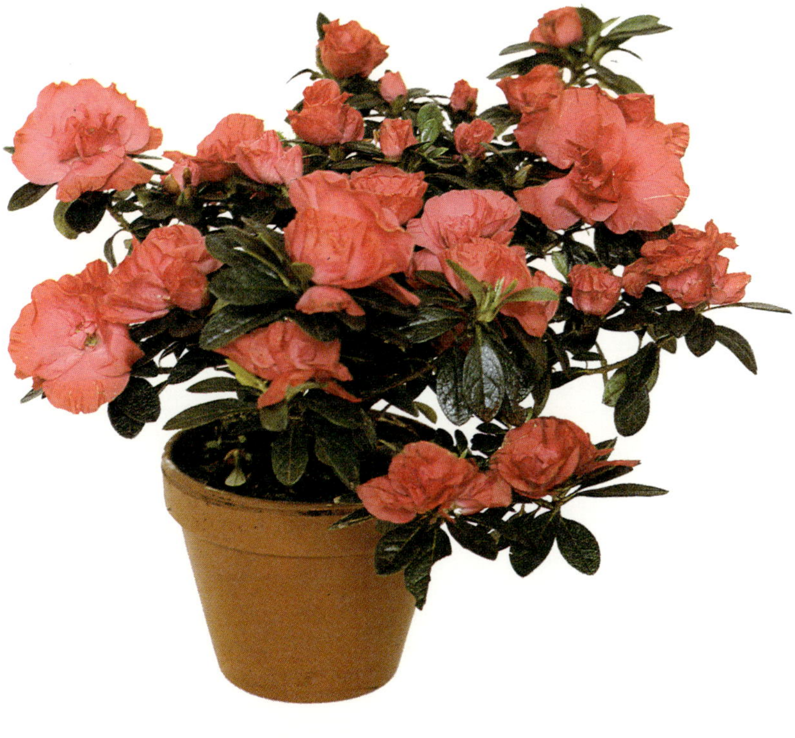

Regular care for healthy plants

The secret of success for getting the very best from your houseplants lies in learning to understand them and their needs; this way they'll always be in peak condition with plenty of handsome new growth and lots of exciting flowers.

There are certain basic ways of looking after plants, and in the following section you'll find lots of helpful advice on the vital aspects of houseplant care — temperature, light, watering, humidity and so on; and in the A-Z section the specific needs of every plant will be laid out in detail for you to follow. However, there are ground rules which apply to almost all houseplants — the basic knowledge you need to help keep your plants in tip-top condition.

Light and temperature guidelines

Both light and temperature are vital factors for the good health of every plant. Many of our houseplants come from hot climates and you must take this into account when you choose where to put them. After all, a tropical plant can't really be expected to thrive in cold conditions.

- KEEP PLANTS AWAY FROM HEAT. Leaves can be badly scorched by fires and radiators, even after a single exposure. Move any plants in danger before you switch on central heating.
- BEWARE OF FROST. Plants left behind curtains on windowsills during cold winter nights run a real risk of frost damage. Move them back into the room.
- KEEP PLANTS AWAY FROM COLD DRAUGHTS. Badly fitting doors and windows channel cold air, making leaves discolour and drop off; and in extreme cases plants die.
- DON'T KEEP HOUSEPLANTS IN THE DIRECT SUN. Most plants like good, bright, slightly shaded light; too much sun scorches delicate leaves. See our A-Z section for the exceptions.
- GIVE YOUR PLANTS GOOD LIGHT IN WINTER. Even though most plants don't grow in winter, they still need to sit in good light to keep their leaves healthy.

Foliage and flowers

To keep your plants looking their very best you must get into the habit of REGULARLY CHECKING them over and tidying them up.

- REMOVE DEAD OR DYING FLOWERS. Snip them off just behind the flower head with a sharp pair of scissors.
- REMOVE DEAD OR DYING LEAVES. Dead foliage looks horrible and also attracts diseases like grey mould, which can go on to attack the rest of the plant. Use a sharp knife or pair of scissors, and cut off the leaf stalk as near as possible to the stem.
- DON'T PANIC IF A LEAF DIES. Most houseplants eventually lose some of their leaves naturally.
- STAKE PLANTS AS THEY GROW. Support growing shoots and floppy stems with string and canes.
- CLEAN PLANT LEAVES. Dust clogs leaf pores and halts plant growth. Sponge leaves clean with water once a month. For hairy-leaved plants use a soft paint brush.

Maintenance guidelines

The table shows when and how often you should be checking your houseplants to see if they need attention. Try to get into the habit of looking at them on a regular basis every few days.

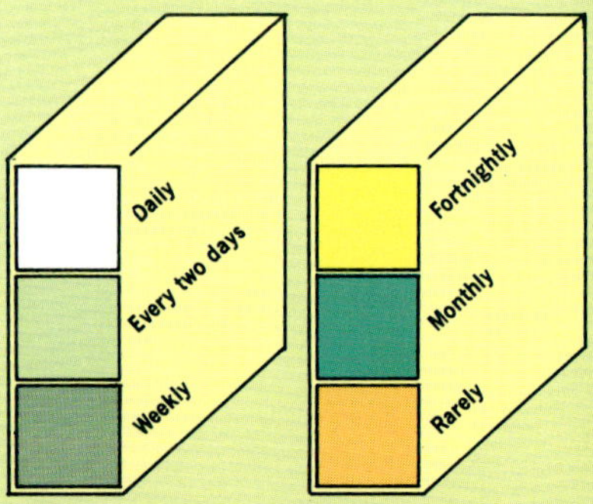

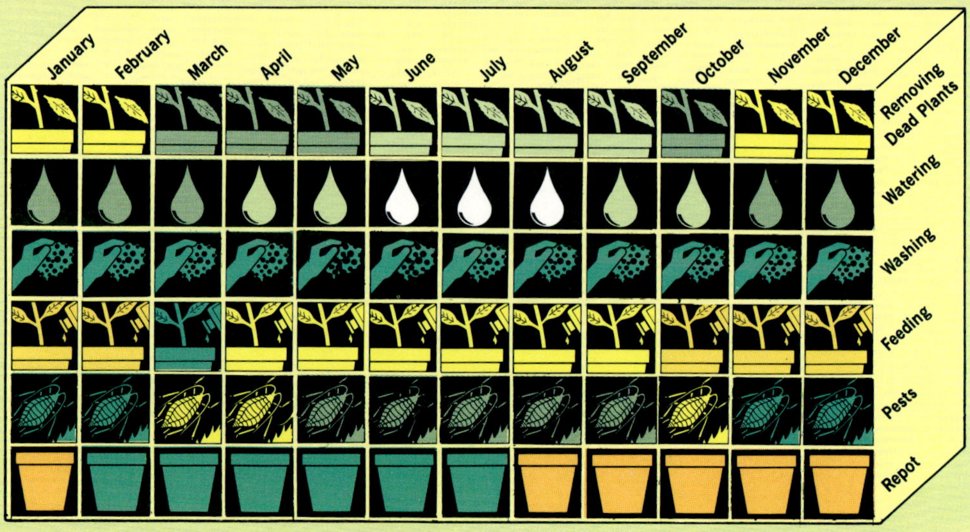

Potting and feeding

Both of these are SPRING and SUMMER JOBS. Potting at the right time is vital for flowering plants because if you do it at the wrong moment they could fail to flower that year. The following points are guidelines to help you decide when to act.

- INSPECT ROOTS. When roots start to poke through the base of the pot it's a sign that your plant needs potting into a bigger pot; do it quickly before the roots have time to grow much further.
- REPOT BEFORE THE MAIN SPRING GROWTH. As a general rule all plants should be repotted as they wake from their winter rest — if you leave it too long you'll run the risk of damaging new shoots and roots when you repot.
- REPOTTING LARGE PLANTS. When a plant is already large enough, knock it out of its pot, tease away some of the old compost and replace with fresh.
- TOPDRESS A REALLY BIG PLANT. When a plant is too big to repot, topdress it by scraping away the top 2-3 in (5-7cm) of compost and replace with fresh.
- FEED PLANTS REGULARLY IN SUMMER. Start a regular feeding routine every 14 days in the summer. Alternatively use solid fertiliser sticks or tablets every six weeks.
- DON'T FEED PLANTS IN WINTER. Stop feeding plants while they are resting in the cold winter months.

Pests and diseases

Trouble once started can spread very fast in the warm, protected environment of your home. Be careful to use only houseplant pesticides and always READ THE INSTRUCTIONS on the packet and follow them carefully.

- CHECK REGULARLY FOR PESTS. Look at the new shoots and under leaves regularly for any sign of trouble. Act immediately.
- ACT PROMPTLY. In the early stages you can just rub the pest off the plant with your fingers; or spray with washing-up liquid and water (except in the case of ferns).
- SEVERE TROUBLE. When trouble is really bad, you have to use chemicals. It is often necessary to repeat the treatment after a few days.

Watering

Regular and correct watering is the main part of your houseplant routine. This can be tricky as the symptoms of OVERwatering are often the same as UNDERwatering — and both can kill your plants, as does NOT WATERING at all. It's impossible to prescribe an exact watering plan as plants differ in their individual needs and because each home has different conditions — humidity, temperature and so on — but the following general rules apply.

- DON'T LET YOUR PLANTS DRY OUT. Most plants need moist compost. Water little and often when the top of the compost feels dry.
- WATER YOUR PLANTS REGULARLY. A regular watering routine helps you keep up with your plants' needs, and means that you are less likely to miss any out.
- MIST SPRAY IN HOT WEATHER. Crisp, brown leaf edges show lack of humidity. Tropical plants especially need the humidity provided by regular spraying.
- DON'T LET YOUR PLANTS SIT IN WATER. Saturated compost leads to root rot and eventually a dead plant. Tip away excess water after 20 minutes.
- WATER MOST IN SUMMER. While your plants are growing they are drinking at quite a rate. If the compost is dry on top, they probably need watering – leave it for a little longer, if the plant likes drying out between waterings.
- GIVE LESS WATER IN WINTER. Plants stop growing and also stop drinking — just give them a drop from time to time to keep going.

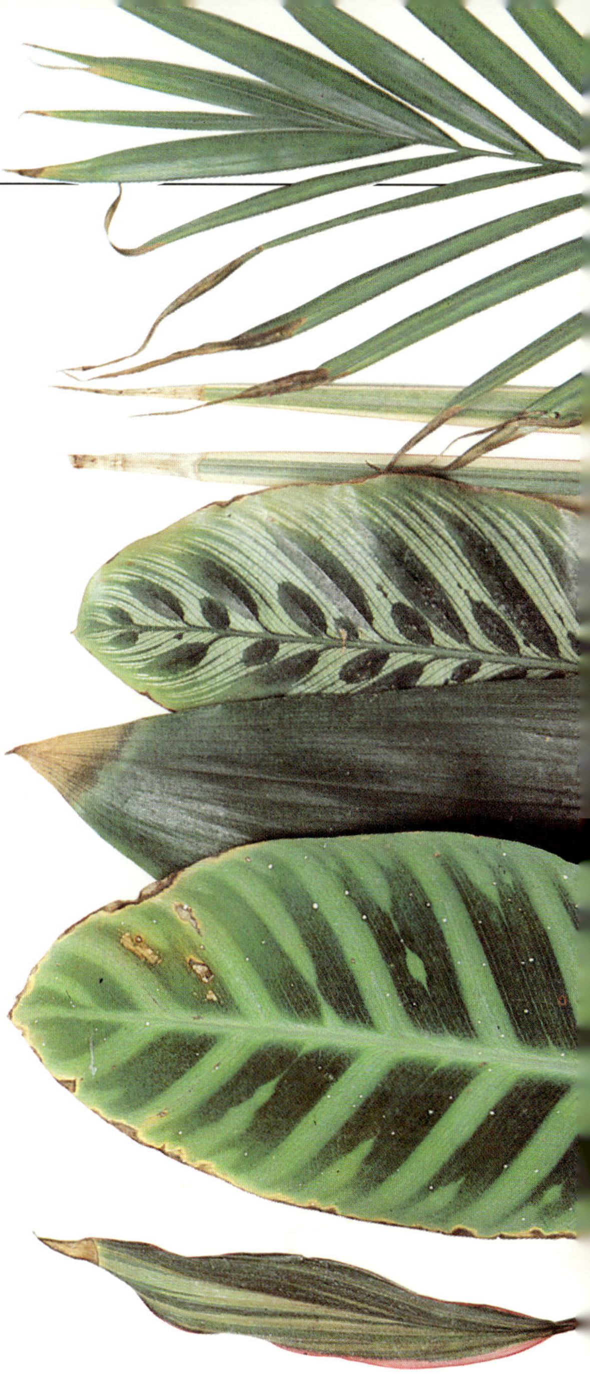

Brown edged leaves are usually caused by underwatering as the leaf tissues dry out. From the top: palm, pandanus, calathea, aspidistra, calathea, cordyline.

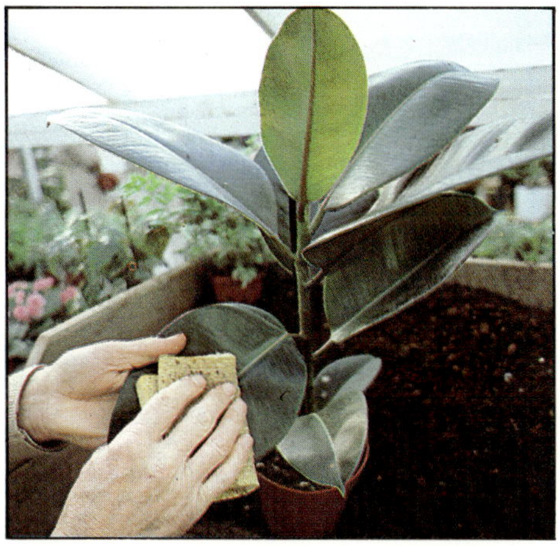

Sponge clean leaves every few weeks with soapy water; never use detergent.

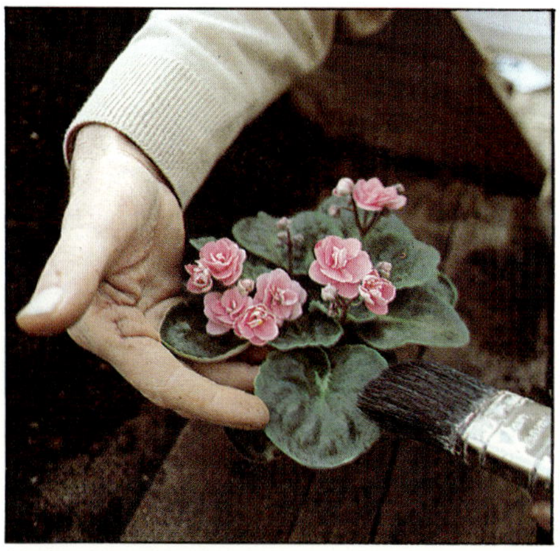

Hairy leaved plants are best dusted with a soft brush.

Basic equipment you need

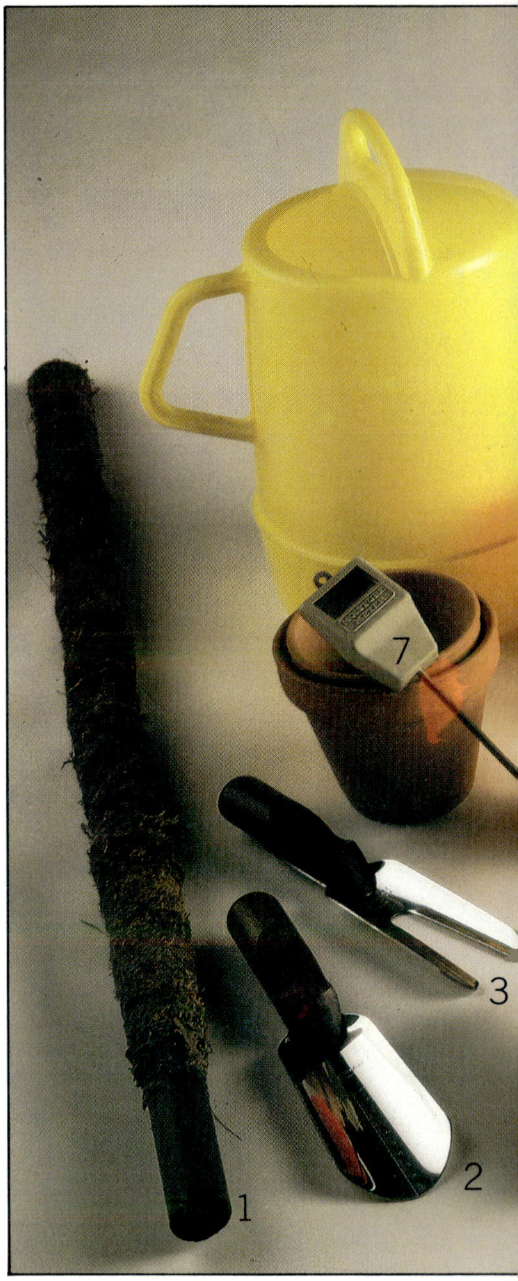

The nice thing about houseplants is that you need minimal equipment to look after them, but if you have the right tools it makes life so much easier. These are just guidelines to help you along with your plants; we'll be dealing with everything in much greater detail later on.

Essential equipment

Although you can use a milk bottle for watering, it's better to invest in a watering can. Look for the kind with a long, narrow spout so that you can easily reach plants which are high up or lurking at the back of groups. Also make sure you get a can which will hold a reasonable amount of water or you'll spend all day running between the tap and your plants.

You will need a good pair of secateurs for pruning back the wiry stems of climbing and shrubby houseplants. For smaller plants where secateurs are too clumsy, get a sharp pair of long pointed scissors so you can snip away faded flowers and leaves without damaging the rest of the plant.

A hand held mist sprayer is a must for keeping plants — particularly tropical ones which need high humidity — healthy and fresh in warm weather. Buy one which gives a fine mist-like spray of water, those that leave droplets do more harm than good.

To handle compost you'll need a small trowel. And a hand fork is useful for stirring the top of the compost of established plants, to prevent moss and green growths living on the surface.

Food and supports

To grow healthy plants you must feed them every 14 days or so in the summer. There are various kinds of plant fertilisers, many of which are for different purposes; we tell you more about them all in the article on pages 90-93. There are concentrated liquids which are diluted with water and then watered into the compost; dry powder that is dissolved into water; or solid fertiliser in the form of sticks or tablets. The last of these are simply pushed into the compost where they slowly release their fertiliser with each watering. They are good for about six weeks before you need to insert some more.

As plants grow you'll find that you need to stake them, even though they may not be climbers. Use bamboo canes cut to various lengths or short split canes which are often dyed green so they hide among the foliage. Tie the plants to the supports with soft twine, raffia or very pliable wire.

Some tropical plants produce roots from their stems which like to cling to supports. For these plants there are special moss covered poles which are pushed into the pot.

Watering

Self-watering planters are ideal for people who can't manage a regular watering routine; they have a reservoir of water at the bottom which the plant is constantly able to draw on when it needs to drink. There's usually a water level indicator which shows how much water is in the reservoir.

Potting and propagators

March and April are the main repotting months, so be prepared. Small plants are grown in 3in (7cm) pots, middling plants in 6in (15cm) pots and large plants in 10in (25cm) pots. You also need potting compost, but buy it only as needed as the quality deteriorates after the bag has been open for a few weeks.

Houseplants thrive in peat-based compost. This has the advantage of being clean and light, so it's easy to carry and particularly useful for hanging baskets. The alternative is a soil based compost — John Innes No 2 is good. And get some plastic plant labels if you have difficulty remembering names.

Cuttings and seeds need protection and warmth to grow and this means giving them a closed environment. A nice and cheap way is to put pots of seeds and cuttings in clear polythene bags sealed at the pot rims with rubber

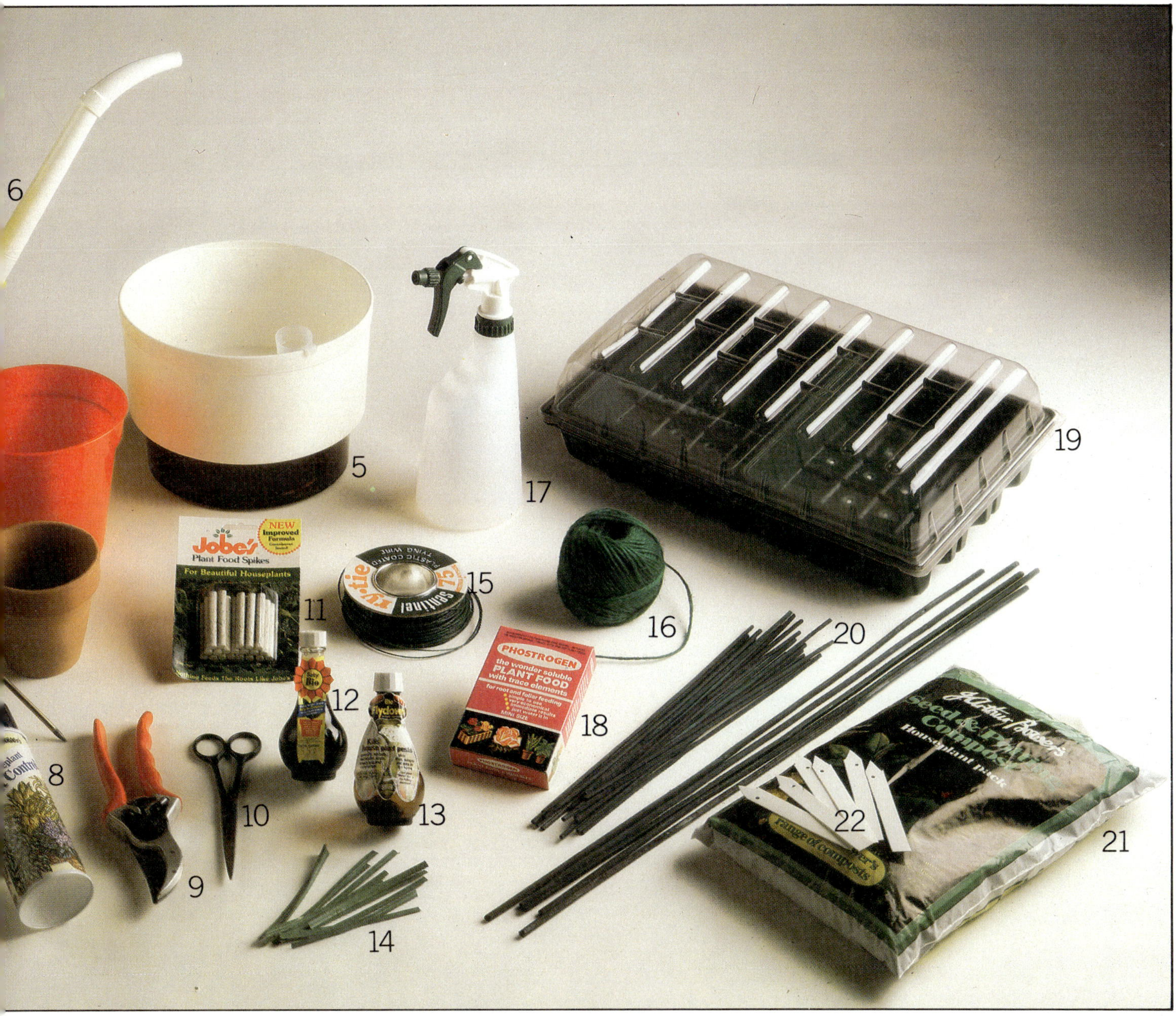

bands. Water the compost gently, seal the pot and leave on a warm windowsill.

If plastic bags aren't to your taste, then you can buy a propagator. Ordinary propagators are just a seed tray with a plastic hood cover. They need to sit on a sunny windowsill to build up the warmth inside. Heated propagators have a sealed electric cable sandwiched inside the seed tray. They are powered from an ordinary electric socket and are economical to run.

Controlling pests and diseases

It pays to be prepared with a houseplant pesticide which you can apply at the first sign of trouble.

Most pesticides are diluted with water and sprayed onto the plant; however, you can get them ready mixed in aerosol form. Make certain you buy a houseplant pesticide and not a preparation for outdoor use, as garden chemicals are too toxic to be used safely within a confined area like a house.

Water meters

If you find it a problem judging when to water your plants you could find a moisture meter helpful; this has a probe which is inserted into the compost and a dial then indicates 'wet', 'moist' or 'dry' so you can act accordingly and be quite confident about watering.

Houseplant equipment:
1, sphagnum moss plant pole. **2**, small hand trowel for repotting. **3**, hand fork. **4**, selection of pots for repotting. **5**, self watering planter. **6**, watering can with a long spout. **7**, water meter. **8**, houseplant pesticide in an aerosol. **9**, secateurs. **10**, long scissors. **11**, solid fertiliser sticks. **12**, liquid houseplant fertiliser. **13**, liquid pesticide to dilute with water. **14**, plastic covered wire plant ties. **15**, strong, pliable plant wire. **16**, soft green twine. **17**, the essential mist sprayer. **18**, powdered houseplant food to dissolve in water. **19**, unheated plastic propagator. **20**, green plant stakes of different lengths. **21**, bag of houseplant potting compost. **22**, plant labels.

Why plants need light

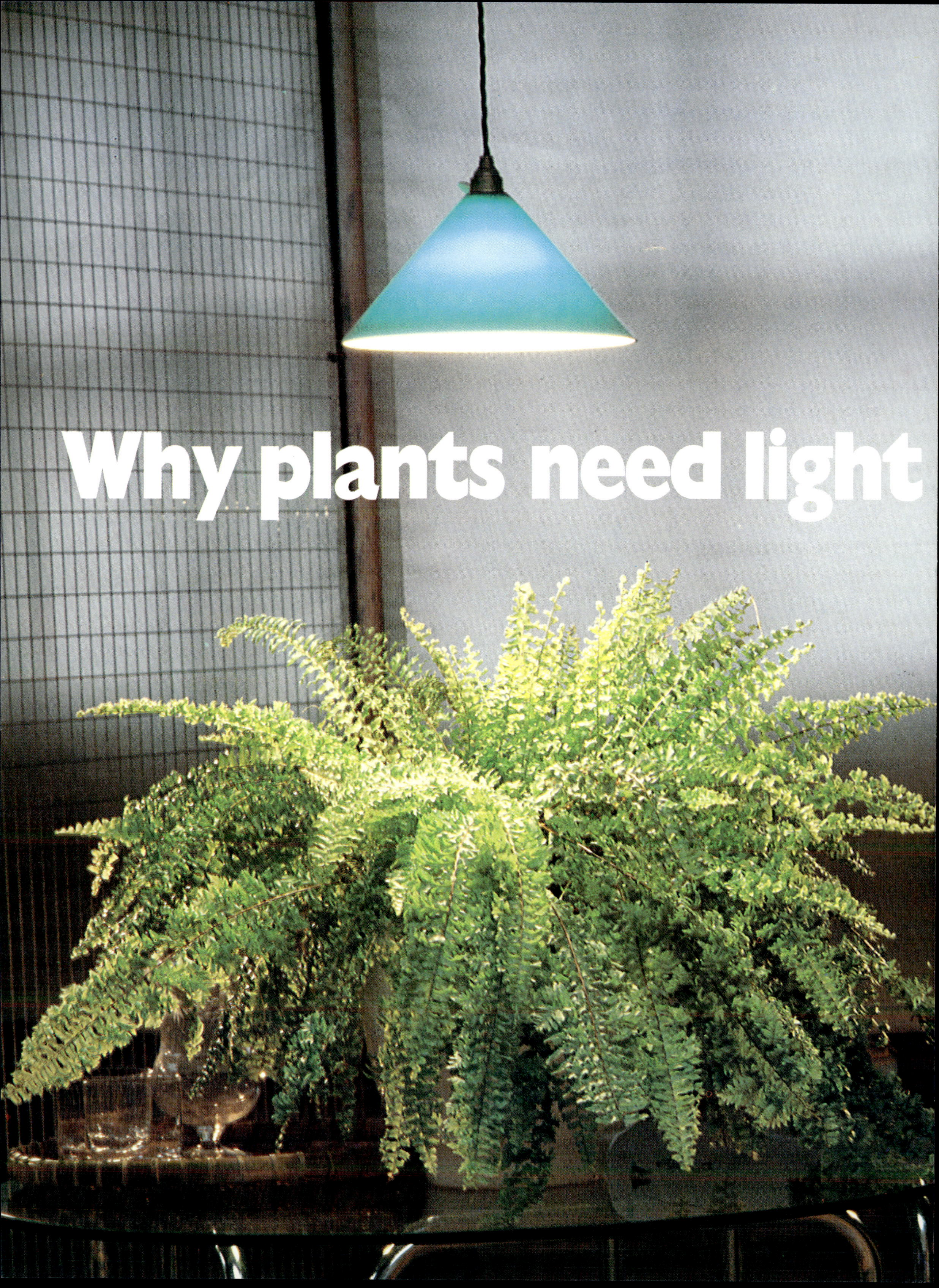

All plants use the sun's light to make the energy required for growth — which is why you can't get houseplants to grow if you put them in the middle of a gloomy room. The more light you give your plants, the healthier and happier they'll be, with lots of lovely colourful, fresh leaves and flowers. If you can't provide enough light, use artificial light instead — your plants will grow just as well.

Different plants need varying degrees of light, depending on how they have adapted their leaves to get the most from the light they receive in their natural habitat. So, for example, a Swiss Cheese Plant,which grows wild in dimly lit tropical American jungles, doesn't need strong light to grow well; but it does have enormous leaves to catch as much light as it can. However, if you give your Swiss Cheese Plant lots of strong sunlight, thinking to do it a favour, you'll scorch it, because the Swiss Cheese Plant doesn't have natural heat protection in its leaves, as in the jungle such insulation isn't necessary.

The complete reverse is true for desert cacti which are used to extended periods of intense heat; they long ago reduced their leaves into spines as protection against absorbing too much of the baking sunshine. So, if at home you put your cactus in a shady position, it won't grow at all because it's not getting the sheer intensity of light it needs to make it grow and flower.

Judging the light

You can see quite easily which parts of your house have good, bright, light and where it's so poorly lit that you won't be able to grow anything. Unless you have a sunroom, the brightest light is on the windowsills; but it's still quite bright 2-3ft (0.6-0.9m) into a room from the windows and, depending on which way the windows face, and whether the sun is blocked by trees or buildings, the amount of light is bright enough for shade-loving plants for a further 6ft (1.8m). After that the light intensity drops rapidly, no matter what your eyes tell you.

Know your plant

Save your sunniest windowsills for plants that need maximum light. Usually when you buy a houseplant, there is a descriptive label which tells you what amount of light your new plant needs.

Adjusting houseplants to light

Once you find the right spot for your plants, you should still adjust their position slightly from time to time for their comfort. For a start, really strong sun can scorch houseplant leaves through the glass; this is most dangerous in spring, when a sudden burst of sunny weather will damage leaves which normally have time to gradually get accustomed to the higher intensities of summer light.

Never put a new plant straight into bright light, even if it needs it — get it gradually accustomed to brighter light over a week or so — unless you are sure it was grown in bright light.

To protect plants from the fierce sun use net curtains at the windows: they are excellent for filtering the sun, but still let through plenty of really bright light for plants to grow well.

Never spray plants in the bright sun; this is because the water droplets on the leaves act like minute magnifying glasses, and concentrate the sun's rays in one spot, creating tiny scorch marks.

Every three or four days give your plants a 45° turn, because otherwise they lean badly towards the light. Indoor plants, unlike garden plants, generally only get light from one direction, which makes a lop-sided plant. The answer is to get into the habit of giving your plants a frequent and regular turn, so that the stem grows straight and the whole plant is well balanced.

A word of warning about turning plants: some flowering plants must not

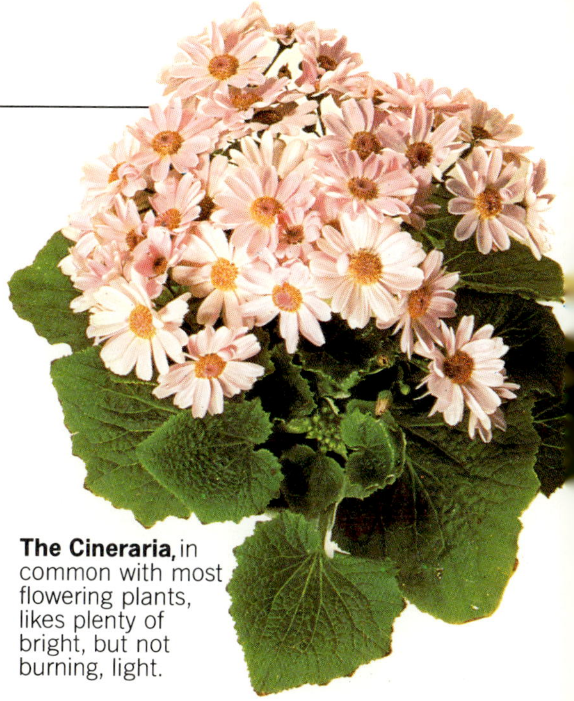

The Cineraria, in common with most flowering plants, likes plenty of bright, but not burning, light.

How plants use sunlight

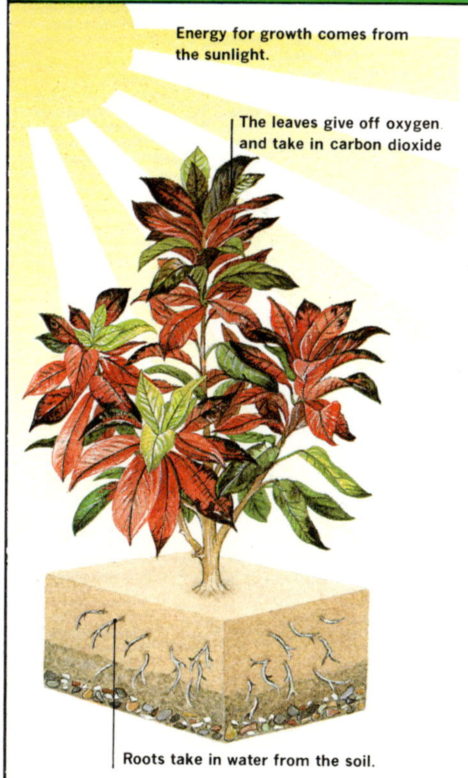

Basically, plants use light to make simple sugars, broadly similar to glucose, which are later turned into the more complex chemicals they need for healthy, vigorous growth. The green colouring of plant leaves — correctly called chlorophyll — absorbs energy from sunlight. This energy is then used to combine carbon dioxide from the air with water to make sugars; the process is called photosynthesis. At the same time the plant is giving off oxygen through its leaves. The sugars are used to form new tissucs — which is how a plant grows.

At night when it's dark, plants stop making the sugars. Their 'breathing' reverses and they take in a little oxygen from the air to turn the stored sugars into energy for growth.

Without sufficient light, the amount of chlorophyll in the leaves is reduced, so the plant can't make enough glucose to grow and will be weak with thin stems and pale leaves.

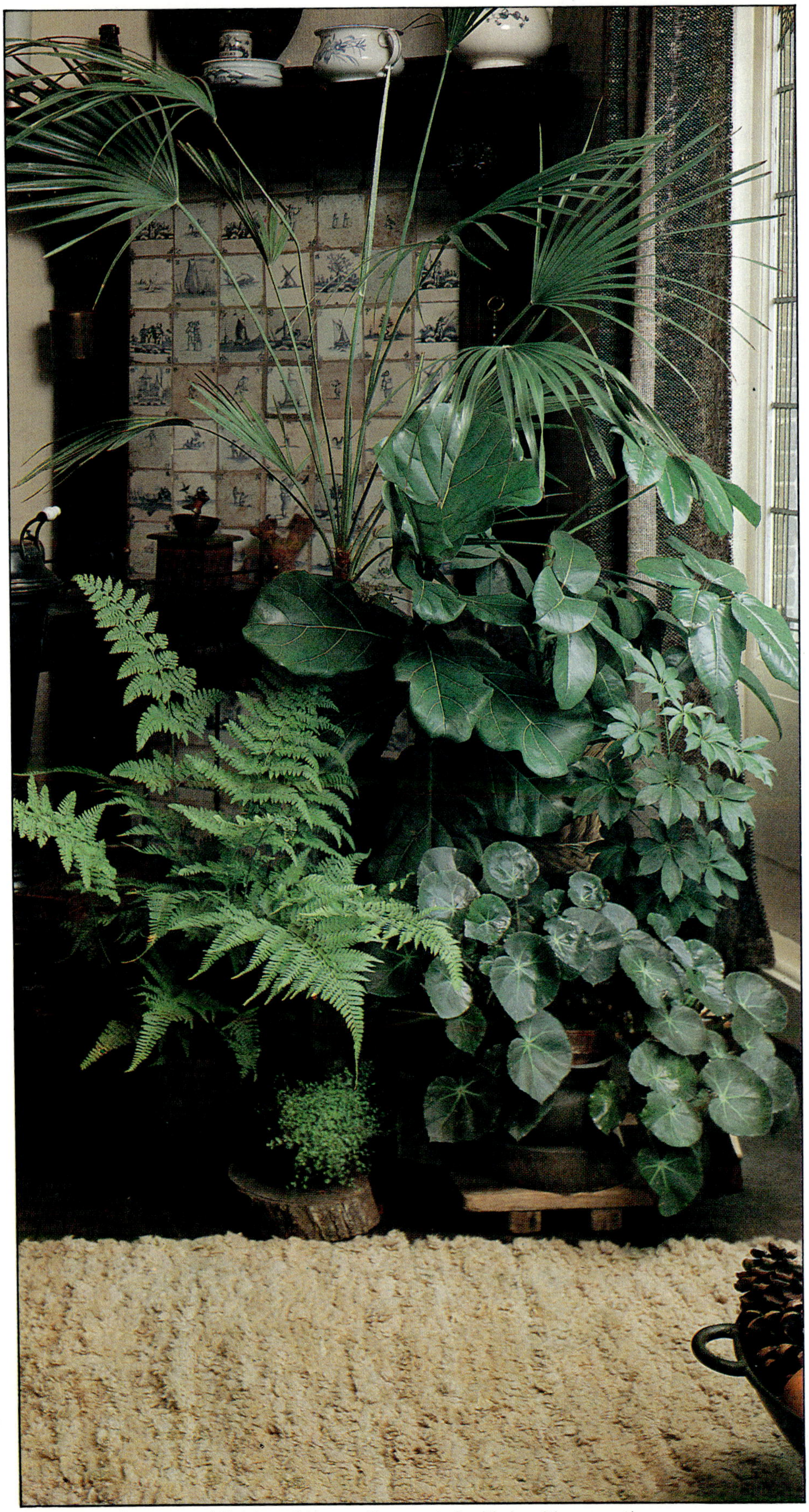

Give your plants good light and they will respond with healthy growth.

be turned while their buds are forming, or they will drop off. By turning the plant you make the flower buds twist towards the light until they drop. Two notorious examples are the Christmas and Easter Cactus — so when you buy such a plant always point the buds and flowers towards the light and don't move them.

Another point to note is that plants with variegated leaves need more light than plants with plain green leaves. If you don't give a variegated plant enough light it will lose its variegation and the leaves will go a plain green. So, while ordinary Ivies put up with poor light, variegated Ivies must have bright light to keep the patterns on their leaves.

If you can, give some of your houseplants a summer holiday in the sun, say between June and early September. Stand them out of doors for a few weeks in good, bright light — it's amazing how much better their growth and leaf colour will be. But be careful not to put them where they get direct, scorching sun — and don't forget to water them regularly as their compost dries out much quicker in the open air.

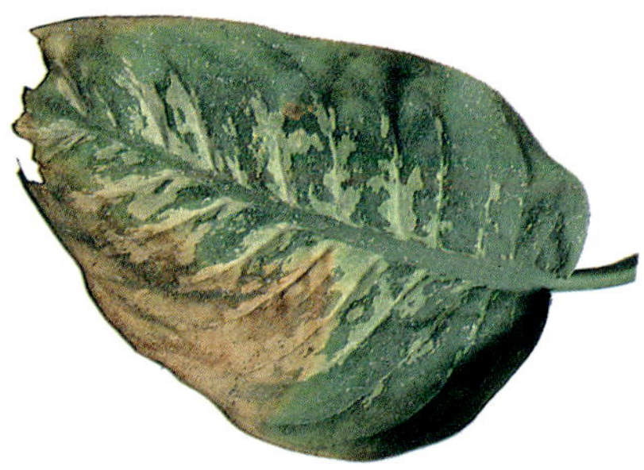

Sun scorched Dieffenbachia leaf

Using artificial light

If you live in a shady house don't despair of ever growing anything other than Ivies and Aspidistras; use artificial light to brighten up your plants and your decor. Ordinary light bulbs don't emit enough light in the red and orange part of the spectrum for plants to grow, so get a special plant-growing bulb which fits into an ordinary light-bulb socket. These have to be fairly close to the plant — within 3ft (0.9m) to be of much use — and kept switched on for 8-12 hours a day to be effective in a really gloomy spot in the middle of a room.

Fluorescent light is much the best form of artificial light for growing plants. The tubes are not difficult to install, but if you are not electrically minded, get a qualified electrician to fit the units.

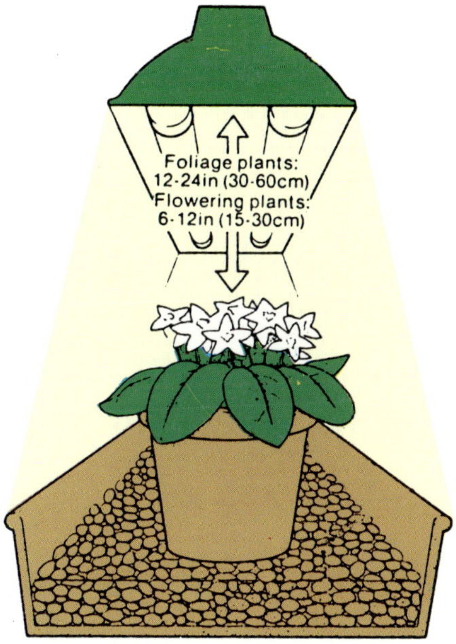

Fluorescent light If you are really serious about growing your indoor plants under artificial light, then arrange your set-up as shown above. Use fluorescent tubes — ideally ones that produce a balanced light output — and suspend them 18-24in (45-60cm) from your plants (depending on type). A pebble tray filled with water will help to maintain high humidity.

Mount the fluorescent tubes in pairs, say above shelves, corner units and in alcoves, and position them 18-24in (45-60cm) above the plants, so that the light shines directly down onto them. Choose 40 watt, cool white or daylight tubes and if possible use a reflecting hood to direct and spread the light downwards. Diffusers can be used to hide the tubes, but of course these slightly reduce light intensity.

Another way to provide artificial lighting and a warm, humid, environment for some of the smaller, more delicate and tricky houseplants is to get a fish tank, complete with cover and built-in fluorescent tube. The tank can then be used as a terrarium for extra special plants.

Health and happiness

So, as you now know, your houseplants need light for their health as well as for their growth. It's not enough to buy a plant and put it in the middle of a room and hope for the best. If it is a plant that needs a lot of light, it simply won't grow. For your plant to thrive, you must give it all the light it needs.

Plants for light and shade

- For the sunniest windowsills, where it gets baking hot close to the glass, trust such sun-lovers as zonal, regal, ivy and scented-leaved Pelargoniums (commonly called Geraniums), the Passion Flower, Jade Plant, cacti, Bougainvilleas and Acacias.
- Where there's good sun for part of the day, grow a Shrimp Plant, Spider Plant, Ornamental Peppers and Tradescantia. But even these may need moving away from the burning sun in the hottest weather.
- Bright but sunless positions are ideal for plants needing lots of light, but which would scorch in the direct sun. Grow the magnificent Flamingo Flower, Indian Azalea, the Finger Aralia, all sorts of different Fuchsias, the Dumb Cane and the Christmas Cactus.

Semi-shade

- There are plenty of attractive foliage plants which thrive in semi-shady positions. Some of the finest are the Mother-in-Law's Tongue, Sweetheart Plant, Aspidistra and lots of lovely ferns.

Gloomy positions

- Really gloomy spots are best left to those ardent shade-lovers, the Ivies, especially the small-leaved, plain green varieties, as well as Aspidistra, the Snakeskin Plant and Baby's Tears.

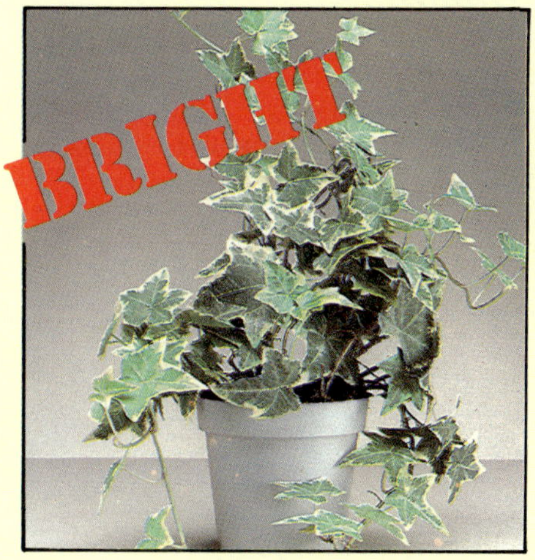

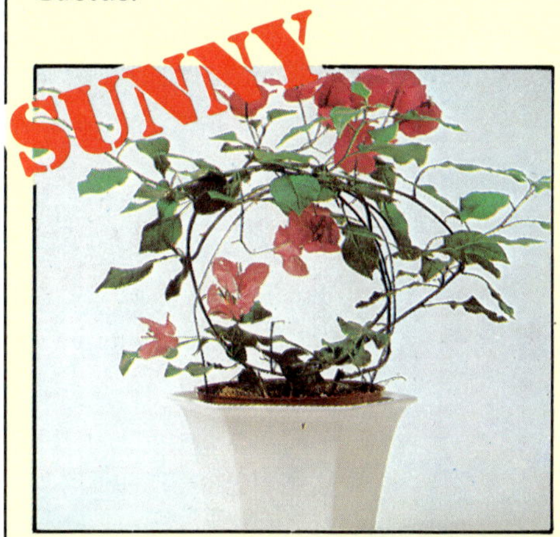

Very few houseplants are as tough as the Bougainvillea, *left*, which can sit safely in the full sun. Most need bright but indirect light, like the variegated Ivy, *above*. Only a few, like the Aspidistra, *below*, are happy in shade.

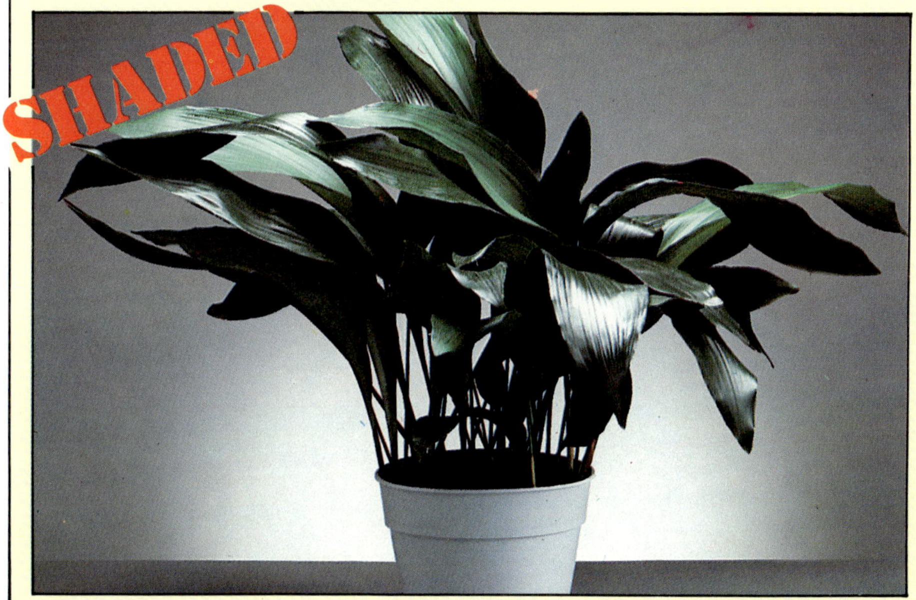

How much water do plants need?

Of all the different aspects of houseplant care, watering probably presents the most problems. Watering itself is easy, but it takes experience to judge how much water a particular plant needs and when. It is a sad fact that more houseplants die through being overwatered than by not being given enough water. Saturated compost deprives roots of oxygen and cold, stagnant water encourages rot to set in. This is often the result of giving your plants 'just a quick splash' of water every day, regardless of temperature and season. Here we tell you everything you need to know about how to judge the exact amount of water to give to your plants.

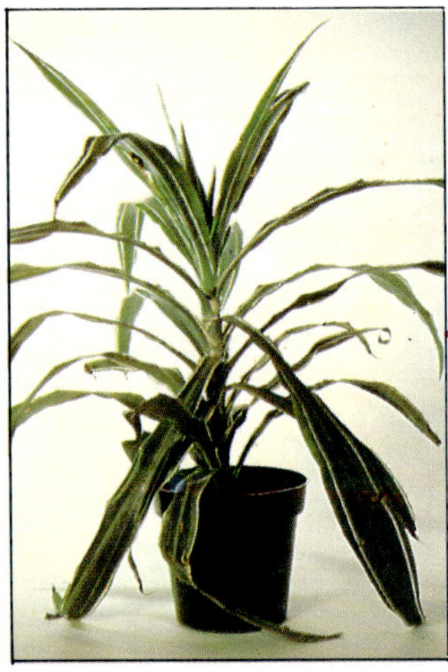

Wilting plant: overwatering can cause root rot which in turn leads to wilting leaves. Rot starts when the plant has been standing for too long in cold, stagnant water. The compost gets waterlogged and prevents the roots getting oxygen so they cannot take water to the leaves efficiently. If the soil stays waterlogged the roots start to rot.

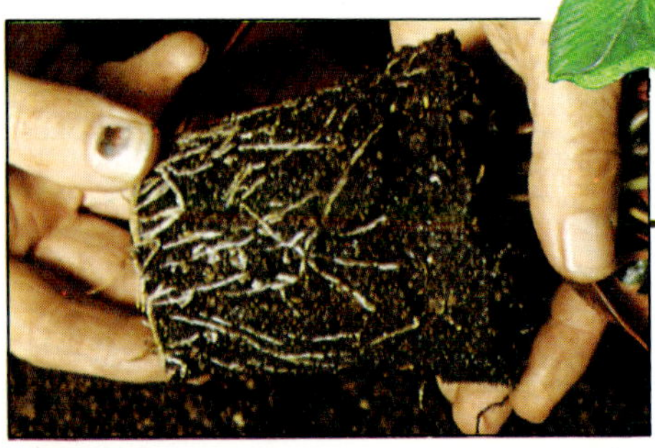

Check for root rot: get the plant out of its pot and tease the compost away from any brown, unhealthy roots. Pull the root gently; if the outer skin comes away easily leaving an inner core, your plant has rot. All you can do is remove the bad roots, dry the soil and hope that your plant recovers.

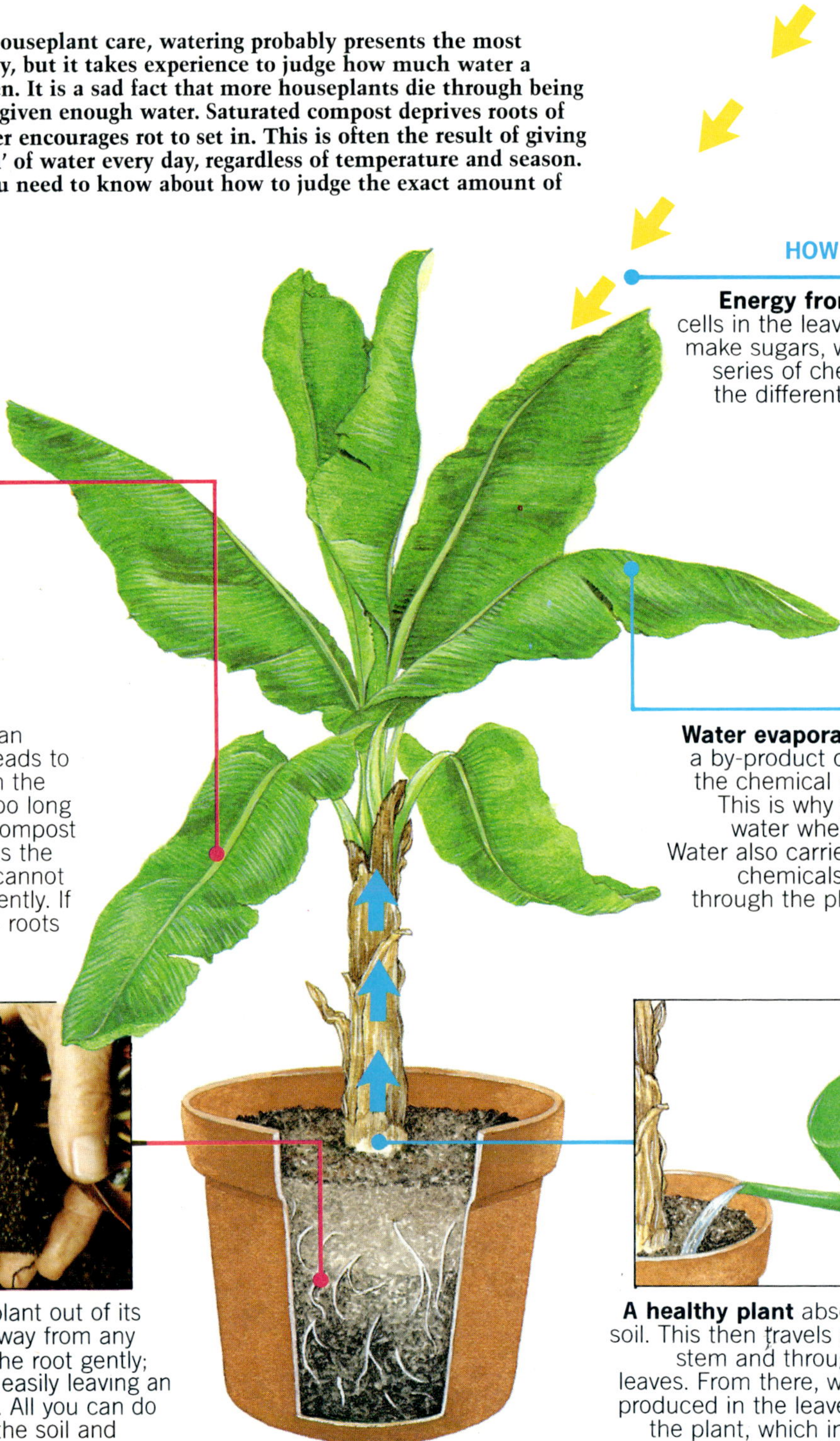

HOW PLANTS USE WATER

Energy from sunlight triggers the cells in the leaves to release oxygen to make sugars, which are changed by a series of chemical reactions into all the different 'building materials' for the plant to grow.

Water evaporates from the leaves as a by-product of respiration and of all the chemical reactions taking place. This is why your plant needs most water when it is growing actively. Water also carries all the nutrients and chemicals that have to be taken through the plant to the parts where they are needed.

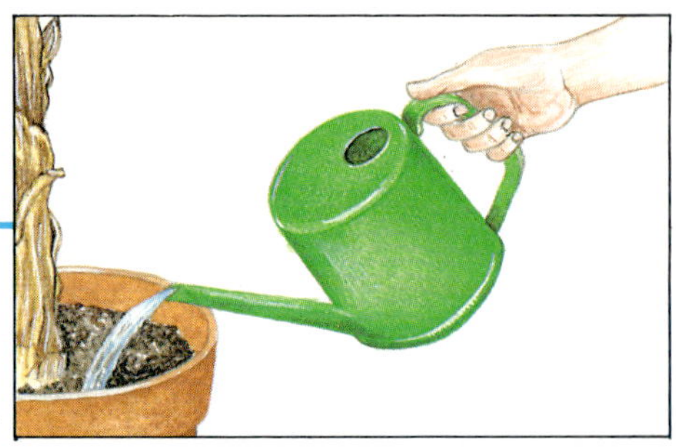

A healthy plant absorbs moisture from the soil. This then travels along the roots, up the stem and through the branches to the leaves. From there, water carries the sugars produced in the leaves to the other parts of the plant, which in turn helps more roots and leaves to grow healthily.

Holiday plant care: it's easy enough to take a few simple precautions to avoid the awful let-down of coming home from a lovely holiday only to find that your plants have dried out. One method is to use a self-watering pot, *right*. This is basically two pots, one inside the other, with the lower one filled with water, **1**. Water gets to the plant through a wick, **2**, and the water is topped up via a tube, **3**. Alternatively capillary matting, *below*, is a good short-term answer. Lay it flat in the sink or bath and dip one end in a large bowl of water on a level above the matting. Water moves by capillary action down the mat to where the plants can take it. (It also works if the water source is *lower* than the plants.) The method works for as long as there is water remaining in the bowl.

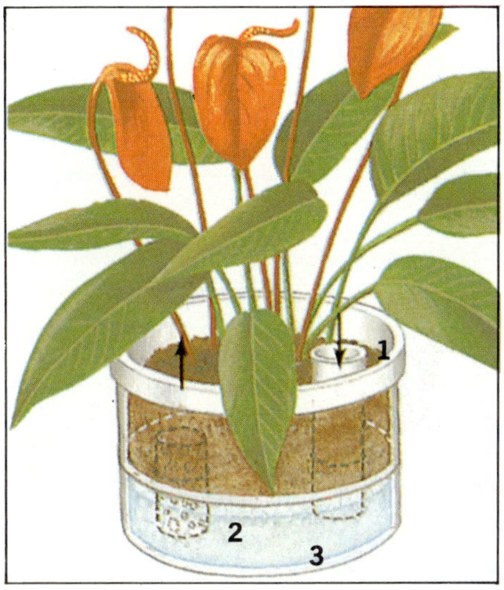

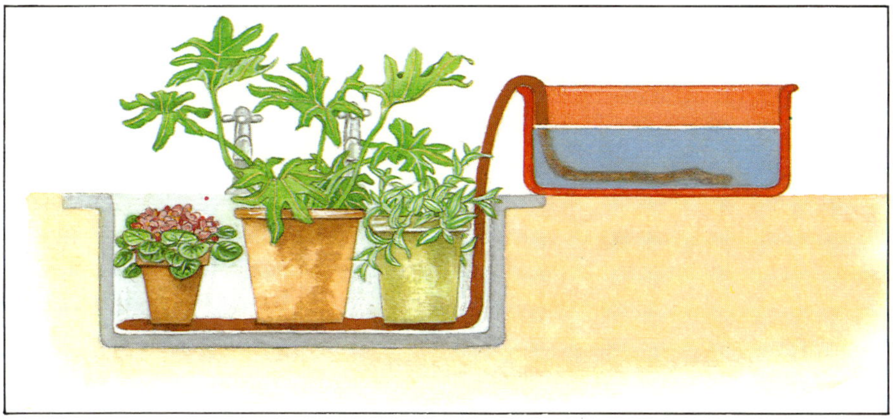

Simple watering tests

- For a plant in a clay pot, fix a cotton reel on the end of a bamboo cane and tap the pot. If you get a ringing sound it means that the clay, and therefore the compost, is dry and needs watering; when you tap the pot and get a dull clunk, then the compost is wet enough already.
- Pick up the plant (whether in a clay or plastic pot): if it feels heavy then the compost is wet; if it feels light, then the compost is dry. This is a reliable test, but it takes a little time to gauge the weights of individual plants and it isn't always practical with large plants.
- Feel the surface of the compost: push your finger down about 1in (25mm) into the compost. If the compost feels dry, then give your plant some water. If it feels damp, play safe and don't water, but test the compost again the following day.
- If you don't feel confident with any of these tests, get yourself a moisture meter. This is a metal probe which is pushed into the compost; on a dial at the top a needle indicates 'wet', 'moist' and 'dry', so you can see at a glance whether to water.

Judging when to water is a skill which comes with practice and appreciation of the way your plants grow. But it's not difficult. There are a few simple rules to remember, and then you'll always be able to get it right.

Plants need most water when they are growing. This is usually during the warm days of spring and summer, especially when they are developing flower buds and blooming.

Give your plants considerably less water in the autumn and winter when the temperature is much lower and the majority of plants are resting. The exception to the rule is when you keep your plants in a hot room, in which case you should water as often as in summer.

A plant which has completely filled its pot with roots needs watering more often than a plant whose roots still have plenty of room for growth.

The type of compost you use affects the frequency of watering; peat-based compost dries out slowly because it's spongy and holds a lot of water. But when peat dries out, it shrinks and is almost impossible to re-wet. Soil-based composts such as John Innes don't hold water so well and therefore dry out much more quickly, but soil doesn't noticeably shrink.

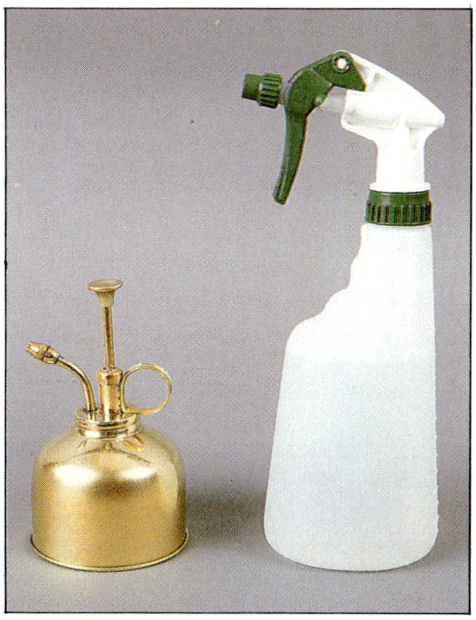

Mist sprayers: regular mist spraying is an important part of houseplant care. The decorative brass sprayer emits a good strong spray but doesn't hold much water. The more practical plastic sprayer holds more water and has an adjustible nozzle — but it doesn't look as pretty!

Plants in clay pots need watering about twice as often than those in plastic pots. This is because moisture is drawn out of the compost by the porous clay, and then evaporates through the sides of the pot.

Watering tips

Try to water your plants in the morning, when the temperature is rising and when the plant's need is greatest. If you water in the evening, your plants will probably stay damp all night, and if the temperature drops this can make them susceptible to the dreaded grey mould and root rot.

Most plants need a winter rest during which time they require little or no watering. Cacti and succulents are the prime examples. In spring wake

How much water do plants need?

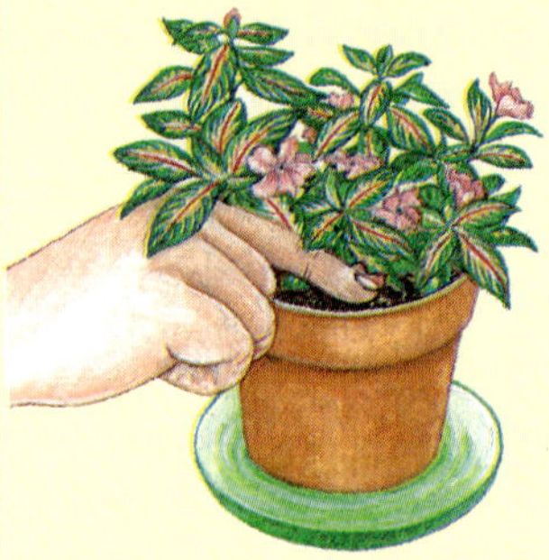

Normal watering: plants such as Busy Lizzie like to dry out slightly. Push your finger about 1in (25mm) into the compost. If it feels dry, then water.

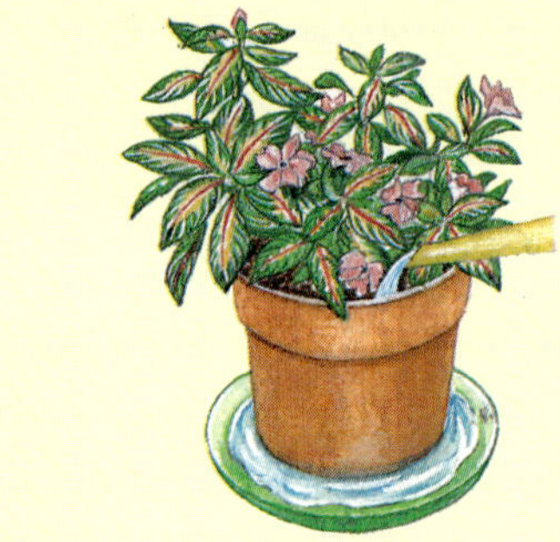

Fill the pot up to the rim with water to thoroughly soak the compost. Wait until water runs out of the pot. Throw the surplus away after 15 minutes.

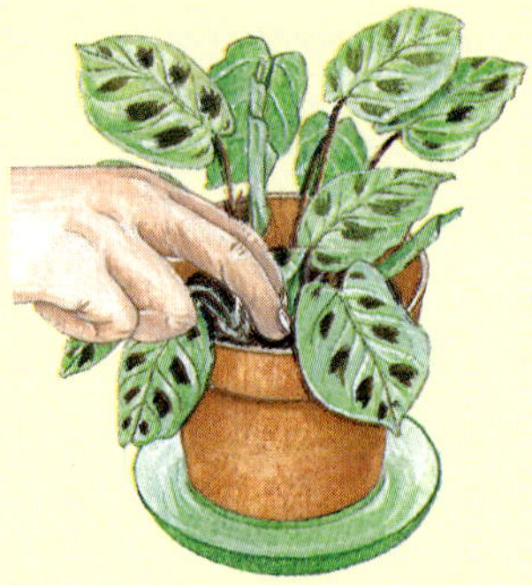

Constant moisture: some plants, like Maranta, need to have their roots moist. Test the compost with a fingertip — if it's dry, the plant needs water.

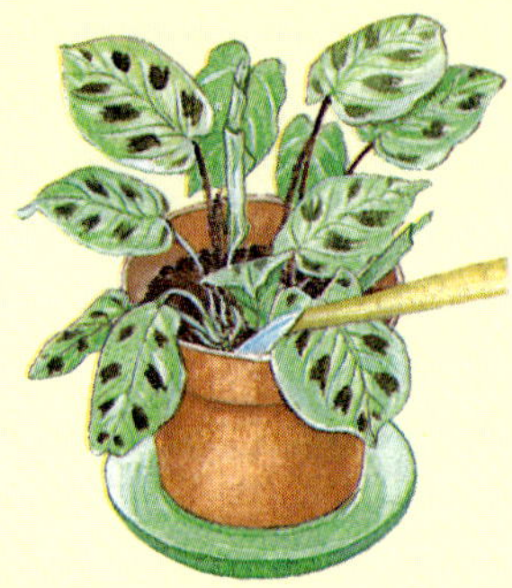

Pour in just a little water — but not enough for any to run into the drip saucer. This way you are watering little and often to keep the compost moist.

Watering problems and cures

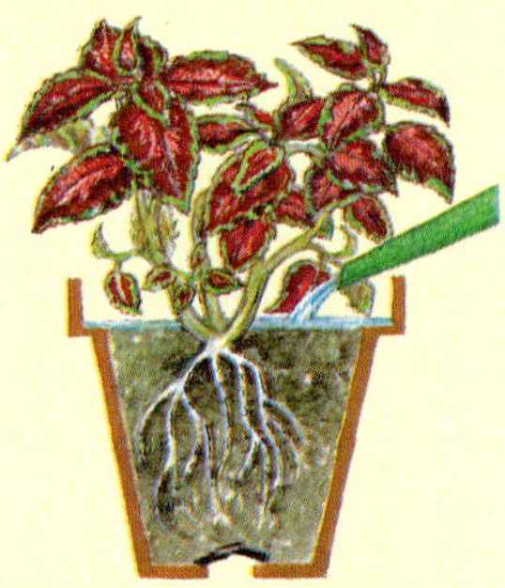

Compacted soil: sometimes the surface of the compost sets hard and solid. Water then remains on top of the surface and doesn't soak through to the roots.

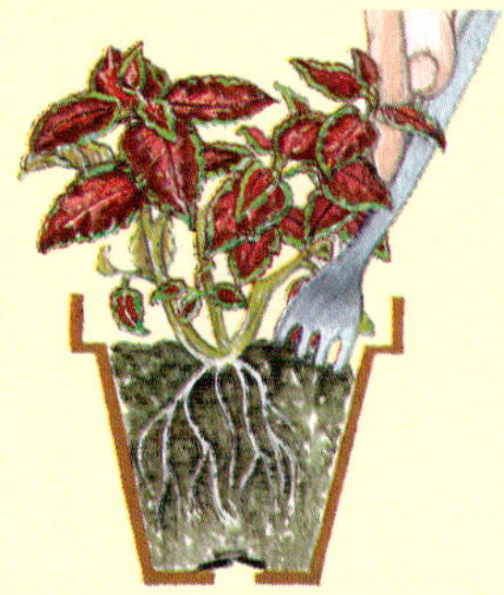

Cure the problem by gently stirring the compost surface with a small cutlery fork. Try not to damage the roots when you poke the fork into the compost.

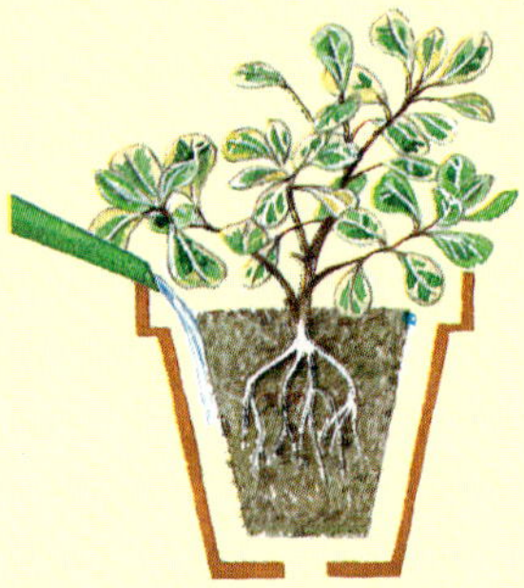

Dried compost: peat shrinks if it isn't kept constantly moist. When you apply water, it just runs straight out of the pot without wetting the compost.

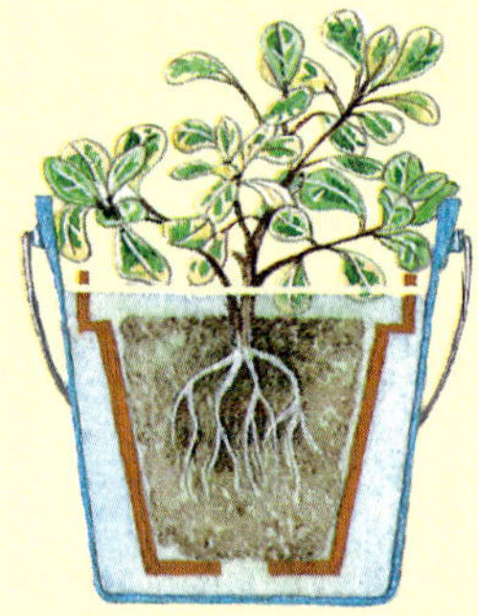

Cure the problem by plunging the plant, pot and all, into a bucket of tepid water. Leave for about 15 minutes or until the compost has swelled. Then drain thoroughly.

your plants up with a good drink. Stand the pots to their rims in a bowl of tepid water until the surface of the compost becomes moist, then remove the pots and let them drain. Do the same if any of your plants have dried out by neglect.

Some plants with woolly or hairy leaves, like African Violets and Gloxinias, hate being watered from above as this wets the leaves and leads to rotting and fungal diseases. Be careful with Cyclamen as well, because water in the centre of the corm can start the leaf and flower stalks rotting. Stand such plants up to their rims in tepid water for five minutes, then let them drain thoroughly afterwards.

Urn plants like bromeliads need the centre of their 'vase' filled with fresh water about once a week. Also the so-called 'air' plants (mostly Tillandsias), which are grown on pieces of wood and coral, benefit from a daily mist spray of water in summer and a spray once a week in winter, despite their name!

Using tap water

Ordinary tap water is fine for most plants even if it is hard and contains chalk. But collect rainwater for Azaleas, Heathers, Urn and Air plants which don't like chalk. If you can collect enough rainwater, use it for all your houseplants, otherwise use cold boiled water for chalk-hating plants.

If you spray your houseplants with hard tap water, you'll find that you are left with unsightly white drying smears on the leaves. These are chalk deposits, but they can be easily removed with a moist soft cloth or sponge.

Providing humidity

Many houseplants must have moist air around their leaves — particularly when it is hot — and for this you may need to create humidity. One way of doing this is to spray the foliage every day.

Another method is to stand pots in trays or saucers containing a layer of gravel or small pebbles sitting in about an inch (25mm) of water.

Yet another way of providing humidity is to stand each pot in a bigger, ornamental container. Fill the space between the pot and the outer container with moist peat up to the pot's rim.

When you're away

A great part of the fun in keeping houseplants is in learning all about them, getting to know your favourites and developing a feel for their particular needs. You'll find that you rapidly become confident about what sort of light conditions and watering they thrive on. But all your patient care may seem to be in vain when you go away for a holiday and are faced with your plants being neglected for several weeks.

A little help from your friends

The best way of all to care for your plants is to have someone giving them exactly the care that you would if you were at home. But take care: if your plant-sitter isn't reliable, you would be better using one of the techniques suggested here.

The commonest fault when friends look after plants for you is not, as you might think, that they forget to water them, but that they are so enthusiastic to do the right thing that they *overwater* them. The best protection against this is to take the trouble to leave a brief list, giving details of your plants' particular needs. Suggest how often they should be watered; which of them, if any, should be sprayed and how often; what light conditions they like — and any 'special points' you can think of. It may take an hour or so of your time, but it'll be well worth it. Even if you've talked your plant-sitter through everything, put it in writing, too — people can be forgetful!

Make sure you leave an appropriate watering-can or jug around, a source of water, and a cloth to mop up spillages. If you group your plants together in the kitchen or the bathroom, there will be less trekking about to be done.

Remember, it isn't just you who'll be delighted when you come home to healthy plants — their temporary guardian will be too!

You must, of course, make arrangements for your plants while you're away, just as you would for your pets. But don't worry unduly — there are several simple precautions you can take to give your plants the maximum care and attention even while you're not there.

The most important thing — as with everything else to do with holidays — is planning. Provided you think ahead, and allow yourself enough time before you leave, getting your plants ready for their holiday treatment shouldn't present any problems.

First of all, there are certain methods of growing houseplants that are naturally very suited to minimal care and these, of course, are ideal for holiday time. They include growing plants hydroponically, where the water level just needs to be kept within certain clearly defined limits and the plants will naturally take just as much moisture as they need. Any sort of enclosed atmosphere calls for very little attention on your part — bottle gardens, terrariums, Wardian cases all have self-regulating environments, which are highly convenient if you're away, or even if you're just forgetful!

So, if you have plants already well established growing in this way, you're in luck. If not, you'll need to work out how your plants will get the necessary watering while you're on holiday.

Weekend breaks

The sort of precautions you must take will depend on how long you're going to be away. If it's just a weekend or a few days, it'll probably be enough to water your plants thoroughly before you leave. Make sure you protect them from very hot sun in the summer: move them

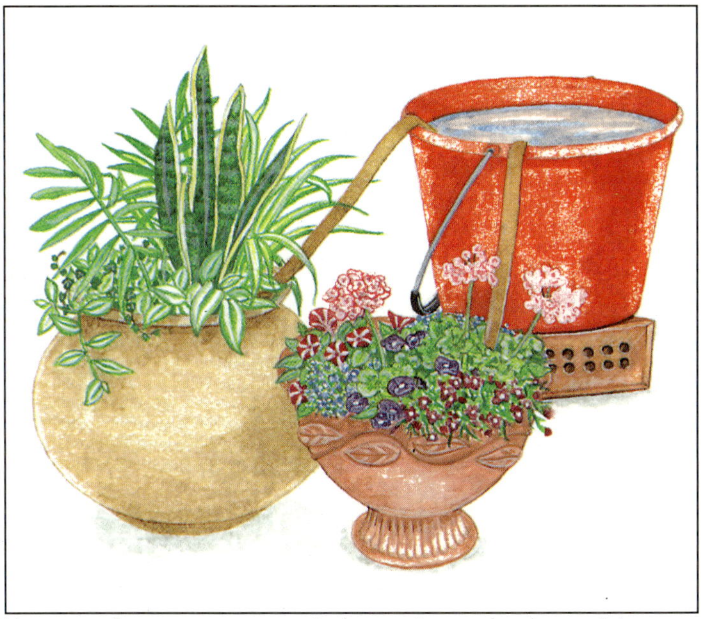

You can rig up your own watering system using lampwick and water raised about 4in (10cm) off the ground.

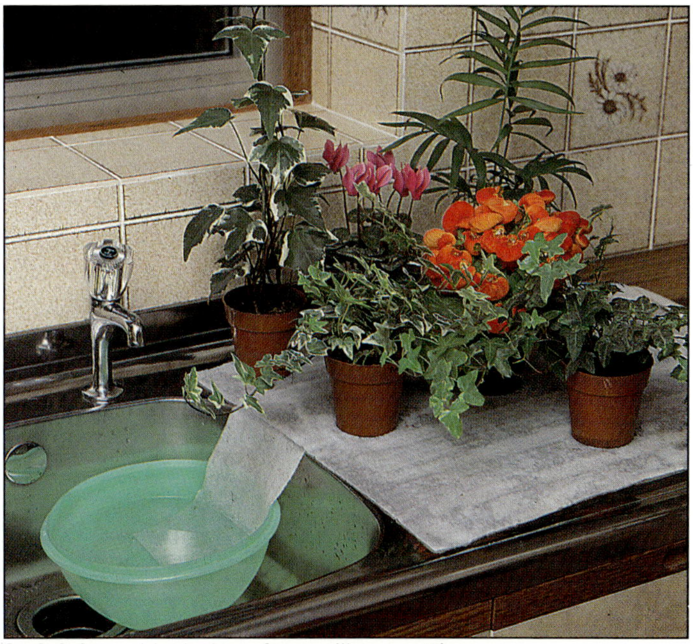

A sink is an ideal place for capillary matting.

away from windowsills, and partly draw curtains at south-facing windows.

In winter you must protect plants from extreme cold: again, don't leave them on windowsills, where the temperature can drop very low at night, but put them in the warmest room in the house — the kitchen, probably, if motorised appliances such as the refrigerator are left on. If the weather's very cold, you could group your plants on top of the refrigerator, where they will benefit from the warmth of the motor.

Even with a short break, if you have a very thirsty plant, or one that likes very high humidity, you may still need to make other arrangements — like the ceramic mushrooms, *right*.

Annual holidays

Surrounding pots with moist peat or wrapping them in moist paper will help to provide a little more humidity for a few days. For very thirsty plants you may need to use one of the watering methods recommended below.

For longer breaks, more action will be needed. It is probably during your annual holiday that your plants will be at their most vulnerable — and this is likely also to be a hot time of the year, when watering is especially important. As a general guideline, if you're away for up to a fortnight, one of the self-watering methods outlined below will probably be adequate.

If you're away for longer, you really will have to co-opt a friend or neighbour. In this case it's a good idea to put your plants together as it will save time and ensure that none gets overlooked.

The bath or the kitchen sink may seem an obvious place to group your plants while you're away. But make sure you protect your furniture. Line the bath with paper towels so that the bases of the pots do not scratch it — don't use newspaper, as some printing inks leach out and cause irreversible staining, especially to acrylic baths. Newspaper is fine in a stainless steel sink, though.

Loss of water from the surface of the compost can be reduced to some extent by lowering the level of available light. Drawing or partly drawing curtains effectively slows down your plant's life processes, and provided you're not away for more than two to three weeks the plant will not suffer. Substantial reduction of light for a longer period would make the plant spindly and straggly and should be avoided.

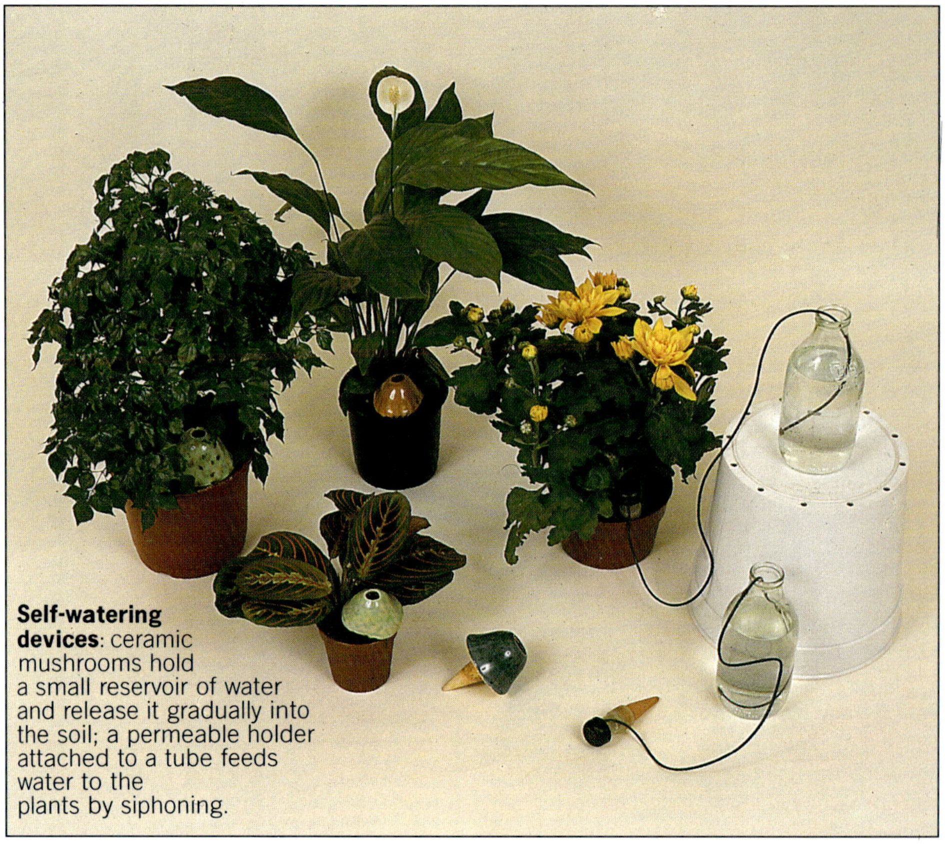

Self-watering devices: ceramic mushrooms hold a small reservoir of water and release it gradually into the soil; a permeable holder attached to a tube feeds water to the plants by siphoning.

Self-watering containers

If you have a few large, specimen plants, you may want to invest in some self-watering containers for them. These consist of a reservoir from which water is passed to the compost by means of a wick or a permeable membrane. You'll need to remove the plant carefully from its existing pot and repot it in the new one, but once you've done that, you've got the benefit of a minimum-care container until you need to pot the plant on. All you'll need to do is to check the water level and top it up occasionally — this will be much less often than conventional watering.

Capillary matting

For a large number of plants, a very simple yet useful self-watering technique is to use 'capillary' matting, which you can buy in any good garden shop or centre. It is a material made of man-made fibres, which acts like a wick in drawing water. You can buy any length of it to order, and it isn't expensive.

For capillary matting to work properly — drawing up water in a steady and controlled way — the source of water must be either lower or higher than the matting itself (the matting usually comes with instructions giving ideal water levels). Lay the matting on a flat, water-resistant surface — a piece of Perspex or vinyl would be ideal — and let the end dangle down. Put the plants in their pots on the matting, and immerse the end of the matting in a bucket of water. The matting will act as a wick, drawing up the water as necessary.

What to avoid

- **Don't give all** your plants a good soaking, then leave them standing in water. Even in summer, plants may be overwatered, and leaving them in pools of water easily causes root rot.
- **Don't just leave** your plants and go away with your fingers crossed. Some *may* be tough enough to fend for themselves with no care at all, but it's a big risk to take, especially in high summer or the depths of winter when temperatures can be extreme.
- **Don't despair** if you do have some casualties. If you take care to do the best you can, most of your plants will be fine. But nobody can predict sudden sub-Arctic weather — or heatwaves! If you have any particularly sensitive plants, it's always best if a friend or neighbour can call in and water them regularly.

Keeping up humidity

Most houseplants come from the tropics where they thrive under conditions that the average human finds almost intolerable. It's not just the heat, it's also the humidity — the amount of water vapour in the air — that counts. When the surrounding air becomes too dry, plants begin to shrivel up.

Plants need a moist environment if they aren't to lose too much water from their leaves. Tiny pores (stomata) open to let in vital gases, but at the same time this allows precious water to escape. It's a process known as transpiration. The more water-laden the surrounding air, the less able it is to accept additional moisture from the plants — so the less water they lose.

Cold air holds only a little water vapour before becoming 'saturated'. On an average winter day, the air is usually moist. Indeed it can be so dense with water vapour that you actually see the moisture hanging in the air, as fog.

As the air warms up, its capacity to hold water vapour increases. It needs more moisture to achieve the same degree of humidity or saturation. In the morning, before the heating system or sunshine has warmed it, a room at a temperature of, say, 50°F (10°C) may be quite humid enough for plants. But, by the time the room is at a respectable 70°F (21°C), it will need twice the amount of water in the atmosphere to achieve the same effect.

Measuring humidity

It's an astonishing fact that a centrally heated room may be drier than the Sahara Desert, when measured on the RH scale. This scale measures 'relative humidity' from 0% (completely dry air) to 100% (completely saturated with moisture). The driest part of the earth, where scarcely any plant life survives, registers only 10%. Many deserts — large parts of Australia, for instance — have an RH value of 20-30%, while on a summer's day in England, the relative humidity will be around 40-50%. At the top end of the scale, humidity in a tropical forest can range from 60-100%.

Plants may enjoy a high humidity, but, on the whole, humans don't. The happy compromise is an RH of between 60-80%, although some plants can put up with a minimum of 40%. You can easily measure the amount of moisture in the air by using one of the inexpensive humidity meters, or hygrometers. This will save you a lot of guesswork when it comes to meeting your plant's moisture needs.

Broadly-speaking, plants fall into three distinct groups: those that need dryish air, those needing moderately humid air and those which prefer a very high humidity. As a general rule, the thinner and more papery the leaf, the higher its moisture requirements.

On page 75 you will find a humidity table which groups some of the most popular houseplants. The majority of houseplants, especially foliage plants, fall into the second category. Most will thrive in normal warm living rooms, provided the air is kept sufficiently moist around them.

For the desert cacti and succulents that need relatively dry air, you may not have to provide any extra moisture. No plant will grow in completely dry air, but it's safe to say that none of your rooms will be entirely free of moisture. These plants need an RH of only 35%.

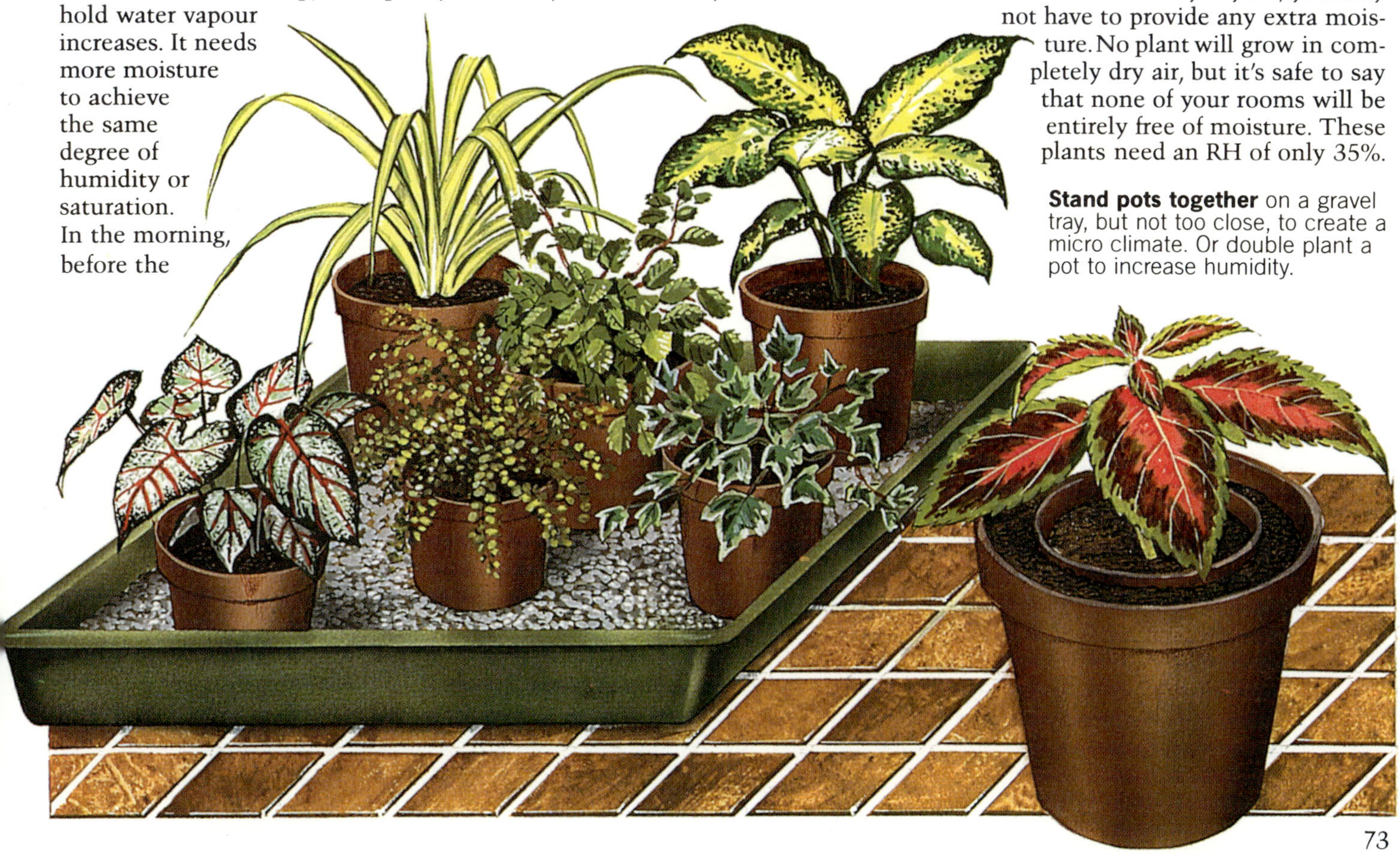

Stand pots together on a gravel tray, but not too close, to create a micro climate. Or double plant a pot to increase humidity.

Useful tips

Strange as it may sound, a fish tank fitted with a fluorescent light in its cover provides a guaranteed method of cultivating the most delicate tropical plants — better than a conventional bottle garden or terrarium. Since the compost at the bottom doesn't dry out very quickly, it's really easy to maintain. And it makes a stunning room feature.

Because the cover is removable, the plants can be sprayed as often as necessary, and if it's kept in a warm room, the atmosphere inside will be very humid.

At the other extreme, it's going to be hard to maintain the kind of conditions that plants in the 'high humidity' category flourish in — but not impossible. Give moisture lovers like Angel's Wings (Caladium) a start by putting them in the bathroom or kitchen — both become pretty humid when in use. Then boost the levels, by providing extra humidity locally. You could well achieve tropical rain forest conditions!

Providing humidity

Because we heat our homes in the winter, creating a moist environment is an all-year-round concern. There's nothing quite like central heating for drying out the air. But whatever the source of heat — whether it be fires, convection heaters or sunshine — the warmer the room, the more attention you need to pay to the atmosphere.

The easiest way to increase the moisture in the air is to provide a constant rate of water evaporation. Bowls of water dotted around the room are simple, effective ways of releasing water vapour into the air.

Humidifiers, which can be clipped on to radiators, work on the same principle. Or you could treat yourself to a free-standing electric humidifier. This works like an electric fan, blowing air over a permanent reservoir of water and vaporising it over a period of hours to create a constant, high humidity. Some are self-adjusting and will turn themselves off and on as required.

All these methods increase the humidity of the air in the room as a whole. But you need to be able to take account of the needs of individual plants as well as your own needs — and many will want a moister environment than you find comfortable. The answer is to provide humidity locally.

Gravel trays

Justifiably popular, gravel trays are a good way of creating a local climate around your plants. Any shallow, plastic, waterproof container will do. Fill it, to a depth of 2in (5cm), or so, with gravel, pebbles or a horticultural aggregate like Hortag. Make sure the granules aren't more than ½in (13mm) in diameter.

Add enough water to reach the top of the gravel, but not to cover it, and place the plant pots on top. Don't allow the pots to stand in water; if the compost in the pots becomes waterlogged, the roots will rot. Top the water up regularly.

Use a container whose width is equal to the spread of the plant, if you can; as the water evaporates, all the leaves will benefit from this vapour 'bath'.

This method is especially good for plants standing above or close to a radiator; the gravel tray has the additional benefit of deflecting the heat away from them. But beware, the trays will dry out more quickly too.

Plunging pots

Plunging pots up to their rims in peat (or Hortag) is a highly recommended way of providing humidity. Just choose a container big enough to leave a large gap all around the plant pot — an ornamental pot holder is perfect for a single, specimen plant. Pack a good, thick layer of peat between pot and container — all around it, as well as underneath. The bigger the outer pot, the better. It works particularly well if the outer container is wide enough to provide a moist surface of peat beneath the spreading leaves. The medium should be kept moist, but not absolutely waterlogged.

Double-planting, as this is also called, has other advantages. It provides a reserve of moisture below the pot, and also insulates the plants' roots, protecting them from sudden temperature changes, keeping them cool in summer and warm in winter.

Creating a micro-climate

Plants always seem to grow much better in groups than in isolation. When close together, they create a micro-climate of their own; the water vapour each transpires tends to be trapped in the foliage instead of being dispersed.

You can stand a number of plants together on a gravel tray, but a group

Danger signs

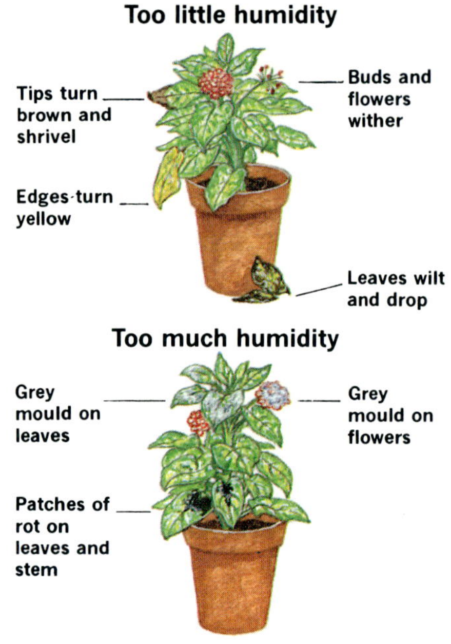

Your plants will give you clear signals if they don't have a sufficiently moist atmosphere around them. The leaves will dry up and shrivel. Or they may turn brown at the edges, making the plants look very unsightly. Flowers and buds may drop, foliage will lack its customary lushness and growth will be altogether poor. Your plants will take on a distinctly jaded air. Take action straight away!

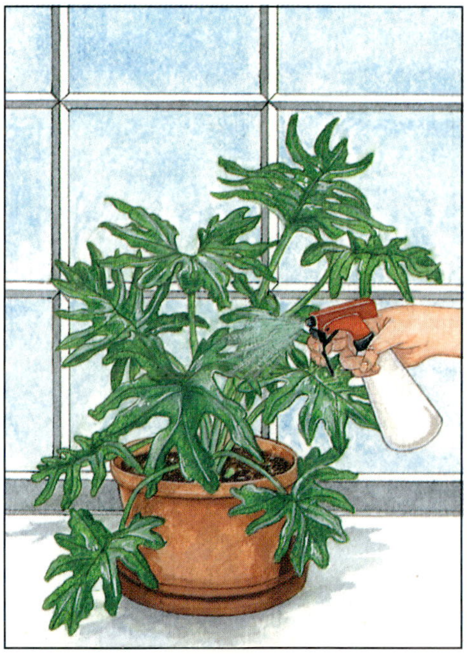

In hot, dry weather mist spray daily; the best time is early morning, and never spray in direct sunlight.

Humidity guide

Plants for dry environments (RH: 35-40%)

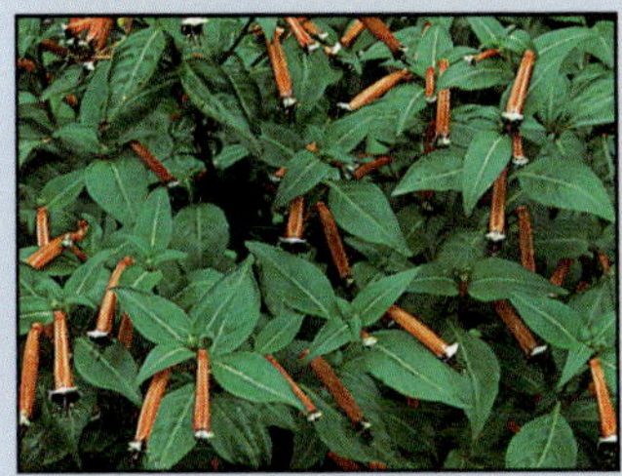
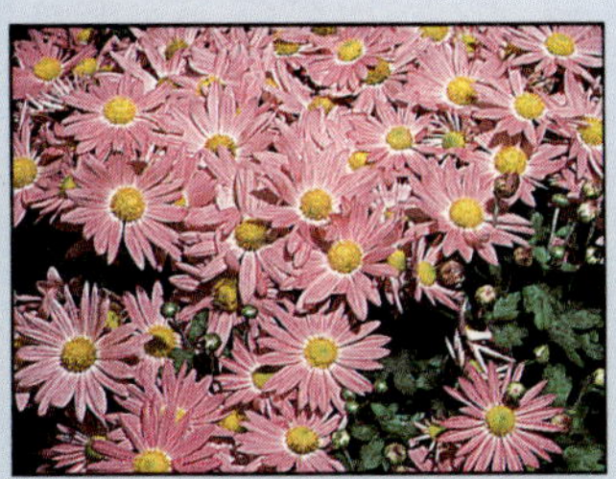
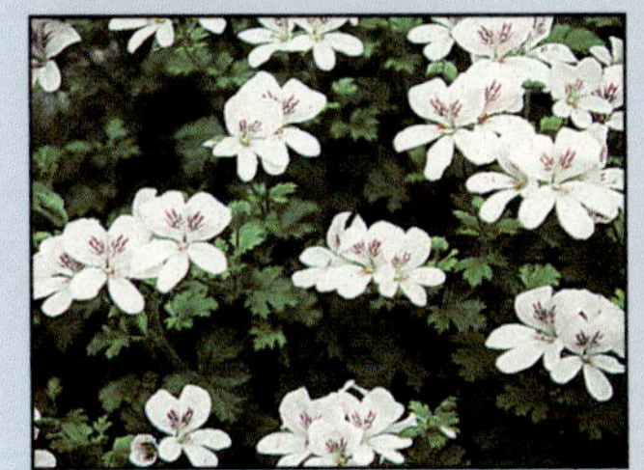
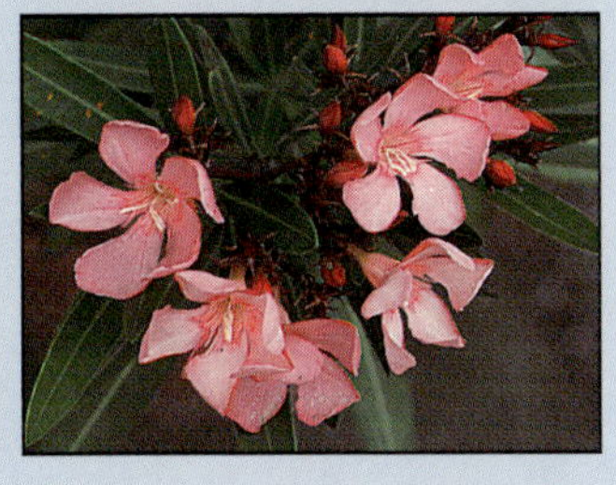

Bead Plant (Nertera)
Cigar Plant (Cuphea), *far left above*
Desert cacti and succulents
Dwarf pot Chrysanthemum, *left above*
Geranium (Pelargonium), *far left below*
Ground Ivy (Glecoma)
Hippeastrum
Jacob's Ladder (Pedilanthus)
Japanese Aralia (Fatsia)
Mother-in-Law's Tongue (Sansevieria)
Oleander (Nerium), *left below*
Ornamental Pepper (Capsicum)

Plants for moderate humidity (RH: about 60%)

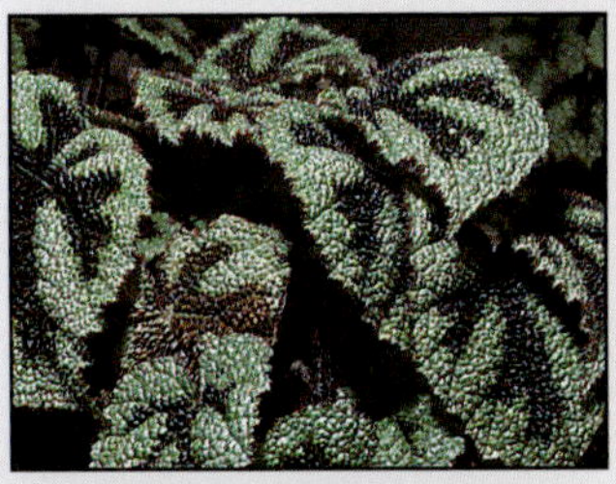
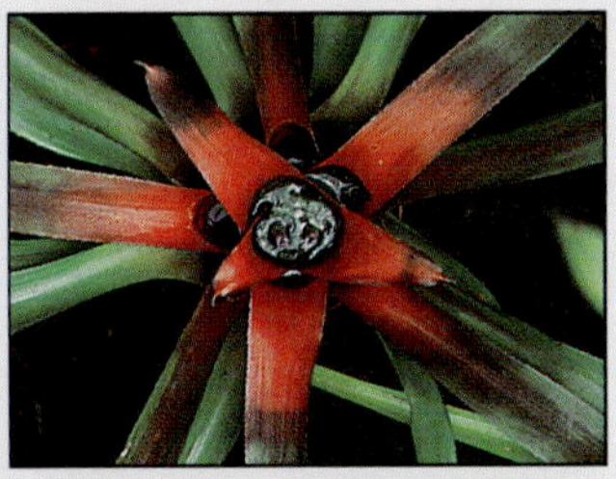
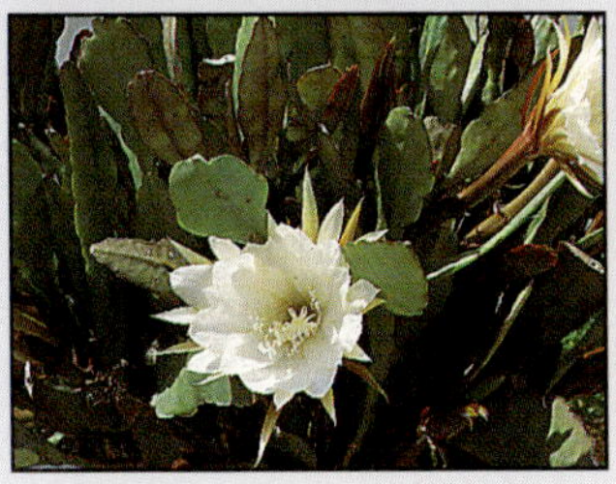
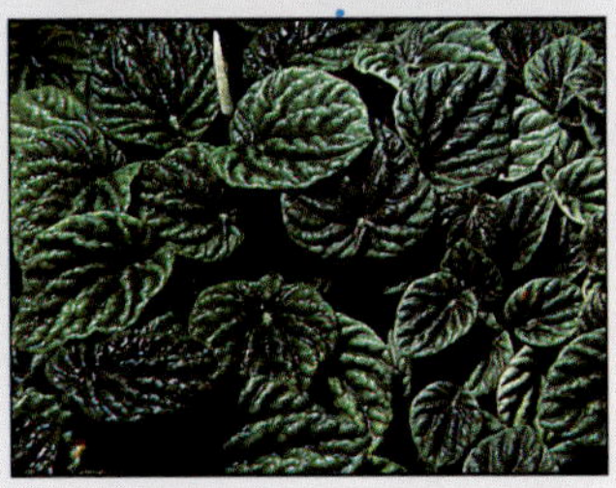

Asparagus Fern
Begonia (particularly the foliage kinds), *far left above*
Bromeliads, *left above*
Cordyline
Croton (Codiaeum)
Dracaena
Dumb Cane (Dieffenbachia)
Ferns
Forest Cacti (e.g. Christmas Cactus and Orchid Cactus), *far left below*
Palms
Peperomia, *left below*
Philodendron
Prayer Plant (Maranta)
Rubber Plant and **Fig** (Ficus)
Swiss Cheese Plant (Monstera)

Plants for very high humidity (RH: minimum 80%)

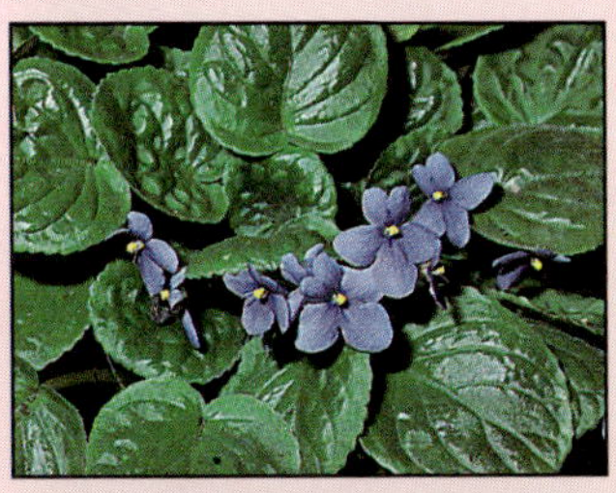
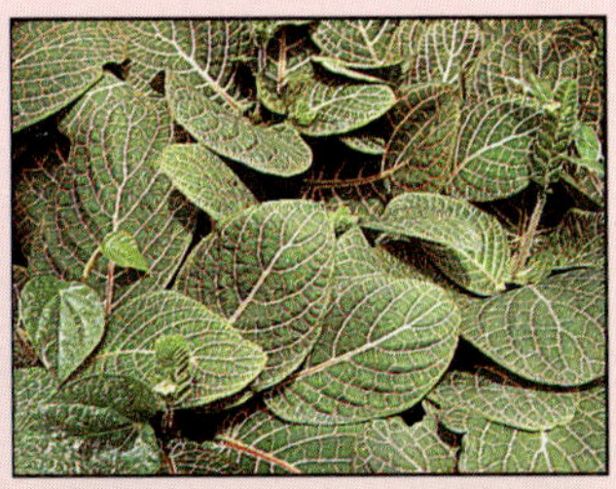
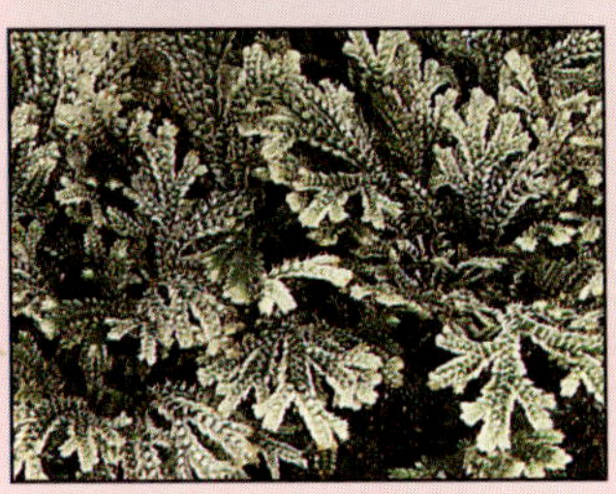
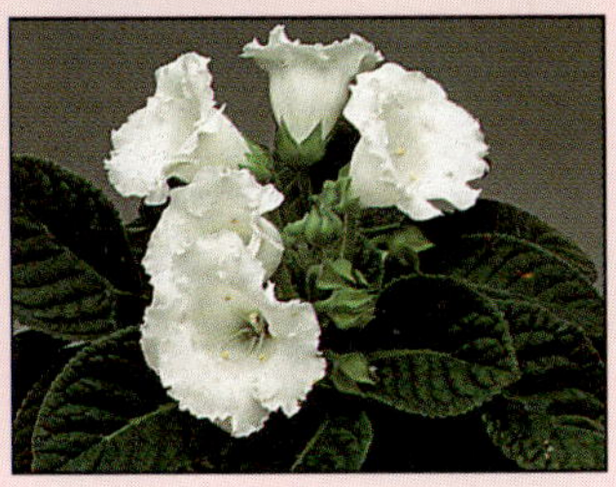

African Violet (Saintpaulia), *far left above*
Angel's Wings (Caladium)
Flame Violet (Episcia)
Net Plant (Fittonia), *left above*
Selaginella, *far left below*
Sinningia, *left below*
Sonerila

planting with pots sunk in peat is probably the best way of creating and maintaining a humid environment. The plants can be arranged attractively together in large planters, or you can plant them in a deep trough.

One word of warning. Occasionally, this can produce too moist an environment, especially if the plants are overcrowded. The tell-tale signs are patches of grey mould — or even rot — on the leaves or stems, or flowers covered in grey mould.

Spraying plants

A fine mist spray of water, from an atomiser gun, may be enough to keep the air around your plants moist enough. But the effects of spraying are short-lived and you may find it tedious work having to spray once and often twice a day. During the hotter months, you will probably have to use other methods as well.

Spraying has another drawback. It's important to spray all around the plants, and, however careful you are, this may damage wallcoverings or furnishings unless you're prepared to move your plants before spraying them.

On the credit side, mist spraying keeps leaves clean, and the coating of small droplets has a cooling effect on hot sunny days, It also discourages red spider mite, one of the houseplants' scourges.

Spray in the cool of the morning, before the atmsophere warms up, so that the foliage dries off before the evening. Never spray in direct sunlight, the small droplets will magnify the rays of the sun and brown scorch marks will appear on the leaves. Use tepid water, preferably from a rain butt. Tap water in many homes is hard, and this may leave a white, chalky deposit on the leaves. Should this happen, sponge off the deposit with tepid rainwater.

Don't spray plants with hairy or woolly leaves — the African Violet (Saintpaulia), for instance. Beads of water will be trapped and may cause the leaves to rot.

It's probably a good idea to rely on one of the other methods, and to reserve the mist spray for boosting humidity during the hotter months of the year. Don't be surprised if you end up using all the methods described here, one way or another. Different plants, and different conditions, will always demand a variety of solutions.

Pots and containers

Gleaming copper coal scuttles, teapots, old china potties and hanging baskets — all can make stunning homes for houseplants. Displaying pot plants well is an art form: if you get the effect right, everyone will notice.

When you buy a plant it comes in a standard clay or, more likely, plastic pot (**1**). The tiniest pot is about 2$\frac{1}{2}$in (6cm) in diameter across the inside rim. Sizes increase by about $\frac{1}{2}$in (13mm) at a time, all the way up to 15in (38cm).

Clay pots are thicker and help to insulate plants against the cold better than plastic. But clay is heavier and likely to shatter if it's dropped. Ornamental terracotta containers (**2**), have the same qualities as clay pots. Glazed terracotta (**3**) is more useful as the glaze stops moisture escaping through the pot and leaving rings on the furniture.

You can grow plants in virtually any ornamental container which will hold soil. Perhaps you have some old china jugs or potties (**4**) you could use. Or even a lovely jardinière (**5**). Much cheaper and easier to find are stylish modern china containers (**6**) which can be bought at department stores.

An economic alternative but just as pretty are baskets (**7**). They can be in natural, mellow colours or bright and shiny with paint and varnish. The disadvantages are that baskets tend to be flimsy and they need a drip tray inside to stop water going straight through.

Cheerful, coloured metal and enamel containers (**8**) are particularly useful if you want bright colours to match your decor. But be wary of unsightly rust.

Glass is traditionally used for bottle gardens (**9**) because it lets through plenty of light at the same time as protecting the plants inside from draughts and cold temperatures. Modern glass and lead terrariums are very attractive (**10**) and an effective way of showing off tiny, tender plants.

Gleaming brass (**11**) and copper pots look absolutely splendid holding leafy green houseplants. The catch, of course, is that you need to get the metal cleaning fluid out almost as often as you have to feed the plant inside it! Before using metal containers, line the inside with kitchen foil so the pot doesn't get ruined by water — it is a good idea to do this with all precious ornamental containers.

When planting direct into any container without drainage holes, provide a good, thick layer of pebbles or pea shingle before filling with compost. This is so that excess water can run away from the plant's roots so they are not at risk from rotting.

If your ceilings are a suitable height (and strength) you can broaden your dimensions by using hanging baskets (**12**). Most useful are the plastic ones with an attached drip tray; with these you won't get water all over the floor. Don't be content with the range of pots and containers offered by your local shops and garden centres. Ingenuity plays an important role in growing plants and it's surprising what you can find if you rummage around in junk shops.

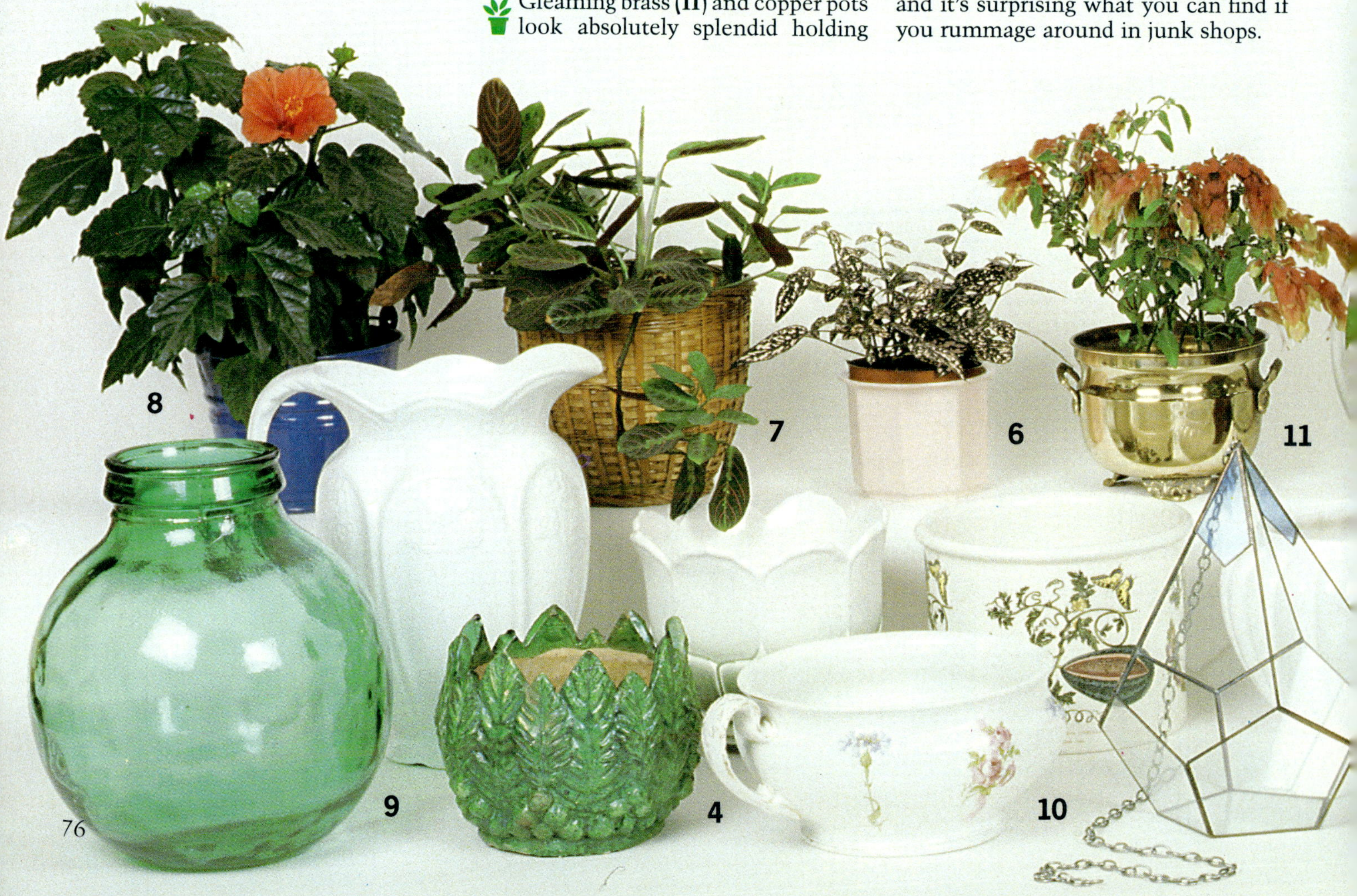

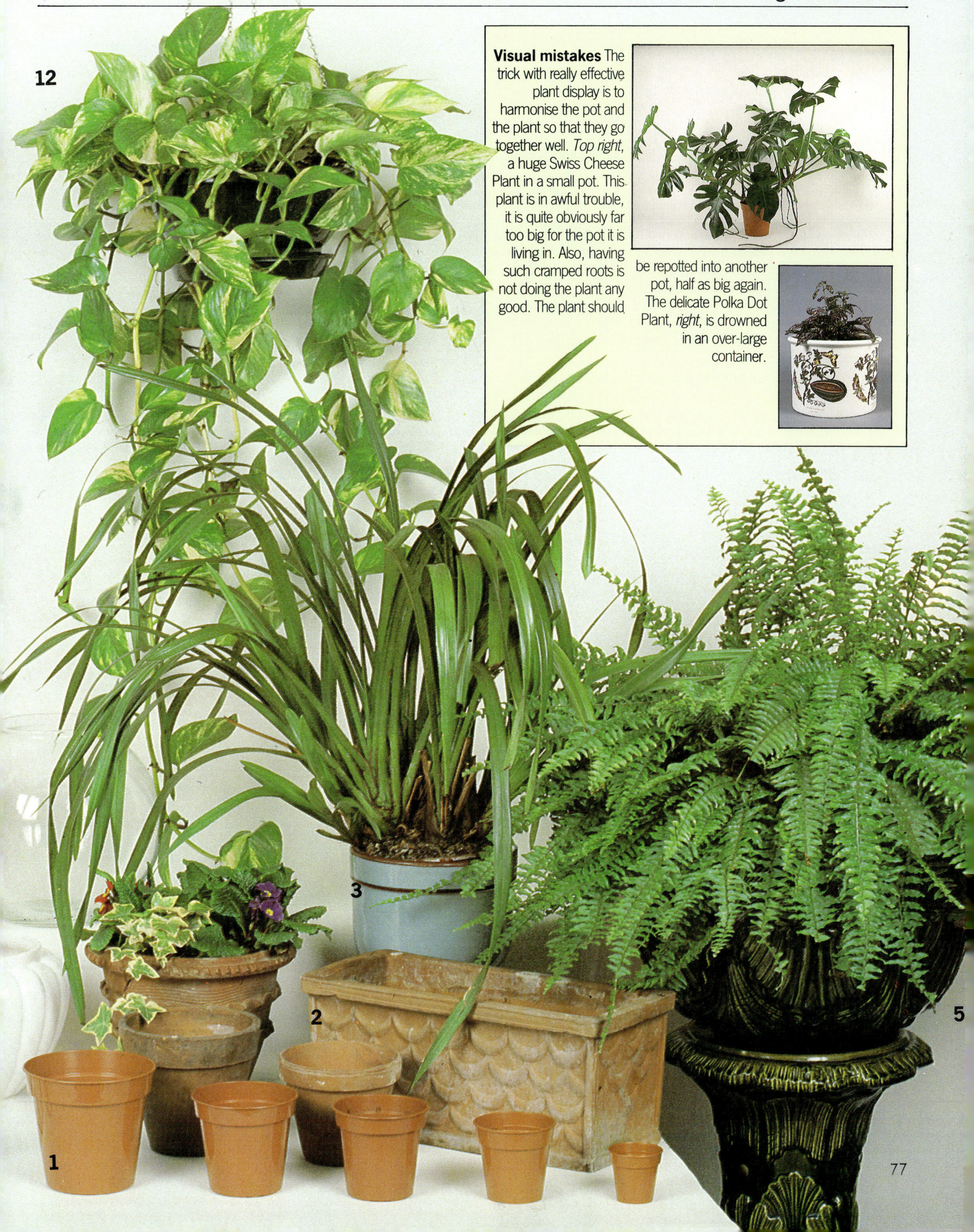

Visual mistakes The trick with really effective plant display is to harmonise the pot and the plant so that they go together well. *Top right*, a huge Swiss Cheese Plant in a small pot. This plant is in awful trouble, it is quite obviously far too big for the pot it is living in. Also, having such cramped roots is not doing the plant any good. The plant should be repotted into another pot, half as big again. The delicate Polka Dot Plant, *right*, is drowned in an over-large container.

The answer's in the soil...

Compost may look uninspiring, but it's wonderful stuff — it's the source from which your houseplants draw essential nutrients and water through their roots, and without which they cannot survive. Healthy compost, composed of the right ingredients, is vital if you want your plants to flourish. Not only does compost feed your plants, it keeps their roots moist, holds air around the roots and secures the plant upright in its pot.

Garden centres offer a huge range of composts — but don't be overwhelmed; many of them are much the same thing, but sold under different brand names — just as similar washing powders appear under a variety of brand names in the supermarket. To help you come to the right choice, we'll describe the various ingredients of compost and tell you which particular type is right for your plants.

The most important rule is not to put your houseplants into ordinary garden soil. Not only will this fail to provide the right mix and nutrients — it will also contain pests and diseases that will attack and harm your plants.

Most composts are composed of either peat or soil (loam), plus fertiliser and sometimes sand as well. Some plants do best in soil-based compost while others prefer one that is peat-based.

Soil-based compost

This is made of sterilised loam (which just means soil), with a smaller quantity of peat and sand, plus fertiliser. The

Compost: What goes in?

The most popular and easily available soil-based composts are the John Innes range, which were researched by the John Innes Institute in the 1930s.

The idea for them came with the discovery that garden soil was not suitable for the artificial conditions in which houseplants are grown. In theory, John Innes compost should be the same wherever you buy it — in practice, of course, it will vary with the quality of the materials.

John Innes potting compost is available in three different types, all carefully designed to promote healthy growth in plants at different stages of their lives. The diagram on the right shows what it is made of. The compost contains seven parts of sterilised loam, three parts of peat and one part of coarse, washed sand. These are measured by volume and mixed together thoroughly. Then a basic fertiliser mix — made up of two parts of hoof and horn meal, two parts of superphosphate and one part of potassium sulphate — is added to the compost by weight: the higher the number of the John Innes compost, the more of this fertiliser mix is in it. Finally, small amounts of chalk or limestone are put in.

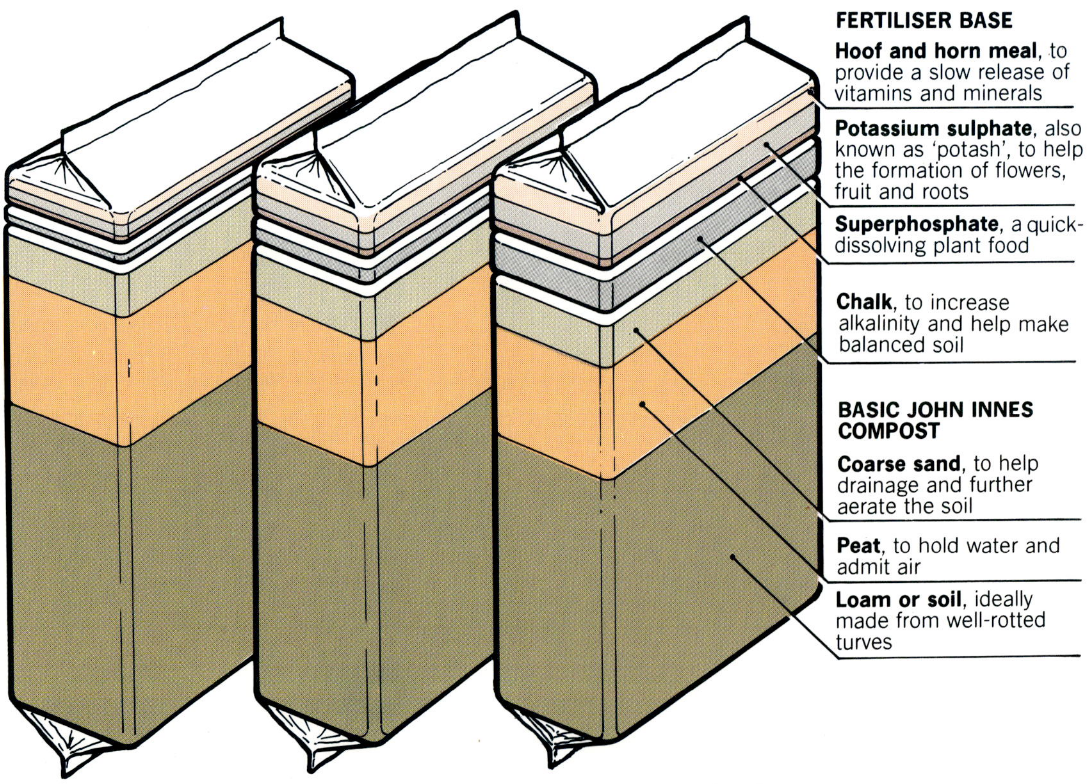

John Innes No 1
For seedlings and cuttings, in small pots up to 4in (10cm)

70lb (32kg) compost
4oz (118g) fertiliser base
¾oz (21g) chalk

John Innes No 2
For mature plants, in medium pots 4-8in (10-20cm)

70lb (32kg) compost
8oz (226g) fertiliser base
½oz (14g) chalk

John Innes No 3
For vigorous and fast-growing plants, in large pots 8in (20cm) and bigger

70lb (32kg) compost
12oz (340g) fertiliser base
2½oz (71g) chalk

widely-used John Innes Composts are based on a mixture — really a recipe — of these four ingredients (see diagram). John Innes Seed Compost is used to give seedlings and cuttings a good start; it doesn't contain any fertiliser, which would 'burn' the tender young roots.

The proportion of each ingredient in the compost is most important: loam is the main ingredient and gives the mixture body and prevents the plant's food from being washed away. Peat holds water well, rather like a sponge does and keeps the roots moist. Sand drains the compost quickly, which prevents waterlogging, and lets air get to the roots. Fertiliser provides the food that plants need for healthy growth.

Soil-based compost holds the fertiliser for about 12 weeks, so you don't need to feed your plant for the first three months after repotting. Don't be tempted to feed repotted plants too soon or to give extra fertiliser to a young plant or a small one; too much of a good thing can kill a plant completely!

Peat-based compost

Peat-based compost is a more recent development, and it's usually the medium your new plant is growing in when you buy it. Nurserymen use it because it's light to carry, and partly because it's cheap to buy and easy to sterilise and unlikely to have weeds or diseases in it.

Most brands of peat-based compost (often also called soilless compost) are a mixture of peat and fertiliser. Or it can be composed of an inorganic material, such as Perlite or vermiculite, mixed in with the peat and fertiliser. Perlite is the brand name for a type of white, irregular shaped granule made from volcanic rock, while vermiculite is expanded volcanic rock — both of them are very light. Fertiliser is released to the plant more quickly from a peat-based compost than from a soil-based one and you will need to feed the plant about six weeks after repotting.

The main disadvantage of peat-based compost is that it can dry out completely if you forget to water the plant in hot weather and be difficult to moisten again thoroughly. The remedy is to stand the pot to over its rim in a bowl of water, until the compost unshrivels, fills out and becomes moist again. If even this doesn't work put a drop or two of Fairy Liquid, or another good quality washing up liquid, into the water, which

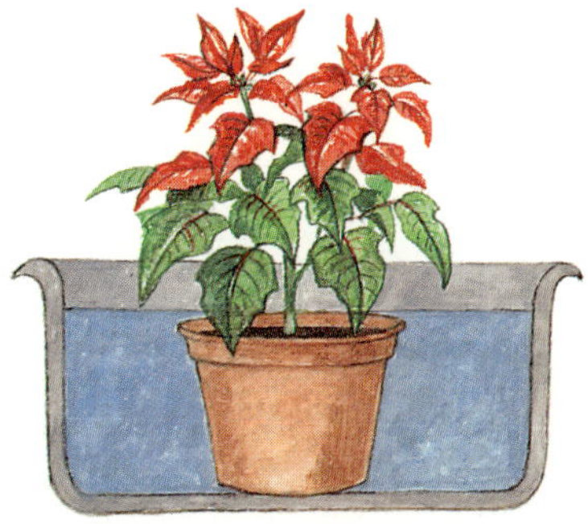

If the compost has dried out, immerse the whole pot in water for 15-20 minutes.

coats the peat and helps it to reabsorb water.

It's a good idea to use plastic pots with peat-based compost as plastic is non-porous and doesn't draw out moisture from around the roots and dry out the compost as quickly as clay.

Top dressing

The term 'top dressing' refers to the method of renewing the top layer of compost in a pot without moving the plant or interfering with its roots. Just take off the top 1-2in (25-50mm) of compost and replace it with fresh compost.

Top dress a plant whenever the compost in its pot has developed a crusty surface, or if you have a large mature plant in a heavy container which is too big to repot easily. Water the new compost thoroughly, and don't feed the plant for at least two months.

Wetting agent

There is a special wetting agent available now that you can add to the compost to help it retain moisture — called acrylic copolymer, it comes in granules that you mix in with the compost. You then don't have to water the plant so often. You can get this wetting agent at gardening departments and garden centres.

Fresh is best

Whatever type of compost you choose, try to use it soon after buying it; an open bag of compost loses its goodness within a couple of months after being exposed to air.

Once you have got your plant growing happily in one type of compost (or have bought a plant already in a particular type of compost) try to stick to it. Plants are like some people — they get used to the place where their roots are and don't take kindly to change!

Special composts

Some plants have rather special needs if they are to do really well. Azaleas and Heathers, for example, hate lime — it pushes the soil balance towards alkalinity rather than acidity.

So for those plants you must make sure you ask for a special compost, called ericaceous compost, which has no lime in it. Other plants need particularly good drainage — if their roots are vulnerable to rot, for example, or if their natural habitat is specially light, airy soil. This is provided by extra amounts of coarse sand, charcoal or Perlite.

Most good garden shops or garden centres will have a range of special composts for the most popular houseplants, but if you're feeling adventurous you can always try mixing your own.

The following are just a few examples of 'recipes' that are worth trying — there are probably as many different recipes as there are keen gardeners!

Cacti need specially good drainage. In a pot, where their roots grow more closely together than in the wild, there's a risk that they may develop rot if the soil stays too damp. Many good garden shops, and all specialist Cacti suppliers, will be able to offer you compost specially designed for Cacti and other succulents.

Mix as follows:	*or*
2 parts John Innes No 1	1 part loam
	1 part peat
1 part coarse sand	1 part coarse sand

Palms should be grown in a soil-based compost. They need good drainage and lots of fertiliser — you can even use a little manure, provided you don't mind the smell in the house!

Mix as follows:

4 parts loam	2 parts coarse sand
1 part peat	3 parts leaf mould

Ferns can belong to two different types: they can be epiphytic, which means they grow on trees; or terrestrial, growing on the ground. Good drainage is important for both, but especially for the epiphytic ferns.

Mix as follows:

For terrestrial ferns	*For epiphytic ferns*
2 parts loam	1 part peat
2 parts peat	1 part coarse sand
2 parts leaf mould	1 part leaf mould
1 part coarse sand	
1 part charcoal	

Potting — do's and don'ts

By growing a plant in a pot you limit its size to suit your home by preventing its roots from spreading. In this way indoor favourites like the Rubber Plant and Tree Philodendron, which grow to enormous heights in their native habitat, are restricted to heights of 4ft (1.2m) or so. But there is a limit to the amount of cramping your plant will put up with; sooner or later it will need a larger pot and fresh compost if it's to thrive.

The mistake that many houseplant owners make is to leave their plants in the same pot for too long. With regular feeding most plants will stay happily in the same containers for many months, but eventually the goodness in the compost will be depleted and the amount of compost steadily dimishes as the roots take up more space. As young plants grow, they're potted on into ever larger pots until they reach their 'final size', and even then you'll still need to renew the compost from time to time.

Reading the signs

Growing plants are started in the smallest possible pots and should be moved on as soon as their roots have filled them. This ensures that there's always fresh compost for the plant's roots to penetrate. But don't repot unless it's really necessary — the process *does* disturb the plant and plants aren't at their best growing in pots which are too large for them. 'If in doubt, don't' is the motto for potting on.

A few plants give very clear signals when they're in trouble — the fat fleshy roots of Chlorophytum, for instance, will push up through the drainage holes — but most plants push a few roots through, so don't automaticially pot on until you've examined the roots. Carefully remove the plant from its pot. If the compost is completely packed with roots, the plant needs moving on. But if there's still plenty of root-free compost visible, pop the plant back into the pot.

Potting

It's well worth while potting up a number of plants in one go. Find a spot where you will have a large surface to work on, and where all the plants, pots, potting compost, etc, can be collected together. Potting is a messy business, so it's a good idea to spread a large plastic sheet or newspapers over your working area. Protect any nearby furniture, too.

Have a selection of potting composts ready. It's best to pot plants on into the compost that they're used to, but if in doubt consult the guide to potting composts on pages 78-79. The night before start preparing; thoroughly water all the plants you want to repot. This will make it easier to get them out of their pots. Soak any new, unglazed clay pots, too, for at least 12 hours, to rid them of any impurities. Clay pots should always be damp before compost is put in them; this stops them drawing water out of the compost too quickly.

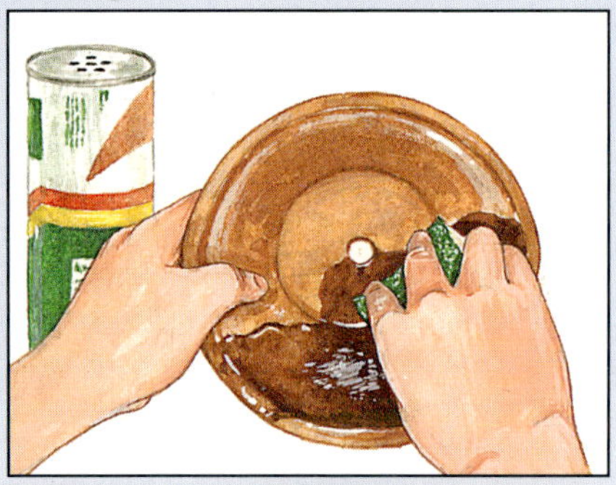

1 Prepare the pots. Scrub your used pots (plastic or clay) with hot water and a household cleaning powder, tackling any lime deposits or other debris with a soft scrubbing brush. Rinse the pots thoroughly in clean water. Leave them until the surface water dries up; if the pots are too wet when you come to use them, the compost may stick to the sides.

Similarly rinse any new clay pots that have been soaking overnight and allow the surface to dry off.

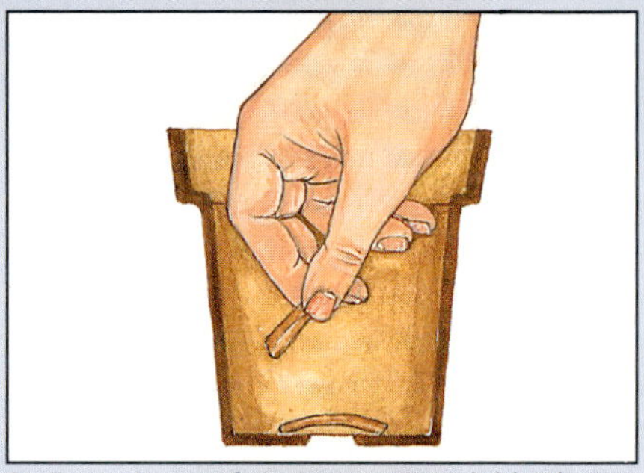

2 Put a layer of drainage material in the bottom of clay pots. (The only exceptions are clay pots that are to stand on any capillary matting or automatic watering tray.) Use broken pot fragments (crocks), if possible. Place one large piece over the hole, and cover it with several smaller pieces. If no crocks are available, use pebbles, but make sure that they don't block the drainage holes and prevent moisture escaping.

Plastic pots, with their numerous small drainage holes, don't usually require 'crocking', but if they are to stand in a saucer or drip tray, it's a good idea to cover the bottom with pebbles. This helps prevent the compost becoming too soggy if water is accidentally left in the saucer.

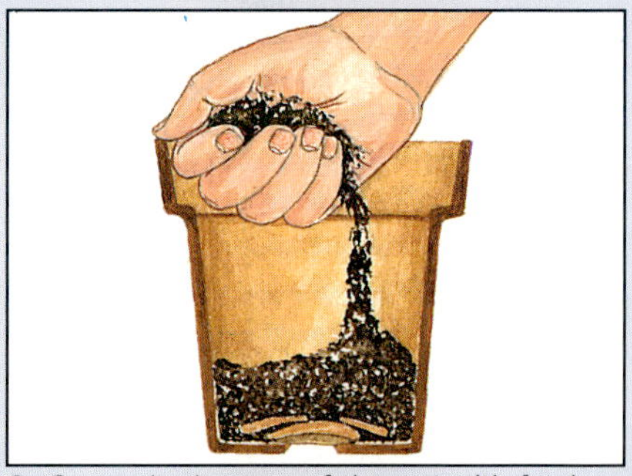

3 Cover the bottom of the pot with fresh, moist compost and firm it lightly, then remove the plant from its pot.

Some plants may be difficult to examine in this way. Large plants, for example, are not so easily removed from their pots and will be dealt with later. You may find that the plant has become so pot-bound that the projecting roots need to be broken off before you can turn the plant out.

Roughly speaking, annual plants raised from seed and other fast-growing plants will need to be potted on several times in the space of a few months. Usually they start off in a 3½in (9cm) pot and are potted on to a final size of 5in (13cm) — or 6in (15cm) for larger plants. The slow growers — which include most of the permanent houseplants — need potting on only once a year, or even less for very slow growers.

Plants with small root systems — Begonias, Bromeliads, cacti and succulents, many ferns, Pepper Elders, Mother-in-Law's Tongue and Saintpaulias — shouldn't be potted on until their pots are well-filled with roots. And some plants actually prefer to be pot-bound — these include the flesh-rooted Clivias and Hippeastrums, which always flower better when their roots are cramped.

When to pot on your plants

Never move plants during their resting season. The roots won't be able to penetrate the new compost, which will in turn become very soggy and cause root rot. Wait until the spring or summer — preferably April for slow or moderate

step by step

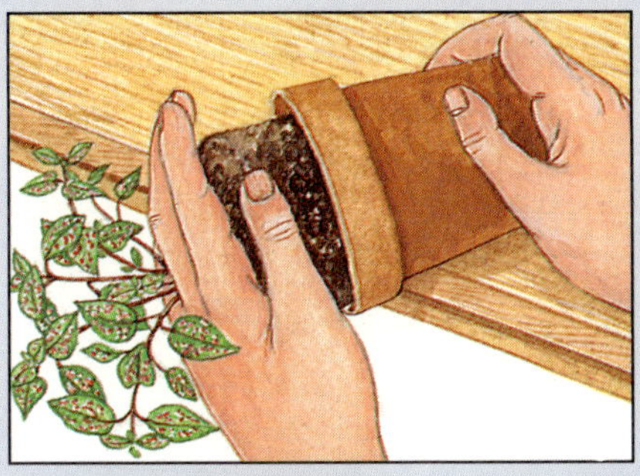

4 Take care when lifting the plant; first slip one hand, palm downwards, beneath the plant's foliage to cover the surface of the compost, with fingers either side of the stem. Turn the pot upside down. Give the bottom some sharp taps, or tap the pot rim on the edge of a table. This should loosen the rootball enough for you to lift the pot away. If there's any difficulty, push a sharp knife down between pot and compost.

Roots coming through the bottom of the pot may stop you removing the plant easily. If you have difficulty, break the pot or cut through it with shears.

Now check the roots. Any that are completely dried up or rotten must be cut off. Gently clear away clinging fragments of drainage material.

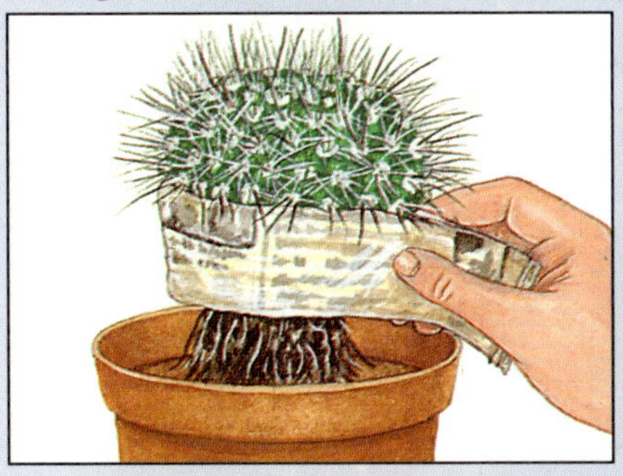

5 Not all plants can be dealt with in that way, though. Prickly plants present their own problems. Gloves can help, but the best way to deal with a cactus, for example, is to 'lassoo' it with a thick band of rolled up newspaper.

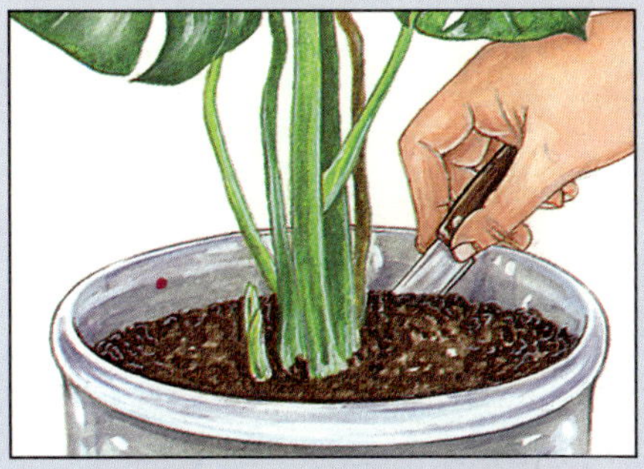

6 Large plants, too, need a slightly different approach – and you may need someone to help you. Lay the pot on its side and tap the rim with a block of wood, at the same time gently pulling at the plant. You may need to run a long-bladed knife around the inside of the pot to release the rootball, or, failing that, break the pot. (The repotting of large plants is covered on page 83.)

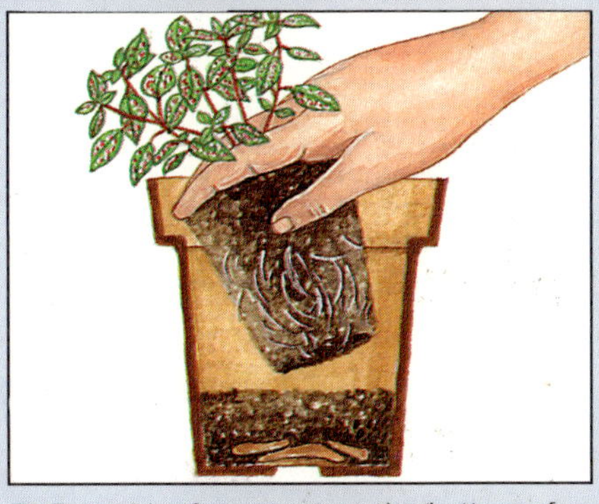

7 Put a bit of compost on the bottom of the pot then stand the plant right in the centre. Be sure to leave room between the top of the rootball and the top of the pot to allow for watering; the top of the rootball should be between ½-2in (1.3-5cm) below the rim depending on pot size (see 'Space for water', below. Remember to allow for a light covering of compost then adjust the layer of compost beneath the rootball accordingly.

Take the opportunity to correct any tilt the plant has been suffering from by building up the compost underneath it.

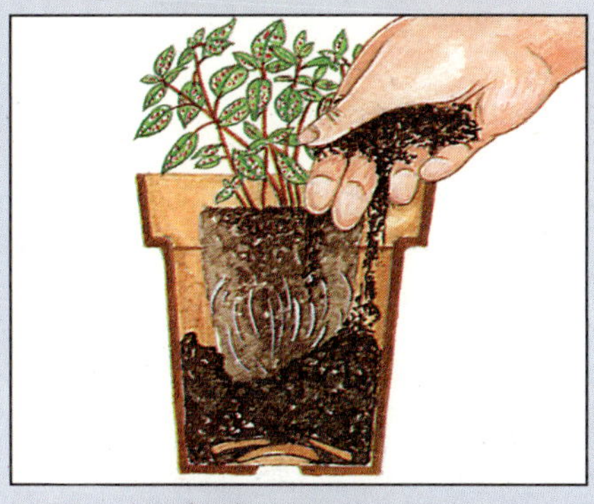

8 Fill in with fresh compost, pouring it down the sides of the rootball so that the plant is firmly supported. Scatter a little over the top; the mixture should completely cover the roots, but shouldn't reach as far as green stem or the lower foliage.

Tap the pot on the table to eliminate air pockets and settle the compost, then push it down with the fingers, gently, just enough to hold the plant secure. But don't firm too much, it may hinder drainage.

John Innes composts need a little more firming than the soilless types.

Space for water

Pot size	Space below rim
Up to 5in (13cm)	½in (13mm)
6-7in (15-18cm)	¾in (19mm)
8-9in (20-23cm)	1in (25mm)
10-12in (25-30cm)	1½in (38mm)
15in (38cm)	2in (5cm)

growers which will just be coming into growth.

Sick plants should never be moved to another pot; the shock may be too much for a weakened plant to bear. So wait until it's on the mend.

Choosing the best pot

Plastic pots deserve their popularity; they are cheap, easy to clean and lightweight. There's a big choice of shape, too. But plastic pots do have disadvantages. Large, heavy plants, may well topple them, for instance, and there can be a risk of waterlogging. Unlike the old-fashioned clay pots, plastic pots can't 'breathe' to allow water (and air) to pass through the sides. So plants in plastic pots need watering less often.

Which pot size?

Existing pot size	Move up by
Up to 4½in (11cm)	½in (13mm)
5-9 (13-23cm)	1in (25mm)
10in (25cm)	2in (5cm)
12in (30cm)	3in (7cm)

For fast-growers, like annuals, double up at least on the above recommendations or you'll be forever potting on. For instance, the usual practice is to move plants from a 3½in (9cm) pot to a 5in (13cm) pot.

Clay pots are ideal for large or top-heavy plants, but they do need a lot more work both in preparation and when they're in use (see overleaf for more details). Clay pots are more fragile, of course, and being porous the compost in them dries out more rapidly, especially in warm conditions, so plants will need frequent checking. But this does mean there's less chance of plants becoming waterlogged.

The size of pot you choose is important. It's no good potting on into too large a pot. If there's too much compost around the roots, it will become very wet and sour, causing the roots to rot.

Pots are usually measured across the top, inside the rim, either in inches or centimetres. You will usually find the measurement imprinted on the base of the pot. A selection of 2½in (7cm), 3½in (9cm), 5in (13cm) and 7in (18cm) pots

Whether you're repotting a flowering plant, Yucca, fern or trailer, it's important to choose the right pot size. And if using plastic pots take care not to overwater.

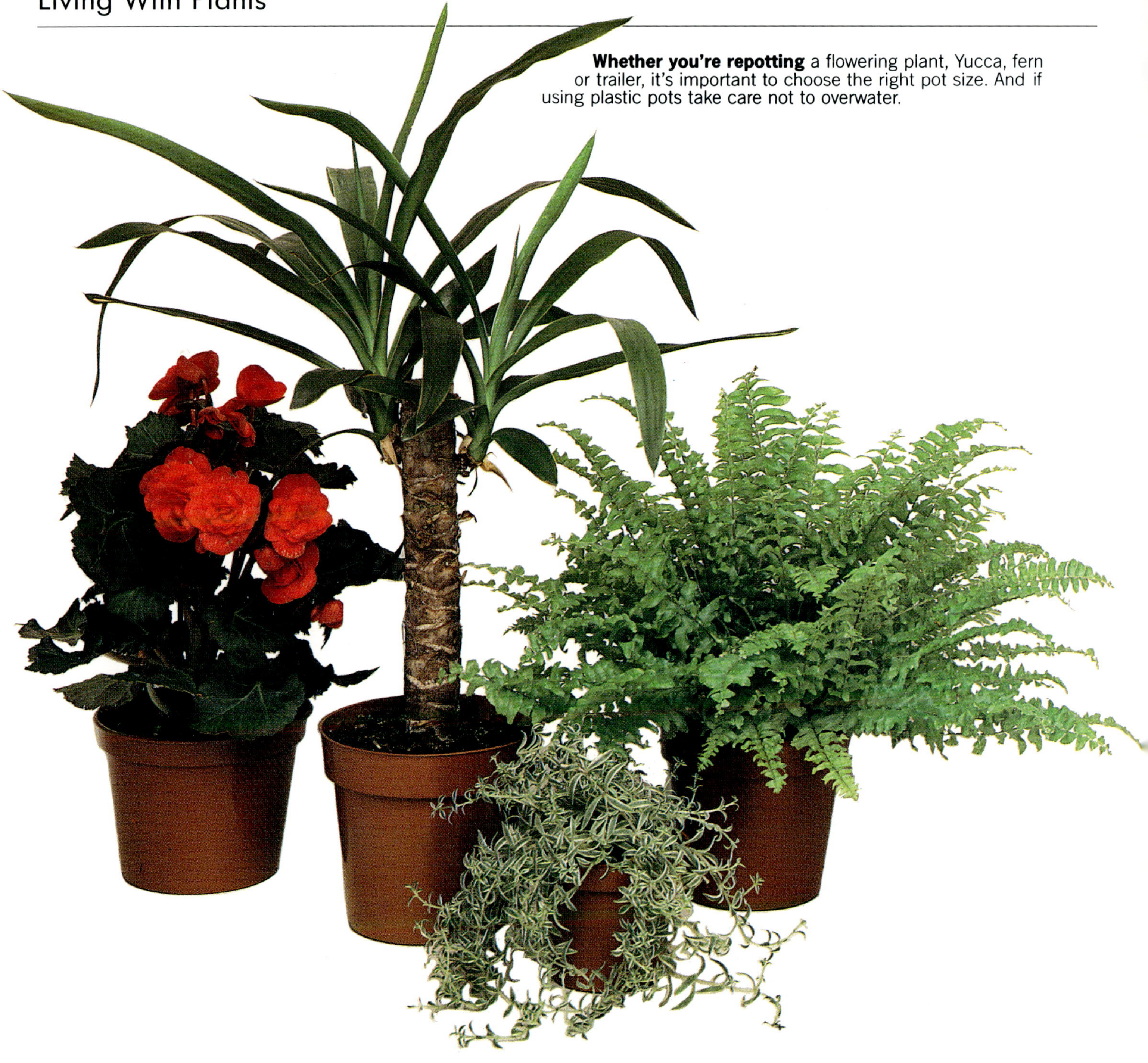

should meet most of your needs with a few larger pots for more mature plants. It's probably worth investing in a few half-pots, too. As the name suggests, these are usually about half the depth of normal pots and are useful for shallow-rooting plants like Saintpaulias, Pepper Elders and Wandering Jews. (See previous page for what size pot to choose.)

Repotting and top-dressing

A plant that's grown as big as you want it — say reaching a final pot size of 12-15in (30-38cm) for large plants — must still be moved. Every second year it will need repotting to give it a fresh supply of compost. Do this in April, just as growth is starting.

Remove the plant from its pot in the usual way. Using an old kitchen fork, or other similar tool, tease away the compost from around the roots. Cut off any roots that are dead or damaged and trim the rootball by about a quarter.

You can use the old pot again, or select a fresh one; either way, prepare it as you would when potting on. Put the plant back in the pot and fill in with compost, checking that the level is correct, just as you would when potting on.

In the years when you aren't repotting you'll need to 'topdress' the plant. To do this you simply remove the top 1-2in (2.5-5cm) of compost and replace it with fresh; depending on what compost was used before, topdress with either John Innes No 3, or a soilless compost with extra fertiliser added, if it comes without. Topdress, too, if the surface of the compost has developed a whitish crust — the result of too much lime in the tap water.

Potting on a large houseplant

It is inevitable that, soon or later, one of your houseplants will outgrow its pot and will need to be repotted into a larger one. This is best done during the growing season, between April and September, when plants are at their most adaptable. If the plant is not too big, it is a fairly simple procedure to remove it from its pot and repot it directly into its new one. A large specimen, on the other hand, is a different proposition and the conventional method of repotting may present difficulties, which often result in the plant ending up either off-centre or at an acute angle, both of which problems can be very hard to correct.

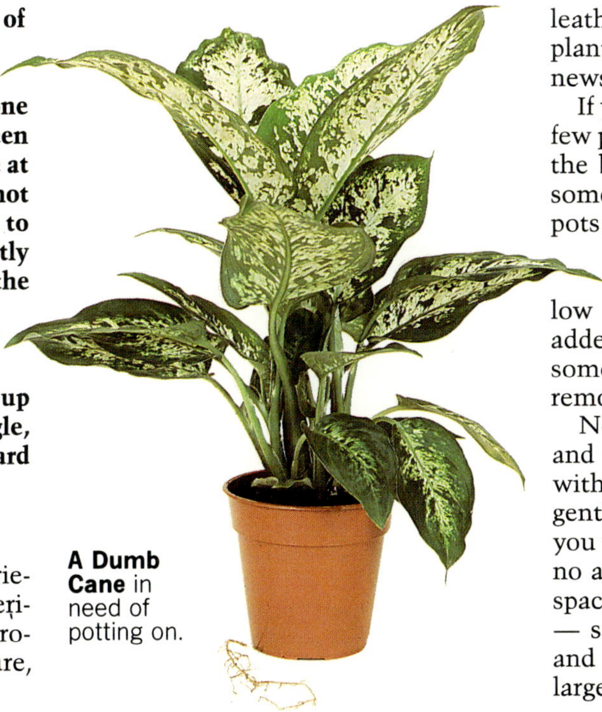

A Dumb Cane in need of potting on.

What you need

First of all, always select a good proprietary compost rather than using unsterilised soil from the garden. This will provide your plant with the correct texture, a healthy balance of nutrients and a growing medium free from pests and diseases.

Choosing the right pot is also important. Buy one that is 2in (5cm) larger in diameter than the old pot, leaving a space of around 1in (2.5cm) between the root-ball and the new pot. Do not be tempted to use too large a pot as a plant can suffer from being over-potted.

Plastic pots are both cheap and clean but terracotta pots are preferable because they are porous. This helps to prevent a build-up of water which can be detrimental to the roots. Their weight also provides a large plant with a greater degree of stability.

What to do

Having selected both new pot and compost, water the plant evenly and tap the old pot gently all around its rim to loosen it — you may need to run a long knife round the edge of the compost. Remove the plant from its old pot, while holding it gently but firmly in position with one hand placed over the surface of the soil. You may need someone to help you to support the plant while you remove the pot. Once you have done this, gently place the root-ball of the plant on some newspaper, taking care not to damage it. (If you are repotting a large cactus with spines, you will need to protect your hands with heavy-duty leather gloves, or even by wrapping the plant up carefully in several layers of newspaper.)

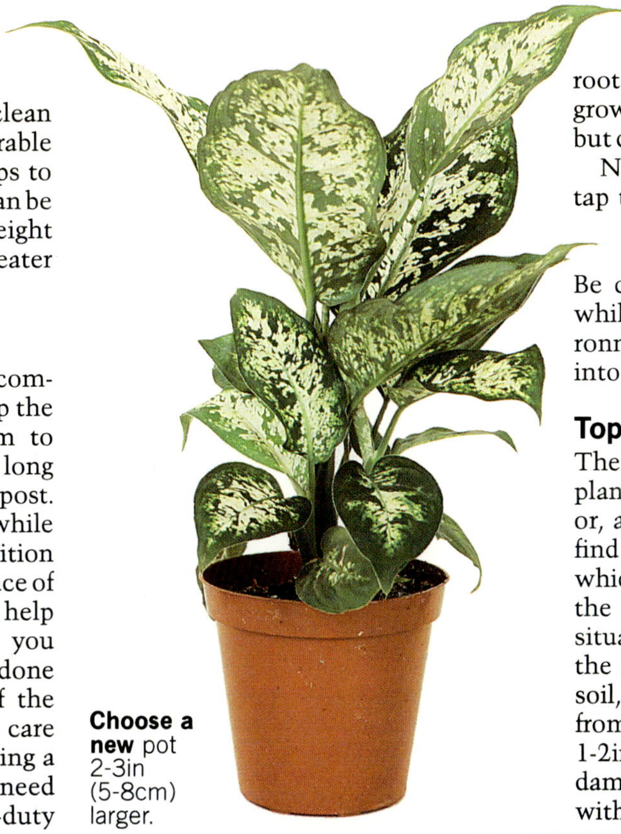

Choose a new pot 2-3in (5-8cm) larger.

If you are using a terracotta pot, put a few pieces of broken earthenware pot in the bottom to aid drainage. Next, add some compost so that the rims of both pots are level when the old one is placed inside the new one. Obviously, if the old pot is too low down more compost should be added; and conversely if it is too high some of the compost should be removed.

Now position the old pot in the centre and fill the gap between the two pots with compost, taking care to firm it gently and evenly with your hands as you work and so ensuring that there are no air spaces. Also take care to leave a space at the top of the pot for watering — say, 2in (5cm) for a 10in (25cm) pot and 3in (8cm) for a 12in (30cm) pot or larger. When this space has been completely filled with compost, gently but firmly push the old inner pot downwards and rotate it slightly before removing it. With a bit of luck, this will have created a mould into which the plant will now fit snugly.

Before repotting, examine the rootball of your plant; if it is too tight, gently tease out some of the roots in order to encourage them to grow into their new growing medium — but do take care not to damage the roots.

Now place the plant in its new home, tap the pot in order to settle the compost around the root-ball and water the new compost sparingly. Be careful not to overwater the plant while it is still adapting to its new environment and making fresh root growth into the new compost.

Top dressing

There may come a time when a large plant either grows too big to be repotted or, alternatively, when it is difficult to find a larger container than the one in which it is currently growing. If this is the case, you can improve the plant's situation to some extent by top dressing the surface. To do this gently rake the soil, removing some of the old compost from the surface to a depth of about 1-2in (2.5-5cm), and taking care not to damage the roots. Replace the compost with fresh.

Encouraging a plant to flower

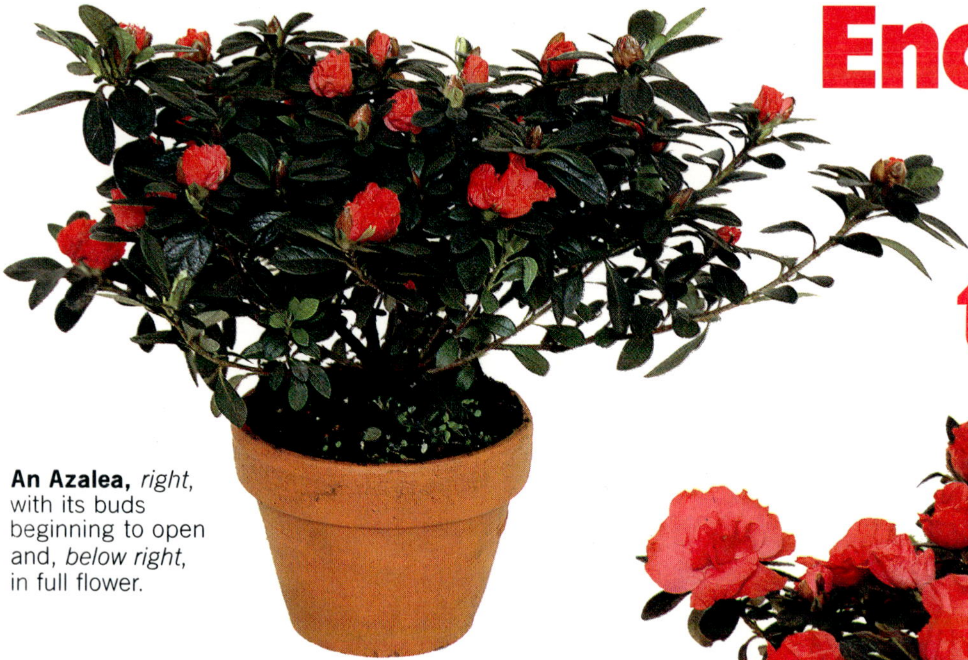

An Azalea, *right*, with its buds beginning to open and, *below right*, in full flower.

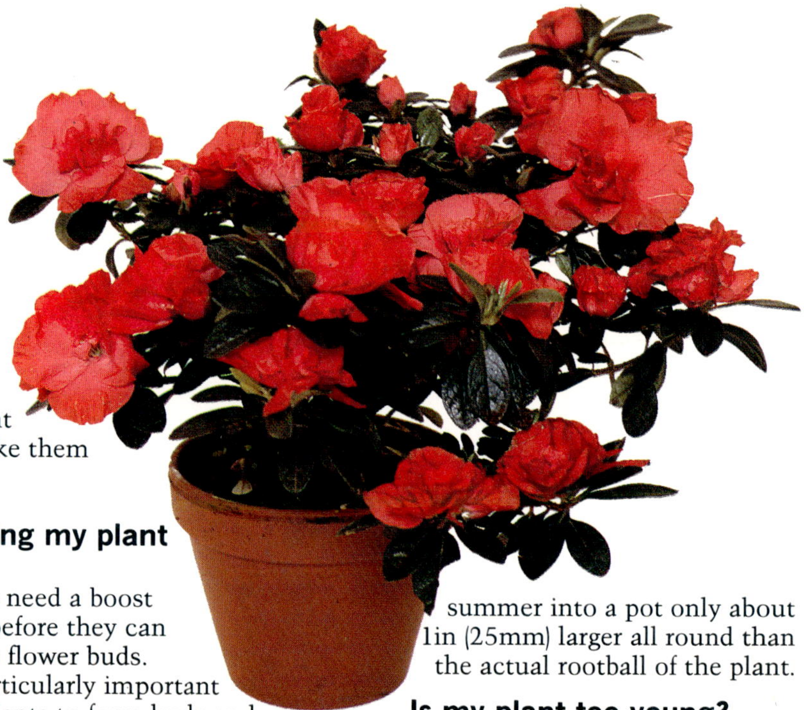

It is terribly disappointing when a much-loved houseplant fails to flower. However this is more likely to be your fault than the plant's — you may be doing something wrong by failing to supply some vital requirement that your plant needs to develop flower buds. But don't worry, it's very easy to solve this problem of lack of flowers by taking a few simple cultural steps.

Sometimes a particular plant won't flower despite all your loving care and attention throughout the year. If this happens ask yourself the following questions.

Is my plant getting enough light?

Flowering houseplants are essentially windowsill plants; they need maximum light all year, but especially when buds are developing and when the plant is in bloom. If you suspect your plant isn't getting enough light, move it to a bright position shaded from direct sun.

Cacti and Succulents from the dry areas of the world are often reluctant to flower and won't do so at all without plenty of sunlight. Don't keep them anywhere but in the brightest light and in as much direct sun as possible.

One solution to the light problem is to supply artificial light. You can use fluorescent tubes or special growing bulbs or lamps; these are similar to ordinary light bulbs but they transmit light in the frequencies that plants use for growing. African Violets respond well to this treatment but you need to give them between 16 and 18 hours of artificial light a day to make them flower.

Am I feeding my plant correctly?

Many plants need a boost of fertiliser before they can start to form flower buds. Potash is particularly important as it helps plants to form buds and flowers. The other major plant foods, nitrogen and phosphorus, are also needed but in much smaller amounts.

During the growing season — from early spring until early autumn — water your flowering houseplants every two weeks with a liquid fertiliser containing a high proportion of potash. Most of the houseplant fertilisers and Phostrogen are fine for this.

Cacti and Succulents, despite popular belief, need regular feeding with a special Cactus fertiliser, such as Cactigrow, to encourage them to flower.

Is my plant's pot too big?

Some plants need to have their roots fairly cramped before they stop growing roots and start producing flowers. Three popular prime examples are Geraniums, African Violets and Clivia. So if you suspect the pot your plant is in is too big for it, repot the plant in spring or summer into a pot only about 1in (25mm) larger all round than the actual rootball of the plant.

Is my plant too young?

Azalea, Anthurium and Clivia, among others, need to be reasonably large and mature before they can produce flowers; the plant's priority is to grow a good root system first to give it the strength to develop flowers.

Some plants, such as the Shrimp Plant, Cigar Plant and Busy Lizzie, only produce a lot of flowers when they are a nice bushy shape with lots of stems for the flowers to appear on. Pinch out the growing tips when the plant is small.

Do the flower buds drop?

Sometimes plants form flower buds that drop before they open. The Christmas and Easter Cactus are especially notorious for this. With these two plants it's lack of light that causes flower drop; the buds twist themselves off the stems in an attempt to reach the light. Keep your plant in a bright window with the buds facing the light.

All about pruning

Many of our houseplants come from tropical rain forests where they are able to run riot — some sprawling all over the place, others reaching enormous heights. Such unrestrained habits can obviously not be allowed in the home and we therefore have to get rid of bare leggy stems , and to encourage plants to make a bushier, neater growth.

Not all houseplants, however, need pruning. Many of the lower-growing perennials, for example — like the Chinese Evergreen *(Aglaonema modestrum)* and the Cast-iron Plant (Aspidistra) — will never get out of hand. And neither will most of the flowering pot plants such as the Clivia. The very fact that these plants are growing in pots automatically restricts their size to some extent.

Those houseplants that do require some degree of pruning can be divided into two groups. The one requires nothing more drastic than a simple technique known as 'pinching' which encourages a bushy, compact growth and, with some plants, also ensures more flowers. The other group of plants needs to be more severely cut back, either to restrict their size or to produce a neater, more compact growth, and this is generally done before, or as soon as, plants enter their growing season — in other words, some time in late winter or early spring.

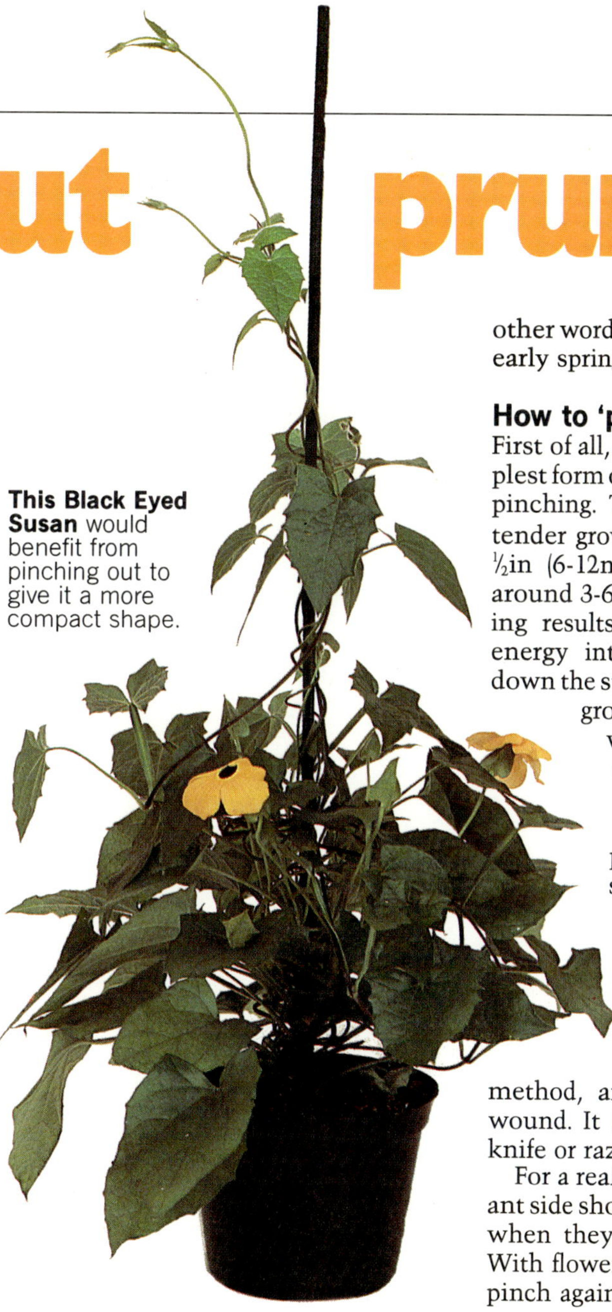

This Black Eyed Susan would benefit from pinching out to give it a more compact shape.

How to 'pinch'

First of all, let us take a look at the simplest form of pruning, which is known as pinching. This involves removing the tender growing tip — i.e. the top ¼in-½in (6-12mm) — from young plants, around 3-6in (8-15cm) in height. Pinching results in the plant diverting its energy into producing shoots lower down the stem, which results in a bushy growth rather than a single stem with a few meagre shoots at the top. In the case of flowering plants you will also find that more flowers are produced, because each side shoot will carry a bloom.

This technique is so-called because the tip of the stem can literally be pinched out between forefinger and thumb. This is not, however, the best method, and can result in a ragged wound. It is far better to use a sharp knife or razor blade.

For a really bushy growth, the resultant side shoots can also be pinched out, when they are about 3in (8cm) long. With flowering plants, however, do not pinch again after the second pinching,

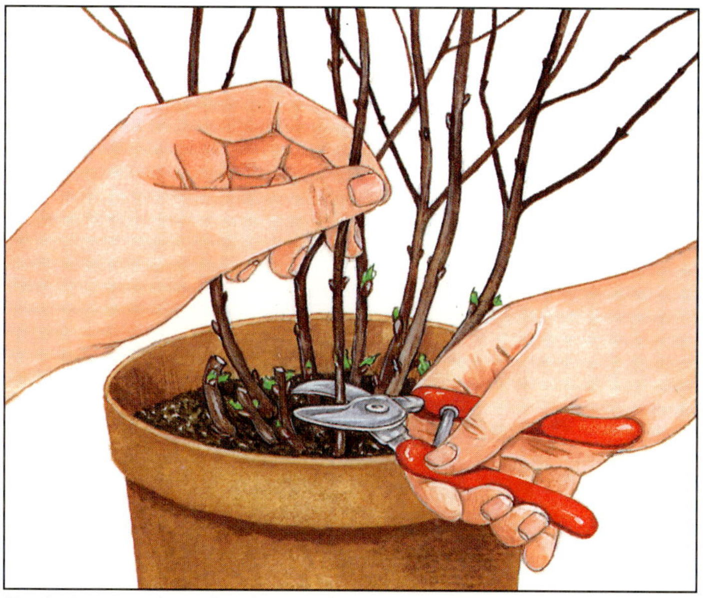

Fuchsias need cutting back after their winter rest.

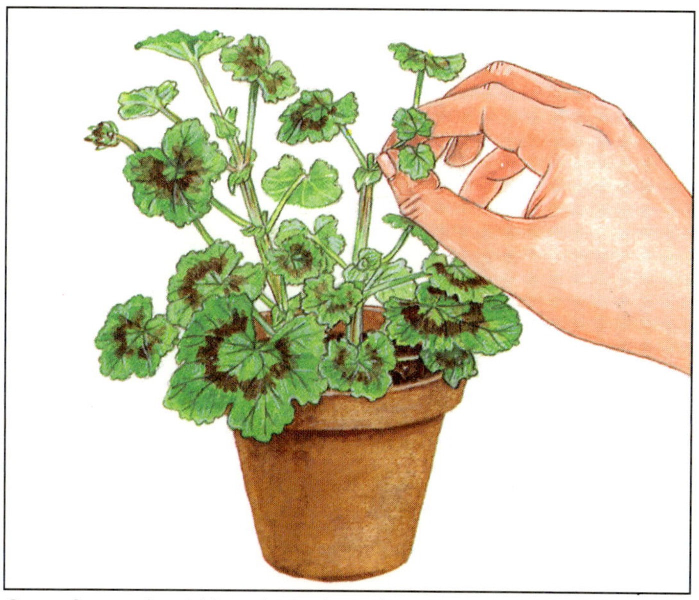

Geraniums should be pinched out between finger and thumb.

Plants to pinch

Foliage plants

Aluminium Plant (Pilea)
Beefsteak Plant (Iresine)
Croton (Codiaeum)
Flame Nettle (Coleus)
Ivy (Hedera)
Japanese Aralia (Fatsia)
Parasol Plant (Heptapleurum)
Polka Dot Plant (Hypoestes)
Purple Heart (Setcreasea)
Swedish Ivy (Plectranthus)
Trailing Fig and **Rubber Plant** (Ficus)
Velvet Plant (Gynura)
Wandering Jew (Tradescantia and Zebrina)

Flowering plants

Black Eyed Susan (Thunbergia)
Busy Lizzy (Impatiens)
Cigar Flower (Cuphea)
Fuchsia
Geranium (Pelargonium)
Shrimp Plant (Beloperone)

Plants to cut back

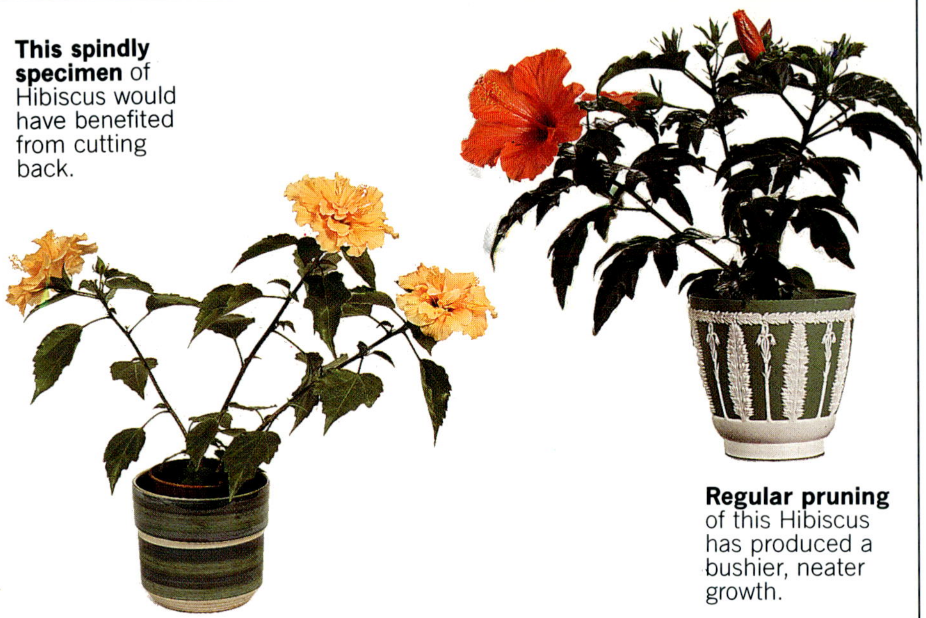

This spindly specimen of Hibiscus would have benefited from cutting back.

Regular pruning of this Hibiscus has produced a bushier, neater growth.

Azalea *(Rhododendron simsii* and *R.obtusum)*: prune in April by cutting back any long shoots by up to half their length.

Begonia Vine *(Cissus discolor)*: cut back the main stems in February or March by half to two-thirds their length, and side shoots to within 2-3in (5-8cm).

Bell Flower *(Campanula isophylla)*: cut the stems back to their base after flowering.

Fuchsia: prune mature plants after their winter rest by cutting back all the previous year's growth to within one or two buds.

Geranium *(Pelargonium)*: cut back all stems or shoots in March by about half their length.

Hibiscus: prune mature plants in February or March by removing all thin spindly shoots and cut back the main stems by half their length.

Jasmine *(Jasminum polyanthum)*: cut back old stems by two-thirds of their length as soon as flowering is over. In summer, pinch out tips of new shoots.

Shrimp plant *(Beloperone guttata)*: this benefits from regular cutting back as well as pinching. Cut back large established plants by half in February or March.

Zebra Plant *(Aphelandra squarrosa* 'Louisae'): cut back the stems by half as soon as flowering is over.

as this would considerably delay flowering. For example, it takes Fuchsias about six weeks to produce flower buds after the second pinching.

How to cut back

When you prune a plant, always make a clean, smooth cut rather than a ragged one, as the former heals over more rapidly, so reducing the risk of disease. Soft-stemmed plants can be pruned with a really sharp gardening knife, say, or with a safety razor blade. Plants with tougher stems, on the other hand, should be pruned with a pair of secateurs. Generally, only lightweight secateurs are ever needed for houseplants.

When you are cutting back a shoot or stem, always make the cut just above a leaf or bud — in other words, just above a leaf-joint or node.

You will find that some plants — like, for example, the Rubber Plant — exude a milky white sap from the pruning cut. You should try to stop this by dusting the cut with powdered charcoal.

Very tall or leggy plants

Most climbers — like the Kangaroo Vine and Grape Ivy *(Cissus)*, Ivy Tree *(Fatshedera)*, Swiss Cheese Plant *(Monstera)* and Philodendron — can all be cut back as required in February or March when they threaten to push their way through the ceiling.

Other plants which are inclined to become too tall — such as the Cordyline, Dracaena, Dumb Cane *(Dieffenbachia)*, Japanese Aralia *(Fatsia)*, and Rubber Plant and other Figs *(Ficus)* — can all be treated in the same way. These plants often become very leggy, with no leaves at the base. When this happens, try cutting the plant back to within 6in (15cm) of the pot, which should result in new bushy growth. As long as the plant is still a reasonably young specimen — say, up to five years old — there is a fairly high chance that it will produce new shoots from dormant buds. The Velvet Plant *(Gynura)* also tends to become leggy and this too should be cut back in February or March by at least half to two-thirds.

Dead flowers and leaves

Dead flowers should never be left on plants. They can become infected with the fungal disease grey mould *(botrytis)*, which can then spread to healthy parts of the plants, and they also encourage the plant to waste its energy on seed formation. So always pick or cut off dead blooms, removing the stalks as well.

The same applies to dead leaves. These should be cut off cleanly, including the stalks, with a knife or secateurs.

Variegated plants

These sometimes produce a plain green shoot with no variegated markings. Green shoots are more vigorous than variegated ones and should always be cut right out at their point of origin as soon as you notice them, before they have time to swamp the entire plant.

Giving support

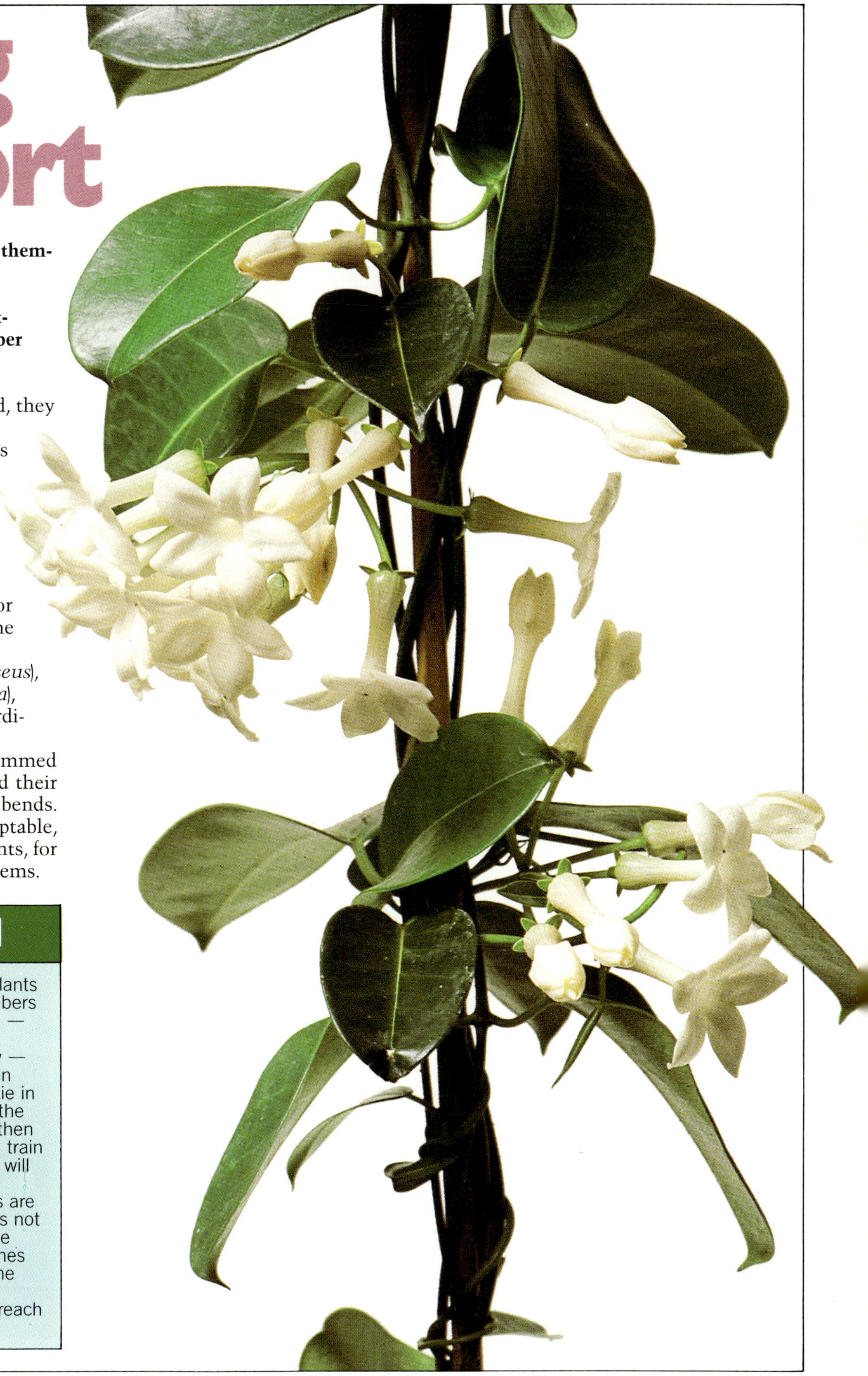

Most of our houseplants support themselves perfectly well without any human assistance, but some — particularly climbers and straight-stemmed plants such as the Rubber Plant — do need a little help.

If climbers were not supported, they would sprawl all over the place. In fact, with some of them this is a perfectly natural habit but an inconvenient one, to say the least, in the home. That said, some climbers can be grown quite successfully as trailing plants in hanging containers or in pots on a shelf or windowsill — examples being the Goose Foot Plant (Syngonium), Asparagus Fern (*Asparagus setaceus*), Kangaroo Vine (*Cissus antarctica*), Grape Ivy (*C.rhombifolia*) and ordinary Ivies (Hedera).

As for many tall, straight-stemmed plants, if these are not supported their stems will develop kinks and bends. Some people might find this acceptable, but most prefer their Rubber Plants, for example, to have nice straight stems.

Useful tips: I

As you get to know your houseplants you will discover that twining climbers such as Stephanotis and Jasmine — i.e. those which wrap their stems around the supports as they grow — twine either in a clockwise or in an anti-clockwise direction. Loosely tie in the tops of the stems and watch the way in which they want to twine, then train them in that direction. If you train them in the wrong direction, they will simply unwind themselves again!

To avoid root damage, supports are best inserted when potting. This is not always possible, however, as in the case of twiggy sticks and split canes for bulbs, for example, or when the plant has outgrown its original support. Supports should always reach the bottom of the pot.

Types of support

There are various ways in which houseplants can be supported — the humble bamboo cane being just one very rudimentary example, and probably the least attractive.

Moss poles. A moss-covered pole is an attractive method of supporting climbing plants which produce aerial roots from their stems. Examples of such plants include the Swiss Cheese Plant (*Monstera deliciosa*), climbing varieties of Philodendron, and Devil's Ivy (*Scindapsus aureus*). Provided the moss is kept moist, the roots will penetrate into it and the plant will therefore support itself.

You can either buy a moss pole from a garden centre, or you may prefer to make your own, which is very easy to do. First of all, you need a broom handle, of the eventual height to which you want the plant to grow. Ideally, a moss pole of the correct height should be inserted when you are potting the plant because the pole is difficult to replace once it is installed and stems have rooted into it, so do think carefully about the eventual height of your plant.

Make sure that the broom handle is long enough to reach the bottom of the pot. Lay out a sheet of ½in (13mm) wire netting on a flat surface and cover it with a 1-2in (2.5-5cm) layer of moss. Then place the broom handle on top of this and roll the whole thing up, securing the edges together with wire.

A refinement is to place a suitably sized plastic pot in the top of the moss pole — with the base resting on top of the broom handle and the rim level with the wire netting, so that it is virtually hidden from view. This device is handy for keeping the moss permanently moist, which is essential if the stems are to root into it. When water is poured into the pot, it trickles down through the moss. Another way of moistening the moss is to mist spray.

Finally, insert your plant in the pot and loosely tie the stems to the pole using soft string.

Wire netting cylinder. A simple cylinder of small-mesh wire netting makes a good support for Ivies. Make up a netting cylinder about half the diameter of a large pot, insert it in the pot and plant three or four young Ivies around it. They will cling to it and soon grow into a thick 'column' of foliage. The cylinder may need to be supported by a few bamboo canes inserted inside it.

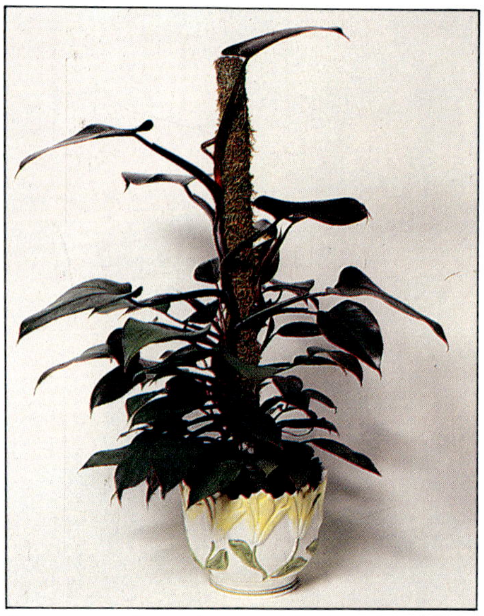

A moss pole makes an ideal support for Philodendron with its aerial roots.

Wire hoops. These make ideal supports for some flowering climbers, such as the Paper Flower (Bougainvillea), Wax Plant (Hoya), Madagascar Jasmine (Stephanotis) and Jasmine (Jasminum). It has been noticed that these plants all flower much more freely if their stems are trained in circular fashion rather than straight up.

Wire hoops are easy to make. All you need is a length of thick, heavy-duty, galvanised or plastic-coated wire. Bend this into a hoop, with the two ends acting as supporting 'legs' by being inserted right down to the bottom of the pot.

DIY trellis. It is easy to make your own trellis for climbing plants, including any of those mentioned above as well as Kangaroo Vine, Grape Ivy, ordinary Ivies and Asparagus Fern. Several bamboo canes can be tied together, with some upright and some cross pieces, to form a fan shape.

Pot trellis. If you do not want to construct your own trellis, you can buy a ready-made pot trellis, which comes in various shapes and sizes and is simply pushed into the pot. It is usually made from plastic-coated steel. It is not available in very large sizes, so is recommended only for small climbing plants — such as Asparagus Fern — and Ivies which can be cut back if necessary.

Wall trellis. Really large, heavy climbing plants — such as the Swiss Cheese Plant and Philodendrons — are sometimes trained against trellis panels mounted on the wall. Suitable panels for indoor use are made of plastic-coated steel and usually come in white. They are available in various shapes and sizes, and are generally supplied with suitable fixing brackets.

Useful tips: 2

Generally speaking, it is best not to start with too large or conspicuous supports. On the whole, young plants should be provided with small supports, and these can be replaced with larger ones as the plants grow bigger. This is not always possible, as with moss poles: once stems have rooted into the moss, it is virtually impossible to detach them.

Single bamboo cane. A single, thick bamboo cane is an adequate support for tall, straight-stemmed houseplants like the Rubber Plant (*Ficus elastica*), Fiddle-leaf Fig (*Ficus lyrata*) and Dracaenas. Such plants should be supported from an early age.

Split cane. Thin canes, varying in length from 1-2ft (30-60cm), are useful for supporting very small plants and also for bulbs such as Hyacinths. With large-flowered Hyacinths, for example, each stem needs a split cane to support the heavy flower head, and this should be placed just behind the stem.

Twiggy sticks. A good way to support Freesias is to push in branched sticks, known as twiggy sticks, between them before they become too tall. The stems will then grow up through them and be well supported. The sticks could be a bit shorter than the flowering height of the plants.

Tying in

Plants need to be tied into their recommended supports and for this you can use soft green garden string, fine plastic coated wire, or raffia. The latter is a cream-coloured natural product.

Plants are tied in by looping the wire in a loose figure-of-eight around both stem and support (see figure **5**) — when using softer ties, make a second figure-of-eight instead of a loop. Never tie in stems tightly — they must have room to thicken. A tight cane can kink or cut into the stem, and can even kill off the part above the knot. Split wire rings are also useful for tying in thin-stemmed plants, as are those paper-covered white ties, the ends of which are simply twisted together to form a loop around both stem and support.

Ways to support your plants

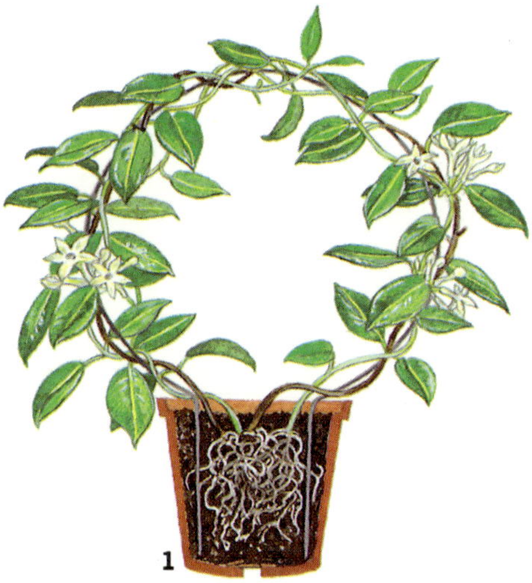

1

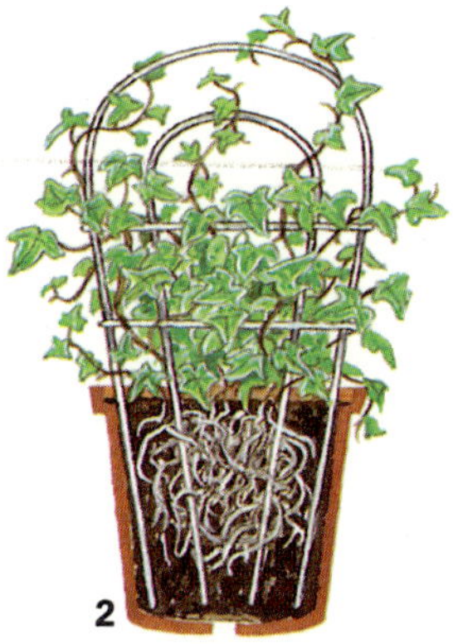

2

1. A wire hoop is ideal for supporting the twining Stephanotis — it produces many more flowers if trained in a circular fashion rather than straight up.

2. Ready-made pot trellis comes in various shapes and is ideal for small climbing plants, or climbers such as Ivy which can be cut back as much as needed.

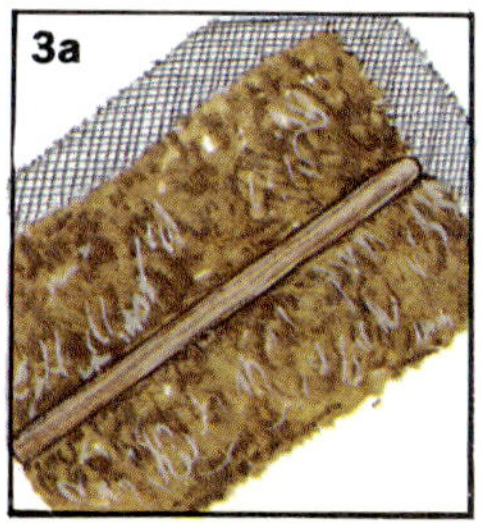

3a

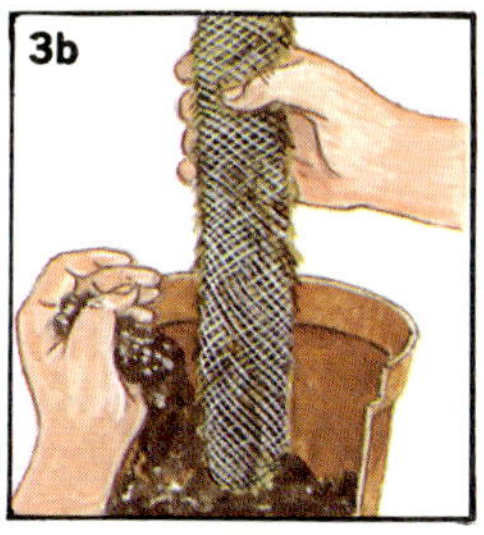

3b

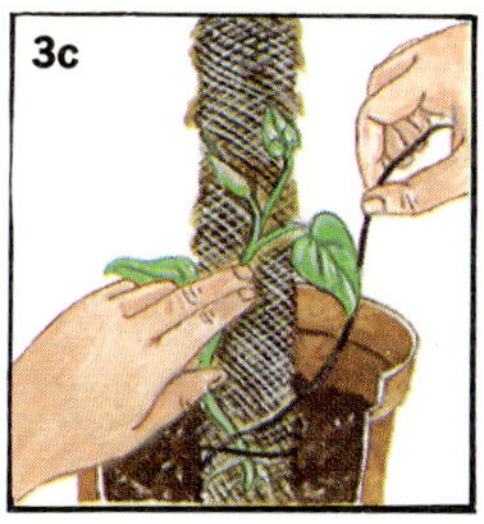

3c

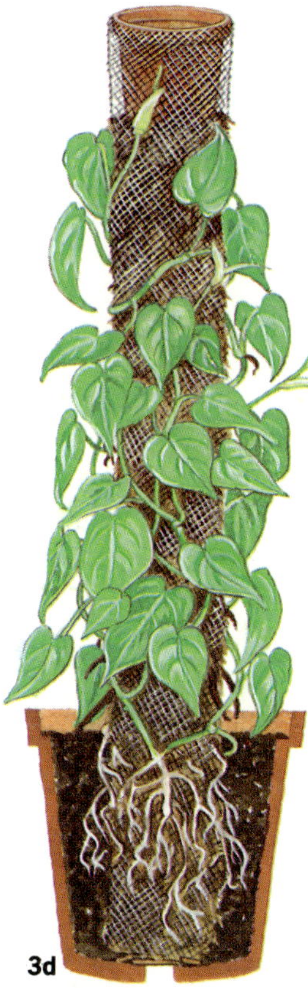

3d

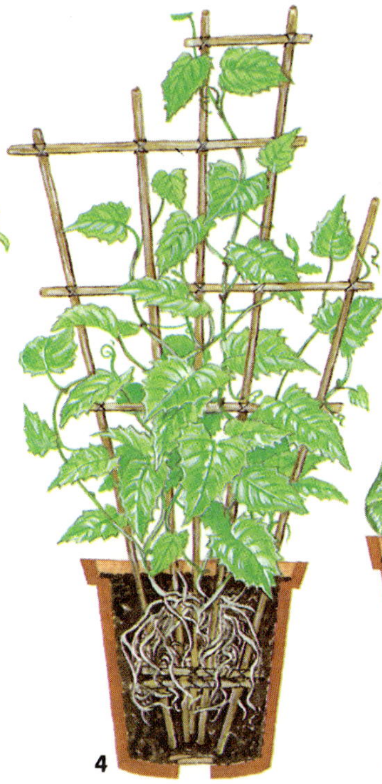

4

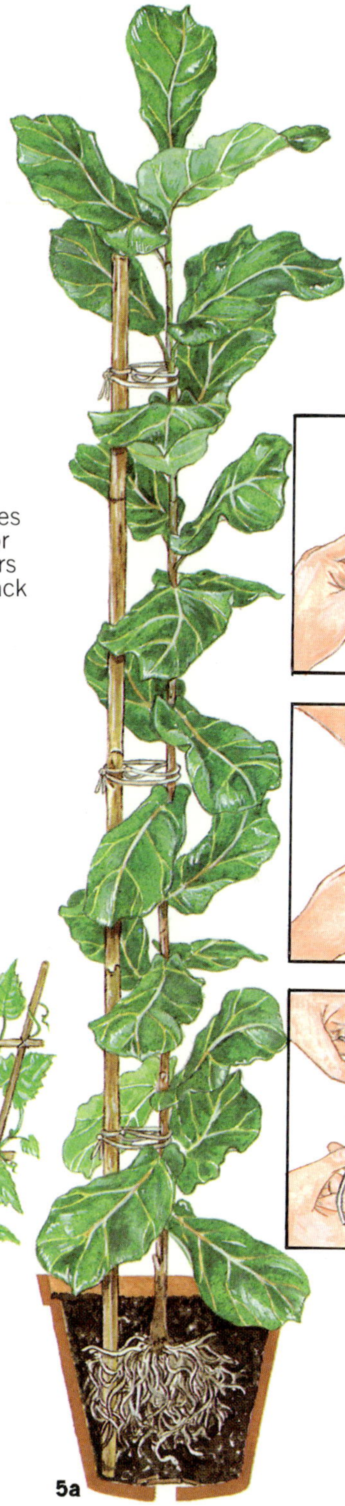

5a

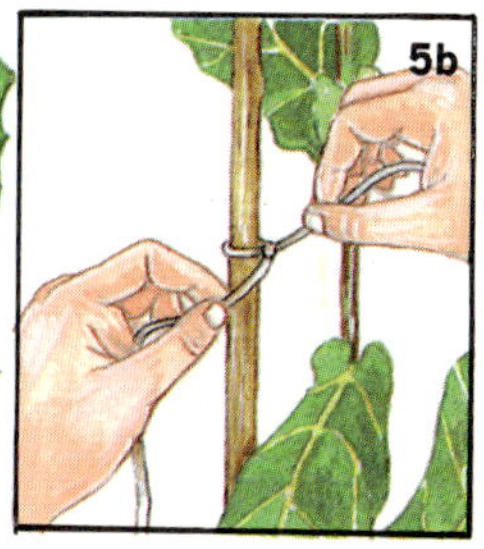

5b

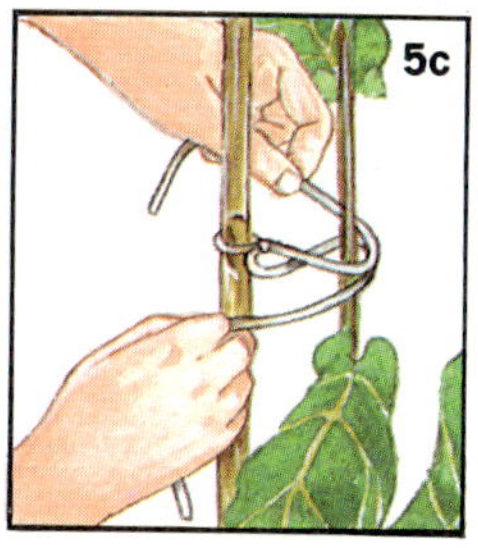

5c

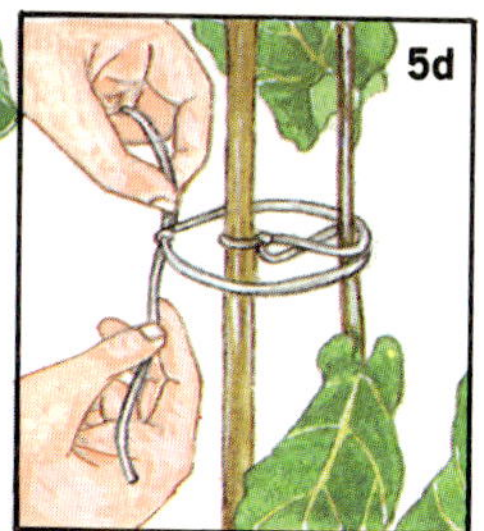

5d

3. When making a moss pole the moss should be flush with one long edge of the netting and fall short on the other to allow for the join. Also leave room at the top for a small pot **(3a)**. Secure the edges of the moss pole and plant it **(3b)**. Tie your plant loosely to the pole **(3c)**, and place a small flower pot into the top of the cylinder **(3d)**.

4. A DIY trellis made from bamboo cane is attractive and easy to make.

5. Tall straight-stemmed plants, such as the Fiddle-leaf Fig, need supporting at an early age. Use a thick cane support and tie in the plant at intervals with plastic coated wire **(5a)** making a figure-of-eight as shown **(5b,c, d)**.

How fertilisers work

Have you been starving your houseplants without even realising it? Unless you're in the habit of using fertilisers — and using them properly — there's a distinct possibility that some of your plants are undernourished.

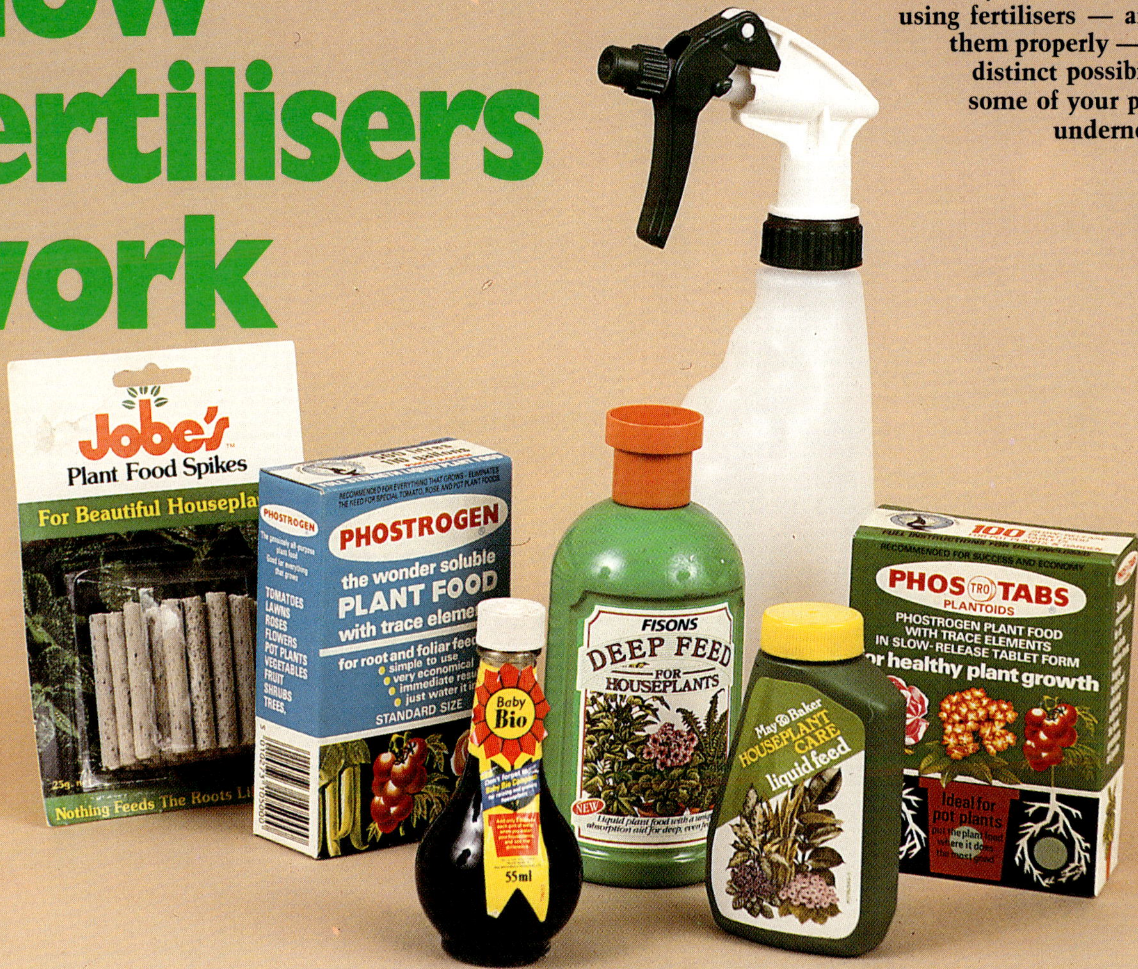

You'd be forgiven for assuming that houseplants can rely on their compost for the nourishment they need, and up to a point that's certainly true. But watering alone will not do; within a matter of weeks, a perfectly healthy specimen may start to decline in vigour, as the natural goodness in its compost is used up, or washed away.

For young plants that have to be moved on to ever bigger pots in the natural course of events, renewing the compost every three to six months is perfectly practicable. Indeed it's actually unwise to add fertiliser to a young plant for fear of burning its root system. But for established plants, it makes more sense to use a fertiliser to replenish the plant's food supply.

Used with a little know-how as part of a good plant-care routine, a fertiliser will keep plants in the best possible shape, ensuring well balanced growth and, for flowering plants, a splendid display. And the joy is that you will be able to direct improvements towards each individual plant's weakness — by choosing the right fertiliser for its needs.

Fertilisers need to be treated with respect; plants may be killed by too much interference far more easily than by too little, so it's wise to err on the side of caution and to add less rather than more.

Remember, too, that more than plants may be at risk. Fertilisers can be dangerous in the hands of children and the unsuspecting. Keep all packets well out of reach and make sure they are clearly labelled. Avoid transferring fertilisers into discarded food containers or bottles.

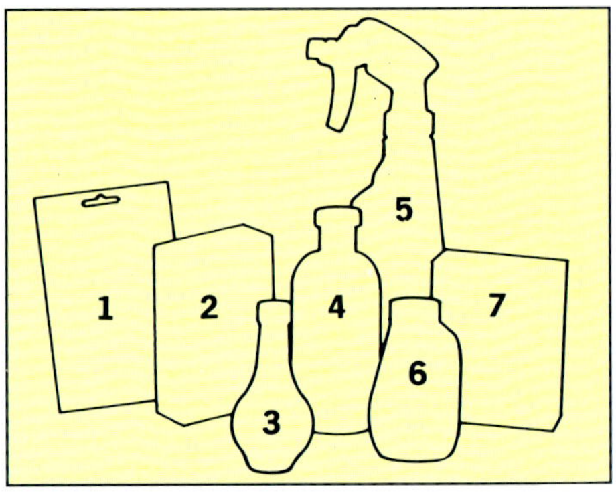

1. Jobe's Plant Food Spikes.
2. Phostrogen, root and foliar feed.
3. Baby Bio, liquid.
4. Fison's Deep Feed, liquid.
5. Spray for applying foliar feed.
6. May and Baker Houseplant Care, liquid.
7. Phostrotabs, tablets.

Choosing and using a fertiliser

Fertilisers come in a wealth of forms, from solutions to powders, sticks or granules. The choice can seem intimidating, but a brief profile of each will put you in the picture.

Whichever you choose, always ensure that the compost is thoroughly damp before applying any fertiliser. Water the plants first, and let the moisture drain right through the compost. Unless the compost is properly dampened in this way, the fertiliser may burn the roots.

Liquids, powders and crystals

If you're in the habit of regularly checking over your houseplants, you'll probably find it easy to establish and stick to a feeding programme using a liquid fertiliser. As these must first be diluted with water before use, they can easily be incorporated into your watering sessions.

The great advantage of liquid feeding is that it gives you far more flexibility than the other methods; you can control exactly when you feed and how much you give your plants. On the other hand, you will have to spend time mixing up the formula, and if you are at all forgetful, you may end up inadvertently neglecting your plants.

These minor shortcomings apart, products like Baby Bio (solution) or Phostrogen (powder) produce very good results, provided you follow a few simple dos and don'ts:

- Do dilute the fertiliser adequately, following the manufacturer's instructions. A plant will *not* grow faster if you feed it with a stronger solution. If you do, you may damage your plant's roots quite severely and scorch its leaves.
- Always use the weakest solution specified on the label if the manufacturer has not specified a strength for houseplants.
- Try not to let fertiliser come into contact with the foliage unless, of course, you are using a foliar feed (see below). This is especially important in sunny weather when leaves may be scorched by the sun's rays coming through the window. Wipe off any droplets with a damp cloth.

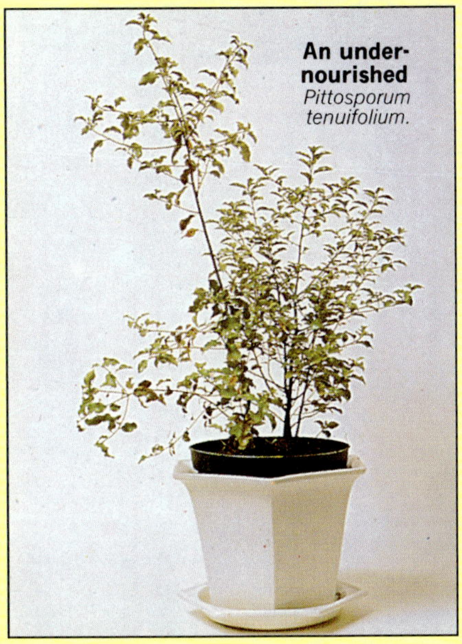

An under-nourished *Pittosporum tenuifolium.*

How often you feed will vary from plant to plant, but as a rough guide you can expect to give each one a minimum of three or four applications of a standard fertiliser during one growing season. In practice, you may find that you need to feed some plants once a fortnight, and really fast-growing plants, like Busy Lizzies and Spider Plants, once a week. Never exceed the manufacturers' recommendations, and if you notice that growth is becoming lush and rather floppy, chances are that you should cut down on the feeding. Another sure sign of overfeeding is poor flowering, although plenty of leaves are produced.

Fertiliser sticks and tablets

If you want as little trouble as possible, these 'solid' fertilisers are ideal. Just poke them into the compost as recommended and your work is over for the next few weeks, as the goodness slowly seeps into the growing mixture.

Although sticks can't give you the flexibility offered by the liquids, individual manufacturers are at last beginning to offer a choice of formulas (like the Jobe range, for instance) to suit different types of plant.

Tablets work in the same way as sticks.

Granules

Fertiliser granules are really only useful when you are making up your own potting mixtures.

Controlled release fertiliser pellets

These can be an absolute boon because they provide long-term nourishment for as much as a year, but, once again, they are designed to be mixed in with a made-up potting compost. Osmocote and Ficote are both well-known, reliable brands.

Foliar feeds

Foliar feeds have revolutionised feeding techniques by breaking the rules. The only fertilisers that can be sprayed directly on to leaves, they make the perfect plant pick-me-up, as they are absorbed into the plant sap and quickly assimilated.

Because of this characteristic, they're marvellous for plants which can't absorb much through their roots — like air plants, for instance, whose roots are surrounded by moss rather than compost.

Use these sprays with a little caution and don't spray near any furnishings.

Don't rely on foliar feeds exclusively. Use a foliar feed as a trouble shooter, then return to the more conventional methods of your regular feeding programme.

When to start a feeding programme

Feeding plants at the wrong time is more than wasteful — it's positively harmful. The golden rule is: only feed plants during their active growing season (which is, roughly speaking, between April and September); for the rest of the time, stick to water.

It's a mistake to try and 'force' growth during the dormant period. All you'll achieve is a spindly specimen with small, pale leaves, for the untapped nutrient salts build up around the roots and actually hinder the plant.

Any plants that have been repotted recently into fresh compost will have enough goodness to last them quite a while. As a rule of thumb, soil-based mixtures like John Innes will hold their fertiliser for up to 12 weeks, while a peat-based variety is likely to be exhausted inside six to eight weeks. Once that time limit is up, you should start feeding.

Where shop-bought plants are concerned, be prepared to start feeding immediately. It's very likely that their supplies will be used up by the time they reach your home.

The tell-tale signs to watch out for are a crop of duller, smaller leaves and, in the case of variegated plants, new leaves without the usual markings. Start feeding at once!

Don't expect any miracles, though; fertilisers are a food, not a medicine. Before stepping up on the feeding, do check for any other possible causes if a plant is failing to respond. Is it being overwatered, or does it prefer a different location? Make sure that it hasn't outgrown its pot, either.

Making the right choice

You can't go wrong with a 'standard' fertiliser — a sort of chemical cocktail of the nutrients which plants require for healthy growth. The nutrients, dissolved in water, are absorbed via the plant's roots.

The 'big three' plant foods are nitrogen, phosphorus and potassium (abbreviated, by international agreement, to the letters N, P and K, respectively). Besides these *macronutrients* (which also include calcium, magnesium and sulphur) are a host of *micronutrients*, otherwise known as trace elements, since only a 'trace' of each is needed. Turn to the chart overleaf to see what part each of these plays in your plants' lives — and what can happen to your plants if there's a deficiency of any of them.

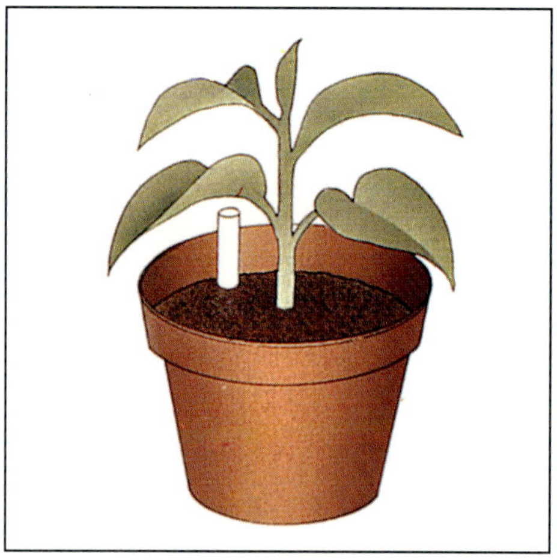

Stick fertilisers cut work down to a minimum; push the recommended number into the soil and for the next few weeks the nutrients will slowly seep into the compost and all you'll need to do is water the plant.

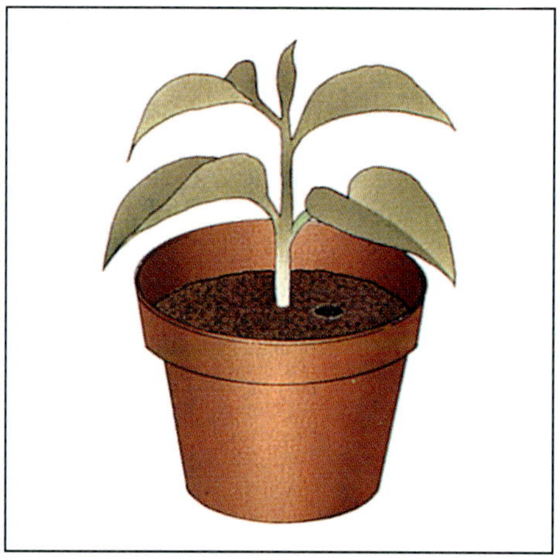

Tablets work in the same way as stick fertilisers and are equally clean and simple to use. In both cases it's important to follow the manufacturer's instructions to the letter.

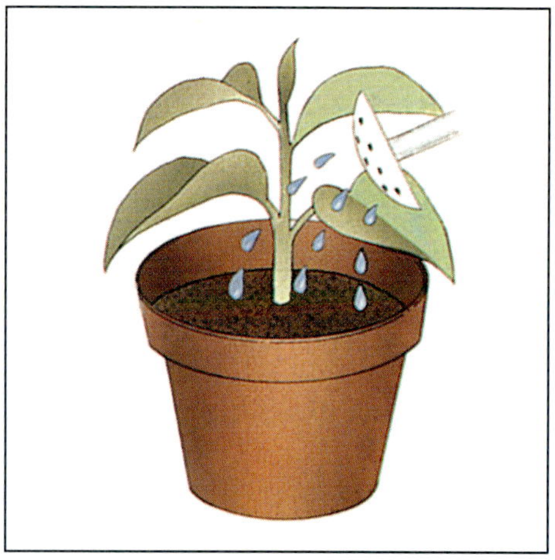

Liquid feeding is probably the most popular method and gives good results; it's slightly more time consuming but has the advantage that you can control exactly how much food your plant gets.

What's in the fertilisers

	What it's for	Signs of deficiency	Source	Special notes
NITROGEN	The most important element for healthy growth, and also for maintaining leaf colour.	Small, pale leaves lacking vigour and lustre.	Can only be absorbed in nitrate form such as ammonium nitrate, potassium nitrate or the more inferior sodium nitrate. Also supplied by organic products like bonemeal and hoof-and-horn.	Always useful for leafy plants, but especially important at the start of the growing season.
PHOSPHORUS	Essential in helping plant metabolism (process of converting nutrients into living matter), it's present in relatively high levels in the growing parts of the plant and is very important in root growth.	Poor root growth; poor plant development; immaturity.	Many different forms. Examples include superphosphate and mono-ammonium phosphate.	Good for plants just before or during flowering. Especially good for roses.
POTASSIUM	Vital to the development of flowers and fruit. Potassium helps stimulate flowering and maturing of fruit.	Plants produce poor show of fruit and flowers, or none at all.	Potassium sulphate, or sulphate of potash, and potassium nitrate.	Especially good for plants that have just finished flowering; helps them in the rebuilding process.
CALCIUM	General growth and development.	Disrupted rate of growth and development; may result in death of developing shoots.	Usually available in most fertilisers.	
MAGNESIUM	Helps to make chlorophyll, the green pigment that absorbs sunlight as an energy source.	Poor, weak foliage and chlorosis (loss of colour in leaves and stems; see also iron, right).	Epsom salts, magnesium sulphate.	
SULPHUR	Needed for photosynthesis — the conversion of carbon dioxide into the sugars the plant needs.	Small, pale leaves, or leaves with a reddish tinge. May make the plant vulnerable to disease.	Sulphates such as potassium sulphate.	

All the main and trace elements, *above*, are vitally important to healthy plant growth, the basic distinction being that the main elements are needed in larger amounts than the trace elements.

Knowing which elements are affecting which aspects of plant growth and development will help you select the best fertiliser for your needs. Consult the A-Z guides for further information on individual plants and also follow any suggestions you get from the shop or nursery.

There are plenty of natural, or 'organic', sources for these elements — bonemeal, fishmeal, hoof-and-horn, dried blood, woodash, seaweed, etc., are all familiar names to the outdoor gardener. However, these organic fertilisers are all very slow-acting because their chemicals have first to be released by the actions of micro-organisms in the compost.

Synthetic products tend to be a better bet for houseplants. They are quicker acting and can be absorbed more or less directly by the root system.

You can buy either 'simple' fertilisers, containing just one or two chemicals, or the more versatile 'compound' or standard fertilisers which provide a balanced mixture of plant foods. All the major elements are usually present, together with

What's in the fertilisers (trace elements)

	What it's for	Signs of deficiency	Source	Special notes
IRON	Vitally important for the production of chlorophyll, the green pigment in plants.	Chlorosis: leaves become blotched with pale green or yellow. Particularly noticeable on young, green growth. Results in poor, stunted growth.	Iron is not readily available to plants and has to be given in the form of iron sequestrene or sequestered iron.	Deficiency affects acid-loving plants in particular.
BORON	Assists in tip growth of roots and shoots.	Unsatisfactory development of roots and growing points, and even of flowers. However, deficiency of this kind is very rare.	Normally present as a trace in standard fertilisers. Directly available from borax (sodium tetraborate).	It is very unlikely that your plants will lack boron, so use with very great caution; it can be toxic if added in excess.
ZINC	Important for satisfactory growth.	Loss of vigour and lack of growth.	Zinc salts in plant compost.	Plants are very unlikely to suffer from lack of zinc. Add with caution; it is toxic if applied in excess.
MANGANESE	Important in photosynthesis (see sulphur, left).	Similar to, though less common than, iron deficiency, but leaves become more mottled.	Manganese sulphate.	
COPPER	General growth.	Growth defects.	Usually available in fertilisers with a quantity of trace elements added to them.	Copper deficiency in plants is very rare and usually confined to plants in a peaty compost.
CHLORINE	Important in photosynthesis.	Any deficiency is most unlikely.	Present in most tap water and most fertilisers.	
MOLYBDENUM	Important in helping plants to use nitrate.	Similar to lack of nitrogen.	Sodium molybdate or ammonium molybdate. Usually available as a trace element in certain fertilisers.	Poinsettia (*Euphorbia pulcherrima*) is one of the few houseplants susceptible to molybdenum deficiency; the leaves turn mottled and yellowish with brown edges.

a few trace elements, and the finished product is often a combination of synthetic and organic products; Baby Bio and Liquinure, for instance, both have a seaweed base.

Each manufacturer makes his product to his own recipe, so if you can learn to read the coded labels on the pack, you will have an advantage.

Reading the labels

Manufacturers are obliged to include a three-number code on their brands. It will look something like this: 6:10:6. The numbers stand for the nitrogen, phosphorus and potassium content in the product concerned, and always in that order. The content is shown as a percentage, so in our example, the nitrogen and potassium content is, in each case, 6 per cent, while the phosphorus is a higher 10 per cent. The chart above reveals that a high phosphate content is good for plants in bloom, or just starting into flower.

Try to avoid those fertilisers with a very high nitrogen content — in a ratio of more than four parts nitrogen to one part each of phosphorus and potassium (written 4:1:1). High nitrogen fertilisers are not suitable for indoor use and will make growth far too lush and soft.

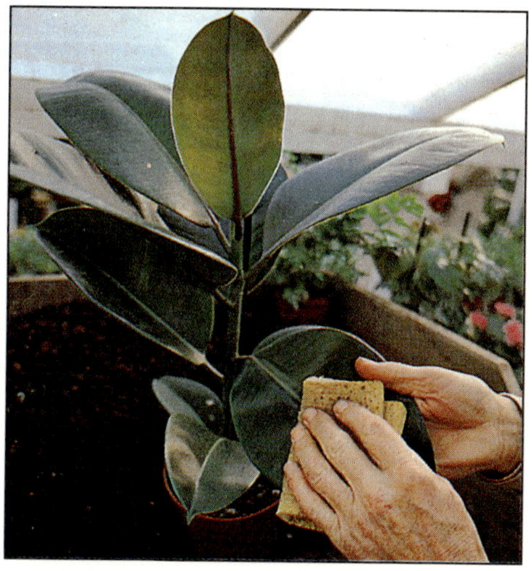

If fertiliser is accidentally splashed on leaves, carefully sponge it off — unless, of course, it's a foliar feed!

Do check the individual A-Z guides for feeding information on your houseplants, as their requirements will vary.

Special purpose fertilisers

Standard fertilisers are perfectly adequate for most houseplant needs, but there may be occasions when a special purpose fertiliser could be worth a try. There is a number of such products on the market, and of these the tomato fertiliser is probably the best known. Don't be put off by the name! When used at a more dilute rate (as recommended on the pack for flowering plants) a tomato fertiliser can be very beneficial to flowering plants and cacti, promoting sturdier growth and a fine show of flowers.

If you want to grow any lime-hating plants — Miniature Orange, Gardenia or Indian Azalea, for example — you could find that some iron sequestrene comes in handy. Plants can find it difficult to get iron from a chalky or limy soil, and lime-haters will be unable to get sufficient supplies if there's the slightest hint of these alkalis in their compost. They may develop a sickness called chlorosis, in which they lose the green pigment in their leaves and stems. Old wives' tales about adding rusty nails to the soil are quite unfounded — the iron must come in an easily soluble form, as in 'sequestered' iron.

Incidentally, there are certain fertilisers that acid-loving plants must steer clear of — bonemeal, hoof-and-horn and superphosphate all contain alkaline calcium salts. You'll find that there are special 'acid reaction' fertilisers available from which any offending alkalis are banished.

KEY

- Symptom
- Cause
- Cure

What's wrong

However hard you try, at some point you are bound to have a houseplant that will, completely out of the blue, wilt, drop its leaves or be attacked by nasty mites or bugs. But don't despair — just identify what's wrong with your plant by checking the picture below; look for your problem, see what the cause is and then you can follow our recommended cure. If you catch the trouble quickly you will be able to stop the problem spreading and help your plant recover fast.

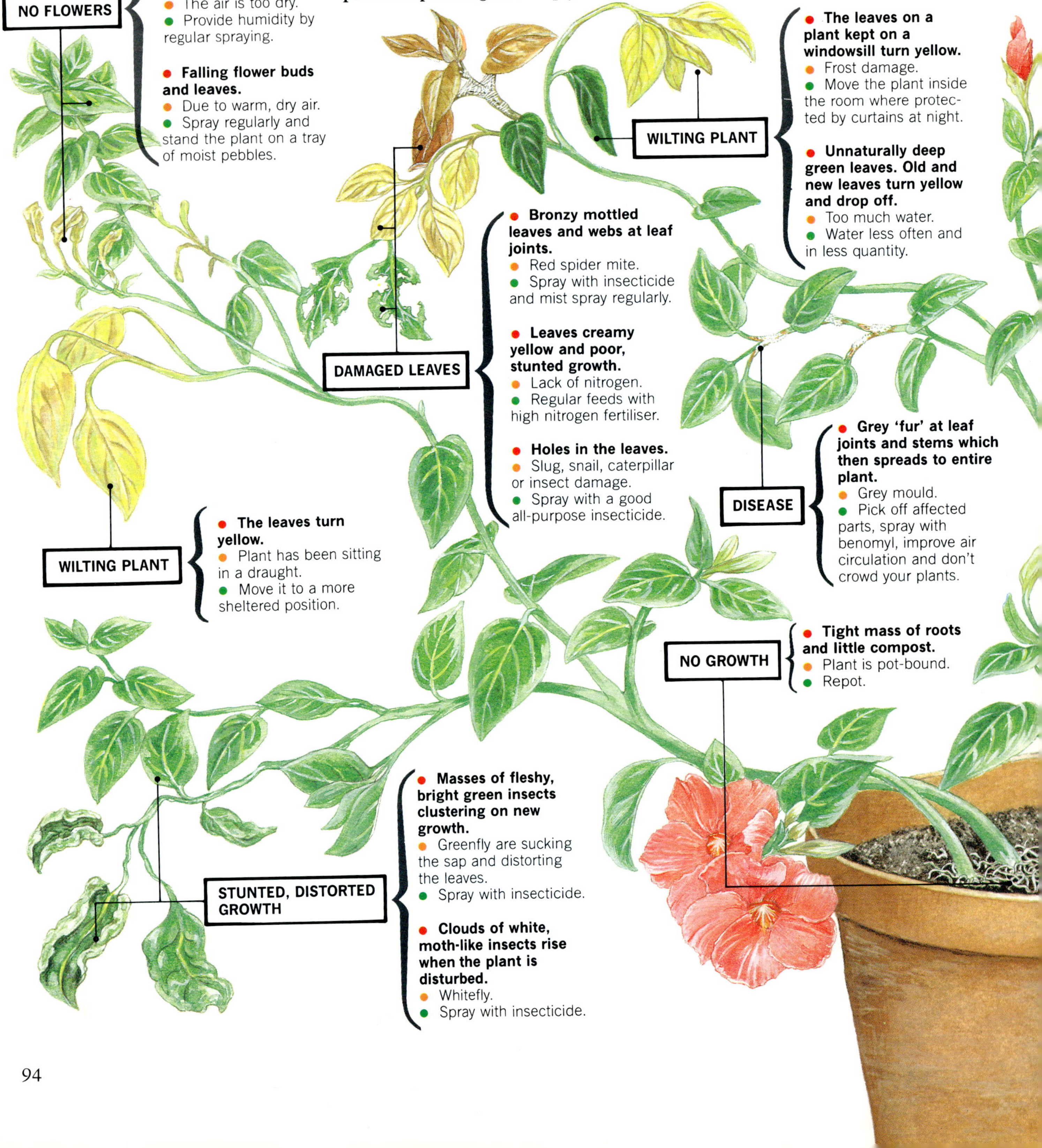

NO FLOWERS

- **Lots of leaves and no flowers.**
- Too much fertiliser.
- Stop feeding for six weeks and then only feed in the growing season.

- **Buds shrivel.**
- The air is too dry.
- Provide humidity by regular spraying.

- **Falling flower buds and leaves.**
- Due to warm, dry air.
- Spray regularly and stand the plant on a tray of moist pebbles.

WILTING PLANT

- **The leaves on a plant kept on a windowsill turn yellow.**
- Frost damage.
- Move the plant inside the room where protected by curtains at night.

- **Unnaturally deep green leaves. Old and new leaves turn yellow and drop off.**
- Too much water.
- Water less often and in less quantity.

DAMAGED LEAVES

- **Bronzy mottled leaves and webs at leaf joints.**
- Red spider mite.
- Spray with insecticide and mist spray regularly.

- **Leaves creamy yellow and poor, stunted growth.**
- Lack of nitrogen.
- Regular feeds with high nitrogen fertiliser.

- **Holes in the leaves.**
- Slug, snail, caterpillar or insect damage.
- Spray with a good all-purpose insecticide.

DISEASE

- **Grey 'fur' at leaf joints and stems which then spreads to entire plant.**
- Grey mould.
- Pick off affected parts, spray with benomyl, improve air circulation and don't crowd your plants.

WILTING PLANT

- **The leaves turn yellow.**
- Plant has been sitting in a draught.
- Move it to a more sheltered position.

NO GROWTH

- **Tight mass of roots and little compost.**
- Plant is pot-bound.
- Repot.

STUNTED, DISTORTED GROWTH

- **Masses of fleshy, bright green insects clustering on new growth.**
- Greenfly are sucking the sap and distorting the leaves.
- Spray with insecticide.

- **Clouds of white, moth-like insects rise when the plant is disturbed.**
- Whitefly.
- Spray with insecticide.

with my plant

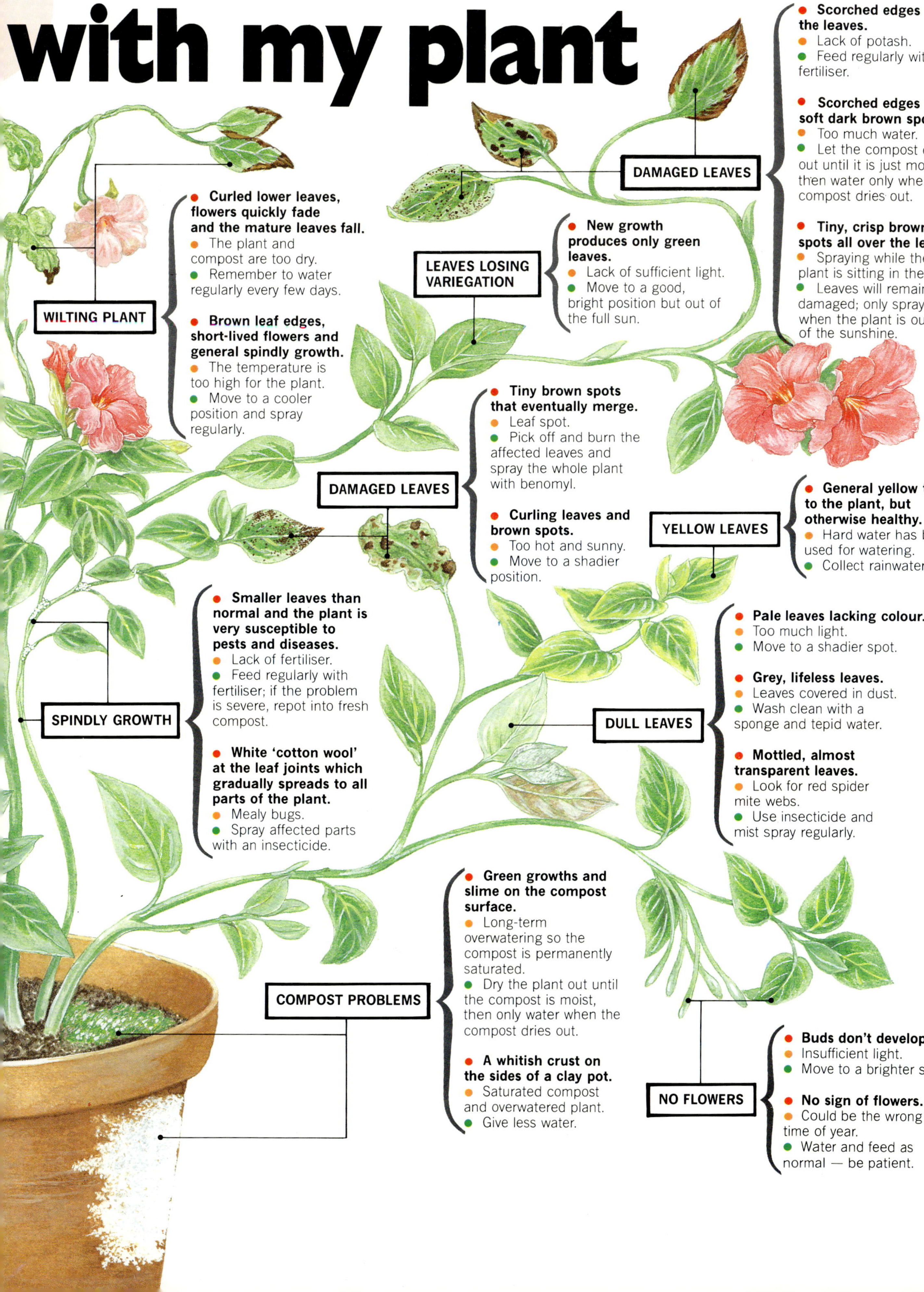

WILTING PLANT

- **Curled lower leaves, flowers quickly fade and the mature leaves fall.**
  - The plant and compost are too dry.
  - Remember to water regularly every few days.
- **Brown leaf edges, short-lived flowers and general spindly growth.**
  - The temperature is too high for the plant.
  - Move to a cooler position and spray regularly.

LEAVES LOSING VARIEGATION

- **New growth produces only green leaves.**
  - Lack of sufficient light.
  - Move to a good, bright position but out of the full sun.

DAMAGED LEAVES

- **Scorched edges to the leaves.**
  - Lack of potash.
  - Feed regularly with fertiliser.
- **Scorched edges and soft dark brown spots.**
  - Too much water.
  - Let the compost dry out until it is just moist, then water only when the compost dries out.
- **Tiny, crisp brown spots all over the leaf.**
  - Spraying while the plant is sitting in the sun.
  - Leaves will remain damaged; only spray when the plant is out of the sunshine.

DAMAGED LEAVES

- **Tiny brown spots that eventually merge.**
  - Leaf spot.
  - Pick off and burn the affected leaves and spray the whole plant with benomyl.
- **Curling leaves and brown spots.**
  - Too hot and sunny.
  - Move to a shadier position.

YELLOW LEAVES

- **General yellow tinge to the plant, but otherwise healthy.**
  - Hard water has been used for watering.
  - Collect rainwater.

SPINDLY GROWTH

- **Smaller leaves than normal and the plant is very susceptible to pests and diseases.**
  - Lack of fertiliser.
  - Feed regularly with fertiliser; if the problem is severe, repot into fresh compost.
- **White 'cotton wool' at the leaf joints which gradually spreads to all parts of the plant.**
  - Mealy bugs.
  - Spray affected parts with an insecticide.

DULL LEAVES

- **Pale leaves lacking colour.**
  - Too much light.
  - Move to a shadier spot.
- **Grey, lifeless leaves.**
  - Leaves covered in dust.
  - Wash clean with a sponge and tepid water.
- **Mottled, almost transparent leaves.**
  - Look for red spider mite webs.
  - Use insecticide and mist spray regularly.

COMPOST PROBLEMS

- **Green growths and slime on the compost surface.**
  - Long-term overwatering so the compost is permanently saturated.
  - Dry the plant out until the compost is moist, then only water when the compost dries out.
- **A whitish crust on the sides of a clay pot.**
  - Saturated compost and overwatered plant.
  - Give less water.

NO FLOWERS

- **Buds don't develop.**
  - Insufficient light.
  - Move to a brighter spot.
- **No sign of flowers.**
  - Could be the wrong time of year.
  - Water and feed as normal — be patient.

Know your enemy

Have you ever wondered why your Poinsettia seems to suffer from flying dandruff, why your Busy Lizzie feels sticky, or why your Joseph's Coat looks decidedly shabby? The answer is probably that some nasty pest and all its relatives are feasting on your beloved plant. Don't ignore signs that all is not well; if these pests are not dealt with promptly, drastic remedies may eventually be necessary.

Your immediate response should be to identify the pest so you know how to deal with it effectively. But prevention is better than cure, so it is only sensible to inspect your houseplant regularly for pests, checking for the first signs of trouble, and to give preventative sprays of insecticide two or three times a year.

When pests are just beginning to trouble your plant you can usually wipe them off with your fingers or wash them off with a sponge and a drop or two of washing up liquid in a bucket of tepid water. For more severe trouble and also as a preventative, use chemicals. Generally these come as liquids, or as dry powder which dissolves in water. There are lots of brands formulated for different pests. Usually a good all-purpose pesticide suffices, but sometimes a particular active ingredient is called for, so look for a product containing that specific chemical. For more information on pesticides see pages 99-100.

ALWAYS READ THE CHEMICAL MANUFACTURERS' INSTRUCTIONS BEFORE USING ANY PESTICIDE. PAY PARTICULAR ATTENTION TO CHILDREN, PETS, WILDLIFE AND FOODSTUFFS WHICH SHOULD BE KEPT WELL AWAY FROM THE CHEMICALS AND ANY TREATMENT.

Thrips

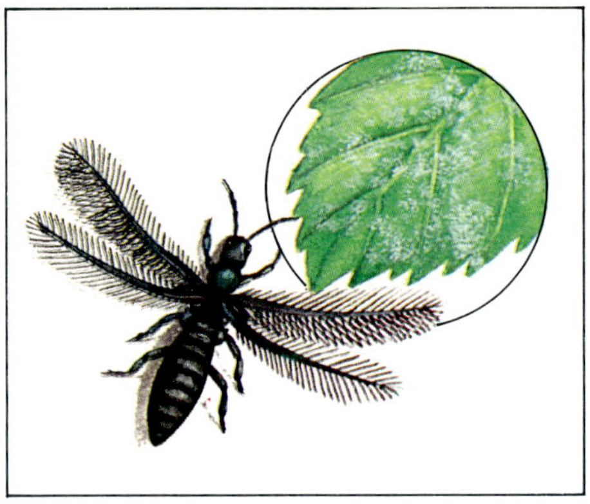

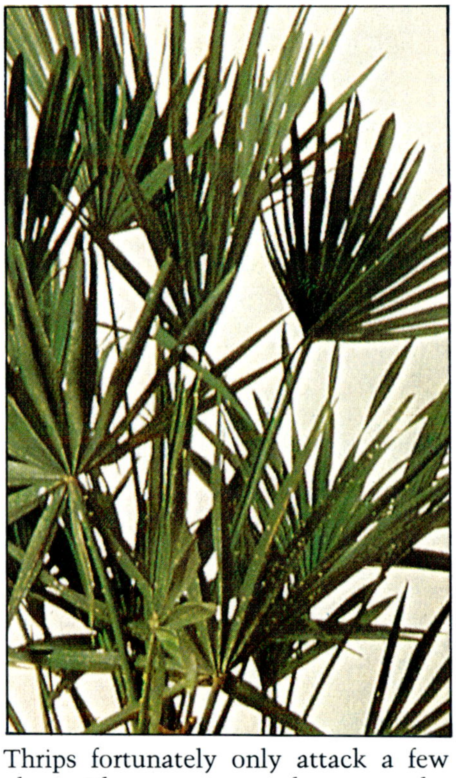

Thrips fortunately only attack a few plants. They cause most damage to the flowers of plants such as Cyclamen by streaking and spotting the petals. Look for tiny, long black insects nestling among the flower petals.

Control by spraying with a pesticide containing permethrin, pyrethrum, derris or malathion and repeat if necessary.

Whitefly

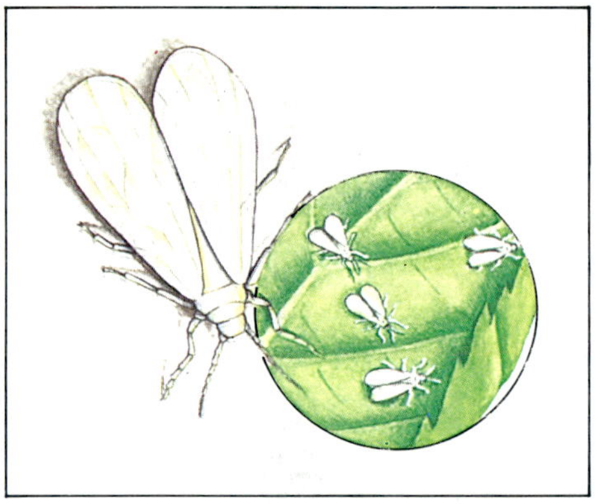

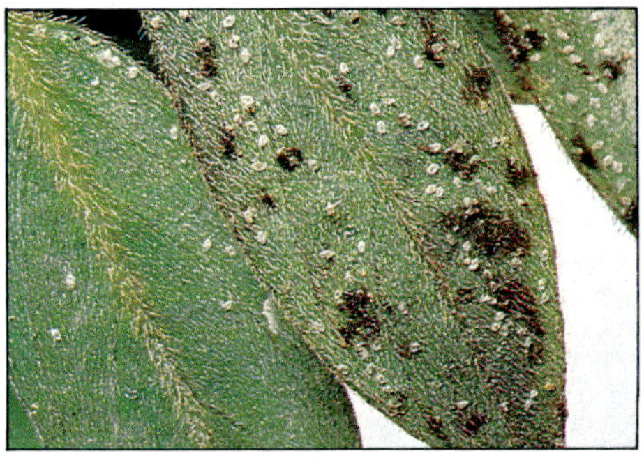

You know your plant has got whitefly if a cloud of tiny flying insects rises from the plant when the leaves are disturbed. They can be a real nuisance and a problem to control. Whitefly thrive in warm, dry conditions but they can still be a problem in the cold — the only difference is that their life cycle takes longer. The flies leave behind eggs and larvae on the undersides of the leaves. The larvae don't cause serious damage, but the presence of the adults, and the fact that the larvae can clearly be seen as tiny, white oval 'scales' that excrete 'honeydew' and encourage sooty mould, makes them a real nuisance. Eventually, masses of larval scales will make the leaves mottle and the plant lose its vigour.

To control whitefly you have to commit yourself to a concerted campaign for up to six weeks. Spray the plant twice a week with permethrin, pyrethrum or malathion.

Aphid

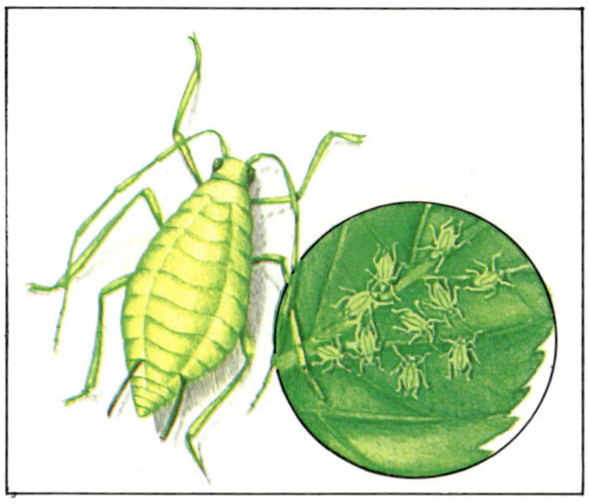

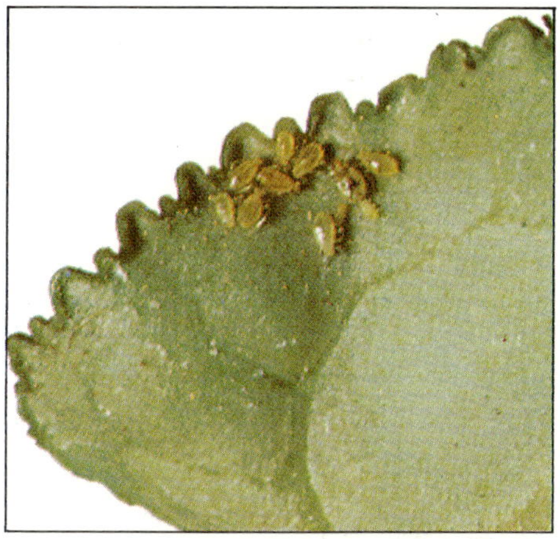

Aphid is the blanket term for the different kinds of black, yellow, pink and greenfly. They all breed prolifically and hundreds can appear almost overnight. They are winged or wingless depending on maturity. Once aphids start to multiply your plant can be severely damaged very quickly. They attack new growth by stabbing a pointed feeding tube into the young cells and sucking out the plant juices. This makes new growth curl with damage until it's severely deformed. The plant may take several weeks to recover.

Aphids also excrete the sticky substance known as honeydew. This drops down onto the lower leaves leaving a sugary deposit. After a short time a fungus called sooty mould may develop and disfigure your plant even more.

A small attack of aphids can be easily rinsed off with tepid water, otherwise spray with permethrin, pyrethrum or malathion once a week for three weeks.

Remove honeydew and sooty mould by lightly sponging the leaves with tepid water containing a few drops of washing-up liquid.

Mealy bug

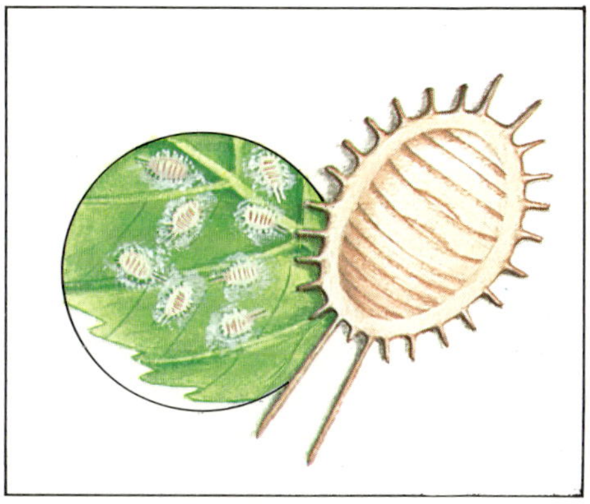

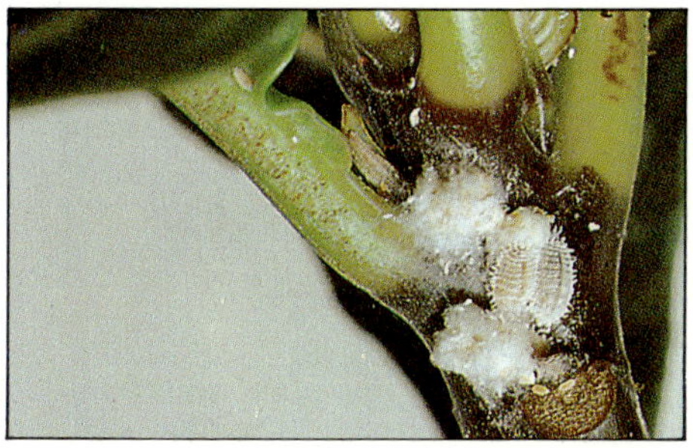

An adult mealy bug looks rather like a flattened wood louse with a white powdery coating that acts as a protective covering. The first sign of mealy bug is little white cotton-wool blobs at the leaf joints and under the leaves near the veins. This is the protective home for the young mealy bugs. When the infestation is really bad they are found in large numbers on young growth, and the damage they cause can be quite severe.

Root mealy bugs are not quite as active, but they are just as destructive. If your plant's growth seems stunted, suspect root mealy bugs at work. Remove the plant carefully from its pot, and look for the bugs clustering around the roots, particularly at the base of the root ball.

A minor infestation of mealy bugs can be dealt with by dabbing them with a small paint brush or piece of cotton wool dipped in methylated spirits. Swab the areas of young and adult mealy bugs.

Treat serious attacks of mealy bug with a spray of malathion or dimethoate, which is a systemic insecticide.

Control root mealy bugs by watering or dipping the root ball into a solution of malathion. For complete control repeat the treatment two or three times at 10-14 day intervals.

Fungus gnat

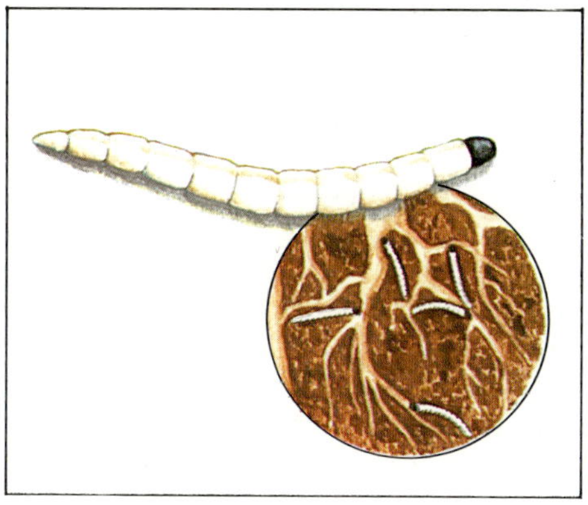

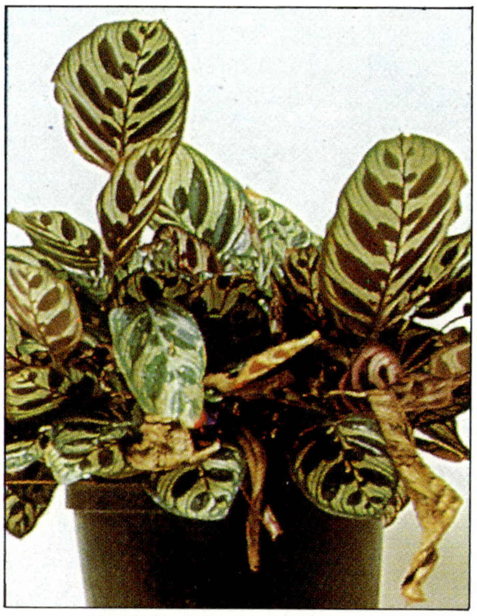

Also called scarid fly; these are not a major problem but they can be a considerable nuisance and damage the roots of plants grown in peat compost. They thrive in warm, moist, humid conditions and can increase to almost plague proportions. The gnats look like tiny mosquitoes and live in the surface compost where they eat dead and decaying matter. They only become obvious when the compost is disturbed and the adults fly up — but it's the small, maggot-like larvae that cause damage. They eat plant roots and succulent stems at, and just below, soil level.

To control them you have to carry out a two-pronged attack. The adults can be effectively dispatched with a spray of permethrin, pyrethrum or malathion. Then, deal with the larvae by watering a solution of malathion into the compost. Give two or three treatments at seven to ten day intervals.

Red spider mite

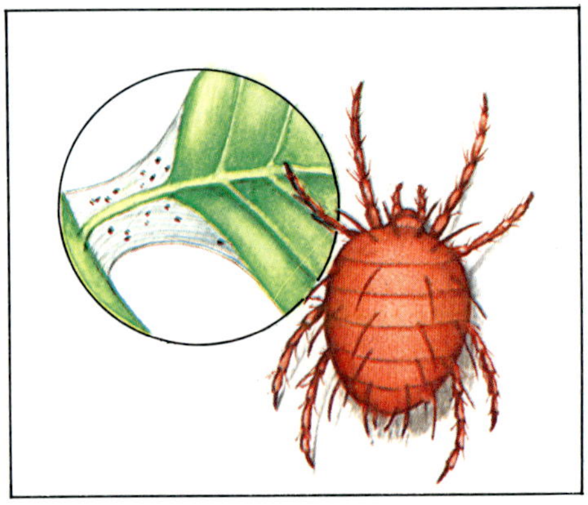

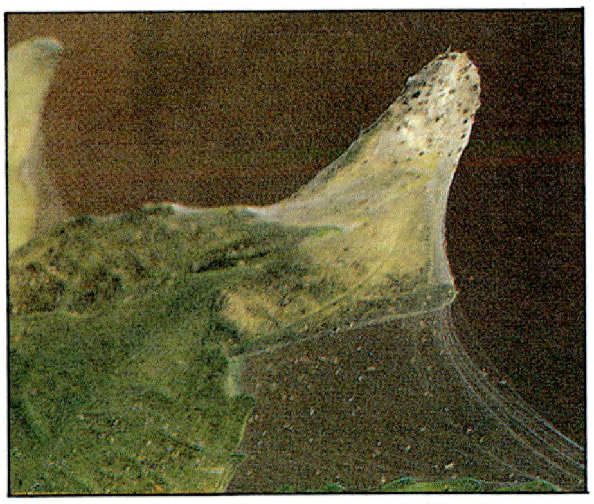

These are one of the most difficult pests to see and one of the most tricky to eradicate. The minute mites are almost invisible to the naked eye and live on the underside of leaves, biting and tearing the leaf tissue. In severe attacks the adult mites are visible as pale, straw-coloured creatures, several of which could fit on a pin head. The mite only turns red when temperatures drop and it prepares to hibernate, but it rarely does this indoors. The damage done to the leaves by the mite causes a distinct loss of green pigment and a dull, yellowish, mottled appearance.

Severe attacks occur when the air is warm and dry, making the leaves curl and turn brown at the edges and then progressively all over. When the damage is this severe the underside of leaves and new shoots show the minute webs.

Discourage red spider mite by regularly misting the foliage — particularly the undersides — with water, but this doesn't kill the mites totally. To kill them you have to use an insecticide such as derris, malathion or dimethoate applied regularly at seven to ten day intervals for about a month in order to catch all stages of the pest.

Scale insect

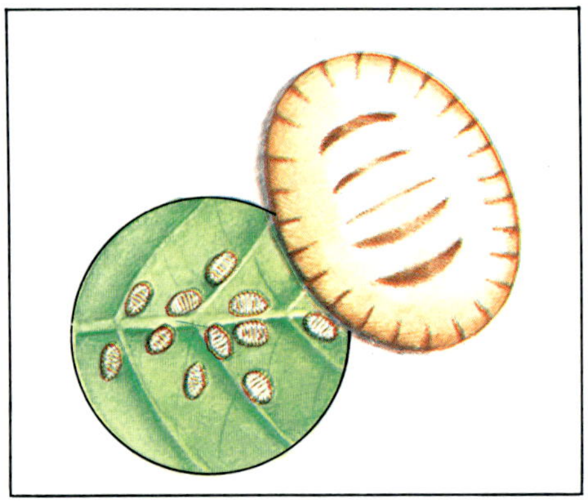

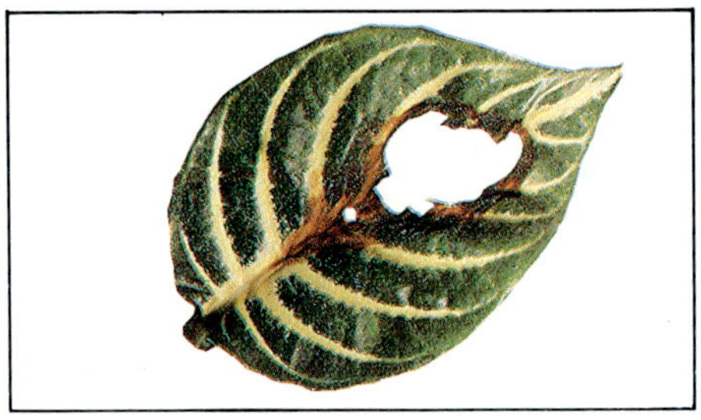

Scale insects are an unusual-looking plant pest. They look like tiny, dark brown blisters or warts on the stems and leaves, and are generally to be found on the underside of the leaves, clustering close to the veins. These blisters are really egg cases; the eggs hatch out inside the case, which then serves as an incubator for the young scale insects and protects them from attack by other insects and chemicals.

The young scale insect is tiny, flat and a pale straw colour, almost to the point of being transparent. When it crawls out of the protective blister, the young scale insect searches for its own feeding position; each one attaches itself to the surface of a stem or leaf and starts to excrete honeydew and consume the plant's fluids.

As scale becomes severe, new growth is deformed and young shoots may be killed off completely. The growth of sooty mould on the honeydew excretion can also become a major problem in bad infestations.

Scale insects are difficult to control, especially as the eggs and very young are protected by the egg case. Deal with it in two ways: firstly, scrape off visible scales with a fingernail or nail file, then spray three times with malathion or dimethoate at 10-14 day intervals.

Slugs and snails

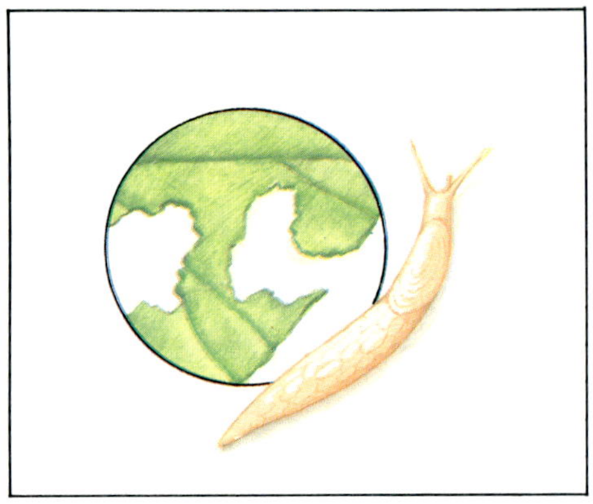

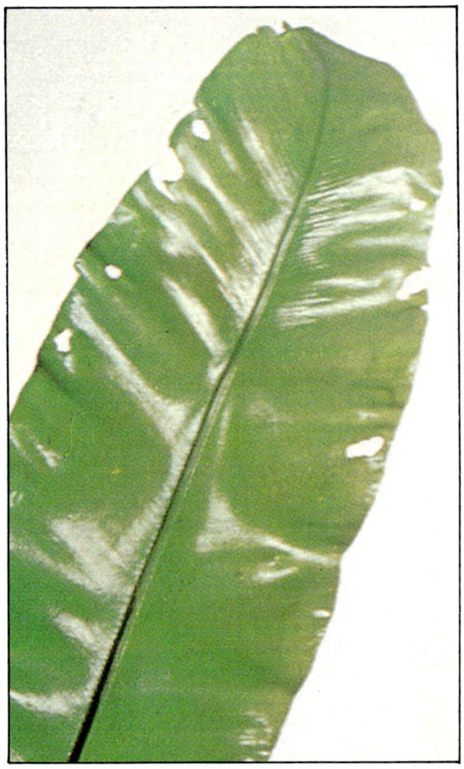

The types of slug or snail that attack houseplants are very different from the garden kind; they are quite tiny and hide during the day in any little crevice they can find, only coming out for a nocturnal feast. They cause severe damage in localised areas where they eat large chunks of leaf. If you can't find the culprit in the pot, look for the tiny tell-tale silvery streaks of slime that slugs and snails leave behind.

Slugs and snails are easily dealt with by a light sprinkling of metaldehyde pellets on the compost surface. The slug or snail will then be poisoned when it eats the pellets.

All about pesticides

The subject of pesticides is a complex one and can baffle even the keenest gardener. Gone are the days when there was only the one chemical, DDT, which could be used for everything. A highly sophisticated armoury is now available to tackle all the different possible fungal infections and other garden pests.

Chemical activity

The term 'pesticide' in fact covers a wide range of chemicals that have a number of different uses. As far as houseplants are concerned, pesticides include all the following.

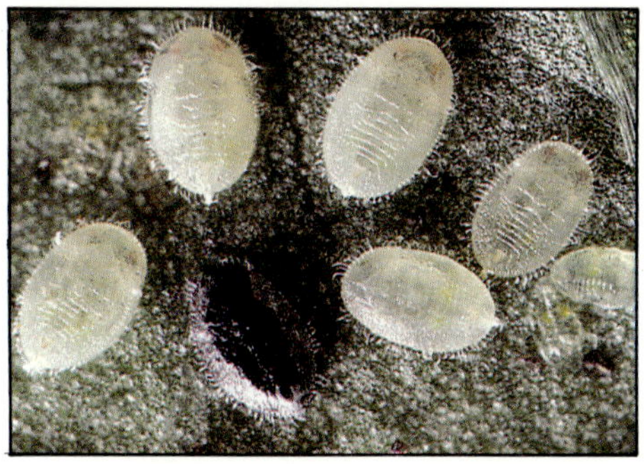

Insecticides. These include many different chemicals and are applied to the plant or compost to control pests such as aphids (greenfly and blackfly), caterpillars, whiteflies (*above*), fungus gnats and other insects.

Acaricides. These are specialised chemicals used for controlling members of the spider family which are particularly dangerous to houseplants and can be difficult to eliminate, such as red spider mite and tarsonemid mite. Specific acaricides tend to be restricted to commercial use, but examples of those that also have wider insecticidal properties include pirimiphos-methyl, malathion and dimethoate.

Nematicides. These chemicals are even more specialised and have been specifically designed to control nematodes (worms) such as eelworms. Eelworms are microscopic worms which live inside the affected plant tissue and, in order to deal with these pests, nematicides are inevitably highly toxic. They are not therefore generally available to members of the gardening public and their use is usually restricted to professional growers.

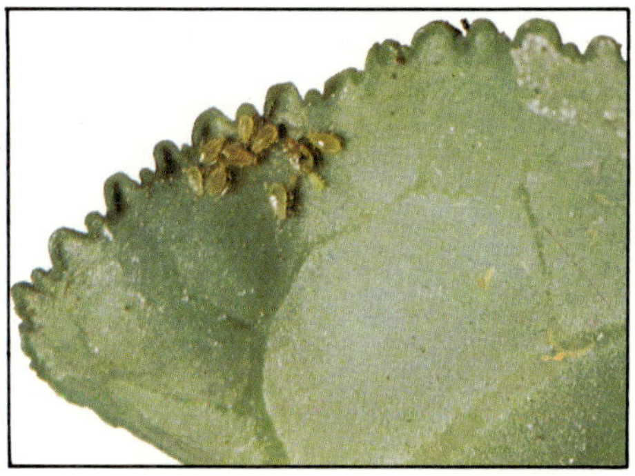

Aphicides. These are targeted at aphids, such as greenfly (*above*) and blackfly. Some are specially formulated to kill only aphids; these are particularly useful for plants in flower that are likely to be visited by perfectly harmless insects such as butterflies and bees or, for that matter, useful ones such as ladybirds that are doing their best to rid your plants of aphids. The best specific aphicide is probably pirimicarb, which acts selectively against only aphids. There are, however, many other aphicides that also act as general insecticides and will control many pests; these include malathion, dimethoate, permethrin and pyrethrum.

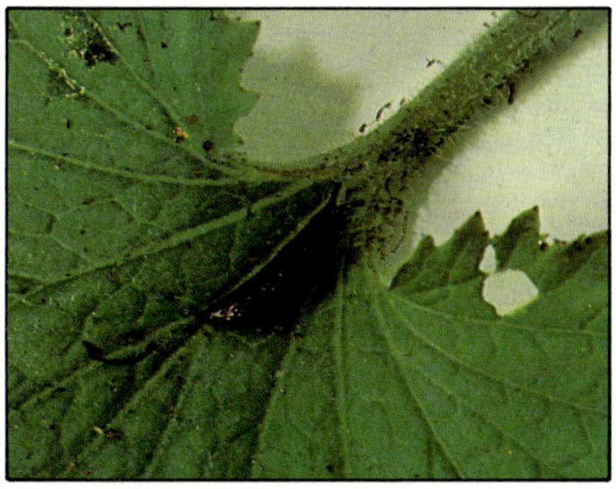

Molluscicides. These are used to control pests such as slugs (*above*) and snails. They are not usually a major threat to houseplants, but some small slugs and snails that seek refuge in crevices in the compost in the daytime and then feast on the plant in the evening can be problematic. Molluscicides, either in the form of a poisonous bait or in liquid form which is coated on to plant tissue, control these particular pests very effectively. Chemicals such as metaldehyde and methiocarb are very efficient.

Fungicides. These are a very useful group of chemicals that prevent and, in some cases, control and kill fungal disorders. The wide range of fungal disorders that affects houseplants includes leaf spot, stem and root rot, mildew and rust. Not all fungi actually kill plants — indeed some will only survive on living tissue — but they can seriously reduce plant vigour and deform growth. Fungicides are generally best applied as a preventive measure.

Methods of application

Although the effect of any particular pesticide depends to a great extent on its actual chemical activity and mode of action, it can also be influenced by the way in which it is applied.

Sprays. These are probably the most common formulation and come in concentrated form, either as a liquid or as a wettable powder, which is diluted according to the manufacturer's instructions and then applied to plants by means of a hand sprayer. Water acts as the chemical carrier and conveys it to the plant in droplets of chemical solution. The water then evaporates, leaving the chemical behind to act on the pest. It is always best to apply pesticidal sprays out of doors.

Drenches. Some chemicals are applied as a drench or watering to the compost. These are used to control soil-borne pests and diseases, unless it is a systemic pesticide, in which case it will be absorbed by the plant. Chemical solutions for use as drenches are usually the same formulations as those used for sprays, as water is once again used as the chemical carrier.

Granules. These are chemicals packed in a granular form and are used in the control of certain soil-borne pests. The granules can either be mixed into the compost or simply added to the surface. On wetting the soil the chemical is leached out into the compost and will start to take effect on the pest or fungal disease. Chemical granules are not often used for the pest control of houseplants and tend to be more widely useful in the garden, where they are regularly wetted by rainfall and thus more easily absorbed, first by the soil and then by the pest.

How they work

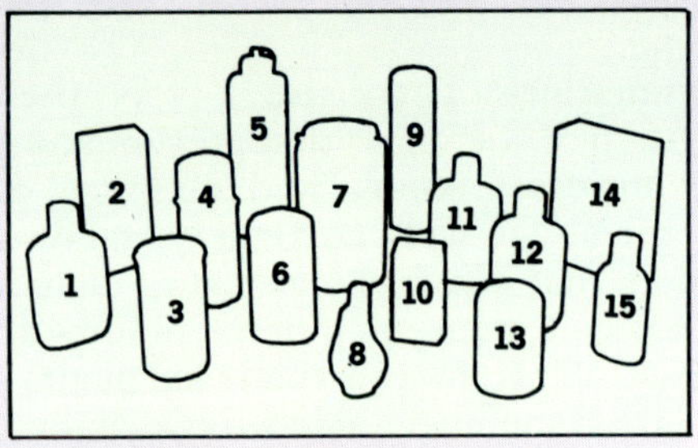

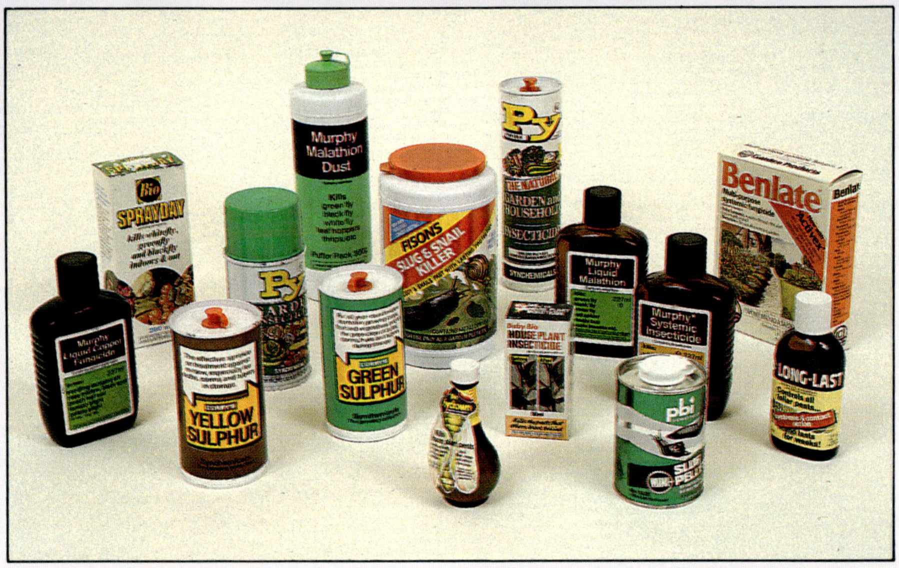

1 Murphy Liquid Copper Fungicide
2 Bio Sprayday
3 Corry's Yellow Sulphur
4 Py Spray Garden Insecticide
5 Murphy Malathion Dust
6 Corry's Green Sulphur
7 Fisons Slug and Snail Killer
8 Bio Flydown
9 Py Powder
10 Baby Bio House Plant Insecticide
11 Murphy Liquid Malathion
12 Murphy Systemic Insecticide
13 PBI Slug Mini-Pellets
14 Benlate
15 Bio Long-Last

Pesticides are complex chemical formulas that may either be derived from a natural source — such as pyrethrum which comes from a plant and will appeal to those gardeners who prefer to use products of natural origin — or they may have been developed by chemists after many years of research.

Although the effect of each chemical varies according to the particular group of chemicals to which it belongs, it can also work quite differently according to how the insect actually receives the poison.

● **Contact pesticides.** These are applied directly on to the pest, which means that good coverage of the infected plant is absolutely essential. The insect may then be poisoned either by the direct effect of the chemical on it, or by eating — or walking over — poisoned plant tissue to which the chemical has been applied. Many of these insecticides have special wetting agents, or surfactants, added to them — as, indeed, they are to many pesticides — in order to improve the chemical's ability to stick to plant tissue. Some contact insecticides also contain fungicides.

● **Preventive pesticides.** The term 'preventive' is applied to those fungicides which help to control fungal diseases such as mildew, grey mould fungus and leaf spot. Preventive fungicides have been in use for many years and may be sulphur- or copper-based. The effect of these chemicals on a plant is to inhibit the germination of fungal spores, which helps to reduce the spread of the disease. Preventive treatment should not, therefore, be applied at too late a stage, when the plant may already be at an advanced stage of infection.

● **Systemic pesticides.** These include both insecticides and fungicides and are a relatively recent innovation in the history of pesticides. They are extremely effective and greatly facilitate the control of many pests. Systemic pesticides may be sprayed or even watered on to plants and then rapidly enter the plant tissue where they are able to move freely to all parts of the plant and thus provide comprehensive protection from pests and fungal diseases — unless, of course, the pest or fungus in question has developed a resistance to that particular chemical. An insect only has to eat some of the poisoned plant tissue to be killed as sap is absorbed into its body. And a fungus may suffer the same fate as it attempts to draw nutrition from the plant carrying the fungicide in its tissue. Products that combine a systemic insecticide with a systemic fungicide are now widely available. Systemic pesticides are a superior alternative to contact pesticides because they do not depend on total coverage of the foliage.

WARNING
Remember to take full account of all the safety precautions recommended by the manufacturer as regards the mixing, use and storage of pesticides.

Dusts. Instead of being diluted in water, a chemical dust uses an inert carrier dust or powder to transport the chemical. Chemical dusts can simply be 'puffed' on to plants in order to control pests or diseases, but they tend to leave an unsightly deposit on foliage which devalues their use indoors.

Aerosols. These are a particularly convenient way of applying a chemical to a plant. The aerosol transports it in minute droplets which provide an effective coverage. Another advantage is that aerosols come in an easy, ready-to-use form.

Misters. Hand mist sprayers containing ready-to-use solutions have recently been introduced to fill the gap between the convenient aerosol and the dilute-yourself concentrate. This combines the advantages of the aerosol with those of the re-fillable mister and is therefore a useful additional pest control system.

Chemical baits. Some pests, such as slugs and snails, cannot easily be sprayed and are therefore more easily dealt with by chemical baits. These both attract their victims and then poison them. They are widely used in the garden and can also be used, in a smaller version, on houseplants.

Chemical vaporisers. These work on the same principle as those chemical vaporising strips that are sometimes hung from the ceiling to control insects such as mosquitoes. They take the form of small plant 'labels' or tabs which are impregnated with a special chemical and which you simply insert in the soil.

First aid

Healthy plants — like healthy people — tend to shrug off disease. But if you detect any sign of disease on your houseplants you should move to the rescue quickly, before the trouble spreads to the rest of the plant or to other plants near by.

The problem with an ailing houseplant is that it's difficult to tell at first whether it is suffering from an illness, or whether it is just weak and listless and very unhappy about the conditions in which you are growing it.

If you are worried about the health of any particular plant, ask yourself whether the plant is getting too much light or warmth, or too little of either. Is the plant waterlogged — or perhaps completely dried out? Is it sitting in a draught?

A plant sitting in the wrong environment for it won't be completely healthy, and will therefore be much more susceptible to disease. And, once it has succumbed, it will go downhill rapidly. Act quickly, both by improving the plant's surroundings and by giving it the appropriate treatment for the disease.

All the chemicals we recommend are available from good gardening shops and garden centres. The chemical ingredients of each product are clearly set out on the packet — read the instructions before you buy to check whether the manufacturer warns you not to use the product on certain plants.

TAKE GREAT CARE WHEN YOU ARE USING ANY CHEMICAL TO KEEP IT WELL AWAY FROM CHILDREN, PETS AND FOOD. READ THE MANUFACTURER'S RECOMMENDATIONS CAREFULLY, AND MAKE SURE THE TREATMENT IS SUITABLE FOR YOUR PARTICULAR PLANT.

Leaf spot

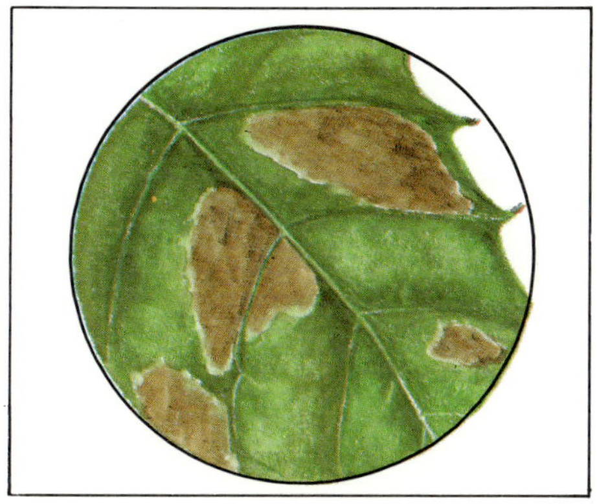

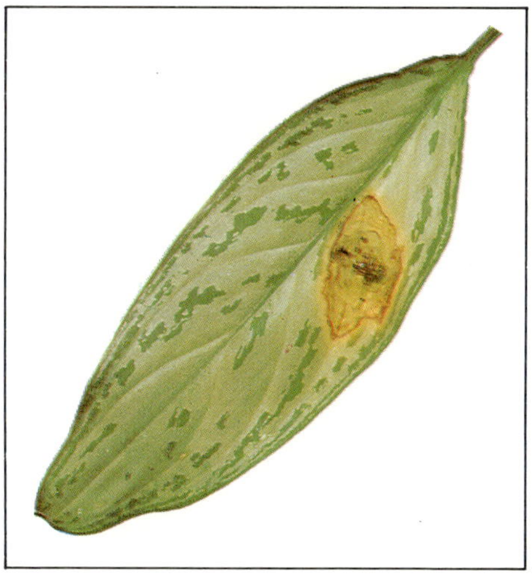

Bacterial spots are rather uncommon and not easy to recognise; they sometimes have a translucent margin and they may occasionally ooze little globules of bacteria. You might find them on Ivies; if so, it's important to remove all the infected leaves.

Fungal spots vary from tiny spots to large patches spreading all over the leaf (the Rubber Plant sometimes suffers from this). The entire leaf may turn yellow and then brown as the cells are destroyed.

To control bacterial leaf spot, spray the plant regularly with a liquid copper fungicide. You can treat fungal leaf spot with a fungicide containing benomyl, such as Benlate, and products containing copper. Remove the affected leaves and burn them. However, by the time you have noticed the spots the fungal spores may already have been released and it may be too late to save your plant.

Root & stem rot

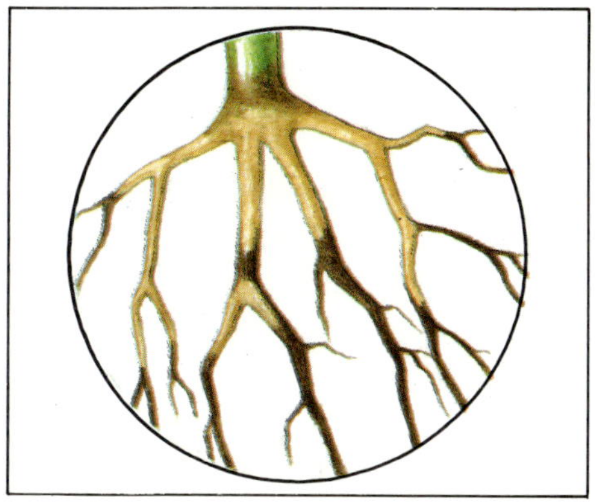

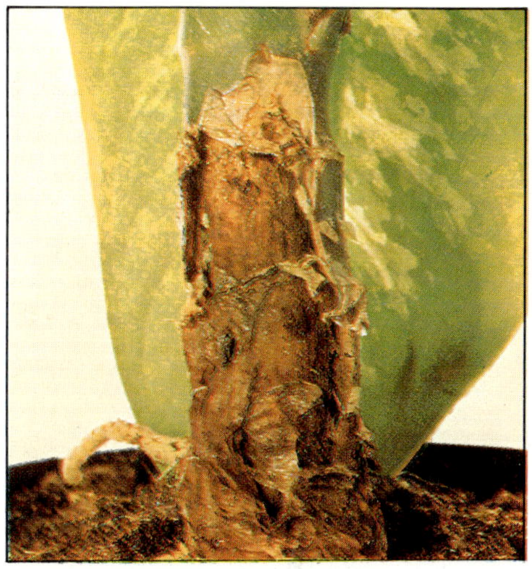

If your pot plants are kept too dank and wet, organisms that live on decaying matter may suddenly attack.

Most houseplants don't like their roots being constantly wet — except for Ferns and Azaleas, which should always be moist. You should suspect that fungal organisms are attacking the root or stem of your plant if the leaves turn yellow, wither and fall off prematurely. Rotting roots are easy to pull apart (healthy roots are usually white and brittle). The stems may also be turning black, and becoming soft.

Watering with a chemical such as benomyl may help if the affected plant is treated early enough. But if the treatment is too long delayed your plant may be beyond saving. To avoid root and stem rot, make sure your plants don't become waterlogged, particularly in cold weather. When watering a plant by placing the pot in water, don't let it sit there longer than 15-20 minutes.

Damping off

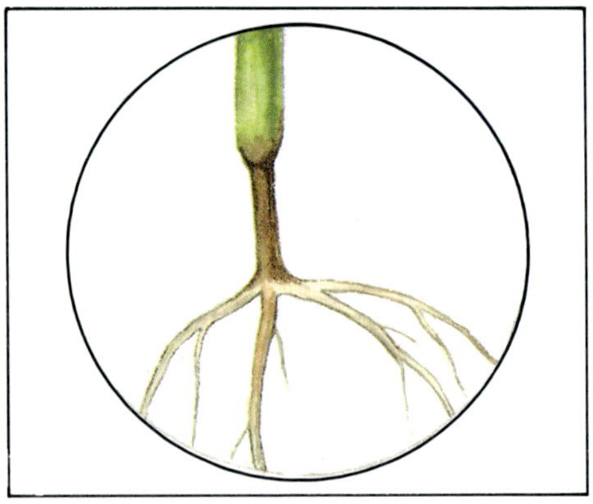

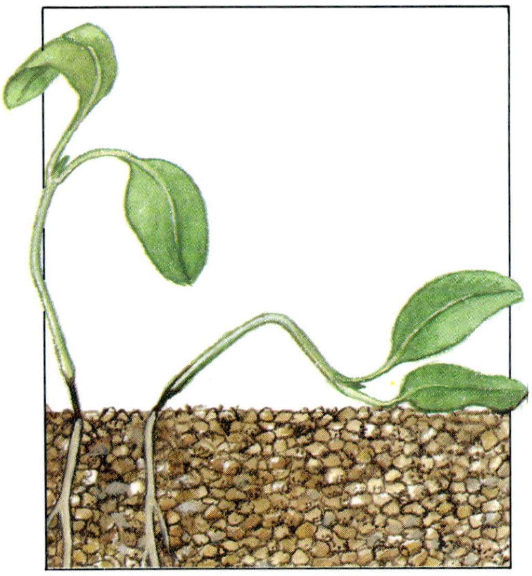

Damping off is a fungal disease caught by seedlings and cuttings. Suddenly, without warning, what you thought was a perfectly healthy cutting or seedling may topple over and die. If you pull the victim up you will see that the base of the stem has withered and gone completely black.

The problem is caused by a minute fungus living in a dirty pot or tray, or possibly in unsterilised or contaminated compost. It might even have come from the water you have been using.

Whatever the cause, there is nothing you can do to save the affected cutting or seedling. Pull it out and throw it away — if possible, burn it. To save the rest of the cuttings or seedlings spray them all immediately with a liquid copper fungicide, or Cheshunt Compound (a fungicide powder that you dissolve in water and spray onto your seedlings).

Mildew

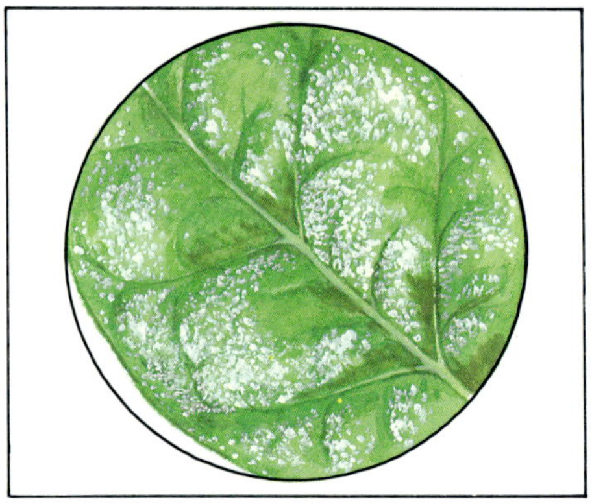

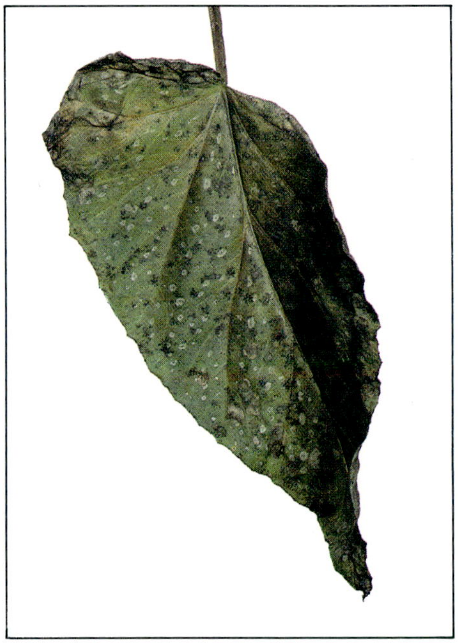

Powdery mildew is a disease that shows up as a fine white powdery dust mainly on leaves but sometimes also on the flowers. It doesn't have fluffy growths like grey mould but it can stop the plant growing healthily. There is also a less common kind of mildew called downy mildew, which has spore-bearing bodies that are easier to see.

Spray the infected plant with a fungicide containing benomyl or triforine at two or three week intervals during the season when the plant is very dry and the fungus is particularly active. You can prevent mildew by dusting the plant lightly with flowers of sulphur every 10 or 14 days — but check the label to see that sulphur won't cause any damage to your plant.

Grey mould

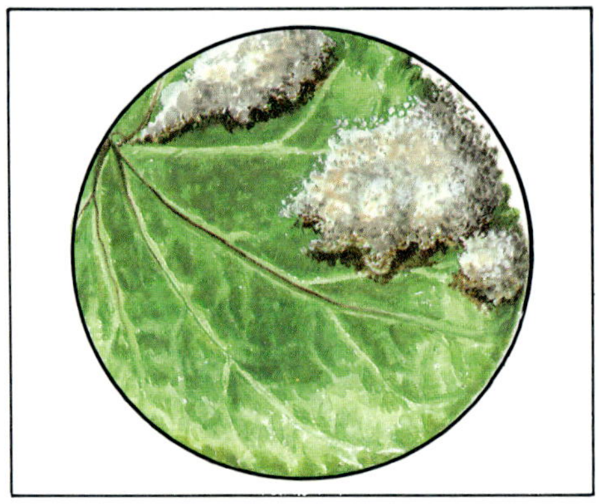

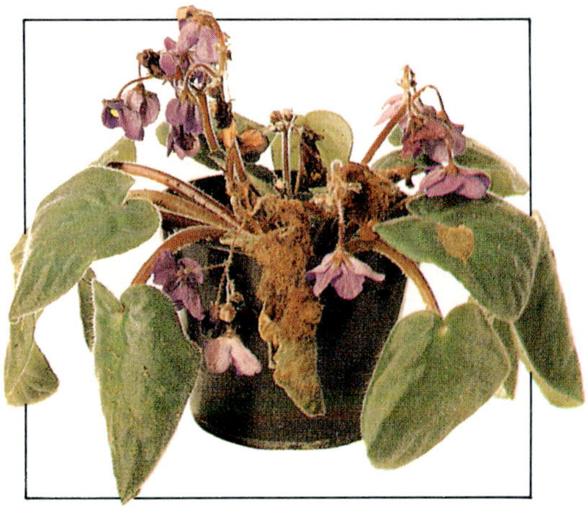

Grey mould, or Botrytis, is a particularly nasty disease that attacks fleshy plants such as African Violet, Cyclamen, Begonia and Gloxinia when they are kept too damp.

The fungus looks greyish-brown and is rather fluffy. It normally starts by infecting pieces of dead and decaying plant tissue, such as old leaves and withering flowers, and when it has used up that source of food it then attacks healthy living tissue.

Grey mould is dangerous and must be treated urgently as soon as you notice it.

First cut away all withering or damaged leaves and dying flowers using a clean sharp knife or tweezers. Don't leave any jagged or broken stems behind; try to remove dead flowers and leaf stalks cleanly, as near to the base of the plant as possible. Make sure that the plant isn't waterlogged and that it has enough fresh air. To prevent the problem occurring again, spray the plant with a fungicide containing benomyl.

Kiss of life

One of the most disheartening experiences for any houseplant owner is to find a favourite plant developing limp, lifeless leaves, or foliage dying when there is no apparent pest to blame. The tendency is to blame yourself — but although you may not have been providing the right living conditions, you shouldn't despair. Look carefully at the situation of the plant and try to assess the likely causes of the problem. Sometimes the treatment will be quite small-scale — merely changing the plant's position or giving it less water — sometimes it will be more drastic, and you may have to use ruthless surgery to trim off dead foliage or branches. Remember, plants that have been sick need time to convalesce, just like people.

The first thing to look out for is the *position* of a sick plant. The natural habitats of your plants are almost certainly very diverse, so it is important that you try and match, as much as possible, their natural growing conditions with those available within your house; the A-Z guide will help you decide the most suitable position for each of your plants. Generally, green foliage plants thrive much better than flowering plants in poor light. So for these areas, Aspidistras and palms are ideal, while the colourful African Violets (*Saintpaulias*) should be given the brightest light that windowsills can afford. Your Cyclamen or Cissus may be suffering from higher temperatures that are more suitable for plants such as Cotyledon or Dieffenbachia. By putting your Araucaria in a hot sunny position it will not only have to endure leaf scorch, but the compost will dry out rapidly, leading to dehydration — and a very sick plant. Be very wary of heat sources such as radiators or stoves; avoid them at all costs — the same is true of draughts.

If the positioning seems right, the next thing to look at is watering. In fact, of all the things that make plants start to lose condition, the most common are problems with watering.

Plants obviously need more water during the periods of active growth, but knowing exactly how much water to give and how often is not easy. Although the plastic pots most commonly used today retain moisture, they are not as porous as the clay ones, and can prevent roots from receiving the aeration they require. Evaporation often takes place unevenly, so while the surface of the compost appears dry, the roots of your plant may still be very damp. You may find yourself tempted to give your plant daily waterings in the belief that it has dried out. But beware — waterlogging beneath the surface of the compost can prevent vital air from getting to the roots. This waterlogging can cause root rot; the roots then cannot take up moisture properly, and so, even though it has been receiving plenty of water, your plant will begin to look dehydrated.

The simplest way of discovering whether your plant needs water is to test the compost by scratching it with your fingertips; provide water if the compost is dry for about 1-2 inches (2.5-5cm) below the surface. For a few foliage plants the compost can be allowed to dry out more — to one-third or even one-half of its depth.

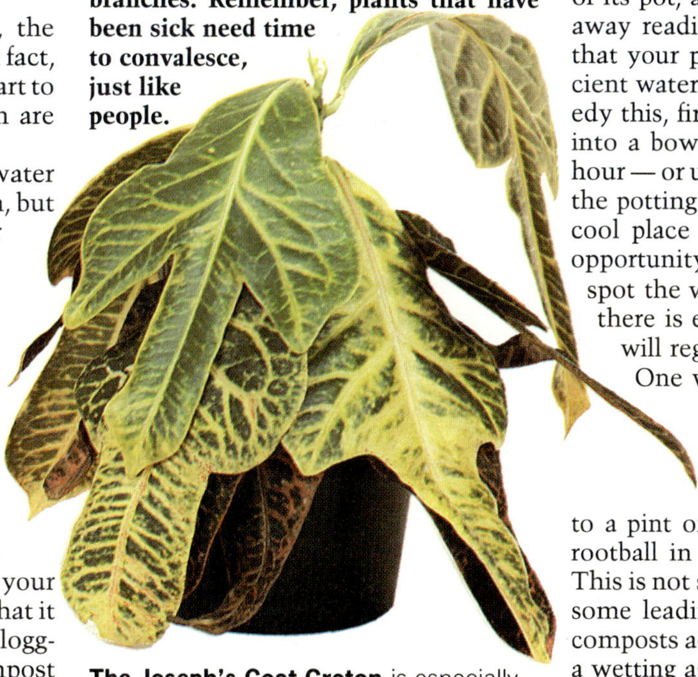

The Joseph's Coat Croton is especially vulnerable to cold — below 60°F (15°C) its leaves will droop and go brown, *above.*

It is important that you never guess your plant's watering requirements. Look them up in the A-Z guide, and, as a simple rule of thumb, when in doubt, don't water. Your plants will probably thank you if you follow this rule!

Overwatering

The symptoms of overwatering are many: rotten areas of foliage; brown and mushy roots; leaves that are limp, curled or prone to dropping off. Try to avoid overwatering at all times, especially during the resting period; watering one to three times a month is generally quite sufficient. However, if you find that one of your plants has been overwatered, you must give it the chance to dry out completely. Carefully ease the whole plant out of the pot and stand it on a sheet of newspaper to help absorb excess moisture.

Underwatering

To confuse matters, *under*watered plants generally have the same symptoms as *over*watered ones. Modern peat-based composts can dry out very quickly and these composts can also be extremely difficult to re-wet. They often will not retain moisture and the result is dehydration. If you think this has happened, take the plant gently out of its pot; a very dry mixture that falls away readily from the roots indicates that your plant has not received sufficient water from the compost. To remedy this, first of all plunge the rootball into a bowl of tepid water for half an hour — or until bubbles stop rising from the potting mixture. Doing all this in a cool place will give the foliage every opportunity to recover properly; if you spot the warning signs early enough there is every chance that your plant will regain its vitality.

One way of helping the compost to absorb moisture more effectively is to add three or four drops of a good quality washing-up liquid to a pint of tepid water, and soak the rootball in this for 20 to 30 minutes. This is not such a surprising method — some leading producers of peat-based composts add a kind of detergent called a wetting agent to their compost.

Correct watering

To water a plant properly, place it on a saucer and water the surface of the compost, allowing the water to drain through the compost into the saucer below. Leave the plant on the saucer for 20 to 30 minutes and then throw away any remaining water. If the surface of the compost is 'caked', preventing the water from draining through, prick the surface gently with a fork. If the moisture has still not been absorbed after 20 minutes or so, the soil is probably so compacted that the plant will have to be repotted in a more porous mixture; remove any rotted brown roots and don't water again until you see signs of renewed growth.

For plants such as Saintpaulia, Gloxinia and Cyclamen, which do not like water on their leaves or crowns, a different technique is necessary. Immerse the pots in tepid water to just below the level of the compost, and allow them to soak for about half an hour, or until the surface glistens.

Summertime

During the hot, dry summer months plants lose much of their moisture through evaporation, and it is important that you provide an adequate supply of water, both to replace the water lost and to enable new growth to appear. Always check the guidelines for each individual plant, however; it is more difficult to correct overwatering than to compensate for underwatering. If any of your plants have suffered a shock to their system caused by either too much, or too little, water they will need considerable care and attention if they are to be nursed back to full health.

A wilting plant has probably been overwatered with the result that the roots have been partially damaged. One solution is to place it inside a temporary mini-greenhouse to aid recovery. You can easily rig this up using a clear polythene bag, supported by a few short canes long enough to keep the polythene clear of the foliage. Before placing your sick plant inside, spray it well with a fine mist of tepid water. Try to avoid direct sunlight (to prevent leaf scorching) and place the mini-greenhouse in as cool a place as possible so that the plant does not completely dry out. (Be careful, of course, to keep polythene bags away from children.)

When your plant begins to look fit again, you can start to wean it away from its protective covering, but remember that it is still in convalescence — try to avoid placing it near draughts and keep a watchful eye out for badly damaged or dead leaves. These have to be cut away cleanly before they rot and cause further problems.

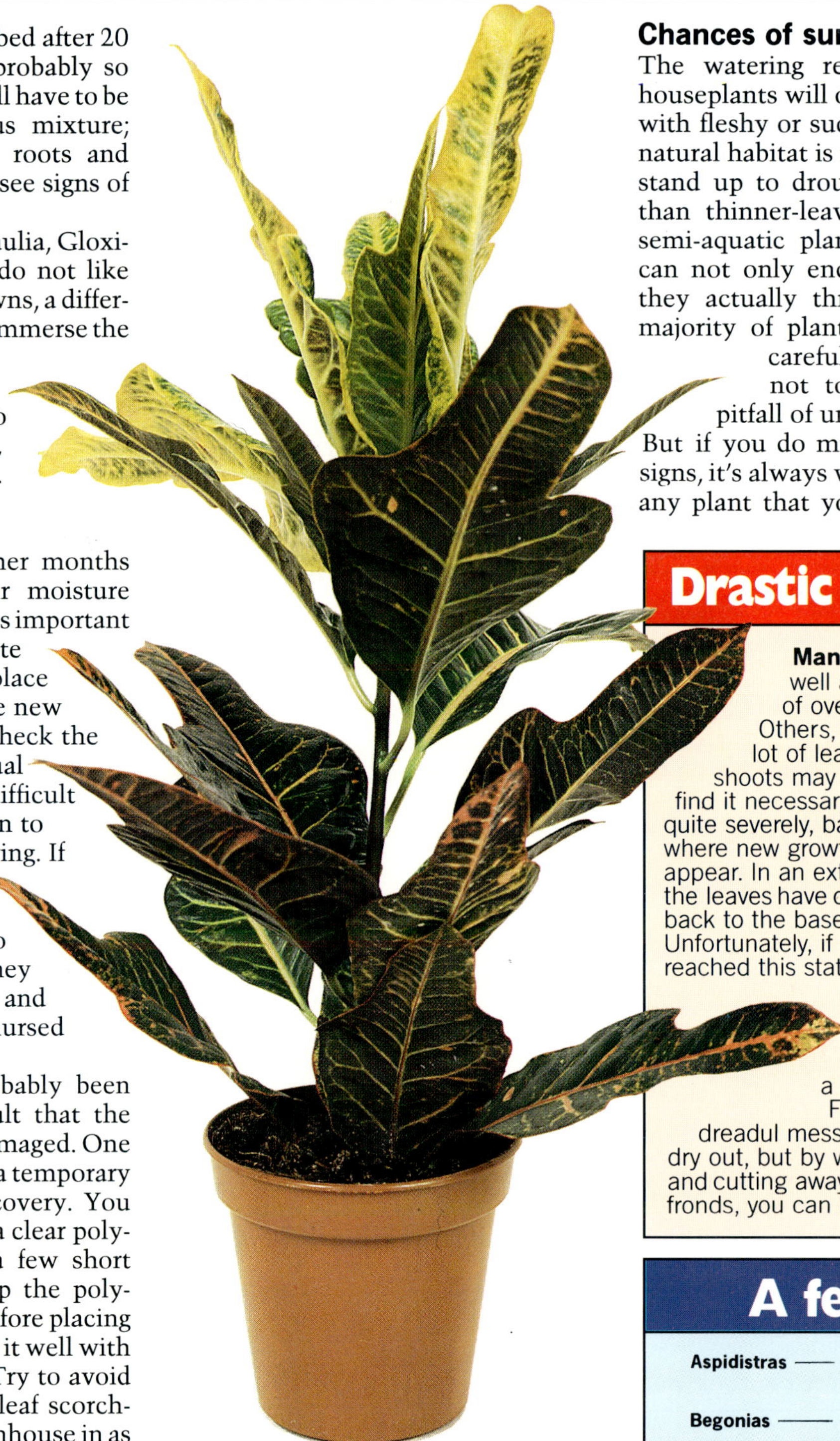

To cure a plant, wrap it in a polythene bag and keep it warm. A healthy plant, *above*, has a strong upright growth.

Wintertime

In the winter months it may take even longer to persuade your plant to pick up again due to the fluctuating temperatures caused by central heating. If you use a mini-greenhouse during this time, keep it at a temperature of 60-65°F (15-18°C), and do not give the plant any water.

Chances of survival

The watering requirements of your houseplants will obviously vary. Those with fleshy or succulent leaves (whose natural habitat is in dry conditions) can stand up to drought more effectively than thinner-leaved plants. Similarly, semi-aquatic plants such as Cyperus can not only endure waterlogging — they actually thrive on it. With the majority of plants, however, be very careful when watering: try not to succumb to either pitfall of under- or overwatering. But if you do miss the early warning signs, it's always worth trying to revive any plant that you're fond of.

Drastic measures

Many plants can recover well after the initial shock of over- or underwatering Others, however, may lose a lot of leaves, or some of their shoots may die back. You might find it necessary to prune your plant quite severely, back to the point where new growth looks likely to appear. In an extreme case, where all the leaves have died, try cutting right back to the base of the plant. Unfortunately, if your plant has reached this state, there is only the slimmest chance of recovery unless you are dealing with a fern. The Maidenhair Fern can become a dreadul mess if it's allowed to dry out, but by watering it thoroughly and cutting away the dead or dying fronds, you can help it recover.

A few tips

Aspidistras	Moderate light; room temperature; moderate watering
Begonias	Bright but indirect light; room temperature; moderate watering
Busy Lizzie *(Impatiens)*	Bright light; room temperature; frequent watering when growing
Dieffenbachia	Good light; warm; frequent watering
Ferns	Indirect light; warm; frequent watering
Fittonia	Shade essential; warm; moderate watering
Geraniums *(Pelargonium)*	Direct sunlight; room temperature; moderate watering
Ivies *(Hedera)*	Moderate light; cool moderate watering
Kaffir Lily *(Clivia miniata)*	Bright but indirect light; cool; moderate watering

Talk to your plants

LUTHER BURBANK, a famous nurseryman from California, developed the spineless cactus (*Opuntia ficus-indica*) in the early years of this century. He spoke to the plants as they were growing: 'You have nothing to fear,' he would tell them, 'you don't need your defensive thorns. I will protect you.' How much influence Burbank's soothing comments had upon the development of the spineless cactus is difficult – if not impossible – to estimate. But like many plant owners, he was convinced he had to win the trust of his plants – and that talking to them was the best method.

Many people talk to their plants just as they do to their household pets or, indeed, their children. Houseplants are regarded and treated by many people in much the same way as dogs, cats or birds. And people's reactions to the health or otherwise of their plants is often out of all proportion to the cost of replacing the plants involved. We really do get upset when our plants are not growing as they should.

Do *you* talk to your houseplants? Do you regularly chat them up, giving them words of encouragement to grow lustily or to start to flower, or do you offer threats of banishment if they don't mend their ways? And do you think your plants take any notice of your words of praise or your warnings?

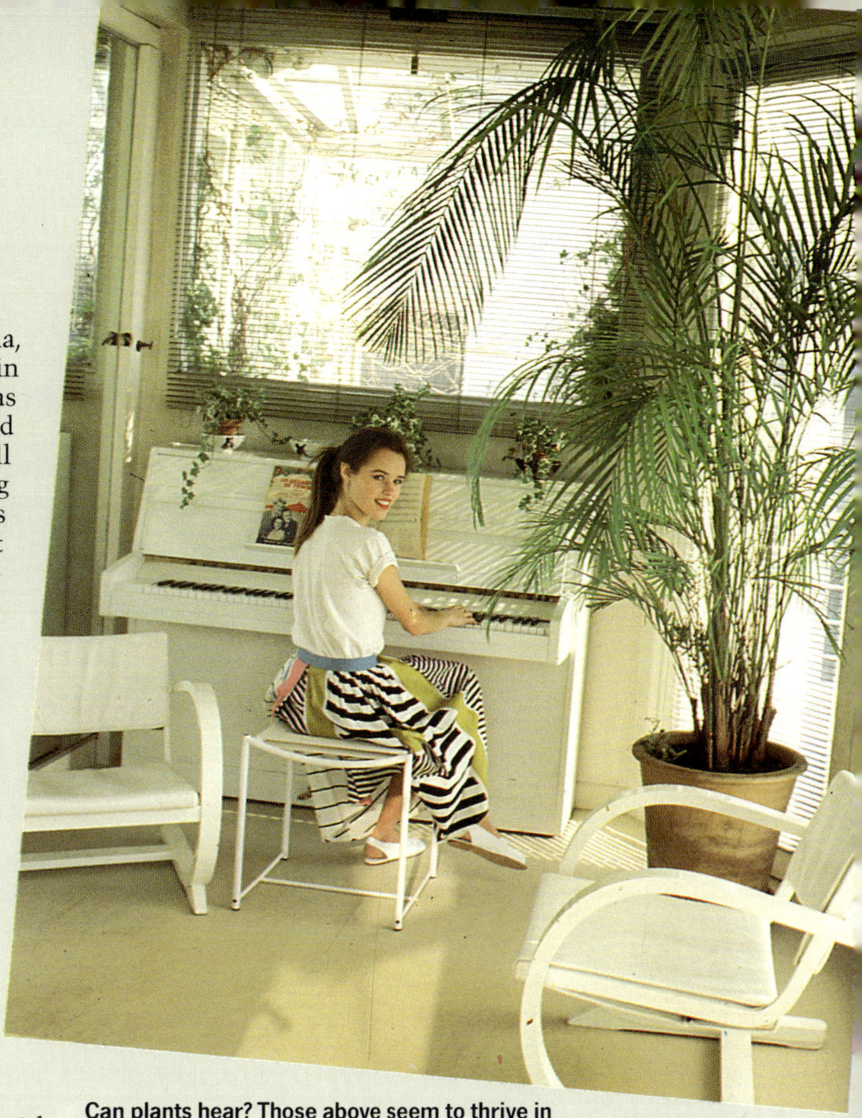

Can plants hear? Those above seem to thrive in a musical environment, while the one on the right below suffered badly when continually exposed to loud rock music.

Some eminent interest

A number of very eminent people deeply involved with plants (Darwin was one) have thought of plants in human terms and over the last few decades extensive research has been carried out into the idea that plants are not indifferent to human beings.

Former CIA employee Cleve Backster connected the electrodes of a lie detector to a Philodendron, and claimed to have evidence that the plant was able to react to his *intention* to maltreat it in some way: he called this seemingly supernatural ability 'primary perception'. In the late 1960s, a student named Mary Retallack in Denver, Colorado, subjected a group of plants to the notes B and D played loudly over and over again 12 hours a day. At the end of three weeks, all the plants had died – except for some African Violets, which flourished. A 'control' group of the same plant types grown at the same time in normal sound conditions all grew in a healthy manner.

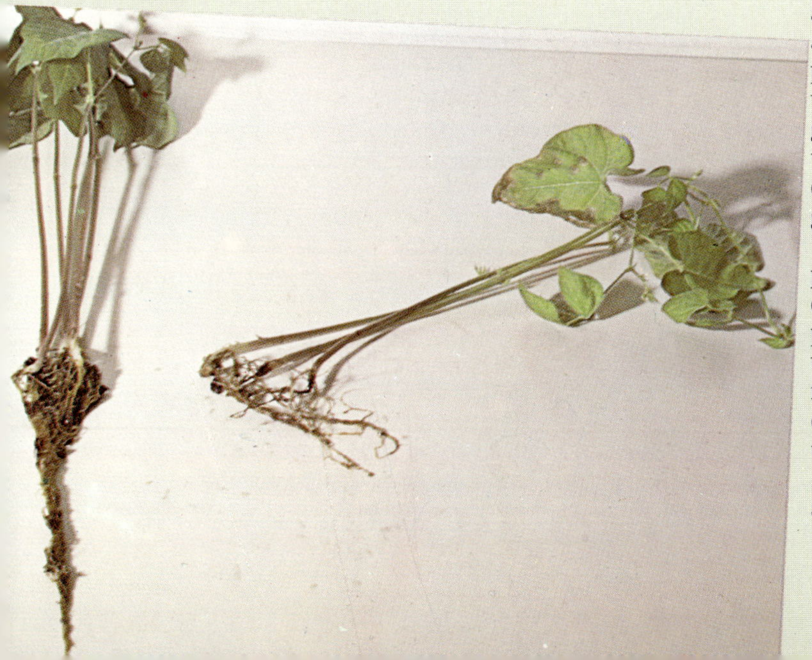

Fact or fancy?

Whatever the results of this scientific (or pseudo-scientific) research, there is one thing that we can probably say about talking to plants: the specific needs of each plant must always be considered, and the person who talks to his or her plants, treats them as individuals and is concerned for their various states of development is by far the most likely to get good results. The single-minded decorator, concerned only with instant effect, placing plants in corners without light or in draughts merely because it suits the room is unlikely to get anything like the same healthy, growing specimens.

Interestingly enough, while the scientific research on plants responding to humans is inconclusive, it has been established over the past few years that humans respond positively to caring for plants. Several major American universities offer degrees in horticultural therapy, a treatment whereby patients with physical or mental problems can find some relief in a close interest in plants. And in this therapy, patients are actively encouraged to talk to plants!

So talk to your plants by all means – it's good for them, and it may be even better for you.

Seasonal spring care

Plants seem to sense the coming of spring long before we do and, just as the first spring bulbs burst into flower on even the coldest, dampest spring mornings, houseplants have also noticed the increasing hours of daylight and have started to put on fresh growth, so signalling a change in care from that required in the long, cold, dark winter months.

The appearance of new growing shoots, new leaves or even flowers are the most common signals to watch out for, all of which herald the change in season. And with this seasonal change comes the need to adjust the care of your houseplants.

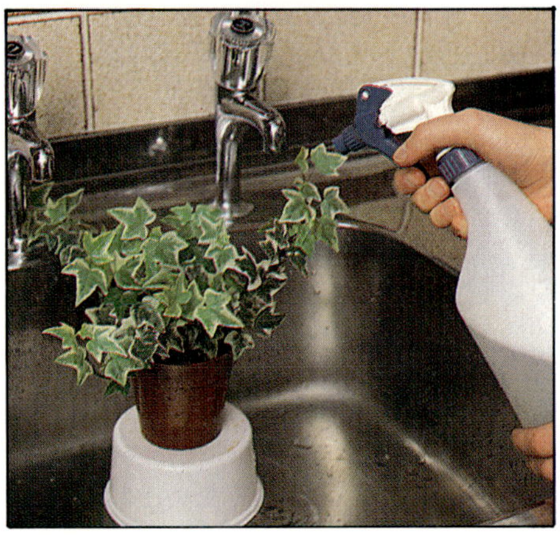

Spring clean foliage by spraying it with tepid water, but take care not to overwater the plant in the process.

Watering

As houseplants start to put on new growth, so their need for water increases. And as daylight hours increase and temperatures rise, so plants become more active in producing plant foods and will lose more water from their leaves, thus increasing their need for water.

Care should nevertheless be taken not to overwater, but only gradually to increase the amount of water supplied. Apart from certain plants — such as Azaleas and Ferns — which should always be kept moist, it is a good practice to allow the compost to dry out a little before re-watering it. Surprisingly enough, houseplants are very susceptible to being overwatered in the spring — particularly as the onset of spring is not always all that it is romanticised to be: a sudden return of a cold snap can slow plants down again and reduce their need for water. Plants can only be overwatered by watering them too often, so it is always a good idea to let them use up most of the moisture they have available before giving them any more.

Feeding

The increase in a plant's growth in the spring necessitates the addition of extra plant nutrients to sustain healthy development. Whatever type of plant food you use, you must give your plant somewhat less at the onset of spring than it will require later on, when at the height of its growing season. Overfeeding encourages lush growth with no stamina in the stems and discourages the production of flowers, and too high a concentration can also damage the plant's root system.

If you are using a liquid fertiliser, for example, do not feed at full strength for the first few weeks but use in a more diluted form, at half or even one-third of the normal recommended rate. It is particularly important not to feed the plant when the compost is dry. It is also important not to feed for six to eight weeks after repotting as the fresh compost will have all the nutrients the plant needs. Then, as the season progresses and the plant's rate of growth increases, so the amount of fertiliser may be increased to the normal recommended dilution rate. The frequency with which you need to feed depends on the type of plant in question: feed those plants that produce a lot of new foliage, such as Ivy (Hedera) or Grape Ivy (*Cissus rhombifolia*) once every one to two weeks; while those plants which produce less foliage, such as Dracaena, Cordyline and Maranta, usually need to be fed only once every three or four weeks.

Repotting

Towards the end of spring, it is time to consider repotting your houseplants. It is important, however, not to repot them too soon, or you might run the risk of losing them.

Plants that are still in a relatively dormant condition after their annual winter rest should not be repotted until they have started into active growth, as the shock of being repotted too soon can kill them. The sudden increase in the amount of water available when a plant has been potted on may prove too much and the plant may be damaged or even killed by this excess. As its need for water increases through the season, however, it will be more tolerant and better able to withstand being moved to a larger pot.

The benefits of repotting are not only that the plant has more room to spread its roots but also that it has an increased amount of plant nutrients available to it during the growing season, more water, and greater stability.

Temperature

As outdoor temperatures rise during the spring, so houseplants become less dependent on central heating. It is, however, important to try to avoid sudden fluctuations in temperature, which can result in leaf drop and may even be fatal.

Houseplants need to be gradually weaned off artificial heating at this time of year in order to enable them to survive the late spring and summer without any artificial heat at all.

It is also important to avoid subjecting your plants to draughts during the early part of the season, particularly if they have grown accustomed to a warm, stable environment. You may find it refreshing to allow a breath of cool fresh spring air to ventilate your home, but your houseplants may not be quite so enthusiastic!

Pruning, training, staking

As houseplants start to grow anew, it is important to ensure that they grow in the way you want them to. Climbers such as Ivy (Hedera), for example, will probably need some sort of additional support in order to guide them in the right direction from the very start of the growing season.

Other plants may need to be trained to ensure a good compact growth. Plants such as Jasmine, for example, need to be trained regularly — around and up a cane, say, or around a hoop — or their growth will soon become

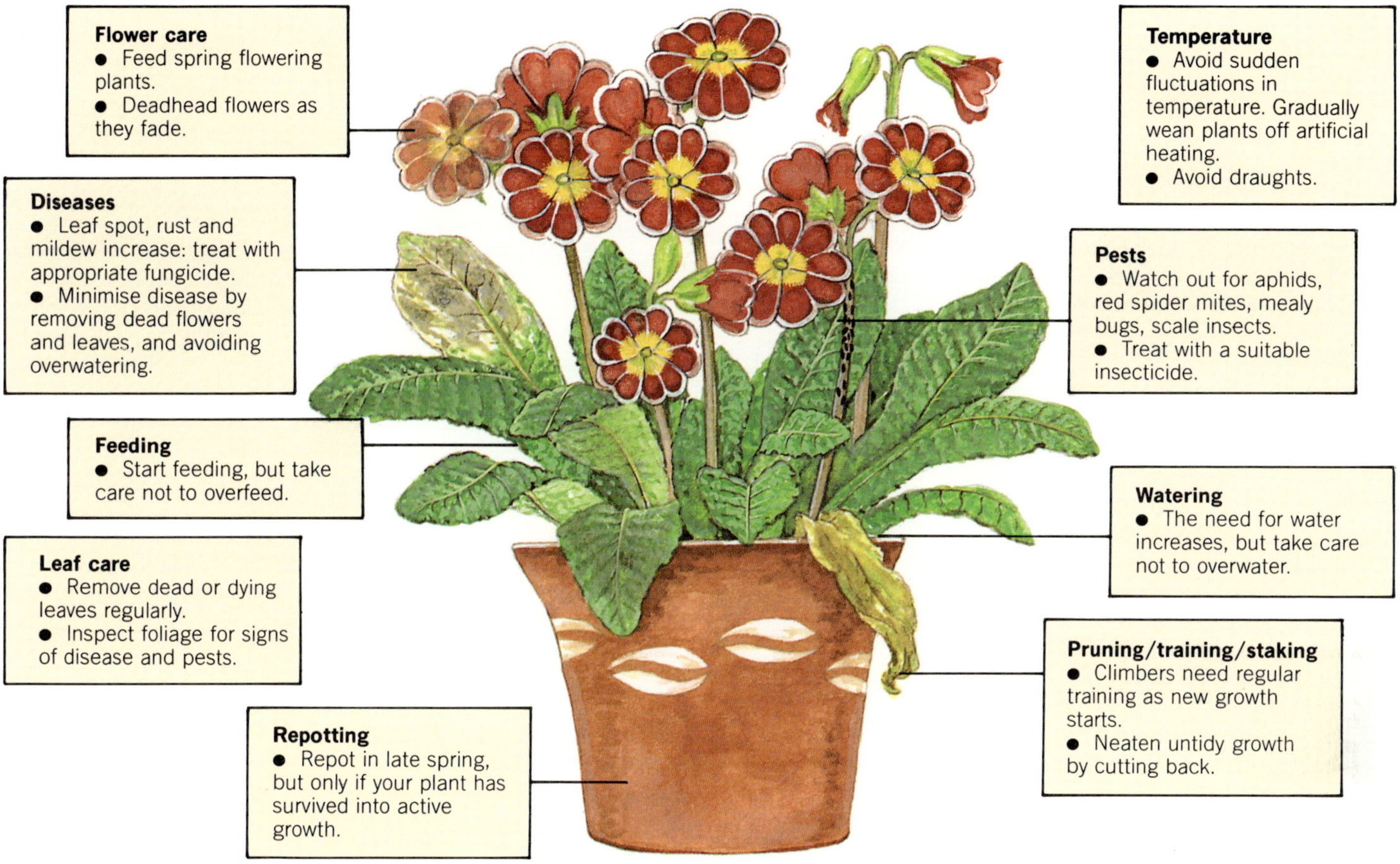

tangled and untidy. While others, like the Shrimp Plant (*Beloperone guttata*), benefit from being cut back in order to encourage a neat compact habit rather than allowing them to become leggy and unsightly.

Flower care

Some houseplants flower in the spring. Jasmine, Easter Cactus (*Rhipsalidopsis gaertneri*) and Primula, for example, are all at their best during this season. It is important with these plants, therefore, to ensure that they are correctly supplied with the right balance of plant foods, with a higher level of potash or potassium, in order to help the development of flowers.

And finally, when the flowers have faded, remove them by regular deadheading in order to make sure that no debilitating disease can set in, and to prevent the plant from wasting its energies on seed formation.

Leaf care

The accumulation of winter dust on your houseplants can suddenly look unsightly when the sun begins to shine on them, and it is worth 'spring cleaning' the foliage at this time of year. Do be wary of oil-based cleaning products, however, as these can sometimes damage more delicate foliage — so use with caution and always read the manufacturer's instructions carefully.

Towards the end of spring, many houseplants will benefit from a light shower of tepid water to remove accumulated dust, but be careful not to overwater the plant during this process.

Pests

Many pests hibernate during the winter, though some — such as scale insect, mealy bug and red spider mite — seem to keep going all year round. But as spring arrives, a new-found energy seems to hit the insect world.

Pest infestations that had up until now been at a low level will suddenly and quite dramatically explode, causing immense damage to houseplants in a relatively short period. Watch out in particular for aphids (greenfly and blackfly), as their rate of reproduction is alarmingly rapid.

Inspect the foliage of your houseplants regularly and look out for aphids on any new shoots and flower buds; red spider mites on the underside of leaves; mealy bugs on the undersides of leaves and in the leaf axils; and scale insects on leaf stems and veins. As soon as you have identified a problem, be sure to deal with it promptly with a suitable pesticide and repeat the treatment as recommended by the manufacturer.

Diseases

Although some diseases, like pests, cause problems throughout the year, spring will bring a new surge of activity in the fungal and bacterial world, though that said, certain diseases such as grey mould (botrytis) and some of the root rots tend to be more prevalent during the late autumn, winter and early spring. But there are some diseases, on the other hand, such as leaf spot, rust and mildew, which will increase as the improved climatical conditions favour their growth and spread.

Care should be taken to control all plant diseases, both by chemical and physical means. Their effect can often be minimised by careful plant management — for example, by removing dead or dying leaves or flowers, and by avoiding overwatering. A close watch should be kept at all times and, at the first sign of disease, appropriate remedial action should be taken as soon as possible.

Seasonal summer care

Although summer is the most active time of year as far as houseplants are concerned, it is also the time when they are usually at their best and probably their healthiest. It is nevertheless a time when their care is vitally important.

Watering

Surprisingly enough, the amount of water required by houseplants can vary dramatically, according to the weather. During periods of prolonged warmth and sunshine, a plant may need to be watered as often as once a day. But during cool wet periods, on the other hand, the amount of water it requires will be much less, and that same plant may not need to be watered more often than once or twice a week. It is therefore important to take note of climatic conditions when watering, as houseplants can just as easily be overwatered during the summer months as they can during the winter.

It is particularly important to ensure that a plant is carefully watered for the first few weeks after repotting, in order to allow the new roots to penetrate the compost. Too much water may prevent this from occurring and can, at worst, kill the plant.

As far as holiday care is concerned, it is important to make special provisions for the care of your houseplants when you are away. Try to ensure that all your plants are adequately watered before you go away and, when necessary, ,make plans for their continued care. This may mean moving plants to a location where their water requirements are reduced, or finding some alternative method of supplying them with water in your absence, such as capillary matting. Alternatively, it may be worth calling on the services of a friend or neighbour to 'plant sit' (see also 'When you're away', page 71).

Feeding

Houseplants require additional nutrients during the summer months, when they are at their most active. Most houseplants should be fed weekly or fortnightly, according to their rate of growth. Use a proprietary liquid fertiliser and follow the manufacturer's instructions. Do not be tempted to feed more often or at a higher concentration than recommended by the fact that the plant seems to be growing so well that you want to encourage it. Overfeeding can cause severe damage to the root system — which can, in turn, lead to the plant's untimely demise. And always water well before feeding a 'dry' plant.

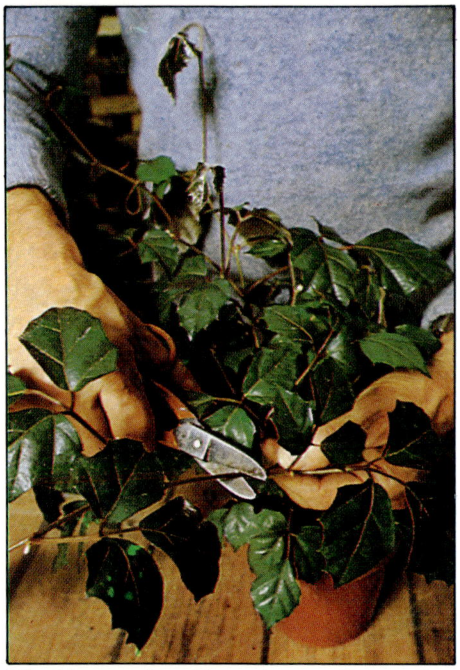

Climbing and trailing plants will benefit from a light trim.

Do not feed for six to eight weeks after repotting, as the fresh compost will contain all the necessary plant nutrients. When you do start feeding, do so at a reduced rate. It may not be necessary to feed at all if the plant is repotted late in the season, or if the compost contains a long-lasting fertiliser.

Repotting

The best time to repot your houseplants was in the late spring, so any plants that have not yet been repotted and would benefit from a bigger container should be potted on now. It is best not to wait until the season is too far advanced.

Temperature

Fortunately, the indoor temperature is probably one of the last things that you will need to worry about during the summer months, as the majority of houseplants will tolerate normal household temperatures during this period. If, however, the temperature drops during cold wet periods, it may be necessary to provide some additional, artificial heat for the more tender plants, such as Angel's Wings (Caladium).

Conversely, during warm dry spells it is essential that some ventilation be provided for many houseplants, such as Ivy (Hedera), Grape Ivy (*Cissus rhombifolia*), Kangaroo Vine (*C. antarctica*) and Cyclamen, all of which prefer more temperate conditions.

Pruning, training, staking

As their rate of growth increases, it may become necessary to prune your houseplants to maintain a tidy shape. Climbing and trailing plants, for example, will clearly benefit from a light trim, which can be carried out with a sharp pair of scissors or secateurs. Plants with softer tissue, such as Pilea or Wandering Jew (Tradescantia), can simply be pinched into shape by the careful use of thumb and forefinger, while pinching out growing tips will encourage bushiness. Climbing plants also need staking to give them adequate support, otherwise their stems may get broken.

When you are tying stems to the support, make sure the ties are not applied so tightly that they could cause damage or restrict growth. Also inspect existing ties to ensure that they too are not causing any damage.

Flower care

Houseplants which produce flowers throughout the summer will benefit from special-purpose flowering plant fertiliser when they are in bud and bloom. Many plants will produce more foliage when they have finished flowering and will then require further nutrition in the form of a conventional houseplant fertiliser.

Dead flower heads should be removed immediately after they have started to fade to ensure that they do not rot and cause subsequent disease, and to prevent the plant from diverting its energies into seed formation.

Leaf care

Certain houseplants benefit from extra humidity throughout the summer. This

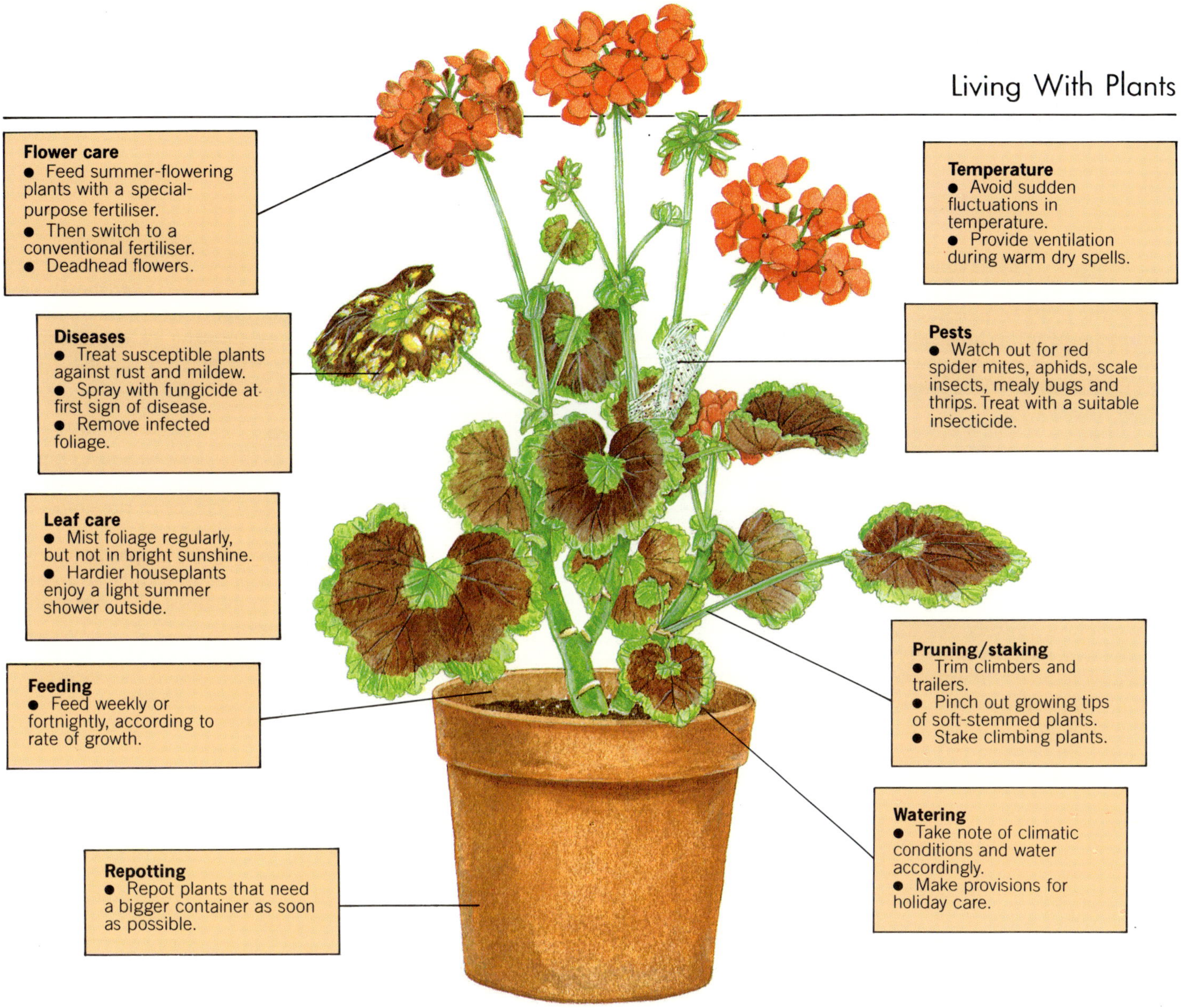

is particularly beneficial to African Violets (Saintpaulia), Prayer Plants (Maranta) and Ferns.

Most plants will benefit from a regular misting on their foliage with tepid water, applied through a fine mist sprayer. Care should, however, be taken to ensure that water droplets are not allowed to remain on the foliage in bright sunshine as they will act as tiny magnifying lenses and may result in scorched leaves.

You should also avoid applying water to those plants, like African Violets (Saintpaulia), which do not like water on their foliage. For plants such as these, it is better to improve the humidity in the immediate atmosphere by surrounding the plant with moist peat or dampened stones in a saucer.

The foliage of many houseplants, including Ficus, Monstera, Palms, Hedera, Philodendrons and many others, enjoys a light, tepid shower to remove any accumulated dust and dirt. This is particularly useful for plants with leaves that are difficult to clean by hand. Some of the hardier houseplants, such as Ivy (Hedera), may even be placed outside during a light summer shower. It is important, however, not to allow the compost to become too wet as a result.

Always remove any damaged, diseased or dead leaves in order to discourage any disease.

Pests

These are particularly active during the summer months and a close watch should be kept at this time of year to ensure that the appropriate remedial action is taken at the first sign of infestation. Red spider mite and whitefly are particularly troublesome now and it is essential to control them by using the appropriate insecticide.

Red spider mites thrive in hot dry conditions, so their activity can be reduced somewhat by regularly misting both surfaces of the foliage with tepid water. Plants which benefit particularly from this treatment include Ivy (Hedera) and Croton (Codiaeum).

Other major pests which you should look out for are aphids, scale insects, mealy bugs and thrips.

Diseases

Rust and mildew are two particularly problematic fungal diseases at this time of year, and control is often best effected by prevention rather than cure. Applying fungicides to prevent these diseases from infecting susceptible plants is better than waiting for the first sign of disease to occur.

With other diseases, however, it is probably better to save spraying all your plants until a problem actually manifests itself. Many fungal and bacterial diseases are localised and can quite easily be controlled by the removal of all infected foliage, which should then be hygienically disposed of to prevent the spread of disease.

Seasonal autumn care

The change in seasons can often be quite difficult to detect. This is particularly true of the critical transition from summer into autumn, as houseplants put the brakes on their rate of growth in readiness for the onset of the long, dark, cold winter months.

Watering

The amount of water your houseplants require will steadily decrease to a minimum at this time of year. Great care should therefore be taken to ensure that you reduce the quantity you give them in line with their needs, which you should follow closely. As the weather deteriorates, so most houseplants automatically reduce the amount of water they can make use of, and it is therefore all too easy to overwater them, which can result in damage either to the root system or to the stem.

Feeding

It is important to discontinue feeding most houseplants from the end of September, as their growth rate slows down and their need for nutrients diminishes. The application of any fertiliser during this period may result in the accumulation of excess fertiliser salts in the compost. This can, in turn, lead to severe root damage and may even be fatal.

Slow-release fertilisers come into their own at this time of year, because the release pattern of nutrients is governed both by temperature and by moisture content. As ambient temperatures decrease and you give your plants less water, so the amount of fertiliser which is released into the soil reduces automatically. Generally, however, most houseplants are now preparing themselves for a condition close to dormancy, with little if any sign of growth, and don't therefore need any fresh supply of fertiliser.

There are, however, some exceptions. These include Poinsettia, Azalea and Cyclamen, which flower late in the autumn, or even later in winter. These do need to be fed, using a fertiliser that is relatively well balanced in its nitrogen, phosphorus and potassium content, with a slight bias — if anything — towards a higher potassium content for good flower development and quality.

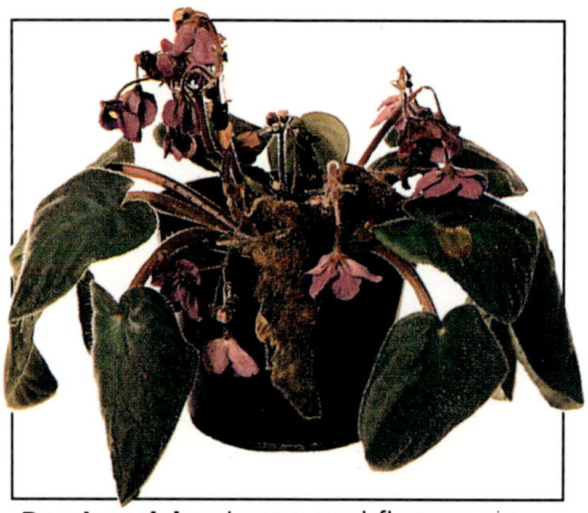

Dead or dying leaves and flowers are breeding grounds for botrytis, to which African Violets are very susceptible.

Repotting

It is inadvisable to repot houseplants at this time of year. The shock could seriously damage or even kill them.

Temperature

It is important to try to maintain a stable, constant temperature at this time of year as houseplants acclimatise to colder conditions. Severe damage may be caused by sudden fluctuations in temperature, particularly if the weather suddenly changes dramatically from a warm Indian summer's day to a cold, frosty night.

Sudden low temperatures, coupled with excessively wet compost, are the principal hazards for houseplants during this season. It is also important to avoid draughts.

Flower care

Continue to remove any dead or dying flowers on those houseplants that are still producing flowers at this time of year. Late autumn and winter flowering plants, such as Azalea and Cyclamen, need to be adequately fed and watered as their flowers develop, otherwise the results will be a great disappointment at a time of year when many houseplants are not at their best.

It is particularly important to note the special care of those plants that are sensitive to day length and, in particular, short-day responsive plants such as the Poinsettia *(Euphorbia pulcherrima)*. In order to obtain a well-coloured display of bracts, the plant must not only be adequately fed and watered but should also be allowed only a natural quota of daylight. Any exposure to artificial light after the natural hours of daylight during the key months of September to November will prevent the plant from producing its colourful bracts.

Leaf care

Little needs to be done to houseplants in the way of leaf care at this time of year — apart, of course, from the continued removal of any dead or damaged leaves. And it is advisable to stop mist spraying plants, or at least to reduce it dramatically. Not only does the atmosphere tend to be more humid at this time, just before the central heating is turned on, but any water which is allowed to remain on foliage may actually be detrimental to a plant's well-being.

Pests

As their peak of activity during the summer passes, many pests will slow down their reproductive rate and become less of a problem. They should not, however, be ignored and remedial action should be continued if necessary.

Aphids may continue to be a nuisance during the early part of the season, particularly if the plant is still flowering. Towards the end of the season, however, they will probably disappear until the spring, when you will see a new upsurge in their activity.

Take particular care to control red spider mite at this time of year, as they will continue to feed quite happily on your houseplants throughout the year, albeit at a reduced rate in line with lessening day length and temperature. Mealy bugs and scale insects will also continue to be active, though again less so than at the height of summer.

Whiteflies will remain a nuisance throughout the winter, in much the same way as red spider mite, and may be particularly difficult to control. Thriving as they do in warm, dry conditions, they delight in the comfortable environment produced by central heating. As they go through several stages of development — from egg to larva and then finally to adult — they are rather difficult to eradicate, especially as they can only really be effectively killed at the adult moth stage. Their control is in

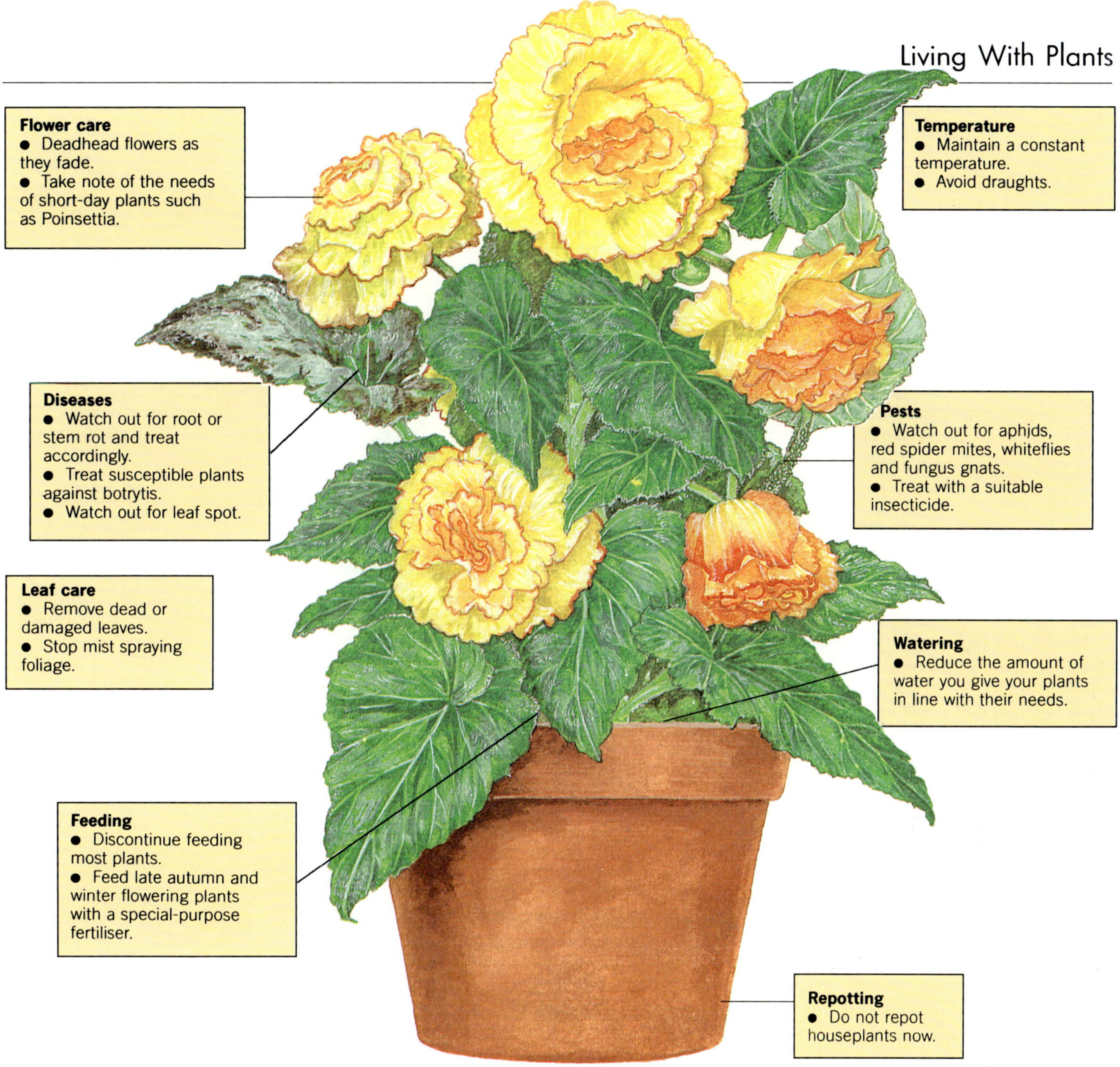

fact more difficult during the autumn and winter months because their life cycle is spread over a longer period, which means you need to treat them regularly over a long period of time to catch the adults as they emerge. A watchful control of whitefly during the autumn will reduce the likelihood of a continuing winter problem, especially on plants like Poinsettia.

Fungus gnats may also be a problem at this time of year. These little insects lay their eggs on the surface of the compost and the larvae then eat dead and decaying organic matter, such as peat and dead leaves and roots. Not only can the insects be a nuisance when they fly up in your face every time they are disturbed, but the larvae are also suspected of aiding the demise of an ailing plant by eating damaged root tissue. With the increased likelihood of this happening in the autumn under the relatively dank conditions that so often exist at this time of year, this pest may be particularly troublesome.

Diseases

Pay close attention to the possibility of root or stem rot, both of which can easily set in at this time, particularly when plants are at risk of being overwatered. If root or stem rot does occur, it will be necessary to use an appropriate fungicide.

It is also important to ensure that any dead or dying leaves or flowers are removed promptly as these are ideal breeding grounds for diseases such as grey mould fungus (botrytis), which produces a fluffy, greyish-brown growth. Having exhausted the food available in dead tissue, the fungus then rapidly multiplies and attacks healthy living tissue, particularly on susceptible plants such as African Violet (Saintpaulia) and Cyclamen. Apart from continued good husbandry, it may also be worth using a fungicide to help prevent the disease from occurring in the first place, rather than waiting to treat a plant that is already affected.

Leaf spot may also be a problem if foliage is allowed to remain wet or if the atmosphere is dank. A general improvement in regular cultural care should reduce the likelihood of the problem.

Seasonal winter care

The winter is a very trying time for houseplants as well as houseplant enthusiasts. Although many plants will by now have slowed down their rate of growth to a virtual halt until the spring, they are nevertheless exposed to an increased risk of damage from a variety of seasonal factors, including low temperatures, overwatering and draughts.

Watering

Great care should be taken throughout the winter months to ensure that houseplants are not overwatered — something to which they are particularly vulnerable at this time of year, probably more than at any other. In general, it is better to keep the majority of plants on the dry side rather than to allow them to get too wet. Even moisture-loving plants such as Ferns and Azaleas can easily be given too much water in winter when drying conditions are slow, and plants that are allowed to sit in cold, wet compost will rapidly fail, though central heating will have a very drying effect.

Some plants, such as cacti and other succulents, can get by with very little water indeed in winter. Depending on the variety, certain cacti actually prefer not to be watered at all in winter and this, coupled with lower temperatures, should in fact encourage the plant to flower the following spring.

The temperature of tapwater will obviously be lower at this time of year and care should be taken not to shock plants by giving them water that is too cold. It is therefore better to allow water to stand in the can for a few hours until it has reached room temperature, or to add just a little hot water from the kettle to the cold tapwater in your can. Do take care, however, not to go to the other extreme and to water with hot water: water that is barely tepid is just right.

Feeding

The majority of houseplants should not be fed at all during this period: being in a dormant state, the plant's nutritional needs are low and any accumulation of fertiliser salts in the compost will probably result in root damage and may even be fatal. There are, however, certain plants that should be fed in winter, including Cyclamen, Azalea and Poinsettia, all of which produce their flowers at this time of year or, in the case of Poinsettia, their showy, colourful bracts.

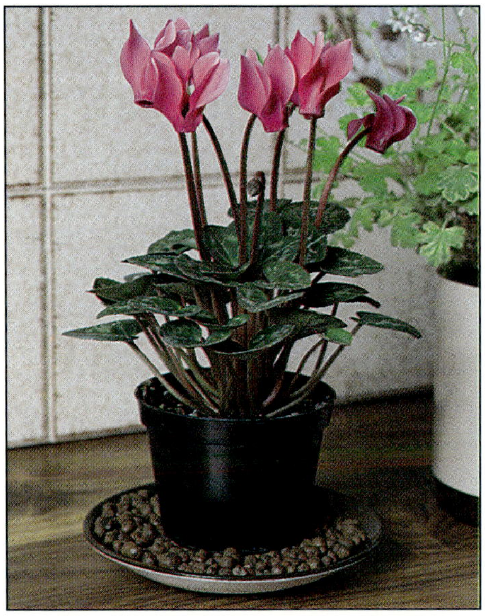

Provide your Cyclamen with a humid atmosphere by placing it on a saucer full of moist pebbles.

These plants should be fed with a dilute feed of a special-purpose liquid fertiliser for flowering plants. A tomato fertiliser may also be used, as long as it is well diluted. The frequency of feeding should not, however, be more than once every two to four weeks, in order to avoid the problem of excess fertiliser salts accumulating in the compost.

Temperature

The temperatures that houseplants have to tolerate in the winter can cause them problems. It is best to aim for as stable a temperature as possible. Sudden fluctuations, from the cosy warm environment during the hours when your heating is on to the inhospitable cold temperatures while you are out at work or overnight — can easily be detrimental to a plant's well-being.

Draughts can be particularly damaging to houseplants and can cause much the same problems as sudden fluctuations in temperature. Rapid leaf drop, for example, can occur with plants such as Croton (Codiaeum) and Weeping Fig (*Ficus benjamina*). Try to ensure that plants that are sensitive to draughts and temperature fluctuations are kept away from windows and doors where problems are likely to be most severe.

Humidity

The humidity level tends to be rather low in centrally heated houses at this time of year because of central and other forms of modern heating which encourage a dry atmosphere. Kitchens and bathrooms tend to be relatively more humid and provide a welcome refuge for plants such as Prayer Plant (Maranta), African Violet (Saintpaulia) and *Begonia rex*, all of which appreciate a humid environment. The use of a humidifier helps to some extent, but not enough to meet the requirements of many plants, while frequent misting can sometimes encourage fungal diseases. It is therefore more practical, if possible, to improve the general level of humidity.

A good way of providing localised humidity is by placing the plant on a large saucer containing dampened pebbles, which will then release evaporated water into the surrounding atmosphere. Alternatively, sink the pot into a container filled with moist peat. This is of particular benefit to relatively low-growing plants, such as Prayer Plant (Maranta), African Violet (Saintpaulia), *Begonia rex* and Creeping fig (*Ficus pumila*). Larger plants will benefit to a lesser degree from this technique, so you may find that you have no alternative but to resort to misting with tepid water. If this is the case, however, you should take care not to overdo it and remember not to spray mist close to furnishings or any electrical equipment.

Flower care

Although there are relatively few houseplants that flower during the winter, it is important for those that do to ensure that they are given a little extra care.

Try to avoid getting water on to the flower petals, which could encourage rot, remove flowers as soon as they start to fade and before they have a chance to rot. This is particularly important for Cyclamen and African Violet — though even Azalea flowers, which tend to be somewhat hardier, can also be affected. It is also advisable, where possible, to

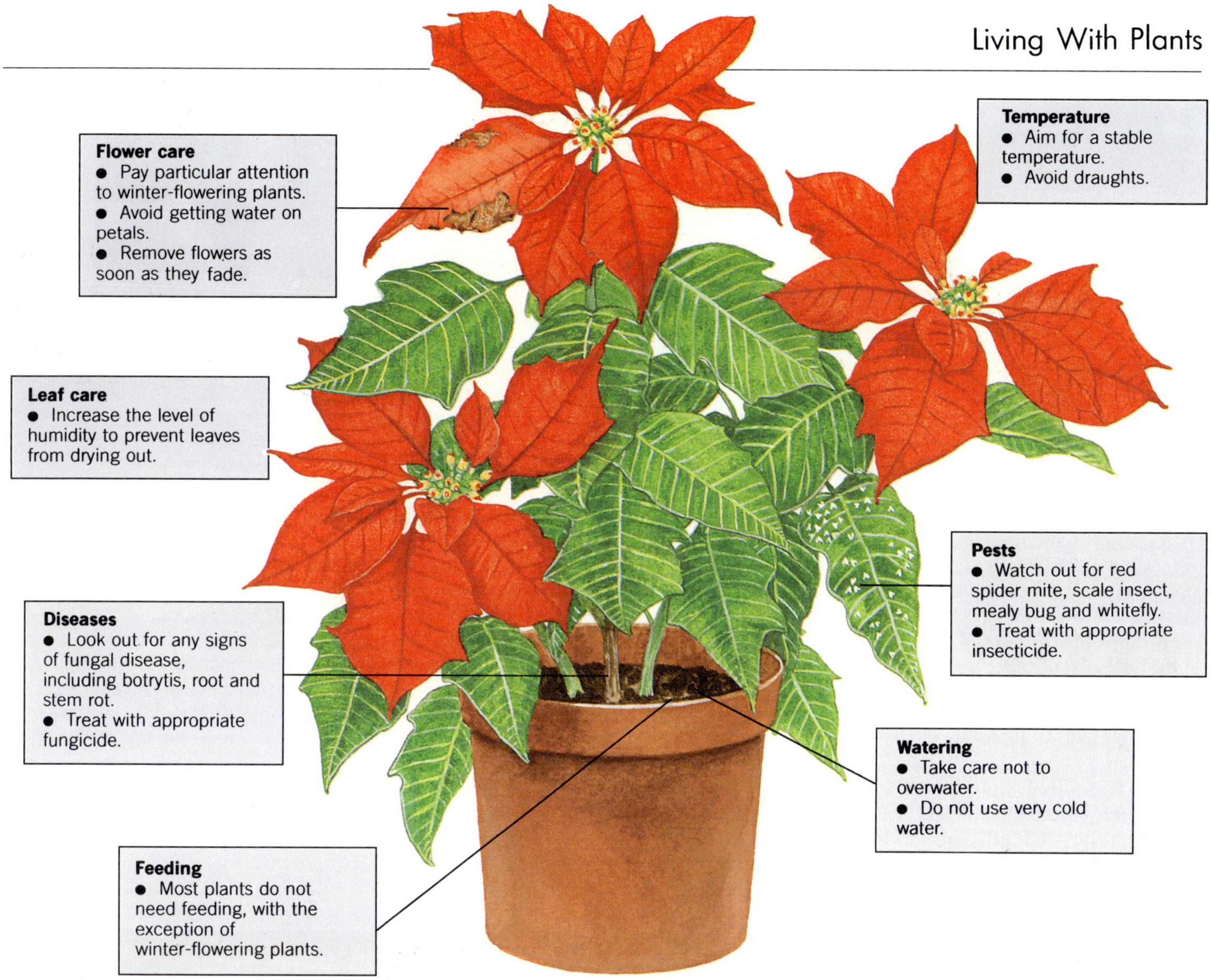

avoid dank conditions for flowering plants as these too can encourage fungal problems and may necessitate treatment with a fungicide, either to prevent or at least to eradicate problems.

Most plants will probably 'rest' after flowering, or at least slow down their growth rate, before bursting into growth again in the spring. Cyclamen will actually die back down to the corm and remain dormant for several weeks.

Leaf care

Something that commonly affects foliage in winter is a brown dessication, or drying out, of the edges and death of leaf tissue. It is usually caused by too dry an environment. Those plants that are most commonly affected are ones with thin leaves such as Maranta, Ferns and Dracaena, although thicker-leaved plants such as Monstera may also suffer the same fate. The problem may be alleviated by increasing the level of humidity in the atmosphere.

Pests

Fortunately, pests are not generally a great problem during the winter, although red spider mite, scale insect and mealy bug will remain relatively active, though less so than in the height of summer. In general, the warmer the temperature the more active the pests. Whitefly can also be a nuisance on some plants, such as Poinsettia, and again this is especially likely if temperatures are fairly high.

In spite of their relatively reduced activity, the control of pests is nevertheless important at this time of year, as it may well help to lessen the problem in spring.

Diseases

Look out for the signs of grey mould fungus (botrytis) which can cause immense damage at this time of year, especially on flowering plants. Look, too, for any signs of fungal disease on the leaves: the tips and edges are often the first place where a fungal infection will take hold, especially when they are grown in a dank environment with fairly high humidity levels. At the first sign of a brown softening of the leaf extremities, treat the plant with a fungicide and, if the infection is limited to only a few leaves, remove these to help avoid the spread of infection.

Also watch out for root and stem rot, both of which can occur at this time when it is all too easy to overwater houseplants. Should you overwater them, you'll need to be prepared to take drastic action to save a seriously ailing plant. The symptoms of overwatering, which can eventually lead to root and stem rot, include limp, wilting foliage.

If the plant is not too wet at the root it may be watered with a fungicide. But if it is too wet, gently remove it from the pot, lay it on its side on some newspaper to absorb the excess moisture and leave for a few days to dry out a little. Then repot and water with a fungicide.

Why plants need a winter rest

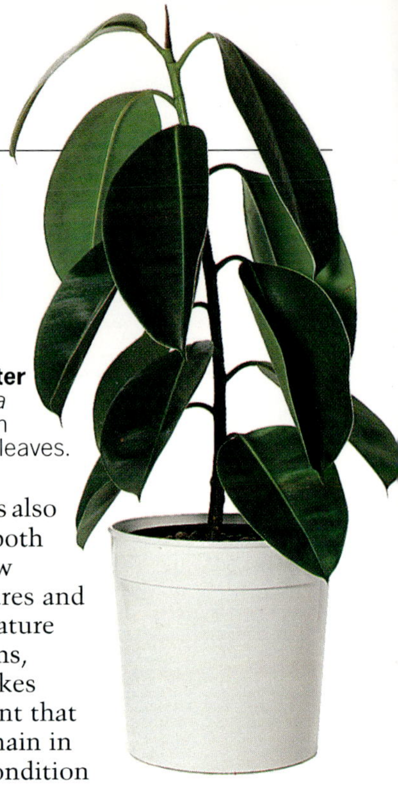

If you overwater a *Ficus elastica* at rest, you can expect wilting leaves.

For many plants, the arrival of winter heralds a period of rest. As light intensity decreases and day length shortens, so most houseplants put the brakes on their rate of growth, thus slowing it down or even calling a complete halt to it.

The care of plants during their rest period is crucial, and it is particularly important to avoid extreme fluctuations in temperature and excessive amounts of water, both of which could damage their health. Plants are at a very susceptible stage at this time of year, in spite of their relative inactivity.

If you encourage a tropical or subtropical plant to grow actively during periods of low winter light, it will eventually suffer, becoming spindly and pale.

Instead of being encouraged to grow in winter, therefore, most indoor plants should be forced to rest. This slows down the plant's growth, until conditions are again right for renewed growth. 'Rest' usually means, quite simply, the restriction of watering, the cessation of feeding, and a lowering of temperature.

Although many houseplants appear to be quite dormant at this time of year, most do continue to require some water — albeit in much lesser quantities. Evergreen plants, which retain their leaves, should still be watered moderately, whereas deciduous plants, such as Fuchsia and Caladium, which lose their leaves, need just enough water to keep the potting compost barely moist.

The benefits

Indoor Jasmine (*Jasminum polyanthum*) will be encouraged to flower in the early spring after a cool winter, with just sufficient water to prevent it from wilting. If it is denied its winter rest and the plant is kept too warm and watered too frequently, it will become lank and will not flower nearly so profusely, if at all. African Violets also benefit from a rest period.

Cacti and succulents have a pronounced rest period, during which watering must be greatly reduced. Water them only when the surface of the soil feels dry and crumbly and the pot feels light when you pick it up, which may happen as rarely as once a month in the winter. They are also more likely to produce flowers if they are kept dry from October until March or early April. They should be watered only very little — perhaps just a couple of times throughout the winter — to prevent total dehydration. With the advent of longer days and increased light, watering may then be resumed. If cacti are deprived of this rest period, they will flower less prolifically — if at all.

Another benefit that plants should reap during their winter rest is that they are not forced into the production of lank, unhealthy foliage, which would be particularly vulnerable to disease. Any new foliage which is produced at this time is also sensitive both to very low temperatures and to temperature fluctuations, which makes it important that plants remain in a stable condition during their rest period.

Following this rest period, houseplants will sense the increase in day length, temperature and light, and will suddenly break into new growth, producing both fresh foliage and, where appropriate, flowers. At the first signs that the winter rest period is drawing to a close it is important to start increasing the amount of water applied — still taking great care, of course, not to overwater — and to resume feeding.

Exceptions to the rule

Not all plants need a winter rest period — some are in fact actively growing during what is, for them, their normal growing or flowering period.

- The Poinsettia (*Euphorbia pulcherrima*) is probably the best-known plant that is active during the winter months. Having developed new foliage between April and September, the plant then produces coloured bracts, which are usually bright red but can also be pink or white. These are produced as soon as the plant senses the shorter day length, from September on. It also produces tiny insignificant flowers over the Christmas period and then ceases to develop any further until the spring.

- The Pot Chrysanthemum or, as it is sometimes called, the All-year-round Chrysanthemum, flowers naturally in the autumn and early winter, and the Christmas Cactus is another example. Similarly, the Silver-leaved Cyclamen also flowers quite naturally in the latter part of the year before taking a rest, when the foliage dies back to the corm for several weeks before being started into growth again — usually by increasing the plant's watering.

- Another plant which is well known for its long period of late colour is the Indian Azalea (*Azalea indica*) which, although it is in active growth from May through until about August, comes into bud in October or November to flower over the Christmas and New Year period. After flowering, the Azalea then rests briefly for just a few weeks at the end of the winter before breaking into renewed growth as fresh foliage develops. Even though it may not be growing actively after flowering, it should nevertheless be kept watered and not allowed to dry out completely.

- It is important to remember that all plants need some sort of rest period. Care that is taken at this time will help to ensure that the plant's transition from dormancy into activity is as smooth as possible, with a better chance of a healthy, vigorous growing period.

PERFECT PROPAGATION

If you've ever wondered about taking cuttings from a favourite plant that is looking a little tired, but decided it would be too difficult, then think again. The fact is that most houseplants are very easy to propagate in this way, and you could be rewarded with a host of strong young plants taken from an established 'parent'.

Some houseplants are best propagated by air layering – again, there is no mystery to this technique, and your rubber plant or monstera could soon look a lot healthier for this treatment. Or you might like to start from scratch and grow your own plants from seed – given the right conditions, you will have the enjoyment of watching your seedlings take form and eventually become sturdy new specimens.

And there's always the fun of growing more unusual plants from ordinary kitchen 'rubbish' – so next time you're about to throw out orange pips, sprouting sweet potatoes or a pineapple top – try planting them instead and see what grows!

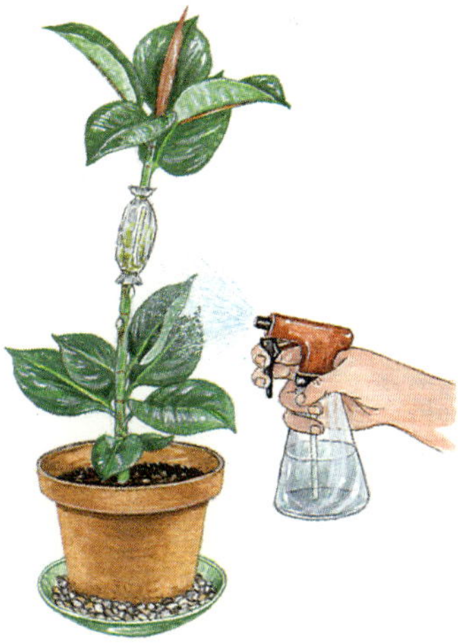

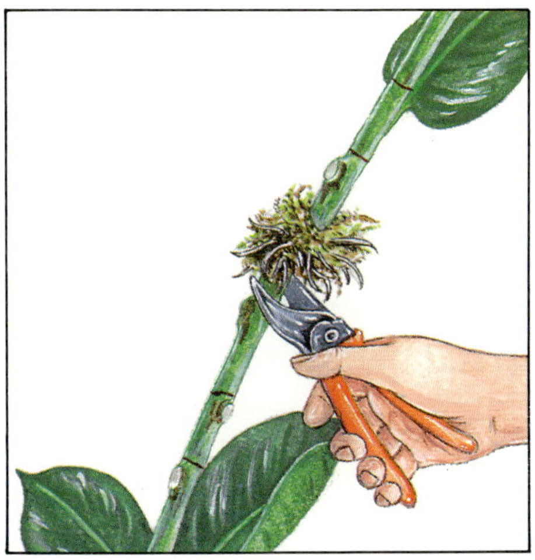

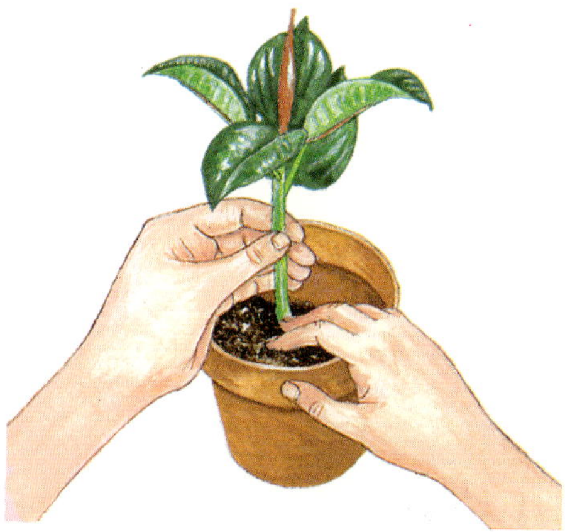

Something for

Many unusual and attractive houseplants can be yours for virtually nothing: all you need is a little ingenuity and a lot of patience! Almost every tropical fruit or vegetable that you can buy at your local greengrocer's — avocados, lemons, pineapples, sweet potatoes and many more — can yield pips, stones or roots capable of germinating and growing into a dramatic plant that will thrive in your home.

Tropical plants grown from pips or roots are no more difficult to care for than any other kind of houseplant; and because many of these plants have luxuriant, exotic foliage a successfully grown specimen can make a distinctive feature for your living room. It's fun to experiment to discover what you can grow, but you'll need lots of patience, since some of the large stones take up to four months to germinate. Remember, too, that it's very unlikely you'll ever get any edible fruit from your plants.

Always use fresh fruit and vegetables. If the fruit has been processed in any way, by being canned or frozen, the seeds will probably be sterile. Don't worry if you have difficulty getting the pips or roots to germinate; try growing a number at the same time and some of them will sprout. The seedlings will need warmth, water, humidity, bright light, good compost and fertiliser.

PIPS

Many kinds of tropical fruit can be grown from their pips so long as plenty of warmth is provided.

The pips of citrus fruits, including those of grapefruit, oranges, tangerines, limes and lemons, all grow into attractive small trees with glossy green leaves and sweet-smelling white flowers. Some of these pips are sterile and won't germinate, but if you grow a number of pips of different types you are bound to get some seedlings.

Plant five or six pips to a 3in (7cm) pot of John Innes Seed Compost. Provide a temperature of 70°F (21°C) until the seedlings are about 3in (7cm) tall, then let the temperature drop a bit. Pot up each seedling into John Innes No 2.

Provide the young plants with good light and plenty of fresh air, and feed them every 14 days during the growing season with a tomato fertiliser. Every two months dissolve some sequestred iron powder (a type of fertiliser that prevents mineral deficiencies) into water and water it into the soil: this prevents lack of iron in the plant, which shows as yellowing between the leaf veins.

Protect your plant from the cold in winter. If you are lucky, after a few years pretty white flowers will appear in summer. You can hand pollinate these with a small paint brush if you wish — but don't expect the resulting fruit to be fit to eat. The fruit will be small and misshapen due to the plant's restricted root growth, but it will look very pretty!

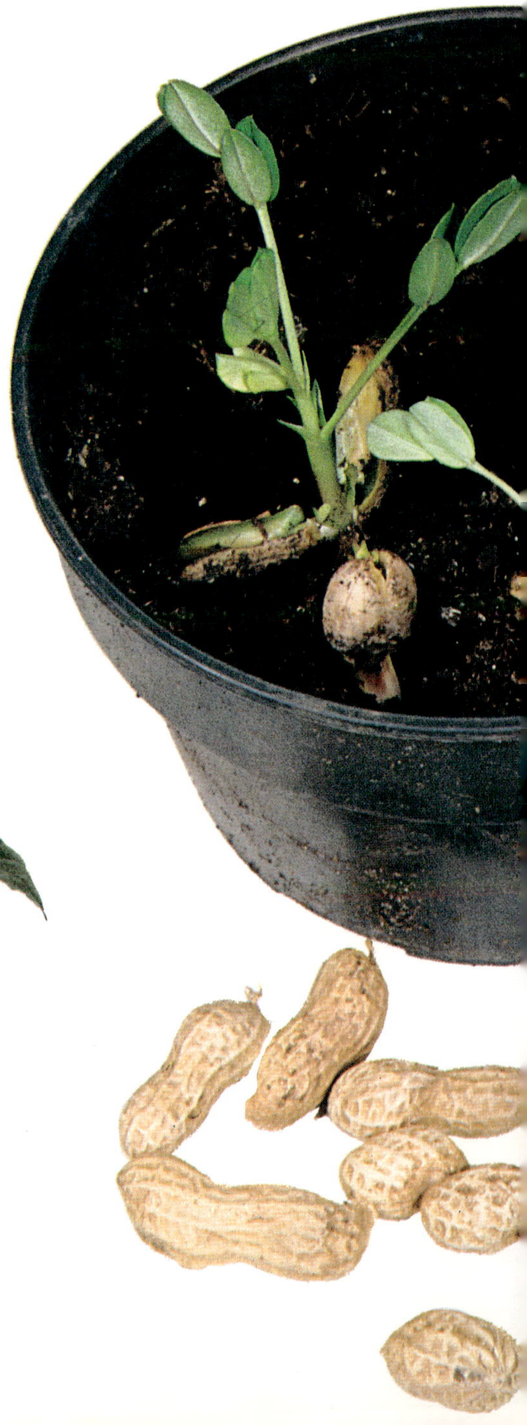

Coffee

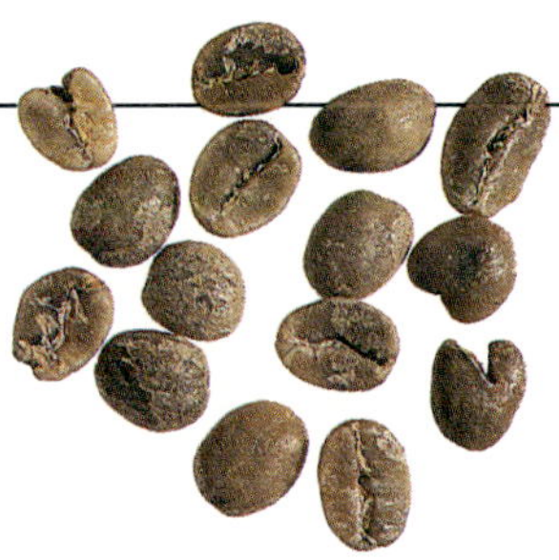

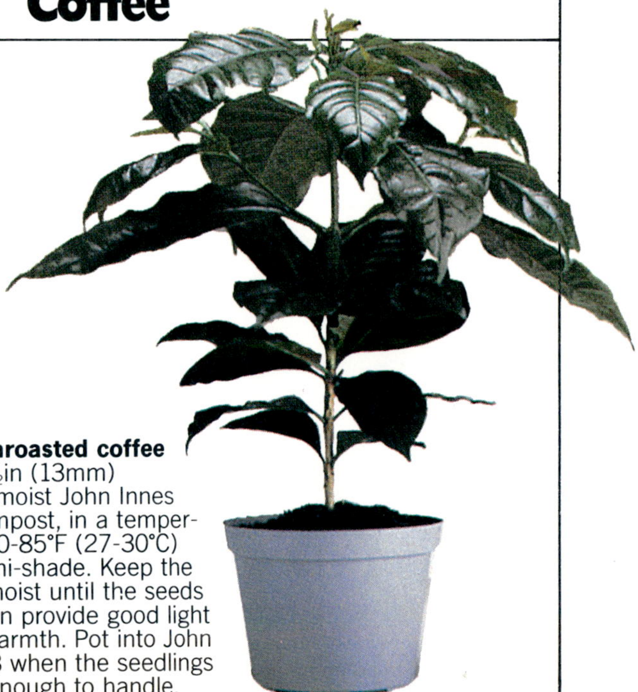

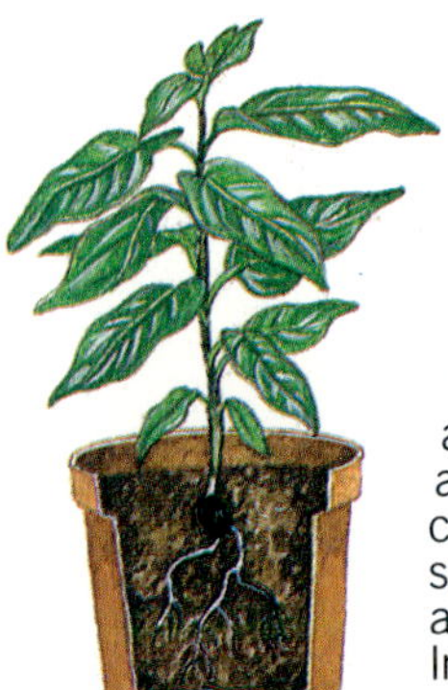

Sow unroasted coffee beans ½in (13mm) deep in moist John Innes Seed Compost, in a temperature of 80-85°F (27-30°C) and in semi-shade. Keep the compost moist until the seeds sprout, then provide good light and less warmth. Pot into John Innes No 3 when the seedlings are large enough to handle.

nothing

The attractive green kiwi fruit is also known as the Chinese Gooseberry and is a vigorous climbing shrub. It has creamy white flowers about 1½in (4cm) across in summer and occasionally, under the right conditions, produces edible fruits. Collect some of the shiny black seeds from fresh fruit and sow them as described earlier.

The pomegranate is a lovely bush with light green leaves and, in summer, 2in (5cm) scarlet flowers. Sow the dry seeds in spring.

The coffee plant has very handsome glossy, dark green leaves but rarely grows more than about 4ft (1.2m) tall in the home. To grow your own specimen, sow fresh unroasted coffee beans into seed compost. It takes several years before it is mature enough to produce its sweet-smelling, small white flowers which are followed by red berries.

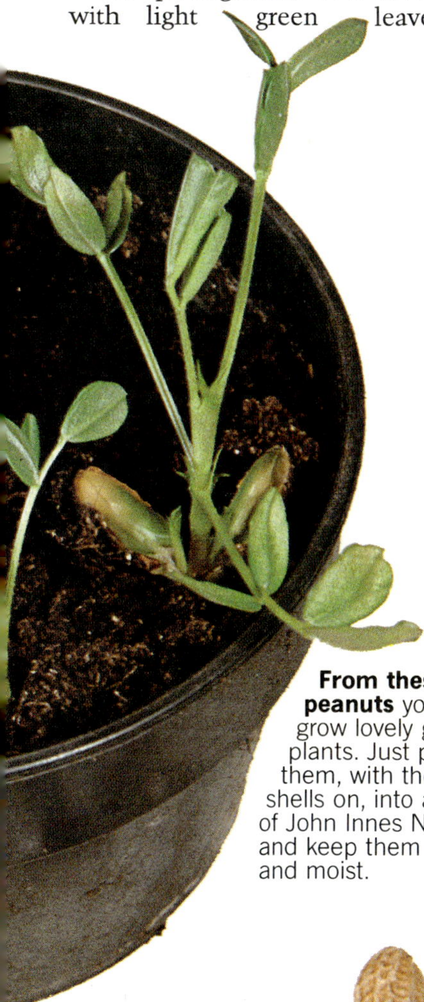

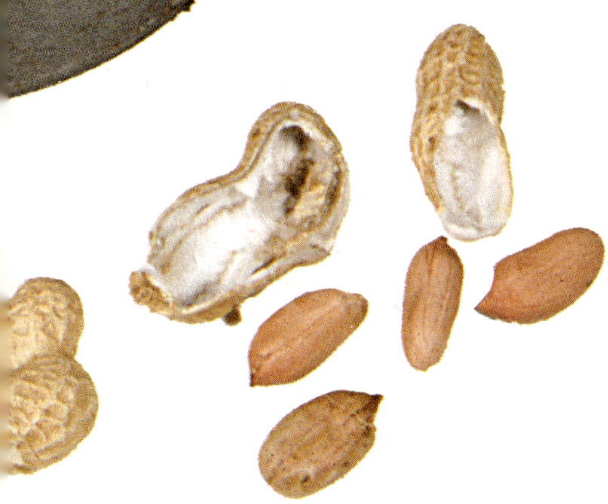

From these raw peanuts you can grow lovely green plants. Just pop them, with their shells on, into a pot of John Innes No 2 and keep them warm and moist.

ROOTS

Lots of interesting plants can be grown from roots.

If you keep a sharp eye open at the greengrocer's you can often find fresh ginger with a few pale green growth buds beginning to sprout from the roots — though the shoots don't have to be showing to grow a plant. The ginger plant, which comes from the East Indies, grows up to 3ft (90cm) high with dark green, strap-like leaves. It produces a thick, aromatic root.

To grow your own ginger plant, take a ginger root and plant it about 2-4in (5-10cm) deep in a large 10in (25cm) pot of John Innes No 2. Keep the pot at about 68°F (20°C) while the root is sprouting and in the growing season. Feed your plant every 14 days with liquid fertiliser and keep the compost moist. In winter your plant will die

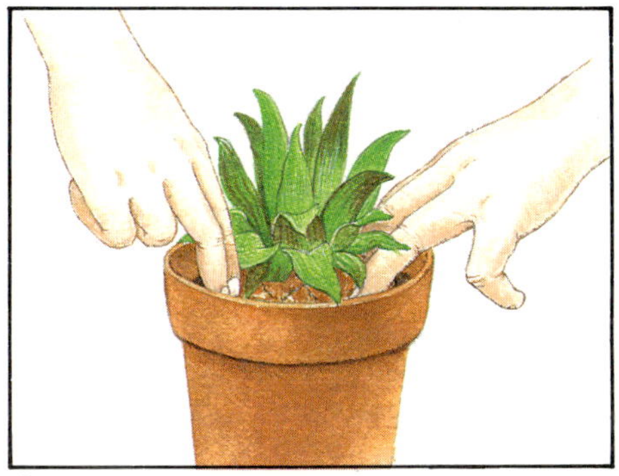

Growing a pineapple
Some crowns can be reluctant to root, so be prepared to try a couple of times. Slice the top of a pineapple off 1in (2.5cm) down from the crown. Let it dry for two or three days.

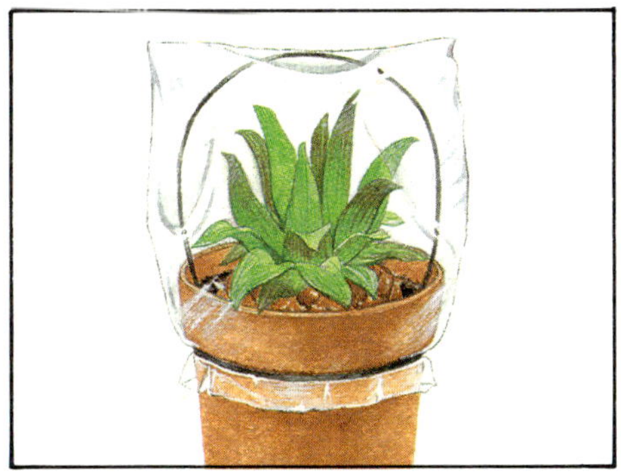

Remove the bottom layer of the leaves and plant firmly on top of the compost. Cover it with a clear polythene bag and stand the pot in a light, warm position with a night temperature of no less than 65°F (18°C).

Sweet Potato

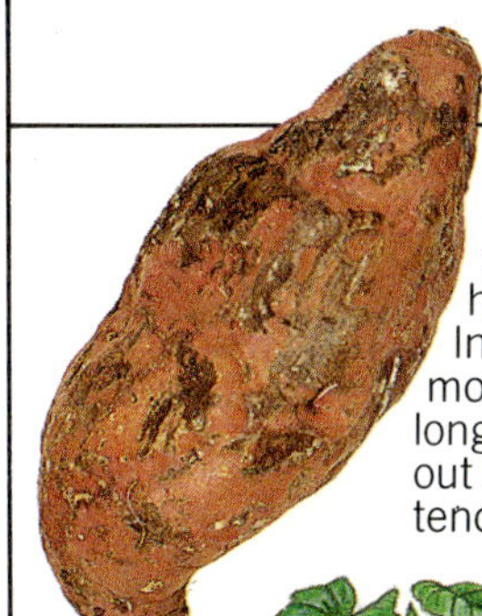

Plant a sweet potato with the narrow end pointing downwards, halfway into John Innes No 2. Keep it moist and warm and long tendrils will grow out of the top. Train the tendrils up a frame of bamboo canes.

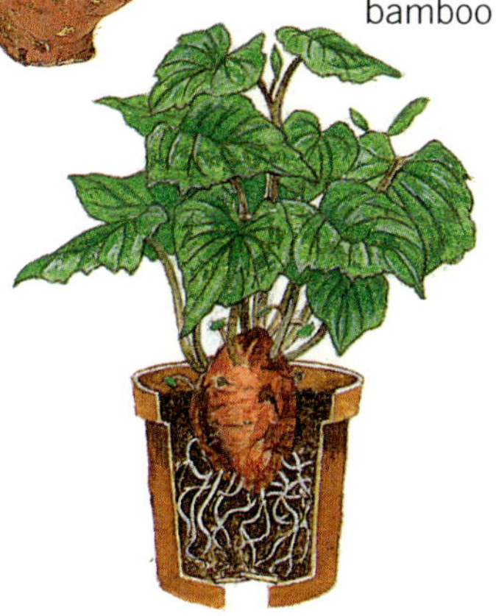

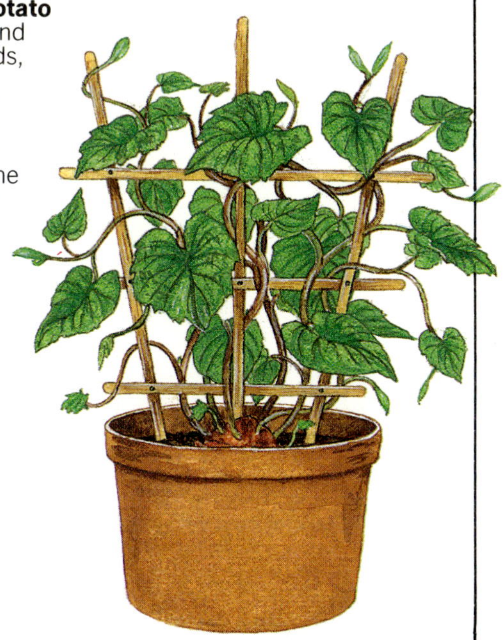

down and you should keep it cooler, about 45°F (7°C) and rather drier; let the compost dry out on the surface before watering again. In spring you can divide your plant to make two plants or simply let it stay as one large plant.

The sweet potato is a type of Bindweed related to Morning Glory. It looks like a large, elongated, fairly smooth-skinned potato with a red or yellowish skin. Plant one in John Innes No 2 in a pot about 10in (25cm) wide with the narrow end of the tuber pointing down. Eventually long tendrils will emerge which you can stake.

A yam root will produce a dramatic large plant with huge leaves. The root has a skin that looks a little like tree bark. It needs a very big container so its roots can spread. Give your yam plenty of light and keep it cool during winter. When the plant gets too big, just cut the tuber in half — you can plant one end and eat the other!

STONES

Some fruit stones, such as those of the avocado, mango, lychee, date and coconut, can be grown into attractive plants. Always carefully wash the stone and remove all fruit before planting.

Almost everyone has had a go at growing an avocado stone, though with varying degrees of success. Properly grown, an avocado is a lovely plant which, in its native habitat of the West Indies, grows to 60ft (18m), but luckily it won't reach anything like that at home!

An avocado has large, elongated oval, dark green leaves on a tall, slim plant. Use a firm, ripe stone (if the brown skin sticks stubbornly to the fruit the stone is not mature enough). You can either suspend the stone over a jar of water, using matchsticks to hold it upright with the base just touching the water surface, or plant the stone in a 3in (7cm) pot of John Innes No 1, leaving one third of the stone above the surface. Give it a temperature of 70°F (21°C). Once it germinates pot your avocado up into a 7in (18cm) pot of John Innes No 2.

When your plant is 8-10in (20-25cm) high, cut off the top 2in (5cm); this will encourage it to make branches. Prune your avocado back in this way whenever the stems get too leggy and you will encourage a nice, bushy shape.

A mango has a flat, oval, almost bearded stone that can be persuaded to sprout in time. It will grow into a dark

Avocado Pear

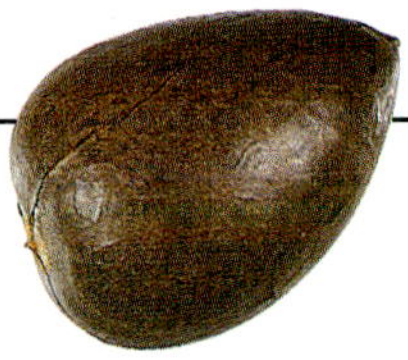

1 Suspend a cleaned avocado stone over a jar of water so the rounded end just touches the water.
2 Roots and a shoot should appear.
3 Plant two thirds into John Innes No 1 and keep warm and moist.

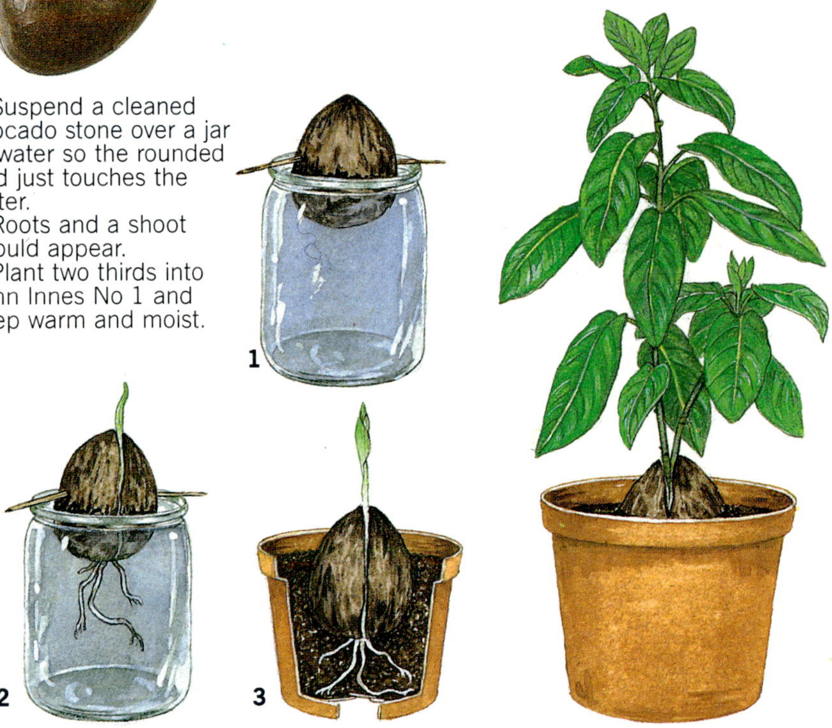

Date

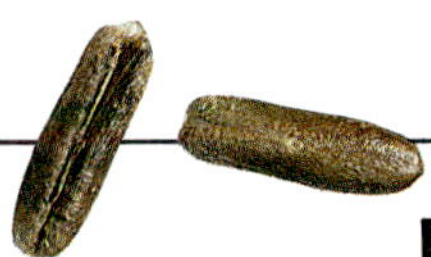

Roughen the date stones with sandpaper.
Sow the stones in John Innes Seed Compost, keep them moist and very warm.

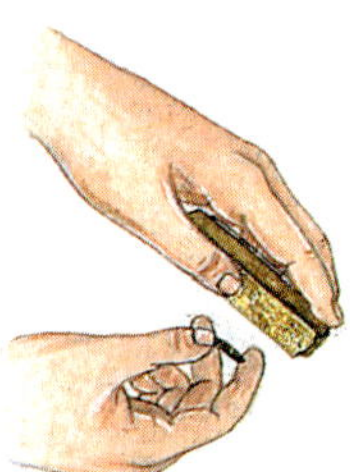

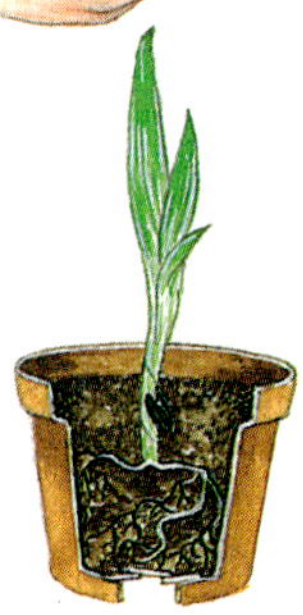

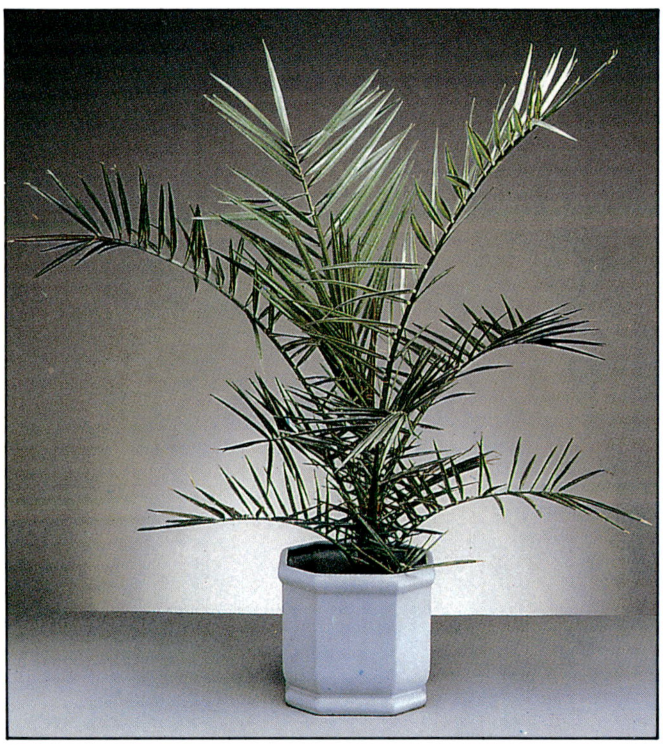

A mature date palm is an attractive houseplant.

green, large-leafed tree but it needs a lot of humidity to do well. As with all tropical plants, if the leaves turn brown at the edges it is a sign of dry air or overwatering, so watch out for this and act accordingly.

The lychee is an evergreen tree with attractive long, hanging leaves; it is a native of Southern China. Use seeds taken from the fresh fruit; they are about 1in (25mm) long, hard, black and oval shaped. They take a while to germinate.

Sometimes you can be lucky enough to find a coconut that is sprouting; this can grow eventually into a large and handsome palm tree. Put the coconut into a large pot of John Innes No 3 and lay it on its side, so that the three black 'eyes' are lying near the compost. Provide light, heat and humidity.

Date stones require more patience than most as even after sprouting they can take up to two years before they produce a leaf that even looks like a palm! Until then they have just a narrow green spike. Eventually a date palm will grow to 5-6ft (1.5-1.8m).

Wash the stones, then lightly sandpaper or file them to help moisture get in and the stone to germinate, which can take months.

An alternative method is to put the stones together in a polythene bag of moist peat, seal it tightly and leave them in a warm, dark airing cupboard. Look at them after about six weeks to check for signs of growth. As soon as any start to sprout, pot them up in John Innes Seed Compost. Keep them moist and at a temperature of 60°F (15°C).

NUTS

All sorts of nuts can be grown into plants but the most successful are fresh peanuts. They are very easy to grow in a warm and sunny position. Sow them still in their shells in John Innes No 2 in a 3in (7cm) pot. Give them a temperature of around 80°F (27°C) to germinate; then keep them on a warm, sunny window. When the pot is full of roots, pot each plant singly into a 10in (25cm) pot. Keep the compost moist and mist spray the foliage every day in warm weather. As your plant grows, long green shoots will appear from the yellow blooms; these will bend over and disappear and burrow into the compost where they will start to form peanuts below the compost surface. You can harvest your peanuts at the end of the growing season.

Citrus

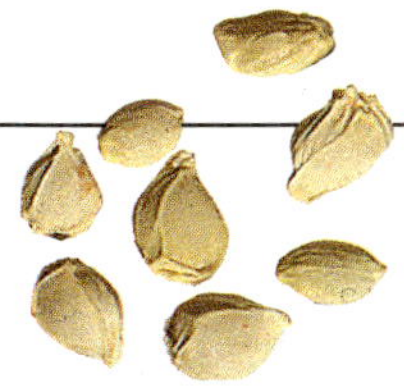

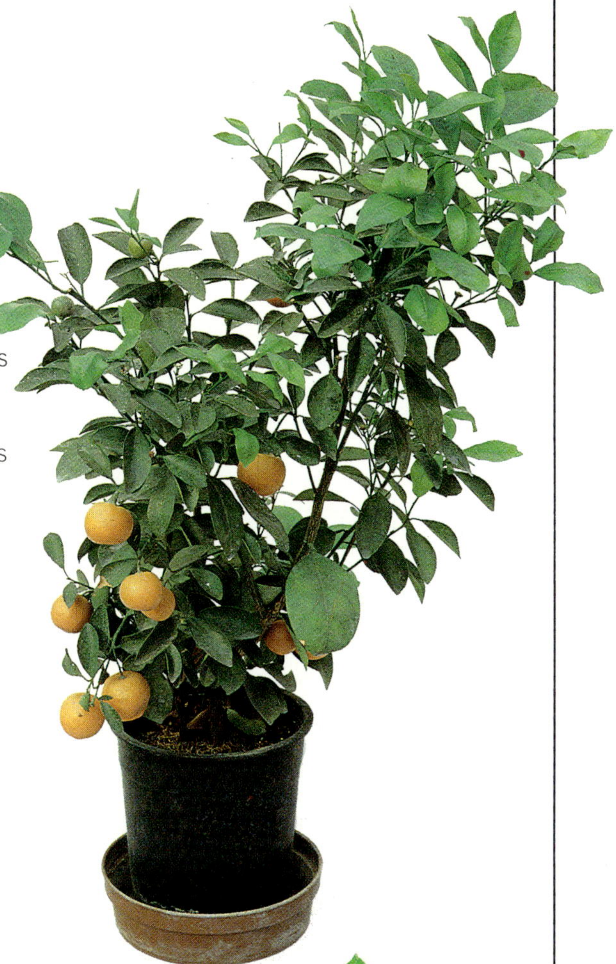

You can grow either orange or lemon trees from pips. Plant a few fresh pips in moist John Innes Compost and keep them warm. Give young seedlings good light and feed every two weeks until they are about 3in tall. Pot them on individually into 3in (7cm) pots of John Innes No 2.

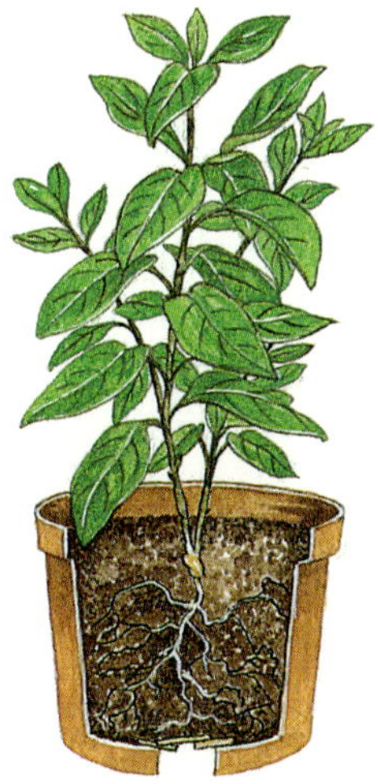

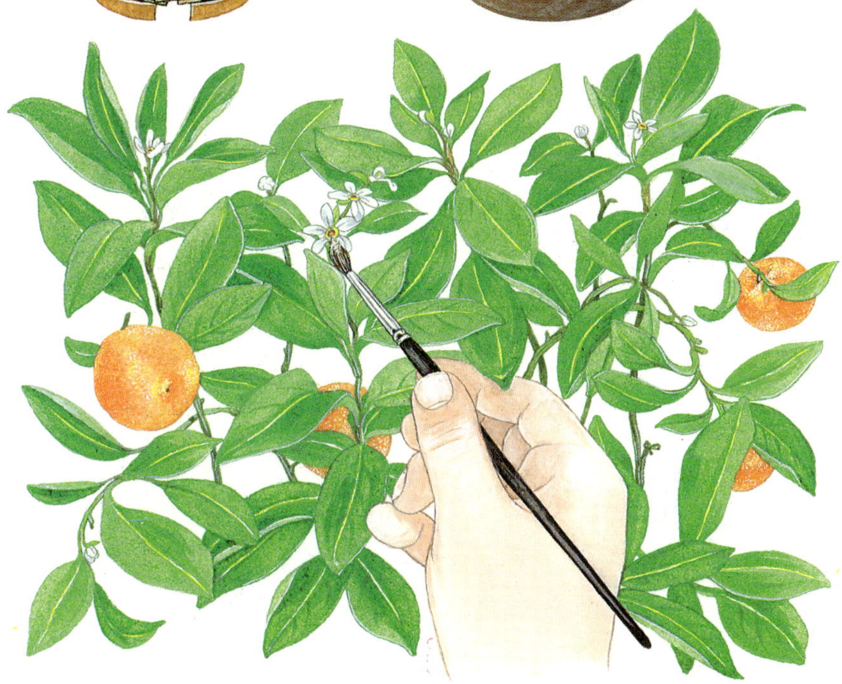

Help your citrus produce fruit by brushing the pollen from one flower to the next.

Take your cut

After you've grown and loved your houseplants for a while, you'll find yourself itching to try your hand at propagating them. The easiest way to increase your favourite plants is to take cuttings in spring and summer. It's a quick, cheap and almost foolproof method and you're guaranteed to get a plant identical in every way to the parent.

Stem cuttings are the easiest cuttings to take but there are other methods which we shall explain later on. Select the plant that you want to take cuttings from and put it on a clean table or surface where you can see it properly. Choose the cuttings from fresh, healthy young stems that don't have any flowers or flower buds; cut the stems from the middle and crowded top of the plant or from a point where you won't ruin the shape of your plant.

To give your cuttings the best possible start buy a small bottle or tube of hormone rooting powder; it contains growth hormones that encourage a cut shoot to grow strong healthy roots.

You can get ready-made peat-based or John Innes Seed Compost or, if you prefer, you can make your own by mixing equal amounts of moist peat and horticultural sand.

Always place your cuttings in small, shallow pots to root — a 3in (7cm) pot is usually right for a few cuttings. Fill the pot with compost then make holes in the compost round the edge of the pot using a sharp pencil or knitting needle.

Warmth and light

Keep your cuttings in a reasonably warm place, well away from draughts, to give them every chance to root. Most cuttings root best when they are kept in a warm, closed environment in good light — but not in direct sunlight where they might get scorched.

A heated propagator is helpful as cuttings will root quickly in its constant warmth and humid atmosphere. An electrically-heated propagator giving a temperature of 65-70°F (18-21°C) is perfect. But if you don't have one, you can improvise successfully by putting a clear polythene bag (not one with holes punched in it) over the pot and sealing it with a rubber band.

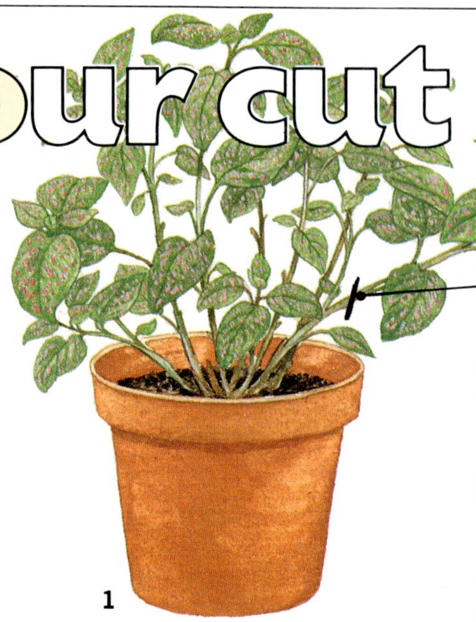

1

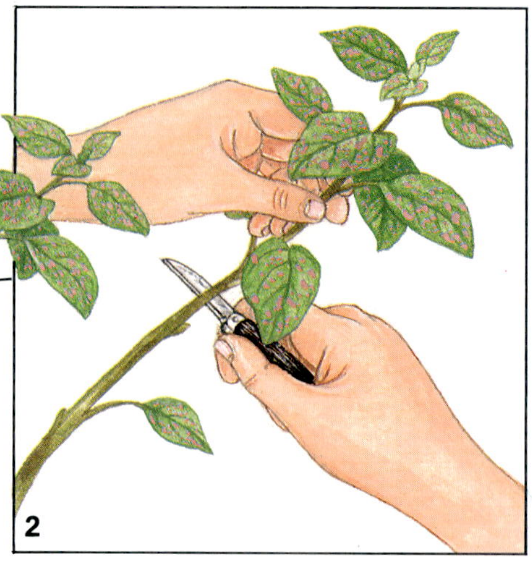

2

1 With a sharp knife cut a piece of stem about 3-4in (7-10cm) long; **2** make the cut just below the bulge where a leaf joins the stem — this is called the node.

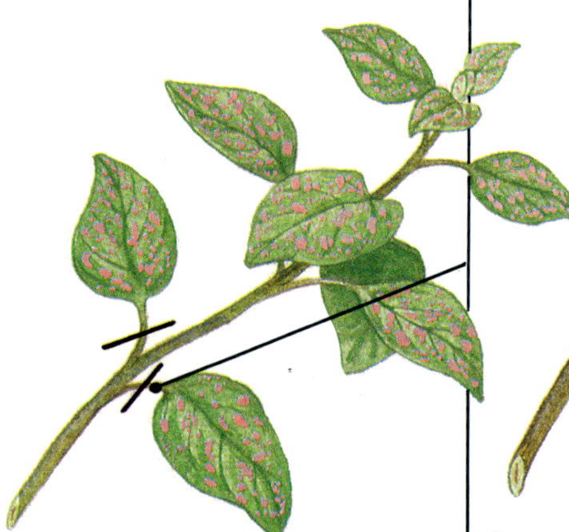

3

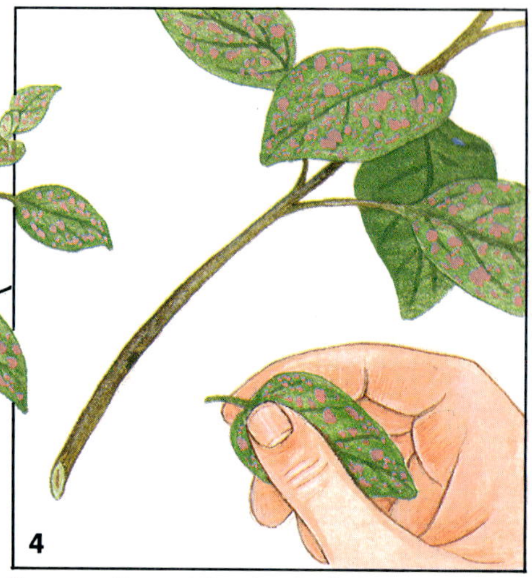

4

Prepare the cutting by **3** slicing and then **4** gently peeling off the lower pair of leaves, being careful not to damage the delicate outer layer of the cutting.

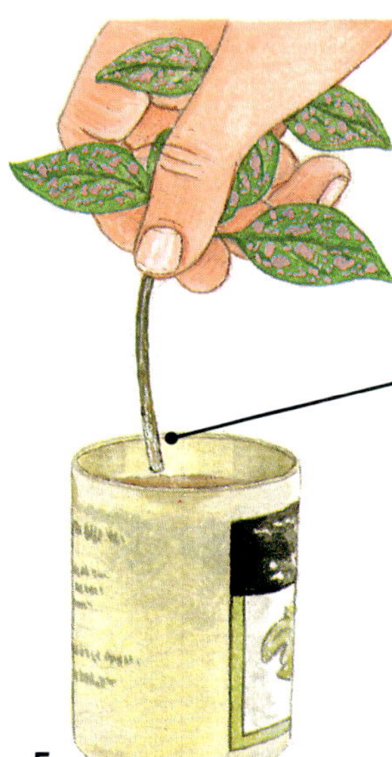

5

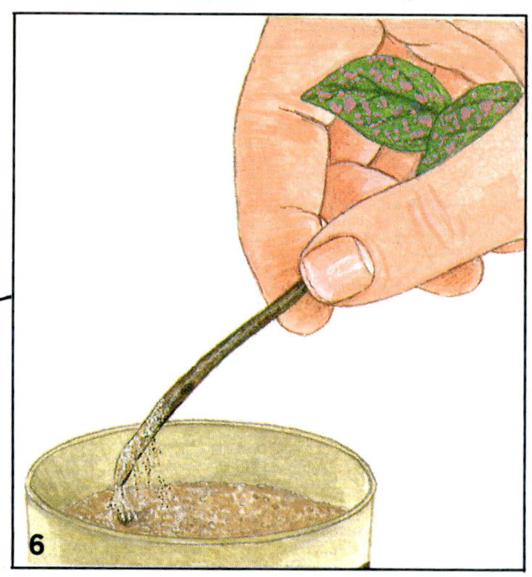

6

5 Dip the cut end, about ¼in (6mm), in hormone rooting powder and then **6** shake off surplus powder to stop the end getting clogged up.

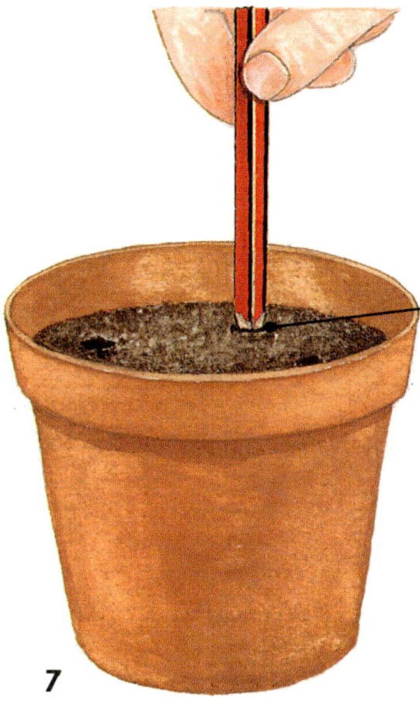

7

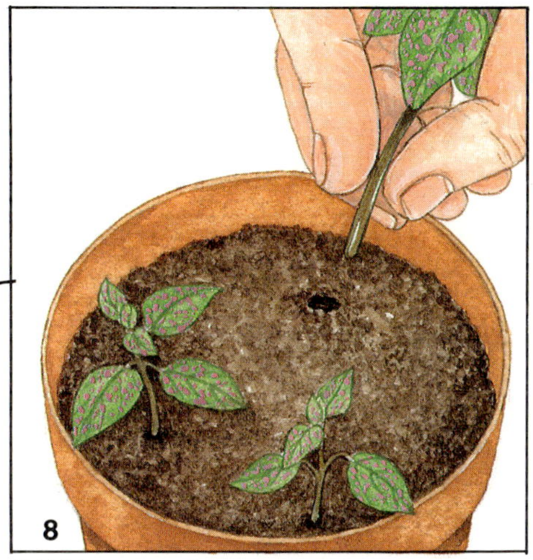

8

7 With a pencil make a hole for each cutting in the compost, near the edge of the pot. **8** Drop a cutting into each hole and firm the compost with your fingers.

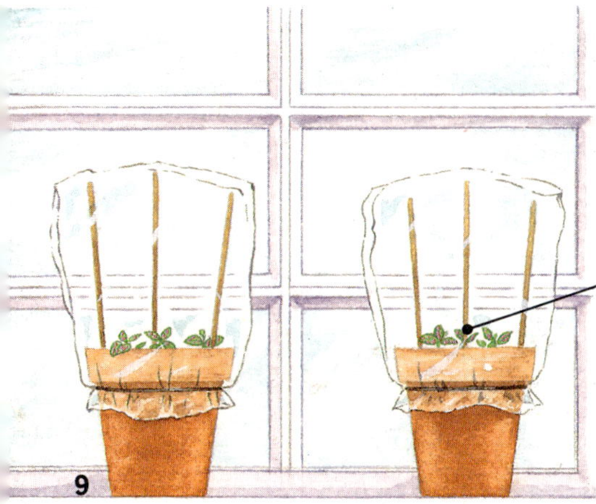

9

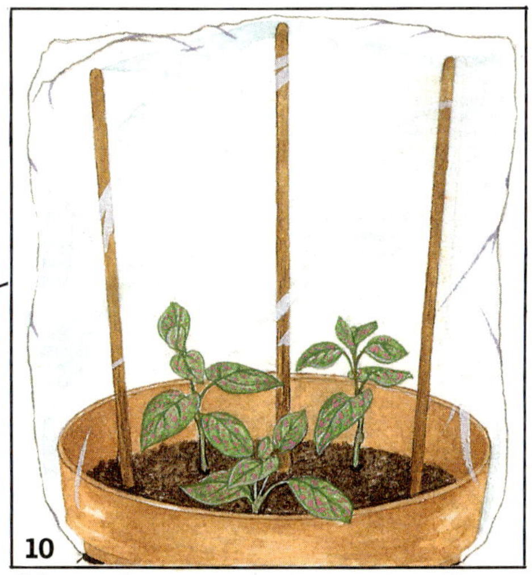

10

9 Improvise your own propagator with a clear polythene bag secured at the pot rim by a rubber band. **10** Use short canes to hold the polythene clear of the cuttings.

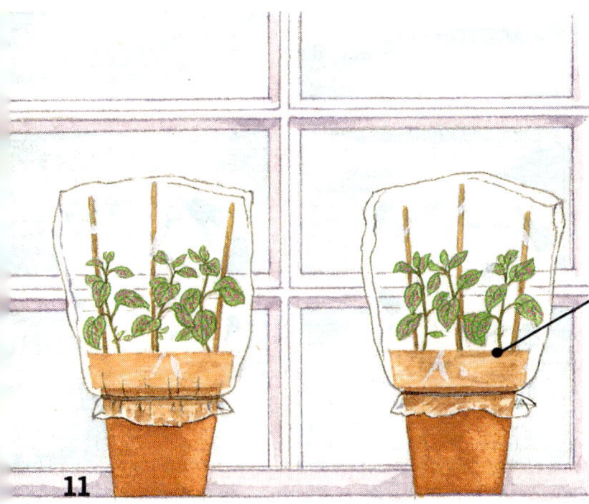

11

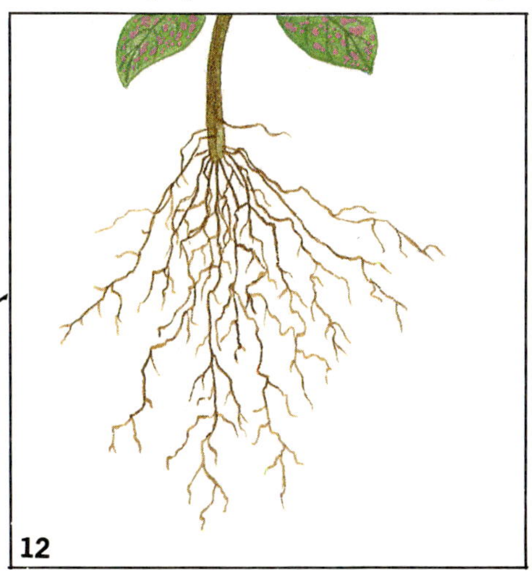

12

11 When the cuttings have grown for about four weeks and are starting to produce shoots, they should have developed a healthy root system **12**.

Watering and rooting

You must check a heated propagator every day to see if the compost needs watering as the heat dries it out very quickly. With cuttings under polythene, or in an unheated propagator, the moisture in the compost will be enough for the cuttings until they root, as the condensation will run off the sides back into the compost.

Open a heated propagator every day to change the air and to wipe away any condensation with a tissue. At the same time check for dead leaves and any sign of black, soggy or rotting stems. Throw away any cutting that looks unhealthy as it can contaminate the others.

Once the cuttings have grown roots they are ready to be moved into individual pots. Wait until you can see that the tips of the shoots have started to grow — then you can be fairly sure that the roots are also growing under the compost. When you think the cuttings have 'taken', lift one up to see if it has good white roots.

Start each rooted cutting in a small 3in (7cm) pot. Don't be too ambitious for it by putting it in too big a pot; young plants grow best when their roots don't have too much room to explore.

Alternative methods

With a plant that has a rather woody stem, such as a Fuchsia, you can take cuttings with a heel of bark. This gives the cutting a head start on rooting. In this case you simply peel off the shoot taking with it a slither of bark from the main stem. After that you treat the cutting in exactly the same way as an ordinary stem cutting.

Some cuttings will root in water as well as compost; try this with Busy Lizzies, Tradescantias, Zebrinas, Coleus, Fuchsias and Crotons. Prepare cuttings in the same way as already described. Use a jam jar with about 1in (25mm) of water in the bottom and stretch a piece of clingfilm across the top; make holes in the clingfilm with a sharp pencil to hold the cuttings. Push each cutting carefully through its hole so that the bottom of the stem just enters the water. Put the pot in a warm, bright place, but not in direct sunlight, and inspect it daily to see if the roots are growing.

When the roots are about 1in (25mm) long they are ready to go into pots of compost. Be extra careful when handling water-grown cuttings as the roots are particularly brittle.

Taking leaf cuttings

Making new plants from leaves is fun: they root easily and quickly and give you more new plants than you could ever expect from stem cuttings. Only a small range of plants is eligible for this treatment, but they include very popular and pretty ones such as the African Violet and Begonias. Because you get so many new plants for so little trouble, leaf propagation would be an enjoyable and inexpensive way to make presents for other people.

Plants to choose

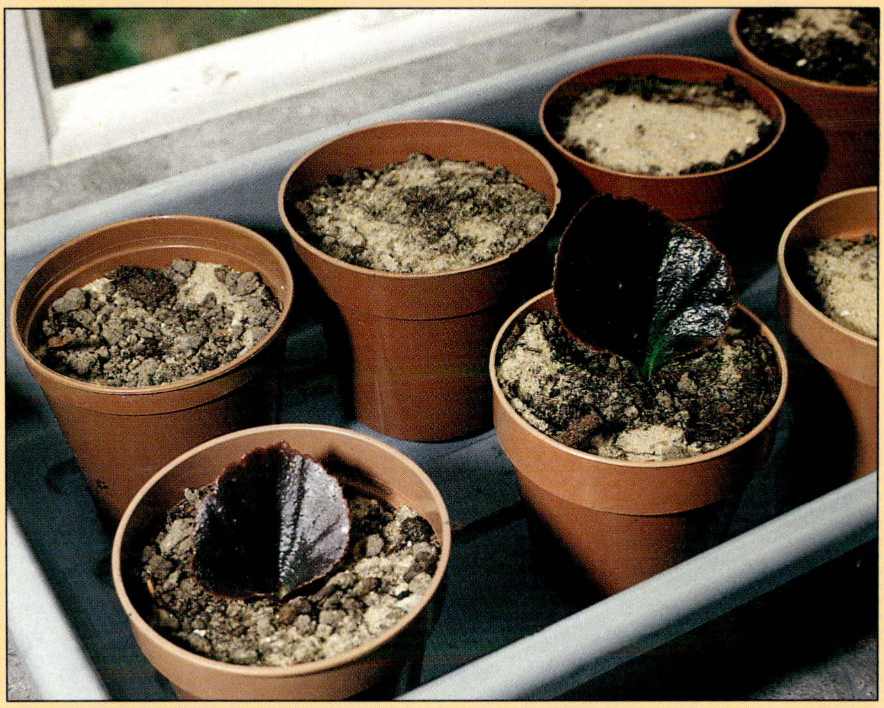

Leaves with stalks
Begonia boweri (Eyelash Begonia)
Peperomia argyreia (Watermelon Peperomia)
P.caperata (Emerald Ripple)
P.griseo-argentea (Silver Ripple)
Saintpaulia ionantha (African Violet)
Sinningia speciosa (Gloxinia)

Whole leaves
Begonia rex, above
B.masoniana (Iron Cross Begonia)
Crassula arborescens (Chinese Jade)
C.argentea (Jade Plant)
C.lycopodioides (Rat Tail Plant)
Echeveria glauca (Blue Echeveria)
E.harmsii (Mexican Snowball)
E.setosa (Firecracker Plant)
Sedum adolphii (Golden Sedum)
S.morganianum (Burro's Tail)
S.rubrotinctum (Jelly Bean Plant)

Leaf sections
Begonia masoniana (Iron Cross Plant)
B.rex
Sansevieria hahnii (Bird's Nest Sansevieria)
S.trifasciata or *S.zeylanica* (Mother-in-Law's Tongue)
Sinningia speciosa (Gloxinia)
Streptocarpus hybridus (Cape Primrose)

The plants with the ability to propagate from their leaves are those in the Begonia, Crassula and Gesneriad groups — these plants all have slightly fleshy leaves. The best time to take leaf cuttings is in early summer, when leaves are strong and mature. In spring they are putting all their energy into growing, while late in the summer their capacity to propagate is reduced. But when leaves are just mature, their surface area is at its maximum, they're at their best in terms of producing food, and they're strong enough to withstand the period during propagation when they are severed from the parent plant. You should always choose a complete and undamaged leaf that has finished growing and that looks completely healthy.

What you need

The most common problem when taking cuttings from a leaf is that it rots before the new plantlets have developed — so make sure that the materials you start with are the best you can get, and that all the equipment you use is completely clean. In the enclosed atmosphere necessary for propagation any disease will develop very rapidly and pests will multiply.

You can root some leaves in water, but most go straight into compost and the right mix is essential. Plants won't establish roots in very packed soil where air and water can't circulate easily, so good drainage must be provided. Use equal parts of good fresh peat, coarse Perlite and Vermiculite, or a proprietary brand of seed and cuttings compost, such as Levingtons or Arthur Bowers, with some extra coarse sand, Perlite or Vermiculite added. Fill a shallow seed tray or individual, wide pots, with this mixture.

For best results you should have a propagator, to keep the temperature warm and constant — 70°F (21°C) is ideal. But you can also get good results by enclosing the pot or tray in a clear polythene bag or covering it with glass, and rooting the cuttings on a lightly shaded windowsill so that they get warmth but not bright sun.

Always water in the leaves with a dilute systemic fungicide containing benomyl, such as Benlate, before you cover them. This will help reduce the chance of pests and diseases damaging the leaves or new plantlets.

Using leaves with stalks

Whole leaves, with a spur of stalk, can be used to propagate several very attractive plants — African Violets (Saintpaulia); all the Peperomias, including the glorious silver and green striped Watermelon Plant *(Peperomia argyreia)*; small-leaved Begonias, including the Eyelash Plant *(Begonia bowerii)*, and Gloxinias *(Sinningia speciosa)*.

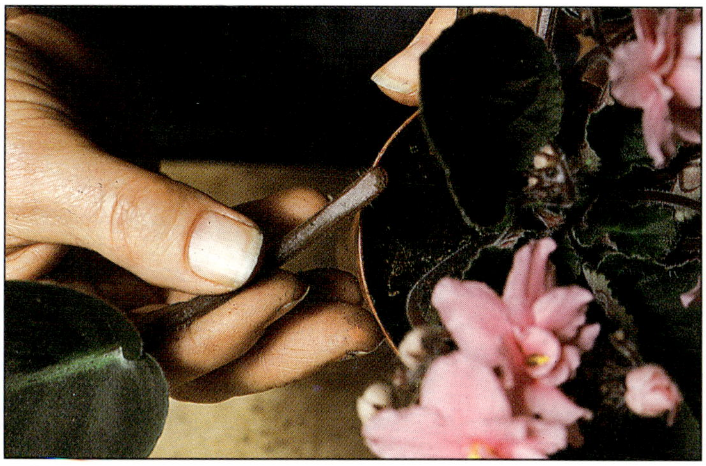

1. Remove the entire African Violet leaf.

Aftercare

Whether you have rooted your new plantlets in water or compost, the cluster that usually forms from each leaf or section needs to be split up as soon as the plantlets are about 1in (2.5cm) tall.

Pot each new plant separately in a 2in (5cm) pot, using a peat based compost, such as Arthur Bowers or Levingtons. Grow them in bright but not direct light, and feed them at every other watering with a fertiliser high in phosphate and potassium, but low in nitrogen – this is the right mix to encourage new, healthy roots. A tomato fertilizer would be ideal (see page 93).

When the young plants are well established, you can treat them as mature plants – see individual details in the 'A-Z of Plants' section.

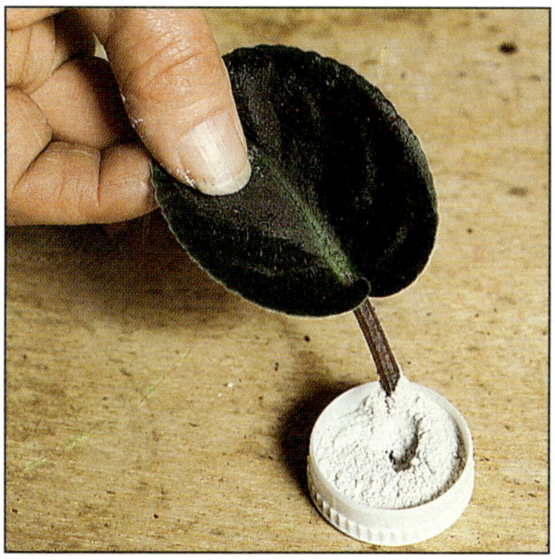

2. Trim the leaf stalk and dip in a rooting powder.

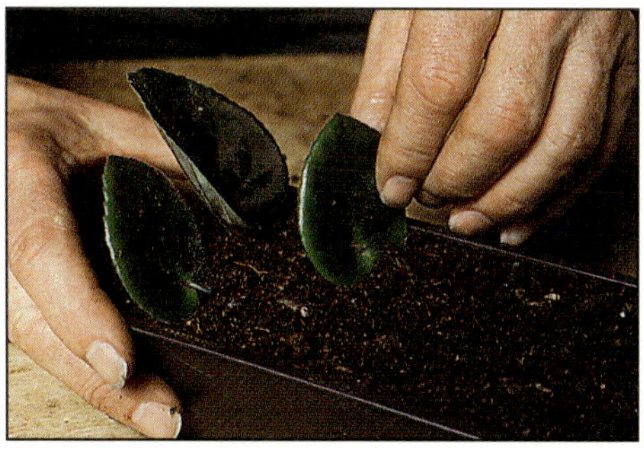

3. Insert the stalk into prepared compost, firm and water in.

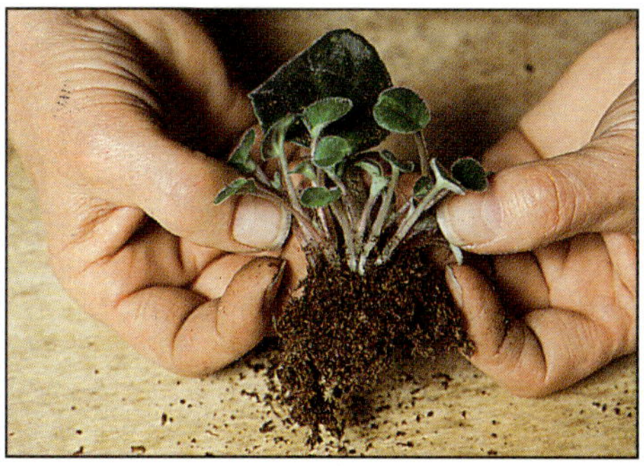

4. The leaves should root in about six weeks.

Slice a leaf from the plant, together with ½-1in (13-25mm) of stalk, using a razor blade or a very sharp knife. Dip the end of the stalk in a hormone rooting powder or gel (such as Fisons Clear Cut) and then insert it into your prepared pot or tray of compost.

Do this with as many leaves as you like, but bear in mind that each leaf will produce several new plants. Firm them gently and water them in, and they will root in about six weeks; shoots will appear in about ten.

You can also root African Violets in water — fill a small jar nearly to the rim with water and cover it with aluminium foil. Make holes for the leaf stalks and pop them through so that the ends are in water. When the shoots have appeared, transplant them into compost.

When the plantlets are about 1in (2.5cm) tall, plant them out in separate pots and treat them as mature plants. It's likely to take about nine months to get to this stage.

Using whole leaves

Succulent plants are easily propagated directly from the leaves. Echeverias, Sedums and Crassulas (which all belong to the *Crassulaceae* family) are all good candidates for this treatment. You simply detach whole, fleshy leaves by slicing them off the parent plant, and allow the gummy sap to dry for a day or so. Then insert them up to a quarter of their length in the compost and water them in, remembering to add the fungicide. Cover the tray or pot with clear polythene or glass, making sure it doesn't touch the leaves, and rooting will start within two to three weeks.

Whole leaves are used in a different way to propagate *Begonia rex* and its

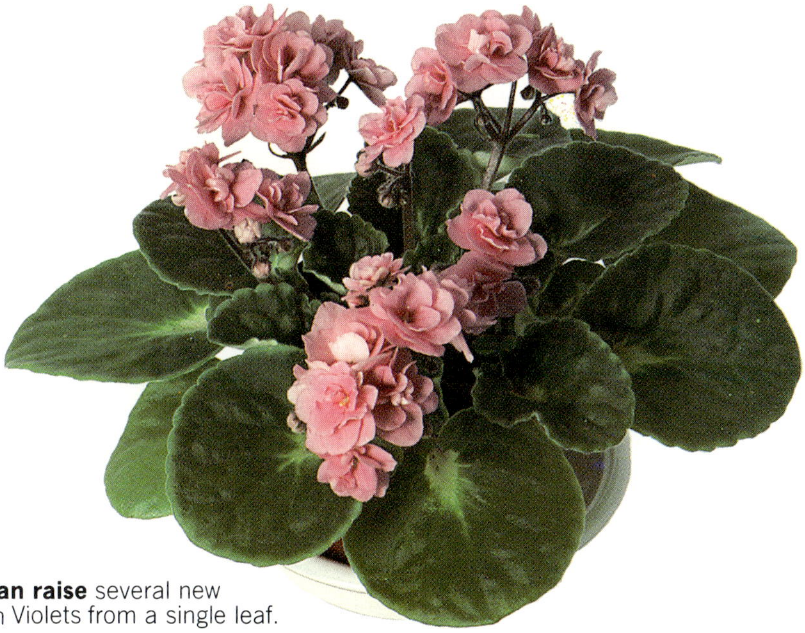

You can raise several new African Violets from a single leaf.

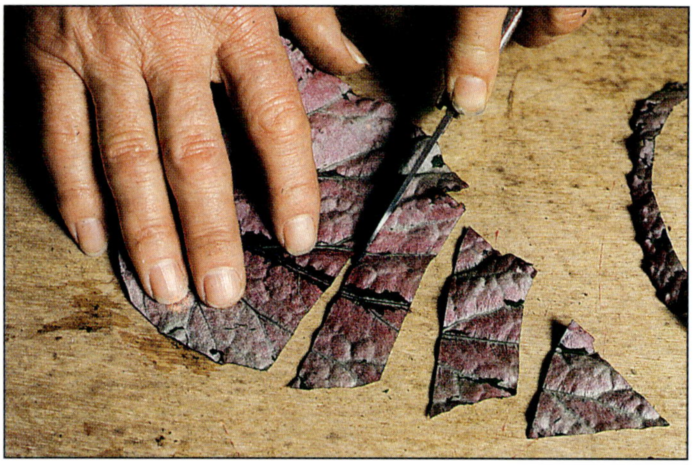
1. *Begonia rex* is easily propagated from leaf cuttings.

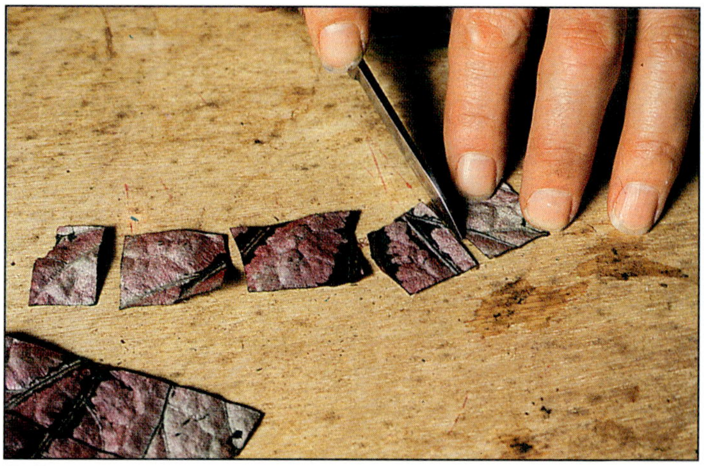
2. Trim the edges of the leaf, then cut up in squares.

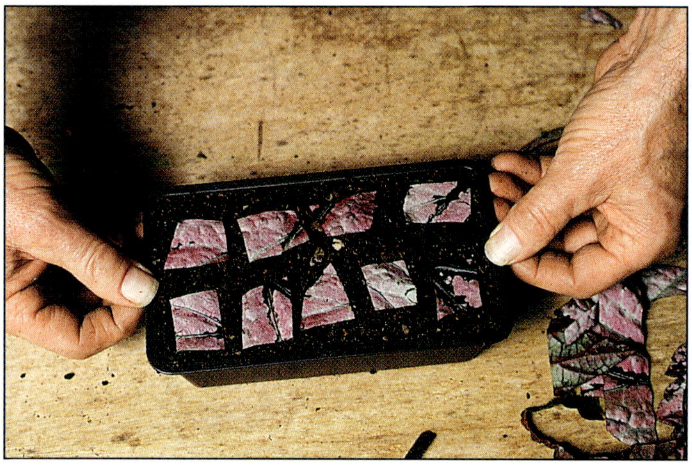
3. Lay the squares on compost, with leaf undersides down.

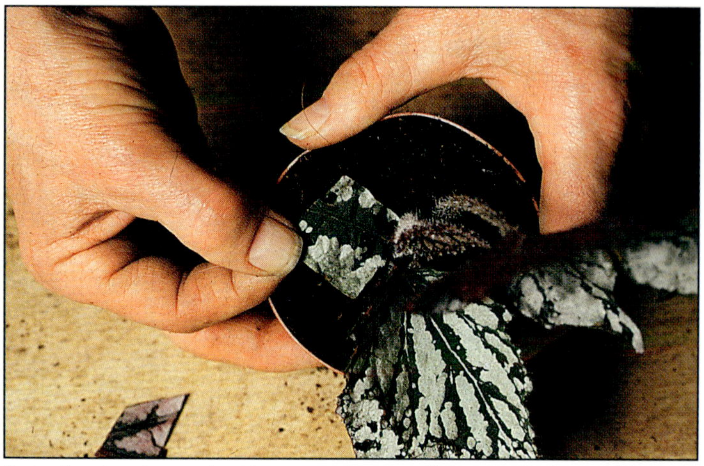
4. In five to six weeks the new plants will be ready for potting.

handsome cousin *B.masoniana.* Slice off a whole leaf (remember that one leaf will give you several new plants) and lay it on a flat surface with the underside facing up. With a razor blade, make cuts through each vein where it joins with another — you'll have half a dozen or more cuts, depending on the size of the leaf. Water the prepared compost so that its surface is slightly damp, and lay the leaf, cut side down, flat on top of the compost, anchoring it firmly in place with one or two wire staples pushed through it. You may need to use more staples with *B.masoniana* to keep it in good contact with the soil.

Water in, and cover the pot or tray with polythene or glass or, even better, put it in a propagator. Keep it at a steady 70°F (21°C), and plantlets will begin to form from each of the cut veins after five to six weeks.

Using leaf sections

To make even more plants at one time, you can cut one leaf of *Begonia rex* or its related species into several small sections. Then you'll get several new plantlets from each section. The principle is just the same as using a whole leaf.

Choose a big Begonia leaf and cut it into squares about 1in (2.5cm) across. This will automatically make the necessary cuts through the veins. You then lay each section flat on the compost as for whole leaves. Because *B.masoniana* leaves are too wrinkled to keep in good contact with the compost when lying flat, it's best to insert each section upright in the compost to about half its length, as you would when using leaves with stems attached. Make sure that the biggest severed vein in each section is inserted in the compost.

This is also the best way to propagate succulents like Sansevierias, which have long leaves with parallel lengthwise veins, and Streptocarpus, which has a single, central vein in each leaf. Gloxinias can also be propagated in this way. In these cases, slicing each leaf into sections straight across its whole width will ensure that you get the necessary cuts in the veins from which new plants will root. However, if you want to try Sansevierias, stick to the green-leaved types — variegations will not come through in the new plants, which will always be plain green.

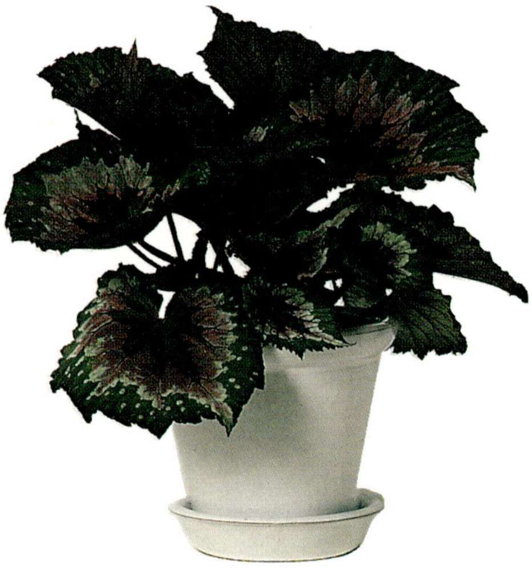
Increase *Begonia rex* from leaf cuttings.

Air layering

Do yourself a good turn: neaten up that straggly, unkempt Rubber Plant and gain a new one — for scarcely any effort. And all for the price of a bag of sphagnum moss, a tray of gravel and a little potting compost.

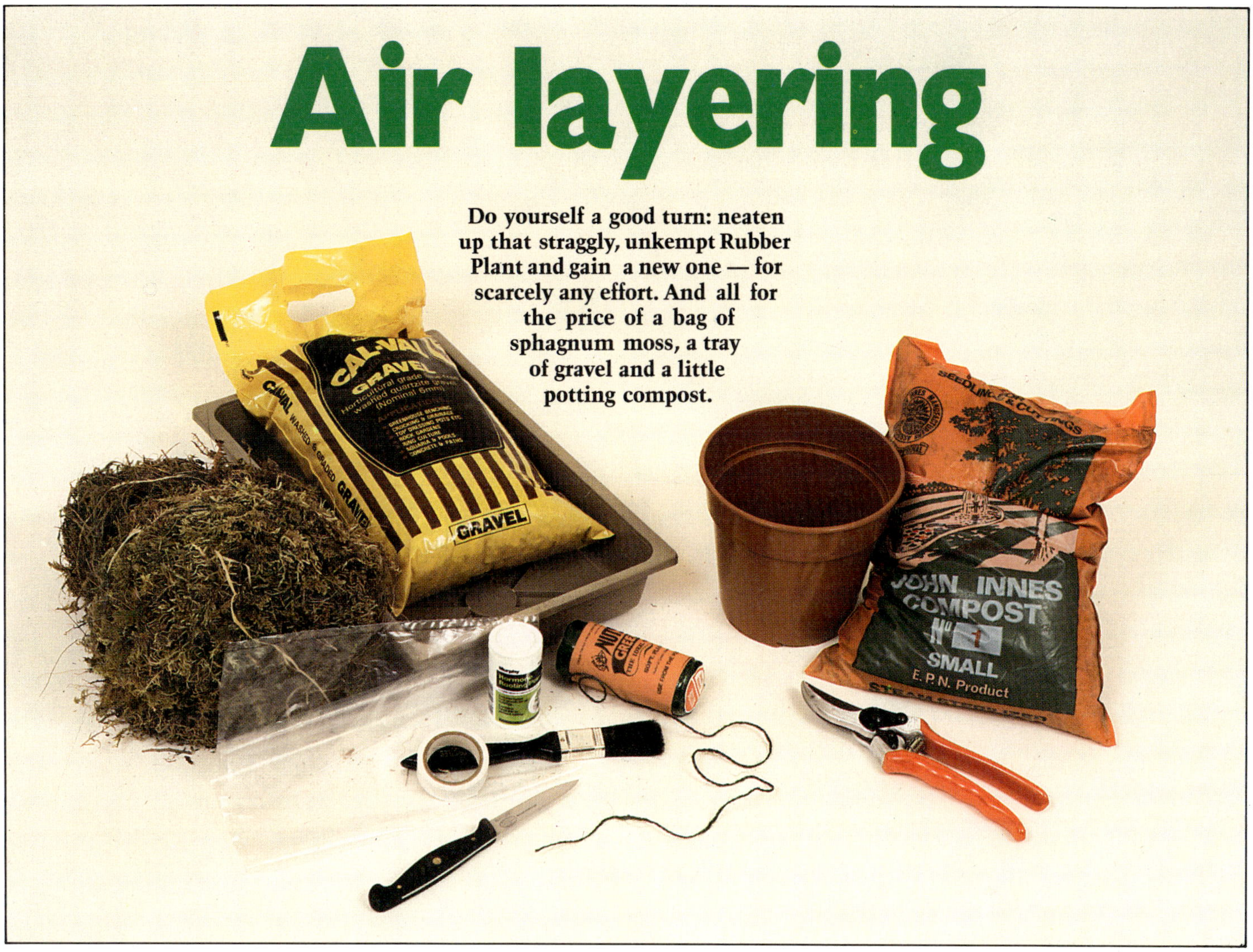

Is your Rubber Plant touching the ceiling? Stiff-stemmed plants like the Fiddle-leaf Fig, Dumb Cane and Swiss Cheese Plant easily get out of hand. They can become tall, ungainly and increasingly unattractive as they get older and lose their lower leaves. When they reach that stage, they don't really deserve house room.

Air layering offers you a chance to grow a fresh new plant, by encouraging part of the stem near the top of the established plant to produce roots. The top is then severed to make a new plant — and the parent plant usually benefits from the trim.

This is one of the oldest methods of raising plants, probably pioneered in China over 4,000 years ago, hence its other name — Chinese layering. It's particularly useful for woody plants, because they can't be 'layered' in the usual way — by bending the stems down to soil level and allowing roots to develop where stem and soil meet. But air layering is also easier and more reliable than taking cuttings — and Rubber Plants and other Ficus species, Crotons and False Aralia are notoriously tricky to raise in that way. Air layering leaves the parent plant fairly undisturbed, so you use this technique without risk of harming your plant. When working with younger plants that are still in good shape, it's best to leave the main stem untrimmed and to use a side shoot.

Don't think of starting until late spring or early summer, though, when plants are in their active growing season and will be more efficient at producing roots. The warmer the weather, the quicker the rooting.

You'll need nothing more sophisticated in the way of equipment than a bag of sphagnum moss obtainable from your local garden centre or florist. Before you begin, check the box, *right*, for what you need.

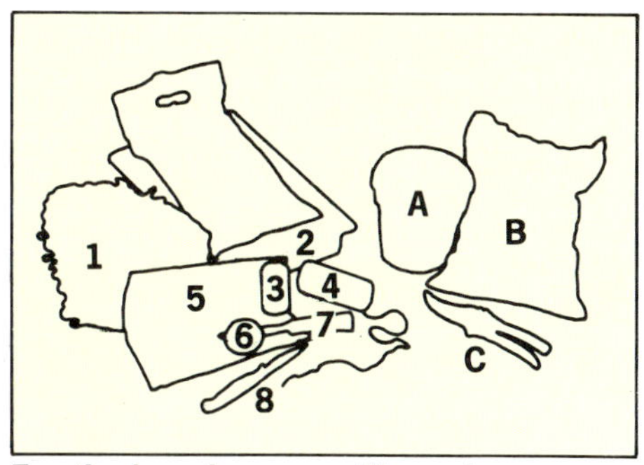

For the layering you will need:
1 sphagnum moss
2 a gravel tray (see text)
3 hormone rooting powder
4 some strong thread (optional)
5 a piece of clear polythene about 2ft (0.6m) × 1ft (0.3m) — a plastic bag cut down the sides will do
6 waterproof adhesive tape
7 a paintbrush (optional)
8 a sharp knife

In addition, for potting up:
A suitable-sized pot
B John Innes No 1 Potting Compost
C sharp secateurs

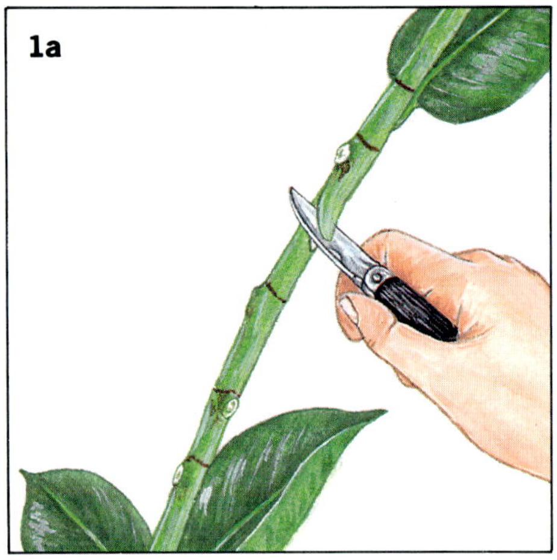

Air layering step-by-step

1a Begin preparations the day before you're going to begin layering, by soaking the sphagnum moss in water overnight.

The following day, select the stem you're going to use, whether it's a main stem or a large side shoot. Near the top, say between 6in (15cm) and 12in (30cm) down, cut away a few of the leaves to give you a clear space of 4-6in (10-15cm) or so to work in.

Now prepare to cut a wound in the section of stem you have cleared, about 3-4in (7-10cm) below the top leaf; it is from the wound that the new roots will grow.

Using a really sharp knife, make a slanting upward cut, about 2-3in (5-7cm) long, but not penetrating more than halfway through the stem. Food and hormones will now begin to build up in the area of this 'tongue', as the plant responds to the wounding.

1b A less risky way of making the wound is to remove a girdle of bark from around the stem. This method leaves the tissues inside the plant undisturbed and therefore means that the stem is not weakened as much.

Scratch out two fine rings in the bark, about ½in (13mm) apart and peel off the area between the lines.

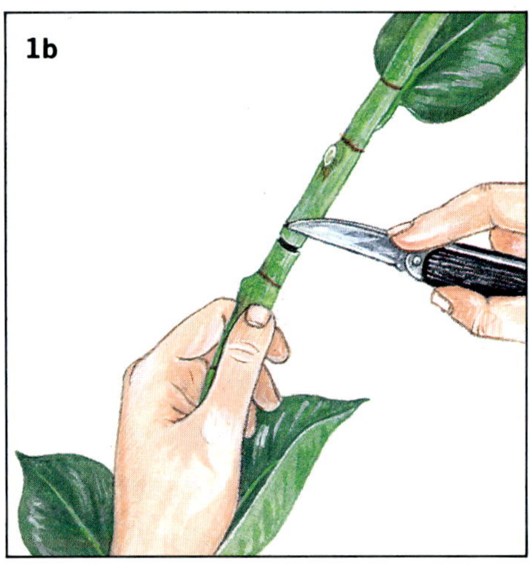

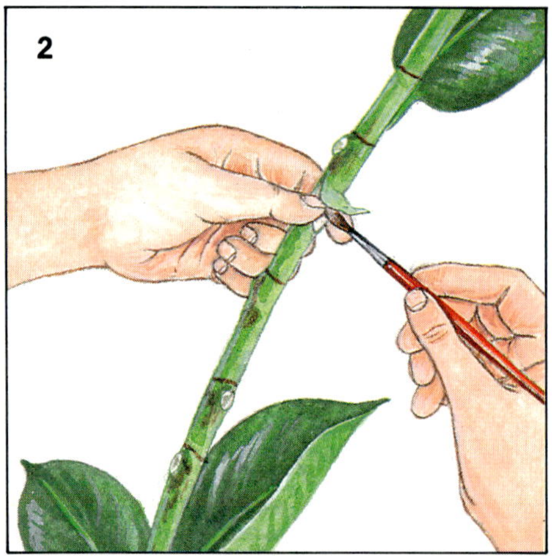

2 To encourage fast rooting and a strong root system, coat the wound with a hormone rooting powder or liquid; use a paintbrush to apply the rooting hormone, and prise the tongue open gently.

3 It is important to keep the wound open, to stop it from healing instead of putting out shoots. So pack the cut with a small, moist wad of sphagnum moss. Some experts suggest using a small pebble, or a matchstick, but these have no advantage and may be trickier to insert without risk to the weakened stem.

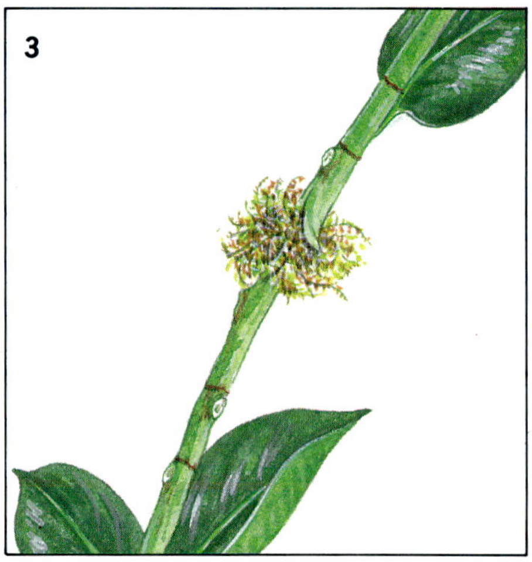

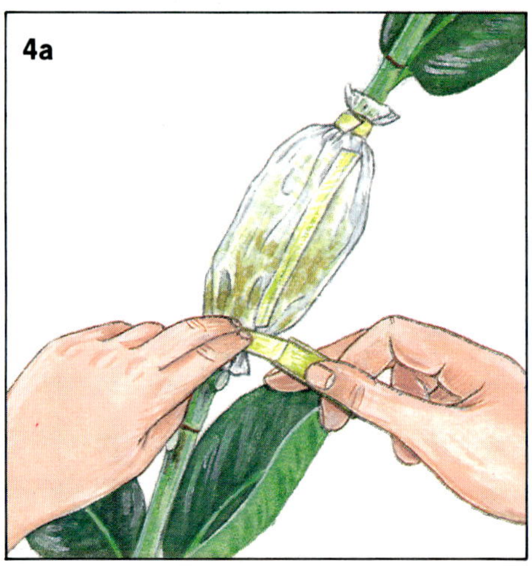

Good candidates

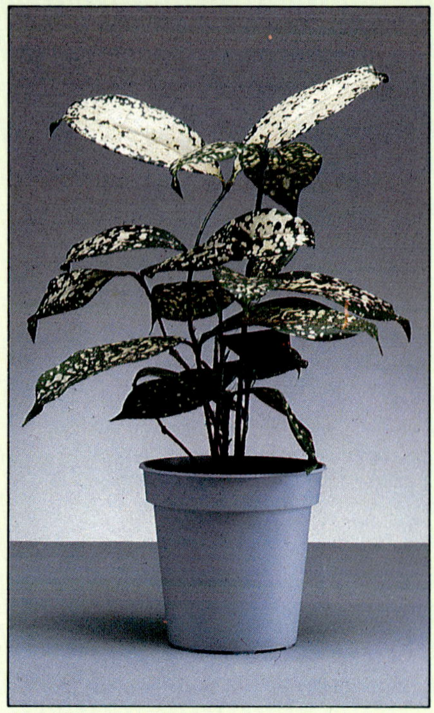

Cordyline
Croton (*Codiaeum*)
Gold Dust Dracaena (*see above*)
Dumb Cane (*Dieffenbachia*)*
False Aralia (*Dizygotheca elegantissima*)
Fiddle-leaf Fig (*Ficus lyrata*)
Philodendron
Rubber Plant (*Ficus elastica*)
Swiss Cheese Plant (*Monstera deliciosa*)
Weeping Fig (*Ficus benjamina*)

*** WARNING**
Be careful when dealing with the Dieffenbachia; the sticky liquid it exudes is poisonous so wash your hands thoroughly afterwards.

4a The wound is now wrapped in sphagnum moss; this is the best rooting medium because it holds water well, is well aerated and easy to handle.

Take a thick pad of the moss (about two handfuls), squeeze out the excess water and work it into a ball so that the fibres are interwoven. Once the ball is about 2-3in (5-7cm) in diameter, divide it in half and press half to either side of the stem, where the wound is. Knead the moss together again at the sides, and secure it firmly with strong thread or sticky tape.

Wrap the polythene sheeting around the stem like a bandage, and seal it, top and bottom, with a few rounds of waterproof, adhesive tape. Seal the overlapping edge with tape, too, so that as little moisture as possible can escape.

4b

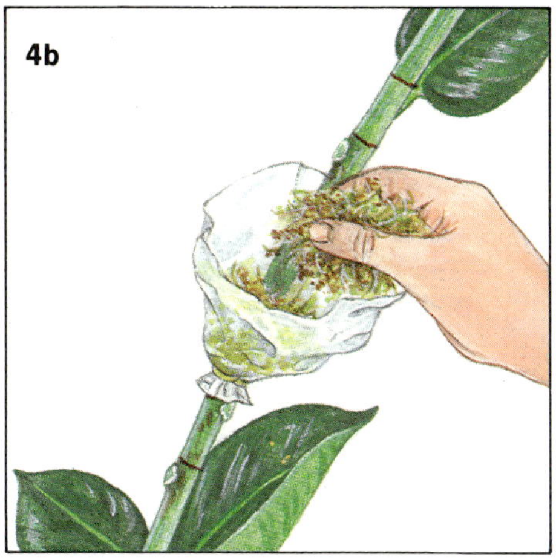

4b As an alternative, you may find it easier to make a 'cup' of polythene first, and then pack the moss in afterwards. Fix on the polythene sheet, securing it at the base and side. Now fill the 'bag' with moss and, finally, seal it at the top.

5 Try to create a warm and humid atmosphere for the plant. If possible, stand it on a dish or tray filled with gravel, pebbles or Hortag (a proprietary gravel) which should be kept moist. If you can, put the plant in your warmest room and spray the foliage daily with a mist sprayer.

5

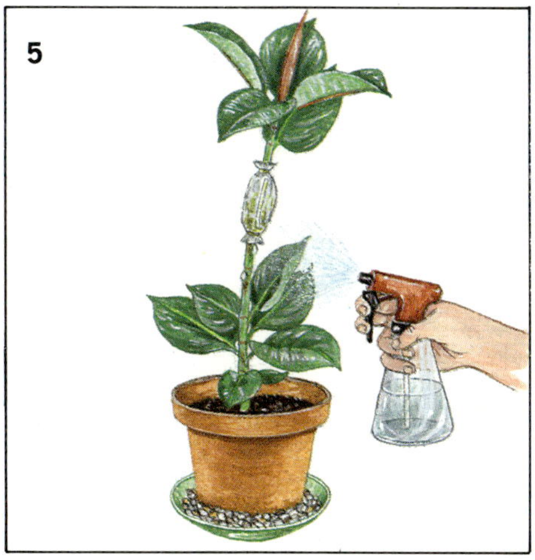

Now all you can do is wait. Inside the sealed polythene, the environment will be warm, dark and moist, and a new root system will begin to develop. How long this takes will depend on the plant — some root more quickly than others — but on average, it will be about eight weeks or so before you'll see any white roots appearing. Not until they are visible should you think or removing the polythene bandage.

When you see that the time is right, choose a suitable-sized pot for the young plant — one that is at least 4in (10cm) in diameter. Because you'll have to make a guess, have one or two larger pots ready, just in case. You will need one that is just a bit larger than the plant's root system, by about $\frac{1}{2}$in (13mm) all round. Half fill it with John Innes No 1, or a similar potting mixture.

6 The rooted stem may now be cut away from the parent plant. First remove the polythene wrapping then make a horizontal cut just below the ball of moss, clear of the new roots, using a pair of sharp secateurs. On no account allow the new roots to become dry; once the plant is separate from the parent, it must be potted up straight away.

7 Leave the sphagnum moss in place. If you try to remove it, you may damage the new roots, whereas putting it into the pot with the young plant can do no harm at all.

Put the young plant into its pot immediately, working more potting mixture in around the sides of the mossy root ball and on top. Firm it down very carefully to avoid damaging the brittle roots. Now water it well.

6

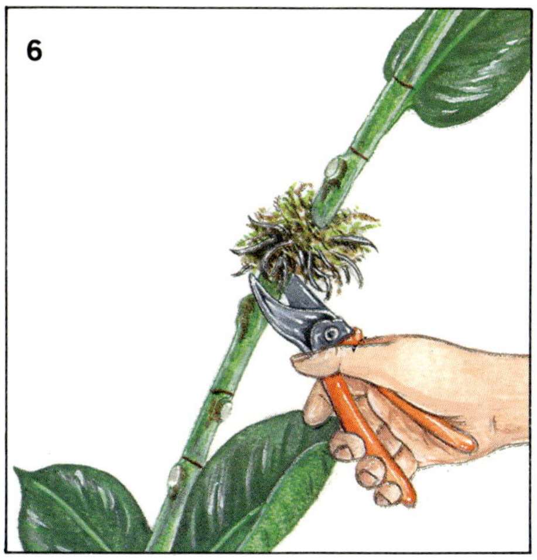

7

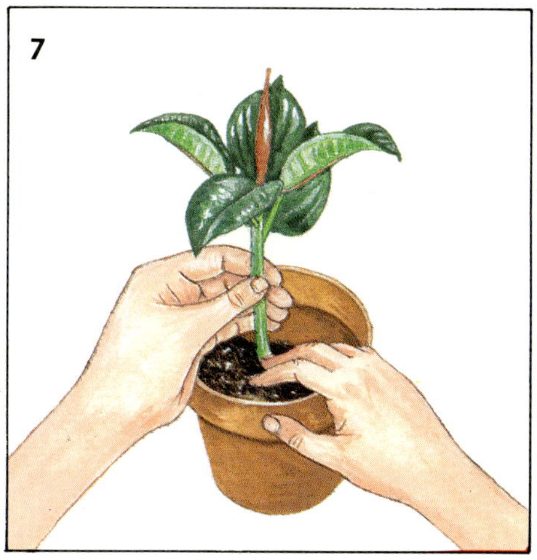

Caring for your new plant

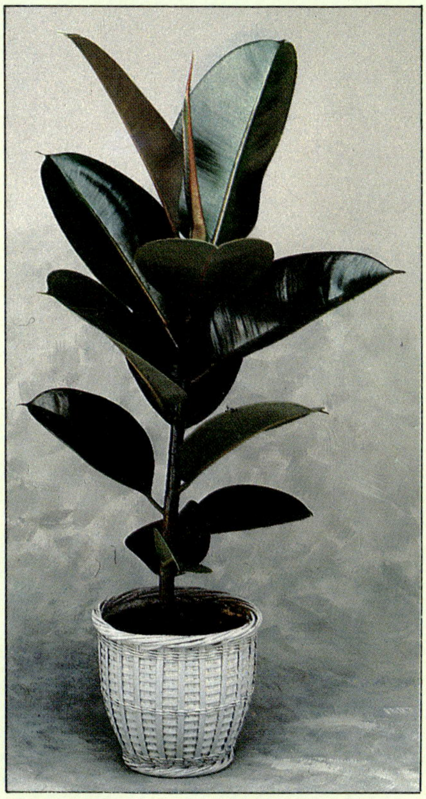

The young plant will need some special attention until it establishes itself. Encourage it to root into the compost as quickly as possible, by keeping it in a warm place until the tip of the stem is starting to grow. Until then, use the gravel tray described earlier to keep the atmosphere humid, and make sure the plant is shaded from sunshine. Water just enough to keep the compost moist, not sodden.

You may find the young plant needs some extra support until it develops more roots; tie it temporarily to a stick pushed in the potting mixture — but take care to avoid the young roots. Once new growth appears, treat the plant like a mature specimen, watering and feeding accordingly. In the following spring it will be ready for repotting.

As to the parent plant, now's the opportunity for some radical reshaping. Don't be nervous — cut the old stem back to a point where new growth will make a more compact, respectable specimen. You can get away with trimming it by as much as two-thirds and you'll be well rewarded with a rejuvenated, bushy plant.

Air-layer your old, leggy *Ficus elastica* to gain a fine, new plant, *left*.

Seed sowing step by step

The cheapest way of getting a large collection of houseplants is to grow them from seeds — and one of the nicest things about doing this is the satisfaction you get from growing plants from scratch. Many seeds germinate very easily and the seedlings pop up out of the soil within a couple of weeks. Other seeds can be trickier; start with the easy ones and progress to those that are slightly harder. Be guided by the seed packets; most of them say how easy or difficult the seeds inside are to germinate and grow.

Where to start

The time to start thinking about seed sowing is in the spring; this is because the weather is beginning to warm up and the summer stretches ahead to give your plants plenty of time to grow and gather strength before the rigours of winter. You can buy seeds and equipment at garden centres and department stores.

Ideally you need a little bit of extra warmth to encourage seeds to germinate; one way to achieve this is to invest in a small, inexpensive propagator. You can get a propagator small enough to sit on a windowsill and progressively bigger sizes up to one that will take three seed trays. Propagators can be unheated or electrically heated, depending on how much you want to spend. An electric propagator will provide a temperature of around 65-70°F (18-21°C), which is warm enough for raising most seeds.

If you only want to grow a few plants or don't want to spend any money, you can still germinate a wide range of seeds on a warm windowsill. Cover the seeds with a clear polythene bag and seal it with a rubber band or piece of string to

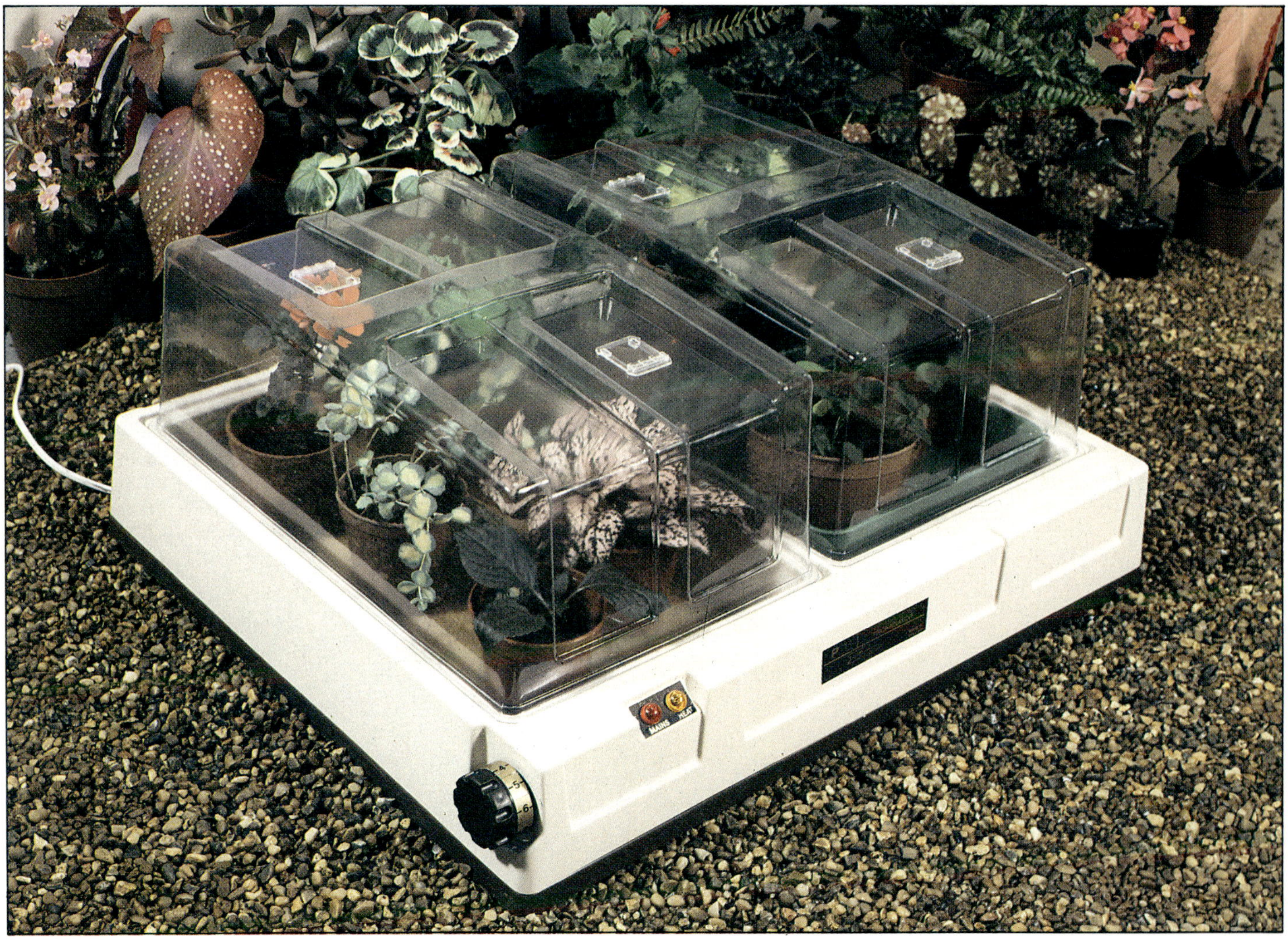

An electric propagator provides the ideal environment for germination and the early stages of seedling growth.

keep the moisture and warmth inside, or use a piece of glass. Or put the seeds in the airing cupboard to give them the initial warmth they need to germinate; if you do this remember to move the seedlings out into the light as soon as they show.

Don't try to economise on compost by using garden soil; it has too many other seeds and bugs in it that will overwhelm your seeds. Buy a good seed compost like John Innes Seed Compost or one of the soilless composts, such as Levingtons or Arthur Bowers, or a multi-purpose compost.

Growing houseplants from seed is a very simple process — just follow our step by step guidelines, *right*, and you will be rewarded with lots of healthy plants of your own — and much cheaper than in the shops!

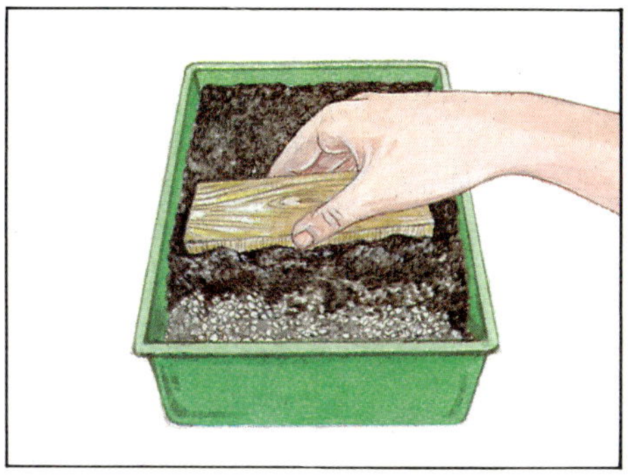

• **Preparing the compost.** If you only have a few seeds you can sow them into a small pot, say 3-4in (7-10cm). But use a tray if you have a lot of seeds. Fill the pot or tray to within ½in (13mm) of the top and lightly firm it. Level and smooth the compost with a flat piece of wood or the bottom of another pot.

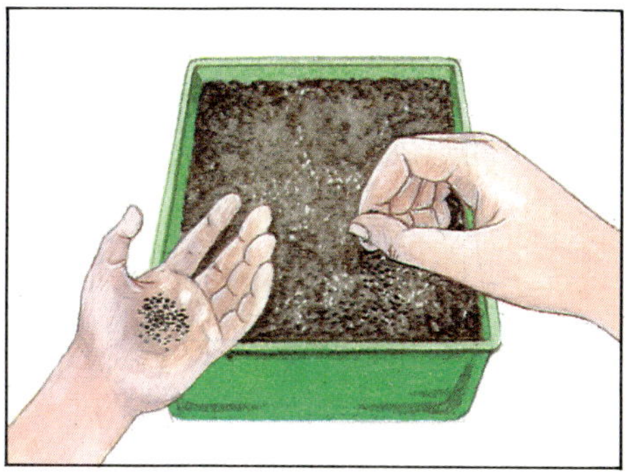

• **How to sow the seeds.** Space out large seeds individually, roughly ½in (13mm) apart, across the compost surface. Sprinkle smaller seeds evenly over the surface using your finger and thumb. Tiny, dust-like seeds can be mixed with a small amount of fine, dry silver sand before sowing to make them easier to handle.

• **Cover the seeds with compost.** Use a fine-mesh kitchen sieve to sift the compost to a fine texture and cover the seeds with an even layer of compost equal to twice their diameter. This helps the seedlings to germinate evenly. Don't cover very small, dust-like seeds with compost or they may not appear at all. Instead, press them into the compost surface using a flat piece of wood.

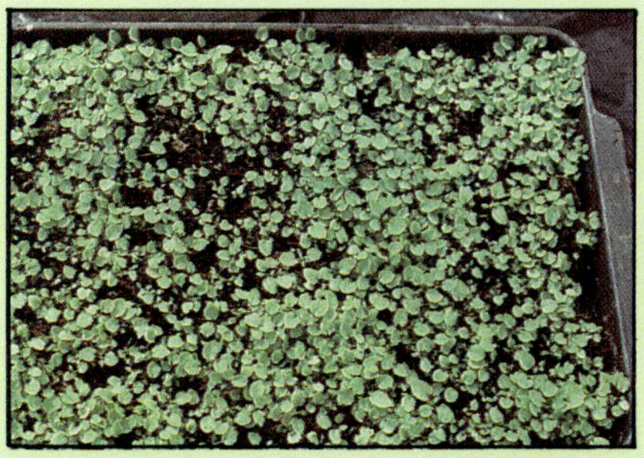

Primula seedlings — before and after

You can have hundreds of plants for less money than you would pay for one in a shop! Sow Primula seeds in spring/summer to flower the following spring. The result should be healthy, fresh green seedlings, *left*.
The following spring you should have lots of lovely, colourful, mature *Primula obconicas* like this one, *below*!

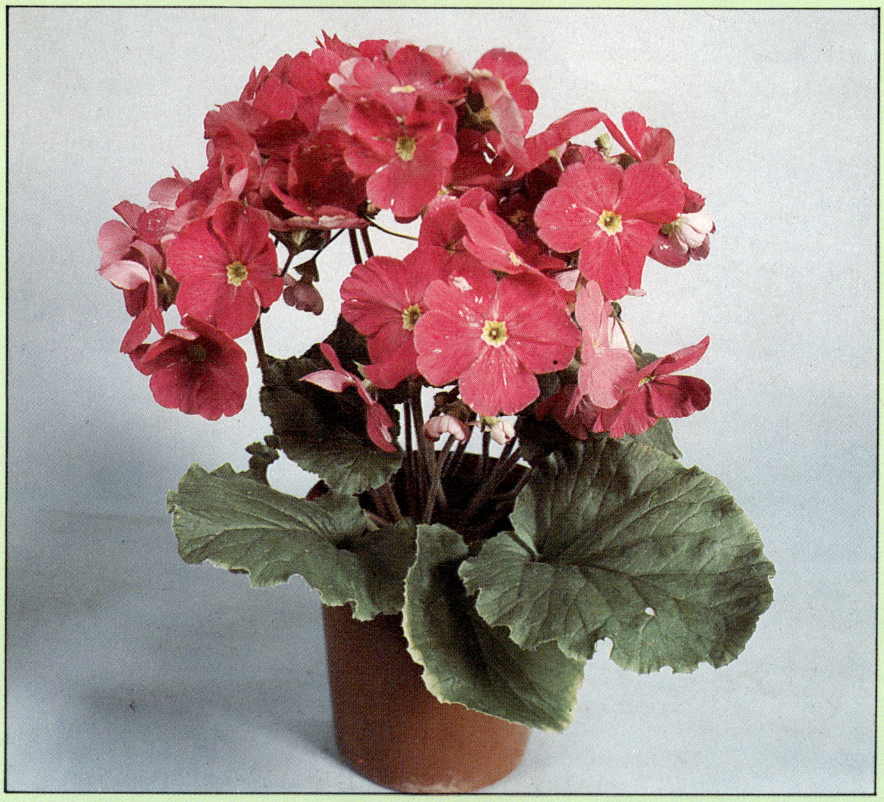

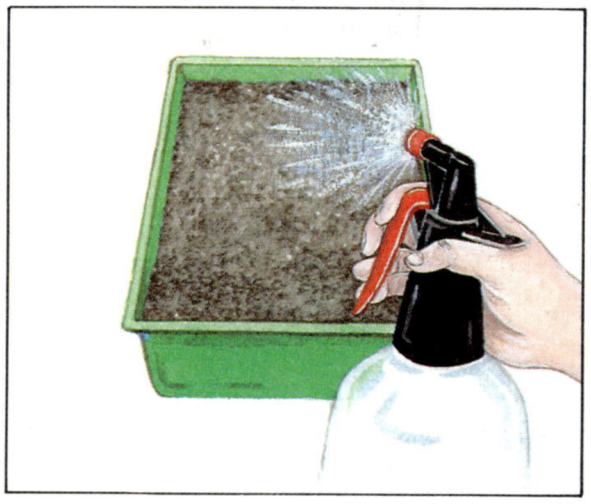

• **Watering the seeds.** Seeds can't swell and germinate without water so the compost must be nice and moist. To avoid the devastating seedling disease known as 'damping off', which causes seedlings to keel over and die, add some Cheshunt Compound powder fungicide, as directed on the tin, to the water. Use a hand mist sprayer and thoroughly dampen the compost, or stand the container up to its rim in tepid water until the surface of the compost becomes moist. Remove the container from the water and let it drain.

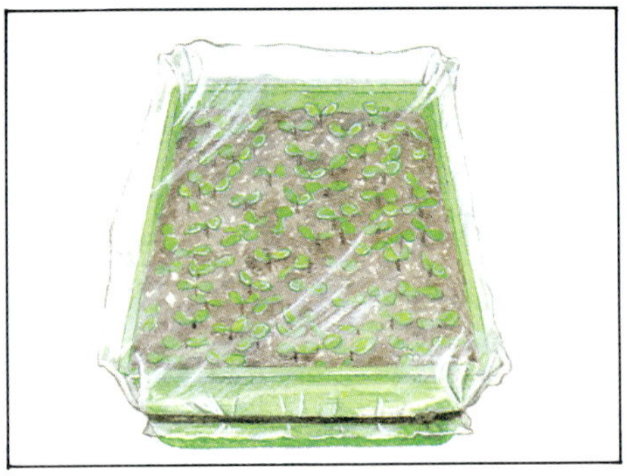

• **Germinating the seeds.** Put the pots or trays in a propagator or cover them with a polythene bag. This gives the seeds warmth and prevents the compost drying out too quickly. Mist spray the compost whenever it looks in danger of drying out.

The time seeds take to germinate varies considerably depending on the plant. Busy Lizzies can appear within a week or two, but Palms can take six months or more.

• **How to treat the seedlings.** As soon as the seedlings appear move them to a spot where they will be in good natural light, but not in direct sun or they will shrivel and die. If seedlings don't get sufficient light they will become very pale, drawn and spindly.

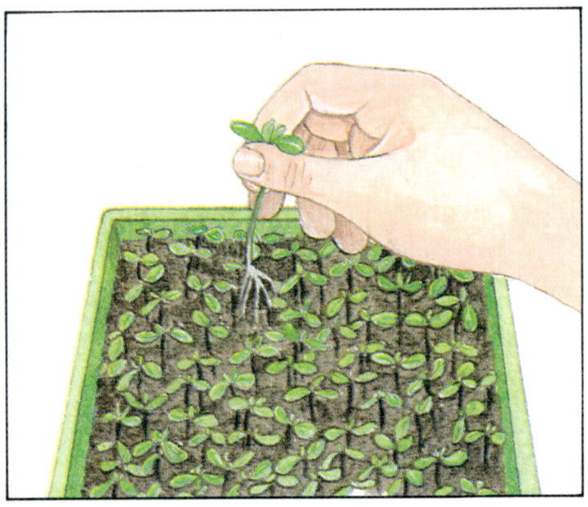

• **Thinning out the seedlings.** When lots of seedlings germinate they can become too overcrowded to grow properly. So keep the seedlings healthy and give them air and room to spread by thinning them out a little. Starting from one end, work over the tray removing the weaker seedlings by pulling each one gently out between your thumb and forefinger, until there are no leaves touching each other. This gives the remaining seedlings plenty of room to grow without the danger of the roots becoming too cramped.

Some plants to grow from seed

Easy	Difficult
Asparagus Ferns	African Violet
Busy Lizzie	*Begonia rex*
Cacti	Calceolaria
Castor Oil Plant	Cape Primrose
Coleus	Cineraria
Myrtle	Ferns
Philodendrons	Figs
Polka Dot Plant	Italian Bellflower
Sensitive Plant	Palms
Silk Oak	Primula
	Umbrella Plant

• **Pricking out the seedlings.** When the seedlings are large enough to handle easily, and before they become overcrowded again, they must be transplanted to other containers.

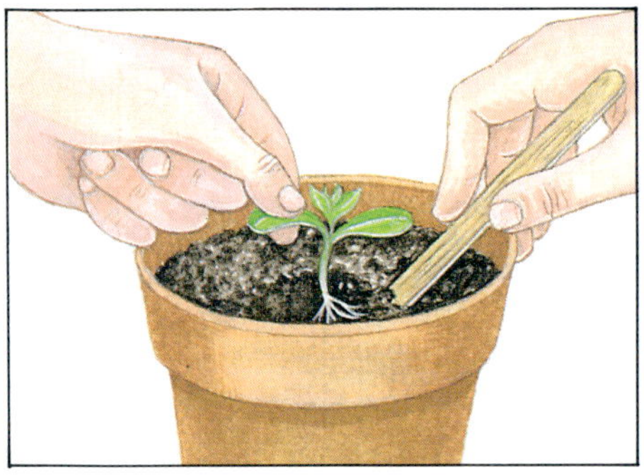

• **Transplanting the seedlings.** Use a soilless peat-based compost or John Innes No 1 and put a little compost in the bottom of a 3in (7cm) pot and firm it gently. Using a plastic plant label or tiny kitchen fork, loosen a few seedlings at a time from the compost. Insert the label well under the roots and gently lift the compost up trying not to snap too many roots as you do so.

Always handle a seedling by its lower two fleshy leaves — in other words the first two leaves that appear. Never touch the stem or you'll strangle and kill the seedling, or the upper leaves, as you may damage the growth point and again kill the seedling.

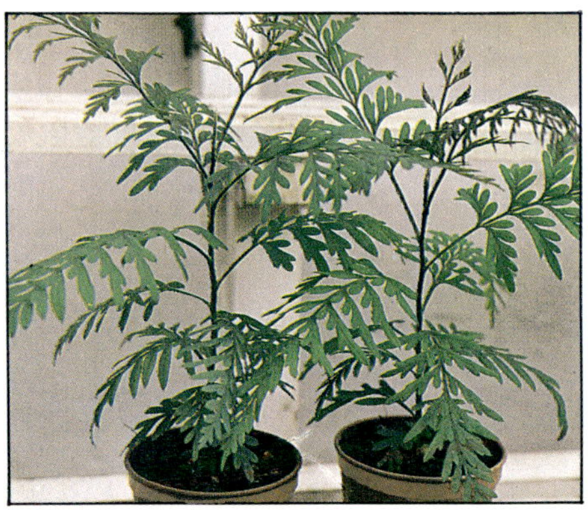

One to two year old Silk Oak seedlings.

Lift and gently shake one seedling at a time away from the compost. Hold the seedling over the centre of the pot so that its roots dangle straight down, and the lower seed leaves are more-or-less level with the pot rim. Trickle compost into the pot up to the rim; give the pot a sharp tap on the table to settle the compost and gently firm it with your fingers. By the time you finish, the compost surface should be about ½in (13mm) below the rim of the pot to allow room for watering and the lower leaves should be just above the compost surface.

• **Establishing the seedlings.** Mix a little Cheshunt Compound fungicide powder into some water and, using an indoor watering can, water the seedlings. Keep them in a warm, light place for a week or two to help them get established in their new compost. Each one can be moved to a position with a temperature suited to that particular plant.

Where to buy seeds

Houseplant seeds can be bought from garden centres and most department stores around the country. They are also available mail order from the major seed companies. You can get seeds in colourfully illustrated paper envelopes as well as foil wrapped. The seeds wrapped in foil will keep for much longer because oxygen won't be able to get at them.

Some packets only contain a few seeds while others contain lots; this depends on the type of plant concerned. If a flower produces hundreds of seeds, then that's what you'll get; at the other extreme, with some Palms and very rare plants there'll only be perhaps three or four seeds in a packet. This regulating of contents also helps the seedsman keep most packets at around the same price.

A very convenient method of raising seeds are the so-called starter packs; these consist of a plastic tray filled with sowing compost or a sterile material called vermiculite. In some packs the seeds are already sown. In many packs the clear plastic lid is lifted off and turned over to make a mini propagator for the seeds. Full, fairly straightforward instructions are always supplied with the packs.

SOMETHING DIFFERENT

Perhaps your home has limited space but you would still like some plant life around – or maybe you already have a collection of ordinary houseplants and feel you'd like the challenge of something new. Here we suggest some possibilities which you may have felt would be too tricky or time-consuming to be attempted: we tell you otherwise!

Cacti always have novelty value, and you can build up an extensive collection of different varieties, or stick to a small but exquisite cactus garden. Have you ever thought of growing orchids? They are a lot less temperamental than they're given credit for, and can make a glorious display. You could establish a bottle garden for minimum-care greenery – or have a go at growing a bonsai tree.

Whatever you decide to do, you can be sure of having a fascinating centrepiece in your collection that is guaranteed to be a talking point for all who see it.

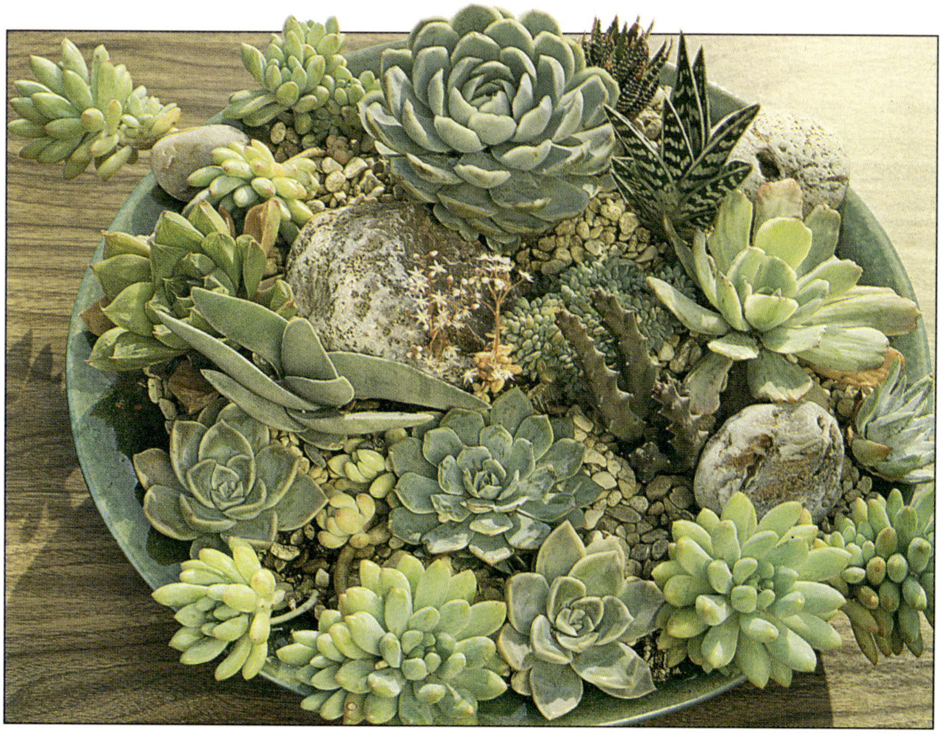

Planting a bottle garden

Creating a beautiful plant arrangement inside a container is not only challenging and great fun — it's also a very practical way to give plants an environment in which they'll thrive and be happy. And glass containers, plain or tinted, look lovely in themselves, as well as providing the perfect setting for a miniature garden.

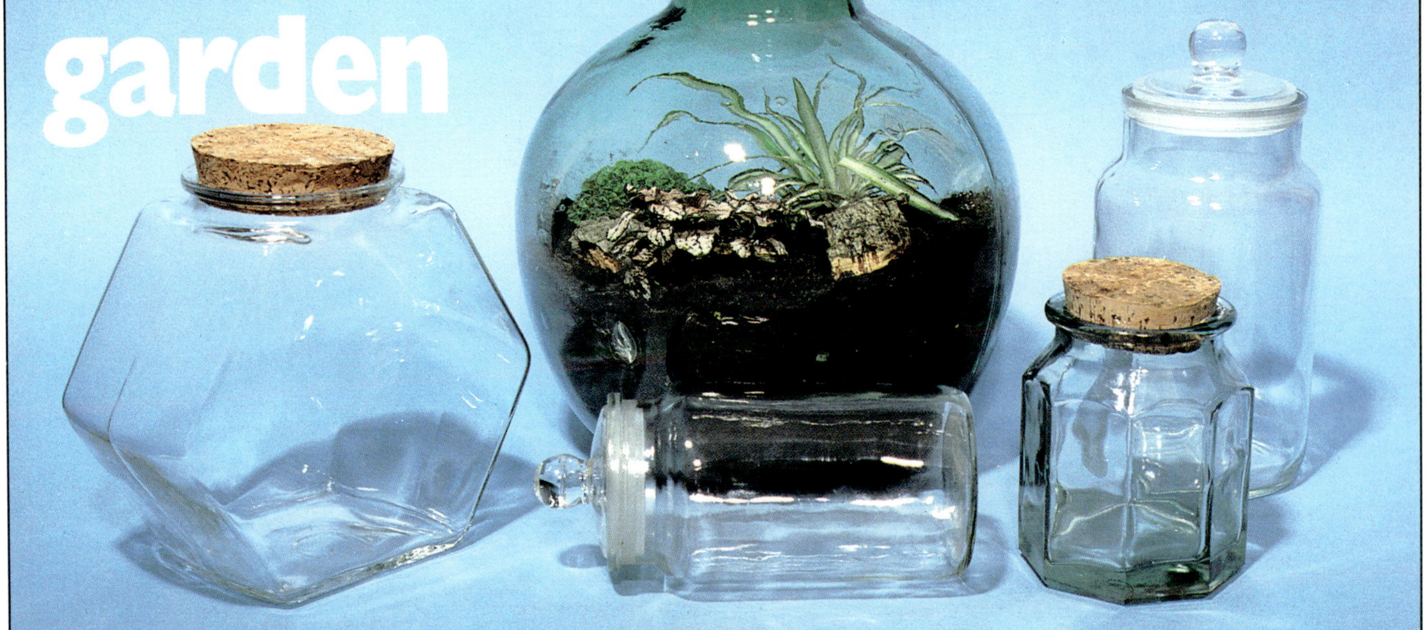

A range of containers: carboys often have attractively tinted glass, but plain storage jars will do just as well.

Bottle gardens have a lot of plus points, and virtually no disadvantages. Obviously you must take care not to have them somewhere where they might be knocked over and broken, so don't put them on the floor near doorways or in parts of the house which get a lot of traffic, and don't risk them on shelves unless they're going to be left undisturbed and are out of the reach of small children.

A bottle garden acts like a miniature glasshouse — its main advantage is that it provides an enclosed, self-regulating atmosphere for the plants to live in. Not only will they do very well, but they require virtually no care or maintenance — essential if you're forgetful or very busy! They are also a boon if you go away frequently, since you needn't worry about the plants drying out, provided the container is sealed properly. They're protected from fumes, draughts and sudden changes of temperature, and can't be knocked or damaged. Pests and diseases won't be a problem either, since there is no way that they can get in from the outside.

Bottle gardens may seem to work by magic, but actually the principle is very simple. Once the compost has been watered and the bottle sealed, water is just recycled inside. It is taken up by the roots of the plants and given off by the leaves; it then condenses on the sides of the bottle and runs back into the compost. There's no risk of underwatering or overwatering your plants, because they'll take just the amount of moisture they need.

The best plants to choose for a bottle garden are those that like moisture and warmth, and that grow fairly slowly. If you plant fast-growing varieties in a bottle you'll be spending all your time pruning them back so that they don't run out of space! On the whole, flowering plants don't do all that well — their petals are vulnerable to mould in the humid atmosphere, and that encourages disease. So it's best to stick to the prettier foliage plants. The one exception to this, however, is the African Violet: all the varieties, with their lovely colours, do very well in an enclosed atmosphere. On the opposite page we give you some ideas about what to choose and what plants look good together.

What container?

Almost any glass jar or container can be used, provided it is large enough for you to plant it comfortably and has a tightly fitting lid or stopper that you can remove easily. Carboys, wine demijohns, sweet jars, bulbous wine bottles — the possibilities are endless. You can buy specially made jars in garden centres, but it's more fun — and cheaper! — to experiment with other containers. You can often pick up lovely things in junk shops. Tinted glass looks pretty, but make sure it isn't *too* dark, or it will stop the light getting to your plants.

If you buy a bottle from a garden shop, it'll probably be ready to plant straightaway. But if you are using a container from any other source, do be sure that you clean it very thoroughly — it could have had something in it that might be damaging to your plants. Wash it with mild, soapy water and rinse it and, just to be on the safe side, sterilise it with a solution such as Milton.

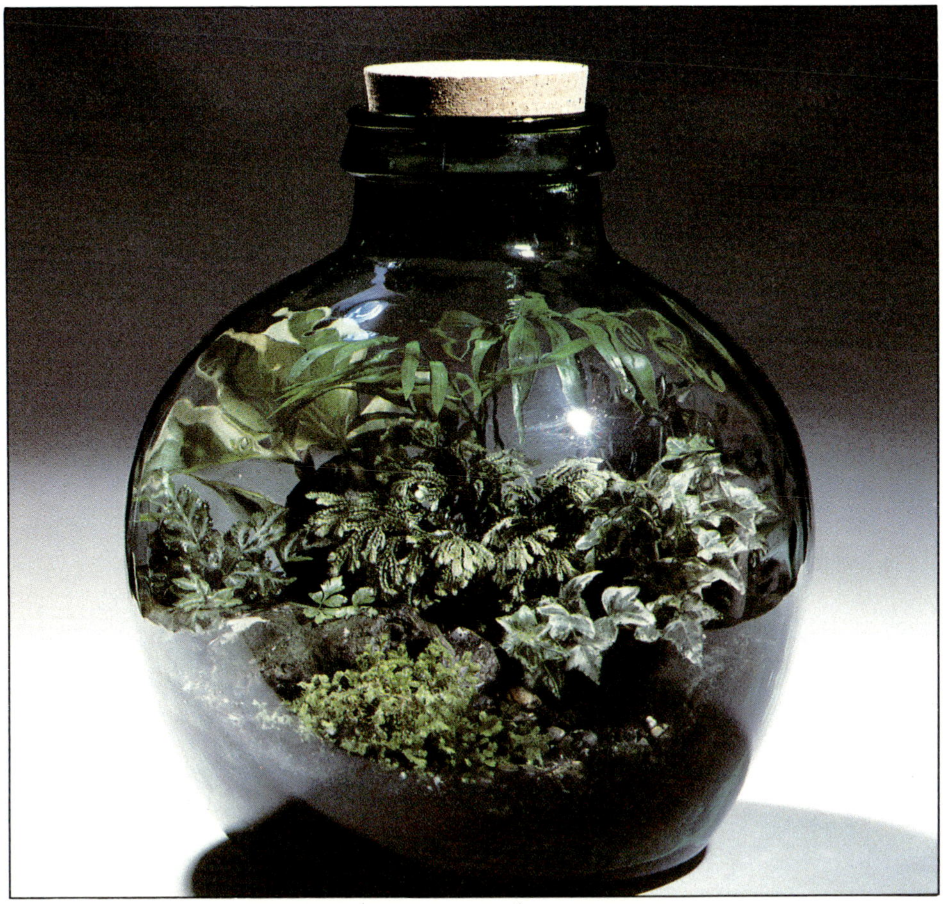

A variegated ivy, some creeping moss, a Silver Lace Fern and a palm provide a wide variety of textures.

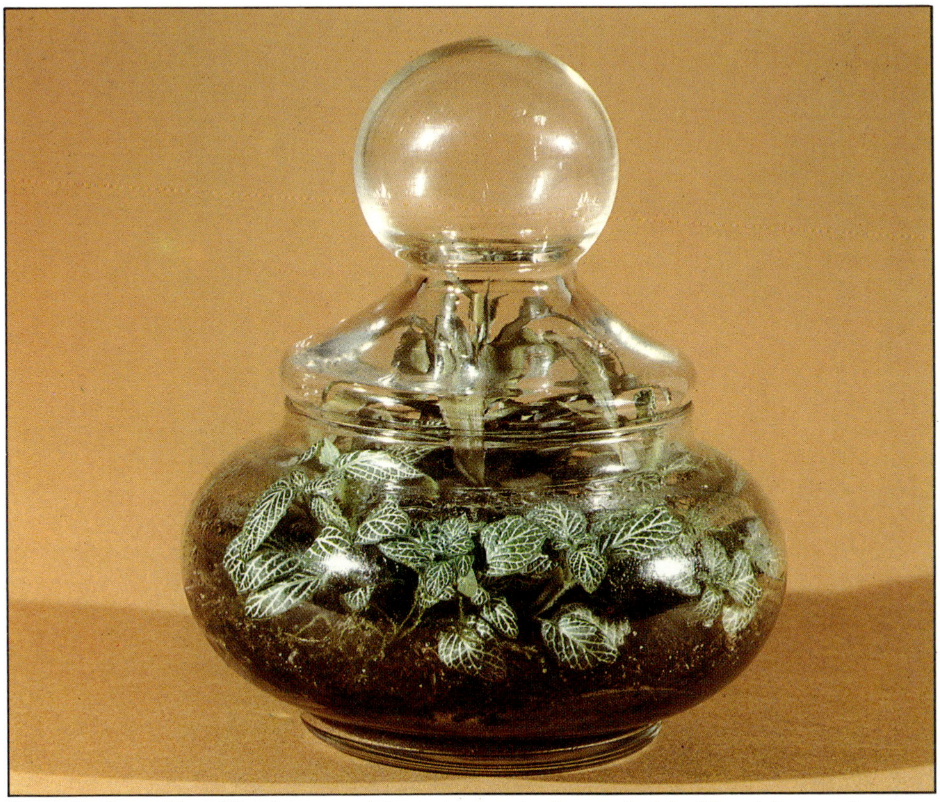

A pretty jar with a fittonia around the edge and a bromeliad to fill out the centre.

Bottle beauties

Acorus gramineus variegatus **Sweet flag**	Fan-shaped tufts of white-striped grassy leaves
Adiantum raddianum **Delta Maidenhair Fern**	Filmy pale green fronds on dark brown stems
Begonia rex	Leaves marked with red, green and russet
Calathea insignis **Rattlesnake Plant**	Leaves with reddish undersides and dark brown bands
Calathea makoyana **Peacock Plant**	Green and white herringbone-striped leaves
Calathea ornata	Leaves with narrow pink or ivory stripes
Calathea zebrina **Zebra Plant**	Dark stripes and a velvety surface
Cryptanthus **Starfish Plant**	Striped with white, brown or red
Cyperus alternifolius **Umbrella Plant**	Tiny umbrellas of slender leaves
Dracaena sanderiana **Ribbon Plant**	Vivid green leaves with white rims
Ficus pumila **Creeping Fig**	Small oval green leaves and wiry stems
Fittonia argyroneura **Snakeskin Plant**	Leaves intricately netted with white
Fittonia verschaffeltii **Mosaic Plant**	Leaves netted with red
Hedera helix **Glacier Ivy**	Creamy variegated leaves
Hedera helix **Little Eva Ivy**	Small leaves rimmed with cream
Hedera sagittaefolia **Needlepoint Ivy**	Leaves with a long pointed lobe
Maranta leuconeura **Prayer Plant**	Broad green leaves blotched with purple
Maranta tricolor **Herringbone Plant**	Red veins and a yellow midrib
Neanthe bella **Parlour Palm**	Elegant and tiny palm with arching stems
Pellaea rotundifolia **Button Fern**	Button-like leaves on slender stems
Pellionia daveauana	Tiny plant with brown-edged golden leaves
Pellionia pulchra	Green leaves with dark brown veins
Peperomia argyreia **Rugby Football Plant**	Heart-shaped leaves with green and silver stripes
Peperomia caperata **Emerald Ripple**	Quilted green leaves and whitish-green flowers
Pilea **Moon Valley**	Greenish-yellow leaves with black veins
Pilea cadieri **Aluminium Plant**	Quilted leaves patched with silver
Pilea involucrata **Friendship Plant**	Reddish leaves with dark veins
Saxifraga sarmentosa tricolor **Mother of Thousands**	Cream and green leaves edged with pink or red

Tools for the job

You'll need some rather unusual tools to plant a bottle garden, but don't worry — you don't need to buy them specially because they can be very easily made up from ordinary household and gardening things.

You'll need a few lengths of thin cane or some supporting stakes, long enough to reach comfortably to the bottom of the jar and leave you enough to hold on to. Tie to the end of three of them:

A a spoon.
B a kitchen fork.
C an empty cotton reel, flat end down.

These will be perfect for making holes for plants, and for loosening and firming the soil.

You'll also need:

D a small sharp knife or a razor blade on the end of a stick for removing dead leaves and pruning back growth.
E some tweezers to help position your plants, and you can make these by splitting the end of a cane.
F two sticks held together can serve as tongs.

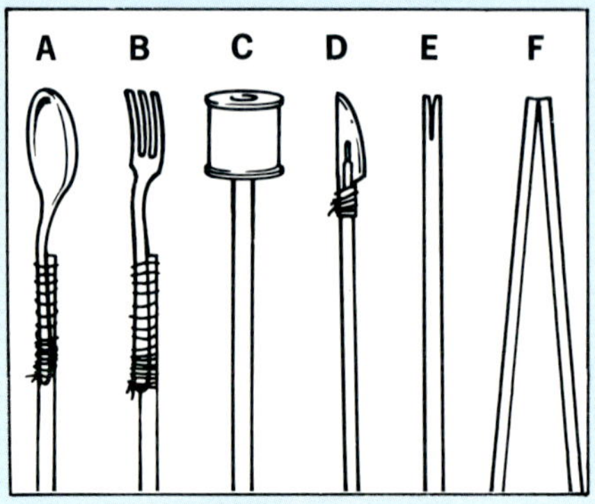

1 First funnel in a 2in (5cm) layer of gravel, to provide good drainage. Then add 3-4in (7-10cm) of potting compost.

2 Starting from the outside of the bottle, put your selected plants gently into prepared holes.

3 When you've positioned each plant, firm the soil around it gently using the cotton reel tied to a cane.

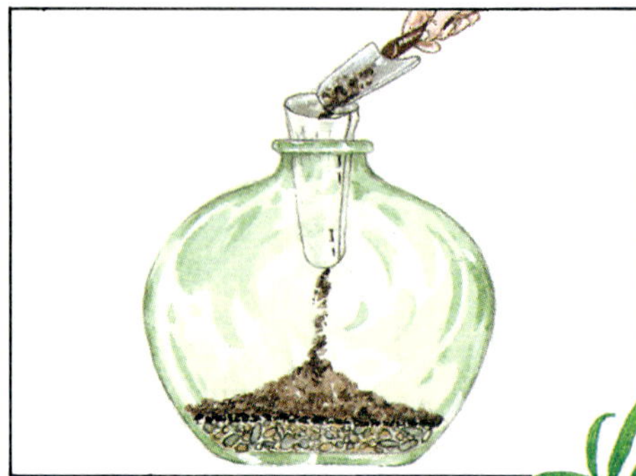

1

Preparing for planting

Because you don't want your bottle plants to grow too fast, the soil in your container must not be too rich. Also, to make sure you don't introduce any pests or diseases, buy the soil ingredients from a supplier who sells them in sealed plastic bags — they ought to be quite sterile. First of all, put in a 2in (5cm) layer of gravel, to provide good drainage. The best method is to pour it in through a funnel made from stiff paper or thin card, so that it goes neatly to the bottom of the jar and does not mess up the sides. Then add ½in (13mm) of charcoal to help keep the soil free from impurities — it will absorb the excess mineral salts and decaying plant matter that can build up in an enclosed atmosphere.

For compost, you could use John Innes No 1, Levingtons Multi-Purpose or Baby Bio Seed and Potting mixture. It's an excellent idea to add one part of Perlite to every two parts of compost — these granules of very light rock help the soil to drain well. You can buy all of these products easily in garden shops. When you've mixed up your compost, funnel it carefully into the jar to a depth of about 3-4in (7-10cm). If you like, you can then use the spoon and fork to make a few little 'hills' in the soil to add interest to the plants and help to set them off. It's a good idea also to bury in the soil a few tablets or spikes of solid fertiliser. This is a convenient way of releasing nourishment to the plants over the next few months.

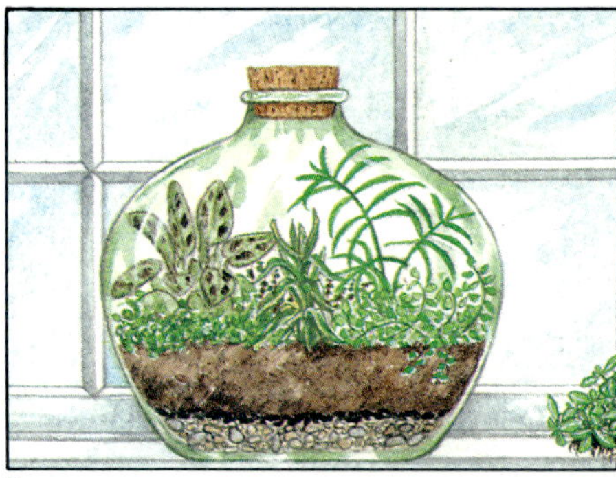

6

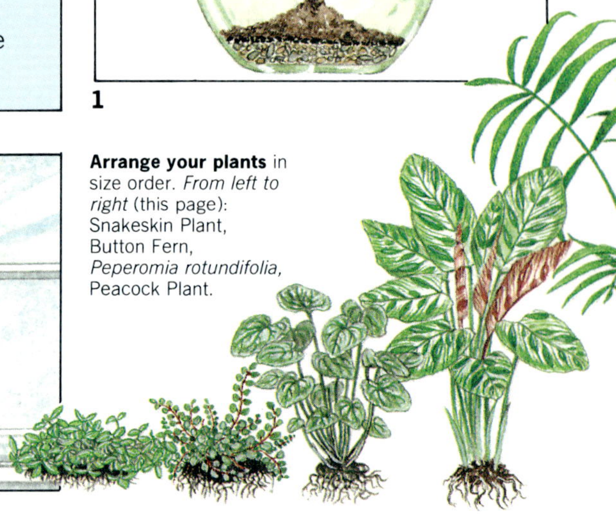

Arrange your plants in size order. *From left to right* (this page): Snakeskin Plant, Button Fern, *Peperomia rotundifolia*, Peacock Plant.

Planting the garden

After all the preparation, you're now ready for the exciting part! Lay out some sheets of newspaper on a table, and experiment with arranging the plants you've chosen. Aim to put taller plants in the middle where they'll have the most space above them; but otherwise just move them round until you're pleased with the effect.

When you've decided where they'll go, use the spoon to make the first planting hole. Always start with the plants on the outside of the jar; if you plant the middle first, you won't be able to reach the outside easily. Put the plant carefully into the cane tweezers (or between the tongs) and lower it into the hole and, with your other hand, pack the soil around the roots with the fork. When the plant feels firmly positioned, ease the tweezers away gently, and then press the soil down firmly around the plant with the cotton reel.

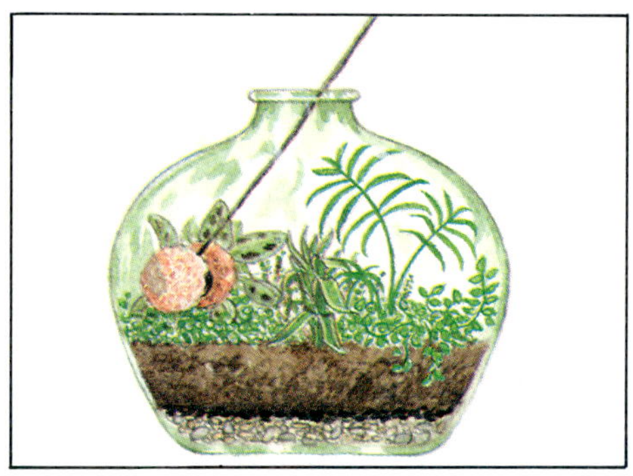

5

When all your plants are in, water them carefully. The best way is to let the water trickle slowly down the side of the jar and seep into the soil, so that it doesn't splash the plants with mud. Add just enough water for the surface of the soil to become dark — if you're in any doubt, go for too little water rather than too much. If there are soil particles or mud splashes on the inside of the jar,

4 When the bottle garden is full, water it carefully, directing the water down the inside of the glass.

5 Clean the inside of the glass of soil or water by wiping with a piece of sponge or cloth.

6 Put the stopper on your completed garden, and position the bottle where it will get lots of light.

Arrangements to try

There are dozens of exciting permutations when it comes to arranging plants in a bottle garden, and you can be as artistic as you like, provided you don't crowd the jar. Try and choose plants with different coloured leaves, so that they contrast with each other. You could have a Ribbon Plant as a centrepiece, set off by an equally tall Parlour Palm, the two of them contrasted with a selection of much smaller plants, such as Ivy (right). Or for smaller plants you could choose the golden-leaved *Pellionia daveauana*, a Starfish Plant and a Friendship Plant. Another pretty group of small plants would be the Aluminium Plant, the Mother of Thousands and the *Peperomia* Emerald Ripple.

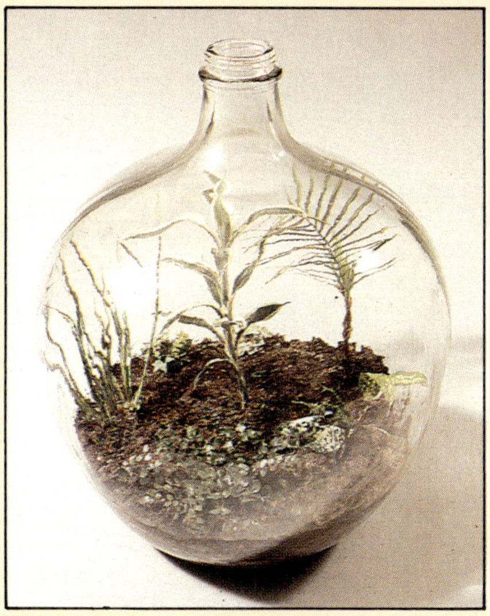

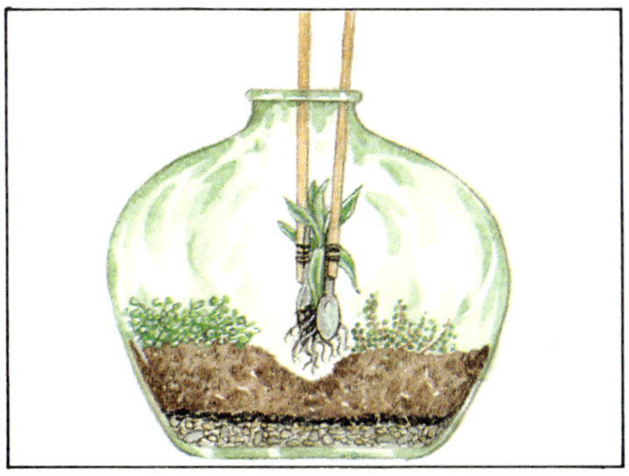

2

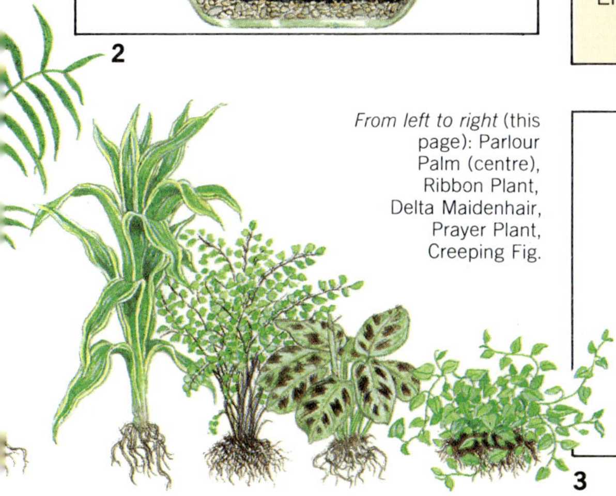

From left to right (this page): Parlour Palm (centre), Ribbon Plant, Delta Maidenhair, Prayer Plant, Creeping Fig.

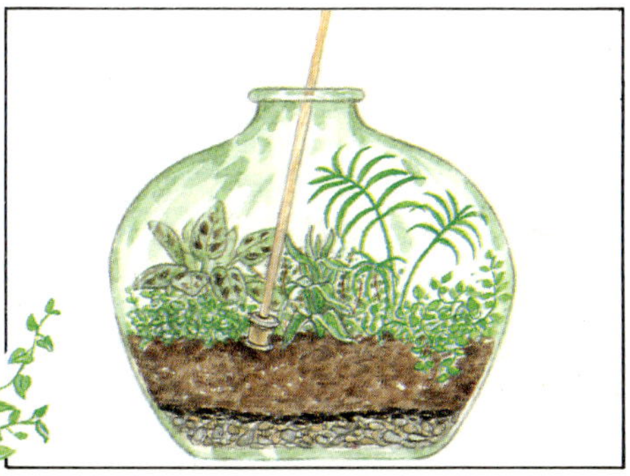

3

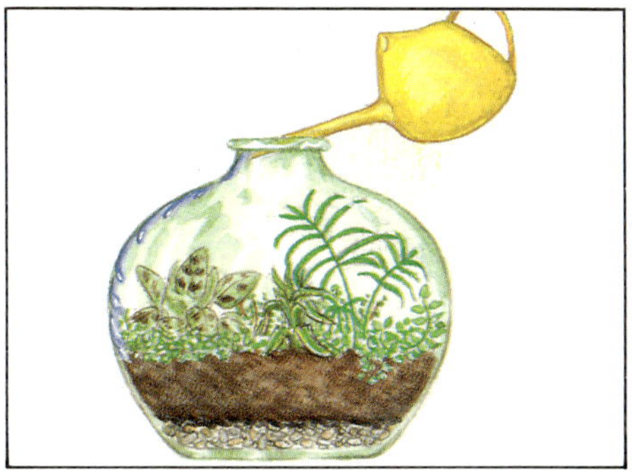

4

clean them off with a piece of sponge or damp cloth attached to a wire — a bent wire coathanger is perfect for the job. Apart from making your bottle garden look attractive, you should keep the insides clean so that water is not trapped by soil particles as it trickles down the sides of the jar into the compost. Now replace the stopper on your bottle and make sure it is a tight fit.

Caring for your bottle garden

Put your bottle garden somewhere where it will get lots of light, but not in direct sun — glass concentrates the sun's rays and the result could be scorched leaves inside the bottle. A north-facing windowsill is ideal. You may find that condensation forms on the inside of the bottle after a few days. This is nothing to worry about — just take off the lid or stopper for a few hours to let the compost dry out a little, then replace it.

Once a week or so, you should have a look at your bottle garden, to check whether it needs any attention. If you see any dead leaves or decaying matter, prune it away carefully. Also remove any leaves the moment you see them becoming discoloured — they'll attract disease spores if they are left to decay further and would eventually ruin the other plants in your arrangement. You may also need to cut away occasional shoots if a plant is growing very vigorously, in case it begins to take up too much room in the bottle.

If all goes well, you shouldn't need to do anything more — your plants will literally look after themselves. Just add a few more fertiliser tablets or spikes every few months to encourage healthy growth. If a disease or pest does manage to get into the garden, it should be quite simple to deal with. If it's a minor problem — such as greenfly, for example — spray a little insecticide into the bottle. But any infestation by mealy bug or red spider mite calls for more drastic action, and it's safer to deal with it outside the bottle. Repeated spraying of strong insecticide into an enclosed atmosphere may be too much for the plants, because it will remain in the atmosphere for a long time, unable to disperse.

Using your tongs, gently prise the affected plant out of the soil and remove it carefully from the bottle. Clean it and dip it in an insecticide solution containing malathion, and then return it to the garden. Repeat the process if necessary.

You'll probably find that your bottle plants don't grow so much in the winter, when light levels are low. This is perfectly normal, but there is a way round it. If you have a bottle with a wide enough neck, and can manage to get a lamp holder to fit it, you can shine a low wattage light bulb (say up to 60 watts) directly into the garden. This will help the plants to grow, as well as make the garden a very pretty feature.

Planning a miniature garden

Miniature gardens can be a lot of fun. Basically, the idea is to group plants in such a way as to create a suggestion of landscaping. This is what sets a miniature garden apart from any other arrangement of plants in a bowl.

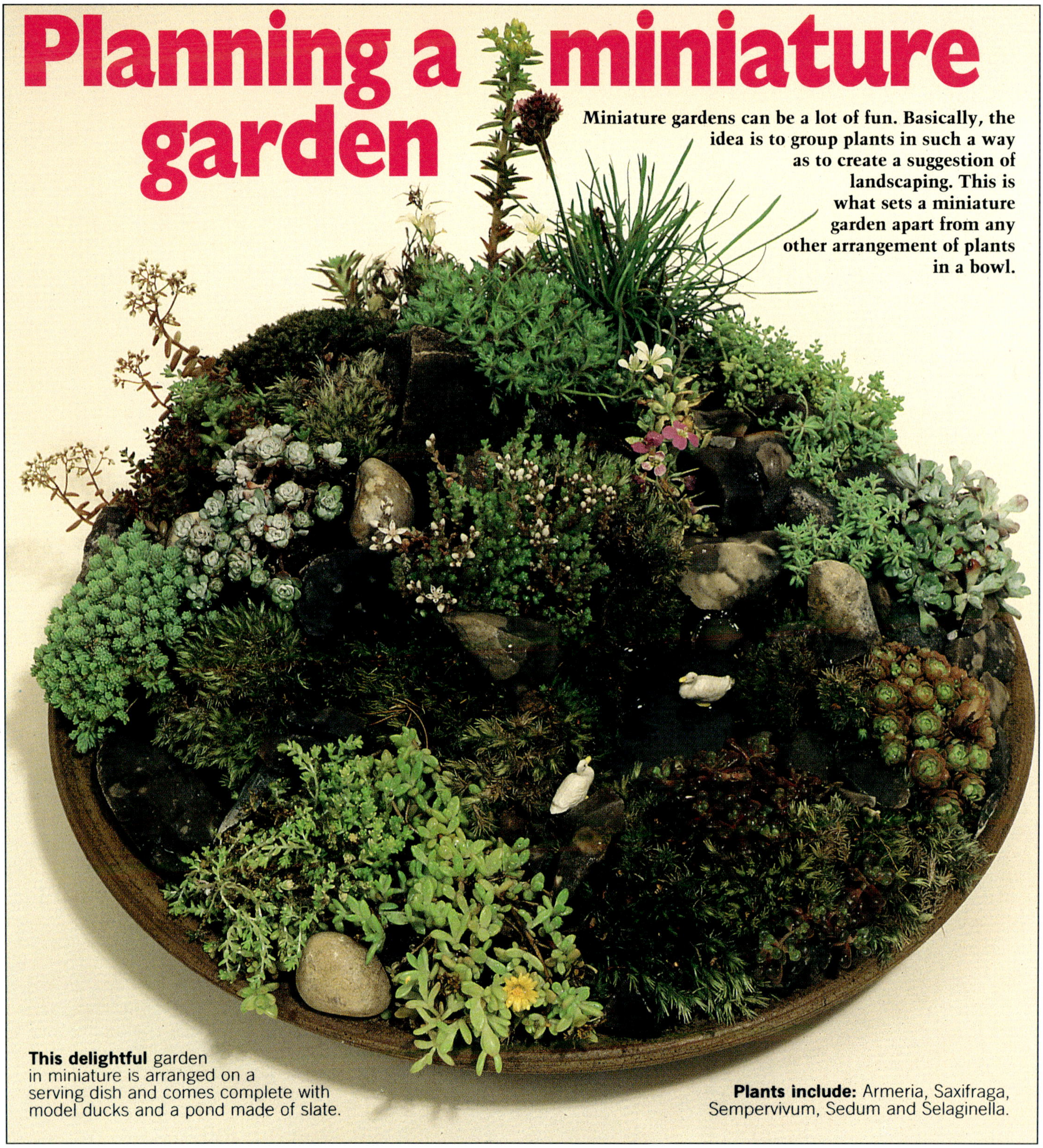

This delightful garden in miniature is arranged on a serving dish and comes complete with model ducks and a pond made of slate.

Plants include: Armeria, Saxifraga, Sempervivum, Sedum and Selaginella.

Properly done, a miniature garden is far more interesting to look at than a single plant, or even a group, because there is so much more detail to absorb. It can be as realistic — or otherwise — as you like, ranging from a miniaturised replica of your garden outside to something one step removed from a Japanese flower arrangement. As you might expect, there is a definite technique for creating a successful miniature garden. And, in just the same way as full-sized landscape gardening, it all starts with careful planning.

First things first

Designing and planning the miniature garden begins by looking carefully at the place in which the finished garden is to go. It is most important to get the relationship between the garden and its surroundings right from the start.

Plants

Choose these with care. Plants should remain small and keep their shape well. Remember to decide on your theme before you start buying new plants, and choose only those which contribute to it.

Go for varieties which replicate the shapes of larger, outdoor plants if you want a realistic miniature garden, or choose ones that represent scaled-down tropical landscape gardens, alpine gardens, or even stylised Japanese gardens.

SMALL AND SLOW

Dwarf Pomegranate *(Punica granatum nana)*
Earth Star (Cryptanthus)
Episcia
Lachenalia
Palm seedlings
Snakeskin Plant *(Fittonia argyroneura nana)*
Look out too for bonsai trained versions of shrubby houseplants or trees.

FERNS

Button Fern *(Pellaea rotundifolia)*
Dwarf Maidenhair *(Adiantum pedatum subpumilum)*
Rose Maidenhair *(A. hispidulum)*

MINIATURE IVIES

Hedera helix 'Ambrosia' — small crimped leaves, variegated
H. helix 'Arran' — mini version of plain green wild Ivy
H. helix 'Aurea' — variegated, lime green leaves marked with dark green splashes
H. helix 'Jubilee' — notable dense variety with tiny vareigated leaves
H. helix 'Spetchley' — stiff upright stems, densely packed with tiny leaves

PLANTS MIMICKING SCALED-DOWN OUTDOOR PLANTS

SHRUBBY
Box *(Buxus sempervirens)* — can be clipped into miniature topiary shapes
Bead Plant (Nertera depressa) low hummocks covered with small red berries
Euonymus
Miniature Rose
Myrtle *(Myrtus communis compacta)* — can be clipped and trained into shape
Resurrection Plant *(Selaginella lepidophylla)*

SPIKY
Mondo Grass *(Ophiopogon japonicus)*
Sweet Flag *(Acorus gramineus)* 'Variegatus'

CREEPING
Creeping Jenny *(Pilea depressa)*
Indian Strawberry *(Duchesnea indica)*

ALPINE AND ROCK PLANTS

These are best grown in a sunny porch before being brought into a cool room for flowering, and then returned outdoors after flowering.
Armeria caespitosa — a mini hillock-forming Thrift, pink flowers
Arenaria purpurascens — mat forming, pink flowers
Cobweb Houseleek *(Sempervivum arachnoideum)*
Dwarf Lavender *(Lavandula spica* 'Dwarf Munstead')
Lewisia cotyledon — rosette-shaped plant, short spikes and stripy pink flowers in summer
Raoulia australis — spreading yellow carpet
Saxifraga aizoon — silvery mounds, pink flowers in spring
S. oppositifolia — bright green mats, purple flowers in spring
Shooting Stars *(Dodecatheon dentatum)*

Spend a few moments really studying the place you have chosen — its shape, whether or not it is enclosed, and so on. Make a mental note of the maximum height the garden can go up to, its width, the background against which the garden will be seen and, most important of all, whether it will be viewed from only one side or all round.

Containers

Now turn your attention to the choice of container. This is the most important single feature of a miniature garden, because it acts as a link, pulling together all the various elements that go to make up the garden. The style of the container sets the scene for the garden more than anything else. Terracotta, glazed porcelain and stoneware are all ideal materials for your container, though good quality plastics may also be used. Neutral colours such as beige, earthy greens and browns look most natural, though there is, of course, no reason why you shouldn't choose another colour if it happens to tone in with your room's colour scheme. Bright colours, though, do not somehow look quite right in the context of a miniature garden. Patterned containers are also difficult to work with.

Containers for miniature gardens need to be wide and relatively shallow. And, since the garden will probably be stood on a polished surface, you'll need a container without any drainage holes in the bottom. You may find something suitable at a garden centre, but the best choice is often found in a florist's shop specialising in unusual vases — the shallow kind used for Japanese flower arrangements is ideal.

Ornaments and other 'props'

This is an area where you are allowed a certain amount of artistic licence. Try to choose tasteful items that pursue the theme of your garden, while remaining on the same scale. The sort of ornaments you might like to use include small figurines, miniature pagodas, models or abstract pieces.

Cut flowers

Another useful way of adding to the illusion of a real-life garden is to use cut flowers or foliage. Then, when you are designing the layout, leave a space for a small water container (such as the containers that rolls of film come in), which should be sunk into the compost. This can then be used for an ever-changing selection of fresh seasonal materials.

Soil and surface cover

Because your container has no drainage holes you'll need to provide an adequate drainage layer and ensure that the soil doesn't go sour. A ½in (13mm) layer of gravel gives adequate drainage, followed by an equal layer of lightly broken charcoal and finally weak potting compost.

Finally, the finishing touch that completes any miniature garden is its surface cover. Like the container, this acts as a link, pulling plants and props together, so that they no longer look like a lot of separate items. It also provides a common background against which everything in the garden can then be seen.

Choose a background appropriate to the type of garden you are making. For example, alpine plants suit a fine gritty background, whereas a tropical garden looks better against a mossy background. And if you are trying to recreate a very realistic garden, use a bit of both to suggest lawns and pathways. Gravel surfaces are in fact best suggested not by gravel itself, but by a scaled-down alternative — sharp sand or the sort of fine grit often sold for cacti. Both are available from garden centres.

Mossy surfaces are best achieved using Helxine or one of the creeping Selaginellas such as *S.denticulata*, which is green, or *S.d. aurea*, which is gold. Alternatively, for a hummocky surface, try *S.krausseana brownii*, which forms bright green mossy mounds, about 4in (10cm) high. Or for a pale, greeny-blue mossy finish, use dried Reindeer Moss, which is available from florists.

The art of bonsai

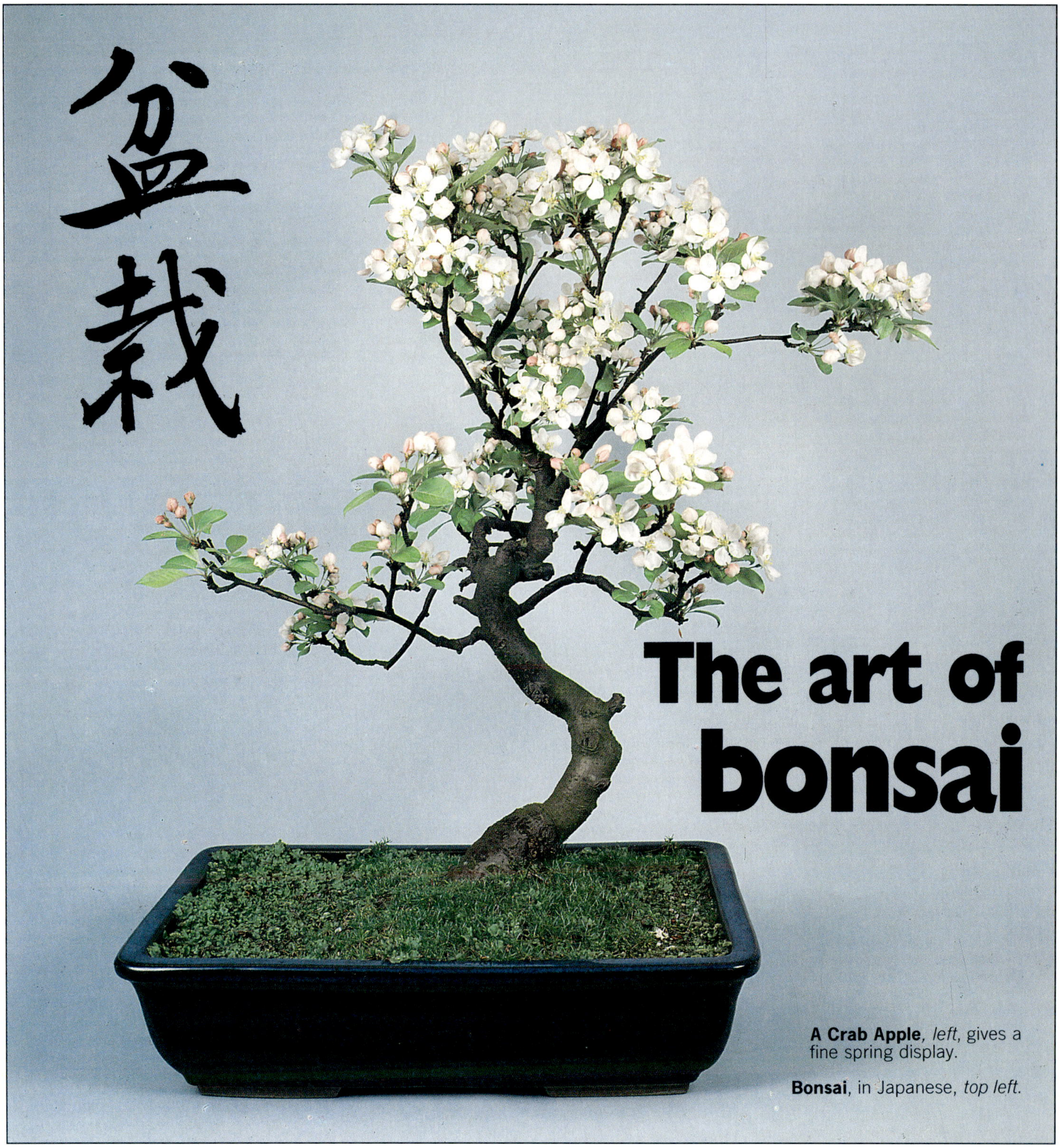

A Crab Apple, *left*, gives a fine spring display.

Bonsai, in Japanese, *top left*.

The ancient art of growing trees and shrubs in miniature is currently enjoying a great increase in popularity. Bonsai — which has been practised for hundreds of years in China and Japan — actually means 'plant in a container', and that is exactly what these fascinating 'doll's house' trees are.

It isn't known for certain how bonsai first originated. It could have been accidental. Deprived of good soil and nutrients, a tree will grow small and stunted — you may have seen one yourself like this growing on a mountainside, for example. If such a tree were brought indoors in a container as a decoration, looked after and given nutrition, it would then start to grow to its normal size, and would need drastic pruning of both roots and shoots to keep it small. What is certain is that the art of miniaturising plants in this way has been known in China and Japan for at least six hundred years.

Many kinds of tree and shrub lend themselves to this treatment. Majestic deciduous trees such as Maple (Acer) and Beech *(Fagus sylvatica)* are chosen for their shape, colour and the variety they afford as they pass through the seasons, with spring blossom, summer fruits and autumn leaf fall. Evergreens such as Juniper (Juniperus) and Japanese Cedar *(Cryptomeria japonica)* are ideal subjects, while shrubs such as Azalea, Cotoneaster and Pyracantha are interesting not only on account of their leaf form but because they flower. The chart describes some more varieties.

You can keep bonsai trees successfully in your home provided you remember a few very important rules. The first one is that most bonsai are not genuine houseplants. They love fresh air, and will not survive if kept indoors all the time. Unless they are tender species which have been specially raised as indoor plants, you should keep them in a sheltered garden, or on a balcony, as a permanent home and just bring them indoors from time to time for short periods as a splendid and unusual decorative feature. If you keep several bonsai trees, you should be able to have one on a table indoors most of the year by moving them around — but it's not a good idea to leave any one specimen indoors for more than a few days at a time. Lack of fresh air and light will make its leaves pale and straggly.

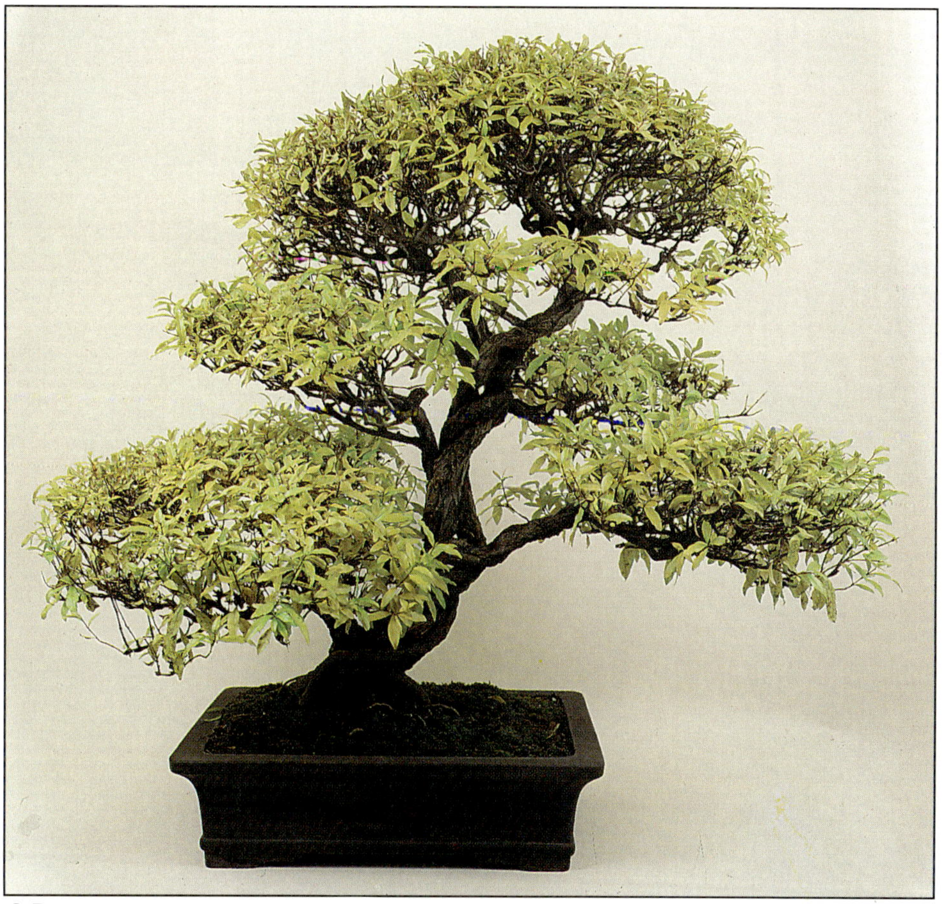

A Pomegranate is a good choice for growing indoors.

Buying a bonsai

The best thing to do if you are a beginner with bonsai is to buy a good, healthy specimen from a reliable garden centre or specialist. It may be a genuine Japanese specimen — grown in Japan and exported — or one grown in this country. Either way, it will be much more expensive even than an exotic houseplant — in Japan bonsai are regarded as heirlooms! But the expense will be worth it: if you take proper care of your tree it should live for more than a hundred years.

When you buy a bonsai tree, you should first establish that it is genuine — there are dwarf conifers now available which, at three to five years old, can look confusingly like bonsai of about ten years old. Look out for a good shape, with no signs of damage, pests or disease. There should be no evidence of crude cutting back of branches, leaves should be glossy and green and any flower or fruit buds should look plump and firm. The older the tree, the better established it is — look out for moss on the trunk which is a sign of age.

Traditional bonsai styles

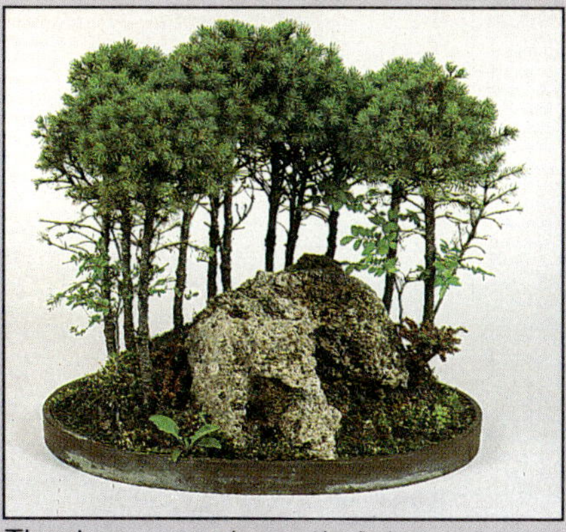

The Japanese shape their bonsai trees in certain specific styles. These are the most common:

Chokkan: upright.

Group plantings: arranged with the tallest trees at the front to create a perspective that suggests a forest grove. (See Spruce and Elm forest, *left.*)

Hankan: gnarled and growing in one direction, to suggest a tree on a windswept cliff.

Ishi-tsuki: tree growing out of a stone, as may be seen on a cliff or mountain.

Kengai: cascade, grown on a tall stand and trained to grow downwards.

Shakan: slanting trunk, or semi-cascade.

Day-to-day care

Bonsai trees should be grown outside most of the time. Choose a semi-shaded position in summer, and protect them from hard frost in the winter by moving them to a shed or frost-free, but cool, place indoors — this is particularly important for citrus trees. Bonsai are especially vulnerable to sudden changes of temperature, so don't move them from a cold outdoor position straight to a centrally heated room in winter.

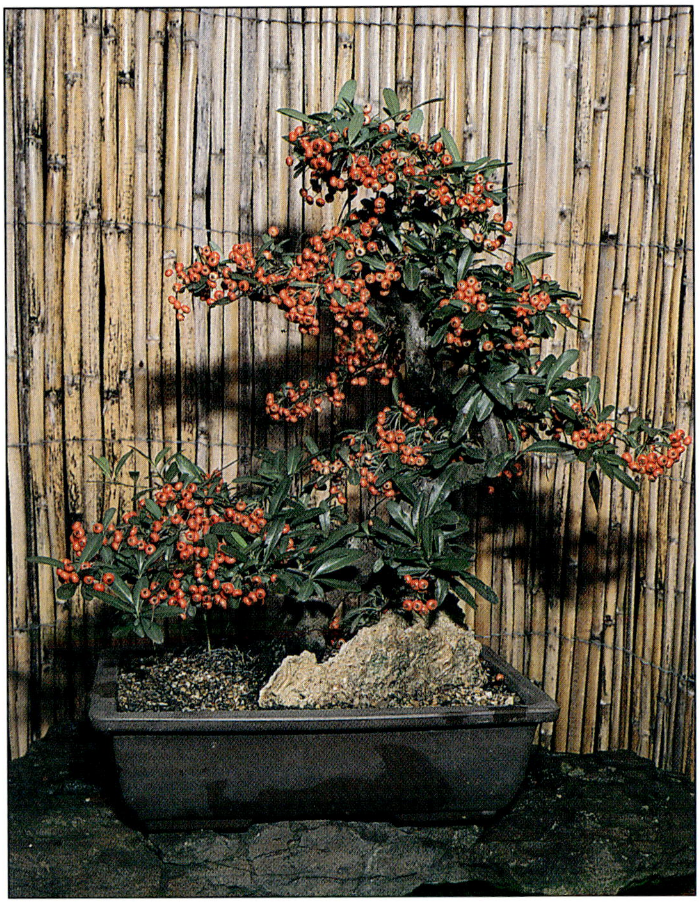

The fruits of *Cotoneaster horizontalis* last for several months.

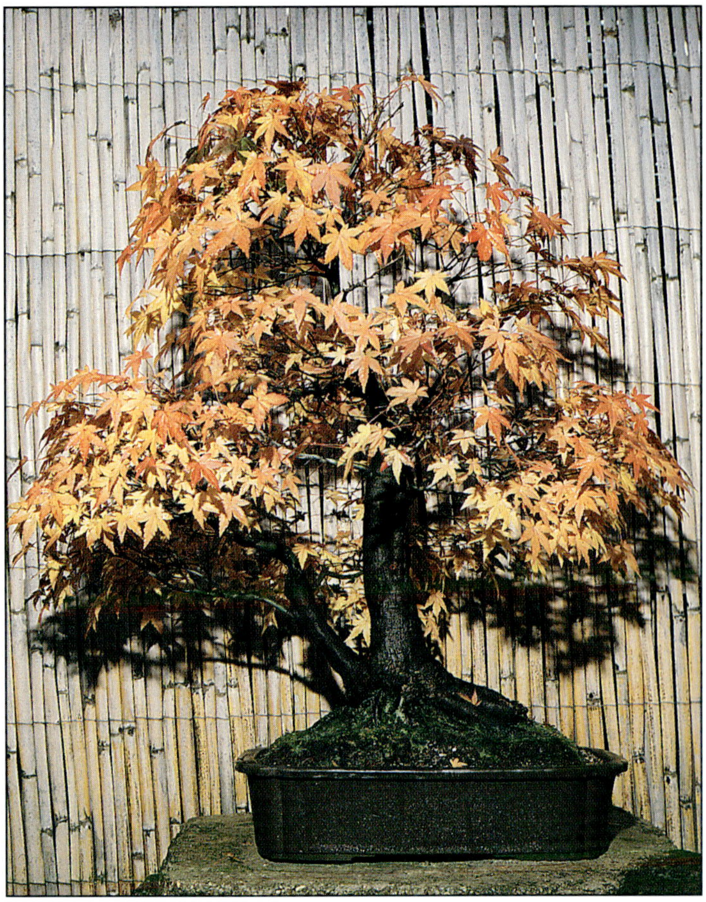

A Japanese Maple *(Acer palmatum)* about 80 years old.

Transfer them in stages through several positions, each one slightly warmer than before, and do the same in reverse when returning them outside.

While they're indoors, they should be given a fairly cool position, free from draughts and with as much natural light as possible. Don't put them in front of a south-facing window, as the direct sun could scorch the leaves.

Water your trees regularly — the compost must never be allowed to dry out completely. Rainfall will usually be sufficient for most of the year while they are outdoors. In summer, and during their stay indoors, water them every few days and spray them with soft water several times a day to reduce the loss of moisture from the leaves. Rainwater is ideal, but if you use tapwater, let it stand for a day first to get rid of toxic gases.

During the growing season in spring and summer it is important to provide the tree with nutrients. Use a liquid fertiliser every two to three weeks, applying it either with the water, or when the plant's roots are well moistened (giving fertiliser when the roots are dry can scorch them). The fertiliser should be a standard one, with equal proportions of nitrogen, phosphorus and potassium. Don't feed the trees after the end of the summer or during the winter.

Potting on

Don't be frightened at the idea of repotting a bonsai tree — it's just the same as with any houseplant. You'll need to repot your tree every one to two years while it is up to ten years old; thereafter repot anything between two and ten years, depending on how fast it is growing. If you don't repot it regularly, the roots will gradually fill the pot and push out all the compost.

With bonsai, there is another reason to repot: it gives you the opportunity to prune the roots, which is necessary to keep the plant small. You may find that some years you don't need to put the tree in a bigger pot, but that after pruning you can replace it in the same one.

The time to repot is in very early spring, before the plant starts into new growth — don't ever repot a plant while it is actively growing because the shock could severely damage or even kill it. Remove the plant from the pot, carefully tease open the root ball and spread the roots out. Using a sharp, sterilised pair of scissors or secateurs, trim off up to a third of the roots.

Prepare the new pot with a few pieces of broken earthenware in the bottom to cover the drainage holes. Then add a sprinkling of sharp horticultural grit to help drainage. Don't be tempted to use garden soil for your bonsai, even though it is a tree. Its roots are contained in an unnaturally small space and it must have a balanced compost to grow in. Partly fill the new pot with John Innes No 2, and put the trimmed plant in, firming it gently with more compost round the roots. Water in thoroughly and leave it to continue growing.

Growing your own

If you want the challenge — and have a lot of patience! — you can try growing your own bonsai from seeds or from cuttings; good indoor specimens can be raised from fresh olive, pomegranate or date pips. You will need to shape and control the growth of the tree's branches — an art calling for some skill, which takes a good many years to achieve.

Pots for bonsai

Containers for bonsai specimens must be very carefully chosen from a point of quality, shape and size. Because they'll spend most of the year outdoors, they must be able to withstand rain and a degree of frost. This means, in practice, that they are usually made of very good quality pottery, which has been highly fired to make it strong. They should be shallow — as little as 1½in (3.75cm) in depth — in order to keep the root growth down, and must have good drainage holes.

Traditionally, Japanese containers are oval or rectangular, and often very old. They are without any ornamentation, and come in beautiful muted colours — blues, greys, browns, greens and cream. Artistically, they are like frames to pictures — the container should enhance the single tree or group, but not distract attention away from it.

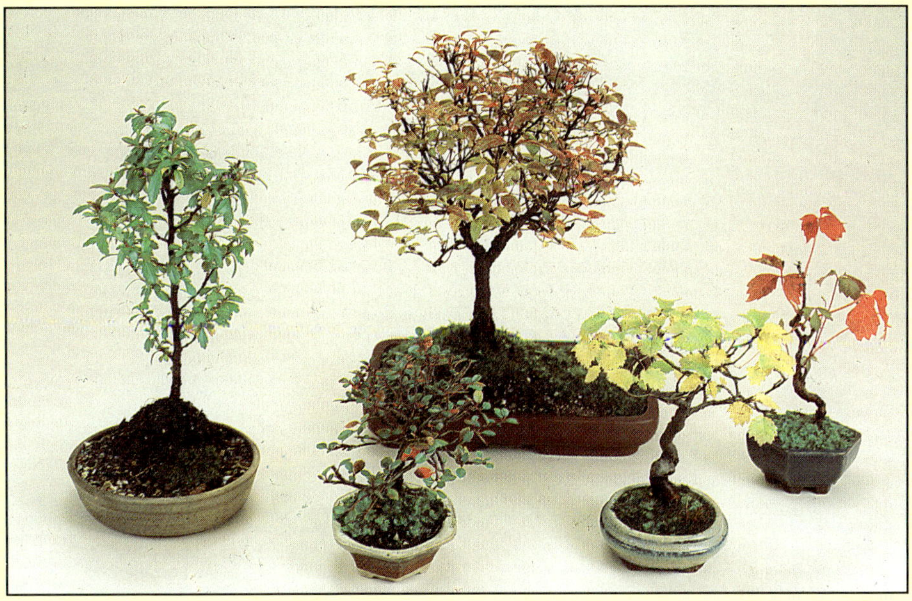

Keeping bonsai in shape

Even with a ready-grown bonsai tree, you'll have to prune it regularly to keep its growth compact and its shape neat and attractive.

Pruning of the tree above the soil is done in early spring, just before the plant starts into new growth — it's best to do this at the same time as you prune the roots. It involves removing any branches or stems that look as though they may overcrowd the plant with foliage, that are beginning to grow in completely the wrong direction or are crossing each other, or that are growing too low down the main trunk. Also any branch that shows signs of disease or damage should be removed.

Using sharp, sterilised secateurs, cut back stems close to the main branch, or to the nearest bud, so that as little as possible of a stump remains. As well as keeping the plant looking attractive, this will help the wound to heal rapidly. It is traditional to cut off alternate branches from the main stem to make the plant well balanced in growth. Once the main shape is assured, you'll just need to prune the tree once a year to keep it nicely shaped.

With deciduous trees, such as Maple, or very young pine trees, the tips of the growing shoots should also be pinched out from time to time to encourage bushy, dense growth. And it's a good idea to remove some whole new leaves in early summer — the tree will then put out more leaves, but they will be finer and smaller. Do this only with the larger-leaved trees or it will not have the right effect.

With flowering trees, such as those which are in the Prunus group (peach, plum, almond and cherry), you should prune back about two-thirds of the branches after they have finished flowering.

With younger specimens, experts twist wire round the branches and bend them to make them grow in the right direction; this is a skilled job and part of the bonsai art. Mature trees will have already been trained to shape and you should only need to prune the top growth and roots. This will keep them looking beautiful and growing healthily for many years.

Varieties to choose

Deciduous trees	Evergreen trees	Flowering and/or fruiting shrubs and trees	
Beech *(Fagus sylvatica)* Oval, wavy-edged leaves with round clusters of green flowers in spring.	**Fir** (Abies) Pyramid-shaped with glossy dark green needles.	**Almond, Cherry, Peach** and **Plum** (Prunus) Lovely blossoms in spring and miniature fruit in season. Deciduous.	**Herringbone Cotoneaster** *(Cotoneaster horizontalis)* Herringbone-shaped leaves and scarlet berries. Deciduous.
Elm (Ulmus) Leaves turn golden in autumn.	**Japanese Cedar** *(Cryptomeria japonica)* Delicate bright green leaves turn crimson in winter.	**Azalea** *(Rhododendron lateritium)* An evergreen with dark pink flowers in June.	**Pomegranate** *(Punica granatum nana)* Vivid orange flowers in May/June, followed by fruit. Semi-evergreen indoors.
Maidenhair *(Gingko biloba)* Attractive foliage turns yellow in autumn.	**Juniper** (Juniperus) Pyramid- or bush-shaped with narrow needles.	**Crab Apple** (Malus) Rose-pink or white blossom in spring, fruit in autumn.	**Winter Jasmine** *(Jasminum nudiflorum)* Bright yellow flowers between November and March. Deciduous.
Maple (Acer) Red-veined leaves turn crimson in autumn.	**Pine** (Pinus) Dark green needles and erect cones.	**Firethorn** (Pyracantha) White blossom and yellow, orange or scarlet berries most of the year. Evergreen.	
Oak (Quercus) Rather rare as bonsai, because leaves stay large.	**Spruce** (Picea) Pyramid-shaped with hanging cones.		

Growing cacti

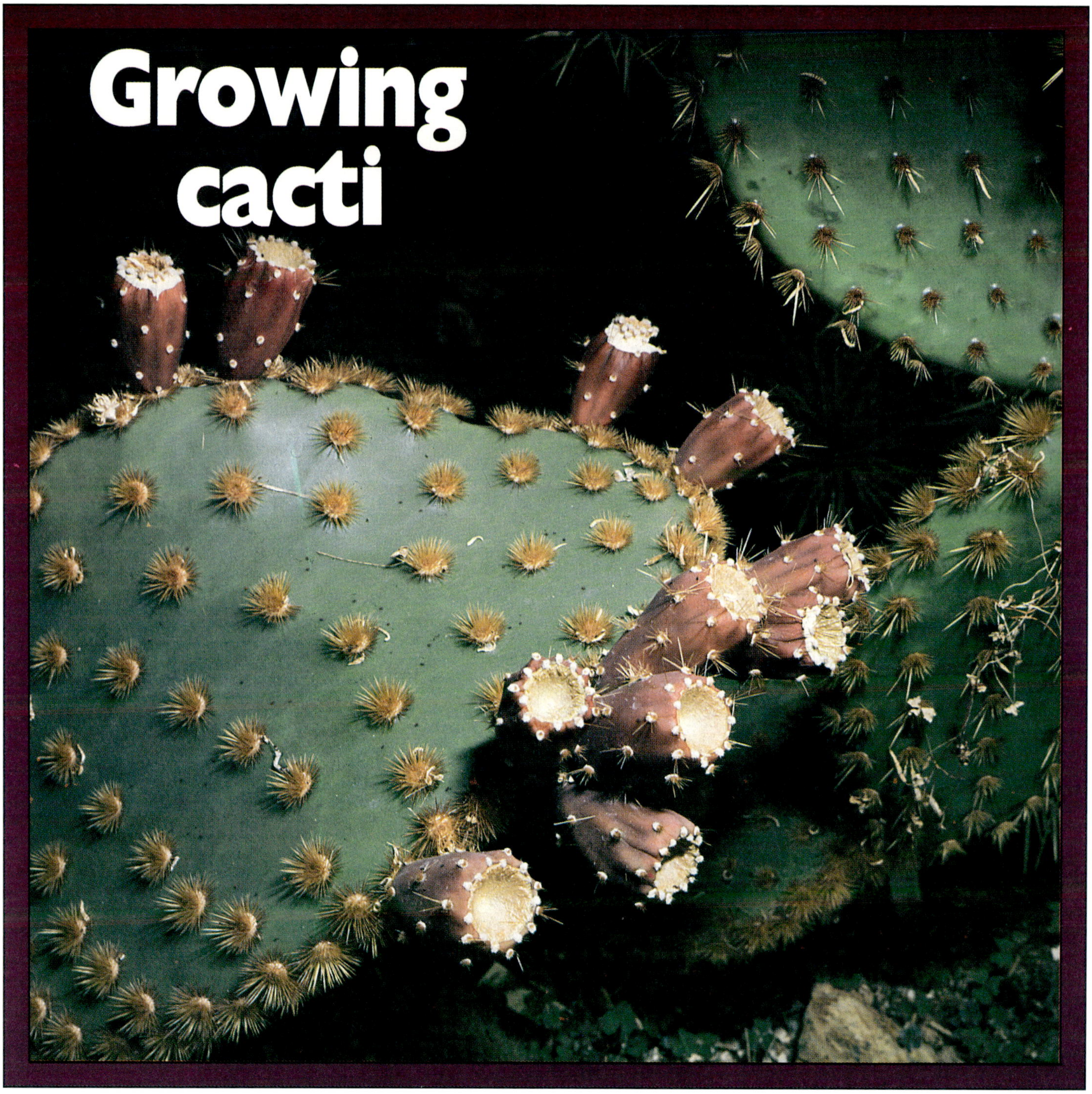

Cacti are among the easiest of houseplants to keep, and among the most rewarding. They come in amazing and bizarre forms — thin columns covered in silky hair, barrel shapes studded with spines, fleshy rosettes and starry shapes. They are always full of interest, and their flowers can be truly breathtaking.

It is a popular idea that cacti thrive if they are neglected — this isn't strictly true! Like all plants, they'll do best if they're looked after properly, but equally they're tough enough to survive being forgotten occasionally. Most of them can tolerate long periods without water or fertiliser, and then, perhaps, repay us with a dazzling display of brilliant, brightly-coloured blooms.

Two kinds of cacti

Cacti belong to a group of plants called succulents. Their main characteristic is that they have managed to adapt to very harsh conditions that would kill other plants; they can withstand extremes of temperature, for example, and go for long periods without water. Cacti have a structure in their leaves, stems or roots which stores water, so that in drought conditions (or if you forget to water them!) they have a source of nourishment to draw on.

Opuntia aciculata bears purple seed pods on flattened leaves.

Desert cacti (easily raised from seed)

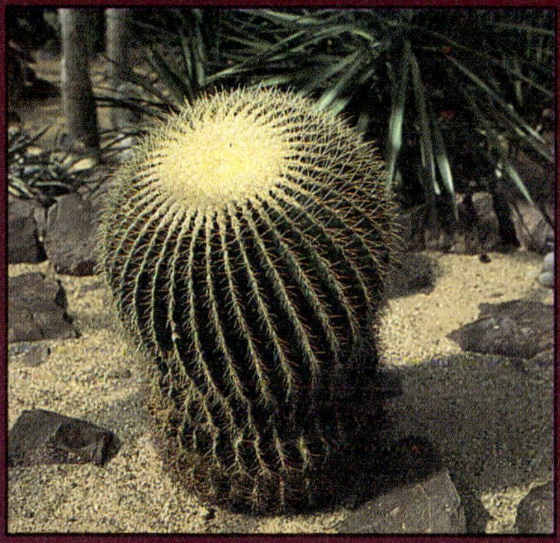

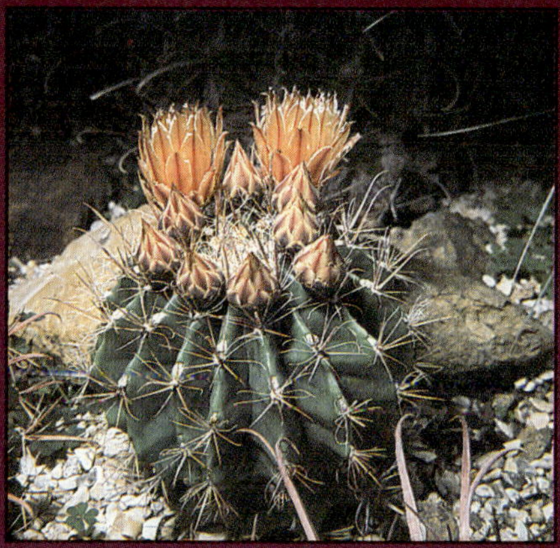

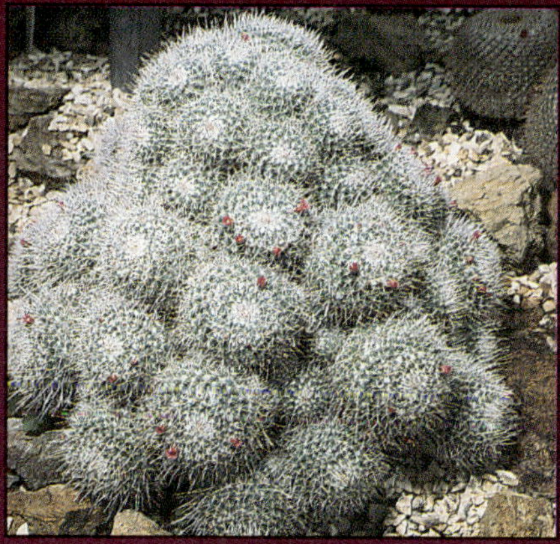

Acanthocalycium
Globe-shaped flowers ranging from white to pink and violet

Ariocarpus
Gnarled rosette shape with pink flowers

Azurocereus hertlinglianus
Unusual sky-blue stems with branches

Cephalocereus senilis **Old Man Cactus**
Beautiful silky-bearded column

Cleistocactus pallidus
Thin columns with yellow flowers

Blossfeldia campaniflora
Globe-shaped with starry yellow flowers

Echinocactus grusonii **Barrel Cactus, *above left***
Enormous globes up to 2ft (0.6m) across with yellow spines

Ferocactus, above: F.townsendianus
Globe-shaped family with hooked spines and red, yellow or orange flowers

Gymnocalycium bruchii
Globe-shaped with shell-pink flowers

Lobivia backbergii
Columnar with ribbed stems and crimson flowers

Lophophora williamsii
Globe-shaped with no spines; blue-green with light pink flowers

Mammillaria **Pincushion Cactus, *above***
Vast family, globe-shaped with pink flowers

Opuntia
Large family, most with flattened, branching leaf pads

Parodia sanguiniflora **Tom Thumb Cactus**
Globe-shaped with hooked red spines and red flowers

Rebutia miniscula **Mexican Sunball Cactus**
Globe-shaped with flowers in a vast range of colours from scarlet through gold to white

Turbinicarpus **Hatchet Cactus**
Distinctive with a ruff of white spines and semi-double cream, pink or magenta flowers

What makes cacti different from other succulents is that their spines and flowers grow from a round or elongated 'cushion' of hairs called an areole. Almost all cacti come originally from the Americas, where they exist in two habitats — deserts and rain forests.

- **Desert cacti** have adapted to growing under an arid, burning sun during the day, and surviving nights that are freezing cold and heavy with dew. The Pincushion *(Mammillaria)* and Bunny Ears *(Opuntia)* are examples — it goes without saying what these look like! Most desert cacti are globe-shaped or cylindrical and have masses of prickles or hooked spines — these are in fact leaves that have adapted to the dry conditions by becoming very thin and hard so that the minimum amount of water is lost from them.
- **Forest cacti** (sometimes called jungle cacti) thrive in completely the opposite extreme, in the rich leaf debris found in the rain forests of tropical America. They have a flatter shape than desert cacti and some of them trail. Christmas Cactus *(Schlumbergera truncata)* and Easter Cactus *(Rhipsalidopsis gaertneri)* are popular types that will do well in the home — their names come from their traditional flowering times, but as houseplants they'll flower any time in spring.

The real king of the forest cacti is undoubtedly the Orchid Cactus *(Epiphyllum)*. A dull plant out of flower, it is a thing of wonder when it blooms, treating you to a marvellous display of brightly coloured, cup-shaped blooms, up to a dozen at a time, each of them as much as 6in (15cm) across. Hybrids are available in a range of colours; the white ones have a ravishing scent.

Find the best conditions

Not surprisingly, given their different habitats, desert and forest cacti require rather different treatment if they are to do well as houseplants. To put it simply, you must aim to copy their natural conditions as closely as possible.

- **Desert cacti** are happiest in full sunlight; a brightly lit, south-facing windowsill is ideal, but they can face north or east, too, provided you feed them with a fertiliser high in potash — such as Phostrogen, Cactigrow or any fertiliser sold for tomatoes — to compensate for the lack of light. If you have double-glazing, you may find that a cactus in a sunny position needs a little shade in high summer, since the sun's rays may be too concentrated by the double thickness of glass.

Most desert cacti enjoy temperatures of 50-55°F (10-13°C) from autumn through to spring, but they can tolerate dropping down to 45°F (7°C). But two types — Old Man Cactus *(Cephalocereus senilis)* and Peruvian Old Man Cactus *(Espostoa lanata)* — like it warmer, and are best kept at around 60°F (15°C). If the night threatens to be particularly cold, you should move your cacti away from the windowsill.

Water cacti only when the surface of the soil is crumbly and dry, and the pot feels light when you pick it up. This is likely to be about once a week in spring and summer, and once a month in winter (when they are not growing actively), but if you have central heating, winter watering may need to be a little oftener.

Desert cacti hate stuffy conditions. Try and give them plenty of fresh air in summer by putting them near an open window on a fine day. But, like all plants, they don't like draughts, so try to avoid putting them in the path of a concentrated blast of cold air — such as you might get from a badly fitting window or an open door.

Pests and diseases

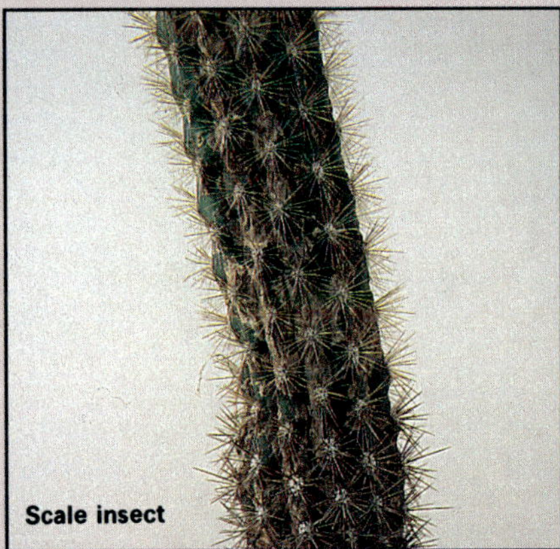

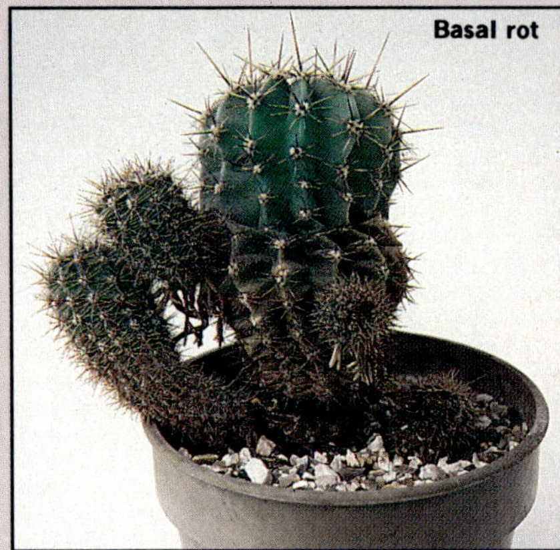

On the whole, Cacti are very easy to keep. But there are a few problems that might cause trouble.

- **Mealy bugs** can be very troublesome if your Cactus gets them. Watch out for the sticky, whitish blobs that look like cotton wool — these are tiny insects that live on the sap of your plant and stop it from growing properly. You should wipe the bugs off with a piece of cotton wool dipped in an insecticide containing malathion or dimethoate.
- **Red spider mite** is a minute pest that also distorts growth; it lives in patches of whitish webbing and discolours your Cactus, turning it a bronze colour. Red spider mite hates humidity, so the first step is to spray the Cactus thoroughly with water. If that doesn't do the trick, try spraying with a solution of malathion or dimethoate.
- **Scale insect** is a tiny, limpet-like creature that sucks sap and weakens growth; it makes the plant turn yellow. You'll have to scrape off the brown scales with a fingernail first, then give the Cactus a good spray with an insecticide containing malathion to protect it for the future.
- **Basal rot** occurs when the base of the plant above the soil begins to rot. If this happens, you have overwatered your Cactus and the roots are already rotten. But you might not have lost the whole plant — if the upper stems still look healthy, cut them off and use them to propagate another plant.

- **Forest cacti** don't like the intense heat enjoyed by the desert variety, so a west- or east-facing windowsill is ideal for them. They like moderate warmth, and they love humidity — so spray a fine mist over the leaves from time to time, or stand the pot on damp gravel so that the plant has a constant supply of moisture to draw on.

Your forest cacti will flower regularly, except during their natural resting periods after flowering, when the temperature is best kept at around 55-60°F (13-15°C) and water withheld. Water them at other times quite frequently, about twice a week.

Propagation

There are two ways you can raise cacti — from seeds and from cuttings. Using seeds is easier but of course you'll have to wait much longer for results. You can get cactus seeds at most good garden shops and garden centres as well as from specialist cacti suppliers. You should have no difficulty growing them provided the seeds are reasonably fresh. Fill 3in (7cm) pots with compost: a good mixture is two parts John Innes Seed Compost to one part of Perlite. The Perlite improves the texture and drainage. Leave a depth of ¾in (19mm) between the surface of the soil and the rim of the pot. Now give the mixture a good soaking by watering the pots thoroughly and letting all excess water drain away.

Scatter the seeds thinly and evenly over the surface, pressing big ones in gently, but do not bury them. To encourage the seeds to germinate, you need to provide them with lots of moisture. The best thing is to cover the pots with a sheet of glass or clingfilm, or put clear polythene bags over them to prevent water loss.

Put the pots in a warm place — about 80°F (27°C) — or in a propagator, if you have one. Germination can take anything from three to eight weeks or longer, so don't worry if nothing seems to happen for a while. At first the seedlings do not need light, but because the seeds may germinate at different times, it's safest to provide moderate light from the beginning. When the seedlings have started to appear — they'll look like little green balls — uncover the pots so that they can get fresh air to help them to grow.

The next stage is to prick them out into individual tiny pots, called thumb pots, which are about 1-1½in (2.5-4cm) across. You do this when they're big enough to handle, say about 1in (25mm) high. But cacti grow very slowly, and it can take between six months and a year before they'll get to this stage. During this time, keep them at room temperature with the right amount of sun depending on their type, and make sure the compost is always slightly moist.

Once they're potted on you can treat your new cacti as mature plants, and, given the right amount of care, they should continue to grow in their slow way to give you years of enjoyment.

Forest cacti

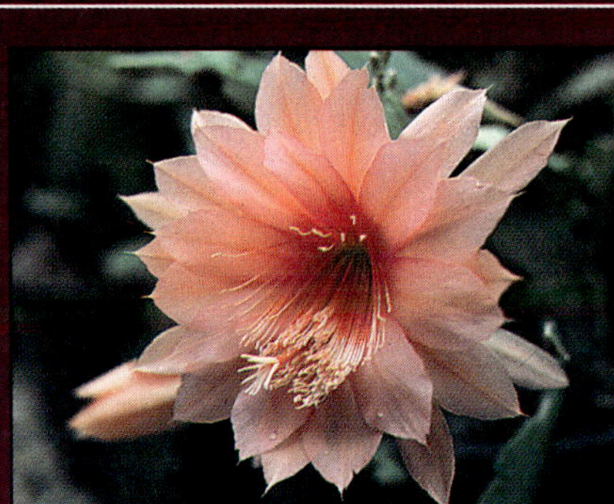

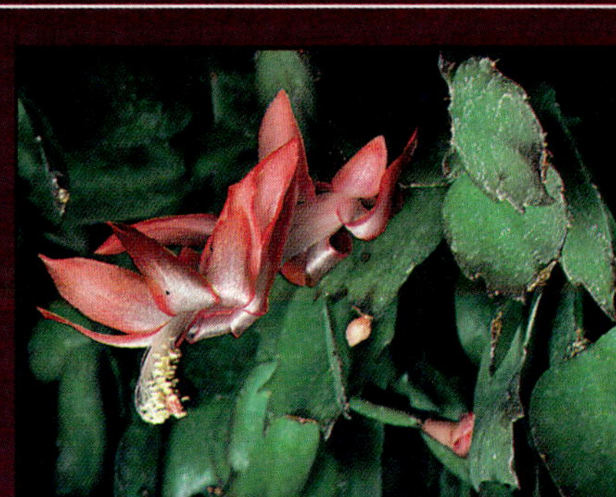

Aporocactus flagelliformis Rat's Tail Cactus
Slender trailing prickly stems; pink flowers

Ephiphyllum hybrids Orchid Cacti, *above*
Leaf-like stems with flamboyant shuttlecock flowers in a range of reds, gold, purple and white, some richly scented

Rhipsalidopsis gaertneri Easter Cactus
Leaf-like stems with scalloped edges and double scarlet flowers

Rhipsalis cassutha Mistletoe Cactus
Thin, branching stems with mistletoe-like fruits following white flowers

Rhipsalis paradoxa Chain Cactus
Branching, triangular winged stems which narrow and twist at intervals

Schlumbergera truncata Christmas Cactus, *above*
Toothed, leaf-like stems; flowers ranging from white through magenta and pink to crimson

Designing a cactus garden

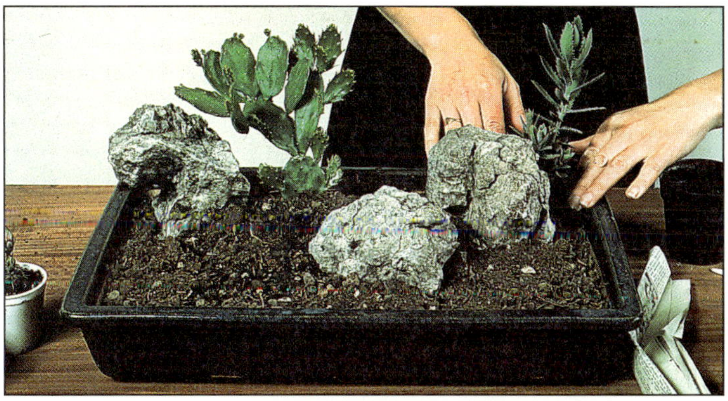

First decide where you want to put your cactus garden. If it's going against a wall, place tall species at the back.

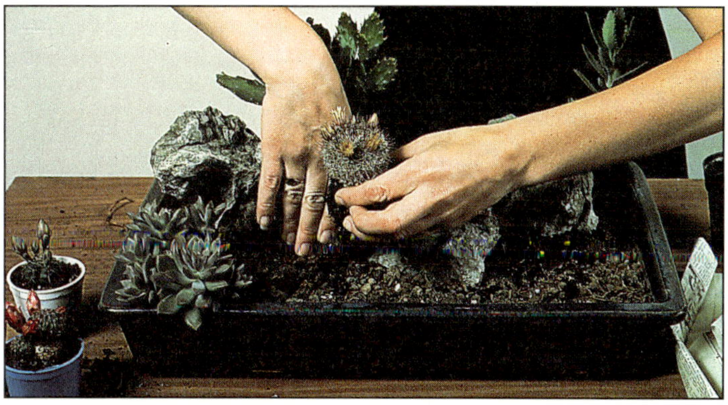

When choosing plants look out for complementary shapes and colours, and choose species with different flowering times.

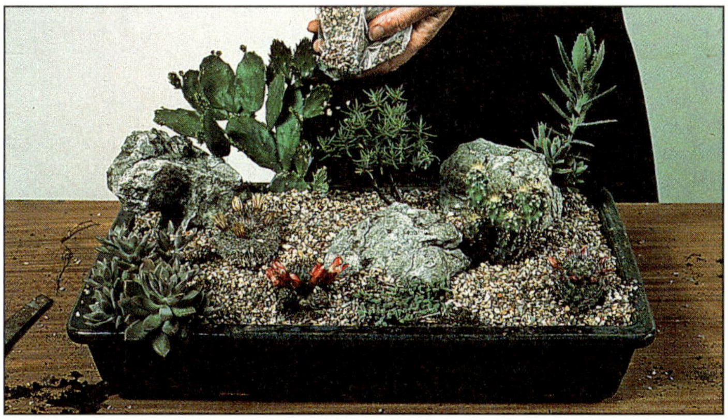

Spaces between plants can be filled with pea gravel which looks most attractive and aids drainage.

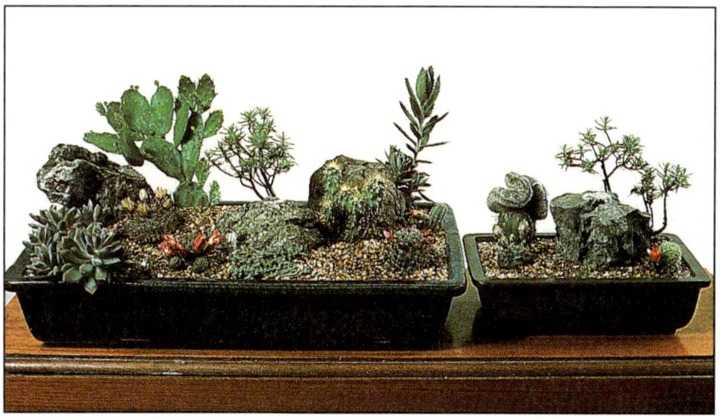

Place your finished garden in a sunny spot and it should delight you throughout the year.

Cacti and other succulents come in such strange shapes, and are so unlike other houseplants, that they usually look their best when grouped together. This enhances their sculptural qualities, and also ensures that the smaller ones, which would look rather odd alone, are well set off in the company of similar or complementary plants. Cacti gardens are also practical: you can keep together all those plants that require the same, rather unusual, conditions.

There are dozens and dozens of cacti to choose for the house (see 'Growing Cacti' page 142, for suggestions on suitable species for growing indoors). Grouping them together to make a suitable landscape – perhaps using small stones and pebbles to suggest a desert scene – is a challenge to bring out the artist in you. But the main thing is to use the tremendous variety of shapes, sizes and colours of the plants to make the most attractive presentation.

Choosing a container

Almost anything will do for a container, new or old — brass troughs, soup tureens, casseroles, even goldfish tanks for larger plantings. However, good drainage is essential for cacti, so the container should have drainage holes. If making holes in an old container would spoil it, cover the base with at least 2in (5cm) of drainage material — crushed charcoal is best because it mops up any impurities in the soil.

Get the compost right

Most cacti thrive in a free draining soil-based compost, but it should not be too rich — two parts John Innes No 1 mixed with one part coarse sand is ideal. Alternatively you could use a proprietary cactus compost. (For more details, see previous page.)

Making a landscape

Whether you're making a small or a big garden, the first thing to create is a focal point, using a tall, dramatic cactus. Then you can fringe this with smaller ones, and plant trailing cacti around the edges, which will in time grow over and conceal the sides of the container.

With a bowl 4-5in (10-13cm) deep and 12in (30cm) across, you could choose a Prickly Pear (Opuntia) with its branching pads as a dramatic centrepiece, with a column-shaped cactus next to it, such

Be adventurous!

Always arrange your chosen plants on a piece of newspaper first, to check that they'll look right before you commit yourself to planting them — and always leave enough room for them to grow. Make sure that you put together only those plants that enjoy the same conditions.

Once you're familiar with the many cacti and succulents available, there's no limit to the variety and number of the arrangements you can make.

as the Silver Torch Cactus (*Cleistocactus straussii*).

Plant around it little groups of smaller cacti, chosen for their exciting shapes. The Goat's Horn Cactus (*Astrophytum capricorne*) is globe-shaped with prominent ribs and wavy spines, while the Pincushion or Powder Puff Cactus (*Mammillaria bocasana*) is prized for its green globe, hooked spines and ring of starry white or red flowers. Choose others from the same type if you have room, bearing in mind their shapes and flower colours. You could intersperse these bigger plants with Living Stones (Lithops) — not cacti but succulents, which look like pebbles, until they burst into flower. To unite all these plants, spread shingle over the compost, and scatter a few real pebbles around.

For the edges of the container, the Rat's Tail Cactus (*Aporocactus flagelliformis*) really comes into its own. It is in fact a forest cactus, but is unusual in that it looks and should be treated just like the others listed above, which are desert cacti. It has prickly green stems with brown spines, which will trail down over the sides of the container, and beautiful bright pink flowers. Burro's or Donkey Tail (*Sedum morganianum*), another succulent which enjoys the same conditions as desert cacti, can keep it company; this has fascinating, tassel-like, waxy, green stems, made of symmetrical 'scales', which trail downwards.

Hanging baskets

You don't have to have your cacti at table or windowsill level. Many varieties are suitable for planting in hanging baskets, trailing from pedestals, or cascading down from flat-backed pots fixed to the wall at any height. These would make a striking feature in a warm, well-lit room — remember that most cacti like as much sun as they can get.

The extraordinary Saucer Plant (*Aeonium tabuliforme*) would make a good centrepiece — with a stem so short that it's scarcely noticeable, the rosette appears quite flat. It should be planted on the slant so that water can run off its packed foliage. It will produce a flower spike that can grow as high as 18in (45cm), with yellow flowers on branches at the tip. Blue Echeveria (*Echeveria glauca*), with its waxy, bluish leaves, would also make an excellent rosette-shaped centrepiece.

One succulent show-stopper is String of Beads (*Senecio rowleyanus*) — an amazing plant with bright green leaves in the shape of tiny globes that trail in strings like necklaces. The strings can grow as long as 3-4ft (0.9-1.2m), so you would need to set the basket pretty high!

The Money Plant or Jade Plant (*Crassula argentea*) would also be a good choice for the focal point of an arrangement, with its shiny dark green leaves on branching stems. It would be beautifully set off by the tree-like *Aeonium arboreum* 'Atropurpureum', with branching stems and lovely deep purple leaves in the shape of little umbrellas. The Tree Aloe (*Aloe arborescens*) is another good upright, tree-like succulent, with striking, toothed leaves.

For a fringe choose the trailing Rosary Vine (*Ceropegia woodii*), with delicate, white-veined leaves on purple stems, interplanted with the Partridge Breast Aloe (*Aloe variegata*) and the Rat Tail Plant (*Crassula lycopodioides*).

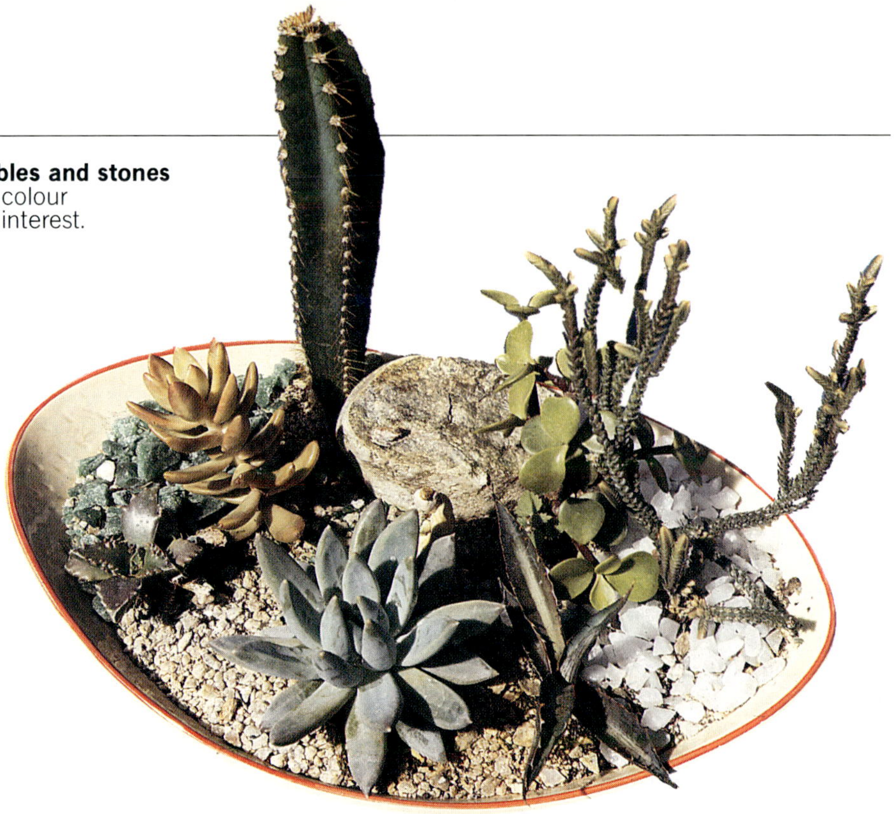

Pebbles and stones add colour and interest.

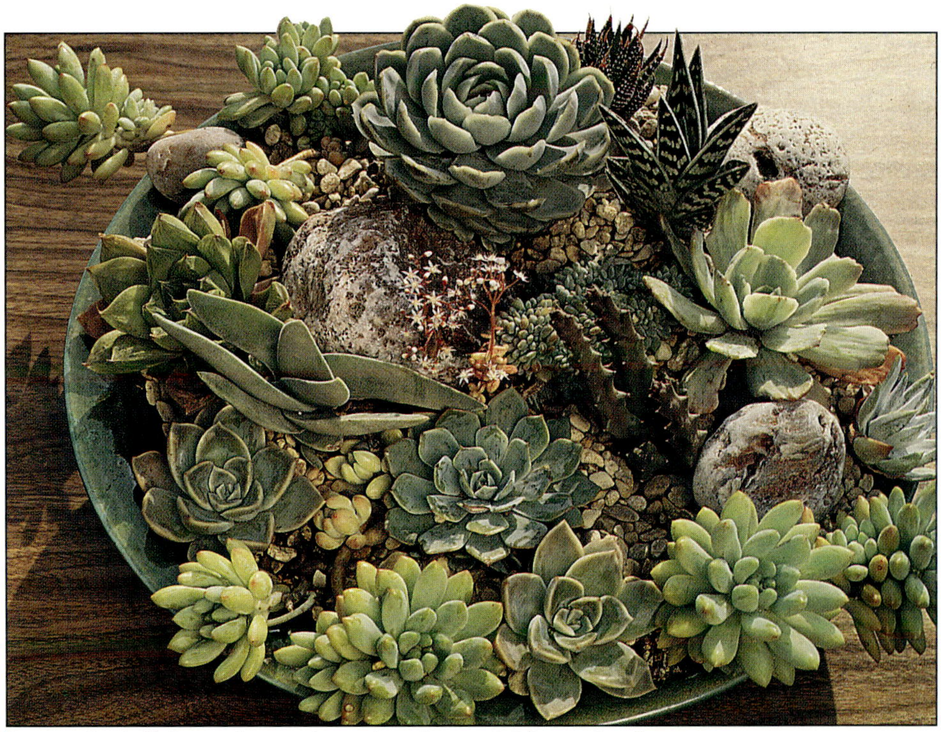

A succulent dish garden makes a handsome table centrepiece.

Easy indoor orchids

If you think you can't grow orchids — think again. Modern plants — hybrids produced by the experts in plant breeding — can be surprisingly undemanding. And the new easy-grow orchids are often even more alluring than their predecessors. They're still exciting and exotic, but, fortunately, they're no longer necessarily expensive to buy or tricky to keep.

The orchid family is vast — probably the largest flowering plant family in the world, with over 100,000 species and hybrids, divided among 750 genera. The figures are staggering. But only a handful of genera have been able to produce tolerant plants which will grow in a variety of surroundings, with a minimum of attention. They can bring flamboyant blooms to your home — often in the darkest, most cruel months of the year.

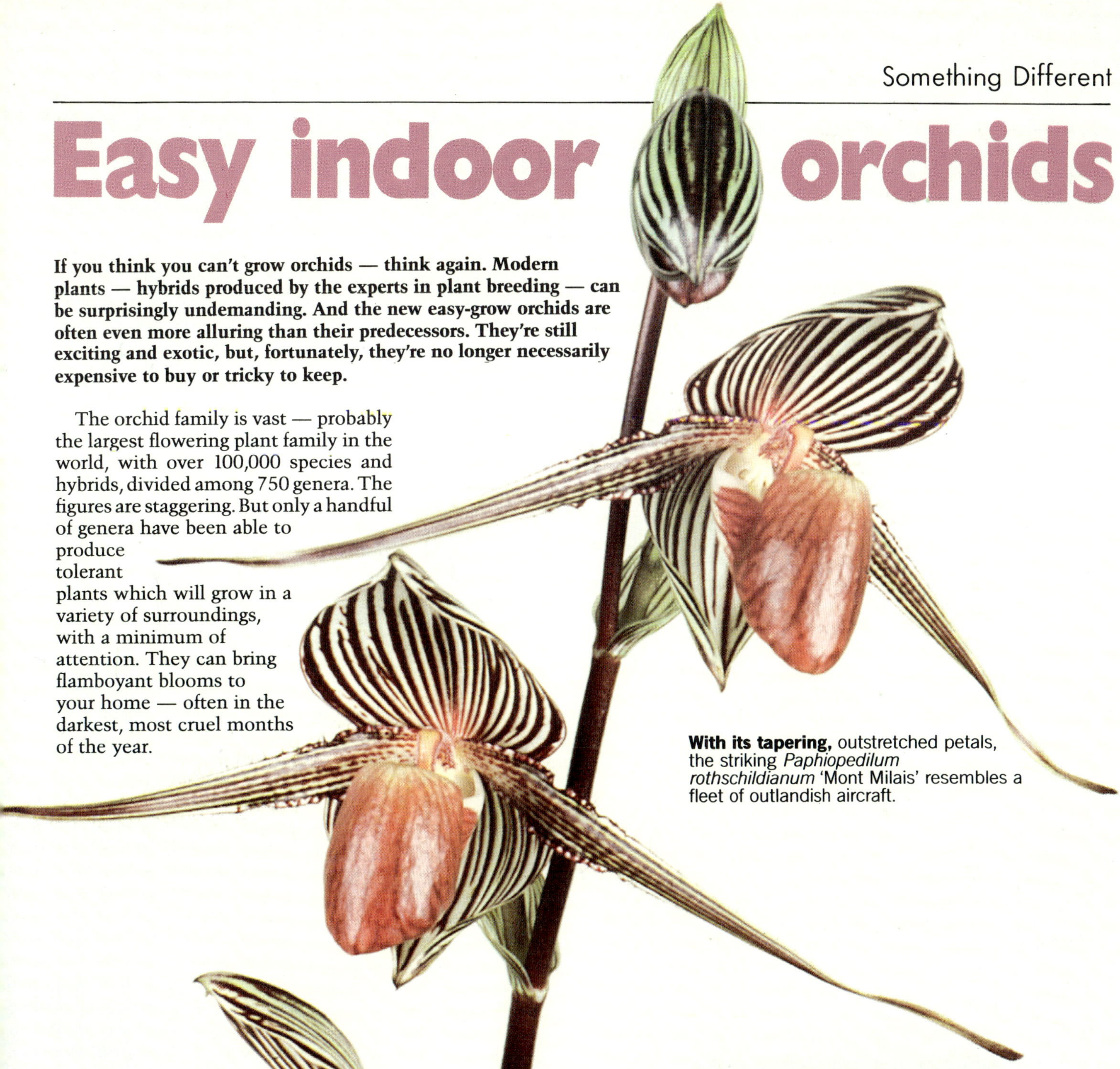

With its tapering, outstretched petals, the striking *Paphiopedilum rothschildianum* 'Mont Milais' resembles a fleet of outlandish aircraft.

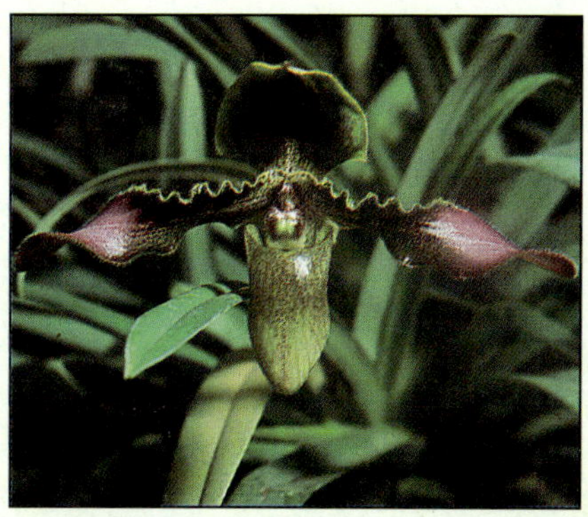

Autumn-flowering *Paphiopedilum hirsutissimum* from Northern India.

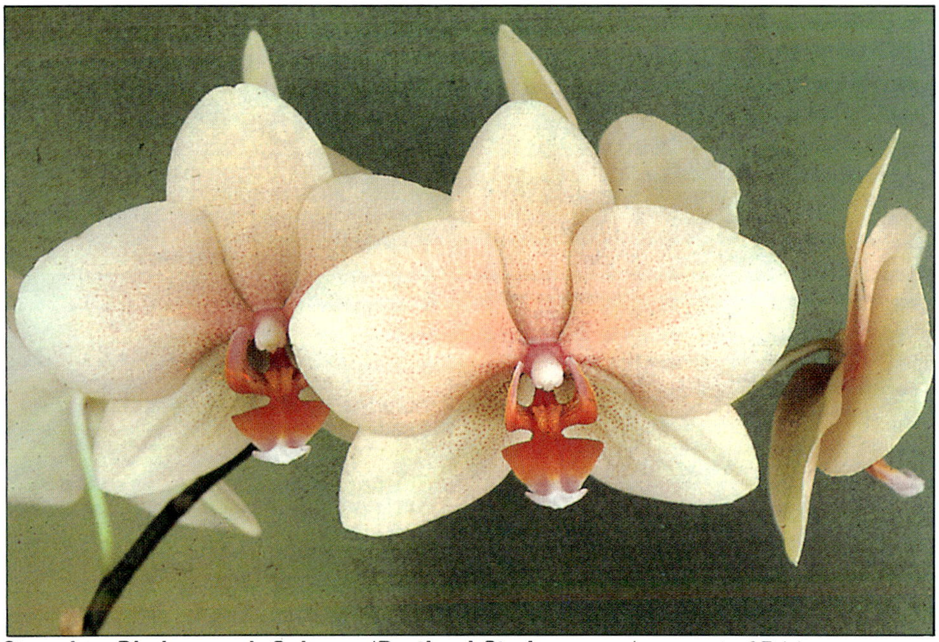

Stunning *Phalaenopsis* Solvang 'Portland Star' can produce up to 15 blooms.

Temperatures

	NIGHT		DAY	
	Winter	Summer	Winter	Summer
Cool	50°F (10°C)	55°F (13°C)	55°F (13°C)	65°F (18°C)
Intermediate	55°F (13°C)	65°F (18°C)	65°F (18°C)	75°F (24°C)
Warm	65°F (18°C)	75°F (24°C)	75°F (24°C)	85°F (29°C)

Orchids grow wild all over the world. The tree orchids, called epiphytes, are native to the tropics, where they cling to trees and shrubs, even rocks, for support, with the aid of their aerial roots.

They aren't parasites, despite popular belief, but are true air plants. Their needs are slight and they get all their water from the moisture in the air, via their aerial roots. Extra nourishment comes from animal and vegetable debris collected amongst the cluster of their leaves. Most of the orchids grown as houseplants are tree orchids. They are ideal for growing on slabs of bark, but most of them grow perfectly happily in pots. Potting will be covered separately.

A few houseplants belong to the other group of orchids — the ground-growers or terrestrials. Terrestrials come from the more temperate climes.They are much less adaptable and usually less attractive than epiphytes and only one type — the Slipper Orchid (Paphiopedilum) — has become relatively common as an indoor plant.

Where to shop

Surprisingly, orchid plants can be bought from chain stores and supermarkets, where they're excellent value. Garden centres and florists also stock them, of course, but for the best choice, contact a specialist orchid nursery.

No orchid is cheap. But remember, most have been carefully nurtured for anything between five and 15 years before they're ready for sale. Hybrids are the best buys, usually. If you stick to those that have a proven track record, you can't go far wrong, and choosing by colour is as good a way as any. Species tend to be a bit more expensive.

There's a guide to the five easiest and most rewarding types given overleaf, but there are a few others you can look out for. They include Cattleyas, Brassias, Dendrobiums, Laelias, Miltonias and Vandas.

Lighting needs

In the wild, orchids prefer bright, but dappled light. They need good light to

Orchid structure

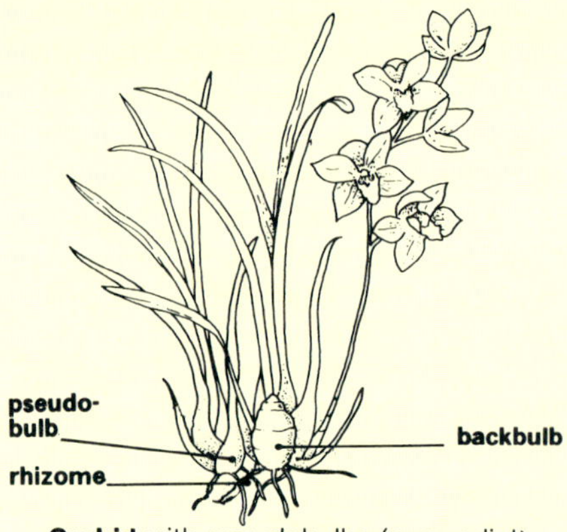

Orchid with pseudobulbs (sympodial)

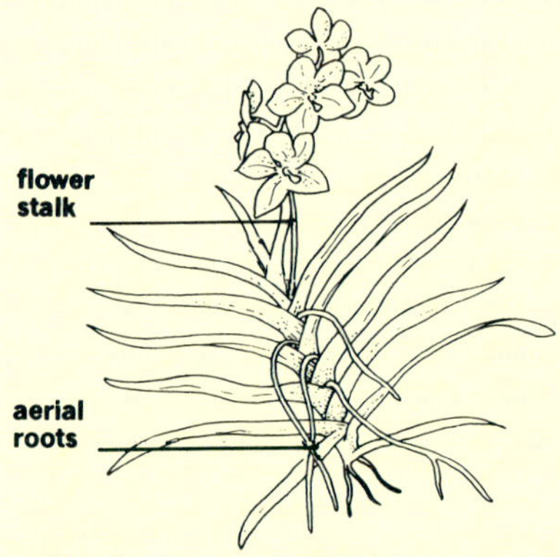

Single-stemmed orchid (monopodial)

Orchids are unusual in more ways than one. Most of those grown as houseplants produce pseudobulbs, or false bulbs, which are like swollen stems. They come in all shapes and sizes, and their job is to carry the new growth. But they have one other important function — to store enough water to get the orchid through a drought.

A long time after their leaves have emerged, the pseudobulb continues to survive. Once its flowers have opened, the pseudobulb, now known as a 'back bulb', begins to die. But its life span can be as long as five years. A plant may carry many pseudobulbs and back bulbs at any time, for new ones develop every year. These are joined to each other by a length of rhizome (stem).

Not all orchids grow in this way. Some epiphytes have just one main stem, which rises from a tuft of roots at the base, and carries leaves (and sometimes aerial roots) along its length. It grows upwards, and can reach 2ft (60cm) or more before producing flower stalks at the top.

The typical terrestrial orchid also has a single stem, rising from thick, fleshy roots or tubers. The terrestrials may rest for a time during the winter months.

Flowers and leaves

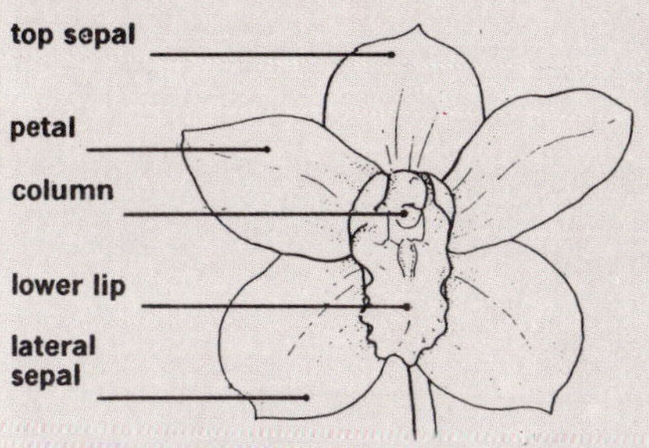

The orchid flower is quite unique. It always follows the same basic design. But no two have quite the same shape: colour and size vary enormously, too.

The characteristic lower lip can be spectacular, often spurred or frilled, and often in colours that startle by their contrasts. Fleshy, waxy blooms may be scented or scentless, noxious or fragrant. They come singly or in clusters, drooping or erect. And they are very enduring. Whether on the plant or in a vase, a flower may last for as long as 12 weeks — though some may last no longer than three weeks.

Foliage can be a bit disappointing. Most leaves are in a single shade of green, and either thick and leathery or thin and papery. Some even fall occasionally. But there are some orchids which make very attractive foliage plants with mottled, two-tone leaves to compensate for the lack of flowers once they have died down.

develop flowers, but they shouldn't ever be exposed to direct sunlight, even through a window. Direct sun can burn them — the foliage becomes yellow and can develop brown or black patches.

The answer is to protect orchids with net curtains and place them, ideally, near an east- or west-facing window. Here the plants will get three or four hours of filtered sun every day.

In winter, good light is even more important for plants about to flower. Unless you can provide them with 10 hours of light a day (and preferably 12), you can't be sure of a good display. Obviously this can present problems. But if weather conditions don't permit, don't give up — an artificial lighting system is a good alternative to natural daylight.

Temperature and humidity

To grow and flower successfully, orchids also need enough (but not too much) warmth and moisture. But getting the temperature right to the last degree isn't crucial.

Orchids fit into temperature categories, as you can see on the chart. Most of those featured here enjoy cool to intermediate conditions. And although they enjoy some fresh air, they don't like cold draughts. If they're on a windowsill, make sure the windows are well-sealed, and move plants away from the windows on frosty nights. In summer months, when temperatures outside are reliable, open the windows, or better still put the orchids outside in a shady spot for a few hours.

A moist atmosphere is vital at all times. To achieve it, fill a dish or gravel tray with pebbles or shingle, which should be kept topped up with water, and put the pots on top.

Gravel trays help to protect the plants from a radiator, too, as these plants can't tolerate too much direct heat.

Mist spraying with a water gun will help keep the atmosphere moist, too, and most orchids will benefit from having their leaves sprayed during the growing season when temperatures rise.

Watering

Orchids prefer rainwater to tapwater, since they dislike lime. If you aren't able to provide this, add one teaspoon of vinegar per gallon (4.5 litres) of tap water, and use this instead.

Never let an orchid stand in water or its roots may rot. The free-draining mixture in which they're grown helps prevent this sort of problem. When watering an epiphytic orchid, soak the mixture thoroughly, making sure the water can drain away. Then leave the plant until the mixture begins to dry out before watering again. This means you probably won't have to water it more than once a week.

During the resting period (see below), water sparingly, giving only enough to stop the compost and the pseudobulbs from drying out completely.

Plants grown in baskets or on bark can be watered by immersing them in a bowl of water for some minutes. Drain them thoroughly before returning them to their usual position. Don't water again until the plant base begins to feel dry.

Terrestrial orchids like more water than tree orchids, so keep their compost steadily moist.

Resting

Some orchids — Odontoglossums, for instance — grow throughout the year, though they'll slow down in autumn or winter. Others, like the Laelias, have a resting phase, when growth all but stops, and some of the leaves may even fall off. This resting period, which follows flowering, lasts no more than a matter of weeks as a rule and during this time plants shouldn't be fed. Water requirements are also minimal.

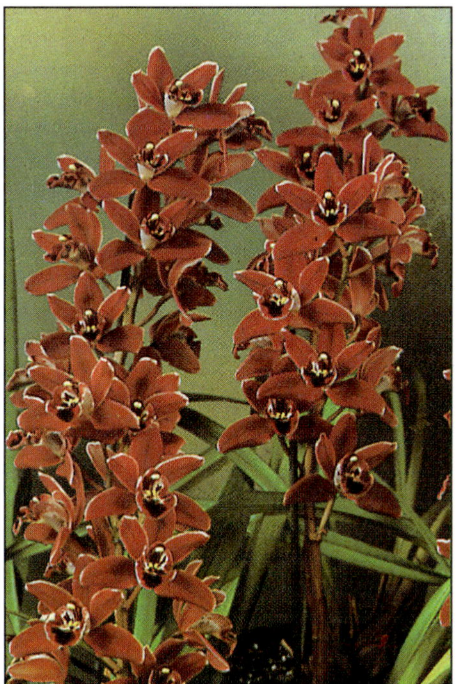

***Cymbidium* Annan 'Cooksbridge'** flowers between late winter and spring.

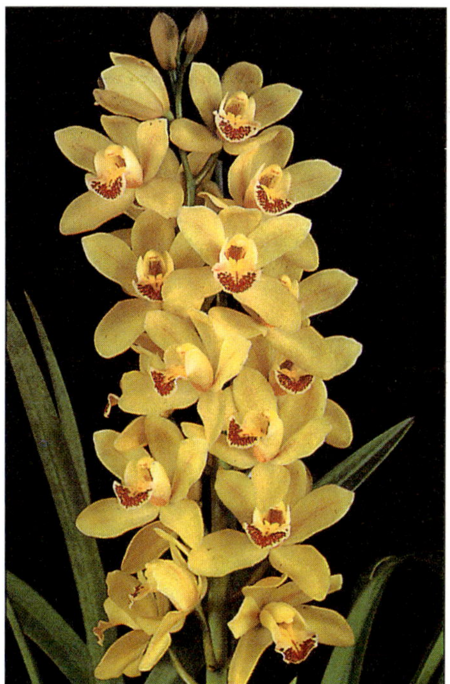

The superb yellow *Cymbidium* Mary Pinchness 'Del Rey'.

Easy orchids to

Name and type	Description	Temperature and humidity	Watering	Resting	Varieties
Odontoglossum Very showy plants, mainly epiphytic, producing pseudo-bulbs. Includes some of the best modern hybrids.	Large, attractive flowers 3-4in (8-10cm) across, often in several colours which form dramatic designs, usually in the form of spots. Plants can produce up to 30 flowers, carried in sprays at the top of several arching flower stems. Flowers are sometimes fragrant, lasting up to 8 or even 10 weeks. They are produced irregularly, every nine months or so, but usually between late autumn and spring.	Cool or intermediate, depending on plant. High humidity; mist spray daily in temperatures over 60°F (15°C). Ensure some fresh air occasionally.	Allow the compost to dry out to half its depth between waterings.	Hybrids have no definite resting period, but slow down after flowering in autumn/winter. Some species have a short rest.	Plants available are mainly hybrids in a wide range of colours. Many are the results of breeding Odontoglossums with more robust relatives. The most popular are Odontiodas, Odontonias, Wilsonaras and Vuylstekearas. Recommended species include: *Odontoglossum bictoniense*, (yellow-green spotted with brown, with a white or pink lip). *O. grande* (Tiger Orchid). (Bright yellow with brown stripes and a creamy yellow lip.) *O. crispum* (white or rose-tinged, or blotched with red).
Moth Orchid *(Phalaenopsis)* Single-stemmed epiphytic orchid which produces aerial roots that may cover surface of compost. Can do well in wooden or wire baskets.	Flowers appear on long, arching stalks, up to 30 at a time, looking like a flight of moths (hence the popular name). Flowers can be 1-5in (2.5-13cm) across, and can appear at any time of year, lasting up to three weeks each. These produce only a few leaves, which are wide and fleshy but not very large. Strong aerial roots.	Intermediate temperatures. High humidity; mist spray daily.	Allow top ½in (13mm) of compost to dry out between waterings. Water in mornings if possible, and wipe off any water that drops on to foliage at once; these plants are particularly vulnerable to fungus and rot.	Growth practically ceases in winter.	Species are naturally either white or pink. Hybrids, which are superior, come in a range of colours and may be striped or spotted. Popular species include: *Palaenopsis amabilis* (white with red-spotted lip and yellow tinge). *P.schilleriana* (pale pink with reddish brown spots). *P.stuartiana* (white, heavily speckled with purple; yellow lip).
Lady's Slipper or Slipper Orchid *(Paphiopedilum)* Terrestrial orchid in an immense range of sizes, shapes and colours. Flowers usually require staking.	Owes its popular name to the pouch-shaped lip. Each flower stem carries just one flower, which may last over 10 weeks, appearing between autumn and spring. Flowers have a waxy, almost artificial look, and the top sepal is often in a contrasting colour to the rest. Thick, fleshy leaves may also be attractively mottled with purple and maroon, though plants of that type tend to need slightly higher temperatures.	Both cool and intermediate growing plants. Mist spray daily in temperatures over 70°F (21°C).	Allow top 1-2in (2.5-5cm) of compost to dry out between waterings.	No resting period, but plants make little growth for six weeks after flowering.	Many colours and combinations available; most plants on offer are hybrids. It is possible to buy species from specialist growers. Recommended species include: *Paphiopedilum fairieanum* (white, veined with purple; green lip with reddish-purple tinge). Flowers in summer and autumn. *P.spiceranum* (yellow-green petals with crimson stripe; white top sepal; crimson lip). Spring flowering. *P.villosum* (glossy, rich bronze). Flowers in winter and spring.
Lycaste Includes some of the easiest of orchids to grow indoors. Those used as houseplants are epiphytic and produce pseudobulbs.	Arching stems each produce one 3in (8cm) flattish, waxy flower. These may be fragrant. Usually spring and summer flowering, but some varieties bloom in winter. Dark green leaves are narrow at base and tip, but very wide in the middle.	Cool growing plants	Allow compost to dry out almost completely between waterings.	Most have long winter rest periods.	Available species include: *Lycaste aromatica* (yellow with reddish spotting). *L.cruenta* (shades of yellow with its lips flushed red). *L.deppei* (green and white with red-streaked lip). There are many hybrids, some of which produce very large flowers.

grow at home

Name and type	Description	Temperature and humidity	Watering	Resting	Varieties
Cymbidiums Easy-to-grow 'beginner's orchid'. Best in miniature form, though standard sizes are also available. Those suitable for growing in the home are all epiphytic and produce pseudobulbs.	Flowers 3in (8cm) across appear along stems, often with as many as 15 flowers per spike. Plants may bloom for up to 12 weeks. Many varieties are autumn and winter blooming. Very wide choice of colours; boat-shaped lip may harmonise or contrast with rest of flower. Leaves are leathery, strap-shaped, about 15in (38cm) long.	Intermediate growers. Plants will survive up to 80°F (27°C). They like high humidity, so mist spray daily in temperatures over 65°F (18°C).	Allow top 1in (2.5cm) of compost to dry out before watering.	Plants may rest briefly in autumn.	Many hybrids and one or two species worth trying. The following are worth considering: *Cymbidium* Annan 'Cooksbridge' (deep pink). *C.* Aviemore 'Lewes' (pale pink). *C.* Stonehaven 'Cooksbridge' (yellow). *C.* Evening Star 'Pastel Princess' (rich cream, with pink lip). *C.devonianum* (olive green, crimson and purple).

Feeding

It's a good idea to give plants a little extra nourishment during the growing season, but take care not to overfeed them — it's harmful. Foliar feeds are ideal for air plants like tree orchids, although liquid feeding is perfectly acceptable — especially for the terrestrials.

Use any general fertiliser, like Phostrogen, at a quarter strength, or buy a special orchid fertiliser from an orchid nursery. These may come in various strengths — for young plants, adult plants or plants approaching flowering.

Give a liquid feed once every two weeks or so, or use a foliar feed at every third or fourth watering.

Caring for your plants

Orchids enjoy a clean, tidy environment. So sponge the leaves of your orchids from time to time, to keep them free of dust. Nip out any black tips that appear — these are just a sign of old age. If a plant loses the odd leaf from time to time, don't be alarmed — it's quite normal. Dead and dying leaves should be removed, in case they cause blemishes on otherwise healthy parts.

When a flower dies always remove it, and at the end of the flowering season cut off the flower stem at the base. Watch out for pests like scale insect or mealy bug, which may be lurking at the base of the old flower stalks, beneath the leaves or on the pseudobulbs. If the atmosphere is not kept sufficiently humid red spider mite can be a problem.

If you look after your plants, you can regard orchids as permanent features of your home which will go on flowering successfully, year after year.

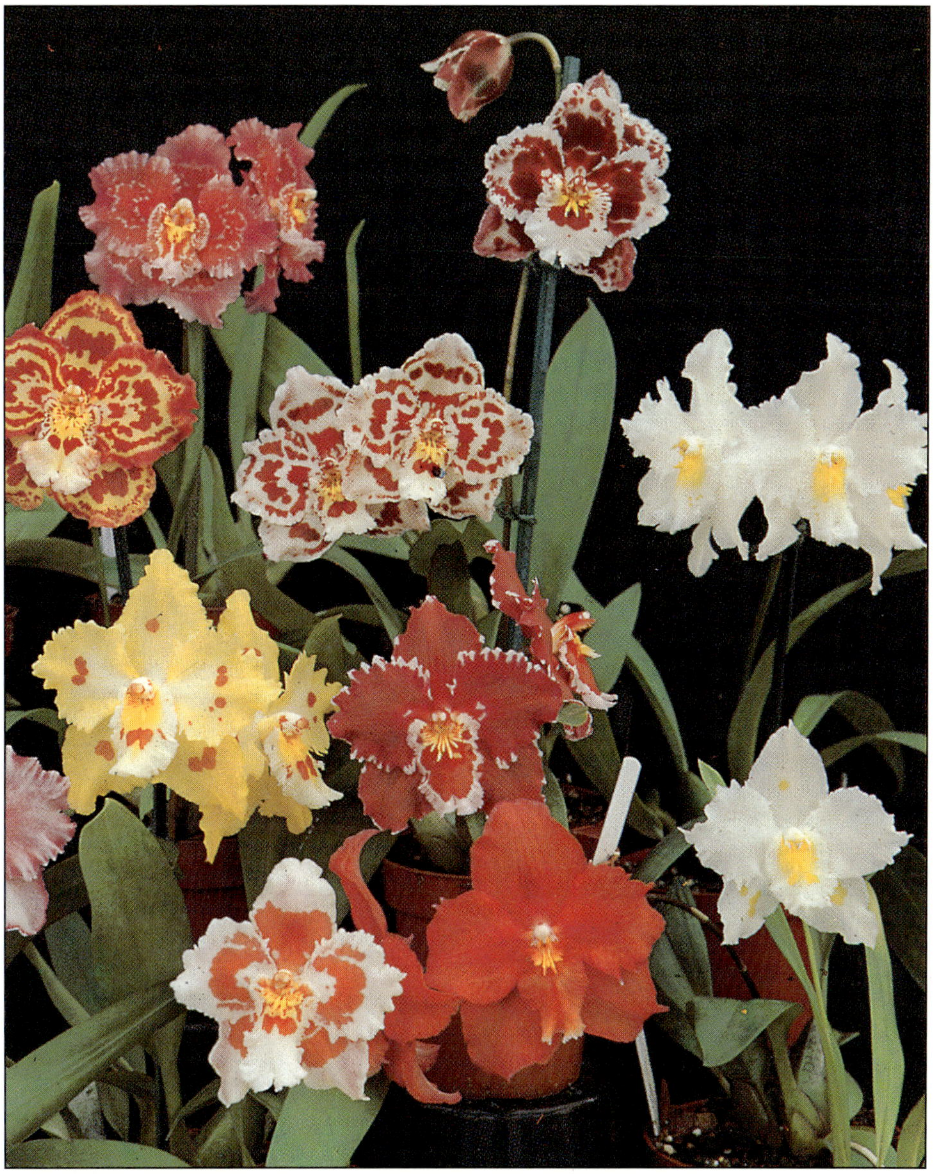

Some of the startling patterns produced by breeding Odontoglossums with other related genera. Mature plants will produce up to 15 flowers on arching stems.

Beautiful bromeliads

Named in honour of Bromel, a seventeenth-century Swedish botanist, bromeliads make up an enormous group of plants, tremendously varied and full of surprises. The best known one is the pineapple. Originally from the humid regions of tropical America, they make excellent houseplants, with stunning flowers, brightly coloured bracts and ornamental foliage. Because they are so exotic and because the way they grow is most unusual, many people assume they are difficult to keep — but nothing could be further from the truth!

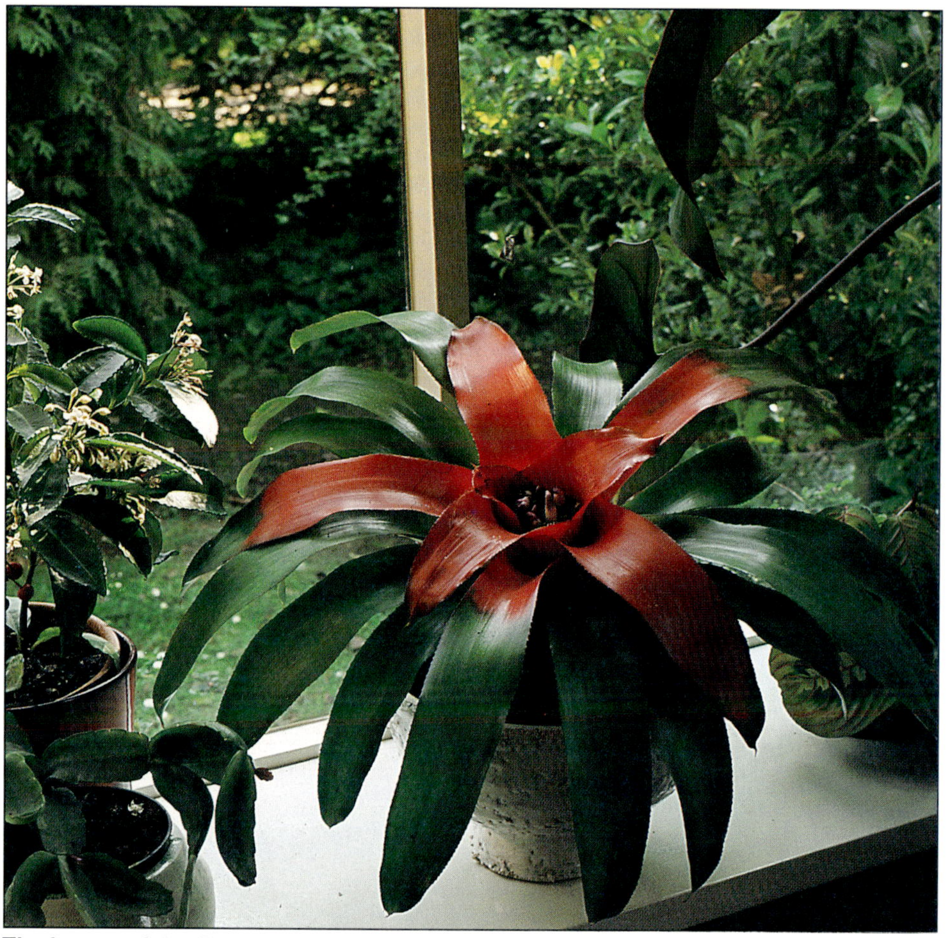

The leaves of the Blushing Bromeliad are suffused with scarlet when it flowers.

Bromeliads can be divided into two categories: the 'epiphytic' ones, which grow on the branches of trees, and the 'terrestrial' ones, which grow rooted in the ground.

Most bromeliads grown as houseplants are epiphytic, although many are adaptable enough to be happy in a pot — except for most Tillandsias. However, their natural method of getting sustenance remains: they draw moisture and nutrition through their leaves directly from the air, and not through their roots, which serve mainly to anchor them. You can arrange to grow them on a piece of bark or tree branch, instead of in a pot, if you prefer!

To assist them in collecting water, bromeliads have developed a little 'cup' at the heart of each rosette of leaves. It is into this cup, if it is big enough, that you pour their water rather than into their compost, although that too should be kept moist. If the cup is very small — as it will be with a young plant, for example — overhead mist spraying is sufficient, because the water will drip down and collect in the cup.

Not only are the leaves of most species thick, glossy and attractively patterned, but some kinds produce magnificent, waxy-textured and startlingly beautiful flowers. The bromeliads that do flower will only do so when they are mature — say, after two or three years — so if you have started with a young one you may have to wait a while.

The flowers sometimes grow half-hidden inside the leaf rosettes, sometimes at the end of long, dramatic spikes. The blooms themselves are in fact no more than ½in (13mm) across, but they grow among brilliantly coloured leaf bracts, usually red or purple. Bromeliads can flower at any time of the year and although the blooms themselves only last a few days, the coloured leaf bracts can survive for much longer, and some varieties produce colourful berries as well.

How to care for them

Apart from the decorative indoor form of the edible pineapple, *Ananas comosus variegatus*, and Earth Star (Cryptanthus), both of which are terrestrial bromeliads which revel in hot, bright sunlight, the rest of the family are happiest in diffused, almost subdued light. This most closely resembles their natural jungle habitat.

They like an average to warm temperature — not less than 55°F (13°C) — but may need extra heat, up to 75°F (24°C), in order to flower. Once the leaf bracts start to deepen in colour, it is a sign that flowering is getting near, so it's a good idea to put them somewhere specially warm for a few weeks and make sure they get constant, very good light, but not direct sunlight. Guard them carefully against draughts and extremes of temperature.

Watering

The best water for bromeliads is soft. If you don't have naturally soft water, use rainwater, water that has been boiled and cooled, or the water you collect when defrosting the refrigerator — but make sure it's come up to room temperature first! You can also add a few drops of vinegar to every pint (0.5 litre) of tapwater to soften it.

With epiphytic bromeliads, the main watering is by filling the leafy cup at the centre of the rosette of leaves. Check this regularly in summer and always keep it topped up and, in addition, replace the water completely once a month. You can do this easily by turning the whole plant gently over to tip out the old water. Every other month you should add liquid fertiliser to the new water. If the plant is in a pot, keep the compost just moist.

With terrestrial bromeliads, such as Ananas and Cryptanthus, you should keep the potting compost fairly moist, but never let the soil get waterlogged.

Mist spray leaves regularly from overhead in spring and summer, and occasionally in the winter. If the leaves ever look pale it's a good idea to spray them with a foliar feed, such as PBI Fillip.

Displaying bromeliads

Because epiphytic bromeliads don't need to be rooted in soil, you can grow them in fascinating ways, such as clinging individually to a piece of bark, cork or driftwood. Or you can arrange several of them on a nicely shaped tree branch about 3-4in (8-10cm) in diameter.

Anchor the branch in a decorative bowl or pot, by packing it round with stones and pebbles and cementing it in with plaster of Paris. Choose half a dozen or more epiphytic bromeliads, such as Tillandsia, Guzmania, Neoregelia and Aechmea. Remove them from any pots, wrap their roots in thick wads of fresh sphagnum moss, and fix this to the branch with loops of plastic-coated wire. Water them and mist spray them regularly just as usual.

With complementing colours and shapes, an arrangement like this makes a stunning feature in a conservatory, where frequent mist spraying can be done without risking any damage to furniture. And if you'd like the branch to be covered with moss, you can make it grow quickly by spraying the branch with milk!

Potting on and propagation

Each rosette of a bromeliad will only flower once and then die, though the bracts will remain attractive for several months. During this period, new offsets will grow up around the base of the plant. When the parent plant has died, you should cut it down to leave room for the offsets to grow up.

With terrestrial bromeliads, the best plan is to leave one, or perhaps two, offsets in the original pot, and remove any others to make separate plants. You'll need to pot the original plant on every year to allow for more root growth, and also more room for the new plants. A pot size of 10-12in (25-30cm) should be the biggest you'll need. Use a peat-based compost, such as Levingtons, mixed with a quarter part of coarse sand or perlite to improve drainage. The compost you use must be lime-free.

To make new plants, remove the offsets carefully and pot them singly in 3-4in (8-10cm) pots, using an open, lime-free, peat-based compost as described above. Keep them in a warm place — at least 55°F (13°C).

You make new epiphytic bromeliads in much the same way: after cutting down the parent plant, separate off a few new offsets, and attach them to separate pieces of bark or wood. You can then treat them as mature plants.

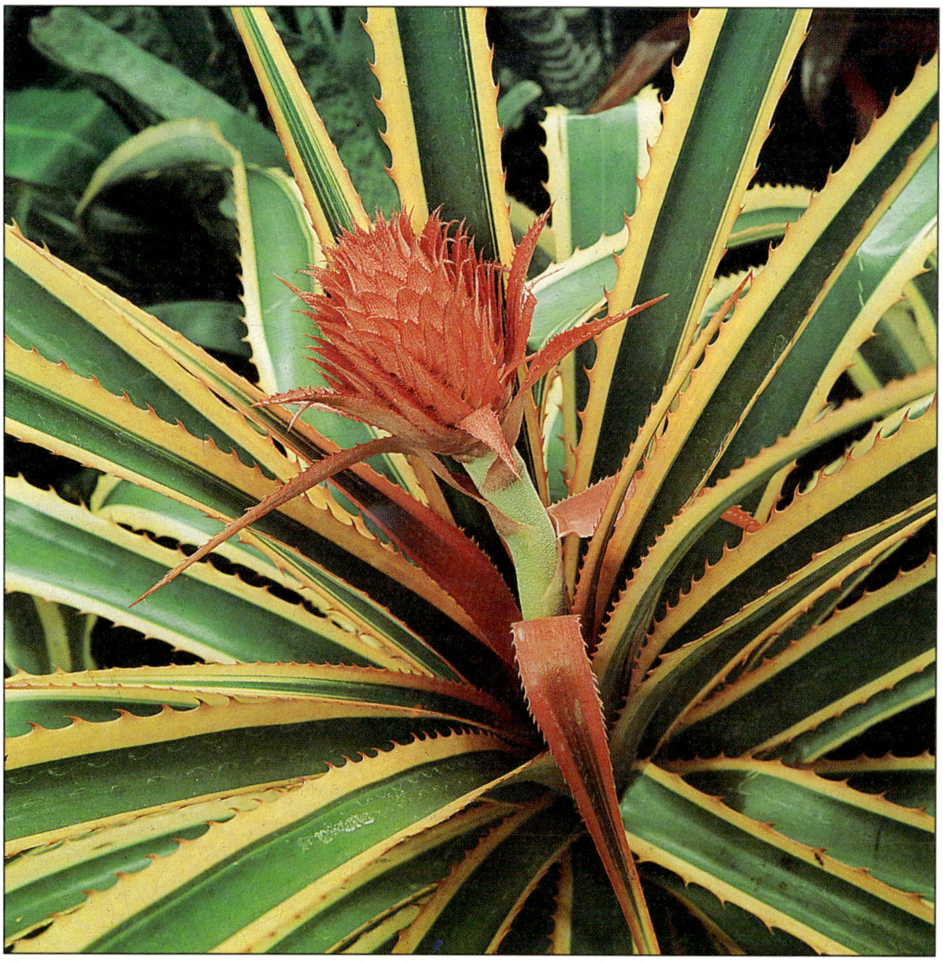

Ananas comosus variegatus is the decorative Pineapple Plant.

Tips on care

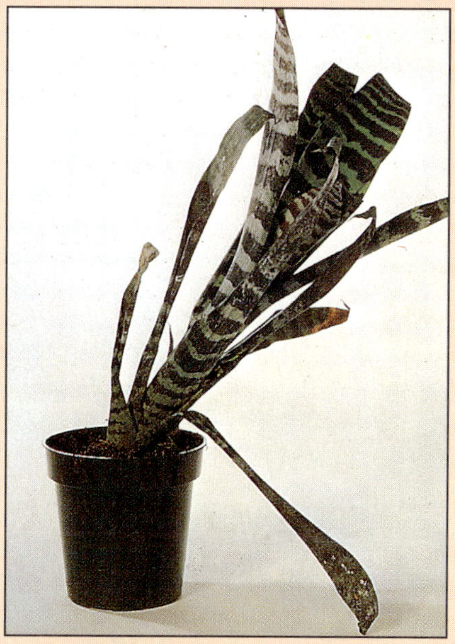

One reason why bromeliads make excellent houseplants is that they are remarkably free from pests. They might suffer from scale insects or from mealy bugs, but both of these can be easily wiped away with a sponge or cloth soaked in a malathion-based insecticide. Always make sure that you keep the central cup filled with water, or your bromeliad will lose strength and die (*above*).

Which ones to choose?

● **The Urn Plant *(Aechmea fasciata)*** is justly popular. It has grey-green, arching leaves, banded with white, from the centre of which appears a long flower spike with a large cone of rosy red bracts around small, pale blue flowers. The flowers gradually turn red, then die, but the bracts remain colourful for several months.

● **The Blue-Flowered Torch *(Tillandsia lindenii)*** has a rosette of long, narrow leaves and a flower stalk up to 1ft (0.3m) long, bearing royal blue flowers inside pink bracts. It looks really exotic, and can bring gasps of amazement from people who see it for the first time.

● The increasingly popular 'air plants', sold on pieces of cork or bark, are members of the Tillandsia group. **Spanish Moss *(Tillandsia usneoides)*** is a curious one, forming long, greyish-green strands that gather into trailing 'beards' several feet long.

● There are others worth seeking out. Specially fine is the **Blushing Bromeliad *(Neoregelia carolinae tricolor)***, whose rosette of green leaves, striped with white or rose-pink, becomes suffused with scarlet at the centre as the plant is about to flower.

● The aptly named **King of the Bromeliads *(Vriesea hieroglyphica)*** is prized above all for its intricately patterned leaves. They grow up to 2½ft (0.75m) long and 3in (8cm) wide, and are bright green with bands of purple. **Flaming Sword *(Vriesea splendens)*** is similar in foliage, but has in addition a long flower spike of brilliant red bracts, from which yellow flowers emerge.

● The plants in the Guzmania group are very beautiful, and usually flower in the winter. ***Guzmania lingulata*** has several forms, usually with smooth green leaves and a flower spike bearing crimson bracts and yellow blooms.

● There are low-growing kinds too, notably **Earth Star *(Cryptanthus)***, a terrestrial bromeliad, which makes a fascinating plant in a terrarium or bottle garden. The leaves, in star-shaped rosettes, are strongly patterned, striped and banded with cream, and often with attractive wavy edges. ***Cryptanthus zonatus*** has brownish-green leaves, cross-banded in white, brown and green.

A good garden centre should stock quite a range of bromeliads. Go along and see what you can find. You certainly won't be disappointed.

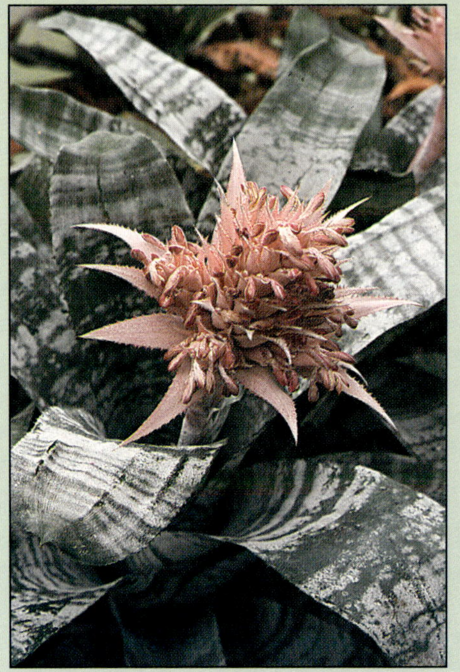

The Urn Plant has a stunning bloom.

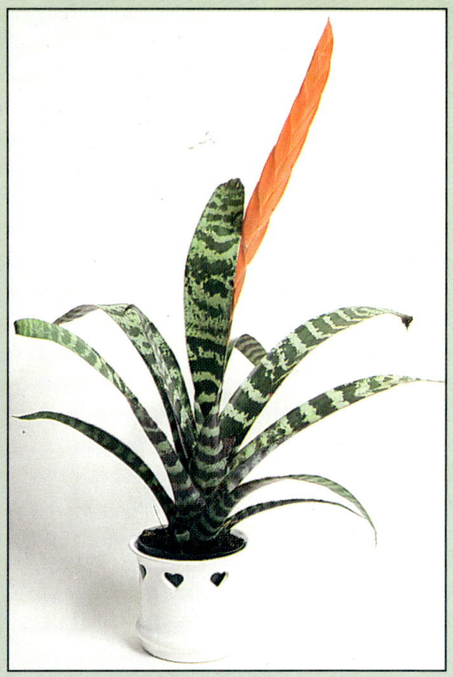

Flaming Sword sums up this flower.

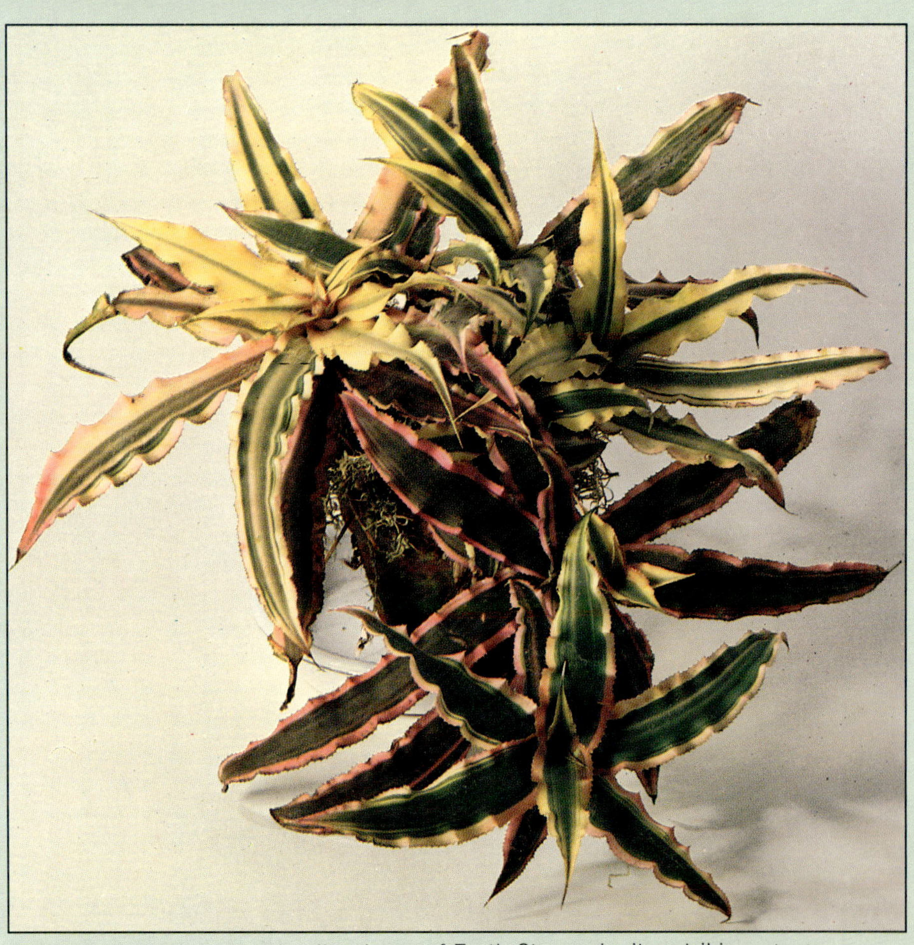

The colourful stripes and spiky shape of Earth Star make it a striking plant.

A-Z OF PLANTS

This unique reference section covers in detail over 150 houseplants, both common and exotic. Each entry begins with an at-a-glance chart which tells you the size of the plant, its light, water and temperature requirements, its relative price and availability. Different species are described and illustrated so you can make a selection of varieties of one plant, if you wish, or choose the best kind for your scheme.

All-year-round care and propagation are described in detail, and step-by-step illustrations will help you to get it right. There are Buying Guides, which advise you on what to look for when selecting a particular plant; and Trouble Shooter panels so you'll know what could go wrong, and how to deal with it.

From Abutilons to Zebrinas – you can be sure of finding a plant to suit any situation. With this guide in your hands you'll have no need to look elsewhere for any information on your houseplants.

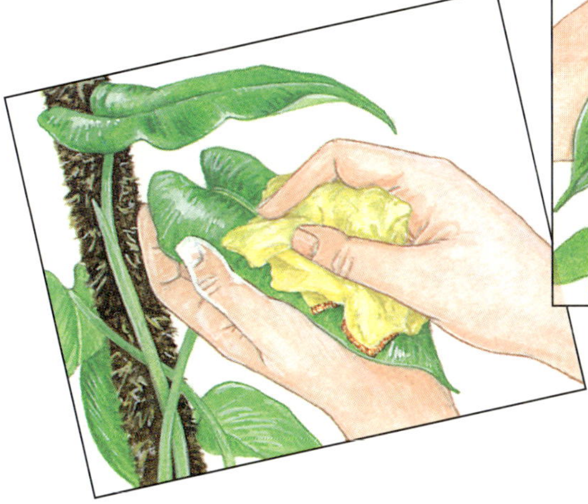

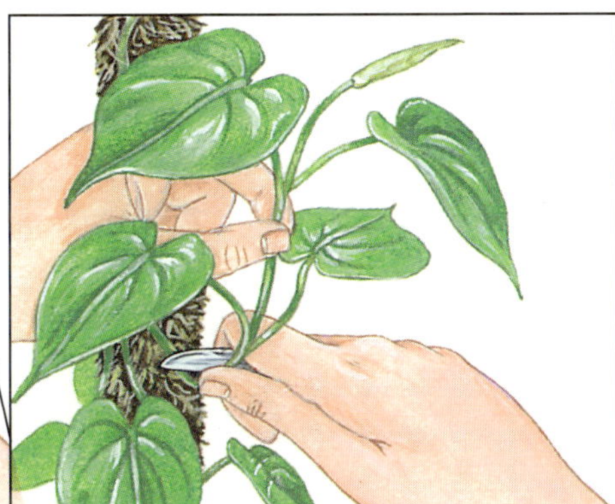

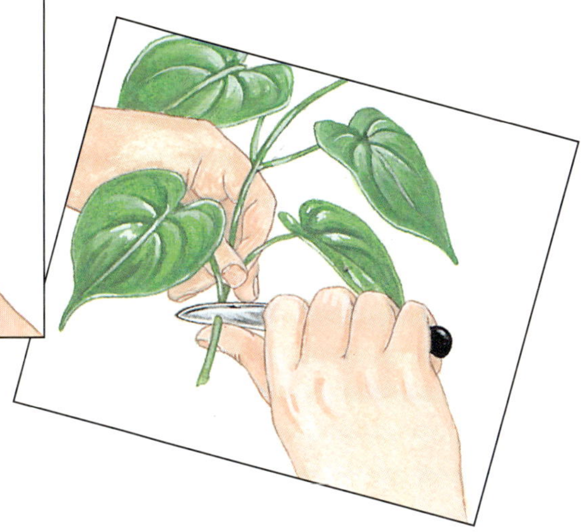

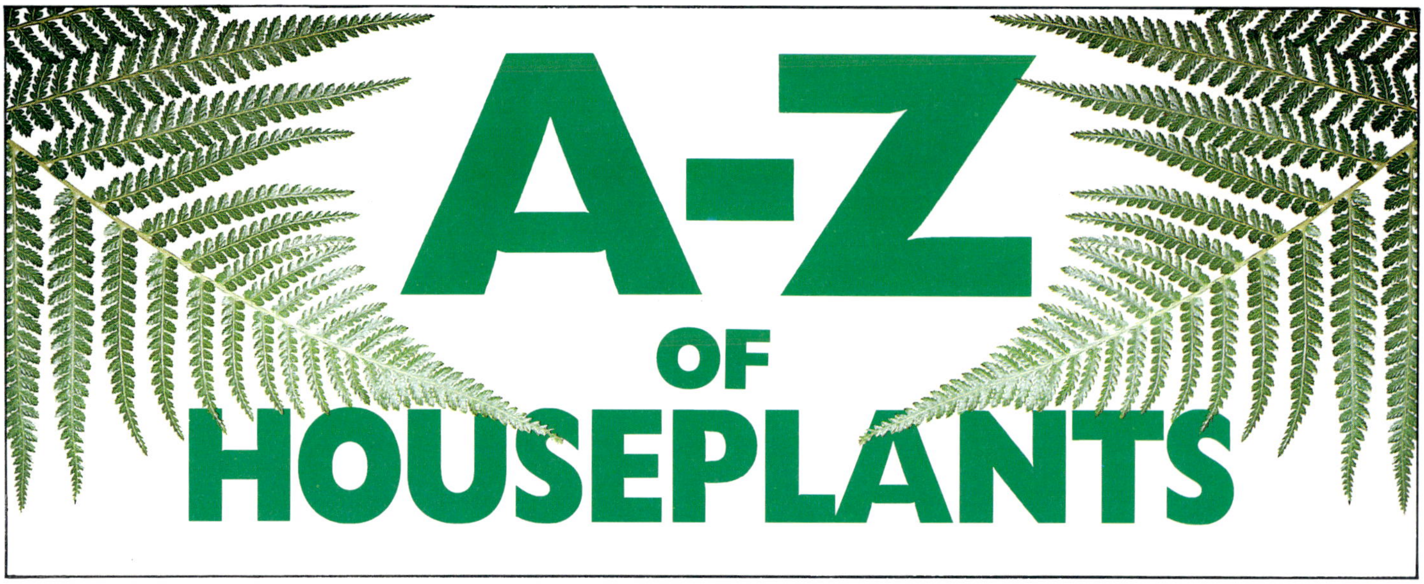

Abutilon

Family name: **Malvaceae**

Common names:
Flowering Maple
Chinese Lantern

Care Easy to grow	**Height** 5ft (1.5m)	**Flower** June-Oct
Light Bright indirect sun	**Spread** 4ft (1.2m)	**Humidity** None
Price Middle range	**Shape** Shrub	**Availability** Garden centres
Temp. Min 40°F (5°C)	Ideal 55°F (13°C)	Max 70°F (21°C)

Abutilons are vigorous shrubs which mostly come from tropical and sub-tropical South America. They grow up to 5ft (1.5m) tall in a pot, and taller still in a large container or soil border. Abutilons develop several slender branches that bear deeply cut, rather maple-like, dark green, soft, velvety leaves, often with attractive yellow mottling. They produce pretty, dangling, bell-shaped flowers in the summer which can also appear throughout the year if you give the plant enough warmth. Flowers vary from white to yellow, orange, pink and red. Look out for the many lovely hybrids such as 'Canary Bird' with its beautiful rich yellow flowers, and 'Apricot' with rich dark green leaves and reddish-orange flowers veined a deeper red. Some Abutilons are hardy in south and west England when grown outside against a sheltering wall.

Spring and summer care

Every year in March repot into John Innes No 2 just before active growth starts. Always keep your Abutilon well watered and never let it dry out completely. Mist spray the leaves with water every day in hot weather. They thrive in temperatures between 50-60°F (10-15°C): the warmer it gets, the

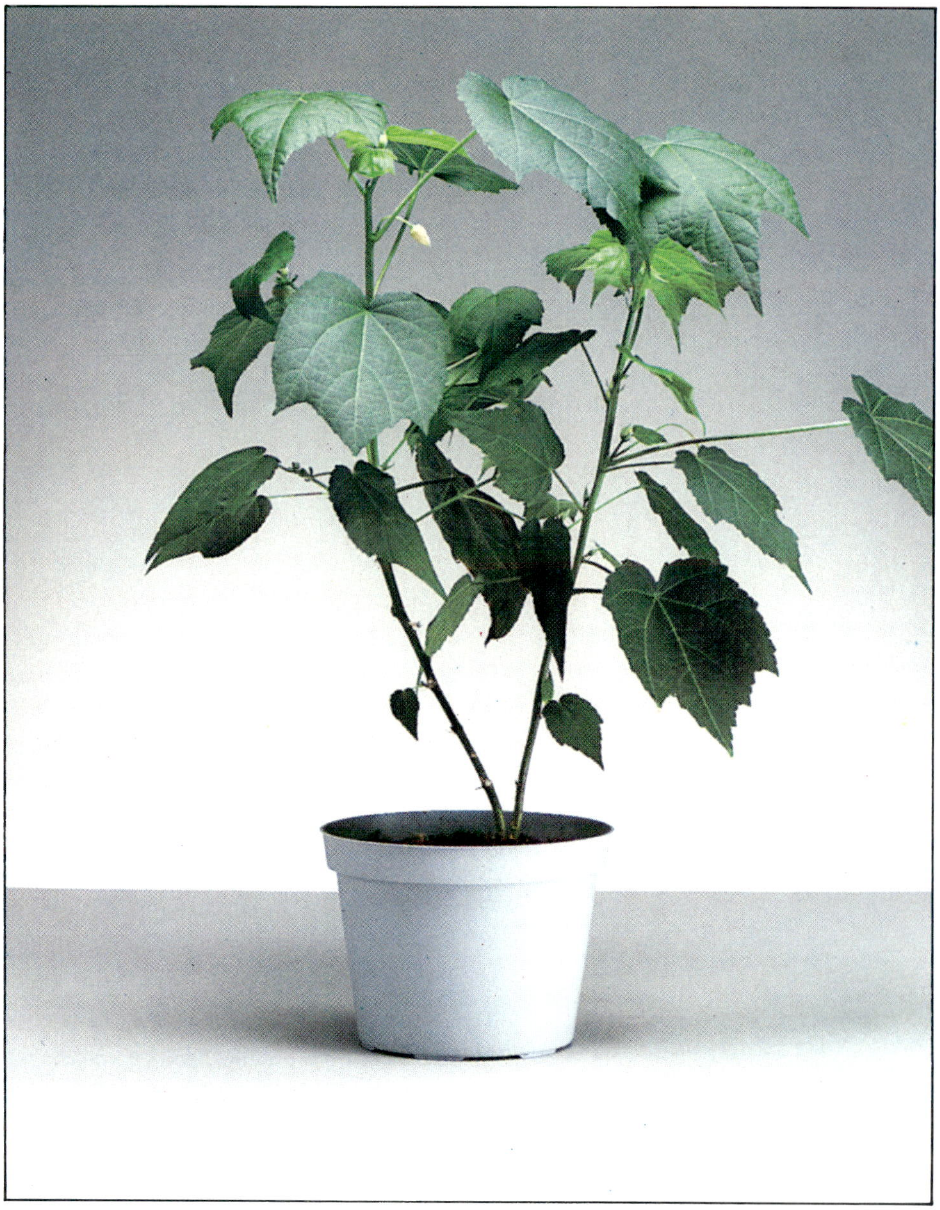

Abutilon thompsonii rapidly grows into a large shrub with careful pruning.

Species

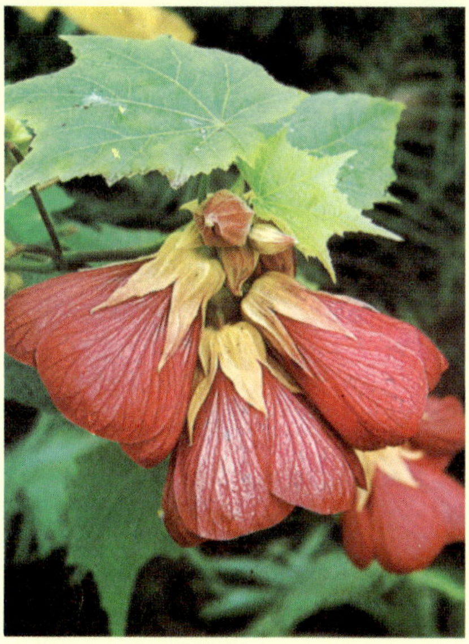

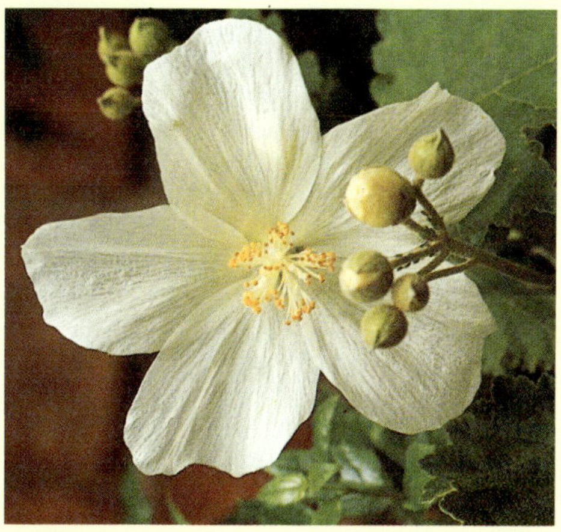

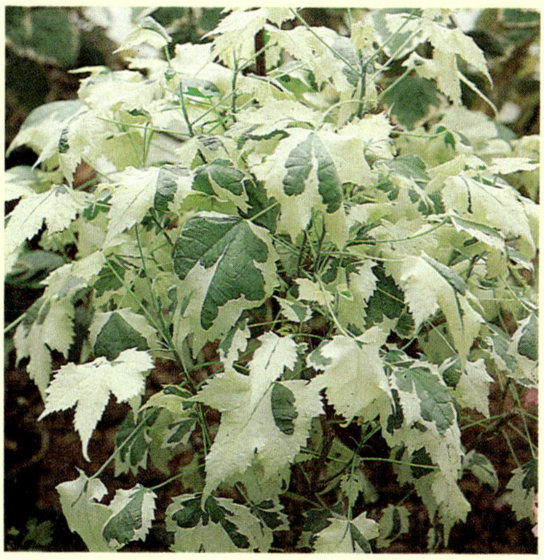

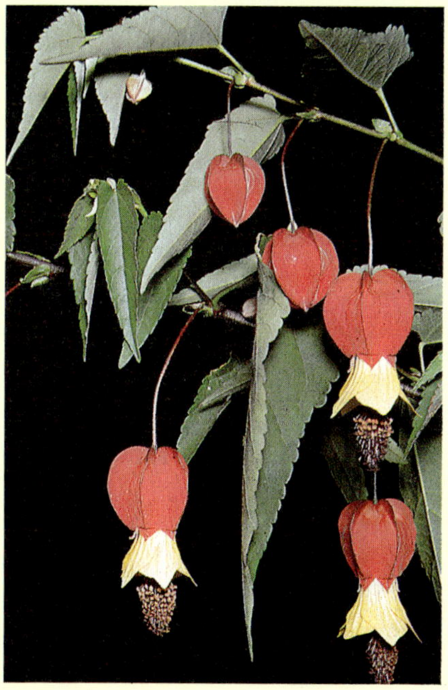

Abutilon thompsonii, *main picture, above and right,* has green leaves sometimes heavily variegated with white. It is the only Abutilon which doesn't have hairy leaves. You must give it really good light to bring out the beauty of its foliage. Its flowers are a lovely orange-salmon, and if given sufficient warmth will appear from late spring through until autumn. It is half hardy in south-west England.

A.striatum is a very similar plant to ***A.thompsonii*** but has lovely orange-red, bell-shaped flowers instead.

A.megapotamicum, *above,* has yellow petals with a bright red inflated calyx above the petals; most unusual.

A.vitifolium, *top centre picture,* grows to 8ft (2.4m) tall with green velvety leaves. Flat flowers open from May to October. A large plant which needs a conservatory.

A.savitzii, the White Parlour Maple, has white leaves, with pretty hanging apricot-coloured flowers.

Trouble Shooter

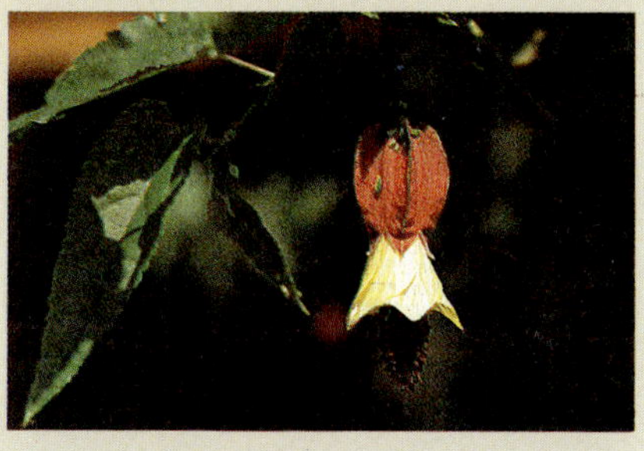

Abutilons are very easy plants to grow and are generally trouble free. The only problem to watch for is greenfly, *above* — spray immediately with a houseplant insecticide containing malathion: do this outside where there's no danger of harmful fumes. The other danger is over enthusiastic pruning which can damage the plant, so take care only to prune in the autumn and spring and never by more than half the stem.

more fresh air they need, especially if they live in a hot room. Abutilons are hungry plants and quickly absorb all the goodness from their compost, so feed them regularly every two weeks with a good liquid fertiliser such as Liquinure.

Give Abutilons good bright light during the growing season in the summer as well as throughout the rest of the year. Heavy shade stops the plant growing. Put your Abutilon outside for the summer if you can only give it a semi-shaded position during winter.

Abutilons are very fast growing and will quickly get straggly. In spring cut back the side shoots by as much as half and support the stems with canes and raffia before growth properly gets under way.

Autumn and winter care

When growth slows down at the beginning of autumn cut your Abutilon back again by as much as half to encourage bushiness. Keep it in a minimum temperature of 40°F (5°C) — any lower and the leaves are likely to drop off. Stop feeding until growth restarts in spring. During autumn and winter water the plant enough to keep the compost just moist — and even in the middle of winter don't let it dry out completely.

Propagation

Abutilons can be increased by cuttings in March and April. Use a sharp knife to take 5-6in (12-15cm) shoots from new top growth. Put the cuttings in sandy potting compost, and keep them warm in a gently airy spot — they should root quickly within a couple of weeks. As soon as they are large enough to handle without getting damaged, move them to a 3in (7cm) pot of John Innes No 2.

Otherwise you can buy seeds quite easily. Sow them in March, ¼in (6mm) deep, into seed trays of sandy seed-sowing compost. Germinate in a temperature of 70°F (21°C) on a warm windowsill or in a closed propagator.

Buying Guide

Look for young bushy plants which have plenty of healthy shoots. Don't buy a leggy plant unless you are going to cut it back hard immediately. Avoid plants which seem to have dried out, or those which have bone dry compost — they'll be difficult to revive.

Acacia

Family name: **Leguminosae**

Common names:
Mimosa/Silver Wattle

Care Easy to grow	**Height** 6 ft (1.8m)	**Flower** Dec-March
Light Full sun	**Spread** 5 ft (1.5m)	**Humidity** None
Price Middle range	**Shape** tree	**Availability** Garden centres
Temp. Min 40°F (5°C)	Ideal 70°F (21°C)	Max 85°F (30°C)

All Acacias are evergreen and the majority become small to large trees. ***Acacia dealbata,*** *right,* is one of the few which makes a good houseplant because with care you can keep it small enough to be manageable. It's grown for its beautiful leaves which, though individually tiny, combine to give the appearance of very dense foliage. If you've restricted the plant's size by pruning, the leaves will almost completely hide its whitish stems and branches. The fern-like leaf fronds are silvery-grey and about 6-9in (15-23cm) overall in length. Thick clusters of small, round, bright yellow, delicately scented pompom flowers appear at the ends of branches from December until about March. Try to stand your plant outside from June to September, but give it a protected position out of cold winds.

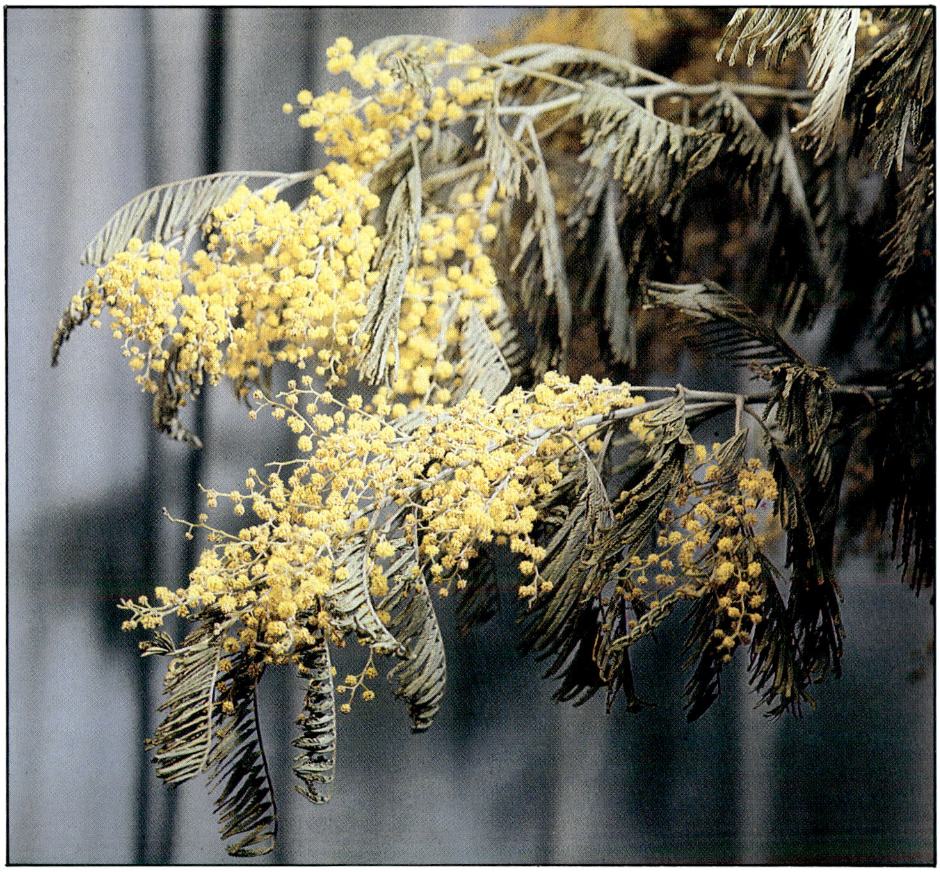

Acacia dealbata produces thick clusters of flowers from late winter until spring.

Spring and summer care

Repot Acacias every year in February or March into John Innes No 2 — or a little later if flowering hasn't stopped. Also, as soon as your Acacia stops flowering, trim it to shape. This will help to control the size of the plant by keeping the new growth close to the stem and making it bushier. As the days warm up in spring give your plant more water and fresh air, until you are watering quite freely by the summer. Feed every 14 days from late spring until August.

Autumn and winter care

A warm winter temperature is most important if you want your Acacia to flower — a minimum of 50°F (10°C) with just enough water to keep the soil moist. Acacias will survive 40°F (5°C) but flowering will be delayed until late spring. The warmer their winter temperature, the sooner they flower.

Propagation

Sow seeds ¼in (6mm) deep into John Innes Seed Sowing Compost in March and keep in a moist, shady position in a temperature of 70°F (21°C). The seeds germinate and grow quickly, so that by the end of their first year they should be 6-8in (15-20cm) tall.

Alternatively, in June or July take 3in (7cm) cuttings from half-ripened shoots — new shoots which are just beginning to get 'woody'. Keep them in a propagator if you have one, or put a clear plastic bag over the pot and seal it with a rubber band. Grow in a mixture of equal parts peat and sand at a temperature of 70°F (21°C), keep them moist and they will root within a couple of weeks.

Mature plants of *A.dealbata* often develop suckers from the base — you can cut these off with a sharp knife and treat them in the same way as cuttings.

Species

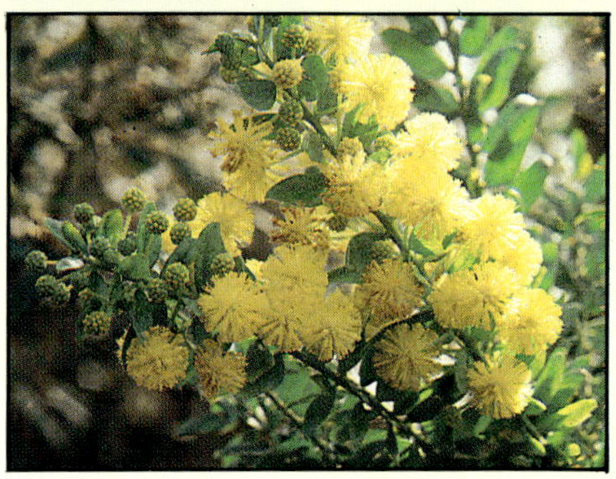

A.armata, the Kangaroo Thorn, *above,* so called because of its bristly stems. The close growing branches are covered with dark green leaves and rounded heads of rich yellow flowers in late spring and summer. The flowers are produced quite close to the stem. This can be a very successful houseplant.

A.drummondii is a dainty species with a rather loose shape. Its leaves are green or grey-blue, and bright golden yellow flowers bloom in the spring.

A.baileyana, *below,* similar to ***A.dealbata,*** with silver-grey leaves and the same yellow pompom flowers. When it's mature it becomes an elegant, rather rounded shrub and an absolute picture in full flower.

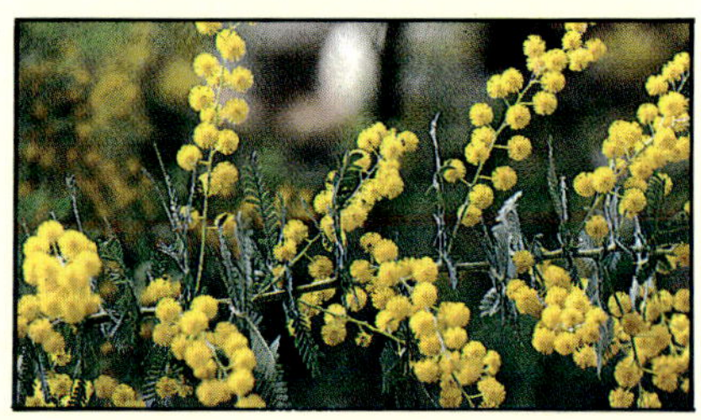

Trouble Shooter

Very few pests affect Acacia though greenfly occasionally attack new shoots; if this happens spray immediately with a houseplant pesticide.

Acalypha

Family name: **Euphorbiaceae**

Common names:
Chenille Plant/Copperleaf

Care Difficult to grow	**Height** 8ft (2.4m)	**Flower** July-Oct
Light Bright indirect sun	**Spread** 6ft (1.8m)	**Humidity** High humidity
Price Middle range	**Shape** Bushy	**Availability** Garden centres
Temp.	Min 45°F (7°C) · Ideal 75°F (24°C)	Max 90°F (33°C)

Acalyphas are colourful, rather large and fast growing woody shrubs from tropical South East Asia and the Pacific islands. One species is grown for its uniquely dramatic tassels of flowers, and the other species for its beautiful foliage. The main growing time is from early spring through until late summer by which time they'll be large bushy plants.

Acalypha hispidia comes from New Guinea and is really showy with its long tassels of chenille-like flowers. It can reach 8ft (2.4m) tall but with autumn pruning can be kept to a more manageable 3-5ft (0.9-1.5m). *A.wilkesiana* is grown for its spectacular large, jagged-edge leaves which are often marked with pink, white or black blotches. The leaves need good bright light to develop their rich colouring but direct strong sun will scorch them. Acalyphas must have high humidity and protection from cold temperatures to do well.

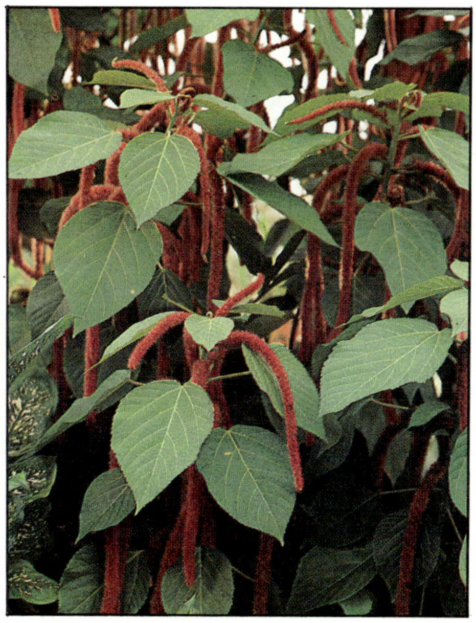

Acalypha hispidia has unique flowers.

Spring and summer care

Repot old plants any time between February and April using a good soil based compost such as John Innes No 2. With plants that are too big to repot completely, carefully scrape away the top 2in (5cm) of soil and replace with fresh compost — this is called 'top dressing'. Regular watering and high humidity are vital — if you forget your plant will lose its leaves, dehydrate and even die. In summer Acalyphas like bright light and temperatures of 70°F (21°C) plus, but keep them out of the direct sun. Don't let the temperature fall below 60°F (15°C) at night. Without sufficient light Acalyphas become spindly, lose much of their colouring and will fail to produce flower tassels. Feed them every 14 days with a good fertiliser such as Phostrogen, which contains the right balance of plant foods.

Autumn and winter care

Cut off any remaining dead tassels. By the end of summer your plant may be too big, so cut it back by as much as half its new growth; or wait until February when it's time to take cuttings. In autumn reduce watering until the compost is kept just moist. Give a minimum winter temperature of 60°F (15°C).

Propagation

Take 5-6in (12-15cm) long cuttings with a small 'heel'. Root in sandy compost at 80°F (26°C). Keep shaded, moist and humid. *A.hispidia* cuttings should flower next year.

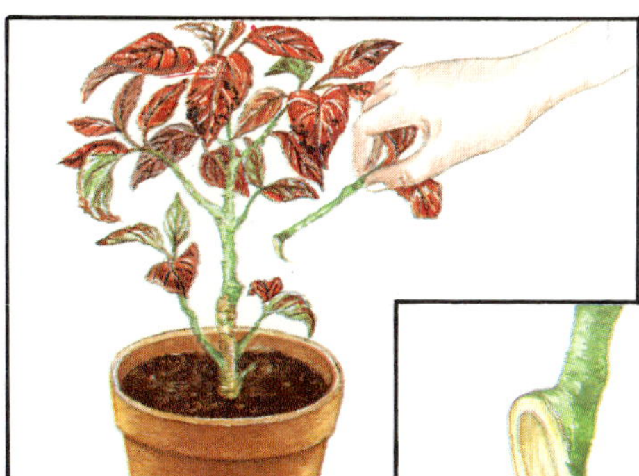

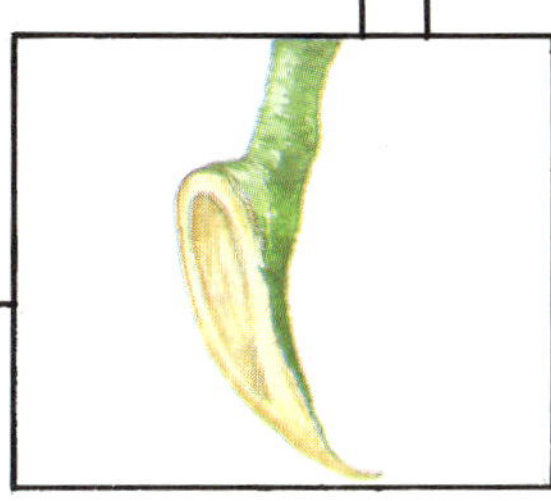

Take short side shoots with a piece of 'heel' *right*, in spring.

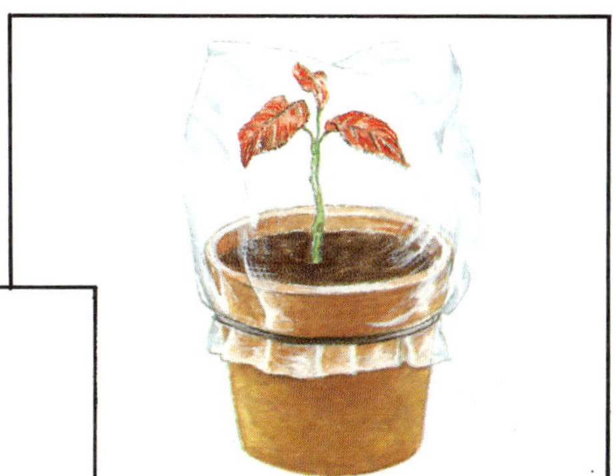

Root the cutting in a warm, moist position on a bright windowsill.

Trouble Shooter

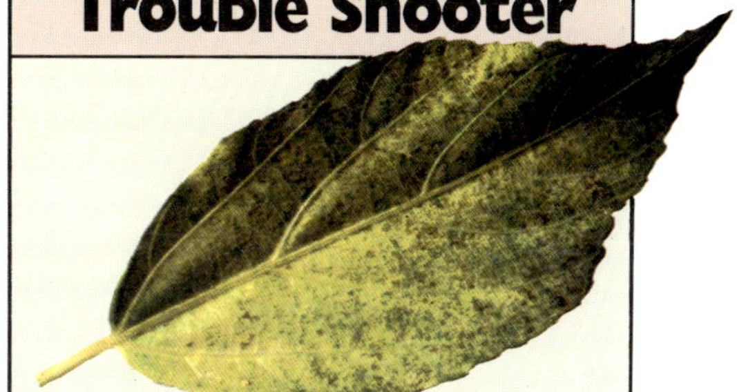

Acalyphas are easy plants to grow and will give you little cause for concern provided you can give them warm winter temperatures. If the leaves start to drop off it's because the air's too dry and you must provide more humidity. Their worst enemy is the red spider mite which appears when the air around the plant is too dry. Mites attack the undersides of leaves and make a fine webbing over new growth. Left alone the mites will totally ruin the appearance of the plant, *see above;* spray with insecticide, and in hot weather make a daily habit of spraying the plant with water.

Species

Acalypha hispidia, *above left,* comes from New Guinea, has bright green, oval, slightly hairy toothed leaves as much as 8in (20cm) long. It's called the Chenille Plant because of the appearance of its hundreds of tiny bright scarlet flowers which hang in spikes as much as 18in (46cm) or more long. They last for quite a long time, but it's a good idea to remove them as soon as the colour starts fading to encourage more flowers to form. You can also get varieties with green or cream tails.

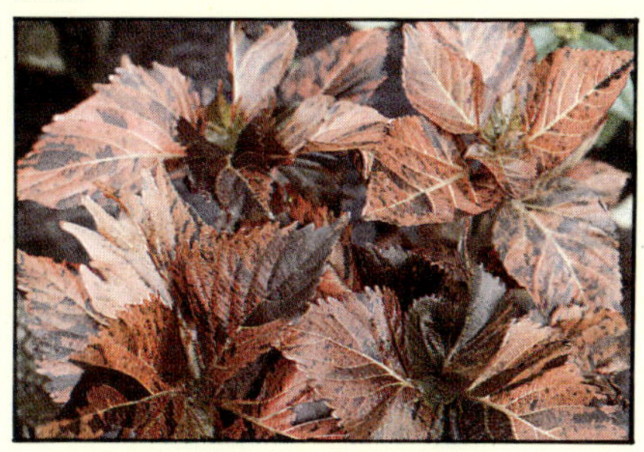

A.wilkesiana, the Copperleaf, *above,* has attractive bronzy-maroon leaves which are up to 6in (15cm) long. Its flowers are quite insignificant. ***A.w.macafeana*** comes from the New Hebrides and has oval red leaves marbled with crimson and bronze. Other varieties have leaf colours in green and cream, pink, orange or red.

A.hoffmannii is completely different, with almost grass-like leaves which are greenish red, tinged white.

Achimenes

Family name: **Gesneriaceae**

Common name:
Hot Water Plant

Care Easy to grow	**Height** 12in (30cm)	**Flower** June-Oct
Light Bright indirect sun	**Spread** 5in (12cm)	**Humidity** Regular spraying
Price Cheap	**Shape** Bushy	**Availability** Common

Temp. Min 40°F (5°C) Ideal 65°F (18°C) Max 80°F (27°C)

These are small, bushy little glossy leaved plants which are smothered in bright tubular flowers throughout summer. Most species come from Mexico and South America. The rather flattish flowers come in a range of colours from white and yellow to pink, red, blue and purple. Individual flowers last for only a few days but follow in quick succession from June through until late September or October. The stems of most species arch attractively which makes them lovely plants for growing in hanging baskets.

Achimenes get their common name Hot Water Plant from the mistaken belief that they should be watered with hot water. Instead, the truth is that they like to have a little warm water in spring to encourage them to start growing. There are lots of pretty hybrids which have been bred together from different species.

Achimenes grow pink or white scaly rhizomes, 1in (2.5cm) long, each of which produces only a single stem — so to get a really bushy display you have to plant a number of rhizomes in the same container. These rhizomes are dormant in winter and send out fresh shoots in spring, but they need warmth and humidity for constant growth. Plants flower from June until mid-autumn when they shrivel and die down for a winter rest until they sprout in the spring.

Spring and summer care

Plant the rhizomes in late February or March 1in (2.5cm) deep into a good compost such as John Innes No 2. Place six to eight rhizomes in a 6in (15cm) pot to get a bushy plant. Carefully give them a little lukewarm water to moisten the compost. After this keep their soil moist all summer — never let them dry out, or conversely, get too wet by sitting in a saucer of water, or you will lose your Achimenes.

Trouble Shooter

Achimenes are ideal houseplants for beginners as they rarely suffer from problems — the few they do have are likely to be because they've been mistreated.

A totally collapsed plant can be due to overwatering, with the result that the rhizomes are rotting; dry the plant out by not watering for a few days until the compost is only just damp. From then on keep the compost just moist and it might recover.

The same result comes from under watering, when the rhizomes have dehydrated to the point where they are unable to grow; give your plant a good drink, then water regularly enough to keep the compost moist.

If your plant fails to flower and only produces brown buds you probably kept it at too high a temperature and in the direct sun; move the plant to another bright spot but out of the direct sun.

Alternatively you could have overwatered — if this is the case, learn to give less water less often.

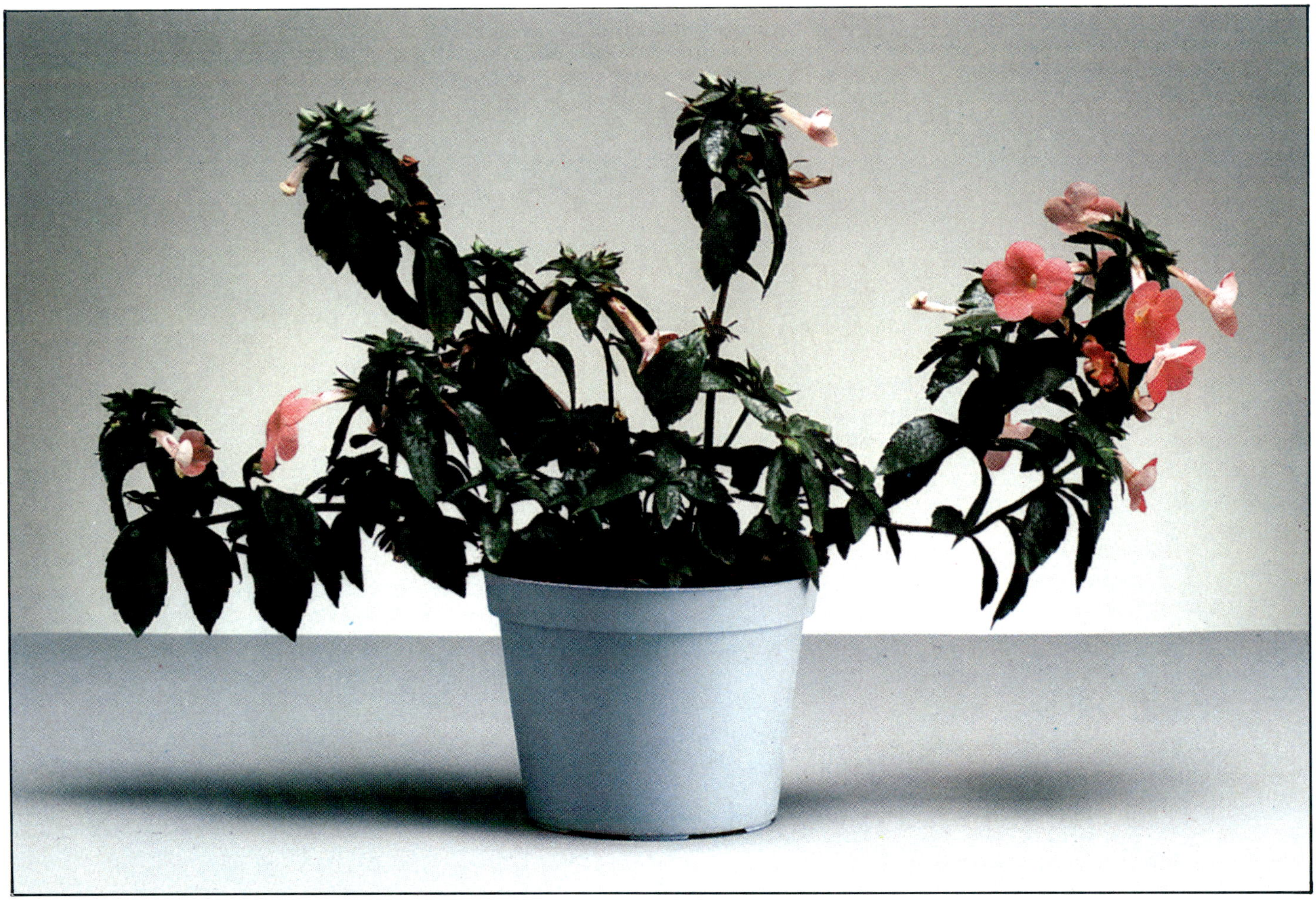

To get an attractive bushy Achimenes plant six rhizomes of the same colour together in a pot.

Start your plants growing in a temperature of 60°F (15°C); this can rise a bit as they grow, but never let it get any higher than 80°F (27°C). Achimenes need plenty of good light, but keep them out of the direct sun. In warm weather, mist spray the air around the plants but don't get moisture droplets on their leaves or flowers. Feed with a high potash fertiliser as made for flowering plants, every two weeks from the time the first flower buds show until flowering finishes in the autumn.

To make your plants bushy, use your forefinger and thumb and literally 'pinch' out the top 1in (2.5cm) or so of the young shoots. Then when the plant grows it will send out two shoots instead of one. Long stems can be supported with raffia and canes.

Autumn and winter care

Give your Achimenes less water as the number of buds decreases in August and September. The leaves will quickly start to wither — when this happens, cut off the stems at soil level and stop watering completely, until you start the rhizomes into growth again in spring. Either leave the rhizomes in their pots or carefully remove them from their compost and store them in dry peat or sand. Keep your plant safe over winter in a frost-free place such as an airing cupboard.

Propagation

This is nice and easy as by the end of the summer each Achimines rhizome produces three to six fresh rhizomes. Pot these up together to get a really bushy plant next season, or split them up at planting time to develop individually.

Seeds can be sown in March into a peat based seed compost with an added handful of sharp sand. Keep them at 70-80°F (21-27°C) during and immediately after germination; then the temperature can fall back to about 65°F (18°C).

Take cuttings from shoots which haven't had flowers in April or early May, and grow them on in gentle warmth — such as on a sunny windowsill — in the same compost mix as for seeds. In fact a good cactus compost has the ideal proportions of peat, loam and sharp sand, plus essential base fertiliser.

Species

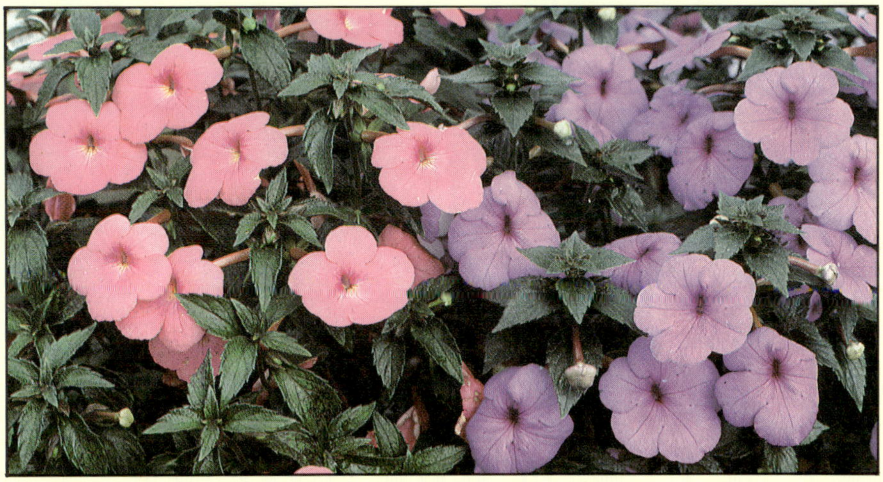

Achimenes grandiflora, *above,* the tallest species, has 2ft (0.6m) arching green or red stems and is ideal for a hanging basket. It's a rather hairy plant with oval, toothed edge leaves with reddish undersides. Large, flat, purplish-red flowers almost 2in (5cm) across appear from the leaf joints from June to early October.

A.longiflora, *main picture and right,* is perfect for a hanging basket. Its growth is variable but generally reaches about 12in (30cm) long stems, often flecked with red. Its small, oval, toothed edge leaves are covered in soft bristles. The violet-blue flowers have long tubes and flat faces. There are a number of good varieties to look out for. 'Alba' has numerous snowy-white flowers with yellow throats spotted purple — often as much as 3in (7cm) wide. 'Major' has metallic green leaves and large 3in (7cm), violet-blue flowers with a golden-yellow throat.

A.candida has the common name Mother's Tears. It is a low growing plant with red-brown wiry stems and rough, greenish leaves with toothed edges. The small flowers are a slightly arched funnel shape and are white and yellow with a purple spotted throat, while the undersides of the petals are a buff colour.

A.skinneri is another good hanging basket plant, but quite loose in shape. The stems produce bulbils (baby bulbs) which can eventually be treated as rhizomes. Its leaves are bronzy-green with pale to medium purple flowers with yellow throats.

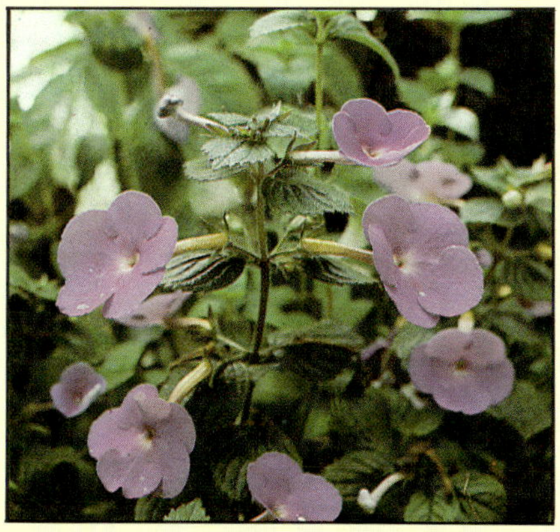

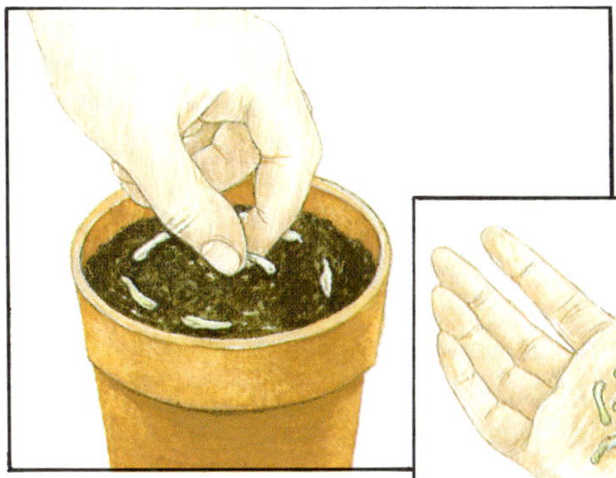

Plant six Achimenes rhizomes in the same pot. They are very small: *right.*

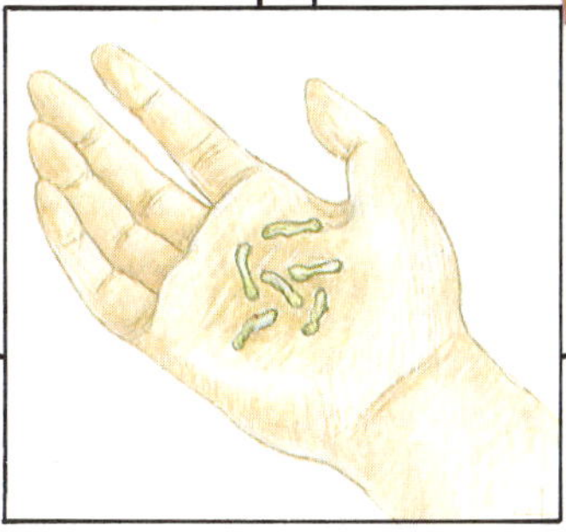

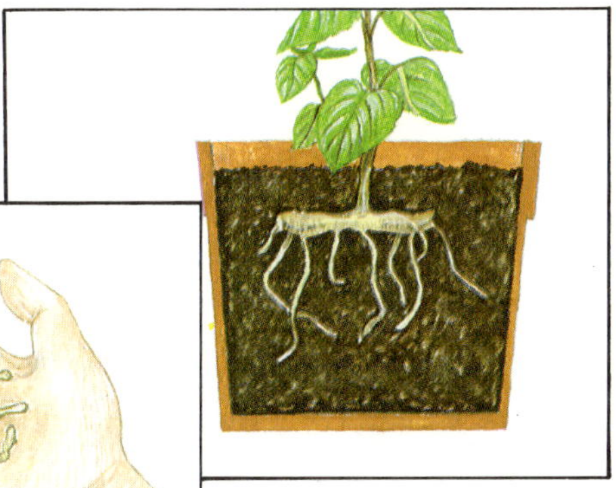

Each rhizome sends up only one or two shoots, so plant a number together.

Buying Guide

Buy Achimenes as rhizomes in the winter. Choose plump, fresh looking rhizomes and buy about six of the same colour to get a bushy plant. For a good selection of hybrids look in a nurseryman's catalogue.

It's much cheaper to buy Achimenes rhizomes than to get a plant when it's in full flower, when you are paying for all the nurseryman's costs of raising the plant as well.

Adiantum

Family name: **Polypodiaceae**

Common name:
Maidenhair Fern

Care Straight-forward	**Height** 10in (25cm)	**Flower** None
Light Shade	**Spread** 20in (48cm)	**Humidity** High humidity
Price Cheap	**Shape** Fern	**Availability** Common

Temp. Min 56°F (13°C) Ideal 65°F (18°C) Max 70°F (21°C)

The Maidenhair Fern is justifiably one of our most popular houseplants as it's so pretty, but it can be temperamental unless you know exactly how to treat it. All the Maidenhairs have delicate foliage with lots of rounded triangular-shaped leaves; these hang in fronds from strong, wiry stalks which supposedly look like a maiden's hair should! They come from all over the world — Europe, Asia, Australasia and the Americas.

The root is really a slender, creeping, underground, fleshy stem, properly called a rhizome, which, given the right treatment, constantly sends up new fronds that unfurl from tight green balls as they grow. The secret of success is to give them warmth and humidity — without either the plant is likely to be disappointing.

Spring and summer care

Pot or repot Adiantums in spring into a good loam based compost like John Innes No 2.

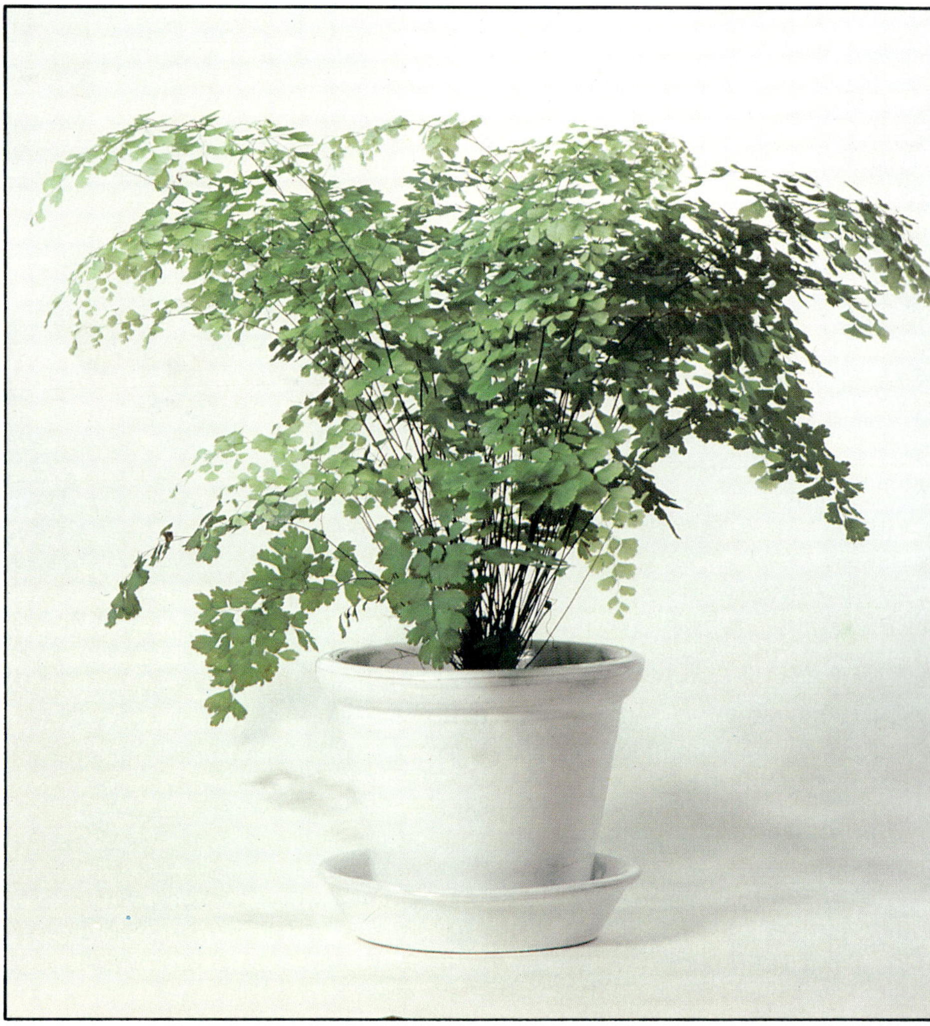

Adiantum capillus-veneris needs warmth and humidity to thrive.

Trouble Shooter

If not cared for properly, Adiantums can be temperamental and prone to a variety of unhealthy conditions.

Shrivelled foliage can result from lack of humidity in conjunction with dry soil and a stuffy atmosphere; give your plants water, high humidity and fresh air for healthy foliage, *right*.

Overwatering is a danger: ferns can drink a lot of water in hot weather but in cooler conditions if you give them too much their roots and rhizomes will rot; stop watering for a few days to let the plant dry out until the compost is only just damp, and then water it only twice a week and you might manage to save it.

If the foliage becomes dry and listless and looks pale and papery, it's probably due to too much sunlight or a lack of fertiliser; move the plant to a shadier position and feed regularly every 14 days.

Adiantums in common with most ferns are very sensitive to fumes which

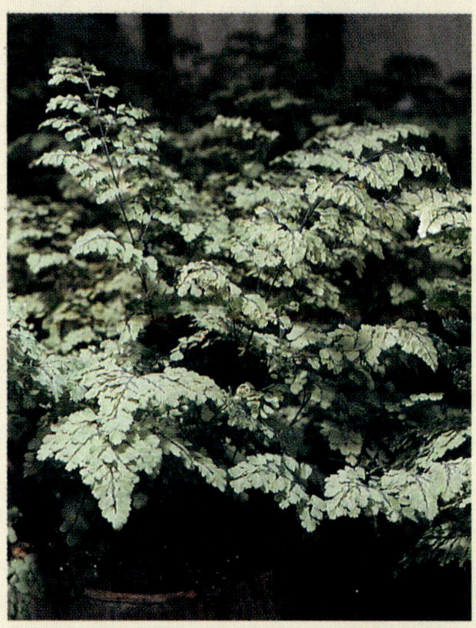

will as a result turn their fronds brown; keep your Adiantum well away from oil and gas heaters.

Whitefly are tiny, white moth-like flying insects which rise in numbers when the leaves are disturbed. Kill them with an insecticide containing pyrethrum; do not use malathion as this can cause problems. Repeat after a few days if necessary.

Mealy bugs rarely attack Adiantums, but when they do they show as white fluffy patches; a touch with a small paintbrush loaded with methylated spirits will destroy them but don't get meths on the foliage.

Scale insects are equally rare but can be a problem. They look like small warts on the underside of the foliage. Don't confuse them with spores — the easy way of telling is that the spores form in regular rows on the underside edge of each leaflet, and never in random patches or on the stalks; scale insects can easily be scraped off, then spray the plant with insecticide to kill off completely any lurking eggs.

You can make your own compost with: 2 parts rough peat; 1 part mixed loam; 1 part silver sand; 1 part charcoal chippings, with just a little added base fertiliser. If the fronds are brown after winter, cut them off at compost level with a a pair of sharp, fine pointed scissors. Give the plant a moderate watering and keep it in a temperature of about 60°F (15°C) to encourage it to start putting out new fronds.

Keep your Adiantum in the semi-shade as sunlight just shrivels up the delicate leaves, and grow it at a temperature of 60-65°F (15-15°C) throughout summer; if it drops to below 56°F (13°C) the chances are that the fern will become dormant and may prove difficult to revive. So the rule is, the higher the temperature, the higher the humidity.

Provide humidity by frequent mist spraying and by standing the pot in a saucer on top of a bed of wet pebbles. Water your plant freely as the weather warms up, but only enough to keep the compost moist — not wet. In warm weather this means watering twice weekly. Feed every 14 days with liquid fertiliser throughout spring and summer.

Autumn and winter care

Keep your Adiantum in a temperature no lower than 56°F (13°C) — otherwise it will become dormant and possibly even die, as it will too if it's kept in a cold draught. Don't provide humidity if the weather is cool, as chilly damp conditions encourage rotting.

Propagation

Divide mature rhizomes every third year in spring and pot them up in the same type of compost as before. Ferns don't flower so there are no seeds to sow, but they do produce spores on the underside of some leaves. These spores are dust-like and are very difficult to grow into plants — really a job for the professional.

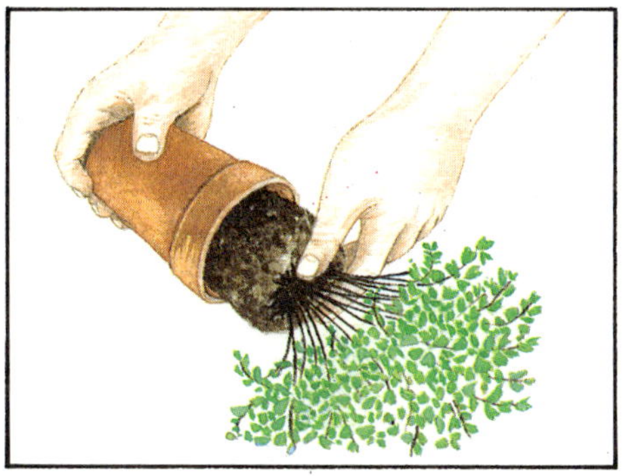

Dividing a Maidenhair fern: support the plant with one hand over the top of the compost, then carefully slip the fern out of its pot.

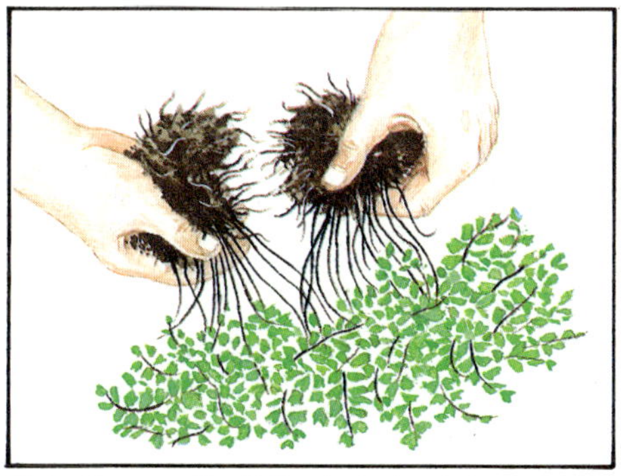

Grip the rootball firmly in both hands and gently tear the plant in half. Grow the pieces individually in the smallest pots which can comfortably contain their roots.

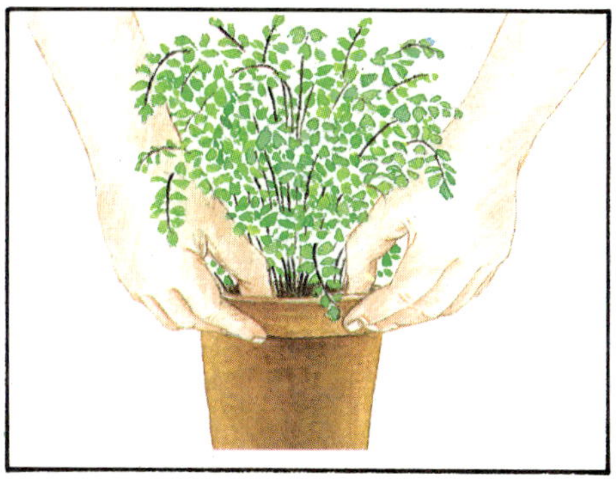

Repot using John Innes No 2; firm the compost around the sides with your thumbs so as not to leave any air pockets. Water the plants well and keep them in the shade.

Species

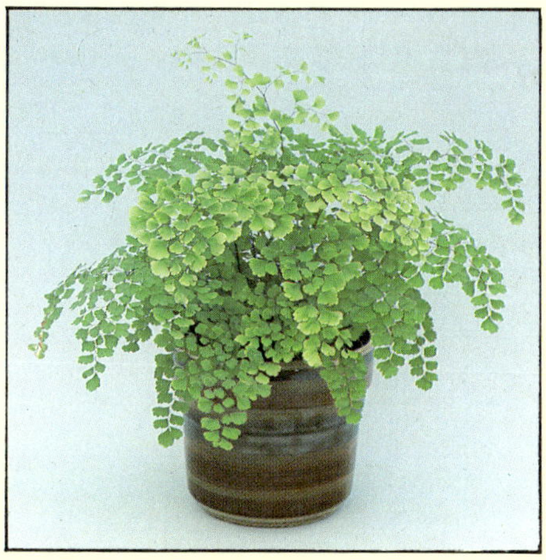

Adiantum capillus-veneris is about the commonest Maidenhair. It has delicate light green fronds on wiry black stalks which rarely grow higher than 12in (30cm), but with really good treatment it can double this size.

***A.raddianum**, above,* is more robust with 20in (50cm) long blackish stalks with finely divided blades of pale green leaflets. As the plant matures there is a tendency for the outer leaf edges to become brownish on the underside where the spores develop in clusters — this does the plant no harm. 'Fritz Luethii' has 20in (50cm) fronds with overlapping curled-edge leaflets which glisten with a steel blue hue. 'Elegans' is strong growing with rather compact fronds, at first reddish-brown but gradually turning yellow-green with time. 'Gracillimum' is a graceful hybrid with masses of tiny leaflets.

A.tenerum is a tall plant with fronds up to 3ft (0.9m) in length. Its leaflets are larger and are often deeply cut with wavy edges. 'Scutum roseum' *below,* has large reddish fronds which mature to a very dark green on shiny black stalks. 'Wrightii' is smaller, but the young fronds are pinkish-red later becoming green with maturity.

A.hispidulum has long, wiry, hairy stalks with thin,leathery leaves.

A.macrophyllum is really eyecatching and is gradually becoming more widely available. It has fronds 12-15in (30-38cm) long on glistening brownish-black stalks — the mature older leaflets can be 2-4in (5-10cm) long, somewhat rounded in shape and papery in texture with finely toothed edges. They are reddish at first but become yellowish-green later.

A.polyphyllum is the largest Adiantum with thick creeping rhizomes and fronds up to 4ft (1.2m) long or even more, on stiff black stalks with leaflets set very close together — almost resembling a comb. The upper edges are slightly toothed.

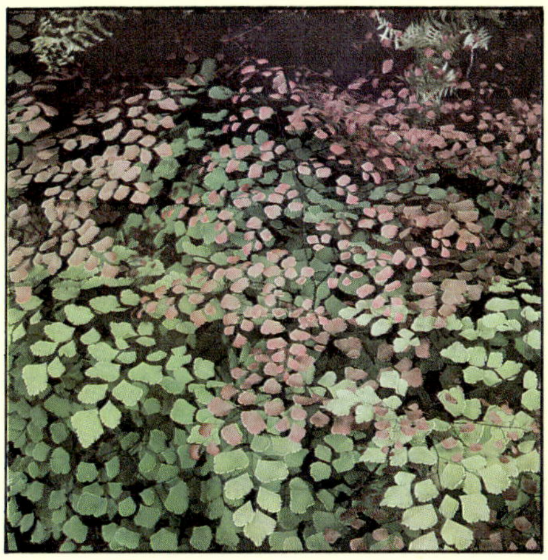

Buying Guide

Look for Adiantums growing in well-moistened compost and reject those which have any dried fronds. Avoid plants which have stood outside in cold winds. Some of the more unusual varieties can be hard to find but persistence pays off!

Aechmea

Family name: **Bromeliaceae**

Common name: **Urn Plant**

Care Easy to grow	**Height** 2ft (0.6m)	**Flower** Blue, pink bracts
Light Bright, indirect sun	**Spread** 4ft (1.2m)	**Humidity** Regular spraying
Price Middle range	**Shape** Bromeliad	**Availability** Common
Temp. Min 55°F (13°C)	Ideal 60°F (15°C)	Max 80°F (27°C)

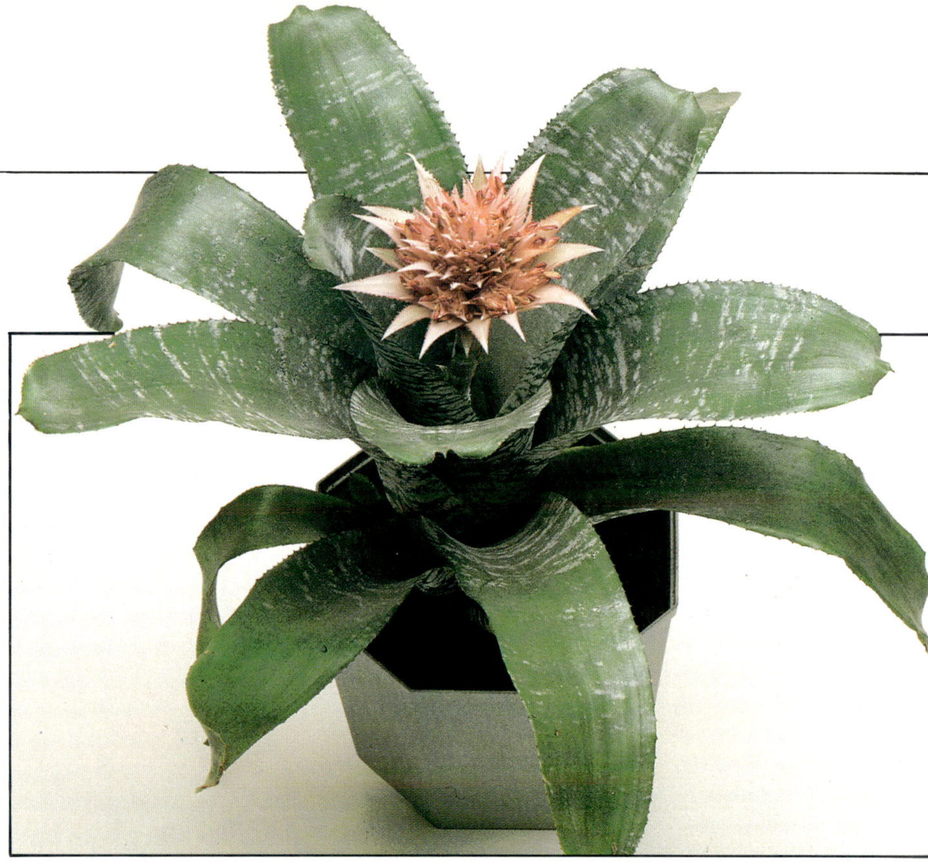

Aechmea fasciata is the easiest of all bromeliads to grow as a houseplant.

Aechmea is one of the largest families of bromeliads. Most are epiphytic — which means they live on jungle trees — and they all come from South America. Aechmeas have large urn-shaped rosettes of tough grey leaves which are designed to catch and channel water down to a central urn. This must always be kept full of water — use rain-water if possible. Mature plants send out a huge head of flowers on a long stem. Aechmeas bloom once and are then thrown away, but meanwhile they will have produced offsets — baby Aechmeas.

Spring and summer care

Pot Aechmeas in the late spring into a peat-based compost such as Levingtons plus a handful of sand and firm them in well. Keep them where they get good bright light and a temperature of over 60°F (15°C), plus lots of humidity. Water well but be careful not to waterlog them. Empty the urn occasionally to change the water as it can get stagnant. Water their soil with half strength liquid fertiliser every 14 days.

Autumn and winter care

Even in winter still keep the soil moist and the urn filled. By late winter the flower head has usually begun to fade; with a sharp knife cut it out carefully close to the base. You'll soon notice baby Aechmeas — offsets — appearing from round the bottom of the plant. These grow and develop quite rapidly and as they do the parent plant will start to fade and die. As soon as the offsets look strong enough, sever the parent just above soil level and throw it away. From then on the offsets can be left in the same container or potted up individually. They will flower in about 12-18 months.

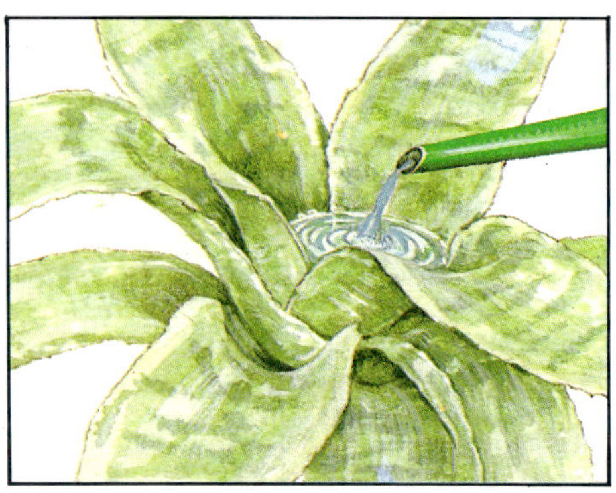

Keep the urn topped up with water and regularly change it completely.

Species

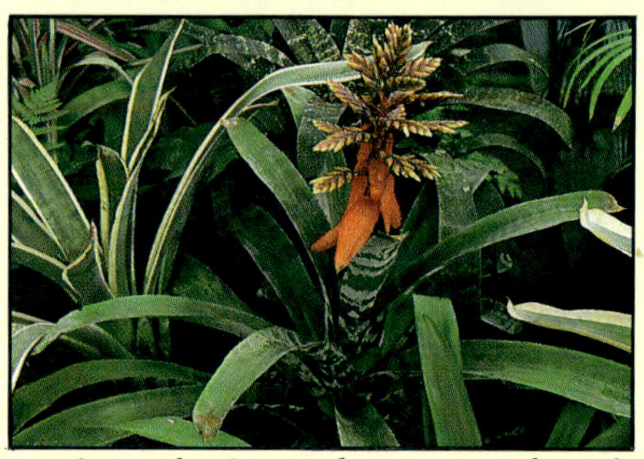

Aechmea fasciata makes an urn shaped rosette of tough, stiff, saw-toothed edge arching leaves, greyish green in colour and cross banded silvery white. The leaves can be up to 2ft (0.6m) long on a mature plant. Around August from the urn in the centre of the rosette appears a long pink stem, topped with a 'ball' of pink bracts (short colourful leaves) from which appear delicate pale blue flowers; these disappear quite quickly but the pink head lasts for about four months.

A. fulgens discolor is an attractive soft leathery-leaved plant, olive green on the upper surface and reddish purple on the underside. The head of flowers is an open spike of oval, reddish berries tipped with purplish flowers.

A.weilbachii has leaves which are coppery green on the top and wine red underneath. Pale lilac flowers appear from a loose head of red bracts.

A.chantinii, *left* is similar to ***A.fasciata***, but has a more open rosette and is bigger. It has leaves with silver bands on both surfaces and a brilliant flower head of orange and bright scarlet. It needs a rather higher temperature — at least 65°F (18°C) and much more humidity than the other Aechmeas.

Propagation

Sow Aechmea seed into a mixture of 2 parts peat to 1 part sand and keep them in a closed propagator at a temperature of 70-80°F (21-27°C). Keep them moist and shaded. When they are large enough to handle they can be potted on individually. From seed they take about five years to flower.

Offsets can be removed at any time of year into small pots using the normal compost.

Trouble Shooter

If the leaves start to lose colour then your air is too dry — give the plant lots of humidity by standing it on a tray filled with water and pebbles, and mist spray every day in warm weather. Leaves are also damaged by draughts and cold — 55°F (13°C) must be the minimum temperature. If your plant seems to be suffering move it to a warm spot quickly and it will probably survive.

Aeschynanthus

Family name: **Gesneriaceae**

Common name: **Lipstick Vine**

Care Difficult to grow	**Height** 2ft (0.6m)	**Flower** July-Sept
Light Bright indirect sun	**Spread** 2ft (0.6m)	**Humidity** High humidity
Price Middle range	**Shape** Hanging	**Availability** Garden centres
Temp. Min 45°F (7°C)	Ideal 70°F (21°C)	Max 80°F(27°C)

All Lipstick Vines that you can get as houseplants are epiphytes, plants which grow without soil high up in the tops of jungle trees, in this case in the Himalayas, Thailand and Malaysia. They produce lots of rather wiry, long trailing stems with well spaced stiffly held dark green leathery elliptic leaves. Grow your Lipstick Vine in a hanging basket to really appreciate its clusters of brilliant orange-red flowers which make this an eyecatching plant in the summer. The individual flowers last for only a few days but they follow rapidly in succession. You must give the plant lots of heat in summer as well as warm winter temperatures to be successful. Look for plants with a good green leaf colour and avoid any where the leaves look withered or shrunken. Aeschynanthus are available only in the summer when they're in flower. To find them go to a good garden centre or specialist nursery.

Spring and summer care

Repot every third year in March using a peat based compost such as Levingtons or Arthur Bowers. Only give a little water at first, then gradually increase the amount as the weather warms up until by the summer you're watering freely and frequently. In the warmest weather they'll appreciate a daily mist spray with water. Feed your plant with weak liquid fertiliser from mid-spring through until mid-autumn. Provide summer temperatures around 70-80°F (21-27°C) and

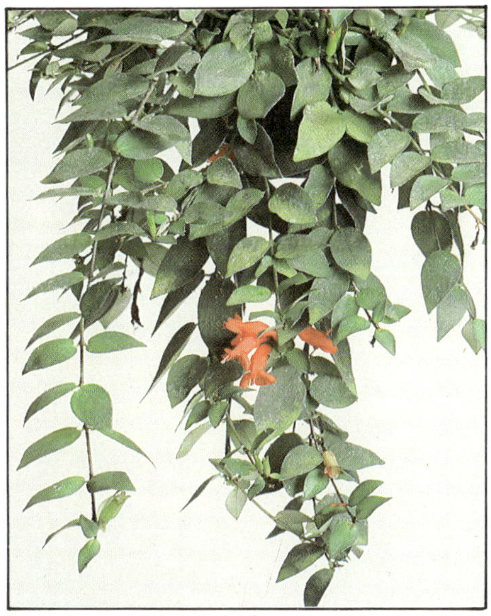

Aeschynanthus lobbianum.

grow the Lipstick Vine where it can get the brightest light, but avoiding long periods in the full sun. As soon as the flowers finish, you can prune back the stems by a third of their length if your plant's getting too leggy.

Autumn and winter care

Stop feeding in mid-autumn and gradually tail off the amount of water you're giving until the plant is kept only just moist through winter. Above all don't let the temperature drop any lower than 60°F (15°C) or the plant will suffer. Continue to provide as much light as possible.

Propagation

In February and March take 3in (7cm) cuttings from firm shoots. Dip the cut ends in hormone rooting powder and pot up in the same compost as the mature plant but with some added sharp sand — 3 parts compost to 1 part sand — to make sure that the water drains away freely. Give the cuttings a high temperature of 80°F (27°C) to root.

Species

Aeschynanthus lobbianum, *left*, has long trailing branches with small elliptic fleshy dark green leaves. The tubular flowers are bright red with a creamy yellow throat and appear in mid to late summer.

A.javanensis, *below*, is very similar to **A.lobbianum** with which it's often confused. It has slightly toothed, small oval,dark green leaves which are inclined to be leathery, borne on long trailing branches. The flowers are scarlet with a bright yellow throat and look like arched tubes, emerging from a silky cup-shaped calyx of purplish red in mid to late summer.

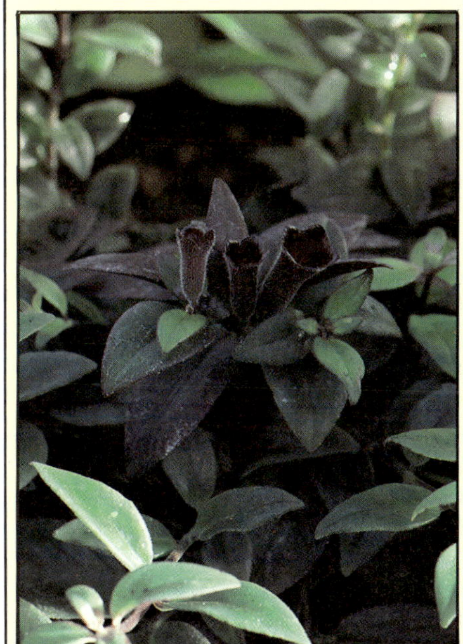

A.marmorata, the Zebra Basket Vine, is a beautiful rarity which can occasionally be found. It has long,waxy dark green leaves which are covered with a network of yellowish-green markings on the top of the leaf and a rich maroon on the underside. The tubular flowers are green with brown spots.

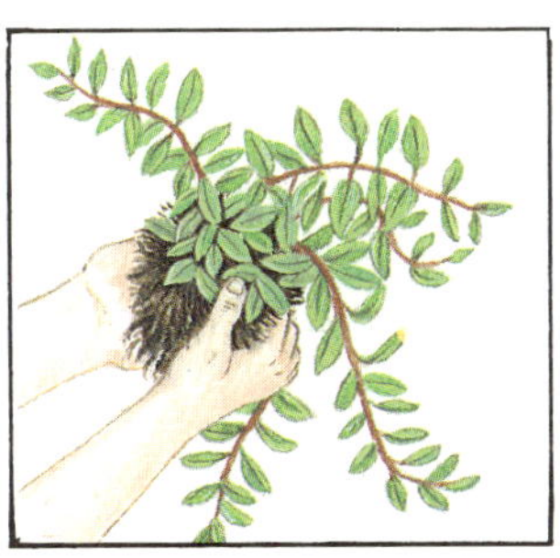

Try something different — grow your Lipstick Vine on a piece of gnarled wood as it does naturally in the jungles of the Far East.

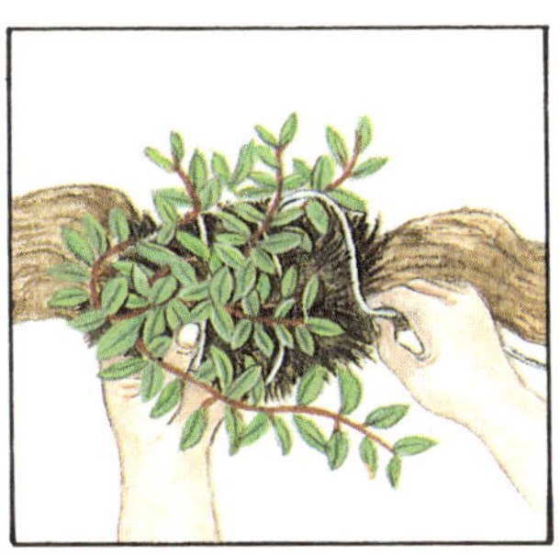

Remove the vine from its pot and arrange it on the wood. Wind soft wire round the roots and wood until the plant is secure.

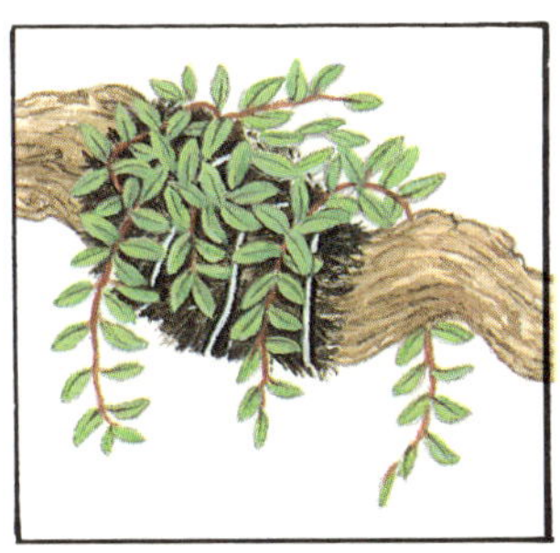

Tuck stray roots in neatly and use sphagnum moss to grow over the wires. Spray in hot weather to keep the plant moist.

Trouble Shooter

This is one of the few plants where greenfly is a rarity, but tell-tale cotton wool-like fluff on the undersides of leaves and at the leaf joints indicates mealy bugs. This is easily remedied by dabbing the fluff with a small paint brush dipped in methylated spirits. Repeat a couple of days later and the problem should disappear.

Agave

Family name: **Agavaceae**

Common name: **Century Plant**

Care Easy to grow	**Height** 1-4ft (0.3-1.2m)	**Flower** Rare
Light Full sun	**Spread** 1-4ft (0.3-1.2m)	**Humidity** Regular spraying
Price Middle range	**Shape** Rosette	**Availability** Garden centres

Temp. Min 45°F (7°C) — Ideal 65°F (18°C) — Max 75°F (24°C)

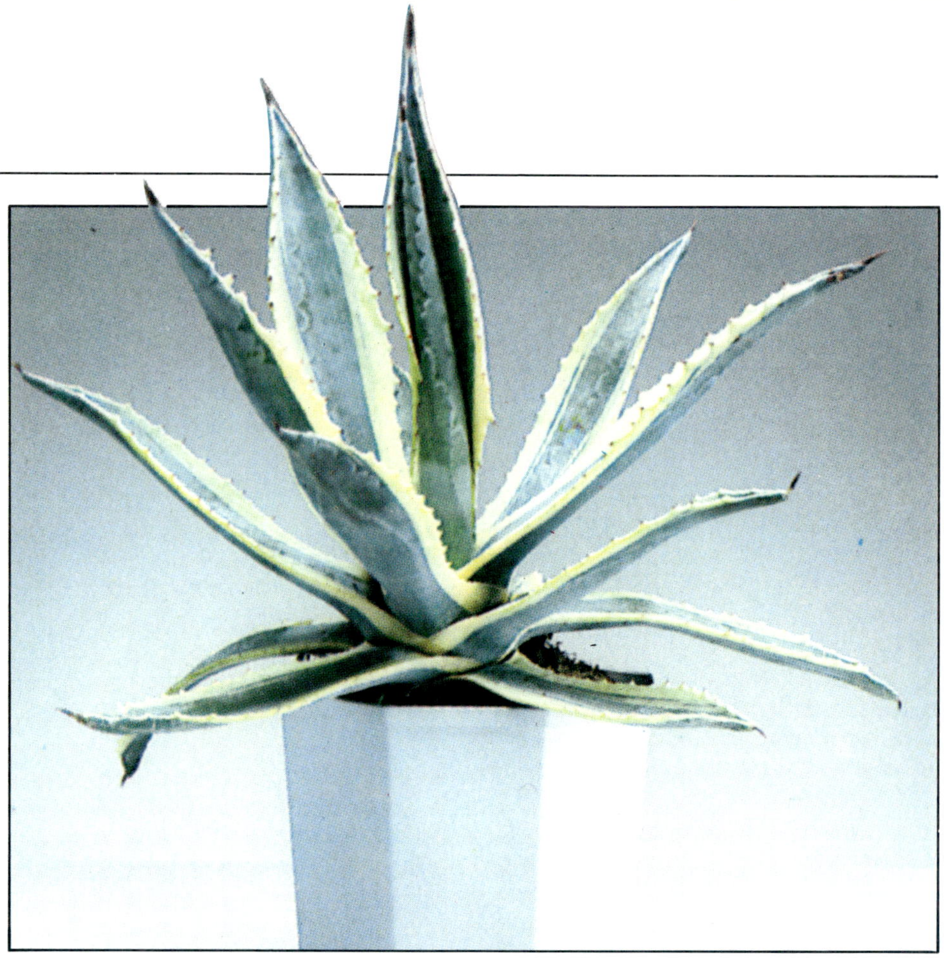

Agave americana marginata is very slow growing but well worth the wait.

The many species of Agave are grown for their dramatic sword-like succulent leaves which are edged with vicious spines. The leaves all grow from a central base point into a symmetrical rosette shape. Agaves come from the Americas and West Indies. The best known species is the Century Plant, *Agave americana*, so called because of the fallacy that it won't flower until it's a hundred years old. The truth is that it takes 10 to 15 years to be mature enough to flower, by which time your plant will have grown far too big to live at home with you. Its rosette will be between 6 and 8ft (1.8 and 2.4m) across and its flower spike up to 40ft (12m) high!

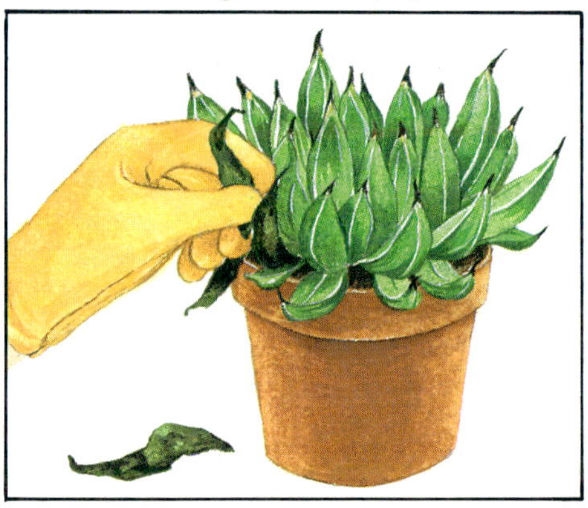

Spring and summer care

Repot your large Agaves in early spring every year and the smaller ones every two or three years using a special cactus compost. Water regularly enough to keep the compost moist, but never so much that the compost remains wet. Feed your Agave every three weeks from April through until October with a special cactus fertiliser or Phostrogen — both contain the correct balance of essential trace elements which guarantee steady, healthy growth. Agaves love sitting in the full sun, but let them get gradually accustomed to it over a couple of weeks if they have most recently been living in the shade. They will also enjoy sitting outside during the summer. By late summer most Agaves have produced offsets — baby plants — around their base; leave them alone until they are large enough to handle without damaging them.

Autumn and winter care

Pull off any leaves which have withered around the base — this is quite natural and nothing to be alarmed about. Continue to give your Agave good light throughout winter. Most species are tough enough to withstand a low winter temperature, but if it falls below 45-50°F (7-10°C) their soil must be completely dry for them to survive.

Propagation

When the offsets are 3-4in (7-10cm) they are big enough to take from the parent plant. Remove them carefully with a sharp knife and pot them separately in cactus compost and grow them at a temperature of 60°F (15°C). Keep them only just moist and not in too much strong sun until they are established.

Trouble Shooter

Agaves are easy to grow and are troubled by few pests. Scale insect looks like tiny brown warts which sometimes become lodged on the underside of leaves. Use a small brush and dab some methylated spirits onto the pest and repeat after a few days.

Overwatering is a constant danger, especially if water gets caught in the centre of the rosette while the weather is cold. If your Agave looks sick and the soil is wet, remove it from the pot and dry it out for a week in a warm place, then repot it.

Species

Agave americana as a young plant has thick, grey-green leaves with sharp, brownish-black spines at the edges and a wicked long black spike at the tip. It grows fast and will outlive its welcome in a few years. ***A.a.marginata***, *top*, has colourful leaves of grey-green with a wide golden yellow margin on both edges. ***A.a.striata*** is similar but with yellow and white stripes running lengthwise near the centre of the leaves. ***A.a.medio-picta***, 'Alba', *below*, has a tighter rosette of paler greyish leaves each with a central silvery-white band running tip to base.

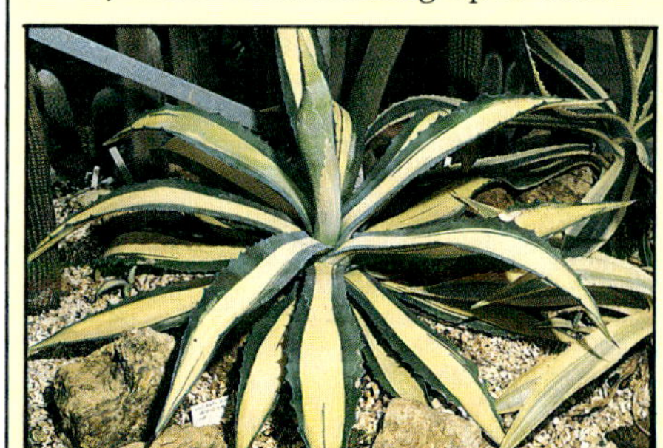

A.stricta has a dense rosette of narrow 14in (36cm) long, green stiff leaves which taper to a point. They mostly stand straight up or are slightly curving in towards the centre.

A.victoriae-reginae has a rosette of numerous grey-green leaves marked with irregular whitish lines. This is the only species which doesn't produce offsets.

Aglaonema

Family name: **Araceae**

Common name:
Chinese Evergreen

Care Straight-forward	**Height** 3ft (0.9m)	**Flower** June-Aug
Light Bright indirect sun	**Spread** 4ft (1.2m)	**Humidity** Regular spraying
Price Middle Range	**Shape** Bushy	**Availability** Garden centres
Temp. Min 60°F (15°C)	Ideal 65°F (18°C)	Max 75°F (24°C)

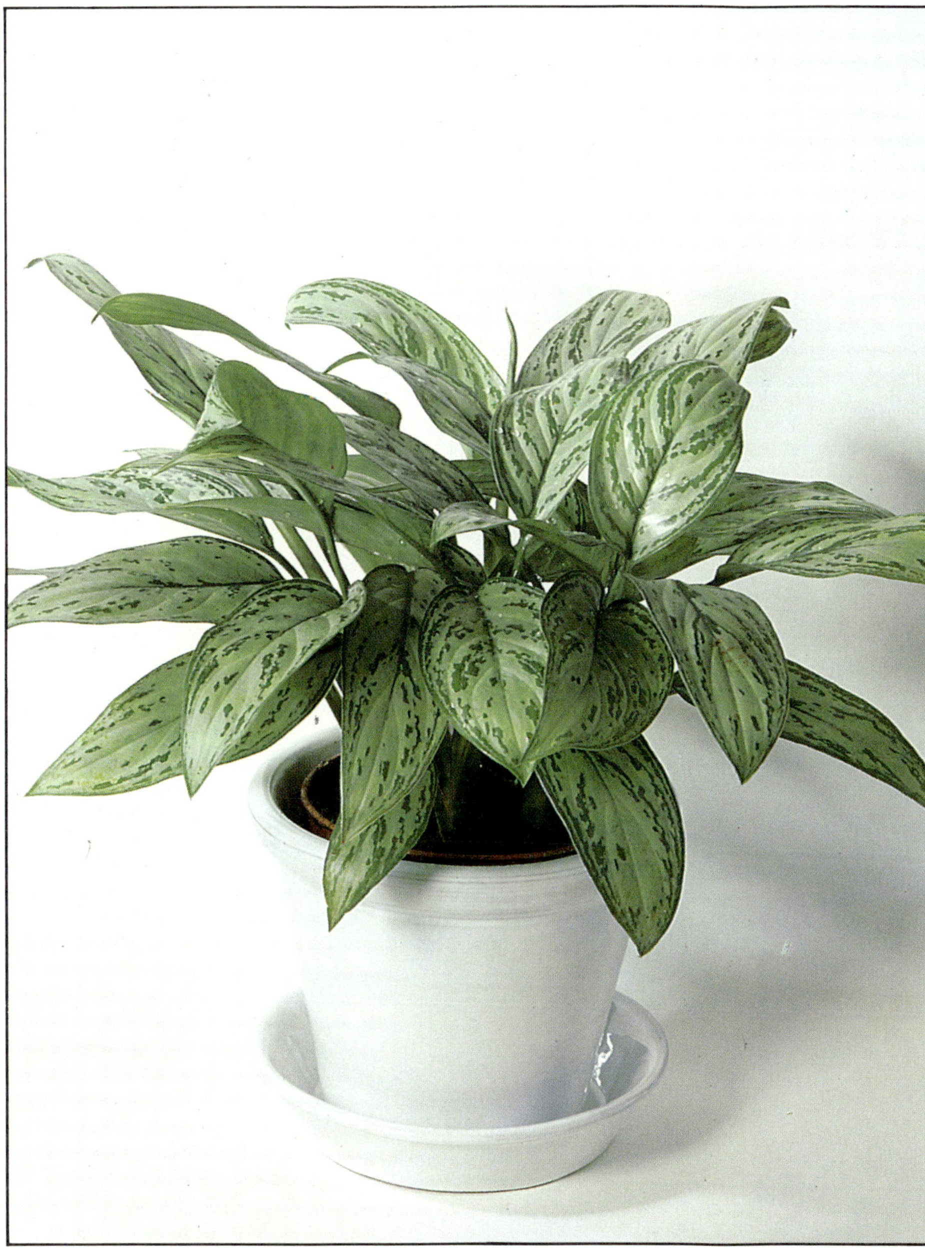

Aglaonemas belong to an exceptionally fine family of plants from South East Asia, the majority of which make excellent foliage houseplants. They are easy to grow provided you give them conditions they like, namely shade, warmth and humidity all year. Their ability to tolerate shade is one of their best qualities, although they do prefer to sit in good light if you can give it to them. Aglaonemas are grown for their lovely, long-stemmed, beautifully mottled leaves which have pointed or partially rounded tips. As a bonus arum-like flowers, called spathes, are produced by mature plants in the summer. They are slow growing, so don't expect a young plant to grow into a magnificent specimen in just one year.

Spring and summer care

Above all give your Aglaonema plenty of warmth in the summer — 65°F (18°C) plus — and you must water freely and regularly, though not so often that the roots and compost remain sodden. As this is a tropical plant humidity is very important. Mist spray at least three times a week in hot weather as this will help to encourage luxurious growth. Provide a liquid feed every 14 days or so in half the strength recommended on the bottle.

With plenty of light and warmth, the foliage of *Aglaonema modestum* 'Silver Queen' will be predominantly silver.

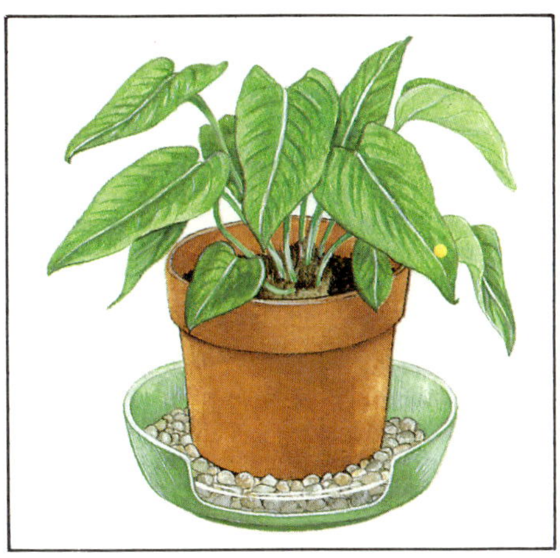

To create humidity, stand your Aglaonema in a pebble and water-filled saucer, but don't let the pot sit in water.

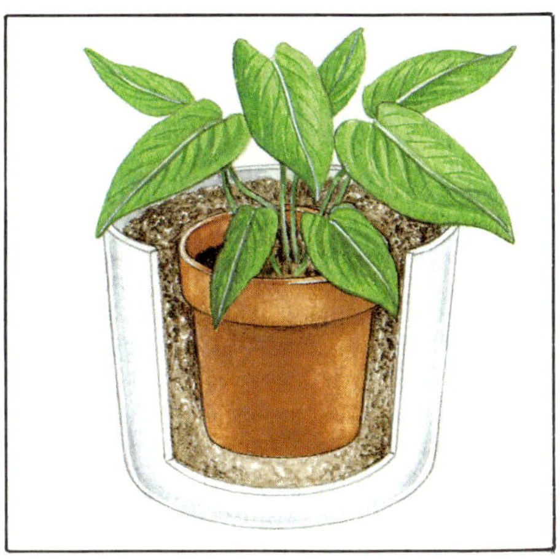

Another way to make humidity is to stand the plant pot inside a bigger pot and fill the gap with moist peat.

Plants like a degree of root restriction but you must remember to feed them regularly. Repot mature plants every three years or so in April in John Innes No 2, but wait until the temperature is 65-70°F (18-21°C) before disturbing them, as they need a steady temperature to get re-established. Be careful not to firm the compost too well as this slows growth.

Autumn and winter care

The most important aspect of winter care is to keep your Aglaonema in a minimum temperature of 60°F (15°C). Keep your plant in the shade or in good light out of direct sun.

Species

Aglaonema modestum, the Chinese Evergreen, slowly grows to about 3ft (0.9m) with waxy green, wedge-shape 6-9in (15-22cm) long leaves on slender stems. The midrib of each leaf is flecked silvery-grey and in time greenish spathe flowers with a creamy-white central spike appear. 'Silver Queen', main picture, *left*, is even more ornamental with long, narrowish 9in (22cm) leaves, grey-green with a silvery greyish-green mottling. If you grow the plant well, silver dominates the foliage.

A.pseudobracteatum, the White Rajah, *below*, is a more sturdy plant with spear-shaped leaves which are a rich green with creamy gold markings, and ultimately whitish spathes.

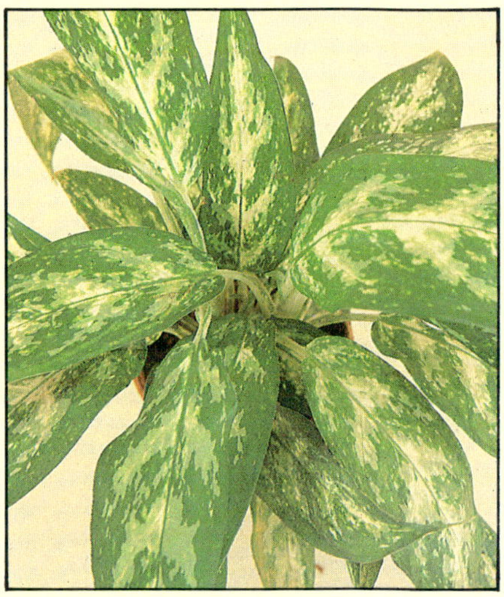

A.crispum, the Painted Drop-Tongue, can reach as much as 3ft (0.9m) tall with large, leathery, somewhat oval leaves with a pointed end. Leaves are silver and greenish grey with the silver effect dominating.

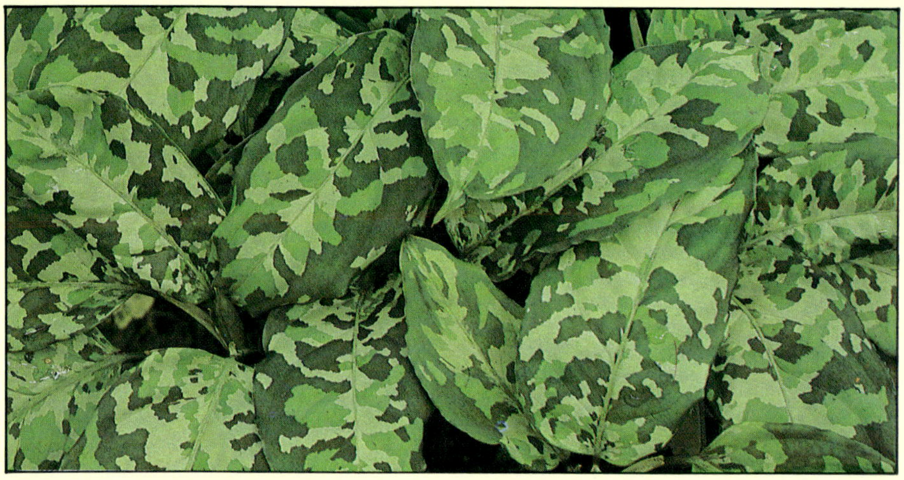

A.versicolor, *above*, is a recent introduction and has strikingly mottled leaves in varying shades of green.

A.costatum is a low growing plant with heart-shaped leaves a rich glossy green, spotted white with a band of white running from tip to base.

A.treubii, *right*, is a slender plant with bluish-green, narrow leathery leaves, sometimes with silvery grey markings.

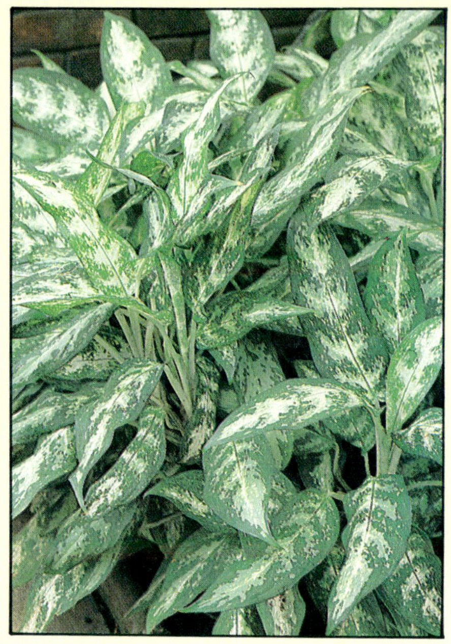

A.oblongifolium is the largest of the species; a slow growing, thick-stemmed plant which grows 4ft (1.2m) or more tall. The leaves are thick, leathery, somewhat oval in shape and bluish-green with whitish-green freckles. The spathe is a rich crimson with a central white spike.

A.angustifolium grows up to about 18in (46cm) with erect, long and slender pointed leaves. The veins are very obvious and slightly sunken into the leaf, giving quite a crinkled appearance.

Water occasionally so as to keep the compost only just moist. Keep out of draughts and away from fumes of any kind.

Propagation

While you are repotting in late April you can carefully divide the root clump. Separate off shoots with three or four new leaves and plenty of roots. Pot the young plants in John Innes No 2 and keep them in a temperature of 70°F (21°C) until they are established.

Another method is to remove the young suckers which appear around the base in summer. Separate them the following spring and make sure that there are at least a few roots attached before potting as before.

Aglaonema seeds are difficult to get hold of, but if you manage to do so you really need a propagator to grow them successfully. Sow in March, $\frac{1}{4}$in (6mm) deep into John Innes Seed Compost. Keep the soil moist and germinate in a temperature of 70°F (21°C).

Trouble Shooter

Trouble arrives if they are not given the conditions they need; too much sun scorches the foliage and makes the leaves curl; so move them out of the sun.

Wilting leaves show that you have under or overwatered your plant; adjust accordingly.

Red spider is one of the few pests which really are a problem; mist spray regularly and use a houseplant insecticide to get rid of them.

Botrytis (grey mould), *below right*, and leaf spot, *above right*, rarely occur, but if they do, use a fungicide.

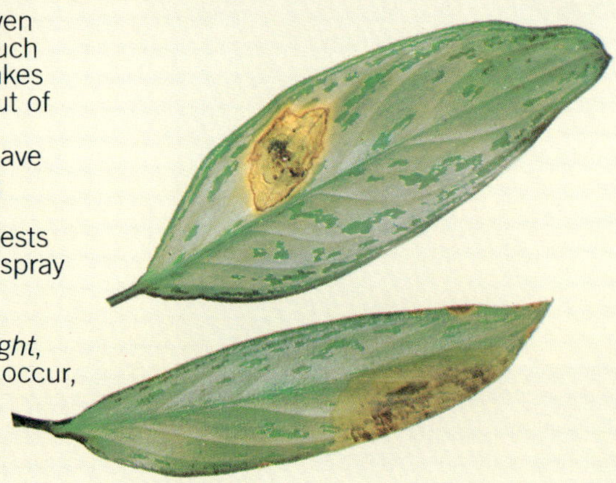

Allamanda

Family name: **Apocynaceae**

Common name:
Golden Trumpet

Care Straightforward	**Height** 10ft (3m)	**Flower** June-July
Light Bright indirect sun	**Spread** 6ft (1.8m)	**Humidity** Regular spraying
Price Middle range	**Shape** Climber	**Availability** Garden centres
Temp. Min 60°F (15°C)	Ideal 80°F (27°C)	Max 90°F (33°C)

The beautiful golden flowered Allamanda is a strong and robust climbing plant from Brazil. If you have the space train it against a wall or across a climbing frame where it will look absolutely magnificent, as it needs plenty of room to grow and do itself justice. It has long, narrow oval leaves arranged in whorls — like the spokes of a wheel — from the woody stems and branches. In June and July large brilliant golden-yellow funnel-shaped trumpet flowers open in clusters at the tips of the branches. Allamanda is very vigorous and can grow up to 10ft (3m) tall in the right conditions; if this is too large you can restrain it with careful pruning. To keep an Allamanda successfully you must give it a warm winter and high humidity.

Spring and summer care

Give your Allamanda plenty of light; however, too much direct sun makes the foliage wilt, so give it semi-shade in the hottest weather. Water regularly throughout the year to keep the soil constantly moist; the bigger the plant the more water it needs in summer, but don't give so much that the compost remains sodden between waterings. Mist spray at least once a day and stand your plant on a tray of wet pebbles in hot weather to create humidity; without this your plant will fail to flower. Give your Allamanda a summer temperature of between 70 and 80°F (21-27°C) with a minimum of 60°F (15°C). As this is such a vigorous plant it must be regularly fed in summer with a weak solution of liquid fertiliser at every watering.

Repot Allamanda any time between late April and late September into John Innes No 2. Be extra careful not to disturb the main clump of roots, as this will stop the plant growing for a couple of months.

Autumn and winter care

Stop feeding in September. Over winter, between late September and late March, the most important thing to do for your Allamanda is to keep it in a temperature constantly above 60°F (15°C). Leave pruning until January or April; this is an essential chore to keep your Allamanda looking tidy — otherwise it can get really out of hand. Prune hard back to the first joint before the main stem to encourage healthy new growth.

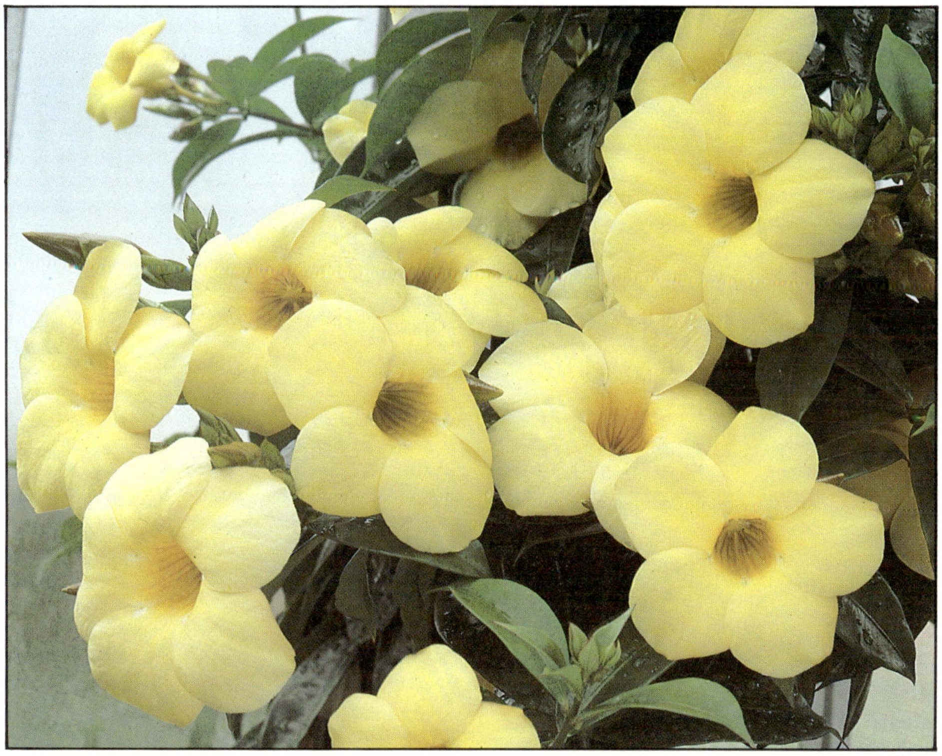

Allamanda cathartica is a magnificent climbing exotic which needs a lot of space.

Propagation

In March or April take 3in (7cm) cuttings from the tips of the branches of last year's growth; use the shoots you've cut off when pruning. Dip the ends in hormone rooting powder and firm them into a compost of equal parts peat and sand; keep them at a temperature of 80°F (27°C). They will root quite quickly and can then be potted into John Innes No 2.

Species

Allamanda cathartica, *above*, has long, 4-6in (10-15cm), leathery, glossy leaves on woody stems and branches. It flowers in summer, usually in June and July. The golden-yellow funnel shaped flowers are about 2in (5cm) deep and 3in (7cm) across. ***A.c.*** 'Grandiflora' is similar but smaller and more compact. It has pale yellow flowers 5in (12cm) across. ***A.c.***'Nobilis', *right*, has purplish branches and bright yellow flowers 5in (12cm) across which are perfumed like a Magnolia. ***A.c.***'Williamsii' is smaller with matt leaves. It has masses of 3in (7cm) scented flowers in shades of yellow with a brownish-maroon throat.

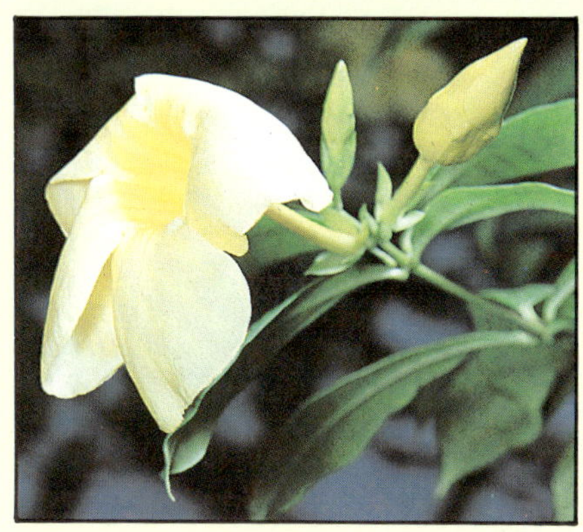

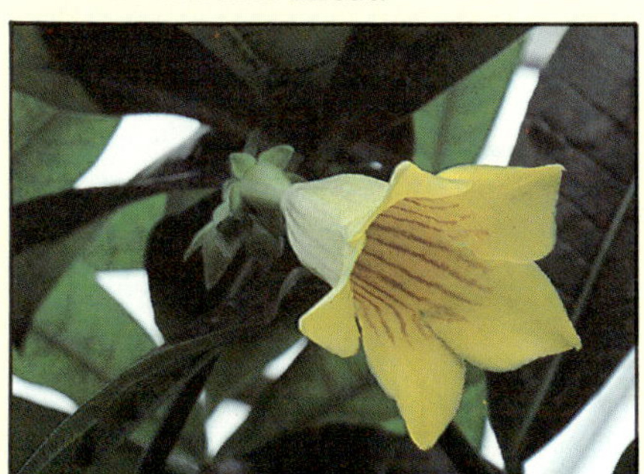

A.neriifolia, *left*, the Golden Trumpet Bush, is an erect shrub with rough, narrow leaves and small 2in (5cm) deep, barely 1in (25mm) wide yellow flowers with an orange-red streaked throat. It flowers intermittently throughout the year and needs a moist, shady and warm position at all times.

A.violacea has slender, clambering branches with oval leaves about 5in (12cm) long. It has brilliant purple or reddish-purple pairs of flowers about 2 in (5cm) long for most of the summer.

Aloe

Family name: **Liliaceae**

Most popular species:
Partridge-Breasted Aloe

Care Easy to grow	**Height** 12in (30cm)	**Flower** March-April
Light Bright indirect sun	**Spread** 12in (30cm)	**Humidity** None
Price Cheap	**Shape** Rosette	**Availability** Common
Temp. Min 50°F(10°C)	Ideal 65°F(18°C)	Max 75°F(24°C)

The Aloes are an enormous family of succulent flowering plants, most of which would make marvellous houseplants if only they were available. Many Aloes come from Africa, Madagascar and Arabia. They are all succulents, which means they come from dry areas where they long ago adapted their leaves and stems to store water so they can survive extended periods of drought. Most Aloes form tightly overlapping stemless rosettes of leaves, sometimes with spines or hooked teeth along their leaf edges. In early spring or late summer they send out a long, slender stalk topped with tubular bell-shaped flowers. The Partridge-Breasted Aloe, *Aloe variegata,* has been a favourite houseplant for over 100 years. It is a strikingly attractive plant with stiff, distinctively marked, fleshy leaves

Spring and summer care

Aloes like to sit in a draught-free but airy position in bright light — only the ones with shiny leaves can sit safely in the full sun. Always water your Aloe regularly but moderately, letting the soil almost dry out between waterings. Be careful not to let water get trapped at the base of the fleshy leaves, as this encourages rot.

Feed your Aloe once a month from April until September with a good liquid fertiliser. Repot every spring into a slightly bigger pot using a really gritty, peat based compost — you can use John Innes No 2 with added grit — making sure to re-plant at the exact depth it was before. The vital requirement is a well drained compost, as Aloes will not tolerate wet feet at any time. To help your plant with drainage, put a layer of grit on the top of the compost so water quickly drains off the surface. Aloes are unsuccessful in bottle gardens, even though they might grow for a while, as the moisture makes the leaves rot.

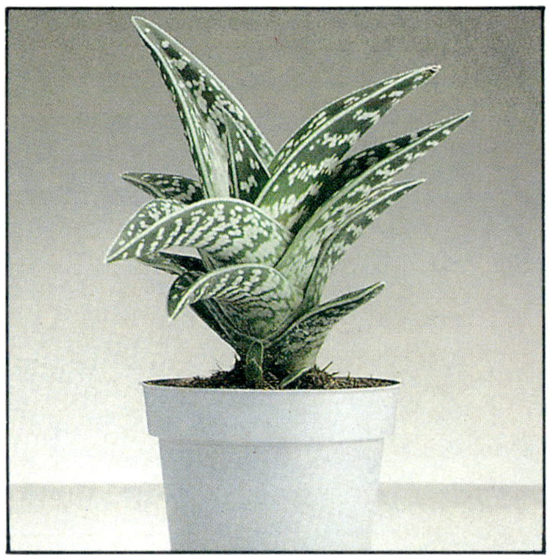

Aloe variegata is an easy plant to grow.

Autumn and winter care

As growth slows down in August tail off the amount of water you're giving your Aloe, until the plant is kept completely dry over winter. Wait until the weather warms up in April and early May before watering again. Still give good light with as much winter sun as possible. Don't, whatever you do, be tempted to give your plant the odd watering even if the weather is unseasonally bright.

Propagation

Sow seeds in a free-draining, sandy seed compost any time from late February to April. Put the seed tray in semi-shade in a temperature of 70°F (21°C) and keep the compost only just moist.

Most Aloes also produce offsets — baby plants — from around their base; these can be removed in late spring and potted separately into a gritty compost; treat them as mature plants once they are rooted.

Trouble Shooter

Root rot starts if the temperature drops below 50°F (10°C), especially if the soil is too moist; move your plant to a warmer and brighter spot where you can dry it out completely and you might save it.

Red spider mite occasionally appear if the air is very still; spray with a succulent insecticide and move the plant to an airier spot.

Species

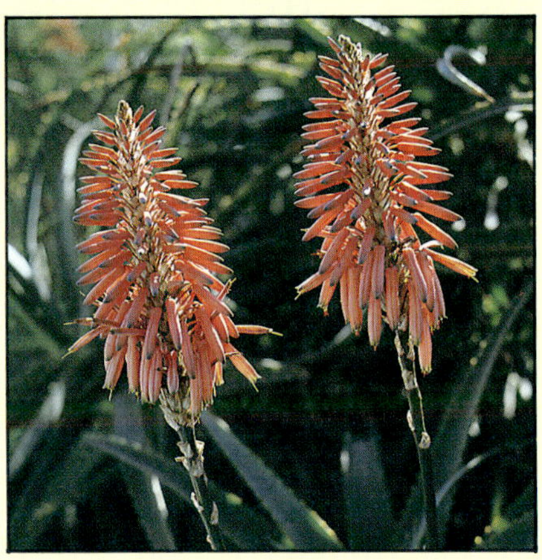

Aloe variegata, the Partridge-Breasted Aloe, *above centre,* is easy to find. It is almost stemless with straight, stiff, slightly inward-curving, tightly overlapping leaves, each with a distinct horny keel for most of its length. The dark green leaves are 12in (30cm) long and irregularly cross-banded, blotched or spotted with white. In March and April a long 12in (30cm) flower spike appears bearing a number of loose pink or scarlet tubular bell-shaped blooms. It freely grows offsets each year. 'Sabra' is a lovely miniature Aloe which produces lots of dainty, bell-shaped, pink flowers in August and September frequently with two or more spikes on a plant. The rosette is made up of about 15 dark green, finely warty, slender 6in (15cm) leaves, covered with numerous whitish spots.

A.barbadensis (also called ***A.vera***) is used for its medicinal qualities. It has a dense rosette of grey-green, initially mottled, very fleshy leaves, about 18in (45cm) tall. A 3ft (0.9cm) stalk bears yellow flowers.

A.aristata, the Lace Aloe, *right,* forms a spherical rosette of dark green leaves, with rows of wart-like whitish tubercles. It often has well over 80 leaves, all with a slightly whitish edge and a slender horny tip. It quickly forms a cushion of plants clustered tightly together about 18in (45cm) in diameter. Orange-red, narrow, bell-shaped flowers appear on 12in (30cm) stems in early summer.

A.rauhii, A.bakeri and ***A.parvula*** are all charming dwarf species from Madagascar which are well worth looking for at specialist nurseries.

A.arborescens, the Candelabra Aloe, *left,* has a tall, bare, woody stem, topped by a loose rosette of long, narrow, toothed-edge mid-green leaves.

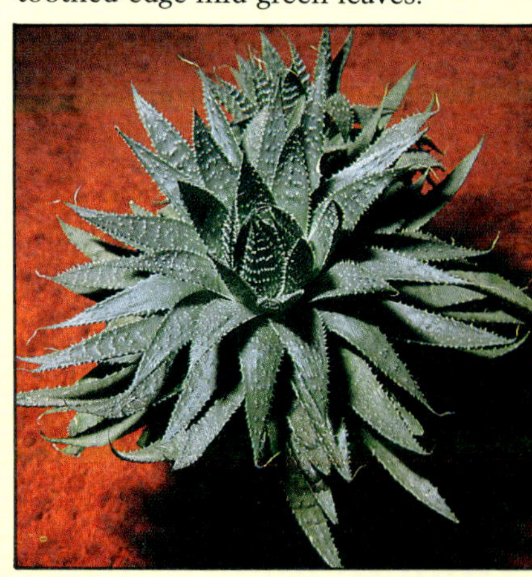

Ananas

Family name: **Bromeliaceae**

Common name: **Pineapple**

Care Easy to grow	**Height** 4ft (1.2m)	**Flower** Any time
Light Full sun	**Spread** 4ft (1.2m)	**Humidity** High humidity
Price Middle range	**Shape** Rosette	**Availability** Garden centres

Temp.	Min	Ideal	Max
	55°F(13°C)	60°F(15°C)	80°F(27°C)

The Pineapple is a surprisingly good houseplant when you consider its exotic Brazilian background — but don't grow it expecting to get a delicious pineapple; you may get fruit from a mature plant, but it's unlikely to be anything other than ornamental! The pineapples we eat come from slow-growing plants with plain, rather dull, viciously spiked, dark green 4ft (1.2m) long leaves; however, shorter, much more attractive Pineapples are easy to find.

The Pineapple plant is a large, stiff, arching rosette with dense heads of bright purple flowers below a thick circular tuft of leaves. The flowers are followed by fruit after about six months. More interesting than the cultivated Pineapple is the variegated kind, which has deeply channelled green leaves edged with whitish-yellow. Mature plants flower very willingly at any time of year; the ripe fruit goes a distinct reddish colour, and at the same time the centre of the rosette also turns slightly pinky-red.

Spring and summer care

Give your Pineapple a temperature around 60°F (15°C) and plenty of good light, in fact the sunnier the better; with the variegated Pineapple this helps produce a pinkish tint to the leaves. Regular watering is very important, but never saturate the compost — let it dry out fairly well between waterings. Mist spray frequently and put a saucer of wet pebbles underneath your plant to provide high humidity in hot weather. Feed with a liquid fertiliser every three or four weeks from late March until October.

Pineapples have shallow roots and only need repotting every other year. Mix your own compost using John Innes No 2 and an equal amount of rough peat. As large Pineapples get top-heavy, weight the bottom of the pot with a good layer of heavy stones.

Autumn and winter care

Unlike most plants the Pineapple does not change much with the seasons, and if you provide good warm conditions it will grow all year round. Nevertheless, the plant's growth does slow down slightly in winter and it needs less regular watering and feeding only every eight weeks. Don't let the plant dry out, and still give it a little humidity, or the leaves may lose their vigour.

Propagation

Remove suckers from around the base of the parent plant in spring and pot them individually. If you keep the suckers warm and treat them well, they will flower and fruit in two years.

Another easy method is to root the crown of the Pineapple. Choose a plump, healthy pineapple and carefully cut the crown from the fruit with a sharp knife; remove the lowest leaves and put the crown in the neck of a jar of water, so that the base just touches the water surface, or is only very slightly submerged. Top up the water to keep it at that same level. Roots will appear within a week, or two weeks at the most; when they are about 1in (2cm) long, carefully pot up the rooted crown in compost. Another method is to let the crown dry up for five or six days until the base is really dry; then firmly set it on (not in) a pot of moist compost, water thoroughly and keep it in a very bright place in a temperature of 70°F (21°C).

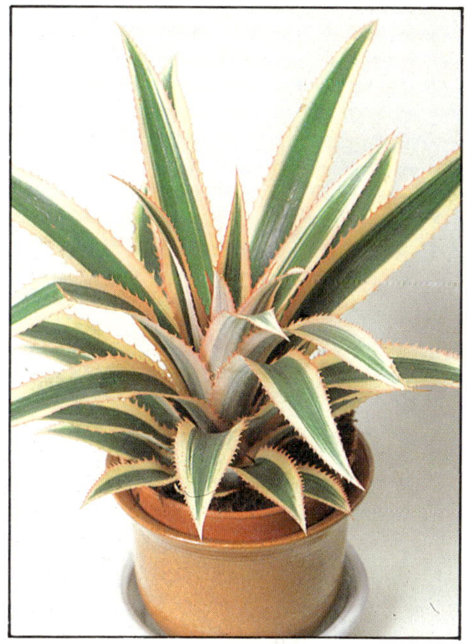

Ananas comosus variegata is an easy, undemanding houseplant.

Species

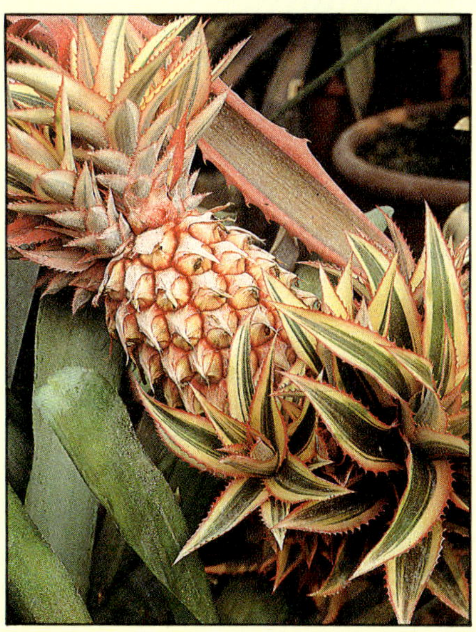

Ananas comosus, the edible Pineapple, has long, sword-shaped, spiny-edged leaves which can grow up to 4ft (1.2m) or more long. ***A.c. variegata***, *left*, the Variegated Pineapple, is more attractive with slightly shorter, 3ft (0.9m) green, white, yellow and pink leaves. It has a red flower-head at the end of a 3ft (0.9m) stalk.

A.ananasoides 'Nana' is a charming dwarf plant with arching, dark green, 18in (45cm) long leaves. It bears non-edible, dark green, very hard fruit, about 1-2in (2-5cm) long. Lots of small plants develop around the base.

A.bracteatus takes eight years to grow to 4ft (1.2m), and occasionally produces lavender coloured flowers followed by large, brownish, edible fruits. ***A.b.striatus*** is similar but with the added attraction of broad, dark green leaves with wide, creamy-yellow edges which have small red spines.

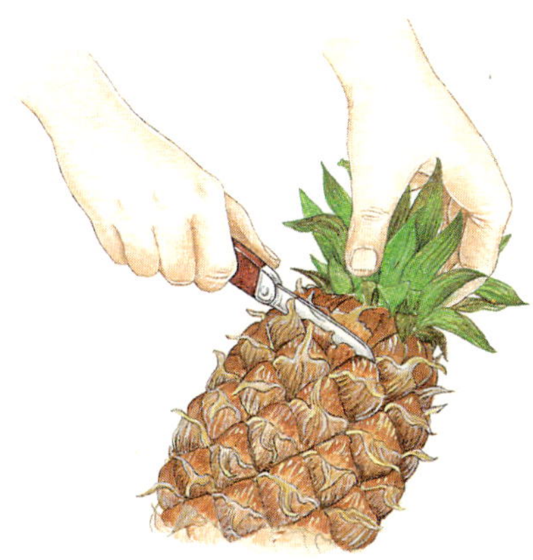

Use a sharp knife to cut the crown.

Trouble Shooter

The whole Pineapple family is very easy to grow as almost no problems occur with pests or diseases. If the plant doesn't thrive, check the information on care above. Perhaps you're doing something wrong.

Anthurium

Family name: **Araceae**

Common name:
Flamingo Plant/Tail Flower

Care Straight-forward	**Height** 12in (30cm)	**Flower** June-Aug
Light Bright indirect sun	**Spread** 12in (30cm)	**Humidity** High humidity
Price Middle range	**Shape** Bushy	**Availability** Common
Temp. Min 60°F(15°C)	Ideal 80°F(27°C)	Max 90°F(33°C)

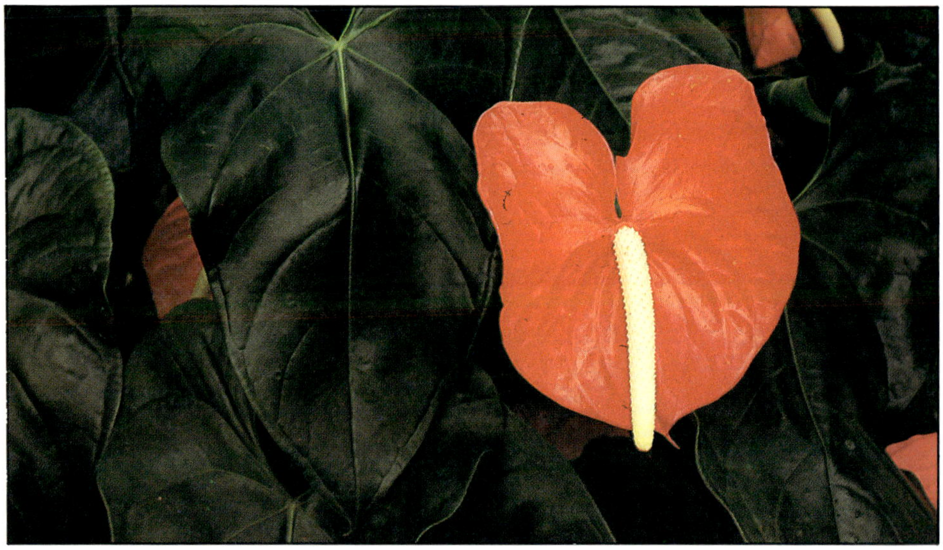

Anthurium andreanum flowers from May through to September.

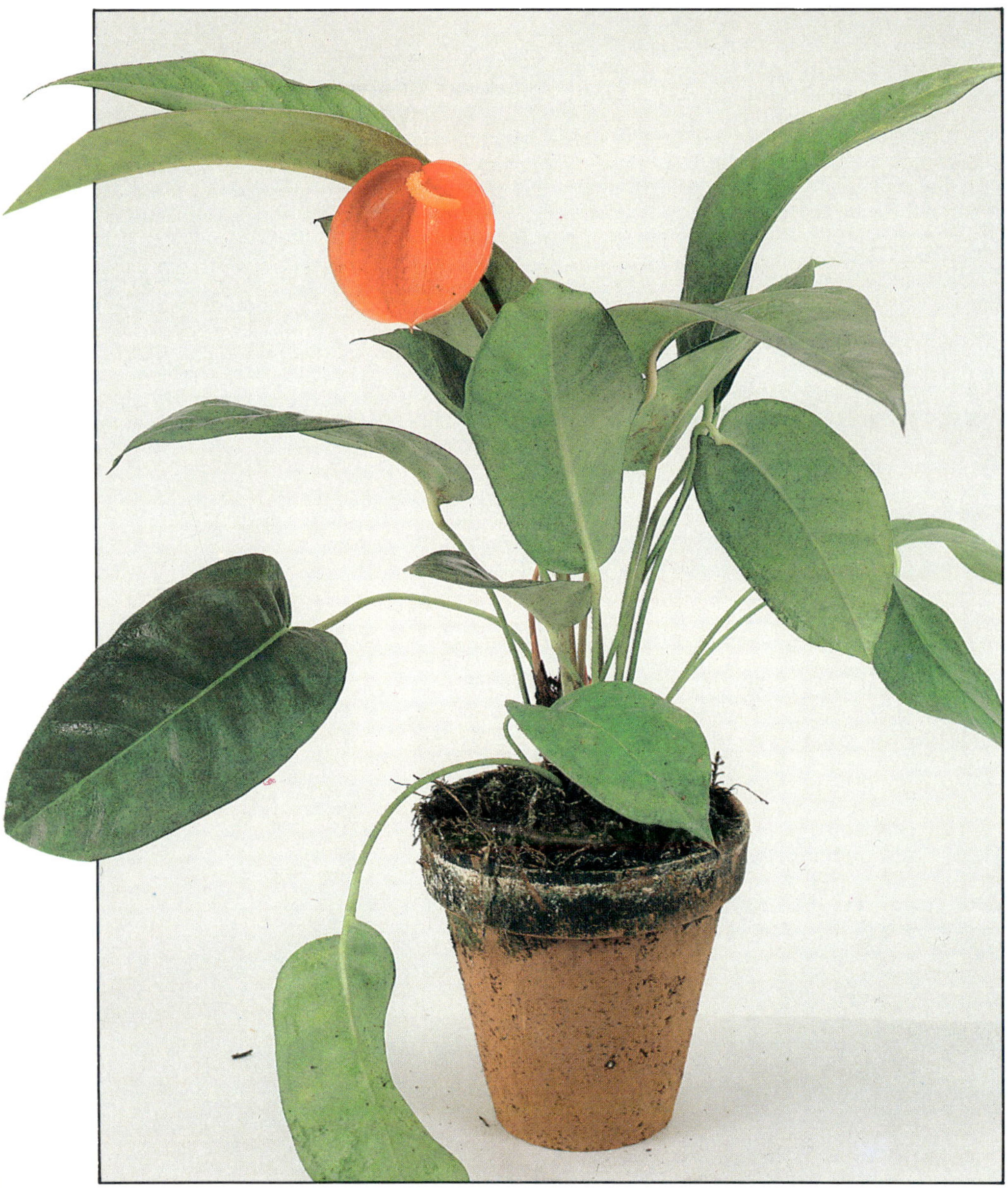

Anthurium scherzerianum needs warmth all year to do really well.

The Anthurium family is a very showy group of superb South American houseplants, which are grown for their amazing flowers and lovely evergreen leaves. The flowers are actually a spathe and spadix; the spathe is a brightly coloured kind of leaf which grows around a small flower spike, properly called the spadix. The stunning Flamingo Plant, *Anthurium scherzerianum* has glossy scarlet spathes, each with a long golden-yellow spadix which curves like a flamingo's neck. Anthuriums flower for eight weeks or so in the summer, but many of them will bloom for most of the year if they are kept at a constant temperature of 70-80°F (21-27°C).

Spring and summer care

Put your Flamingo Plant in a good light spot protected from the full sun — it will be happiest in a bright shady spot, but don't be afraid to move it about until you find its ideal position. Water your plant generously without waterlogging it, and use rainwater if possible; never let it dry out completely. Anthuriums enjoy high temperatures around 80°F (27°C) in the summer and lots of humidity. Stand your plant on a saucer of wet pebbles and mist spray twice a day in hot weather in the mornings and evenings, rather than in the heat of the day.

Repot in March every other year using a good peat-based compost such as Arthur Bowers; add one part chopped up sphagnum moss and a few charcoal chippings to three parts compost. Start to feed your Flamingo Plant with liquid fertiliser once or twice a week from April until late September; this will make the plant flower and the leaves flourish. As the flowers are top heavy, carefully cane the stalks, to support and hold up the flower heads. Also, sponge the leaves clean occasionally to free them of dust.

Autumn and winter care

Remember that your Flamingo Plant comes from the tropics, so it needs a winter minimum temperature of no less than 60-65°F (15-18°C). At this low temperature only give your plant enough water to keep the compost moist, and don't feed until the warmer weather arrives in spring. Continue to protect your plant from the deep sun, though not so much that you put it in the shade.

Propagation

It is possible to propagate the Flamingo Plant if you have a propagator, though it's not easy as you need constant high temperatures and humidity. Sow seeds in early spring and germinate them at a temperature of 75°F (24°C) in the same compost mix as for potting. Keep them shaded, then, as the seedlings appear, give just a touch of fresh air and gradually increase this as they develop.

Mature plants can be divided successfully in February or March using a very sharp and spotlessly clean knife. But this is a risky operation as the plant might not recover from the shock of being cut.

Trouble Shooter

Wilting yellow leaves are caused by draughts and over as well as under-watering; likewise cold or wet conditions. Move your plant to a warmer spot and try drying out or warming up.

If the flowers fail to open or don't even appear, you probably haven't been feeding your plant; start doing so regularly. Lack of humidity also causes flowers to shrivel, even though they might form.

Fungus can attack under various conditions but primarily when the plant is not warm enough or is too wet; use a liquid fungicide.

The worst pest is mealy bug which becomes obvious when fluffy white patches appear under the leaf or at the leaf joints. Deal with this by removing them with a small paint brush dipped in methylated spirits.

Aphids sometimes cluster on new shoots, flowers and leaves making them sticky. Spray with houseplant insecticide.

Buying Guide

For the more unusual Anthuriums you'll have to go to a specialist nurseryman, but the Flamingo Plant is easy to find at most places which sell houseplants.

When buying a plant always check that the leaves are firm and clean — almost with a sheen.

Get a plant that is already flowering, and just as important, find one that is well established in its container.

Species

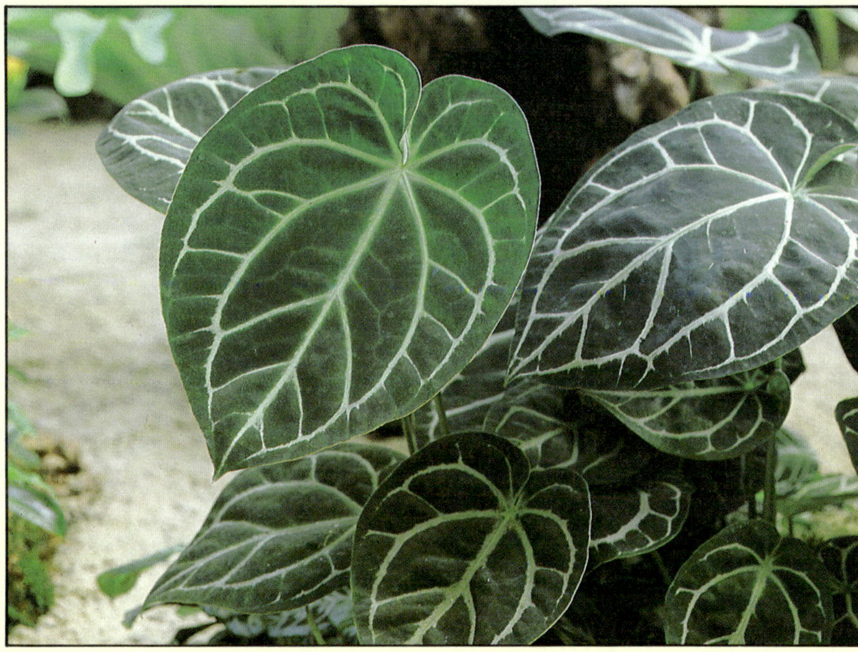

Anthurium scherzerianum, the Flamingo Plant, is the commonest member of the family. It has glossy, brilliant scarlet, oblong spathes, each about 3-4in (7-10cm) long, with a red, orange or golden-yellow twisted spadix. The plant grows 12in (30cm) high with a spread of about twice as much. Glossy green leaves are carried on short wiry stalks and clustered together at the base of the plant. 'Album', *right*, has a white spathe and yellowish spadix but is otherwise exactly the same.

A.andreanum grows to about 18in (45cm) tall with a girth about 12in (30cm). It carries erect dark green, heart-shaped leaves on long stalks and waxy crimson or coral red puckered spathes about 5in (12cm) long and 3in (7cm) wide with a white or yellow spadix. 'Album' has rounded heart-shaped white spathes with a hanging spadix which is yellow at the tip, purplish-pink in the centre and white at the base. 'Giganteum' boasts a pinkish-red spathe and a white or yellow spadix. 'Guatmala' flowers prolifically with crimson-red waxy spathes and a small yellow spadix.

A.crystallinum, *above*, is strikingly handsome and is grown for its large, heart-shaped leaves which are a soft, almost velvety-green and lined with silver. It has green, rather narrow spathes.

A.veitchii, the King Anthurium, is a really magnificent plant with very large, bluish-green leaves often 3ft (0.9m) in length, which look almost quilted. They are heart-shaped at the base with curved and sunken veins and a pale midrib. The spathes are greenish-yellow.

A.warocqueanum, known as the Queen Anthurium, has long, greenish, velvety leaves with ivory-white veining. The leaves are about 3ft (0.9m) long. The spathes are greenish-yellow.

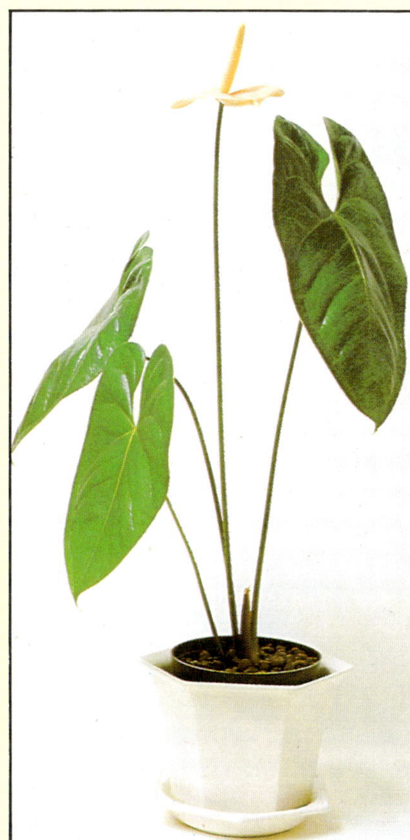

Aphelandra

Family name: **Acanthaceae**

Common name: **Zebra Plant**

Care Straight-forward	**Height** 30in (76cm)	**Flower** June-Sept
Light Bright indirect sun	**Spread** 30in (76cm)	**Humidity** Regular spraying
Price Cheap	**Shape** Bushy	**Availability** Common
Temp. Min 60°F(18°C)	Ideal 70°F(21°C)	Max 80°F(27°C)

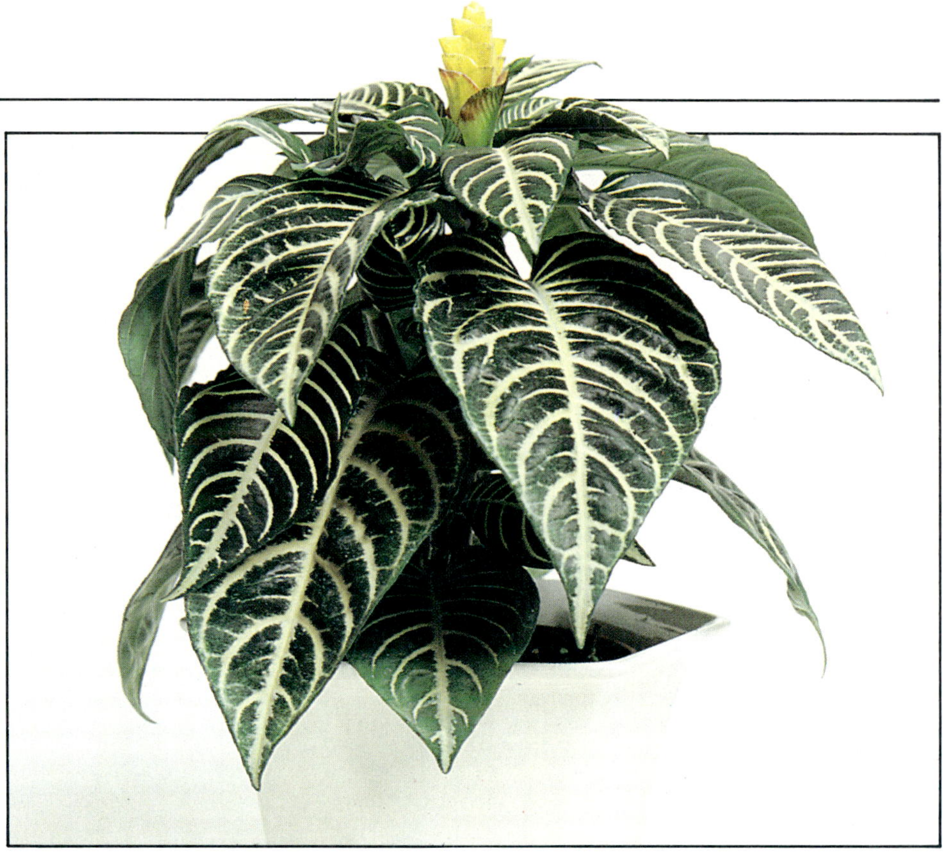

Aphelandra squarrosa has most attractive and unusual leaves.

The Zebra Plant is an eyecatching houseplant all year because of its striking leaves, but it also has the bonus of brilliant summer flowers. It is a small, rather stiff shrub from Central and South America which rarely grows higher than 30in (76cm). The Zebra Plant gets its name from the heavy, white, zebra-like markings on its dark-green leaves. From the tips of the stems in summer come 2in (5cm), spiky pyramids of fiery-yellow scaly bracts (false leaves) from which small tubular flowers emerge; these wither fairly quickly but the bract lasts a couple of months before fading. The Zebra Plant is easy to grow and flower, provided you can give it warmth, a humid atmosphere, moist compost and reasonably bright light all year round.

Spring and summer care

If the stems are leggy, prune your plant right back to within a few shoots in February, to encourage healthy new growth. You must always remember to water your Zebra Plant regularly; if it dries out the leaves will wilt and even drop off, so watch the soil to make sure it's constantly moist. Use your mist sprayer frequently, especially when the temperature rises above 75°F (24°C). For extra humidity stand the plant on a saucer of wet pebbles or put it, pot and all, into a large container and fill the gap between the pots with damp peat so moisture rises around the plant's leaves.

The Zebra Plant needs a fairly high summer temperature of between 65-70°F (18-21°C), and a bright spot out of the direct sun and draughts. Feed regularly every 14 days in summer with a liquid houseplant fertiliser; this encourages the plant to put out lots of healthy new leaves and flowers and stops the plant becoming lanky. Then, when the flower spikes emerge, add a drop of fertiliser with every watering. Snip the flowers off as they fade.

Autumn and winter care

Reduce watering as the weather gets cooler and use tepid water. Continue to give as much bright light as possible. Unless you can manage to keep the temperature above a winter minimum of 60°F (18°C) it will produce listless blooms and maybe even die. Only feed your Zebra Plant in winter if you can provide temperatures around 75°F (23°C). Draughts are fatal.

Propagation

Use a sharp knife to take 3-4in (9-10cm) cuttings from the tops of new stem growth in Spring. Dip the ends in hormone rooting powder and grow in a mix of rough peat and sharp sand at a temperature of 70°F (21°C): use a propagator if possible or root the cuttings on a warm windowsill in a pot covered with a clear plastic bag. After rooting, pot them in John Innes No 3 to get them growing quickly.

Trouble Shooter

Lost leaves usually mean you have not given enough water, the temperature is too low or the plant doesn't get enough light.

Watch out for greenfly on the leaves and flower buds; spray immediately with a houseplant insecticide.

Species

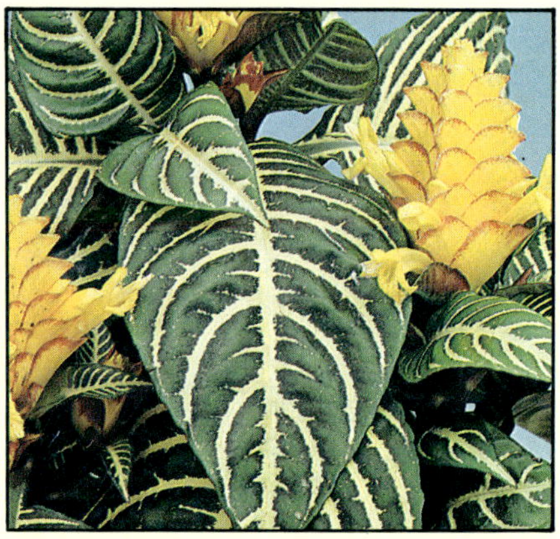

Aphelandra squarrosa is the most popular species with its deep dark green leaves with prominent white veins and fiery-yellow bracts which appear from July to September. 'Dania' still has the pronounced white veins but has paler leaves and grows to only about 12in (30cm) high and 9in (22cm) wide. 'Louisae', *left*, is sturdier and more robust and reaches 30in (74cm) high. Its stems and roots are very fleshy and it has very shiny and firm dark green leaves quite often without the white veining. The bracts are yellow, streaked with red.

A.aurantiaca, the Fiery Spike, has oval, green leaves with greyish veins and a brilliant, showy, orange-yellow bracted spike with bright scarlet flowers and an orange throat and tube.

A.chamissoniana, the Pagoda Plant, has closely-held slender, pointed leaves with silver veining. The spike bears bright yellow bracts with green tips and clear yellow flowers.

Aporocactus

Family name: **Cactaceae**

Common name:
Rat's Tail Cactus

Care Straightforward	**Height** 3ft (0.9m)	**Flower** April-May
Light Full sun	**Spread** 12in (30cm)	**Humidity** None
Price Middle range	**Shape** Trailing	**Availability** Garden centres
Temp. Min 50°F(10°C)	Ideal 60°F(15°C)	Max 70°F(21°C)

In spring the slender trailing stems of Aporocactus are covered with dazzling flowers which are particularly spectacular if you grow the plant in a hanging basket, so that their tails can dangle over the sides. The few species in this family are all natives of Mexico and Central America. The Rat's Tail Cactus is the commonest Aporocactus and gets its name from the khaki colour and length of its stems, which can be over 3ft (0.9m) long. These stems are covered with tiny cushions known as areoles, from which grow clumps of 15 to 20 small, fine, hairy brownish-red spines and, in April and May, trumpet-like crimson flowers. In the wild Aporocactus clings to plants and rocks for support, so guard your other plants from what looks like an innocently dangling stem!

Spring and summer care

Wake up your plant from winter dormancy in April with a little gentle watering; increase this as the weather warms — but be careful not to give too much. Aporocactus can be grown in pots, but because of the length of their stems they are much happier in a hanging basket. Give your plant plenty of good light, and even full sun as long as the heat is not too intense. As soon as the flower buds put in an appearance, add a drop of fertiliser, such as Phostrogen or Cactigrow or a tomato fertiliser, with each watering, to stimulate your plant and encourage lots of flowers.

You must water your Rat's Tail regularly throughout spring and summer. Another advantage of growing this cactus in a hanging basket is that it can easily get rid of surplus water, so there's no danger of waterlogging. The compost must never be wet, only just moist, and the plant needs to be almost dry before water is given again. If you grow your Rat's Tail in a pot never leave it standing in water — after about 20 minutes tip away any excess water.

Autumn and winter care

From late autumn through to early April keep your plant completely dry and don't give it any fertiliser. You can keep your cactus at quite a low temperature during this time, but don't let it get less than 50°F (10°C) for safety. Repot your plant annually at the end of the dormancy period, in late March or beginning of April. If you're using a hanging basket, line it with sphagnum moss before filling it with a good brand of cactus compost or a John Innes No 2 with a little added grit.

Propagation

Sow seeds into a good cactus compost with a little added grit, any time from late January through to April. Keep the compost slightly moist and at a temperature of 70°F (21°C) and put the container in an airy place in good light, out of full sun.

Take cuttings from the tails in early spring; don't just chop off the ends as this will ruin the look of your cactus. Instead take a length of tail and cut it into sections 3in (7cm) long — keep track of the growing end so you know that is the end to push into the compost. Let the pieces dry off for a week then put them in the same moist compost mix as for seeds; push them in 1in (2cm) deep and give them air and good light at a temperature of 70°F (21°C). The cuttings should start to root after two or three weeks; when they are strong enough to move, pot them up in the original compost.

Trouble Shooter

Overwatering at any time of the year causes root rot which works its way back up through the stems.

Too low a temperature in winter is also harmful — never forget that Aporocactus are tropical plants, so keep them nice and warm.

Occasionally scale insect and mealy bug develop — use a systemic malathion based insecticide watered into the soil; the plant absorbs the chemicals and prevents the pests from nesting. If your cactus has a really bad dose then spray with an insecticide such as Murphy's Systemic.

Buying Guide

Most Aporocactus are easy to get hold of provided you go to a cactus nursery, of which there are a number. Look in the advertising section of gardening magazines for specialist addresses.

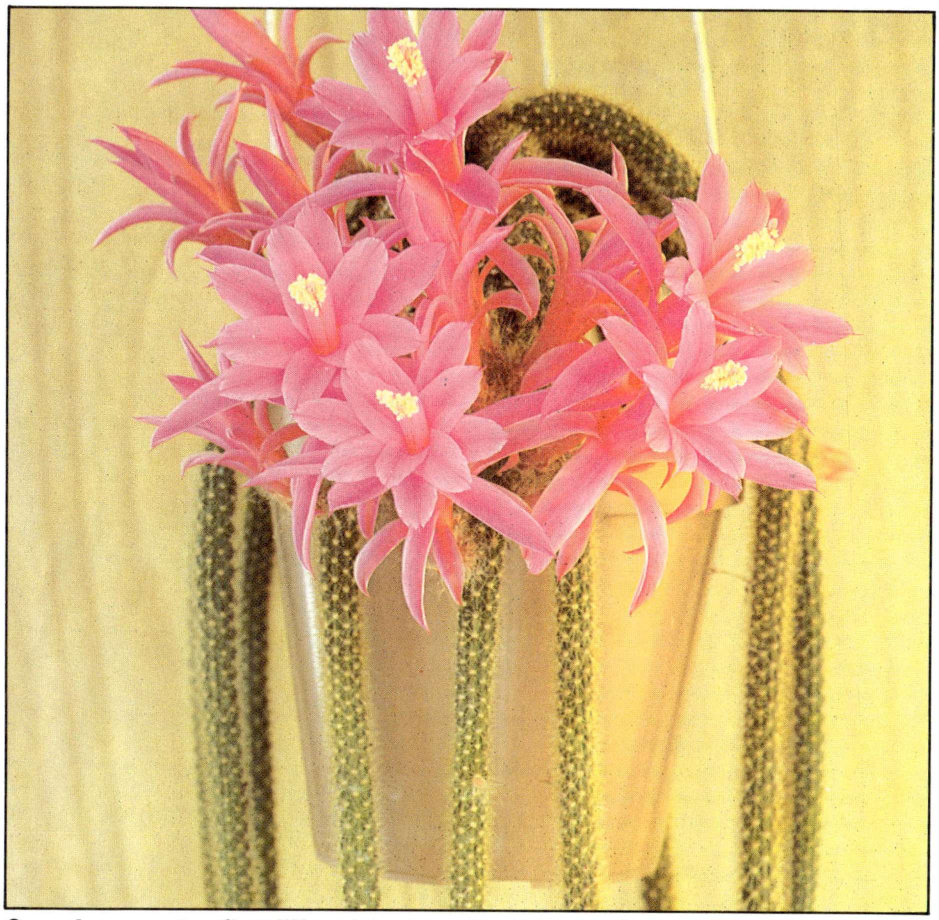

Grow *Aporocactus flagelliformis* in a hanging basket so it can trail happily.

Ardisia

Family name: **Myrsinaceae**

Common names: **Coral Berry Jet-Berry Tree**

Care Straight-forward	**Height** 3ft (0.9m)	**Flower** April—September
Light Bright	**Spread** 12-18in (30-45cm)	**Humidity** None
Price Expensive	**Shape** Small tree	**Availability** Garden centres

Temp. Min 50°F(10°C) — Ideal 70°F (21°C) — Max 75°F (24°C)

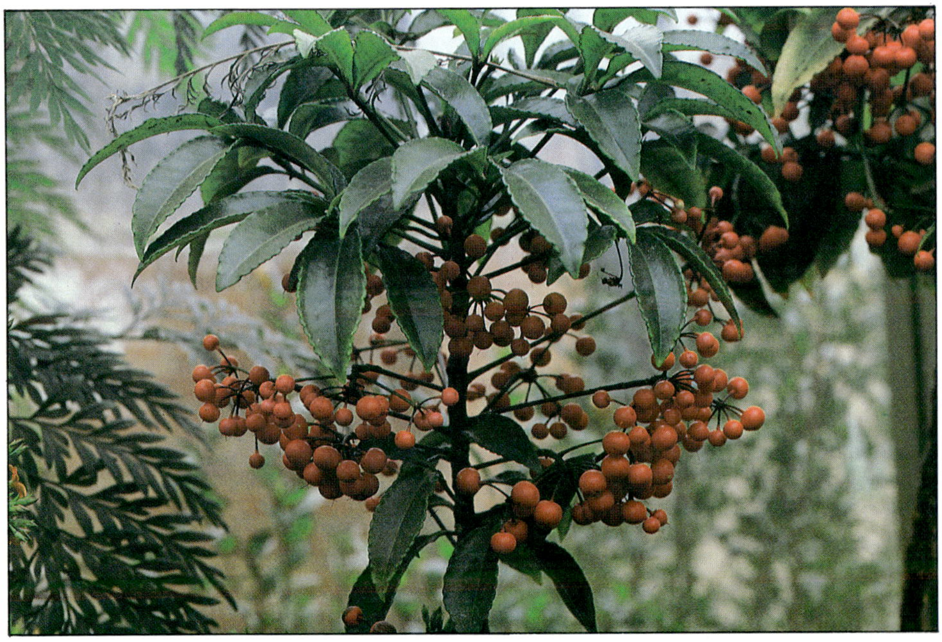

A well grown *Ardisia crenata* carries scarlet berries for most of the year.

These shrubby plants with colourful berries are all very slow growing — which means that once you've got one it is unlikely to outgrow your home for many years to come. The Coral Berry you are most likely to find is *Ardisia crenata* (also known as *crispa*) which comes from Japan. It is a tall, fairly narrow, somewhat spindly evergreen shrub with stiffly held, thick, leathery, crinkle-edged leaves. It has clusters of small, white, star-shaped flowers followed by glossy scarlet berries that stand out around the middle of the plant like a delicate red skirt. In fact, you can have berries on the lower branches with flowers on the top ones at the same time — which creates a most unusual effect. It is not a particularly tricky plant to grow — the greatest difficulty is in getting hold of one in the first place, but it is well worth making the effort to find one.

Spring and summer care

In March prune any straggly shoots back to the stem to tidy up the shape of your plant. Start watering regularly and often, from April through until late September; this is very important as the compost must never dry out or the plant will suffer. Also add a drop of liquid fertiliser with each watering. Give your Coral Berry good light and fairly warm conditions; about 70°F (21°C) is ideal. If the temperature gets much hotter the leaves start to wilt and the berries are liable to shrivel and drop. Clean the glossy leaves with a moist sponge whenever they get dusty.

Pot in February or April using John Innes No 2 or 3. However, because the Coral Berry is so slow growing it only needs repotting every three or four years, and then only pot it into the next size pot — don't give its roots too much room.

Autumn and winter care

Stop feeding in September and water rather less; let the top of the compost dry out a little each time, but still keep the soil slightly moist.

Your Coral Berry needs good light, even sun whenever possible, and a temperature around 55-60°F (13-15°C) to get safely through winter.

Propagation

Steady, high temperatures are necessary for growing your own Coral Berry plants and for this you really need a propagator. If you haven't got one, grow the seeds or cuttings on a sunny windowsill in a pot covered with a clear plastic bag.

Growing from seed is a slow, tedious business, but if you want to have a go you can buy seed from specialist seedsmen. Sow seeds in spring $\frac{1}{4}$in (6mm) deep into John Innes No 2, at a temperature of 75°F (24°C) in moist compost. The seedlings are very slow to appear, but when they do, drop the temperature to 60°F (15°C). The seedlings may only be 1in (2cm) tall after a year's effort!

Another method is to remove side-shoots in March with a small heel of bark attached Dip the cut end in hormone rooting powder and push the shoot into John Innes No 2. Always keep the compost moist and at a temperature of 75°F (24°C) and they should root within six to eight weeks. Cuttings take much longer, and may not root at all, if you can't provide them with enough bottom heat to start the roots growing.

Trouble Shooter

Problems start if you let your Coral Berry dry out, if you forget to feed it, or if you let it get cold.

Greenfly are attracted by juicy young leaves and shoots; spray with a houseplant insecticide. Fluffy white mealy bugs sometimes attach themselves to the ripe berries; use a spray insecticide containing pyrethrum to get rid of them. To avoid pests altogether, it's a good idea to use a systemic insecticide three or four times a year.

Species

Ardisia crenata (or ***crispa***) has deep green, crinkly-edged, long, pointed, leathery leaves. The plant can take years to grow to its full height of 4ft (1.2m). In late May or June, clusters of small white, fragrant flowers appear, each about $\frac{1}{2}$in (13mm) across and sometimes tinged with pink. These are followed by long-lasting glossy, scarlet berries.

A.solanacea, the Jet-Berry Tree, has reddish-brown branches and narrow, pale green, leathery leaves 4-5in (10-12cm) long. Its flowers are an inconspicuous rose-pink or violet, but they turn into clusters of berries each about $\frac{1}{2}$in (13mm) across, at first reddish-pink, then shiny black.

A.humilis comes from Asia and has dark green, soft leathery leaves 2-5in (5-13cm) long. It has hanging flat clusters of charming, small, pale rose flowers, followed by reddish berries, which in time turn glossy black.

Buying Guide

Ardisias can be hard but not impossible to find — especially the unusual species. Look in good garden centres and go to specialist nurserymen — look for their advertisements in gardening magazines. A large Ardisia is quite expensive as it is so slow growing.

Aristolochia

Family name: **Aristolochiaceae**

Common names:
Dutchman's Pipe / Birthwort

Care Straight-forward	**Height** 10ft (3m)	**Flower** July—September
Light Semi-shade	**Spread** 6ft (1.8m)	**Humidity** Regular spraying
Price Middle range	**Shape** Climber	**Availability** Specialist
Temp. Min 50°F (10°C)	Ideal 75°F (24°C)	Max 85°F (30°C)

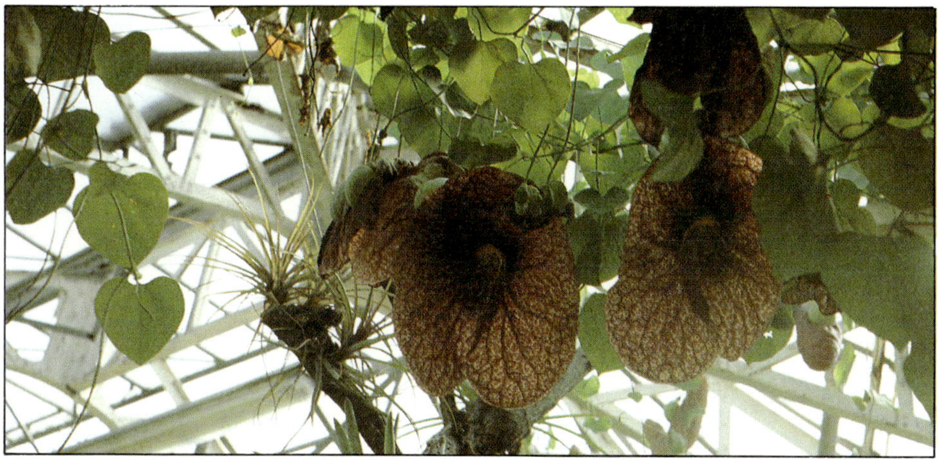

Aristolochia elegans is an easy-to-grow climber that produces pipe-like flowers.

This is an amazing family of plants which are fascinating for the beautiful 'ugliness' of their almost grotesque flowers. The family includes a number of shrubs and climbers, many of which come from Brazil, but only the latter are grown here. The more vigorous climbers are best grown in a conservatory or sun room where they have plenty of room to spread. *Aristolochia elegans* is the one most often grown as a houseplant; it is a graceful climbing plant with kidney-shaped leaves on long twining stems. The flower hangs from a long stalk and consists of an inflated yellow tube that turns upward into a whitish 'cup' with purplish streaks — the plant's common name, 'Dutchman's Pipe', comes from the shape of the flowers, which look very like carved meerschaum pipes. The inner edge of the cup is purplish-brown in colour with white markings. This family is most unusual in that the flowers have no petals, only a widely spreading calyx which reveals the mottled interior.

Spring and summer care

Grow your Aristolochia in a bright but semi-shady position where the foliage and flowers can grow toward the sun. Give it summer temperatures of 70-75°F (21-24°C) or even higher. Every year in March pot it into a good soil-based compost such as John Innes No 2 or 3. A mature Aristolochia will be top-heavy, so give it a good size container — 10-12in (25-30cm) — and weight it with stones to prevent it toppling over. Better still, if you have a greenhouse or sun room, grow it in a soil border where its roots will have plenty of room to spread.

Water often enough to keep the compost moist without waterlogging it. Mist spray regularly in hot weather and provide humidity by standing the pot in a tray of wet pebbles. As new growth starts and flower buds appear this plant gets very greedy as well as thirsty; so feed every 10-14 days with a good liquid fertiliser.

As Aristolochia is a climber, you must give it a trellis or some sort of framework to cling to. The ordinary Aristolochia isn't rampant, but it does have a number of branches to tie in. Train them in a zig-zag to the top of the frame and, if necessary, encourage them to trail back down again. However, if you want to keep your plant more compact, use your finger and thumb to pinch out the end 2-3in (5-7cm) of the shoots.

Autumn and winter care

In winter give your Aristolochia a temperature around 60-65°F (15-18°C), and keep it out of draughts. Stop feeding and mist spraying until the warmer weather of spring. Prune back any untidy shoots in autumn or wait until spring.

Propagation

Aristolochia seeds can be bought from specialist seedsmen. Sow them in March or early April, ¾in (19mm) deep in John Innes Seed Compost with a little added sharp sand to provide good drainage. Use a propagator if possible or a pot enclosed in a clear polythene bag. Keep the seeds moist and in a temperature of 75°F (24°C).

Alternatively in February take 3-4 in (7-10cm) long cuttings from ripe shoots (you can use some of the bits you've pruned off), preferably with a heel of wood. Dip the ends of the cuttings in hormone rooting powder and grow them in the same way as the seeds.

Trouble Shooter

Wilting or faded leaves are due to dry conditions or inadequate feeding: spray regularly and provide extra humidity by standing the pot in a tray of wet pebbles, and feed every 10-14 days.

Greenfly sometimes cluster at the base of the flowers: spray carefully with insecticide.

Species

Aristolochia elegans is a tall, fairly vigorous evergreen climbing plant. It has 2-3in (5-7cm) long, kidney-shaped leaves on long twining stems. Flowers open from July to September. Each flower has a long stalk with an inflated yellow U-bend tube about 1½in (38mm) long with an expanded, whitish streaked purple, cup-shaped mouth about 3in (7cm) across. The inner surfaces of the petals are mostly purplish-brown with white markings.

A.durior, Dutchman's Pipe, is a woody, vigorous, deciduous vine which can grow to 20ft (6m) or more. It has small, pipe-shaped yellow and brown flowers in May and June. Given reasonable protection it is quite hardy and so will grow well in a cold conservatory or porch.

A.brasiliensis is another of the vigorous climbers with soft, velvety leaves and enormous mottled flowers in varying shades of purple, carried on a long, curved tube.

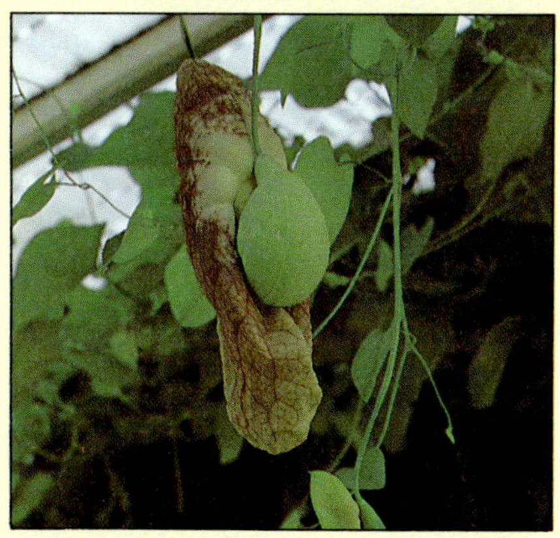

A.gigantea, *above,* comes from Brazil and has the largest flower of all. It is a vigorous clambering vine and really needs a conservatory to grow in. It has deeply veined, heart-shaped, leathery leaves. The flowers have a golden-yellow throat.

Asparagus

Family name: **Liliaceae**

Common name:
Asparagus Fern

Care Straight-forward	**Height** 12in (30cm)	**Flower** June—July
Light Semi-shade	**Spread** 2ft (0.6m)	**Humidity** Regular spraying
Price Cheap	**Shape** Ferny	**Availability** Common
Temp. Min 45°F (7°C)	Ideal 60°F (15°C)	Max 80°F (27°C)

Grow Asparagus Ferns for their lovely, frothy, green foliage which will brighten up any shady corner in your home. They are a family of very adaptable, ornamental plants with spreading or climbing foliage. Grow them in a hanging basket for a jungle effect, or train the climbing species onto a trellis where you can really appreciate their beauty.

Originally from South Africa, most Asparagus grow very quickly if you give them the sort of conditions they love — warmth, semi-shade and high humidity. Some Asparagus have swollen roots which they developed to survive extreme cold or drought. They all have wispy, intertwining stems and pretty, fresh green foliage, which leads them to be mistaken for ferns when, strictly speaking, they are lilies. *Asparagus densiflorus* 'Sprengeri' is probably the commonest Asparagus Fern with slender, delicate branches covered in fresh green, glossy, needle-like leaves. As with many Asparagus species, mature plants produce tiny, slightly fragrant, star-like, pinkish-white flowers which are followed by bright red berries in late summer.

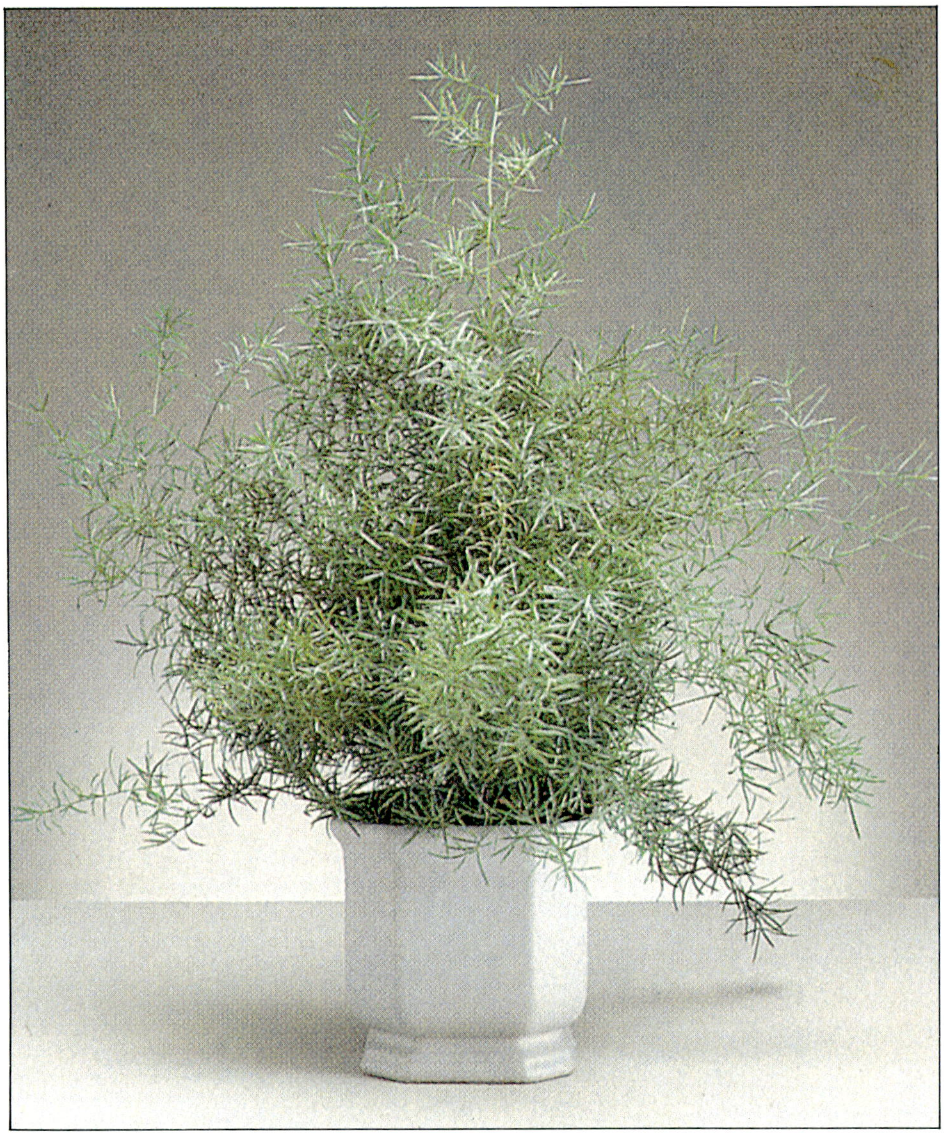

A well-shaped *Asparagus densiflorus* 'Sprengeri' is a lovely sight.

Spring and summer care

In March, before your Asparagus starts to grow again, use a sharp knife to cut off any dead or faded branches right back to the base. Then, if the soil has dried out, plunge the plant into a bucket of tepid water to get it going again. Give the plant warmth and let it settle for a couple of days, then repot your plant if it needs it, using John Innes No 2.

Put the plant in a bright but slightly shaded spot. Your Asparagus will be happiest in temperatures around 55-60°F (13-15°C) but make sure your plant has shade and good ventilation — stuffy air soon ruins the plant. Water thoroughly every couple of days in warm weather and feed with liquid fertiliser every 14 days throughout the growing and flowering season. Spray the foliage in warm weather, or provide constant humidity by standing the pot on a saucer of wet pebbles.

Autumn and winter care

Though your Asparagus can stand cold temperatures, it is safer not to let them drop lower than 45°F (7°C). If temperatures do get this cold, water less often and stop feeding until the warmer days of spring. Give your plant good light or the needles will fade and drop.

Propagation

Sow seeds in late March or April into John Innes No 2 with a little added sharp sand for extra drainage. Keep them moist and airy and at a steady temperature of 70°F (21°C). Seedlings should appear within three or four weeks; when they are 2-3in (5-7cm) tall, pot them into 3in (7cm) pots of John Innes No 1. After a couple of months the seedlings will bush out and start to look like mature plants. Pot them again, but this time into John Innes No 2. Wait for six weeks or so before starting regular but weak liquid feeding.

Alternatively, split mature plants in March. Gently break the swollen roots apart and trim off any damaged roots. Pot into John Innes No 2 and keep them shaded and moist at a temperature of 60°F (15°C). The roots will be established within three or four weeks.

Trouble Shooter

Brown, falling leaves covered at the base with fine webs show that your plant has red spider mite; the air has got too dry, so use a spray insecticide and provide more humidity.

Sticky, small, brown, circular blisters along the stems are actually scale insects; spray with a pyrethrum-based insecticide and, if necessary, repeat 7-10 days later.

Buying Guide

Always buy young Asparagus plants which are growing into a good, bushy shape. Avoid any with yellow leaves and bare stalks.

Species

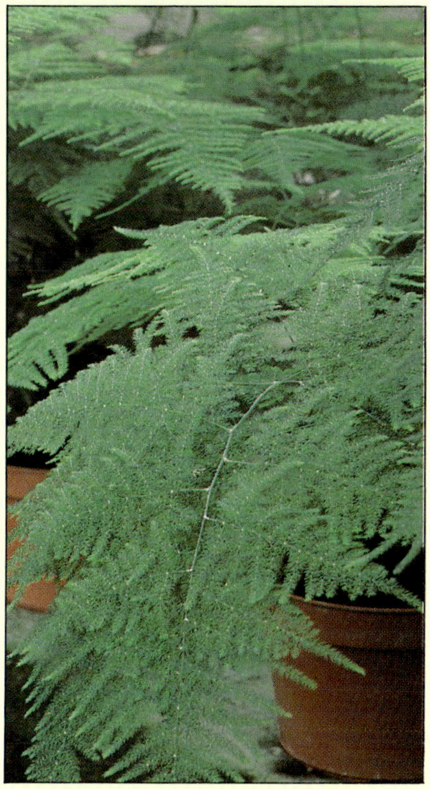

Asparagus densiflorus 'Sprengeri' has thick, fleshy roots, from which grow slender branches covered with fresh, glossy green, needle-like leaves. Tiny, slightly fragrant, white or pinkish flowers in summer are followed by red berries. 'Myersii' (Meyerii), the Plume Asparagus, *below*, has upright or gently-curving, thick, plume-like branches 2ft (0.6m) or more long. Small, fragrant flowers are followed by reddish berries. This plant grows best in a hanging basket.

A.asparagoides is a scrambling, twining vine with slender, almost thread-like stems up to 6ft (1.8m) in length. It has small, glossy green, heart-shaped leaves about 1in (25mm) long. Tiny, white, scented flowers open in pairs under the leaves. 'Myrtifolius' is identical but with smaller leaves and is the Asparagus used by florists in flower arrangements. 'Aurea' is similar to the parent, but with pale green leaves.

A.setaceus (plumosus), *left*, has vigorous, evergreen, fern-like foliage on stems up to 10ft (3m) long. Despite this, it is a delicate plant and has slender, wiry stems and lace-like leaves in horizontal tiers. It has scented, white, rather inconspicuous, flowers. Grow it on a climbing frame to see it at its best.

A.falcatus is one of the taller species and comes from Sri Lanka and parts of tropical Africa. The long, wiry branches are slender and armed with vicious $\frac{1}{4}$in (6mm) spines. The 2in (5cm) long leaves are flat and narrow and tipped with a small spine. This plant has sweetly scented clusters of white flowers followed by orange, berry-like fruits. It is an elegant long-lasting plant and well worth cultivating.

A.declinatus (crispus). A rather weak and straggling, climbing plant with small, white, fragrant, star-like flowers followed by reddish berries. The stems rarely grow longer than 3ft (0.9m).

A.scandens is a scrambling, climbing plant with rounded stems that freely branch out towards the top. It has slender, curved, pale green leaves about $\frac{1}{2}$in (13mm) long. 'Deflexus' has rather unusual stems which grow in a zig-zag fashion.

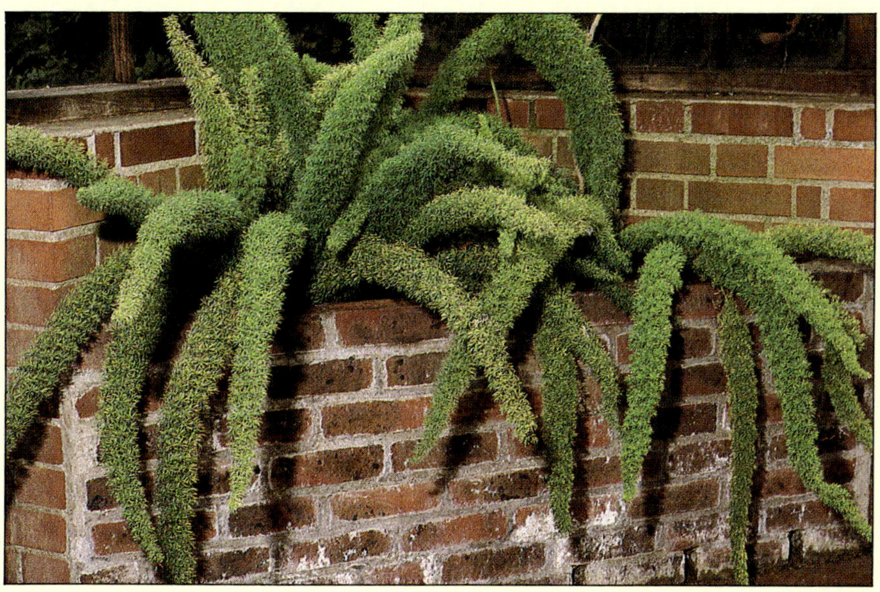

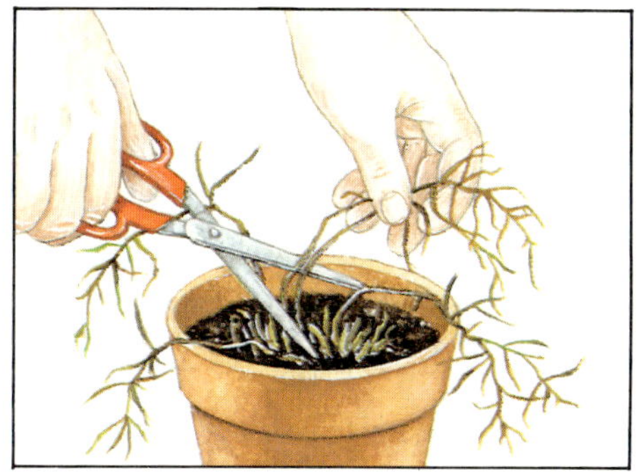

Reviving an Asparagus Fern: if your plant has dried out and lost much of its foliage during winter, give it a boost to get it going again in spring. Use a sharp pair of scissors and cut the wiry stems right back almost to the level of the compost. Be careful of the tiny thorns which can catch your fingers.

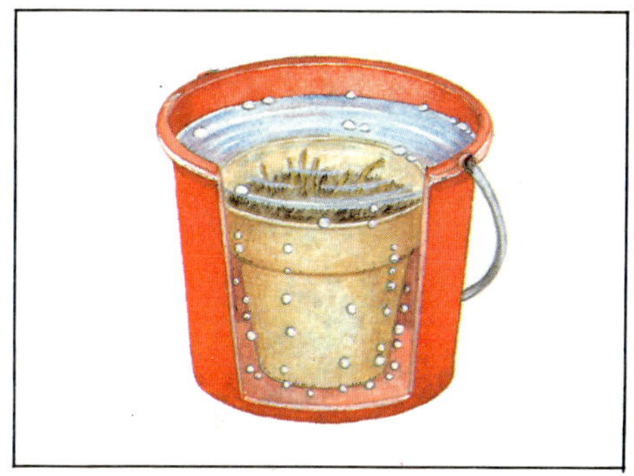

Plunge the whole plant, pot and all, into a bucket of tepid water. The idea is to saturate the compost until water gets right through to the roots and revives them so that they start to grow again. After about 20 minutes take the pot out of the water and then allow it to drain thoroughly.

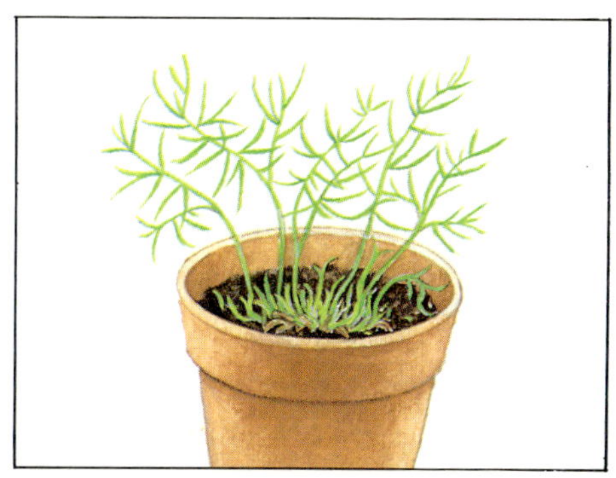

Place your Asparagus Fern where it can get plenty of warmth — about 60°F (15°C) — good ventilation and bright light but out of the direct sun. After a few days you can repot the plant if its roots have filled the pot, or leave it to grow undisturbed for another year. Fresh shoots will appear within a few weeks.

Aspidistra

Family name: **Liliaceae**

Common names:
Cast Iron Plant / Parlour Palm

Care Easy	**Height** 12in (30cm)	**Flower** Occasion-ally
Light Bright, indirect	**Spread** 2ft (0.6m)	**Humidity** Regular spraying
Price Expensive	**Shape** Bushy	**Availability** Garden centres
Temp. Min 45°F (7°C)	Ideal 60°F (15°C)	Max 70°F (21°C)

No houseplant has held its own against all-comers as well as the Aspidistra. A Victorian home wasn't complete without one, though even then it was neglected and forgotten, which is how it earned the nick-name of Cast Iron Plant. If you treat your Aspidistra well it will be a friend for life; nobody knows how long they live — but certainly more than 100 years.

The familiar, old-fashioned *Aspidistra elatior* comes all the way from China and is really a kind of lily with tough, leathery foliage. It has long, dullish-green ribbed leaves and sometimes, in summer, fleshy-pink, star-shaped flowers lurking right at the base of the stalks. These are easily missed if you are not specifically looking hard for them.

There is also a variegated variety with attractive green and white banded leaves; it is slightly more fussy than the ordinary kind as it needs good light. Aspidistras are painfully slow growing — careful attention can result in as many as four or five new leaves a year!

Spring and summer care

Repot every two or three years in March if the roots have completely filled the pot, using John Innes No 3. Big, mature plants can be top dressed instead; remove the top 2-3in (5-7cm) of compost and replace with fresh. Water regularly in warm weather — this can mean twice a week in summer. Feed with half-strength liquid fertiliser once a month during the main growing period, but no more or the leaves will split. Don't ever use leaf shine products as they damage the leaves even though they seem tough enough to take the effect of the polish.

Give your plant temperatures around 55-60°F (13-15°C) and bright indirect light. Ordinary Aspidistras tolerate shade, though don't expect them to grow well, but the variegated kind needs good light to keep the markings on its leaves. Mist spray frequently to keep the leaves fresh and to provide a little humidity. Carefully clean the large leaves with a moist sponge, as often as necessary to clear them of dust.

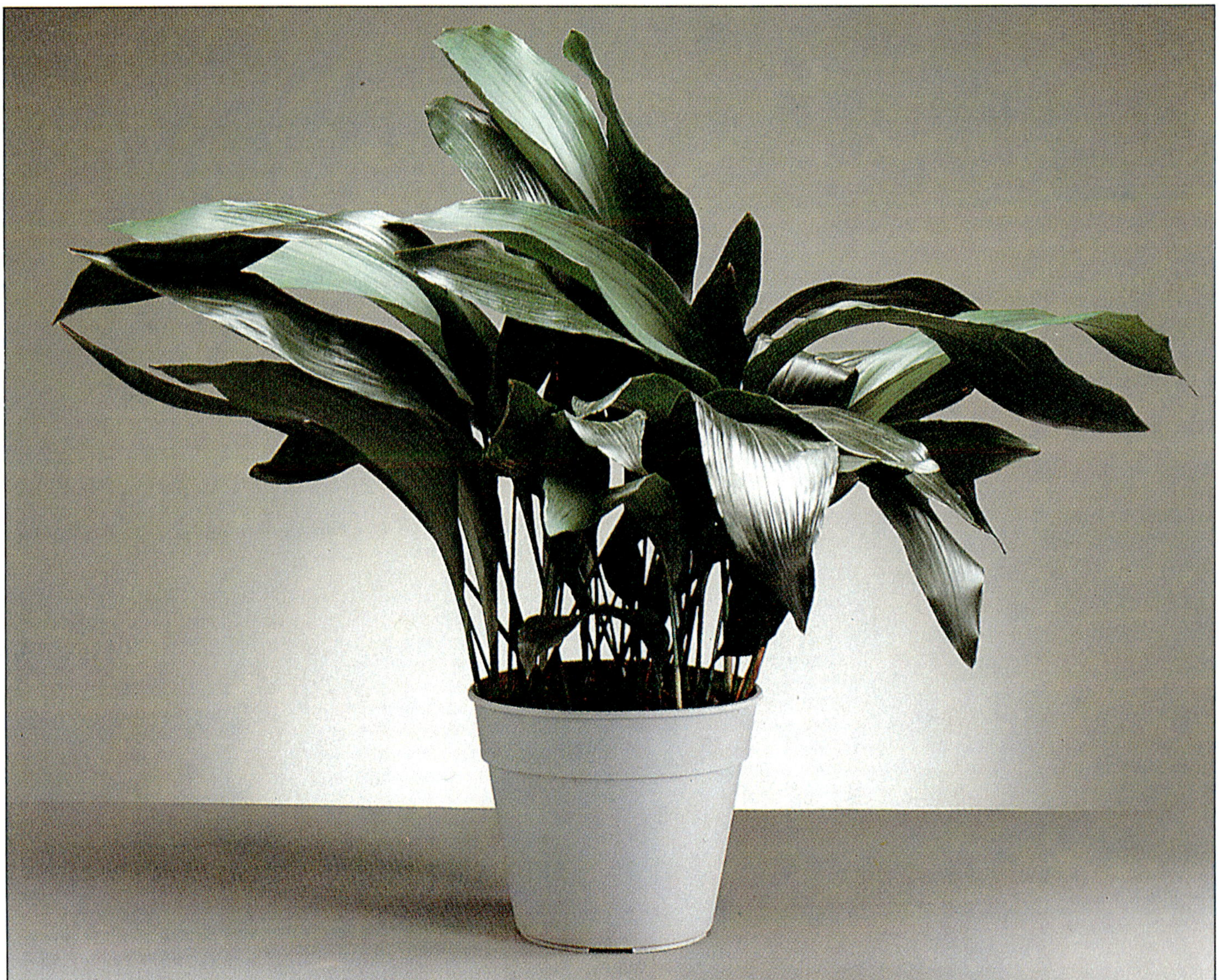

An Aspidistra takes years to grow a good clump of leaves, but as it lives for over a hundred, it has plenty of time to grow!

Species

Aspidistra elatior (also called ***lurida***). The fleshy roots produce a narrow, channelled stalk with fresh green leaves that turn blackish-green and slightly shiny with age. The leaves are fairly narrow, and about 30in (75cm) long when mature. In mid-summer stalkless, fleshy, bell-shaped flowers appear at compost level.

'Variegata', *below*, is similar but with varying widths of green and white bands on its leaves. 'Maculata' is thought to come from Japan, and is a smaller plant with blackish-green leaves spotted and marked with numerous white dots.

A.longifolia comes from the northern hills of Assam in India. It has slender 1-2in (2-5cm) wide and 2-3ft (0.6-0.9m) long leaves and small flowers about ½in (13mm) across.

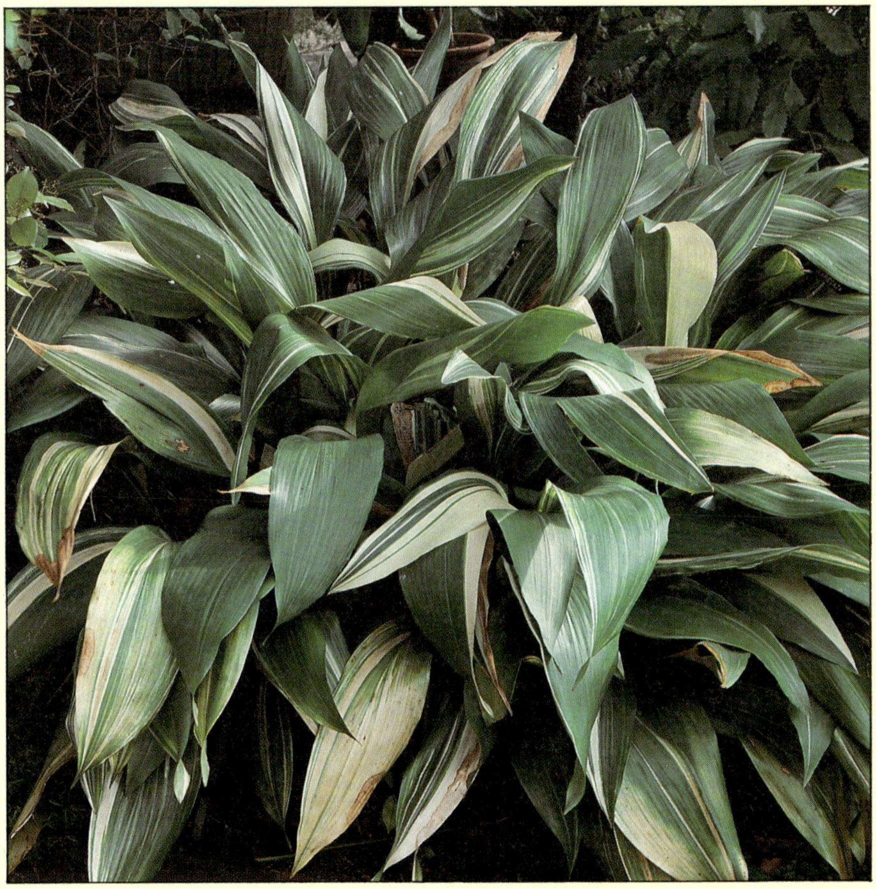

Trouble Shooter

Split leaves are caused by over-fertilising; don't feed for a couple of months, then only give half the recommended strength once a month in summer.

Scorched leaves show that your Aspidistra has been sitting in too much sun; move it to a shady position. Brown marks on the leaves indicate that the plant has been overwatered.

Yellow spotted leaves can mean your Aspidistra has scale insects. Look underneath the leaves for tiny brown blisters; use a systemic malathion-based insecticide such as Murphy's Systemic.

Red spider mite and mealy bug can both appear on a neglected plant if it is too dry. Treat in the same way as scale insects; and as an overall preventative give doses of systemic insecticide three or four times a year.

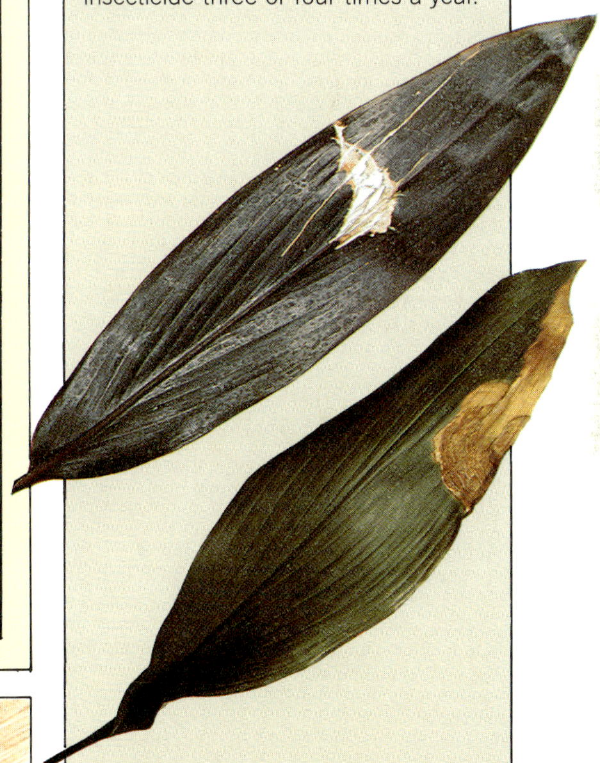

Damaged leaves: splits, *top*, show that your plant has been overfed. The brown mark, *above*, was caused by direct heat from a radiator.

Autumn and winter care

Your Aspidistra won't noticeably alter for winter, but you should change the way you treat it. Stop feeding altogether until the warmer days of spring, and reduce the amount of water. The compost can virtually dry out between times. The Aspidistra can stand a drop in temperature down to 45°F (7°C) without lasting harm; though, to be really kind, give your plant a temperature of 50°F (10°C), in moderate light away from draughts, fumes and smoke.

Propagation

Divide the roots in spring by carefully cutting off a small section of swollen root with four or five attached leaves. Plant firmly in John Innes No 3 and keep the plant moist in a temperature of 60°F (15°C) until it is well established, which takes a few months.

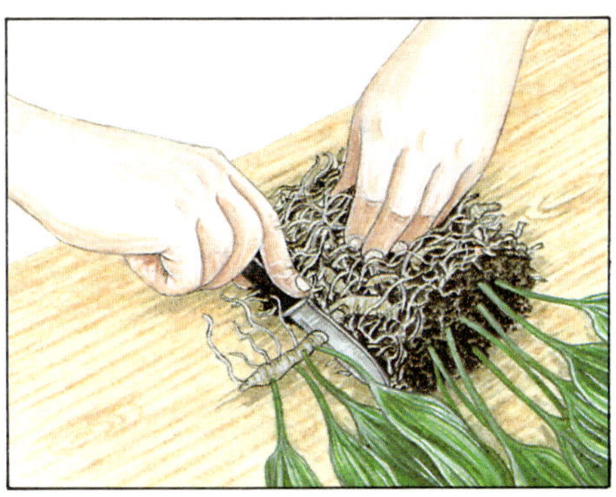

Propagating an Aspidistra: brush away some of the compost from the root. Use a sharp knife and cut off a small piece of fleshy root with a few attached leaves. Plant into John Innes No 3.

Buying Guide

Aspidistras are getting easier to find as they are enjoying renewed popularity. Don't necessarily buy the largest plant; instead look for one with fresh young shoots or leaves, as it shows the roots are vigorous and the plant is growing well.

Asplenium

Family name: **Polypodiaceae**

Common names:
Bird's Nest Fern
Hen and Chickens Fern

Care Straight-forward	**Height** 3ft (0.9m)	**Flower** None
Light Shaded light	**Spread** 3ft (0.9m)	**Humidity** Regular spraying
Price Cheap	**Shape** Fern	**Availability** Common
Temp. Min 55°F (13°C)	Ideal 65°F (18°C)	Max 75°F (24°C)

Aspleniums come from many parts of the world and almost without exception they are shade lovers. This makes them very good houseplants, as well as being splendid for their decorative value. The commonest species is the Bird's Nest Fern, *Asplenium nidus*, which comes mainly from northern Australia. It has a large rosette of shiny, leathery, apple-green, narrow leaves which grow 3ft (0.9m) or more long. Each frond uncurls from a dense crown of blackish scales, which look rather like a bird's nest and from where it gets its common name.

Aspleniums are wonderful shapely houseplants when mature and are easy to grow provided you give them constantly high temperatures of around 65°F (18°C) or higher, with plenty of humidity. The other secrets of success are to grow your plant in a good, constantly moist, peat-based compost in a shady spot, with regular feeding.

Spring and summer care

Pot your Asplenium every year in March or April into a good peat compost such as Levingtons or Arthur Bowers. Firm the plant well. Keep it in a lightly shaded spot, ideally at a temperature of 65°F (18°C). Feed every three weeks or so, with a half-strength liquid fertiliser. With the right conditions it will grow fairly rapidly. In warm weather water two or three times a week to keep the compost moist, but not waterlogged.

Provide your Asplenium with humidity by regular mist spraying — if possible use rain-water. If the air gets very dry your Asplenium will be happier with the constant humidity created by standing the pot on a saucer of wet pebbles. Once a month gently wipe mature leaves clean of dust — but never use leaf shine. At the same time use secateurs to cut off damaged or dry fronds.

Autumn and winter care

In autumn reduce the amount of water you give your Asplenium — give it just enough to keep the compost slightly moist. Try to see that your room temperature doesn't fall below 55°F (13°C).

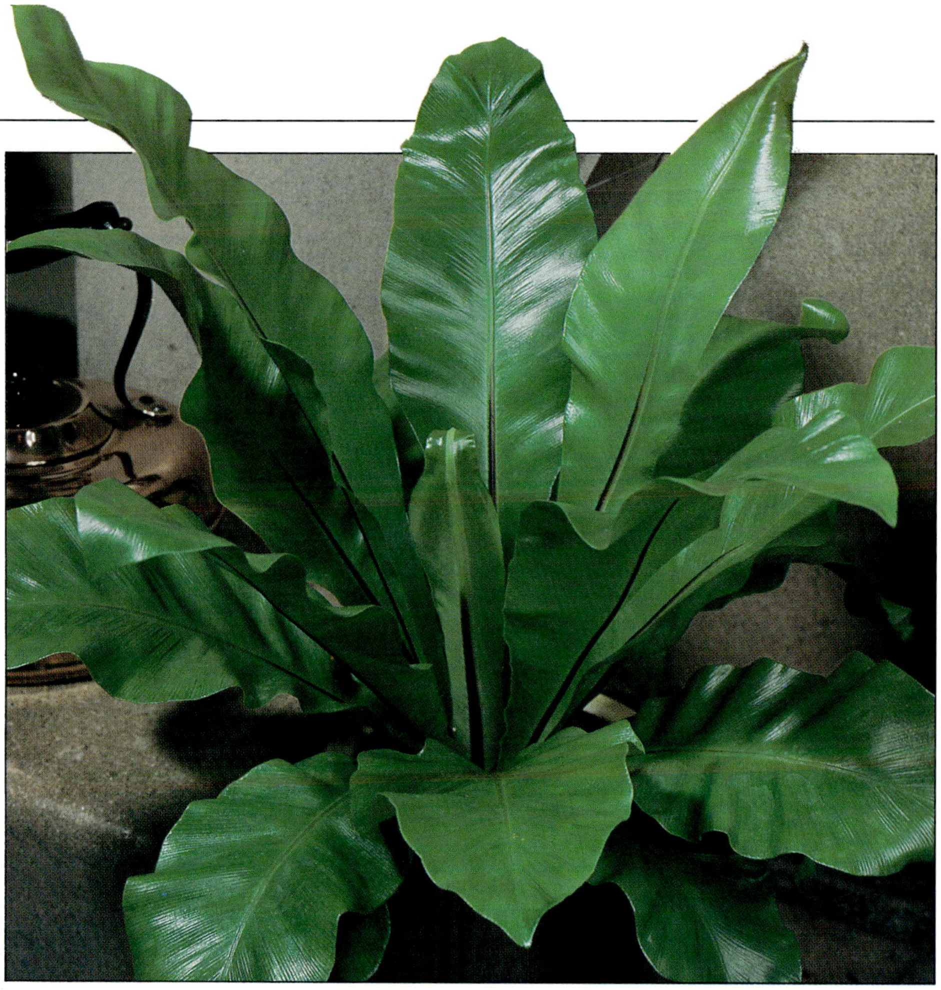

To appreciate the beauty of a Bird's Nest Fern it should stand alone.

Species

Asplenium nidus, the Bird's Nest Fern, comes mainly from northern Australia. It has large, shiny, apple-green, leathery, leaves which can grow 3ft (0.9m) or more long. Each frond has a raised, brownish-black mid-rib. It does best when it has a constant temperature of 65-75°F (18-24°C).

A.bulbiferum, the Hen and Chicken Fern, comes from New Zealand and India. Slender, black stalks up to 2ft (0.6m) long carry green, deeply-cut fronds, which actually look very like carrot leaves. Plantlets develop on the edge of mature fronds and these gently weight the frond, giving it a graceful, arching appearance. Each plantlet is capable of growing into a young plant. It is almost hardy and so is a good plant for a cold house. Give it a summer maximum of 65°F (18°C).

A.viviparum, the Mother Fern, comes from Mauritius and develops small bulbils. It is a tufted, rather loose-looking plant with dark green, arching fronds about 18in (45cm) long and small, very fine, lace-like segments which produce the bulbils.

A.lucidum, the Leather Fern, from New Zealand, is a graceful plant which grows quite quickly. Greyish stalks carry shiny-green fronds. It has narrow, leathery leaflets about 6in (15cm) long with serrated edges.

Propagation

The Bird's Nest Fern can be grown from spores, but it's a very tricky operation and best left to professionals.

A much easier method you can also use with other Aspleniums is to pick off the baby plants (plantlets) from mature fronds. Set them firmly in peat and sand compost and keep them shaded and moist at 60°F (15°C), enclosed in a propagator or polythene bag.

Trouble Shooter

Wilting leaves show that the air is too dry; mist spray regularly.

Scale insect attacks along the underside veins of the foliage. Water a systemic insecticide into the soil two or three times a year as a preventative — or if scale has got a hold, use a spray insecticide immediately.

Azalea

Family name: **Ericaceae**

Common name:
Indian Azalea

Care Straight-forward	**Height** 18in (46cm)	**Flower** Early in spring
Light Shaded light	**Spread** 18in (45cm)	**Humidity** Light spraying
Price Middle range	**Shape** Bushy	**Availability** Common
Temp. Min 45°F (7°C)	Ideal 55°F (13°C)	Max 65°F (18°C)

The colourful Indian Azalea makes a very welcome appearance in winter and is a great favourite around Christmas time. Frilly single or double flowers which come in a wide range of subtle or vibrant colours are its great attraction. The Azalea is a type of Rhododendron, and the plants which cheer up our winter are mostly varieties of *Rhododendron simsii*, a Chinese species.

Azaleas flower naturally in spring, but commercial growers force them into bloom early so we can enjoy them all through winter. The flowers can be virtually any shade of red, orange, pink, white and multi-coloured on small, rounded, 18in (45cm) high, semi-evergreen plants. Azaleas are long lasting and most of them are hardy, so when they have finished flowering they can be planted outside in the garden — either permanently if you have rich, peaty soil or just for the summer.

Spring and summer care

The correct type of soil is vital for your Azalea: it must have good, peaty soil so use pure peat or one of the peat-based compost brands. Watering is also important: use soft water or collect rainwater if you live in a hard water area. Keep your plant wet, not just moist — this means watering every day in warm weather. Good, shaded light is also essential — full sunlight can burn the leaves and have a disastrous effect.

By the middle of spring your Azalea is likely to have finished flowering. Remove all the remains of dead flowers and any very long, untidy stems by pruning back to a nice fat bud or cluster of leaves. Only give it a light trim, as over-enthusiastic pruning can spoil the development of next year's flowers. During summer your Azalea can live indoors or outside in the garden. If you put it outside, find a good, shady corner and plunge the plant, in its pot, into the soil up to the rim. Make sure it stays very moist all summer and then lift it and bring it back indoors in late September before there is a danger of frost. If you keep it indoors, find a bright, cool spot and remember to water it well.

Autumn and winter care

Keep your Azalea cool, in good light but not sunshine. Provide temperatures between 45-55°F (7-13°C), or even up to 60°F (15°C), but any higher will do more harm than good. If it gets too hot, and worse still, dry, the flowers will open before they are really ready and die off very quickly. Keep the compost wet, but not saturated. Provide good ventilation and a light overhead spray with soft water if the temperature rises. Feed with a liquid fertiliser every two weeks during the flowering season.

Buying Guide

Always buy a plant with plenty of fresh-looking leaves and flowers, plus a number of fat buds. If any leaves are wilting, pass it by!

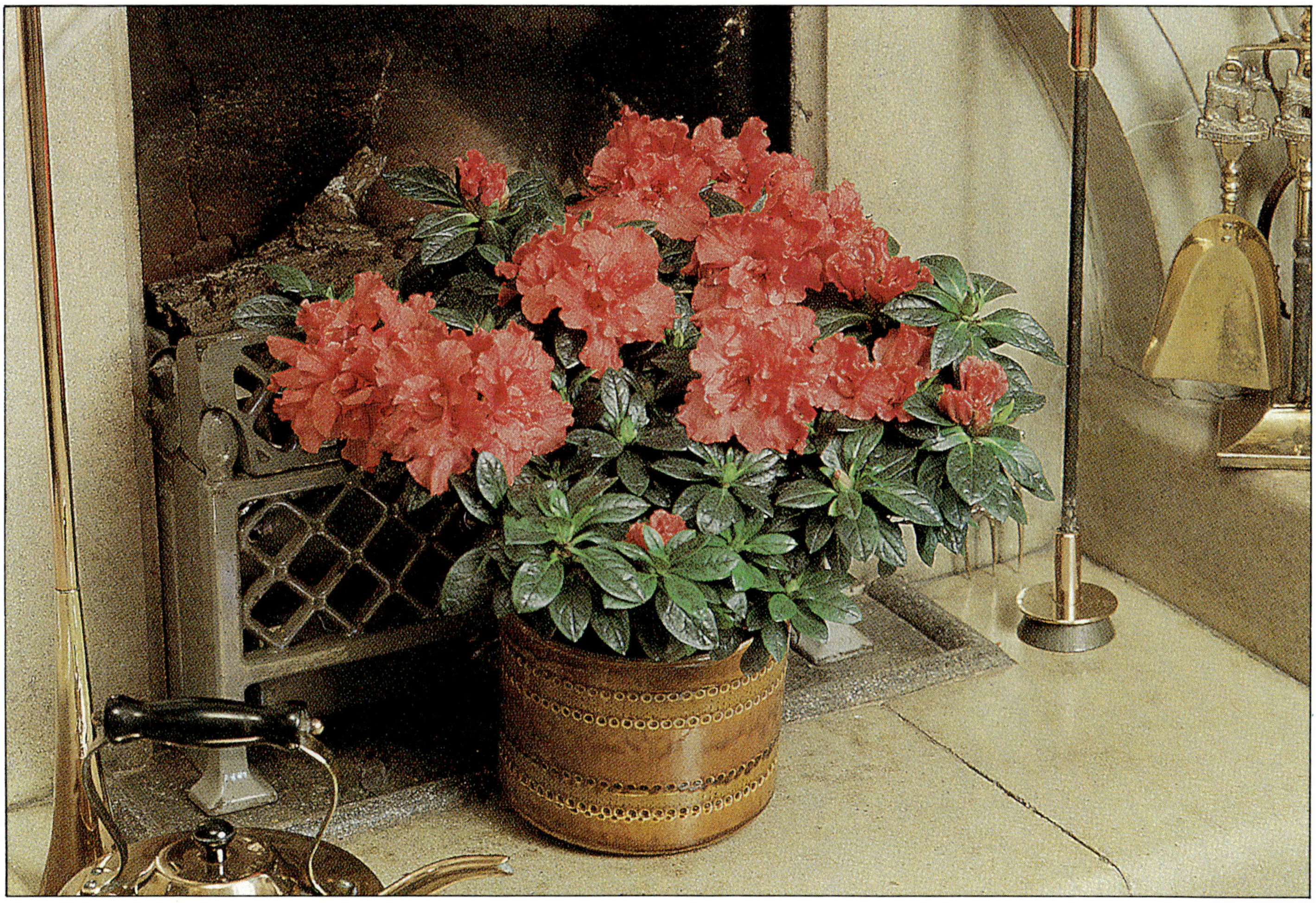

An Azalea provides a bright splash of winter colour at a time when few other plants are flowering.

Trouble Shooter

Wilted or falling dry, brown leaves and flower buds show the temperature is too high and that your plant isn't getting enough water; plunge the entire pot in tepid water for 20 minutes or so, *see below*, and give the foliage a good overhead spray. Then water the plant regularly.

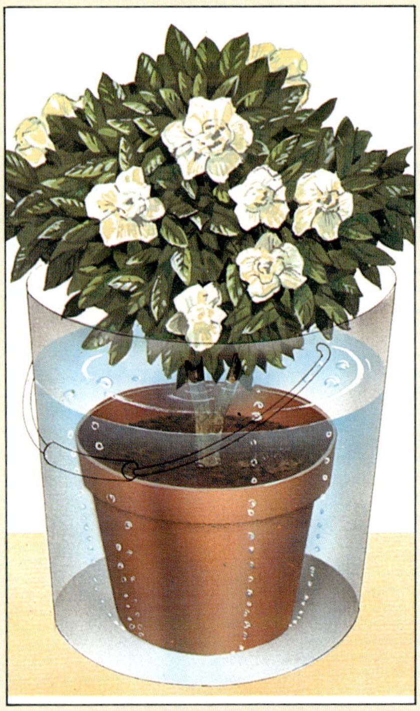

Let the plant drain, then move it to a cooler position and remember to water regularly.

Falling green buds and undeveloped flowers indicate that your plant is sitting in a draught, or that the compost has become saturated; move the plant and water more carefully.

Long, whitish marks in the leaves are a sure sign of leaf miner; use a systemic insecticide watered into the soil, or use a spray containing malathion.

Species

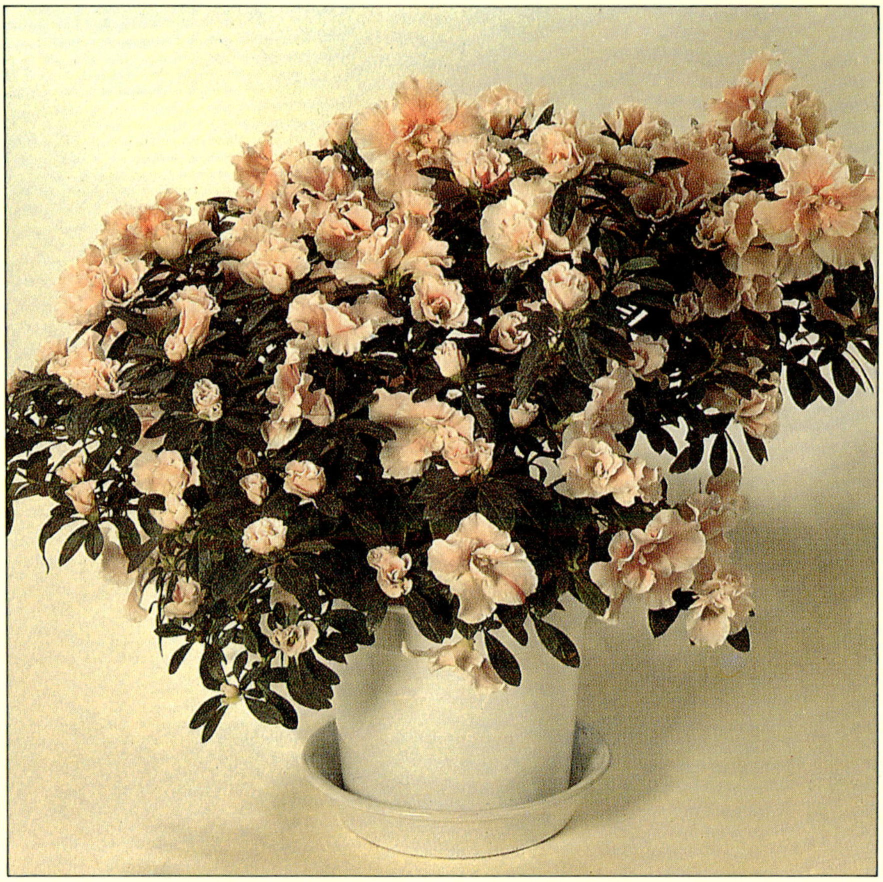

When buying a plant get one with some open flowers and lots of buds.

Azalea indica, the Indian Azalea, *above*, is actually a group name for all the colourful cultivated varieties of Azalea. Many owe their origin to ***Rhododendron simsii***, a Chinese species with semi-evergreen foliage and 2-3in (5-7cm), hairy, reddish, funnel-shaped flowers. There are lots of attractive varieties, all with small, oval, dark green leaves and single or double flowers in a wide range of colours. This Azalea is not fully hardy, so you run the risk of losing it in severe weather if you grow it outside.

Rhododendron obtusum, the Kirishima Azalea, comes from Japan and is a densely-leaved, bushy plant with small, tough, dark green leaves and small, reddish, funnel-shaped flowers open in late March through to May. Many lovely varieties have been developed and they also come in a wide range of colours. These varieties are completely hardy, and can happily live outside in the garden after they have finished flowering indoors.

Propagation

Any time between July and October, take 3in (7cm) long stem cuttings with a small heel of bark. Grow them in a propagator if possible, otherwise in a pot covered with a clear polythene bag, in a mixture of one part peat to three parts sand. Keep the cuttings at an even temperature of 50-55°F (10-13°C) and moderately moist. Rooting takes three to six weeks.

Seeds are less successful as you get variable results in flower colour and in the vigour of the plants, but if you have the seeds it is certainly worth a try. Sow seeds in March onto the surface of a sand and peat compost mix, then cover them with a light layer of gritty sand. Keep the compost just moist and at a temperature of about 60°F (15°C).

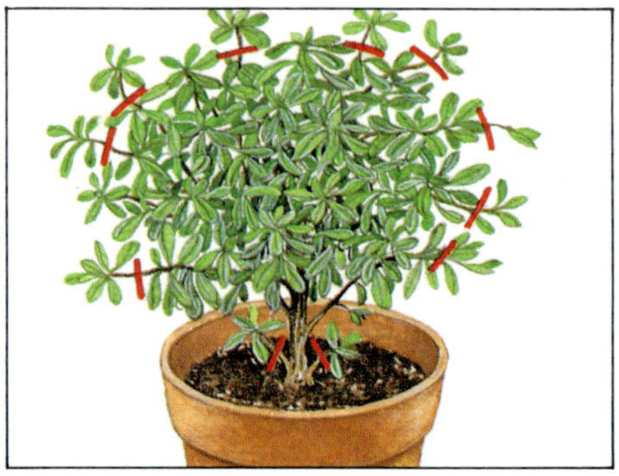

Tidying up an Azalea: in spring trim your plant back to shape, not forgetting the suckers growing from the base.

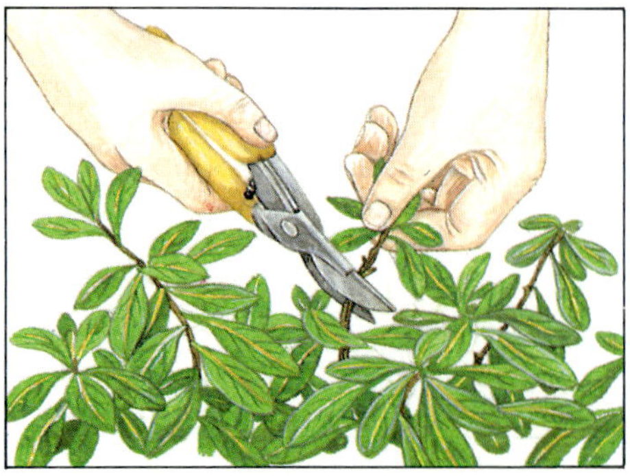

Use sharp secateurs to make a diagonal pruning cut just above a nice fat bud or cluster of healthy leaves.

Beaucarnea

Family name: **Agavaceae**

Common names: **Ponytail Plant Bottle Plant**

Care Easy	**Height** 3ft (0.9m)	**Flower** None
Light Full sun	**Spread** 3ft (0.9m)	**Humidity** None
Price Expensive	**Shape** Small tree	**Availability** Garden centres
Temp. Min 45°F (7°C)	Ideal 70°F (21°C)	Max 80°F (27°C)

The Ponytail Plant is an unusual and spectacular 'feature' houseplant. The main stem is thick and fleshy and gradually develops a swollen base of quite substantial proportions, giving the impression of a sturdy bottle. The leaves are clustered together at the top of the trunk and curve out like a pony's tail. The ordinary Ponytail Plant is called *Nolina recurvata*, but it has been called Beaucarnea for so long that we are treating it as such here, along with the real, very similar, Beaucarneas.

The Ponytail Plant comes from the hot, dry, desert regions of Mexico where it grows over 30ft (9m) tall. At home though, in a pot, it is unlikely to get much higher than 3ft (0.9m). It is a very easy houseplant to keep, provided it doesn't get too cold in winter.

Spring and summer care

The Ponytail Plant is happy in full sun or good, bright light: if you give it too much shade it won't grow. Summer temperatures can rise to 70°F (21°C) and above without harm. Water your plant well, then let the soil get almost completely dry before watering again. Feed twice a year with Cactigrow or Phostrogen in liquid form; once in spring, just as growth starts, then again at the very end of summer. Repot in April only if your plant is beginning to outgrow its container. Use John Innes No 2.

Autumn and winter care

Continue to give your Ponytail Plant the best possible light, and be careful to keep it well out of draughts. Provide a temperature of about 50°F (10°C) and don't water from late October until late March. The plant needs this winter rest so it can live off the stored water in its swollen base. Give it just a drop of water towards the end of winter. If your plant is exposed to temperatures in excess of 60°F (15°C) during winter, you must continue watering as usual — but this is not ideal.

Propagation

Sow seeds in February or March using a good seed compost. Grow in a temperature of 65-70°F (18-21°C), if possible with bottom heat for quick germination. When the seedlings are 2-3in (5-7cm) tall, pot them up individually in John Innes No 2.

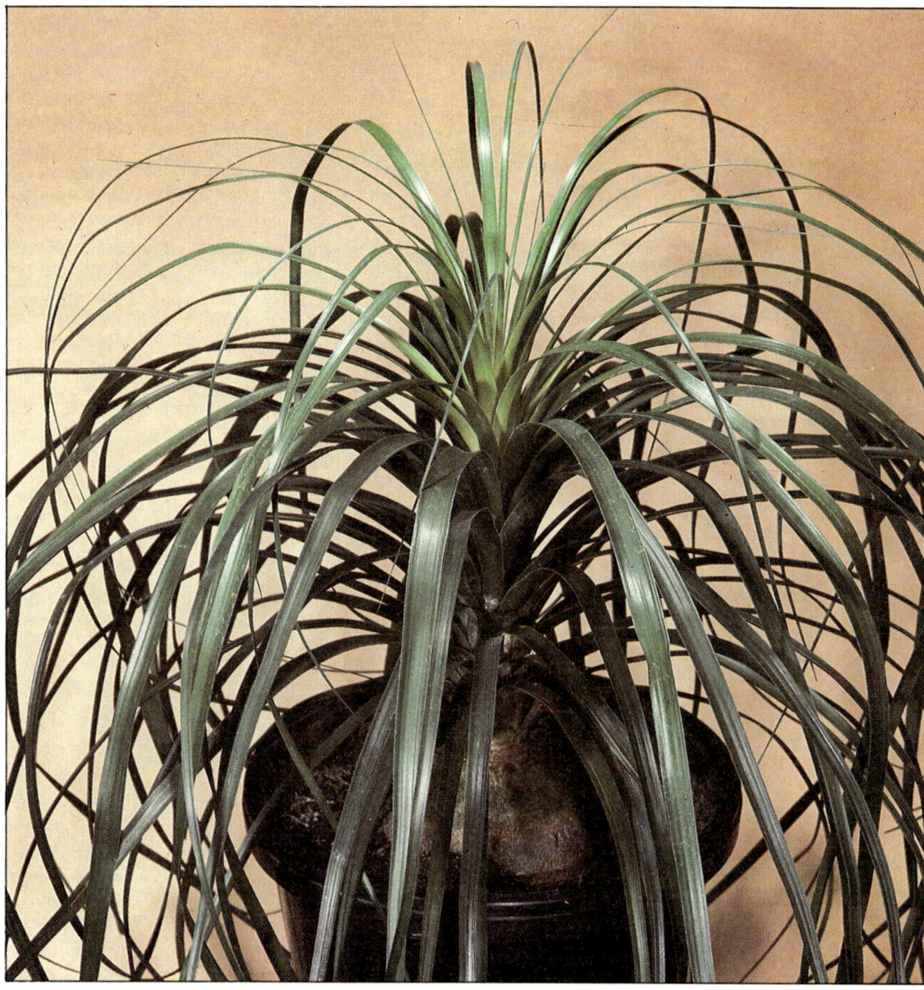

The Ponytail Plant loves the warm, dry air of central heating in winter.

Trouble Shooter

Happily troubles are few and far between: mealy bug can sometimes prove a nuisance, but these white, fluffy patches can be wiped away with a brush dipped in methylated spirits.

Too much water in winter, especially if the conditions are cold, will start rot within the root. This will extend into the trunk — there is no cure.

Buying Guide

You'll have to search around to find a Ponytail Plant — they sometimes appear at garden centres as small young plants. Go to a specialist cacti and succulent nursery to be sure of finding one. Specialists also supply Beaucarnea seeds.

Species

Nolina recurvata, Ponytail Plant, has a thick, fleshy, grey-brown stem which swells at the base with stored water. Long, slender, arching leaves grow in a plume from the top. White clusters of inconspicuous flowers appear on mature plants but this is rare indoors.

N.longifolia has thin, firm, spreading and hanging leaves growing from a dense crown. Each leaf can be over 4ft (1.2m) long and is about 1-1¼in (25-31mm) wide at the base and tapers to a point at its tip.

Beaucarnea gracilis is very similar to ***N.longifolia***, with a swollen, bottle-shaped trunk and a crown of leaves. The leaves are greyish-green, about ½in (13mm) wide and anything from 20-30in (50-75cm) long with rough edges. It has clusters of whitish-pink or almost red flowers at the top of the plant.

B.stricta is again very similar to ***N.longifolia***, but the leaves are very stiff and spreading, each one about ½in (13mm) wide with rough edges.

Begonia

Family name: **Begoniaceae**

Common name: **Begonia**

Care Easy	**Height** 9-24in (23-61cm)	**Flower** March—Feb
Light Bright indirect sun	**Spread** 9-18in (23-45cm)	**Humidity** Regular spraying
Price Cheap	**Shape** Bushy	**Availability** Common
Temp. Min 50°F(10°C)	Ideal 65°F (18°C)	Max 75°F(24°C)

There are, astonishingly, over 1,000 types of flowering and ornamental Begonia. Their exotic flowers and foliage make them favourite and well-established houseplants. Some Begonias are grown for their foliage and some for their flowers.

There are three main groups of Begonia, divided by root type into rhizomatous, tuberous and fibrous. A rhizome is a swollen root, like a thickened stem, that grows horizontally above or below the surface of the soil with finer roots growing down from it. It looks rather like stem ginger and stores water and nutrients for use in dry conditions.

A tuber is a swollen section of a main root, with roots continuing and dividing into ever smaller roots below the tuber. A tuber is also a food reserve and similar to a potato in shape and texture.

Fibrous roots are like the fine ordinary roots that start thick and then branch off into tinier and tinier ones as they get further away from the soil's surface.

The rhizomatous group are grown for their colourful leaves, the prime example being *Begonia rex*, which originally came from India. The leaves cover a huge range of bright and stripy colours on large, pointed, oval-shaped, and corrugated leaves.

The tuberous group are mostly colourful hybrids with large single or double flowers in summer. They are dormant in winter, when they die right back to the tuber. Tuberous Begonias look particularly good in hanging baskets but the more upright kinds are pretty in a simple pot.

The fibrous group are evergreen, though some lose a few leaves in winter. They are the tallest Begonia group, some growing 3ft (0.9m) high. They have asymmetrical, heart-shaped leaves, which in some species are very hairy. Some fibrous-rooted Begonias are

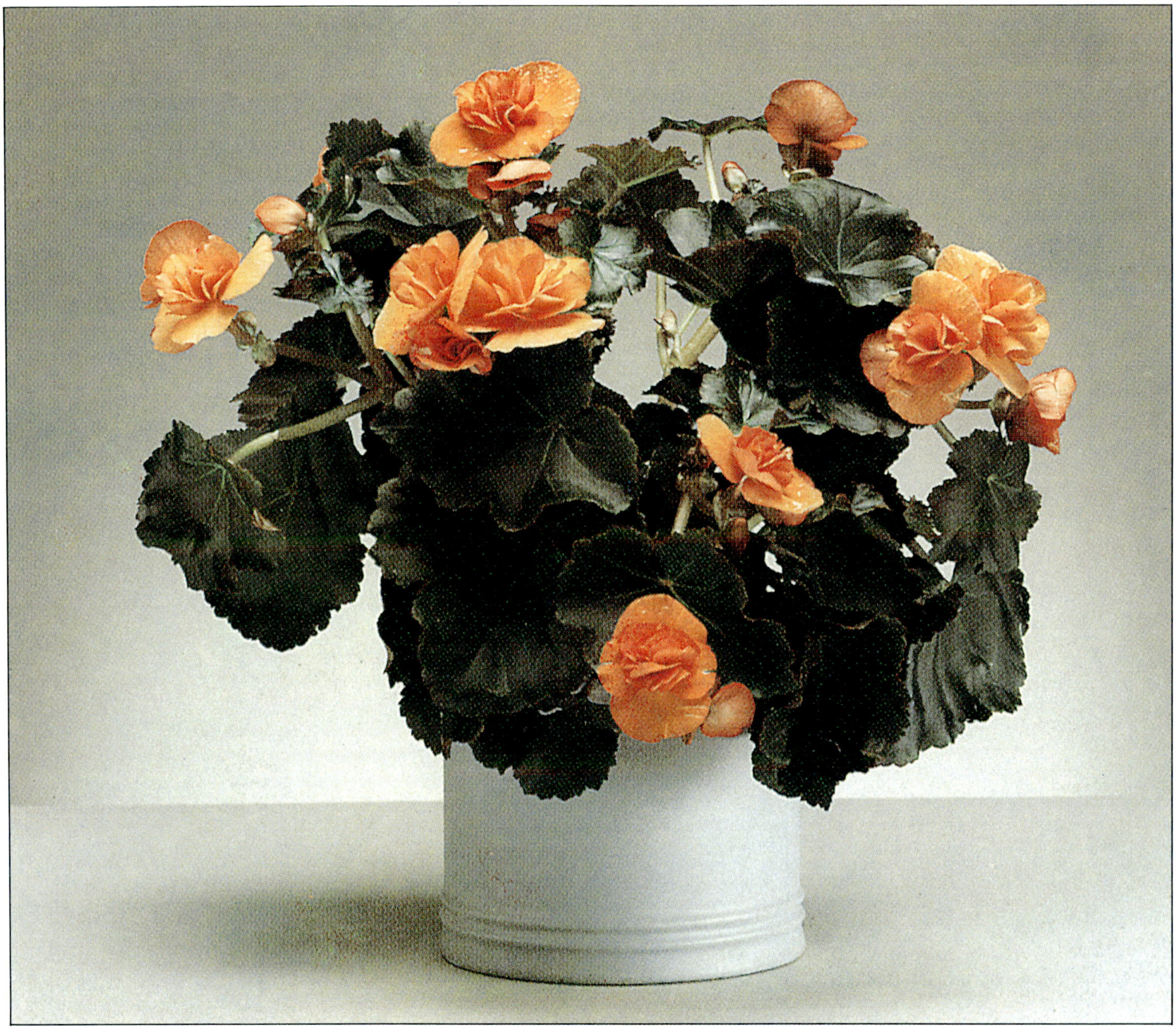

The tuberous Begonia is a reliable houseplant with a wide colour range and a very long flowering period.

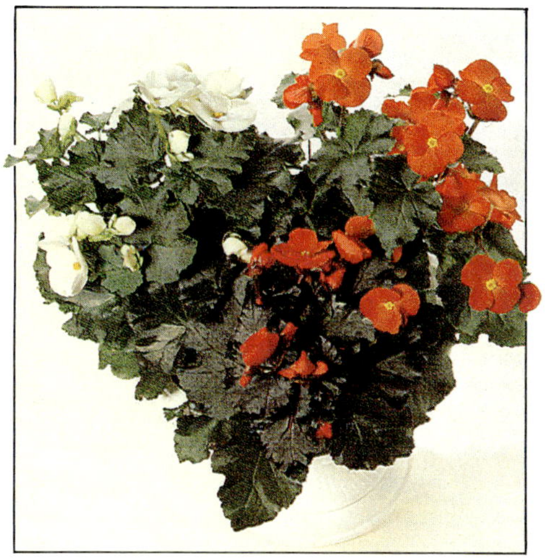

Fibrous Begonias are one of the most popular of all houseplants and can be either double flowered, or single flowered, *above*. These Begonias flower for months on end until they are exhausted, and then thrown away.

bushy and some trail, but they all produce lots of pretty clusters of flowers.

Spring and summer care

Rhizomatous Begonias: like a temperature of 60°F (15°C) throughout the year. For colourful foliage and flowers they need bright light — three to four hours of direct sunlight a day if you want flowers, but out of direct sunlight if you prefer the foliage.

Tuberous Begonias: give your plant bright but filtered light. If temperatures go over 65°F (18°C), stand your plant on a saucer of wet pebbles to give it more humidity. Water moderately, letting the surface of the compost dry out between times. Use a liquid fertiliser containing potash every two weeks during the growing season. Water less as the plant approaches its dormant period in late autumn.

Fibrous-rooted Begonias: remove dead leaves and flowers immediately they appear; if left on the plant they will rot or blemish other leaves they touch.

In March step up your watering to encourage new growth; water once or twice a week, giving the plant more in really hot weather. Leaves droop and flowers fall if you don't give your plant enough water — but don't overwater it. Return to watering moderately once flowering stops. Feed with liquid fertiliser every two weeks from April to September.

It is important that your plant gets good light, but not full sun as it burns the leaves and flowers. Provide a temperature of 60°F (15°C) — give extra but not dense shade if temperatures soar, but try to keep to a 70°F (21°C) maximum. Make sure the room is well ventilated but not draughty.

Humidity is essential but be careful if you mist spray not to spray the flowers as it 'spots' them. Also spray before the sun's rays reach the plant as the droplets will cause scorch marks to appear on the leaves.

Autumn and winter care

Rhizomatous Begonias: water your plant moderately in winter, letting the surface of the soil dry out between waterings. Keep in a shady spot where the atmosphere is not too dry. Don't feed in the winter. Repot, if necessary, during winter into a peat-based, completely soilless compost, such as Levingtons, adding one part sharp grit or sand per three parts compost.

Tuberous Begonias: stop watering when the plant's leaves start to drop in autumn. Keep a dormant plant in a temperature of 55°F (13°C) and provide bright but filtered light. Semi-tuberous hybrids should be kept just moist during winter. Repot in a peat-based compost, ensuring good drainage by placing bits of broken pot in the bottom.

Fibrous-rooted Begonias: if your plant is straggly, prune it back to give a nice shape, removing any unhealthy growth. Repot into John Innes No 2 before the growing season in February if the plant has filled its pot. The ideal temperature for your Begonia is 60°F (15°C). Adapt watering to your conditions: if temperatures are cool, water less — and never overwater.

Propagation

Rhizomatous Begonias: leaf cuttings are the best way of propagating *B.rex*. Cut through the veins on the underside of the leaf with a clean, sharp knife (or cut it into squares as shown on the right) and lay the leaf, underside down, on a tray of firmed half peat, half sand compost. Keep the cuttings shaded from bright light and give them a moist, humid atmosphere. Tiny plants will sprout from the cuts. Give more light as they develop.

Tuberous Begonias: collect the small tubers (bulbils) that form at the leaf joints in autumn. Keep the bulbils in a container at 55°F (13°C) until spring. Plant each bulbil in its own smallish pot, just covering it with moistened, peaty potting compost. Keep the compost just moist and place the pots in bright but filtered light. As the bulbils develop, gradually give them more water. When they are about 3in (8cm) high they can be treated like mature tuberous Begonias, although they will not flower properly for two years.

Fibrous-rooted Begonias: sow the seeds in January or February when indoor temperatures are 65-75°F (18-24°C). Spread the seeds evenly over the surface of John Innes Seed Compost and cover with a light layer of fine sand. Keep the compost moist and in a shady place until the seeds germinate. A propagator is best but otherwise seal the seed tray in a clear, polythene bag and keep it warm. As the seedlings grow, gradually give more light, but not full sun, and reduce the temperature to 65°F (18°C), providing good ventilation.

Leaf and stem cuttings 2-3in (5-7cm) long root easily in spring and summer; using John Innes No 2, dip the ends in hormone rooting powder and insert each into its own pot of moist compost. Keep semi-shaded, moist but not wet, and in a temperature of 65-70°F (18-24°C).

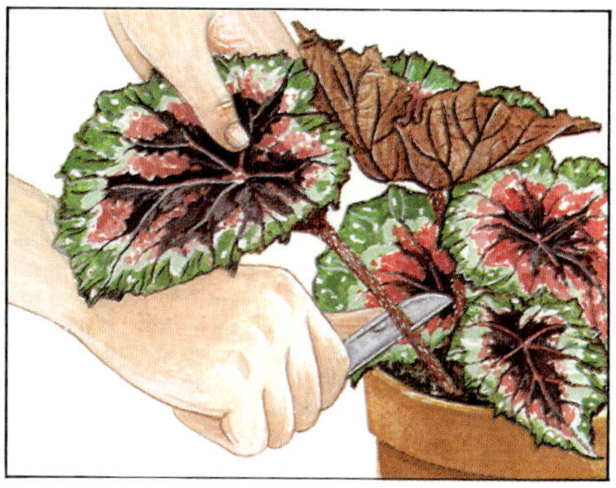

Propagating a *Begonia rex*. Select a good healthy leaf and sever it from the plant near the base using a sharp knife.

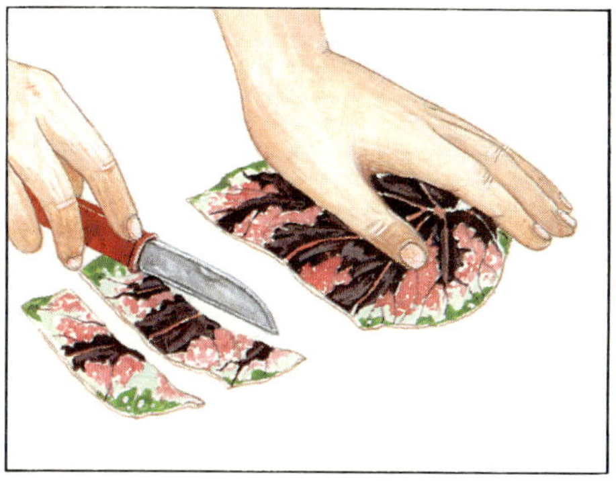

Remove the stalk, then carefully cut the leaf into strips about 1in (25mm) wide.

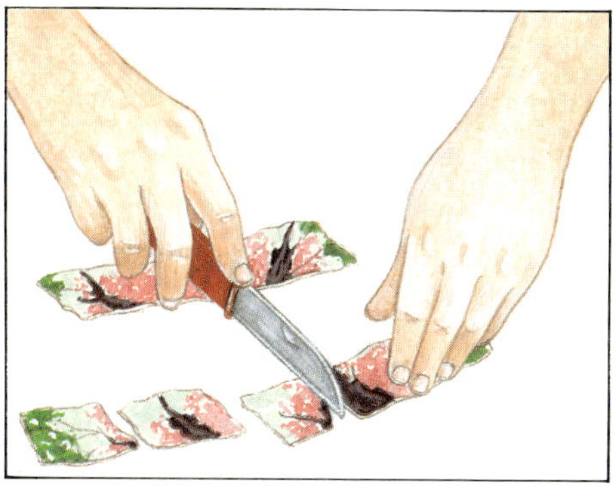

Trim the jagged edges off the leaf and cut the leaf sections into squares.

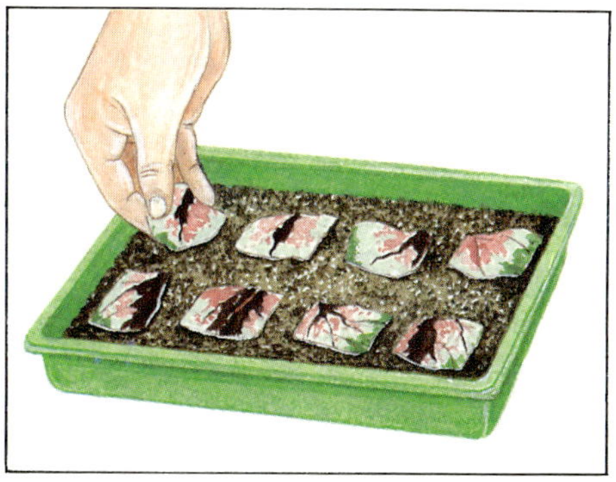

Lay the leaf pieces right side up on top of the compost, spacing them well.

Species

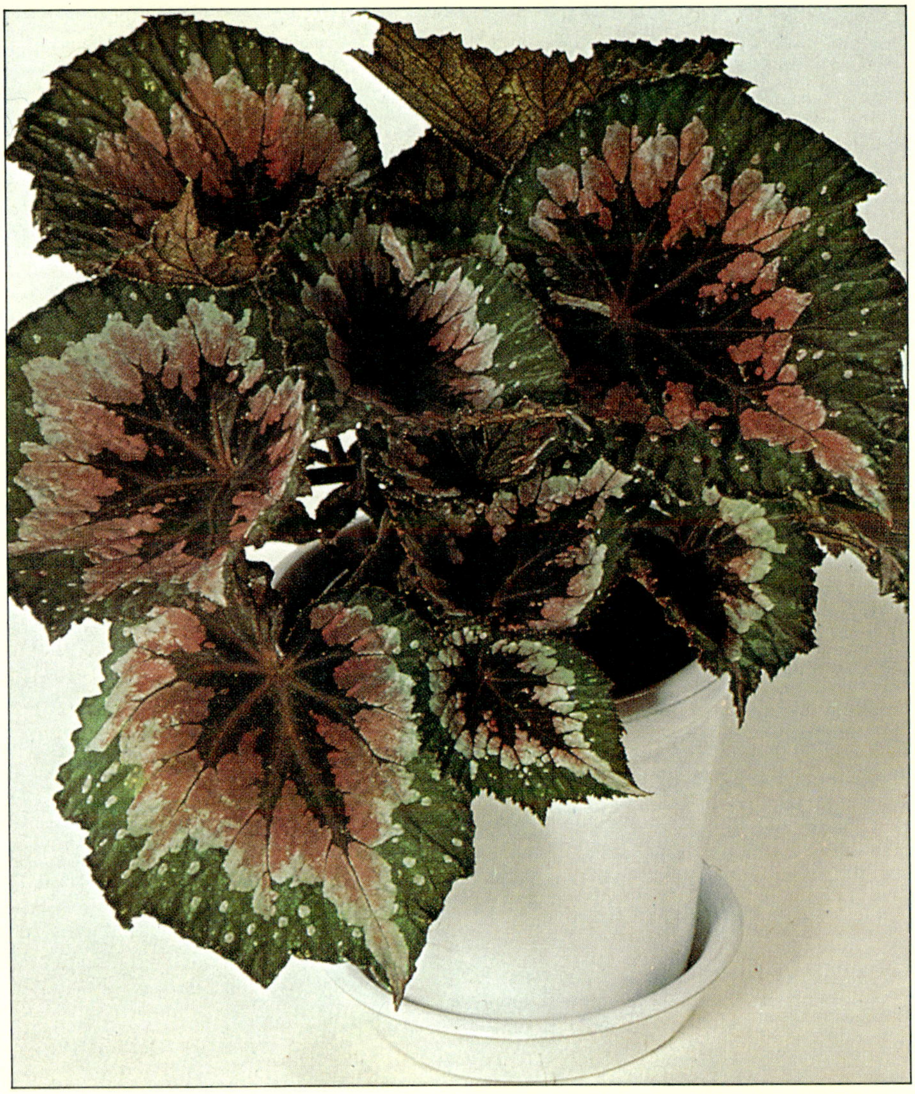

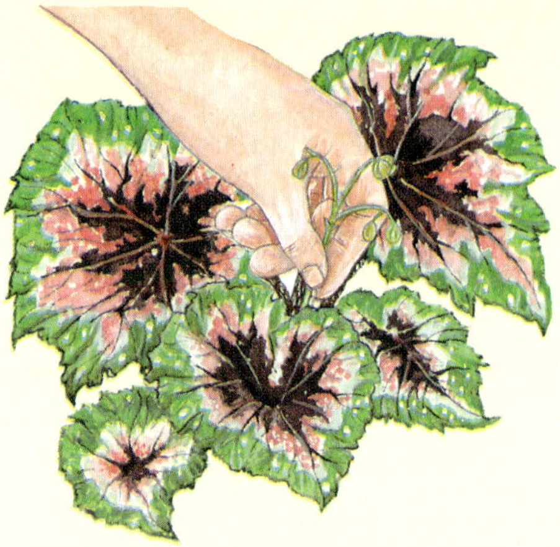

Carefully pick off the flowering stems of *Begonia rex* to encourage the plant to produce more spectacular leaves.

Rhizomatous Begonias
B.rex, *above*, comes from Assam, India. There are lots of different hybrids showing the vast range of Begonia leaf colours, mostly on small, 9in (23cm) high plants. The insignificant flowers are best removed to encourage more leaves. 'Her Majesty' has very wide, deep reddish-purple leaves with olive green zones and silvery-white mottling. 'Silver Queen' has silvery-grey leaves with blue-green central veins. 'Merry Christmas' has smooth leaves with a vivid purplish-red central zone, areas of silvery-pink and deep green, edged with pinkish-lilac. 'Helen Teupel' is bushy with long, pointed, oval leaves that are purplish-red with blue-green veins. The veins separate silver and pink zones, and the edges of the leaves are a rich purple colour.

B.masoniana, *right*, the Iron Cross Begonia, comes mainly from China. It has quilted, deep green hairy leaves with distinctive purplish-brown iron cross markings. It is a robust plant and has thick, fleshy, red stems covered in tiny white hairs. Greenish-white flowers with little reddish hairs on the petals' undersides appear in March to June.

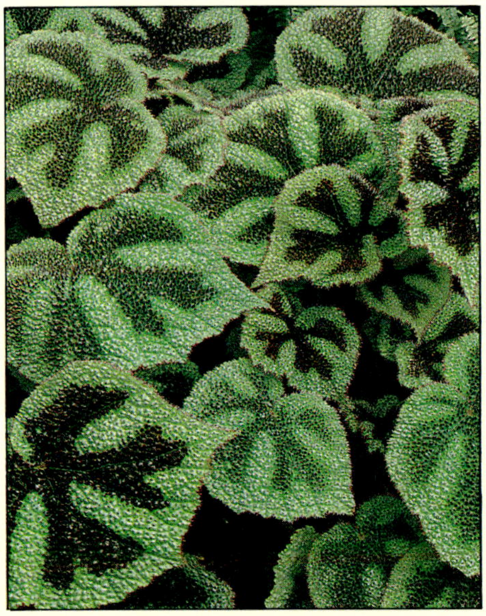

B.versicolor, the Fairy Carpet Begonia, is a small, attractive plant from China. The leaves are dark green with silvery-white, bright green and bronze patterns and are round, thick, puckered and covered with thousands of tiny, reddish hairs.

Tuberous Begonias
B.clarkei, from South America, has pale pink flowers in the summer months and is one of the main parents of all the lovely hybrids that are available.

B.pearcei, from South America, produces striking red flowers in the summer and is the other parent of the wide range of hybrids.

Fibrous-rooted Begonias
B.venosa, from Brazil, is a succulent that can grow 2ft (0.6m) high. Its thick stems are erect and have slightly cupped, dark green leaves and both leaves and stems are coated with a greyish-white felting. It has white flowers.

B.incana, from Mexico, is another succulent. Its thick, fleshy, erect stems are covered with tiny whitish scales. The leaves are shield-shaped with dense, fine white hairs on their upper surfaces with a pale green colouring underneath. It produces drooping white flowers in the summer.

B.metallica, from Brazil, has pointed, oval, metallic-green leaves with sunken purplish veins that are red on the

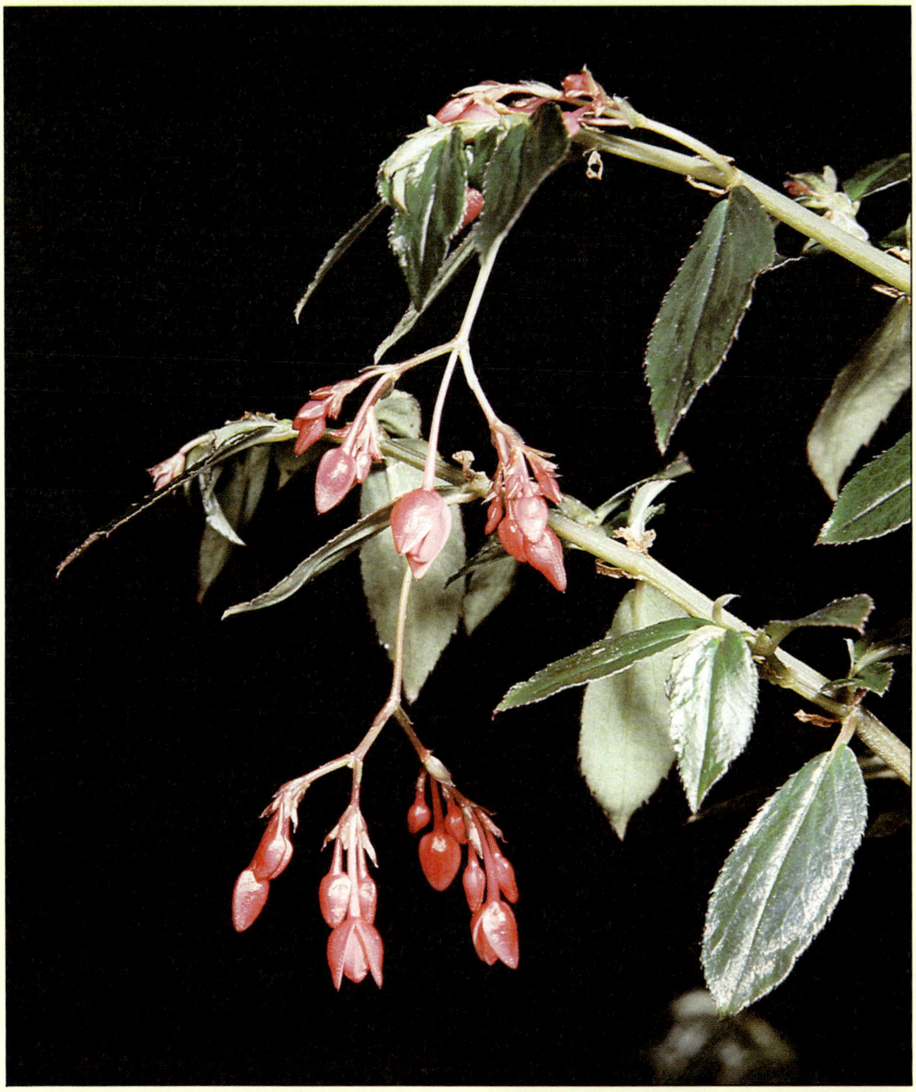

underside of the leaf. A sturdy and decorative species, it has rose-pink, slightly hairy flowers.

B.fuchsioides, *above*, is from Mexico. From late spring through summer it produces lovely red or pink fuchsia-like flowers that hang from long, slender stems with small, glossy, oval leaves.

B.scharffii (or haageana), *right*, Elephant's Ear, from Brazil, is an upright plant that grows to about 2ft (0.6m). The leaves are silky and a very dark yellowish-green with completely red undersides. Clusters of pale pink flowers appear towards the tips of the stems.

B.limmingheiana (or B.glaucophylla), the Shrimp Begonia, is suited to hanging baskets as the stems trail. The leaves can be pale to glossy dark green and have wavy edges. Its rose-pink to orange-red flowers hang from the trailing stems.

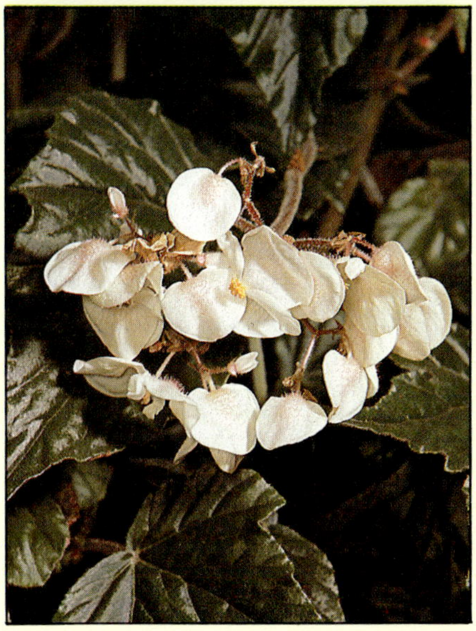

Trouble Shooter

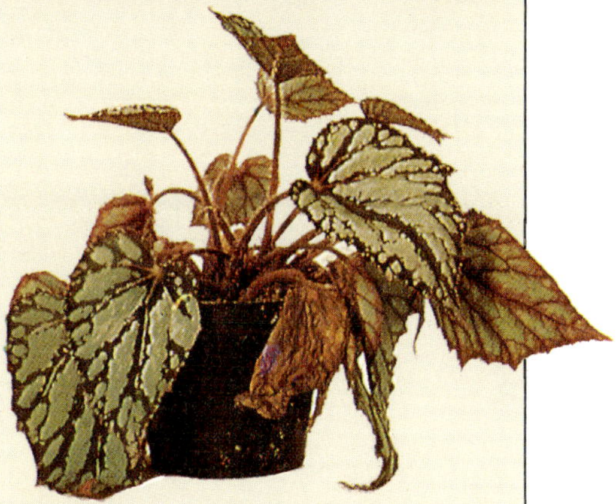

A collapsed plant means you have been overwatering and have exposed it to too much heat; move it to a cooler spot and let the surface of the soil dry out before watering again.

Grey mould (botrytis), *above* and *below*, appears underneath leaves in blackish blotches;

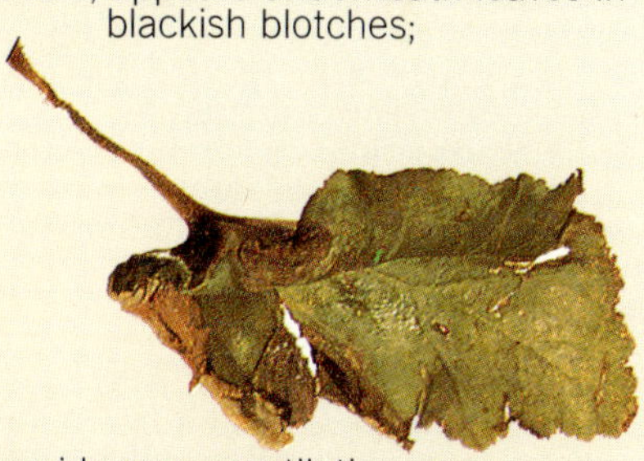

provide more ventilation.

Mildew affects stems and the undersides of leaves; let the plant almost completely dry out, increase ventilation, but avoid draughts, and treat with a fungicide, such as Benlate.

Water in a systemic insecticide two or three times during the growing season to prevent attacks of the few pests Begonias are prone to — aphids and eelworms. Use a systemic insecticide if an attack occurs.

Scorching, *below*, can be avoided by keeping your Begonia out of strong full sun; this will also prevent excessive drying out which is certain to kill your plant.

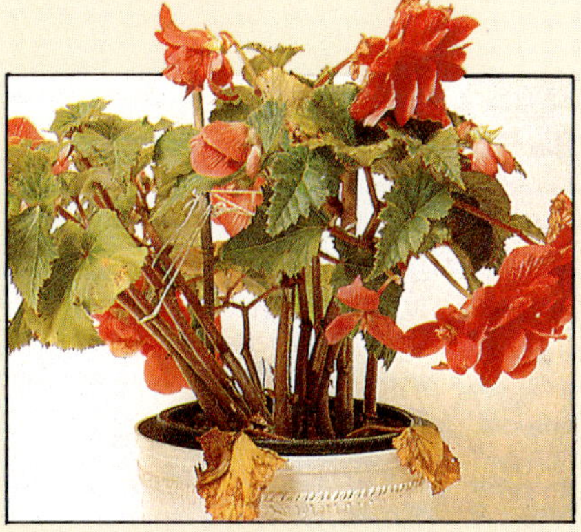

Beloperone

Family name: **Acanthaceae**

Common name: **Shrimp Plant**

Care Easy	**Height** 2ft (0.6m)	**Flower** April—Dec
Light Bright indirect sun	**Spread** 1ft (0.3m)	**Humidity** Regular spraying
Price Cheap	**Shape** Bushy	**Availability** Common
Temp. Min 45°F (7°C)	Ideal 60°F (15°C)	Max 70°F (21°C)

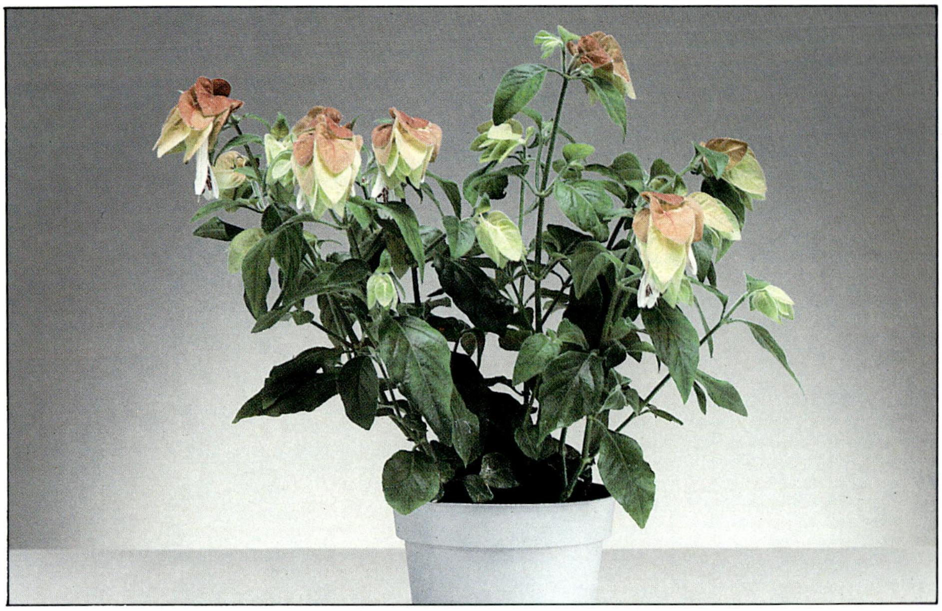

Beloperone guttata is a handsome, easy to care for plant.

Decorative and very popular, the Shrimp Plant gets its name from the intriguing arrangement of its reddish-brown false leaves (bracts), which overlap and gently arch as they hang from the branches, looking very like the curved, scaly bodies of shrimps. From these bracts small tubular flowers appear in summer — the bracts, though, last for about eight months making the plant interesting for most of the year.

Usually when you buy a Shrimp Plant it is a neat, compact little shrub but it grows very fast when it is happy in its environment and will soon out-grow its pot, so you will need to repot it at least once a year.

Spring and summer care

The Shrimp Plant flowers in summer and so needs to be kept well watered — but not so it's wet. Feed with a liquid fertiliser every two or three weeks during the growing season. The plant will not be harmed if temperatures rise, but 75°F (24°C) is the maximum temperature it will tolerate. Provide lots of humidity if it gets hotter by putting your plant on a tray of wet pebbles or by mist spraying occasionally.

Autumn and winter care

Water your Shrimp Plant moderately — every two weeks is just enough to stop it drying out but will also give it a winter rest. For the same reason do not feed until spring. Your plant will be able to stand temperatures as low as 45°F (7°C). Give it plenty of fresh air but don't let the plant sit in a cold draught. Repot towards the end of the coldest months into John Innes No 2, making sure that you do not disturb the root ball. Firm the compost well. If your plant has lost its shape and has some spindly branches, lightly clip it back into shape. If the branches are really weak, prune them back to within 3in (7cm) of the soil's surface and they should sprout again in spring.

Propagation

In March or April take 3in (7cm) long cuttings with a heel of bark and pot in a half peat, half sand compost. Keep the compost just moist and give cuttings a temperature of about 70°F (21°C) — if you have a propagator so much the better as this will help the cuttings to root faster. Pinch off any flower buds on young cuttings as flowers take energy away that should be used for building up a root system and growing leaves.

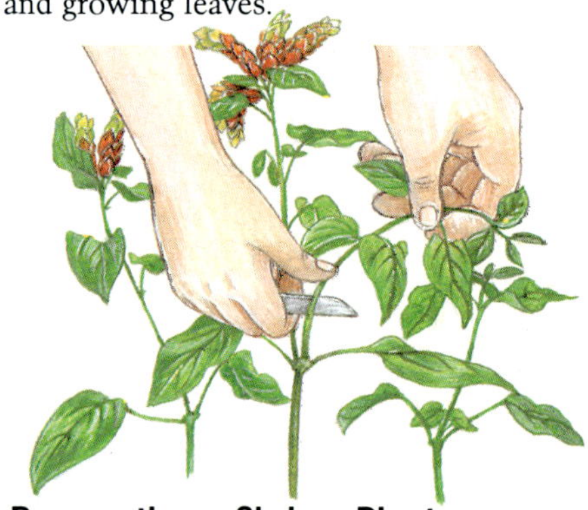

Propagating a Shrimp Plant: use a sharp knife and cut off a non-flowering shoot. Trim, leaving a shoot about 3in (7cm) long.

Trouble Shooter

Leaves losing colour is either due to overwatering or to lack of nutrients; let the plant dry out and pick off any dead or dying leaves, then feed it every two to three weeks with a liquid fertiliser from spring until autumn.

Leaves dropping off is either caused by the plant being too dry or by a cold draught; water your plant well in summer, moderately through the winter and give it plenty of fresh air but keep it out of draughts.

If the bracts are yellowish the plant has too much shade; give it plenty of good, sunny light.

Sticky, oddly-shaped leaves and stems signal greenfly or red spider mite; use a systemic insecticide, watering it into the soil once or twice in the growing season.

Species

Beloperone guttata (or ***californica***), from Mexico, is a sprawling plant with thin, wiry, rather weak stems, but as a pot plant it can be kept in check by pruning — left to its own devices it will easily grow over 2ft (0.6m) tall. The leaves are rough, hairy and almost arrow-shaped. The small whitish flowers have purple dots on their larger petals and hang from showy, heart-shaped and overlapping reddish-brown bracts, of which there are about two to three clustered together at the ends of the branches. The bracts last much longer than the flowers. 'Lutea' and 'Yellow Queen', *below*, vary only in that the bracts are yellow.

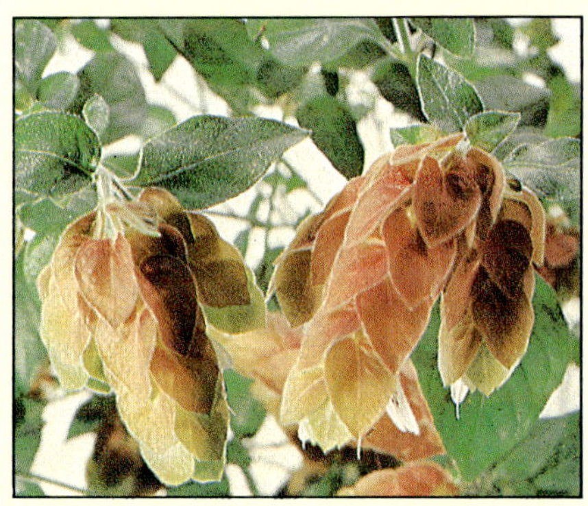

B.violacea, from Colombia, has long, hairy leaves about 3in (7cm) long. Its bracts are coppery brown, the individual scales being smaller than those of the ***B.guttata***, and it has mostly purple flowers with only a few white ones.

B.carnosa comes from Mexico, and has brownish-red bracts that form a compact 'tail' and yellow flowers with distinctive red markings.

Billbergia

Family name: **Bromeliaceae**

Common names: **Angel's Tears Queen's Tears**

Care Easy	**Height** 20in (50cm)	**Flower** June—Sept
Light Bright indirect sun	**Spread** 20in (50cm)	**Humidity** Regular spraying
Price Middle range	**Shape** Bushy	**Availability** Specialist
Temp. Min 50°F (10°C)	Ideal 70°F (21°C)	Max 80°F (27°C)

Unlike its other bromeliad relatives, which mostly grow in nooks in the branches of trees, this family of plants includes several species that grow quite happily on the ground. Billbergias come from southern Mexico and South America, as far south as northern Argentina. *Billbergia nutans,* the most popular houseplant of all the species, most likely earned its common name, 'Angel's Tears' or 'Queen's Tears', from the delicate, long, drop-like flowers, carried on stems with several pink false leaves (bracts). It is a 'funnel plant' that, due to the rosette arrangement of its leaves, can keep water in the urn that the leaves form. This helps create the humidity that the plant needs.

Billbergia leaves are dark green, narrow and long with hundreds of tiny spines along the edges. Angel's Tears is not very difficult to grow and even quite young plants produce flowers. The inner petals are green with blue edges, the outer petals reddish with green and blue mottling. This plant readily produces baby plants around its base (offsets) so, although the flowering rosettes die back soon after they have flowered, there are plenty of new plants to take their place.

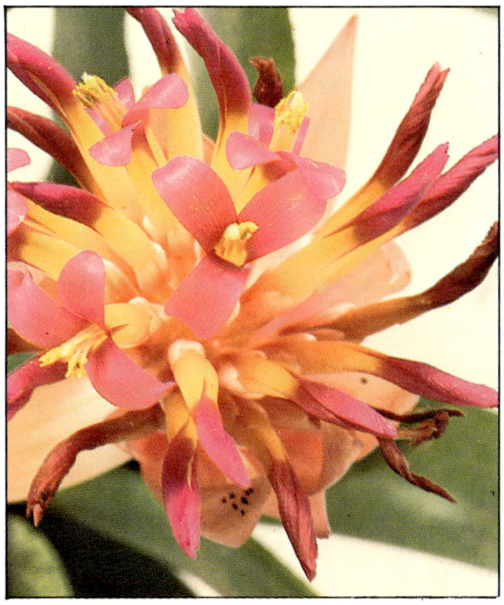

Billbergia pyramidalis, the 'Summer Torch', has a spectacular flower.

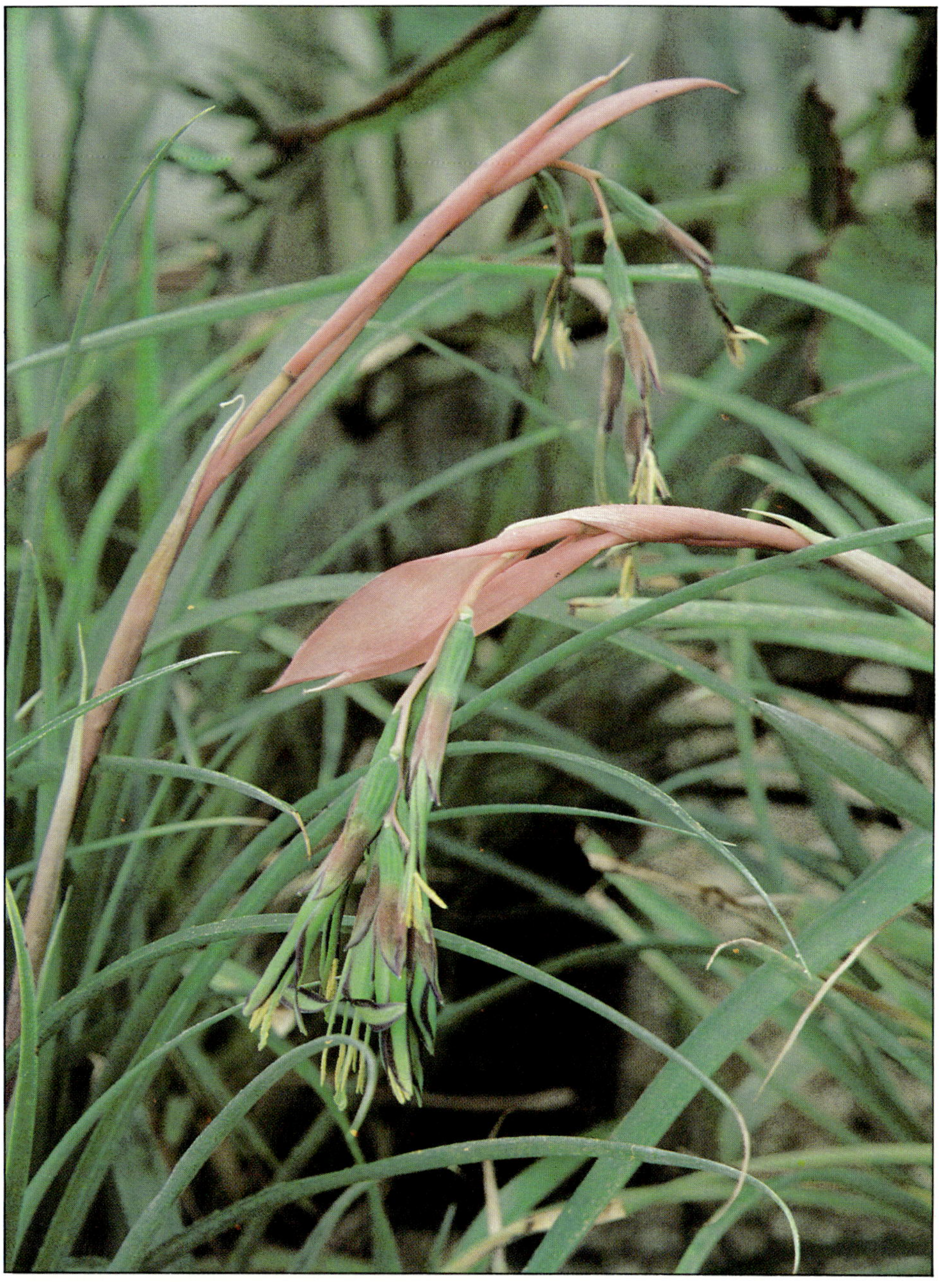

Billbergia nutans gets the name Angel's Tears from its elegant, arching flowers.

Trouble Shooter

If your plant fails to thrive, it may have root rot. Leaf and root rot result from the plant being exposed to cold and/or overwatering; keep your plant warmer than 50°F (10°C) in winter, or, if you can't, keep it on the dry side.

Scorched or dead leaves are caused by exposure to direct sun; move to bright but filtered light.

White, fluffy-looking mealy bugs can be dealt with by just wiping them away with a soft cloth or paintbrush dipped in methylated spirit.

Red spider mites only affect plants when the atmosphere is not humid enough and too hot, so avoid these conditions and you should have no trouble; treat with a systemic insecticide if you have an infested plant, or if you only have a few red spider mites, wipe them and their webs away with a cloth soaked in warm water. Mist spray regularly to keep the air humid.

Scale insects, which look like tiny brown warts, multiply rapidly if not dealt with; water the soil with a systemic insecticide or spray thoroughly with a liquid malathion insecticide.

Spring and summer care

Your Billbergia will be happiest in a bright, semi-sunny position with temperatures of 50-70°F (10-21°C), a humid atmosphere and regular watering. Provide humidity by regularly mist spraying or by standing the plant on a saucer of wet pebbles, especially in hot weather. Keep water in the plant's urn all the time but empty it out every month and fill with fresh, otherwise it will become unpleasantly stagnant. Allow the compost to dry out on the surface between waterings. Feed every two weeks with half-strength liquid fertiliser, watering it into the soil and into the urn, especially when the flower buds show as this will encourage your plant to put on a good display.

From April until late September is the main growing season; during this time keep the plant warm — 70-75°F (21-24°C) is ideal. Good, bright but filtered light will bring out the spectacular colouring of the leaves — full sun or deep shade will scorch or kill the plant's leaves.

Autumn and winter care

Some species continue to flower in the winter so don't let temperatures drop below 50°F (10°C). Cold causes the leaves to rot, and this is even more likely if the room is badly ventilated. Don't let your plant stand in a pool of water; in fact it usually grows vigorously if the soil is almost dry before it is watered again.

Propagation

Sow seeds fresh from the plant and while still moist in seed compost (old, dry seeds are unlikely to germinate). Spread a layer of fine, gritty sand over the top of the compost and keep in a constantly moist, humid atmosphere in temperatures of between 75-80°F (24-27°C) and in a semi-shaded position. Seedlings should start to show four to six weeks after planting.

In late March or early April you can take 4-6in (10-15cm) tall offsets from the base of the mature plant. Keep a piece of root attached to the offset and pot up singly in a peat-based compost with an open texture, like Levingtons, with a little added grit. Keep the offsets just moist until they start to grow and well away from full sun because this dehydrates the roots. When the plants have rooted — in about eight weeks — they can be treated like mature Billbergias.

Buying Guide

There are many different Billbergias and specialist nurseries will be able to give you detailed information about all the more exotic kinds, which can reward the search for something really different.

Billbergias are increasingly available at good garden centres and specialist seedsmen will supply seeds of the more unusual species.

Species

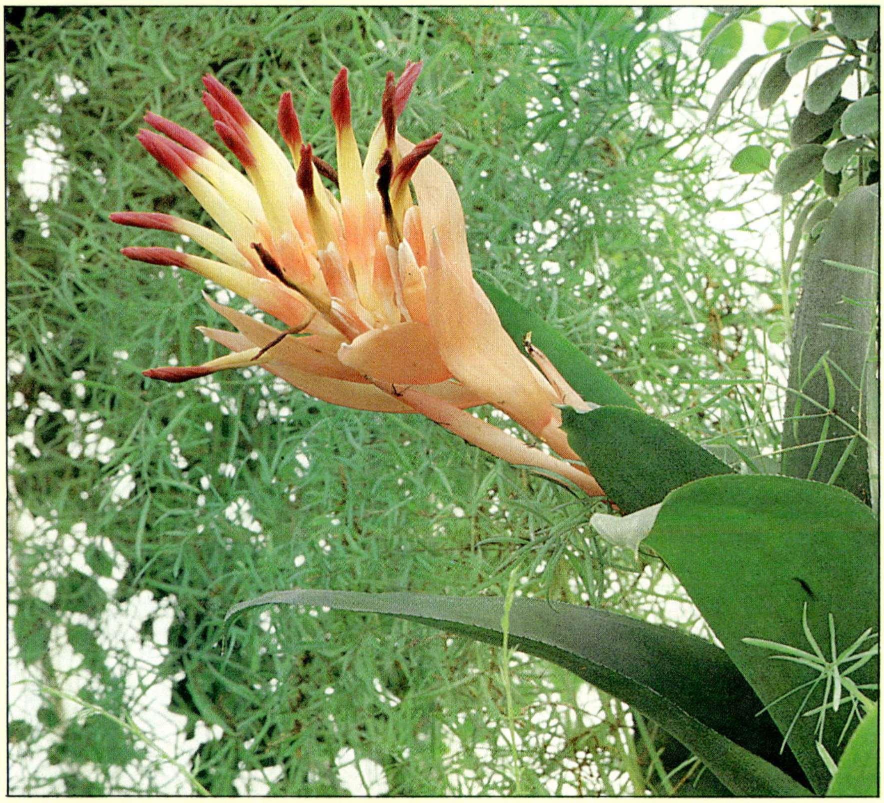

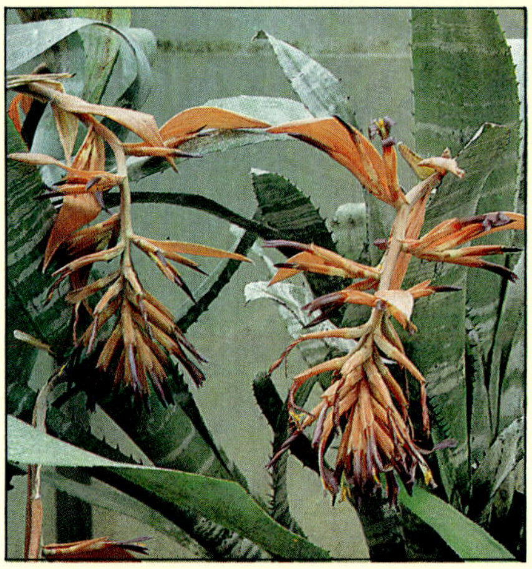

Billbergia nutans, Angel's Tears or Queen's Tears, has dark green, narrow leaves, 15-20in (38-50cm) long, with prickly edges. The stems have long, pink, false leaves out of which the drop-like flower emerges. The inner petals are green with blue edges, the outer petals reddish, mottled with green and blue. The leaves form a funnel shape vase in which the plant stores water.

B.pyramidalis, Summer Torch, *top*, lives in trees but grows very well in a pot. It has a wide, funnel-shaped rosette with green or grey-green leaves, each about 12in (30cm) long and 1in (2cm) or so wide, tapering to a pointed tip. Its exquisite flower has a soft white stem with large, scarlet and yellow false leaves at the end, out of which come carmine red, violet-edged flowers. 'Concolor' has wider, fresh green leaves, red false leaves and totally red flowers; 'Striata' has slender leaves with yellow stripes and red flowers in autumn or early winter.

B.zebrina, *left*, is one of the tallest species: it has a long tube-like rosette, which can grow up to 3ft (0.9m), with purplish-bronze or dark-green leaves, heavily cross-banded in silvery-grey. The leaves have a white, scaly coating and spines along the edges. Its flowers are very similar to those of the *B.nutans* but they are deep purple and the inner petals are pointed with green edges.

B.saundersii has incredibly colourful foliage: it has narrow, bright green leaves with reddish-brown edges, paler bands of colour across the leaves and yellow and reddish mottling. Its flowers are yellow at the base and purplish-blue from the middle to the curly tips and hang in clusters from slightly arching stems that have red and whitish scales. 'Fantasia' has dark green leaves, with creamy white blotches and spots, and rose-pink false leaves, out of which poke its purplish-blue flowers. 'Muriel Waterman' is a stunning, compact, tubular plant with stiff, plum-coloured leaves, cross-banded in silvery pink, with false leaves and green-blue flowers.

Blechnum

Family names: **Polypodiaceae/ Blechnaceae**

Common name: **Hard Fern**

Care Straight-forward	**Height** 2-3ft (0.6-0.9m)	**Flower** None
Light Shade	**Spread** 2-2½ft (0.6-0.75m)	**Winter** Needs protection
Price Middle range	**Shape** Fern	**Availability** Specialist nurseries

This is a large group with over 200 evergreen species and is widely distributed over both northern and southern hemispheres. Despite its common name, these ferns are by no means all hardy, but there are a few species that will thrive outdoors, making a most attractive pot for a balcony or small garden where there is some measure of shade. And there are a few more that will thrive in a porch or unheated greenhouse and others that make excellent houseplants.

A popular choice for growing in a container outdoors is *Blechnum pennamarina*, a hardy, mat-forming species from New Zealand and Tasmania with deep green, lance-shaped fronds and growing to a height of about 2ft (0.6m). Equally popular is the British native *B.spicant, below*, which is similar but somewhat larger and more erect.

Spring and summer care

Grow your Hard Fern in partial shade all the time – never in full sun. These plants are moisture lovers and should be watered freely. During the growing season from May to September give a weak liquid feed every month, using half the amount recommended by the manufacturer. To provide humidity, mist spray in dry weather, daily when the weather is very warm. These ferns are appreciative plants and respond readily to careful attention given to them while they are growing in the summer months.

Autumn and winter care

From October to March water sparingly, so that the compost is only just moist, but be sure not to let the soil dry out. As in summer, make sure your plant is always shaded and never in full sun. Pot or repot every February or March, using a good peat-based compost with a handful of sharp sand added. Alternatively, for an ideal compost make up a mixture of equal parts of loam, peat, leaf-mould and sharp

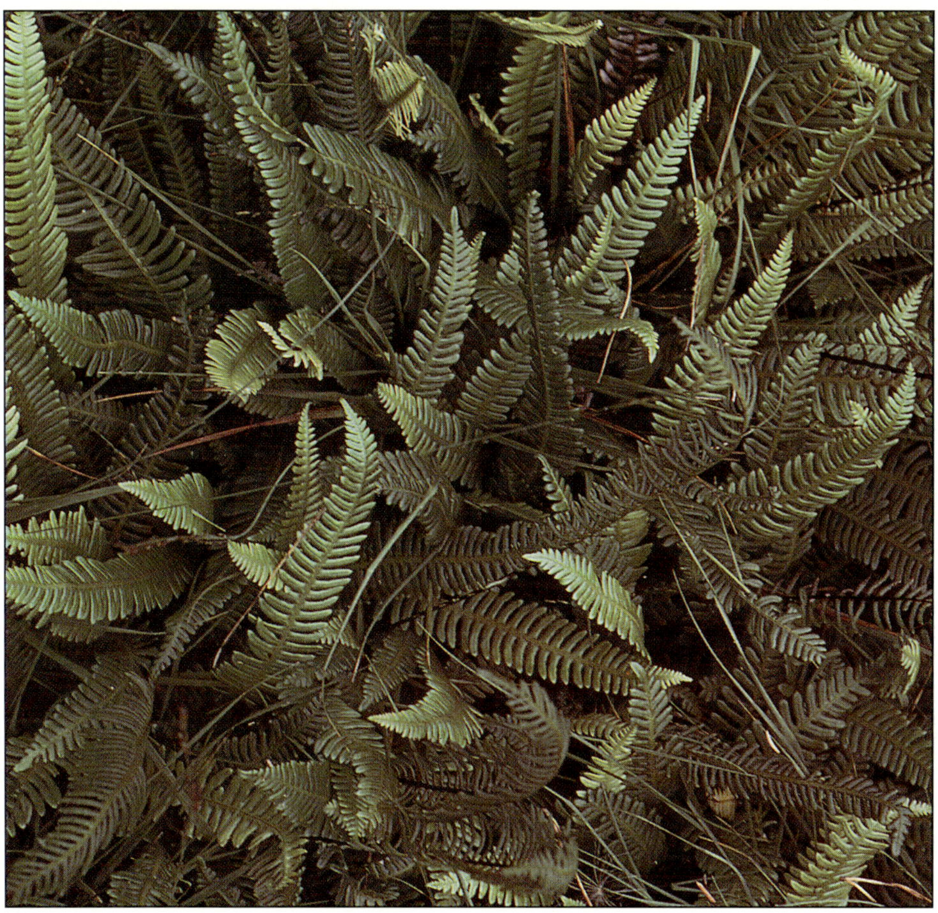

***Blechnum spicant* with its** lance-shaped fronds is native to Britain.

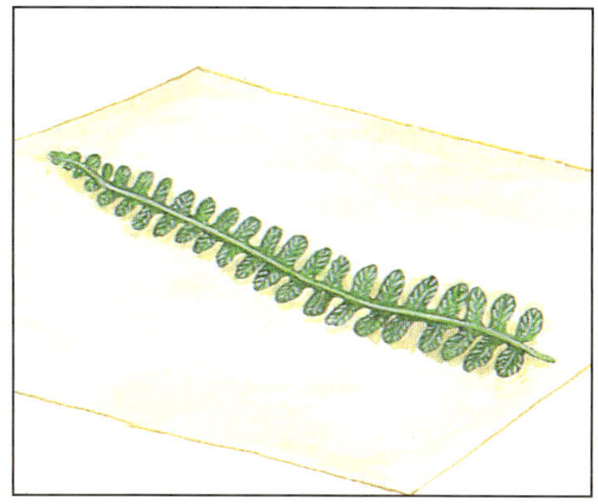

Propagation by spores. Place a pinna (segment of frond) underside down on a piece of paper in a warm spot.

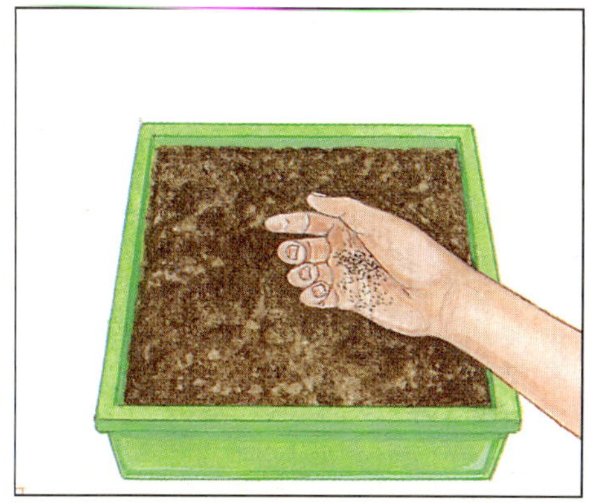

Fill a seed tray with moss peat and after a day collect the released spores and spread them over the surface.

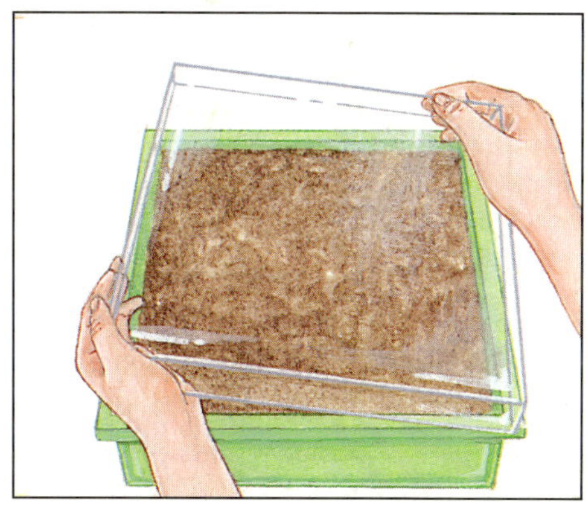

Keep tray in a propagator until spores have germinated, or cover tray with a sheet of glass and keep in warmth.

Buying Guide

If buying Hard Ferns in spring, make sure that the plants you choose have not been damaged by the frost. Check also that the roots aren't too dry because if they are the tips of the fronds are also likely to dry up.

Always try to pick a plant which is well-balanced with a symmetrical outline.

sand. Repot spreading species every year and other types every two years. *B.penna-marina* and *B.spicant* are best grown in half pots, starting with a 5-6in (13-15cm) pot and potting on to a final 12in (30cm) pot size. Grow other types in the same diameter pots but make sure you use standard pot depths.

Half hardy species, such as *B.gibbum*, will need to be placed under cover during winter. Hardy types are best given the protection of a south- or west-facing wall during the coldest months; if frost does attack their leaves, turning them brown, plants should recover.

Propagation

Spreading types with creeping rhizomatous roots can be divided when potting. Other species are best raised from spores. Fill a seed tray with a mixture of two parts moss peat and one part sharp sand, then moisten it thoroughly before spreading the spores over the surface. Place the tray in a propagator and keep it shaded at a temperature of 70-75°F (21-24°C) until the spores have germinated – this should take about five to six weeks.

After germination, uncover the tray and move to a lightly shaded spot, but maintain the warmth until seedlings are about 2in (5cm) high and can be handled with ease. Then transfer to 3in (8cm) pots of the usual compost. Grow them on indoors for a year by which time they should be sizable plants, 6-7in (15-18cm) tall, and ready and sufficiently mature for placing outside.

Trouble Shooter

Pale leaves that begin to go brown along the edges and the tips are an indication of too much sun. Trim off the brown parts and move the plant to a more shaded position. Brownish marks will also appear if the situation is too cold. Again trim off the brown bits and provide protection.

Pests are unlikely, though red spider mite may attack if conditions are too dry; treat with a malathion-based insecticide. To prevent future attacks, mist spray regularly to deter this pest, or use a systemic insecticide as a deterrent applied according to the manufacturer's instructions.

Species

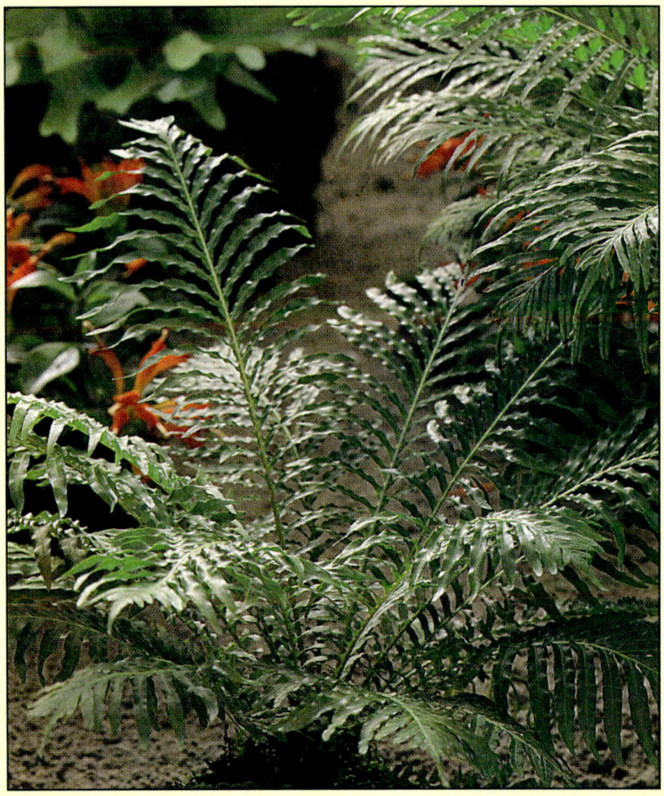

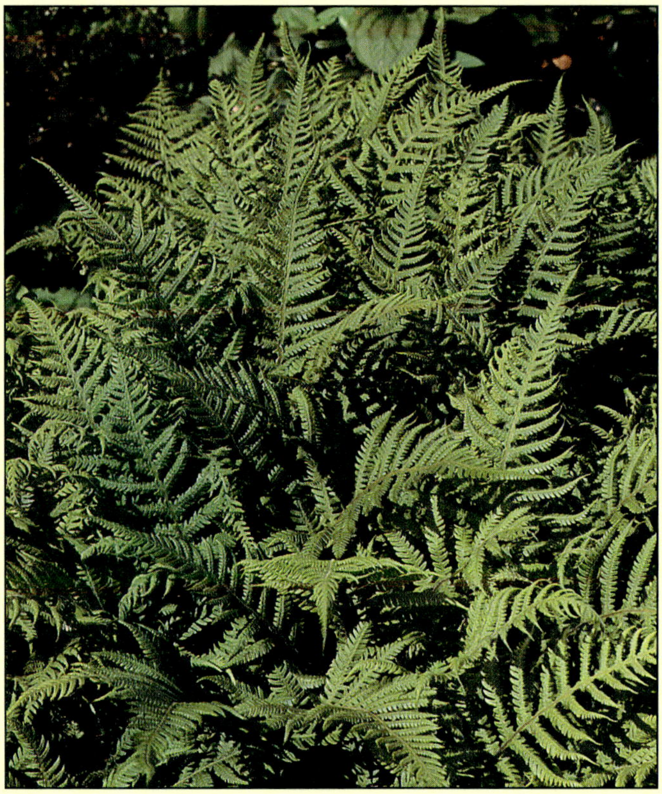

Blechnum spicant is a native of Great Britain, and similar to *B.penna-marina*, but somewhat larger.

B.brasiliense, from Peru and Brazil, is a most elegant and beautiful plant. The bright green, somewhat leathery fronds are bedecked with wavy, overlapping pinnae and set in a fascinating rosette formation. A mature plant is almost tree-like, over 3ft (0.9m) tall and with a scaly trunk. The form 'Crispum' has leaves with curly edges. Like *B.occidentale*, this species is best suited to greenhouse cultivation.

B.penna-marina, *above right*, a hardy plant from New Zealand and Tasmania, is a dwarf species with creeping rootstock and spreading habit, making a dense carpet of deep green fronds. The fronds are narrow and lance-shaped, 2-8in (5-20cm) long, arranged in spreading rosettes up to 2ft (0.6m) high.

B.gibbum, *above left*, from New Caledonia, is half hardy. It makes a striking, tall plant reaching 3ft 9in (1.1m) in height. It forms a trunk with a rosette of graceful fronds branching out from the top. This plant is not fully hardy and it is advisable not to leave it outside during the winter months.

B.occidentale, from Chile, is not as hardy and requires a minimum temperature of 50°F (10°C), so is best suited for growing in a greenhouse or indoors. The spear-shaped fronds are arranged symmetrically on scaly stalks, and can be up to 16in (40cm) long, with slender pointed leaflets arrayed along a pale midrib. The roots are of a spreading kind, so this species can be propagated by division.

Bletilla

Family name: **Orchidaceae**

Common name: **Bletilla**

Care Straight-forward	**Height** 1ft (0.3m)	**Flower** June-August
Light Bright, indirect	**Spread** 12-15in (30-38cm)	**Winter** Needs protection
Price Middle range	**Shape** Tufted	**Availability** Garden centres

This small group of terrestrial orchids from eastern Asia is almost hardy and in the south of England can be grown outdoors given the protection of a south- or west-facing wall. Otherwise it is best grown indoors in a cool greenhouse or sun porch if frost is likely.

Bletilla striata, right, is the only species readily available. It is a deciduous, summer-flowering orchid, which bears a delicate flower spike of 10-12 rosy-pink blooms, with rich purple ridges on the lips. The flowering period is very long, with buds appearing June or July, and gradually opening through July and August. The leaves grow in a slender rosette about 1ft (0.3m) high, and are pleated along their length. 'Alba' is a charming white variety.

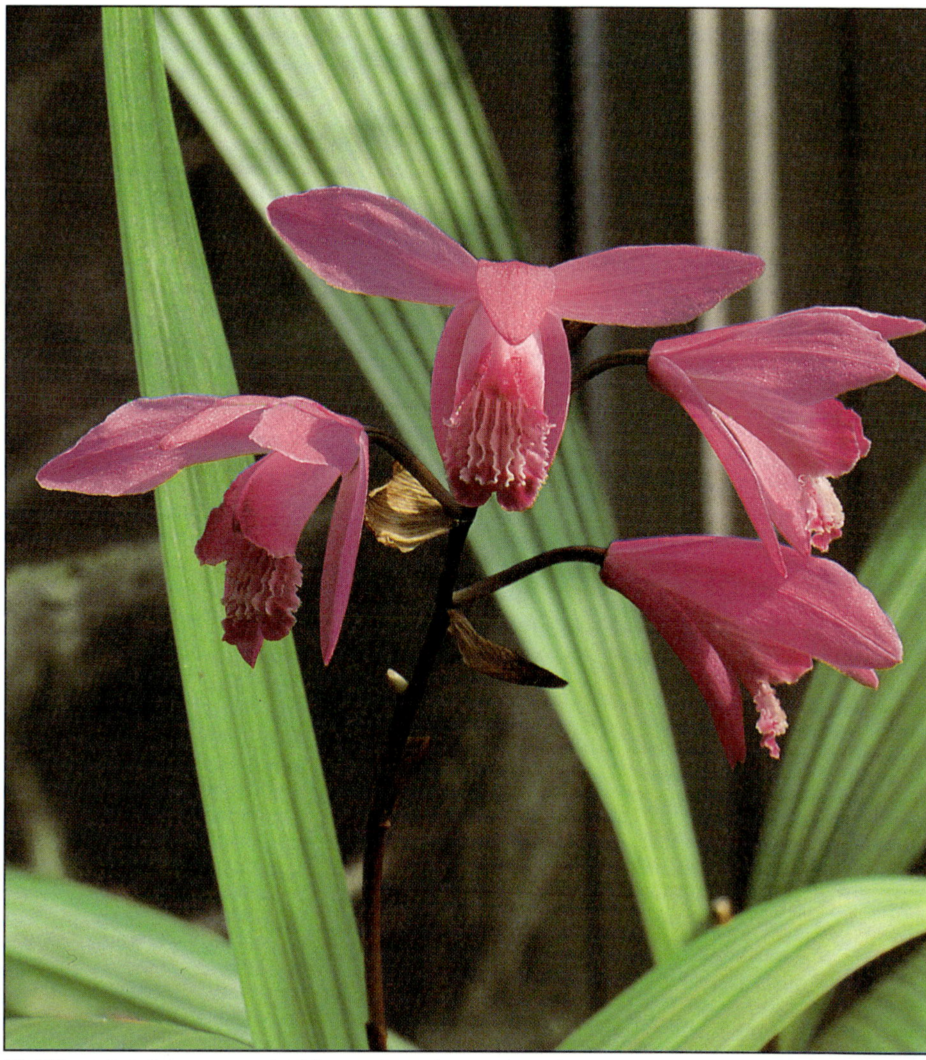

***Bletilla striata* bears** rosy-pink blooms from June to August.

Spring and summer care

Repot in very early spring – March or early April – before leaves come into growth, or immediately after flowering in September. Start off in a 5-6in (13-15cm) pot and completely cover the pseudobulb-like tuber with compost. A good potting mixture can be made from three parts fibrous loam with one part each of moss peat, well-rotted leaf-mould and sharp sand. Bletilla flourish when their roots are cramped, so only pot on when really necessary.

Ideally you should place your Bletilla in a bright, but partially shaded area – though some full sun is not harmful. To start the plant into growth after its winter rest, find a warm, sheltered position which will provide minimum temperatures of around 55-65°F (13-18°C). When leaves begin to grow in late April or early May start watering, and keep the plants moist at all times. Give a weak feed every three to four weeks, using a liquid fertiliser at half the recommended strength.

Autumn and winter care

Your Bletilla is best brought inside during the winter months and placed in the brightest position you can find. Though it can withstand quite low temperatures, it can't be trusted to survive the frost, so do make sure the temperature doesn't fall below 40°F (4°C). If you really have nowhere to store the plant indoors, cover the soil with straw and tie some sacking round the pot. It is important that the soil doesn't dry out, so water occasionally, keeping the compost just moist.

Propagation

Propagation is by division and this is best done when the foliage has died down in autumn. Divide the tuber carefully with a sharp knife, then dust the cut surfaces with a fungicidal sulphur powder. Pot up into the usual compost, keep moist and at a minimum temperature of 50°F (10°C) until your plant has become established. Then from October onwards, give the normal winter treatment.

Species

Bletilla striata (also known as *Bletia hyacinthina*) comes from Japan and parts of China. It is a deciduous species which forms a slender rosette with three to five narrow, pleated leaves, about 12in (30cm) in length. In late June a dainty flower spike, 12-18in (30-45cm) tall, emerges from each rosette, carrying up to 10-12 rosy-pink to deep purplish-pink flowers, each measuring up to 2in (5cm) across. The three-lobed lip of the blooms is ridged in rich purple. The variety 'Alba' is similar; some are white, others may be suffused with pink.

Trouble Shooter

Soft, limp leaves are an indication of too shady a position; move the plant to a brighter location if these symptoms appear. Failure to keep the compost moist, both in summer and winter, may cause the root system to dry up and be fatal to your plant. On the other hand, you need to be careful not to overwater – especially during the colder months; never leave the pot standing in water or the roots may rot. Greenfly may attack young leaves and perhaps also the flower buds; should this happen treat immediately with a malathion-based insecticide.

Bougainvillea

Family name: **Nyctaginaceae**

Common name: **Paper Flower**

Care Straight-forward	**Height** 6ft (1.8m)	**Flower** June—Sept
Light Full sun	**Spread** 6ft (1.8m)	**Humidity** Regular spraying
Price Expensive	**Shape** Climber	**Availability** Garden centres
Temp. Min 45°F (7°C)	Ideal 70°F (21°C)	Max 90°F (33°C)

People think of the Bougainvillea as an exotic, rambling, climbing outdoor plant with beautiful flowers and foliage. It is, but there are also lots of varieties that make lovely and much more manageable houseplants. All the plants come from Brazil, the sub-tropics and coasts around the Mediterranean. *Bougainvillea glabra* is the best-known with its colourful, bright purple false leaves (bracts). Its stems and branches are woody and mature plants grow sharp thorns. The thin, papery bracts form clusters towards the ends of the thorny branches, surrounding tiny, cream-coloured flowers, which contrast strikingly with the glossy, dark green leaves. The colourful bracts appear in spring and summer and the plant flowers in the summer months.

Spring and summer care

Your Bougainvillea needs bright light all year round, and in the summer it needs full sun and regular feeding and watering. If the roots have filled the pot your plant needs repotting; do it in early spring using John Innes No 3. A mature plant in the right conditions may grow up to 6ft (1.8m) so, in early spring, prune back by about a third to encourage the plant back into a nice, bushy shape.

Temperatures can reach 70°F (21°C) or more without harming your plant.

Water your Bougainvillea moderately two to three times a week so that the soil is constantly moist, but not so that the plant gets 'wet feet'. Feed every two weeks during the summer with a fertiliser containing potash so that the plant keeps flowering and producing its bright bracts.

Autumn and winter care

In the winter, water your plant only when its compost is almost completely dry. Temperatures can fall to 45°F (7°C) — even slightly lower — without harming the roots, but it will drop its leaves. If this happens, prune the branches to neaten the plant's shape, keep it in an airy, bright position and it will grow again in mid to late spring. Then, gradually give it more water and warmth.

Propagation

In March or April take 3in (7cm) cuttings of young shoots, cutting so that each has a heel of bark; dip the cut ends in hormone rooting powder and insert in sandy compost. Keep your cuttings at 70-75°F (21-24°C) in a propagator, in good but filtered light, and provide plenty of humidity. Alternatively put the pot into a sealed polythene bag and place it on a sunny windowsill. When roots form, in about eight weeks, pot into John Innes No 3.

Trouble Shooter

Pests can be prevented by watering in or spraying with a systemic insecticide when your plant starts growing, then two or three more times during the growing season.

Falling leaves or flowers not forming are due to overwatering or positioning the plant in heavy shade. Make sure your plant is well-drained and gets plenty of full light.

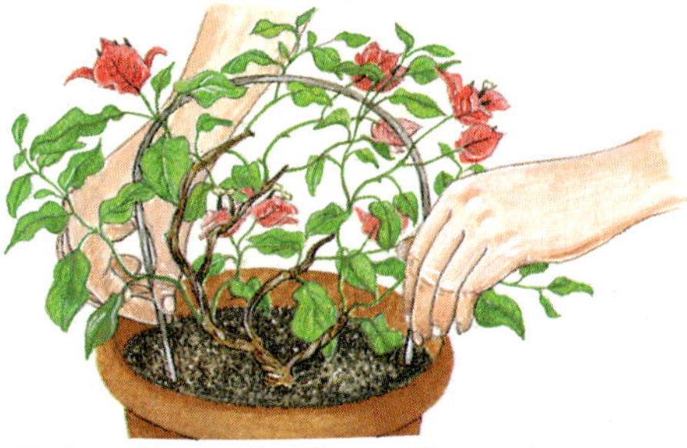

Train a Bougainvillea with a wire or cane hoop. Twine the stems gently round and tie them loosely to the arch.

Species

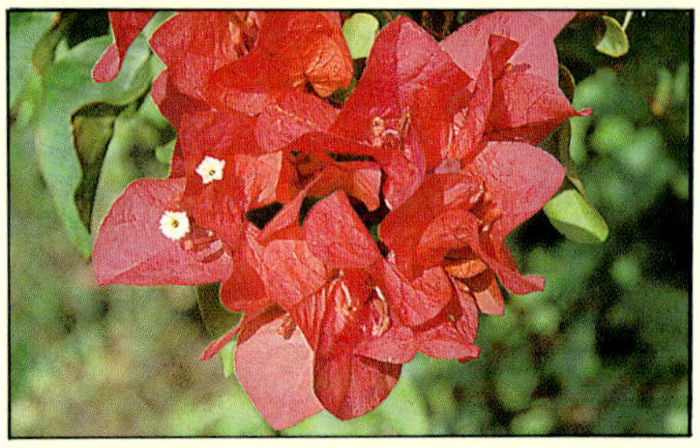

***Bougainvillea glabra* (or *brasiliensis*)**, commonly called the Paper Flower, has woody branches with dark green leaves and clusters of papery bracts at the ends. There are several hybrids — the ones without hairy leaves seem to make the best houseplants. They come with white, yellow, pink, orange through to red and purple bracts and some are also variegated.

B.spectabilis is a strong climber. The bracts are deep purple and the leaves are slightly hairy. This is the parent of many other Bougainvilleas, giving a huge array of colours, *above*, but only a few make suitable houseplants.

B.peruviana is a smaller-leaved species with exquisite pale pink false leaves. 'Mrs Butt' ('Buttiana'), also called 'Crimson Lake', has cascades of crimson bracts and is more bushy than most Bougainvilleas. 'Harrisii' is a good variegated variety: it has bright green leaves with creamy markings, and rich purple clusters of bracts with tiny white flowers.

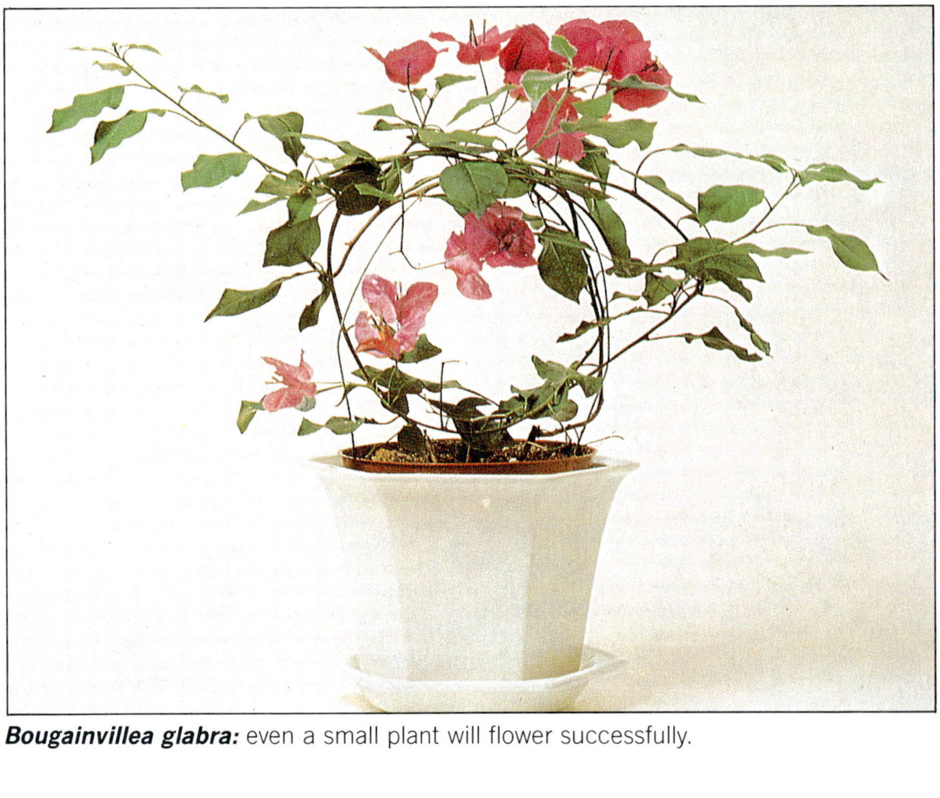

Bougainvillea glabra: even a small plant will flower successfully.

Bouvardia

Family name: **Rubiaceae**

Common name: **Jasmine Plant**

Care Straight-forward	**Height** 3ft (0.9m)	**Flower** Oct—Dec
Light Bright indirect sun	**Spread** 4ft (1.2m)	**Humidity** Regular spraying
Price Middle range	**Shape** Bushy	**Availability** Garden centres
Temp. Min 55°F (13°C)	Ideal 60°F(15°C)	Max 70°F(21°C)

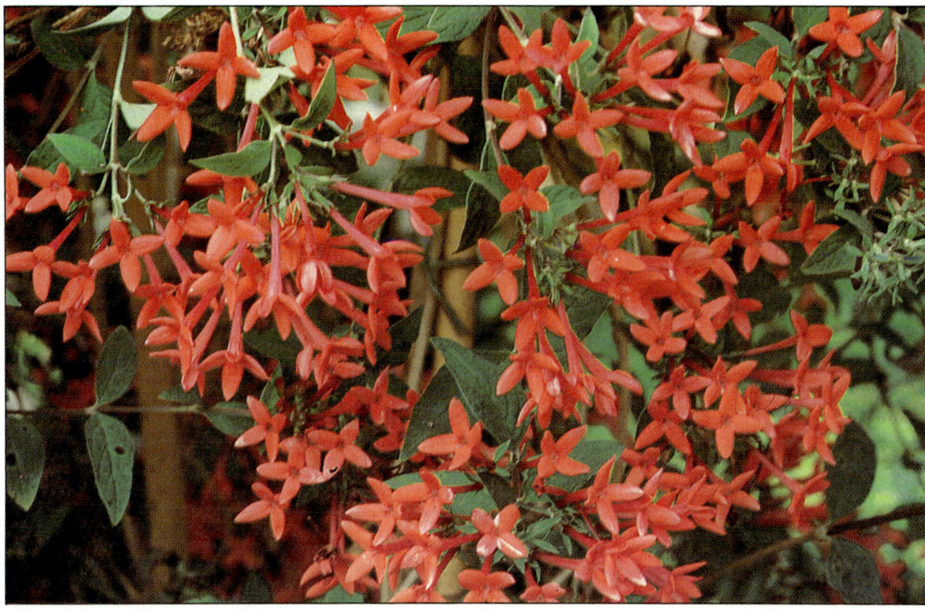

'President Cleveland' has sweetly scented flowers between June and November.

Bouvardia belongs to a small family of very attractive flowering plants that originally came from Mexico and South America. The Bouvardias that are grown as houseplants are all small, shrubby evergreens about 2-3ft (0.6-1m) high with flowers of different colours according to species, mostly sweetly scented. *Bouvardia longiflora*, from Mexico, is the most popular houseplant. Its stems are woody with many slender branches bearing smooth, bright green leaves. The white, tubular flowers are over 2in (5cm) long and beautifully scented — not only that, but it flowers in autumn, providing a lovely show of colour when most other plants have stopped flowering. 'President Cleveland' is the most popular houseplant Bouvardia with its highly scented scarlet flowers.

Spring and summer care

In spring, water moderately and feed with a half-strength liquid fertiliser regularly every 14 days from May to late October. Your plant will enjoy sitting in a good, bright spot in filtered sunlight. Repot in March if the roots have filled the pot; this should be only every two or three years if you feed it moderately. Use a loam-based compost such as John Innes No 2.

Summer treatment varies because, although flowers mainly appear late in summer, they may continue well into the winter months. Temperatures from late January until September of 60-75°F (15-24°C) and regular, moderate watering and feeding help to prepare your plant for flowering. During midsummer, give your plant plenty of air — even stand it outside — but keep it out of the sun, and water freely if it is hot.

Autumn and winter care

Give your Bouvardia as much light as possible all winter. From September to January keep it in a temperature between 55-60°F (13-15°C) and water just enough to keep the compost moist. From October to February, continue watering moderately giving less water in the coldest months. In January or February, prune the previous year's growth severely, down to within 3-4in (7-10cm) of the plant's base. The growing period starts soon after this, so new branches and foliage will quickly appear.

Propagation

Plant seeds in John Innes Seed Compost in late February or March and keep them at a temperature of 65-70°F (18-21°C). Provide shade and keep them constantly moist until they germinate, then move the seedlings into good light — but not direct sun.

In February or March take cuttings of young shoots, 2-3in (5-7cm) long. Grow in a mixture of sand and peat compost. You can also propagate by dividing the roots of your Bouvardia, planting the divisions in normal potting compost.

Trouble Shooter

Aphids can attack young growth, especially the shoots and buds; use a systemic insecticide or spray with a malathion-based product to get rid of them.

Never overwater at any time or you run the risk of rotting the roots and causing leaf and flower drop.

Species

Bouvardia longiflora, the Jasmine Plant, comes from Mexico. It has long, woody stems with lots of slightly arching, slender branches carrying glossy, mid-green leaves. At the ends of the branches in October to December are loose clusters of long, white, tubular flowers which have a beautiful scent. 'Mary', *right*, has pretty pale pink flowers.

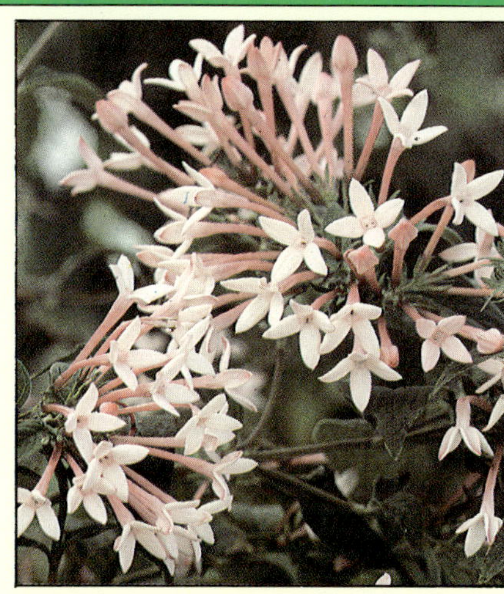

B.humboldtii is considered a variety of *B.longiflora*. The flowers though are, in general, larger and snowy white. Only rarely do plants exceed about 2ft (0.7m) tall, even when grown in a soil border or large pot, and they can be restricted to a 5-6in (13-15cm) container without difficulty by pruning regularly.

B.ternifolia, the Scarlet Trompetilla, is a rather straggly Mexican species with slightly hairy leaves which grow opposite each other along the branches, rather like a ladder. It has clusters of deep scarlet flowers, each slightly longer than 1in (2cm). 'White Joy' is a lovely pure white flowering variety that is in bloom much of the year. It has smaller flowers than the species, but in heavier clusters. 'Giant Pink' has clusters of large pink flowers.

B.augustifolia is a lovely flowering species from Mexico. It is a very bushy plant and has bright green foliage and rich, scarlet flowers.

B.jasminiflora is a winter-flowering species that is found in many parts of South America. It has quite small leaves and sweetly scented white flowers.

Browallia

Family name: **Solanaceae**

Common names: **Sapphire Flower/Amethyst Flower**

Care Easy	**Height** 2ft (0.6m)	**Flower** July—Sept
Light Bright indirect sun	**Spread** 2ft (0.6m)	**Humidity** Regular spraying
Price Cheap	**Shape** Bushy	**Availability** Garden centres
Temp. Min 50°F (10°C)	Ideal 60°F (15°C)	Max 80°F (27°C)

Although most Browallias are perennials they are often treated like annuals because seeds planted in the spring produce flowers that same year. All come from South America and make excellent houseplants. 'Blue Troll' is about the most popular as it is smaller and easier to look after than most Browallias. Its small, glossy, pointed leaves and rich bluey-purple flowers with white centres make it a very attractive flowering pot plant. Grow Browallia in a hanging basket so you can really enjoy the brilliantly-coloured flowers on its gently arching stems.

Spring and summer care

From March until late summer, keep plants in a temperature of 55-65°F (13-18°C) — though if it gets any hotter your plant will not suffer. Feed as soon as flower buds form and then every two weeks until the end of summer. Always give your Browallia good light and, when flowers appear, a little bright sunlight. Give your plant plenty of fresh air.

Autumn and winter care

In the winter you can either treat your Browallia like an annual and let it die after it has finished flowering or treat it like a perennial by pruning the dead bits back hard and keeping the soil just moist. Give it a temperature of 50-55°F (10-13°C) and wait for it to sprout again around March — it is unlikely, though, to be as vigorous in its second season.

Propagation

Sow seeds in February, using a propagator if possible or you can put the seed tray in a clear polythene bag and keep it warm on a sunny windowsill. Use a good seed compost such as John Innes or Levingtons that has a light, open texture, and carefully push each seed about ¼in (6mm) down into it. Keep moist and give plenty of fresh air, in a temperature of 55-65°F (10-13°C) until seedlings are large enough to handle. Pot them into John Innes No 3 and give good light, and a little water, until they have grown a few leaves. Treat the plants well and they will reward you with colourful flowers in July.

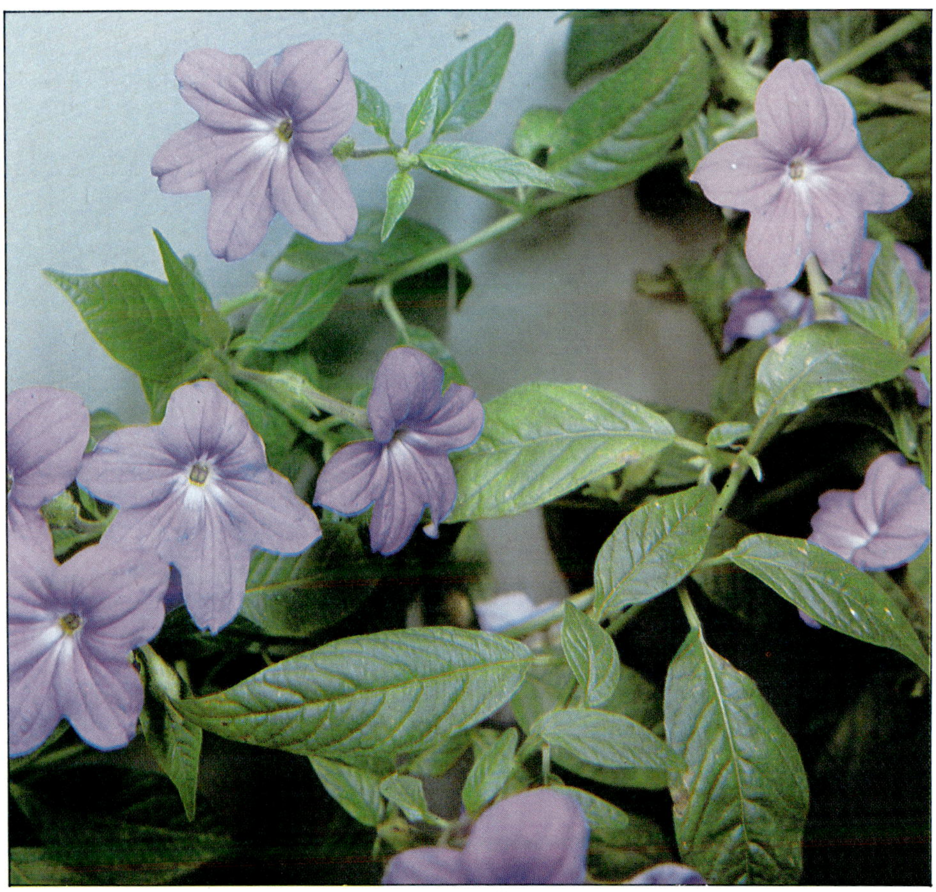

Browallia speciosa is the large parent plant of the many smaller hybrids.

Species

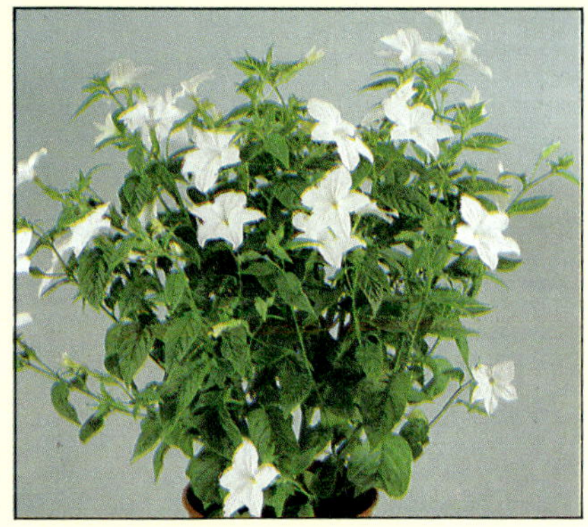

Browallia speciosa, from Peru, is shrubby with slender, spreading branches. It can grow to 2ft (0.6m) but can be kept compact by pinching out the growing tips in spring and throughout the growing season. Small, glossy, pointed leaves are set off by lots of very pretty blue or purplish-blue flowers about 2in (5cm) across. 'Blue Troll' is a smaller version with small leaves and rich bluey-purple flowers with white centres. 'Marine Blue' has darker blue flowers while 'White Troll', *above,* has white flowers and grows to about 10in (25cm) high.

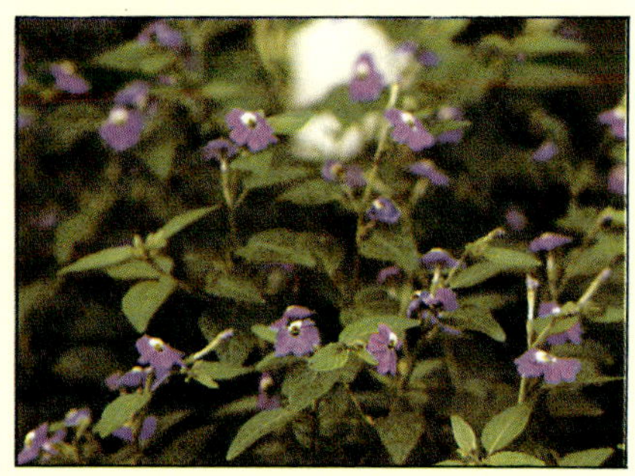

B.viscosa, *above,* from Colombia, can grow 1-2ft (0.3-0.6m) tall. Its stems and branches are slightly sticky and it has rich bluey-purple flowers. 'Sapphire' has deep blue flowers with white centres.

Trouble Shooter

Rotting roots show that you have been overwatering; always water moderately.

Sticky, dirty leaves indicate greenfly; spray with a pyrethrum-based insecticide. Take preventative action by using a systemic insecticide in spring and then again three or four times during the growing season.

Drooping, withering and unopened leaves signal that the air is too dry; provide good ventilation throughout the year and extra humidity by mist spraying occasionally or standing the plant on a tray of wet pebbles if the atmosphere is particularly dry.

Brunfelsia

Family name: **Solanaceae**

Common names: **Yesterday, Today and Tomorrow Morning, Noon and Night**

Care Straight-forward	**Height** 2ft (0.6m)	**Flower** May—Oct
Light Bright indirect sun	**Spread** 2ft (0.6m)	**Humidity** Regular spraying
Price Middle range	**Shape** Bushy	**Availability** Garden centres
Temp Min 50°F (10°C)	Ideal 70°F (21°C)	Max 85°F (30°C)

This is a group of glamorous flowering plants, which is, surprisingly, closely related to the ordinary potato. There are over 30 species which all come from tropical America and the West Indies and are either shrubby plants or, occasionally, smallish trees. All have brilliantly coloured flowers that change from violet-purple when they first open, fading to pale lavender-blue and finally to white — which is how the plant got its common name as its colour changes from one day to the next. The pale flowers have a strong fragrance at night, but the others have almost no scent at all. *Brunfelsia calycina* from Brazil and Peru is the most common houseplant species. It grows quite tall with dark green, glossy leaves and magnificent large, deep-purple flowers all through the summer and often on into autumn.

Spring and summer care

Since these plants come from hot, humid countries, it is essential that you provide a constant temperature of around 70°F (21°C), although some species like 75°F (24°C). You must give your plant good filtered sunshine during the growing season, to help leaves and flowers grow healthily. Provide your plant with the humidity it needs by standing it on a tray of wet pebbles and mist spraying during the hottest weather. From early spring through to late summer water sufficiently for the soil to be moist, but not wet. As flower buds appear, feed your Brunfelsia every three weeks with a liquid fertiliser to keep it healthy and happy.

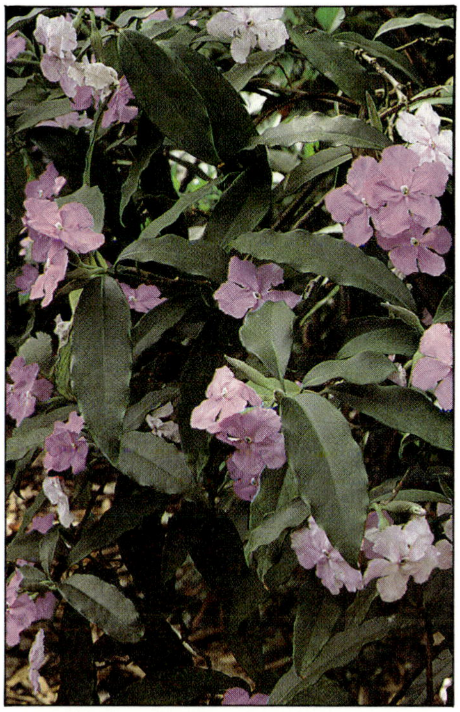

Brunfelsia calycina flowers all summer.

Autumn and winter care

In the winter keep the temperature between 50 and 55°F (10-13°C) and water so that the soil is barely moist. Prune as soon after flowering as possible to encourage compact growth and, if your plant needs repotting, this should be done at the same time. Brunfelsia likes a peat-based compost with a little loam mixed in, such as John Innes No 2 or 3.

Propagation

Take cuttings 3-4in (7-10cm) long in late spring; dip the ends in hormone rooting powder and insert them in a half peat, half sand mixture. Keep moist and humid with a temperature of 70°F (21°C) in a slightly shaded spot, preferably in a propagator, as bottom heat is helpful, or a pot covered with a clear polythene bag and kept on a sunny windowsill. Roots should appear in two to three weeks.

Trouble Shooter

Troubles can occur if you overwater your plant during the winter, especially if temperatures are below 50°F (10°C), as this can cause root rot or wilting of the leaves; water less often and keep your Brunfelsia in a warmer part of the house.

Scale insects can attack and cause discolouring of the leaves; wipe them off with a cloth or paintbrush dipped in methylated spirits.

Greenfly can also be a nuisance; the best way to deal with them, and all pests, is to water in a malathion systemic insecticide once a month throughout the growing season — this should protect your plant for the whole year.

Species

Brunfelsia calycina grows to 2ft (0.6m) and has glossy, dark green, lance-shaped leaves. It produces large, deep-purple blooms about 3in (7cm) across with wavy edges, opening in spring and carrying on throughout the summer and often into the autumn as well. 'Macrantha' is a glamorous variety from the tropical parts of Chile, and has huge, deep lavender to pale purple flowers.

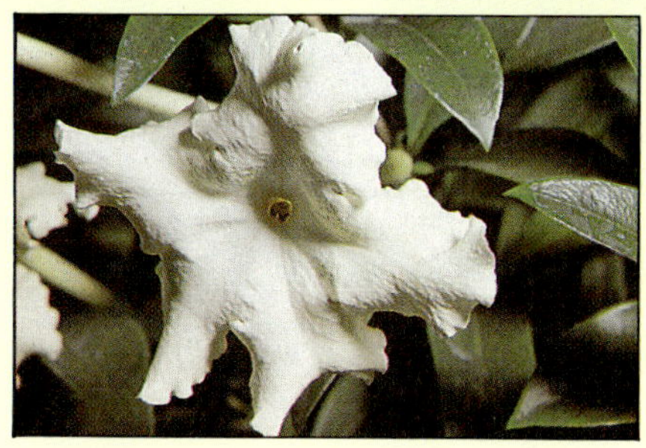

B.undulata, *above*, from the West Indian islands, is rather rare but occasionally available. It grows to about 3ft (0.9m), has elegant slender leaves and fragrant white flowers.

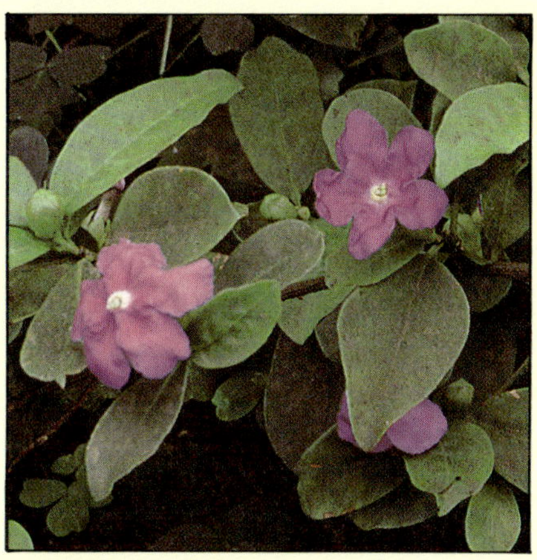

B.latifolia, *above*, is from tropical South America. A bushy shrub, it grows 2-3ft (0.6-0.9m) high and has long, broad leaves 4-5in (10-13cm) long that are slightly hairy on the underside. In late winter and spring, it freely produces highly scented, lavender-coloured flowers that have a white centre when they open, but gradually the flower becomes completely white.

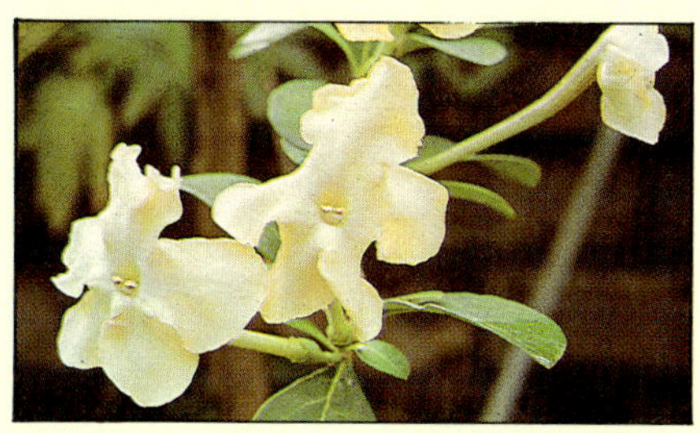

B.americana, *above*, from the West Indies, is commonly called Lady of the Night because its flowers have a wonderful fragrance at night. In its native habitat it can grow to 6ft (1.8m) tall. An evergreen, its leaves are 4-5in (10-13cm) long and oval in shape; it has large, pure white flowers that turn creamy-yellow. The flowers are about 3in (7cm) across and open from slender tubes over 4in (10cm) long.

Caladium

Family name: **Araceae**

Common name: **Angel's Wings**

Care Straight-forward	**Height** 9-15in (23-38cm)	**Flower** None
Light Shaded	**Spread** 20in (50cm)	**Humidity** Mist spray regularly
Price Middle range	**Shape** Arching	**Availability** Garden centres
Temp. Min 60°F (15°C)	Ideal 70°F (21°C)	Max 75°F (24°C)

Caladiums have some of the most colourful and interesting foliage of all houseplants. They get their common name from the shape of their leaves — which do have a very ethereal quality, particularly the large white, green-veined ones. There are many different kinds of Caladium, all from tropical South America and the West Indies. They are about 9-15in (23-38cm) tall and have heart-shaped leaves in a wide range of colours. There are many hybrids that have their own particular colourings and leaf markings, and they can be easily found in garden centres and nurseries.

Caladium bicolor is a parent of most of the hybrids and is itself a distinctive plant. It comes from the southern West Indies, Guyana and Brazil and grows in shady places near to rain forests. The *bicolor*'s leaves are mostly dark green with dark red veins and white mottling. Caladiums lose their leaves in late autumn and die down completely for winter but sprout again in spring.

Spring and summer care

Repot dormant tubers if necessary in March into a rich, quite acid soil — Levingtons or Arthur Bowers compost is suitable, but add a little extra sand to make sure it drains well.

Spring through summer is the Caladium's growing season. Water moderately at the beginning of spring, giving the plant more water as it starts to grow vigorously, but be careful not to overwater as this will damage the roots. Let the surface of the compost dry out a little before watering again. Give the plant a good foliar feed with a mist spray every other week to keep the leaves healthy.

To grow your Caladium successfully it is essential that you give it humidity and a constant temperature of 70°F (21°C) or higher. Because it comes from a rain-forest

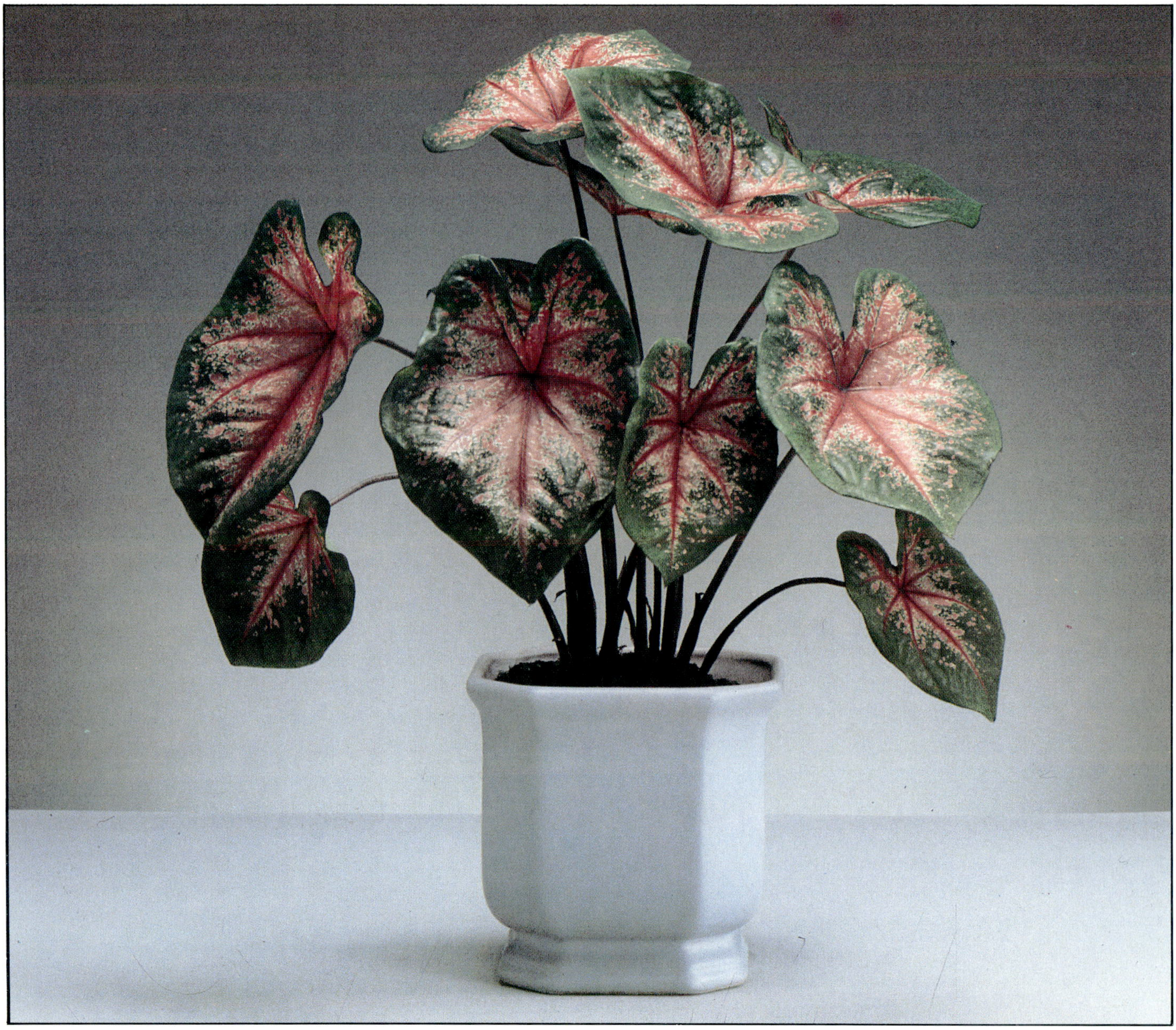

Caladium bicolor is a good example of just how colourful Caladium leaves can be.

environment, your Caladium will love semi-shade and hate bright sunlight.

Autumn and winter care

The leaves die down completely during mid to late autumn. From then until late spring, the tubers must be kept completely dry — don't water at all. Keep the plant in a constant temperature of at least 60°F (15°C) — a cold spell will kill it, so do keep it warm.

Propagation

In late February or March tubers usually produce offsets; you can remove these carefully from the pot. Dust the tuber with sulphur powder if you happen to cut it as you remove the offsets so as to prevent rot. Plant each offset in Levingtons or Arthur Bowers peat-based compost and add a little sand, to make sure it drains well. Keep at a constant temperature of 70°F (21°C).

Trouble Shooter

Wilting or shrivelling leaves show that you have either not watered your Caladium sufficiently or have not given it enough humidity; a cold draught also has this effect. Let the surface of the compost dry out between waterings — and keep the plant well away from draughts.

Unhealthy-looking foliage results from keeping the plant too cool; move your plant to a warmer spot or it will die.

Aphids attack new leaves; spray with a pyrethrum insecticide or, alternatively, water a systemic insecticide into the compost in spring as a preventative measure.

Buying Guide

Late March or early April is the best time to buy a Caladium as the foliage will be colourful, and you will be able to choose one that is growing vigorously. Look out for a plant that has several new shoots sprouting round the base as this is a healthy sign.

Some of the more unusual Caladiums can be hard to find but specialist nurseries that stock bulbous and tuberous-rooted plants should be a good hunting ground.

Species

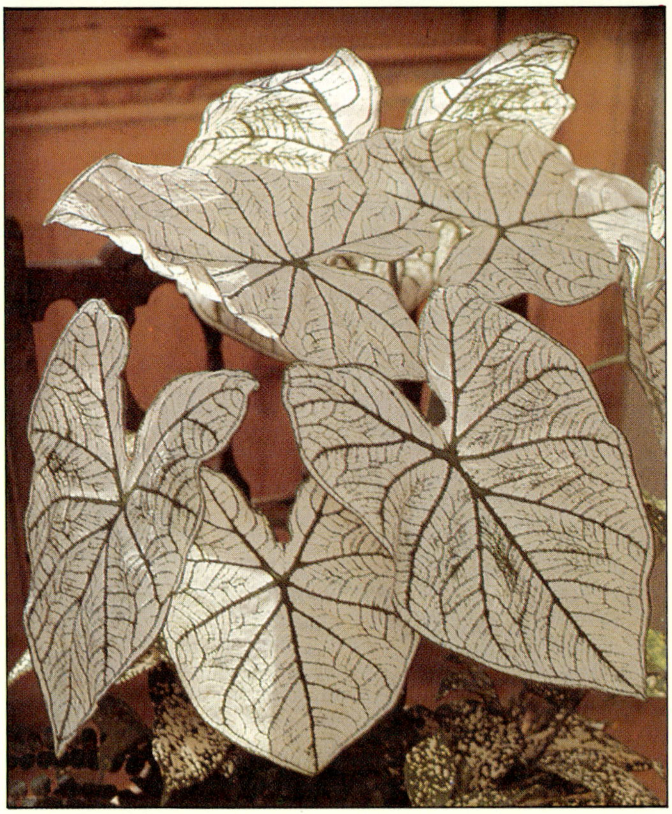

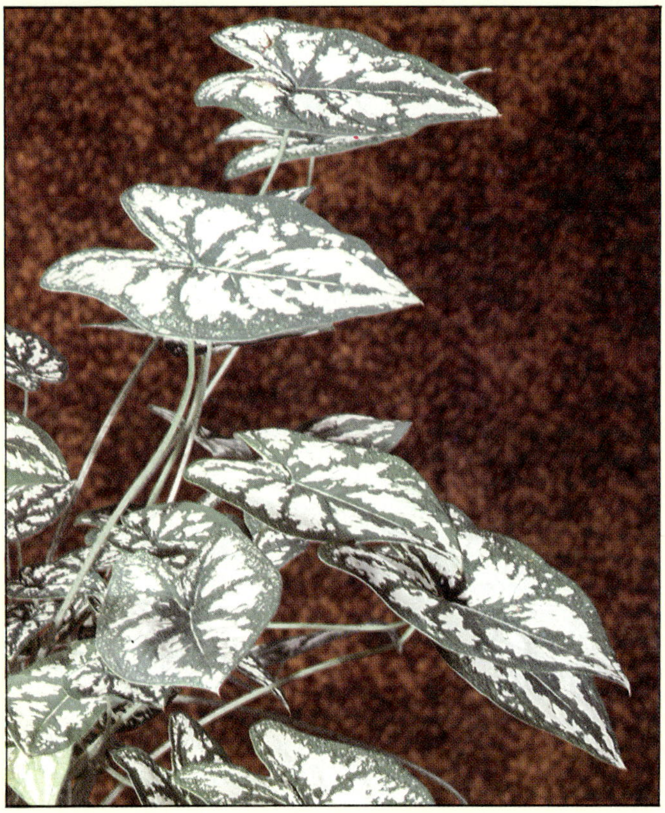

Caladium bicolor, Angel's Wings, from the south West Indies, Guyana and Brazil, has heart-shaped leaves that are dark green with dark red veins and white mottling. It has yellowish-white spathe-like flowers with green tips. The leaves grow fresh from the tuber each spring.

C. x hortulanum 'Candidum' and 'Silver Leaves', *above left*, have very thin greyish-green leaves with striking dark green veins. 'Freda Hempel' is a compact, bushy plant with red-centred leaves, edged with dark green. 'Lord Derby' is bushy with pale rose-pink leaves that have green veins and dark green edges.

C.humboldtii (argyrites), *above right*, is only about 9in (23cm) tall with small, distinctly arrow-shaped leaves that are a rich green colour with almost transparent blotches between the veins.

***C.picturatum* (or *sagittifolium*)** has green, white-veined leaves that are longer and narrower than the other species. It is also available in other leaf colours — from reddish to buff-coloured to green. Most types have undulating edges to their leaves.

C.steudnerifolium, from Colombia, is a very colourful species that is not difficult to grow. The leaves are mostly bright green, waxy and heart-shaped. The upper surfaces are mottled with whitish grey but the undersides of the leaves are green. The stems are grey-brown in colour, cross-banded in silver.

Calathea

Family name: **Marantaceae**

Common name: **Peacock Plant**

Care Straight-forward	**Height** 2ft (0.6m)	**Flower** None
Light Shaded	**Spread** 12-18in (30-45cm)	**Humidity** Spray daily
Price Middle range	**Shape** Shrubby	**Availability** Garden centres
Temp. Min 65°F (18°C)	Ideal 70°F (21°C)	Max 80°F (27°C)

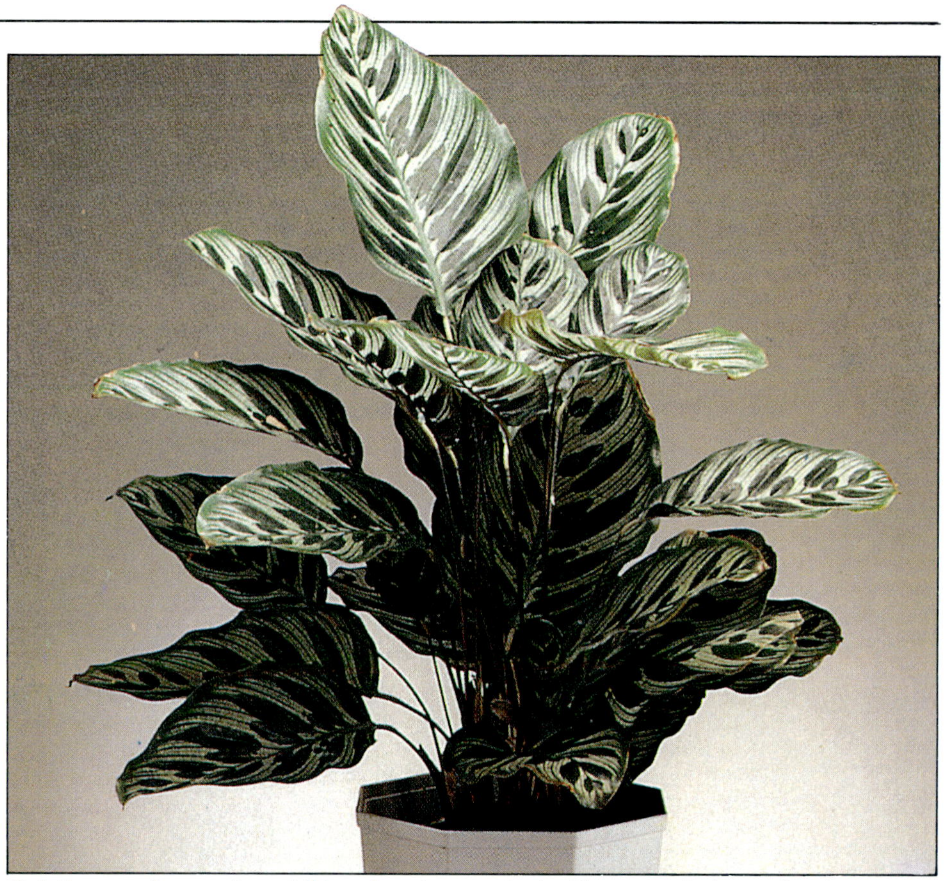

Calathea makoyana is a striking, handsome plant with unusual, decorative leaves.

Calathea makoyana is probably the most commonly found member of this family. It is the distinctive leaves that make it such an attractive plant to grow. They are a full, oval shape and artistically patterned in shades of green, yellow and yellowish-green on the upper surfaces, this pattern being repeated in reddish-purple on the undersides, providing a lovely contrast. It is this intriguing design that gives the plant its common name, as the shapes on the leaves look like peacock feathers. Calatheas do need humidity and high temperatures but will reward careful looking after with a profusion of handsome, colourful leaves. Some Calatheas also have pretty flowers.

You may find that some of these plants are called Maranta in the shops. This is because many Calatheas were at one time part of the very similar Maranta family, but they have since been reclassified.

Spring and summer care

Repot, if your plant has filled its pot with roots, at the start of the growing season in March into a loam-based compost such as John Innes No 2 or 3 — the fresh compost will give the plant a boost of nutrients. Never let the temperature drop below 65°F (18°C) and keep your plant in a humid, shady spot — high temperatures will not harm your plant so long as it is shaded and the atmosphere is kept humid. Stand your Calathea on a tray of moist pebbles and mist spray daily to keep the humidity high. Water freely from April to September and feed with liquid fertiliser every two or three weeks.

Autumn and winter care

Water enough to keep the compost moist but not as freely as during the summer. Shade and a moist atmosphere are vital during the cooler months, as is a constant temperature of 65°F (18°C).

Propagation

In late March or April divide an overcrowded plant and pot the divisions into John Innes No 2 or 3. It is important to keep them in a temperature of 70°F (21°C), or even slightly higher, to encourage the plants to send down new roots. Water carefully, shade them and provide high humidity.

Species

C.makoyana, the Peacock Plant, from Brazil, is a bushy 2ft (0.6m) tall plant with 6in (15cm) long oval leaves. It has very fine patterns in green, yellow and yellowish-green on the tops of its leaves and a mirror image of these in reddish-purple on the undersides. The leaves are carried on long, slender stems.

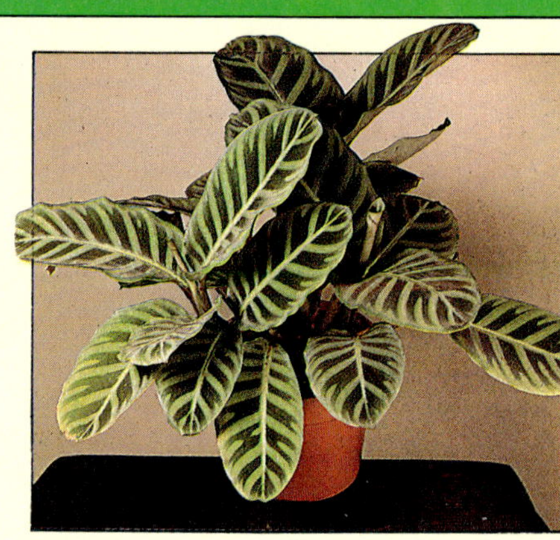

C. zebrina, *right*, the Zebra Plant, comes from Brazil and grows to about 2ft (0,6m) high. It has bright green leaves with pale veins and purple undersides. It needs a lot of warmth and humidity to thrive.

C.grandiflora, from Brazil, has glossy green, puckered leaves about 12in (30cm) long. It has the added attraction of colourful flowers. They are almost tubular spikes, yellowish in colour and carried on thick stems.

C.ornata, from Colombia and Equador, is 12-24in (30-60cm) tall with thin, papery leaves on long stalks. The leaves are either white or striped in white when they are young, turning greenish-bronze with reddish undersides as they age.

C.insignis **(or *lancifolia*)**, *above*, from Brazil, is called the Rattlesnake Plant because of its long, narrow leaves which have dark-green horizontal markings that are alternately long and short on a plain yellowish-green background. The undersides are a rich maroon and the edges of the leaves undulate. It is a bushy plant that grows about 4-5ft (1.2-1.5m) tall in the wild, but as a houseplant it will grow to about 12-14in (30-36cm).

C.veitchiana, from Peru, is also called the Peacock Plant. It has stiff, leathery leaves that are an elongated oval shape, about 12in (30cm) long. The leaves are patterned in various shades of green with greyish-green feather-like and brownish-green arch-shaped markings, like a peacock's feather.

Callistemon

Family name: **Myrtaceae**

Common name: **Bottle Brush**

Care Easy	**Height** 5ft (1.5m)	**Flower** June
Light Sun/bright light	**Spread** 4ft (1.2m)	**Humidity** None
Price Expensive	**Shape** Shrubby	**Availability** Garden centres
Temp. Min 45°F (7°C)	Ideal 65°F (18°C)	Max 80°F (27°C)

Callistemons are renowned for their extraordinary flowers, which are made up of hundreds of bright red or pink stamens with yellow tips radiating out from the end of the stem — just like bottle brushes!

Callistemons come from Australia and New Caledonia and love the sun. They have attractive, lance-shaped, mid-green leaves, and their distinctive flowers appear at the ends of branches in June. Most of them are shrubby and a few grow to tree-like proportions in their natural habitat. They are quite tolerant about watering, soil and temperatures which makes them very good houseplants for a wide range of conditions and ideal for a houseplant novice.

Callistemon citrinus is the best Bottle Brush to grow indoors as it rarely gets higher than 5ft (1.5m) tall, and has an attractive deep-red flower spike with a distinctly lemony scent. The Bottle Brush is pretty easy to grow and if you look after your plant, regularly pruning, repotting and feeding, it should give you colour for many years.

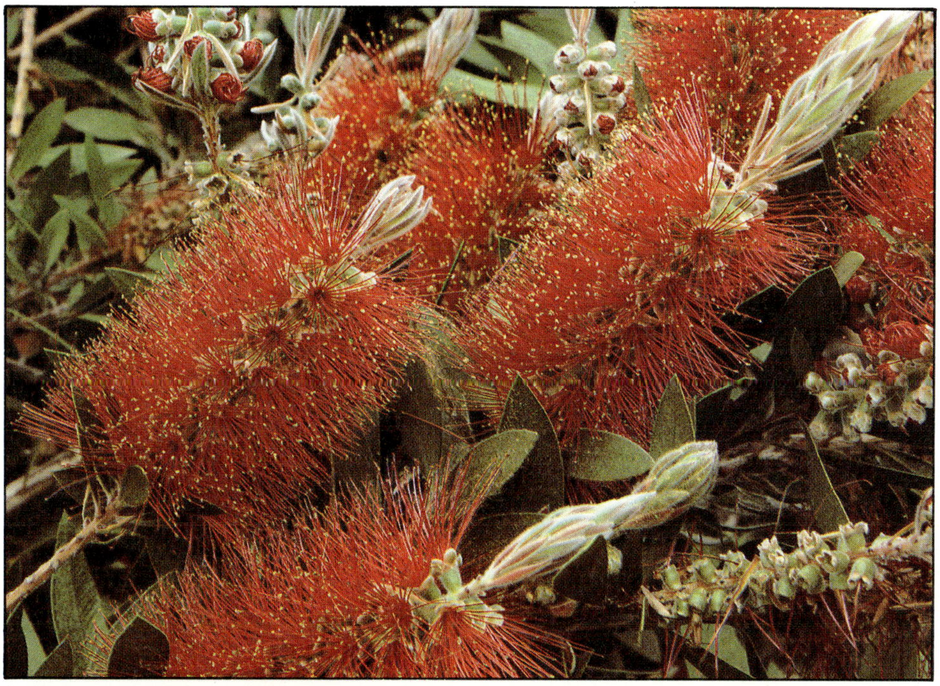

***Callistemon citrinus* 'Splendens'** in full, brilliant flower.

Spring and summer care

Repot in April or early May at the latest if your Bottle Brush has become pot bound, using John Innes No 3. Put a good layer of pebbles in the bottom of the pot to weight it and provide good drainage. As this is a sun-loving plant, temperatures can rise to 65 or 70°F (18 or 21°C) without damage. Water freely from April to the end of September. Feed with liquid fertiliser every two weeks.

Autumn and winter care

Keep temperatures above a 45°F (7°C) minimum — 50-55°F (10-13°C) is ideal during the winter. Put your plant in the brightest natural light you can find in the house, but don't let it sit in strong, cold draughts. Water your Bottle Brush occasionally to keep the compost moist, letting it dry out partially between times. The Bottle Brush is inclined to be straggly, so clip it back to a neat shape in early autumn.

Propagation

You can sow seeds in March or April, but you will need to be patient with them as it can be three or four years before you can expect to have flowering plants.

Alternatively, in summer take 3-4in (7-10cm) long cuttings with a heel of bark from non-flowering shoots. Dip the cut ends in hormone rooting powder and poke into a tray filled with half peat, half sand compost. Keep the compost just moist and give the cuttings a temperature of 60 to 65°F (15 to 18°C) and plenty of fresh air. Using a propagator is the best way of getting the roots growing but, instead, you can simply fasten a clear polythene bag over your container and keep it on a sunny windowsill.

Once the cuttings have rooted, pot them on into small pots filled with John Innes No 3 and stand in bright but filtered light. Keep watering them well and give them plenty of fresh air during the summer.

Species

***Callistemon citrinus* (or *lanceolatus*)** comes from eastern Australia and will rarely grow taller than 5ft (1.5m). The branches have a coating of fine silky hairs and the leaves are about 3in (7cm) long, grey-green, thickish, stiff and lance-shaped. The striking lemon-scented 'bottle brush' flower spikes appear in June, are about 2½-5in (6-13cm) long and a deep red colour. 'Splendens' is a glamorous plant with its slightly larger flower spikes in bright crimson.

C.salignus is harder to find. It has yellow flowers 2-3in (5-7cm) long in autumn and the variety 'Alba' has white flowers. Both usually grow to about 5-8ft (1.5-2.4m) and both have interesting leaves — they are a beautiful bright red when they first appear, gradually changing to a deep green colour.

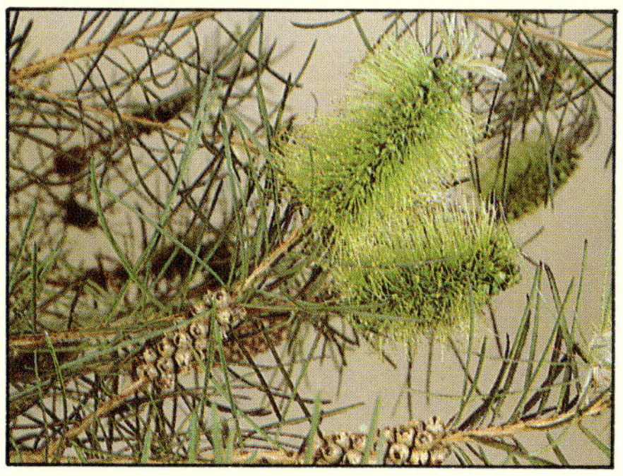

C.pinifolius, *above*, also a rare plant, is from New South Wales and is smaller — only growing to about 3-4ft (0.9-1.2m). It tends to be straggly with long, slender leaves. The flower spikes are pale green and about 2-3in (5-7cm) long.

Trouble Shooter

An unhealthy-looking plant usually results from sitting it in dense shade; move it to a sunny window.

Wilting followed by dying leaves is caused by overwatering; never let your Bottle-Brush sit in water.

Mealy bugs attack new leaves and stems; clean them away with a brush or cloth dipped in methylated spirits. As a preventative, use a malathion-based systemic insecticide two or three times in the growing season.

Campanula

Family name: **Campanulaceae**

Common names: **Italian Bellflower/Star of Bethlehem**

Care Easy	**Height** 6-8in (15-20cm)	**Flower** Summer
Light Indirect sun	**Spread** 8-12in (20-30cm)	**Humidity** Mist spray regularly
Price Middle range	**Shape** Trailing	**Availability** Garden centres
Temp. Min 45°F (7°C)	Ideal 60°F (15°C)	Max 70°F (21°C)

The Italian Bellflower is a pretty little houseplant whose garden relatives include Canterbury Bells and over 200 others. Many of these Campanulas are perennials and most of them come from Europe. The popular Italian Bellflower, *Campanula isophylla*, comes from northern Italy and is smothered with little star-shaped flowers for most of the summer. It is one of the finest of all houseplants with its slender stems and fresh green leaves. Lilac blue or pure white bell-shaped flowers appear in clusters towards the tips of the stems in summer. The Campanula is an ideal plant for a hanging basket as it grows very quickly, dangling its long stems over the edge, producing an array of attractive flowers.

Spring and summer care

Give your Italian Bellflower bright indirect sun all year round to encourage bushiness and flowering. Without sufficient light your plant will get leggy and flower sparsely.

Pot on your plant into John Innes No 3 in early spring only if it really needs it. The Italian Bellflower flourishes in a temperature around 60°F (15°C) but can stand a drop to 45°F (7°C). Water freely, as often as daily in warm weather, and spray regularly to provide humidity. Your plant will die back badly and stop flowering if you let it dry out. Water in a liquid fertiliser every 14 to 20 days. Pick off the flowers as they die to encourage more buds to form; this will make your plant flower all summer.

If you grow your Italian Bellflower in a hanging basket, line the basket first with a good padding of sphagnum moss and soak it well. The damp moss will help to create a humid atmosphere.

Autumn and winter care

Winter temperatures can safely fall to around 45°F (7°C); provide only enough water to prevent the compost completely drying out. Give your plant a good light but not winter

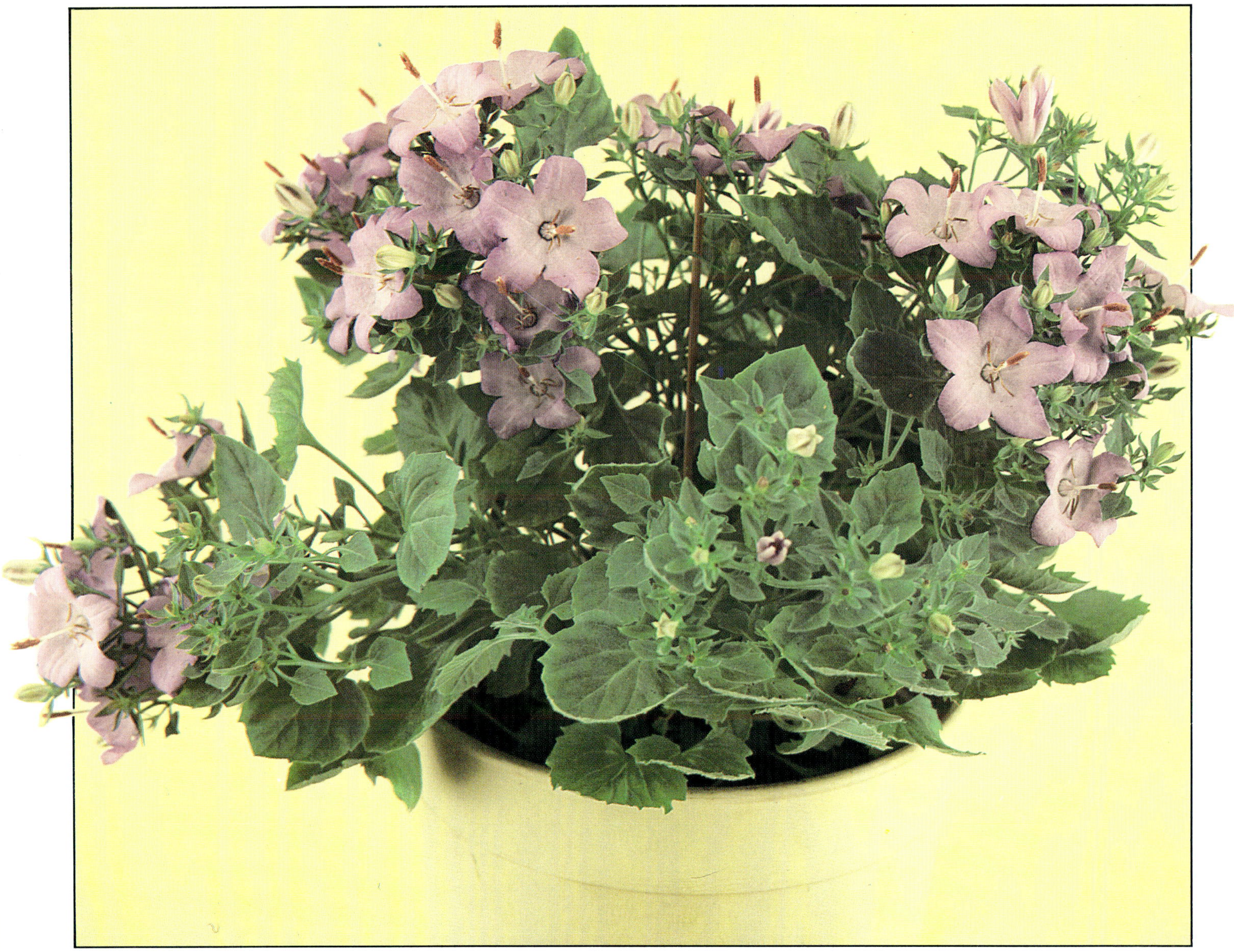

Campanula isophylla is a perennial with pretty, star-shaped flowers.

Trouble Shooter

Wilting, pale, shrivelled leaves and dead, dried out flowers and buds indicate that you have let your plant dry out; cut back all the dead foliage and spray and water regularly.

No flowers and a sad, collapsed plant show that you have been overwatering and that the roots are rotting; cut back badly affected shoots and don't water again until the compost is only just moist.

A light webbing between the leaves and buds is a sure sign of red spider mite, which often occurs if the plant is too dry; spray with a malathion-based systemic insecticide. As a preventative you can also apply this to the soil two or three times a year.

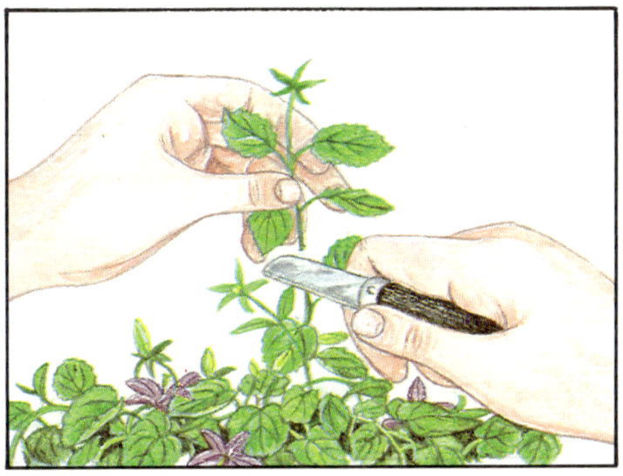

Taking a cutting: slice off a new shoot with a sharp knife.

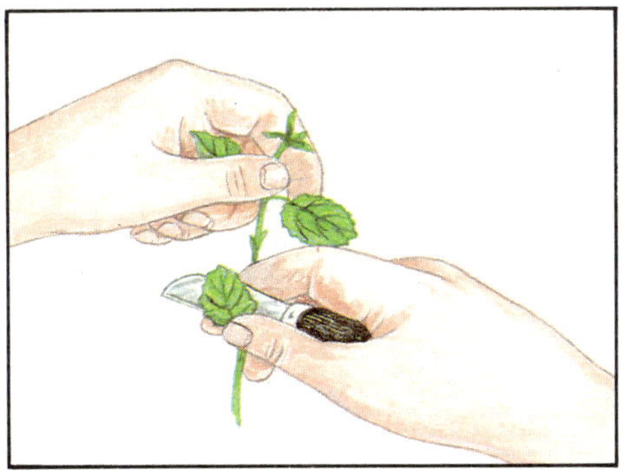

Trim the cutting, holding the shoot gently, so it is 3-4in (7-10cm) long.

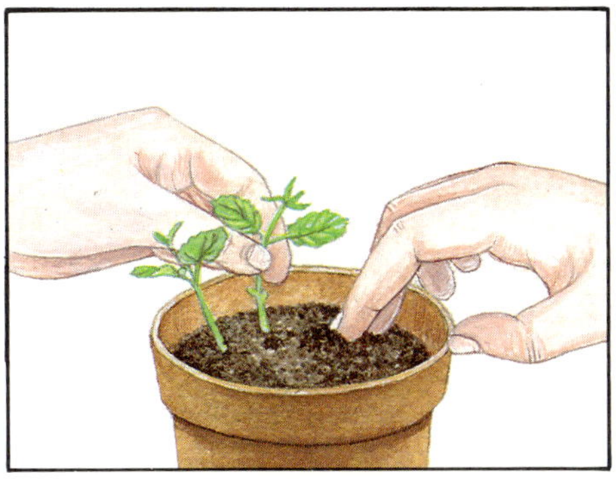

Dip the cut end in hormone rooting powder, plant and keep warm.

Species

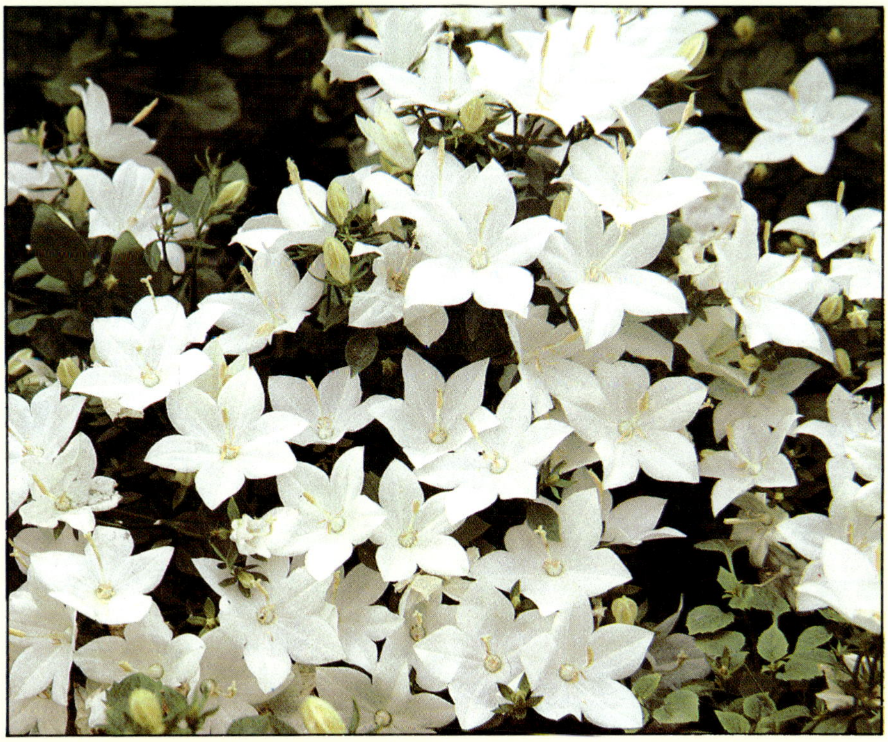

Campanula isophylla, the Italian Bellflower, has a slightly woody framework from which grow bright green, brittle shoots and round, serrated edge leaves both of which ooze a white sap when cut. It rarely grows more than 6-8in (15-20cm) high but the stems can dangle about 18-24in (45-60cm). Lilac blue bell-shaped flowers each about 1in (25mm) across follow each other in profusion from late spring through to the end of summer. 'Alba' is slightly sturdier and has pure white flowers, as does 'Kristel', *above*. 'Mayi' has mauve flowers above grey-green, finely hairy leaves.

***C.tomentosa* (or *rupestris*)** comes from the Greek mainland and islands where it grows in the full sun on the cliff sides. It has rounded, grey-green, silky leaves that grow out from the centre of the plant in a rosette. The flowers grow almost horizontally from this rosette each with a brilliant blue, bell-shaped flower about 1in (25mm) across with a few greyish leaves behind it. Grow it in a hanging basket with a little added lime in the compost. It is available through specialist alpine suppliers and can, if protected, survive outdoors.

C. vidalli comes from the Azores and is a shrubby plant with thick stems and attractive pink or white bell-shaped flowers. It is important to keep this plant free from frost at all times.

sunshine as this is too strong. At the end of winter prune your plant severely to about 2 or 3in (5-7cm) above the compost. Keep the shoots you cut off for cuttings.

Propagation

Sow seeds into a good seed compost in August. Keep the mixture moist, reasonably humid and at a minimum temperature of 60°F (15°C). Within three months the seedlings will be ready for potting singly into pots of John Innes No 3.

Alternatively, take 3-4in (7-10cm) cuttings (or use the bits you've pruned off) in early spring. Dip the cut ends into hormone rooting powder and pot the cuttings into a compost containing a good proportion of sharp sand. Keep the cuttings in a temperature of 60°F (15°C), constantly moist and in a lightly shaded spot. The cuttings will root quickly, after which you can pot them up into John Innes No 3.

Buying Guide

The Italian Bellflower appears in garden centres and shops when it is in flower, or seeds can be bought through mail order from most seed merchants. Select a sturdy plant without blemishes of any sort on the foliage, with plenty of buds still to open. If the leaves are even slightly yellowish select another plant.

Capsicum

Family name: **Solanaceae**

Common name: **Ornamental Pepper/Christmas Cherry**

Care Easy	**Height** 12-15in (30-38cm)	**Flower** June
Light Good	**Spread** 12in (30cm)	**Humidity** Regular spraying
Price Cheap	**Shape** Bushy	**Availability** Common
Temp. Min 50°F (10°C)	Ideal 60°F (15°C)	Max 70°F (21°C)

Ornamental Peppers are unusual house-plants because they are grown for their decorative fruits rather than their flowers or foliage. These fruits generally start green then turn shades of yellow, orange and eventually red. Unlike culinary peppers these are not for eating — they are, in fact, poisonous! Capsicums are small, dark green, bushy plants about 12-15in (30-38cm) tall and appear for sale in the shops in early winter when there are fruits on the plant. Earlier in the year they are covered in small white flowers, which later develop into the fruits. Ornamental Peppers are annuals and so are thrown away in early spring after fruiting has finished. There are many attractive hybrids that have varying colours and fruit shapes.

Spring and summer care

In summer your plant will be growing towards maturity. Small, white, rather insignificant flowers appear in June. If you need to repot your plant use John Innes No 3. Give your Ornamental Pepper good bright light, especially when the fruits are ripening, and keep the temperature between 50 and 70°F (10-21°C). Always keep your plant well watered throughout the growing season, especially when the temperature soars, but let your plant dry out slightly between applications. Add a good liquid fertiliser to the water every week or so, particularly as the fruits are beginning to form. Once the fruits are fully developed, stop feeding.

Autumn and winter care

This is when your plant is at its most ornamental so you must keep it in a minimum temperature of 50°F (10°C) or it will deteriorate. Provide a good circulation of fresh air, but avoid cold draughts. Water enough to keep the compost barely moist. When the fruits start to shrivel and drop off in early spring, throw the plant away.

Propagation

Sow seeds in February or March, using a good seed compost. Keep them moist and in a temperature of 65-70°F (18-21°C). Try to give them a little fresh air to stop them damping off. When the seedlings are large enough to handle, in late March or April, move them into individual pots of John Innes No 3.

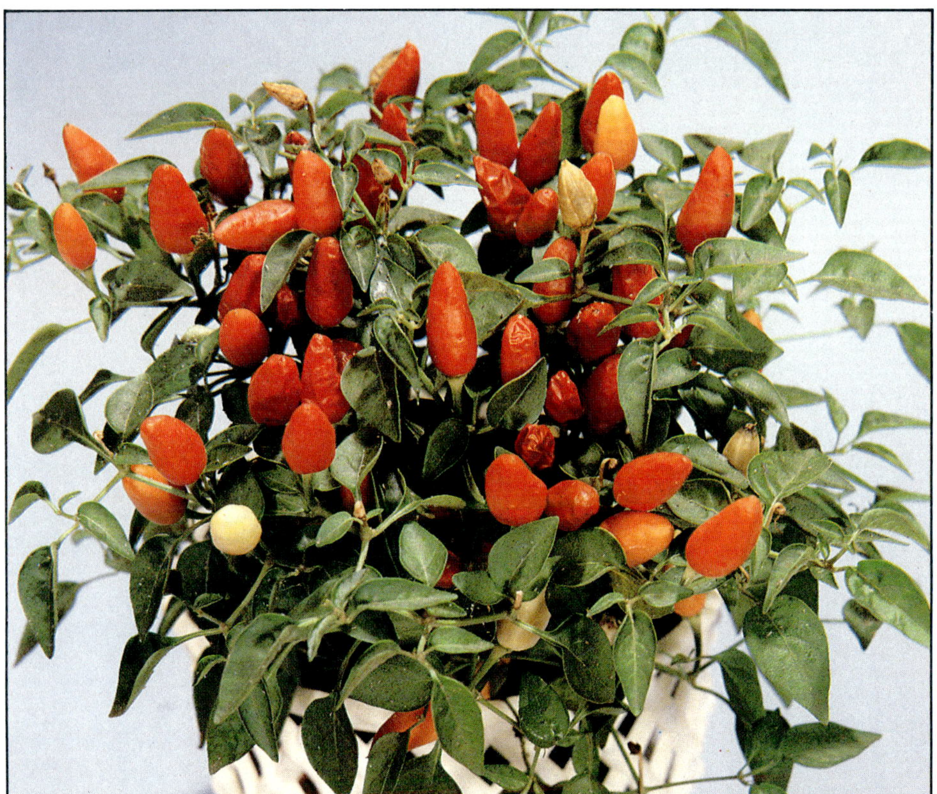

Capsicum annuum's bright red fruits and green leaves make a very handsome plant.

Trouble Shooter

Drooping and wilting leaves show that you are not watering correctly, or that the plant is not getting enough light, that the temperature is badly wrong or you've forgotten to feed your plant; adjust accordingly.

Small, white, moth-like insects that fly up in clouds when the plant is disturbed are whitefly; use a systemic insecticide.

Tiny webbing between the shoots is a sure sign of red spider mite, which only appears when the air is very dry; use a systemic insecticide and increase the humidity by regular spraying.

Species

Capsicum annuum comes from many parts of South America. It is a shrubby little plant about 12-15in (30-38cm) high, with bright green, narrow, lance-shaped leaves about 1½in (38mm) long, densely arranged to give the plant a very compact shape. The flowers are small and white and appear in June. They are followed by decorative red fruits that look like cones, although hybrids come in other shapes like the 'Hotbed round', *below.*

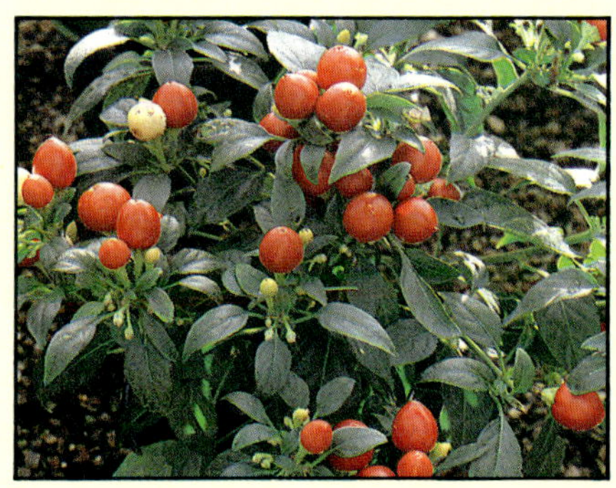

C.frutescens also comes from South America where it grows over 3ft (0.9m) tall. It has white flowers at the tips of the stems in summer which give way to 1in (25mm) long, red or yellow fruits.

The many hybrids are all crosses between these two species. 'Fips' is a charming little plant not more than 6in (15cm) high. It is very compact with dense foliage. The fruits start green then gradually turn to orange and eventually deep red. 'Bonfire' is very similar but with yellow and red fruits. 'Fiesta' has erect, tapering 2in (5cm) fruits, which start life cream then turn yellow to orange and finally red. If you want an Ornamental Pepper to eat, get 'Longum' or 'Red Chile', which are not poisonous, but don't eat the others!

Ceropegia

Family name: **Asclepiadaceae**

Common names: **Rosary Vine/ String of Hearts**

Care Middle	**Height** Trailing to 3ft (0.9m)	**Flower** September and October
Light Sunny	**Spread** 8-10in (20-25cm)	**Winter** Indoor protection
Price Middle range	**Shape** Trailing	**Availability** Garden centres

There are some 200 species of Ceropegia, mainly tuberous-rooted, succulent plants with twining upright or trailing stems bearing very decorative foliage and small, appealing, lantern-shaped flowers. Their distribution is widespread, from Arabia to China and Australia, but most of the better-known plants originate from southern Africa and the Canary Isles.

The species most often seen is the Rosary Vine or String of Hearts (*Ceropegia woodii*), *below*, from southern Africa. The common names refer both to the small, succulent, heart-shaped leaves and to small tuberous growths which are produced here and there along the slender, purple, thread-like stems. These can trail to a length of 3ft (0.9m) and make the Rosary Vine a most effective choice for a hanging-basket, though they can also be trained upwards on miniature trellises. A popular choice as a house plant or easily grown in a cool greenhouse, it can be very impressively displayed outdoors, producing delicate, pale purple flowers in September and October. However, while it will tolerate quite low temperatures, it is not a hardy plant and will need to be brought inside during the winter.

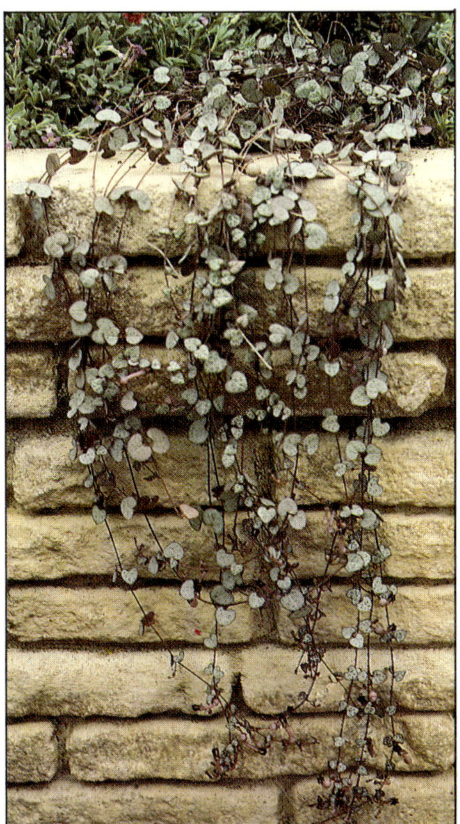

The beautiful Rosary Vine is superb when allowed to trail freely.

Spring and summer care

Grow your plant in a proprietary cactus compost, or make up your own mixture using equal parts of loam, peat, leaf-mould and sharp sand; always crock the pots well to ensure good drainage. Plant the tuber quite shallowly, only $^1/_2$in (1cm) or so below the surface of the compost. Pot small plants on in the spring to a container one size larger; mature plants will thrive in a 3-4in (8-10cm) pot for several years. For a hanging-basket, use a few Ceropegias planted roughly $1^1/_2$-2in (4-5cm) apart.

For healthy growth and good leaf colouring, good light is essential; a south- or west-facing position gives the best results. From April to late September, water moderately so that the compost is just moist, then allow the top two-thirds to dry out before watering again. During this active growth period add a weak liquid fertiliser to the water every two to three weeks – use half the recommended amount.

Autumn and winter care

While Ceropegia will withstand quite low temperatures, it is definitely not frost-hardy; it should be kept at a minimum of 45-50°F (7-10°C) for safety, so it is best brought inside during the coldest months. Give it the lighest possible position and keep it free from cold draughts. Water very sparingly from October through to March, giving just enough water to prevent the compost from drying out completely. Cold, wet compost is a certain recipe for disaster.

Propagation

New plants are easily raised from cuttings or by planting the tuberous growths which are produced along the stems. Remove stem tubers or take 3-4in (8-10cm) stem cuttings in early spring, cutting just below a leaf joint. Leave them a few days for the cuts to callus over then set them in a mixture of equal parts of peat and sand. Keep lightly shaded, at a temperature of 60-65°F (16-18°C), and water very sparingly until new growth indicates that rooting is established; this may take eight weeks or so, but after that growth is quite quick. Pot up in the usual compost and treat as mature plants (see 'Spring and summer care').

Trouble Shooter

Leaves will start to shrivel and fall if plants receive too little water in summer; give your plant a good soaking, allowing it to drain before setting it back in place, and it should recover. Conversely, overwatering in winter may result in lasting damage and cause the whole plant structure to rot. Leaf colouring will be impaired and the gaps between pairs of leaves extended if plants have too little light; give your plant the brightest possible position. Regular feeding is important, too; plants will loose their vigour and may fail to flower if this is neglected.

Mealy bug may be a problem; wipe the leaves with a cloth or paintbrush dipped in methylated spirit, or spray with a malathion-based insecticide if the infestation is severe.

Species

Ceropegia woodii, the Rosary Vine or String of Hearts, from southern Africa, is the best known species. Slender, thread-like, purplish stems grow out of a hard, woody, tuberous base, to a length of 3ft (0.9m) or so – though plants can reach as much as 8-9ft (2.4-2.7m). These carry opposite pairs of fleshy, heart-shaped, $^1/_2$in (13mm) long leaves, dark green marbled in white with purple undersides. Inch-long (2.5cm) flowers are borne in late summer from the leaf axils; they consist of a small, rounded, purplish-brown base with a narrow tube of pale purple lobes, joined at the tip.

C.radicans, also from southern Africa, is another trailing plant, with small, thick, ovate leaves, dark green in colour. The $1^1/_2$-2in (4-5cm) long upright flowers are in the form of a long and slender tube, swollen at the base, the lobes joined at the tip, with colourings of green, white and purple.

C.fusca is an erect, rather cane-like species from the Canary Isles, which is well suited to pot-growth. The grey succulent stems, often tinged with purple, carry small, short-lived leaves and short, brownish flowers.

C.dichotoma is also from the Canary Isles, with stout, erect, pale green stems up to 3ft (0.9m) in length. Leaves are small and narrow and short lived; pale yellow flowers.

Chamaedorea

Family name: **Palmae**

Common name: **Parlour Palm**

Care Straight-forward	**Height** 1-9ft (0.3-2.7m)	**Flower** None
Light Filtered sun	**Spread** 1-6ft 0.3-1.8m)	**Humidity** Mist spray regularly
Price Expensive	**Shape** Arching	**Availability** Common

Temp. Min 50°F (10°C) Ideal 65°F (18°C) Max 75°F (24°C)

Buying Guide

It is possible to buy Parlour Palms from about 8in (20cm) high to almost mature height but the bigger the plant, the bigger the price! It is very satisfying — as well as cheaper — to buy a small plant and grow it to maturity yourself.

Trouble Shooter

Wilting or unhealthy plants mean you are not giving them the right attention; follow the watering, feeding and temperature directions given below and your plant should abound with health!

Yellowing leaves usually indicate the presence of red spider mite — look for their minute webs on the undersides of the leaves; spray with a malathion-based systemic insecticide.

Mealy bug and scale insect can occur; water in a malathion-based systemic insecticide three or four times a year to deter them or you can just spray to clear up an outbreak.

The Parlour Palm has an enduring appeal and is one of the best of the many types of palms you can grow in the home. *Chamaedorea elegans bella*, or *Neanthe bella*, is the most popular variety. It is a miniature Palm and so grows more slowly than some other varieties. The stems are slender but tough, forming a compact and graceful rosette of narrow, thin, feathery fronds. The main stem gradually forms from the short, older fronds as they die, the new leaves growing meanwhile from the centre of the crown. Flowers do appear on young plants, but although they are interesting, they are rather insignificant. Grow a Parlour Palm on its own so you can admire its shape or, when it's small, in a bottle garden, where it will look attractive grouped with other plants; in time your Palm will outgrow the bottle garden and then it can become a feature in its own right.

Spring and summer care

Repot your Parlour Palm only when it has become root-bound — usually every other year or so — in March. Use John Innes No 1 with some added decomposed, granulated leaf mould (three parts compost to one part leaf mould or granulated peat) and firm the plant in well.

Water your Parlour Palm freely during the warmer months but don't overdo it — make sure that the soil is kept constantly moist, perhaps watering it two or three times a week. Use a half-strength liquid fertiliser specially formulated for foliage plants and feed your Parlour Palm every two or three weeks. Temperatures can rise without harm, but if you can keep an even temperature of 65°F (18°C) your plant will be very happy!

Because the Parlour Palm is a forest plant it prefers filtered sun or bright but shaded light — certainly not direct, full sunlight as this will scorch the leaves. Provide draught-free ventilation and some humidity by mist spraying or sit the plant on a tray of wet pebbles.

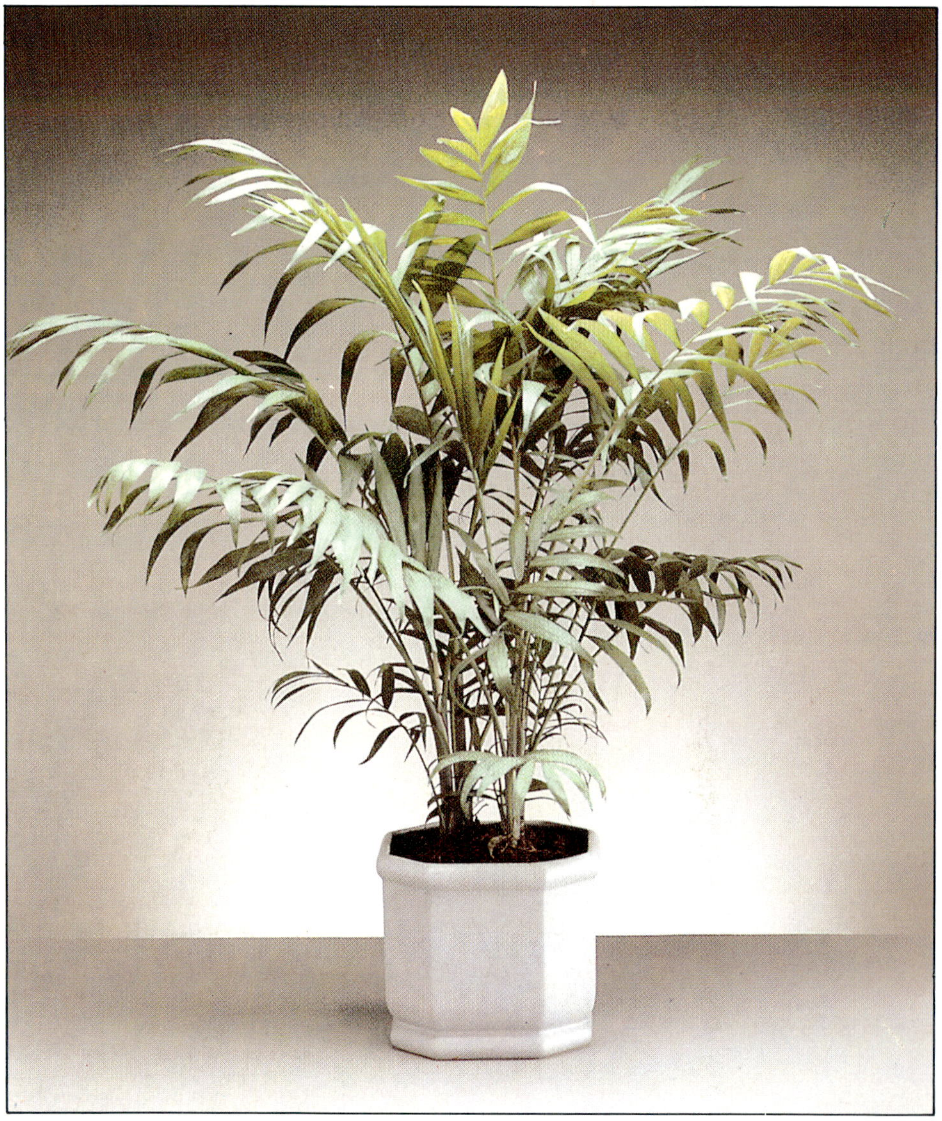

Chamaedorea elegans has graceful, elegant green fronds.

Autumn and winter care

Water your Parlour Palm much less in the winter months, just enough to keep the compost moist. Once a week should be sufficient, but this depends on the temperature of the room. Keep your Palm in bright but filtered light — don't keep it too far from a window for any length of time as it will become spindly. Keep it out of draughts and mist spray, especially if your plant is in a very warm room, to maintain humidity. Clean the leaves from time to time with a damp cloth to free them of dust; this will also help keep up humidity. It is

Species

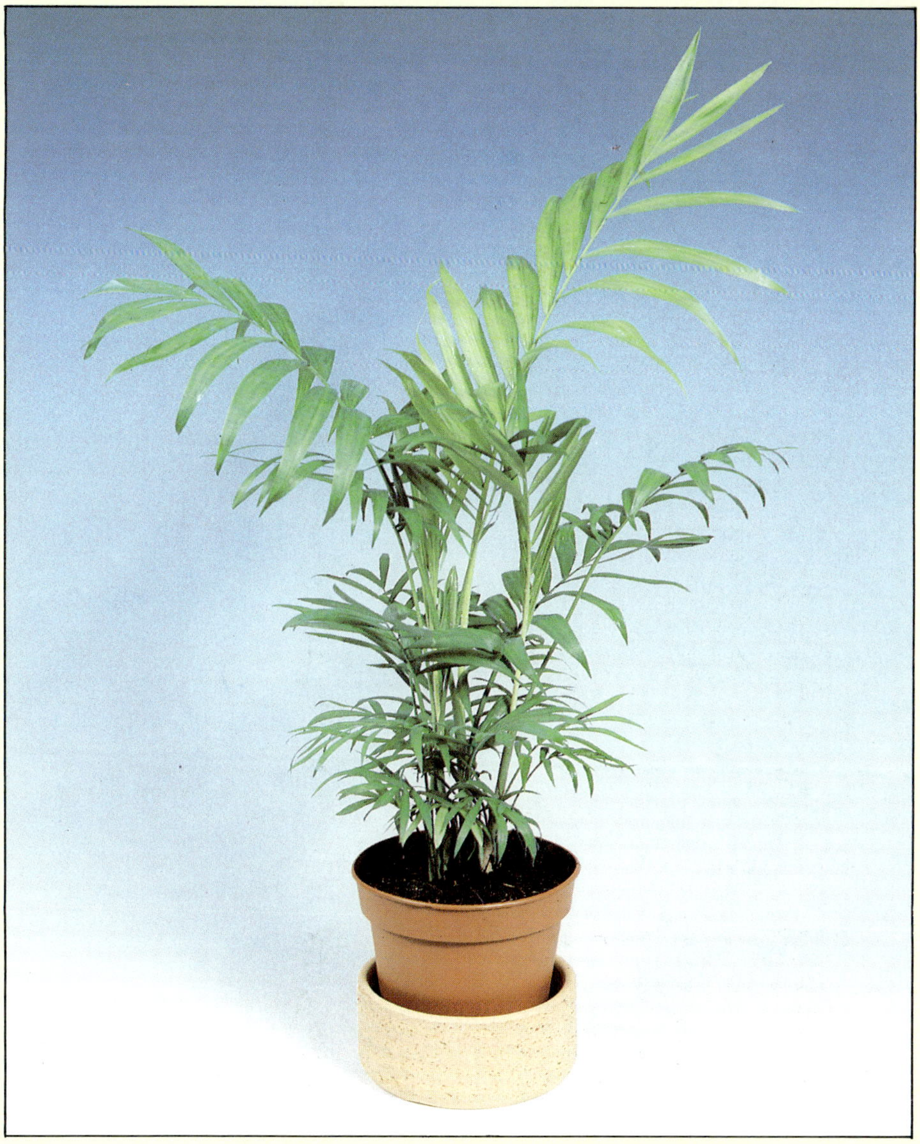

***Chamaedorea elegans* (or *Neanthe elegans*)**, from Mexico, grows fast for a Palm, reaching 8-9ft (2.4-2.7m) in six or eight years. It has a long slender stem, topped with clusters of lance-shaped leaves. The leaves can vary in length but are approximately 18-24in (46-61cm) long and about 1in (2.5cm) wide. The popular variety 'Bella' (or *Neanthe* 'Bella') differs in that it is a natural miniature and grows slowly. It originally came from the mountainous forest regions of eastern Guatemala and has tough, slender stems that form a compact, graceful rosette of narrow, thin, feathery fronds. Young plants produce insignificant flowers.

***C.metallica* (or *tenella*)**, from Mexico, develops a sturdy but slender trunk, about 2-3ft (0.6-0.9m) long, with the individual 'leaves' in each frond joined together, only separating at the tips to form a sort of toothed fan-shape. When it is young it flowers at the tip of a short stalk.

C.elatior, from the forest of Chiapas in south Mexico, makes a very good houseplant. Its stems are slender and reed-like and it has widely separated dark green leaves.

C.cataractarum, *left*, has been popular in the USA for many years and its popularity is spreading. It is a dwarf plant with a greenish, white-spotted trunk and grows steadily to produce a very compact shape with a heavily-leaved crown of dark green feathery fronds. Flowers appear on young plants and are followed by reddish berry-like fruits.

important to maintain humidity around your Palm's leaves, otherwise they brown.

Propagation

Using a moistened half peat, half sand compost, plant the seeds 1in (25mm) into the compost. Alternatively, just lay the seeds on the compost surface until they start to germinate and only then push them in — the latter option is probably the better as you can see instantly how they are progressing! Ensure that the seed tray is kept at a temperature of 75-80°F (24-26°C) and that the compost is kept constantly moist.

When they have grown their first set of leaves, pot the young Palms individually into 3in (7cm) pots of John Innes No 1 with some decomposed, granulated leaf mould mixed into it as before. Keep the seedlings in a temperature of at least 65°F (18°C), keep them moist and provide a humid atmosphere.

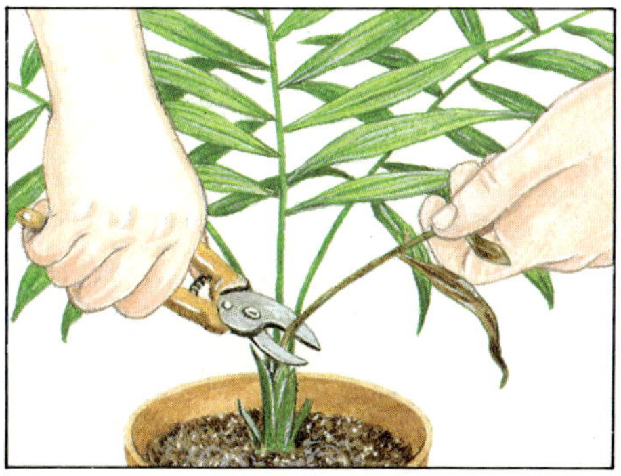

Tidying up your Palm: if a frond has turned brown and dry, simply clip it off with a pair of secateurs where the frond branches out from the stem. To avoid this happening again, stand your Palm on a tray of wet pebbles to provide more humidity.

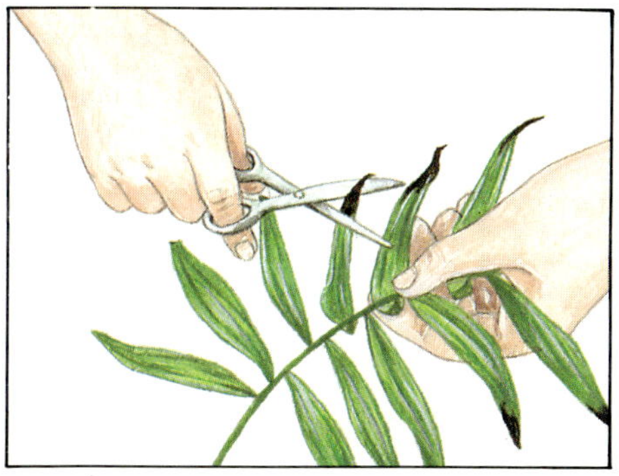

If only the tips of the fronds have shrivelled and browned, you don't need to remove the whole branch — just cut off the ends neatly with a pair of scissors. Stand your plant on a tray of wet pebbles and mist spray regularly to give it the humidity needed.

Chlorophytum

Family name: **Asphodelaceae**

Common names:
Spider Plant/ Ribbon Plant

Care Easy	**Height** 10in (25cm)	**Flower** All year
Light Semi shade	**Spread** 12in (30cm)	**Humidity** Mist spray regularly
Price Middle range	**Shape** Rosette	**Availability** Common
Temp. Min 45°F (7°C)	Ideal 65°F (18°C)	Max 75°F (24°C)

Spider Plants are enormously popular and there are lots of different, very attractive varieties to choose from. The foliage is the real focus of interest, since it has numerous, elegant, long, arching, green and white leaves. All Spider Plants produce little white flowers and some of the less common species have really lovely flowers that are a charming feature of the plant.

Chlorophytum comosum variegatum is the most common Spider Plant. Its graceful, arching, strap-like leaves grow out from a central rosette and have different thicknesses of white running the length of the leaves. Long, fleshy, whitish stalks sprout from the middle of the rosette, carrying the flowers from which little plantlets form. You can cut these off and pot them on separately or leave the plantlets attached to the plant and put the parent plant on a high level so the plantlets hang at different levels, creating a very attractive waterfall effect. Mature Spider Plants look very good in hanging baskets, especially if you leave the stems with plantlets to arch over the edge of the basket — they help to make a spectacularly dense display of coloured foliage providing a pretty variation on the waterfall idea. Alternatively, you can wind the plantlet stems round a hoop, making a lovely arch of little plantlets.

Spring and summer care

Summer temperatures can rise to 80°F (26°C) or higher without damaging your plant. Should there be a heatwave, however, do not leave your plant in direct sunlight; find it a bright but shaded location where there is a degree of humidity — a little sunshine though is good for it. Water freely from spring to late summer, adding a drop of liquid fertiliser to the water each time.

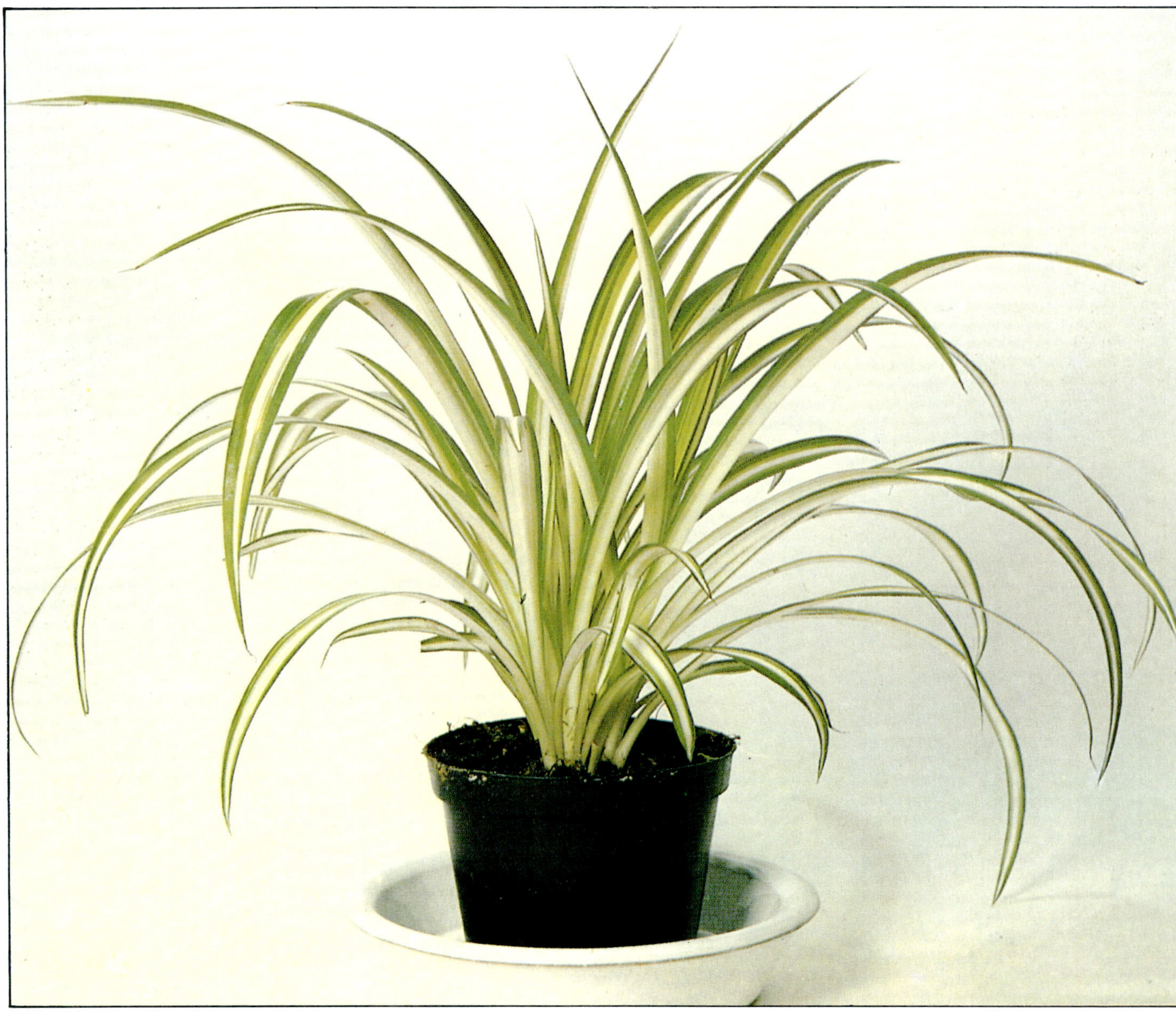

A Spider Plant has attractive arching fronds and looks good on its own or grouped with other plants.

Trouble Shooter

Unhealthy leaves and root rot may occur if you overwater your plant or let it stand in a pool of water for any length of time as this affects the fleshy root tubers; water more carefully and let the compost dry out between waterings.

Dry brown leaf tips are a sign that you haven't been watering enough; water freely during spring to late summer and moderately in autumn and winter.

Red spider mite or mealy bug occasionally attack Spider Plants; spray with a malation or systemic insecticide — the systemic spray will also act as a long-term deterrent.

Autumn and winter care

Do not let the temperature fall below 45°F (17°C), and provide non-draughty ventilation. Repot in late winter, using John Innes No 2 or a similar loam-based mixture. A pot-bound Spider Plant will perform the extraordinary feat of pushing itself out of its pot if it is left pot bound for any length of time as the roots just keep on growing. If you turn it out of its pot you will see a line where the compost ends and the roots kept growing! Spider Plants also grow widthways, so it is wise not to leave one pot-bound in a fragile pot for too long, as the pot may crack or shatter.

Give your plant the best possible light throughout the winter months — if you keep it too shaded, in time the leaves will lose their variegation altogether.

Propagation

Sow seeds in March and April, and pot them on when the seedlings are large enough to handle and then treat them in the same way as you would a mature Spider Plant. Plantlets can be grown very easily. Cut off plantlets or leave them attached to the parent plant and pot into John Innes No 2. If you have left them attached to the parent plant, sever them when they start sending roots of their own down into the soil. Plant them in John Innes No 2 and keep shaded until they have rooted, then treat them like mature Spider Plants.

It is quite a good idea to leave plantlets attached as the fleshy stem acts like an umbilical cord, sending on nutrients to the plantlets. Alternatively, you can pop plantlets into jam jars of water where they will quickly put out roots. Pot them on when they have lots of roots — usually within about six weeks — following the same procedure described before.

Since Spider Plants grow so quickly they can soon become pot-bound; either repot into a larger container or divide the plant carefully and plant the divisions.

Species

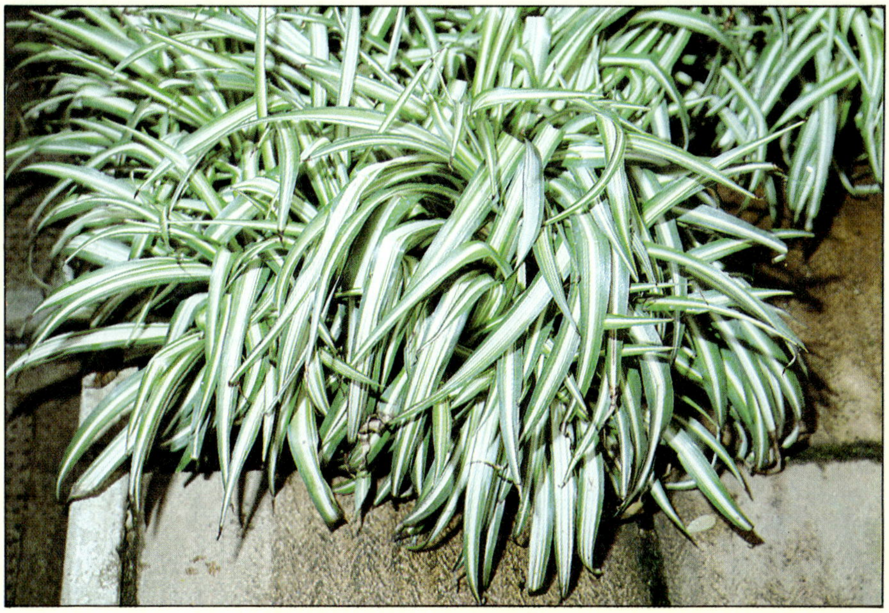

C.comosum comes from the mountainous forests in the Cape Province in South Africa. The leaves are green with decidedly wavy edges and grow from a rosette close to the ground. Long white stems grow out from the rosette and carry lots of small white flowers, from which tiny plantlets form once the petals have fallen off. The variegated variety is the popular Spider Plant and has the familiar, gracefully arching, strap-like leaves with bands of white in varying widths running the length of them. The long stems carry insignificant whitish flowers which produce plantlets.

***C.capense* (or *elatum*)** has an elongated rosette of deep green leaves and flowers at the tips of its long stems. Like the other species, it also produces plantlets. The variegated variety, *above*, has lovely green and white leaves.

C.undulatum from south-westerly parts of the Cape Province grows to about 1ft (0.3m). It has narrow, firm leaves with slightly roughened edges. A spike grows out from the centre of the rosette and carries attractive white flowers, about 2in (5cm) in diameter, with dark red prominent ridges running up the undersides of the petals.

C.laxum from Ghana and Northern Nigeria is a bushy little plant with strap-like, glossy green leaves springing up from a rosette. The leaves are daintily edged with white and at the ends of the stems little white flowers are clustered together.

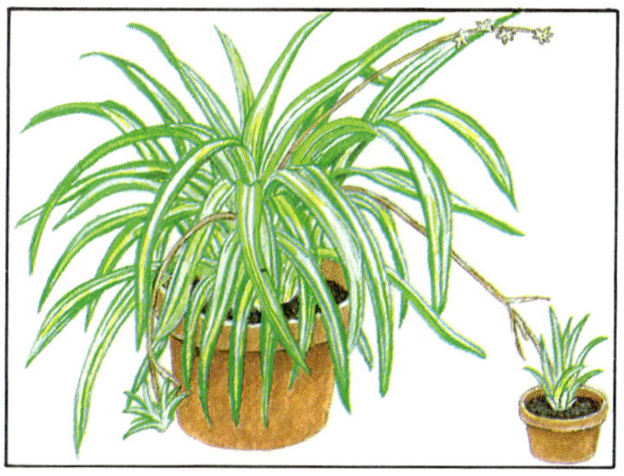

Propagating a Spider Plant: pot a plantlet; sever from parent when rooted.

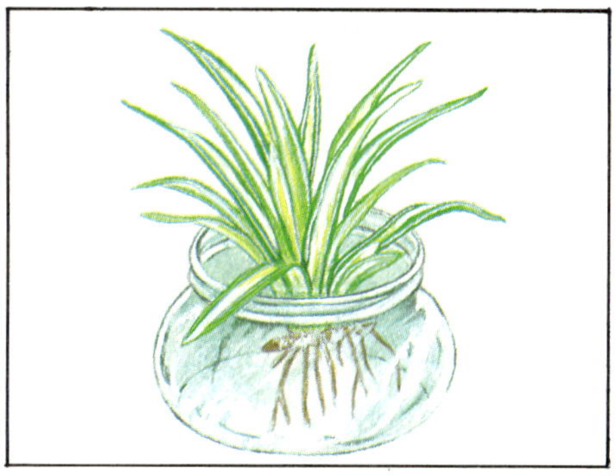

Or put a plantlet in a jar of water and pot when it has lots of healthy roots.

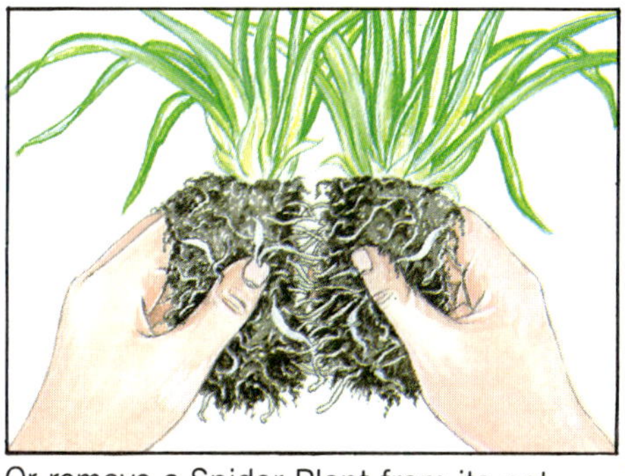

Or remove a Spider Plant from its pot and carefully expose the roots. Divide to make two plants and pot each separately.

Chrysanthemum

Family name: **Compositae**

Common name:
Pot Chrysanthemum

Care Easy	**Height** 12in (30cm)	**Flower** May-October
Light Bright indirect	**Spread** 12in (30cm)	**Humidity** Mist spray regularly
Price Cheap	**Shape** Shrubby	**Availability** Common
Temp. Min 40F (4°C)	Ideal 55°F (13°C)	Max 70°F (21°C)

The Chrysanthemum family encompasses so many different types of plant and flower that to describe even a proportion of the popular kinds would take a long time. However, it is the Pot Chrysanthemum that is grown as a houseplant — others are only seen as cut flowers in the home as they need patient attention in greenhouse conditions.

Pot Chrysanthemums are in the shops all year round, but they are at their best in autumn and winter. Although it is only temporarily in the home, the Pot Chrysanthemum has won enormous popularity in the past few years because it's so easy to grow and can be relied on to flower attractively. Commercial growers treat their Chrysanthemums with a special dwarfing chemical that restricts their growth, so they are always nice and compact plants with even-sized flowers that all open at much the same time — which makes them ideal when you want to cheer up a room with a burst of colour.

Chrysanthemum flowers are either single or double and come particularly in autumnal colours, like yellow, orange, red, rust, pink and white. One of the parents of the Pot Chrysanthemum, *C.morifolium*, has been grown in China and Japan for at least 3,000 years! It is a branching perennial that grows to 3ft (0.9m) or so. But when it's grown as a Pot Chrysanthemum it is much smaller — anything from about 12-18in (30-46cm) — and is usually treated as an annual and thrown away after flowering. It is possible to keep a Pot Chrysanthemum to grow on and flower in future years, but you'll have to grow it outside in the garden, as it will revert to its proper height and be too unwieldy to have in the house. Its flowers will not be such good quality.

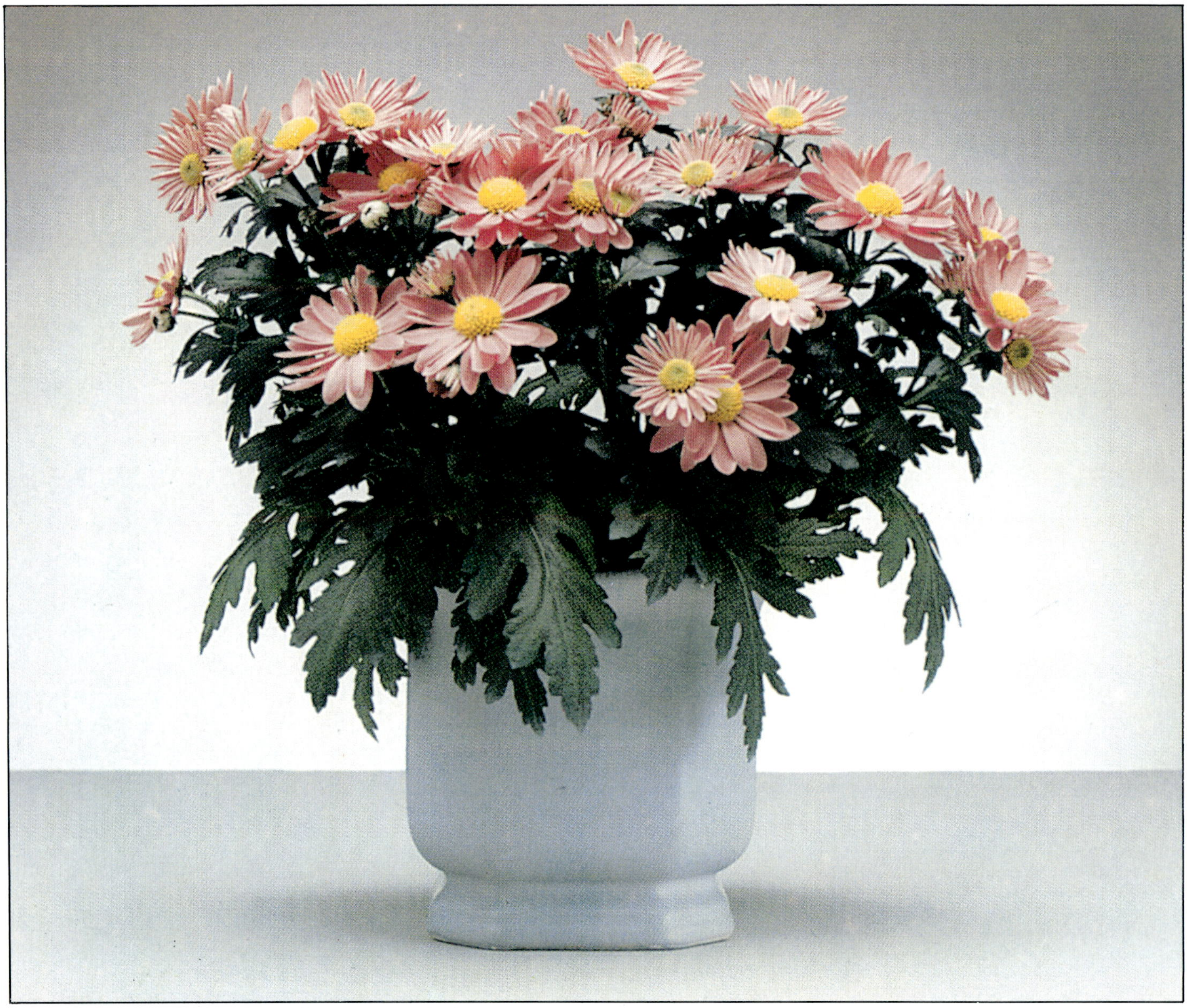

A Pot Chrysanthemum blooms in autumn and winter and is easy to grow successfully. This one has lots of colourful single flowers.

Trouble Shooter

Chrysanthemums rarely suffer from plant diseases but they can be prone to greenfly and whitefly, which particularly like juicy young leaves and leave a sticky coating on the foliage. Red spider mite spin tiny webs between the leaves which make them turn yellow; thrips are tiny black insects that jump from leaf to leaf, leaving silvery streaks that spot and distort the flowers. All these bugs can be eliminated fairly easily; as soon as you see any signs of trouble, apply a fine spray insecticide containing pyrethrum or malathion, or spray or water in a systemic insecticide that contains either of these.

Spring and summer care

In the summer, if you have a potted plant still in bloom, keep it cool and away from excessive sun. Make sure that it's constantly moist and has a good supply of fresh air with plenty of humidity. When flowering is over either throw the plant away or put it in the garden.

When growing Chrysanthemums from cuttings or seeds the most important element is a good growing medium. The compost should retain moisture but also drain well; John Innes No 1 is excellent for the first potting on while the plant is young; subsequently you will need to add in a little extra peat. Don't feed your plant until it starts to grow buds, then use a liquid fertiliser every three weeks or so.

Autumn and winter care

Pot Chysanthemums normally flower for eight to ten weeks from late autumn to early spring, but this also depends on where you keep your plant. It will be happiest in bright filtered light, not direct sunlight, and where it can get plenty of air. Give your plant a temperature around 55-65°F (13-18°C). Don't give the plant too much shade or the buds are unlikely to open. Water regularly to keep the compost constantly moist and mist spray your plant every few days so the leaves and flowers are fresh — especially if the plant is kept in a heated room. Your plant will flower for much longer if you keep it in a cool room. It won't need feeding unless you are planning to keep the plant for outdoor flowering.

When you are growing your plants from cuttings or seeds, temperature is important — as is the amount of light. Oddly-shaped flowers can occur if the temperature is above 60°F (15°C) and the light not bright enough. Generally, Chrysanthemums prefer cool conditions — from 40-50°F (4-10°C) — and, given these, they will live longer and will produce more flowers of better quality — if it is too warm the flowers die quickly.

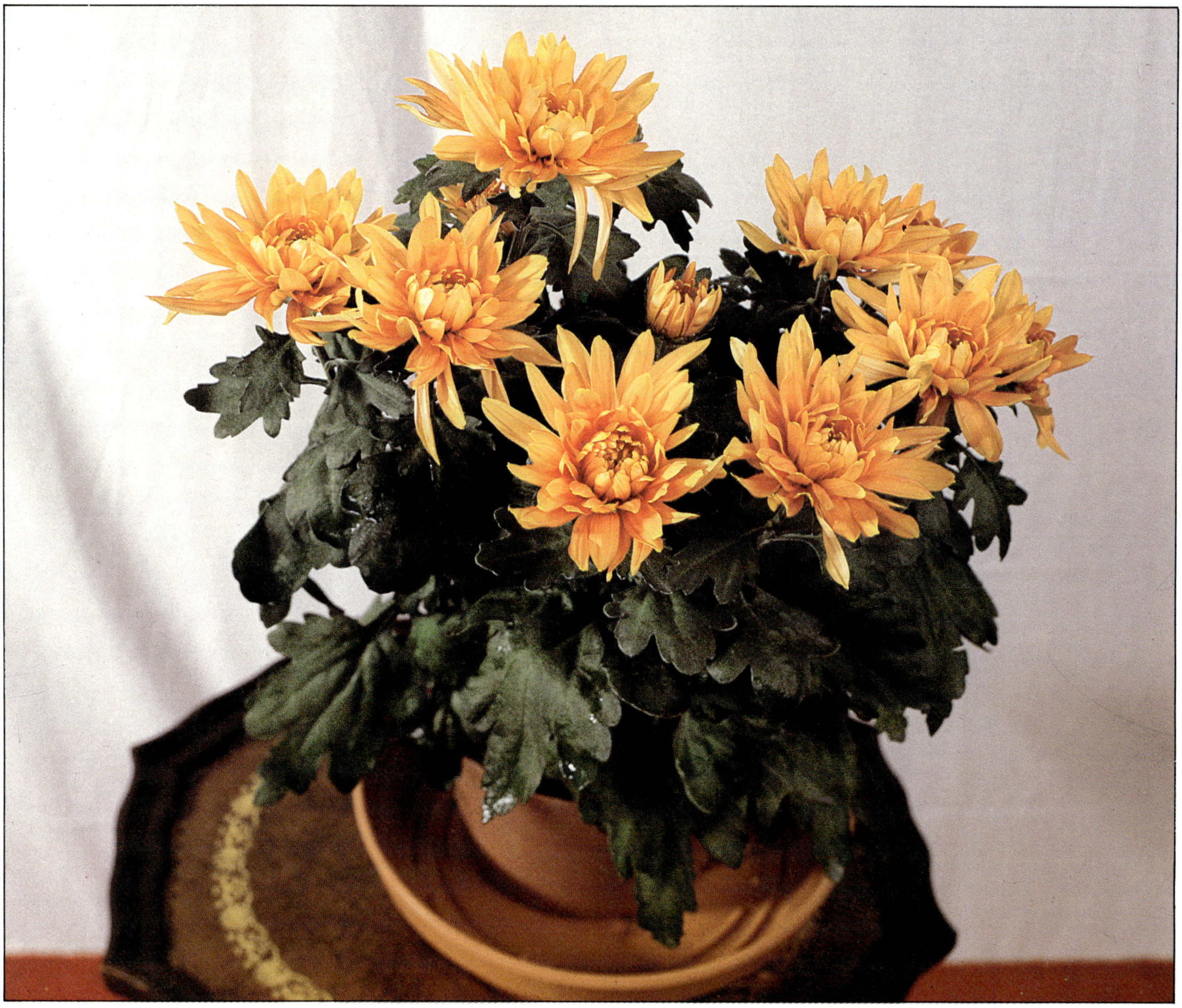

Most Pot Chrysanthemums have double flowers and can be found in a wide range of autumnal colours.

Species

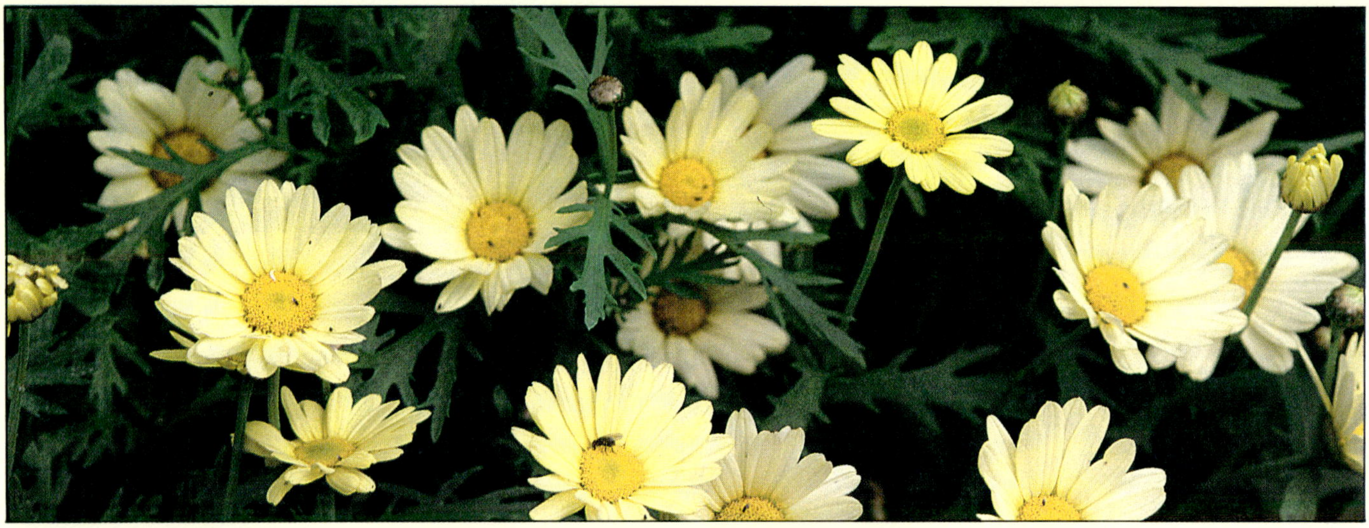

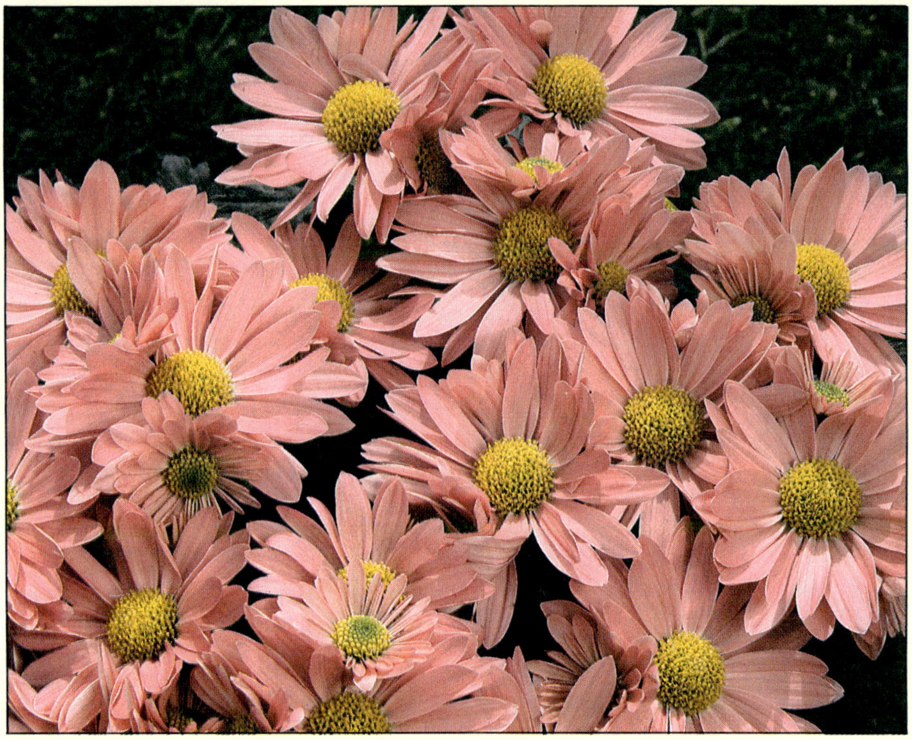

Chrysanthemum indicum, from China, is the parent of a lot of the 'Japanese' varieties used for exhibitions as well as being the parent of the many houseplants.

C.frutescens, *above*, is an annual from the Canary Islands, and produces masses of very pretty white or yellow flowers in summer when it is sold as a Pot Chrysanthemum. A pink variety is also available. It is a vigorous growing plant reaching up to 3ft (0.9m) high, so you will need to control it carefully — when it is sold flowering it is usually about 18in (46cm) high. Prune from time to time to keep it reasonably compact.

C.morifolium, *left*, from China and Japan, is a perennial, branching plant that can reach heights of 3ft (0.9m) or more, but when sold as a Pot Chrysanthemum it is about 12in (30cm) high. The leaves are soft, slightly hairy, strongly scented and grey-green. It flowers in late autumn and early winter but is induced to flower all year round by commercial growers. The flowers (all grown as cut flowers) come in all kinds of exotic colours and shapes — incurved, pompons, decoratives, singles, Japanese, anemones and cascades.

Propagation

Pot Chrysanthemums are best bought fresh each year. Cuttings and seeds root and grow easily, but they will grow into big plants even when taken from a small Chrysanthemum. This is because the cuttings won't have been treated with dwarfing compound.

Take cuttings in early spring with a heel of bark, dip the cut end in hormone rooting powder, and insert into pots of John Innes No 1. Keep the compost moist and in a temperature of 50-55°F (10-13°C).

When the cuttings root, pot each one singly into a 3in (7cm) pot of John Innes No 1. Move each plant to a slightly bigger pot as soon as the current pot is full of roots, until it's large enough to treat as a mature plant.

Sow seeds in a fairly light compost in March and keep in a temperature of 65°F (18°C). Pot up the seedlings individually when they are large enough to handle. Keep the seedlings constantly moist and gradually reduce the temperature to about 60°F (16°C) — they should be about 3-5in (7-13cm) tall by this time. Provide filtered light, fresh air and humidity.

As the plants grow, keep them well watered and in a position where they get plenty of fresh air. The young plants do not need to be fed until buds begin to form.

Buying Guide

When buying a Chrysanthemum, look at the leaves; they should be a fresh, healthy green — any yellow or decaying leaves are a sure sign of an unhealthy plant. Choose a plant with a nice compact shape as it is more likely to flower evenly. Always buy a plant with buds already showing colour, as sometimes they can fail to open if they are too tightly shut.

Cissus

Family name: **Vitaceae**

Common name: **Kangaroo Vine**

Care Straight-forward	**Height** 1-6ft (0.3-1.8m)	**Flower** None
Light Shaded	**Spread** 1-3ft (0.3-0.9m)	**Humidity** Mist spray regularly
Price Middle range	**Shape** Climbing	**Availability** Common

Temp.	Min	Ideal	Max
	45°F (7°C)	65°F (24°C)	85°F (30°C)

A native plant of Australasia, Africa, Asia and the Americas, the Cissus is a lovely climber with curly tendrils that it uses to anchor itself as it climbs. The Cissus is a popular and adaptable houseplant that is ideal for shady and cool positions. Some types have almost grotesque, thick trunks and are in fact a type of succulent. The most popular Cissus, *Cissus antarctica*, is a very handsome and vigorous plant with bright green, glossy, heart-shaped leaves carried in profusion on narrow, wiry stems. Mature plants produce inedible black fruits after flowering, but they are most unlikely to flower in the home.

The species *C. discolor* has exotic, decorative leaves with silvery-white variegations of rich violet and purplish-red, surrounded with a delicate shade of green. It is far more demanding than the others though, needing high temperatures and humidity. There are a number of species and varieties that have differently shaped leaves, colouring and so on, but all climb and are fairly easy to look after.

Spring and summer care

If you have a young plant give it a support to climb up or let it trail naturally. Carefully push a cane or two into the compost (trying not to damage the roots), deep enough to provide a secure framework to keep your plant upright. Train your Cissus by hanging the tendrils on the canes or tying the branches neatly to them to form an attractive shape. Be careful not to strangle the stems by tying the string too tightly. When your plant is mature and growing rapidly, you will need to replace the original canes with longer ones or a lattice-like frame for the more numerous branches to cling to.

Late spring is the best time to give your Cissus a tidying prune, but a vigorous plant may well need to be trimmed at other times during the growing season. Your Cissus will enjoy a temperature of around 65-75°F (18-24°C) but if you have a *C.discolor* it needs higher temperatures of 80-85°F (27-30°C), otherwise it loses its colourful leaves.

Late March to late August is the growing season; during this time, water freely, keeping the soil constantly moist, but no wetter as the roots can easily rot. Feed with liquid fertiliser every two to three weeks, watering it into the soil. Give your plant plenty of fresh air and humidity with regular mist spraying or, better still, sit your plant on a tray of wet pebbles to provide constant humidity.

Autumn and winter care

Winter care varies slightly from one species to another. For most a cool atmosphere of 40-45°F (4-7°C) is sufficient. *C.discolor* is slightly more demanding, requiring a minimum ideal temperature of 55°F (13°C). If this temperature is not maintained the plant will suffer and the leaves will lose their colour and fall. This species also needs good light — bad light will make its colour fade, but on the other hand, full sunlight will scorch it. The other types of Cissus mentioned will live in shady places without damage.

Water your plant moderately in winter, just enough to stop it drying out; it will also appreciate an occasional light mist spray. Do not feed from September until March to give your Cissus a rest; this will help it to grow healthily and vigorously in the spring.

Trouble Shooter

Drooping or wilting leaves show that it is too cold for your Cissus; move it to a warmer part of the house.

Damaged and scarred leaves are caused by overwatering; let the plant dry out for a short while and then water just enough to keep it moist.

Sluggish growth is the result of the plant not getting the nutrients it needs — this plant grows so vigorously it quickly exhausts the supplies in the soil; feed regularly with liquid fertiliser.

Wilting, followed by brown and falling leaves, indicates overexposure to sun or heat; provide light shade and suitable temperatures (*C.discolor* needs more heat than *C.antarctica*).

A six or seven year old Cissus will sometimes collapse suddenly and die; the cause is simply old age.

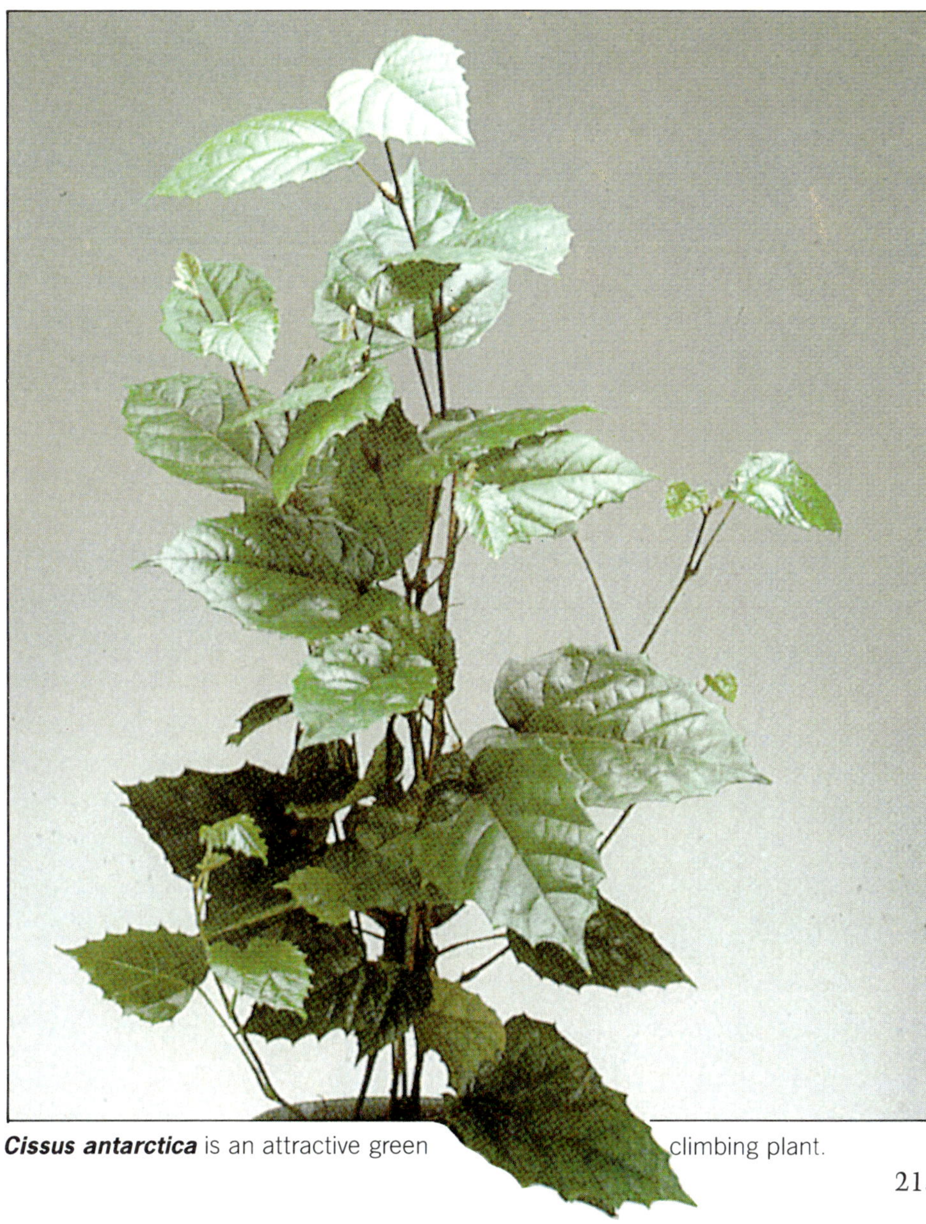

Cissus antarctica is an attractive green climbing plant.

Species

Cissus antarctica, from New South Wales in Australia, has masses of glossy, dark green, heart-shaped leaves about 4in (10cm) long and 2in (5cm) across, with light brown veins. It is a vigorous climber and mature plants can produce little black inedible fruits after flowering, but this is rare indoors.

C.discolor, the Begonia Vine, *right*, from Java and Cambodia, looks very like *Begonia Rex*. Its leaves are about 6in (15cm) long and seem quilted with sunken green veins and silvery-white raised ridges with variegations in violet, purplish-red and green. The undersides of the leaves are a uniform maroon-red. It is a sturdy climber but needs a temperature of 70°F (21°C) and high humidity to maintain its colourful foliage. Put it in a large container and let it grow freely. It rapidly forms a dense column of foliage about 4-6ft (1.2-1.8m) high. Overwatering can damage the leaves.

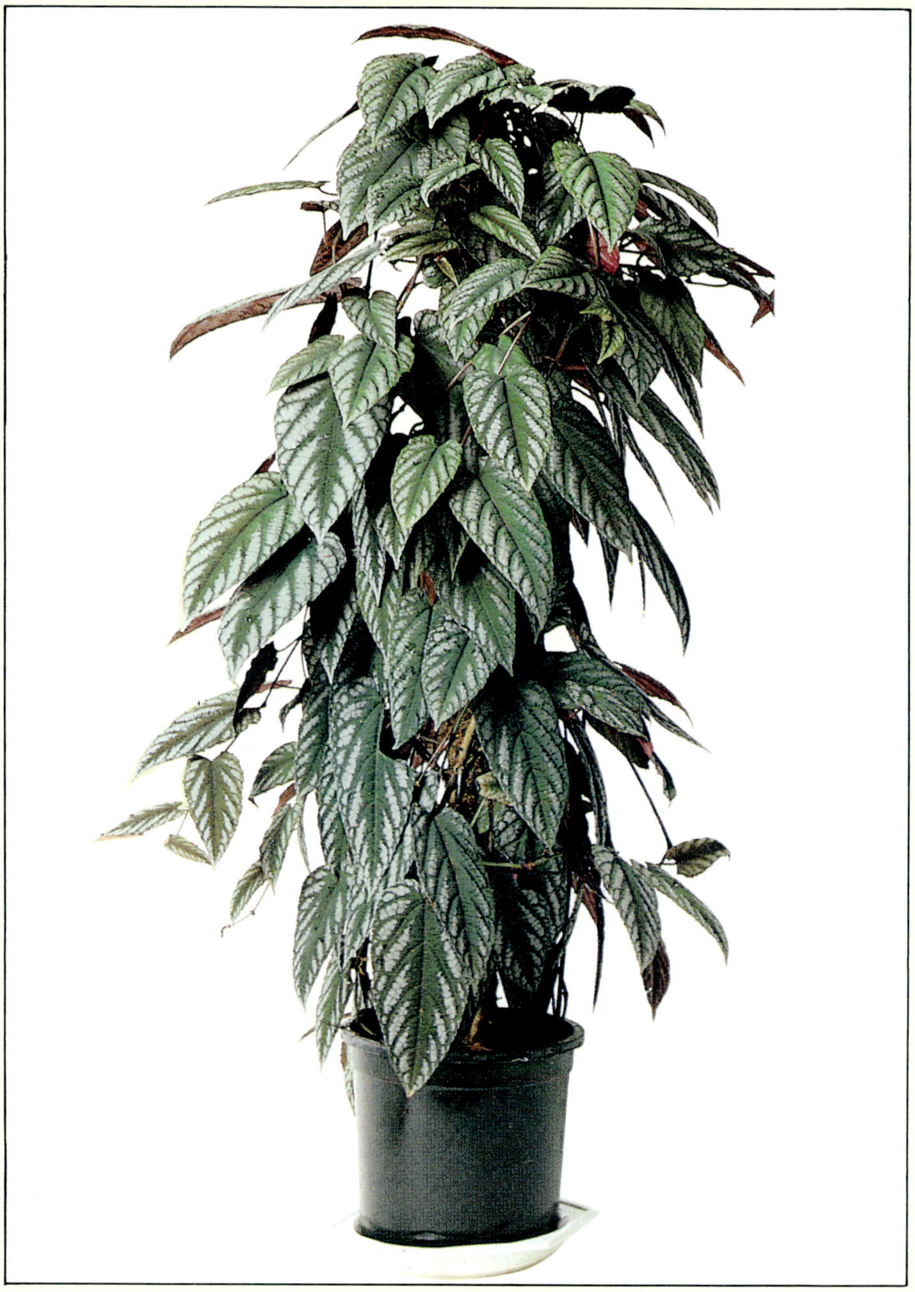

C.rhombifolia **(or *Rhoicissus rhomboides*)**, the Grape Ivy, from South America and the West Indies, has long, brown, hairy branches with lots of clinging tendrils and dark green, velvety, three-lobed leaves. Each lobe is slightly diamond-shaped. 'Mandaiana', although slightly rarer, is slightly easier to grow. Its stems are thick and sturdy, with grape-shaped glossy, dark green, quite fleshy and firm leaves. It is a very erect plant, compact, densely leaved and elegant.

C.quadrangularis, from Somalia and East Africa, is a succulent climber with lots of tendrils to secure it as it climbs. It has unusual stems that have four prominent ribs running almost the complete length of the stems and branches. The leaves are heart-shaped, fleshy, with three lobes and coarsely serrated edges.

C.hypoglauca, from Australia, is a handsome, shrubby climber with lots of tendrils and can reach heights of 6ft (1.8m) or more. Its leaves are brownish-green, thick and leathery, and are divided into five, glossy, toothed leaflets.

Propagation

Take 2-3in (5-7cm) long cuttings of young shoots with a heel in late spring. Dip the cut ends in hormone rooting powder and insert them into a half sand and half granulated peat compost. Keep the compost moist, the atmosphere humid and the temperature at about 75-80°F (24-26°C) until they root, which should be in two to three weeks. A propagator will speed this up as it provides a constant ideal temperature, but a seed tray in a clear polythene bag on a warm windowsill should have the same effect. When the cuttings have rooted, pot them on using John Innes No 2 compost. Keep them shaded, moist and in a good, airy position and they will grow very rapidly.

Certain rarer species can be obtained as seed from specialist seedsmen. The seeds are large and need to be sown ¼in (6mm) deep in half peat, half sand compost, covered with a layer of sharp sand. Treat them in the same way as cuttings and the seeds will germinate in five to six weeks. When they are larger, pot up in John Innes No 2.

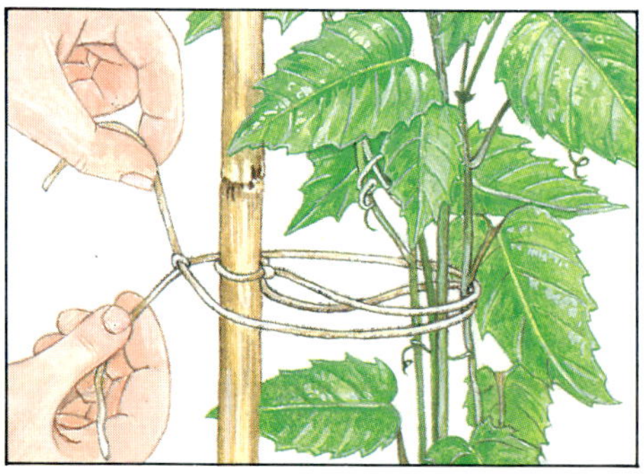

Training your Cissus, *right*. Tie the stems loosely but firmly to a sturdy cane.

Citrus

Family name: **Rutaceae**

Common name: **Orange/Lemon**

Care Straight-forward	**Height** 2ft (0.6m)	**Flower** June-Sept
Light Sun/bright light	**Spread** 1½ft (0.4m)	**Humidity** Mist spray regularly
Price Expensive	**Shape** Shrub-like tree	**Availability** Garden centres

Temp. Min 55°F (13°C) Ideal 70°F (21°C) Max 80°F (27°C)

The Orange and Lemon are exotic plants, yet they are easy to grow and look after in the home. In addition, they may bear fruit, which will add a splash of colour to the room, although most are purely decorative as they tend to be a little too acid-tasting. The Orange and Lemon are large-growing shrubby trees with lots of beautiful dark green, shiny leaves.

Citrus mitis, the most commonly grown Citrus, is a small shrub-like tree, rarely growing more than 2ft (0.6m) or so tall. In summer or, if the weather is warm enough, throughout the year, the Citrus produces fragrant, attractive white flowers. These are followed by fruits about 1½in (4cm) across that start green and gradually turn orange as they ripen. A Citrus grows slowly but flowers and fruits even when it is young. Sit your plant in a bright spot, water and feed it regularly and you should have a healthy, very handsome plant for many years.

Spring and summer care

Repot in early spring using a loam-based compost, such as John Innes No 2. Make sure the compost drains well by putting a 1-2in (3-5cm) layer of small pebbles or bits of broken clay pot into the bottom of the container. This also makes the plant less likely to tip over in a sudden gust of wind when you put it outside.

Summer is normally the Orange's flowering period, during which time it may well need to be watered every day. Be careful, though, not to overwater as it cannot stand having 'wet feet'.

Feed every 10-14 days with a liquid fertiliser — this is especially important when the flowers appear. Mist spray regularly on the hottest days to stop the leaves drying out.

As summer warmth becomes reliable, stand your plant outside to get plenty of fresh air and sunshine.

Autumn and winter care

The Orange must be coddled slightly in the winter. Keep it in a temperature as near to 55°F (13°C) as possible and water sparingly from October through to March. Place it in the best light and make sure that it is not exposed to any cold draughts. The Orange also dislikes fumes and smoke.

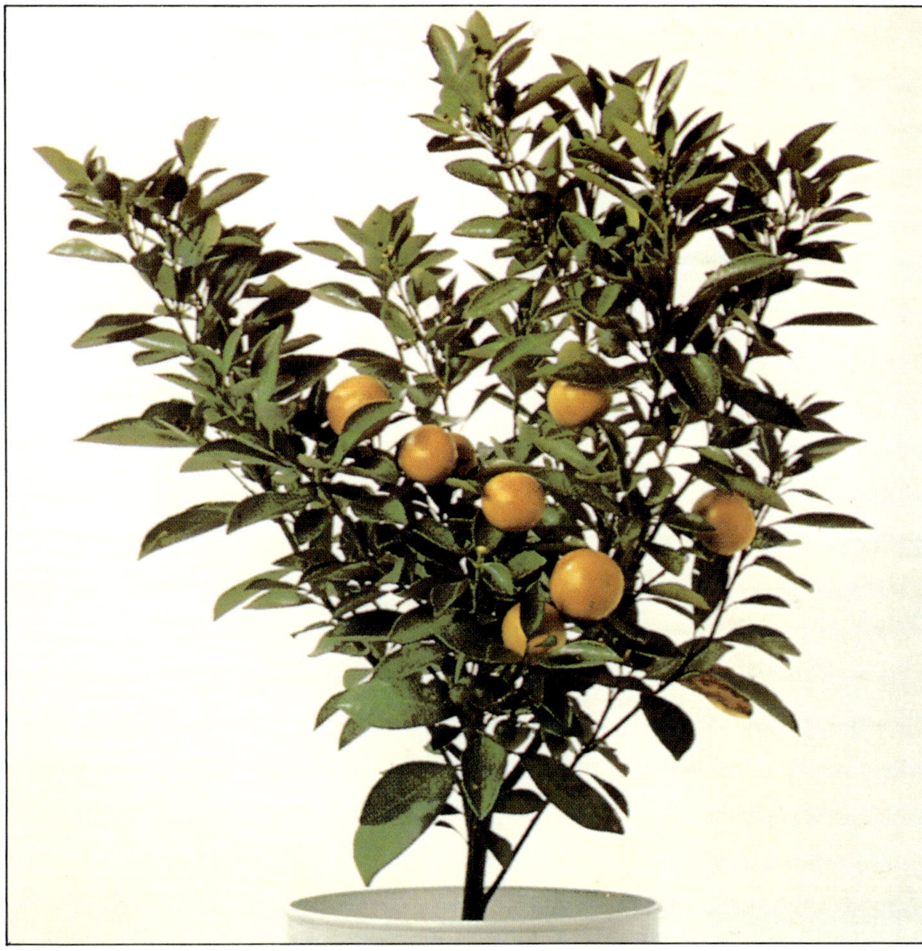

A Calamondin Orange will produce fruit while it is still quite young.

Propagation

You can grow an Orange tree from seed but it will be, at best, several years before it flowers or bears fruits.

Sow seeds in John Innes Seed Compost in March and keep at a temperature of 61°F (16°C). When the seedlings are large enough to handle, pot them on into John Innes No 2, keeping them at the same temperature, and pot on into gradually larger pots as they grow.

Take cuttings in June or July for quicker results. Dip the cut ends in hormone rooting powder, plant in John Innes No 2 and firm the compost around each cutting. Keep the cuttings just moist and slightly shaded from full sun, provide a temperature of 65-70°F (18-21°C) and give them plenty of fresh air. The cuttings should root within six weeks and then they can be potted up singly in John Innes No 2.

Species

Citrus mitis, the Calamondin Orange, comes from the Philippines.It is a small, shrubby tree with glossy, dark green, oval, leathery leaves and grows no higher than about 2ft (0.6m) tall. Its fragrant white flowers are followed by fruits that start dark green and ripen to a true orange.

C.limon, the Lemon, *right*, makes a very good houseplant. It has large, dark green oval, leathery leaves and highly scented flowers in spring and early summer. Fruits follow the flowers and are very dark green at first, taking several months to ripen.

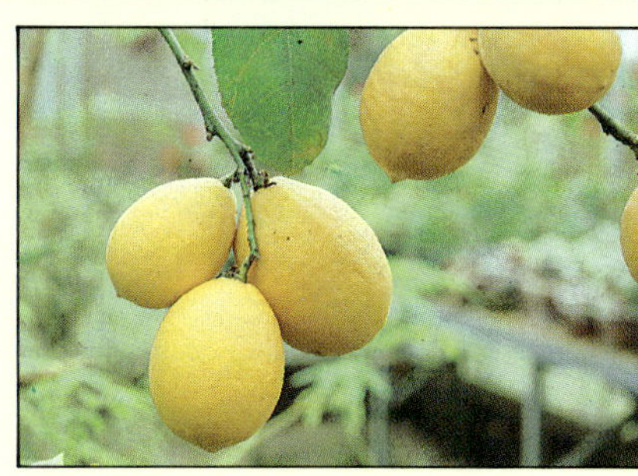

C.taitensis, the Otaheite Orange, from China, is a dwarf plant with lots of dark green leaves and waxy, pinkish white flowers that have a beautiful scent. After the flowers die, fruits develop but are, unfortunately, too acid to eat.

Clivia

Family name: **Amaryllidaceae**

Common name: **Kaffir Lily**

Care Easy	**Height** 18in (45cm)	**Flower** March-August
Light Bright	**Spread** 4ft (1.2m)	**Humidity** Occasional mist spray
Price Expensive	**Shape** Fan-shaped	**Availability** Garden centres
Temp. Min 45°F (7°C)	Ideal 65°F (18°C)	Max 75°F (24°C)

The Kaffir Lily has been an enormously popular houseplant for many years as its magnificent heads of orange flowers make it a particularly eye-catching plant. The thick, fleshy, strap-like leaves grow in a most unusual way by arching out and overlapping each other at the base from either side, with new leaves sprouting from the centre to form a flat, fan-like shape. In early spring a thick flower stalk grows, slightly off-centre, and in a few weeks a pompon head of pretty, slightly tubular flowers in shades of orangey-red opens up. More rarely the flowers are apricot or pale yellow. These individual flowers only last a few days, but dead flowers are soon replaced with fresh ones for several weeks.

The Kaffir Lily produces very large roots and will soon fill its pot, but it flowers better when it is in this state. Also, the plant regularly develops offsets (baby plants) around the base. These develop into full-size plants which, if left in place, will turn your Kaffir Lily into a large clump of dark green leaves and make it a particularly spectacular sight when in flower.

Spring and summer care

Only repot your plant once every three or four years when it has outgrown its pot and the surface compost is covered in roots. Use John Innes No 3 and transplant into a heavy pot, so that your plant is less likely to tip over when it is mature.

Summer temperatures of 70°F (21°C) or so will not harm your plant so long as it is not left in direct sun; place it where it can receive bright light for part of the day.

Water your Kaffir Lily freely all through the summer until September, then water less so that the soil is kept only just moist until the flower buds develop. During the growing season, feed with a liquid fertiliser every 14

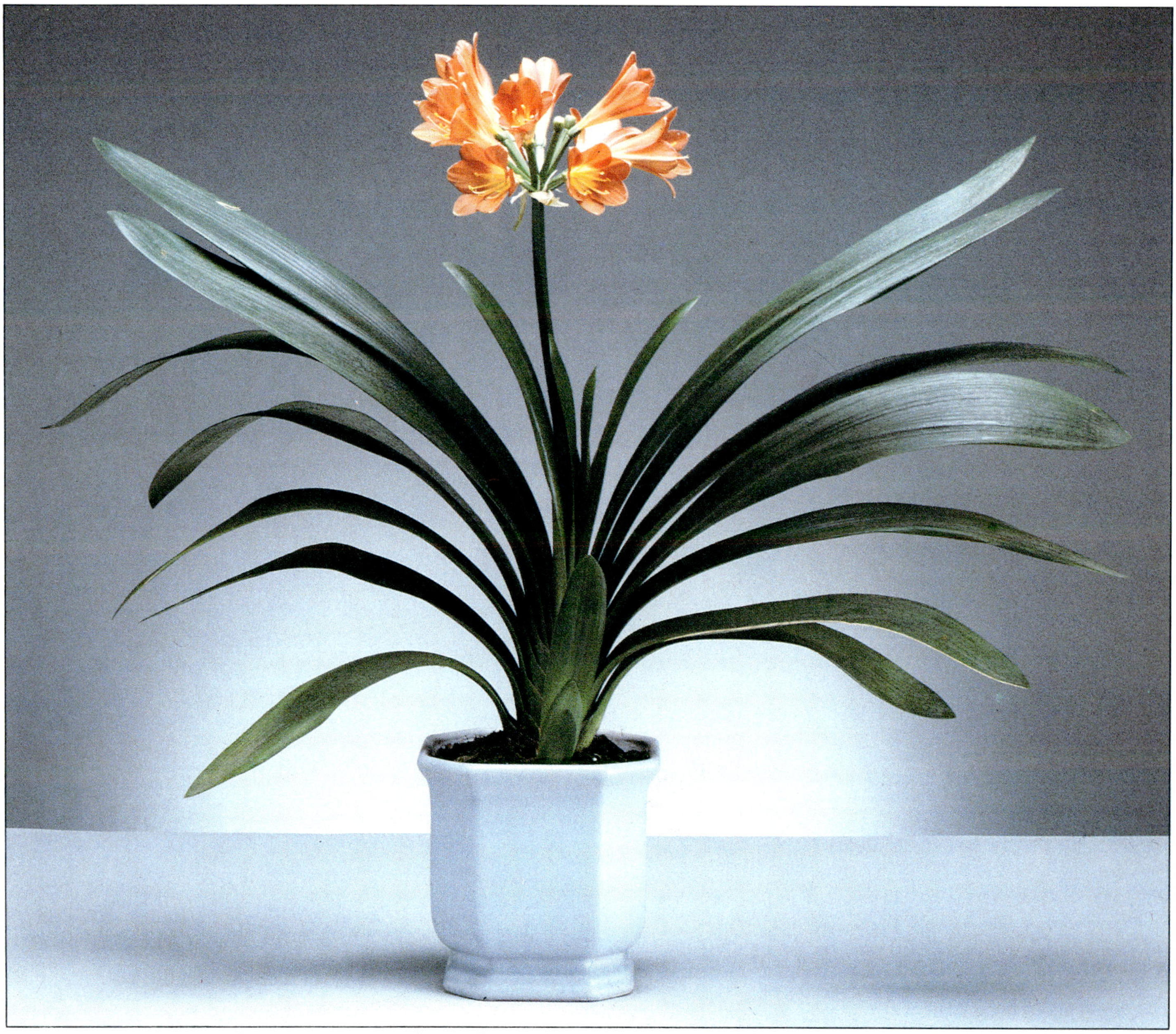

Clivia miniata has beautiful trumpet-shaped flowers from early spring until August.

days or so — this will give the plant the strength it needs to flower the following spring. Cut off the dead flower heads after flowering is over.

Autumn and winter care

Keep your plant cool in early winter at a temperature of about 50°F (10°C). The temperature can rise as your plant develops flower buds in February, but don't let the temperature climb above 65°F (18°C) or flowering will be forced and over too quickly.

At this time try to keep your plant in a constant temperature of 60°F (15°C). Water it regularly while the flowers continue and through the growing season that follows immediately afterwards. Carefully pull off the flower stalk when flowering finishes.

For the rest of spring and summer put your plant in a really well-lit spot, but not in direct sunlight, which can scorch the leaves.

Propagation

Your plant will look more spectacular if you leave it alone to grow into a clump, but it is easy to propagate from offsets if you wish to.

At the same time as repotting in February, carefully remove the offsets from the parent plant with a sharp knife. Try not to disturb the roots more than you have to. Plant each offset into a 3-5in (7-13cm) pot of John Innes No 3 with a little added peat and sharp sand. Keep the soil just moist and put the pot out of direct sunlight, giving the offsets a little more light once they have rooted. When established, treat the offsets as mature plants and they should flower the following year.

Alternatively, sow seeds in March into seed compost with a little added sharp sand and keep in a temperature of 70°F (21°C). Water enough to keep the compost just moist. It will be about eight years before your seedlings are mature enough to flower.

Trouble Shooter

Shrivelling or off-colour leaves appear when you underwater or overwater; if the compost feels bone dry when you rub it between your fingers, water it moderately and regularly. If the compost clumps together and is wet when you rub it between your fingers, let it dry out almost completely and water less than you have been but regularly from then on.

Fluffy white blobs underneath the leaves or at the leaf joints are mealy bugs; wipe them away with a cloth or paintbrush dipped in methylated spirits; repeat after a week if necessary.

Species

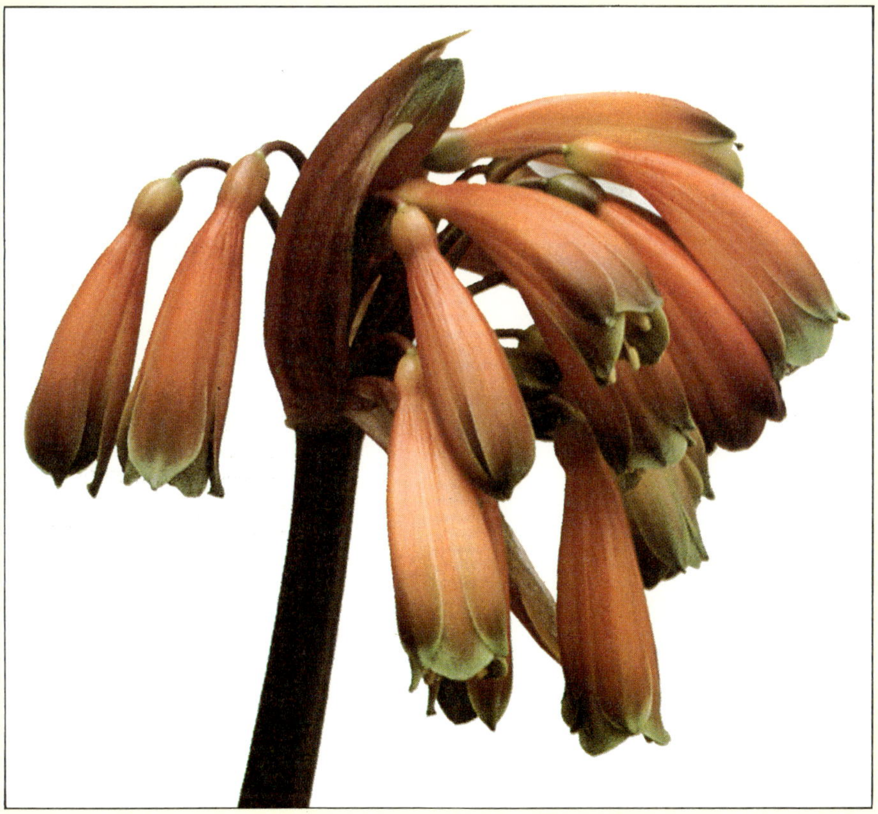

Clivia miniata, the Kaffir Lily, comes from the Transvaal and Natal in South Africa and has thick, fleshy, dark green, strap-like leaves about 2ft (0.6m) long that gently arch out from each side of the plant to form a spreading fan-shape. A flower stem grows out slightly off-centre from under the leaves, often reaching 18-24in (45-60cm) long, with a pompon of apricot, trumpet-shaped flowers at the top.

C.nobilis, *above*, is a South African plant that grows 12-18in (30-45cm) tall. Its reddish flowers are tipped with green and hang down from the flower spike and last from late April until July.

C.gardenii, from the bush and wooded areas of the Transvaal and Natal, often has 12 or more 2ft (0.6m) long leaves that grow ladder-like from the bulb. A short stout stalk sprouts from the centre of the plant and several yellowish-orange flowers tipped with green hang in a halo round the top in May.

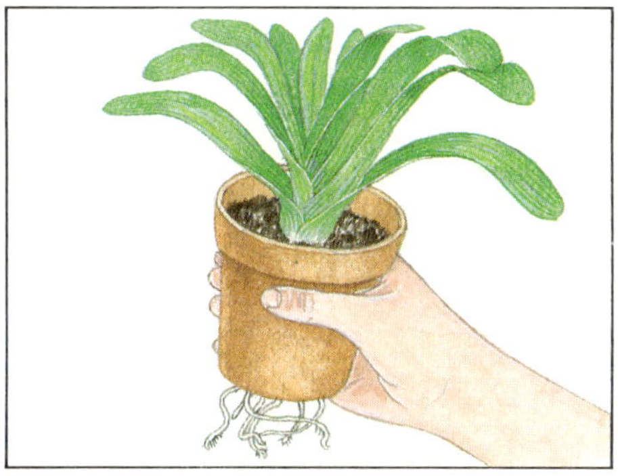

Repotting your Kaffir Lily: repot only when the roots fill the container.

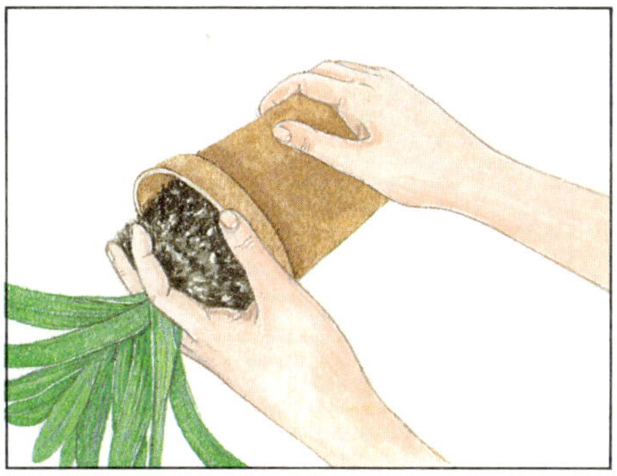

Carefully knock the plant out of its pot, supporting the bulb in one hand.

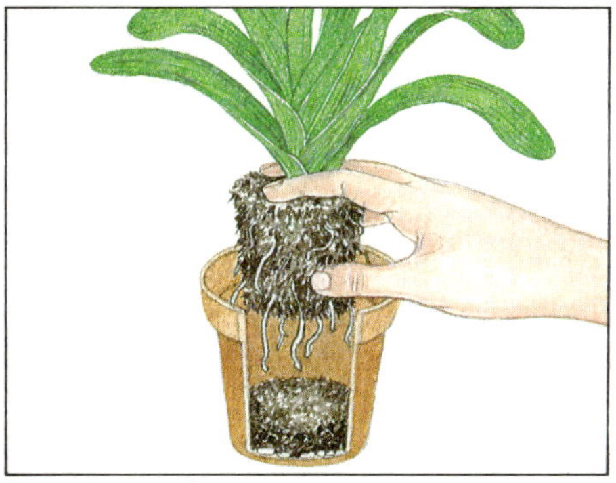

Put a layer of compost in a pot 1in (2cm) larger than the rootball; pop in the plant and gently firm more compost around the side.

Codiaeum

Family name: **Euphorbiaceae**

Common names:
Croton/Joseph's Coat

Care Tricky	**Height** 24in (60cm)	**Flower** None
Light Bright indirect	**Spread** 12-18in (30-45cm)	**Humidity** Regular mist spraying
Price Middle range	**Shape** Shrubby	**Availability** Common

Temp. Min 60°F (15°C) Ideal 65°F (18°C) Max 70°F (21°C)

The Croton is a familiar, and much loved, colourful foliage houseplant, which has a wide range of leaf shapes, colours and markings.

Codiaeum variegatum pictum is the Croton you're most likely to see in the shops in all its many variations. The ordinary Croton has medium-sized, stiff, oval, dark green leaves with the veins attractively picked out in yellow and rose-pink. Some varieties have leaves with three rounded lobes, others have leaves with red undersides or yellow and pinkish-red markings as well as coloured veins.

All Croton varieties grow into fairly substantial plants of 3ft (0.9m) or more high, but if you prune them back each spring you can make your plant more compact.

To grow a Croton successfully, you must give it constant warmth all year round or it will shed its leaves and die. Also provide good, bright light to bring out the full beauty of its extravagant leaves.

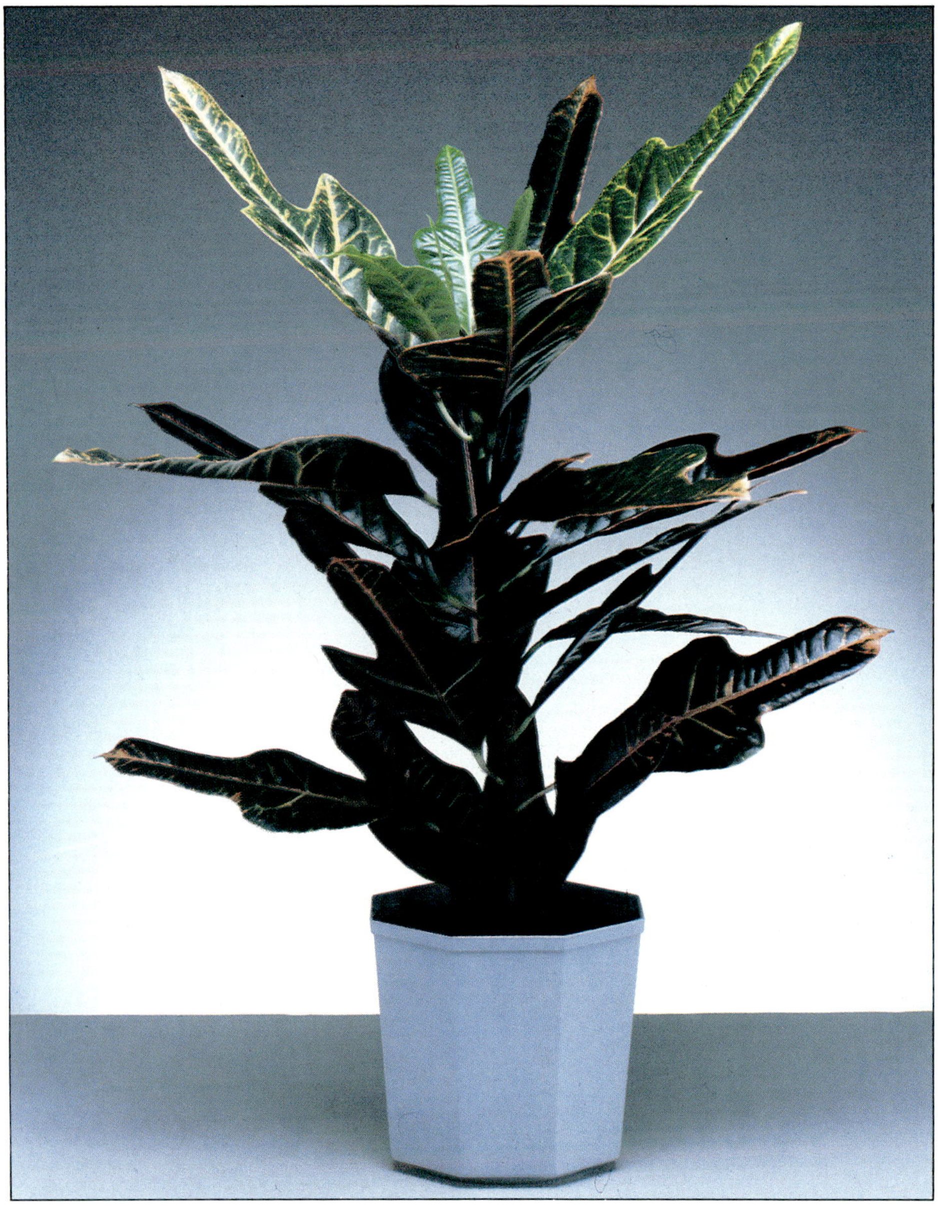

Codiaeum variegatum pictum needs heat and humidity to thrive.

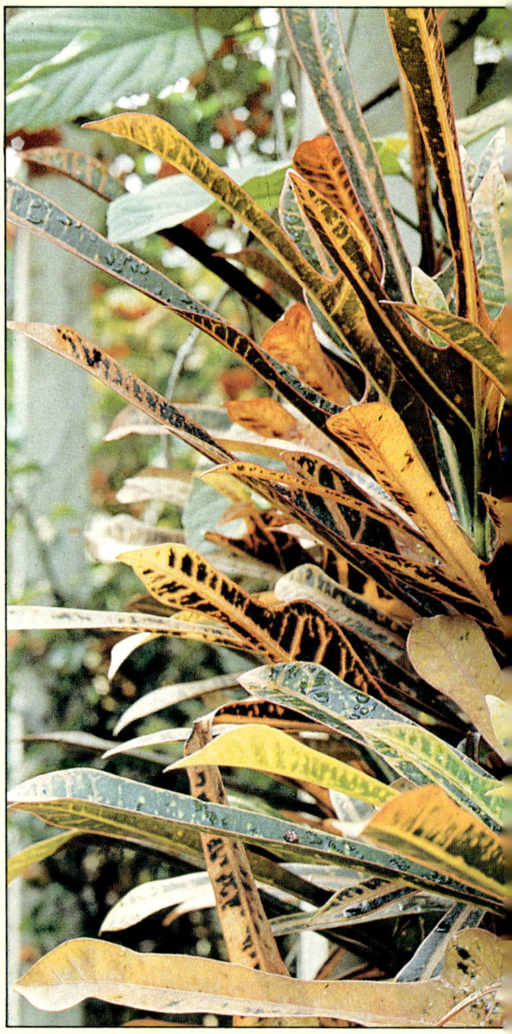

Codiaeum variegatum pictum comes from Malaysia, southern India and Sri Lanka and has dark green evergreen leaves that are quite thick and leathery with attractively coloured veins in shades of yellow and pink. There are numerous varieties to choose from with different leaf colours and shapes; the following are some of the best.

'Disraeli', *above,* has dark green leaves with an attractive three-lobed shape. The lobes are mottled with yellow and the veins too are yellow. The undersides of the leaves are a brick-red colour.

'Reidii', *above right,* is generally reckoned to have more consistent leaf colouring than most Crotons. The leaves are dark green with yellow to pinkish-red shading and dark yellow veins. It is a compact plant and the quite large oval-shaped leaves make it a handsome foliage plant.

'Black Prince' has blackish-green, broad, oval leaves that are stiff and a little leathery and sometimes flecked with yellow, orange and scarlet.

Species

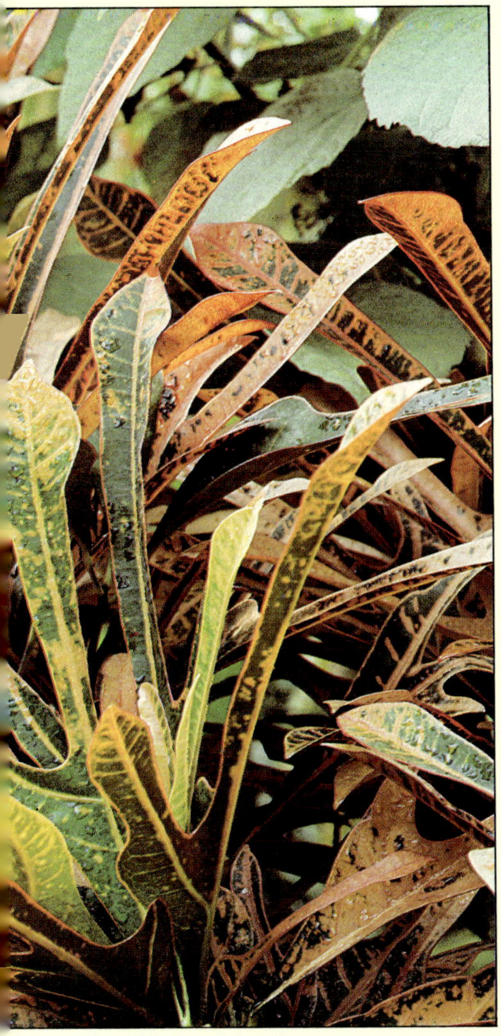

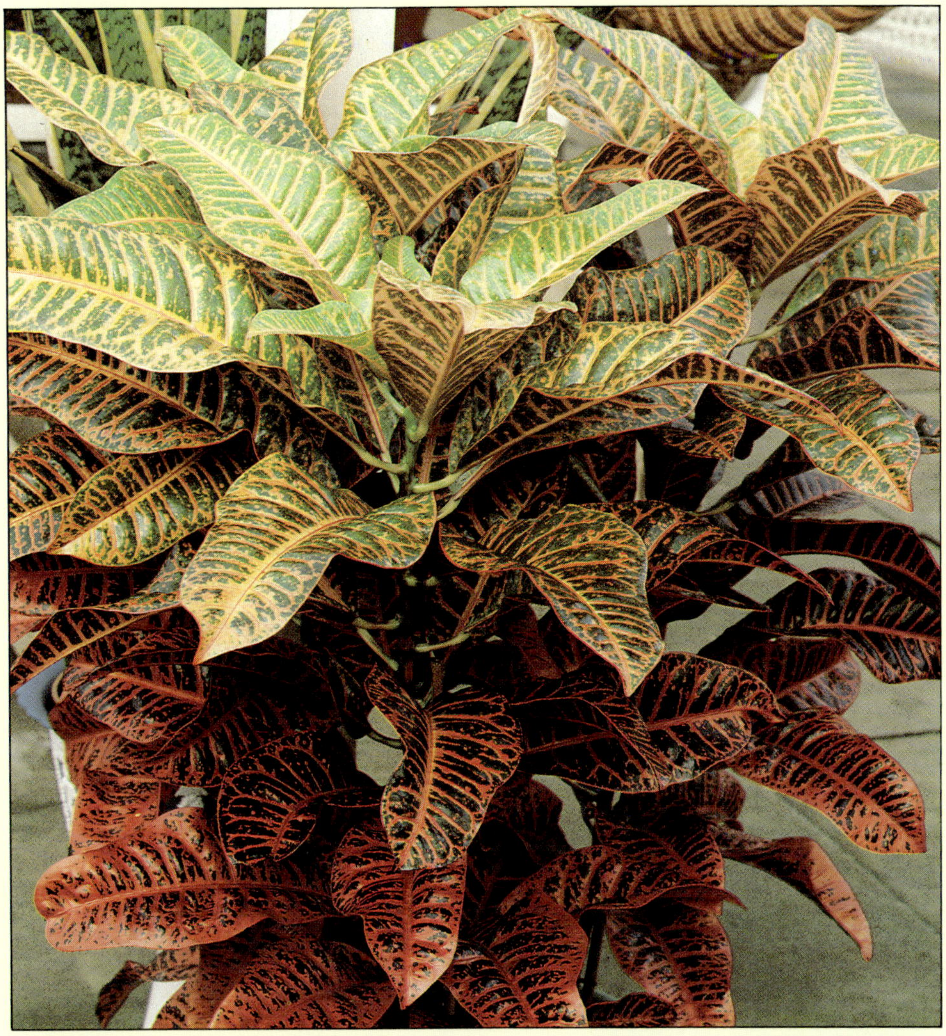

C.spirale comes from Malaysia and is a quite compact and bushy shrub. Its leaves are stiff and narrow with markings and veins in green, yellow and orangey-red. The leaves are unusual in that they curve gently in on themselves to form a slight spiral.

C.warrenii , *right,* from Malaysian jungle country, is taller and more tree-like than the species so far mentioned. The leaves are long and narrow, twist slightly and hang down a little from the branches. Reddish with yellow markings, the leaves have brownish edges.

C.bogoriense has long, oval, dark green leaves with bright yellow markings. It is a compact plant with slender stems.

C.aucubaefolium is sturdy and easy to grow with leaves that look very like those of the variegated Laurel. They are a bright, glossy green, about 4-6in (10-15cm) long, thick and leathery with irregular mottling in yellow.

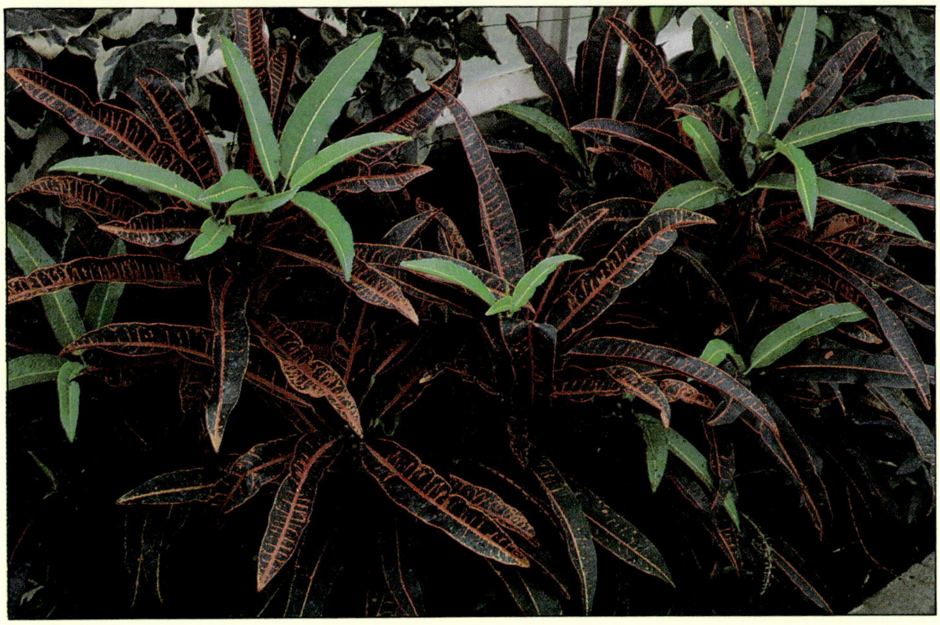

Trouble Shooter

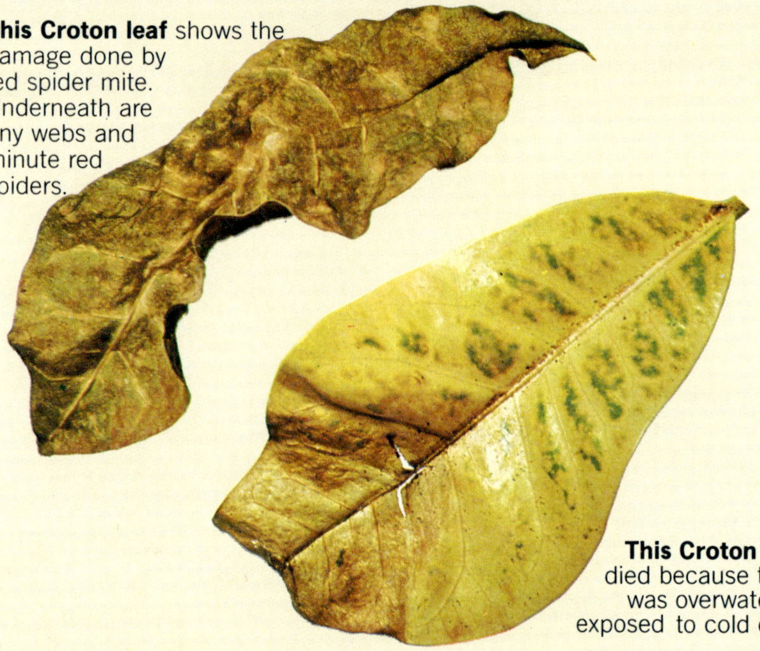

This Croton leaf shows the damage done by red spider mite. Underneath are tiny webs and minute red spiders.

This Croton leaf has died because the plant was overwatered and exposed to cold draughts.

White, fluffy patches on the undersides of young leaves or at the leaf joints are mealy bugs; carefully wipe away the bugs with a paint brush dipped in methylated spirits.

Little wart-like lumps on the stems and undersides of leaves are scale insects; wipe them away with a paint brush that has been dipped in methylated spirits. Alternatively, spray mealy bugs or scale insects with a malathion-based insecticide. You can deter both these pests by applying the insecticide to the soil two or three times during the growing season.

Red spider mite is evidenced by tiny webs underneath the leaves and at the joints of leaves and stems; treat your plant with a malathion-based insecticide. Since a very dry atmosphere is often the cause of red spider mite, increase and maintain a more humid atmosphere by regular mist spraying and you should not be troubled again.

Fading, falling leaves show that you are not watering enough, watering too much, keeping your Croton in dense shade, not feeding it enough, or that the room is too cold for it; check all these factors, follow the plant care directions given previously and your plant will recover, provided you have not neglected it for too long.

Scorched leaves are caused by too much exposure to direct sun; keep your Croton semi shaded and it will be much happier.

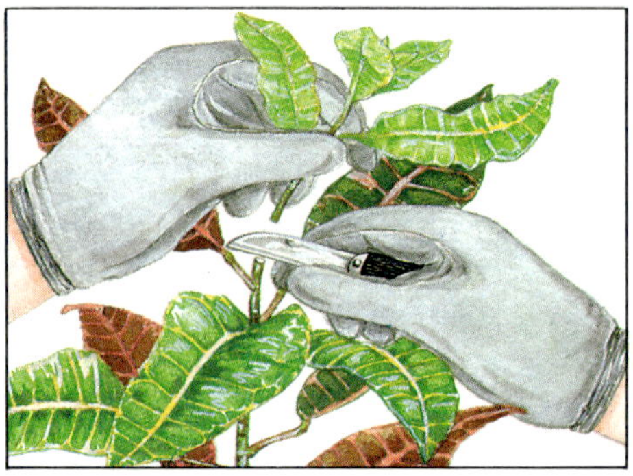

Taking Croton cuttings: choose a young stem with two pairs of leaves and a shoot.

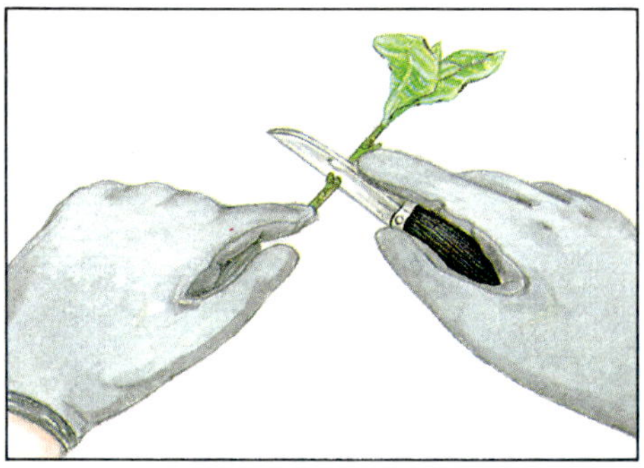

With a sharp knife, trim the cutting to about 3-4in (7-10cm) long.

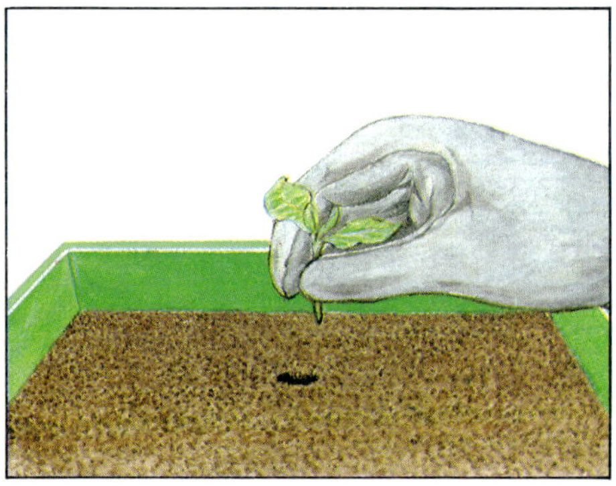

Dip the cut end in hormone rooting powder and insert the cutting in moist peat and sand compost.

Spring and summer care

Towards the end of the plant's winter rest — in about February — repot your Croton if its roots are cramped. Use a loam-based compost such as John Innes No 2 or 3.

In March, if your plant has become a bit straggly or lopsided, prune it carefully to bring it back to shape. You'll find that when you cut the stems they will bleed a white sap; to stop the flow and seal the cut ends, dust them with a little sulphur powder or powdered charcoal. The Croton grows from March until October during which time try to keep the temperature at about 65°F (18°C). Put your plant in an airy spot in bright light, but not full sun, which can scorch the leaves. Regularly mist spray your plant in the mornings.

A happy Croton will grow rapidly, so make sure there are plenty of nutrients in the soil for it to use to produce healthy growth. To do this add a few drops of liquid fertiliser to the water every 10-14 days. Start to tail off feeding towards October, however, to prepare your plant for its winter rest.

Autumn and winter care

For your Croton to be healthy during the winter it must be kept at a temperature of 65°F (18°C). Water less in the winter and stop feeding your plant as it will not be growing very much; more than moderate watering will be more than it can manage and could lead to root rot. Make sure there is fresh air in the room, but no draughts, and sit your plant in good light.

Propagation

Take 3-4in (7-10cm) cuttings in spring with a least one pair of leaves attached and, ideally, two pairs of leaves and a shoot. Dip the cut ends in hormone rooting powder and insert the cuttings in a compost mix of half and half John Innes No 2 and sharp sand. Moisten the compost thoroughly and keep it that way while the cuttings root. Keep the cuttings in a constant high temperature of 75°F (24°C) and in a semi-shaded spot. If you are using a propagator, make sure you take the cover off for a few minutes two or three times a day to ensure that the cuttings do not rot, or keep the ventilators fully open all day. The cuttings should develop roots in three or four weeks after which they can be potted into John Innes No 2 or 3.

Specialist seedsmen sell seeds for a few of the species. Sow these in January or February in the same compost mixture as for cuttings. As soon as the seeds sprout, give them plenty of fresh air and a temperature of 70°F (21°C). Pot the seedlings on individually into 3in (7cm) pots, or smaller, of John Innes No 2 as soon as they are large enough to handle.

Coffea

Family name: **Rubiaceae**

Common name: **Coffee Plant**

Care Straight-forward	**Height** 4ft (1.2m)	**Flower** Midsummer
Light Bright	**Spread** 2ft (0.6m)	**Humidity** Regular mist spraying
Price Middle range	**Shape** Shrubby	**Availability** Garden centres
Temp. Min 55°F (13°C)	Ideal 70°F (21°C)	Max 75°F (24°C)

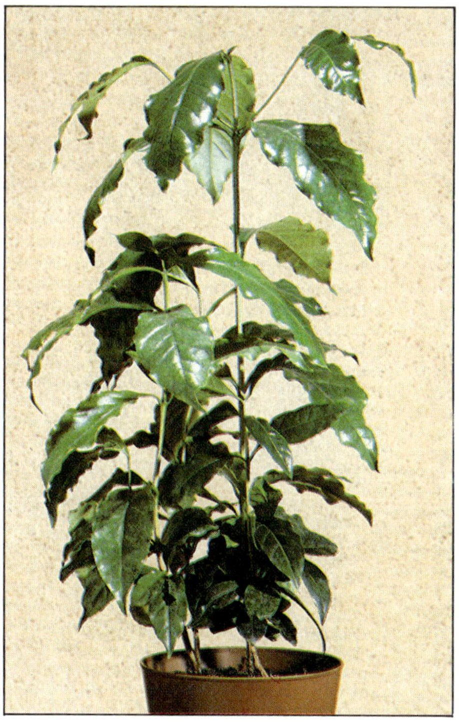

Coffea arabica is a handsome plant.

There are about forty different types of Coffee Plant, mostly from Africa originally, but now grown in many tropical areas of the world to provide the various kinds of coffee bean. The plant itself is an evergreen shrub and makes a very handsome foliage pot plant. *Coffea arabica* is the most widely grown as a houseplant and can grow as high as 15ft (4.6m) in its natural habitat, though rarely much more than about 4-5ft (1.2-1.5m) in a pot.

The Coffee Plant has lovely, slender branches with very ornamental, glossy, dark green, oval 6in (15cm) long leaves with undulating edges. Fragrant, star-shaped white flowers bloom in clusters at the leaf joints in midsummer. Sometimes when the flowers die, though rarely in the home, vivid scarlet berries appear. Each berry contains two seeds which are the coffee beans themselves.

Trouble Shooter

Lack-lustre leaves often result if temperatures fluctuate a great deal; the solution is to maintain the ideal temperature for this plant of 65°F (18°C). Although the Coffee Plant will tolerate a higher temperature, if it should rise to 80-85°F (27-30°C), give your plant more shade.

Wilting or dropping leaves show that you have been overwatering; let your plant dry out for a few days. Then knock the plant out of its pot and put some bits of broken clay pot or small pebbles in the bottom of the pot before repotting; this will help the soil to drain quickly.

Mealy bug and scale insect attack new growth and can be found by looking underneath young leaves and at the leaf joints; dispense with such pests by spraying with a malathion-based or systemic insecticide.

Species

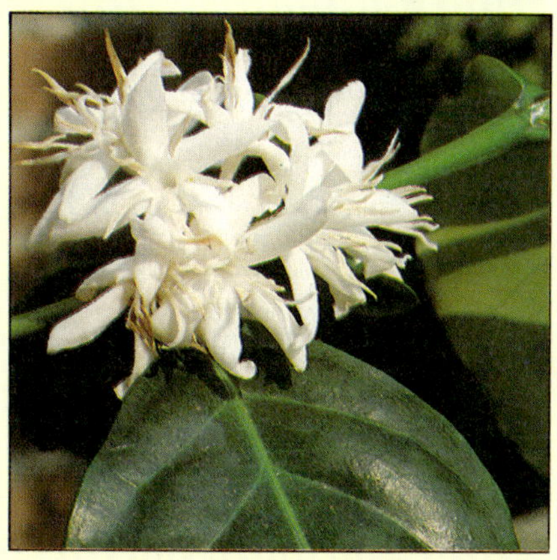

***Coffea arabica**, above*, the Coffee Plant, comes originally from the lower slopes of the mountains in Ethiopa, where it grows to a height of 15ft (4.6m). Slender stems and branches carry dark green, glossy, oval-shaped leaves about 6in (15cm) long with undulating edges. In midsummer clusters of lovely, fragrant, white star-shaped flowers appear where the leaves join the stems.

C.robusta, from Zaire, is a very compact foliage plant with waxy, dark green, pointed leaves. The flowers are fragrant, pure white and very pretty.

C. liberica, from West Africa, has wide, glossy dark green leaves about 12in (30cm) long. It also has the characteristic, sweetly scented white flowers.

Buying Guide

The Coffee Plant can sometimes be hard to find, but most good garden centres will have one.

If you can't track a plant down, try growing your own from seed. All good seedsmen supply Coffee seeds, but you might have to send for some mail order if you can't find a good local supplier.

Spring and summer care

Repot your plant in late spring using John Innes No 3 compost. Don't pot on into a much larger pot — choose one only about 1in (2cm) bigger all round; it is much better for the plant if its pot size increases gradually. At the same time you can clip your plant back to shape if it has got straggly or is in danger of growing too big to manage.

Give your Coffee Plant good bright light, but not full sun as this scorches the leaves — filtered sunlight is best; equally, do not sit your plant in dense shade as the foliage will soon become dull and lifeless. Water your Coffee Plant freely and regularly but don't let it stand in water for any length of time. Mist spray once or twice a week at the height of summer to provide humidity and to keep the leaves clean and healthy.

Feed according to the size of your plant: give a young plant a drop of liquid fertiliser with each watering in summer. A mature plant in its final size pot can have a stronger solution, as directed on the bottle, once a week in summer.

Autumn and winter care

Keep your plant in an even temperature of 65°F (18°C) and water less but just enough to keep the compost moist. Make sure your plant receives plenty of fresh air but is not sitting in a draught.

Propagation

In March sow seeds about ½in (13mm) deep in John Innes Seed Compost or a peat-based seed compost. Keep the seeds in a temperature of 80-85°F (27-30°C), in a semi-shaded position; make sure that the compost is constantly moist and that the air is humid until the seeds germinate. When the seedlings appear, move them into good, filtered light and reduce the temperature and humidity. Pot the seedlings individually into 3in (7cm) pots of John Innes No 3 as soon as they are large enough to handle.

Take cuttings of firm shoots in early summer; if you are pruning some unruly branches at the same time, you can use the offcuts. The cuttings need to be 4-6in (10-15cm) or so long and have a few leaves with a young sprouting tip. Insert the cuttings into a half peat and half sand compost and keep them in a temperature of 65°F (18°C) and constantly moist. If you provide these conditions and fairly good light the cuttings should root within a few weeks. When they have rooted, pot the cuttings on into 3-4in (7-10cm) pots of John Innes No 3.

Coleus

Family name: **Labiatae**

Common names:
Coleus/Flame Nettle

Care Easy	**Height** 2-3ft (0.6-0.9m)	**Flower** Summer
Light Bright	**Spread** 1-2ft (0.3-0.6m)	**Humidity** Regular mist spraying
Price Cheap	**Shape** Shrubby	**Availability** Common
Temp. Min 55°F (13°C)	Ideal 60°F (15°C)	Max 80°F (27°C)

Trouble Shooter

Wilting, yellow or falling leaves indicate a lack of humidity, underwatering, or both; water your Coleus freely in summer and mist spray regularly when it is hot and dry. Keep the soil just moist during autumn and winter.

A rotting stem, which can be seen as a dark; shrivelled ring just above the soil, is evidence of overwatering; let your plant dry out for a few days and you might save it; in future reduce the amount of water you give your Coleus so the compost is just moist.

Undeveloped leaves and sluggish growth are signs of lack of nutrients in the soil or insufficient light; feed your plant every 14 days or so and provide brighter light.

Loss of leaf colour occurs if you keep your plant too shaded; give it the brightest light in the house.

Your plant will collapse in a soggy heap if you expose it to low temperatures or cold draughts; cut back the bedraggled stems and keep it in a minimum temperature of 55°F (13°C) and well away from draughts.

Greenfly, thrips and mealy bug can occasionally attack young growth; spray greenfly and thrips with a pyrethrum-based insecticide or, in the case of mealy bugs, remove them with a small brush dipped in methylated spirits. Apply a systemic insecticide to the soil in spring and every four to six weeks after that until September.

The Coleus is much prized for its superbly colourful and decorative leaves which hint at its origins in the tropical parts of Africa and Asia. The Coleus we most often see are hybrids, each of which puts on a slightly different leaf display in combinations of pale green, bronze, purple, reddish purple, crimson, dark green and various shades of yellow and orange. The leaves themselves also vary, from a full heart shape or an elongated, pointed oval to quite deeply indented with wavy edges.

Coleus blumei is the main parent of most of the hybrids. It is a shrubby plant, about 2-3ft (0.6-0.9m) tall when mature, and has pale green, coarsely serrated, heart-shaped leaves with bronze or reddish-purple bands of colour — rather like contour lines — ringing the leaves. This plant also produces small, rather indifferent spikes of white or purple flowers. Other varieties have blue flowers but they are all best removed to encourage more and better leaves

Despite its exotic foliage, the Coleus is one of the easiest of all houseplants to grow, but to get the very best from them, grow fresh plants each year.

Spring and summer care

Your Coleus is a sun-loving plant that needs good light to produce its vivid leaf colours — so make sure you give your plant the brightest light in the house. On really hot days provide a little light shade to prevent the leaves from being scorched; given some shade, your plant will be quite safe even when temperatures rise to 75°F (24°C), or higher, although its ideal temperature is about 60°F (15°C).

Your plant will look best if it has a nice, bushy shape; to achieve this, regularly pinch out the growing tips of each branch as soon as the ends start to get straggly. Also, it's a good idea to pinch out the flower buds as they begin to form because the flowers are not particularly interesting and this helps your plant channel its energies into producing more leaves.

During the summer your Coleus needs plenty of food and water — simply stick to the following routine and you should have no trouble. From April to September, when your plant will be growing most vigorously, water it freely and feed with a liquid fertiliser every two or three weeks.

Keep your plant in a reasonably humid atmosphere, but also make sure that plenty of fresh air circulates. A mist spray every few days helps to create a humid atmosphere, but spray early in the day as unabsorbed droplets of water magnify the sun's rays, causing ugly scorch marks on the leaves.

Autumn and winter care

By the end of summer your Coleus is likely to be looking a bit sad and leggy, as well as missing a lot of leaves from around the base. You can keep your plant over winter but it is so cheap and easy to raise new plants from seeds each spring that you should really consider sowing them yourself. However, if you want to keep a favourite plant, maintain winter temperatures above a minimum 55°F (13°C) and make sure that the compost is kept

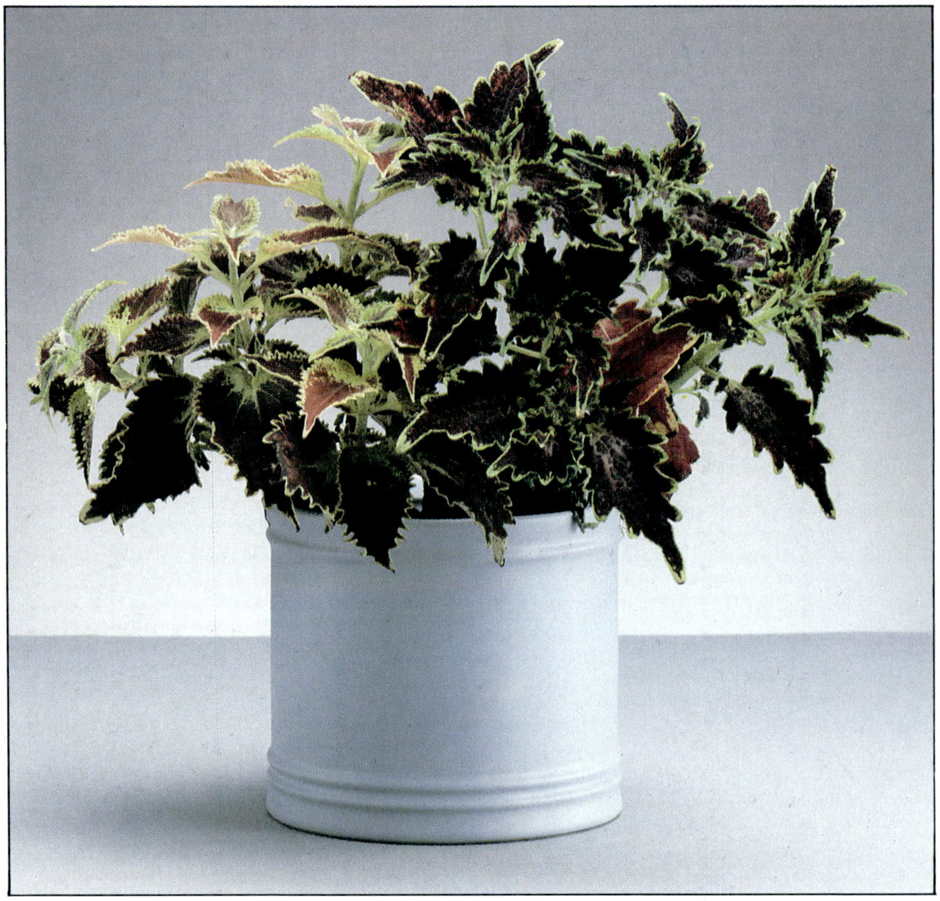

Coleus blumei remains colourful all year and is easy to grow from seed too!

just moist, though never wet. Give your plant good light, but keep it free from chilly draughts. Don't feed or mist spray your plant until the warmer days of spring when growth is just starting up again.

In early spring your Coleus should start sprouting new shoots from around the base and lower stem. Trim back any straggly stems above this growth and your plant will grow up again quickly and fill out into a nice rounded and bushy shape.

Propagation

Sow Coleus seeds in January or February. Push them 1/16in (2mm) deep into some John Innes No 2 with a little added sharp sand. Keep the compost moist and in a temperature of 70°F (21°C). A propagator will give constant warmth. Alternatively you can simply fasten a polythene bag over the seed tray and keep it on a sunny windowsill to give the seeds a warm, enclosed, humid environment.

Buying Guide

Look for nice bushy little plants in spring and choose a plant with attractively marked and coloured leaves. Avoid straggly plants completely.

Take 3-4in (7-10cm) cuttings of young shoots any time between April and September. Dip the cut ends in hormone rooting powder and insert the cuttings into John Innes No 2 with a little added sharp sand to provide good drainage. Keep the compost moist and provide a temperature of 65 to 70°F (18-21°C). Keep the air around the cuttings humid, but at the same time give adequate ventilation. Pot each plant individually when the cuttings have strong, healthy roots and sprout new growth.

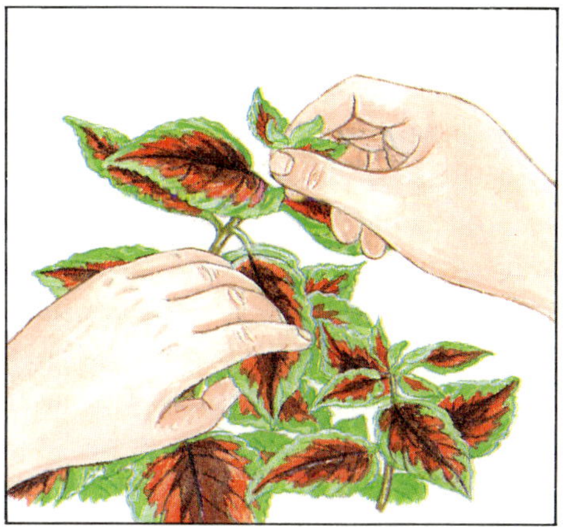

Make your Coleus bushy by pinching out the growing tips every few weeks. Remove the flower buds regularly in the same way to strengthen your plant.

Species

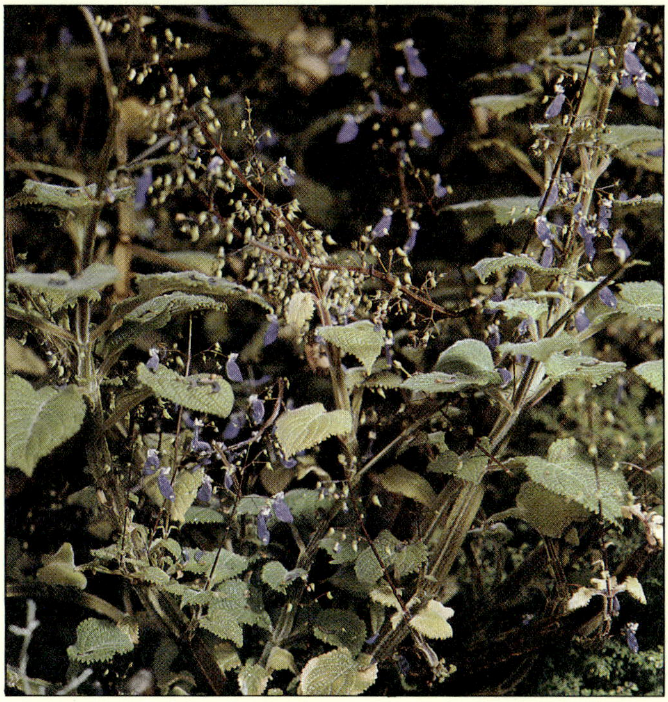

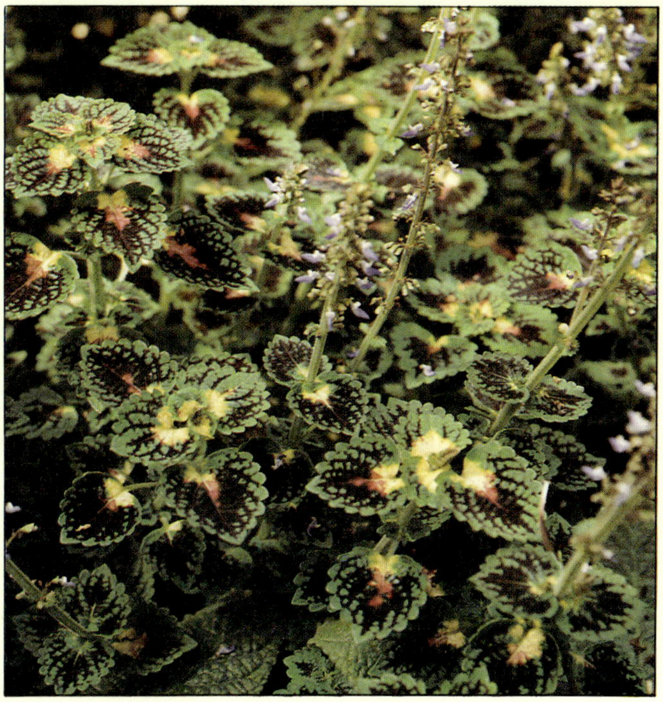

Coleus blumei, the Flame Nettle, from Java, is a shrubby plant that grows about 2-3ft (0.6-0.9m) tall. Its pale green, oval leaves are patterned with reddish-purple or bronze soft bands of colour with coarsely serrated edges. This is the parent of most of the hybrids of which there's a very long list; the following are some of the most decorative.

'Carefree' is about 12in (30cm) tall and has oak-leaf shaped leaves. The leaves are dark red, brownish-pink and greenish-yellow in the centre and green round the scalloped edges. 'Rainbow', as its name suggests, comes in a wide range of colours; the most attractive version has rich crimson-coloured leaves with darker red veins and leaf edges of an almost black red. 'Sabre' grows about 12in (30cm) tall and produces lots of branches from its base, making a very compact and bushy plant. The leaves are lance-shaped and patterned with red, green and yellow.

C.frederici, *above left*, comes from Angola and has dark green leaves with prominent veins and serrated edges. Unlike other Coleus, this plant's most distinctive feature is its pretty purplish-blue flower, small clusters of which are carried on short stems at the top of a longish spike.

C.rehneltianus, *above right*, from Sri Lanka, is more of a creeper than a shrub. The nettle-like, tooth-edged leaves are brownish-purple in the centre and have a wide band of green round the edge.

C.verschaffeltii is also from Java but is even more brightly coloured! It has large, crimson leaves, about 4-6in (10-15cm) long, with a large purple splash in the centre. The edges of the leaves are dark green with reddish-purple undersides.

Columnea

Family name:
Gesneriaceae

Common name: **Goldfish Plant**

Care Tricky	**Height** 2-3ft (0.6-0.9m)	**Flower** November-April
Light Indirect sun	**Spread** 1-2ft (0.3-0.6m)	**Humidity** Regular mist spraying
Price Middle range	**Shape** Trailing	**Availability** Garden centres
Temp. Min 60°F (15°C)	Ideal 70°F (21°C)	Max 80°F (27°C)

Species

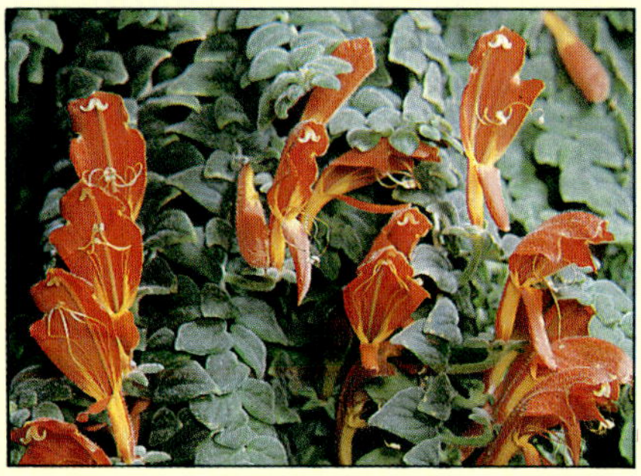

Columnea banksii (or ***C.hirta***), the Goldfish Plant, comes from the rain forests of Central and South America. It grows on the jungle trees where it anchors itself firmly with its long roots. Long, trailing stems carry small, fleshy, oval, dark green leaves which grow opposite each other in pairs. Vermilion flowers with orange-yellow markings appear from the leaf joints in late winter and early spring.

C.gloriosa, *above*, from Costa Rica, is also a trailing plant. Its leaves are more oblong in shape, though slightly smaller and covered with tiny reddish hairs. The 3in (7cm) long flowers are bright red with yellow in the throat. This plant must be kept warmer than *C.banksii.*

C.microphylla, also from Costa Rica, is a very popular variety. It has small, brownish-green, hairy leaves on long hanging stems and yellow-throated orange-red flowers.

C.crassifolia is an unusual succulent species from the forests of southern Mexico and Guatemala. The stems are thick and fleshy and semi-upright with long, narrow, fleshy, green leaves. The orange-red flowers are tubular.

The Goldfish Plant is grown for its extraordinary, bright orange, open-mouthed, tubular flowers which give the distinct impression of a wide-mouthed goldfish. These flowers stand out at a sharp angle from the plant's stem, usually appearing in late winter and early spring.

In the tropical rain forests of South America, the Goldfish Plant grows on trees by holding onto the bark with roots that grow out along the length of the trailing stems. The plant lives by absorbing moisture from the heavily humid air, as well as from rain showers and heavy dews.

Columnea banksii is the commonest Goldfish Plant. Its long, trailing stems carry dark green, oval-shaped, rather fleshy leaves that grow in opposite pairs. Its vermilion flowers have yellow throat markings and appear at a sharp angle from the leaf joints in winter and early spring.

To grow a Goldfish Plant well you must give it plenty of humidity and warmth or it is liable to drop its leaves and fail to flower.

Spring and summer care

Your Goldfish Plant will be happiest in a hanging pot or basket where its stems can trail freely. Trim an untidy plant immediately after flowering in spring; otherwise leave your plant to grow undisturbed.

Fill the pot with John Innes No 2, plus a little added sharp sand to make the compost drain well. If you want to grow your Goldfish Plant in a wire basket, line it with a layer of sphagnum moss about 1in (2cm) thick before filling it with the compost.

From March to September make sure your Goldfish Plant has constantly moist, though not wet, compost. Feed every three or four weeks with a half-strength liquid fertiliser to encourage plenty of flowers. Summer temperatures can rise to 75 or 80°F (24-27°C) as long as the air is humid and you do not expose your plant to the full sun.

Autumn and winter care

In winter make sure your plant is given a minimum temperature of 60°F (15°C) — if it is exposed to colder temperatures, it will shrivel up and die. Keep your Goldfish Plant well away from draughts. Give your plant good light but shade it just a little from winter sunshine. Only provide a very little water during the cold months of the year.

Propagation

In March or February, sow seeds in a compost mixture of half peat and half sand and provide a temperature of 75-80°F (24-27°C); keep just moist and semi-shaded. Seedlings should appear in about three or four weeks.

You can take 3-4in (7-10cm) cuttings of firm shoots at any time of the year, so long as you can give them a high temperature. Insert the cuttings into a compost mixture of two parts John Innes No 2 and one part sharp sand. Keep the cuttings constantly moist, provide a temperature of 75°F (24°C) and semi shade until they have rooted.

Trouble Shooter

Botrytis, or grey mould, occurs if you overwater and can, if far enough advanced, kill the plant; if botrytis is in its early stages, let the plant dry out for a while, trim off the affected parts and treat with Benlate.

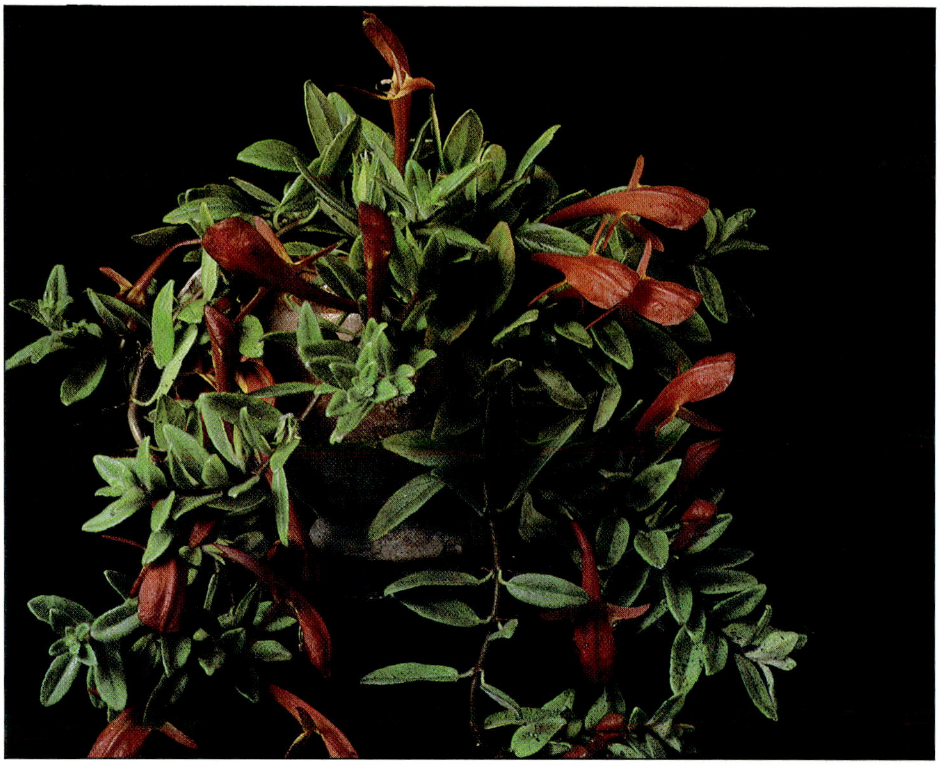

Columnea banksii blooms with unusual, goldfish-like flowers in spring.

Conophytum

Family name: **Mesembryanthemaceae**

Common name: **Mimicry Plant**

Care Tricky	**Height** ¾-2in (19-50mm)	**Flower** August-November
Light Bright/sun	**Spread** ½-3in (13-75mm)	**Humidity** None
Price Cheap	**Shape** Clump	**Availability** Garden centres
Temp. Min 55°F (13°C)	Ideal 60°F (15°C)	Max 80°F (27°C)

The fascinating Mimicry Plant's common name originates from the intriguing shape of its leaves, which grow in smooth, thick, fleshy pairs; these look very like pebbles — especially if you come across them growing in the wild. In summer a mature Mimicry Plant will produce pretty daisy-like flowers in white, yellow, orange, pink, violet or red.

Conophytum louisae is the most common of the many species and comes from Namibia in south west Africa. It is quite compact as the 'pebbles' are only ½-¾in (13-19mm) long and under ½in (13mm) wide. Each pebble is smooth, greyish to greenish-blue and pairs up with another one to form an elongated heart shape. These pebbles grow together in clumps. In late summer each plant produces beautiful pale or bright yellow flowers about 1in (2cm) across, which open in bright sunlight and close up at night.

The secret of success with a Mimicry Plant is bright light and careful watering at the right times of the year.

Spring and summer care

Your Mimicry Plant will be happiest in a very porous compost. There are several very good composts for Cacti or you can make your own mixture of two parts John Innes No 2 to one part sharp, gritty sand; this will ensure that the compost drains well.

In spring your Mimicry Plant will begin its dormant phase — you can tell when it starts, because the pebbles develop a papery skin. During dormancy new leaves gradually form within the old ones so that by the end of April or early May all that remains of the old leaves is papery skin enclosing the new leaves. Water lightly at this time so that the new leaves do not dehydrate and die.

From mid May to July do not water your Mimicry Plant at all, then, from August to early October water regularly as before. From July to October feed your plant with liquid fertiliser once a month.

Late summer is the plant's most active growth period and during this time you should water your plant lightly, so that the compost is always just moist. The new leaves will swell and eventually break through the papery covering, shedding it rather like a snake sheds its old skin.

Autumn and winter care

Pay careful attention to watering; from October through to April give your plant only just enough water to prevent the compost getting too dry. Keep your plant in a temperature of 55-60°F (13-15°C), give it the best light and keep it away from draughts.

Propagation

From mid March to late April sow seeds in a mixture of two parts John Innes No 2 and one part sharp sand. Keep the seeds just moist and in a temperature of 60-70°F (15-21°C). Provide plenty of humidity but give more fresh air once the seeds have germinated. You will need to be patient as the seedlings are very slow growing.

Take cuttings of individual leaves in May or June, but make sure that a little bit of stem is attached; allow the cut end to dry out until the cut has calloused over. Insert the cut end into a pot of the same compost mix as before, keep the cuttings in a temperature of 65°F (18°C) in barely moist compost. When the cuttings have rooted treat them in the same way as a mature Mimicry Plant.

Trouble Shooter

Rotting roots are caused by over-watering and can extend to the whole of the plant if not dealt with quickly; knock the plant out of its pot and inspect the roots. If the roots are brown and limp, they are rotting. Let your plant dry out for a few days and then water lightly.

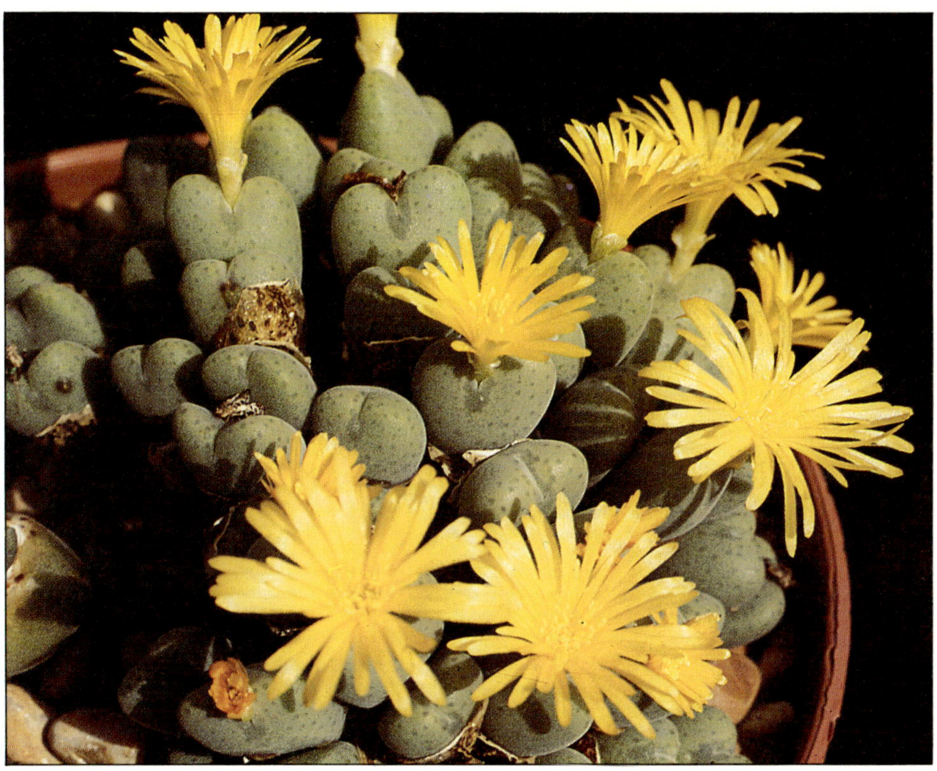

Conophytum louisae, showing new growth surrounded by the old, dead leaves.

Species

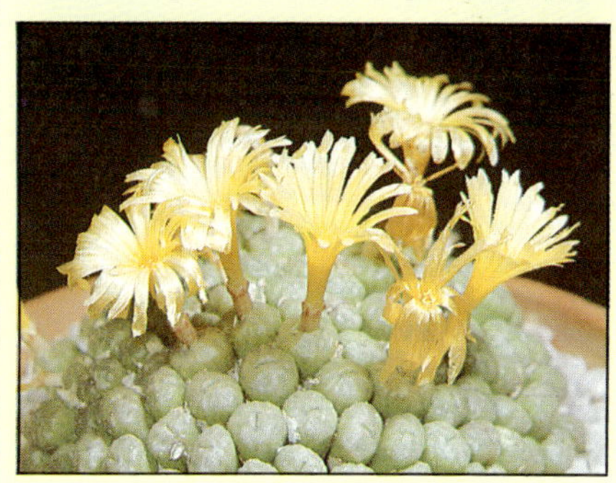

Conophytum louisae, the Mimicry Plant, is from Namibia. Each leaf is about ½-¼in (13-19mm) long and ½in (13mm) across. The pairs of thick greenish-blue leaves form an elongated heart shape. The daisy-like flowers are yellow and about 1in (2cm) across.

C.tischeri, *above*, comes from Namibia and has leaves that are distinctly heart shaped. Each leaf is about ½in (13mm) long, grey-green in colour and dotted with a darker green.

Cordyline

Family name: **Agavaceae**

Common name:
Cabbage Tree/Ti Plant

Care Easy	**Height** 3-10ft (0.6-3m)	**Flower** None
Light Indirect sun	**Spread** 1-8ft (0.3-2.4m)	**Humidity** Regular mist spraying
Price Cheap	**Shape** Rosette	**Availability** Common

Temp. Min 55°F (13°C) Ideal 70°F (21°C) Max 80°F (27°C)

Various members of the Cordyline family grow in Asia, though Australasia is their main homeland. The Cordyline is a tree-like, slightly shrubby plant with little or no trunk. The long, lance-shaped evergreen leaves can be either narrow or wide, with plain green or striking red, pink or bronze shading, edges or markings.

Cordyline terminalis is one of the most popular species with lovely bronze, green and pinkish-red leaves, that are a pale crimson colour when young. It comes originally from Polynesia and India and can reach a height of 10ft (3m) or more; but if you restrict the roots by not repotting your plant too often, it can be kept to a more manageable 3ft (0.9m) high.

Two very colourful and popular varieties are 'Tricolor', which has pink, red and cream stripes on a dark green background and 'Firebrand', which has spectacular, reddish, curving leaves.

The Cabbage Tree gets its common name from the New Zealander settlers who ate the young leaves of *Cordyline australis* as a vegetable. Some Cabbage Trees look very like the separate species Draceana and this can lead to confusion.

The Cordyline grows quite slowly, so there is no need to worry about it outgrowing the space available for a good few years. The Ti Plant's only real fault is that it loses its lower leaves with age, which can make some plants look straggly. But, in return for moderate watering, feeding and good light you will have a very handsome, long-lasting foliage plant!

Spring and summer care

In March, if you suspect that the roots of your plant are cramped, knock the plant out of its pot to see if the compost is thick with roots; if it is, repot with John Innes No 2 or Levingtons, adding one part sharp sand to every three parts compost, to make sure that it will drain well.

From late March to late September temperatures can rise to 75-80°F (24-27°C) without harm, but any higher will not do the plant any good. Put your plant in bright but filtered light; strong sunlight will scorch the leaves. Water your Cordyline twice a week in warm weather and throughout the growing season feed with liquid fertiliser every two or three weeks when you water. Your plant will enjoy plenty of fresh air and a mist spray once or twice a week.

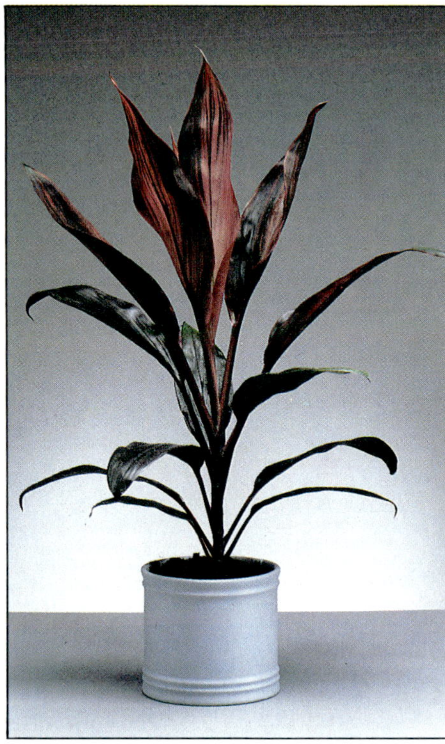

Cordyline terminalis 'Firebrand'.

Autumn and winter care

From late September to March keep the temperature above 55°F (13°C) and, ideally, between 60-70°F (15-21°C). Water once a week and don't let your plant stand in water as this leads to root rot. The Cordyline also hates cold draughts. When winter sunshine warms the room, your plant will appreciate a light mist spray to create a little humidity and keep its leaves fresh.

Trouble Shooter

Drooping, falling leaves are a sure sign that you have kept the plant in too dry or too hot an atmosphere; the Cordyline needs some humidity, especially at the hottest times of the year, so mist spray once or twice a week in summer. Provide a little light shade if temperatures exceed 80°F (27°C).

Rotting roots are caused by a combination of overwatering and exposure to cold; let the compost dry out for a few days and keep the plant warmer, then follow the care directions.

Scale insect can attack the undersides of the leaves and leaf joints; use a paintbrush dipped in methylated spirits and dab each insect or spray the plant with a malathion-based insecticide. As a preventative, spray or water into the compost a systemic insecticide each spring; repeat half-way through the summer and again in September. This also deters red spider mite and aphids.

Propagation

In late February or March plant seeds 1in (2cm) deep in a compost mixture of two parts John Innes No 2 and one part sharp sand. Keep the seeds in a steady temperature of 80°F (27°C) to help them germinate properly — ideally use a heated propagator. However, you can achieve much the same effect by tying a clear polythene bag over the seed tray and keeping it in a warm place — such as on a sunny windowsill. If the seeds are kept at a lower temperature they are likely to rot.

Take cuttings in March by cutting a length of stem into 3in (7cm) sections; insert the sections into moist compost and keep at a constant temperature of about 70°F (21°C).

Species

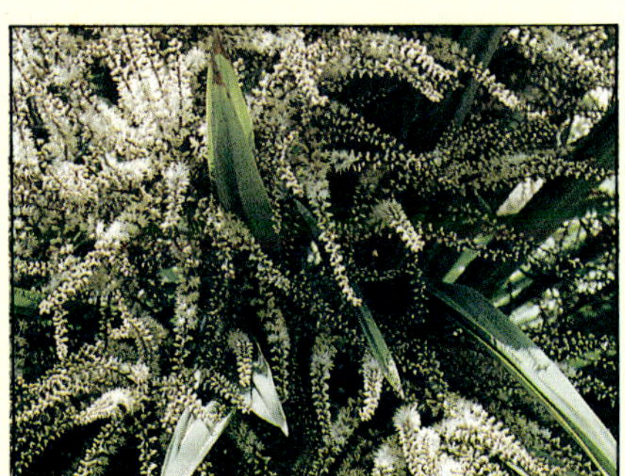

Cordyline terminalis, Ti Plant, comes from Polynesia and India where it grows 10ft (3m) high, but it is much more compact in a pot. Sword-shaped leaves are about 12-14in (30-36cm) long and bronze-green with pinkish-red shading around the edges. The leaves are usually pale crimson when they first emerge. 'Tricolor' has multicoloured leaves, variegated in pink, red and cream on a dark green background; 'Firebrand' has curving reddish leaves; and 'Red-edge' is compact with bright reddish-purple leaves and green markings with a very prominent midrib.

C.australis, *left*, the Cabbage Tree, comes from Australasia and is an evergreen tree-like plant. It has sword-shaped, arching green leaves about 2-3ft (0.6-0.9m) long and 2in (5cm) wide. These sprout out like a fountain to form a dense crown of foliage. Fragrant white flowers bloom in clusters, though they very rarely occur in the home.

Cotyledon

Family name: **Crassulaceae**

Common name:
Pig's Ears/Silver Ruffles

Care Straight-forward	**Height** 9-12in (23-30cm)	**Flower** June-August
Light Full sun	**Spread** 12in (30cm)	**Humidity** None
Price Cheap	**Shape** Shrubby	**Availability** Garden centres

Temp. Min 50°F (10°C) · Ideal 70°F (21°C) · Max 80°F (27°C)

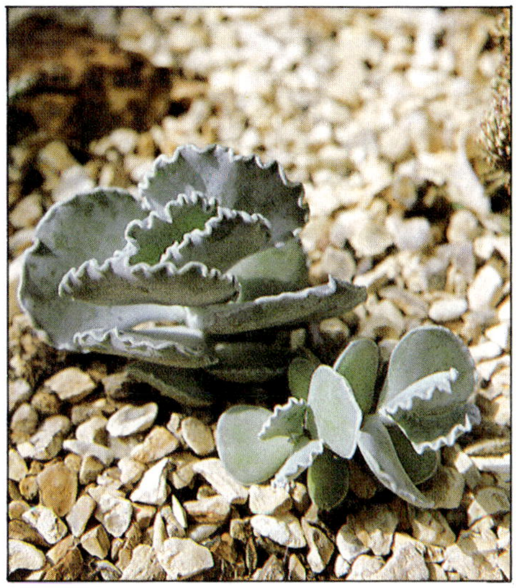

Cotyledon undulata has shell-like leaves.

The Cotyledon's large, flat leaves suggest the plant's rather unfortunate nickname of Pig's Ears! The much more glamorous common name, Silver Ruffles, comes from the greyish-green colouring of some of the species and the attractive undulating edges of the leaves.

Cotyledons are attractive succulent plants mostly from the dry parts of Africa, southern Saudi Arabia and the Yemen. They are all rather shrubby with rounded, oval-shaped leaves that grow opposite each other along the stems. Red, yellow or orange-red tubular flowers hang down from the stems in clusters in late spring and summer.

The fleshy leaves and stems of all Cotyledon species store water so they can survive successfully through the long, dry seasons in their natural habitat. This means that if your plant gets too much water throughout the year, it will rot; the plant is not able to cope with excess water.

Cotyledon undulata is perhaps the most widely grown Cotyledon with its compact shape and thick, white, powdery coating on the leaves and stems; the leaves are shaped just like scallop shells, right down to the wavy edges! Orange-yellow flowers with red-tinged tips cluster in groups of twelve or more at the top of a long stalk in summer.

Spring and summer care

Your Cotyledon will be quite happy in temperatures up to and a little beyond 70°F (21°C); provide plenty of fresh air, but watch out for harmful cold draughts. From March through to September your plant will appreciate being watered well; drench the compost, allow the surplus to drain away and wait until the compost is dry before watering again. Feed your plant with a liquid fertiliser every three or four weeks when you water.

Autumn and winter care

Do not water your Cotyledon at all from November to March while it is dormant. Provide a temperature of around 50°F (10°C). As autumn approaches, gradually decrease the amount of water you give your plant, until by early November you have stopped watering completely. Provide lots of bright light, even full sun, whenever possible. In March you can start watering again, gradually increasing the amount of water — but be very careful not to overwater.

Propagation

Take stem cuttings in spring and grow them in sandy compost. Keep the cuttings in a temperature of 60-65°F (15-18°C); make sure that the compost is constantly moist and provide a little shade. Treat the rooted cuttings in the same way as mature plants.

Leaf cuttings are a reliable method of propagation. Snap the leaf off at the leaf joint (axil), push into sandy compost leaving two thirds of it above the surface, and then treat in the same way as stem cuttings.

Sow seeds in March using a Cactus compost or John Innes No 2 with a little added sharp sand. Keep the compost constantly moist and provide a temperature of 70°F (21°C). When the seedlings are large enough to handle, move them on individually into 3in (7cm) pots.

Trouble Shooter

Falling leaves and rotting stems are caused by overwatering, especially if you water in winter; remember that this plant stores water, so the compost should dry out between waterings and then be left completely dry between November and March while the plant is dormant.

Cottonwool-like patches are mealy bugs; clean them away with a brush dipped in methylated spirits. To avoid pests altogether, treat your plant with a systemic insecticide (one that doesn't contain the chemical malathion as this would damage your plant) three or four times during the growing season.

Buying Guide

The commonest Cotyledons are widely available at garden centres and high street shops. For a wider selection go to a cacti and succulent specialist.

Species

Cotyledon undulata, Silver Ruffles, comes from South Africa and is a distinctive, shrubby plant about 18-20in (45-50cm) tall. Its wide, fleshy stem, branches and scallop-shaped, wavy-edged leaves have a thick, powdery white coating. In late spring and summer orange-yellow flowers with yellow tips appear in clusters at the ends of long stalks.

C. orbiculata, Pig's Ears, from South Africa, Namibia and the Natal, is a shrubby plant that can grow 2ft (0.6m) high, or a little more. Large silvery-grey, red-edged leaves crowd together at the tips of the branches; they are about 5in (13cm) long and 2-3in (5-7cm) wide. Yellowish-red, bell-shaped flowers are carried in clusters at the end of a stalk.

C. ladismithiensis, from Cape Province, is a shrubby dwarf plant, only 6-8in (15-20cm) tall. Its rounded leaves are 1-2in (2-5cm) long, with blunt, tooth-shaped indentations at the tip. They are very fleshy and the whole surface is covered with tiny white hairs. Flower stalks grow in the spring and summer and bear slightly drooping, reddish or brownish-red flowers in clusters at the ends.

C.papillaris, *below*, has fleshy green leaves edged with a thin red line. The bell-shaped flowers bloom in summer.

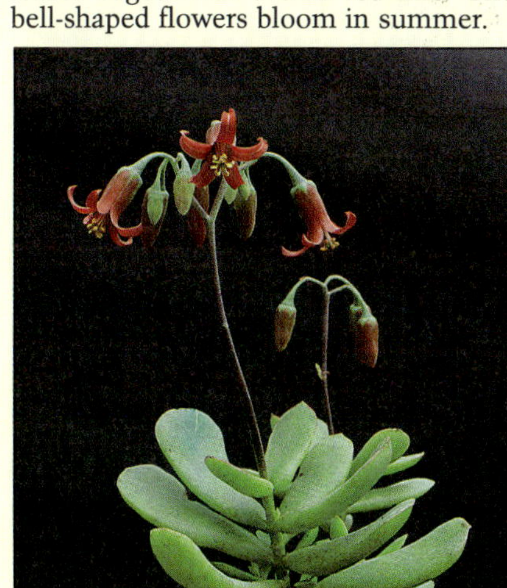

Crassula

Family name: **Crassulaceae**

Common names:
Jade Plant/Concertina Plant

Care Easy	**Height** 1-3ft (0.3-0.9m)	**Flower** May-July
Light Full sun	**Spread** 12-18in (30-45cm)	**Humidity** None
Price Cheap	**Shape** Shrubby	**Availability** Common
Temp Min 55°F (13°C)	Ideal 70°F (21°C)	Max 80°F (27°C)

Crassulas are succulent, water-storing plants that come in all sorts of shapes and sizes — most of them are upright but there are also shrubby, creeping and trailing Crassulas.

The commonest member of the family is the Jade Plant or *Crassula portulacea* (formerly called *C.argentea*). It has a tree-like shape which makes a mature plant look rather like a Bonsai. The Jade Plant grows to about 3ft (0.9m) high and has robust stems and branches thickly covered with fleshy, pale to dark jade green, oval leaves, sometimes with reddish edges. In early spring dense heads of pink, star-shaped flowers appear at the ends of flower stalks.

Another favourite is the similar species, *C.arborescens* — sometimes called the Silver Jade Plant. This differs from the Jade Plant in that it has silvery grey-green leaves — hence its common name — with wider and darker red edges and little reddish dots over the surface.

The Concertina Plant looks completely different; *C.perforata* is a straggly, small shrub with small leaves growing opposite each other up the stems in such a way as to look a little like a fully extended concertina. The grey-green leaves are covered with tiny red dots. Confusingly, *C.rupestris* also has the common name Concertina Plant. Its small oval leaves are greyish-green with red margins and grow opposite each other on slender stems. Yellow flowers cluster together at the ends of flower stalks.

Spring and summer care

Repot your Crassula in spring if the plant has completely filled its pot with roots. Use John Innes No 2 or 3 with a little added sharp sand or use a good Cactus compost; whatever mixture you use, make sure that it is porous to let water drain away quickly.

In April, gradually start to increase the amount of water you give your Jade Plant, until by May you are watering freely. Water only when the compost is dry to the touch; soak the compost thoroughly, let it drain and then water again in a few days when the soil is dry. Be careful to avoid waterlogging as the plant can develop root rot.

Temperatures of 70°F (21°C) or more will not harm your plant so long as you do not water during the hottest part of the day. The Jade Plant does not object to lack of humidity and will be unhappy and prone to moulds if you mist spray it. From April to August feed your plant once a week with a drop or two of liquid fertiliser added to the water.

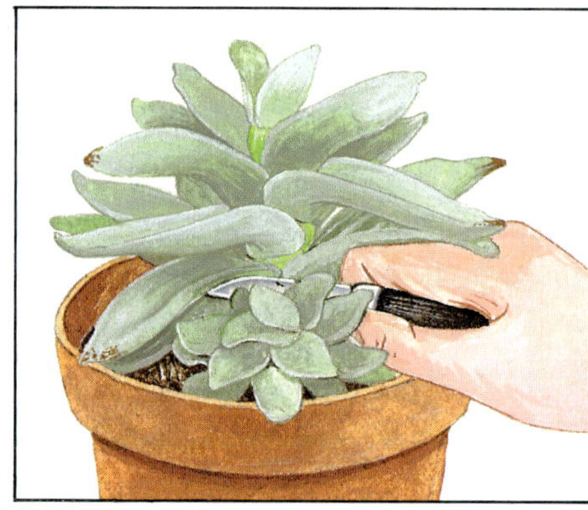

Dividing a Crassula: carefully cut an offset (baby plant) away from the parent plant in spring.

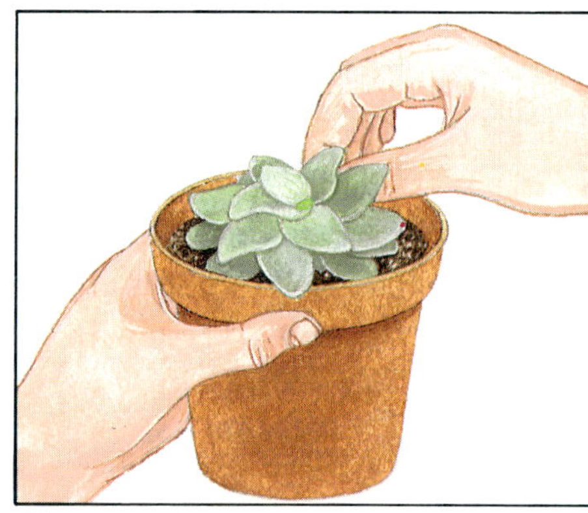

Plant the offset in half peat half sand. Keep moist and moderately warm in bright, filtered light, and feed each month — it will root easily.

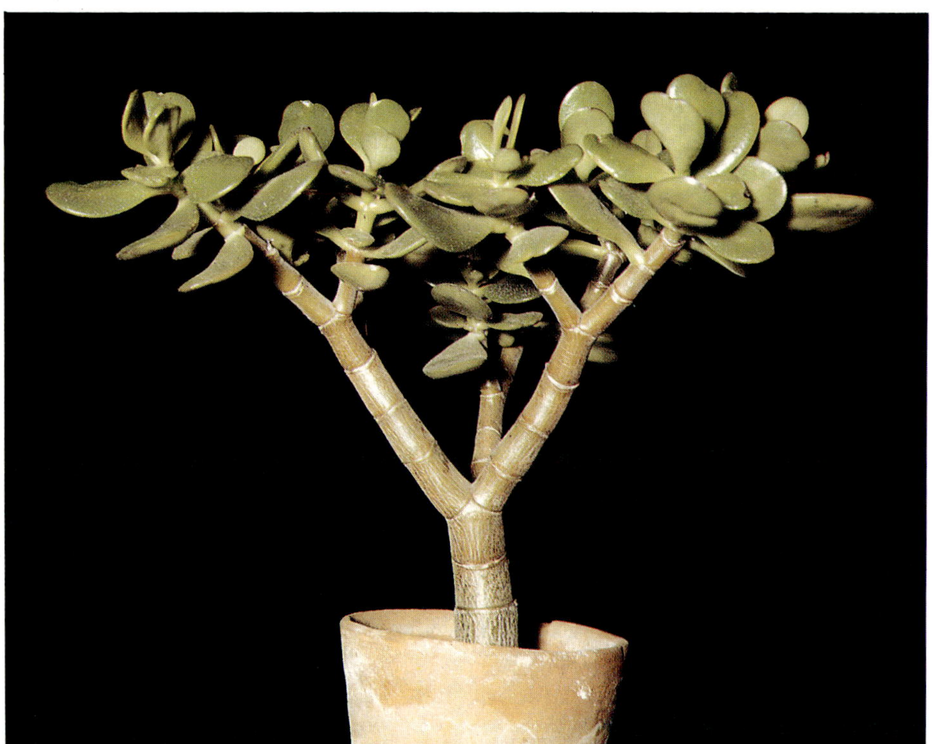

Crassula portulacea is an unusual, tree-like succulent — almost like a natural Bonsai.

Autumn and winter care

In September start to tail off the amount of water and food you give your plant and stop feeding altogether from November. Keep your plant quite dry from mid-November until mid-March.

In winter provide your Jade Plant with a temperature of around 55°F (13°C); this is especially important if you want your plant to flower in early spring. The Jade Plant likes bright light throughout the year and hates to sit in a draught.

Propagation

Take 4-5in (10-13cm) long stem cuttings, with two or three pairs of leaves, from May to July. Let the cuttings dry off, then plant them about 2in (5cm) deep in a peat and sand compost. Keep them at a temperature of around 70°F (21°C) and make sure that the

Buying Guide

The Crassula species and varieties mentioned can be bought from most good garden centres, but a specialist succulent plant nursery will have an even greater selection if you are after a real novelty!

Species

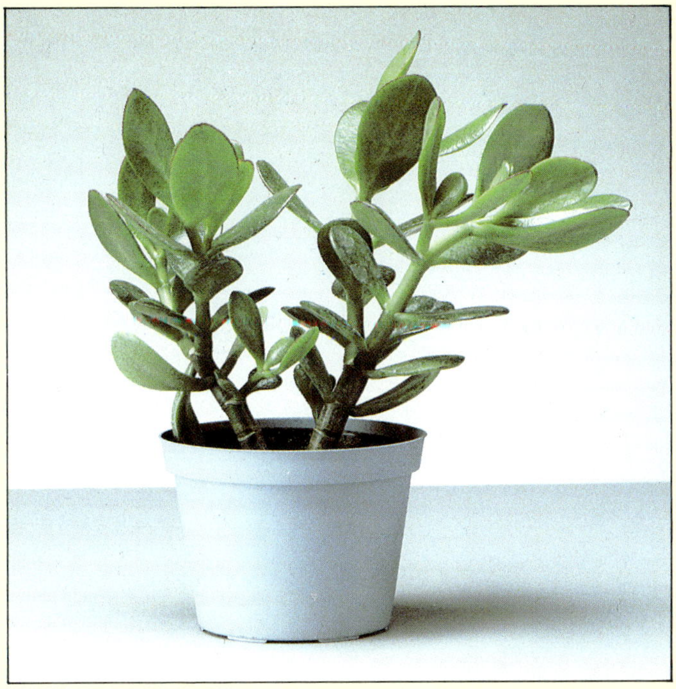

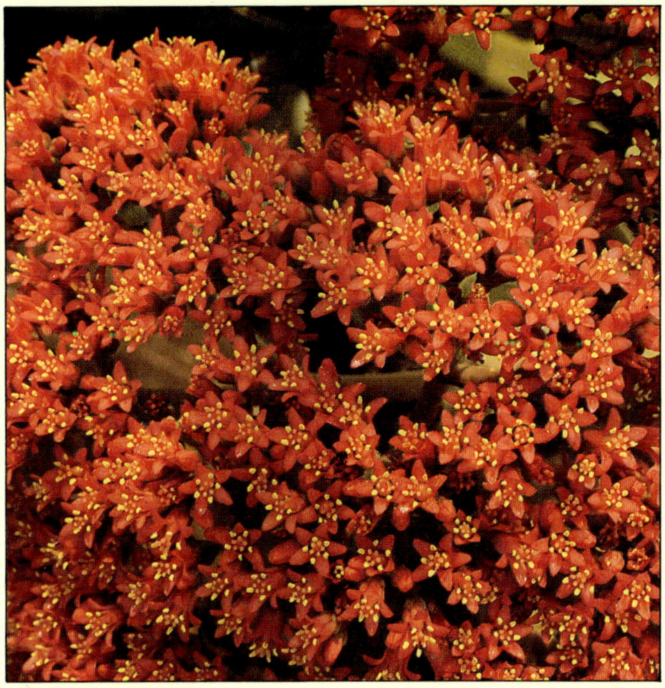

Crassula portulacea (or ***C.argentea***), the Jade Plant, comes from the dry areas of the Cape Province and southern Africa up to Natal. It grows to about 3ft (0.9m) and has thick stems, often at least 3in (7cm) thick at the base. It has lots of thick, fleshy branches covered with oval, fleshy leaves that are pale to dark green with reddish margins. Pink or whitish-pink, star-shaped flowers appear in clusters at the beginning of spring.

C.arborescens, the Silver Jade Plant, *above*, is very similar to *C.portulacea* but its leaves are silvery grey-green with small reddish dots and darker red edges. It grows to about 2ft (0.6m) high.

C.rupestris, the Concertina Plant, *right*, is a small, shrubby plant with slender stems and little oval, rounded leaves that are grey-green with reddish edges. The flowers are yellow and grouped in clusters.

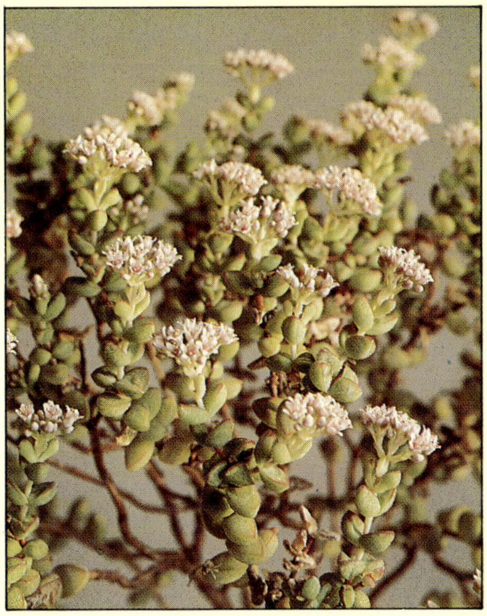

C.falcata, *above*, the Airplane Propeller Plant, from Cape Province in South Africa, may consist of a single long stem that grows to about 12in (30cm) or so. It has pointed, blue-green leaves, and orange-red clusters of flowers appear from June to August. The variety 'Minima' is one of the many pretty hybrids cultivated from this species.

C.lycopodiodes, from Namibia, is a semi-shrubby plant that grows about 9in (23cm) high. Its erect stems are covered with tiny fleshy leaves packed so tightly that the stems look four-sided. In spring and summer this plant produces minute flowers. All the varieties of this plant are fairly similar to the parent.

C.perforata, the Concertina Plant, is a straggly, small shrub with tiny leaves set opposite each other in pairs along the branches. The leaves are grey-green and dotted with small red spots.

compost is kept only just moist. When the cuttings have taken root, treat them like mature Jade Plants.

You can also propagate Crassulas from offsets (baby plants) — see the illustrations on the previous page.

Sow seeds in March or October in a tray of sandy compost, and cover them lightly with a fine dust of compost. Keep the compost just moist and provide a temperature of 60-70°F (15-21°C). When the seedlings begin to sprout, give them good light and a very little water. When the seedlings are large enough to handle, pot them up individually in John Innes No 2 or 3.

Trouble Shooter

White, fluffy patches, particularly at the stem and leaf joints, are mealy bugs; wipe them away with a small brush dipped in methylated spirits. Other pests can be dispatched by using a spray or systemic insecticide. Do not use a malathion-based insecticide as this chemical is toxic to Crassulas.

Rotting stems and leaves indicate that you have been overwatering; never let your plant stand in water, especially in cold weather, and let the compost dry out between times.

Wilting and falling leaves are due to exposure to cold or draughts; keep your plant warm and out of cold draughts.

Crossandra

Family name: **Acanthaceae**

Common name:
Firecracker Flower

Care Tricky	**Height** 2ft (0.6m)	**Flower** March-October
Light Bright indirect	**Spread** 12-18in (30-45cm)	**Humidity** High humidity
Price Middle range	**Shape** Bushy	**Availability** Garden centres
Temp. Min 60°F (15°C)	Ideal 70°F (21°C)	Max 80°F (27°C)

This beautiful, exotic plant well deserves its common name of Firecracker Flower with its fiery orange blooms.

Originally from Asia, Africa and Madagascar this plant gets its shrubby shape from its large, glossy green, spear-shaped leaves. The *Crossandra infundibuliformis* (or *undulaefolia*) is the most popular Crossandra for a very good reason — it is very pretty! It is an attractive, shrubby, shiny green plant that rarely grows taller than 2ft (0.6m) high; its crowning glory is the display of long-lasting orange-red flowers that emerge from a flower spike made up of decorative green bracts (false leaves).

The variety 'Mona Walhed' is a particularly fine plant that has been developed to show the best qualities of the species. It is more compact, only about 12in (30cm) high, and has the characteristic glossy, dark green leaves, but its flowers are a delicate shade of salmon pink instead of fiery orange-red.

The only trouble with the Firecracker Flower is that it is quite demanding in its needs; at home in the semi-tropical forest, it is shaded, warm and constantly humid, and it really needs these conditions to thrive in your home.

Spring and summer care

Repot at the beginning of March, but only if your plant is pot-bound; use a loam-based compost such as John Innes No 2 and put a few pieces of broken clay pot in the bottom of the container to help the compost drain well.

Your Firecracker Flower will be growing and flowering from March to October when you need to increase the temperature to at least 70°F (21°C); temperatures higher than this will benefit the plant as long as you sit it in semi-shade and provide plenty of humidity. Always keep your plant out of full sun, but make sure that it receives bright indirect light. Full sun damages the plant's leaves and will stop it flowering properly.

Water your Firecracker Flower about once a week, just enough to keep its compost moist; it hates wet compost but, equally, hates to be dry. Feed your plant with liquid fertiliser added to the water every two weeks during the growing season.

Autumn and winter care

In winter it is very important to provide your Firecracker Flower with a temperature of at least 60°F (15°C); higher temperatures are even better, provided you keep the atmosphere humid and the plant away from winter sun. The best situation for your plant is in slightly shaded, filtered light, well away from draughts.

Water moderately with tepid water during winter. Remove any dead leaves or flowers immediately to prevent rot and mould developing.

Propagation

You can get Firecracker Flower seeds quite easily from good garden centres and specialist seedsmen. Sow the seeds in March into a light compost of equal parts peat and sand. Give the seeds a constant temperature of 80°F (27°C) to ensure good germination — a propagator is ideal, but a good alternative is to seal a clear polythene bag over the pot and keep it on a warm windowsill. Keep the compost moist and shaded, and give the seedlings fresh air for an hour each day.

In March take 3-4in (7-10cm) long stem cuttings; dip the cut ends in hormone rooting powder and plant in compost of equal parts peat and sand. Keep in a temperature of 70°F (21°C). Pot on when they've rooted.

Species

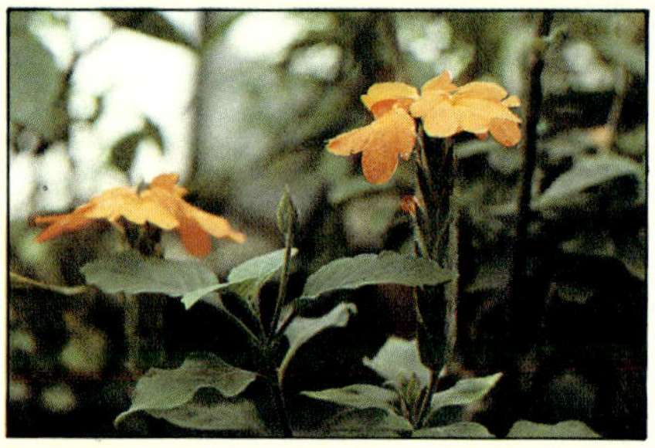

Crossandra infundibuliformis (or ***C.undulaefolia***), the Firecracker Flower, comes from India and Malaysia and grows to a maximum of 2ft (0.6m) high. It has wide, glossy green leaves about 2in (5cm) long and orange-red flowers. 'Mona Walhed', a lovely variety cultivated in Sweden, is very similar, but smaller, with shiny, dark green leaves and pretty soft salmon-pink flowers.

C.nilotica, *above*, from Tanzania is taller than the other species, 2ft (0.6m) or more high, with long glossy, dark green leaves and rich orange flowers.

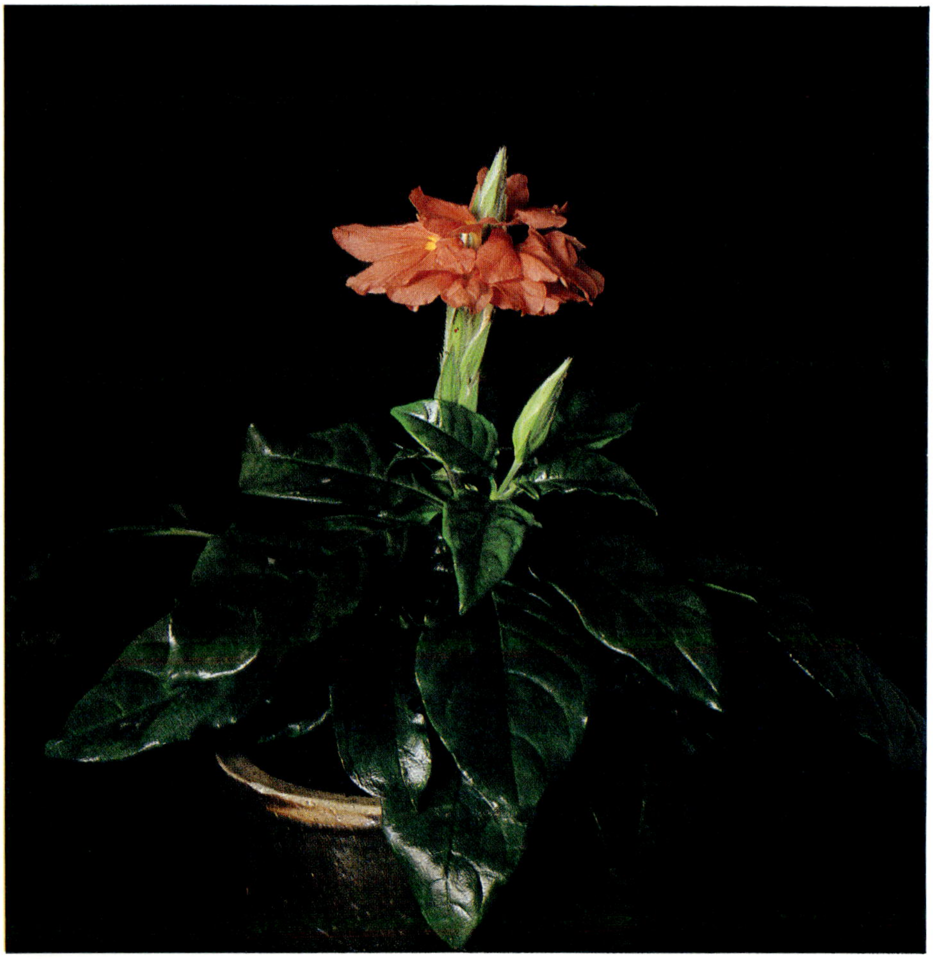

Crossandra infundibuliformis is an exotic, shrubby plant with fiery orange flowers.

Cryptanthus

Family name: **Bromeliaceae**

Common names:
Earth Star/Starfish Plant

Care Easy	**Height** 6-8in (15-20cm)	**Flower** None
Light Any situation	**Spread** 8-12in (20-30cm)	**Humidity** Regular spraying
Price Cheap	**Shape** Star-shaped	**Availability** Specialist

Temp. Min 60°F (15°C) — Ideal 70°F (21°C) — Max 80°F (27°C)

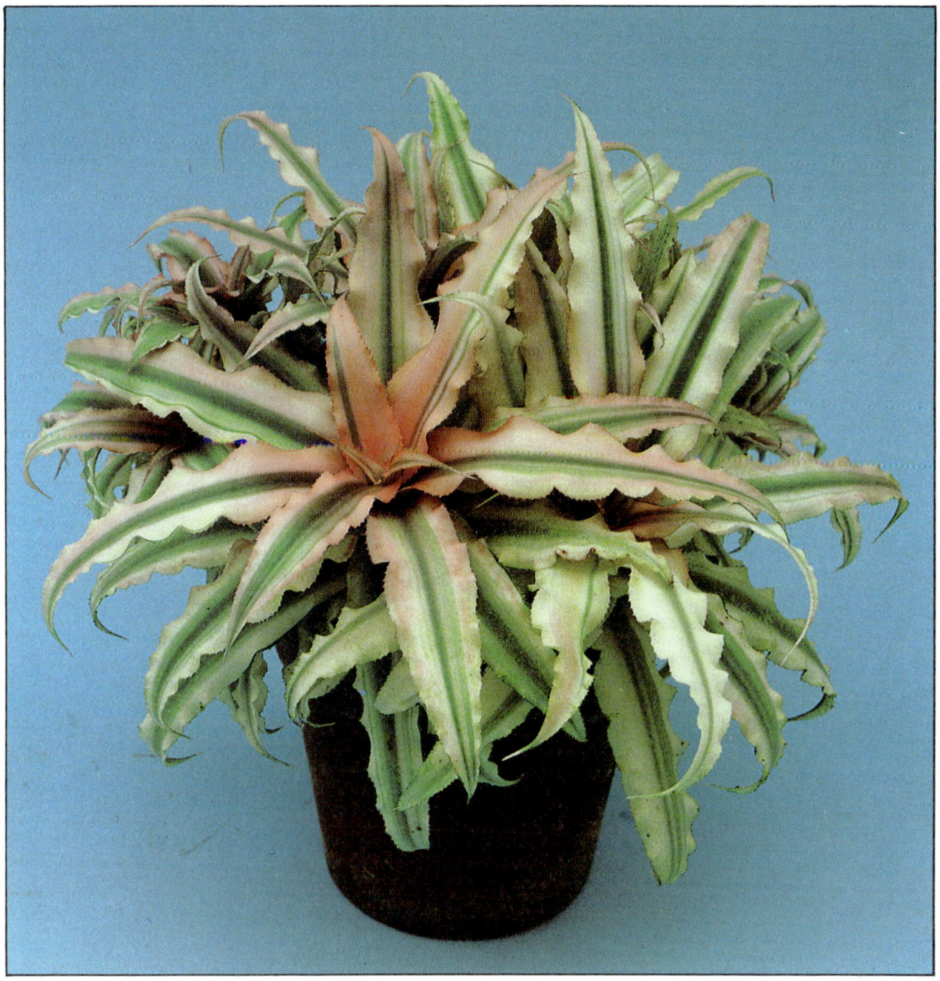

Cryptanthus bivittatus soon produces a little colony of plants as you can see!

Earth Star is an unusual Bromeliad because it lives on the ground rather than up in the trees like most other Bromeliads. Most Earth Stars do not have stems so the short, arching, lance-shaped leaves form a neat rosette close to the soil. This plant is grown for its brightly marked leaves that show wonderful colour variations in stripes, banding or mottling. Most of the species come from the Brazilian jungle where occasionally hundreds of Earth Stars appear in various colours and markings, forming a dense carpet on the forest floor — a really amazing sight!

Cryptanthus bivittatus is one of the most popular species, although there are many types of Earth Star to choose from. It looks a bit like an exotic Spider Plant with green, light green and greeny-white striped leaves arching out from the crown; the edges are crinkly and the leaves can have tinges of pink or brown in the stripes.

The Earth Star is not a fussy plant — it will tolerate full sun or shade, moist or dry conditions — but it does need warmth of not less than 60°F (15°C). This is a very adaptable plant; you can grow it in a pot, or it will settle down happily in a bottle garden attached to a clump of moss or piece of cork bark.

Spring and summer care

Water your plant about twice a week — just enough to keep the compost constantly moist. To keep the bright leaf colours, mist spray regularly every couple of days in the hottest weather. Feed the leaves directly every six to eight weeks during the growing season by adding a couple of drops of liquid fertiliser to water and mist spraying. No other feeding is necessary. In summer small white flowers appear, but they are rather insignificant compared with the leaves.

Autumn and winter care

Repotting can be done at any time of the year as long as you can provide a temperature of 70°F (21°C) until the fibrous roots establish themselves in the new compost. Use a good peat-based compost, such as Levingtons, and add a little sharp sand to help it drain well. Alternatively, you can make your own mixture as follows: two parts totally decomposed and shredded leaf-mould, one part granulated peat and one part sharp sand.

Temperature is so critical that your Earth Star will not survive if it drops below 60°F (15°C). Water so as to keep the compost moist — once a week should be just right.

When some autumn or winter sun appears, give your plant a foliar feed by adding a couple of drops of liquid fertiliser to the water in your mist sprayer and give the plant a light overhead spray.

If your Earth Star is living in a bottle garden, keep it out of the direct sun and grow

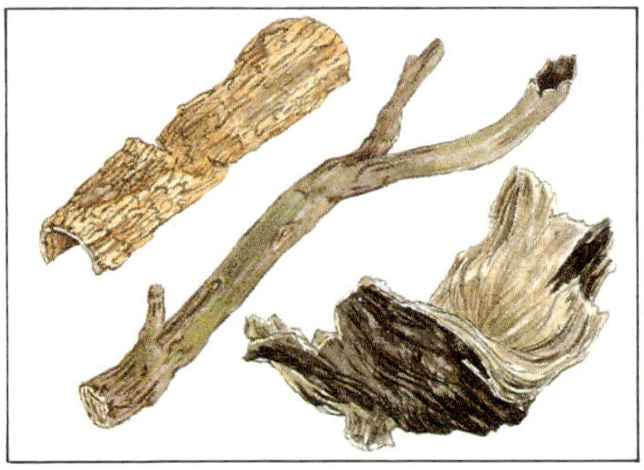

Planting an Earth Star in bark: find a nicely-shaped piece of bark.

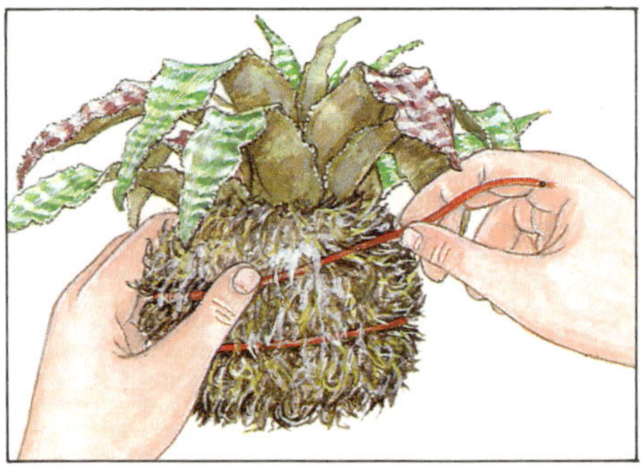

Wrap the rootball with moist sphagnum moss and tie it on.

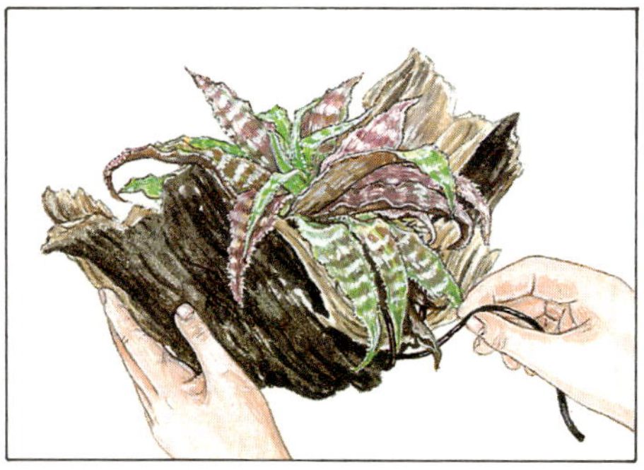

Bind the plant to the bark and just spray to keep the rootball moist.

Species

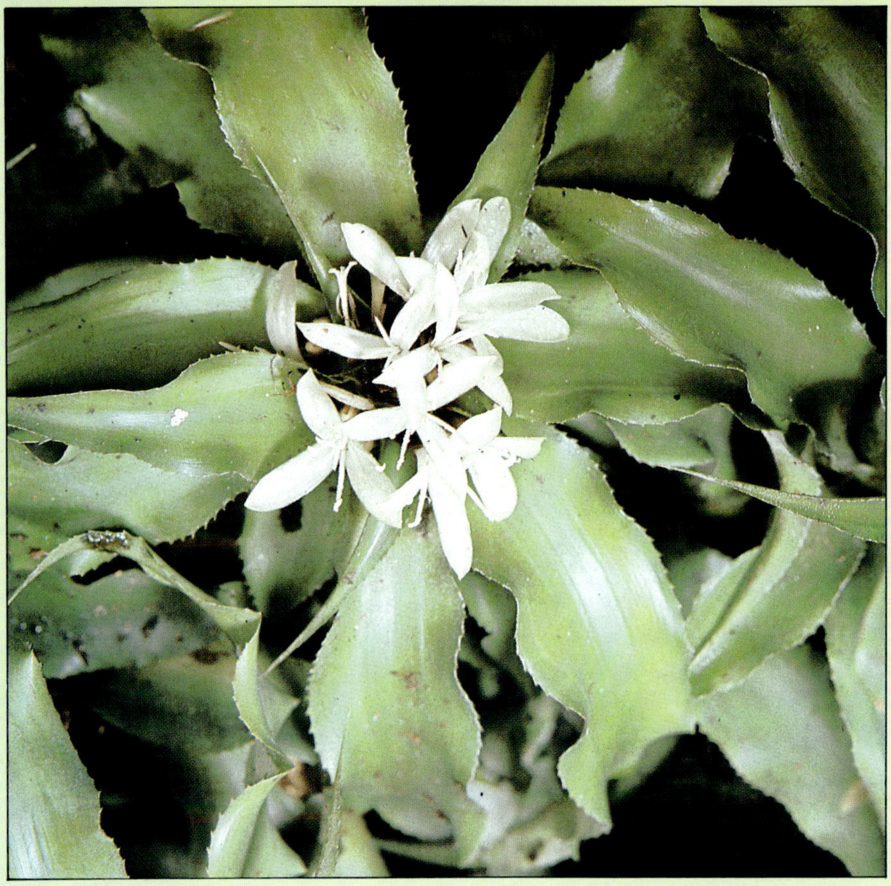

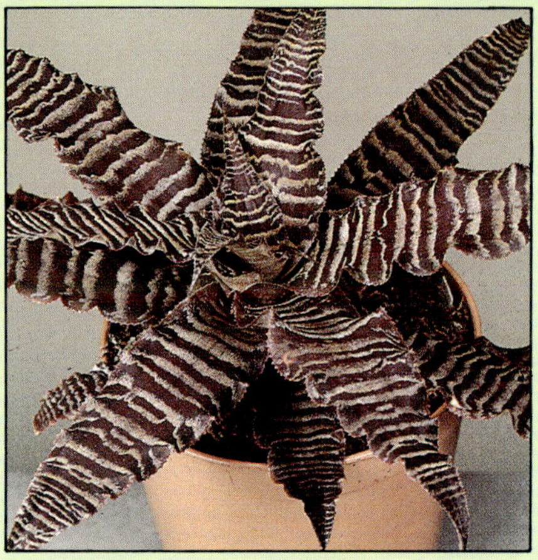

C.fosterianus, *above*, has deep magenta or coppery coloured leaves with greyish crossbanding on the upper surface and a thick layer of grey scales on the undersides. The edges of the leaves are wavy and lined with minute spines.

Cryptanthus bivittatus, Earth Star, has crinkly-edged, lance-shaped striped leaves that arch out from a ground-level rosette. There are numerous attractive varieties, and some of the best are: 'Atropurpurea', which has purplish tinged leaves that makes the stripes almost indistinguishable — it is a compact plant and very adaptable; 'Minor', a small olive green plant with reddish-brown bands of colour; and 'Tricolor', which is larger with narrow, leathery leaves about 8in (20cm) long that are mainly olive green and have creamy-white edges shaded with soft salmon-pink.

C.acaulis, *above*, the Starfish Plant, has very wavy leaves with unevenly toothed edges, pale green on top and scaly and white on the underside. It quickly multiplies to form groups. It has the best of all the Cryptanthus flowers — white, 1in (25mm) across and scented.

C.lacerdae looks a little ragged as its leaves have densely toothed and very wavy edges. The leaves are dark green with silver-white edges and whitish lines running down their length; the undersides are covered with whitish scales. 'Minima' is a miniature form.

C.zonatus is like *C.fosterianus* in that it has 6-8in (15-20cm) long strap-like leaves, but they are grass-green on top with grey-green bands across the width and almost white undersides, due to a thick layer of greyish-white scales.

C.beuckeri has spoon-shaped leaves that form a much flatter rosette. It is small, only 6in (15cm) high, and the leaves are green, marbled with white and flushed with rose-pink. The wavy edges are toothed, and the undersides are scaly and greyish-white.

C.bromelioides has a large rosette out of which grows a stem that then takes root and produces a new plant, so if you give it a large container you will soon have a small colony of them. The leaves are soft, a little fleshy, about 8in (20cm) long, green on top and white and scaly underneath. 'Tricolor' is very eyecatching. Its green leaves are striped lengthways with creamy-white lines, flushed slightly with pale pink, and they have densely but finely toothed edges in reddish-maroon.

it in a mixture of sphagnum moss and peat with a little shredded bark. Make sure that water doesn't collect around the roots; just give it as much moisture as it can absorb and water again when the mixture is dry.

Propagation

The easiest method of propagation is to divide the plant. Most Earth Stars produce offsets (baby plants) that sprout around the base. Knock the plant out of its pot, and carefully pull an offset away from the main plant by gently teasing apart the roots. Plant the offset in its own pot of compost. Keep the compost moist and provide a temperature of 70°F (21°C) or higher until the plant's roots start growing, then look after it in the same way as a mature plant.

The rarer species are harder to find and generally need to be grown from seeds, which you can buy from a specialist. Lay the seeds on a tray filled with the recommended compost and lightly cover them with a fine layer of compost. Keep the seeds constantly moist, in a shaded place, and provide a temperature of 80°F (27°C). Use a propagator if you have one and open it up to give the seeds some fresh air each day. If you do not have a propagator, put the seed tray in a clear polythene bag in a shaded but warm place and, similarly, open up the bag to ventilate the seeds each day.

Trouble Shooter

Leaves browning at the tips and eventually dying altogether are a sign of excessive dryness; do not leave your plant without water for any length of time — but do not go to the other extreme and overwater.

Leaves can lose their colour if the plant sits in shade for too long; bright light from a sunny window will keep the leaves colourful.

Cycas

Family name: **Cycadaceae**

Common name: **Sago Palm**

Care Straightforward	**Height** 3-4ft (0.9-1.2m)	**Flower** None
Light Bright indirect sun	**Spread** 4ft (1.2m)	**Humidity** High humidity
Price Expensive	**Shape** Palm-like	**Availability** Specialist

Temp. Min 60°F (15°C) — Ideal 80°F (27°C) — Max 90°F (33°C)

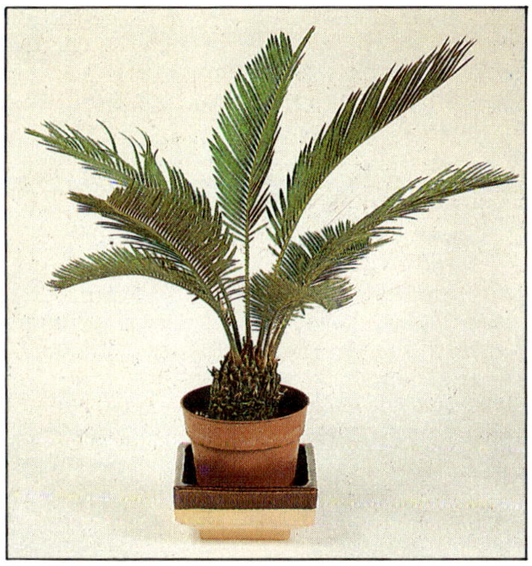

Cycas revoluta has arching fronds.

The Sago Palm is a primitive form of plant that has remained almost unchanged since prehistoric times. Despite this impressive pedigree, the Sago Palm adapts well to living indoors where it makes a very handsome and unusual houseplant; and the fact that the plant in your living room is virtually identical to plants that existed along with dinosaurs millions of years ago is quite something to think about!

The most popular species is *Cycas revoluta*, a native of Indonesia and Japan. It is very slow growing with a thick trunk — young plants look rather like a pineapple until the trunk starts to grow. Palm-like fronds, each about 3ft (0.9m) long, arch out from a central crown; each frond is composed of many tightly-packed narrow leaflets, making the fronds look like large green feathers. A mature plant may produce a spectacular flower cone in the centre of the crown, but this is very unlikely in the home.

Quite similar, but harder to find, is the *Cycas circinalis* from Madagascar and India. Although it is a tropical plant, it is not difficult to look after; give it a bright but semi-shaded position and its fronds will show a lovely depth of colour.

Give your Sago Palm plenty of warmth and humidity to encourage it to grow well — even though this will be painfully slowly!

Spring and summer care

Your Sago Palm is a very slow-growing plant and will only need repotting every three or four years when the roots completely fill its pot. It is very important that this plant has quick-draining compost so that its roots don't sit in water for any length of time; put some pebbles or broken pieces of clay pot in the bottom of the container and use John Innes No 2.

The Sago Palm enjoys temperatures of 75-80°F (24-27°C) and higher; water your plant freely in summer and, provided the compost drains well, it will be happy. In the hottest weather water as often as two to three times a week. Add liquid fertiliser to the water every six to eight weeks to keep up the supply of nutrients; do not feed more often as overfeeding makes the plant grow too fast and lose its shape. If possible put your plant outside from June to September, but shelter it from strong sun.

Autumn and winter care

Water just enough to keep the soil moist, but no more, and keep your plant in a temperature of 60-65°F (15-18°C). If you cannot provide these temperatures, water your plant even less. Even in winter make sure that your plant gets a little fresh, circulating, but non-draughty, air.

Propagation

March to May is the best time to sow seeds; lay the large seeds on the surface of a tray filled with a mixture of John Innes No 2 and sharp sand. Keep the seeds in a constant temperature of between 75-80°F (24-27°C); use a propagator or put the seed tray in a clear polythene bag and keep it on a warm, sunny windowsill and mist spray every day, even twice a day if temperatures rise higher. When each seed germinates it produces a fleshy root; throw away the seeds that don't sprout when the others do and gently push the germinated seeds into the compost.

If your plant produces offsets you can carefully remove them at any time of the year and grow them on in pots of John Innes No2. Provide a temperature of 75-80°F (24-27°C) and, when they have taken root, treat them as mature Sago Palms.

Species

Cycas revoluta hails from Indonesia and Japan; it has a thick trunk and dark green palm-like fronds. The leaflets of each frond curve under slightly at the edges and grow out of a central spine. The plant grows to about 3-4ft (0.9-1.2m) in the home — very slowly!

C.circinalis comes from Madagascar and India and is similar to *C. revoluta*, but each frond is flat and the effect is generally more graceful.

The following all make very good houseplants and, even though they have different names, they belong to the same family. They are, however, not easily available so you will need to go to a specialist nursery to find them:

Dioon edulis, the Mexican Palm, *below left,* from Mexico, is very similar to *C. revoluta* but has grey-green fronds that are definitely more feathery. It is also very slow growing.

Encephalartos, *below,* from South Africa, and ***Macrozamia***, from Australia, are both very similar to the Sago Palm and are occasionally sold as such.

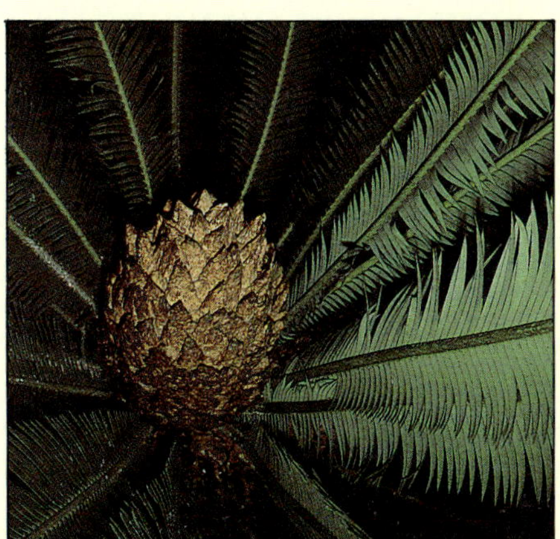

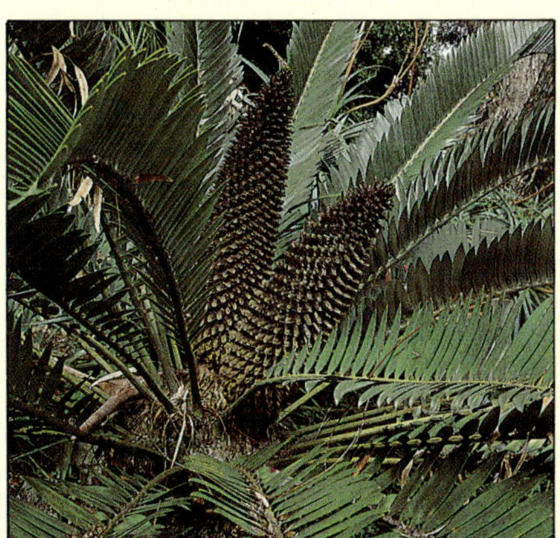

Trouble Shooter

Mealy bug and scale insect sometimes attack the Sago Palm; wipe them away with a brush dipped in methylated spirits.

Brown leaves occur if you do not water your plant enough in the summer, or if it is exposed to cold in winter (especially if you overwater as well); take the appropriate action and your Sago Palm should recover.

Cyclamen

Family name: **Primulaceae**

Common name: **Cyclamen**

Care Straight-forward	**Height** 12in (30cm)	**Flower** November-March
Light Bright indirect sun	**Spread** 12-16in (30-40cm)	**Humidity** None
Price Middle range	**Shape** Bushy	**Availability** Common
Temp. Min 40°F (5°C)	Ideal 55°F (13°C)	Max 65°F (18°C)

The Cyclamen is one of the most popular houseplants of all, partly due to the fact that it flowers from late November all the way through to March, so it brightens up a room when a lot of other plants are uninteresting.

The Cyclamen grows from a corm — a thick, oval, fibrous disk — rounded on the bottom where the roots grow from, with a dip in the top where the stems grow. In the wild some of the corms are starchy and edible, but they are not eaten by people — pigs are rather partial to them! In the areas where this happens, Cyclamen is sometimes called Sowbread. Another interesting fact about Cyclamen is that in the wild the seeds are distributed by ants.

The species you are most likely to see in the shops is *Cyclamen persicum* or one of its many offspring. The shuttlecock-shape flowers unfurl from the base of the plant in continuous succession throughout winter on long 9in (23cm) stems in shades of white, pink, red or purple. Some varieties have attractively ruffled petal edges. The heart-shaped leaves are very attractive and have distinctive silvery grey-green patterns on a dark green background.

If you treat your Cyclamen well it will live for three or four years and, as a bonus, each year it will produce more flowers than the year before, until it declines in vigour.

Spring and summer care

Since the main period of activity for Cyclamen is from November to March, summer care is minimal. The Cyclamen actually dies down in late spring and is dormant all summer.

As the stems shrivel and dry out in late spring gently pull them out from the corm. Aim to break them away right at the surface of the corm as otherwise stumps can rot and kill the plant; if you wait until the stems are dead and dry they will pull away cleanly. Simply keep the soil around the corm moist by watering occasionally — don't overwater and don't let the soil dry out. As soon as new growth starts to appear, give your plant a little more water.

Autumn and winter care

Water your Cyclamen just enough to keep the soil constantly moist; do make sure that your plant never stands in water as this will rot its roots. Water your Cyclamen by pouring the water into the plant's saucer, let it sit for about 20 minutes then pour away any water not absorbed by the compost. If you water a Cyclamen from the top, you run the risk of the water lodging in the dip of the corm and rotting the plant at the base.

Flower buds should start to appear in late September or October and your plant will continue to produce flowers right through to April. While your Cyclamen is growing actively, give it a temperature of 50-60°F (10-15°C) and sit it in bright light, but not full sunlight. Try to keep it in a cool room as central heating will dry it out and cause the flowers to fade quickly. Feed your plant with liquid fertiliser every two or three weeks by adding it to the water; this will help the leaves and flowers to develop properly.

Your Cyclamen will enjoy a breath of fresh air and some humidity while it's flowering. Provide humidity by standing your plant on a tray of moist pebbles so moisture can evaporate around the leaves when it is warm. Be careful to check that this does not make your plant too wet, however, as it is very prone to rot. Remove dead flowers immediately by sharply twisting them off so that the stalk snaps at the base of the corm; do the same with dying leaves.

As the flowers and leaves begin to fade in late spring, gradually reduce the amount of water you give your plant so that you do not force it to keep growing but encourage it into dormancy. Then keep the compost just short of dry, giving it very little water..

After flowering, if your Cyclamen has filled its pot tightly with roots, repot it when the leaves have died down. You might have to repot every year, but don't do it unless the roots are really tightly packed, as your Cyclamen will flower best when it is slightly pot-bound. Use John Innes No 2 and put a few pieces of broken clay pot in the bottom of the container as this will help the compost to drain well.

Propagation

If you are a keen gardener, try growing your own Cyclamen plants from seed any time from July to September. Sow them in John Innes No 2 with a handful of added sharp sand and keep in a temperature of 65-75°F (18-24°C). Put the seed tray in a dark, warm place and check it every day to make sure the compost is just moist. The seeds should germinate in five or six weeks.

When the seedlings are large enough to handle, pot each one individually into a 2in (5cm) pot; keep the compost moist and provide a temperature of 60-65°F (15-18°C). Repot as necessary when each little plant fills its pot, until by the following May or early June it is in a 4 or 6in (10 or 15cm) pot. Feed the plants every six weeks, provide an even temperature and flowers should appear from October onwards. Then you can treat them as mature plants.

To divide a corm, see illustrations opposite.

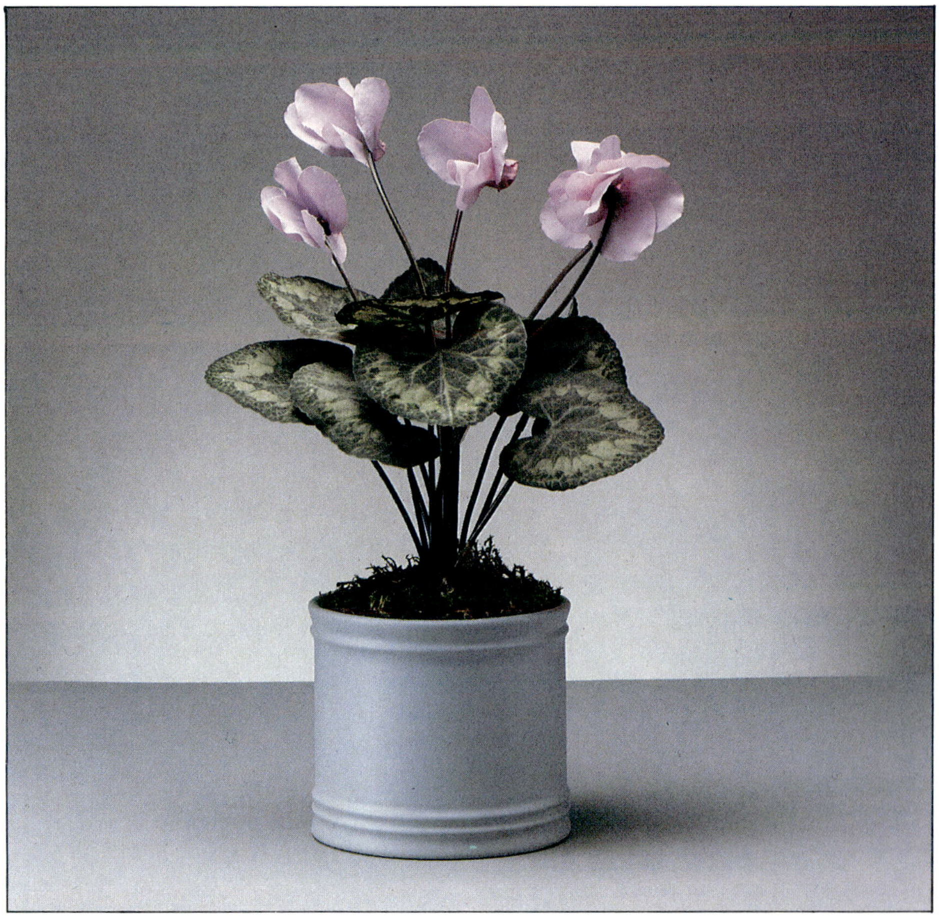

Cyclamen persicum has decorative leaves and flowers from November until March.

Species

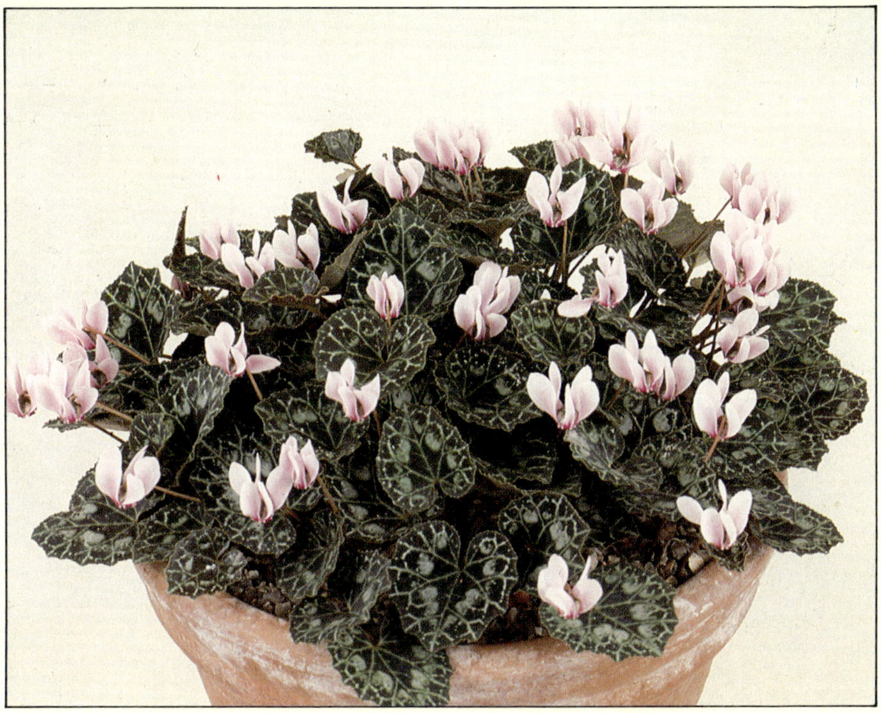

Cyclamen persicum, from North Africa, the Middle East and Crete, has rounded, heart-shaped leaves with grey or silver-green markings on dark green. The flowers appear at the tops of long stalks and come in white, pink, red or purple.

The many varieties are grouped under the name *C.persicum giganteum*. Some pretty plants are 'Candlestick' with soft pink flowers, banded with reddish pink; 'Bonfire' is a neat compact plant with bright scarlet, glossy flowers and attractively marked leaves; 'Rococo' has pink or pinkish-red flowers with slightly fleshy petals that have frilly edges and the centre in a deeper reddish colour; and 'Vogt's Double' has double flowers in shades of pink.

C.graecum, *above*, from Greece and the Greek islands, has flowers that vary in colour from pale pink shades to salmon-pink and appear in September. It has heart-shaped, quite velvety leaves, patterned with silver-white and with thicker, stiff edges.

C.libanoticum, *above right*, from the Lebanon, has dark green leaves, often with yellow markings, and various colours on the undersides of the leaves. The flowers are quite large, purplish-pink and speckled.

C.balearicum, *right*, from Majorca and neighbouring islands, flowers from March to April. The flowers are small, numerous and a delicate pinkish-white with a pink throat and a slight scent.

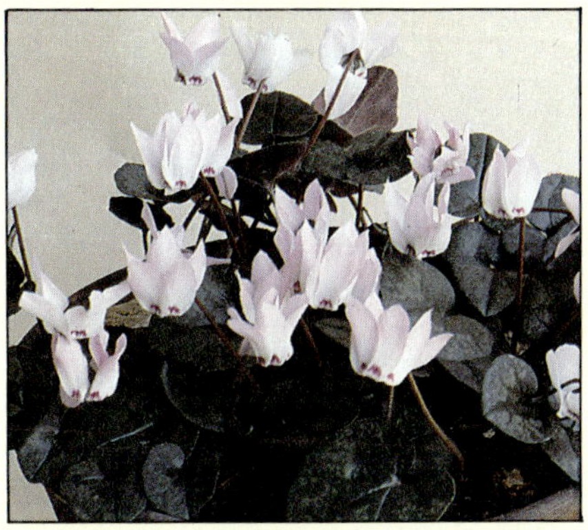

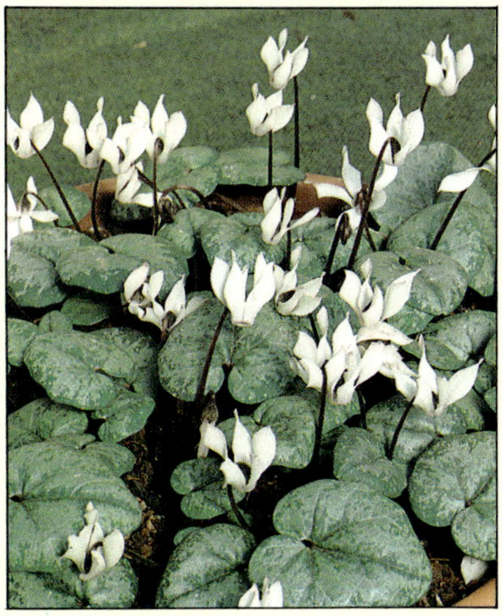

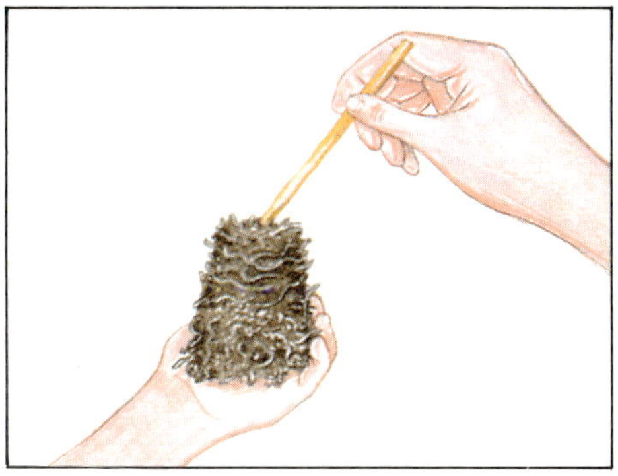

Dividing a corm: in late spring remove the soil from around the roots.

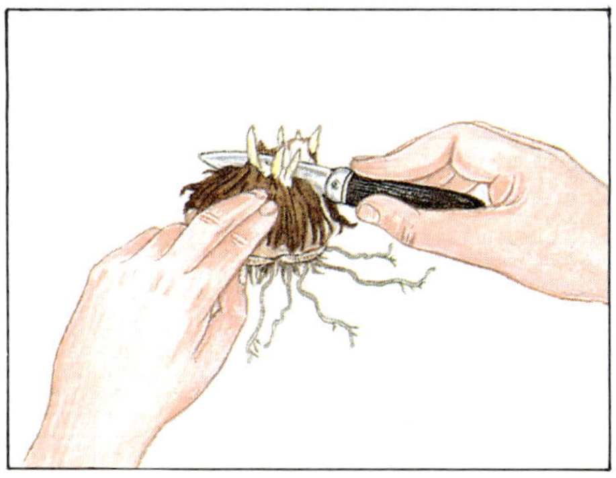

Cut the corm so each half has leaf buds. Dust the cut with sulphur powder.

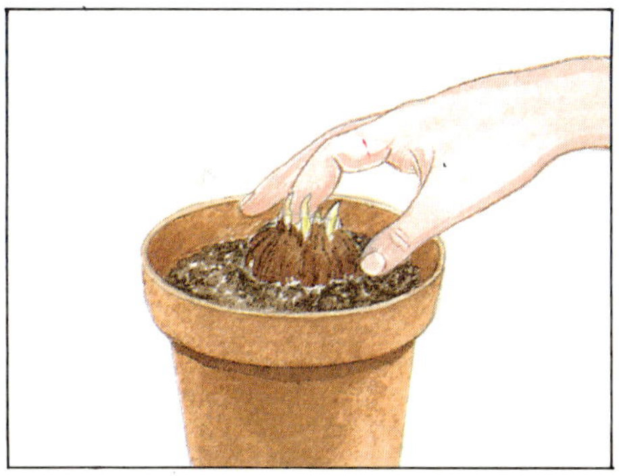

Plant each half in John Innes No 2 and keep in a cool place.

Trouble Shooter

Discoloured leaves and eventually root, corm and stem rot are encouraged very easily by overwatering; give your plant a drier and more airy spot to live in, remove the affected leaves and spray the plant with dichloran. Always water into a Cyclamen's drip tray, not directly onto the compost.

Shrivelling, yellowing leaves are a signal that the air is too dry and the temperature too high or that the plant has been exposed to full sun; move your plant to a more shaded place, but where it will still receive good light, keep the compost moist and provide temperatures of 60 to 65°F (15-18°C).

Cymbidium

Family name: **Orchidaceae**

Common name: **Cymbidium**

Care Straight-forward	**Height** 15in-4ft (38cm-1.2m)	**Flower** November-March
Light Bright indirect sun	**Spread** 2-4ft (0.6-1.2m)	**Humidity** Regular spraying
Price Expensive	**Shape** Arching	**Availability** Garden centres
Temp. Min 60°F (15°C)	Ideal 70°F (21°C)	Max 80°F (27°C)

If you adore Orchids but don't have a hot house, a Cymbidium is absolutely perfect for you as it is an exceptionally pretty plant. The great virtue of this Orchid is that it is a very tolerant and easy to grow plant; it happily accepts a little neglect and still manages to flower magnificently! However, it will respond to a bit of love and attention by producing truly spectacular flowers.

In its native habitat, the Cymbidium grows in the trees as well as on the ground, in either the semi-desert or rain forest areas of Australia and the Far East. All the houseplants, though, are the type which, in the wild, grow in trees.

The popularity of Cymbidium has led growers to develop many hybrids and these have flowers in a wide variety of colours — from pure white to deep purple, pink to pinky red and often with another colour staining the centre of the flower. As many as 15 flowers each 3in (7cm) across can be produced on a single flower spike and a plant can have three or more flower spikes in a season and each flower can last about six weeks.

The slender leaves are evergreen and sometimes quite graceful, and look rather like giant blades of grass growing from a flat bulb at compost level. When not in flower a Cymbidium is not a remarkable plant, but it more than makes up for this when it is!

Cymbidium hybrids are divided into two groups: 'standards' that are large arching plants 4ft (1.2m) or more high and 'miniatures' that grow to a maximum of about 15in (38cm) tall. Miniature Cymbidiums make the most successful houseplants as they are a more manageable size.

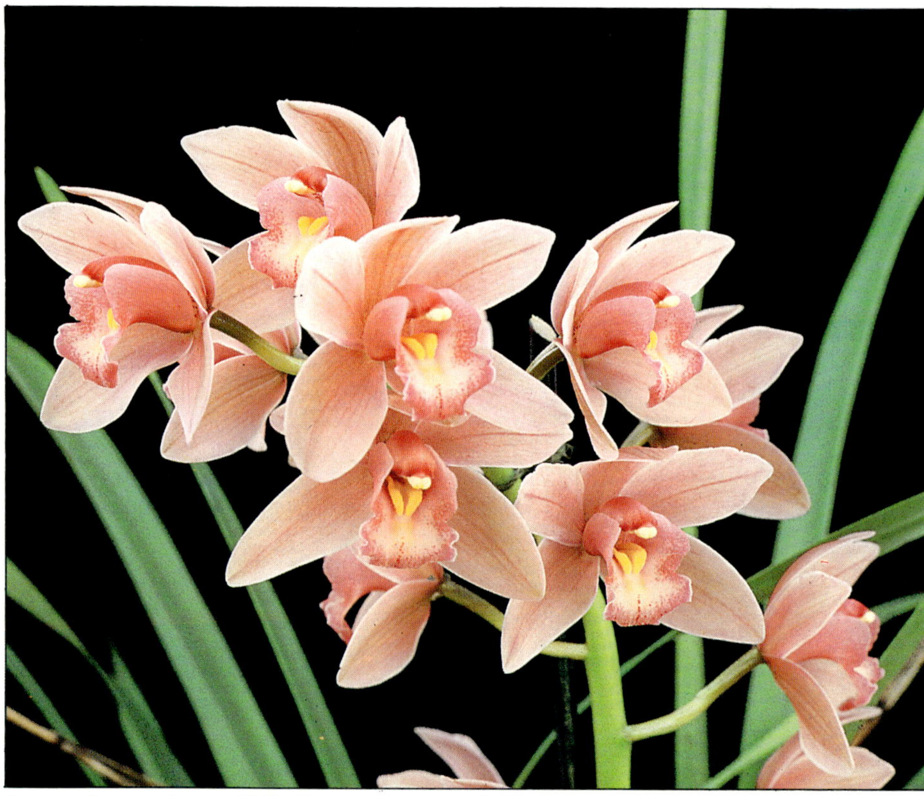

A pink-flowered Cymbidium — just one of the many magnificent varieties.

Spring and summer care

Orchids only need repotting every three or four years in spring. Good Orchid composts can be bought from garden centres or, alternatively, you can make your own by mixing together one part fibrous loam, two parts sphagnum moss peat and one part washed river sand. Make sure that the pot will drain well by putting a few bits of broken clay pot or a handful of small pebbles in the bottom of the container. This also weights the pot, which is useful as the plant can get top heavy.

From April to September water your plant freely but let the compost dry out almost completely between waterings — too much water will rot the roots. Every two weeks throughout the growing season add a few drops of a liquid fertiliser high in nitrogen to the water — or you can buy special orchid fertiliser. Towards the end of summer change to a fertiliser high in potash.

Cymbidiums like a humid atmosphere, so mist spray regularly when the weather is hot, though not in full sun. In fact, your plant will be happiest in a bright spot that is out of direct sun as the sun's rays will scorch and eventually kill the plant's leaves. The ideal temperature during the summer months is within the range of 60-75°F (15-24°C). When temperatures outside are reliably warm you can put your Cymbidium outside in a lightly shaded spot to enjoy the fresh air.

Autumn and winter care

Many Cymbidiums flower from late autumn until early spring and they need special care during this time. A temperature of between 60-65°F (15-18°C) is the ideal range for the winter months, though this can fall to about 55°F (13°C) overnight as long as it gets warmer during the day. Your plant will grow better if you provide good air circulation, but guard against draughts. Keep your Cymbidium in a really bright position, though not full sun nor deep shade, especially when your plant is in flower.

Collect rain-water if you can, otherwise use tepid tap water; water freely each time and then wait until the compost is dry before watering again — never water when the compost is still moist.

In late September or October your plant will probably form flower spikes, but will take two or three months before producing flowers. When the flower spikes are quite tall, tie them loosely but firmly to thin stakes so that they will stay upright — sometimes the weight of the flowers causes the flower spikes to keel over. Do be careful to insert the canes into the soil gently, feeling for the roots as you go.

Trouble Shooter

Red spider mite will attack if you keep your Cymbidium in too dry an atmosphere or forget to water it for some time; spray with derris to kill the spider mite and, from then on, water your plant when it is dry to provide some humidity — but beware of going to the other extreme and overwatering your plant, which is equally bad for it.

Buying Guide

Cymbidiums can seem expensive to buy, but they are well worth the money. When well cared for, they flower for months at a time and will grow successfully for many years.

Choose a plant while it's in bloom so that you can see the colour of its flowers If you go to an Orchid specialist you will have a greater range of colours and shapes to choose from.

Propagation

The only practical way to increase your Cymbidium is by division, but be warned, your plant is unlikely to flower the year after being split into two plants. Divide your plant in the following way: knock it out of its pot, shaking off the compost. See where the plant divides into two naturally and then pull the plant apart along this division. You will need to be firm but try to tease the roots apart in such a way as to cause the least amount of damage.

Plant the divisions separately into rough sphagnum peat in a pot only a little bigger than the roots need. Keep the compost moist and the plants in a shaded but warm place until they start to grow roots. When the divisions start to put down roots of their own, transfer them to pots, again only slightly bigger than the roots, fill with a good Orchid compost or a mixture of one part fibrous loam, two parts sphagnum moss peat and one part washed river sand. Provide good drainage by putting some pebbles or pieces of broken clay pot in the bottom of the containers. Then you can treat them like mature Cymbidiums.

Species

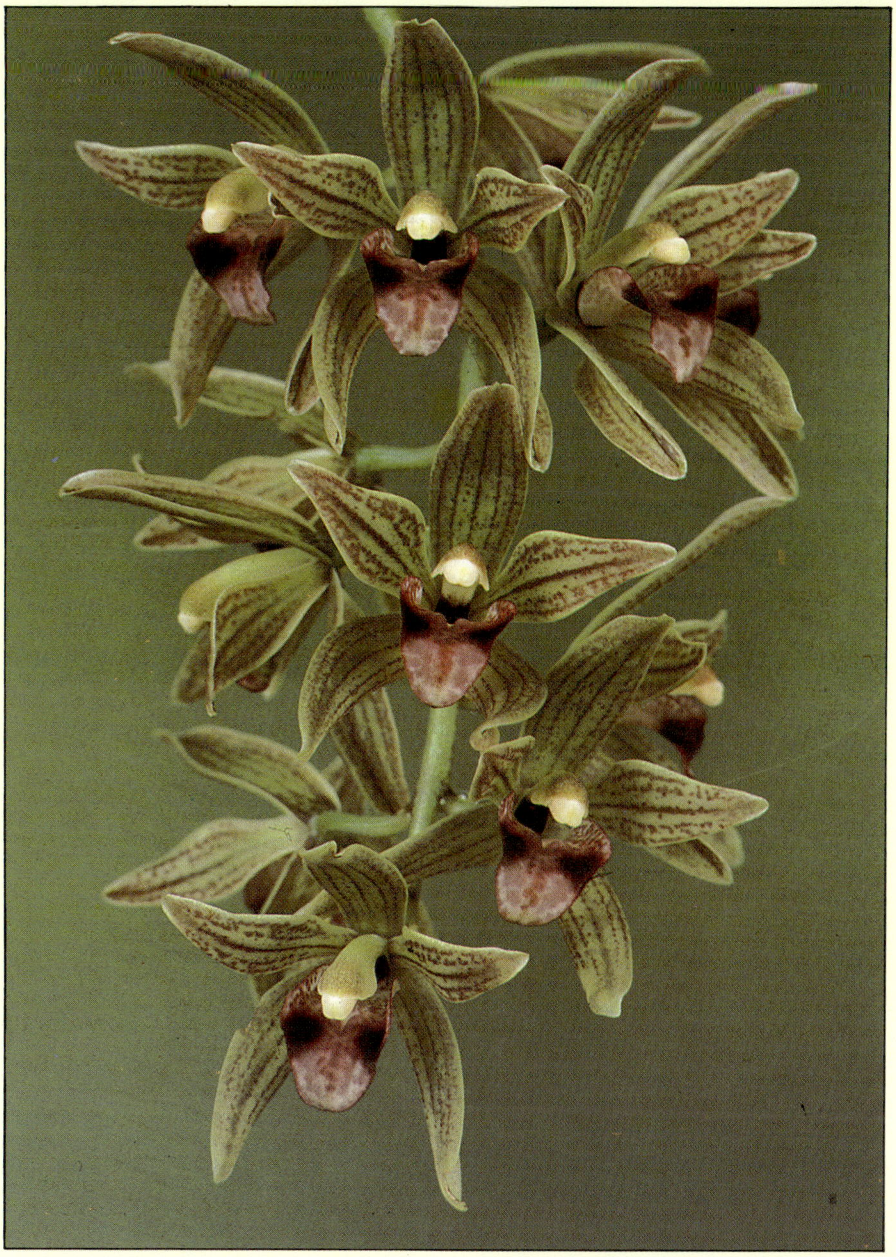

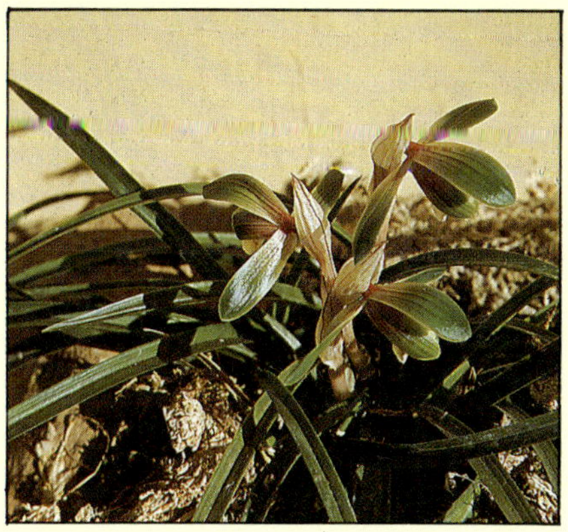

Cymbidium pumilum, from south China, is a terrestial (meaning it grows on the ground) Orchid. It has long, strap-like bright green leaves about 12in (30cm) long. The waxy flowers are reddish-brown and yellow and each about 2in (5cm) across.

This species is the main parent of many of the hybrids, which are either 'standard' or 'miniature'. 'Albo-marginatum' has white-edged leaves and reddish-brown flowers that have a white lip with red spots. It flowers in August and September and produces more flowers for several weeks after the first ones appear. 'Flirtation' is a true miniature and a very compact plant. Its flowers come in various shades of greenish cream, pink or brownish purple but all have a white lip spotted in dark maroon. 'Mary Pinchess Del Ray', from America, is a very popular yellow-flowered Cymbidium.

C.virescens, *above*, from Japan, is a very pretty miniature with slender leaves and small, very fragrant, green and red flowers with a white lip spotted with red. 'Angustifolium' has vivid green flowers with delicate purple stripes, a yellowish-white lip shading to yellow and purplish markings or mottling.

C.devonianum, *left*, from Assam and Sikkim in India, has deep yellow-green flowers with crimson spots and a purplish-red lip. The flowers are 1-1½in (25-38mm) across and are produced very freely.

C.tigrinum, from Burma and India, doesn't grow very tall as its leaves are only 6in (15cm) long. Each flower spike produces three to seven flowers, about 2in (5cm) across. The flowers are yellowish - green with a three-lobed lip — the centre one is white with red spots, the two either side are at an angle to the centre and yellow with reddish markings. This species is a parent of many of the hybrids.

C.grandiflorum, from the eastern Himalayas, is a standard Cymbidium. The leaves are up to 2ft (0.6m) long and six to twelve flowers, each 3-4in (7-10cm) across, bloom on every flower stalk. The flowers are a little fleshy and sweetly scented, mostly green with a yellow lip that has red markings or speckling.

Cyperus

Family name: **Cyperaceae**

Common name: **Umbrella Plant**

Care Straightforward	**Height** 18-24in (45-60cm)	**Flower** July-Sept
Light Bright	**Spread** 9-12in (23-30cm)	**Humidity** Regular mist spraying
Price Expensive	**Shape** Umbrella	**Availability** Specialist
Temp. Min 55°F (13°C)	Ideal 70-80°F (21-27°C)	Max 85°F (30°C)

This eyecatching and unusual type of grass is a native of South America, Africa, Asia and Europe where it grows in the semi-marsh areas. *Cyperus alternifolius* is the most often seen Umbrella Plant, the common name referring to the shape of its narrow, green leaves, which radiate like the ribs of an open umbrella from the top of a long, narrow stalk. Pale green and brown grass-like flowers radiate similarly from among the ribs and stand above the leaves like a halo. However, the flowers themselves are unremarkable.

There are some interesting naturally occurring variations of this plant as well as the beautiful common Umbrella Plant. There is, for instance, a miniature version, which is very pretty, and a very striking variegated variety that has creamy-white horizontal bands on the leaves.

Cyperus esculentus from the Punjab in India has lovely slender arching leaves and produces tubers (rounded sections of root that act as food stores for the plant) that are edible and called Tiger Nuts.

The most remarkable plant in this family is *Cyperus papyrus* from which paper was made by the ancient Egyptians. It still grows naturally in the watery margins of the banks of the river Nile. Papyrus is very tall and elegant and is becoming increasingly popular as a houseplant.

To grow an Umbrella Plant successfully you must give it gentle warmth in winter and keep it constantly moist — in fact this is one of the very few houseplants that it's almost impossible to overwater as it loves to have its feet in water all the time!

Trouble Shooter

Leaves wilting, then turning yellow show you have not been giving your plant enough water; remember that this plant grows in swamps and must be watered freely, especially in warm weather, and given high levels of humidity.

The same thing can also happen if the temperature is too low in winter; cut the stalks down to within 2in (5cm) of the soil level, keep in a temperature above 55°F (13°C) and water enough so the compost is moist.

Greenfly sometimes attack Cyperus; spray with a suitable insecticide, such as pyrethrum.

Spring and summer care

Repot your plant, if it has filled its pot with roots, at the beginning of the growing season, in about March, before it starts to grow actively. Use John Innes No 2 and, since Cyperus loves moisture, mix some charcoal chippings into the compost to keep it fresh. Charcoal will prevent the water becoming stagnant.

Your Umbrella Plant will enjoy temperatures of 70-80°F (21-27°C), provided it gets lots of humidity and regular mist spraying every day; any higher than this and you need to give your plant a little shade or move it out of direct sun.

This is the one plant you can water generously; indeed, keep 2-3in (5-7cm) of water in the drip tray so your plant can drink freely. Add a half-strength liquid fertiliser to the water every two weeks from March until September. Cut the occasional dead leaf stalk right back to the base of the plant.

Autumn and winter care

Keep your plant in a temperature of between 55-60°F (13-15°C), but remember if it gets hotter, to increase the level of humidity proportionally. It is essential to keep the compost really moist, but not wet, even in winter. If you cannot keep your plant in the recommended temperature range, lessen the amount of water you give it, but make sure that it is kept nicely moist.

Propagation

In spring you can divide your plant into two. It's advisable to do this job outside, as this is a particularly messy business due to the very moist compost! Knock the plant out of its pot, supporting the stems with one hand, and shake off the compost. Look for a natural division in the roots and then carefully but firmly pull the plant into two sections, taking care to snap as few roots as possible. Tidy up the rootball a little by cutting off any old woody roots. Plant the sections in pots filled with John Innes No 2 with some charcoal chips mixed in with it. Water the compost thoroughly.

Alternatively, you can cut off a matured flower head with leaves, retaining a few inches of the stem. Then trim the leaves back with a pair of scissors, cutting off about half the length of each leaf. Turn the cutting upside down and rest the 'umbrella' on the surface of either a jam jar of room temperature water or a tray of moist sand. Keep the

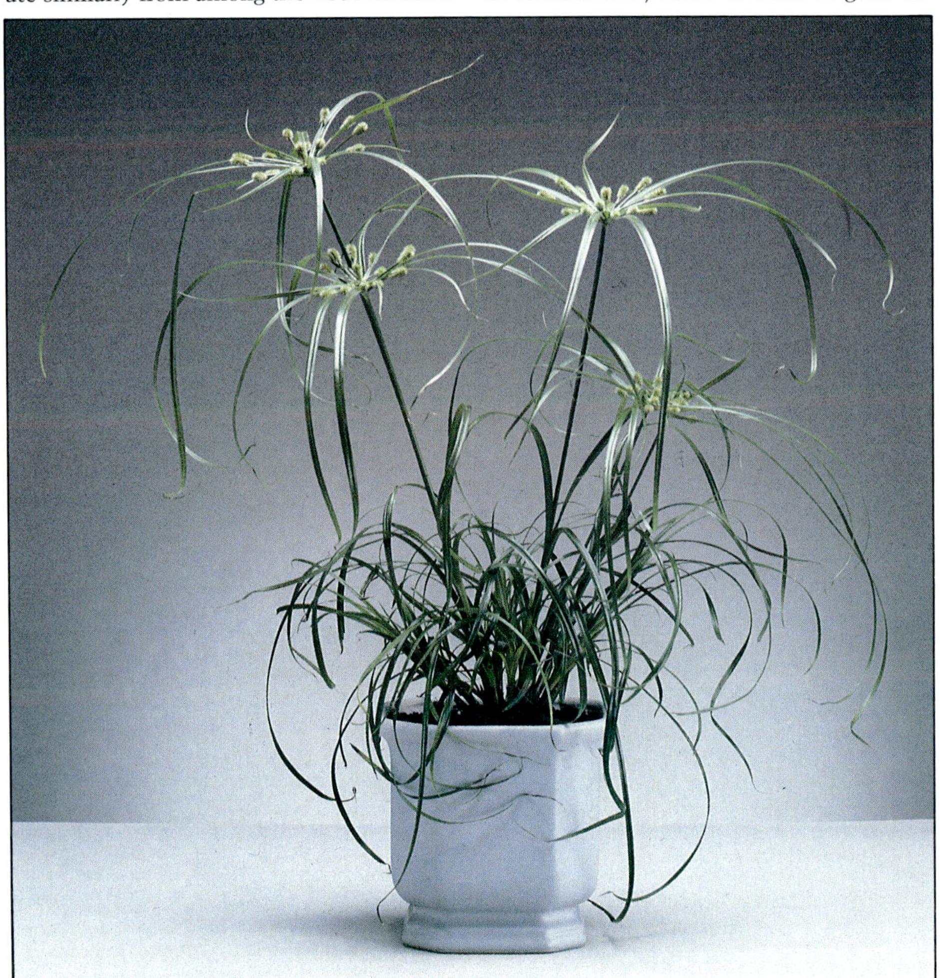

Cyperus alternifolius is an unusual, attractive, moisture-loving plant.

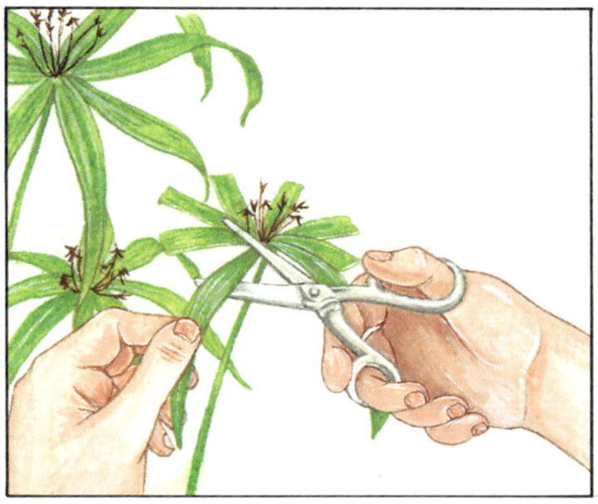

Taking Cyperus cuttings: cut off a stem with a matured flower head and trim the leaves back to half their length.

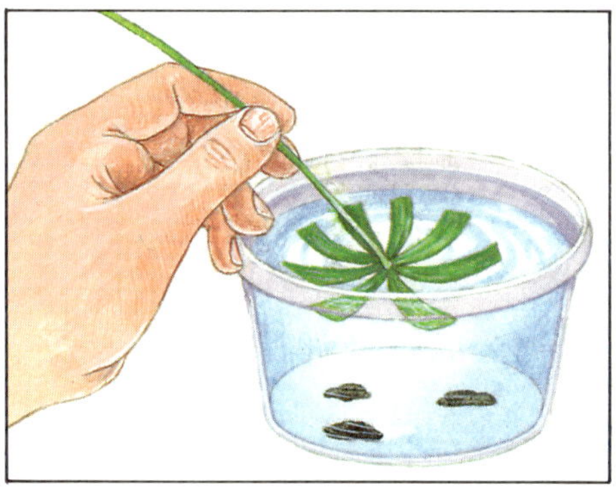

Rest the cutting stem up in a jar of tepid water, placing a few charcoal chippings in the bottom.

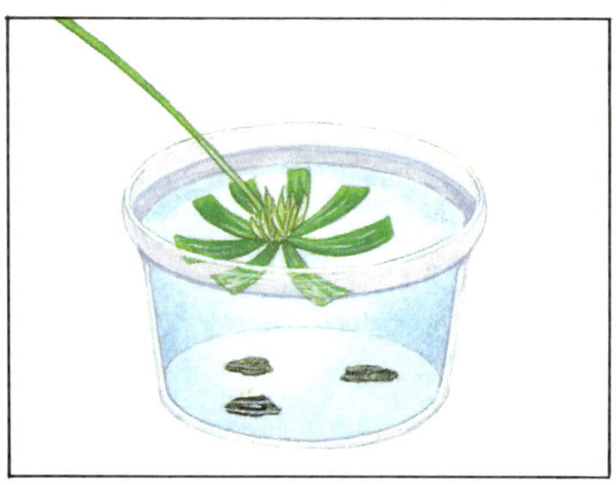

Keep in a warm place and change the water each week. When 3-4 shoots appear, pot in John Innes No 2 with some charcoal chippings mixed in.

cutting in a brightly-lit spot and in a temperature of 70°F (21°C). If you have used a tray of moist sand, keep the sand damp. When the cuttings have taken root, plant them in pots filled with John Innes No 2 with added chips of charcoal mixed in — this will prevent the compost developing a stagnant odour.

Sow seeds in March or April in shallow seed trays filled with peat, with an added handful of sand to ensure that it drains well, and keep them in a temperature of 65-70°F (18-21°C). Keep the compost constantly moist and partially shade the seed tray while the seeds germinate. If you would like one of the rarer Cyperus plants, growing from seed is often the easiest way of obtaining one!

Species

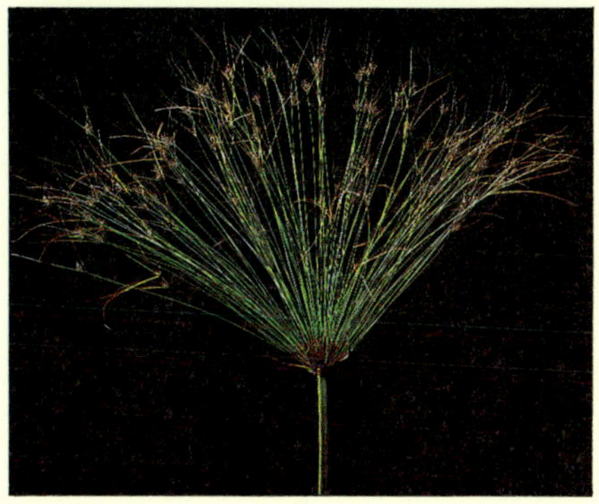

Cyperus alternifolius, the Umbrella Plant, from Madagascar, grows about 18-24in (45-60cm) high, with long slender leaves that grow out umbrella-like around the top of thin green stalks. It has tiny flowers at the ends of short stalks that sprout out from the centre of the 'umbrellas'. You can also get a variegated version of this plant with horizontal creamy-white bands on the leaves. The variety 'Gracilis', from Australia, is a miniature form, rarely growing more than 15-18in (38-45cm) tall.

C.papyrus, *left*, the Egyptian Paper Plant, from Egypt, has very long stems and can grow to 6ft (1.8m) or more. The leaves are narrow and hang down slightly from the tops of the stems. It produces thick clusters of silky thread-like spikelets.

C.diffusus comes from Mauritius and reaches 2-3ft (0.6-0.9m) in height. It has dark green leaves and flower heads up to 12in (30cm) across, made up from pale brownish spikelets. *C.albostriatus* is similar and may be the same plant. There is also a delightful variegated form of this plant with yellow and cream striped leaves.

C.esculentus comes from the Punjab in India, but also grows in Africa and America. It grows to about 12-15in (30-38cm) and has very slender, arching leaves with small groups of yellowish-brown or yellow spikelets. This species produces edible tubers called Tiger Nuts.

C.rotundus, *below*, from India, is very like *C.esculentus* but grows taller, to about 3ft (0.9m) or so.

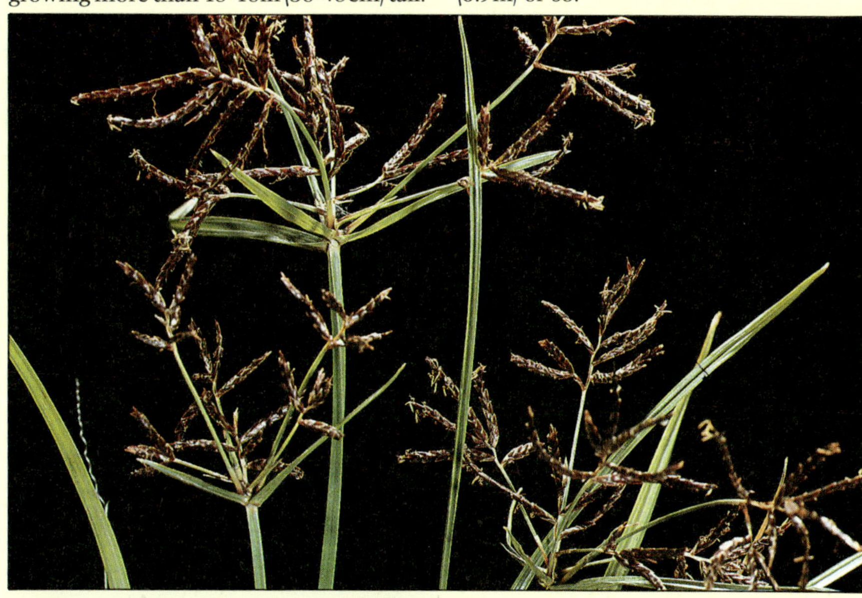

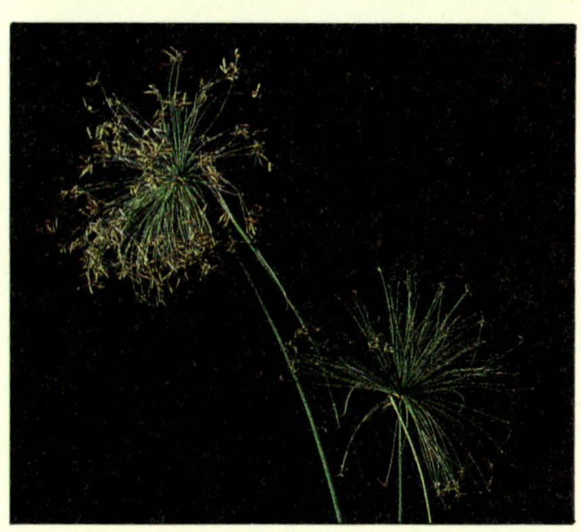

C.haspan, *left*, comes from Indonesia, India, the Americas and other warm swampy regions of the world and is a medium to large plant. The stout and sturdy stems, which are often three sided, especially towards the ends, grow about 10-40in (25-102cm) high. Its leaves are fairly short and a dense flower head of reddish spikelets grows out from the top of the stem.

C.brevifolius grows in the tropical parts of America. It grows about 3ft (0.9m) or more tall and is very bushy. The stems are triangular in section and have only three leaves branching out at the top.

Cyrtomium

Family name: **Polypodiaceae**

Common name: **Holly Fern**

Care Easy	**Height** 8-12in (20-30cm)	**Flower** None
Light Bright	**Spread** 1-2ft (0.3-0.6m)	**Humidity** Regular mist spraying
Price Middle range	**Shape** Fern	**Availability** Garden centre
Temp. Min 50°F (10°C)	Ideal 60°F (15°C)	Max 65°F (18°C)

The Holly Fern is a very easy plant to grow and is useful for interior decoration as its distinctive, spiky, dark-green leaves are extremely attractive. It will tolerate poor conditions and yet still remain handsome and shiny — even through the winter!

Cyrtomium falcatum is the best-known Holly Fern and it will grow in environments that other houseplants would soon start to collapse in. Like other plants in the fern group it has fronds; a central spine is lined either side with small, holly-like, pointed leaflets. The leaflets are glossy, dark green and last a long time. The variety 'Rochfordianum' is even more robust than the species — so you really shouldn't go far wrong with it — and has broader fronds.

Although the Holly Fern will survive most stages of neglect, it will grow significantly better if you sit it in good, bright light — but not direct sun — and give it moderate warmth, a good level of humidity and don't overwater it.

Spring and summer care

If your Holly Fern has filled its pot with roots, repot it in March. Use a good peat-based compost and put a few pebbles or broken pieces of clay pot in the bottom of the container to make sure that it will drain well. Keep your plant in a minimum temperature of 55°F (13°C) and spray fairly frequently to maintain humidity.

Your plant will be happiest with a maximum summer temperature of 65°F (18°C); if the weather is hotter than this, give your plant some shade, water it regularly and provide quite high humidity by mist spraying regularly or standing the pot on a tray of moist pebbles. Make sure you do not overwater but also don't let it dry out completely as this will damage the root system — water when the surface of the compost is dry.

Feed your plant with half-strength liquid fertiliser every week during the growing season, adding it to the water.

Autumn and winter care

Winter need not be a dormant season. If you keep your Holly Fern in a temperature range of 55-65°F (13-18°C) it will continue to grow. If you cannot provide temperatures as high as these, keep it in a minimum of 50°F (10°C). Even at this temperature it will not shed its leaves, though it will be in a semi-dormant state, and you will still need to water it just enough to keep the compost slightly moist.

It is important to keep your plant away from any cold draughts as this can damage the fronds, as will exposure to cold generally.

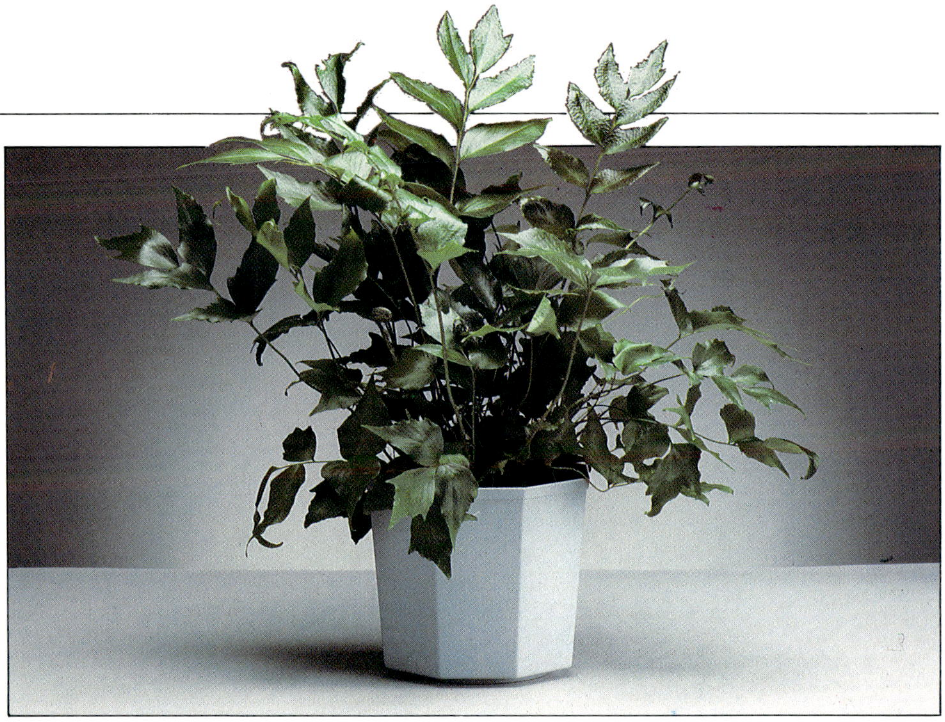

Cyrtomium falcatum is a very attractive fern that is also easy to grow.

Propagation

In March, divide a mature plant by taking it out of its pot and pulling it apart so that you have two halves. Each half should have a fleshy root (rhizome) with 2-3in (5-7cm) of fine roots attached and three or four fronds. It is not always easy to see the rhizomes, but search carefully through the masses of fine roots and you should find them.

Plant the divisions in pots of moist, peat-based compost, setting the roots just below the surface of the compost. Sit the pots in bright, filtered light, keep the compost just moist until the divisions start producing shoots and, from then on, treat like mature Holly Ferns.

Trouble Shooter

A wilting plant is the result of overwatering at any time of the year, but especially during winter, and if the temperature falls below 50°F (10°C) let the plant dry out for a few days and your plant should recover.

Scorched fronds occur if your plant sits in hot, direct sun and the sun will also dehydrate the roots; make sure you give your plant some shade when the sun is hot.

Small, warty blisters in the nooks and crannies of your plant are scale insect; if there are only a few, remove by wiping them off with a damp cloth. If there are a lot of them, spray with a malathion-based insecticide and an hour later spray with fresh water to rinse the insecticide from the fronds.

Species

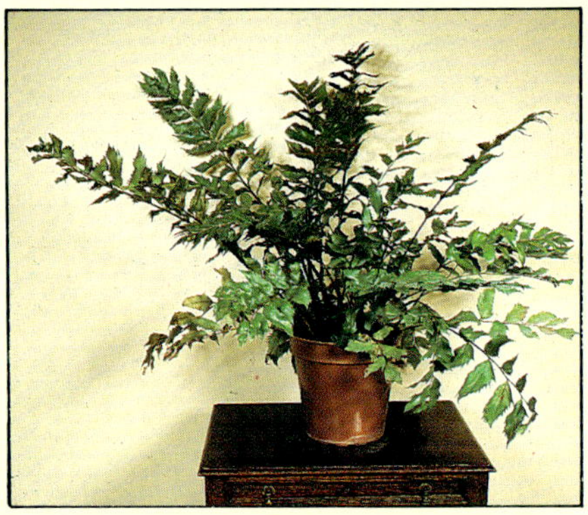

Cyrtomium falcatum, Holly Fern, from China and Japan is a very well-known, quite hardy, dark green, glossy plant. It has holly-like leaflets, about 3in (7cm) long, that grow out from each side of a brown stalk. The variety 'Rochfordianum' is more robust than the species and has broader fronds with slightly larger leaflets that are thicker with wavy, serrated edges.

C.caryotideum, *left,* is similar to *C.falcatum* and is also from Japan. It has slender, drooping fresh green fronds. Its leaflets are narrower than those of the *C.falcatum*, have toothed edges and grow close together along the stalks.

C.fortunei, also like *C.falcatum*, is a compact plant with tufted, green, but not as shiny, evergreen fronds.

Datura

Family name: **Solanaceae**

Common name: **Angel's Trumpet**

Care Straight-forward	**Height** 6ft (1.8m)	**Flower** August
Light Sunny/bright	**Spread** 5ft (1.5m)	**Humidity** None
Price Expensive	**Shape** Bushy/tree-like	**Availability** Specialist
Temp. Min 45°F (7°C)	Ideal 75-80°F (24-27°C)	Max 85°F (30°C)

The Angel's Trumpet is a truly exotic plant, though a very poisonous one, from South America. You can easily see how the large whitish flowers with horizontal green veins got their common name. Some of the Angel's Trumpet's relations are not so glamorous: the humble potato is one, as well as an extremely poisonous plant known as the Thorn Apple or Deadly Nightshade, which grows wild in most parts of the world.

In the home your *Datura arborea* may grow to 6ft (1.8m), although in Peru, its native country, it can reach 9ft (2.7m) tall. Angel's Trumpet is a very vigorous bushy plant and needs lots of space for its roots. If you have a pretty tub available this is the ideal plant to put in it.

The Angel's Trumpet has lots of white flowers in August, in the shape of large hanging funnels with delicate little points turned out like a well-laundered handkerchief. The leaves are soft, green and slightly hairy.

You must give your Angel's Trumpet quite a lot of warmth to grow it successfully, because it comes from a tropical climate. If you have a glazed porch or sunroom, your Angel's Trumpet will provide you with glorious flowers in the summer and a pretty tree-like shape the rest of the year.

Spring and summer care

Keep your Angel's Trumpet in a warm, sunny room — even as high as 80°F (27°C). Water the plant freely every couple of days and feed it every two weeks during the growing and flowering season by putting liquid fertiliser into the water. If you have a garden, your Angel's Trumpet will be delighted to be left in the open between June and September on warm summer days; it likes the fresh air and doesn't mind full sunlight.

Autumn and winter care

Your Angel's Trumpet must be kept at a temperature well above freezing — the real minimum is 45°F (7°C) — so this is not a plant for you if your house gets cold in winter. It doesn't need very much watering between September and April; although on bright days you can give a little water just to moisten the soil.

Prune the rather woody branches right back to a healthy shoot at the end of September if you want to keep your plant fairly small, taking them almost back to the main framework of the plant. If you want to let your plant grow as tall as possible, just prune the straggly branches back lightly in the autumn to encourage bushy new growth in spring.

When pruning be very careful not to get the highly poisonous sap on your hands — wear gardening gloves as a precaution if necessary.

Propagation

Take cuttings of half-ripe shoots 6-7in (15-18cm) long in May, again taking care not to get the poisonous sap on your hands. Dip the ends of the cuttings in hormone rooting powder and put them into a compost that is equal parts sand and peat, keeping the temperature about 75°F (24°C). Keep the cuttings moist and slightly shaded until they are rooted, then they should be potted into John Innes No 2 compost.

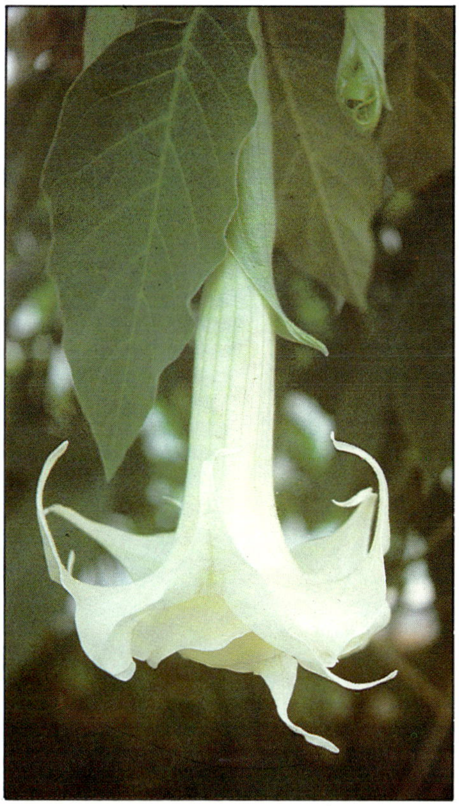

Datura arborea's lovely exotic flower.

Trouble Shooter

Clouds of tiny white flying insects clustering around the leaves are whitefly, which attack in the warmer months; spray with a malathion-based insecticide or a systemic insecticide added to water. As a precaution do this every four or five weeks in summer anyway. If your Angel's Trumpet is in the garden, lightly hose it down to drive the whitefly away.

Species

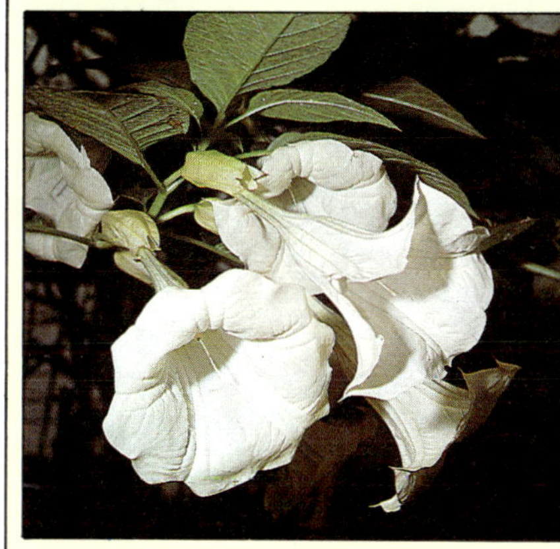

Datura arborea, the Angel's Trumpet, is from Peru. It has large, funnel-like, 'double' white flowers with green markings, and soft green oval-shaped leaves. It is a tree-like plant, reaching 6ft (1.8m) as a houseplant.

D.suaveolens, *above*, is very similar, also from Peru and also, confusingly, commonly called Angel's Trumpet. Its flowers are white funnels with delicate green markings, but single petalled, and appear in August.

D.mollis comes from Ecuador, and is a shrubby plant, with pale or salmon-pink flowers often with an attractive yellowish-orange sheen.

D.chlorantha is Peruvian and is easy to grow. It has spectacular yellow trumpet flowers, which smell sweetly.

D.sanguinea, *below*, from Peru has rich orange-red, bell-shaped trumpet flowers and very decorative, soft, almost velvety foliage. The leaves have wavy edges and are mid-green in colour. It grows to 4-5ft (1.2-1.5m) tall.

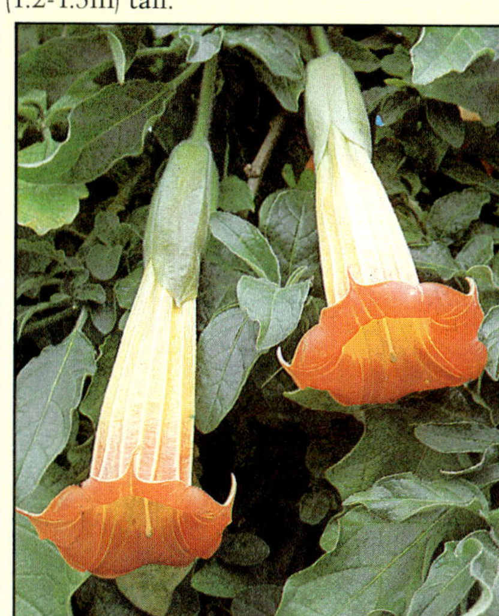

Davallia

Family name: **Polypodiaceae**

Common name: **Hare's Foot Fern**

Care Easy	**Height** 12-18in (30-45cm)	**Flower** None
Light Good indirect	**Spread** 8-12in (20-30cm)	**Humidity** Regular mist spraying
Price Cheap	**Shape** Fern	**Availability** Common

Temp. Min 50°F (10°C) Ideal 65°F (18°C) Max 75°F (24°C)

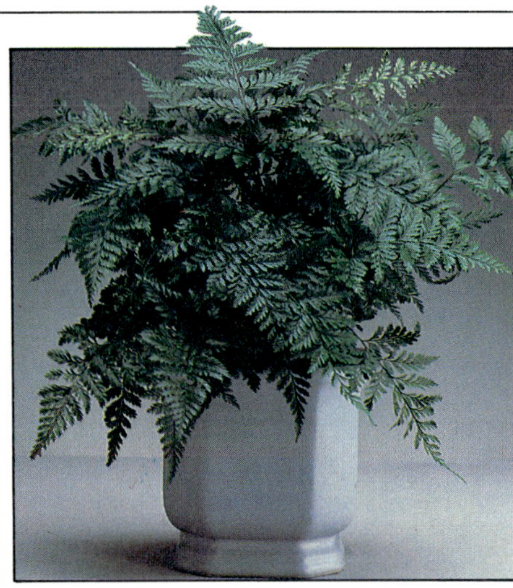

Davallia canariensis is easy to grow.

The ferns in this group are splendid, luxuriant plants which seem to grow literally right out of their pots and are wonderful candidates for hanging baskets, dripping luxuriantly down and creating a complete fern 'ball'. They are epiphytic plants (they grow in trees) from the forests of Australia, Japan, Indonesia, north-west Africa and the Canary Islands. As houseplants they extend their slender, furry rhizomes — which are fleshy roots — to quickly grow over their plant pots to hide the sides. Davallias are one of the easiest ferns to grow as they don't need high humidity.

The Hare's Foot Fern *(Davallia canariensis)* comes originally from the Canaries where it grows over trees and rocks. Its creeping rhizome root is covered with golden brown scales and tipped with white, like a hare's paw. The fronds are about 1ft (0.3m) tall — each wiry stalk is topped with strong mid-green, finely divided, feathery leaflets, giving the whole frond a triangular shape.

Spring and summer care

Keep the soil moist all the time and your Davallia won't mind if the heat goes up to 70°F (21°C). Add liquid fertiliser to the water every three to four weeks and spray regularly every day or two. If your Davallia is in a hanging basket you may need to buy a device for watering plants high up; you can get a long-handled spray from your garden centre or good department stores. To get your plant down for watering and tidying up once a month, you might find that a pulley-system for raising and lowering is a more practical alternative.

All Davallias require a well-drained compost that must be made firm enough for the fleshy roots to get a secure hold. To make up a hanging basket put a thick layer of sphagnum moss around the whole of the inside of the basket, firm this as much as possible, then fill it with a mixture of two parts granulated peat, one part loam, one part decomposed leaf mould and one part washed sand.

Autumn and winter care

For good looks all winter long keep your Davallia at a temperature of 60°F (15°C). If you do have to keep it in a lower temperature, don't let it fall below 50°F (10°C), and water more sparingly. Otherwise, water your Davallia when the compost begins to dry out, by immersing your plant in a bowl of water and then letting it drain thoroughly before replacing it in position. Keep your Davallia in good light but not in full sunlight, which would burn the fronds.

Propagation

In February, before growth starts again in spring, take 3-4in (7-10cm) tip-cuttings from the rhizomes, set them in peaty compost and keep them warm and moist. Within a few weeks your cuttings will root.

Another method is to sow spores on the surface of compost made from peat and sand, keep them warm, between 60-75°F (15-24°C), and moist, in a propagator if you have one. If you don't have a propagator try putting a polythene bag over the tray of damp compost to keep the spores warm and muggy. But your young ferns won't look like mature plants for a couple of years grown this way.

Trouble Shooter

Falling brown fronds are caused by dehydration — they may tolerate a short drought, but not for long! Cut off the dead fronds, immerse the whole plant in water and once you have put it back in place remember to water and spray regularly in future and keep your plant well away from draughts.

Buying Guide

When you buy a Davallia, choose a small plant. Not only will it be cheaper but it is more likely to have crisp, fresh green leaves without brown edges. Also the fleshy rhizomes should then be in good condition; do not buy a Davallia if the tips of the rhizomes are damaged as the plant is likely to be in poor condition generally.

Species

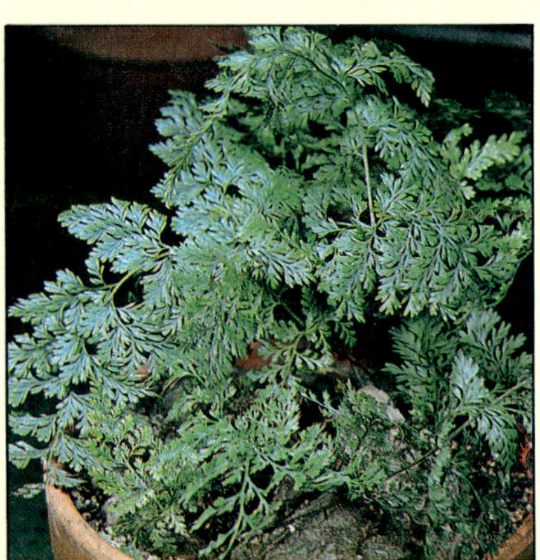

Davallia canariensis, the Hare's Foot Fern, is from the Canary Islands. Its fronds are about 12in (30cm) long, mid-green and triangular and when grown in a pot or basket, they hang down over the sides. The fleshy roots are covered with pale brown scales and grow out from the main plant by creeping along the surface of the compost and then out of the pot altogether.

D.mariesii, *left*, also known as *D.bullata*, the Squirrel's Foot Fern or Ball Fern, is a Japanese plant, with slender, light brown, hairy rhizomes and fine lace-like fronds of bright green which tend to become bronze-coloured when they are mature.

D.fijiensis, *right*, the Rabbit's Foot Fern, is from the Fiji Islands. The fleshy roots are soft brown and 'woolly'. In the wild it grows up in the trees. 'Plumosa' is a more common variety, from Polynesia. The rhizomes are slender and soft, with arching fronds of plume-like leaflets.

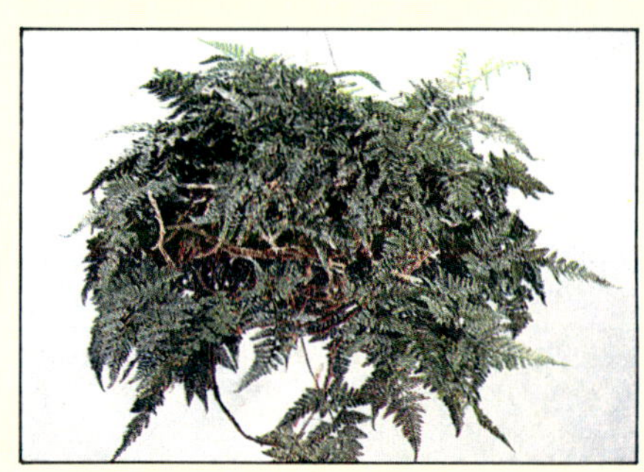

Dieffenbachia

Family name: **Araceae**

Common names:
Dumb Cane/Leopard Lily

Care Easy	**Height** 4-6ft (1.2-1.8m)	**Flower** Sometimes in summer
Light Bright indirect	**Spread** 2-3ft (0.6-0.9m)	**Humidity** Regular mist spraying
Price Middle range	**Shape** Upright/ compact	**Availability** Common
Temp. Min 60°F (15°C)	Ideal 75-85°F (24-30°C)	Max 90°F (33°C)

One of the most decorative and exotic of houseplants, the Dumb Cane, or Dieffenbachia, is actually easy to grow! The wide variety of intriguing marbled leaf patterns has made this plant very popular, whether it is grown in a group arrangement or on its own as a dramatic focal point.

The Dumb Cane, depending on the variety, can grow quite tall; sometimes it has thick, robust stems, sometimes it is compact with elegant, slender stems.

Dieffenbachia is called Dumb Cane for a good reason: the sap is poisonous and, if it is swallowed, causes severe inflammation of the mouth and throat which makes it very difficult to speak. You also have to be careful to keep sap away from any tender part of the body, such as eyes, nose or any skin wounds. It is a wise precaution to wash your hands thoroughly after handling the plant and to wear gloves if you take cuttings or trim it at all. As long as you know this and take a little care, however, there is no reason why you shouldn't enjoy this attractive plant.

The most outstanding and commonly available Dumb Cane is the *Dieffenbachia picta*, or, more correctly since it has now been renamed, *D.maculata*. It is from the tropical areas of Brazil and has oval, slightly lance-shaped leaves that are glossy green with ivory-white mottling. It does not always flower, but if it does the bloom is in the form of a green blade or spathe, typically like an Arum Lily.

Spring and summer care

Repot if necessary in early spring, just before the main growing season. The compost in the new pot should be John Innes No 3 or a mixture of your own, using two parts of a

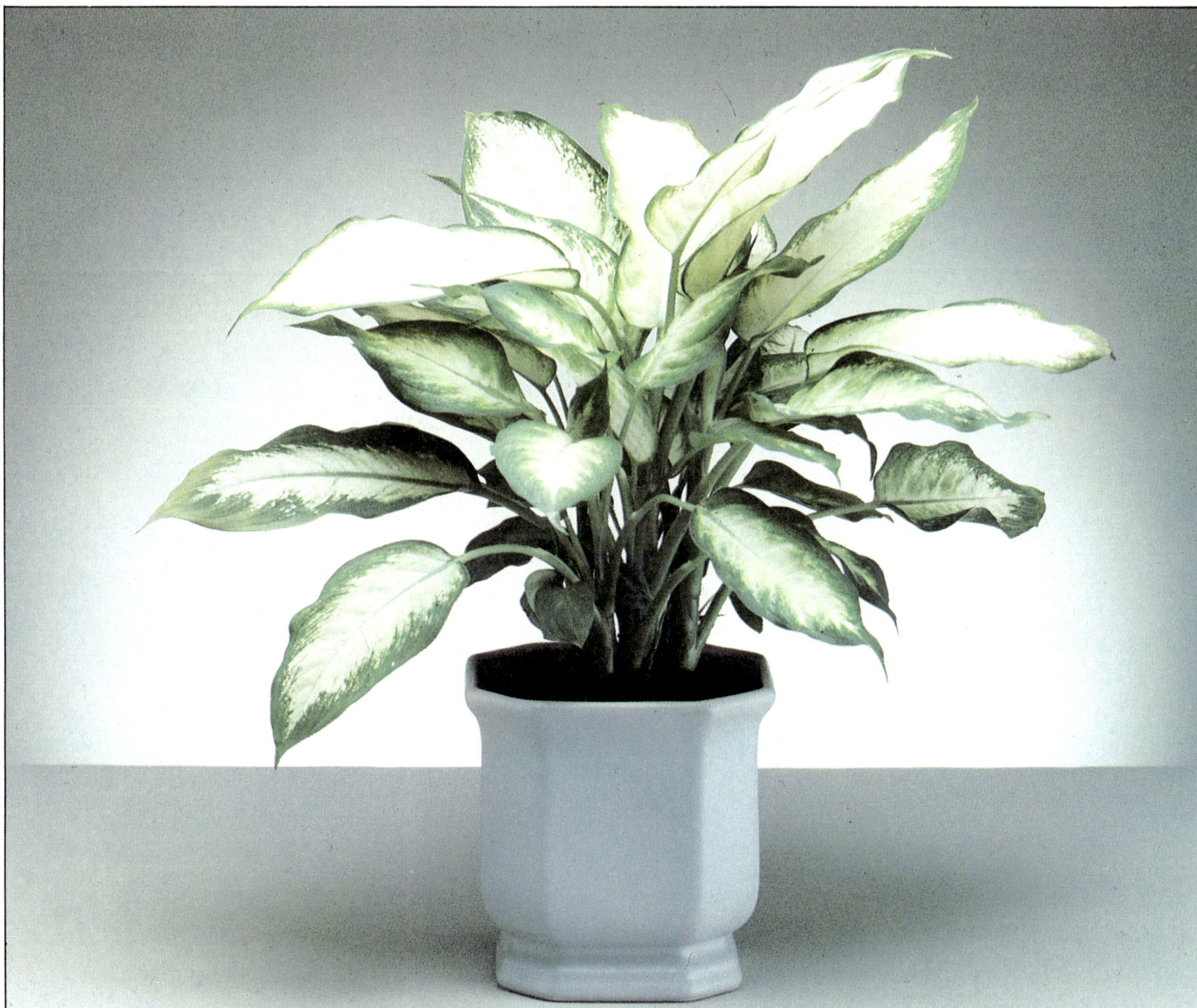

***Dieffenbachia picta* 'Exotica'** is a popular plant because of its exotic, highly decorative leaves.

good quality loam, one part of peat, one part of decomposed leaf-mould and some washed sharp sand. Firm it well and keep it moist.

Your Dumb Cane is fond of warmth, liking temperatures well over 70°F (21°C), even as high as 85°F (30°C). Give it a light position but not in the full summer sunlight, which might scorch the leaves. It needs lots of indirect light otherwise the beautiful variegated markings will disappear.

Your Dumb Cane needs to be in moist soil all the time, but should not get 'wet feet' by being left to stand in water. Between April and September give it a liquid fertiliser added to the water. Keep the atmosphere as moist as possible by spraying the leaves with rain-water if you can manage to collect some!

Autumn and winter care

Your Dumb Cane may survive if the temperature gets too low, but it won't flourish. The ideal minimum is between 60-65°F (15-18°C) and it still likes a light position. Don't let it get dried out — just keep the soil moist all the way through the winter by watering it lightly once a week or so and, on very bright days, giving it a light spray. But do beware of cold draughts: your Dumb Cane likes a little air circulating around it, but doesn't like to be too cool.

Propagation

Take stem cuttings 2-4in (5-10cm) long, including the leaf joint (the part where the leaf joins the stem), in early spring. Remember that your Dumb Cane, though very attractive, is poisonous and you should wear gloves when handling it, particularly when cutting it up, as you might accidentally get the sap on a skin wound or rub it into your eyes by mistake.

Treat the cuttings with a hormone rooting powder by sprinkling a little on the cut ends, then let them dry off for a day or two. Set them firmly in pots of potting compost with a little sand added, to help the water to drain

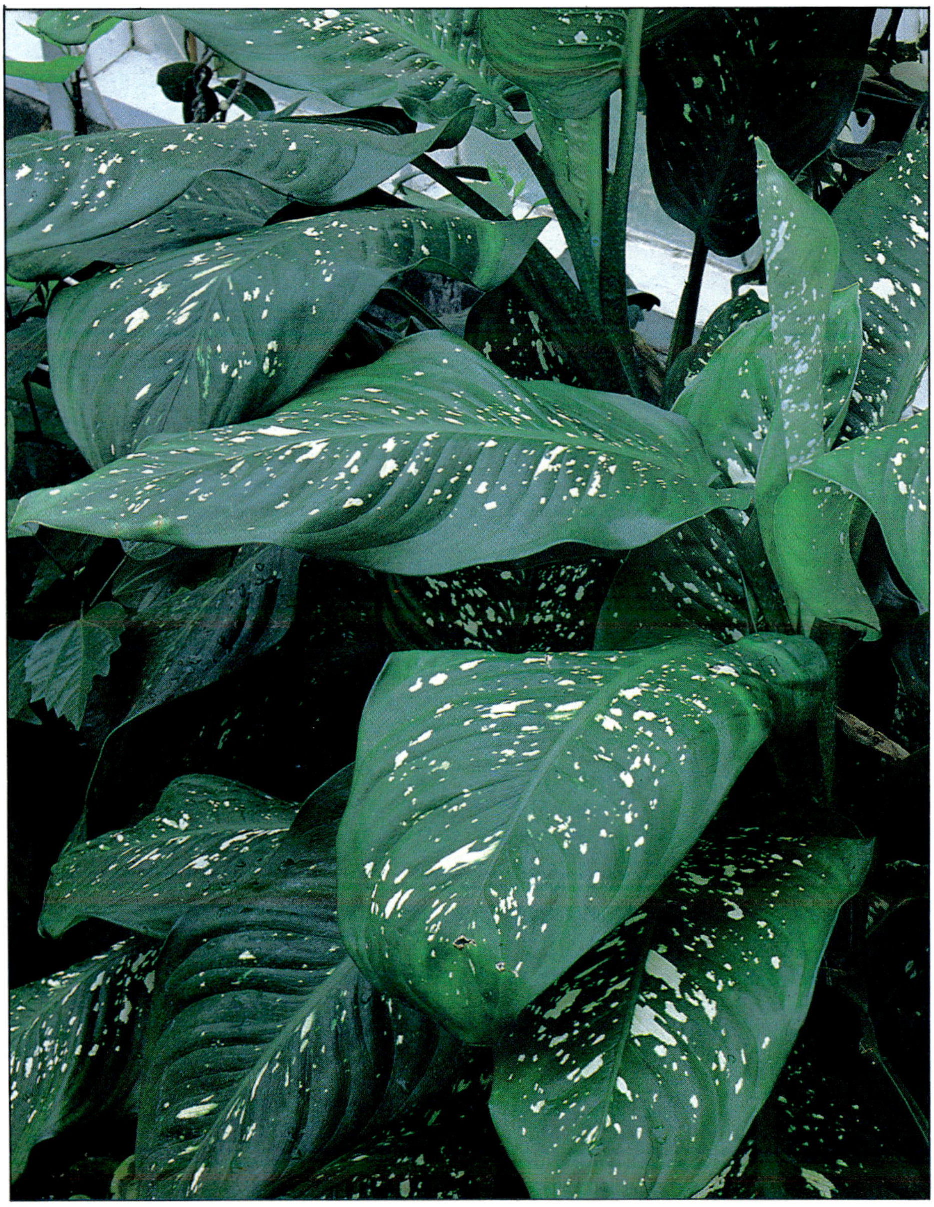

***Dieffenbachia picta* 'Splendens'** is also a popular variety but has greener leaves.

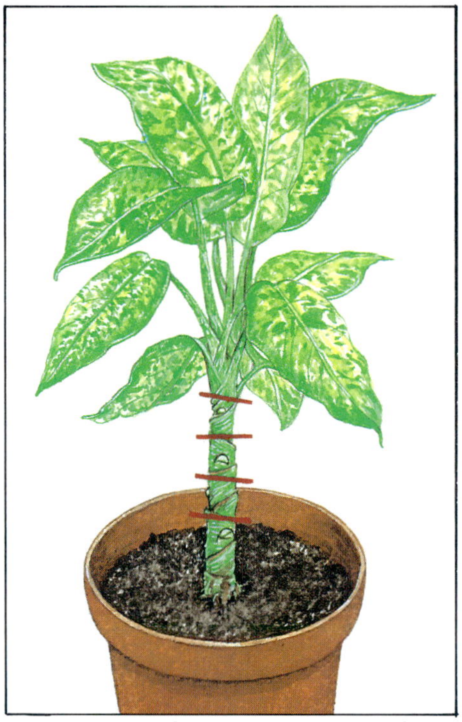

Taking Dumb Cane stem cuttings: in spring cut a section of stem about 2-4in (5-10cm) long with a leaf joint — ideally the sections between the red lines.

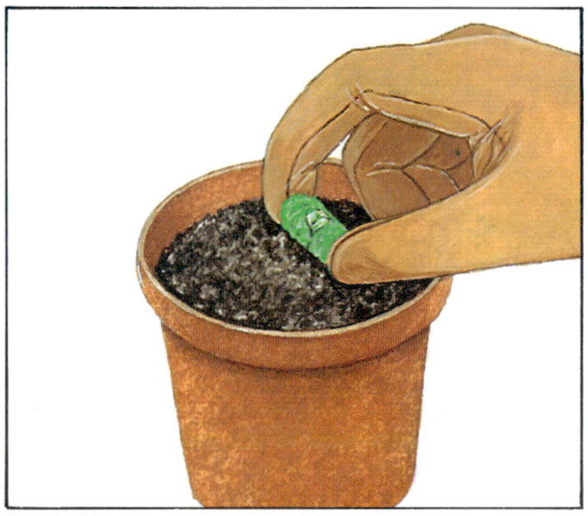

Sprinkle hormone rooting powder on each end of the cuttings: plant in compost and keep warm and moist — in a propagator or a polythene bag.

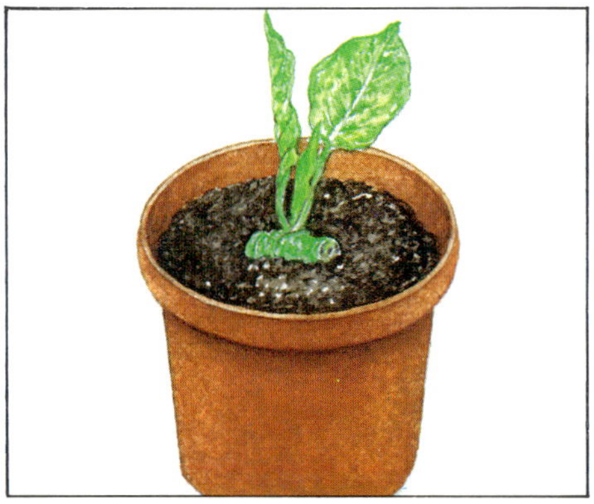

When a couple of leaves have grown, pot on in John Innes No 3.

away, and keep them constantly moist and warm — 75-80°F (24-27°C) — in a propagator if you have one, or with a polythene bag stretched over the pots if you haven't. Open up the propagator or the polythene bag each day to freshen the air inside. Cuttings will root within a few weeks and then you can move them into pots of normal compost — John Innes No 3 or the mixture described in the 'Spring and summer care' section.

Dumb Cane seeds are sometimes available from seedsmen, but they must be used when fresh; after about two months they become stale and won't grow. Put the seeds about ½in (13mm) deep in potting compost with added sand and keep them in a propagator. Keep the seeds moist all the time at a very warm temperature, 75-80°F (24-27°C), in a shaded place until they germinate — for example the airing cupboard, which is warm and dark. Don't forget about them though or the compost will get too dried up. When the seedlings start to grow, move them into a light position so that they start turning green, and once they are big enough to handle give them individual 3in (7cm) pots. When your seedlings are 5-6in (13-15cm) tall give them slightly bigger pots. All the way through this growing period they need lots of warmth and lots of moisture.

Buying Guide

To ensure that you buy a healthy Dumb Cane, look for two things: firstly, the stem must be firm and upright — avoid a plant with a drooping or discoloured stem. Secondly, choose a plant with undamaged leaves that have good, even patterning and colouring.

Trouble Shooter

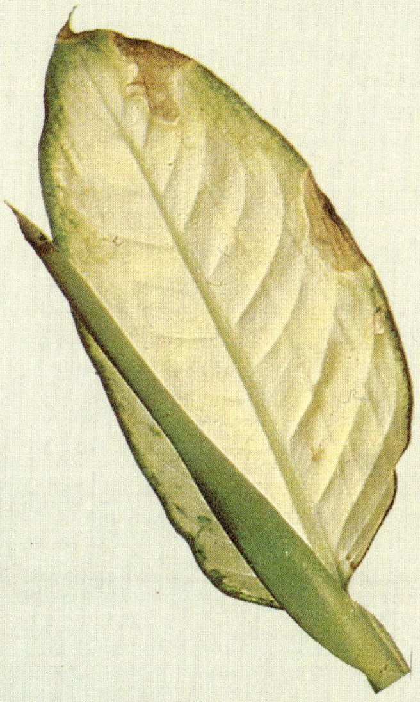

This leaf shows all the signs of overwatering. Remember to water less in winter, *right*.

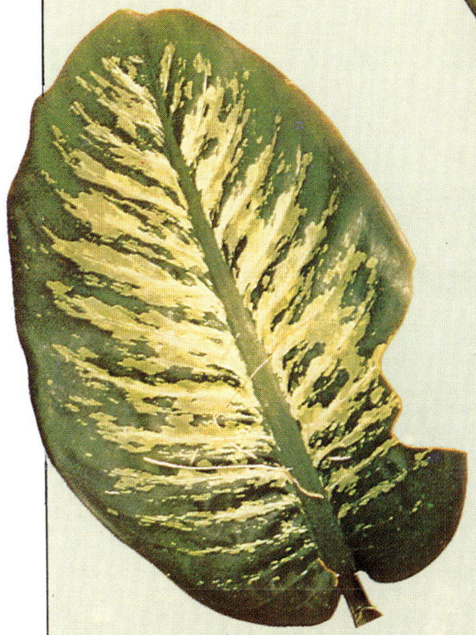

A scorched leaf. Keep your plant away from radiators and out of direct sun, *left*.

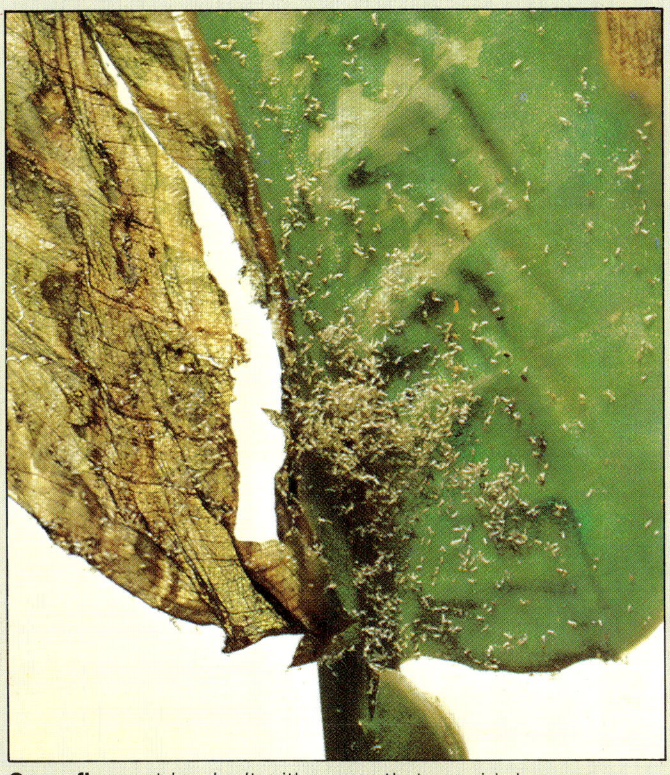

Greenfly must be dealt with promptly to avoid damage.

Leaf wilt or droop, loss of colour or even leaf fall is caused by too much damp or too little heat or both; if your plant is waterlogged take it out of the pot (wearing gloves to avoid the poisonous sap), put it on newspaper to absorb the excess moisture and let it dry out. Repot it and keep it in a warm place.

Leaf scorch happens if your plant sits too near a window or in bright sun for too long; move to a less sunny spot or away from the radiator.

Slow growth or lack of colour and variegation in the leaves comes from underfeeding in the spring and summer or possibly from lack of light. Feed your Dumb Cane every two weeks during the growing season with a liquid fertiliser added to the water, and keep it in good light, but not direct sunlight, all year.

A bronzy mottled stain on the leaves, which turns red when the temperature is cold, is red spider mite; get rid of the mite by spraying with malathion or a systemic insecticide, or add insecticide to the water. The mite is encouraged by a dry atmosphere so mist spray your plant regularly.

White blobs like cotton wool on the underneath of leaves or where the leaves join the stems are mealy bug; wipe the bugs away with a brush dipped in methylated spirits which dissolves the white fluffy coating, killing the bugs. Or use a malathion spray or a systemic insecticide.

Clusters of green around the leaves mean an infestation of greenfly; spray with a systemic insecticide. As a prevention it's a good idea to spray the soil early in the growing season with a systemic insecticide and then to repeat the spraying every six weeks until late September.

WARNING
Dumb Cane is a poisonous plant: the sap can irritate your eyes, nose or mouth or any skin wound. When you take cuttings you *must* wear gardening gloves. If you handle it at any time with bare hands, wash them very thoroughly afterwards.

Species

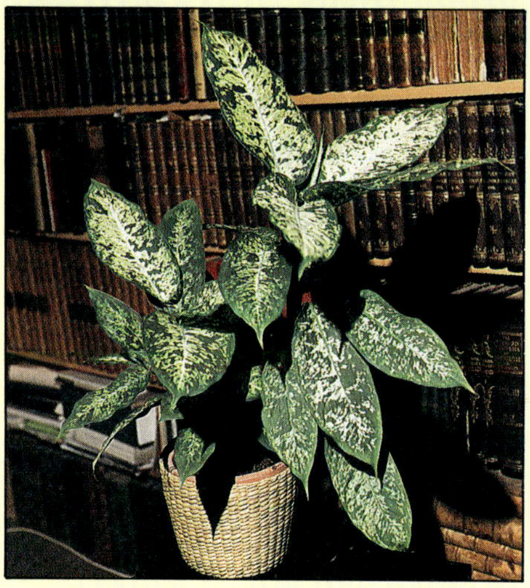

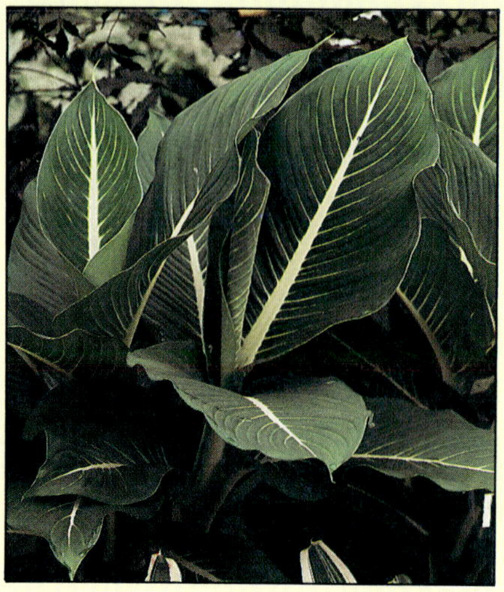

Dieffenbachia picta (or more correctly, ***D.maculata***), the Dumb Cane or Leopard Lily, comes from the tropical parts of Brazil. It grows to 4-6ft (1.2-1.8m) high, and has oval-shaped leaves, rich glossy green with ivory-white marks and mottling. Sometimes, though not every summer, it has a green Arum-type flower. 'Splendens' is a variety with rich velvety bronze-green leaves, spotted and mottled with pale green and creamy-white with an ivory stripe down the middle. 'Exotica' has almost totally creamy-yellow leaves with a thin edge of pale green, and is quite a slender, neat plant. This is the most popular Dieffenbachia but there are also many other varieties available.

D.bausei, *near right*, is a charming plant whose parents are *D.maculata* and *D.weirii*. It has oval, pointed leaves of yellowish-green with dark-green edges and over the whole leaf there are dark green and white spots. The leaves are up to 1ft (0.3m) long and 6in (15cm) wide, growing out from 8in (20cm) long stalks.

D.oerstedii, *above far right*, from Costa Rica and Guatemala, is an interesting large plant with blackish-green, oval leaves, on slender stalks, with a very striking ivory line down the centre.

D.amoena, from Costa Rica and Colombia, is a robust plant with a thick stem that is very sturdy and gives the plant a compact shape. It grows to about 2-3ft (0.6-0.9m) high. The huge leaves can be 2ft (0.6m) long and as much as 9in (23cm) wide! The mottling and bands on the leaves are creamy-white on a rich deep green background. 'Tropic Snow', *right*, is a variety with stiffer, more leathery leaves, and pale cream and green variegations radiating out on glossy dark green leaves. 'Pia' is a common variety with a compact shape, with pale green creamy-yellow variegations and a deep green central strip.

D.imperialis is a large plant, one of the tallest of the Dieffenbachias — in its native Peru it's almost a tree! The leaves are very large and leathery, oval, with a paler green and creamy-yellow midrib and flecks of silvery-grey on a dark green background.

D.fosteri, a Costa Rican plant, is a good example of a small-scale Dumb Cane. It won't grow much above 2ft (0.6m) high. It has slender graceful stems and deep green leathery leaves very close together, which really glisten and are not very variegated.

D.wallisii is a tall plant, growing up to 15ft (4.3m), so beware! It has very distinctive lance-shaped leaves of bronze-green with a greyish-cream central area. Seeds are sometimes offered by garden centres, though it's rare to find a ready grown pot plant.

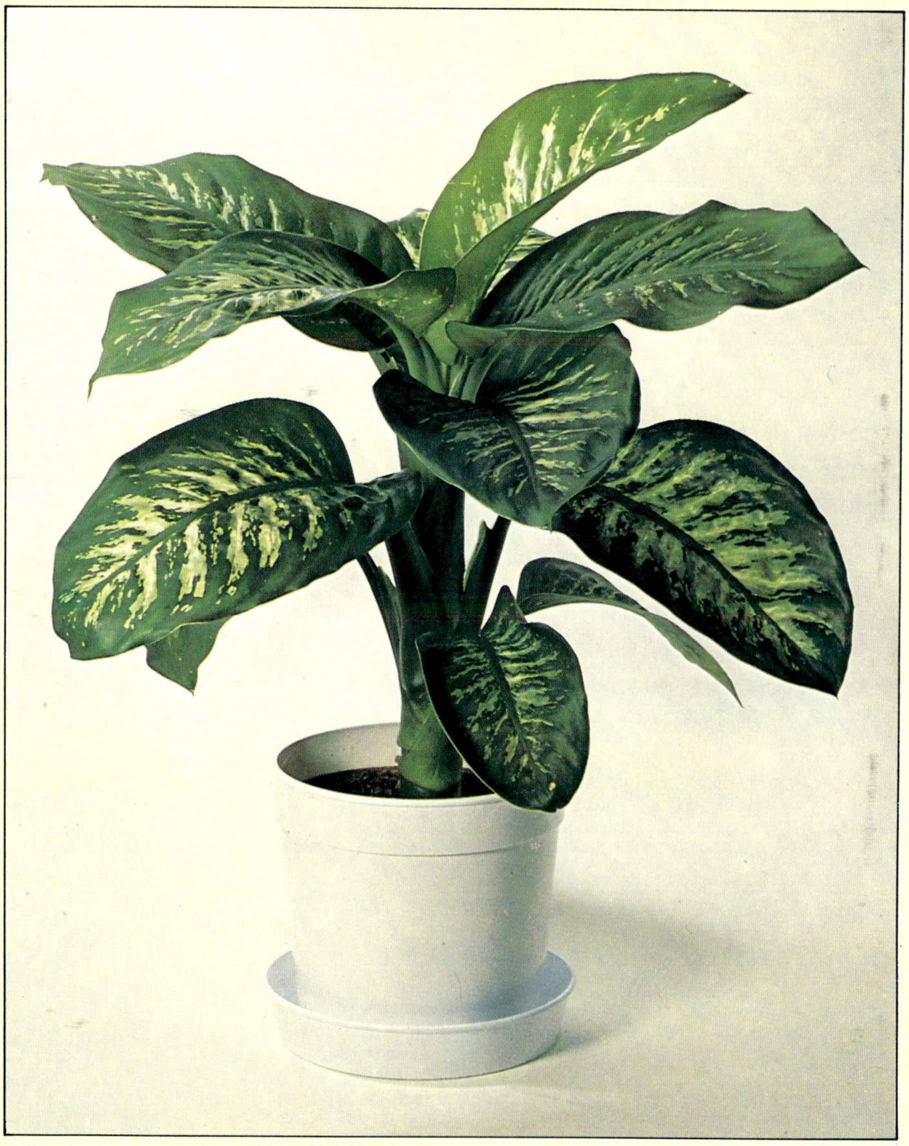

Dionaea

Family name: **Droseraceae**

Common name: **Venus Fly Trap**

Care Tricky	**Height** 6in (15cm)	**Flower** July-August
Light Bright indirect	**Spread** 1ft (0.3m)	**Humidity** High
Price Expensive	**Shape** Branching	**Availability** Specialist
Temp. Min 45°F (7°C)	Ideal 55-65°F (13-18°C)	Max 70°F (21°C)

If you want to try your hand at a really exotic plant — a real conversation-stopper! — you should try keeping a Venus Fly Trap, the commonest of the carnivorous plants available as a houseplant. It is a most exciting plant to grow, as it takes its nourishment partly from insects that it swallows whole: as a side-effect it also has the distinct advantage of keeping your room free of bluebottles and irritating insects in the warm summer months. If insect life is short, you can even feed the plant little titbits of meat or fish and then watch its fascinating trap mechanism at work. Mind you, it doesn't have an inexhaustible appetite, so you shouldn't overfeed it: each 'mouth' can only swallow about five times before it dies.

The *Dionaea muscipula* is the only species in its group, a most remarkable plant that comes from the south eastern states of the USA. Its natural habitat is the moist, mossy places in Carolina where the soil is acid and doesn't contain all the nutrients the plant needs. This is why it has developed insect-eating powers; the insects provide the necessary extra nourishment.

The Venus Fly Trap must be kept rather warm and moist, even during the winter, and must never be allowed to dry out. This makes it quite a difficult plant to grow, but it's worth taking some trouble with it because it is so exciting to have around! It is a very suitable plant to keep in a well-regulated, warm environment, such as in a propagator or a glass case, for example a Wardian case, which will encourage the humidity essential for it to thrive. If you grow it in a closed case all the year round and it is short of natural insect life, you can give it the occasional fly or titbit in the summer months — it doesn't need this nourishment in the winter when it isn't growing.

The plant consists of a fleshy root and a loose ring of leaves. Each leaf has a stalk with two 'half leaves' at the end, turned slightly upwards and equipped with teeth. When an insect touches the spread-out bottom leaf, both leaves snap shut and the teeth interlock, trapping their prey inside. Inside the 'mouth' formed by the trap, digestive glands secrete juices that destroy the insect, breaking it down into food. Flowers are star-like, white and appear in July and August.

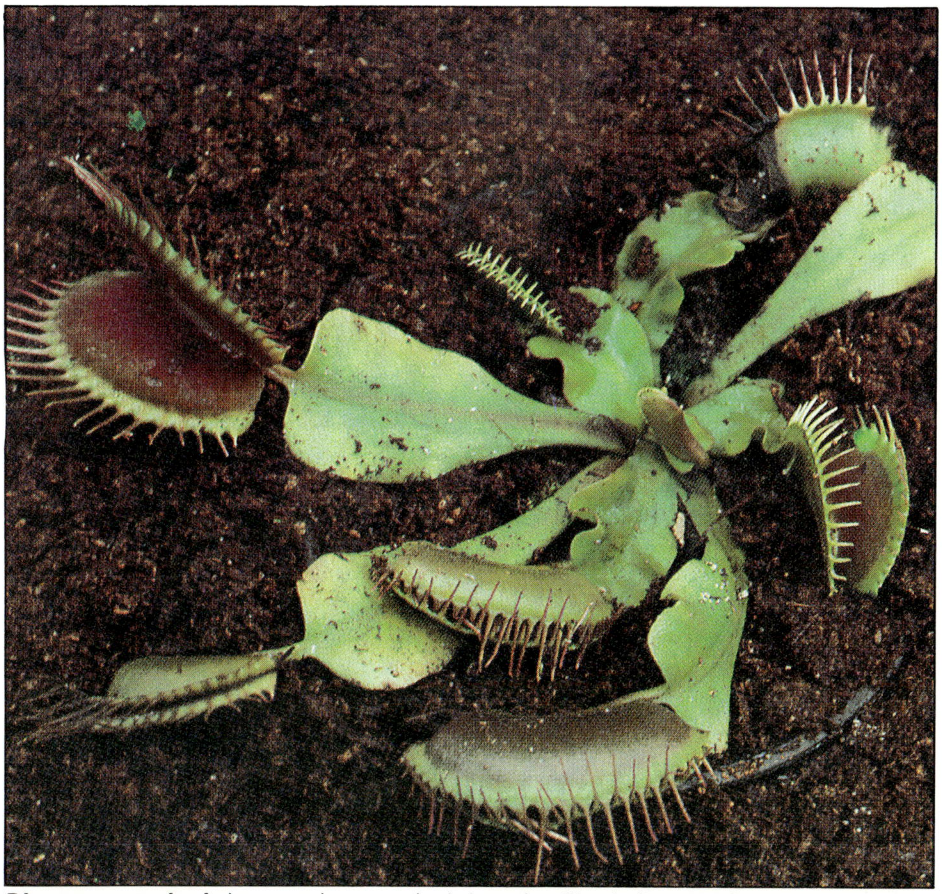

Dionaea muscipula is a carnivorous plant, trapping flies in its open jaws.

Spring and summer care

Use compost that is equal parts peat and live sphagnum moss (ask for fresh moss at a garden centre), and check that the compost never gets dried out. Double-pot your plant by putting the Venus Fly Trap's pot inside another one, with a layer of moss in it. This insulates your plant from the cold and helps to keep the compost moist. Summer temperatures should be 55°F (13°C), or higher, and your plant should be kept moist. Feed it once a month or so with a liquid fertiliser, especially if it isn't getting much live food.

Autumn and winter care

You must not let your Venus Fly Trap get colder than 45°F (7°C) in the winter and it will still need plenty of moisture. If you're worried about lack of warmth in your house, keep the plant in a glass case or a propagator during the winter. The Venus Fly Trap does not need feeding in the winter.

Propagation

Divide your plant in late March or April. Plant the divisions in the same mixture of peat and sphagnum moss and follow the double-potting procedure described in spring and summer care. Keep the new plants in a shady place and as warm as possible.

Sow seeds in March or April, if you feel adventurous — it's not too difficult. Take fresh seeds (if they are more than six weeks old they won't grow), set them in a mixture of fresh sphagnum moss and peat and keep them at 55°F (13°C).

Species

Dionaea muscipula, Venus Fly Trap, is the only species in the group. It comes from the Carolinas in the USA and is a carnivorous plant. The leaves are oval-shaped, with tooth-like fringing, and joined together in pairs at the tops of stalks. When an insect lands in the open 'jaws' the two halves of the leaf close together, trapping the insect, which is then dissolved by the plant's digestive juices. This process supplies the plant with nutrients. It grows about 6in (15cm) tall and has white, star-like flowers in July and August.

Trouble Shooter

The Venus Fly Trap gets rid of insect attackers very dramatically, so you won't have a problem with pests! If the plant wilts, it is likely to be cold or too dry, and it probably won't revive. Learn from the mistake and, if you have other Venus Fly Traps, make sure you keep them warm and damp — ideally in a glass case as this will almost certainly provide the right environment for them.

Dipladenia

Family name: **Apocynaceae**

Common name: **Pink Allamanda**

Care Straightforward	**Height** 4-10ft (1.2-3m)	**Flower** June-Sept
Light Bright, indirect sun	**Spread** 18in (45cm)	**Humidity** Mist spray regularly
Price Expensive	**Shape** Climber	**Availability** Garden centres
Temp. Min 55°F (13°C)	Ideal 65°F (18°C)	Max 75°F (24°C)

The Dipladenia is a leafy, evergreen, flowering climber that gives any room a really tropical, exotic look. Its large, showy flowers span a range of brilliant colours, and appear in large numbers, even on plants that are still quite young.

In its native jungle habitat in South America, some types of Dipladenia grow rampantly and can reach heights of 25-30ft (7.5-9m), so only a few of the 40 or so Dipladenia species are suitable as houseplants — unless you have a lot of space.

Dipladenia sanderi is the species most commonly grown as a houseplant. It is a woody-stemmed plant with a natural inclination to trail and climb and, left to itself, it can grow to 10ft (3m). However, with regular and careful pruning it can be persuaded not to exceed 3-4ft (0.9-1.2m). Its attractive, pale pink, trumpet-shaped flowers are borne in profusion in summer.

You may find that some suppliers now refer to the Dipladenia as Mandevilla; this is because the family has — rather confusingly — been reclassified. But as the plant is still widely known as Dipladenia we are using this name here.

Spring and summer care

A young Dipladenia should be supported by a stake, which can be replaced with a wire trellis (in the shape of a cone or a globe) for the plant to scramble over as it gets larger. Take care as you push the ends of the stake or trellis into the compost not to damage the roots.

Repot your Dipladenia every two years or so in early spring. Put a ½in (13mm) layer of broken pieces of clay pot in the bottom of the container to ensure good drainage. Then fill up the pot with a peat-based compost, such as Arthur Bowers or Levingtons.

The Dipladenia enjoys a hot, humid atmosphere and plenty of bright light — though it objects to direct sun. If a plant is to thrive and produce plenty of flowers, the temperature should never fall below 65°F (18°C).

Water your plant freely so that the compost is always moist (but not waterlogged) and add some liquid fertiliser to the water every two to three weeks. Make sure the atmosphere is constantly humid by mist spraying the leaves daily or by standing your plant on a saucer of wet pebbles.

Autumn and winter care

Prune your Dipladenia in October when it has finished flowering, cutting away most of the current year's growth. This will encourage your plant to grow into a nice bushy shape, and to produce plenty of flowers the following year. Water your plant moderately and give it an occasional mist spray to keep up the humidity level. Provide good — but draught free — ventilation and an even temperature of 55-60°F (13-15°C).

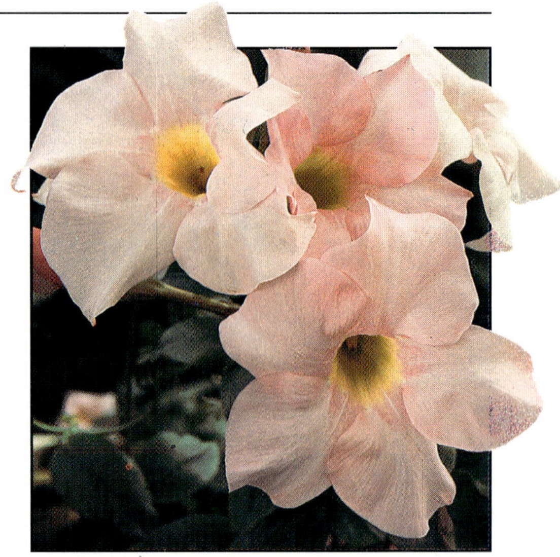

Dipladenia sanderi has lovely flowers.

Propagation

Take cuttings from your Dipladenia in spring. Cut 3in (7cm) lengths from new shoots and dip the cut ends in hormone rooting powder. Root the cuttings by growing them in a tray or pot of moist cuttings compost (you can buy this or make your own by mixing equal parts of peat and coarse sand together). If possible, put the tray or pot into a heated propagator, but if you don't have one, cover the container with a clear polythene bag and keep it in a warm place, ventilating it for a few minutes each day. Make sure the compost is kept moist and provide a temperature of 75-80°F (24-27°C); the cuttings should root in a week or two, and some of them may even flower the same year.

Species

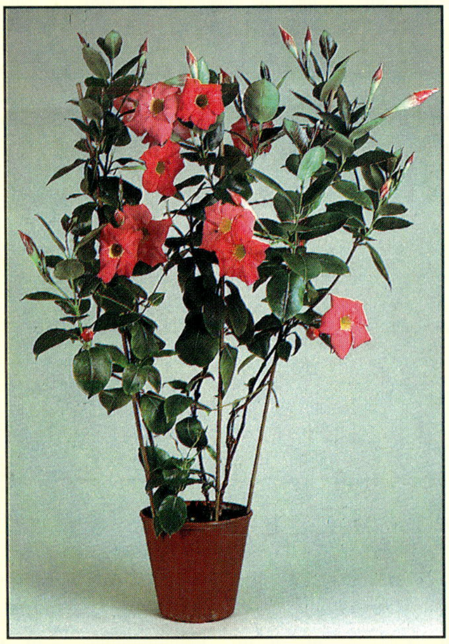

Dipladenia sanderi, Pink Allamanda, from Brazil, is a fast-growing evergreen climber. It has small, leathery, 2in (5cm) long, pointed, oval leaves that are bright glossy green on top and brownish-green on the underside. They grow in pairs opposite each other along the woody stems. The beautiful pale rose to salmon-pink trumpet-shaped flowers are about 3in (7cm) long and have bright yellow throats; they bloom in large numbers throughout the summer.

D.splendens, *left*, also from Brazil, has stems that are covered with fine hairs. The large, handsome, rich green leaves are oval-shaped and up to 8in (20cm) long and 4in (10cm) wide. The exotic trumpet-shaped flowers in shades of white, red and purple are 3in (7cm) across. Each flower lasts from three to four days.

D.boliviensis, from Bolivia, has smaller flowers, about 2in (5cm) across, that are white with a bright orange-yellow throat. They are sweetly scented.

Trouble Shooter

Drooping leaves, particularly in winter, indicate that your Dipladenia is suffering from too cold a temperature; move your plant to a warmer spot — about 70°F (21°C) in the summer and not lower than 55°F (13°C) in the winter — and it should perk up.

Brown spots on the leaves are leaf scorch, which occurs if your plant is too dry or gets too much direct sun; water your plant freely and move it out of direct sunlight to avoid further damage.

Reddish mottling and tiny webs underneath the leaves are red spider mite; spray with a malathion-based insecticide to get rid of them. As this pest thrives in dry atmospheres, and Dipladenia likes humidity anyway, mist spray daily to discourage them and benefit your plant at the same time!

Cotton-wool like patches underneath the leaves and at the leaf joints are a sign of mealy bug; wipe them away with a paintbrush dipped in methylated spirits.

Dizygotheca

Family name: **Araliaceae**

Common name: **False Aralia**

Care Straight-forward	**Height** 2-4ft (0.6-1.2m)	**Flower** None
Light Bright, indirect sun	**Spread** 12-18in (30-45cm)	**Humidity** Mist spray regularly
Price Expensive	**Shape** Shrubby	**Availability** Garden centres
Temp. Min 65°F (18°C)	Ideal 75°F (24°C)	Max 85°F (29°C)

The False Aralias are a small group of extremely elegant foliage plants that come from the tropics. The one most commonly grown as a houseplant is *Dizygotheca elegantissima,* a leafy plant with slender upright stems each carrying a rosette of long, arching leaflets. Each rosette is, in fact, a single leaf, deeply indented to form long, thin, notched leaflets, which are such a dark browny-green they look almost black.

False Aralias do need a little dedication to look after as they require quite high temperatures throughout the year and a bright position that is out of direct sunlight. But if you give them loving, careful attention they will reward you by adding a note of distinctive elegance to your home.

Trouble Shooter

Excessively drooping leaves result if conditions are too cold or too wet or too dry; move your plant to a warmer spot and always keep the compost moist rather than wet. Ensure adequate humidity for your plant by mist spraying every other day.

Tiny, brown, blister-like bumps on the stems or underside of the leaves are scale insect; scrape as many off as you can then spray your plant with a malathion-based insecticide. If there are still some live scale insects after 10 days spray lightly again.

Spring and summer care

If your False Aralia has outgrown its pot, which should only happen every two years or so as it is a slow-growing plant, repot it in early spring. Use a soil-based compost, such as John Innes No 2, and pot on into a pot one size larger than its previous one.

If your plant is getting a bit untidy, prune it in spring, cutting away any straggly growth.

Because the False Aralia is a tropical plant, it needs a warm, humid atmosphere. The ideal summer temperature is 75-80°F (24-27°C) and you will need to water your plant regularly to keep the compost moist. Every two weeks add a couple of drops of liquid fertiliser to the water. Mist spray your plant every day and stand the pot on a tray of wet pebbles to provide humidity.

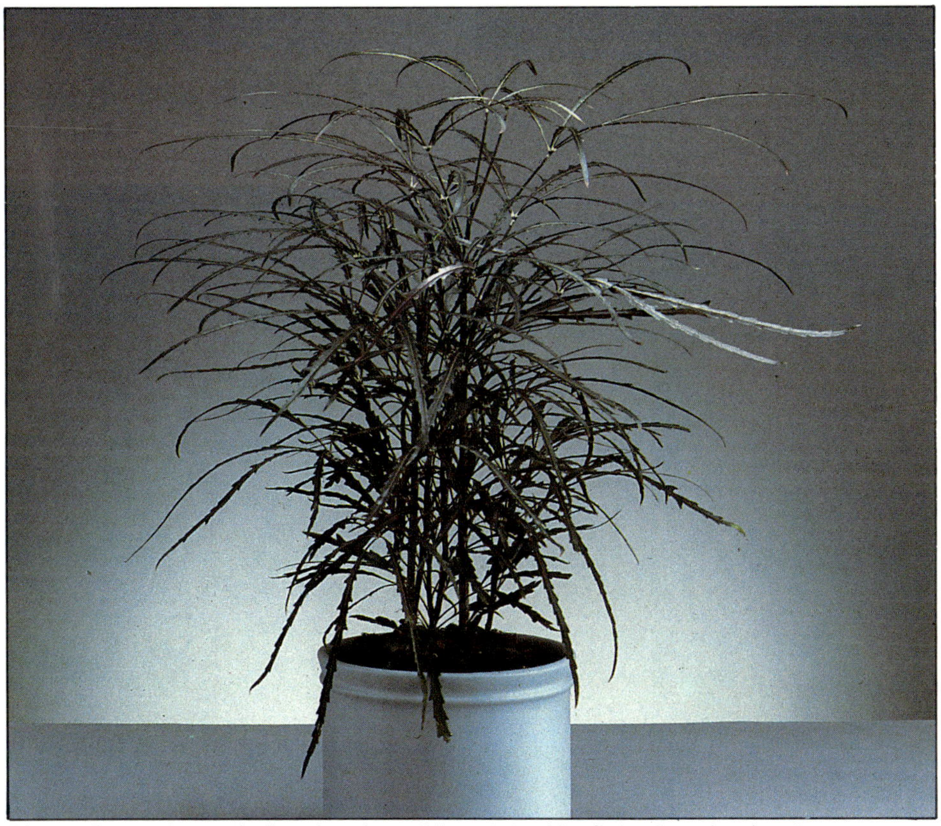

Dizygotheca elegantissima has long thin notched leaflets atop slender stems.

Species

Dizygotheca elegantissima, False Aralia, from the New Hebrides, is a decorative foliage plant, growing no more than 4ft (1.2m) high. Its leaves are rather like a spread out hand in shape, with long thin leaflets radiating out from the top of each stem. The leaflets have notched edges and are each about 3-4in (7-10cm) long and ½in (13mm) wide. The young leaflets are a deep coppery colour, but this gradually turns to a dark, blackish green as they mature.

D.veitchii, from New Caledonia near Australia, is also a slender, graceful plant with leaves similar in shape to those of *D.elegantissima* but the leaflets are a little wider and have slightly wavy toothed edges. They are glossy brown-green with pink midribs.

Autumn and winter care

Even in winter your False Aralia needs to be kept in a warm and humid atmosphere to stay looking healthy. Water only slightly less than in summer to keep the compost moist and mist spray every other day with tepid water to maintain humidity. Do not let the temperature fall below 65°F (18°C) and keep your plant in a good bright position but out of full sun.

Propagation

Sow seeds in March or April in a mixture of two parts peat and one part washed sharp sand. Water the compost well and keep the seed tray in a shaded place. Keep up a good level of humidity and make sure that the temperature stays within the range of 75-80°F (24-27°C). Ideally a propagator should be used but otherwise you can try covering the seed tray with a sheet of clear polythene and keeping it in a warm place. When the first pair of true leaves have grown, pot the seedlings on individually into 3in (7cm) pots.

It is easier, and quicker, to propagate False Aralias by taking stem tip cuttings in spring. Cut a 4in (10cm) length from the tip of a stem, making sure that it has a growing tip and a couple of pairs of leaves. Dip the cut end in hormone rooting powder and insert it in a mixture of equal parts peat and sand, submerging about half its length in the compost. Keep the cutting in a temperature of 70°F (21°C) — in a propagator, if you have one, ventilating it for a few minutes each day — in a shaded spot and keep it moist. It will root very quickly and when the tip has grown new shoots, pot the cutting into a 3in (7cm) pot filled with John Innes No 2. When the cutting has grown sufficiently to be potted up into its final container, it is a good idea to put several plants into one pot as this creates a nicely bushy effect.

Dracaena

Family name: **Liliaceae**

Common name: **Dragon Tree**

Care Easy	**Height** 3-4ft (0.9-1.2m)	**Flower** Late April-Oct
Light Bright, indirect sun	**Spread** 15in (38cm)	**Humidity** Mist spray regularly
Price Middle range	**Shape** Shrubby	**Availability** Garden centres
Temp. Min 60°F (15°C)	Ideal 70°F (21°C)	Max 80°F (27°C)

Less expensive than the palms and more elegant in appearance than the yuccas, the Dragon Tree is often the ideal solution as the dramatic centre-piece of a plant arrangement. Buy it as a single stem topped by a tuft of arching leaves, or as a beautiful plume of foliage rising straight out of the pot — the type you choose really depends on the height you want and what you can afford.

The Dragon Tree comes mainly from tropical Africa and is often confused with its Australasian relation, the Cordyline, which is on the whole slightly less tough. It's worth remembering that one species is often misnamed by suppliers; if you are offered a *Dracaena terminalis*, look up *Cordyline terminalis* to see how to look after it.

The most commonly available Dragon Trees are the varieties of *Dracaena deremensis.* They will grow slowly to a height of about 4ft (1.2m) or more and have long, pointed lance-shaped leaves with white stripes running down their length. The plant grows upwards as new leaves unroll from the centre and old ones at the base die and fall off, leaving a lengthened palm-tree-like bare stem. The Dragon Tree is mainly grown for its attractive leaves, though a really healthy, mature plant may have large cream or white flowers through the summer. Another common species is *D.draco*, which is one of the long-lived Dragon Trees — there is one famous example in Tenerife that is thought to be over 1,000 years old! The sap of this plant is red and is called dragon's blood.

Spring and summer care

Repot into a bigger pot (one size up) in the spring every second year — or every year if your plant is growing quickly. The Dragon Tree is not fussy about soil types; use some fresh peat or soil-based potting compost over a layer of broken clay pot and coarse gravel.

The ideal spot for a Dragon Tree is out of direct sunlight in a room with plenty of windows — a sitting room, bathroom or landing rather than a hallway. It loves a warm, humid atmosphere of 60-80°F (15-27°C); the hotter it is the more humidity it needs, so mist spray the leaves daily when it's hot. Keep the soil damp, but don't let it become waterlogged.

Add a couple of drops of liquid fertiliser to the water twice a week and water it into the soil. The roots of your Dragon Tree like a fair amount of space — a 2ft (0.6m) plant will be happiest in a 6in (15cm) pot.

Autumn and winter care

As the temperature drops, stop using fertiliser altogether and water the plant less often — though don't let the soil dry out completely. The winter temperature should not fall below 60°F (15°C) if the plant is to stay healthy and mist spray weekly to ensure adequate humidity.

Propagation

Some seed catalogues offer a range of Dracaena species so why not make a collection of the different types. Sow the seeds in seed compost in March; they need a steady temperature of about 80°F (27°C), so a small electric propagator is ideal, but you can keep the seed tray in a clear polythene bag on a sunny windowsill if you don't have a propagator. As soon as the seedlings are large enough to handle, transfer each one into a 3in (7cm) pot and keep them at 70-75°F (21-24°C) and draught-free, sheltered from direct sunlight.

Take stem tip cuttings in spring, following the steps illustrated on the facing page.

Take some stem cuttings from an overgrown plant in April to make new plants. Cut off an unwanted side-branch and trim it into 3in (7cm) lengths, removing any old leaves. Dip the ends in hormone rooting powder and lay the pieces of stem lengthwise in a tray of compost in your propagator or a polythene bag at a temperature of about 75°F (24°C). Once the cuttings have taken and leaves have appeared, transfer them to 3in (7cm) pots filled with ordinary soil-based potting compost. For the first few months, the new leaves will be plain green — they develop white markings as they mature.

Buying Guide

Look for plants with healthy, unmarked leaves. If you want a tall specimen on a stem, buy the height you want as most of these species are slow-growing plants.

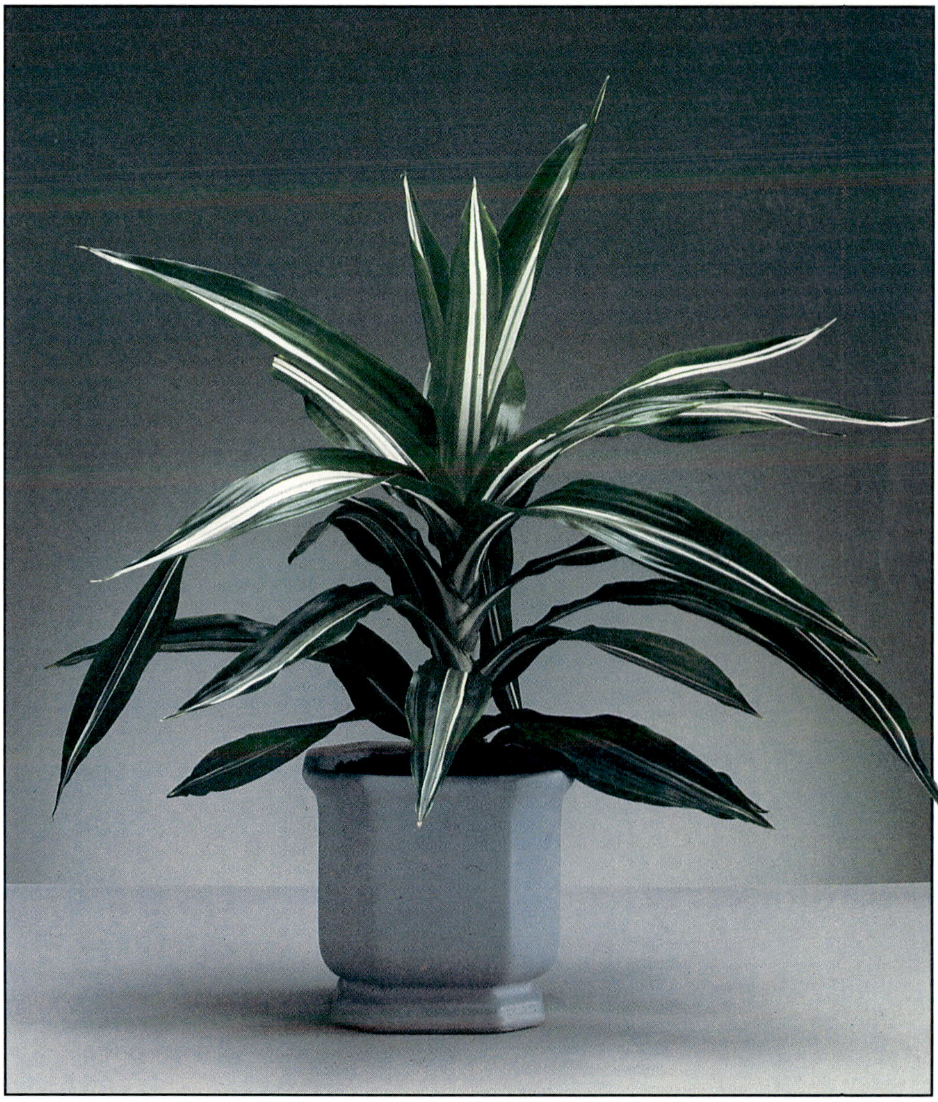

***Dracaena deremensis* 'Bausei'** makes a lovely houseplant with its attractive leaves.

Species

Dracaena deremensis comes from tropical Africa and grows to about 4ft (1.2m) as a houseplant. The slim, dark-green leaves with a whitish green midrib grow from rather stiff, upright stems. There are several very attractive varieties that differ mainly in the type of white markings; 'Souvenir de Augustus Schryer' has a rosette of glossy green leaves edged with broad, cream-coloured bands; 'Bausei' is more stripey with a central pale-green band and 'Warneckii' has two stripes.

D.sanderiana, *right*, Ribbon Plant, from Cameroon, grows about 2-4ft (0.6-1.2m) tall. The leaves are slender, spear-like, and green with wide white margins and arranged in rosettes. The edges have an attractive twist in them.

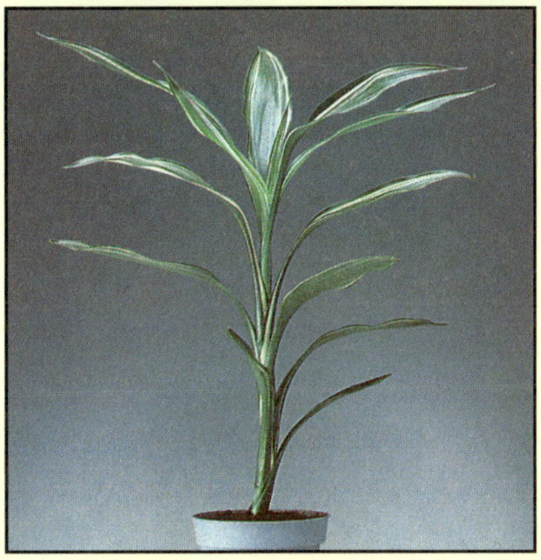

D.marginata, Madagascar Dragon Tree, is one of the easiest Dragon Trees to grow. Its thin, elegant stems carry plumes of delicate, arching green leaves edged with red. The variety 'Tricolor' is the same as its parent in every respect, but is more colourful as it has a fine cream stripe on the leaves as well.

D.godseffiana (or ***D.surculosa***), the Gold Dust Dracaena, from Zaire, is quite different to the other commonly available Dragon Trees. Its yellow-spotted leaves are 3in (7cm) long and oval rather than the more characteristic strap-shape. They are arranged in groups of three and carried on thin, wiry stems to make a rather bushy plant of about 3-6ft (0.9-1.8m) in height with a spread of about 15in (38cm). It is a shade-loving plant. 'Florida Beauty' is a dwarf variety with leaves that are heavily spotted with yellow and white, *below*.

D.draco, Dragon Tree, from the Canary Islands, is one of the largest Dragon Trees and lives for a long time. Its deep to blue-green leaves are thick and fleshy, often with red-tinged edges. This plant also has beautiful, slightly green flowers, even on quite young plants.

D.fragrans, from tropical Africa, comes in a very popular, robust form called 'Massangeana' that is often nicknamed the Corn Palm. It has a chunky, woody stem carrying large rosettes of yellow-striped dark-green leaves that droop gently downwards.

D.goldieana, from southern Nigeria, has a long, slender stem with dark-green leaves that have pale green and silver-grey bands of colour across them. It also has clusters of pure white flowers in the centre of the rosette.

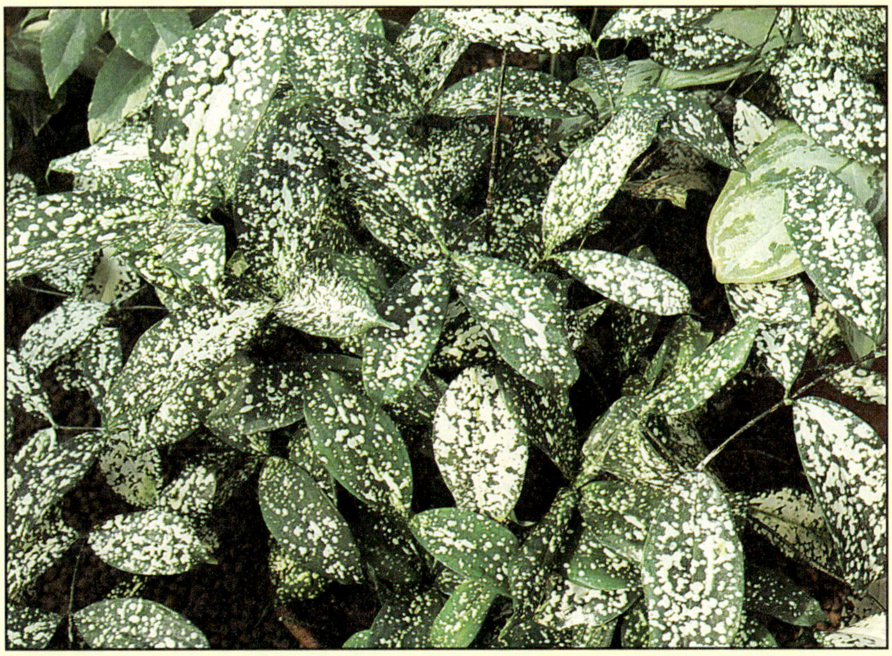

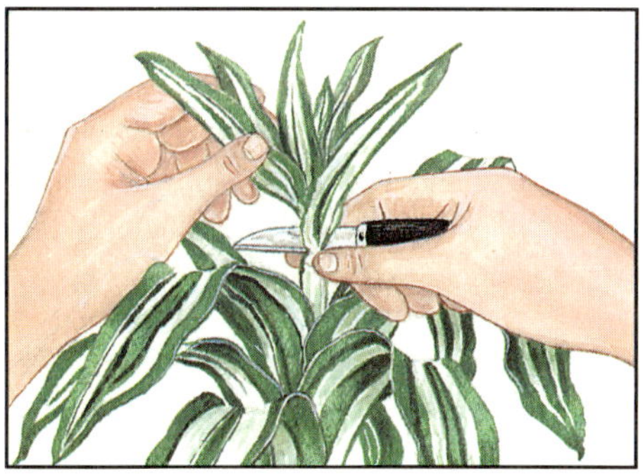

Taking Dragon Tree stem tip cuttings: slice off a shoot with two pairs of leaves and a growing tip. Trim the stem and remove the lower leaves. Dip the cut end in hormone rooting powder.

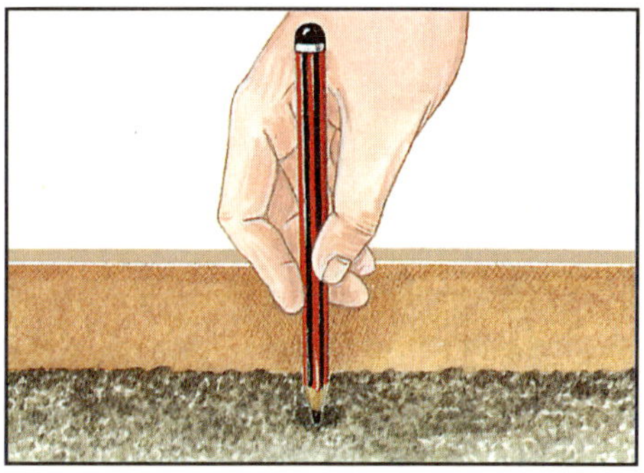

Make a little hole in the compost with a pencil and plant the cutting in it.

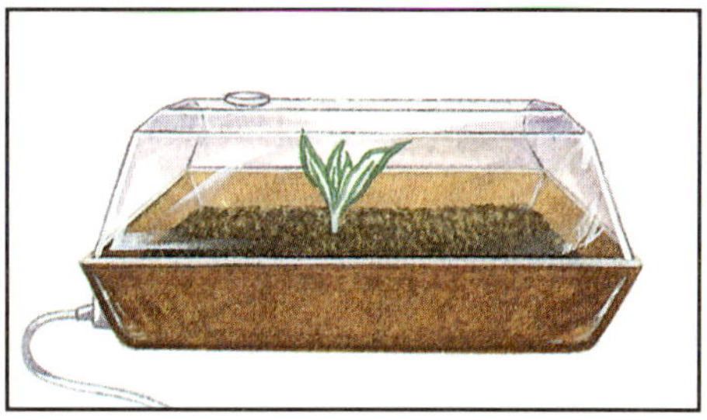

Water well and keep in a propagator (or covered with polythene supported with wire) at 75°F (24°C). Ventilate a few minutes each day and keep moist. After three weeks pot on the rooted cutting.

Trouble Shooter

Wilting leaves that droop prematurely can indicate that either the plant is too dry or that it is waterlogged; test the soil to feel if it is dry or wet and adjust your watering accordingly. Low temperatures (especially combined with overwatering) can have the same effect so move your plant to somewhere a bit warmer.

Tiny insects, appearing as small bumps on the underside of the leaves, are a sign of either scale insect or, more rarely, mealy bug; treat with a malathion-based systemic insecticide. As a preventative, water a systemic insecticide into the soil three or four times during the growing season.

Echeveria

Family name: **Crassulaceae**

Common name: **Painted Lady**

Care Easy	**Height** 3-12in (8-30cm)	**Flower** Intermittently April-Oct
Light Full sun	**Spread** 3-7in (7-18cm)	**Humidity** None
Price Cheap	**Shape** Rosette	**Availability** Common
Temp. Min 45°F (7°C)	Ideal 65°F (18°C)	Max 75°F (24°C)

A collection of these fascinating star-shaped plants makes an ideal feature for a sunny windowsill. They come originally from Central and north-westerly parts of South America where they often have to tolerate very wide extremes of temperature. In fact, it is this ability to put up with extremely hot days followed by very cold nights that makes the Echeveria one of the most easy-going houseplants you can grow.

The most popular species is *Echeveria derenbergii*, nicknamed the Painted Lady. Like many other Echeverias, its thick, fleshy leaves are arranged in a tightly-packed rosette. Unlike some of its relatives though, the tips of the Painted Lady's pale grey-green leaves are tinged with red, and in early spring bright orange-yellow, lantern-shaped flowers push their way upwards between the leaves.

Spring and summer care

Repot your Echeveria, if necessary, in April every year, using a good cactus potting compost or John Innes No 2 with some added coarse sand. Take care not to overwater your plant; water it thoroughly once a week, allowing the compost to dry out between waterings. The Echeveria's closely-packed, fleshy leaves are likely to rot if water gets trapped between them, so avoid wetting the leaves. If your plant fills its container it is a good idea to stand it in a saucer of water for a few minutes so that the compost can draw up the moisture it needs from below. To keep your plant growing healthily, add a few drops of liquid fertiliser to the water every four weeks.

Many types of Echeveria are covered with a delicate powdery dust; this is quite normal and healthy and should not be washed or rubbed off. If you do splash the leaves or get them dirty, use a dry, soft artist's brush to gently clean them up.

Tough though this plant is, it grows best in temperatures ranging between 60-70°F (15-21°C). If your plant is growing in a spot that gets the midday sun in high summer, it's a good idea to move it or shade it slightly to prevent it getting overheated.

Autumn and winter care

In the colder months, water your plant very sparingly — the colder it gets the less water it will want. If temperatures fall much below 45°F (7°C), move your plant to a slightly warmer spot in bright light.

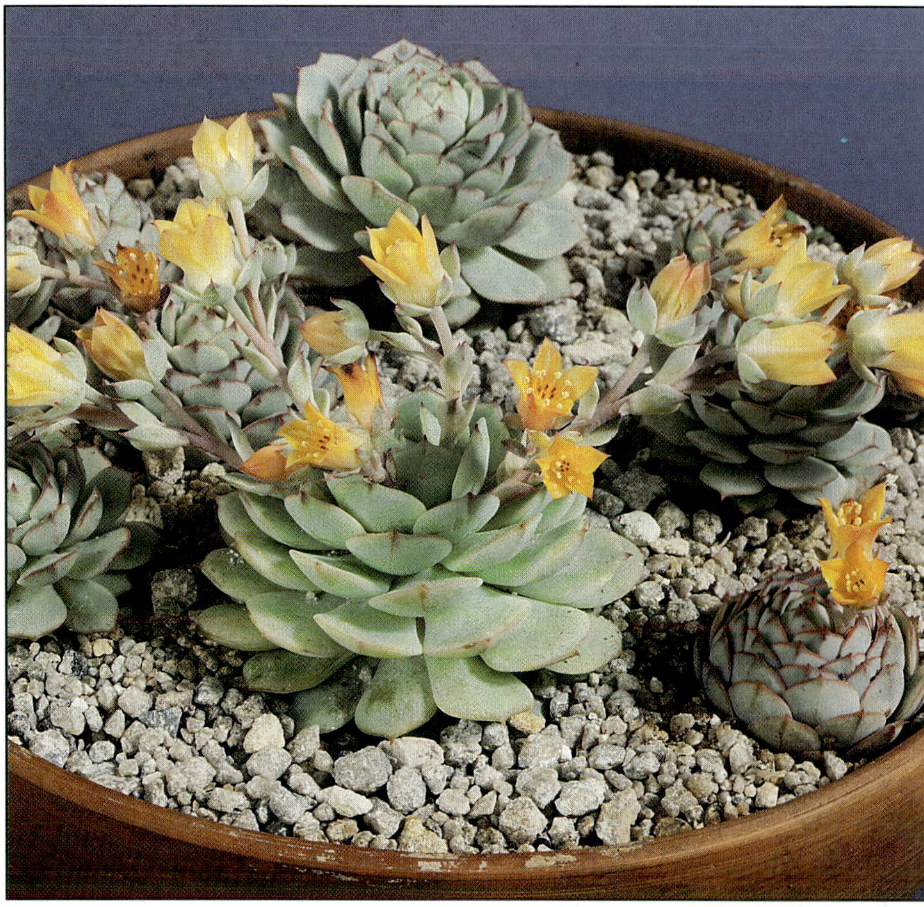

Echeveria derenbergii forms groups easily and has pretty flowers in spring.

Propagation

Sow seeds in John Innes Seed Compost and cover them with a little sharp sand. Keep the soil moist and the temperature between 50-60°F (10-15°C) and put a clear polythene bag over the seed tray or pot until the seeds have sprouted. When the seedlings are large enough to handle, pot them up individually using John Innes No 2 compost.

To take a leaf cutting, gently pull a leaf away from the stem and insert the leaf base in a pot of moist John Innes No 2. Keep the cutting in bright light; you do not need to cover it. Water enough to stop the compost drying out and maintain a temperature of 60-65°F (15-18°C). New shoots will soon appear from the base of the shrivelling leaf and when the plantlet has reached a manageable size, pot it up and then treat it as you would a mature Echeveria

One of the easiest ways to grow a new plant is by potting up an offset. Offsets are miniature rosettes that grow around the base of mature plants or on stems. In March, carefully remove an offset and let it dry out for a day or so; this lets the cut surface harden over, avoiding the possibility of rot developing. Plant it in a pot filled with John Innes No 1, mixing in a little coarse sand and also cover the surface of the compost with a thin layer. The offset should have taken root within two weeks.

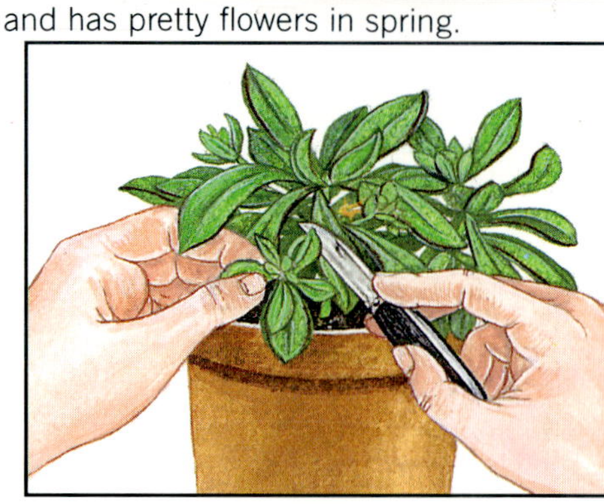

Propagating an Echeveria offset: simply cut off a healthy rosette, trim the stem and let it dry out for a day.

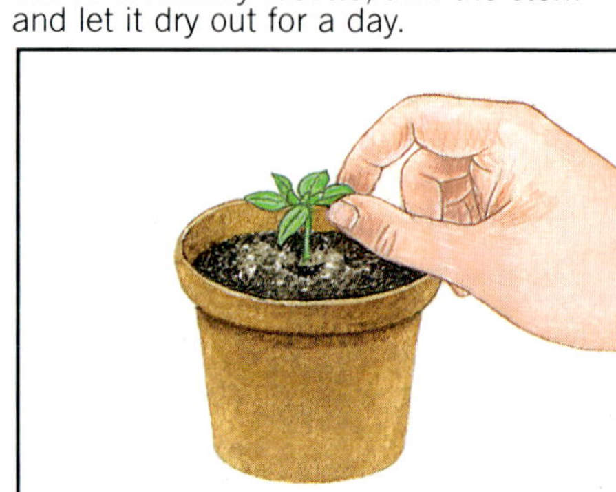

Plant the offset in John Innes No 1, covering the surface of the compost with coarse sand.

Species

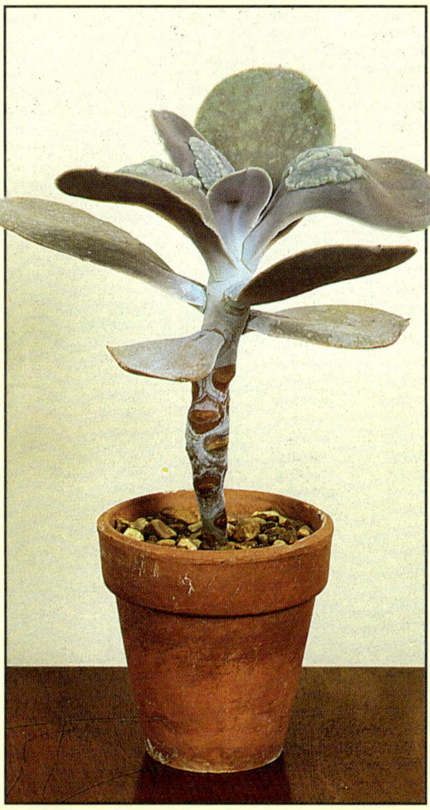

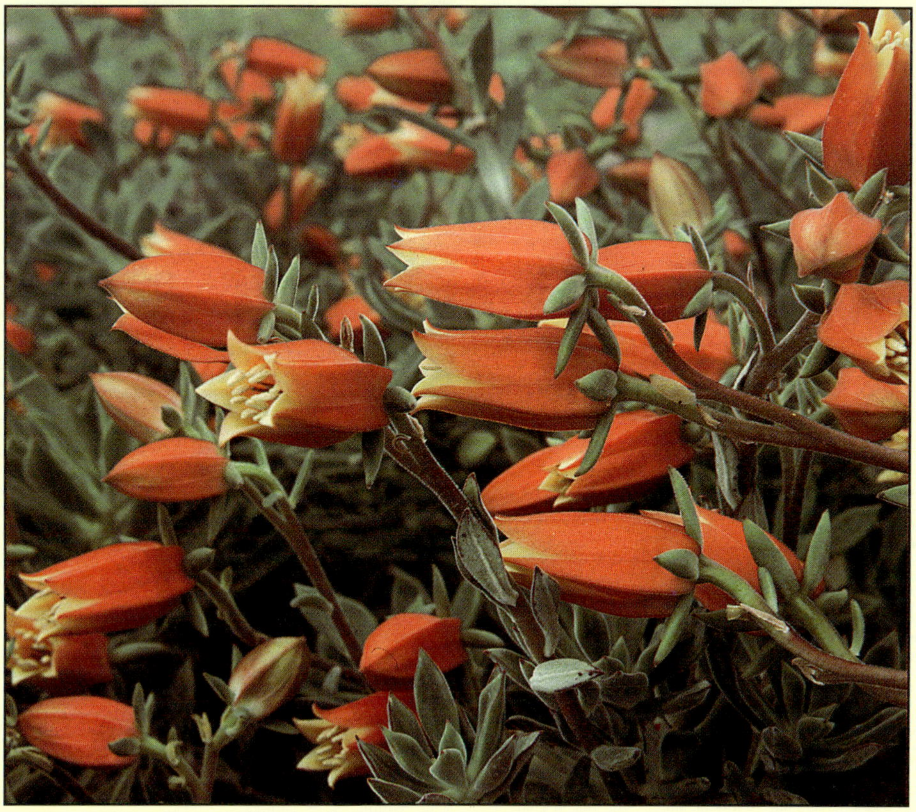

Echeveria derenbergii, Painted Lady, from southern Mexico, is a small, leafy, rosette plant, about 3in (7cm) in diameter. It has smooth, grey-green leaves and orange-yellow flowers in spring. The variety 'Dorosa' forms a larger rosette, about 7in (18cm) across, and has pale green leaves with red tips and slightly hairy edges. 'Worfield Wonder' is a very free-flowering variety that can even survive a mild winter outside in a sunny, sheltered position.

E.gibbiflora, *above left*, comes from Mexico and is one of the taller species. It grows to about 2ft (0.6m) and its bare stems and branches carry rosettes of large, fleshy, spoon-shaped, grey-green leaves, often with a pink tinge. Its huge red and yellow flowers are borne on tall stems and usually appear in the autumn. The variety 'Carunculata' has similar flowers, but its leaves have irregular bumps on their upper surface. 'Metallica' is another variety; it has the ordinary smooth leaves of the species but, as its name suggests, is a metallic pinky-bronze colour.

E.zahnii has grey-green leaves that are slightly pink-spotted on the upper surface. The rather loose rosette is usually carried on a short stem. It has small, orange-yellow, bell-shaped flowers on 5in (13cm) stems. 'Hoveyi' is an unusual variety with large, fleshy leaves that are about 2in (5cm) long and grey-green with pink stripes running along their length.

E.harmsii (or ***Oliversanthus elegans***), *above right*, Mexican Snowball, is a small, branched shrub with mid-green, lance-shaped leaves forming a loose rosette. It has large scarlet flowers 1in (2.5cm) long, carried individually or in small clusters round a tall spike.

E.setosa, Firecracker Plant, is another stemless, compact rosette plant. It has dark-green leaves that are covered in fine white bristly hairs and produces orange flowers in late spring.

E.glauca, Blue Echeveria, has green-blue leaves that form a dense rosette. As the leaves mature they often develop a reddish tinge round the edges. The flowers are carried on tall spikes each bearing up to 20 vivid red blooms.

Buying Guide

Look for well-shaped plants with no lopsided growth and healthy-looking unmarked leaves. Rosettes should be perfect, with no missing or broken foliage. Take great care when handling the plants not to crush their leaves and stems since they snap very easily. Use a small cardboard box to carry the plant home.

Trouble Shooter

Stem, root and leaf rot, and plants that grow out of shape, are all the result of overwatering; in summer water only when the soil is dry and in winter hardly water at all.

Lower leaves dying and falling off, revealing a short stem, result from neglect or simply old age. Cut the head of the plant off close to the bottom leaves, allow the leafy rosette to dry out for a day or so, and pot it up in John Innes No 2, covering the surface of the compost with sharp sand. This job is best done in March.

Mealy bug like the nooks and crannies provided by the Echeveria's closely-packed leaves — look for white patches on the foliage; dab the bugs with a paintbrush dipped in methyated spirit.

Echinopsis

Family name: **Cactaceae**

Common names:
Sea Urchin Cactus/Thistle Globe

Care Easy	**Height** 3-6in (8-15cm)	**Flower** June-Sept
Light Full sun	**Spread** 3-5in (8-13cm)	**Humidity** None
Price Cheap	**Shape** Global	**Availability** Garden centres
Temp. Min 45°F (7°C)	Ideal 60°F (15°C)	Max 75°F (24°C)

The Echinopsis is renowned for its beautiful, sweetly-scented flowers, which usually open in the evening. This is a large family of South American cacti and all its members are easy to grow and will flower freely if they are given bright, sunny light.

The Echinopsis is a typical cactus shape — globular, with a number of ribs edged with prickles that run right down from the crown to the base. The prickles and the rounded shape give the Echinopsis its characteristic appearance rather like a hedgehog — in fact, its Latin name is derived from the Greek for hedgehog!

The *Echinopsis multiplex* is the best-known species and the most commonly available one. It is a globular shape with 14 or so ribs that run from the top to the base of the plant. Along the ribs are little raised cushions, called areoles, out of which grow clusters of spines, each cluster forming a star shape. When the cactus is about three years old it will produce large, truly magnificent flowers. In early summer several blooms emerge from the areoles — they are a beautiful shade of pink with a sweet perfume and, though each flower only lasts a day, more flowers keep appearing to replace them at intervals so that you'll have a succession of flowers throughout the summer.

The Echinopsis needs the maximum light you can give it throughout the year and positively revels in sunshine. Most types of Echinopsis are night-blooming and the flowers normally open about half an hour after dusk; the flowers will last throughout the night and all through the following day.

Spring and summer care

You should repot your plant in early spring if it has become potbound, using a good cactus compost or John Innes No 2 with some added coarse sand.

Summer temperatures between 60-75°F (15-24°C) are ideal for your Echinopsis. Water your plant thoroughly when the compost is dry, then wait until it dries out before you water it again. Like all desert cacti your Echinopsis will hate being waterlogged so be careful never to let it stand in water. Feed with a liquid fertiliser every three to four weeks from April to September, adding a few drops to the water. Keep your plant in the brightest light possible and preferably in full sunlight.

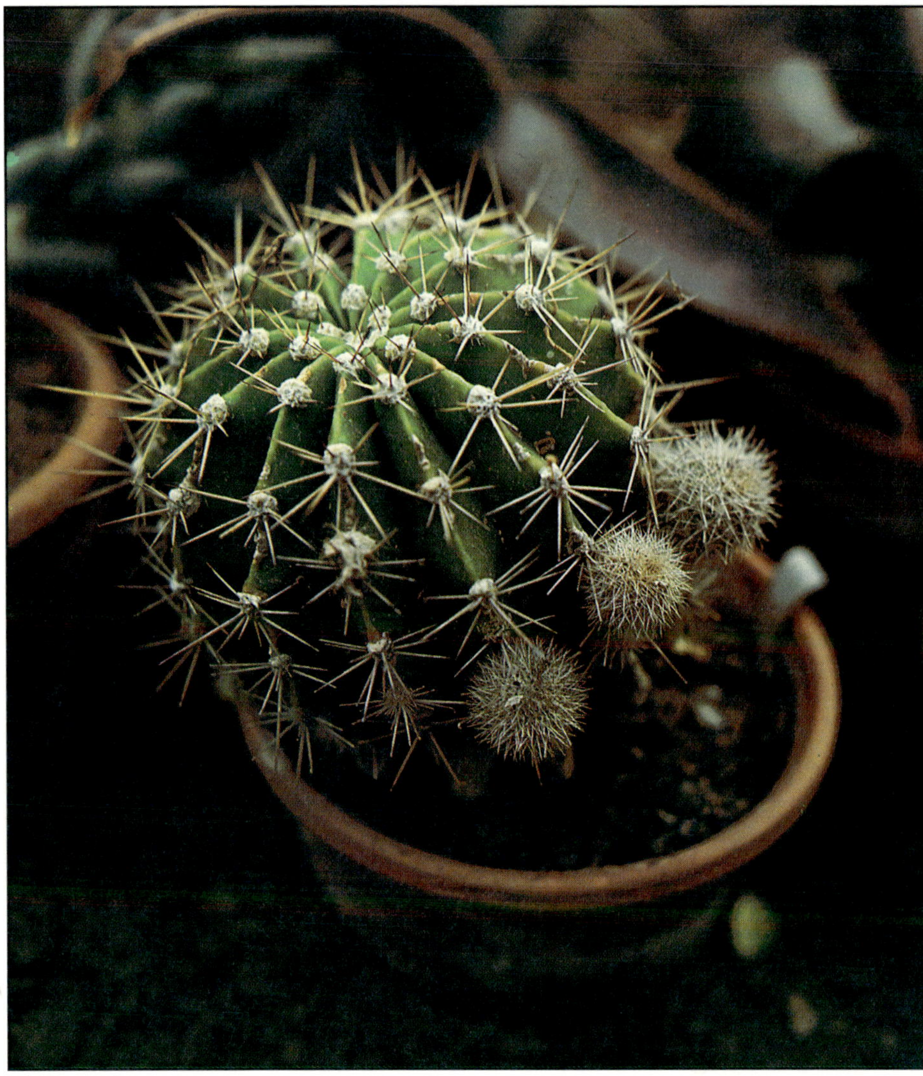

Echinopsis multiplex can easily be propagated from its offsets.

Autumn and winter care

To ensure that your Echinopsis flowers well it needs a winter rest period when it is kept in a temperature of 45-50°F (7-10°C). Water very sparingly from November to March — just enough to prevent the compost from becoming completely dry. Sit your plant in good light at all times and full sun whenever it shines.

Propagation

Sow Echinopsis seeds in March or April. Cover the seeds with a light layer of cactus compost or John Innes No 2 and keep moist and partially shaded until they germinate. Keep the seed tray in a temperature of 65-75°F (18-24°C).

Easier than growing plants from seed is to propagate by severing offsets (little plants that grow around the base of the main plant) from the parent plant with a sharp knife; do this in spring and early summer. Let the cut dry for a week before potting the offset in compost. If you remove an offset and it has roots attached, you should not let it dry out; you can plant it straight away, but keep the compost fairly dry for two to three weeks as this will prevent rot developing.

Trouble Shooter

Wrinkled, soft plants signal root rot, which results from overwatering; let your plant dry out and then let the compost dry before each watering.

A plant that does not flower and has become deformed is one that does not get enough light; this can't be corrected, so remove any young offsets growing around the base of the plant, treat as given in the Propagation section and keep them in bright light all year round, simply discarding the parent plant.

Small, fluffy, white blobs are mealy bugs; wipe them away with a soft brush dipped in methylated spirit.

Species

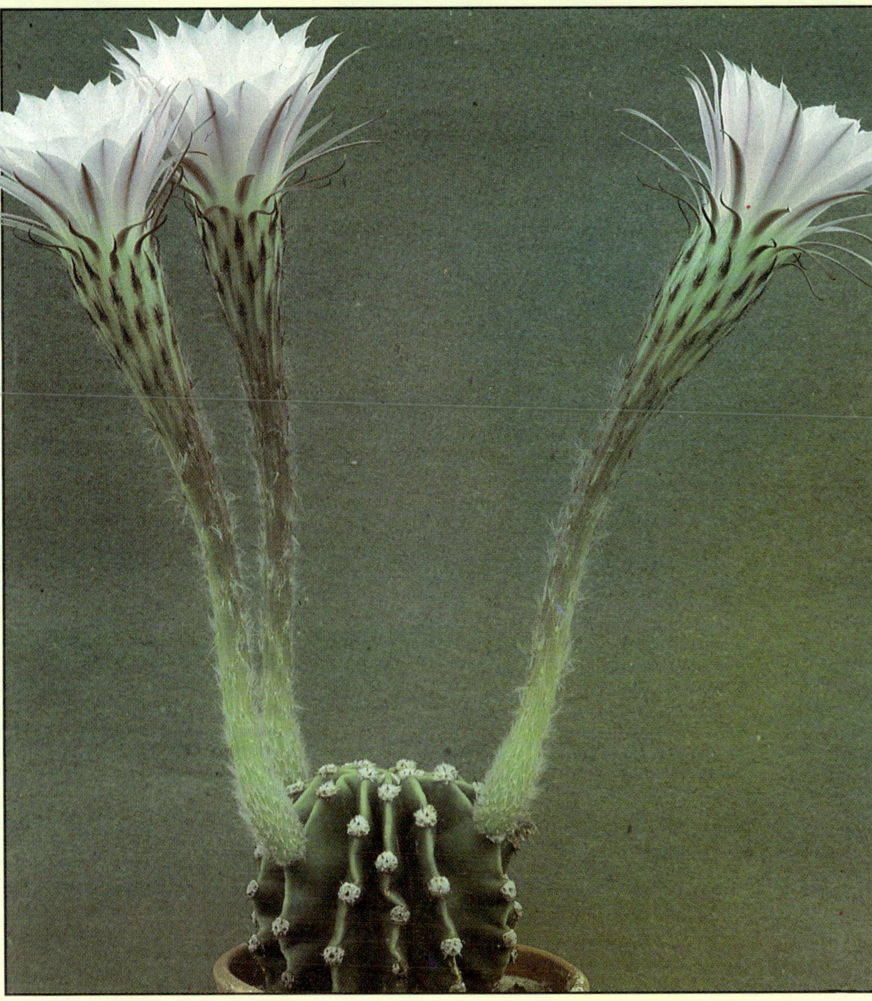

Echinopsis multiplex, Easter Lily Cactus, comes from Brazil and is the most popular and spectacular of this species. It has globular stems, which tend to elongate when they are fully mature. A series of ribs (about 12-14) run from the crown to the base of the plant and at intervals clusters of stout brownish spines radiate from raised cushions. Throughout the summer the cactus blooms with pale pink, very fragrant flowers each 7-8in (18-20cm) long and 5in (13cm) wide.

E.eyriesii, *above*, from Brazil, Argentina and Uruguay, is sometimes called the Sea Urchin Cactus. It has large, sweetly scented, almost pure white flowers 8-10in (20-25cm) long and 5in (13cm) wide. They start to open at dusk and are fully open all of the next day. The body of the plant is dark green with about 15 ribs, carrying clusters of very short spines.

E.tubiflora, *right*, from Brazil and Argentina, is more or less globular in shape with prominent wavy ribs with black spines about ½in (13mm) long.

E.spachianus *(or* ***Trichocereus spachianus)*** is usually available when it is 2-3in (5-7cm) tall, but after a few years it is 3-4ft (0.9-1.2m) tall. It is bright green with many ribs that produce clusters of yellowish-brown spines. The flowers are very large — about 10in (25cm) long — and white except for the outer petals, which are a rich red.

E.silvestrii, from Argentina, also has very large flowers, even when it is quite young. Unlike most of the other species it rarely produces offsets so it often grows as a solitary, grey-green globular plant, reaching about 6in (15cm). It has many ribs, over 20, each with yellowish-grey spines. In late spring and early summer, large, white, trumpet-shaped flowers appear.

E.aurea, from Argentina, is more or less globular in shape and tends to produce lots of offsets around its base to form groups of plants. It is very free-flowering, producing exotic lemon-yellow flowers. The variety 'Aurantiaca' is similar in most respects; the body of the plant is brown-green, spiny and forms groups extremely easily. Its flowers are handsome and brownish-orange in colour.

E.huascha *(or* ***Trichocereus huascha)*** is a sprawling plant with long, spiny stems about 3in (7cm) long. They have many ribs and fairly closely set areoles from which grow numerous yellowish-brown spines. The flowers vary in colour; the species has bright yellow flowers while the variety 'Rubriflorus' has reddish-orange flowers, for example.

E.oxygona is globular when it is young, becoming more cylindrical as it gets older, when it can reach a height of 12in (30cm). The ribs are very evenly arranged with large cushions regularly spaced along them with long, curved spines growing out of them. The flowers are 6-8in (15-20cm) long, trumpet-shaped and white suffused with pink on the inner petals, deep pink on the outside.

NOTE

As well as the many species there is a number of popular hybrids and crosses between Echinopsis and Lobivia. Most of these flower during the day and produce peach, orange, scarlet or purplish flowers readily.

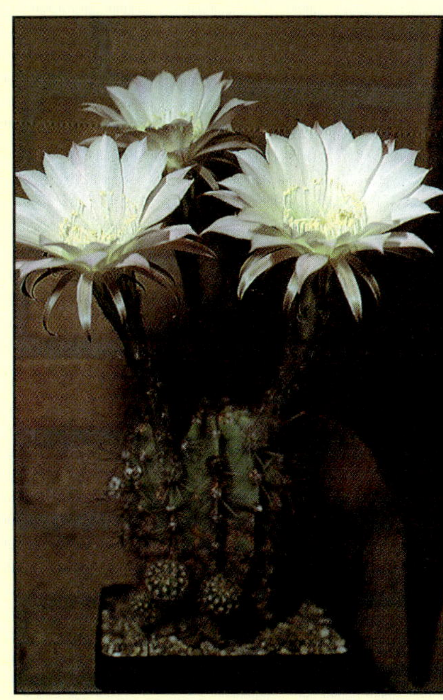

Epiphyllum

Family name: **Cactaceae**

Common name: **Orchid Cactus**

Care Straight-forward	**Height** 15-36in (38-90cm)	**Flower** April-July
Light Bright, indirect sun	**Spread** 8-12in (20-30cm)	**Humidity** Mist spray occasionally
Price Middle range	**Shape** Shrubby	**Availability** Specialist nurseries

Temp. Min 50°F (10°C) Ideal 60°F (15°C) Max 75°F (24°C)

In the wild the Epiphyllum grows in the tropical forests of Central America and looks as exotic as its origins would suggest. The stems are flattened and strap-like and the large, very beautiful flowers open at the ends of them, either during the day or at night. Strictly speaking, species Epiphyllums are not common plants as nearly all those generally grown are hybrids — mostly bred from *Epiphyllum crenatum*. For nearly a century, specialist growers have been working to produce better and better, more colourful flowers so that today you can buy an Epicactus — as this group of hybrids is now called — with flowers in almost every imaginable colour, except blue and pure green.

Spring and summer care

Repot your plant every year in spring, using a peat-based potting compost.

Your Epiphyllum will be happiest in good, diffused light rather than full sun, say on an east-facing windowsill. April to late July is the time flowers generally appear. Water your plant generously to keep the compost thoroughly moist and feed with liquid fertiliser, adding a few drops to the water every 10 days or so during the flowering season.

In the hot weather your plant will benefit from being put outside in a shaded spot, although it can put up with quite high summer temperatures indoors.

Autumn and winter care

The minimum temperature for your plant in winter is 50°F (10°C) and you should give it good bright light at all times, though not any direct winter sun.

From October through to March keep the compost just moist, never letting the roots become completely dry, and gradually increase the amount of water as the buds begin to form. Start to feed your plant with liquid fertiliser at this point to encourage the development of flower buds.

Propagation

In late July or August, after the flowers have finished, take a cutting of a 5-6in (13-15cm) length of stem and let it dry off for a day or two. Then plant the cutting in good soil-based compost, such as John Innes No 2, keep the compost moist and the cutting shaded. Provide a temperature of 70°F (21°C) and fresh air so don't cover the cuttings. In two to three weeks the cutting should send down roots and can then be cared for in the same way as a mature Epiphyllum.

Sow seeds in John Innes No 2, covering them lightly. Keep the seed tray moist and shaded and at a temperature of 70-75°F (21-24°C). When the seeds germinate, thin them out and then, when the seedlings are large enough to be handled safely, pot them on into their own pots filled with cactus compost or equal parts of John Innes No 2 and coarse sand. Put the young plants in a light position but out of direct sun and treat like mature plants. A point to note when growing from seed is that, if you have collected the seeds from a hybrid, the seedlings and, eventually, the mature plants may in no way resemble the parent.

Trouble Shooter

White, fluffy patches are mealy bug; wipe them away with a small brush dipped in methylated spirit or spray with a malathion-based insecticide.

Wilting stems and rotting roots are often a sign of overwatering — especially if it is winter time — so always remember to keep the compost moist but not wet and in winter, when the plant is resting, water only enough to keep the roots from drying out.

Scorched leaves result from overexposure to bright, direct sunlight; make sure your plant is in a semi-shaded position.

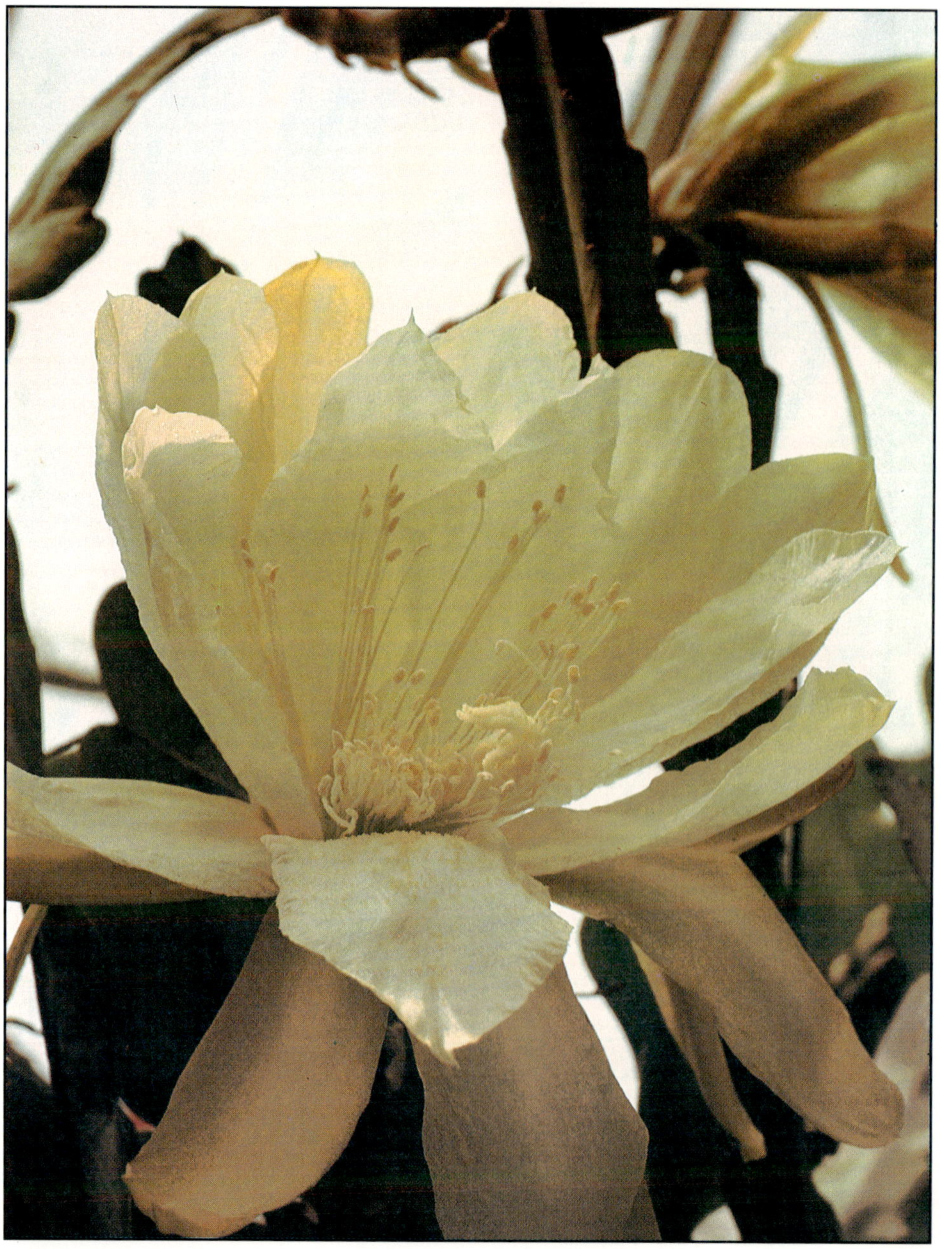

Epiphyllum crenatum has stunning creamy-white flowers.

Species

Epiphyllum crenatum, from Guatemala and neighbouring Central American states, is a day-flowering species. It can grow to about 3ft (0.9m) and is upright and branching. Its stems are round at the base and then flatten out into greyish-green, fleshy, leaf-like shapes with slightly notched edges. When fully open, the creamy-white trumpet-shaped flowers are 8-10in (20-25cm) long and about 6in (15cm) across. Very many of the popular Epiphyllum hybrids have been bred by crossing this species with others. The hybrid varieties are usually easier to grow and flower more readily than the parent. Flower colours include scarlet, purple, white and yellow. 'Cooperi' and 'Kimnachi' both have lovely white, scented flowers that open at midday but only last for 24 hours. Other types have longer-lived flowers, each bloom surviving for four or five days. 'Queen Anne' has yellow, frilly flowers and 'Reward', *below right,* is another good yellow variety. Multicoloured flowers are also available; 'Impello' has flowers that fade from shades of red through violet to pink; 'Dreamland' has pinkish-orange flowers with deep pink throats; 'Pegasus' has orange petals, edged with metallic violet. Look out for the large-flowered varieties like 'King Midas' with magnificent 7in (18cm) golden blooms and 'Space Rocket', *below left,* whose buds open to reveal giant crimson flowers edged with pink.

E.ackermanni, *right,* is extremely popular and easy to grow with masses of beautiful, elongated, trumpet-shaped flowers in bright scarlet.

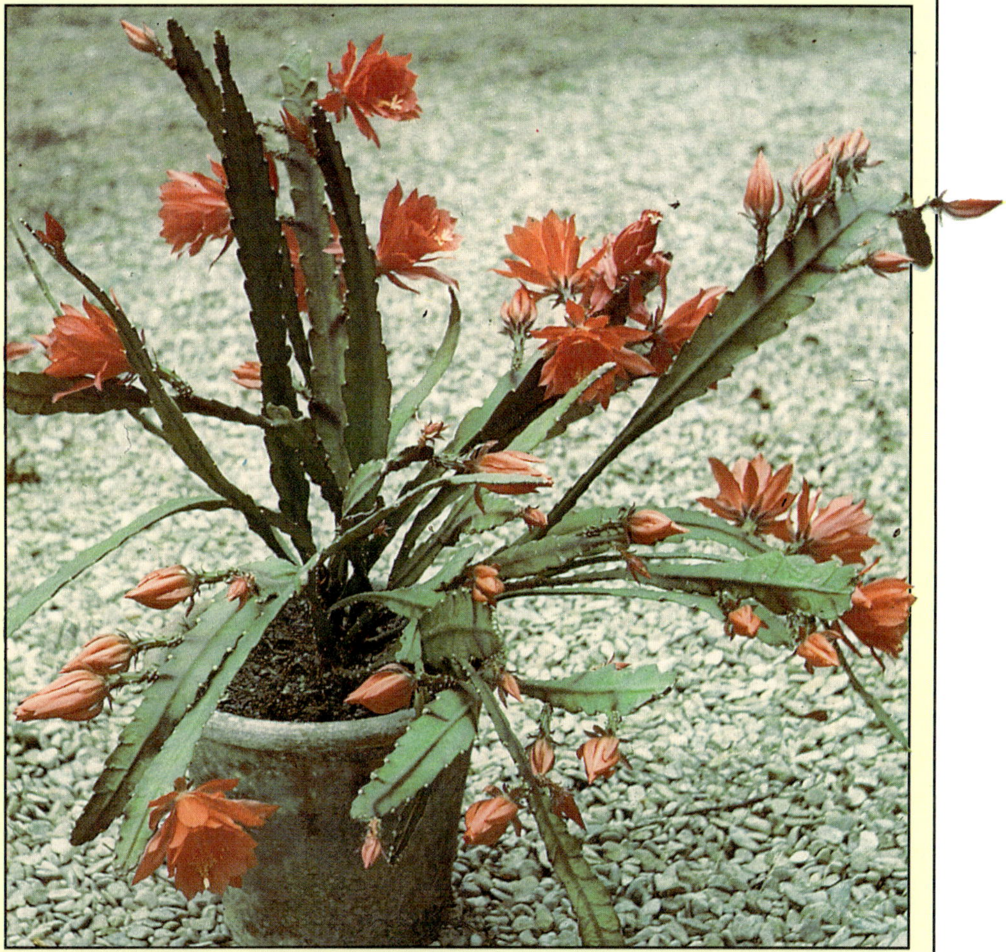

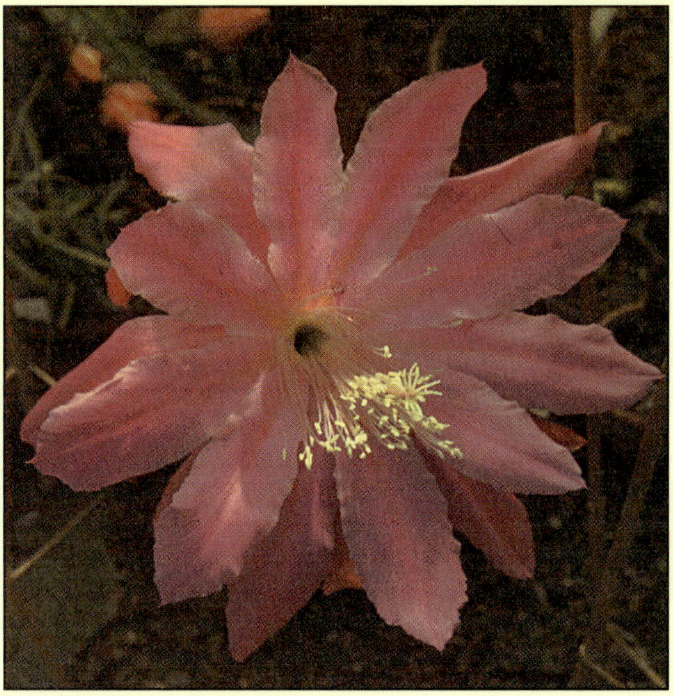

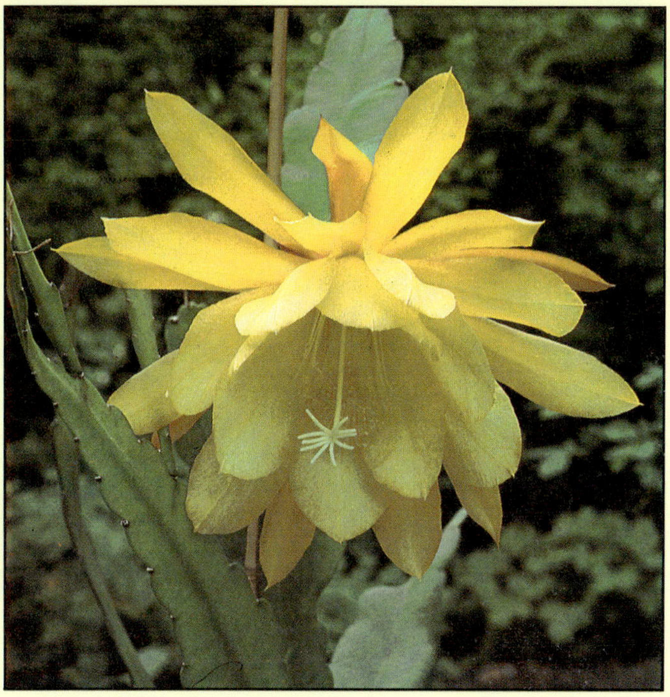

Euphorbia

Family name: **Euphorbiaceae**

Common names: **Poinsettia/ Crown of Thorns/Milkbush**

Care Easy	**Height** 2-5ft (0.6-1.5m)	**Flower** Mostly Nov-Jan
Light Indirect sun	**Spread** 6in-18in (15-45cm)	**Humidity** None
Price Cheap/ medium	**Shape** Bushy	**Availability** Garden centres
Temp. Min 55°F (13°C)	Ideal 65°F (18°C)	Max 75°F (24°C)

The Euphorbia group includes an amazing variety of plants, ones that don't look as if they could possibly be related at all: there's the familiar red-leaved Poinsettia, the Crown of Thorns, which looks more like a cactus with its sharp spines and fleshy stems, and the Milkbush, a spindly, multi-branched plant — to name but three.

Euphorbia pulcherrima, commonly known as the Poinsettia, is the most popular and well-known species of Euphorbia. Originally from Mexico, in its natural surroundings it will grow into a very large, bushy shrub, but the descendants and hybrids of this original form have been developed to be much more compact. The Poinsettia has lots of pointed oval, bright-green leaves, but it is noted for the rosettes of scarlet flower-like bracts (false leaves) that grow at the ends of the branches, surrounding almost insignificant, small, creamy-yellow flowers. The bracts start to form in late autumn and the growers make sure they are at their finest during Christmas time. You can buy varieties now that have pale yellow, white or pale pink bracts and these can look very attractive grouped together.

Crown of Thorns or, to give it its proper name, *E.milii*, looks a lot like a cactus with its fleshy stems armed with long spines, but unlike cacti it also has leaves. A mature Crown of Thorns plant will be quite bushy, with lots of bright green oval-shaped leaves at the tips of the branches, and very small flowers surrounded by red or yellow bracts that are small enough to be easily mistaken for petals.

Not only do these plants look very different from each other, they also have their own particular needs. So that you can easily see how to look after your particular Euphorbia, we have divided the Care and Propagation sections into the three types of Euphorbia; Poinsettias, other shrubby Euphorbias like *E.fulgens* and the succulent Euphorbias (*E.milii, E.tirucalli, E.trigona, E.flanaganii*).

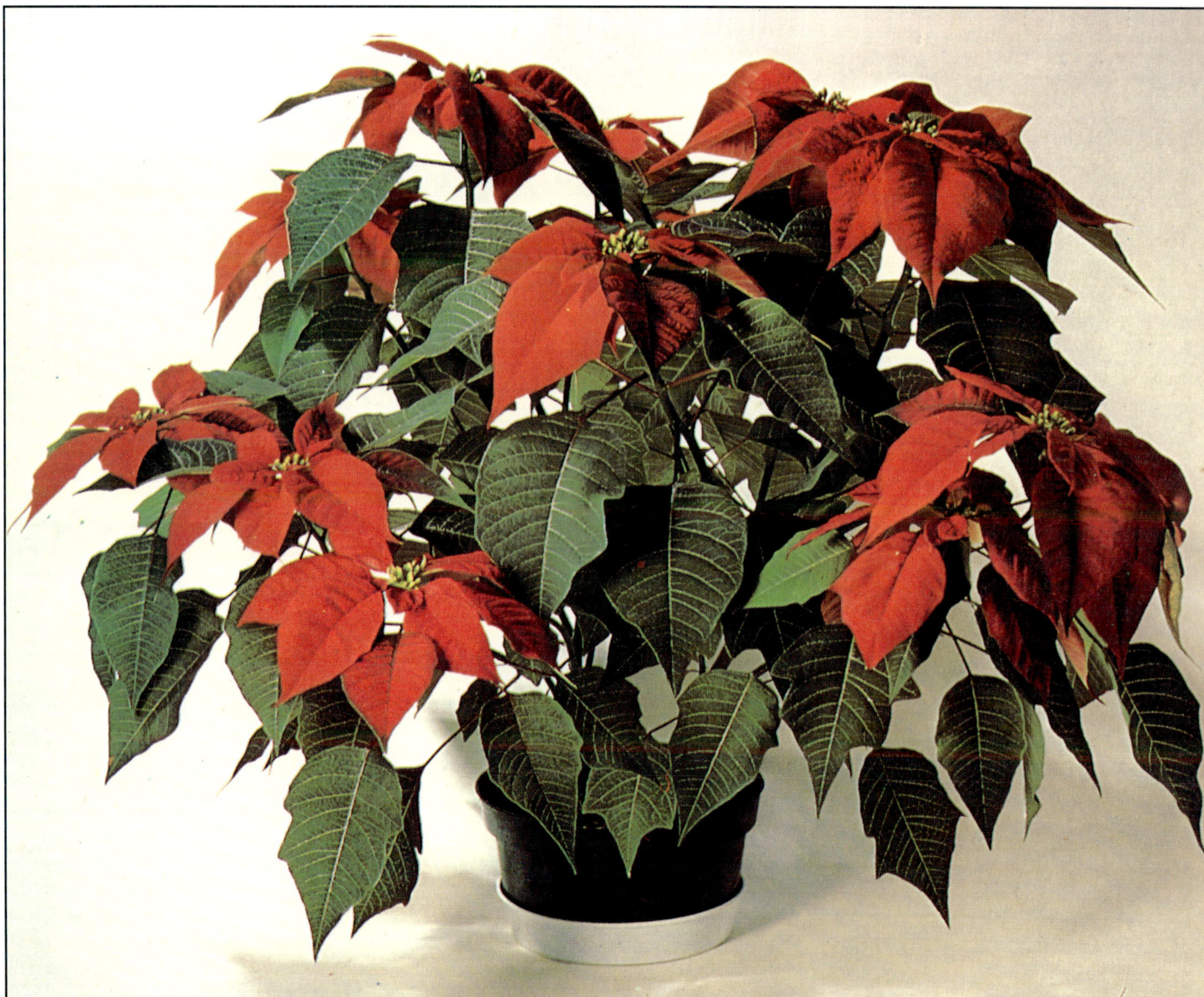

Euphorbia pulcherrima makes a splendid eye-catching feature.

Spring and summer care

Poinsettia: many people discard their Poinsettia after the bracts have faded but it is not difficult to encourage it to produce bracts again. After the bracts have faded cut your plant back hard to the base, leaving just 4in (10cm) of stem. The compost should be almost but not completely dry. Keep the plant at normal room temperatures and put it in bright, indirect light for about a month. Then drench it with water — this will start it growing again.

When your Poinsettia does begin to grow — about May — repot it into fresh soil-based compost like John Innes No 2. Don't put your plant in a bigger pot otherwise it will produce lots of stems and no flowers or bracts.

Keep it in bright, indirect light and water thoroughly every time the compost becomes dry, though never let it dry out completely. Add a couple of drops of liquid fertiliser to the water every two weeks from late May to September.

Prune away any excess growth, keeping five or so stems — this ensures strong bushy growth. You can propagate from the shoots you prune away, by treating them as cuttings (see Propagation).

Other shrubby Euphorbias (eg *E.fulgens*): pot on these plants in late spring, using moistened John Innes No 2 mixed with an equal amount of damp coarse sand or, instead of repotting, raise new plants each year from cuttings (see Propagation).

These plants like normal room temperatures, 65-75°F (18-24°C), a humid atmosphere and bright light but no direct sun. Water your plant thoroughly allowing the compost to get slightly dry before watering again. Add a liquid fertiliser to the water every two weeks from June to September.

To make a compact, bushy plant cut the stems back to 6in (15cm) after potting.

Succulent Euphorbias: *E.milii, E.trigona, E.tirucalli* and *E.flanaganii* all prefer a dry atmosphere, a bright sunny position and ordinary room temperatures. Repot them each spring into a mixture of equal parts John Innes No 2 and coarse sand — and be sure to put a layer of broken pieces of clay pot under the compost.

Water regularly so that the compost is moist, but allow it to dry out slightly between waterings. Add a few drops of a liquid fertiliser to the water every two weeks.

Autumn and winter care

Poinsettias: at the end of September you will need to regulate the light you give your plant strictly in the following way so that it will produce its red bracts. You will find that the resultant plant will be taller than when you bought it as the growers generally treat poinsettias with a dwarfing chemical.

Put your Poinsettia in a black polythene bag for 14 hours a day — from early evening to early morning — and do this every day for eight weeks. Then sit your plant in good light and in a normal room temperature. Water sparingly and don't feed. By Christmas time it should have several of its characteristic red bracts and small creamy-yellow flowers.

Other shrubby Euphorbias: while the plant is flowering keep the compost only slightly moist then reduce the watering still further until the spring when you can take cuttings. Winter temperatures should not fall below 55°F (13°C).

Succulent Euphorbias: after flowering, water your plant less often — the cooler the temperature the less water it should have, although the soil should never be allowed to dry out completely. Don't let the temperature fall below 55°F (13°C) and keep in a bright, sunny position away from cold draughts.

Propagation

Poinsettia and other shrubby Euphorbias: water the parent plant in the spring to restart growth. Cut a young shoot when it is 3-4in (7-10cm) long. Dip the cut surface into water to stop the flow of sap. Pot up each cutting into separate 3in (7cm) pots of equal parts of peat and coarse sand. Cover the pots with clear polythene bags and keep them at a steady temperature between 64-70°F (18-21°C) until new leaves have started to grow. Then pot up the cuttings into bigger pots and treat as you would mature plants.

Succulent Euphorbias: stem tip cuttings can be taken in spring and summer. Cut 3-4in (7-10cm) off the tip of a growing stem. Dip the cutting immediately in a glass of water then spray the plant's cut stem — this will stop the milky sap from seeping out of the plant. Leave the cutting to dry out for a day before potting it up into a 3in (7cm) pot containing a mixture of equal parts peat and coarse sand. The compost should be only slightly moist or the cutting will rot before it can produce roots. Place the uncovered pot in bright, indirect light and away from draughts. A steady temperature of 65°F (18°C) is ideal.

In a month or so new growth should be visible; pot on the cutting into a mixture of equal parts John Innes No 2 and coarse sand and treat as you would the mature plant.

Trouble Shooter

If botrytus, *below,* has attacked your plant, the infected leaves will give off a fine dust when disturbed.

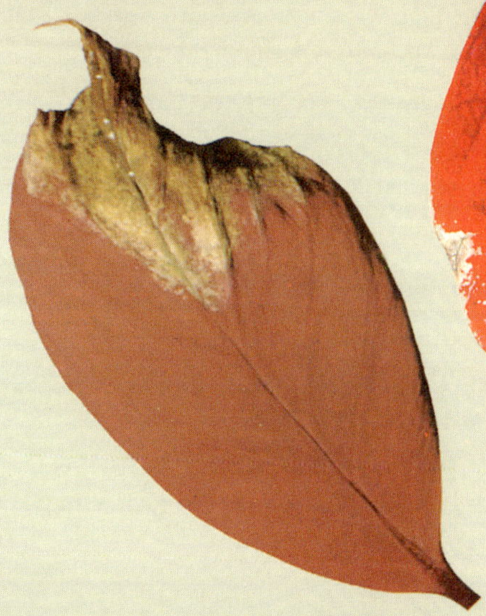

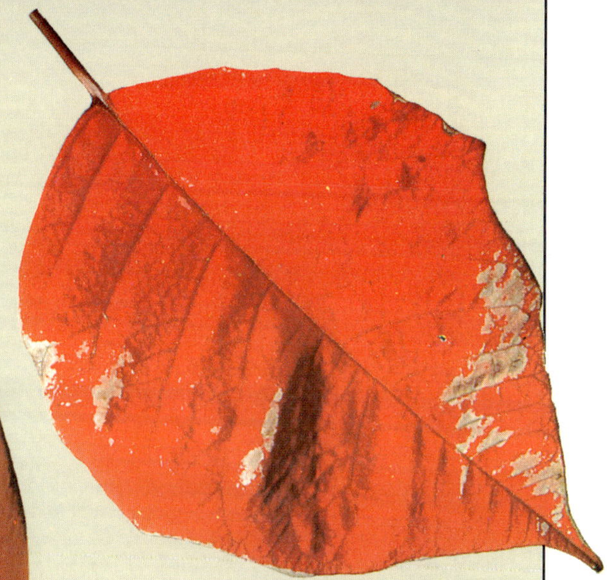

Unhealthy patches, *above,* are often a sign of overwatering.

Poinsettia and other shrubby Euphorbias may suffer from yellowing leaves which eventually fall off. This is often due to cold draughts or gas fumes. Move the plant to a more favourable position. Discolouration of leaves and bracts is a sign of overwatering. If the plant remains sodden the roots will rot and the leaves and bracts will fall off. Dry out the plant before watering again.

Clusters of greenfly around new growth will distort the leaves. Get rid of them with a malathion-based insecticide sprayed all over the plant. This spray will also deal with scale insect which can attack the plants and suck the sap from young growth; check for small, flat blisters on leaves and stems and spray the plant before the insects do too much damage. Poinsettias can sometimes be infected by a fungus disease called botrytus. Look for greyish-looking patches, particularly on the lower leaves and bracts. Remove the infected parts and spray with a fungicide.

Succulent Euphorbias are prone to rotting stems, leaves and roots. Cut away the affected part, move the plant to a less humid position and reduce the watering.

Species

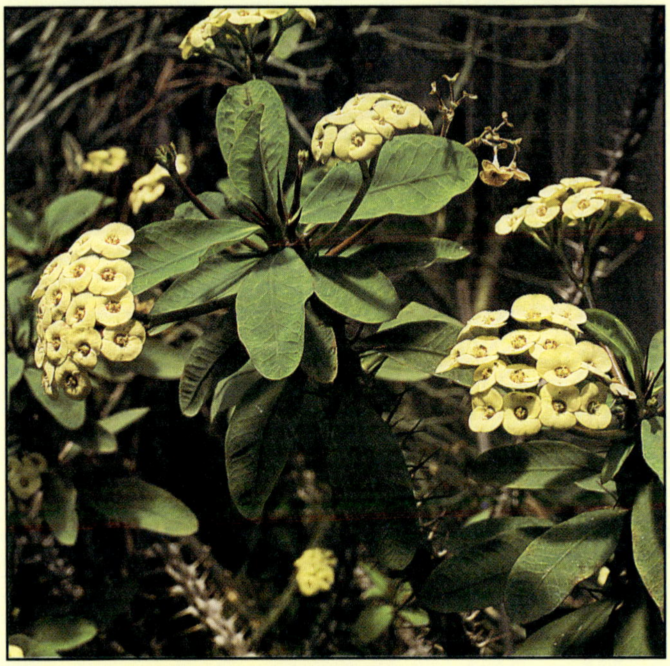

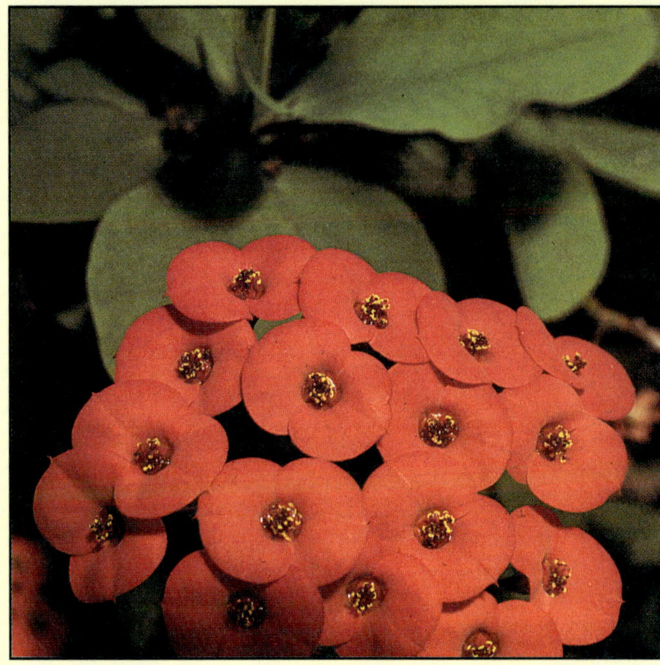

Euphorbia pulcherrima, more usually known as Poinsettia, is a deciduous shrubby plant from Mexico which can grow to a height of 4-5ft (1.2-1.5m) as a houseplant. It has bright green, slightly lobed leaves carried on thin branching stems. The small yellow flowers appear in winter (though they can be artificially forced to appear at any time). The flowers are surrounded by large brightly-coloured bracts that look rather like a cross between leaves and flowers. The bracts are cream, crimson, scarlet or pink, depending on the variety.

E.milii (also called ***E.splendens***), the Crown of Thorns, is a semi-succulent tree-like plant — though it should be treated like a succulent Euphorbia. It has very thorny stems which carry leaves at their tips. The plant grows to about 18in (45cm) and has small yellow winter flowers surrounded by larger, bright red bracts, *above right*. The variety 'Tananarivae', *above left*, has yellow bracts.

E.tirucalli, commonly called the Milkbush because of its white sap, can reach 4ft (1.2m) tall. It has round fleshy stems, only very tiny leaves at the tips of the stems and rarely has flowers; so it has a rather strange naked appearance.

E.fulgens is another shrubby species. It is also known as *E.jacquinaeflora*. It has narrow lance-shaped leaves and arching stems and can grow to a height of 4ft (1.2m). Clusters of red bracts appear with the flowers in winter.

E.trigona is from tropical southern Africa. It is an upright, branched succulent plant which grows up to 3ft (0.9m) tall with thick ridged stems in dark green, marbled with whitish markings. Flowers rarely appear.

E.flanaganii is a fascinating-looking succulent plant from South Africa. It has several rather thin fleshy stems of 6-8in (15-20cm) — these occasionally produce numerous flowers with yellow bracts.

WARNING

The milky sap of many Euphorbias is poisonous, so take care — especially when taking cuttings — to wash the sap off your skin.

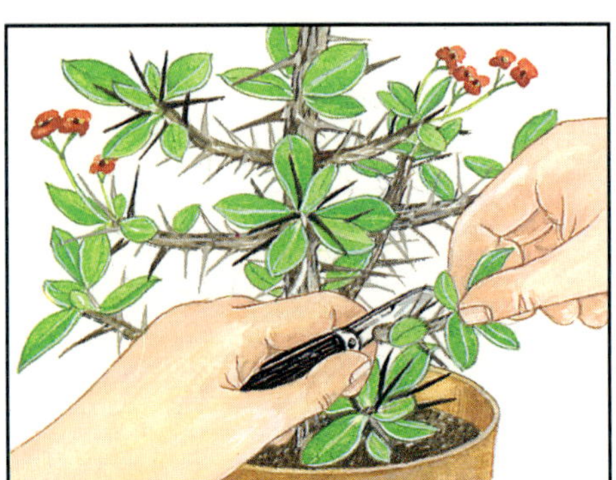

Propagating *Euphorbia milii*: using a sharp knife, take a 3 in (7cm) cutting from a stem tip.

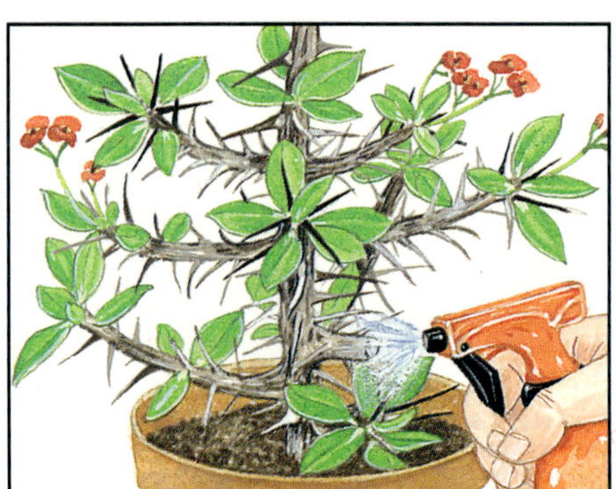

Dip the cut end of the stem in water and spray the cut stem on the plant. This will stop the flow of milky sap.

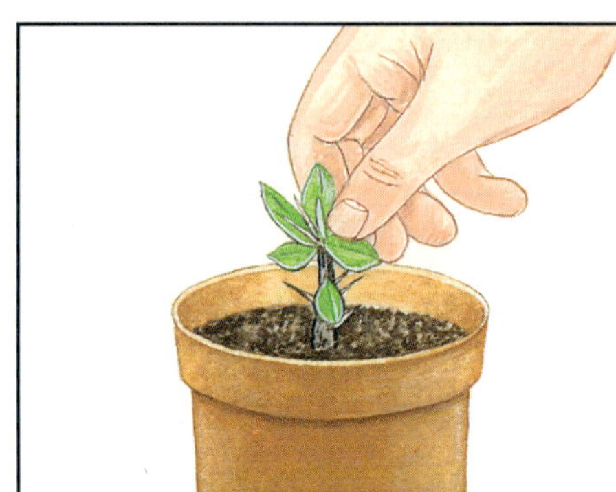

Insert the cutting into a slightly damp mixture of equal parts of John Innes No 2 and coarse sand.

Exacum

Family name: **Gentianaceae**

Common name:
Mexican Violet/Persian Violet

Care Easy	**Height** 6-10in (15-25cm)	**Flower** June-August
Light Indirect sun	**Spread** 6-10in (15-25cm)	**Humidity** Spray only in hot weather
Price Cheap	**Shape** Bushy	**Availability** Garden centres
Temp. Min 60°F (15°C)	Ideal 70°F (21°C)	Max 85°F (30°C)

Only one member of this small group of plants is suitable as a houseplant — the Mexican Violet (*Exacum affine*). Despite its common name, it is actually a native of the Islands of Socotra in the Indian Ocean. This neat, trouble-free little plant makes a 6-10in (15-25cm) high bush, and would be an ideal table decoration in summer when it is a mass of delightful, scented, lilac-coloured flowers.

Though the plant is really a perennial and, with careful treatment, should survive from year to year, it's far easier to treat it as an annual and grow plants from seed each year.

Spring and summer care

The Mexican Violet likes warm temperatures — a minimum of 60°F (15°C) — and a humid atmosphere. The best spot for it is out of direct sunlight in a sunny room — bathrooms are often the ideal place. Keep the soil damp but not soggy. The best way to water a Mexican Violet is to stand the plant in a tray of water for a few minutes so that water is drawn up through the soil from below — don't leave it standing in water for hours on end though or its roots may start to rot. Once a week add a couple of drops of liquid fertiliser to the water. Always remember too that your plant will flower for longer if you carefully pinch out the blooms as they die.

Autumn and winter care

If you want to keep your plant through the winter, reduce the watering once your plant has finished flowering, but never let it dry out completely. Stop using fertiliser and make sure the room temperature never falls below 60°F (15°C).

Propagation

It's so easy to raise Mexican Violets from seed that it hardly seems worthwhile trying to keep plants from year to year. Sow seeds in late summer or spring; autumn sowing gives you flowers earlier in the summer the following year, but spring-sown plants will continue to flower later into the autumn so it's a good idea to sow some seed in October and then some more in March.

Sow the seeds very thinly on the surface of a tray of moistened seed compost. Keep the tray at a steady temperature of about 75°F (24°C) in a shaded position. A small propagator is ideal for raising plants from seed, but if you don't have one put the tray in a clear polythene bag and place it on a warm windowledge, shading the tray from bright light with a piece of paper.

As soon as the seedlings are large enough to handle, use a pencil or a small fork to loosen the seedlings and transfer them to 3in (7cm) pots filled with John Innes No. 2 or 3. Keep the pots of seedlings away from draughts and out of direct sunlight. Make sure the compost stays moist and turn the pots around regularly to keep the seedlings growing straight.

When the seedlings are 2-3in (5-7cm) tall pot them into larger pots, putting a layer of gravel and pieces of broken clay pot in the bottom. For a really bushy-looking plant, carefully pinch out the growing tip of each of the seedlings and plant five seedlings together in a 5in (13cm) pot or bowl. Remember that autumn-grown seedlings need to be kept at a temperature of between 65-70°F (18-21°C) right through the winter months.

Buying Guide

Look for bushy plants with glossy leaves and lots of flower buds. Don't buy a plant that's already in full flower — it won't have a great deal more to offer.

Species

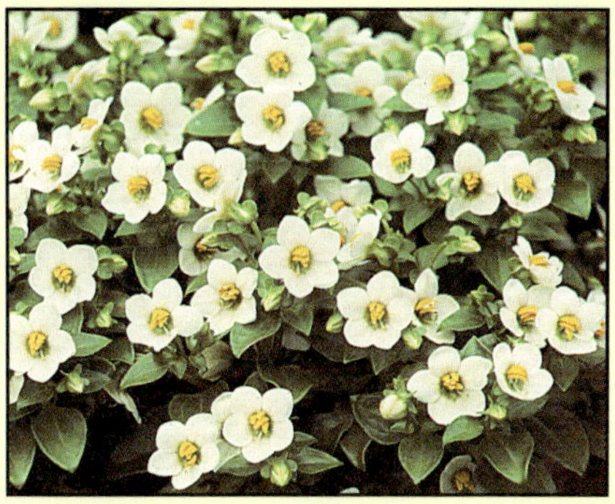

Exacum affine, the Mexican Violet, from the Island of Socotra in the Indian Ocean, has small glossy, oval leaves set opposite one another along branching stems. It makes a small rounded bush 6-10in (15-25cm) across and has violet-coloured flowers with bright yellow stamens in the centre, and there is also a pretty white form, *above*.

E.zeylanicum is occasionally found in seed catalogues or garden centres. It grows to about 2ft (0.6cm) and flowers from late August to October.

E.macranthum is another of the rarer species. It has smaller, purplish-blue flowers in summer.

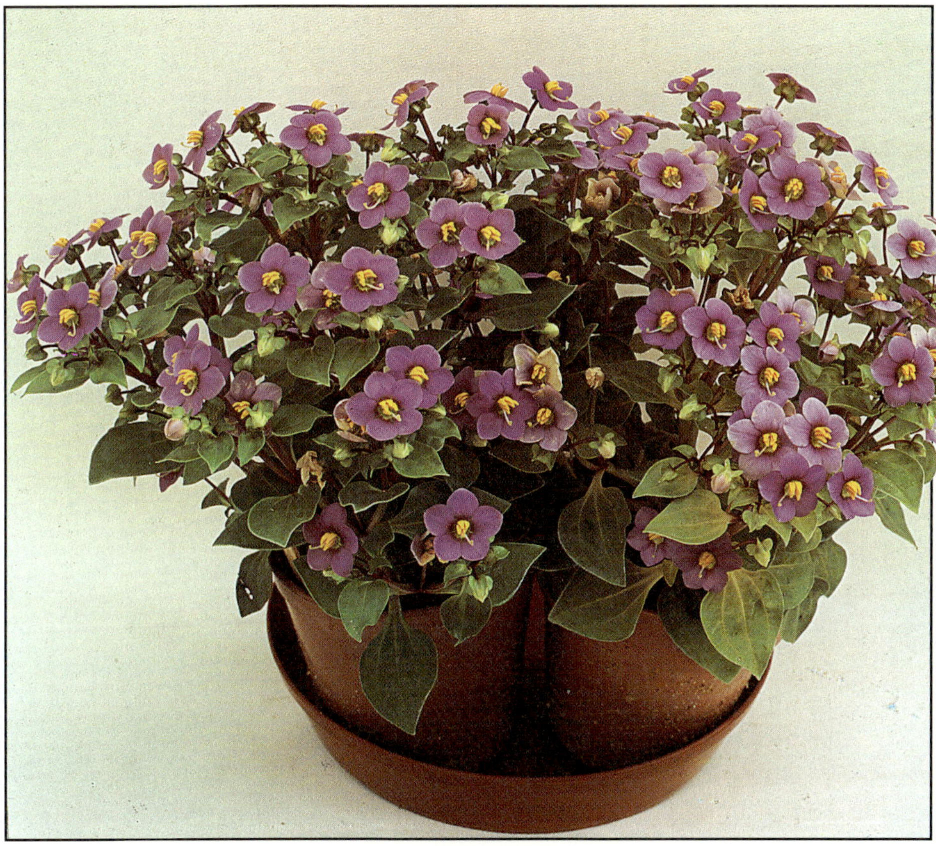

Exacum affine is a delightful little flowering bush.

Fatshedera

Family name: **Araliaceae**

Common names: **Ivy Tree, Miracle Plant, Fat-headed Lizzie**

Care Easy	**Height** 2-6ft (0.6-1.8m)	**Flower** Oct-Nov
Light Bright indirect sun	**Spread** 1-4ft (0.3-1.2m)	**Humidity** Occasional mist spray
Price Medium	**Shape** Shrubby climber	**Availability** Garden centres

Temp. Min 45°F (7°C) — Ideal 60°F (15°C) — Max 75°F (24°C)

This eye-catching evergreen is one of today's most useful houseplants. It's tough, will stand the dry atmosphere of a centrally heated room yet can also survive temperatures only a few degrees above freezing, and it isn't plagued by pests or plant diseases.

As the name suggests, Fatshedera is a hybrid of two well-known plants: Ivy (Hedera) and Fatsia. It has some of the leaf shape and climbing nature of the Ivy combined with the glossy rich colouring and upright shape of the Fatsia. It can be grown as a bush like Fatsia; all you have to do is pinch out the growing tips each spring. Alternatively, you may prefer to grow your plant like an Ivy and allow it to trail or climb. When left to its own devices, Fatshedera is a semi-climbing shrub with upright shoots which tend to trail as they mature.

In September and October the plant has clusters of small star-shaped, pale green flowers. There is also a variegated Fatshedera which is extremely attractive, but it does need brighter light in order to thrive.

Spring and summer care

You can repot your Fatshedera every year in spring. If roots are encircling the rootball inside the pot, transfer into a container one size larger. Use John Innes No 2 or 3 for repotting.

Water your plant regularly so that the compost is kept moist but not sodden, and add a couple of drops of liquid fertiliser to the water every two weeks. Don't leave the pot standing in a saucer of water, though, or the leaves will become discoloured. Mist spraying the leaves with water is a good idea — particularly when the weather is hot and dry.

If the temperature exceeds 75°F (24°C) indoors, move the plant outside to a shady spot

The large glossy leaves can get quite dirty so dust them regularly or wipe them with a damp cloth — or you may find it easier to put your plant under a shower for a few minutes.

Fatshedera will grow best in bright but indirect light. However, your plant will do fairly well in quite a shaded position.

To ensure that your plant grows into an attractive bushy shape, pinch out the tips of the stems when it begins to look too tall.

Autumn and winter care

During the winter months, when your plant will make little or no growth, keep it, ideally, at a temperature of around 45°F (7°C) and water sparingly — enough to keep the soil just moist. In a centrally heated room, however, it needs a little more water and will appreciate a spray of water on its leaves.

Propagation

Take 6-8in (15-20cm) cuttings from the tips of the shoots during the spring and summer. Plant them in pots of moist John Innes No 2 or 3 mixed with a little sharp sand, and put the pots into clear polythene bags, making sure the cuttings don't touch the polythene. Keep the compost moist and at a temperature of about 60-65°F (15-18°C).

Once the cuttings show signs of new growth, remove the bag. Keep the plant away from draughts and bright sunlight and otherwise treat as you would a mature Fatshedera.

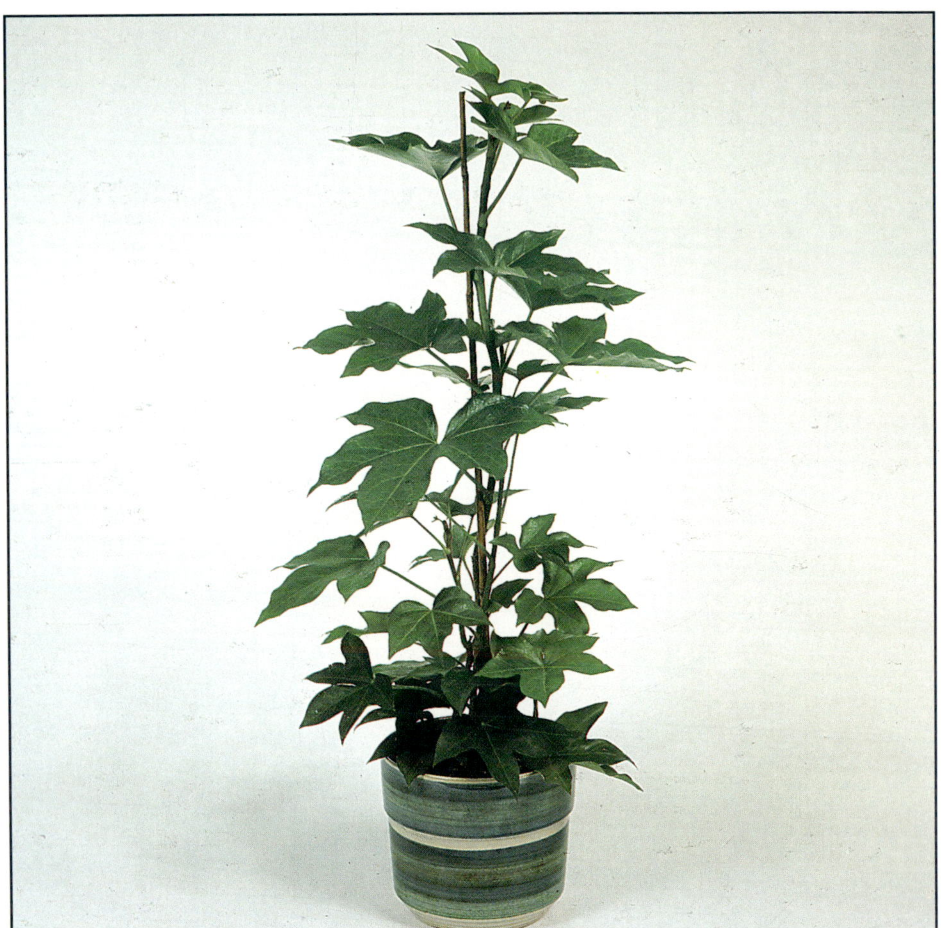

Fatshedera lizei can be grown as a climber like Hedera, or a bush like Fatsia.

Species

Fatshedera lizei is, strictly speaking, a hybrid and not a member of a group of species. As a result the plant is infertile and cannot be propagated from seed. It has lush, green, leathery leaves, shaped rather like a small fig leaf or a large ivy leaf, and pale green autumn flowers carried in clusters on a stem. When grown as a bushy plant, Fatshedera can grow as high as 6ft (1.8m) and as wide as 4ft (1.2m). 'Variegata', *below*, is a very handsome variegated form with creamy-yellow markings.

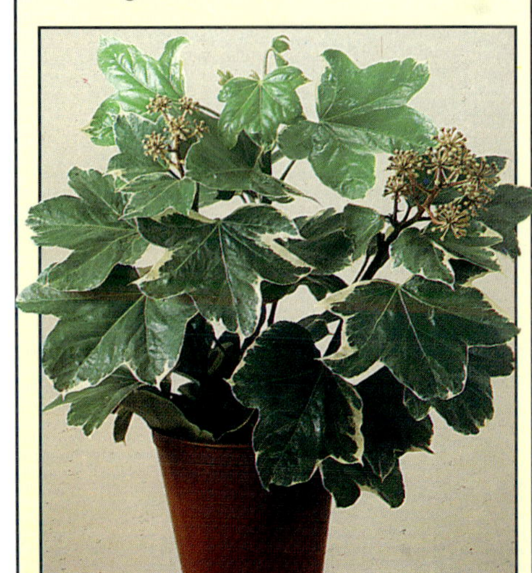

Fatsia

Family name: **Araliaceae**

Common name:
Figleaf Palm

Care Easy	**Height** 4-15ft (1.2-4.5m)	**Flower** August-October
Light Bright indirect sun	**Spread** 1-3ft (0.3-0.9m)	**Humidity** Regular mist spray
Price Medium	**Shape** Shrubby	**Availability** Garden centres
Temp. Min 45°F (7°C)	Ideal 65°F (18°C)	Max 70°F (21°C)

Originally from Japan and Taiwan, this large, impressive evergreen has been a popular houseplant for over one hundred and fifty years. A striking feature of this elegant plant is its large glossy green leaves which look rather like huge hands and can measure between 6-18in (15-45cm) or more across. Fatsias have been known to reach heights of over 15ft (4.5m), but drastic pruning can curb your plant's growth if it begins to take over the house! Its tolerance to a wide range of conditions makes it the ideal plant for those with little experience of houseplants.

Fatsia japonica (or sometimes called *F.sieboldii*) is the only species. Extremely fast-growing, it can reach 4-5ft (1.2-1.5m) in two to three years. Large clusters of white flowers appear in autumn, but these are seldom seen on indoor plants, except on very mature specimens kept in cool conditions.

If size is a problem, *F.j.moserii*, which grows at a slower rate, will give you a smaller, more compact plant.

Spring and summer care

To encourage your plant to grow bigger, pot on in early spring, using John Innes No 2 or 3. You can prune at the same time if your Fatsia's growth has got out of hand — just trim back the straggly shoots.

Keep your plant in bright indirect light, ideally at a temperature of 65°F (18°C). If the temperature rises above this, make sure there is plenty of fresh air circulating round the plant, or put it outside in the shade.

Water regularly to keep the compost moist, but take care not to overwater. Liquid fertiliser can be added to the water every two or three weeks. As Fatsias like a humid environment, overhead spraying will keep your plant free from dust and in tip top condition.

Autumn and winter care

Your plant should be kept at a temperature of 50-55°F (10-13°C) in a bright, but not sunny, position. Water it sufficiently to keep the compost just moist, but if the temperature drops below 50°F (10°C), keep the soil on the dry side. Treat your plant to an overhead spray once a week.

Propagation

The most effective way to propagate the Fatsia is to take 2-3in (5-7cm) stem cuttings of firm shoots. Dip these in hormone rooting powder and plant in 3in (7cm) pots. Cuttings are best taken in early spring or late summer and grown in a mixture of two parts peat and one part sand at a temperature of 70°F (21°C).

Species

Fatsia japonica (or ***F.sieboldii***) is a native plant of Japan and Taiwan. It can grow to 15ft (4.5m) if given unlimited root space. Its large shiny green leaves are usually 8-12in (20-30cm) wide and lobed. In late summer and early autumn, outdoor plants produce large heads of white flowers. *F.j.variegata, below,* is the variegated form and has white or cream colouring on the leaves. *F.j.moserii* is a compact, bushy, slower-growing form.

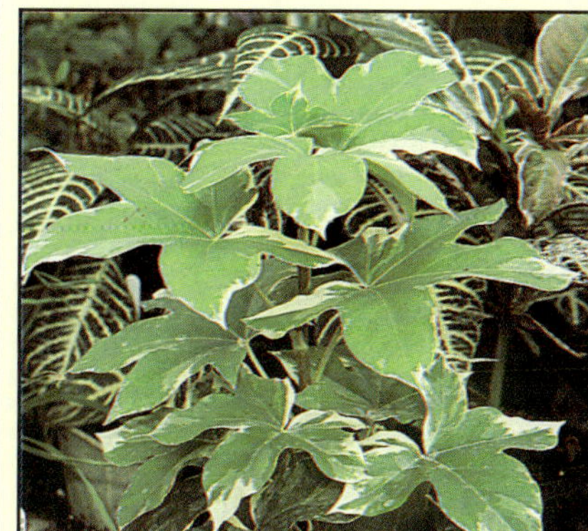

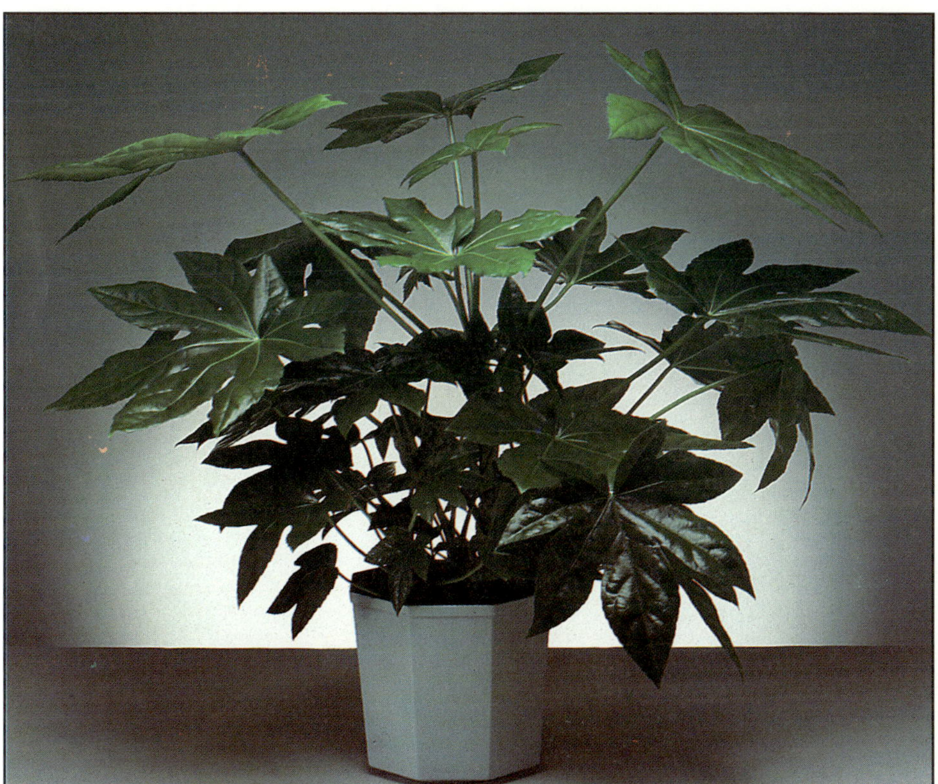

Fatsia japonica is a large, handsome plant with an easy-going nature.

Trouble Shooter

White fluffy patches are mealy bugs, which can be cleaned away with a small brush dipped in methylated spirit. Other pests likely to attack are the red spider mite and greenfly. Both can be destroyed by spraying a malathion-based insecticide directly onto the plant every few weeks until it begins to look healthy again.

Shrivelled leaves can occur if your plant is kept in a hot environment and becomes too dry; on the other hand if you overwater, the plant will look less vigorous and the leaves will become floppy. Keep an eye out for these symptoms and adjust your watering accordingly.

Buying Guide

Choose a plant with bright, glossy green leaves. Fatsias are popular houseplants and can be bought at most good garden centres. Since Fatsias grow quickly, you can save money by buying a small plant.

Ficus

Family name: **Moraceae**

Common names: **Rubber Plant, Weeping Fig, Creeping Fig, Mistletoe Fig, Fiddle-leaf Fig**

Care Straight forward	**Height** 2-6ft (0.6-1.8m)	**Flower** None
Light Bright, indirect sun	**Spread** 18in-2ft (45-60cm)	**Humidity** Regular mist spray
Price Medium/ expensive	**Shape** Tree-like shrub	**Availability** Garden centres
Temp. Min 60°F (15°C)	Ideal 75°F (24°C)	Max 85°F (30°C)

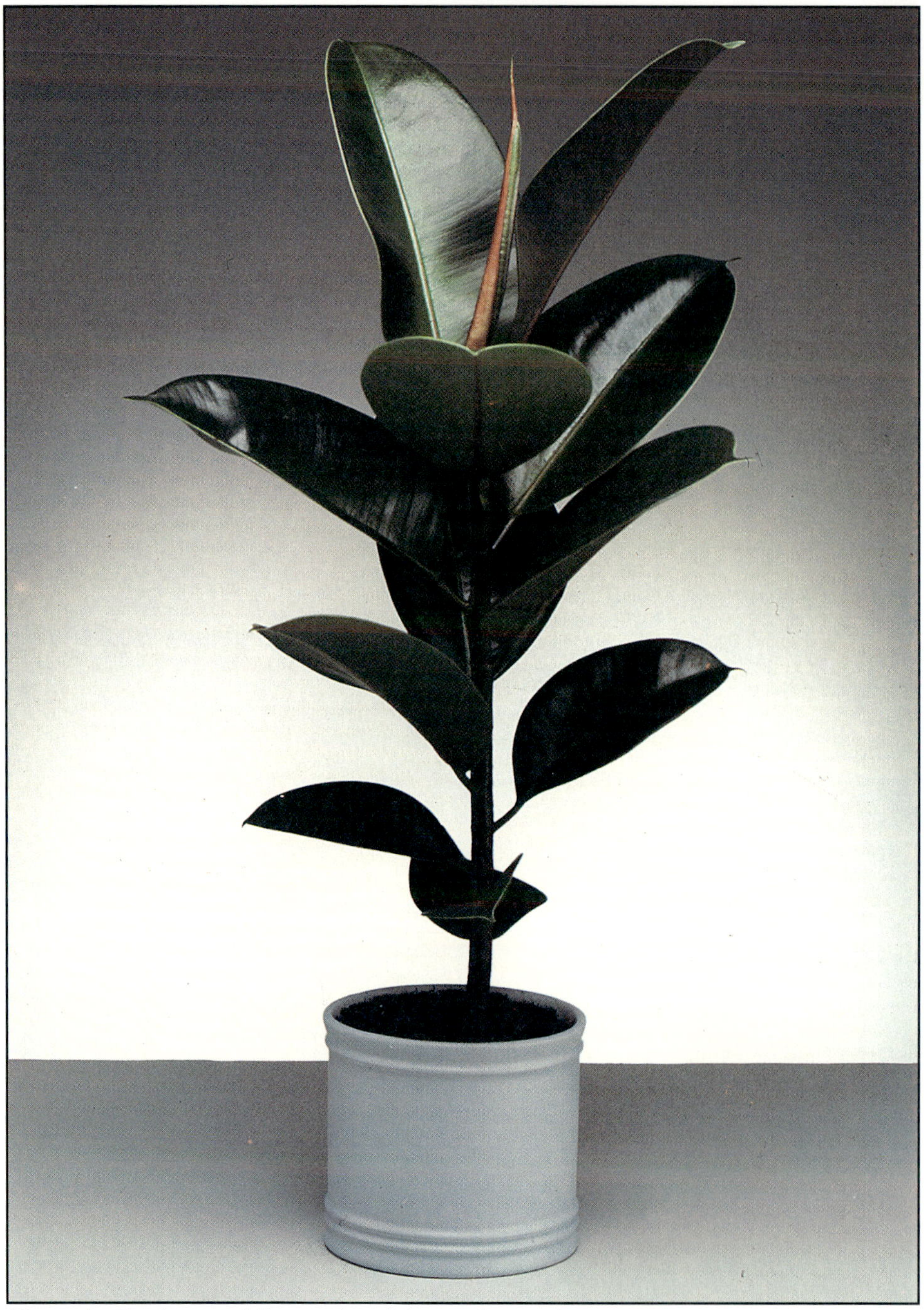

Ficus elastica is one of the most well-known houseplants.

Ficus means fig in Latin but as well as edible fruit trees the group includes a wide range of showy foliage plants, such as that old favourite the tall, shiny leaved Rubber Plant. With over 800 species, this genus is one of the largest with a varied selection of shrubs, trees and climbers; the range is so wide that there is probably a suitable Ficus for any situation in your home.

Ficus species come from many corners of the earth — America and the West Indies, tropical and South Africa, Australasia and many of the Pacific islands. The most popular houseplant is the Rubber Plant, *Ficus elastica*, from Malaysia and India. This handsome tree, which grows to about 4ft (1.2m) or more when grown as a pot plant, reaches a height of 100ft (30m) or more in its natural habitat.

Spring and summer care

Pot on every second year in April using a potting compost such as John Innes No 2 enriched with leaf-mould, at the rate of one part leaf-mould to four parts compost.

Water freely from April to September and never allow plants to dry out. Most Ficus species are forest plants and thrive in humid conditions; so spray regularly, and, in the hottest weather, spray overhead daily — but don't ever spray in the heat of the day and especially not in full sun, or leaves could become scorched or badly marked.

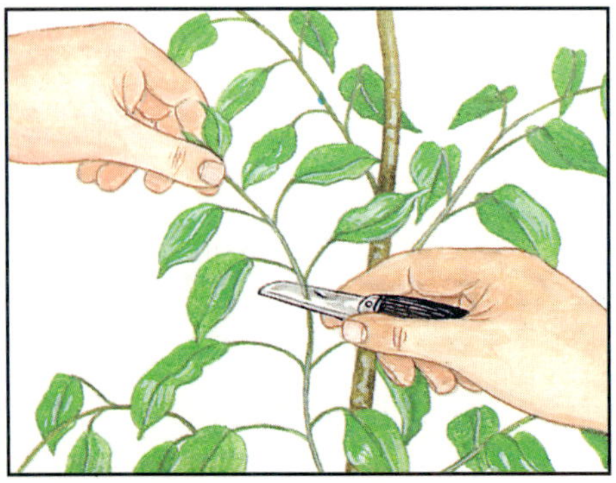

Taking cuttings of Weeping Fig. Remove 4in (10cm) from the stem tip.

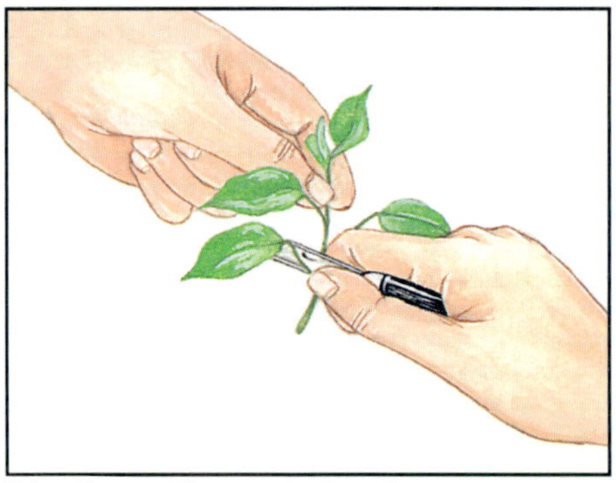

Trim the cutting and allow it to dry out overnight.

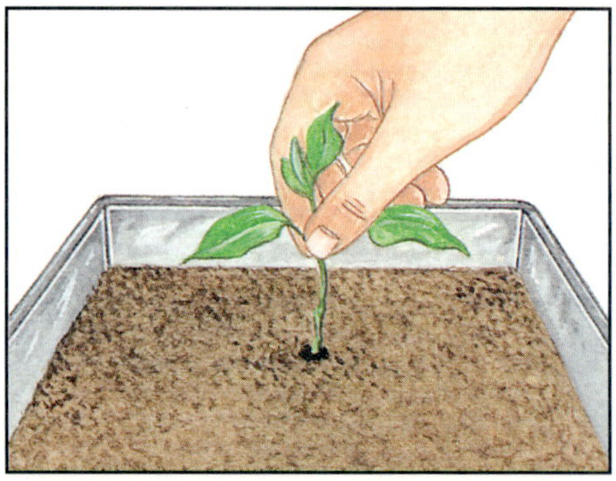

Put the cutting into a mixture of equal parts sand and John Innes No 1.

Trouble Shooter

An overwatered *F.elastica* plant often has wilted leaves.

This plant, *F.pumila,* has not had enough water.

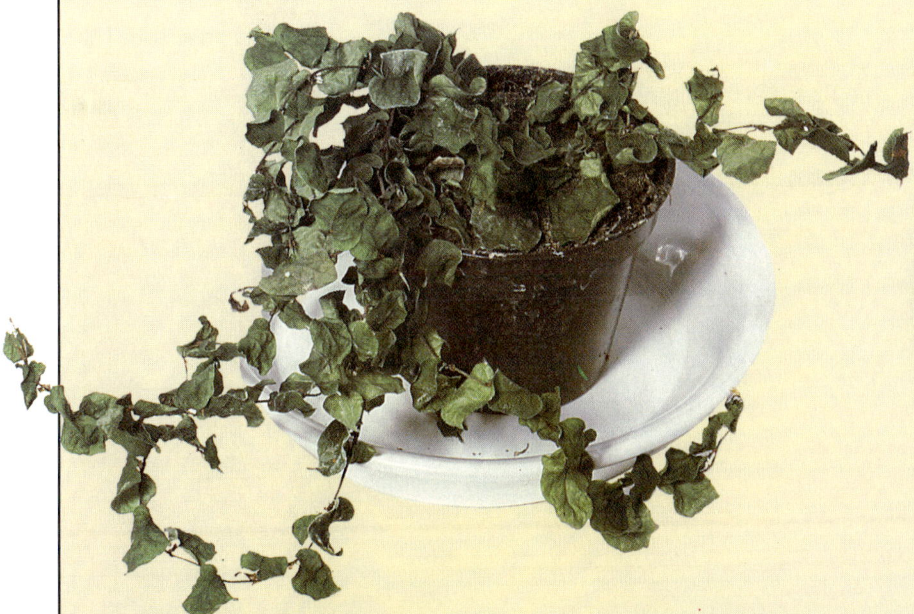

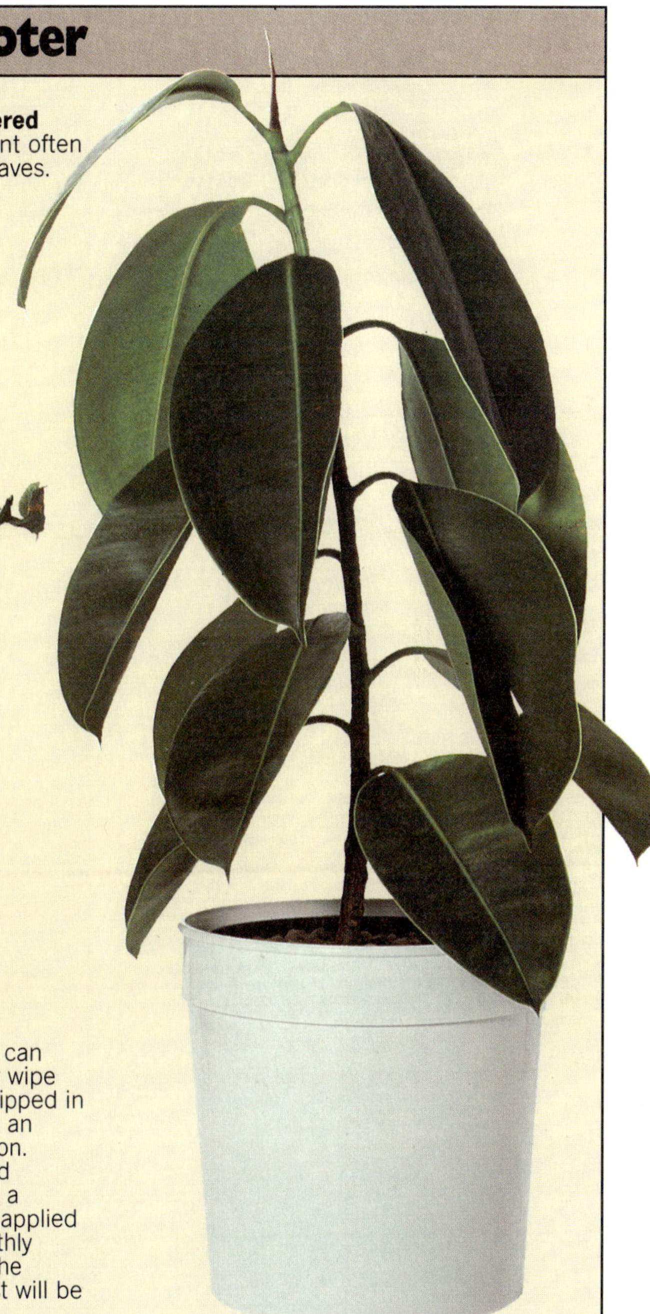

Too little water can result in leaves shrivelling or wilting and dropping. Overwatering, especially if the pot is left standing in water for any length of time, will result in wilting, a change of leaf colour and eventually leaf fall, and the root system may rot. If you notice any of these symptoms, adjust your watering accordingly.

Red spider mite may attack foliage; increase humidity and spray with a malathion-based insecticide.

Scale insect and mealy bug can also prove troublesome; either wipe over the leaves with a brush dipped in methylated spirit or spray with an insecticide containing malathion.

Pest control is important and prevention is better than cure; a dimethoate-based insecticide applied directly to the soil at two-monthly intervals will be absorbed by the plant's system so that any pest will be killed as soon as it attacks.

Buying Guide

Check the stem tips of tree types like the Rubber Plant and the Fiddle-leaf Fig. The growing point should be undamaged. Weeping figs are especially vulnerable to draughts and extreme changes in temperature — in fact just the conditions you might find in a shop during the winter months. It's always wise to buy plants — if you possibly can — in the spring or summer, when there are few cold draughts and no central heating.

Most Ficus plants enjoy heat, and temperatures may be allowed to rise to 80-85°F (27-30°C), with the exception of *F.elastica* which doesn't like temperatures much higher than 70-75°F (21-24°C).

On the whole, tree types such as the Rubber Plant and Weeping Fig should have good light but not direct sunlight — although the Rubber Plant will tolerate some direct sun for short periods. Bushy types, such as the Mistletoe Fig, and trailing types, such as *F.pumila* are best in a partially shaded site.

Sponge down the leaves of shiny-leaved types regularly to keep them free of dust. For really polished looking leaves you can buy a proprietary leaf shiner — but don't be tempted to use it more than once a month.

Autumn and winter care

Water moderately, keeping the soil moist but never sodden. Continue spraying.

Feeding is not usually necessary in winter unless you notice any new growth; in this case your plant will benefit from an occasional liquid feed. Keep temperatures above 60°F (15°C) — 65°F (18°C) is ideal.

Propagation

Increase single-stemmed tree types, such as *F.elastica, F.benghalensis,* and *F.lyrata,* by taking leaf cuttings with a small piece of stem attached in spring. Allow the cut surface to dry off overnight then insert the cuttings in equal parts of peat and sand, and support with a small stake. Keep the cuttings moist at a temperature of 75°F (24°C), and in a lightly shaded spot. When the cuttings have rooted — in about eight weeks — pot up into a mixture of four parts John Innes No 2 to one part leaf-mould.

Creeping and climbing types, such as *F.pumila* and *F. villosa*, can be layered during the growing season. Select a stem and pin it down to the compost at the leaf joint. When the stem has rooted, sever it carefully from the parent plant.

For bushy and branching tree types, like *F.benjamina*, and the more tender epiphytic and succulent species, take stem cuttings 4-6in (10-15cm) long from the tips of branches. Dry off the cut surface overnight, then insert in equal parts John Innes No 1 and sharp sand. Treat as for leaf cuttings but maintain a temperature of 70°F (21°C).

An alternative method of propagating *F.elestica, F.lyrata* and *F.benjamina* is by air-layering in spring — this technique is covered in detail on pages 125-127.

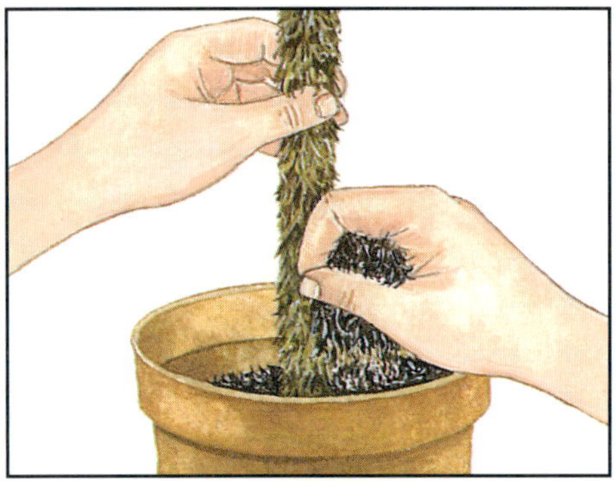

A mossy pole provides an attractive support for a climbing *Ficus*.

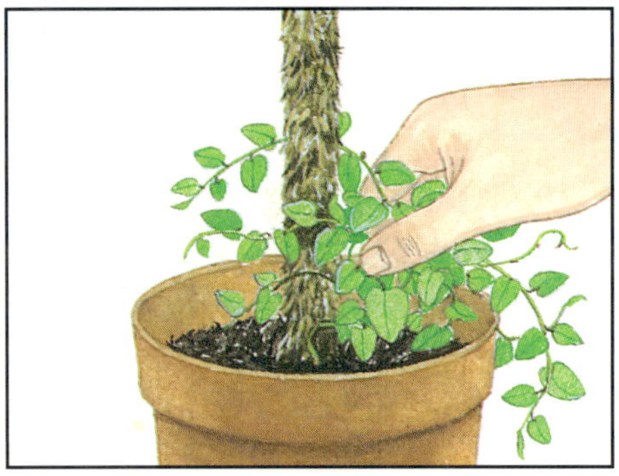

First plant the pole firmly, then plant a climber, such as *Ficus pumila*, beside it.

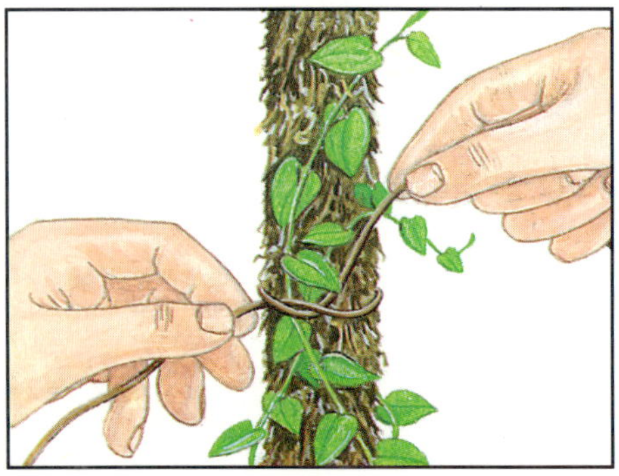

Attach each stem to the pole, using soft twine or hairpins.

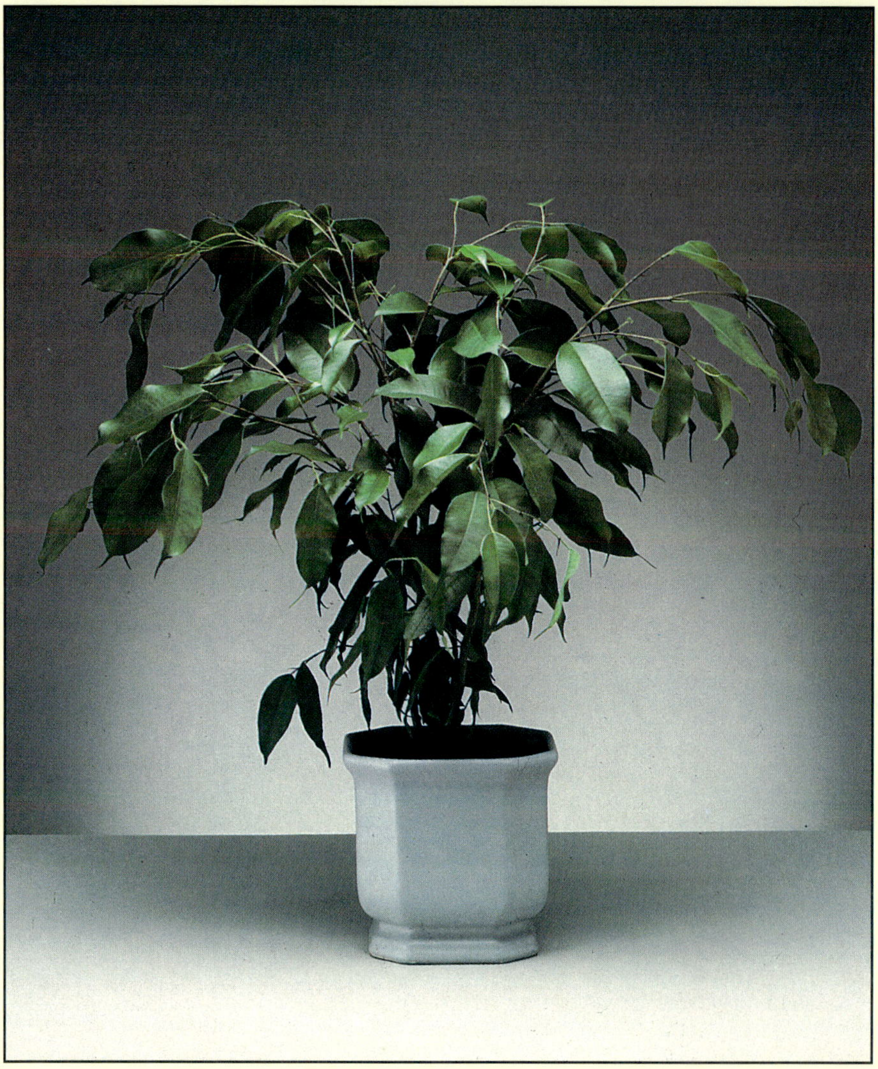

Ficus elastica, the Rubber Plant, comes from Malaysia and India. When grown in a pot this tree usually forms a single, unbranched stem. Large, shiny, leathery, oval leaves, up to 12in (30cm) long, grow directly from the main trunk on short leaf stalks. The variety 'Decora' is the most popular; it is bolder and sturdier than the species with glossy, deep green leaves with an ivory midrib. 'Schrijvereana' is a variegated form. 'Robusta' is similar to 'Decora' but with more rounded leaves and is more robust. 'Rubra' has reddish leaves; 'Abidjan' has very dark green, almost black leaves; and 'Variegata' has silver-grey and white markings.

F.benjamina, *above*, the Weeping Fig, is another Asian species which makes a freely-branching tree shape normally between 2-6ft (0.6-1.8m) tall, with graceful arching habit. The shiny, deep green, oval leaves are slightly pointed and 4-6in (10-15cm) long. Mature plants bear insignificant flowers which give way to deep red berries. 'Hawaii' is variegated with yellow or white margins and markings.

F.palmeri is the only Ficus that can be classed as a 'stem succulent' and is found around the gulf of California. It is a freely branching tree with a swollen, succulent trunk which grows to about 12ft (3.6m). The young branches stay white for some time and are covered in velvety hairs. The thick, heart-shaped leaves, about 3in (7cm) in length, are deep green with tiny hairs on the top and white and thickly felted on the underside. Small greenish white flowers may occasionally be borne in summer and are followed by pairs of fleshy fruits in the leaf axils.

F.petiolaris is a Mexican plant similar to *F.palmeri* in that it has a swollen main trunk. It is smaller — up to 6ft (1.8m) — with heart-shaped,. blue-green leaves veined in pale pink or red.

Species

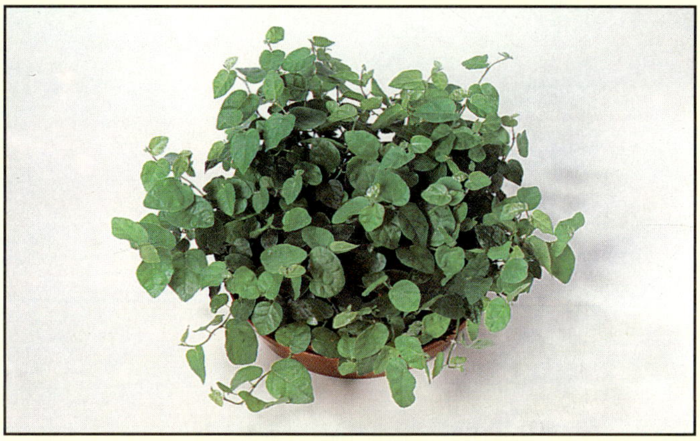

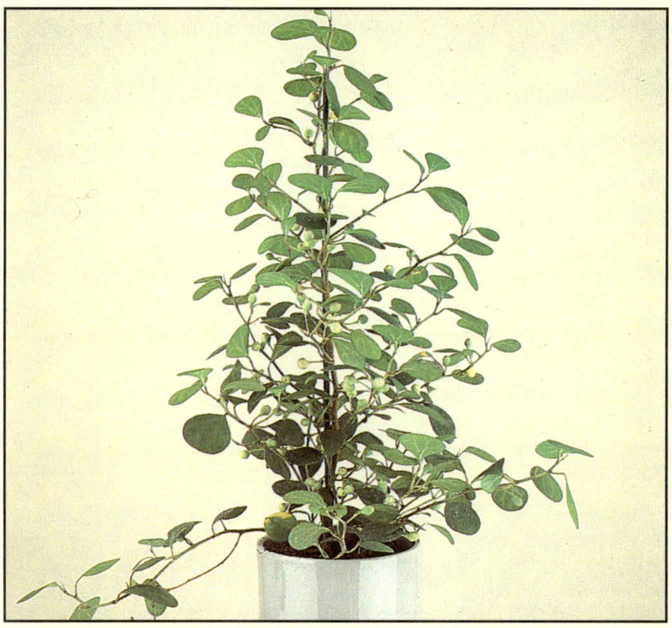

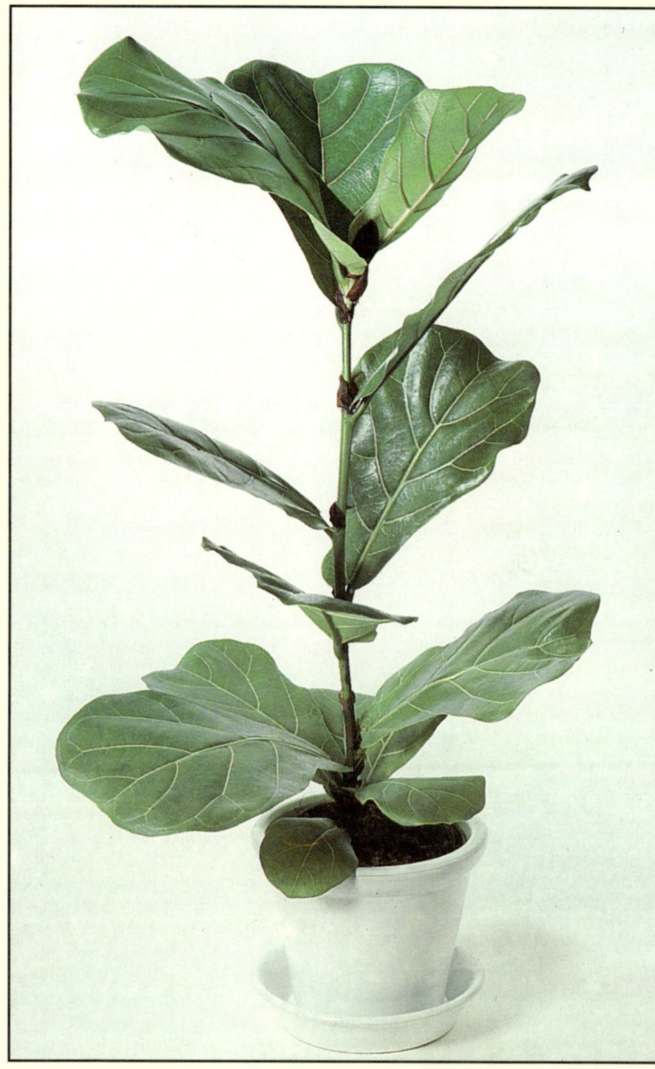

F.pumila, *top* , also known as *F.repens* or *F.stipulata* and commonly called the Creeping Fig, is a rampant creeper with small, heart-shaped, dark green leaves less than 1in (2.5cm) long. It produces aerial roots and clings readily to a wall where it will continue to climb. It also has separate flowering stems with stiffer, longer leaves about 3-4in (7-10cm) in length. It is suitable for hanging baskets or for ground cover in an indoor garden. 'Minima' is the variety most commonly available for growing indoors; it is a useful, compact little houseplant with tiny leaves only ½in (13mm) long. 'Variegata' has 1in (2.5cm) leaves marbled and lined in green and cream.

F.diversifolia, *bottom*, commonly called the Mistletoe Fig, is a rare species from Malaysia, Indonesia and India. It is a compact, shrubby plant which can grow to anything from 2-9ft (0.6-2.7m). Its attractive oval leaves are very firm, dark green with brown speckles on the upper surface and pale green on the underside. A profusion of small clusters of yellow-grey fruits are an added bonus. The demands of the Mistletoe Fig are few and it is probably more difficult to obtain than it is to keep.

F.villosa, also known as *F.barbata*, is a creeping and climbing species from Malaysia. It climbs along whatever support it can find with the help of aerial roots, set along the slender, brownish, hairy stems. Leaves are oval, pointed, about 3-4in (7-10cm) long, dark green and hairy, and set in two alternate rows on either side of the stem. Small clusters of red berries follow the insignificant flowers.

F.sarmentosa from Japan is a slender, thin-stemmed creeper with aerial roots. The leaves are small, more or less oval in shape, about ½in (13mm) long, and provide dense cover for the entire plant.

F.lyrata, *above*, also known as *F.pandurata*, is a native of tropical West Africa and vies for pride of place with the Rubber Plant. Commonly called the Fiddle-leaf Fig, it has large violin-shaped leaves up to 15in (38cm) long and can reach a height of 30-40ft (9-12m) in its natural habitat. Leaves are dark, waxy green, puckered and veined with a paler, yellowish green. On mature plants insignificant flowers are followed by greenish-pink or reddish fruits covered with white spots.

F.benghalensis, or the Banyan Tree, is one of the most robust of the genus and, in its native India or Sri Lanka, can grow to over 12ft (3.6m) tall. At this point the upper branches develop aerial roots which grow downwards and eventually reach the ground below, becoming thicker as they descend until the roots become secondary trunks. The leathery leaves are about 8in (20cm) long, dark green with distinctive yellow-green veinings.

Fittonia

Family name: **Acanthaceae**

Common names:
Painted Net Leaf, Snakeskin Plant

Care Easy	**Height** 12-15in (30-38cm)	**Flower** Very occasionally
Light Shade	**Spread** 4-6in (10-15cm)	**Humidity** Regular mist spray
Price Medium	**Shape** Shrubby	**Availability** Garden centres
Temp. Min 65°F (18°C)	Ideal 75°F (24°C)	Max 85°F (30°C)

These delightful foliage plants are ideal for standing in front of taller, leggy plants; their low-growing, spreading shape will disguise the bare stems behind and their attractive, neatly-overlapping, patterned leaves will add a point of interest and colour to the arrangement. One of the most commonly available is *Fittonia verschaffeltii* or the Painted Net Leaf, from Colombia and Peru. It has quite large, rounded leaves and, like other Fittonias, the veining is picked out in a contrasting colour (pink in the case of Painted Net Leaf) so each leaf looks as if it is smothered in a fine network of webbing.

Species

Fittonia verschaffeltii, from Colombia and Peru, has thin hairy stems and 3-4in (7-10cm) long dark green oval leaves with pink veins.

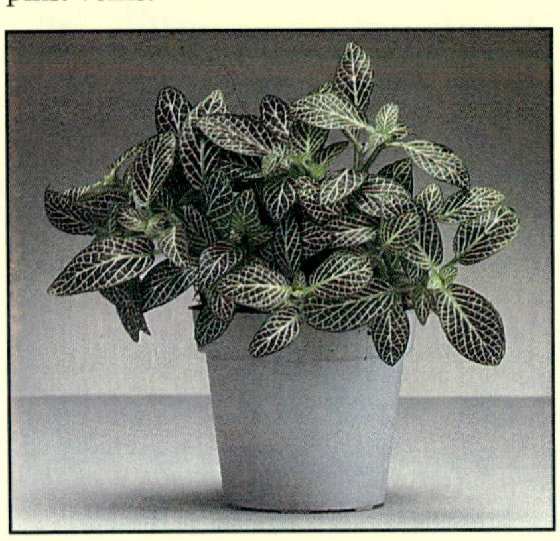

F.argyroneura, from Colombia, Peru and Bolivia, has vivid green oval leaves netted with silvery-white veins. The variety 'Nana', *above*, is a miniature Fittonia. Its leaves are about 1in (2.5cm) long, with a pointed oval shape and white veins.

This plant is becoming very popular since it is easier to grow as a houseplant than other Fittonias.

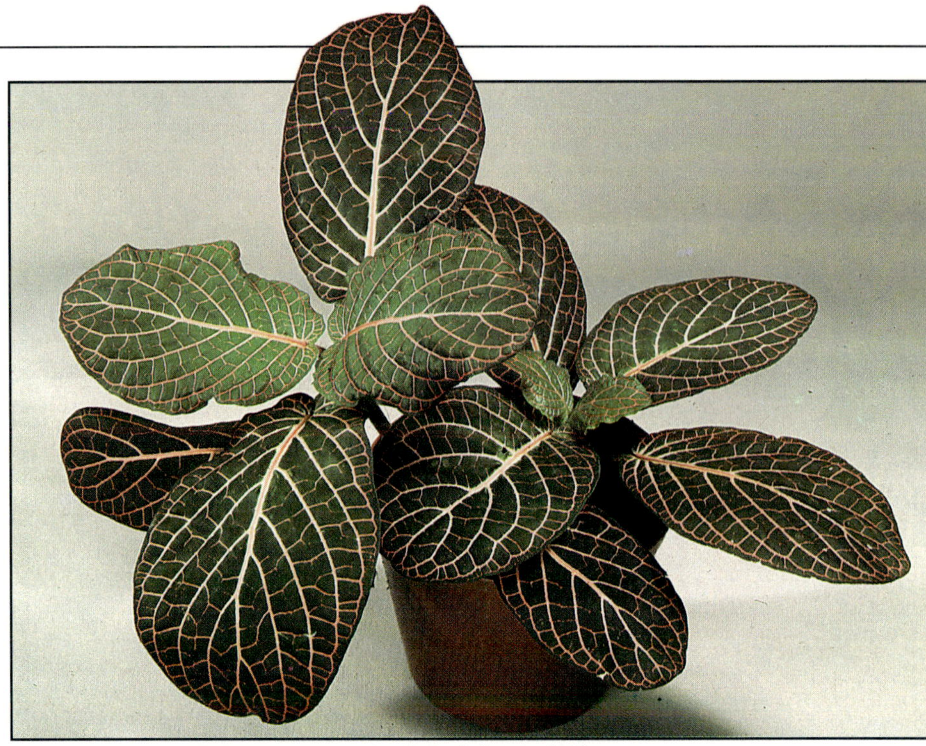

Fittonia verschaffeltii is a delightful little foliage plant.

Spring and summer care

Using a peat-based potting compost, repot your Fittonia in spring, if the plant has completely covered the surface of its pot. They are not deep-rooting plants so choose a shallow flower pot or bowl. Provide good drainage with an extra-deep layer of drainage material under the compost — about a quarter of the depth of the pot filled with crocks or gravel should be enough.

Fittonias like plenty of water but you must take great care not to waterlog the soil. They enjoy a humid atmosphere — so spray the leaves daily with tepid water when the weather is very hot, and in addition place the flower pot on a bowl of damp pebbles. Feed every two or three weeks with half-strength liquid fertiliser.

Unusually for variegated leaved plants, Fittonias need a shaded position so they'll do well growing in the shadow of taller plants. Summer temperatures of 75-80°F (24-27°C) are ideal. Occasionally, small yellow flowers are produced under the foliage. If you spot these snip them off, since they add nothing to the plant's appearance and deprive the leaves and roots of nutrients. Since Fittonias are creeping plants, stray stems will fall over the edge of the pot. While in some ways this adds to the plant's charm, too many cascading stems can look untidy, so prune them off with a sharp pair of scissors.

Autumn and winter care

In the colder months, make sure the temperature does not fall below 65°F (18°C). Reduce the watering but never let the compost dry out completely. Keep the plants out of direct light and away from cold draughts from doors and windows.

Propagation

The stems of Fittonias make roots very easily — in fact, if you inspect your plant closely you may find that some of the stems have dipped down into the soil, rooted themselves and begun to grow into new plants. In spring or summer carefully sever these from the parent plant and repot the plantlets individually into containers of peat-based compost. Keep the plant at 70°F (21°C) until new young leaves are visible.

Cuttings can also be taken from the stem tips. Nip off a shoot just below the fourth pair of leaves. Remove the lowest pair of leaves and put the cut end of the stem into a pot containing a moist mixture of equal parts of peat and coarse sand. Keep the cuttings at a temperature of 70°F (21°C) until they root.

Once they are established, pot up several cuttings in one pot — five or six cuttings in a 5in (13cm) pot will make an attractive display.

Trouble Shooter

If the soil dries out for even a short period the leaves will wilt and then shrivel. If the soil is too wet the leaves may lose their colouring and fall off and the stems may rot. So always remember that the compost should be kept moist but not sodden.

If temperatures drop too low or plants are subjected to draughts, the leaves may turn yellow and fall. If the weather is hot and the air dry, it is essential that the plant is shaded from direct sun and that humidity is increased by mist spraying.

Greenfly sometimes infest Fittonias. They cluster around the tips of stems where new leaves are formed and suck the sap from the cells, deforming the growth. A few greenfly can be gently rinsed off with water. For large numbers spray once a week with an insecticide containing pyrethrum.

Freesia

Family name: **Iridaceae**

Common name: **Freesia**

Care Easy	**Height** 18in (45cm)	**Flower** April/ August
Light Sunny	**Spread** 6-8in (15-20 cm)	**Winter** Needs protection
Price Cheap	**Shape** Leafy clumps	**Availability** Garden centres

Freesias are renowned for the fragrance and beauty of their large, funnel-shaped blooms borne on one side of wiry stems, in a wide range of colours.They are widely grown for the flower trade and one of the most popular of all cut flowers.

The genus contains some 20 species, all of them cormous plants of South African origin. But the Freesias most commonly found are the hybrids of *Freesia x kewensis*, mainly developed from a cross made at Kew Gardens at the end of the last century, between the pale, creamy *F. refracta, right,* and the pink and yellow *F. armstrongii.*

They are not really very hardy plants and are only completely reliable outdoors in favoured areas such as the Scillies and the Channel Islands. Specially-prepared corms, however, are generally available which have been treated for the British climate, and will thrive in a sheltered, sunny spot. They can be planted out in April to provide a bright display of sweetly-scented blooms in late summer, with a flowering period that can last for several weeks, making a colourful display.

Spring and summer care

Grow Freesias in John Innes No 2 or make up your own mixture of four parts loam, one part leaf-mould, one part moss-peat and one part sharp sand. Use individual 5in (13cm) pots of John Innes No 2, or try four or five corms together in a window-box; make sure the container is well-crocked, to provide adequate drainage. For growing outdoors in mild areas, plant ordinary (unprepared) corms in August or September to flower the following April or May; otherwise use specially prepared corms, planting in April, for flowering in August and September.

Buying Guide

When buying corms in spring, avoid those that are shrivelled and dry. And corms damaged by frost during winter will be soft. Both should be avoided.

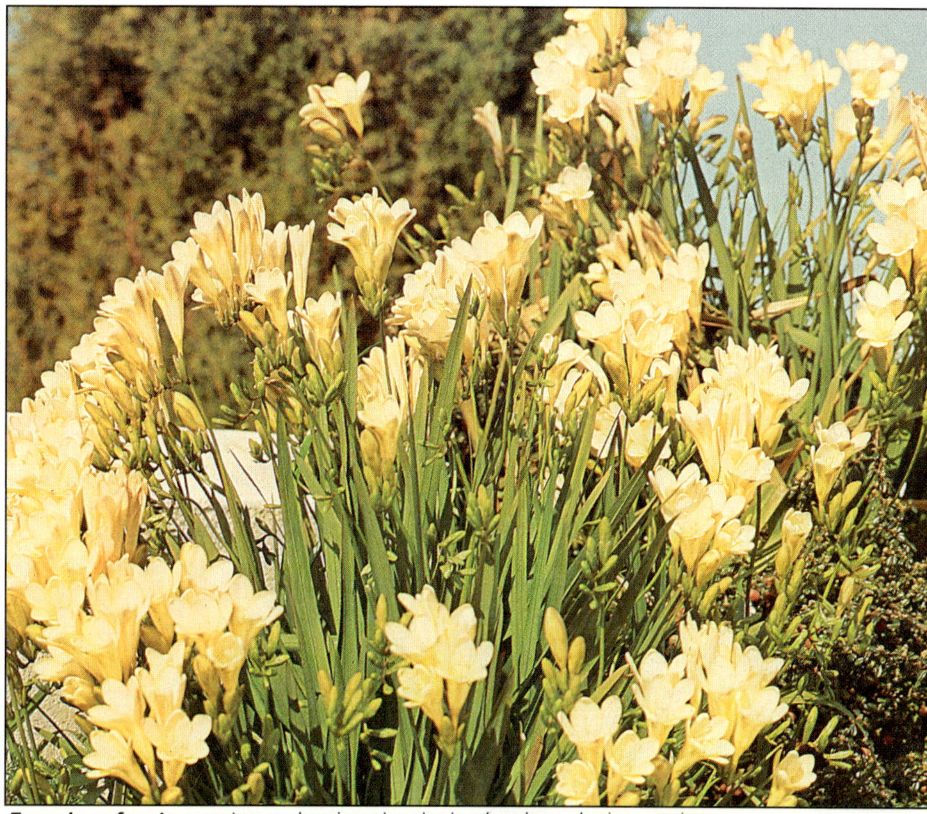

Freesia refracta creates a dominant splash of colour during spring.

The ordinary corms may be left in their containers to flower again in subsequent seasons; the prepared corms will flower outdoors in their first season, after which they should be lifted and stored, for planting the following season as ordinary corms. Corms multiply quite freely if left in their containers; they will need to be lifted and divided, and repotted every three or four years to avoid congestion (see 'Propagation'). In years when not repotting, topdress annually in spring, replacing the top 1-2in (2.5-5cm) with fresh compost.

Freesias grown in pots will need some support; the easiest method is to insert light canes or small pea sticks. For best results your plants should have a really bright position, with adequate shelter from strong winds. Careful watering is important; give only enough to just moisten the soil until growth becomes apparent, then water quite freely – though never to saturation point. Add a weak liquid fertiliser to the water (use half the recommended amount) every three weeks, when the flower spike shows and until flowers begin to fade. After flowering, gradually decrease watering and keep the compost completely dry once the foliage dies down.

Autumn and winter care

Once the foliage has gone, the corms should be protected and the compost kept completely dry. If they are left outdoors then cover the soil completely with a good layer of moss-peat or ashes, so that neither rain nor frost can affect them. If

Trouble Shooter

Care with watering is important. Too much water when plants are actively growing can be dangerous – they will certainly never thrive with 'wet feet'. Never water at all while corms are dormant as they are likely to rot, especially when temperatures are very low.

Greenfly, *below*, is likely to infest stems and leaves, especially as new leaves appear; spray with a pyrethrum-based insecticide immediately they are noticed.

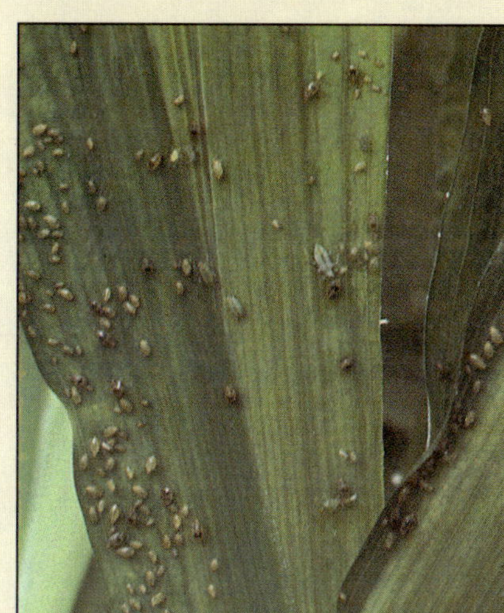

Species

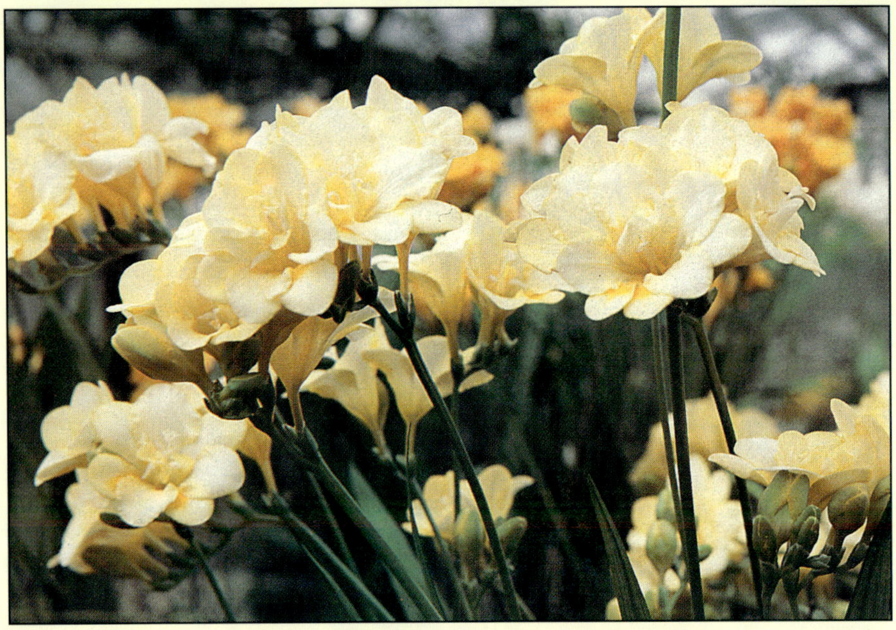

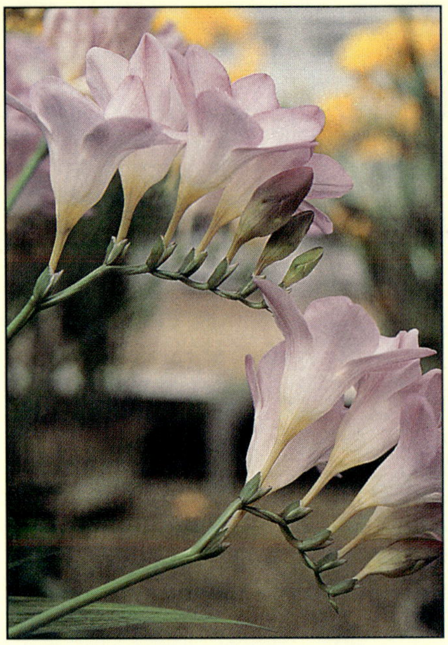

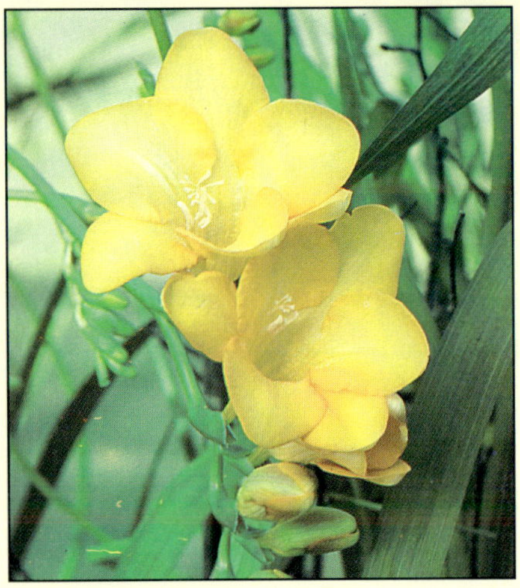

Freesia refracta is the most popular of the true species. It is quite a tall-growing plant, reaching a height of 1½ft (0.45m) when in bloom. It produces five or six long, slender leaves which appear before the characteristic colourful, sweetly-scented, funnel-shaped flowers, borne on one side of wiry stems; there is usually just one, or sometimes two, stems to a single corm. Normally appearing in April, they are about 1¼in (3cm) long, in an array of pale colours – white or greyish-white, greenish-yellow or yellow-orange – often with a few violet lines and a purple tinge to the exterior of the petals. Opening in succession, the flowers usually appear over a period of four to five weeks, making an eye-catching display.

F. armstrongii is a smaller-growing species, to a height of 10-15in (25-38cm). It is otherwise very similar to *F. refracta*, except for the flower colouring – rosy pink, with a yellow tube.

F.x kewensis is the name given to the familiar florists' Freesias, hybrids developed from crossing *F. refracta* with *F. armstrongii*. These reach a height of 18-24in (45-60cm), with narrow, lance-shaped, mid-green leaves and thin branching stems carrying one-sided spikes of flowers set among small bracts. Rather larger than those of the species, the fragrant flowers are found in a wide range of bright colours, including 'Cloe', *top left*; 'Prince of Orange', *left*; and 'Blue Heaven', *top right*.

weather conditions are particularly severe, it's also a good idea to wrap the container with sacking or similar material. Uncover the container in March and water very sparingly, to keep the compost just moist, until growth becomes apparent.

Alternatively, corms may be lifted and stored over winter, for safety, in a dry, frost-free place. With both prepared and ordinary corms, wait until the foliage has completely died down, and leave them as long as possible, to mature, until the first frosts, after which remove for planting the following year.

Propagation

Propagate by removing and replacing offsets. Do note that the treatment given to specially prepared corms will not be passed on to their offsets, which will behave just like ordinary corms. Specially prepared corms must be bought fresh each year, to plant in April.

Lift mature plants and remove the offsets that have formed on the corms, at potting time. Pot up individually in the usual compost and treat as established Freesias (see 'Spring and summer care'); most will flower the following year.

Freesias can also be raised from seed. Sow seeds sparingly into a 5in (13cm) pot in March or April, sprinkling them evenly over a mixture of equal parts of loam, peat and sharp sand and cover with a fine layer of sand. Keep moist, lightly shaded and fairly cool, at a temperature of 45-50°F (7-10°C). Don't transplant seedlings the first year, even though they are quite likely to flower; instead, thin them out, to leave five or six strong seedlings to a 5in (13cm) pot.

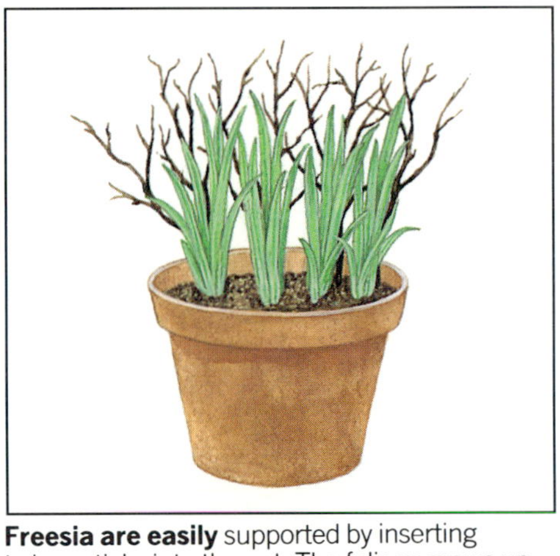

Freesia are easily supported by inserting twiggy sticks into the pot. The foliage grows up and through them.

Fuchsia

Family name: **Onagraceae**

Common name: **Lady's Eardrops**

Care Easy	**Height** 3-6ft (0.9-1.8m)	**Flower** July-October
Light Bright indirect	**Spread** 2-3ft (0.6-0.9m)	**Humidity** Mist spray
Price Middle Range	**Shape** Bushy	**Availability** Garden centres

Temp. Min 40°F (5°C) — Ideal 65°F (18°C) — Max 75°F (24°C)

Fuchsia is an enormous group of beautiful, flowering, deciduous plants. Originally from central and South America and New Zealand, they come in all shapes and sizes and range from shrubs to small trees and trailing plants. These garden and greenhouse favourites are becoming increasingly popular as houseplants. They thrive if they have good ventilation and are kept moist.

Fuchsia fulgens with its heart-shaped leaves and long drooping scarlet flowers is a parent of many of the hybrid Fuchsias now available. The plants are chiefly grown for the beauty of their pendulous flowers like the variety 'Winston Churchill' whose large, bell-like flowers have sepals of deep pink and rich purplish-blue petals.

Spring and summer care

Repot your plant in February using John Innes No 2 compost. Trim plants into shape in March — you can cut away up to a third of the growth. Always keep the compost moist during the growing season, but not waterlogged. Feed your Fuchsia with liquid fertiliser every fourteen days to encourage new growth and buds. Regular spraying, particularly during the height of summer, and temperatures of 55-65°F (13-18°C) will ensure your plant remains in excellent condition. It's important for all Fuchsias to have good light but do not put them in direct sunlight.

Autumn and winter care

During the resting period Fuchsias lose their leaves. They should be stored in a frost-free greenhouse or somewhere cool, like an unheated spare room, in good indirect light. Temperatures around 45-50°F (7-10°C) are ideal. The soil should be kept barely moist with only the occasional dampening.

Propagation

Cuttings 4in (10cm) long can be taken from young shoots in March and April or August and September. Plant these in a 3in (7cm) pot containing a mixture of three parts John Innes No 2 to one part sharp sand. Cover the cuttings with clear polythene and keep them slightly moist at a temperature of 60-65°F (16-18°C). When they have started to grow pinch out the tips to develop a nice bushy plant, then pot on into a bigger pot and treat as a mature plant.

Fuchsias can also be grown from seed. Sow in March or April; use the same potting mixture as for cuttings above, and barely cover the seeds with it. Keep moist and shaded in a temperature of 60°F (16°C) until the seeds have germinated, then give more light. When large enough to handle, plant individually in John Innes No 2 in 3in (7cm) pots.

Trouble Shooter

Few flowers and flower buds, and leaves falling prematurely indicate too much or too little water. Direct sunlight and a hot dry atmosphere can have the same effect. Remember that Fuchsias like cool temperatures, bright but indirect light and, during the growing season, moist soil — this means you will have to water more often in hot weather and less often when it's cool. If fertiliser is not given the plant may be slow to produce flowers.

Discourage insect pests — like greenfly — by using a systemic dimethoate-based insecticide watered directly on to the soil in April, June and September.

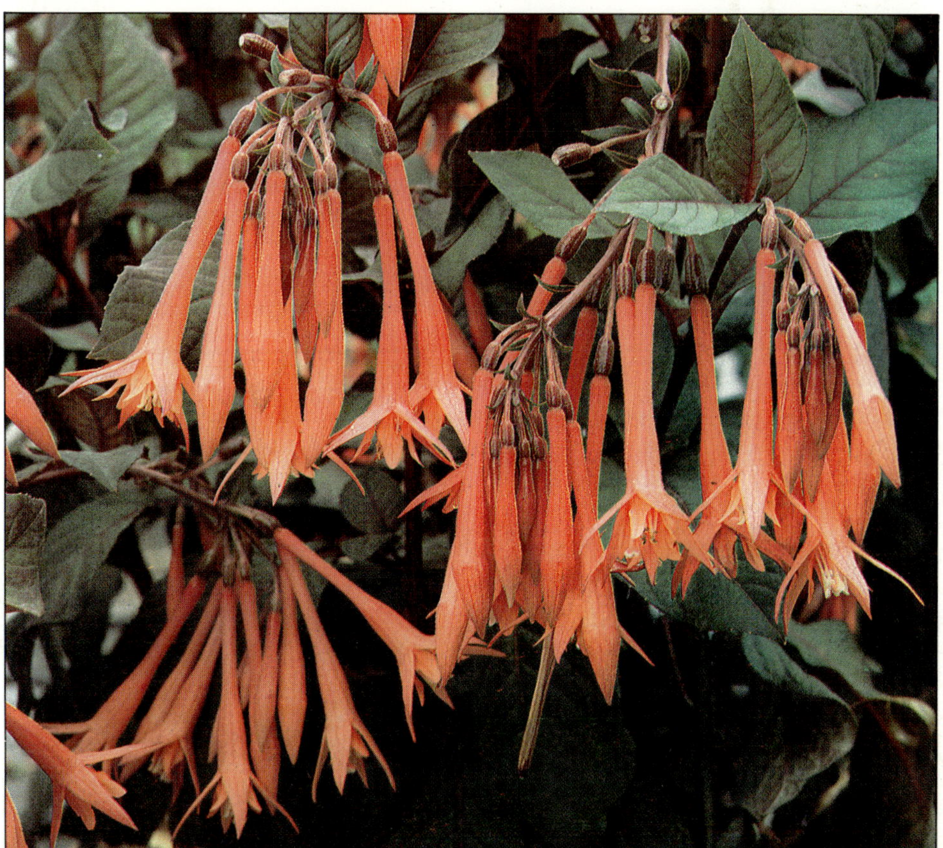

Fuchsia fulgens has rather elegant tubular flowers.

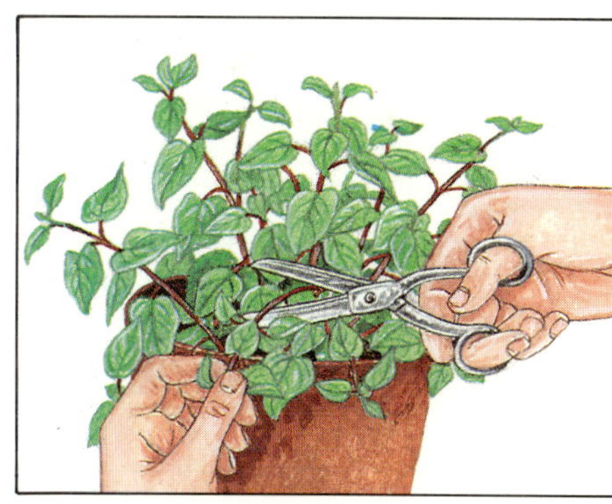

To take a Fuchsia cutting, snip a stem 4in (10cm) from its tip.

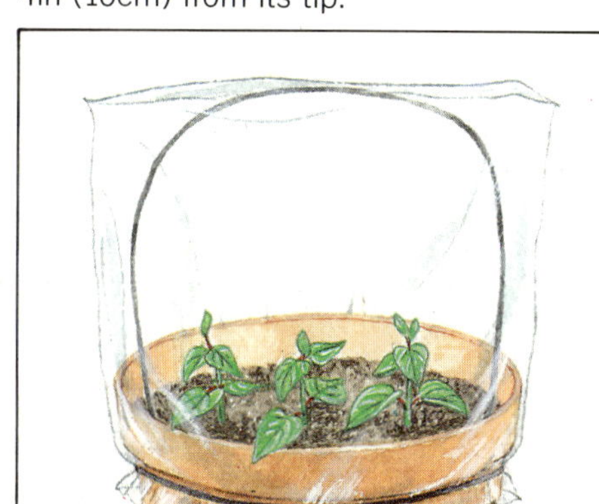

Remove the lowest pair of leaves and insert the cuttings into a pot of compost. Cover the pot with clear polythene supported by a wire hoop.

Species

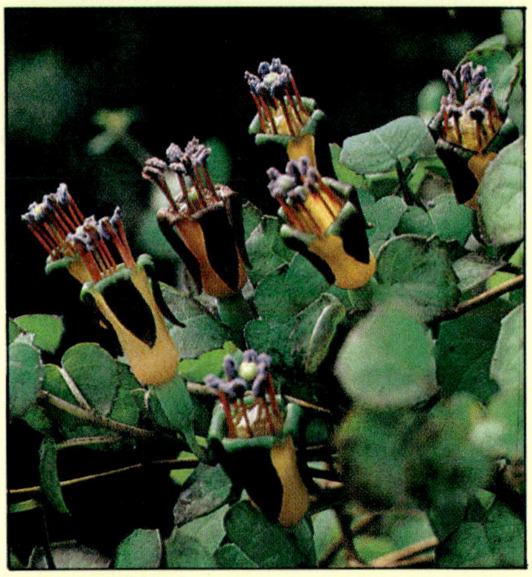

Fuchsia fulgens is one of the commonest members of this genus. Originally from Mexico, this tender shrub-like plant has soft red stems and often grows to 3-6ft (0.9-1.8m) tall. It has heart-shaped leaves of pale to mid-green. The drooping scarlet, rather tubular flowers which appear from July to October, are carried in clusters.

F.hybrida is the heading under which most of the hybrids are placed. Very many beautiful types have been and continue to be developed; 'Cascade', *below right,* is an extremely lovely one with large pale and dark pink flowers ; 'Winston Churchill', *above right,* is an old favourite, with large full flowers of purple surrounded by pink.

F.magellanica comes from Peru and Chile. This bushy shrub is the hardiest of all the Fuchsias and is often used for hedging in Cornwall and parts of Ireland where it reaches heights of 8-10ft (2.4-3m). The plant has small oval leaves about 2in (5cm) long and the drooping flowers are purple and crimson with long stamens. 'Alba' has bright green leaves and pale pink flowers and 'Versicolor' boasts crimson and purple flowers set off against variegated leaves of grey-green, white or yellow, tinted with delicate pink.

F.corymbiflora, from Peru and Ecuador, is a tall shrub with arching stems which can grow to 8ft (2.4m). The long thin flowers are a deep rich red. The plant has pale to mid-green leaves which are pink veined.

F.procumbens, *above,* is a trailing plant from New Zealand with oval-shaped leaves and small orange and purple flowers. Its slender creeping stems make this an ideal species for a hanging basket but unfortunately it is quite hard to come by.

F.triphylla from the West Indies is a small shrub growing to about 2ft (0.6m). It has large, orange-red, pendulous flowers and bronze-green, serrated leaves.

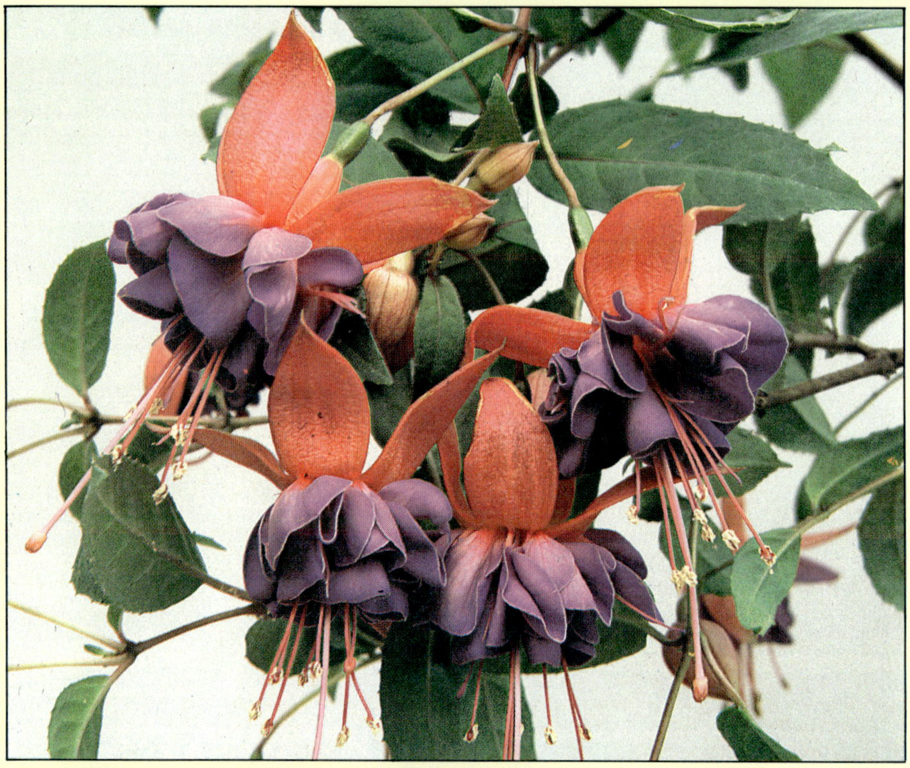

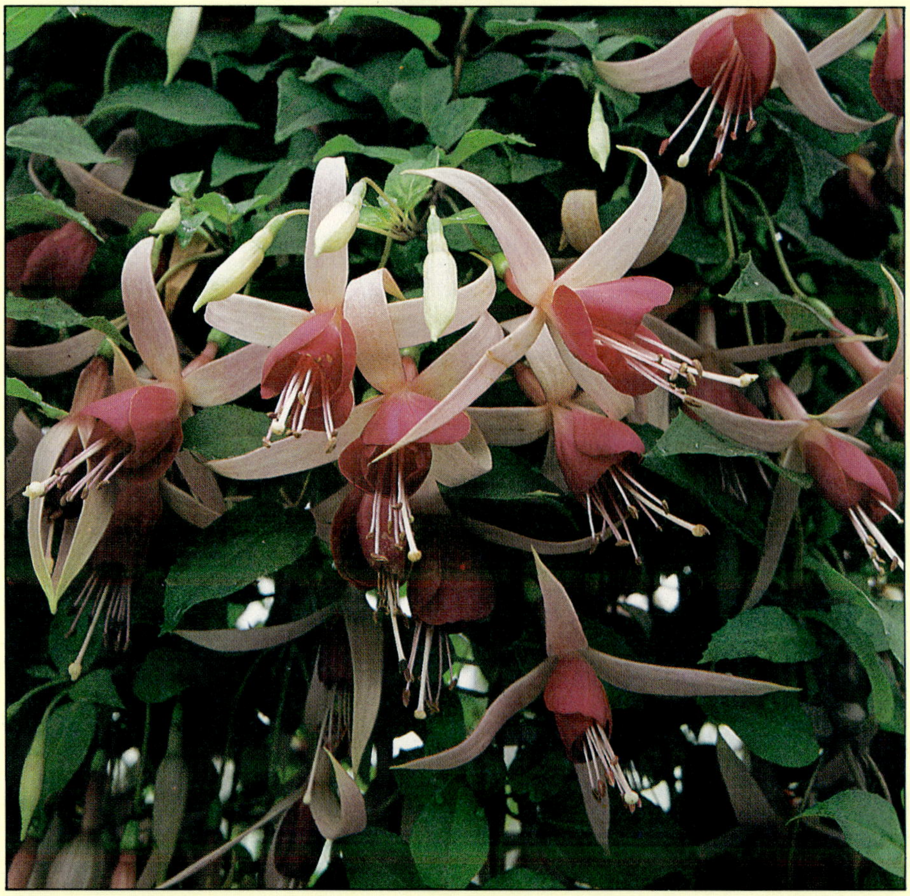

Gardenia

Family name: **Rubiaceae**

Common name: **Cape Jasmine**

Care Tricky	**Height** 2-4ft (0.6-1.2m)	**Flower** Summer or winter
Light Bright indirect	**Spread** 2-3ft (0.6-0.9m)	**Humidity** Mist spray
Price Middle Range	**Shape** Bushy	**Availability** Garden centres
Temp. Min 55°F (13°C)	Ideal 65°F (18°C)	Max 75°F (24°C)

With its sensitive nature the Gardenia is not the easiest of plants to look after, but if you persevere and treat it with care, you will be well rewarded. This beautiful plant has everything: glossy, dark green leaves, which last all the year round, set off perfectly the creamy white flowers with their exotic scent. Outside, in its natural environment, it can grow to 6ft (1.8m), but as a houseplant it seldom exceeds 2-4ft (0.6-1.2m). Most plants bloom in the summer months, but some varieties of Gardenia will flower in winter or early spring. Take care not to handle the blooms, or get them wet, since they're easily bruised.

Gardenia jasminoides, the Cape Jasmine, is the most commonly grown of all the Gardenias. This sturdy bush, from China and Japan, has dark green, lance-shaped leaves about 4in (10cm) across and in spring and summer produces big, heavily scented, white flowers. The double-flowered Gardenia, 'Veitchii', grows into a more compact bush with smaller leaves. It flowers in winter and early spring.

Spring and summer care

Repotting should be done in March or April, but be very careful not to disturb the roots in the process. Gardenias like a lime-free soil so use a peat-based compost or you can make up your own soil-based one. Use one part sterilised loam, one part very well rotted manure, one part peat, adding to this a small amount of sand and charcoal chippings.

These delicate plants prefer slightly warm, lime-free water, so if you live in a hard water area, use boiled water with a few drops of vinegar added. Water freely as the compost must be kept moist at all times. During the growing season add a weak fertiliser.

Your plant will thrive in bright indirect light at normal room temperatures, but if the temperature rises above 70°F (21°C), keep the plant shaded from bright light.

Autumn and winter care

Make sure your plant is kept warm — the temperature should not be allowed to drop below 55°F (13°C). Water enough to keep the soil moist. If yours is a winter-flowering variety, add a weak fertiliser as the flowers develop.

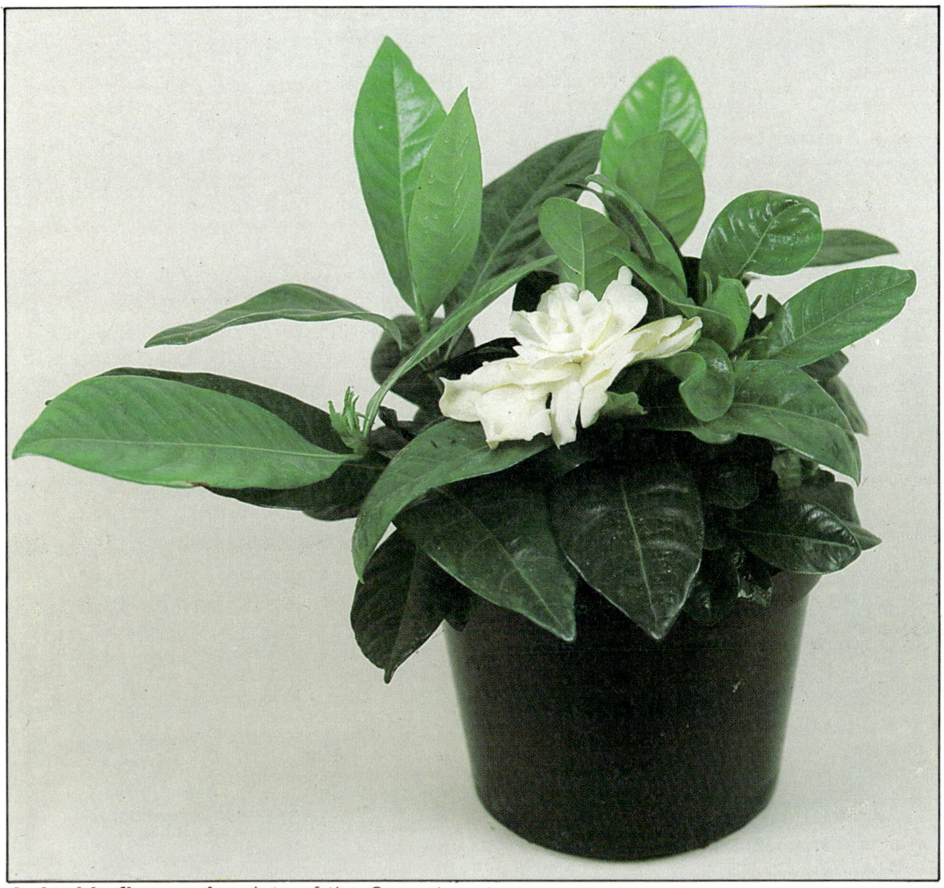

A double-flowered variety of the Cape Jasmine.

As Gardenias like a humid atmosphere, overhead spraying is advisable, but only on the leaves; if you spray the flowers, they tend to turn yellow. Gardenias need to be kept in good light, shaded from direct sun, in an airy, but draught-free, position.

Propagation

This can be done by taking 3in (7cm) cuttings from firm young shoots from January to March. Dip your cutting in a rooting hormone and plant it in a peat-based compost mixed with an equal amount of coarse sand. Gardenia cuttings are best rooted in a propagator at 65-70°F (18-21°C), shaded from full sun, in soil that is kept just moist. Plants grown from cuttings should flower in two to three years.

Trouble Shooter

Leaves will lose their glossy appearance and flowers fall away if the plant is kept too dry or does not have enough light.

In dry air the plant may attract red spider mite. If this happens spray with a dimethoate-based insecticide. This will also deter other pests such as mealy bug and scale insect. To increase humidity, stand the plant pot on a tray of moist pebbles and mist spray regularly.

Species

Gardenia jasminoides, the Cape Jasmine, in spite of its name, comes from Japan and China and not South Africa. It is a bushy plant with woody stems and attractive, shiny, dark green leaves and white perfumed flowers in spring and summer. 'Veitchii' is a more compact bush with a profusion of double white flowers.

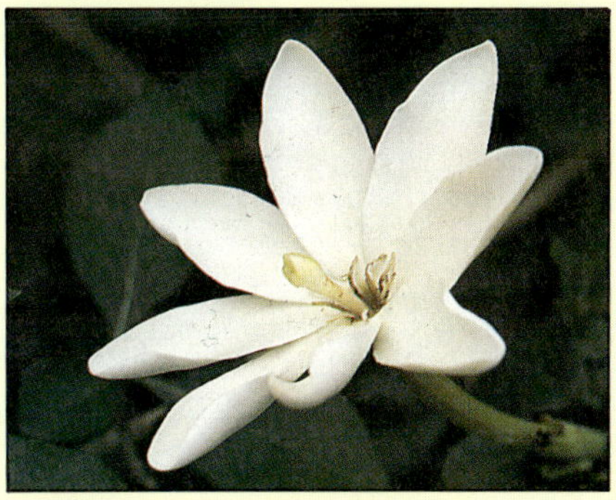

***Gardenia thunbergia**, above,* comes from South Africa. It is a compact, shrubby bush or small tree with large, glossy 6in (15cm) long leaves. The large, fragrant, creamy-white flowers, which appear in autumn and sometimes in winter, are followed by greyish, oval-shaped fruits.

Gerbera

Family name: **Compositae**

Common name: **Transvaal Daisy/Barbeton Daisy**

Care Easy	**Height** 8-15in (20-38cm)	**Flower** Summer
Light Bright indirect	**Spread** 12-18in (30-45cm)	**Humidity** Spray in hot weather
Price Cheap	**Shape** Leafy clump	**Availability** Garden centres
Temp. Min 50°F (10°C)	Ideal 70°F (21°C)	Max 85°F (30°C)

This attractive plant with its beautiful, long-lasting flowers is an ideal plant to bring a touch of colour to your sunniest rooms.

Originally from Africa and Asia, there are over a hundred different types of Gerbera. Most of them have quite large oval-shaped leaves, deeply serrated and slightly silky to the touch — their most striking feature though is their lovely flowers; they are large and daisy-like with coloured petals surrounding a central disc. The velvety petals come in a wide range of colours; soft pastels of lemon and pink, vivid oranges and reds, as well as browns and purples. The most popular houseplant species is *Gerbera jamesonii*, the Transvaal Daisy, from South Africa.

Spring and summer care

In the spring, if your plant has completely filled its pot, it will need dividing and repotting (see Propagation).

Always make sure your plant is in a bright, sunny place where there is good air circulation but no cold draughts.

Gerberas can stand very high temperatures provided that their compost is never allowed to dry out. Water your plant freely from May to late October so that the compost is kept moist but not sodden. Add a drop or two of liquid fertiliser to the water every two weeks to prolong the flowering season — use only half the recommended dose on the bottle. Also, remember to dead-head the flowers once they're past their best; cut their stems down to compost level with a sharp knife.

Autumn and winter care

During the winter months give your Gerbera just enough water to keep the soil from drying out. Make sure that the temperature doesn't drop below 50°F (10°C) and keep your plant in a sunny, draught-free position.

Propagation

A plant that has grown too big for its pot needs dividing and repotting in April. Remove it from the pot and divide the root ball carefully into two halves, removing any dead roots and leaves at the same time. Pot up the divisions in John Innes No 2, water them, and keep them somewhere warm for a week or two — a temperature of 70°F (21°C) in indirect light would be ideal, then once they are growing you can treat them as mature plants.

In March, sow Gerbera seeds into a mixture of equal parts moist peat and sand and maintain a temperature of 55-60°F (13-15°C). Just cover the seeds with compost, keep them moist, and shaded from direct light until they have germinated in 2-4 weeks. Then pot them up individually into 3in (7cm) pots and keep them in bright indirect light.

Trouble Shooter

Gerberas can suffer badly from greenfly, so it's a good idea to protect your plant from being attacked: spray regularly with a systemic insecticide containing dimethoate.

Wilting is usually a sign of water shortage. If the compost around your plant is dry, give the plant a good soaking, but don't forget to check it after half an hour and tip away any excess water.

Species

Gerbera jamesonii, the Transvaal Daisy (also sometimes called the Barbeton Daisy), comes from South Africa. Its deeply lobed leaves, which are rather woolly underneath, form a dense clump about 8-9in (20-23cm) high. From May until August daisy-like flowers on 12-15in (30-38cm) stems tower above the foliage. The outer petals vary in colour — white, yellow, orange, red, pink in many different shades according to the variety — but the central disc of the flower is always yellow. 'Rosea' has beautiful pastel pink blooms 4-5in (10-13cm) across.

G.aurantiaca looks very similar to *G.jamesonii* but has hairier leaves and its scarlet or orange flowers have a central disc of red or dark purple.

G.linnaei (sometimes called ***G.asplenifolia***) again looks rather similar to *G.jamesonii* but it has fern-like leaves, and flowers that are maroon on the under-surface and rich cream on the top.

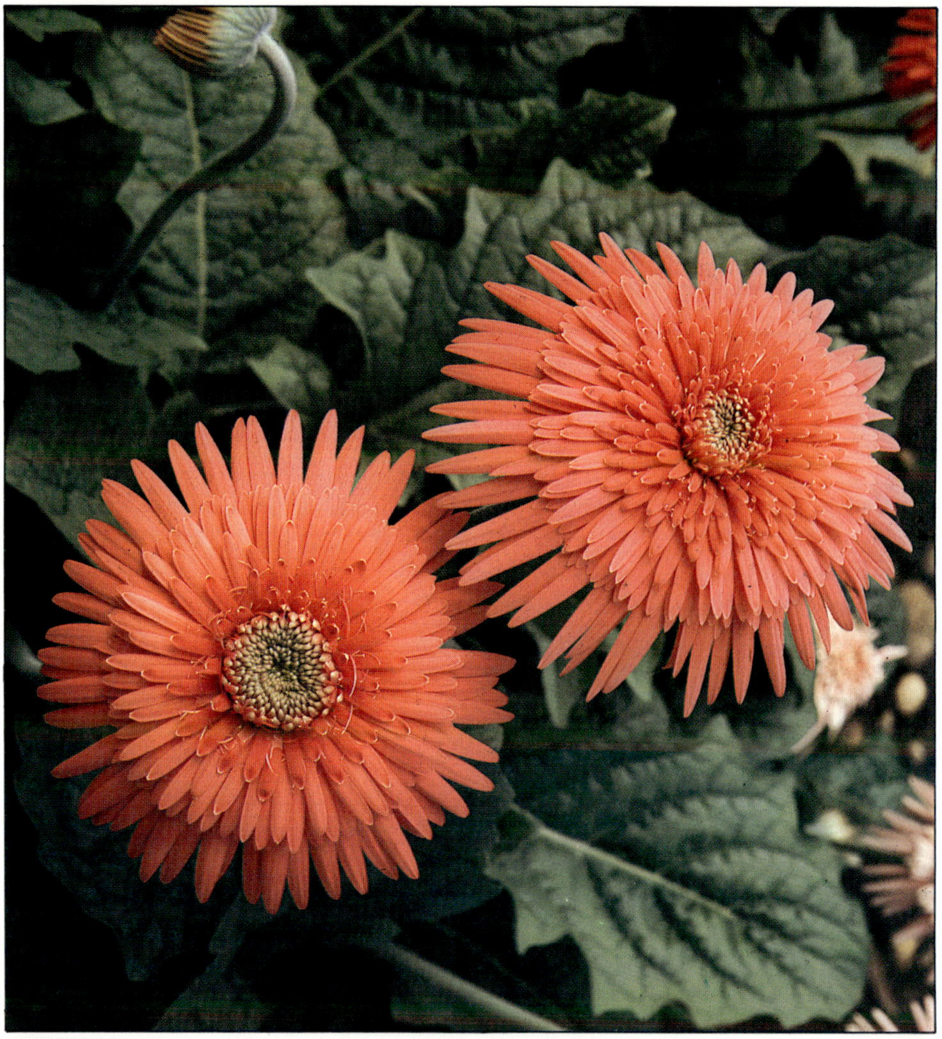

Some varieties of *Gerbera jamesonii* have more than one row of petals.

Grevillea

Family name: **Proteaceae**

Common name:
Silk Oak

Care Easy	**Height** 3-6ft (0.9-1.8m)	**Flower** Summer
Light Bright indirect	**Spread** 2-3ft (0.6-0.9m)	**Humidity** Spray in hot weather
Price Middle Range	**Shape** Tree	**Availability** Garden centres
Temp. Min 40°F (5°C)	Ideal 70°F (21°C)	Max 80°F (27°C)

All Grevilleas are evergreen and although in their natural habitat some grow into sizeable trees of 80ft (24m) or more, careful pruning of your plant will produce an attractive miniature tree or small shrub of 2-6ft (0.6-1.8m) which will be perfectly manageable and very attractive as a houseplant.

There are over two hundred different species of Grevillea, all from Australia and New Zealand. In spite of its origins, the plant is extremely easy to grow here, prefering shade to sun, and tolerating quite a wide range of temperatures; Grevilleas are mainly grown for their beautiful foliage; their arching branches carry feathery, frond-like leaflets of deep green.

Grevillea robusta, the best-known species, is a native of Queensland and New South Wales. The leaves are fern-like, often growing to 18in (45cm) long, rich green and silky to the touch. The plant rarely blooms indoors, but when it does, it produces decorative rich golden-yellow flowers. This is an extremely easy to grow, trouble-free plant and it can be restricted to a manageable bush or small tree of 2-3ft (0.6-0.9m).

Spring and summer care

Repot your plant annually in spring using a lime-free potting compost. If you want your plant to grow bigger, pot it into a larger container. To control the size and shape of your plant prune it carefully after potting in April before the start of the growing season.

In summer Grevillea likes a light position out of direct sun and temperatures of 65-70°F (18-21°C), but keep it out of the direct sun. Water freely from April to September so that the compost is moist but not sodden, and allow the plant to dry out between waterings. Every 3-4 weeks add a few drops of liquid fertiliser to the water. Mist spray only during very hot weather.

Autumn and winter care

Reduce watering in the autumn, giving your Grevillea only enough to avoid the soil drying out completely. Keep your plant in a bright position, but shaded from direct sunlight and draughts. Winter temperatures should range between 45-55°F (7-13°C).

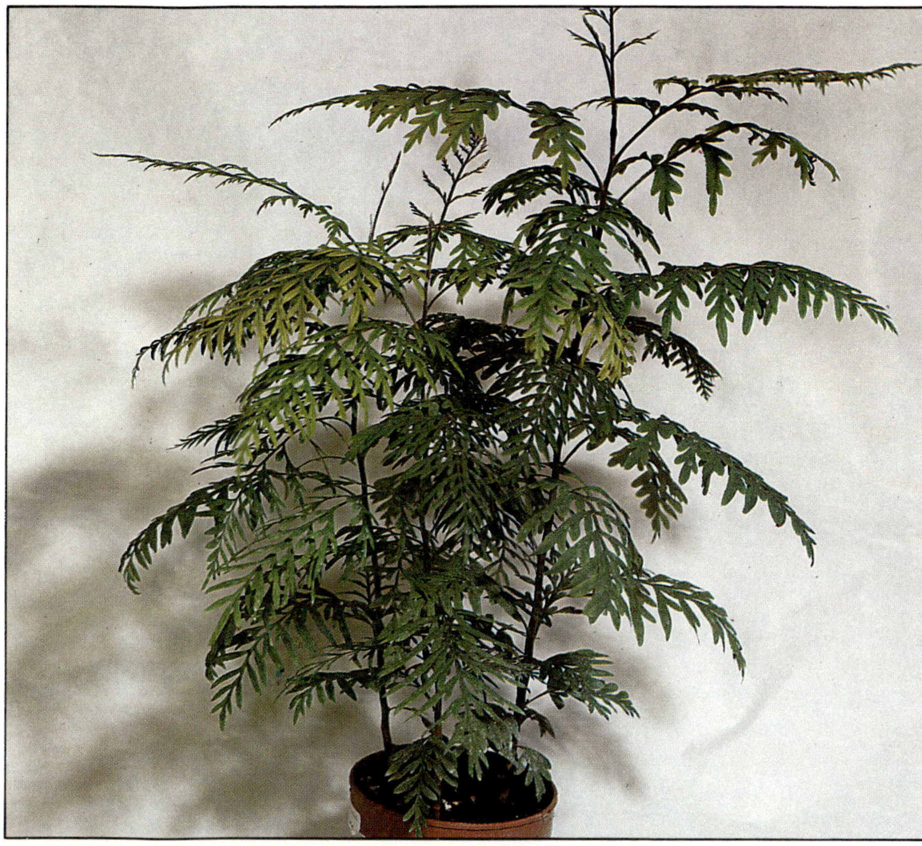

The Silk Oak is a very attractive and easy-going houseplant.

Propagation

Take 2-3in (5-7cm) heel cuttings of young shoots in April or May. Remove the cutting so that a small portion of the woody stem is attached to the base of the cutting. Treat with rooting hormone and plant in a lime-free potting compost. Cover the cuttings and keep them moist in a temperature of around 70°F (21°C) in a propagator if possible.

Grevillea can be grown from seed. Sow seeds in March or April in moist lime-free potting compost mixed with a little coarse sand. Germinate in a temperature of 65-70°F (18-21°C) and keep the seed tray shaded until the seedlings are visible. Keep the compost moist and when seedlings are large enough to handle prick them out into individual 3in (7cm) pots and treat as mature plants.

Species

Grevillea robusta, Silk Oak, from Queensland and New South Wales, can grow up into a sizeable 80ft (24m) tree in its natural habitat, but as a houseplant it's more likely to remain a small tree 3-6ft (0.9-1.8m) in height. Its deep green, fern-like leaves can be 12-18ft (30-45cm) long. These are covered with silky hairs. Flowers seldom appear on small plants.

G.rosmarinifolia, from New South Wales, can grow 6ft (1.8m). Bushy in shape, its long leaves are mid-green on top and pale green underneath. It has red flowers from May to September.

G.banksii, *right,* from Queensland, grows into an attractive tree-like shrub about 3-6ft (0.9-1.8m) tall with hairy branches and rich, green foliage which is white and silky on the underside. It has brush-like pink-red flowers in summer.

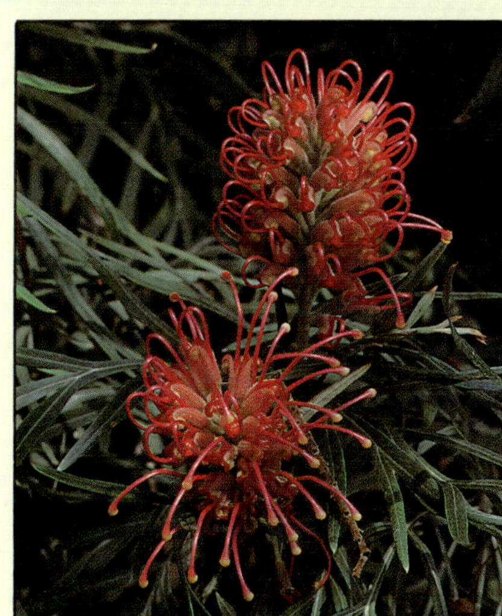

Guzmania

Family name: **Bromeliaceae**

Common names: **Scarlet Star, Striped Torch**

Care Easy	**Height** 12in (30cm)	**Flower** Summer
Light Shade	**Spread** 12in (30cm)	**Humidity** Mist spray
Price Middle Range	**Shape** Rosette	**Availability** Garden centres
Temp. Min 60°F (16°C)	Ideal 70°F (21°C)	Max 80°F (27°C)

This eye-catching group of exotic, tropical plants comes from the jungles of the West Indies and north-westerly parts of South America. They belong to the Bromeliad family — sometimes known as the Urn Plants. Like all Bromeliads the leaves of the Guzmanias grow in the form of a rosette; the bases of the leaves are curved inwards and overlap one another so that a round water-holding cup is formed at the centre of the plant.

The chief attractions of these plants are their spear-shaped, glossy green leaves and their long-lasting, colourful bracts which surround the short-lived flowers. Each leafy rosette only flowers once — so you'll need to pot up offsets from the base of the parent plant if you want flowers again another year.

Guzmania lingulata, the Scarlet Star, is one of the most popular species in the group. It has a very large flower head of scarlet bracts and small yellow flowers.

Spring and summer care

Repot your offsets in March every year (see propagation). Guzmanias are acid-loving plants and like a free-draining soil so use a peat-based compost mixed with a little coarse sand.

Keep your plant in a humid environment — stand the pot on a tray of moist pebbles and spray the foliage with water daily from April until October.

If you live in a hard water area water your plant with rain water if possible, or use boiled water with a few drops of vinegar added. Keep the urn topped-up with water — rather than watering the compost. Add a few drops of a liquid fertiliser to the water every four weeks.

Temperatures can rise to 75-80°F (24-27°C) but remember that even though your plant likes warmth, it is a forest plant and does not thrive in direct sunlight — preferring a shaded position.

Autumn and winter care

Even in winter don't let the temperature drop below 60°F (16°C). Maintain a high level of humidity by spraying the plant twice a week and keep the rosettes filled with lime-free water. For flowers next year the rosettes that flowered this summer should be cut down — this will encourage its offsets to grow (see Propagation).

Propagation

Guzmanias only flower once, but they do produce offsets which will flower next year. In the late autumn after flowering, your plant's foliage will begin to wilt and turn colour. Cut down the flowered rosette to about 2in (5cm) of the base of the plant, taking care not to damage the young offsets, then follow the 'Autumn and winter care' programme.

In the spring, carefully detach the offsets and pot them up individually into 4in (10cm) pots, using a peat-based potting compost mixed with an equal amount of coarse sand. Place in a lightly shaded, draught-free position, keep the urns topped up.

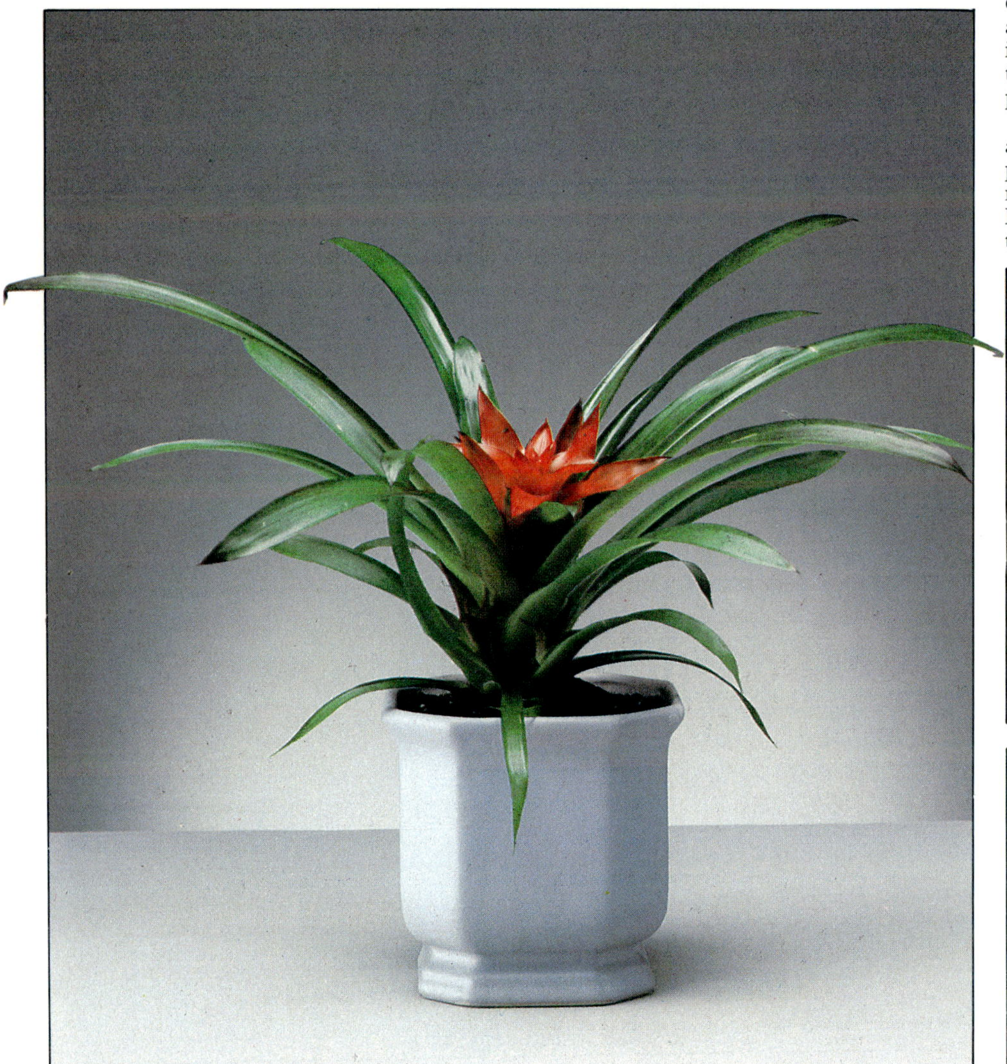

The scarlet bracts of ***Guzmania lingulata*** last for many weeks.

Trouble Shooter

Fortunately, Guzmania is a very easy plant to look after and, providing you get the watering right, it won't suffer from problems often. Brown leaves indicate rotting roots — the consequences of overwatering — take care to water the urn and not the soil as well.

If greenfly attack your plants — look for them on young growth, flower bracts and offsets — spray with a pyrethrum-based insecticide or use a systemic insecticide containing dimethoate — just water it on the soil.

Buying guide

For the best value for money, look for a plant with a fresh, young-looking flowerhead. Check also for signs of offsets forming around the base of the plant — the more there are the more plants you'll have for the next year. Before buying, be sure to check the plant carefully for pests and diseases. Avoid straggly plants completely.

Species

Guzmania lingulata, the Scarlet Star, grows to a height of 12in (30cm). In the centre of the plant, the arching spear-shaped, metallic-green leaves overlap to form a stemless rosette. The flowerhead emerges during the summer; it has a rosette of large red bracts surrounding small yellow flowers.

G.monostachya is sometimes called the Striped Torch because of its poker-like flower spike. This can reach 15in (38cm) long and has white summer flowers with greenish-white bracts striped with purple lines and tipped with orange or red. The narrow arching leaves form a rosette of about 18in (45cm) in diameter.

G.zahnii, one of the most beautiful of all the Guzmania group, forms a large rosette plant which can grow to about 2ft (0.6m) in summer when it's in full flower. The centre of the rosette is a strong coppery-red and the yellow or white flowers are surrounded by reddish bracts. The slender olive green leaves are striped with fine lines on both upper and lower surfaces. 'Omer Morobe', *top*, is a variety grown for its beautiful pink, striped leaves.

G.sanguinea has a flat, broad rosette of thick leaves about 12in (30cm) long. The inner leaves are red from the tips to about half way down, then towards the base they change to yellow or orange spotted with green. The summer flowers, which grow deep in the rosette, are white.

G.musaica, from Colombia, has beautifully marked leaves; pale green with dark red and dark green lines running across the surface, with the underside of the leaf a reddish-purple. The rosette of leaves grows to about 12-18in (30-45cm) tall and in the summer a magnificent flower head emerges from its centre — it has pinkish-red bracts surrounding masses of golden-yellow flowers.

G.conifera, makes a large rosette 3ft (0.9m) high, of stiff tongue-shaped leaves. Its late summer flowerheads are large and cone-shaped; bright red bracts tipped with orange surround the small flowers, *right*.

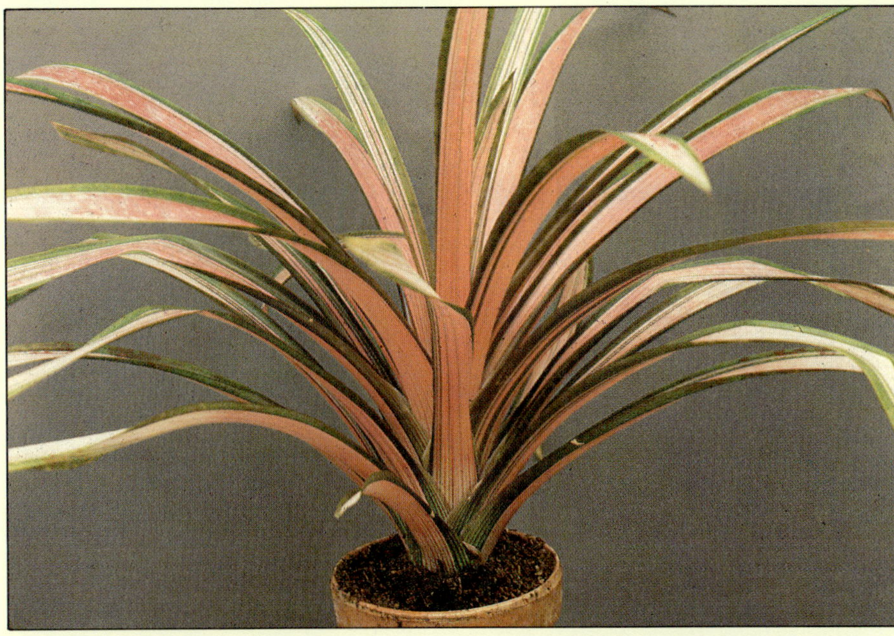

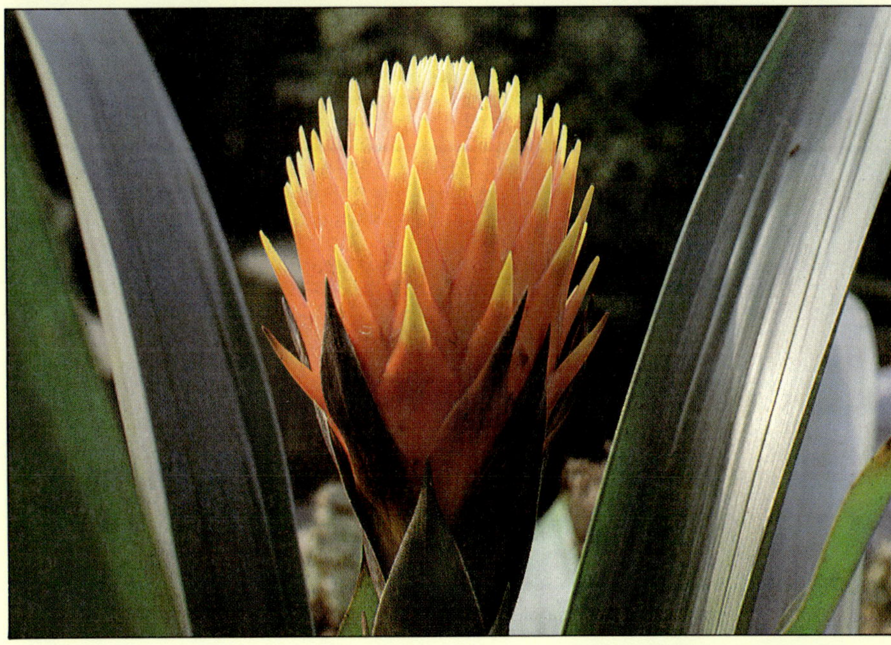

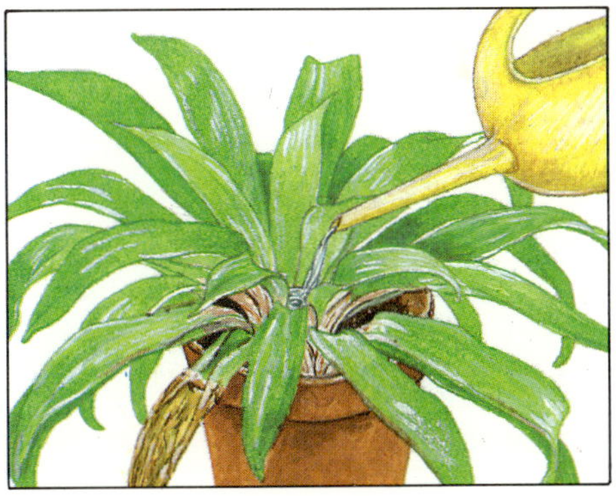

Like all the Urn Plants, water Guzmania by filling the centre of the leafy rosette. Don't use hard water on these acid loving plants.

Remove damaged or rotten leaves — snip them off with a pair of scissors. In the late autumn, leaves wither and die quite naturally. When this begins to happen, cut the plant right back to within 2in (5cm) of the compost, taking care not to damage the young offsets. Detach these in the spring and pot them up individually. You can throw away the parent plant since it won't flower again.

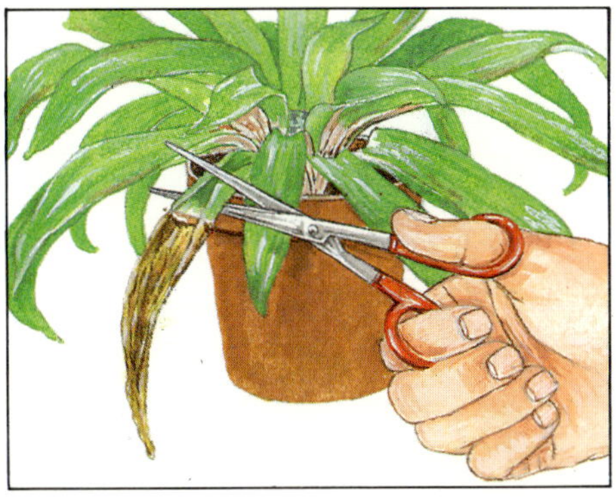

Gynura

Family name: **Compositae**

Common names: **Velvet Plant/ Purple Passion Vine**

Care Easy	**Height** 4-5ft (1.2-1.5m)	**Flower** Spring
Light Bright indirect	**Spread** 1ft (0.3m)	**Humidity** Spray in hot weather
Price Middle Range	**Shape** Trailing	**Availability** Garden centres
Temp. Min 50°F (10°C)	Ideal 70°F (21°C)	Max 80°F (27°C)

Gynuras are easy plants to look after, and if you keep your Velvet Plant in a place where it gets plenty of light, it will provide you with an extremely decorative houseplant.

This attractive plant is grown mainly for its exotic leaves; these are soft and velvety to the touch and covered with tiny purple hairs which give the plant its rich violet colour — and its common name. The younger the plant, the stronger the colour.

Some Gynuras develop into small bushy plants and others into climbers which look particularly effective in a hanging basket. All are rapid growers. One of the most popular members of the family is *Gynura sarmentosa* with its slightly fleshy, nettle-like leaves covered in soft, purple hairs. A creeper from West Africa and India, this plant makes a useful climbing or trailing houseplant .

The small orange flowers which appear early in the year are insignificant and can be picked off before they open, as they do nothing to enhance the look of the plant — and besides, some people don't like their smell! *G.aurantiaca* is a similar, but a more compact, bushy species from Indonesia.

Spring and summer care

Pot on every two years in spring; use a soil-based compost such as John Innes No 2, or, for an ideal growing medium, make up your own potting mixture with equal parts of good loam, peat, decomposed leaf-mould and sharp sand. If your plant is getting out of hand, you can prune it into a more compact shape in spring before the growing season. Gynuras are thirsty plants so water well from June to September. Mist spray in the hottest weather, but be sure to do this early in the day, and never in full sun. Give a weak liquid feed every three or four weeks. Very good light is needed to keep the leaves at their best, and Gynuras appreciate some full sun. Temperatures of 65-70°F (18-21°C) are ideal.

Autumn and winter care

In winter , when your plant makes little or no growth, water very sparingly — only enough to keep the soil just moist. Give as much light as possible and do not allow the temperature to drop below 50°F (10°C).

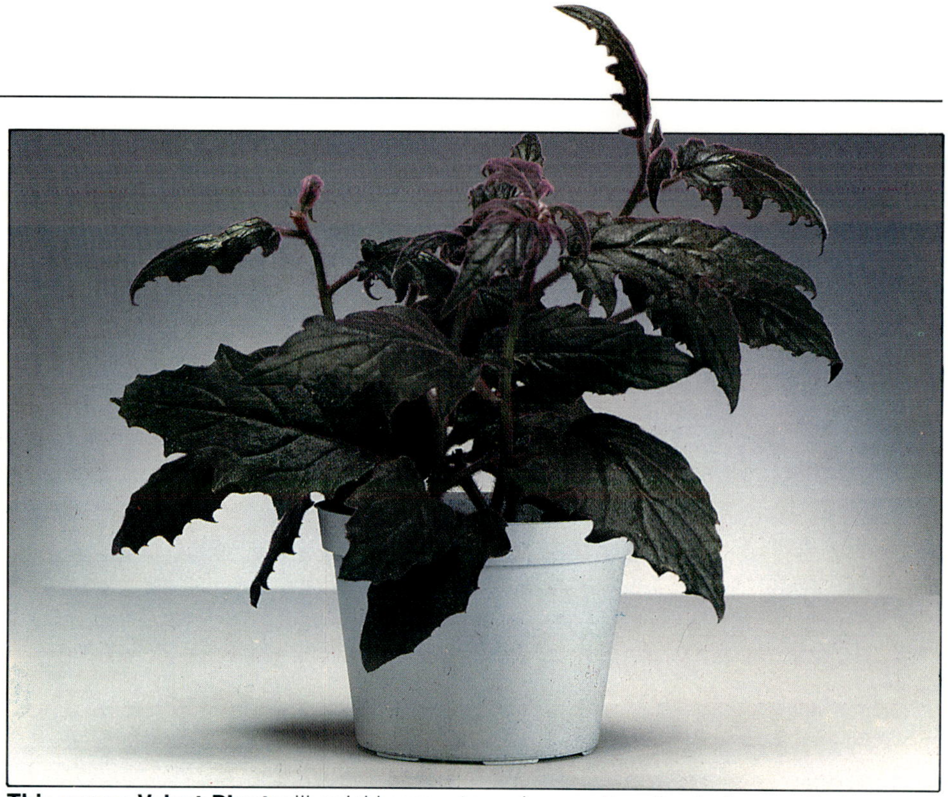

This young Velvet Plant will quickly grow to make an attractive trailer or climber.

Propagation

In April, take cuttings of stem tips 3-5in (7-13cm) long. Plant in a mixture of equal parts of peat and sand, keep moist and root at a temperature of 65-70°F (18-21°C). If you don't have a propagator place the cuttings in a polythene bag and make sure they don't touch the polythene. When you see signs of new growth — in two to three weeks — plant the cuttings in pots of John Innes No 2.

Gynuras can be raised from seed sown between February and early April. Fill a seed tray with a mixture of equal parts peat and sand and sow the seed on the surface. Keep moist and shaded from direct sun, and germinate at a temperature of 70-75°F (21-24°C) — ideally in a propagator.

Trouble Shooter

While Gynura is an easy plant to look after, leaves will quickly turn brown if it's left for too long without water. When mist spraying, spray before the sun is at its hottest as the leaves can blister or become covered with black patches. If your plant is short of light the leaves will lose their rich purple gleam and begin to look less attractive. Pests seldom trouble the Gynura, but if green-fly attacks your plant, spray it with pyrethrum.

Species

Gynura sarmentosa, from India and West Africa, is similar in appearance to the *G.aurantiaca*, but is a more sprawling plant, with long trailing stems. The fleshy, slightly toothed leaves are deep-green and covered with deep purple hairs. Loose clusters of pale orange flowers appear in March and April.

G.aurantiaca, *right*, from Indonesia, grows up to 3ft (0.9m) with a spread of 18in (45cm). It has erect stems which later become more sprawling. The nettle-like leaves and the stems are covered in fine, purple hairs which feel velvety to the touch. Clusters of small, orange flowers appear in February.

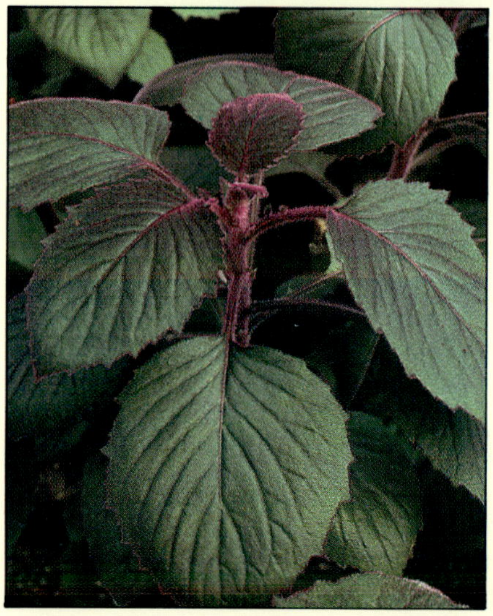

G.bicolor, from Indonesia, has leaves 6in (15cm) long, bluish-green in colour, with a fine down of purple hairs on the upper surface and dark red underneath.

Haemanthus

Family name: **Amaryllidaceae**

Common name:
Blood Lily

Care Straight forward	**Height** 18in (45cm)	**Flower** June
Light Some direct sun	**Spread** 12-18in (30-45cm)	**Humidity** Occasional mist spray
Price Middle Range	**Shape** Fan-shaped	**Availability** Garden centres
Temp. Min 50°F (10°C)	Ideal 60°F (15°C)	Max 75°F (24°C)

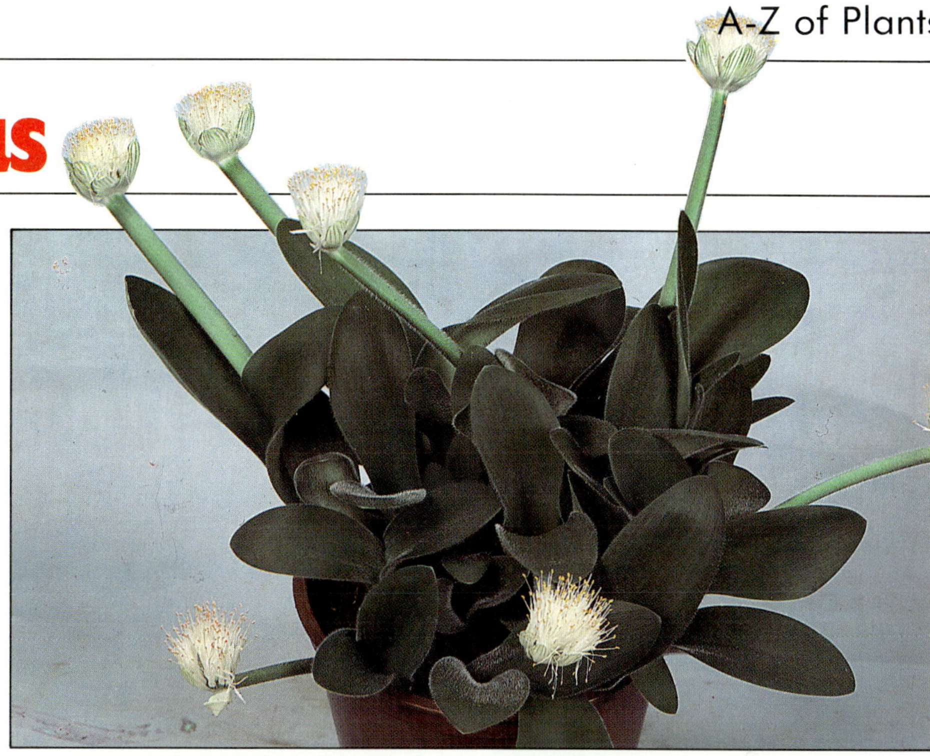

The unusual blooms of *H.albiflos* look rather like shaving brushes.

This exotic group of beautiful flowering bulbs comes from tropical Africa. Some species are deciduous while others are evergreen. They have thick, strap-shaped leaves and rounded or cup-shaped flower heads made up of a mass of 1in (2.5cm) long, stamens, sometimes surrounded by large showy bracts. The flower heads vary considerably in size and colour from deep scarlet to a greenish-white. They appear between April and September, according to species.

Haemanthus albiflos is the most popular species, with brush-like heads of small white flowers, surrounded by green bracts. The flowers are held above the leaves on rather thick, 9in (23cm) long stems.

Spring and summer care

Pot new bulbs in March, using John Innes No 2, covering the necks of the bulbs so that only the tips are showing. Haemanthus are best not disturbed — too frequent repotting can upset regular flowering, so only pot on if the roots are starting to appear on the surface or the bulb is getting very close to the sides of the pot. Otherwise, topdress by sprinkling a little fresh compost on to the surface, in March or April.

A temperature of around 60-65°F (15-18°C) is ideal — and avoid anything lower than 50°F (10°C). For the best results always place the plant in a bright position, where it will receive some direct sunlight every day.

Water moderately throughout the summer and add a little liquid feed every two weeks or so to encourage flowering. As their flowers fade, they are replaced by rich, scarlet berries. When these are past their best, cut the stems right back to the base. The leaves of deciduous plants will shrivel away; with evergreens, cut off the older leaves as they turn brown.

Autumn and winter care

Whether they are deciduous or retain their leaves, always keep the plants totally frost-free, ensuring a minimum temperature in autumn and winter of 50°F (10°C) for safety; try to keep them in a bright spot.

Water evergreen species just enough to keep the soil from drying out; give the deciduous plants only a very occasional watering, to ensure that the mixture does not become totally dry. This way the plants won't have to start all over again to develop their very fleshy roots when growing recommences. Keep the soil more moist from about the beginning of February, then water more freely as growth appears.

Trouble Shooter

Leaves will drop and lose their lustre and flowers may fail to appear if the soil around your plant is allowed to remain too dry for too long. Equally, if you overwater and plants are left standing for long periods in water, the bulbs are likely to rot.

Watch out for occasional fluffy white patches on the leaves — the sign of the mealy bug. They can easily be removed with a paintbrush dipped in methylated spirit.

Propagation

Generally, Haemanthus is propagated by removing offsets and potting them individually in John Innes No 2. Water sparingly for the first few weeks, then treat them as mature plants. Young offsets will take about two years to reach flowering size.

Some species, such as *H.coccineus* and *H.katharinae*, are reluctant to produce offsets and usually need to be propagated from seed. Take the ripe berries and press them lightly into the potting compost, but don't cover them with soil. Until they germinate, they'll need to be kept at a constant temperature of 65-70°F (18-21°C), but out of direct sun. Keep the soil just moist and when leaves start to appear, pot up the plants individually.

Species

Haemanthus albiflos, an evergreen species from South Africa. It has thick, fleshy dark green leaves which are retained all year round. The unusual blooms appearing in June consist of a cup-shaped head made up of many small white flowers.

H.coccineus, known as the Blood Lily, is another native of South Africa. In August or September, each short mottled stem bears a round tufted head of small pinkish flowers, surrounded by showy, deep red, petal-like bracts. The leaves only fully develop after the flowers have died, remaining throughout the winter and spring to die down in the summer.

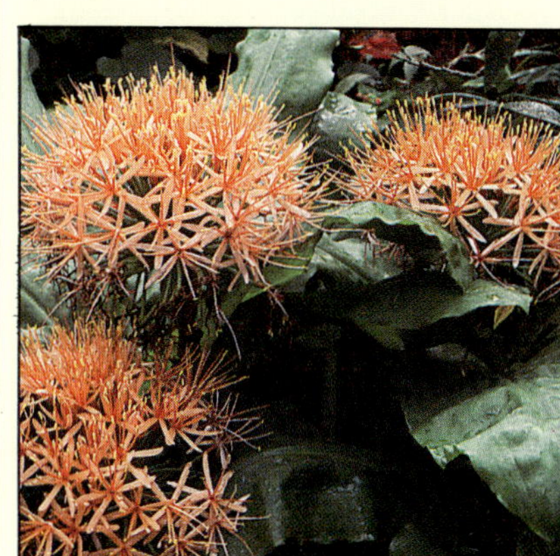

H.katharinae,*above*, is deciduous and has a thick fleshy stalk up to 2ft (60cm) long, carrying long waxy, green leaves. Bright-red, globe-shaped flower heads, up to 8in (20cm) across, are borne in July.

Haworthia

Family name: **Liliaceae**

Common names: **Pearl Plant, Star Window Plant**

Care Easy	**Height** 6-10in (15-25cm)	**Flower** Insignificant
Light Bright indirect	**Spread** 4in (10cm)	**Humidity** None
Price Cheap	**Shape** Tall rosette	**Availability** Garden centres
Temp. Min 40°F (5°C)	Ideal 75°F (24°C)	Max 80°F (27°C)

This group of small succulents provides some of today's most useful plants. They are so easy to care for that you can hardly go wrong, in fact they will tolerate a surprising amount of neglect. A collection of these fascinating little plants would be ideal for children starting to grow their own indoor garden.

Apart from being easy to look after, Haworthias are popular as houseplants because of their interestingly shaped and coloured foliage. Nearly all grow as a stemless rosette of patterned, overlapping, fleshy leaves. *Haworthia reinwardtii* is an exception though. This popular succulent has rows of overlapping leaves completely coating an upright stem — so it looks like an elongated rosette. Although all the Haworthias flower, their flowers are rather small and insignificant, so many people remove them as soon as they appear.

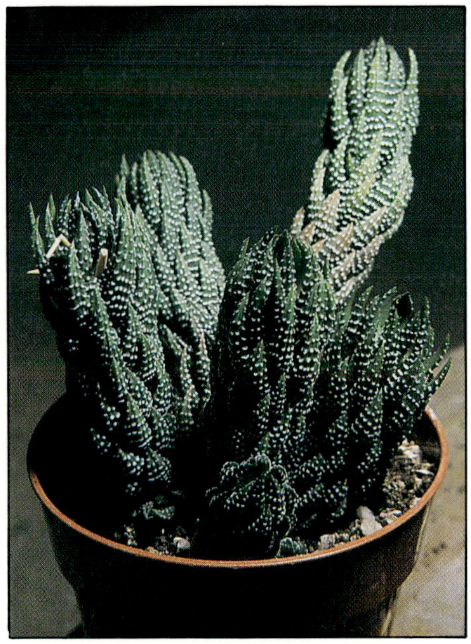

The unusual, bead-coated, tall rosettes of *Haworthia reinwardtii.*

Haworthias originally come from arid areas and like cacti have evolved in such a way that they can store water and nourishment for weeks and even months. So water your plants only when the compost has become dry and make sure it has a warm position with bright, indirect light.

Spring and summer care

If the pot becomes crowded, repot in March before the main growing season using a cactus potting compost or John Innes No 2 mixed with a little sharp sand. From late March to October water regularly, but leave your plant to dry out between waterings. A few drops of a liquid fertiliser can be added to the water once a month. Good light is vital for your plant — even occasional full sun. A temperature of 75°F (24°C) is ideal, although these plants are quite happy in normal room temperatures.

Autumn and winter care

During the winter months your plant will need hardly any water, just enough to prevent the soil drying out completely. Keep it in a good light and try to maintain a temperature of around 50°F (10°C). Although Haworthias will survive at slightly lower temperatures this shouldn't be allowed to drop lower than 40°F (5°C).

Propagation

Carefully detach offsets from the base of the main plant in March or April and leave them to dry for a few days. These can then be potted up using a cactus compost or equal parts of John Innes No 2 with coarse sand added. Spray the offsets with water daily, until they feel securely rooted in their pots (this should take only 2-3 weeks) and then treat as mature plants.

Haworthias can also be grown from seed in spring and this is a good way to build up a collection, particularly of the rarer species. Put some gravel into the bottom of the pot to ensure good drainage and then fill with cactus compost or John Innes No 2 with coarse sand added. Sprinkle seeds carefully over the compost and water gently. Put the seeds in a warm spot sheltered from direct sun and cold draughts. Plant up the seedlings as soon as they are large enough to handle.

Trouble Shooter

Fortunately these are very good-natured plants and will tolerate a certain amount of neglect from their owners. Brown mushy leaves mean too much water. Not enough light will make your plant look straggly and out of shape.

White woolly patches on the leaves are mealy bug. These can be wiped off with a small brush dipped in methylated spirit and your plant can then be treated with a dimethoate-based insecticide watered directly on to the soil. This is a good pest deterrent and can be used three to four times during the growing season.

Buying Guide

Look for undamaged rosettes with no unhealthy or missing leaves.
Take care not to crush the plant as you carry it home.

Species

Haworthia reinwardtii looks quite different from many other Haworthias. It has an elongated rather than a round or flattened rosette of leaves. The stem is stiff and about 6in (15cm) long and thickly covered with overlapping fleshy, dark green leaves spotted with white, bead-like growths. Like all the plants in this group, the greyish-white flowers are small and insignificant.

H.cymbiformis is a compact plant with greyish-green leaves each about 1-2in (2.5-5cm) long, ridged at the tip. Like all Haworthias, these are thick and fleshy and formed into a rosette. The leaves of some varieties such as *H.c.translucens* are decorated with deeper green vein-like lines running from the base to the tips of the leaves.

H.margaritifera, the Pearl Plant, has lance-shaped, dark green leaves, thickly spotted with white bumps which give the plant a pearly-beaded appearance. The fleshy leaves form broad rosettes about 5-6in (13-15cm) across.

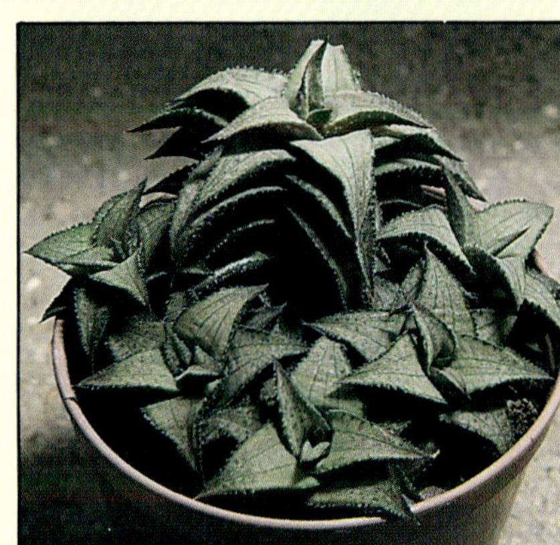

H.tessellata, the Star Window Plant, *above,* is so called because of its small, 2in (5cm) high, star-shaped rosette. This consists of thick, greenish-brown leaves, triangular in shape with very pointed tips. Squarish markings cover the leaves. *H.t.parva* is a more compact version and *H.t.obesa* is more rounded but with pointed leaves.

Hedera

Family name: **Araliaceae**

Common name: **Ivy**

Care Easy	**Height** Unlimited	**Flower** Insignificant
Light Bright	**Spread** 1ft (0.3m)	**Humidity** Mist spray regularly
Price Cheap	**Shape** Climber	**Availability** Common
Temp. Min 40°F (5°C)	Ideal 65°F (18°C)	Max 80°F (27°C)

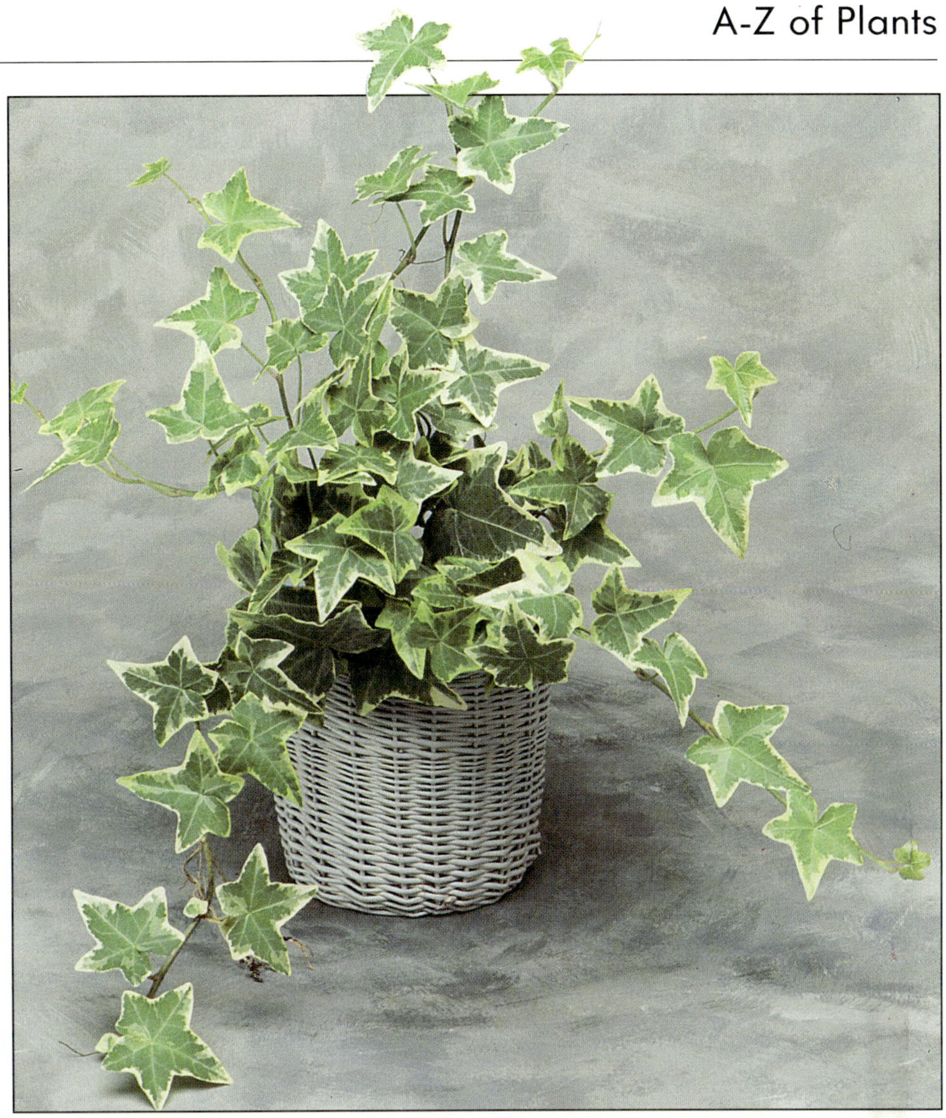

One of the many charming, small-leaved varieties of *Hedera helix*.

Ivies are among the most rewarding of all house plants. These hardy evergreen climbers are highly decorative and quick growing, and with a little care will live for a long time. The few species that make up the Hedera group have spawned countless varieties, with leaves that range in size and shape from tiny diamonds to long pointed stars, and colourings from plain green to complex patterns of gold and silver, yellows, greens, creams and greys.

Most of the varieties have been bred from *Hedera helix* — English or common ivy — a vigorous climber that will easily grow to 50-100ft (15-30m) or more, outside. Its glossy dark-green leaves are typically ivy-shaped, with 3 or 5 pointed lobes. A handsome plant, it's probably outshone now by its varieties, such as 'Glacier', which has variegated leaves of silver-grey with a cream margin, and the charming golden-yellow 'Goldheart'.

These plants are rapid climbers. With aerial roots attached to the stems that will cling to any suitable surface, they quickly work their way up walls or woodwork. More modestly, inside the house you can train them up canes or tie the stems to a trellis. Alternatively, you can encourage them to trail over the edge of a tub or from a hanging basket; try three or four varieties trailing from a single basket for a really decorative effect. If you want a bushy compact plant, pinch out growing tips regularly. And you can cut your plant back rigorously, if it threatens to get out of hand.

These ivies are reasonably easy to grow and shouldn't present any problems if you provide the right conditions. Give them a light, fresh, airy atmosphere, not too hot and not too dry, and your plants will prosper.

Spring and summer care

Repot your ivy every two or three years in 4-6in (10-15cm) pots of John Innes No 2. In the years when you're not repotting, topdress by scraping away an inch or two of compost and replacing it with fresh. Early spring is also the time for any pruning; if your plant is leggy or overgrown, you can cut it back now by as much as half.

Ivies are tough plants; they will put up with a certain amount of neglect and tolerate quite a wide range of temperatures, but you can't expect them to thrive on it. What they particularly dislike is hot, dry air. Their ideal summer temperature is around 60-65°F (15-18°C). Anything over that can cause problems and you'll need to provide extra humidity. During spring and summer try and mist spray at least twice a week. If they don't get adequate light your plants may become rather spindly, with large gaps between leaves, so place them in a good, bright position. The variegated forms, in particular, need good light or their foliage may revert to plain green. But do be sure to keep them out of direct sunlight during summer.

Water moderately — just enough to keep the compost moist — and take care not to overwater. Feed with a weak liquid fertiliser every two or three weeks during the growing season, using half the dose recommended.

Autumn and winter care

Winter requirements vary only a little from those of the growing season. As houseplants, ivies can weather very low temperatures and will survive at 45°F (7°C) or even lower, but they will hardly prosper. It's better to keep them at a room temperature of around 50°F (10°C). Try and provide as well-lit a spot as possible — too much shade might eventually affect the growth and leaf colourings.

Water sparingly during winter, especially if temperatures are low, but never let the compost dry out. Give your ivy as good air circulation as you can. Don't let the air get too dry and spray if the room is heated.

Propagation

Ivies are easy to propagate, whether by layering or by taking cuttings (pages 120-121). In summer, take tip cuttings, about 4in (10cm) long, cutting the shoots just above a leaf bud. Place three or four of them in a 3in (7cm) pot of John Innes No 2 mixed with an equal amount of sharp sand. Keep them moist and warm — 60-65°F (15-18°C) — in a propagator or enclosed in a clear polythene bag, and provide bright indirect light. Rooting should take about a fortnight, after which you should uncover the plants, water them moderately and give them a weak liquid feed once a month. When roots start to come through the drainage holes, pot up individually into containers of John Innes No 2 and treat them as adult plants.

Alternatively, the cuttings will quickly develop roots if you keep them in a glass of water at room temperature in bright indirect light. When the roots are about 1in (25mm) long pot up the cuttings into containers of John Innes No 2.

Species

Hedera helix, the common ivy, is the principal species. A native to England, it is widespread throughout English woodlands, growing 50-100ft (15-30m) or even higher. The plants grow attractively dense and bushy, with glossy dark-green leaves, often freckled with silver along the veins. The leaves have three or five lobes and grow to 4in (10cm) or more.

H.helix has endless varieties, including many decorative smaller-leaved types which are ideal as houseplants. One of the most popular is 'Chicago' — possibly because it is also one of the sturdiest. It grows well either as a climber or a trailer, and has small, medium-green leaves; in one form, 'Chicago Variegata', these come with a creamy-yellow edge. 'Glacier', *bottom right*, is another popular variety. It has small variegated leaves of silver-grey with a creamy-white margin. For a good bushy growth it will need pinching out two or three times a year.

'Sagittaefolia' is an eye-catching variety. It has small, leathery greyish-green leaves, shaped like an arrow-head, with a long, triangular central lobe. There is a variegated form with pale green and yellow markings. This makes an excellent trailing plant and good ground cover; for a dense bushy growth, pinch out regularly. Other plants include 'Goldheart', *bottom left*, which has small leaves of yellow and cream on a deep-green background, and really dense growth, and 'Little Diamond', *top left*, which bears diamond-shaped leaves, greyish-green in colour, with creamy-white variegations.

H.colchica, Persian ivy, is found in Iran and parts of the USSR and is an extremely robust plant. Fast-growing and high-climbing, its heart-shaped, glossy green leaves are the largest of all the species, up to 10in (25cm) long and 6-8in (15-20cm) wide. Among its varieties, *H.c.aurea* has rather smaller leaves, variously marked with yellow and creamy-green splashes, while *H.c.dentata, top right*, has thin,dark-green leaves, sometimes with a purple tint, sometimes variegated.

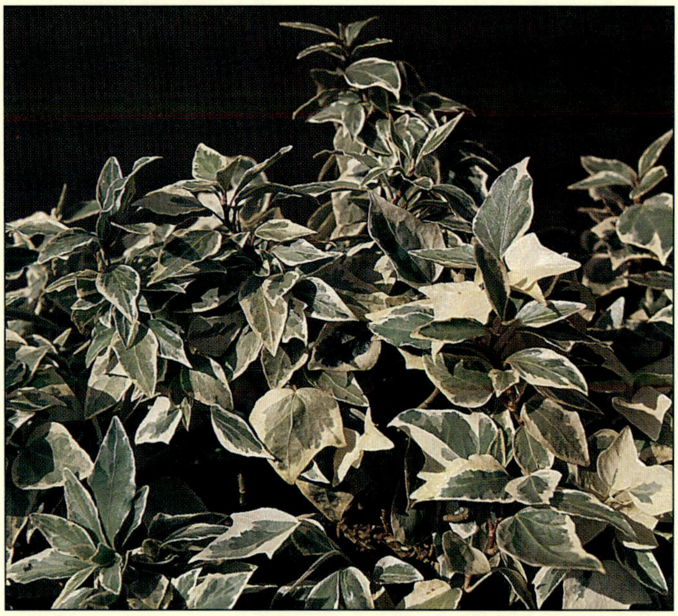

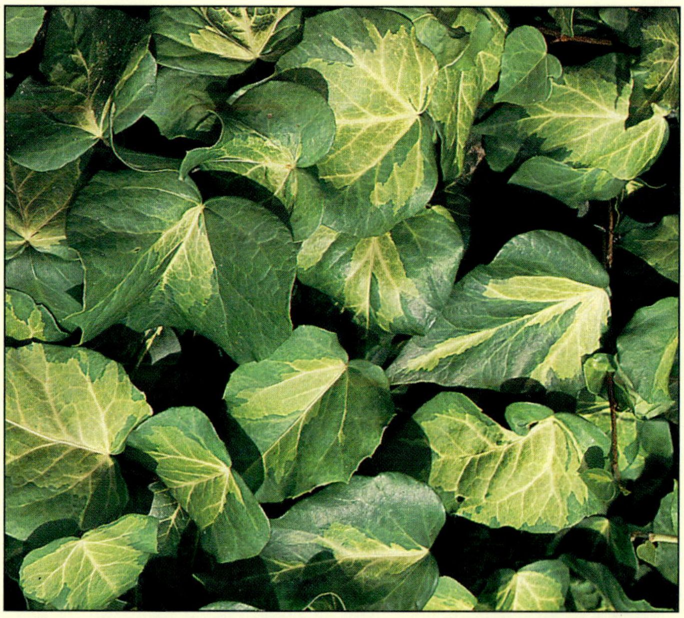

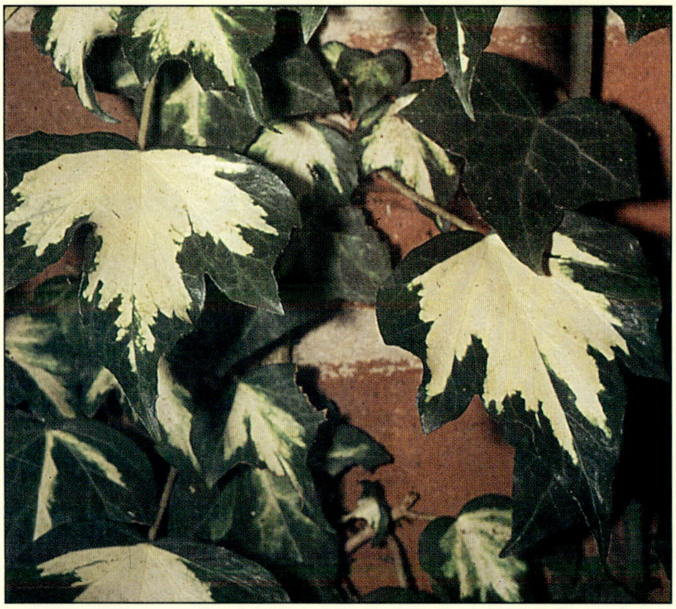

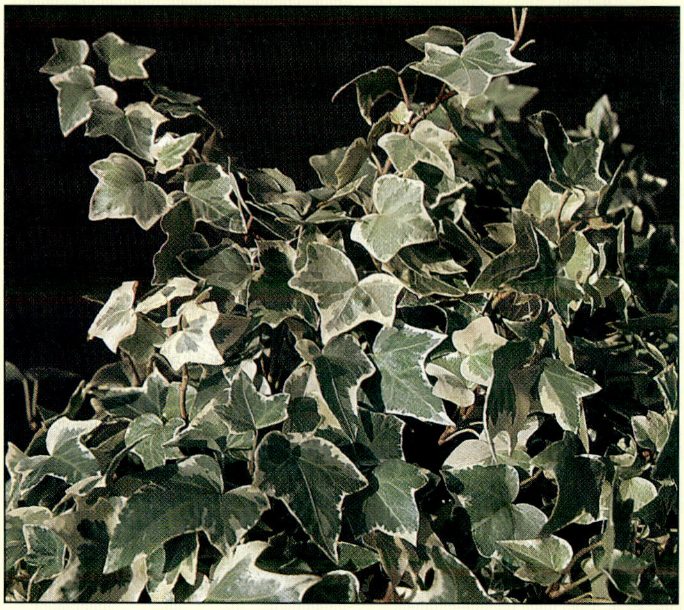

Species

H. canariensis, the Canary or Algerian ivy, is a handsome species from the Canary Islands and north-west Africa. It has large leathery leaves, about 5in by 6in (13cm by 15cm), which are slightly lobed with a heart-shaped base. They are a glossy dark-green with pale-green veins and reddish stalks and stems. More tender than *H.helix*, it is still very well suited to growing as a houseplant. Its smaller-leaved, variegated form, 'Gloire de Marengo', *below*, is an attractive plant with leaves that go from dark-green in the centre through silver-grey to a bold creamy border; 'Variegata', *right*, is larger leaved and similarly variegated.

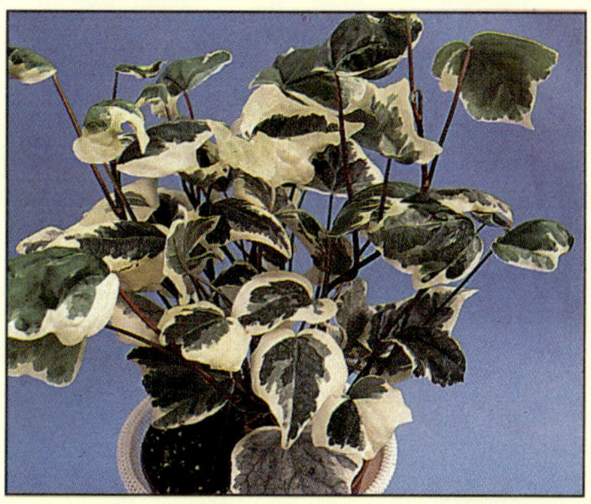

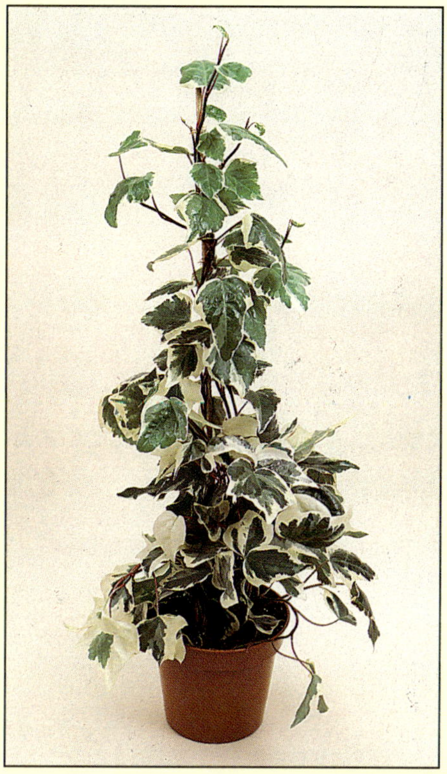

Trouble Shooter

Too dry an atmosphere can cause the leaves to wither and drop, as can too much sun; give the plant a thorough soaking and it may recover. Loss of variegation, distorted growth and shrivelled young leaves, *right*, may be caused by insufficient water and a lack of nutrients. Water and feed your plant more regularly. Blackish marks may appear on the leaves and this can develop into a fungul infection; dry out the soil, then treat the plant with a fungicide such as Benomyl.

Ivy can be susceptible to attack by a number of pests. Hot, dry air will encourage red spider mite; at first signs, spray with a malathion-based insecticide. Overhead spraying with water once or twice a week is a good deterrent. Greyish markings on the young leaves are a sign of thrips; spray with a malathion-based insecticide and remove affected leaves if infestation is severe. Aphids may attack growth; spray with pyrethrum. Scale insects are best removed with a cotton bud dipped in methylated spirit. Keep pests at bay by using a dimethoate-based systemic insecticide, applied in late March, June and then September.

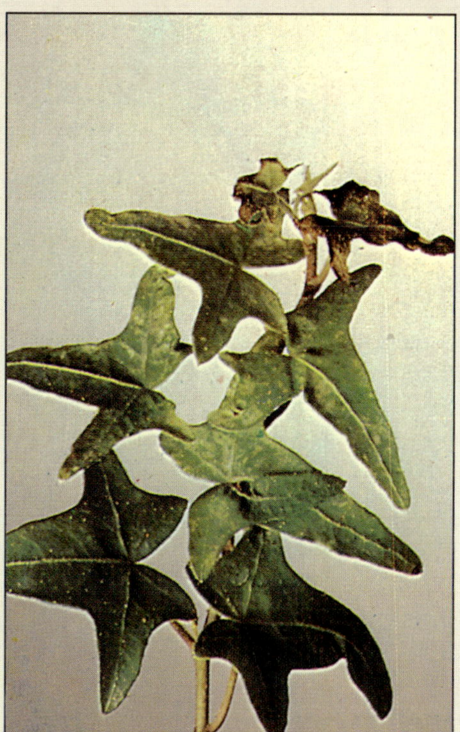

Buying Guide

Ivies are widely available and generally inexpensive, though variegated forms may be slightly dearer. Look for bushy plants which are showing new growth, and avoid anything dehydrated-looking, with bare stems or with dead leaves around the base.

Select a plant with leaves that are uniform in colouring and if you're buying a variegated form, make sure it isn't showing a lot of plain green foliage.

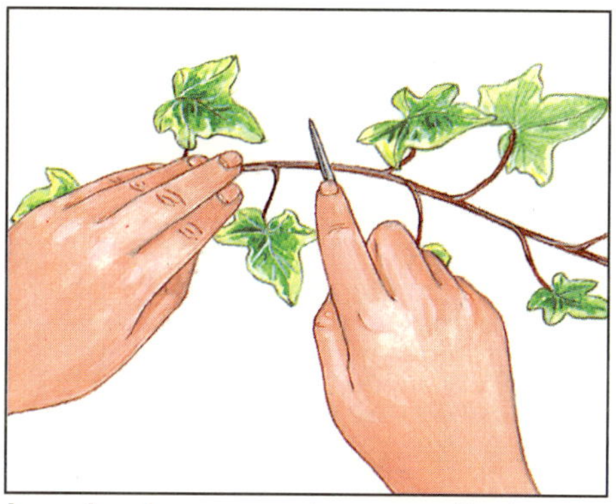

Layering in summer is an excellent way of propagating ivy. Select a strong stem and nick the surface below a leaf joint.

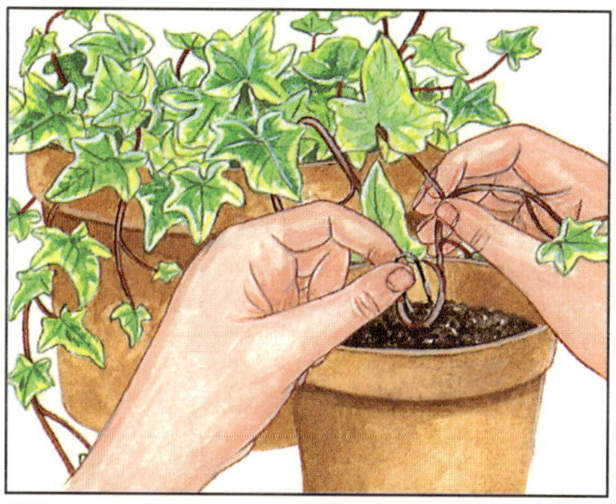

Fill a small pot with John Innes No 2. Bend the stem so that the cut lies on the compost and peg down at this point.

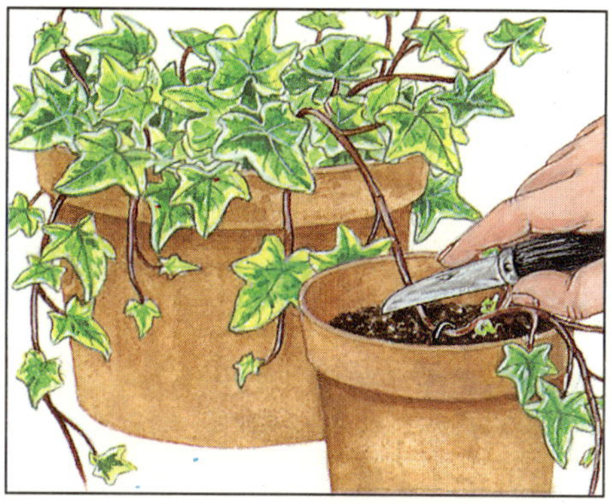

Keep well watered and in a few weeks roots will grow from the cut. When rooted, sever new plant from its parent.

Helxine

Family name: **Urticaceae**

Common names: **Baby's Tears/ Mind Your Own Business**

Care Easy	**Height** 3-4in (7-10cm)	**Flower** Insignificant
Light Bright, indirect	**Spread** Unlimited	**Humidity** Mist spray in hot weather
Price Cheap	**Shape** Cushion	**Availability** Garden centres
Temp. Min 40°F (5°C)	Ideal 65°F (18°C)	Max 80°F (27°C)

This is what might be termed a good 'carpeting' plant. A native of Corsica and Sardinia, it is also reasonably hardy in Britain, at least in the south.

Helxine solierolii is a creeping, trailing plant with masses of tiny, glossy green leaves borne on very thin stems. It grows rapidly to form thick mats or cushions of dense foliage and discerning eyes will spot minute greenish flowers in the leaf axils. Helxine is good as ground cover and if placed in a shallow, wide container it will soon fill it and spill over the sides. This attractive little plant is suitable for planting in pots for table decoration or displaying in hanging baskets.

Spring and summer care

For strong, healthy plants Helxine is best divided every spring — see 'Propagation' for details. Replant into wide, shallow, containers filled with John Innes No 1 or a peat-based potting compost.

Helxine is easy to care for and makes few demands. The most important of these is that it must be kept moist throughout the year, calling for regular watering. It does not even seem to mind being saturated to the point of standing in water at times. It is tolerant of both shade and full sun as long as the root system is supplied with ample moisture.

Autumn and winter care

Variations in temperature do not cause problems but watering must be adjusted accordingly. Extreme cold — especially if frost conditions are likely — means withholding excess water in order to avoid frozen roots.

Propagation

This is a simple matter of dividing up a clump into chosen sizes and potting them up separately in pots of peat- or loam-based compost. This is best undertaken in spring though it is possible to divide at almost any time of year, always providing that care is taken not to break or disturb the root system too badly. Maintain regular watering so as to ensure that the compost remains moist both during and after the operation. Your divided plants may look a little untidy at first but they'll soon settle down.

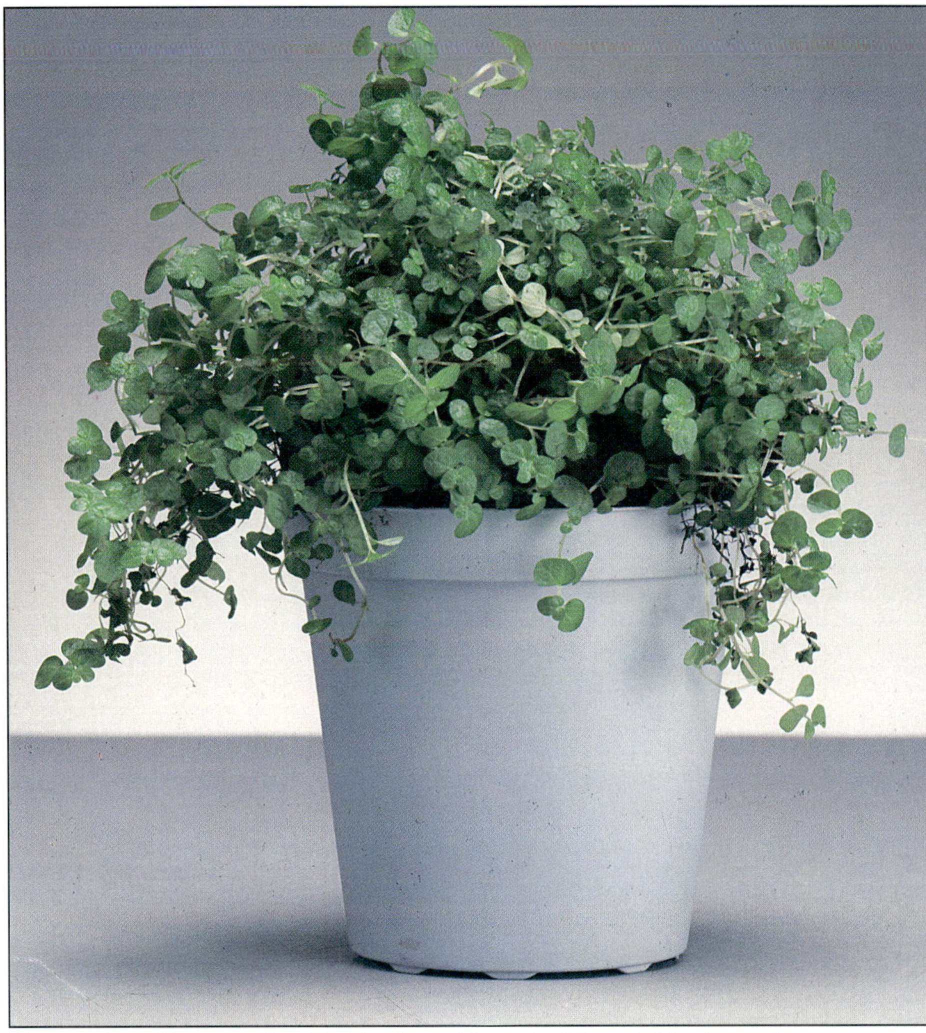

Compact and low growing, Helxine is an ideal plant for a table decoration.

Trouble Shooter

Problems are virtually non-existent. The only possible cause of trouble — even death — is if plants are left to dry out completely. Pests are unlikely to attack.

Buying Guide

Weeds are very difficult to remove from Helxine's dense growth, so make sure before you buy that there are no weeds growing among the tiny leaves.

Species

Helxine solierolii is the plant most commonly seen in people's homes. It is a creeping, trailing plant which soon forms a thick carpet of dense, tiny, glossy leaves. 'Aurea', *right*, is an ivory-white or pale yellowish form which, like the species, forms a dense mass of more colourful leaves and tends to be less invasive. There is also a more unusual variety, 'Argentea', which has appeared in garden centres in recent years and is a delightful miniature with the same habit and growth as the species but with silvery white foliage.

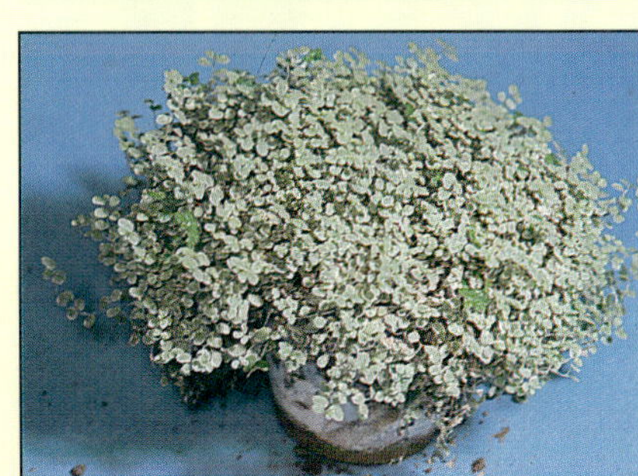

Heptapleurum

Family name: **Araliaceae**

Common name:
Parasol Plant

Care Easy	**Height** 8ft (2.4m)	**Flower** None indoors
Light Bright, indirect	**Spread** 2ft (0.6m)	**Humidity** Mist spray regularly
Price Middle range	**Shape** Upright bush	**Availability** Garden centres
Temp. Min 55°F (13°C)	Ideal 75°F (24°C)	Max 80°F (27°C)

This is one of those botanical groups which, the botanists have decided, should be merged with another. The Heptapleurums now officially belong to the genus Schefflera. However as most suppliers still call them Heptapleurums, we keep to that name.

The common name, Parasol Plant, comes fromthe way the leaves are held. Each leaf is subdivided into at least seven leaflets - these fall gracefully downwards, radiating from the tip of an upward pointing stem, so giving the appearance of a parasol. Left to its own devices, the plant makes an 8ft (2.4m) tall, unbranched tree covered in these very decorative parasols. If you don't want such a tall plant you can simply pinch out the growing tip and it will become bushy and branching.

Quick-growing and easy to care for, this plant makes an ideal choice for an elegant eye-catching feature, either standing alone in the corner of a room, or grouped together with other plants.

Spring and summer care

Repot every spring into a pot size up if you want to encourage your plant to grow bigger. Use John Innes No 3 potting compost. If your plant becomes too large to repot easily, then topdress instead; use a kitchen fork to loosen and remove the top 1-2in (2.5-5cm) of compost, then replace with fresh compost.

Parasol plants do not like direct sun but make sure they get plenty of bright light.

Water your plant regularly, allowing the top surface of the compost to dry out between waterings. Add a few drops of liquid fertiliser to the water every two weeks. They enjoy humidity; so stand the pot in a large saucer of damp pebbles and remember to mist spray regularly, especially in hot weather. You can use a proprietary leaf-shiner to keep the leaves looking healthy — but don't be tempted to use this more than once a month.

The ideal temperature during the growing season is 75°F (24°C), though the plant will thrive in temperatures of 65-80°F (18-27°C).

Autumn and winter care

Decrease watering and humidity slightly and stop using a fertiliser altogether. Keep your plant in bright, indirect sunlight and don't let the temperature fall below 55°F (13°C).

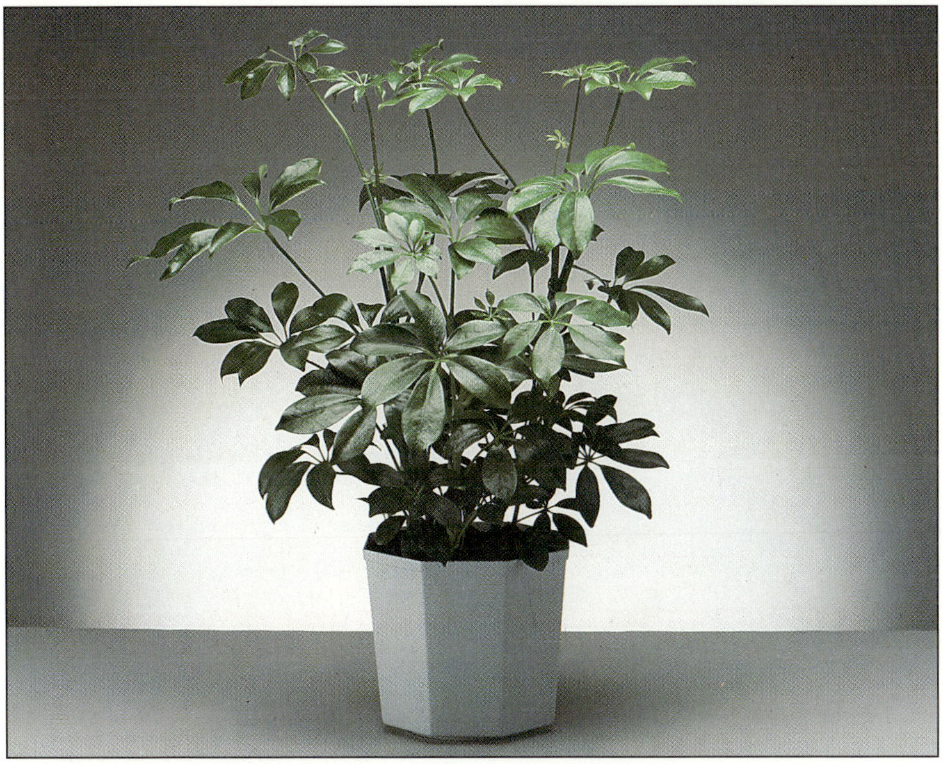

Parasol Plants will reach the ceiling unless, as here, you pinch out the stem tip.

Species

Heptapleurum arboricola, (also called *Schefflera arboricola*) the Parasol Plant from south-east Asia, is a fast-growing plant that can reach 8ft (2.4m). It has an unbranched main stem and leaves which are subdivided into at least seven leaflets, all carried at the tip of a leaf stem. The leaflets are thick and leathery. The variety *H.a.variegata, below,* has yellow-splashed leaflets. 'Hayata' has soft green leaflets with pointed tips. 'Geisha Girl' has dark green leaflets with rounded tips. This plant does not flower indoors.

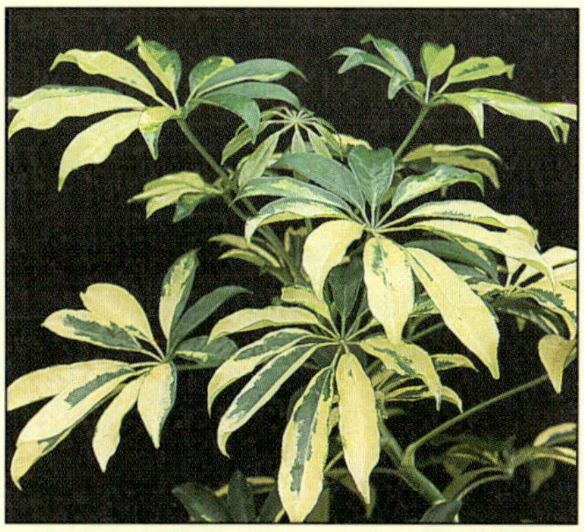

Propagation

Take a tip cutting 3-4in (8-10cm) long in the spring. Cut the stem tip just below a leaf joint then strip off the mature lower leaves. Dip the cut end into rooting powder and insert it into a 3in (7cm) pot filled with equal parts of peat-based potting compost and coarse sand. Put the pot into a clear plastic bag or propagator, and maintain a temperature of 65-75°F (18-24°C) in bright indirect light.

In three to four weeks new growth should be visible. Uncover the plant and water it so that the compost is kept barely moist, add a few drops of fertiliser to the water once a month. When two or three new leaves have grown and a fine mesh of roots has appeared on the surface of the compost, pot the plant on into a pot containing John Innes No 3 and treat the cutting as a mature plant.

Trouble Shooter

Greenfly can sometimes infect Heptapleurums. They cluster around the tip of the plant and distort new growth. Spray the plant with a spray containing pyrethrum.

Wilting, yellowing or dropping leaves are all signs of faulty watering. Remove yellow leaves and test the soil; if it feels wet, allow it to dry out and water it less often; if it feels dry then stand it under a shower for a few minutes and allow the excess water to drain away.

Hibiscus

Family name: **Malvaceae**

Common name: **Rose of China**

Care Straight forward	**Height** 5ft (1.5m)	**Flower** Spring and summer
Light Bright indirect	**Spread** 4ft (1.2m)	**Humidity** Mist spray regularly
Price Middle range	**Shape** Bushy	**Availability** Garden centres
Temp. Min 50°F (10°C)	Ideal 70°F (21°C)	Max 80°F (27°C)

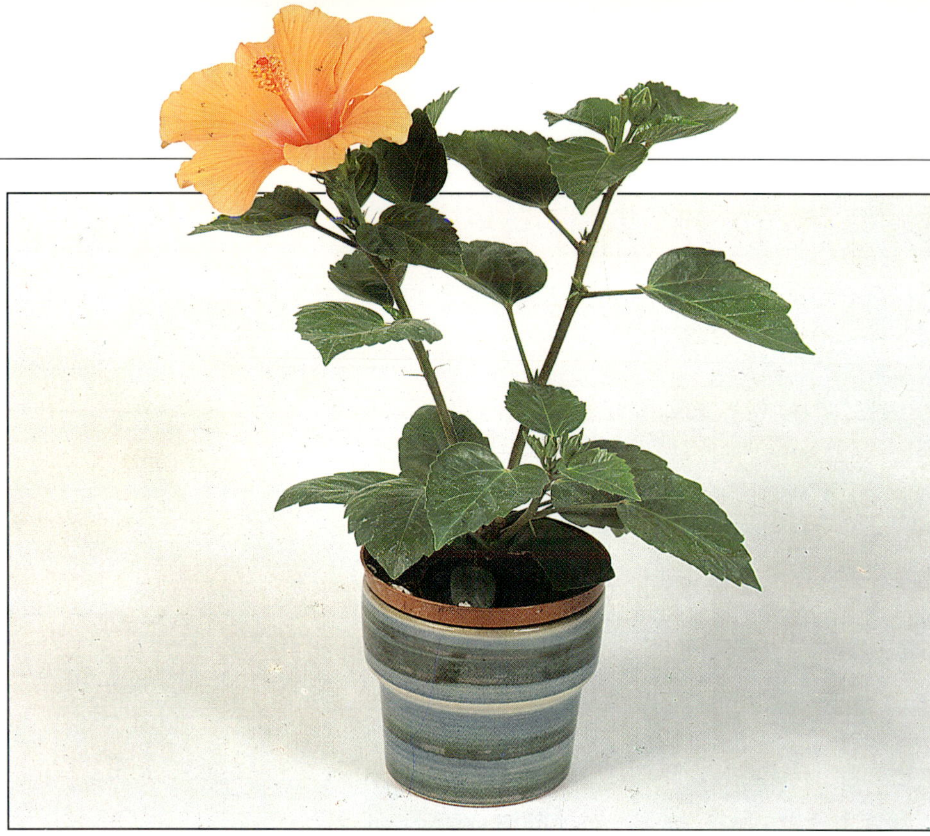

One of the many varieties of the Rose of China.

There are nearly 300 different types of Hibiscus and many of them make excellent houseplants. They are prized mainly for their glossy green leaves and exotic funnel-shaped blooms which come in a wide range of colours.

Hibiscus rosa-sinensis, from China, is the most widely grown as a pot plant. This evergreen, perennial shrub grows to about 5ft (1.5m) if not kept in check. The leaves are glossy green with serrated edges, and from spring to late summer the plant produces its large, papery, crimson flowers, 5in (13cm) across, with long golden stamens. While blooms last only a day or two, with proper care your plant will produce them in great numbers over its long flowering season. The bushy annual, *H.trionum*, bears delightful yellow or creamy-white flowers with bright maroon centres, and is another popular choice.

Spring and summer care

Perennial Hibiscus. Repot annually in March using John Innes No 3, potting on to a larger pot size if necessary. Prune your plant if it has become straggly or too large; it can be cut back hard to 6in (15cm) or so from the base without harming the plant. After potting, place your plant in good indirect light, but be sure to avoid direct sunlight. In summer, temperatures can safely rise to 75°F (24°C), but you'll need to ventilate the room if they rise much higher.

Water freely, especially in hot weather, to keep the roots constantly moist. Mist spray two or three times a week to provide humidity and keep the leaves free of dust. Every two or three weeks feed with a liquid fertiliser.

Annual Hibiscus. In May pot up seedlings individually into pots of John Innes No 1, then treat as for shrubby Hibiscus.

Species

Hibiscus rosa-sinensis, the Rose of China, comes from China and many other parts of Asia. This perennial shrubby plant grows to 5ft (1.5m) and has oval, dark green leaves. From June through to September deep crimson, funnel-shaped flowers, measuring 5 in (13cm) across, are produced in large numbers. Among the many popular varieties are 'Cooperi' with foliage variegated in green, white, pink and crimson, with small, brilliant scarlet flowers; 'Mist' bears single or double bright yellow flowers. 'Alba' has exquisite pure white blooms.

H.schizopetalus comes from Kenya and other parts of tropical Africa. This shrub has slender stems and glossy green leaves. 2in (5cm) wide, orangey-red flowers with backward curving petals appear from August to September.

H.trionum, *right* , from Africa, is an annual which makes a bushy plant about 2-3ft (0.6-0.9m) high. Throughout August and September it bears an abundance of yellow or creamy-white flowers with bright maroon centres.

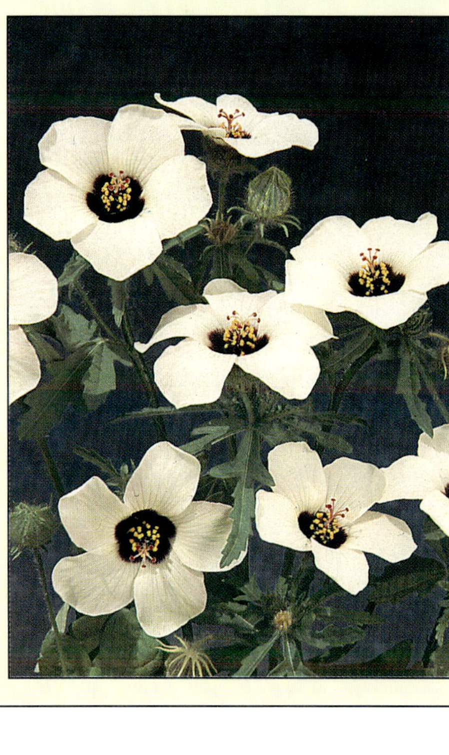

Autumn and winter care

Keep in very good, indirect light and try to keep the temperature at 50°F (10°C) or higher. Water about once a week — enough to prevent the soil from drying out. Mist spray occasionally with tepid water and keep your plant out of draughts.

Annual Hibiscus die after flowering.

Propagation

Perennial Hibiscus. Take 4in (10cm) heel cuttings any time between April and August. To do this, carefully pull a shoot from the parent plant with a small piece of the older stem attached. Trim the edges of the cutting and dip in a hormone rooting powder. Pot up singly in John Innes No 2 mixed with a little coarse sand. Keep the cuttings moist at a temperature of 70°F (21°C). Place the cuttings in a propagator or cover the pot with a polythene bag to keep the atmosphere humid, and place in good, indirect light. When rooted — in about three months — pot up as for mature plants, using 4in (10cm) pots.

Annual Hibiscus. Sow seeds thinly in March into trays of seed compost and germinate at a temperature of 55-61°F (13-16°C). When 3-4in (7-10cm) tall, pot up individually into pots of John Innes No 2 mixed with coarse sand. Treat them as mature perennial Hibiscus and they will grow quickly and flower the same year.

Hippeastrum

Family name: **Amaryllidaceae**

Common name: **Amaryllis**

Care Easy	**Height** 2ft (0.6m)	**Flower** Winter or spring
Light Bright	**Spread** 15-18in (38-45cm)	**Humidity** Mist spray in hot weather
Price Middle range	**Shape** Bulb	**Availability** Garden centres
Temp. Min 40°F (5°C)	Ideal 65°F (18°C)	Max 70°F (21°C)

These beautiful spring-flowering bulbs come originally from South America. Each year they flower, produce leaves and then become dormant.

Plant breeders have produced a huge number of Hippeastrum hybrids, mostly derived from *Hippeastrum vittatum.* They all have huge, stunning, trumpet-shaped flowers in white, pink,scarlet, dark red or orange, many with white stripes. Each bloom can be up to 5in (13cm) long and 6in (15cm) across at the tip. Two to four flowers are supported at the top of a hollow 2ft (0.6m) stem — one bulb producing one, or sometimes two, stems. The flowers last about four weeks then they die and their stems shrivel. The arching, strap-shaped leaves continue growing and make food for the bulb.

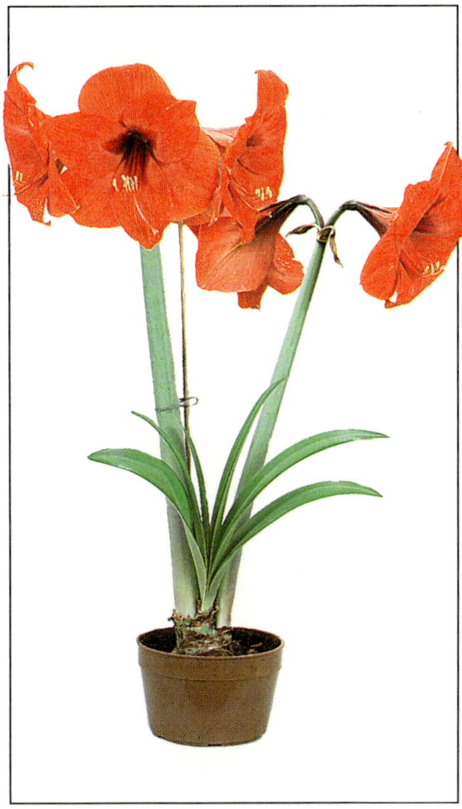

The flower stalk of this *Hippeastrum vittatum* has been staked for support.

Spring and summer care

Hippeastrums do not like to be disturbed, so repot fully-grown bulbs every three or four years in the spring using John Innes No 3 and adding plenty of drainage at the bottom of the pot. The bulb should be planted in a 6in (15cm) pot so that its neck and shoulders are out of the compost. Water the compost so that it is slightly damp. Also water those that have not been repotted to start them into growth.

Put the bulb in a dark, warm place — like an airing cupboard — for a few days. The flower bud should appear first; when this happens put the bulb in a bright lit position, preferably one which gets a few hours of direct sun during the day, and increase the watering, always allowing the surface of the compost to dry out between waterings.

The ideal temperature during the growing season is 65°F (18°C) — any higher and the flowering life will be shortened. During and after flowering add a liquid fertiliser to the water every two weeks. Dead-head by removing each flower once it is past its best — leave the flower to die back naturally.

Autumn and winter care

The bulbs need a rest period, usually in autumn or winter, if they are to flower again. Gradually stop feeding and watering completely. When the leaves have died back remove the dried foliage and keep the bulb in its pot in a light, frost free place.

Propagation

At repotting time small bulbs, which can be seen around the base of the parent bulb, can be detached with their roots from the main bulb. Treat in the same way as fully-grown bulbs, but pot them on every year until they are fully grown. They probably won't flower for two or three years.

Hippeastrums can be raised from seed, although flowers may not be produced for three to five years. Sow the seeds in spring in a mixture of equal parts of John Innes No 1 and coarse sand, just covering the seeds with the compost. Put the seed tray in a clear plastic bag, shade the tray from bright light and keep it at a temperature of 70°F (21°C). Once the seedlings are large enough to handle pot them up individually into 3in (7cm) pots. Do not give the seedlings a rest period, grow them continuously until they reach their flowering size, potting them on each spring, then treat them as mature plants.

Trouble Shooter

These bulbs are generally trouble-free and very easy to look after. Sometimes mealy bug infests the plant. Remove these fluffy white patches with a brush dipped in methylated spirit. Failure to flower is usually due to poor treatment after flowering the previous season.

Make sure the plant is watered and fed regularly after flowering and that the leaves get plenty of bright light.

Species

Hippeastrum vittatum is often mistakenly called Amaryllis - mistakenly since the true Amaryllis belongs to a completely different group of plants. *H.vittatum* has 2ft (0.6m) strap-shaped leaves and large flowers carried on 1-2ft (0.3-0.6m) stems. The flowers are trumpet-shaped and 6in (15cm) across at the tip, and the petals are white with purple stripes. Very many hybrids have been developed from this species: 'Red Lion' is a giant red-flowered variety; 'White Lady' has white flowers tinged with green on the inside; 'Picotee' has a white flower with pink-edged petals; 'Minerva' has white flowers veined with red. Shades of orange and pink are also available.

H.puniceum (also called *H.equestre*), *right*, comes from the West Indies. It has a 2ft (0.6m) flowering stem which carries two to three trumpet-shaped flowers of pinkish-red.

H.rutilum from southern Brazil is slightly smaller than the other species, it is 1ft (0.3m) high with bright red flowers slightly tinged with green.

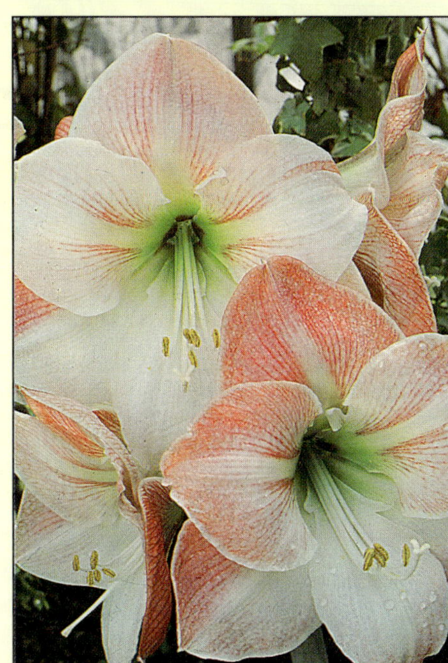

Howea

Family name: **Palmae**

Common names: **Kentia Palm, Sentry Palm**

Care Easy	**Height** 10ft (3m)	**Flower** Rarely
Light Bright	**Spread** 10ft (3m)	**Humidity** Mist spray in hot weather
Price Expensive	**Shape** Arching	**Availability** Garden centres

Temp. Min 55°F (13°C) Ideal 70°F (21°C) Max 80°F (27°C)

These popular palms owe their family name to their original home on Lord Howe Island in the South Pacific, between Australia and New Zealand.

The Kentia Palm (*Howea forsteriana*) is probably the best of all palms for easy culture — attractive and elegant, it's happy in a vast range of light conditions and will show itself to advantage even without much care or attention. It will grow up to about 10ft (3m) tall indoors and can spread to as much as 10ft (3m), too — so when fully grown it will take up a lot of room.

The very similar Sentry Palm (*H.belmoreana*) has upright growth and its fronds are more arching. It will reach the same height as the Kentia Palm, but its spread is not likely to be more than about 6ft (1.8m). Apart from this difference in the way they grow, the appearance of the two species is very similar — they both have single stems and dark green, arching fronds divided at their tips into leaflets about 1½in (3.7cm) wide and up to 2ft (0.6m) long.

Both palms are fairly slow growers (the Kentia a little quicker than the Sentry), and it will take several years to establish a really good specimen plant if you begin with a small one. But during this time they will provide you with very attractive and interesting foliage plants, whose main advantage is that they are very easy to care for. They are happy in virtually any position from direct sun to shade, though if you have them in a really shady place, it's best to move them into a sunny location for a couple of hours every other day. The ideal position for them indoors is good indirect sunlight, but they are remarkably tolerant. In the hottest months they will benefit from standing outdoors in a bright position, but out of direct sunlight.

These palms are quite attractive to pests, so you should take preventive action (see Trouble Shooter). To get rid of dust, mist spray them with tepid water from time to time, or stand them outdoors during a light shower in summer. Don't ever use a commercial product for cleaning or shining the leaves — this may damage the foliage irrevocably.

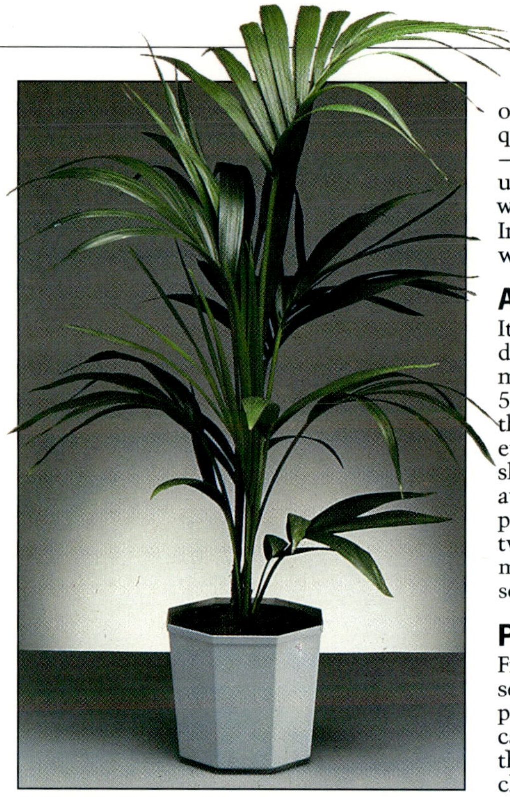

A Kentia Palm adds elegance and style to any room — yet it's easy to care for.

Spring and summer care

Repotting will probably be necessary every two to three years, using one size bigger pot each time. Repot in early spring, and try not to disturb the root system. Use John Innes No 2 and add some peat and extra sand to make it more porous — and make sure the pot or tub has good drainage holes.

During spring and summer, temperatures of 70-75° (21-24°C) are ideal. Water quite frequently but never let the pot stand in water — if anything, these palms prefer to be underwatered rather than overwatered. Feed with a liquid fertiliser every fortnight or so. In high summer spray the plants regularly with tepid water to provide humidity.

Autumn and winter care

It isn't a good idea to let the temperature drop below 60°F (15°C) even in the coldest months. The Kentia Palm might just tolerate 50°F (10°C), but the higher the temperature the better. Give a really bright location wherever possible to keep the foliage healthy and shiny. Good air circulation is required, but avoid cold draughts at all costs. If 60°F (15°C) plus is maintained then water palms every two to three weeks to keep the compost just moist, and mist spray them once a week or so, otherwise keep them on the dry side.

Propagation

From late February to early April sow fresh seeds about 1in (2.5cm) deep in the usual potting mixture (see Spring and summer care), but with even more sand added. Keep the compost moist and use a propagator or a clear plastic bag to help keep the temperature at 80-85°F (27-30°C). Be sure to keep the seed tray out of full sun. Germination can be a little erratic, but when small leaves begin to appear, give some fresh air by opening the vents on your propagator. When the seedlings are big enough to handle, pot them separately in the recommended compost mixture. Howea seeds are very slow-growing, so patience is essential — it could take up to six years to grow a sizeable palm from seed!

Species

Howea forsteriana, the Kentia Palm, has graceful, arching foliage with waxy-green, leathery leaflets. The leafstalks are bare up to 3ft (0.9m) tall, then they support fronds with leaflets that droop from either side of the stem, spaced along it at intervals of about 1in (2.5cm). These stems arch over until they are almost horizontal — it's this characteristic that gives the species its wide spread. In its natural habitat this palm can reach a height of 50ft (15m), but in cultivation it is usually only 8-10ft (2.4-3m) tall. On mature specimens, flowers and fruits form in clusters though this rarely happens when this plant is grown indoors.

H.belmoreana, the Sentry Palm, is rather upright and handsome, and can grow up to 25ft (7.5m) in its natural habitat. It has fronds of narrow leaflets, each very delicately pointed. They grow very close together and give the foliage a leafy, graceful and arching appearance. The stalks are usually reddish-tinted. As the plant ages, its stem forms a short trunk. Like the Kentia Palm, flowers and fruits are rarely produced.

Trouble Shooter

Brown leaves, especially at the top, may be due to overwatering, lack of humidity or cold draughts; let the compost dry out and reduce watering, mist spray regularly and make sure the plant is kept out of draughts, especially in winter. If new growth fails to appear during the growing season, the plant probably needs repotting or isn't getting enough nutrition; repot in spring to a container one size bigger, and feed every couple of weeks during the growing season.

Whitish-brown bumps on the leaves, looking like warts, are scale insects; wipe them off with a small brush dipped in methylated spirit. Silvering or blackening of the leaves is a sign of thrips; tiny pinky-red coloured insects are red spider mite — both of these will respond to spraying with a systemic dimethoate-based insecticide, and in the case of red spider mite the humidity should be increased. It's a good idea in any case to use a systemic insecticide as a deterrent every three months during spring and summer.

Hoya

Family name: **Asclepiadaceae**

Common name:
Miniature Wax Plant, Wax Plant

Care Easy	**Height** 1ft (0.3m)	**Flower** Summer
Light Bright indirect	**Spread** 1ft (0.3m)	**Humidity** Mist spray regularly
Price Middle range	**Shape** Trailing	**Availability** Garden centres
Temp. Min 50°F (10°C)	Ideal 70°F (21°C)	Max 80°F (27°C)

This enormous group of plants has something like 200 different species. Most of them are climbers, a few are bushy and shrub-like and a few are trailers. Relatively trouble-free, they have most attractive star-shaped waxy flowers, which appear every year and last for the whole summer.

The Miniature Wax Plant (*Hoya bella*) has dark green, pointed oval leaves and fragrant flowers that grow in clusters of eight to ten. The flowers are waxy-white with a crimson-purple centre. The plant has upright growth until it is about 1ft (0.3m) tall, and then trails, making it a very pretty choice for a hanging basket. Its title *'bella'* means beautiful and that exactly sums it up!

The Wax Plant (*H.carnosa*), originally from China and Australia, is a fast-growing climber with oval, glossy leaves and clusters of very fragrant pinkish-white flowers, also with a red centre. The flower clusters are much bigger than those of the Miniature Wax Plant, with up to 20 blooms on each. The leaves, too, are bigger, up to 3in (7cm) long. Its vigorous stems — which can grow up to 15ft (4.5m) long — must be attached to some form of support, such as a stake or a trellis.

Spring and summer care

If your plant has outgrown its pot, pot on in March, using John Innes No 3. Don't repot, however, unless your plant is very cramped.

Temperatures in summer may rise to 75-80°F (24-27°C), provided the plant is in a bright, but not directly sunny position.

This is the main growing season, so water very regularly, making sure you never let the compost dry out (this is particularly important for the Miniature Wax Plant). Don't allow your plant to become waterlogged. Provide humidity by mist spraying every week, or daily in very hot weather, and make sure there is good air circulation. Add liquid fertiliser to the water every three to four weeks from April to September.

Autumn and winter care

Give good light at all times, but not full sun. The temperature should not drop below 50°F (10°C). Water very occasionally — just enough to keep the compost from drying out completely. Provide good air circulation but take care to avoid draughts. Mist spray once a week both for humidity and to keep the leaves clean and free of dust.

Propagation

Sow seeds in a peat-based compost or John Innes No 1 in late March or early April. Keep them in a propagator at 75°F (24°C) in the shade, and keep the compost moist. When the seedlings begin to appear, uncover them, then when they're big enough to handle transfer them to individual pots.

Take stem cuttings in June. Snip the stems just below a leaf joint, dip the ends in a rooting powder, and set them in a mixture of equal parts of John Innes No 3 and coarse sand. Keep them in a propagator at 75°F (24°C) until they show signs of new growth, which will normally be in six to eight weeks, then treat them as mature plants.

Buying Guide

A few years ago only a couple of Hoya species were easily available — now there are many more. You can get them from good garden centres or, for more variety, from specialist nurseries.

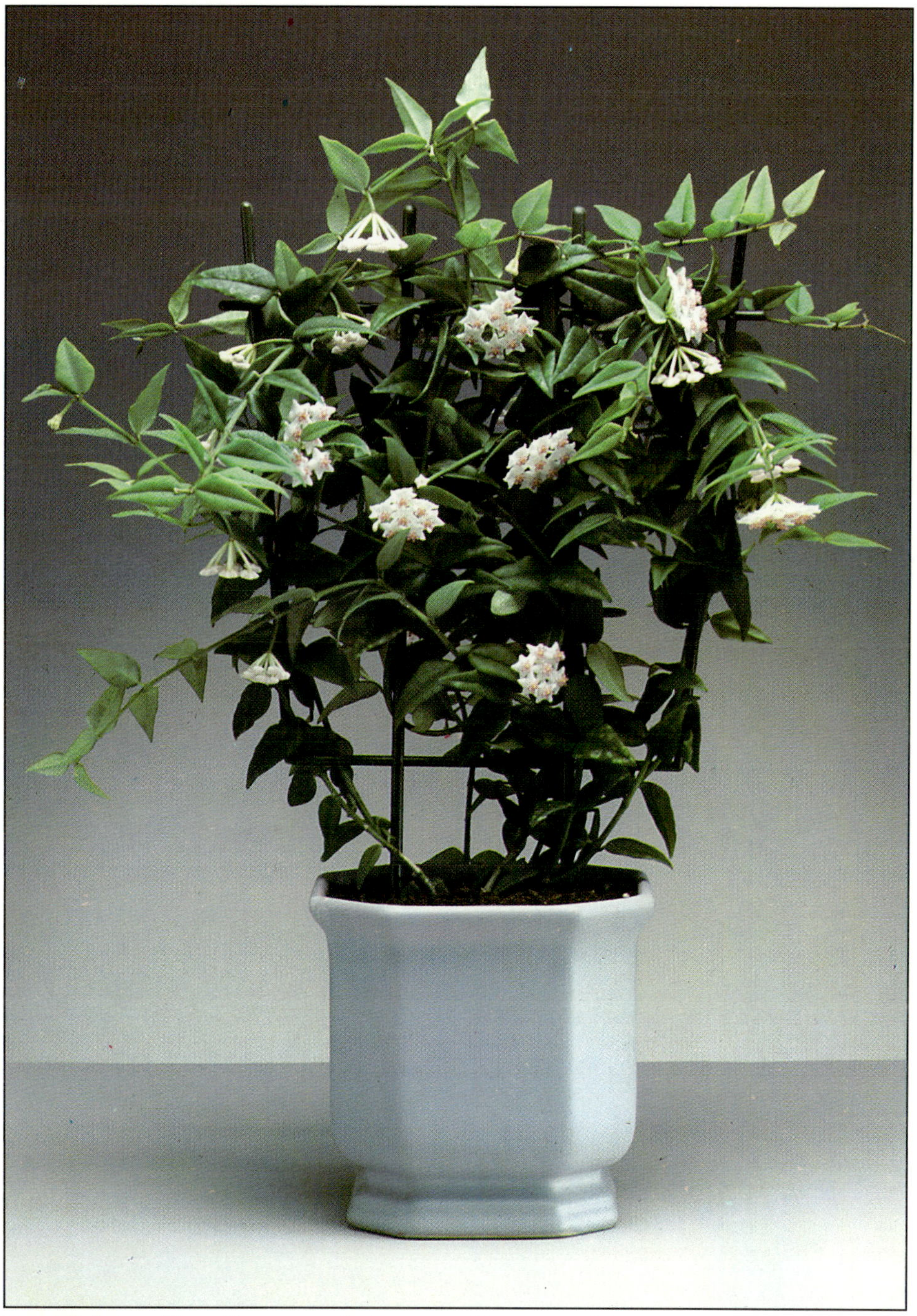

The Miniature Wax Plant can climb up a trellis — or trail from a hanging basket.

Species

***Hoya bella**, right,* the Miniature Wax Plant, is a trailing plant native of India, Burma and Indonesia. It has slightly fleshy leaves, and small, waxy, white summer flowers with red centres, growing in clusters of eight to ten. The leaves are oval and grey-green, about ½in (13mm) wide and 1in (2.5cm) long.

H.carnosa, the Wax Plant, has bigger oval leaves, 1in (2.5cm) wide and 3in (7cm) long, dark green and glossy. Flowers are produced any time from May until September. There are up to 30 flowers in each cluster, whitish-pink with a red centre, and sweetly fragrant. A fast-growing climbing plant, it needs the support of canes or a trellis. Varieties include 'Variegata', *below right,* with green leaves broadly marked with creamy-yellow or pink along the margins, and 'Exotica', whose leaves are light and dark green with centres blotched with deep yellow and pink. The flowers of both these are similar to the species. Another very attractive variety is 'Compacta', with leaves that are peculiarly curled and slightly smaller than those of the species; its growth is dense and compact, as its name suggests.

***H.multiflora,** below left,* is from the Malacca Straits, and can be either climbing or compact and bushy. The leaves are dark green and leathery, and the flowers, produced in summer, are straw-coloured with a brown centre. There are often as many as 25 flowers to a cluster.

H.purpureo-fusca, Jungle Garden, is from Malaysia and Indonesia and is a fast-growing climber. Its leaves are similar to those of *H.carnosa,* but slightly longer and irregularly splashed with silver. Its flower clusters appear in summer; they are most attractive — maroon or purple, finely edged with white and with pinkish-white centres.

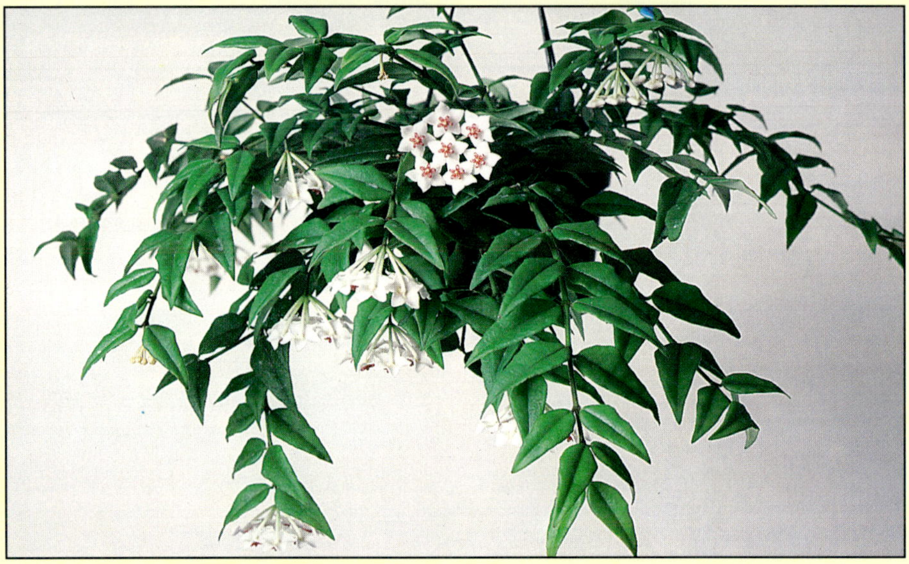

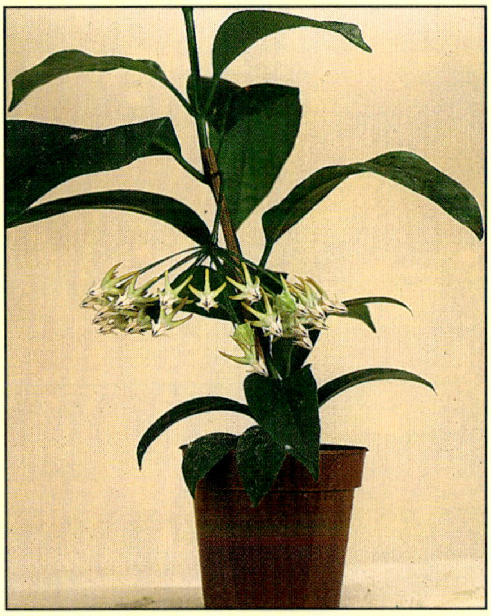

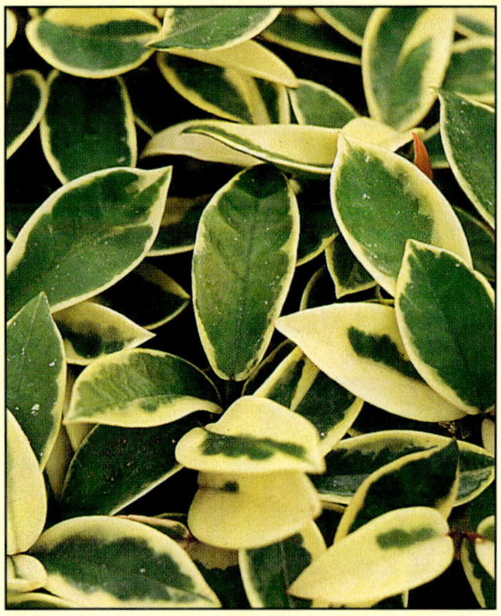

Trouble Shooter

Hoyas are, happily, free from most problems. Yellowish leaves mean overwatering; let the compost dry out and reduce watering in the future. Brown, scorched foliage may result from direct sun; give a bright position, but not direct sun, and never mist spray during the heat of the day. Wilting or falling leaves are a sign of inadequate watering; make sure the compost is always moist in the summer. White, fluffy-looking mealy bug may be brushed off with a small brush dipped in methylated spirit.

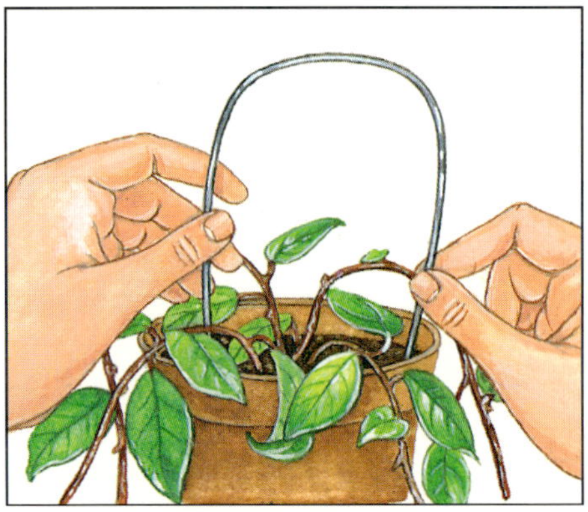

For an attractive leafy mound, train your Hoya over a wire hoop. Carefully wind the stems around the wire.

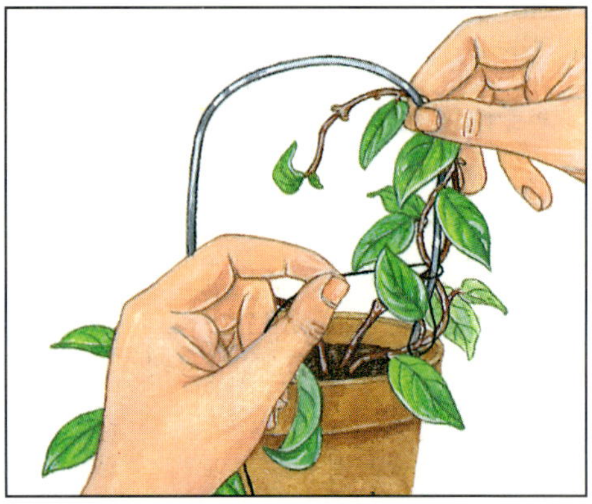

To keep the stems in position, use soft twine to tie them to their support — take care not to tie too tightly.

Hyacinthus

Family name: **Liliaceae**

Common name: **Hyacinth**

Care Easy	**Height** 9-12in	**Flower** Winter or Spring
Light Bright	**Spread** 6in	**Humidity** Not necessary
Price Cheap	**Shape** Bulb	**Availability** Common
Temp. Min 40°F (5°C)	Ideal 65°F (18°C)	Max 70°F (21°C)

These ever-popular bulbs are a delight in the garden in spring — and, if you buy specially treated bulbs for forcing, their wonderful scent and pretty pastel colours can bring a touch of cheer indoors to the last days of winter, too.

The species from which most varieties have been bred is *Hyacinthus orientalis*, a plant which is now, in fact, rarely grown. A group of *H.orientalis* hybrids known as the Dutch Hyacinths have come to represent the species. They have large flowerheads, about 4-6in (10-15cm) long, and come in a wide range of colours.

Spring and summer care

The type of bulbs you use will make a difference to their flowering season. If you pot up bulbs suitable for outdoor use your Hyacinths will flower in spring — their usual flowering time. If you want winter flowers you'll need to buy bulbs which have been prepared specially for forcing. Whichever type you choose, Hyacinth bulbs can only be made to flower successfully once indoors, so you'll need to buy new bulbs each year. However, there's no need to throw away your bulbs after they have flowered inside; planted outside, 6in (15cm) deep, they'll flower again year after year.

Autumn and winter care

For flowers at Christmas, plant fresh prepared bulbs in September using bulb fibre or John Innes No 2. For flowers in May, plant unprepared bulbs in January. You can plant into a bowl with no drainage holes, provided that you take care when watering not to waterlog the soil. Put a layer of compost in the bottom of the container and place bulbs on the compost — quite close together, so that they are almost touching. Fill the gaps around the bulbs with compost and leave the tops of the bulbs just protruding out of the surface of the compost. Put the bowl or pot of bulbs somewhere cool, dark and damp — in a box or outside — and bury the container under 6in (15cm) of peat. When the leaf tips appear on the surface of the peat, move the bulbs to a bright position with a temperature of about 50°F (10°C), gradually rising to about 65°F (18°C). Once the bulbs are inside, water them regularly.

Buying Guide

Buy bulbs marked 'prepared' for early flowering indoors. Make sure the bulbs feel firm and are still dormant. When planning to grow several bulbs in one container, it's wise to choose the same variety, since this ensures that they will appear together.

Hyacinth bulbs can be made to flower when grown in specially designed glass jars filled with water. Fill the container so that the base of the bulb is just in the water. Keep the bulb in a dark cool place until the bulb's leaves are about 1in (2.5cm) long, then bring them into the light and normal room temperatures. Once the roots have formed there is no need to top up the water level to meet the base of the bulb, just ensure that the roots are always covered. Bulbs forced into flower in this way are unlikely to flower again.

Species

Hyacinthus orientalis, from eastern Europe and western Asia originally, has been the subject of much attention by the plant breeders. The true species is now rarely available, instead there are numerous varieties of Dutch Hyacinths in many shades — white, yellow, pink, red, mauve and blue. The flowerheads are 4-6in (10-15cm) long, and carried on a short 4in (10cm) stem. They are strongly scented and appear in the spring, or earlier when forced. 'Jan bos' is a bright red variety; 'Delf Blue' is pale blue; 'City of Haarlem' is cream-coloured. Another group of hybrids are the Roman Hyacinths, *H.o.albulus*. They are very similar to the Dutch type but slightly smaller — up to 6in (15cm) high — and available in white, pink or blue. They can also be made to flower between December and May.

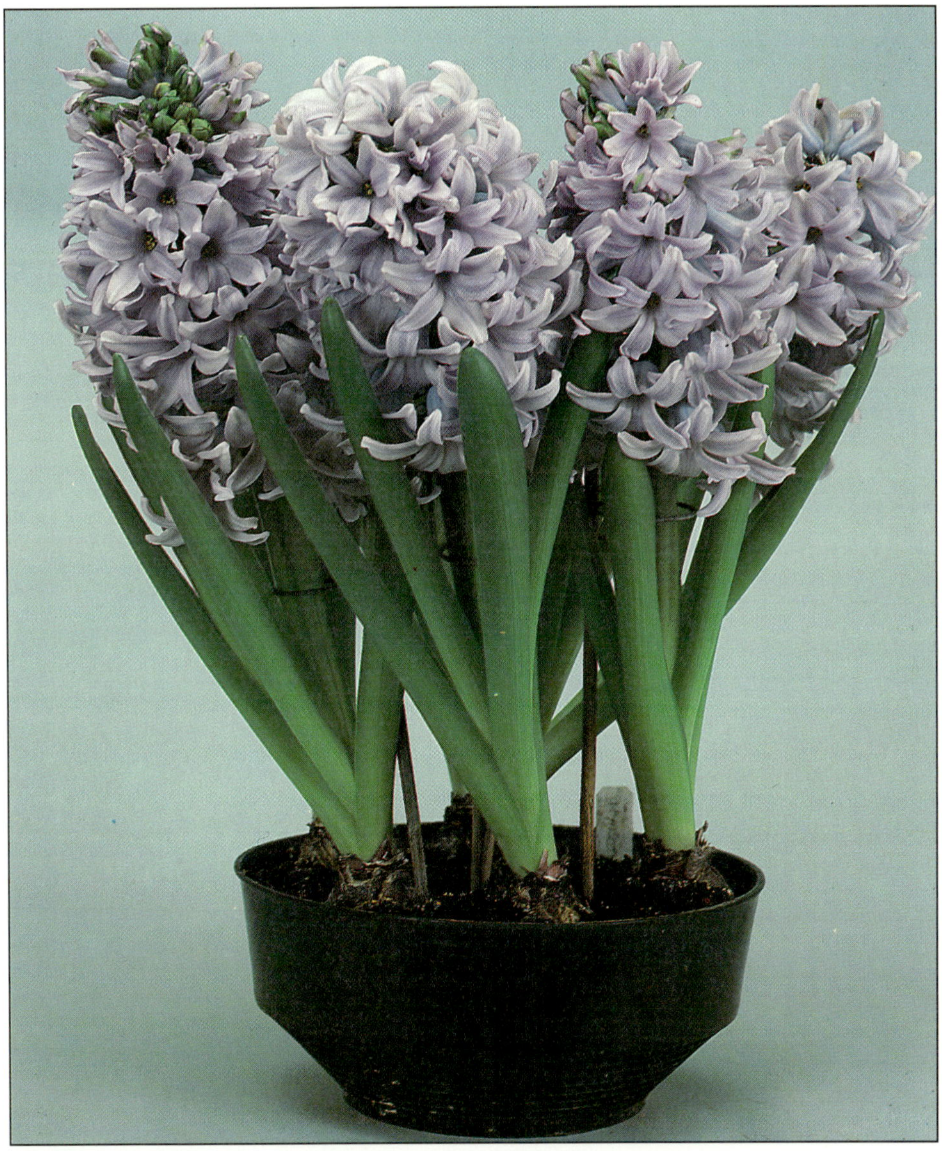

Hyacinth varieties with very large flowerheads may need staking.

Hydrangea

Family name: **Hydrangeaceae**

Common name: **Hydrangea**

Care Easy	**Height** 1-2ft (0.3-0.6m)	**Flower** Spring
Light Bright indirect	**Spread** 1-2ft (0.3-0.6m)	**Humidity** Regular mist spray
Price Cheap	**Shape** Bushy	**Availability** Garden centres

Temp. Min 40°F (5°C) — Ideal 60°F (15°C) — Max 70°F (21°C)

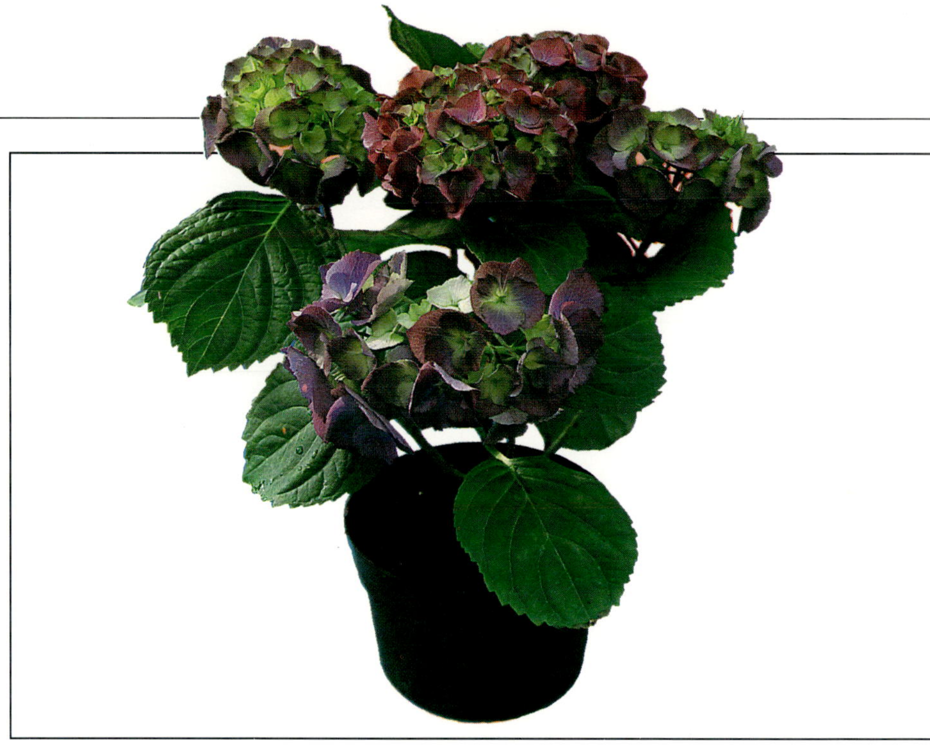

As a houseplant, a Hydrangea makes a delightful, small, flowering bush.

These most attractive and popular plants form a group of about 80 species, native to Asia and central and south America.

Hydrangea macrophylla, from the Himalayas and China, is the species best suited to growing indoors. In its natural habitat it reaches over 6ft (1.8m), but neat low-growing plants have been bred which are ideal as houseplants. A framework of short woody stems supports large flower heads, up to 9in (23cm) across, made up of delightful small flowers in white, pink, red, purple or blue.

Although Hydrangeas are often planted outside or even thrown away after flowering, with care they can be carried over to provide a spring display year after year.

Spring and summer care

For the best results, keep your plant cool, especially during flowering. This will come to an abrupt end if temperatures rise above 70°F (21°C). Aim for a temperature of not more than 60°F (15°C) and the blooms should last six weeks or more. Give your hydrangeas good bright light, but avoid direct sunlight.

It's most important to keep the compost moist at all times; it must never be allowed to dry out. Make sure your plant gets thorough watering, every day if necessary, from spring to autumn. Add a liquid fertiliser to the water once a week during flowering. A regular mist spray will help to extend the flowering period and encourage new growth.

Ideally, when the flowers are past their best, your plant should be moved outdoors for the rest of the summer; stand it in as sheltered a spot as you can, and continue to water and feed as above.

Autumn and winter care

Towards the end of September, as it loses its leaves, your plant should be cut well back. Prune all of the shoots, to leave the lowest pair of buds on each stem. After pruning, repot your plant into fresh compost. Hydrangeas always grow best in lime-free compost. The colour of blue-flowered varieties can be enhanced by adding a proprietary bluing compound to the compost when repotting. Some people add limestone to the compost of pink-flowered hydrangeas to improve the colour, but this is not recommended.

Give the plant a winter rest, in a cold but frost-free room — temperatures should not fall below 45°F (7°C). Water sparingly throughout this dormant period, so the soil is barely moist. Around the end of January, move to a brighter, warmer room — about 55°F (13°C) — and increase watering.

Propagation

Take 5-6in (13-15cm) cuttings from the tips of the stems in August or September, after flowering. Dip the cut end into rooting hormone and set in a mixture of peat and sand. When rooted, pot the cuttings individually into 3in (7cm) pots of John Innes No 2 and pot on into larger containers as they grow. Keep moist and shaded, and grow on at a temperature of 60-65°F (15-18°C), for successful flowering plants in the spring.

Trouble Shooter

Leaves turning brown at the edges and starting to curl under is a sure sign of underwatering; keep the soil always nicely moist. If it gets too dry, the whole plant will shrivel up — immersing the pot in water should revive it.

Use a systemic dimethoate-based insecticide once a month during the growing season to deter pests.

Buying Guide

Plants are best bought in the spring when in tight bud. Avoid those plants which look weak or straggly, or have discoloured foliage.

Species

Hydrangea macrophylla is the species most commonly grown as a houseplant. A deciduous flowering shrub, it is the parent of many beautiful varieties that do very well indoors. These compact, rounded plants, usually 1-2ft (30-60cm) high and wide, carry shiny, light-green oval leaves 4-6in (10-15cm) long, and flowers in shades from pink to blue or in white, which appear in spring and early summer. The varieties are divided into two groups: Hortensias, sometimes called Mop Heads, have large, showy, rounded flower heads, each measuring 6-8in (15-20cm) across and made up of a mass of small flowers; and Lacecaps, *right*, with rather flat, open flower heads, 4-6in (10-15cm) across, of numerous unopened buds, surrounded by large, wide-open flowers, giving a very pretty, lacy effect.

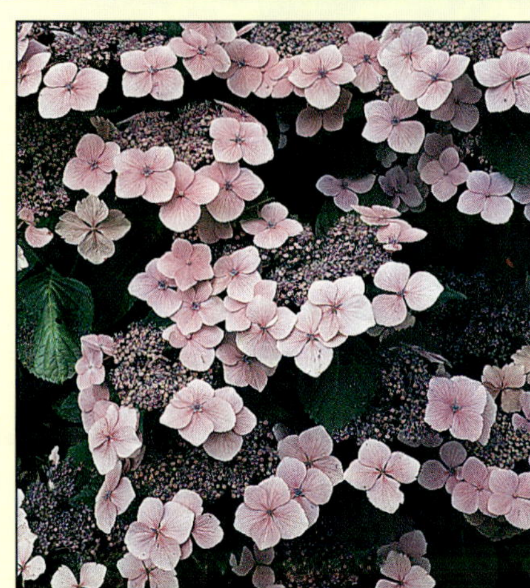

Hypocyrta

Family name: **Gesneriaceae**

Common name:
Clog Plant

Care Straight forward	**Height** 6-8in (15-20cm)	**Flower** Summer
Light Bright indirect	**Spread** 6in (15cm)	**Humidity** Regular mist spray
Price Middle range	**Shape** Arching	**Availability** Garden centres
Temp. Min 55°F (13°C)	Ideal 65°F (18°C)	Max 75°F (24°C)

Among this small group of plants from central and south America, some are creepers which, in their native forests clamber over moss-covered trees, rooting themselves as they grow; others are quite small, bushy plants. All of them, though, have unusual-looking and long-lasting flowers with a pouch-like structure on the underside.

The best known houseplant species is *Hypocyrta glabra*. In its natural habitat it is a semi-trailing plant, so its arching branches make it an ideal choice for hanging baskets — its bright orange flowers peeping out from beneath glossy, dark green foliage.

Spring and summer care

Repot your plant each spring — into a bigger pot if its roots are encircling the root ball inside the pot. Use a peat-based compost with a little coarse sand added.

Temperatures of about 65-70°F (18-21°C) are ideal. Always keep the compost moist, so during hot weather you'll need to water more often — but don't let the pot stand in water for long periods. A few drops of fertiliser in the water every two weeks from April to October will help prolong the flowering season. Mist spray every few days, ideally with rainwater. Hypocyrta will tolerate some shade and a certain amount of direct sun but your plant will grow best in a position that gets bright indirect light.

Autumn and winter care

Maintain a minimum temperature of 55°F (13°C), stop using a fertiliser and reduce the watering to keep the compost only just moist. Mist spray occasionally — especially if the temperature rises. Ideally, keep your plant in bright indirect light.

Propagation

Take 3-4 in (7-10cm) stem tip cuttings in March or April. Treat the cut ends with rooting hormone and then insert into a peat-based potting compost with a little sharp sand added. Keep the temperature at a steady 65-70°F (18-21°C) and make sure the compost is always moist but not sodden. If you put the cuttings in a plastic bag or propagator, be sure to remove the cover for a few minutes every day to give the plants some fresh air. As soon as growth is apparent, pot up the cuttings individually and treat them as mature plants.

Buying Guide

Look for bushy plants rather than unbranching lanky ones. It's best to buy early in the season — ideally in April — so you can enjoy the whole flowering season.

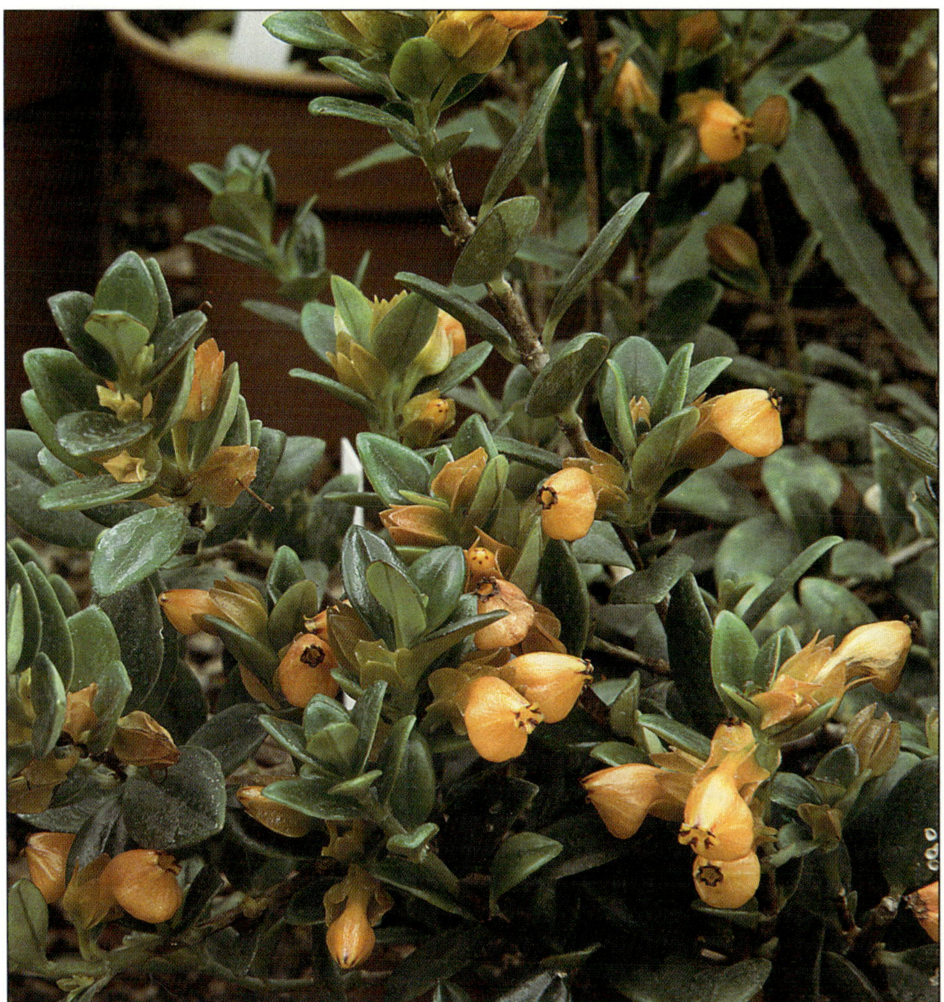

The unusual, lobed flowers of *Hypocyrta glabra* peeping from under the leaves.

Trouble Shooter

Withered leaves are a sign of underwatering — especially if the plant has been exposed to direct sun.

Leaves lose their lustre if the atmosphere is too dry — these plants need regular mist spraying — especially in hot weather. A humid atmosphere will also help to deter red spider mite — but if they do attack your plant, spray with a malathion-based insecticide.

Brown leaves are a sign of overwatering — the compost should be moist and not sodden.

Species

Hypocyrta glabra, the Clog Plant, *left,* is a bushy plant with arching branches and glossy oval-shaped dark green leaves. It has bright orange, lobed flowers. The flowering season lasts from April until October.

H.nummularia, from Central America, is a creeping plant with branching stems covered with red hairs. The leaves are dark green and hairy, oval-shaped with scalloped edges. The summer flowers are red with yellow lobes.

H.teuscheri, from Ecuador, is a creeping plant. It has hairy stems, and pale green leaves with white veining and maroon on the underside. The flowers are bright yellow with red lobes and appear in summer.

Hypoestes

Family name: **Acanthaceae**

Common names:
Freckle Face/Polka Dot Plant

Care Easy	**Height** 1-2ft (0.3-0.6m)	**Flower** Insignificant
Light Bright	**Spread** 1-2ft (0.3-0.6m)	**Humidity** Regular mist spray
Price Cheap	**Shape** Bushy	**Availability** Garden centres
Temp. Min 60°F (15°C)	Ideal 70°F (21°C)	Max 80°F (27°C)

These small evergreen shrubs are mostly grown for their attractive patterned leaves. Of the few Hypoestes suited to growing indoors, the favourite is *Hypoestes sanguinolenta*, from Madagascar, with its attractive, pink-freckled leaves. Its slightly trailing shapes make this plant particularly useful for hanging baskets or wall pots.

Spring and summer care

Repot each year in early spring using John Innes No 2 or 3, transferring the plant to a larger pot if its roots appear congested. After potting, prune back any straggly stems.

The ideal summer temperature is about 70°F (21°C), but it can rise higher without damaging the plant as long as you give extra water. During the spring and summer the compost should feel moist at all times. Give a weak liquid feed every three weeks, using only half the dose recommended on the bottle. Hypoestes like a humid atmosphere so stand your plant in bowl of damp pebbles and mist spray regularly.

Flowers sometimes appear in summer; unless you find them attractive, pinch them out since they will only deprive the leaves of nutrients.

Keep your plant in a very bright, well-lit position but out of direct sun.

Autumn and winter care

These plants do not like cold temperatures and draughts in particular should be avoided. Do not let the temperature fall below 60°F (15°C) and remember that the compost should not be allowed to dry out. Your plant will appreciate regular mist spraying.

Propagation

Take 3in (8cm) stem tip cuttings in spring. Set the cut end into a pot of John Innes No 1 mixed with a small amount of coarse sand. Put the pot into a propagator or plastic bag and maintain a steady temperature of 70-75°F (21-24°C) in a shaded position. Keep the soil moist but not sodden. Once growth is visible, pot up the cuttings individually or, for a dense mound of foliage, plant three rooted cuttings 6in (15cm) apart in the same container.

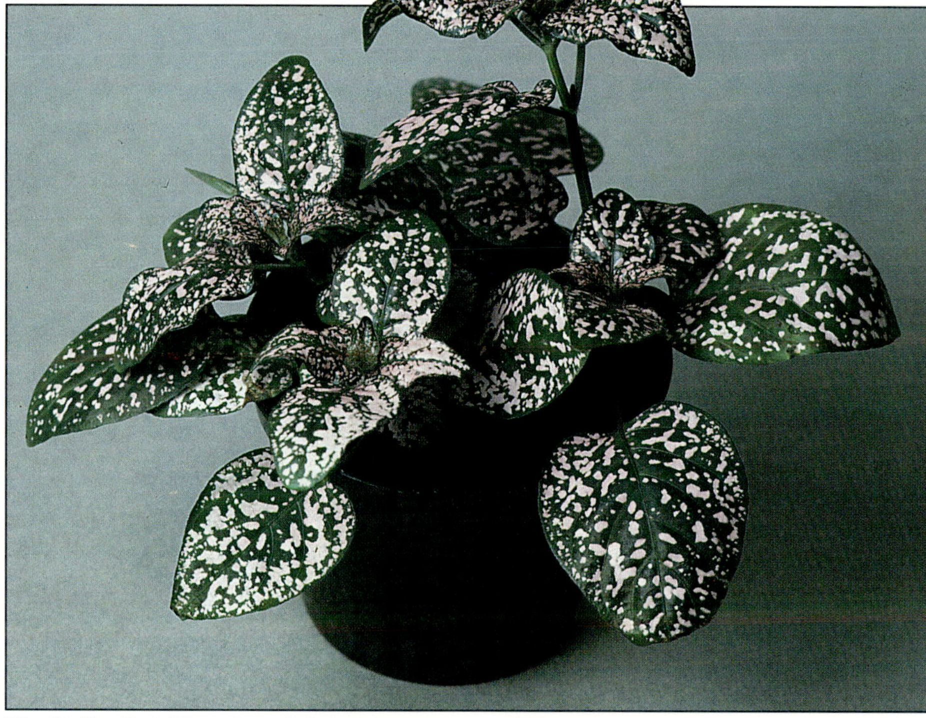

The Polka Dot Plant is a delightful, easy-going little plant.

Buying Guide

Always buy a small plant — not only are they cheaper but, when brought home and subjected to different growing conditions, a young plant will adapt more quickly to the change. Look for plenty of young healthy leaves.

Trouble Shooter

If leaves lose their patterning, give the plant more light. Wilting leaves are a sign of chilling, over- or underwatering; check for draughts and adjust watering. Mealy bugs and scale insects can both be removed with a brush dipped in methylated spirit.

Species

Hypoestes sanguinolenta (sometimes called *H.rotundifolia*), Freckle Face or the Polka Dot Plant, is a low-growing, slightly trailing bush which can grow to 2ft (0.6m) as a houseplant. It has dark green, downy leaves, marked and speckled in rosy-pink. 'Pink Splash' has more and lighter markings of pale pink. Insignificant pale lilac flowers appear in summer.

H.aristata (or *H.antennifera*), *right*, the Ribbon Bush from Natal, is a more upright growing species. A rounded shrub, growing to about 3ft (0.9m) as a houseplant, it has oval leaves emerging usually in groups of three at the same point along the stems. This plant has attractive mauve flowers in summer.

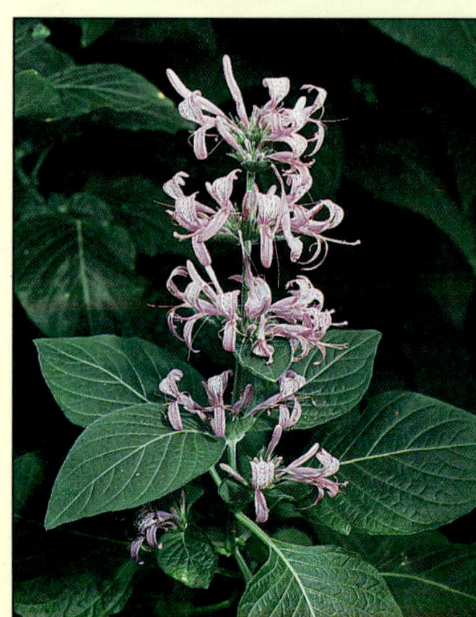

H.taeniata, a forest plant from Madagascar, is similar to *H. aristata* but it has dark pink autumn flowers that are held above the plain green leaves.

Impatiens

Family name: **Balsaminaceae**

Common name:
Busy Lizzie

Care Easy	**Height** 1-2ft (0.3-0.6m)	**Flower** Summer
Light Bright	**Spread** 1-2ft (0.3-0.6m)	**Humidity** Occasional mist spray
Price Cheap	**Shape** Bushy	**Availability** Common
Temp. Min 55°F (13°C)	Ideal 65°F (18°C)	Max 75°F (24°C)

These delightful-looking plants really deserve their popularity; easy to care for, quick to mature and trouble free, they will more than reward you for your efforts, with masses of colourful flowers right through the summer.

By far the most common Impatiens on offer are the hybrid strains of *Impatiens wallerana* — more commonly known as Busy Lizzie. The true species is rarely available as a houseplant. It comes from tropical east Africa and is taller than its hybrids and has bright red flowers. The variegated form of *I.wallerana* is occasionally sold, though even this one has been superseded by variegated hybrids. It has large scarlet flowers and green leaves edged with white. The hybrids come in a wide range of flower and leaf types; flower colours range from white, through pinks and oranges to bright scarlets and dark purples; striped ones are available too. Blooms can be quite simple with a single layer of petals or have a frilly appearance with several layers. Leaves also vary in shape and colour; they can be oval or heart-shaped, plain or variegated, pale green, dark green or bronze-coloured.

Spring and summer care

Impatiens flower better when their roots are slightly cramped, so pot on in spring, but only if your plant is really bursting out of its pot. Use John Innes No 1 or 2 or a peat based potting compost.

The ideal temperature for your plant is about 65°F (18°C), though it will put up with higher. Water your plant so that the compost is always kept moist — though don't let the plant pot stand in a saucer of water for long periods. Mist spray only in very hot weather but don't saturate the leaves since they are prone to fungus diseases in damp conditions. A better way to maintain a humid environment is to stand it in a tray of moist pebbles. Add liquid feed to the water every week between May and September.

Keep your plant in an airy room in bright light — they can tolerate direct sun but not at midday. Prune your Busy Lizzie anytime during the summer.

Autumn and winter care

If you can, continue to maintain a temperature of 65°F (18°C), that way your plant will continue to look attractive during the winter and may continue to flower. At this temperature, reduce watering, humidity and feeding only slightly, but remember if you do let the temperature fall, allow the compost to become slightly drier and stop feeding. Do not allow the temperature to fall lower than 55°F (13°C).

Propagation

Busy Lizzie cuttings are very easy to take. Anytime from April to October, snip off sideshoots about 4in (10cm) long, remove the lowest pair of leaves and stand the cuttings in a glass of water. In a few days roots will appear, then carefully pot the cuttings up into individual pots of moist compost — peat-based or John Innes No 1 or 2 — and keep them out of bright light for a week or two until the roots have established themselves. When there are signs of fresh growth, you can treat them as mature plants. As the cuttings grow, pinch out the tips to keep the plants bushy and compact.

Busy Lizzies can also be grown easily from seed — a useful method if you want a large number of plants. Sow your seeds in the early spring in trays of seed compost. Just cover with compost, then moisten and put the seed tray somewhere warm and dark. Once the seedlings are just visible, give them some light — although they should be shaded from very bright light. Once they are large enough to handle, pot them up separately.

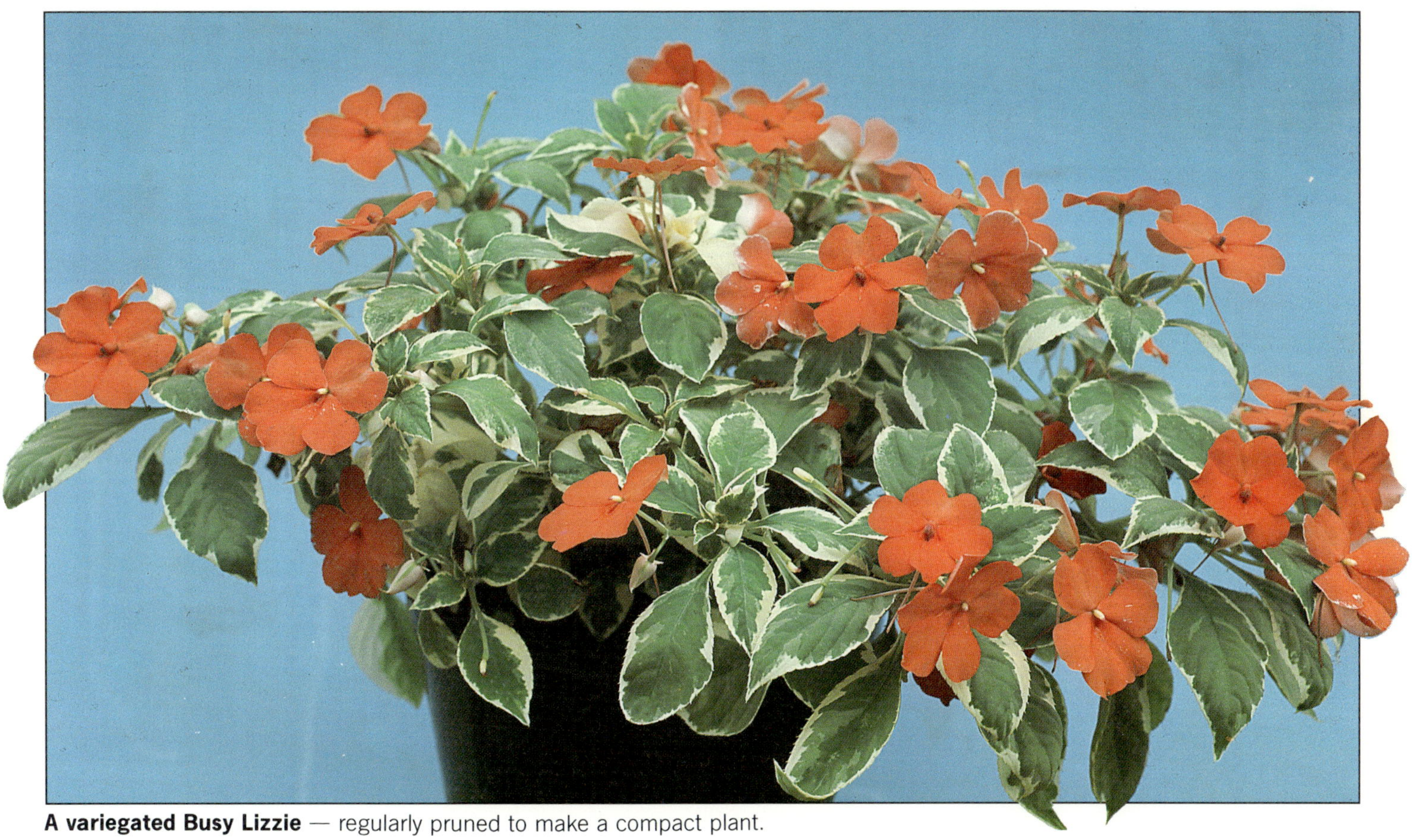

A variegated Busy Lizzie — regularly pruned to make a compact plant.

Species

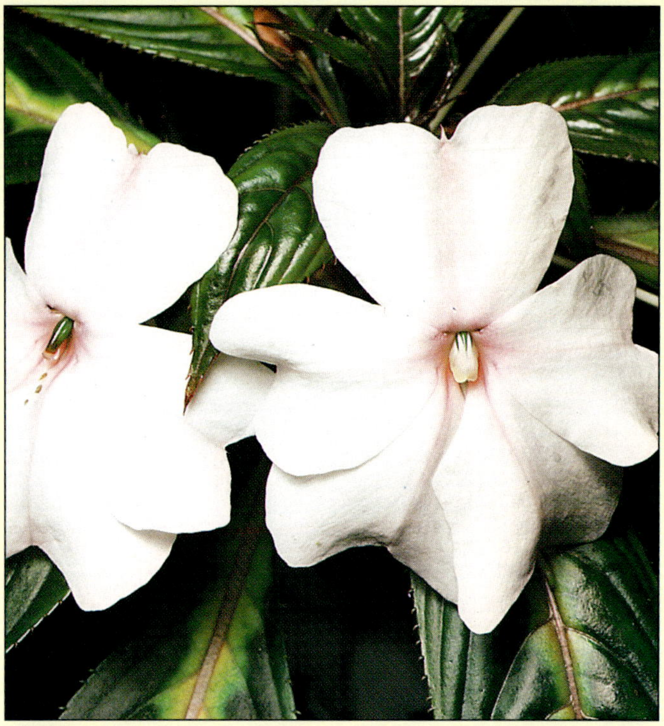

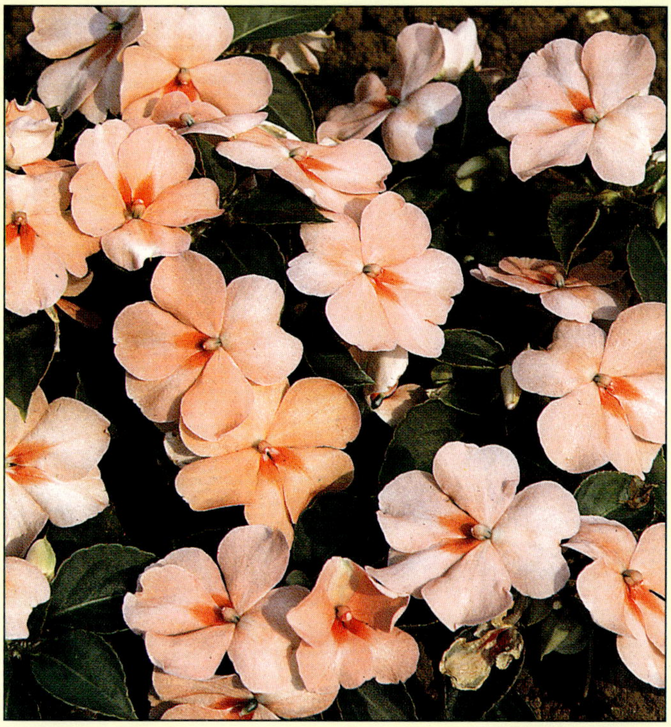

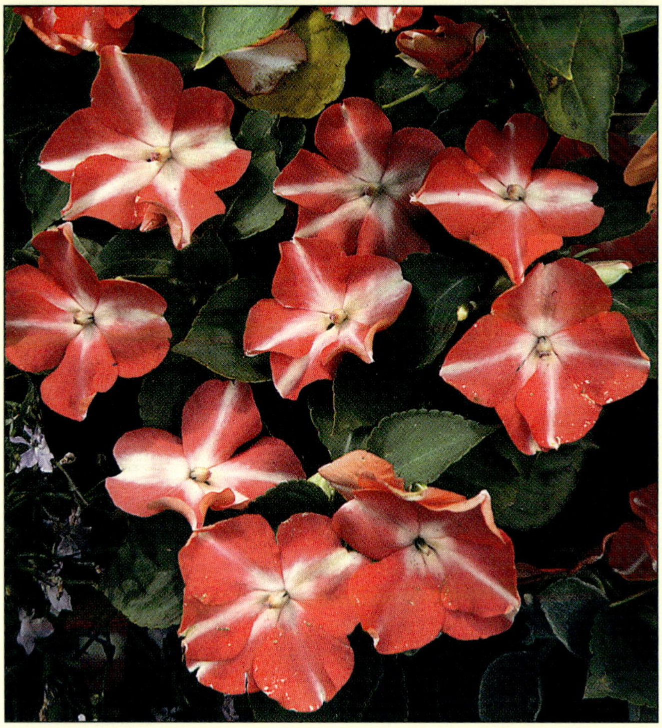

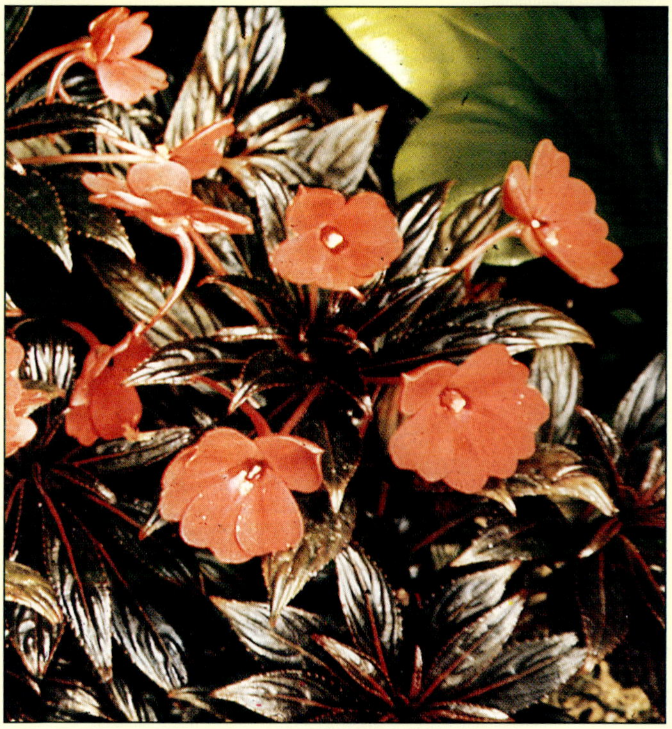

Impatiens wallerana (sometimes called *I.holstii*), Busy Lizzie, from tropical east Africa, grows to about 18in (45cm). It has green or bronzy coloured leaves and fleshy stems, faintly striped with red. The red summer flowers are about 1½in (38mm) across with a small spur at the back. *I.w. 'Variegata'* has scarlet flowers and green leaves edged with white. Very many hybrids are available: 'Arabesque', *top left,* has bronze-green leaves with red and yellow veins, and flowers in white and shades of pink. 'Supernova', *top right*, has pretty pink flowers tinged with red; 'Rose Star', *above left*, has red flowers, crossed with white.

I.petersiana*, above,* is a branching bush that grows to about 18in (45cm). It has rich burgundy-coloured leaves and bright red summer flowers.

Species

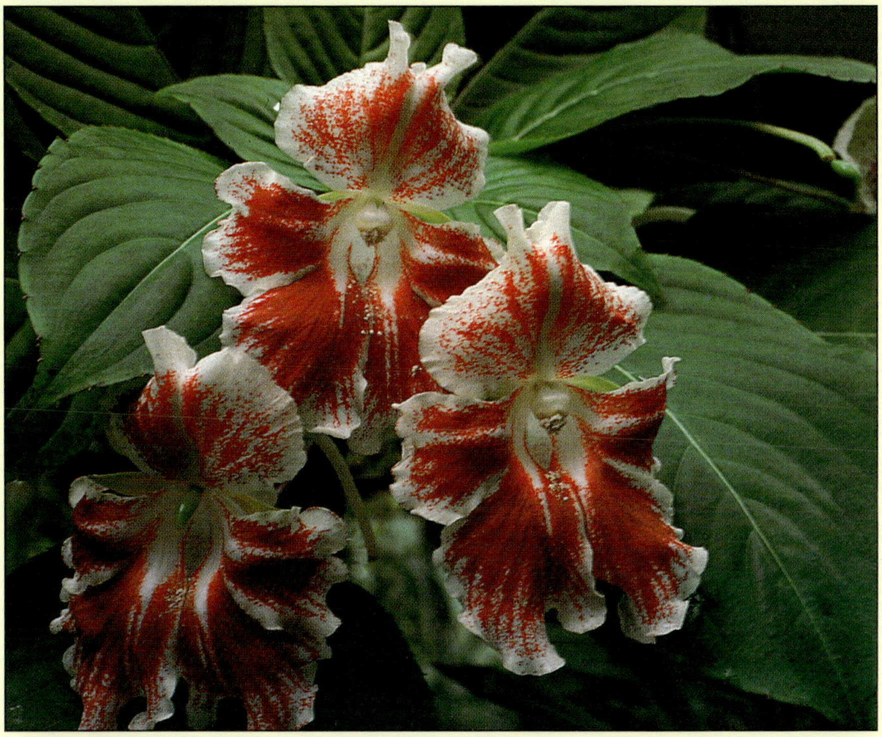

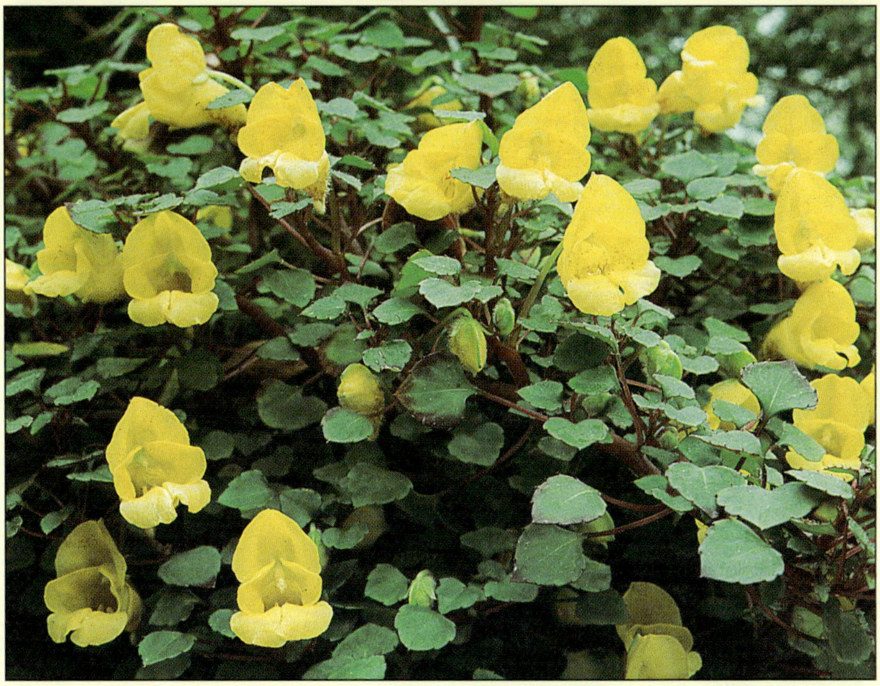

I.hawkeri, from New Guinea, is about 18in (45cm) high with purple stems, and green leaves with a red central vein. The flowers are usually white at the centre. There are many hybrids — they are known as the New Guinea Hybrids — with variously coloured and patterned leaves and large flowers in summer in shades of pink, red and white.

I.repens, *above*, is a low-growing, creeping plant, ideal for hanging baskets. It has golden-yellow summer flowers.

I.hookeriana, *top*, from Sri Lanka is a fleshy-stemmed plant that grows to about 2ft (0.6m). It has plain green leaves and large flowers that vary from white through shades of pink to red.

Trouble Shooter

Busy Lizzies are trouble-free plants given regular basic care and the growing conditions they like. If temperatures fall too low in winter or if they're left in a cold draught, leaves may wilt, turn yellow and fall.

Fungus disease can develop on the leaves and flowers if the plant is kept too damp or cold or in poor light. Spray the plant thoroughly with a fungicide when disease is apparent, alternatively protect your plant from attack by watering a systemic fungicide on to the soil once a week.

If the atmosphere becomes too dry, red spider mite may infest your plant — if you notice delicate brownish webs and curling leaves then spray your plant with a malathion-based insecticide. Greenfly often attack the soft young growth at the tips of branches — spray the plant with a pyrethrum-based insecticide. If you notice whitefly flying away from your plant when it's disturbed, then spray once a week with malathion. A monthly treatment with a systemic insecticide based on dimethoate will protect your plant from attack from most insect pests.

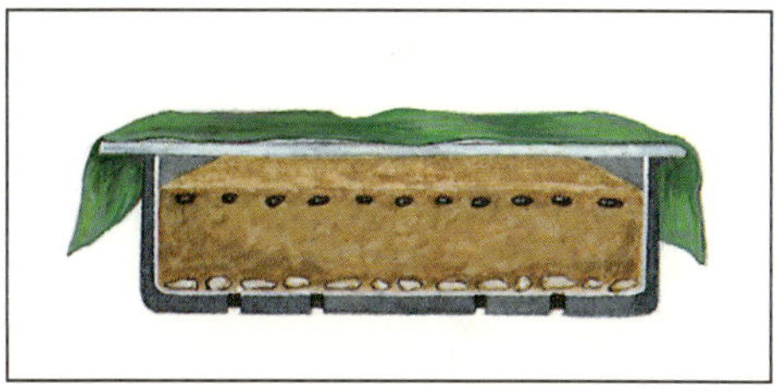

Sprinkle compost over the seeds, then place a cloth over the tray.

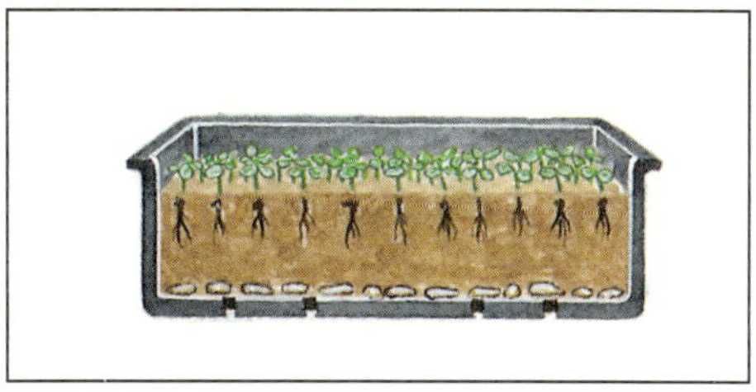

When the seeds have germinated, remove the cover.

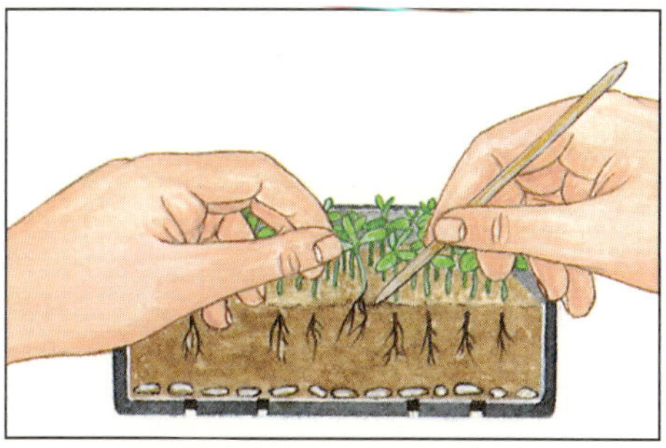

Once the seedlings are large enough to handle, pot them up individually.

Iresine

Family name: **Amaranthaceae**

Common name:
Beefsteak Plant

Care Straight forward	**Height** 12-18in (30-45cm)	**Flower** Rarely
Light Bright direct	**Spread** 12in(30cm)	**Humidity** Mist spray daily
Price Middle range	**Shape** Bushy	**Availability** Garden centres
Temp. Min 55°F (13°C)	Ideal 65°F (18°C)	Max 80°F (27°C)

More people should grow these unusual plants, with their vivid, dark pink foliage; in a sunny room, growing among green-leaved plants, they make an eye-catching contrast.

Iresine herbstii, the Beefsteak Plant, is the most popular indoor species in this group. This bushy evergreen from southern Brazil grows to about 12-18in (30-45cm) in a pot. Soft, succulent, crimson stems carry 3in (8cm) long heart-shaped leaves that are a remarkable deep wine-red, with pale red veins.

These are sun-loving plants and good light is essential. Make sure they're in a bright, sunny position, such as a south-facing window, for healthy, colourful leaves.

Spring and summer care

Repot in February or March, moving plants to a pot one size larger if necessary. Iresine grows rapidly when young and you may need to pot on twice during the growing season. These plants like a rich soil-based potting mixture, such as John Innes No 3, or, better still, make your own with equal parts of peat, loam, decomposed leaf-mould and sharp sand. Pinch out the tips of growing shoots every two months or so, to encourage a more bushy plant.

Ordinary room temperatures, around 60-65°F (15-18°C) say, are fine for these plants. What they do need is a really bright, sunny setting otherwise plants become straggly and their colouring may fade. Should this happen it's best to replace your plant.

The compost should be kept thoroughly moist, so water plentifully but never let the pot stand in water. Humidity is essential: mist spray the leaves daily if you can with tepid water. Once every two or three weeks throughout the growth period, feed the plant with a liquid fertiliser.

Autumn and winter care

As in the summer months, normal room temperature suits Iresines perfectly well. Keep your plant in the lightest, sunniest position possible, to help maintain the rich colouring of the foliage. Water in moderation between October and March — just enough to prevent the compost from drying out.

Propagation

Propagate from cuttings, either in the spring or the autumn. Take tip cuttings of fresh shoots, about 4in (10cm) long, treat them with rooting hormone and set them in a mixture of equal parts of sand and peat. Keep the mixture moist and maintain a temperature of 70-75°F (21-24°C), in a propagator or enclosed in a clear polythene bag. The cuttings will root in two or three weeks, after which they should be uncovered and fed with liquid fertiliser every two weeks. About two months after the start of propagation, pot the cuttings into a rich soil-based potting compost (see 'Spring and summer care') and treat as mature plants.

Trouble Shooter

Any problems with Iresines tend to centre on water and light. Under- or overwatering can cause the leaves to wilt, lose colour and drop. Never allow the compost to dry out for any length of time; equally, don't saturate the plant so that the roots become waterlogged. These sun-loving plants need a really bright spot; too shaded a position and the foliage will lose lustre and colour. Greenfly which cluster round the stem tips, is the only likely pest. It can be quickly dealt with by spraying with a pyrethrum insecticide.

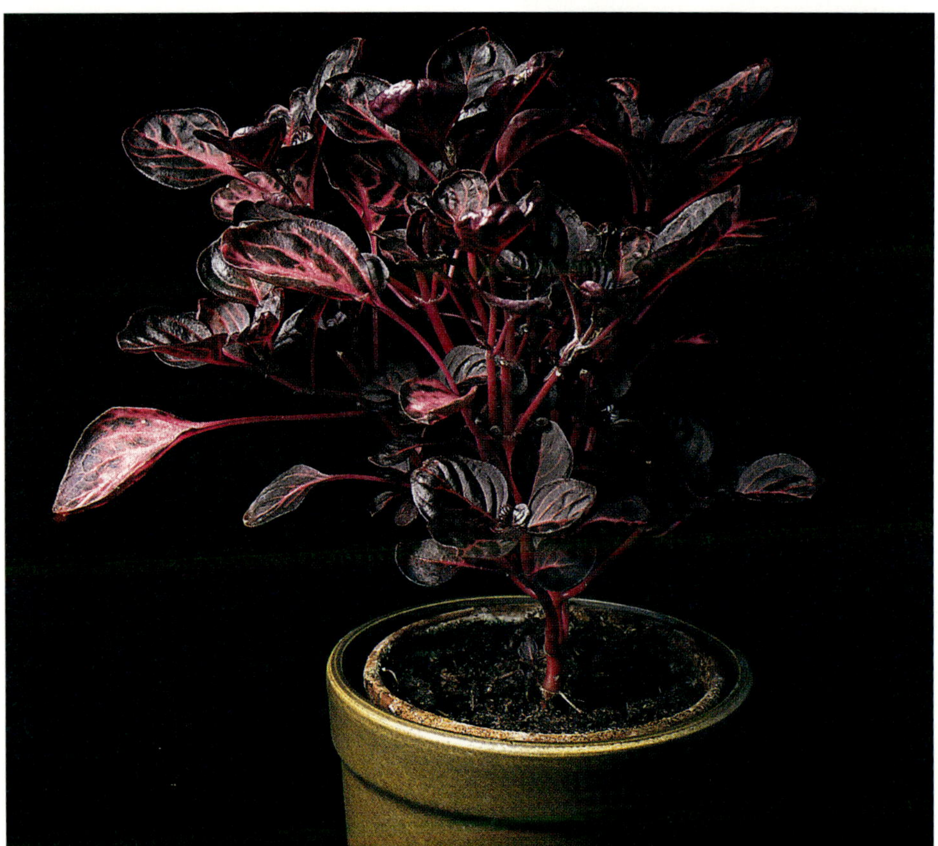

The Beefsteak Plant has vivid, dark pink leaves and stems.

Species

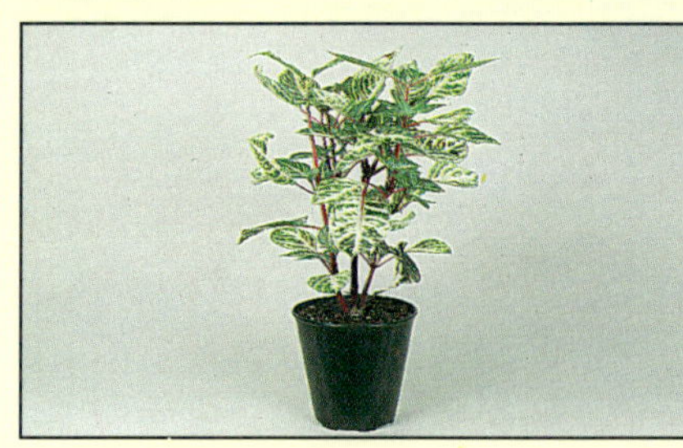

Iresine herbstii, also known as the Beefsteak Plant, is the member of this group of South American plants which is most widely grown indoors. Grown in a pot, it forms a small, shrubby plant, reaching a height and spread of about 2ft (0.6m). The soft, red stems carry notched, heart-shaped leaves up to 3in (8cm) long and 2in (5cm) wide, with 1-2in (2.5-5cm) long leaf-stalks, in a rich wine-red with paler red veining. Its flowers are small and insignificant and rarely produced indoors. There is a highly colourful variety, *I.h.aureo-reticulata, above*, which rejoices in the common name Chicken Gizzard. It's similar in shape to the parent plant, but the leaves have a strong green tinge, with broad yellow veins, while the stems are bright red.

Ixora

Family name: **Rubiaceae**

Common name:
Flame of the Woods

Care Tricky	**Height** 3ft (0.9m)	**Flower** Summer
Light Bright	**Spread** 2ft (0.6m)	**Humidity** Mist spray regularly
Price Expensive	**Shape** Bushy	**Availability** Garden centres
Temp. Min 60°F (15°C)	Ideal 70°F (21°C)	Max 75°F (24°C)

This group of evergreen tropical shrubs are prized for their large exotic clusters of brightly-coloured, fragrant flowers. They are generally grown as greenhouse plants, but with careful treatment they can be made to thrive in the house.

Ixora coccinea, the Flame of the Woods, makes the most successful houseplant of this group. It grows to about 3ft (0.9m) with glossy, thick, dark-green leaves and large dense clusters of rich scarlet, tubular flowers, 4in (10cm) or more across. Properly cared for these blooms will last throughout the summer months.

Ixoras are not the easiest of plants to grow. They don't like being moved and they react very quickly to any adverse conditions. But care and attention is amply rewarded, and the result is well worth the effort.

Spring and summer care

Pot plants on every year in March using John Innes No 2 or No 3, moving up one pot size every time to a maximum of 6 or 7in (15 or 18cm). After the final pot size is reached, topdress instead of potting on, replacing the first 1-2in (2.5-5cm) with fresh compost. Take care when potting to provide good drainage. March is also the time for any pruning, to keep your plant in shape.

Ixoras need warmth and enjoy a summer temperature of 65-70°F (18-21°C) or higher. Always keep your plant in a brightly-lit spot, but be sure to shade it from midday sun in summer.

Water fairly freely so that the compost is never dry, but avoid overwatering; the soil should never be saturated for any length of time. Add liquid fertiliser to the water every two to three weeks from April to September, and mist spray the leaves regularly — daily if possible — with tepid water.

Autumn and winter care

Winter temperatures should never fall below 60°F (15°C) in winter; about 65°F (18°C) is ideal. Keep the plant free from draughts and give it plenty of light. Water more moderately during winter — just enough to keep the compost from drying out — but continue to provide a degree of humidity with light overhead spraying of tepid water two or three times a week.

Propagation

Take firm young stem tip cuttings, 3-4in (8-10cm) long, in March or April. Treat them with rooting hormone and set them in a mixture of two parts compost to one part sand. Enclose the cuttings in a clear polythene bag or, ideally, a propagator, at a temperature of 70-75°F (21-24°C). Rooting should occur in six weeks. When new growth can be seen uncover and water moderately, adding a liquid fertiliser every two weeks. Pot on as the plants grow out of their pots into John Innes No 2 or No 3.

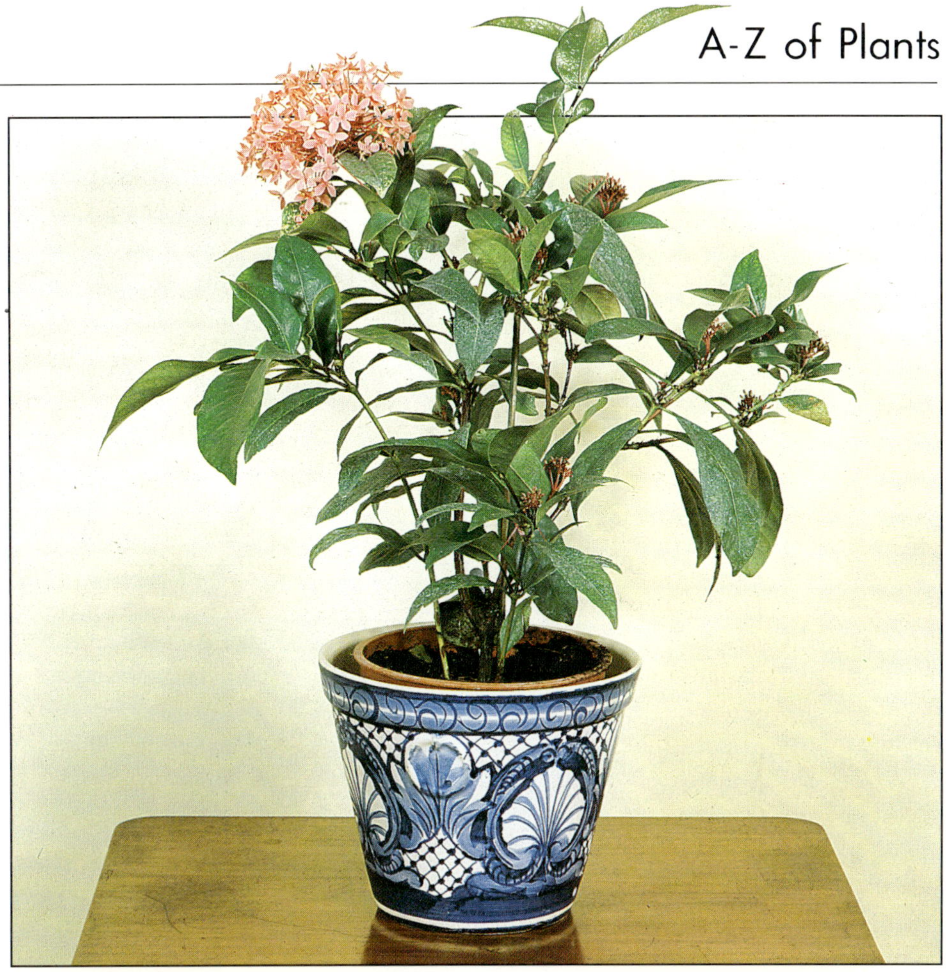

A pale-pink flowered variety of *Ixora coccinea.*

Trouble Shooter

Leaves will quickly wilt and flowers fail to develop if the compost is allowed to get too dry or there is too little humidity. Overwatering can cause root rot; it's important that the soil is properly drained. Use a systemic dimethoate-based insecticide regularly to prevent greenfly, mealy bug and red spider mite; red spider mite should only be a problem if humidity is not provided.

Species

Ixora coccinea, the Flame of the Woods, from Malaysia and India, is a woody, much-branching plant which grows to about 3ft (0.9m) in height. It has thick, shiny, dark green leaves — often bronze-coloured when new — up to 4in (10cm) long and 2in (5cm) wide. From late spring through to autumn it bears large, dense clusters of fragrant, scarlet flowers, which open at the mouth into four widely-spreading petals. There is also a number of varieties of *I.coccinea, right,* with different-coloured flowers in shades of orange, yellow and pink.

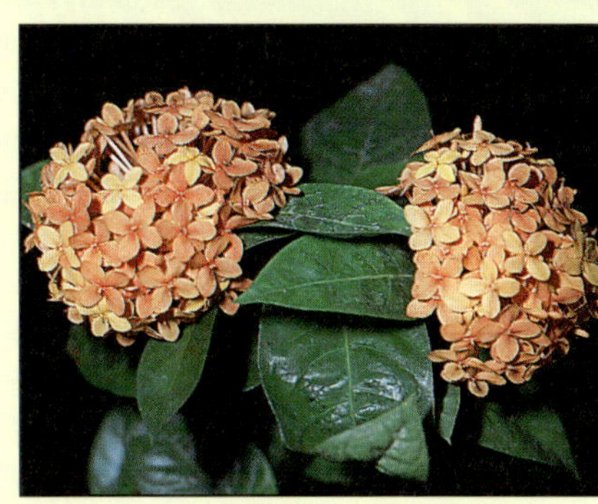

Jacaranda

Family name: **Bignoniaceae**

Common name:
Fern Tree

Care Straight forward	**Height** 3-4ft (0.9-1.2m)	**Flower** Rarely
Light Bright direct	**Spread** 15-18in (38-45cm)	**Humidity** Regular mist spray
Price Expensive	**Shape** Tree	**Availability** Specialist nurseries
Temp. Min 55°F (13°C)	Ideal 70°F (21°C)	Max 80°F (27°C)

These are graceful, elegant shrubs and small trees, with brilliant colourful flowers and a very decorative fern-like foliage. *Jacaranda acutifolia* (also called *J.mimosifolia*), the only species commonly found indoors, makes an excellent houseplant. Given plenty of room in its pot or tub, this elegant, tree-like plant reaches 3-4ft (0.9-1.2m). In the wild it can grow to 30ft (9m) and bears large clusters of beautiful, silky, lavender-blue flowers throughout the summer. In ideal conditions, a plant of five years old or more may produce flowers indoors but, as houseplants, they are generally grown for their very attractive foliage of delicate, lacy, bright green leaves. Jacarandas sometimes lose their leaves in winter — these are quickly replaced with new ones.

Although they are something of a rarity, these plants are not at all difficult to grow and are a perfect choice for a heated, sunny room.

Spring and summer care

Repot each spring, using John Innes No 2, in a pot two sizes larger, up to a maximum of 8-10in (20-25cm); from then on, topdress each year, scraping away the top inch or two (2.5-5cm) of compost and replacing it with fresh. At the same time, prune carefully to keep your plant a neat and compact shape.

Jacarandas are happy at ordinary room temperatures, but a summer temperature as high as 75-80°F (24-27°C) is perfectly alright; you can stand them outdoors in the hottest periods. Give them as light a position as possible, including full sunlight.

Water fairly freely throughout this period, but don't allow pots to stand in water for any length of time. Mist spray the leaves every two or three days to provide a humid atmosphere and feed with liquid fertiliser every two weeks from March to the end of September, for bright-looking, healthy foliage.

Autumn and winter care

Aim for a winter temperature of 60-65°F (15-18°C) — it shouldn't be allowed to fall below 55°F (13°C) — and keep your plant in a bright spot. Water only moderately from October to March, to keep the compost just moist. Mist spray the leaves occasionally.

Trouble Shooter

If they are overwatered or if winter temperatures are too low, these plants will start to deteriorate, but otherwise you are likely to have very few problems with them. For red spider mite, the most likely pest, spray with a malathion-based insecticide or apply a dimethoate-based systemic insecticide as a preventative, two or three times during the growing season. Mist spraying the leaves regularly will discourage them.

Species

Jacaranda acutifolia (also known as *J.mimosifolia*) is normally the only species grown as a houseplant. A small tree, reaching a height of 30ft (9m) in the wild, it usually grows to 3-4ft (0.9-1.2m) indoors. In summer it bears large, silky, lavender-blue flowers, but these are rarely produced in the house and it is grown instead for its delicate, fern-like foliage, with bright green, feathery, frond-like leaves up to 15in (38cm) long and 4in (10cm) wide.

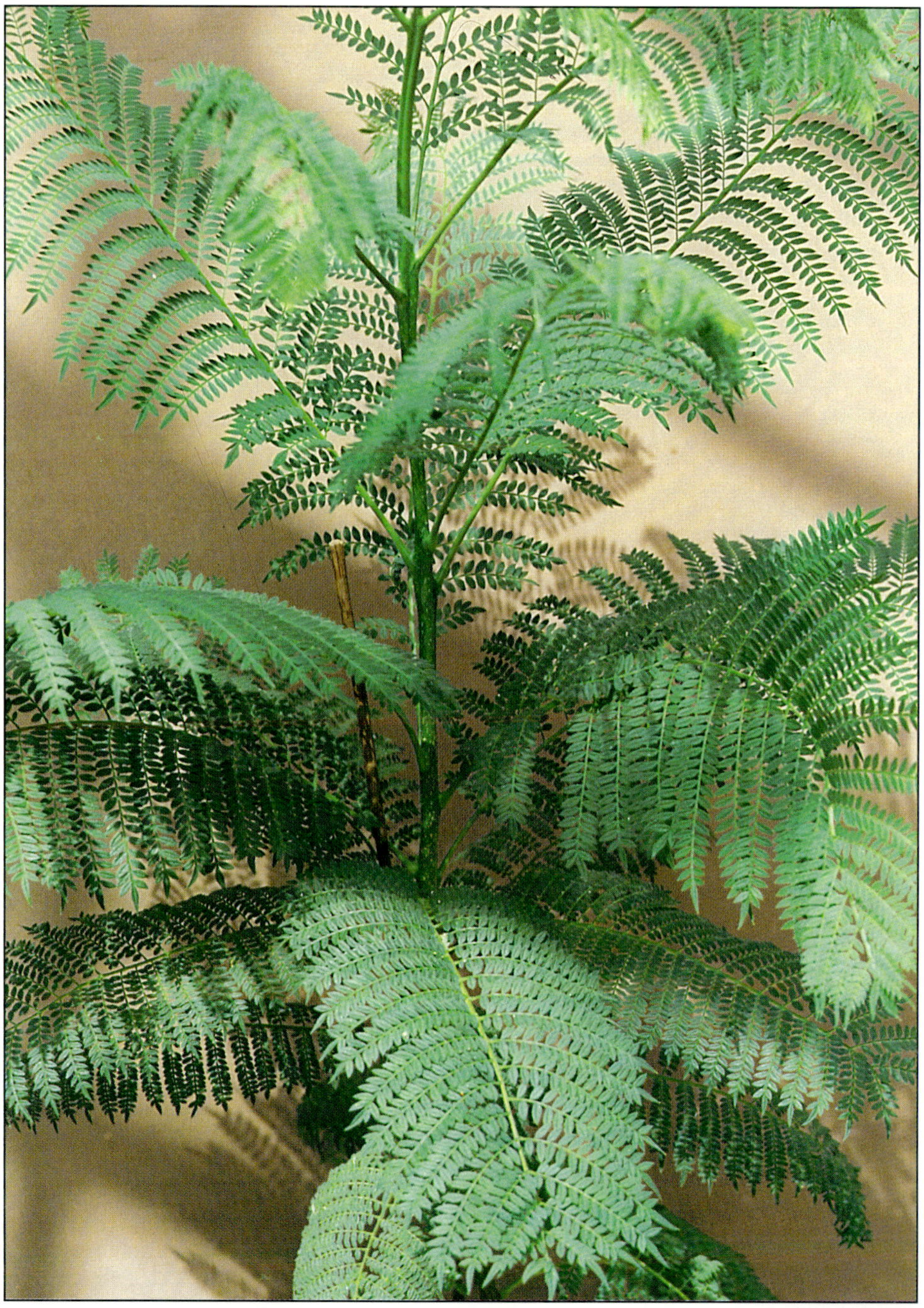

The delicate, ferny foliage of *Jacaranda acutifolia.*

Jacobinia

Family name: **Acanthaceae**

Common names:
King's Crown/Brazilian Plume

Care Easy	**Height** 4ft (1-2m)	**Flower** Summer
Light Bright, indirect	**Spread** 2ft (0.6m)	**Humidity** Mist spray regularly
Price Middle range	**Shape** Bushy	**Availability** Garden centres
Temp. Min 55°F (13°C)	Ideal 65°F (18°C)	Max 75°F (24°C)

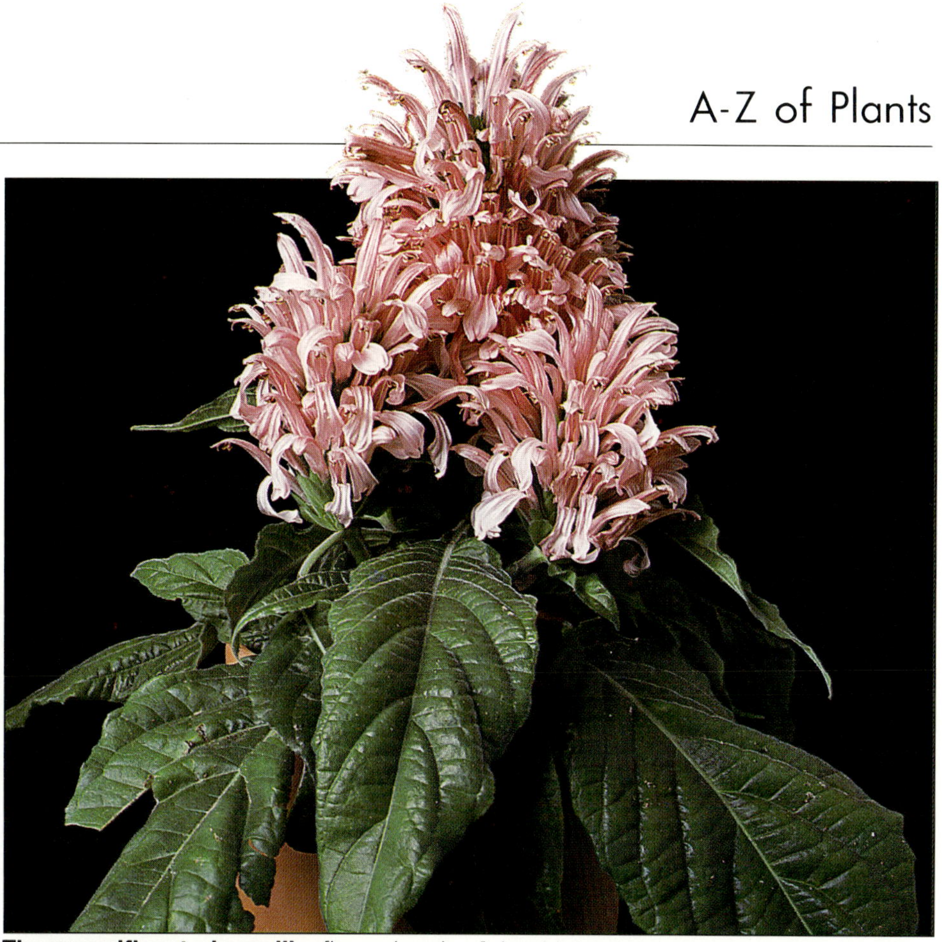

The magnificent plume-like flower heads of *Jacobinia carnea.*

Their profusion of charming colourful flowers, held in large, cone-shaped flower heads or in delicate, small clusters, make Jacobinias a popular choice for indoors. The most widely grown is the tropical evergreen shrub, King's Crown or Brazilian Plume *(Jacobinia carnea)*, with plume-like flower heads, up to 6in (15cm) high of long, deep pink, tubular flowers, set off by large, dark green leaves.

King's Crown is a vigorous plant which can reach 4ft (1.2m) or more if left to grow unchecked. But properly pruned, it makes a neat, bushy houseplant which will go on producing its appealing flowers for years.

Spring and summer care

Repot your plant in spring every two or three years, into John Innes No 2, making sure the pot is well-drained. Topdress when not repotting, replacing the top 1-2in (2.5-5cm) of compost with fresh. Jacobinias will quickly become very straggly-looking if not kept in shape, so prune vigorously in March; pinch out all the growing tips for a bushy, compact, well-shaped plant.

Keep your plant quite warm, about 65°F (18°C) rising to around 75°F (24°C) at the height of summer and give it as bright a position as you can, but avoid direct sunlight during the hottest months.

Jacobinias need moist, humid conditions to thrive. Water freely so that the compost is kept thoroughly moist at all times (though pots should never stand in water) and mist spray the leaves frequently to provide high humidity. Add a liquid fertiliser to the watering every two weeks from April through to September.

Autumn and winter care

In early autumn, when flowering has finished, prune the stems right back to within 4in (10cm) of the base; growth will recommence after only a few weeks. Winter temperatures should be around 60°F (15°C) — avoid anything below 55°F (13°C). Keep the plant in the brightest possible position. Water sparingly — just enough to keep the compost from completely drying out.

Propagation

In the spring, take 3-4in (8-10cm) stem cuttings; treat the cut ends with rooting hormone, set them in a mixture of equal parts of peat and sand, and enclose in a clear polythene bag or, ideally, a propagator. After two or three weeks the cuttings should have rooted; uncover them, keep the mixture just moist and maintain a temperature of 70-75°F (21-24°C). About two months from the start of propagation, pot the cuttings individually into 4in (10cm) pots of John Innes No 2, moving them on to slightly larger pots as they grow, to a final size of 8in (20cm).

Trouble Shooter

This is a robust plant, but its leaves will wilt and discolour and flowering will suffer, if winter temperatures fall too low; aim for around 60°F (15°C). Overwatering can cause problems, especially in winter; good drainage is most important, otherwise root rot can develop, giving drooping, yellowish leaves. Red spider mite is liable to affect plants if humidity is too low; use a malathion insecticide to remove them. To prevent red spider mite, mist spray with water regularly and apply a systemic dimethoate-based insecticide, according to the manufacturer's instructions.

Species

Jacobinia carnea (also known as *Justicia magnifica)*, the King's Crown or Brazilian Plume, is a tropical evergreen shrub from Brazil. A vigorous grower which quickly reaches 4ft (1.2m) or more, it carries pointed green 6in (15cm) long leaves, sometimes with red undersides. Large plume-like clusters of rosy pink flowers appear from July to September.

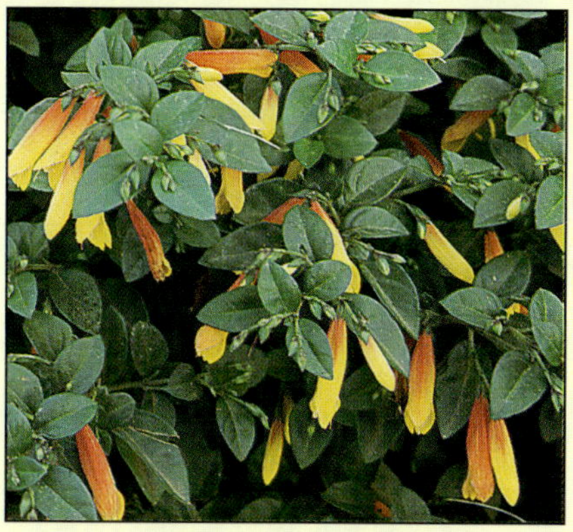

J.pauciflora, *right*, from Brazil, grows to about 2ft (60cm), with small and narrow mid-green leaves. Small clusters of long, drooping, tubular flowers in scarlet and yellow, begin to appear in October and continue throughout the winter.

Jasminum

Family name: **Oleaceae**

Common name:
Jasmine

Care Easy	**Height** 10ft (3m)	**Flower** Winter
Light Bright, indirect	**Spread** 2ft (0.6m)	**Humidity** Mist spray regularly
Price Cheap	**Shape** Climber	**Availability** Garden centres
Temp. Min 50°F (10°C)	Ideal 65°F (18°C)	Max 75°F (24°C)

The Jasmines include some very pretty spring- and winter-flowering evergreen climbers, several of these ideal for growing as houseplants. The most popular suitable species is *Jasminum polyanthum*, a vigorous climbing plant with beautiful, star-like white flowers and a wonderful, sweet scent.

Spring and summer care

Each year, using John Innes No 2 potting compost, pot winter-flowering species in spring and spring-flowering species in September. Be sure to put plenty of crocks under the compost for good drainage. Provide support — canes, trellis or a wire hoop for your plant to clamber over. Prune both spring- and winter-flowering types after repotting; just cut back the stems to shape the plant.

Keep your plant in a bright position but out of direct sun. Make sure the compost is always moist and feed with a fertiliser every two weeks. Temperatures of about 65°F (18°C) are ideal. Mist spray regularly — especially during hot weather. From June to September you can stand your plant outside in a sheltered spot, but this is not essential.

Autumn and winter care

Aim for a temperature between 50-55°F (10-13°C) for winter-flowering species and about 60°F (15°C) for spring-flowering ones. Keep your plant in bright light, and away from draughts. The soil should be only just moist all the time. Add a weak liquid fertiliser to the water every two weeks, using half the recommended dose. Mist spray regularly and try to avoid wetting the flowers and buds.

Propagation

Take cuttings in spring for winter-flowering species and in October for spring-flowering types. Snip 4-6in (10-15cm) from stem tips and, having removed the lowest pair of leaves, treat them with a hormone rooting powder. Set them into John Innes No 2 mixed with a little coarse sand. Keep the cuttings at about 65-70°F (18-21°C) — ideally in a propagator. Make sure the compost is always moist but not waterlogged. Once growth starts you can pot up the cuttings and treat them as mature plants.

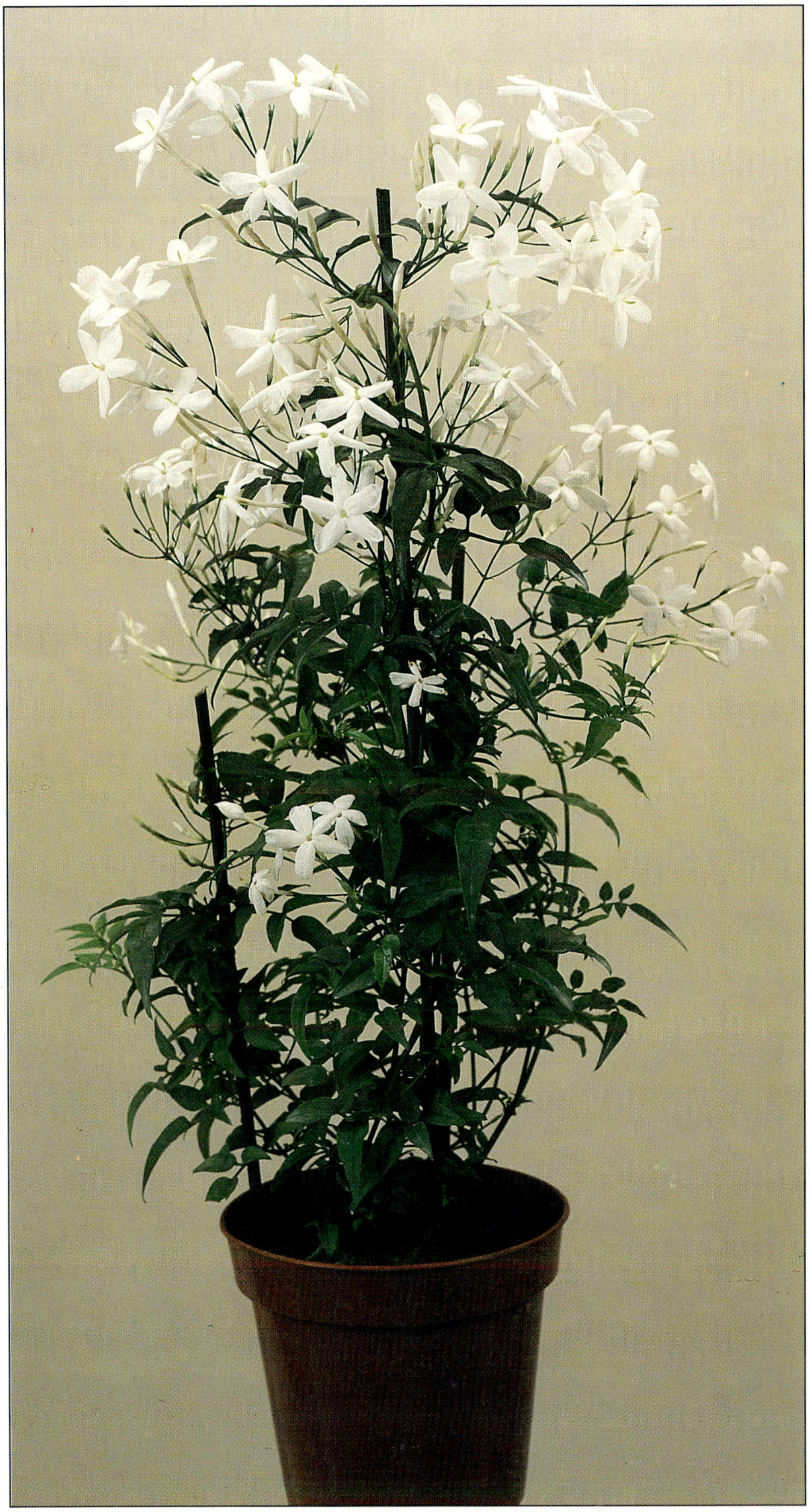

Jasminum polyanthum scents the air through the winter months.

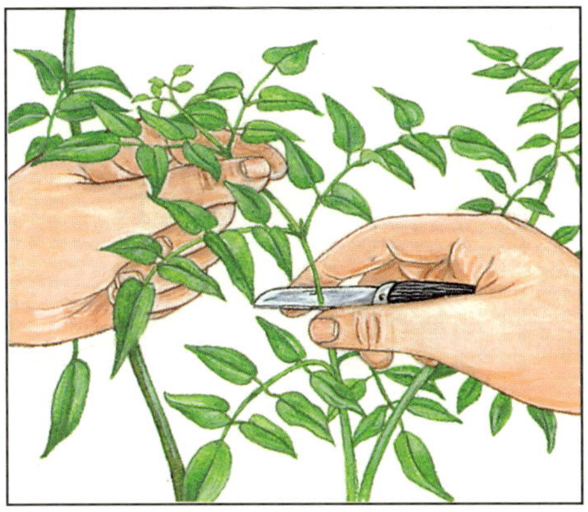

In spring, propagate winter-flowering jasmine by cuttings. Snip 4-6in (10-15cm) from a stem tip — using a sharp knife or a pair of secateurs.

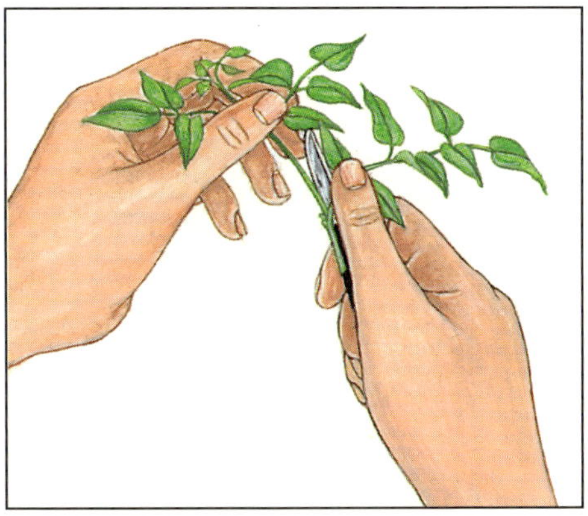

Each sprig of leaflets is, botanically speaking, a single compound leaf. To prepare cuttings remove the lowest pair of true leaves.

Trouble Shooter

Wilting and shrivelled leaves can mean under- or overwatering; check to see how the compost feels and adjust your water accordingly. Flower buds may turn brown and fall if your plant is exposed to direct light; find a more shaded position. Very few flowers may mean too much warmth; winter-flowering species need a temperature no higher than 55°F (13°C) and spring flowering types 60°F (15°C).

Greenfly often cluster around the tips of Jasmine stems — spray your plant with a pyrethrum-based insecticide if you see them.

Species

***Jasminum polyanthum**, right,* is a fast growing evergreen climber from China, that can reach as high as 10ft (2.5m). Its leaves are divided into tiny leaflets, giving the plant a slightly ferny appearance. The flowers, which appear in winter, are white, beautifully scented and nearly 1in (2.5cm) across. They are carried in large clusters of 20 or more.

***J.mesnyi**, below right,* sometimes called *J.primulinum,* is also an evergreen climber which grows to about 10ft (2.5m), but it flowers in spring. Its unscented flowers are yellow, about 2in (5cm) across, and darker towards the centre.

***J.rex**, below left,* from Thailand is a fairly rare species. Also an evergreen winter-flowering climber, it has large, white perfumed flowers, about 2in (5cm) across. The oval leaves are arranged in opposite pairs on smooth green climbing stems.

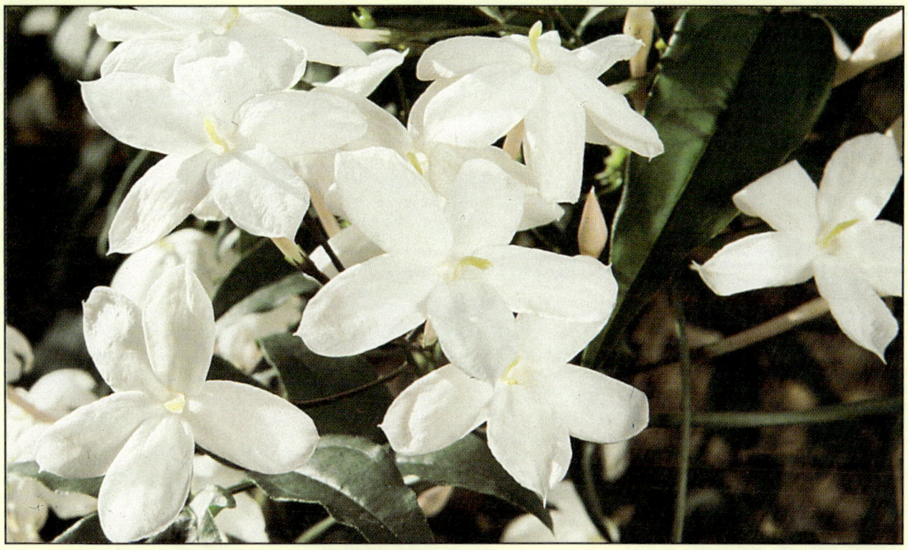

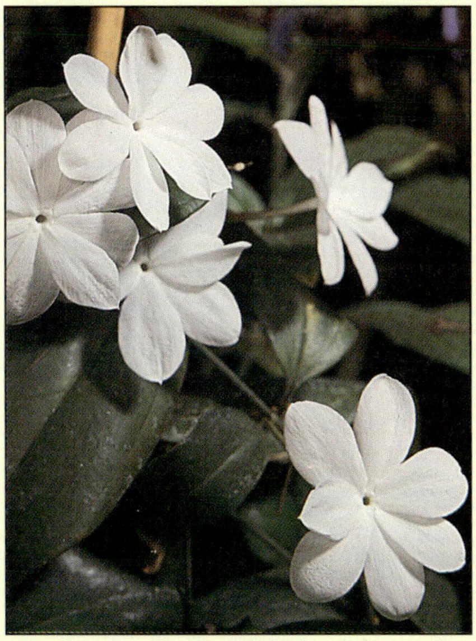

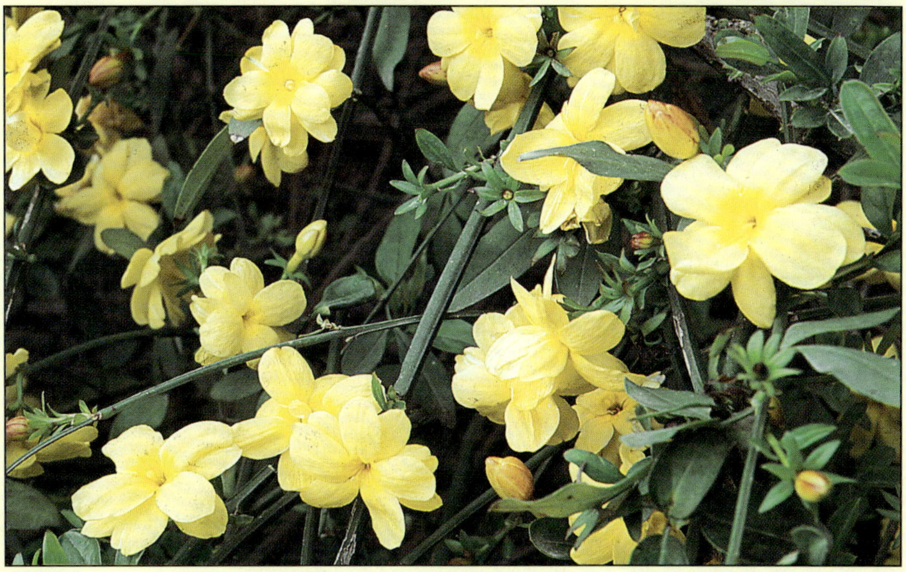

Kalanchoe

Family name: **Crassulaceae**

Common names:
Flaming Katy/Mexican Hat Plant

Care Easy	**Height** 12in (30cm)	**Flower** Winter or spring
Light Bright, indirect	**Spread** 9in (23cm)	**Humidity** Mist spray unnecessary
Price Cheap	**Shape** Leafy clump	**Availability** Garden centres
Temp. Min 50°F (10°C)	Ideal 65°F (18°C)	Max 80°F (27°C)

Among this group of succulent species are some fascinating houseplants; some grown for their attractive leaves and others for their easily produced, colourful flowers. Their best known species is *Kalanchoe blossfeldiana, (right)*, or, as some people call it, Flaming Katy. It makes a neat rosette of thick, glossy, lobed leaves crowned by large clusters of brightly coloured flowers — in pink, red, orange or yellow, depending on the variety. Even though their true flowering time is spring, nurserymen often force them into flower for Christmas, by artificially exposing them to shorter and shorter days — and this triggers their flower development.

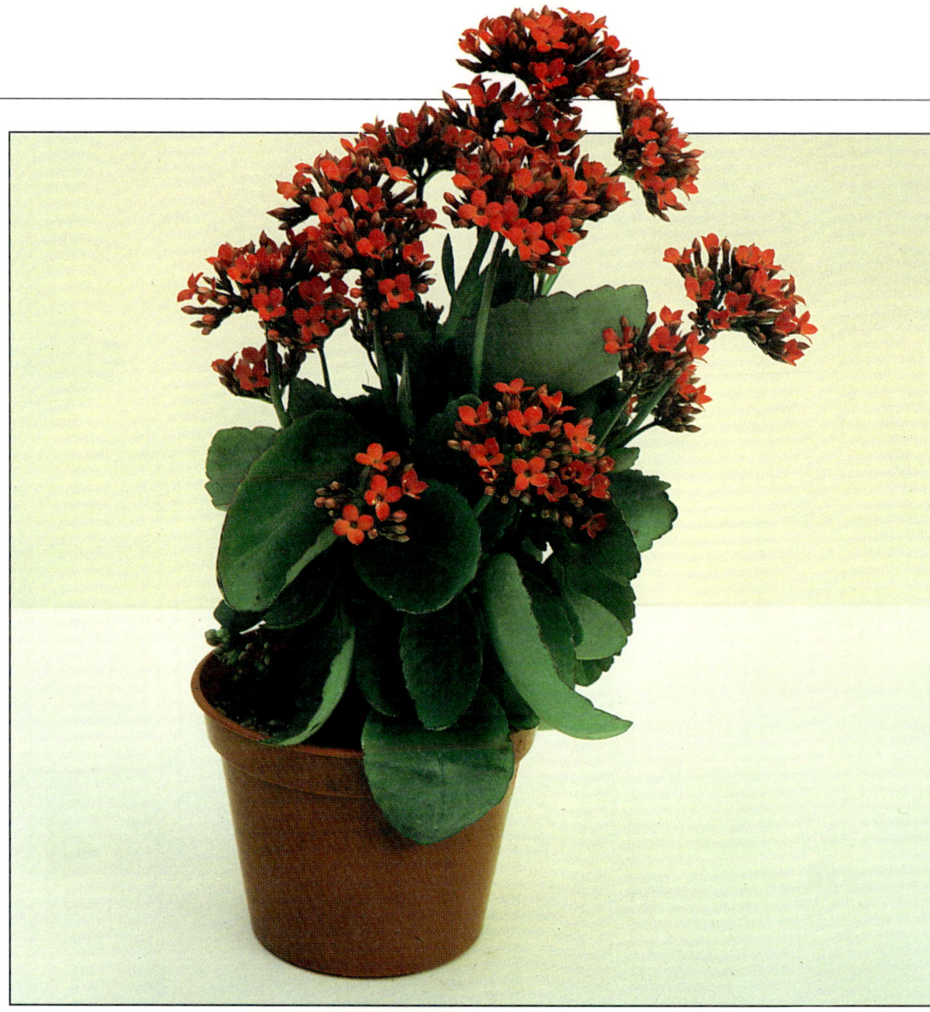

These charming succulents have long-lasting flowers in many colourful shades.

Spring and summer care

Very often Kalanchoes are thrown away after flowering — but there's no reason why they shouldn't be kept to flower year after year, though they'll flower in the spring rather than in winter. After flowering, cut the spent flowering stems to just above the first pair of leaves, then repot your plant. Use a pot one size larger if the roots are encirling the root-ball inside the pot. A proprietary cactus compost is best for potting Kalanchoes.

Water your plant thoroughly throughout the spring and summer, but allow the compost to dry out between waterings. Add a fertiliser to the water every four weeks. Keep your Kalanchoe in bright light but not direct sun, and at normal room temperatures.

Autumn and winter care

Reduce the watering — so that the soil is just moistened, and allow it to dry out between waterings. Add half-strength liquid fertiliser to the water every two weeks. Keep your plant in bright light — direct sun is fine in winter. Don't allow the temperature to fall below 50°F (10°C) — ideally keep it between 55-60°F (13-16°C).

Propagation

Sow seeds any time from February until April, in cactus compost plus a little sharp sand. Keep the compost just moist and the seed tray out of bright, direct light and at a temperature of 70°F (21°C). Once the seedlings are large enough to handle, pot them up individually into cactus compost, moving them on to slightly larger pots as they grow.

Kalanchoes can also be propagated from cuttings. Snip 3-4in (8-10cm) from a stem tip, leave it to dry out for for two days. Dip the cut end in hormone rooting powder then insert it into a pot of cactus compost mixed with a little coarse sand. Keep the cutting at a temperature of about 70°F (21°C) and out of strong light until growth is apparent, then treat them as mature plants.

Some Kalanchoe species, such as *K.daigremontiana*, the Mexican Hat Plant, develop tiny plantlets on their leaf edges. These can be carefully removed and potted up to make new plants. Place them on the surface of some damp cactus compost and keep them shaded until they start to grow.

Trouble Shooter

Overwatering quickly leads to fatal leaf and root rot; Kalanchoes can tolerate underwatering more readily — so, if anything, err towards less water. Mealy bug sometimes attacks these plants — look out for small cottonwool-like tufts and brush them away with a small paint brush dipped in methylated spirit. Never use a malathion-based insecticide on plants belonging to the Crassulaceae family.

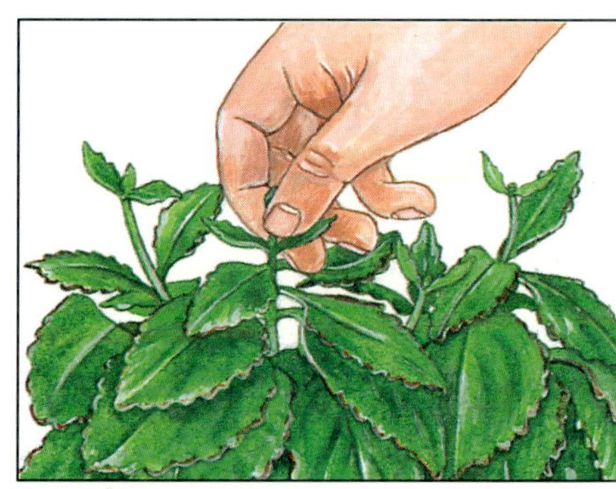

Pinching out the growing tips of young plants will help to keep them bushy and compact.

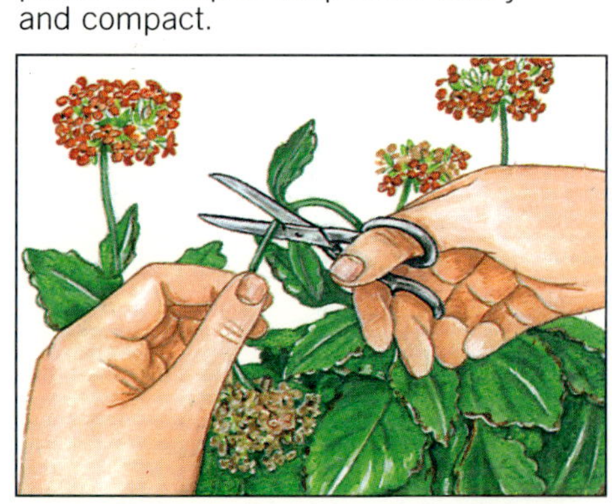

Snip off flower heads once they're passed their best; cut just above the first pair of leaves.

Species

Kalanchoe blossfeldiana, or Flaming Katy, comes from Madagascar. It grows to about 12in (30cm) and has thick, succulent, dark green leaves, about 3in (8cm) long, that are scalloped and sometimes tinged with red around the edge. The flowers appear in spring (or winter, when forced). They are carried in large, flattish clusters held above the foliage and last for about six weeks or more. Very many shades are available.

K.pumila, also from Madagascar, makes an excellent hanging basket plant, with its slighting trailing branches and arching flower heads. It has beautiful, fleshy, grey leaves, about 1in (25mm) long and covered with a fine white powder. The pinkish-violet flowers are carried in clusters in the late winter.

K.marmorata, *below right,* from Ethiopia, sometimes called the Pen Wiper plant, is grown for its attractive fleshy leaves. Pale green at first then, as they mature they turn purplish-grey with rich brown blotches on both surfaces. This is an upright bushy plant and grows to about 15in (38cm) high. White flowers are produced in spring.

K.daigremontiana, *top right,* or Mexican Hat Plant, from Madagascar, is an upright succulent species that grows to about 3-4ft (0.9-1.2m) tall. Its fleshy leaves are triangular and, around the edge of the leaf, new plantlets form. Clusters of greyish-purple flowers appear in late spring.

K.beharensis, *top left,* can reach a height of 10ft (3m) — though it can easily be kept much smaller by cutting back the growing tips each spring. It is grown for its attractive large leaves; these are triangular in shape, shallowly lobed, wavy-edged and 4-8in (10-20cm) or more long. The dense yellowish-brown hairs that cover the leaves give them a soft, velvety appearance. The spring flowers rarely appear on small houseplants; if you let your plant grow to its full height they are carried in clusters on long stems and are yellowish white, tinted with purple on the inside.

K.tomentosa, *below left,* from Madagascar, is a rather upright plant that grows to about 18in (45cm). Its fleshy leaves and stems are coated with dense whitish hairs — making them look rather like felt. The flowers are insignificant.

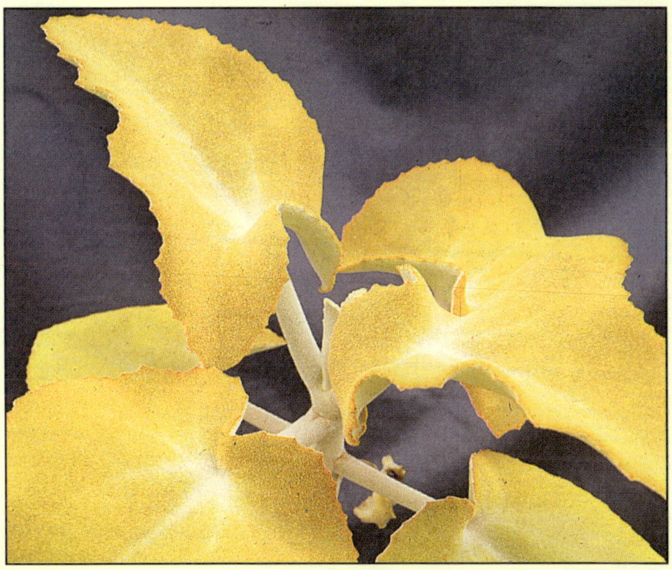

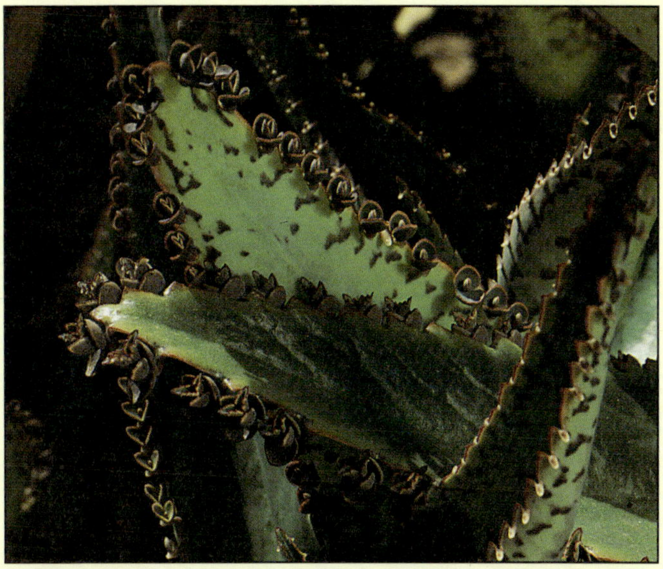

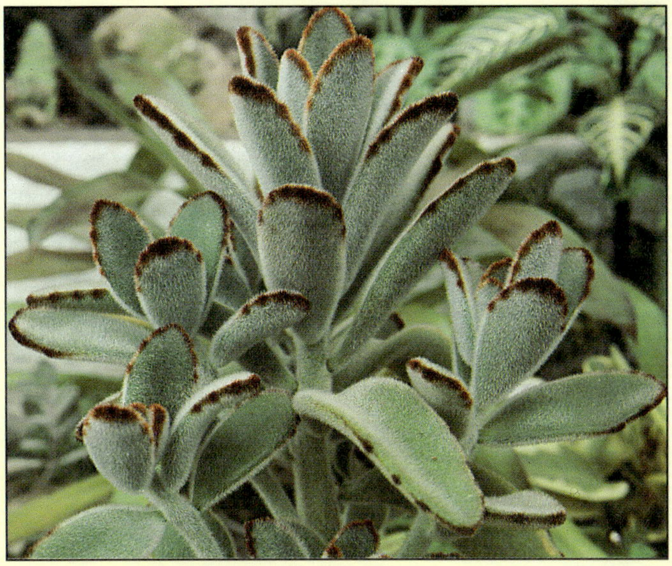

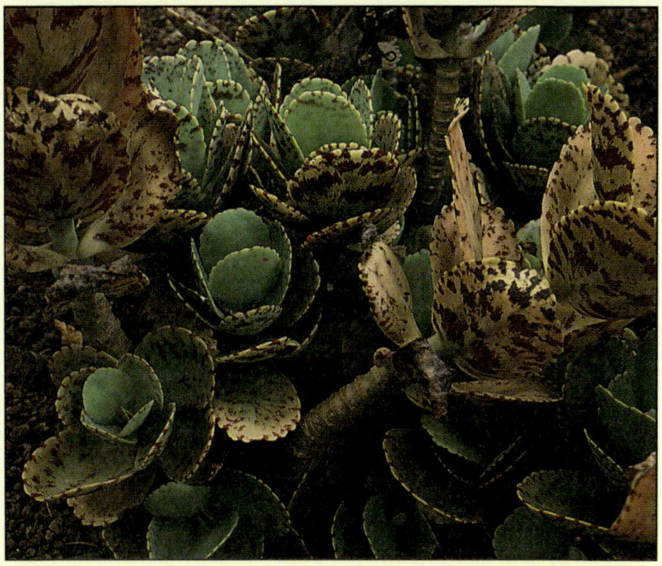

Lantana

Family name: **Verbenaceae**

Common name: **Yellow Sage**

Care Easy	**Height** 4ft (1.2m)	**Flower** Summer
Light Sunny	**Spread** 1ft (0.3m)	**Humidity** Spray in hot weather
Price Middle range	**Shape** Bushy	**Availability** Garden centres

Temp. Min 50°F (10°C) — Ideal 65°F (18°C) — Max 75°F (24°C)

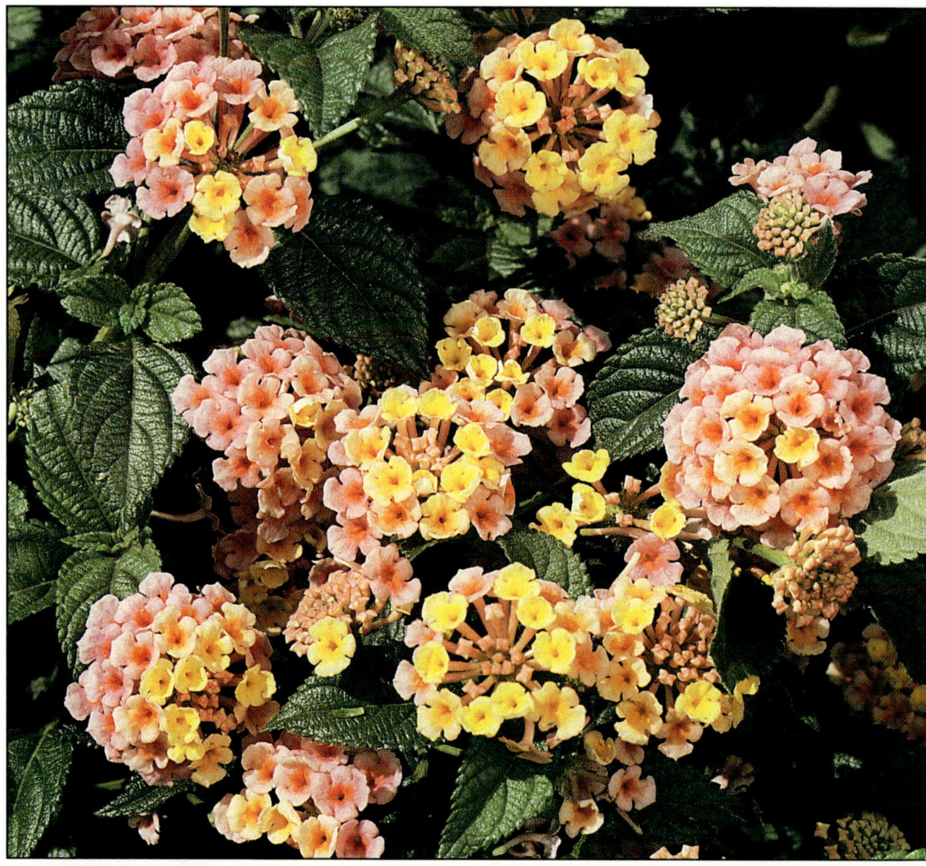

The unusual, multicoloured flower heads of Lantana, the Yellow Sage.

These evergreen shrubs have particularly attractive clusters of small, fragrant flowers. The remarkable feature of *Lantana camara,* which makes the most successful houseplant of this group, is the way each tiny flower changes colour, usually darkening, as it ages, to give a multi-coloured flower head.

Sometimes known as Yellow Sage, in the wild it grows into a rather open, sparse bush up to 4ft (1.2m) or more in height. But it is far more attractive and free-flowering if kept trimmed to 10-15in (25-38cm), and properly pruned it will flourish for years and produce an abundance of flowers.

Spring and summer care

Potting is best done every March, into John Innes No 1, adding some crocks under the compost to ensure good drainage. Move small plants up to a pot one size larger, to a final size of 6-8in (15-20cm), then topdress every year, scraping off the top 1-2in (2.5-5cm) of compost and replacing it with fresh.

Keep your plant at a temperature of 60-65°F (15-18°C), in a really bright, sunny position, where air circulation is good. With too little sunlight, your plant may not flower, but you'll need to shade it from the midday sun during the hottest months.

Water freely from April to October to keep the compost thoroughly moist and add liquid fertiliser every week or two between May and September. Mist spray the leaves in hot weather to provide humidity.

Autumn and winter care

Winter temperatures should be kept at around 50-55°F (10-13°C). Give your plant the best possible light, including full sunlight. Water only moderately between October and April, just enough to prevent the compost drying out. Your plant will need to be well pruned in late winter; cut it right back in February to within 4-6in (10-15cm) of the base to keep the shape neat and compact and encourage it to flower well.

Propagation

Take 3-4in (8-10cm) cuttings of young shoots in March or April, dip the cut ends in a rooting hormone and set in John Innes No 1 with some sharp sand added. Enclose the cuttings in a clear polythene bag or in a propagator, then uncover when new growth is apparent, usually after two or three weeks; keep them moist and slightly shaded from bright light, at a temperature of 65-70°F (18-21°C), throughout. When the cuttings are showing 2-3in (5-8cm) of new growth, pinch out the tips to encourage a bush plant, then pot up individually into 3in (7cm) pots of John Innes No 1 and treat as mature plants.

Trouble Shooter

Lantanas can survive underwatering, although foliage will begin to deteriorate if they are left dry for too long. Overwatering can damage the root system and fungus may develop. They are particularly susceptible to whitefly and may also be attacked by red spider mite; for either pest, spray with a malathion-based insecticide as a deterrent, according to the manufacturer's instructions.

Buying guide

The best time to buy Lantana is in the spring. Look for a neat, bushy plant, with plenty of flower buds and healthy-looking foliage that shows no sign of pests and diseases.

Species

Lantana camara, Yellow Sage, from the West Indies, carries rough-textured, dark green, pungent-smelling leaves on prickly stems. From May to October densely-packed clusters of fragrant flowers appear. These change in colour as they age, from pink or yellow through to orange and red or other shades depending on the variety.

L.montevidensis, *below,* is a spreading plant from Uruguay, sometimes known as the Trailing Lantana and particularly well-suited to hanging baskets. It flowers at any time but especially during the summer, producing a mass of bright, rosy-lilac flowers with yellow centres.

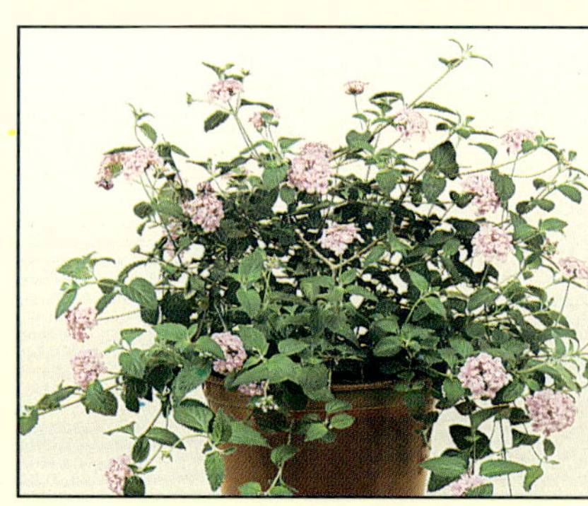

Laurus

Family name: **Lauraceae**

Common names:
Bay Tree/Bay Laurel

Care Easy	**Height** 10-18ft (3-5.4m)	**Flower** Insignificant
Light Sunny	**Spread** 10-15ft (3-4.5m)	**Humidity** Mist spray regularly
Price Middle range	**Shape** Tree or bush	**Availability** Common
Temp. Min 40°F (5°C)	Ideal 65°F (18°C)	Max 75°F (24°C)

A popular choice for patios and terraces, the Bay Tree *(Laurus nobilis)* is not often thought of as a houseplant but, with a little looking after, this attractive and useful plant will thrive indoors.

Bay is an evergreen with dark green foliage. Its aromatic leaves are used in cooking, for flavouring soups, stews, fish and other dishes. In their natural habitat, Bay Trees can grow to 18ft (5.4m) or more, but grown in a pot they are usually kept trimmed to about 3-4ft (0.9-1.2m). You can trim your plant into any shape you like, from an oval or pyramid-shaped bush to a round-headed miniature tree, or you can trim it to keep it as a natural-looking compact bush.

Bay Trees are fairly easy to grow. Give them a bright, sunny spot, with good air circulation, protect them from frost and take care when watering, and you'll have a plant that will survive successfully for many years.

Spring and summer care

Although they grow slowly, bays like plenty of root space so repot in the spring every two years, into John Innes No 2, moving your plant into a pot two sizes larger each time up to a final size of 10-12in (25-30cm).

Ordinary room temperatures are fine; what is important is to find your tree a really bright spot but out of direct sun. The Bay likes plenty of fresh air, too, and doesn't mind draughts, so you can stand it outdoors in the summer. Water moderately from April to October, adding fertiliser to the water every two or three weeks, and mist spray the leaves regularly — especially during hot weather.

Trim your plant to shape, any time between May and July, then give the plant a thorough spraying after trimming, to freshen up the foliage.

Autumn and winter care

Cool winter temperatures suit Bay Trees very well, but make sure you protect your plant from frost. Give it the best light you can, preferably full sun whenever possible. Guard against overwatering during winter; water very sparingly during the coldest months and if the temperature falls below about 45°F (7°C) don't water at all.

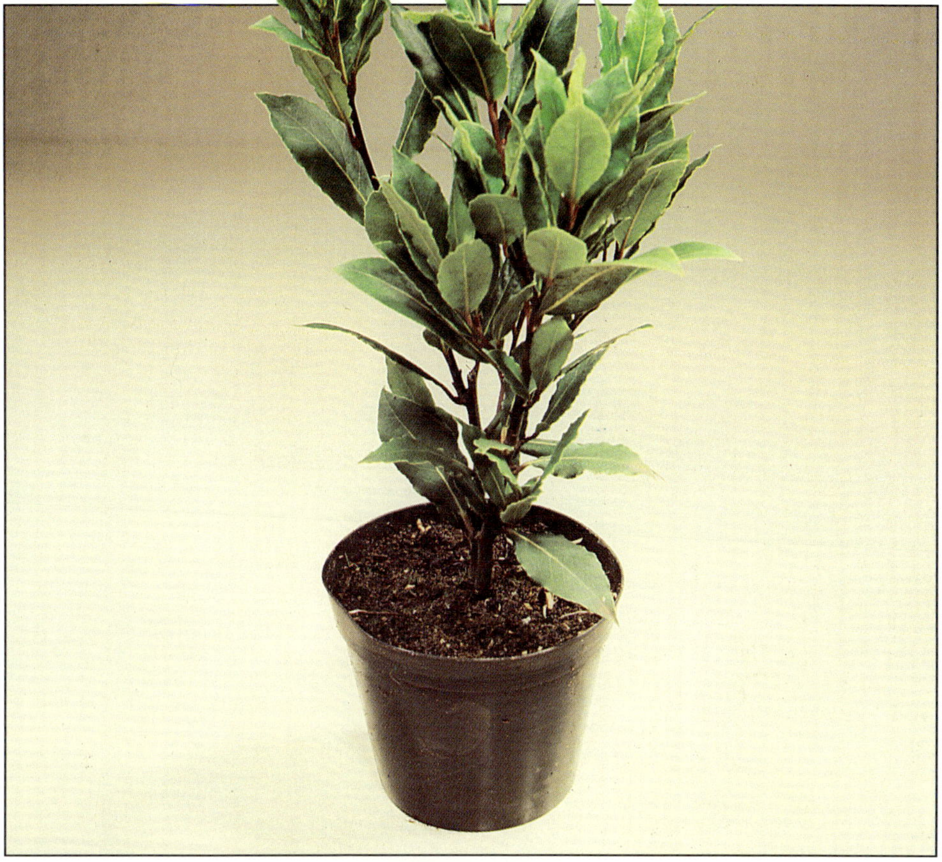

A young Bay Tree showing plenty of fresh new growth.

Trouble Shooter

Troubles are few. The most common cause of failure is overwatering during winter. Be sure to keep your plant frost-free; a severe frost can cause leaves to brown or even kill the upper growth completely. Yellowing and falling leaves in summer — usually from the lower branches — indicate underwatering. Remember to feed every two to three weeks — especially if you're removing a lot of leaves to use for cooking.

Scale insects — usually detectable as tiny brown discs on the undersides of leaves — are a likely attacker: wipe them away with a cotton bud dipped in methylated spirit.

Propagation

This is a straightforward but lengthy process. Take 4-5in (10-13cm) long cuttings of shoots between late July and September. Treat the cut ends with a rooting hormone, then set them in a mixture of half-sand, half-peat in a shaded place, at a temperature of about 60°F (15°C). The cuttings should not be disturbed until they are properly established, with strong, new growth showing, which may take a year or more. Repotting is best done in the spring, in John Innes No 2, then treat as a mature plant.

Species

Laurus nobilis, the Bay Tree or Bay Laurel, is an evergreen shrub with dark green, pointed oval leaves. Insignificant yellow flowers appear in April and dark purple berries form on female plants. Unrestricted, Bay Trees can reach a height and spread of 10-18ft (3-5.4m), but when grown in a pot they are usually kept trimmed to 3-4ft (0.9-1.2m). The aromatic leaves are used for flavouring soups, stews and fish dishes. There are also some varieties including *L.n.aurea*, which is one of the most attractive. Its leaves are a similar shape and flavour to the main species, but it has beautiful golden-yellow foliage. *L.n.angustifolia*, has very narrow, slightly longer leaves.

Buying Guide

Bay Trees tend to be expensive. For the best value choose a plant about 10-12in (25-30cm) high that has plenty of leafy branches. If you want to train your own plant to make a standard tree, look for a plant with a clearly defined main stem.

Lithops

Family name: **Aizoaceae**

Common names:
Living Stones/Pebble Plants

Care Easy	**Height** 1in (2.5cm)	**Flower** Late summer
Light Sunny	**Spread** 2in (5cm)	**Humidity** No mist spraying
Price Cheap	**Shape** Rounded	**Availability** Specialist nurseries
Temp. Min 50°F (10°C)	Ideal 70°F (21°C)	Max 80°F (27°C)

These fascinating little plants are aptly described by their common name, because of their extraordinary resemblance to the stones of their native desert. Among the most interesting of all succulents, they are of southern African origin and consist of a single pair of swollen, mottled leaves, attached to a short stem which is buried in the soil. The leaves are almost completely fused together to form a short, thick body, 1-1½in (2.5-4cm) in diameter, divided across the top. From this division between the leaves a single, daisy-like flower is produced in late summer or early autumn, usually yellow or white in colour, depending on the species.

The plants, which look amazingly like small, smooth pebbles, readily form into small clumps resulting eventually in a pot full of 'stones'. Individual flowers last up to a week and a good-sized group can flower for a month or two in succession.

Lithops lesliei is one of the best known species. It has flat-topped leaves up to 1½in (4cm) thick, that vary in colour from pinkish-grey to a brownish-green. In September it produces large, golden yellow flowers, 1in (2.5cm) or more across. Although virtually identical in shape, the many species present a remarkable range of colours and patterns to choose from and it is very satisfying to build up a collection of different plants.

Spring and summer care

Repot in April every third year using 3in (7cm) pots of cactus compost with some sharp sand added or a mixture of John Innes No 2 and sand in equal parts, adding some crocks under the compost to ensure good drainage.

Normal room temperatures are fine and they can rise as high as 80°F (27°C) without causing any harm. What is important is to give your plant the best possible light — a sunny position is essential.

Water sparingly from late spring until the flower dies in early autumn — just enough to make the compost barely moist. Add weak liquid fertiliser (use half the recommended amount) to the water every four to six weeks, from May to September.

Autumn and winter care

Keep your plants at a temperature of around 50°F (10°C) in the brightest spot you can, with full sun if possible. Start reducing water in September so that by October they are allowed to become completely dry, and they should remain so the whole winter. During this period the leaves will begin to shrivel up and a new pair appear between them, increasing in size until, by April or early May, they are fully formed and the old ones completely dried up. Remove the old leaves now and start watering again.

Propagation

In early summer divide up overcrowded clumps, leave the cuttings to dry for three or four days, then pot up individually in the normal compost (see 'Spring and summer care') and treat as established plants.

Trouble Shooter

Discolouration and poor growth is due to overwatering or watering at the wrong time; eventually, plants will become bloated and may rot. Prolonged exposure to low temperatures is also harmful — aim to provide a minimum of 50°F (10°C). Keep pests at bay with a dimethoate-based systemic insecticide applied at half the recommended amount in May and September.

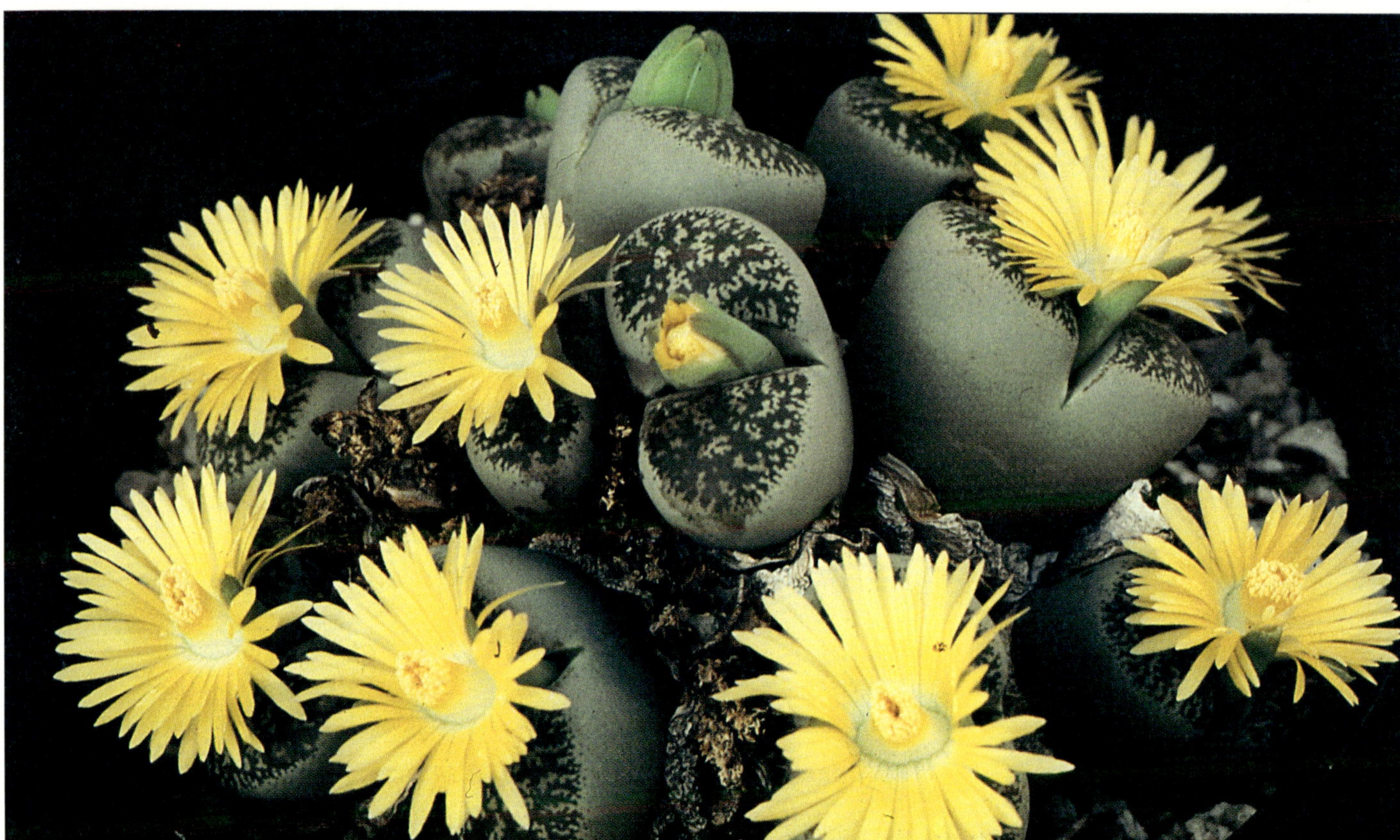

Brightly coloured flowers push up between the two thick, fused leaves of Living Stones.

Species

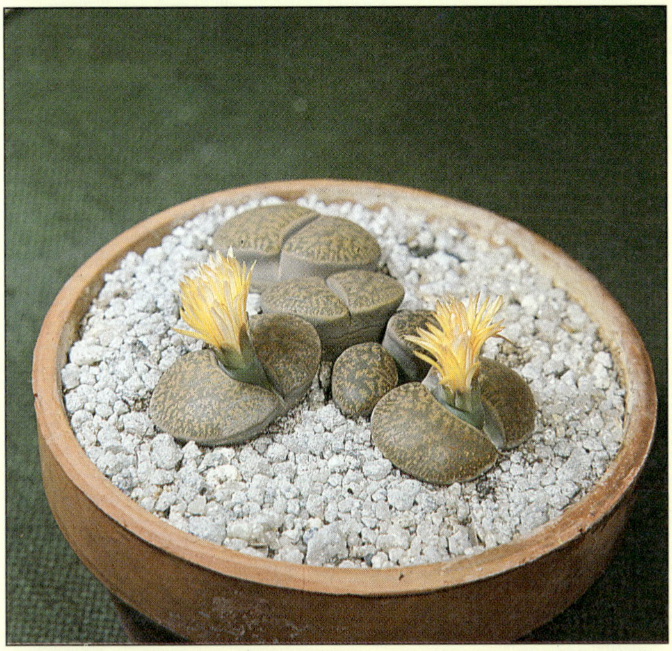

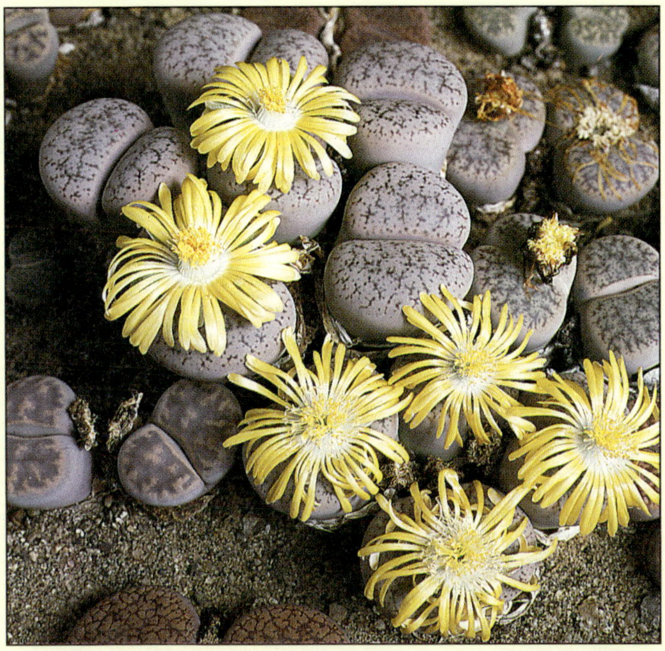

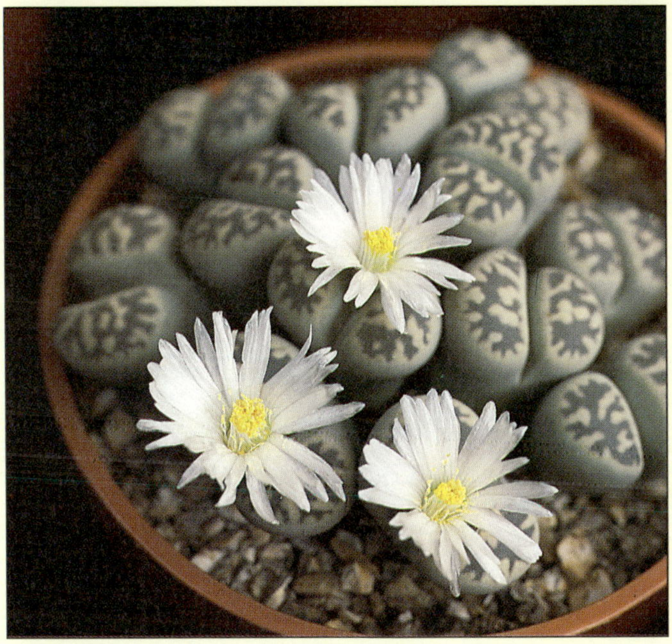

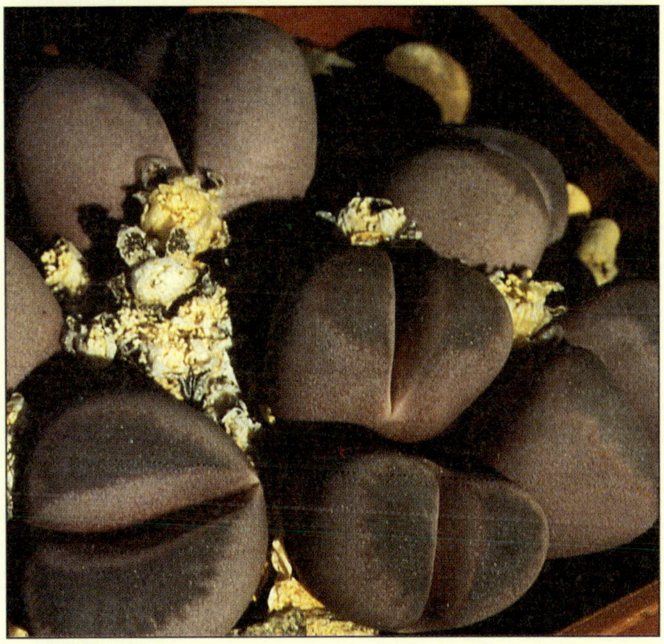

***Lithops lesliei**, top left,* is one of the most popular species, with flat-topped leaves up to 1½in (4cm) thick, that vary from pinkish-grey to a brownish-green, and reddish-brown markings on the upper surface. Large daisy-like flowers, over 1in (2.5cm) across, appear in late summer, golden yellow in colour, with pink shading on the underside of the petals.

***L.aucampiae**, top right,* is one of the largest-bodied plants growing to 1½in (4cm) or more in height, with a similar diameter. Its leaves are a reddish-brown with greenish markings on their flattened surface, and in late August or September it produces large, bright yellow, daisy-like flowers, 1in (2.5cm) or more across.

***L.bella**, bottom left,* is found only on granite mountain slopes, which is reflected in its mottled greyish colouring. It forms clumps readily and produces pure white, daisy-like flowers, around 1in (2.5cm) in diameter, in late summer and autumn.

L.optica is readily distinguished by the deep cleft between its grey-green leaves. Its white flowers appear in November and December, so summer watering and temperatures have to be maintained until then. Not a common species, it is mainly found as the purple-red variety *L.o.rubra, bottom right.*

L.fulleri stands about 1½in (4cm) high, with grey sides and a grey-green mottled top. Its white flowers appear in the autumn.

Lobivia

Family name: **Cactaceae**

Common name:
Lobivia

Care Easy	**Height** 4-5in (10-13cm)	**Flower** Summer
Light Sunny	**Spread** 2in (5cm)	**Humidity** None
Price Cheap	**Shape** Cushion	**Availability** Common
Temp. Min 50°F (10°C)	Ideal 70°F (21°C)	Max 80°F (27°C)

Among the best-known and most popular cacti, Lobivias are easy to grow and require very little special attention, making them a perfect choice for a beginner. They are particularly valued for their spectacular, highly-coloured flowers. Though flowers are short lived — in most species flowers last for between two and four days — the flowering period can last for much of the summer, the plants almost dwarfed by a profusion of large, exotic blooms.

The name Lobivia is, in fact, an anagram of Bolivia where many of these plants are found in the wild, at altitudes as high as 9000ft (2750m) or more. They are compact, rounded or cylindrical cacti, 3-6in (8-15cm) high, usually with many prominent ribs bristling with spines, and most species will readily produce clusters of offsets. *L.famatimensis* is one of the best known species, producing golden-yellow, cup-shaped flowers, some 2in (5cm) across; it has many very popular and colourful varieties.

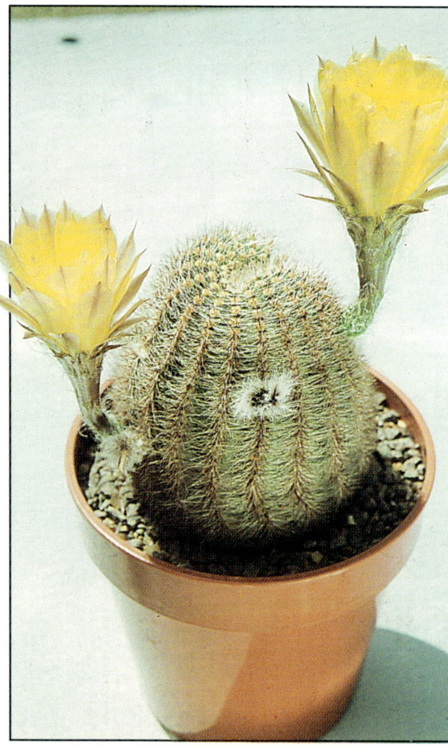

Although each flower is short-lived, Lobivias continue to bloom for months.

Spring and summer care

Pot on in spring, when plants start to make new growth. You only need to do this if the roots have filled the pot or offsets are crowding it out. Alternatively, offsets can be removed and potted up individually (see 'Propagation'). Use a proprietary cactus compost or mix two parts John Innes No 1 to one part coarse sand for potting.

Normal room temperatures are fine, and they can rise as high as 75°F (24°C) or more without causing any harm. What is important is that your plant has a really bright position, with as much full sunlight as possible; try to provide good air circulation as well.

Take care not to overwater; water enough to get the compost thoroughly moist then wait until it begins to dry out before watering again. Add a liquid fertiliser — ideally a proprietary cactus fertiliser — to the water every three weeks or so in summer between May and September. Do not mist spray Lobivias since this can cause rotting.

Autumn and winter care

Give your plant a rest during the winter by keeping temperatures down to about 50°F (10°C), but place it in the sunniest possible position and out of cold draughts. Reduce watering from early autumn and give none between November and March. As the temperature rises gradually increase watering.

Propagation

Lobivias can easily be raised from seed. Sow them in February or March into a cactus compost with sharp sand added; sprinkle the seeds lightly on the surface and cover with a thin layer of coarse sand. Moisten thoroughly and place in a propagator or polythene bag; keep in a shaded place at a temperature of 70-80°F (21-27°C).

The seeds should germinate within three or four weeks — they'll look like tiny green balls; remove them from the bag and bring them into a lighter place, at a temperature of 60-65°F (15-18°C), watering often enough to keep the compost moist. The plants are quite slow developing and it's best to wait until the following spring before moving them on; pot them up individually into 2in (5cm) pots of cactus compost and treat as established plants.

Alternatively, in spring or summer, detach offsets from the parent plant. Some will have a well-developed root system and can be pressed straight into individual 2-3in (5-8cm) pots of cactus compost; otherwise, leave offsets to dry for two or three days before potting, then treat as established plants.

Trouble Shooter

Troubles can be easily avoided. Don't overwater — the roots will rot and the whole plant will become rotten throughout. Plants will become pale and misshapen if they are in too shaded a position; always provide the best possible light. All cacti are susceptible to mealy bug; brush away the fluffy white patches with a paintbrush or cotton bud dipped in methylated spirit, or spray with a malathion-based insecticide if the plant is badly infested. Root mealy bug, which attacks the root system, is a real danger; this never surfaces — so look out for whitish deposits on the roots when repotting. As a preventative, use a systemic dimethoate-based insecticide, according to the manufacturers' instructions.

Species

Lobivia famatimensis comes from northern Argentina, where it grows at altitudes as high as 9000ft (2750m). A compact plant, growing to 4-5in (10-13cm), it is column-shaped with a number of ribs running down its length, covered in whitish spines. Large golden flowers, about 2in (5cm) long and funnel-shaped, are freely produced during the summer; though each flower lasts only a few days, the flowering period can last for many weeks. Popular varieties include *L.f.albiflora* with white flowers and *L.f.aurantiaca, above,* whose flowers are bright orangey-yellow, while those of *L.f.leucomalla* are yellow with a white throat.

L.saltensis produces offsets very readily. It is a pale green, globular plant, with many ribs and numerous spines; bright red, funnel-shaped flowers are borne from the sides of the stem.

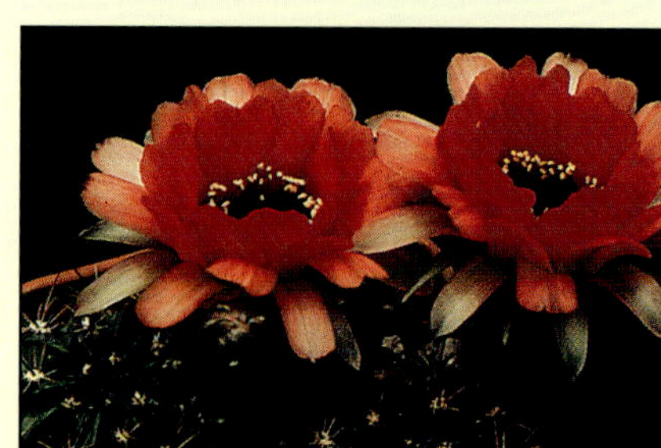

***L.jajoiana**, above,* is another well-known species, from the same region and altitude. Globular in shape, becoming a little taller with age, it usually remains solitary or forms only one or two offsets. Its many ribs bristle with pale red spines and it produces beautiful flowers, about 2in (5cm) long, wine-red or tomato coloured with a blackish-blue shaded throat.

Mammillaria

Family name: **Cactaceae**

Common name: **Cushion Plant/ Pincushion Cactus**

Care Easy	**Height** 2in (5cm)	**Flower** Summer
Light Bright, indirect	**Spread** 2in (5cm)	**Humidity** None
Price Cheap	**Shape** Cushion	**Availability** Garden centres

Temp. Min 50°F (10°C) Ideal 65°F (18°C) Max 80°F (27°C)

For many years this group of plants has captured the imagination of very many cacti enthusiasts. Mostly native of the USA and Mexico, there are more than 400 recognisable species — almost all very easy to grow. So a collection of these plants can make an undemanding yet attractive and interesting feature on a windowsill or in a conservatory.

The Mammillarias are all desert cacti. They are quite small, leafless plants — either column-shaped or squat, like a cushion. Many produce offsets — so they quickly become a clump rather than a solitary plant. The most obvious feature that distinguishes Mammillaria from many other cacti is the body of the plant; it is covered in small nodules, sometimes called tubercles, each with a tuft of spines or hairs at its centre. One of the favourite species is *M.zeilmanniana, right*, a small, slightly woolly, cushion-shaped cactus, mainly grown for its beautiful, reddish summer flowers. Another very popular plant is *M.bocasana*. It forms a mass of small, dark bluish-green cushions covered in stiff white spines. The yellowish flowers almost encircle each cushion in summer.

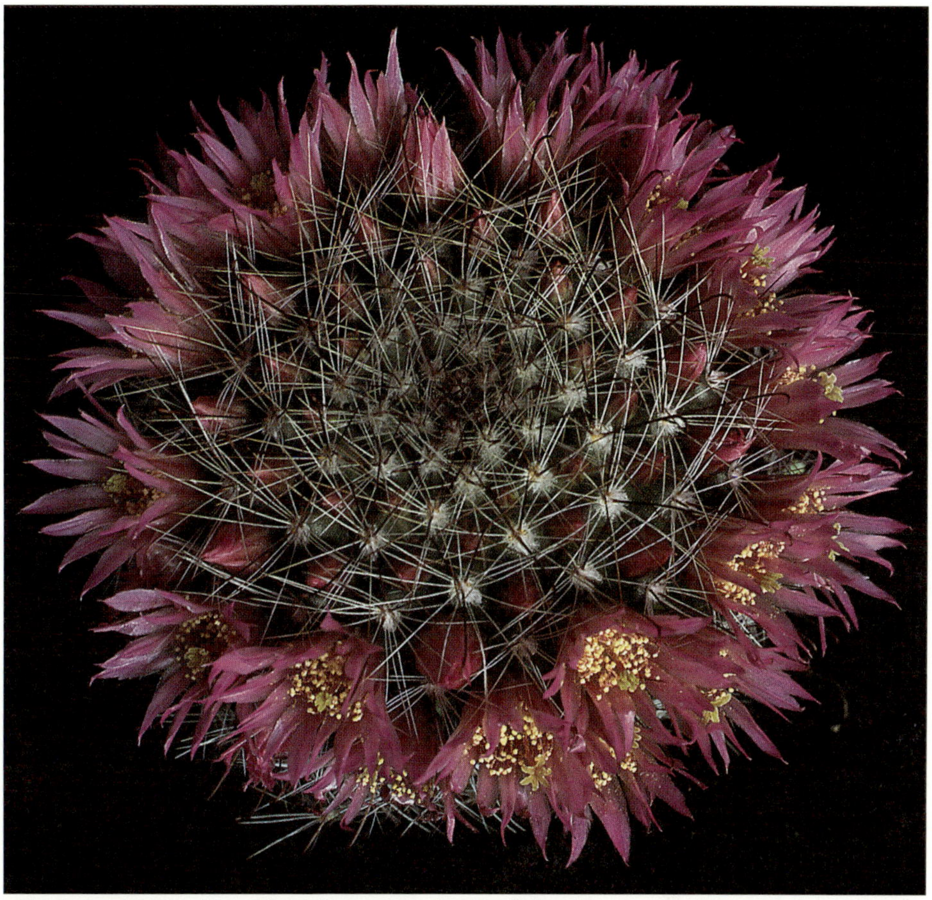

This beautiful Cushion Plant flowers profusely during the summer.

Spring and summer care

March is the best time to pot on your plant. If it has completely covered the surface of its pot, you can divide the plant (see 'Propagation'), or pot it into a pot one size larger. Use cactus compost or mix two parts John Innes No 1 with one part coarse sand for repotting.

After potting gradually bring your plant out of its rest period; water just occasionally at first, then, as the temperature rises, increase the watering. Always allow the surface of the compost to dry out between waterings. Feed your plant every three to four weeks during spring and summer — using a proprietary cactus fertiliser.

Keep your Mammillaria in a very bright position, but out of direct sun, ideally at a temperature of about 65-70°F (18-21°C); higher temperatures are fine, as long as the plant is kept in an airy position.

Autumn and winter care

Keep a minimum winter temperature of 50°F (10°C) — though a little higher would be ideal. At these low temperatures keep your plant completely dry — but if temperatures rise as high as 60°F (15°C) then water very occasionally. At this time of year the compost should never be wet. Make sure your plant gets plenty of bright light — direct sun is fine in winter — and is kept away from cold draughts.

Propagation

Most Mammillarias produce offsets — some more readily than others. These small plantlets can be removed in spring at potting time, and then transferred to their own pot to make a new plant. If your Mammillaria is a spiny one, wear rubber gloves for this job. Carefully cut the offsets away from the parent plant using a sharp knife. Leave the cutting to dry out for a few days, then set it in a small pot of cactus compost and treat it as a mature plant. It should take root quite quickly — within a few days.

You can grow Mammillaria from seed very easily — and this will give you the chance to grow some more unusual ones, or even breed some new hybrids of your own. Make sure your cactus produces fertile seed by pollinating its flowers yourself with a small paintbrush. When the flowers are fully open gently dab the brush on to the centre of each of the flowers. If you want to try and develop a new hybrid, brush the pollen from the flowers of one Mammillaria on to those of another type. If you are very lucky, some of the new plants that grow from the seeds of the cross-pollinated plant may look different from either of its parents.

To collect the seed, wait for the berries to ripen — their colour will darken — then use tweezers to pick them off your plant. Leave the berries to dry off; you can speed up this process by squeezing the seeds out of the berries on to a piece of blotting paper.

In March sow the seeds evenly over the surface of a mixture of equal parts coarse sand and cactus compost then just cover them with a little coarse sand, and moisten the compost thoroughly. Keep the seed tray in a polythene bag or propagator, at a temperature between 65-70°F (18-21°C), and in a shaded position. When seedlings are visible, remove the tray from the bag or propagator and bring it into brighter light.

Don't pot the young seedlings up until they develop into recognisable miniature cacti — this is a slow process and may take as long as a year. During this time apply a weak cactus fertiliser every two to three weeks — using half the dose recommended — and make sure the temperature does not fall below 60°F (15°C), otherwise treat them as established plants.

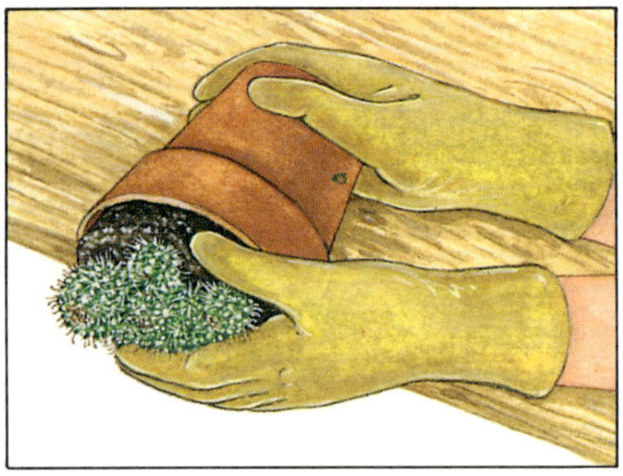

When your plant has covered the surface of the compost, knock it out of its pot. Wear gloves when handling cacti since spines can irritate the skin.

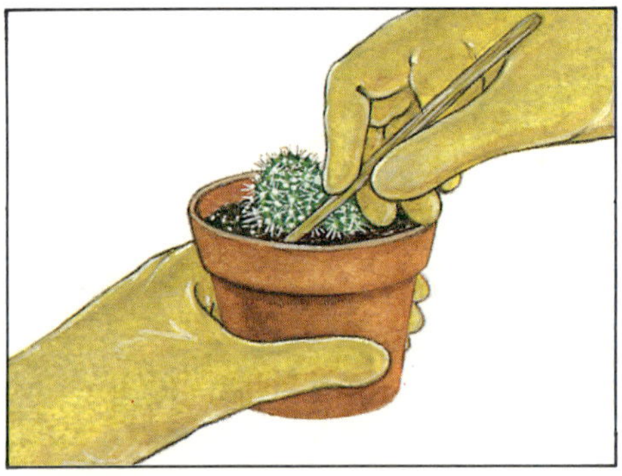

Divide the plant and pot the portions separately, firming down the compost.

Trouble Shooter

These cacti are relatively trouble free. Overwatering, especially in winter, causes rotting which makes the flesh of the plant look bruised and mushy; also take care not to splash water over the body of the plant, since this can cause localised rotting in winter. Carefully remove any bruised-looking material with a scalpel or small sharp knife, then dust the wound with a fungicidal sulphur powder.

Keep the plant dry, in a light position and away from cold draughts. A distorted, pale-looking plant is due either to poor light conditions or a lack of fertiliser.

Mealy bug can be dealt with by dabbing them with methylated spirit. If your plant looks generally rather sickly, lift it out of its pot and inspect the roots for mealy bug. If you see small white tufts clustered around the roots, wash the rootball gently to remove the pest and then repot in fresh compost. It's a wise precaution to protect your plant with a systemic dimethoate-based insecticide applied to the soil three or four times during the growing season — following the manufacturer's instructions. The plant will take this up into its system and protect itself from pest attack.

Species

Mammillaria zeilmanniana, *top,* from Mexico, is a rounded, dark green cushion about 2in (5cm) high. Like all Mammillarias, it is covered with small tubercles, but in this case they are oval and carry tufts of fine white hairs. The beautiful reddish flowers which are about 3/4in (19mm) across, are long-lasting and appear in profusion during the summer. The variety *M.z.alba* has white flowers.

M.bocasana readily forms a mass of dark bluish-green, rounded cushions, each about 2in (5cm) in diameter when they're mature, and covered with white bristly hairs. The ½in (13mm) yellowish flowers have a brown stripe down the centre of each petal, they appear in summer and form almost a complete ring around the body of the plant. *M.b.splendens, bottom,* is smothered in fine, white hairs.

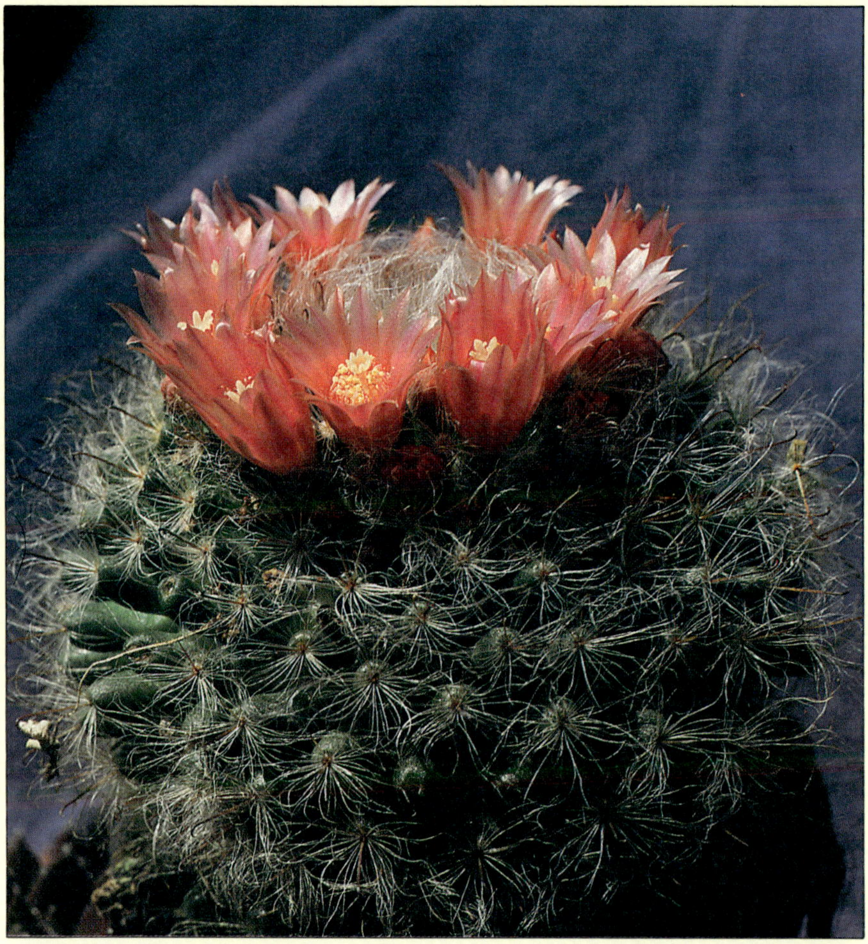

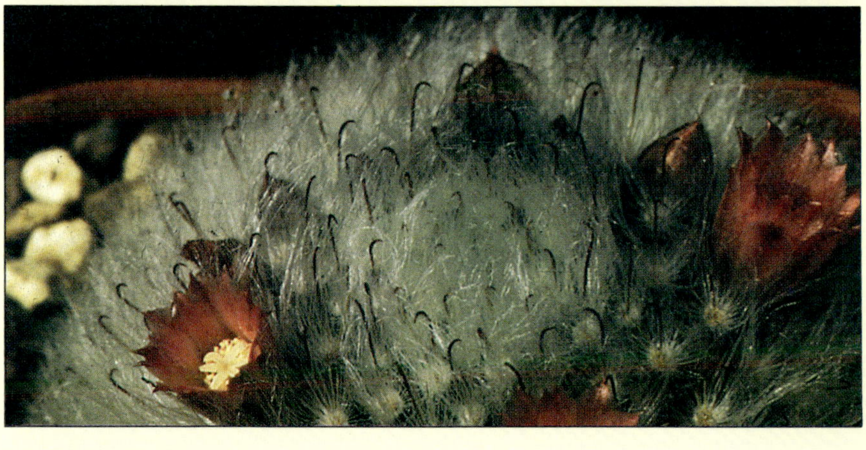

Species

M.mystax, from southern Mexico, is cylindrical in shape and can reach 6in (15cm) high and 4in (10cm) across, and has brown spines. Reddish-pink flowers encircle the crown of the plant in summer followed by crimson fruits.

M.spinosissima, *below left*, from central Mexico, forms a thick column almost 12in (30cm) tall and 5in (13cm) across. It is dark green and covered with fine woolly tufts of hair-like spines which vary in colour depending on the variety; *M.s.auricoma* has white spines, those of *M.s.rubens* are deep reddish brown. The flowers form a ring around the top of the plant — in carmine, pink or white.

M.oliviae has long-lasting, pinkish-red summer flowers. It is a cushion-shaped plant about 4in (10cm) high and covered with white spines. This species prefers a shaded position.

M.rhodantha, *below right*, again from Mexico, is column-shaped and grows to 12in (30cm) tall and 3-4in (8-10cm) across. It has stiff pink or brownish spines and reddish coloured flowers that encircle the plant during the summer months.

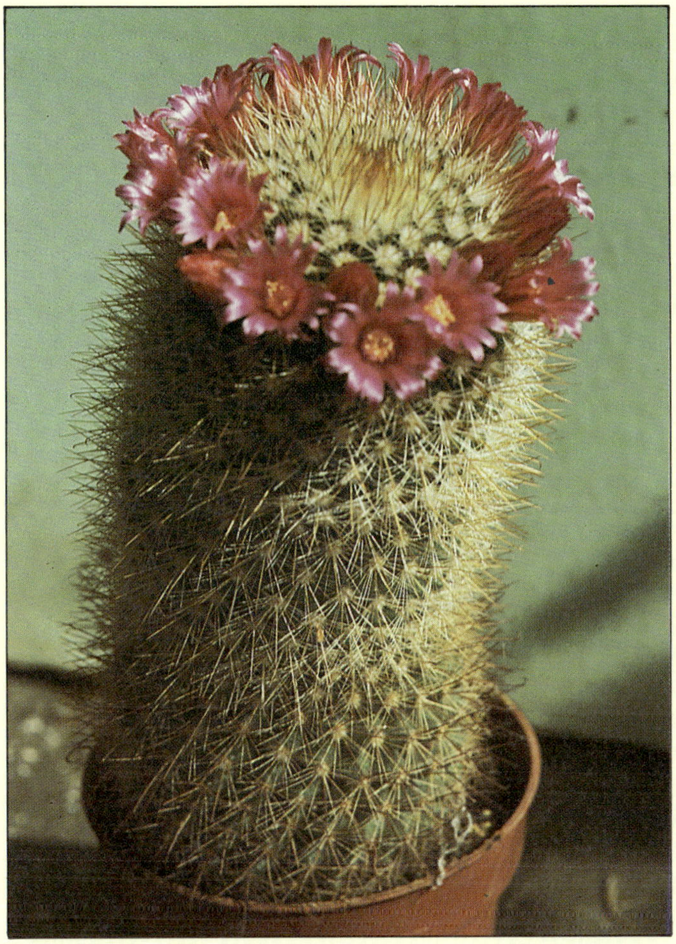

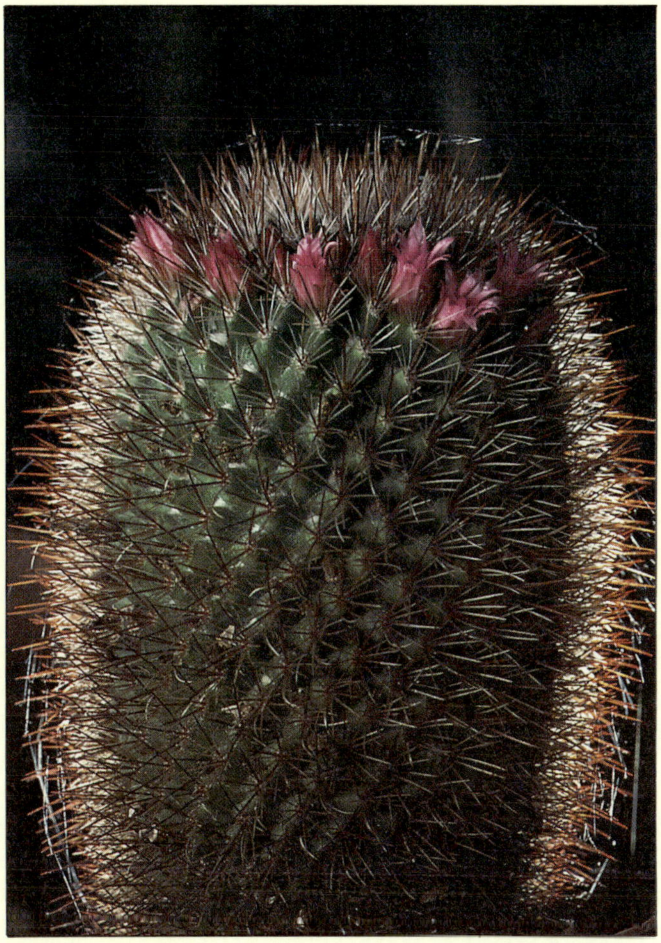

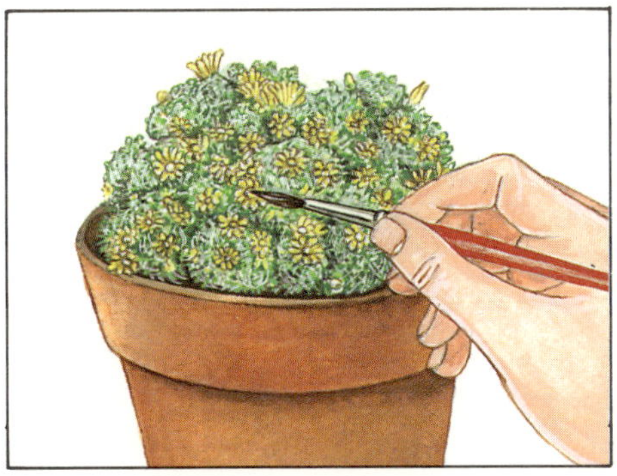

Instead of buying seeds, gather your own. Fertilise the flowers by transferring pollen with a small brush.

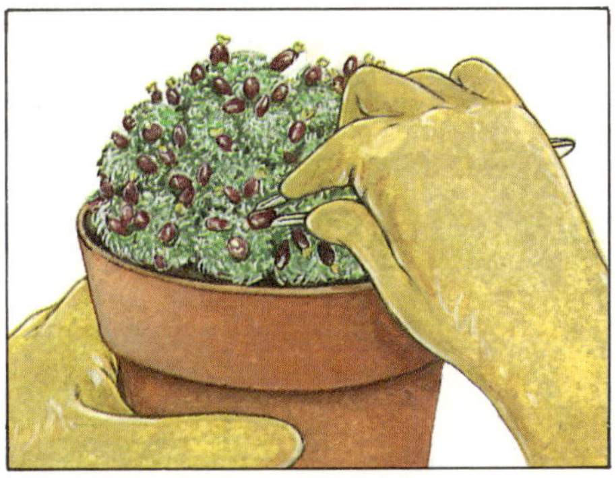

After flowering the fruits will develop. Pick them off your plant when their colour darkens.

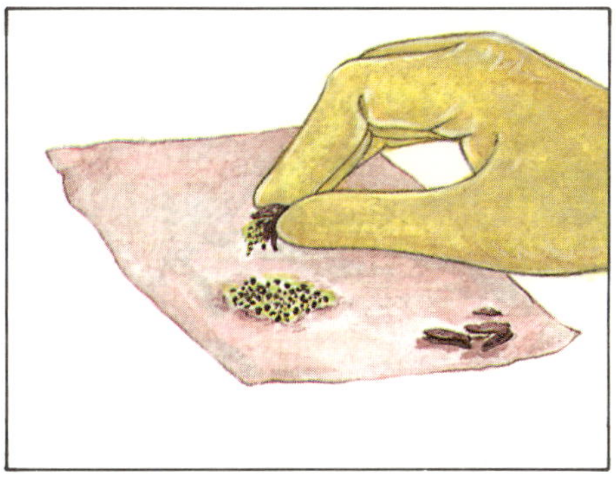

Release the seeds by squeezing the berries on to a piece of absorbent paper, then let them dry off.

Maranta

Family name: **Marantaceae**

Common names: **Prayer Plant, Rabbit Tracks**

Care Easy	**Height** 8in (20cm)	**Flower** Insignificant
Light Shady	**Spread** 12in (30cm)	**Humidity** Mist spray regularly
Price Cheap	**Shape** Bushy	**Availability** Common
Temp. Min 50°F (10°C)	Ideal 70°F (21°C)	Max 80°F (27°C)

Marantas are prized for their foliage, beautifully and distinctively marked in a wide range of patterns and colours. They are also known for their curious habit of folding their leaves together and holding them upright at night like hands in prayer — hence the common name, Prayer Plant.

Maranta leuconeura, right, is the only species of these South American evergreens commonly grown indoors. It is a bushy, low-growing plant, rarely exceeding 8in (20cm) in height, with 3in (7.5cm) long, oval leaves delicately patterned in emerald green, with dark green or light brown markings, looking almost hand-painted. A number of extremely attractive varieties are also available, with varying leaf size, pattern and colouring.

These useful and highly decorative plants are the perfect choice to brighten up a shady spot since, unusually for such brightly-coloured plants, that is where they thrive. And, despite their striking, exotic appearance, they are surprisingly easy to grow.

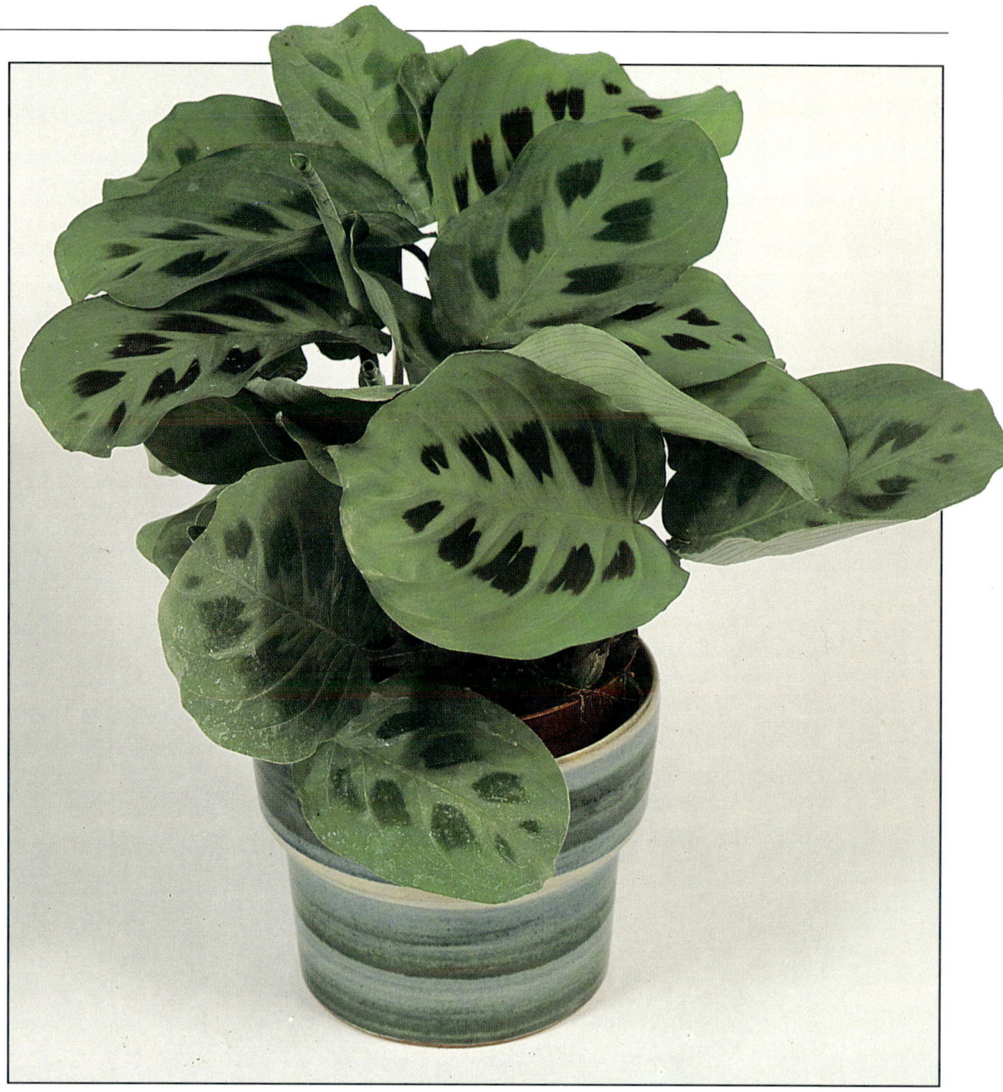

Marantas are attractive, leafy plants, useful for cheering up shady corners.

Spring and summer care

Marantas grow quickly and young plants may need frequent potting on to a final pot size of 5-6in (13-15cm), into John Innes No 2, after which repot in spring every two years. Snip off any dead or shrivelled leaves, at the same time, to make way for new growth.

Temperatures of around 65-70°F (18-21°C) are ideal; they can rise as high as 80°F (27°C) without harm. The most important thing is to protect your plant from bright light, especially direct sunlight; for healthy leaves with good colouring keep the plant in quite a shady position from April to September.

Water freely as much as is necessary to keep the compost thoroughly moist at all times; these are thirsty plants, so watering may be frequent — add a liquid fertiliser to the water every two or three weeks from May to September. Mist spray regularly to maintain a humid atmosphere; with temperatures of 70°F (21°C) or above you'll probably need to spray the leaves daily.

Autumn and winter care

Winter temperatures should not fall below 50°F (10°C), preferably a little higher. Move your plant to a slightly brighter spot during the dullest months, but avoid full sunlight still. Water fairly sparingly to keep the soil just moist, but mist spray the leaves every few days to maintain a high humidity.

Propagation

Propagate by division (see below) in February or March; gently pull the plant apart, taking care not to damage the tubers, and pot up the divisions separately.

Alternatively, take 3-4in (8-10cm) cuttings from the stem tips, with two or three leaves attached, from May to August and set them in 3in (7cm) pots — up to three per pot — of equal parts peat and sand. Enclose in a clear polythene bag — don't allow the leaves to touch the polythene — and keep in a shady place. When the cuttings have rooted, within four to six weeks usually, pot them on individually into John Innes No 2 and treat as established plants.

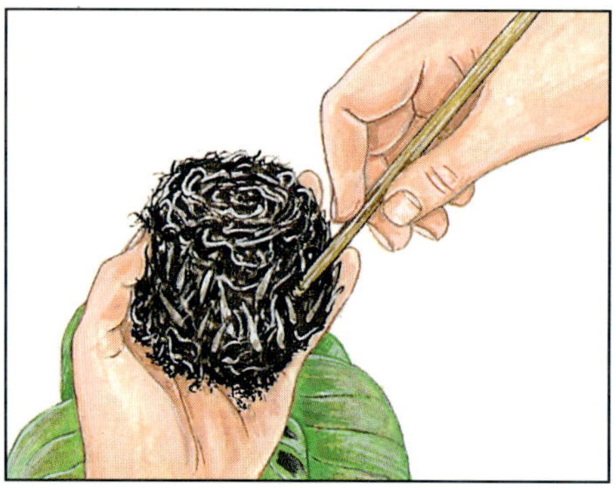

Divide your Maranta in the spring. Gently tease out the fleshy roots taking care not to damage them.

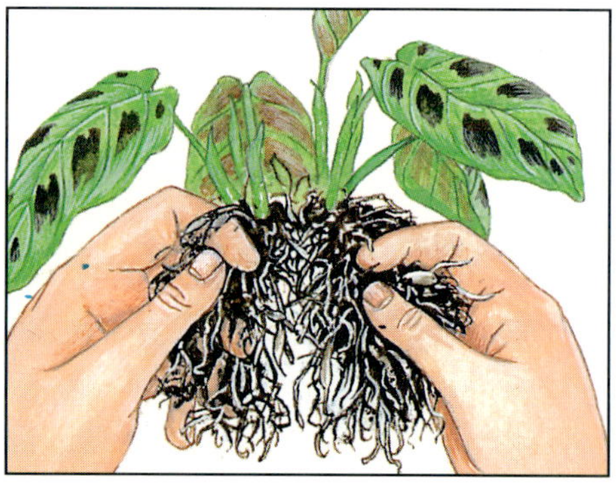

Pull the plant carefully into two halves and pot them up separately using John Innes No 2.

Trouble Shooter

Warmth in winter is vital. Leaves will shrivel and turn brown if temperatures fall too low; new leaves should appear with warmer conditions. Leaves may become bleached and faded if exposed to too much light — full sunlight particularly, which may scorch the leaves; the plant should be moved immediately. For the best leaf colouring and variegation, shade is essential. Leaves falling or leaf tips turning brown indicates that the air is too dry — these plants need high humidity; remove any dead growth and be sure to mist spray regularly.

Low air humidity increases the chances of attack from red spider mite; spray with a malathion-based insecticide to remove them. Mealy bug is a likely pest, usually gathering around the leaf axils and the underside of the leaves. Wipe away the tell-tale fluffy white patches with a cotton bud or paintbrush dipped in methylated spirit or spray with a malathion-based insecticide, if more persistent. Applying a systemic dimethoate-based insecticide is a good overall deterrent; always follow the manufacturers' instructions.

Species

Maranta leuconeura, the Prayer Plant, is a low-growing evergreen from Brazil, with very decorative foliage. A bushy, compact plant, it rarely exceeds 8in (20cm) in height, with a spread of up to 12in (30cm). It has broadly oval, satiny, 3in (7.5cm) long leaves in emerald green, with dark green or light brown blotches, which darken as the plant matures; the underside of the leaf is grey-green shot with purple. This is the only species of Maranta commonly grown indoors, but it has a number of well known varieties with varying leaf size, pattern and colouring.

Among the most popular is *M.l. kerchoveana, top,* known as Rabbit Tracks after the heavy brown blotches on its light green leaves; these markings turn dark green with age. *M.l.tricolor, bottom,* (also known as *M.l.erythrophylla*) has distinctively marked leaves: vivid red veins on a deep olive-green background, with greyish-green margins and bright-green jagged marking along the midrib. A rather similar pattern is found on *M.l.massangeana*, but this has a slightly smaller, blackish-green leaf, with pale-green margins, jagged, silvery marking along the midrib and a fine herringbone pattern of silvery veins.

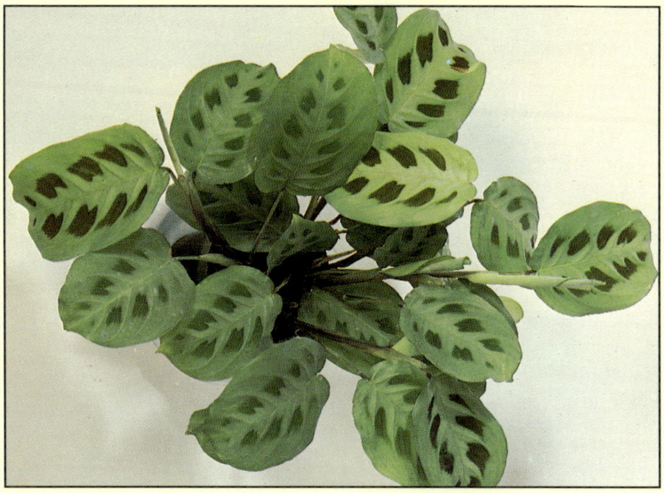

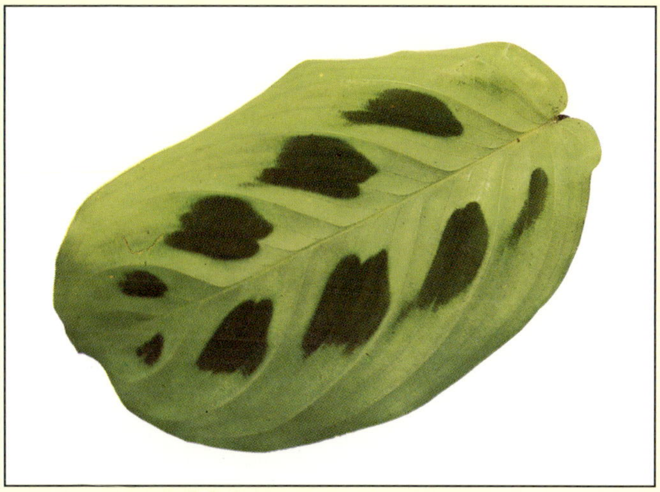

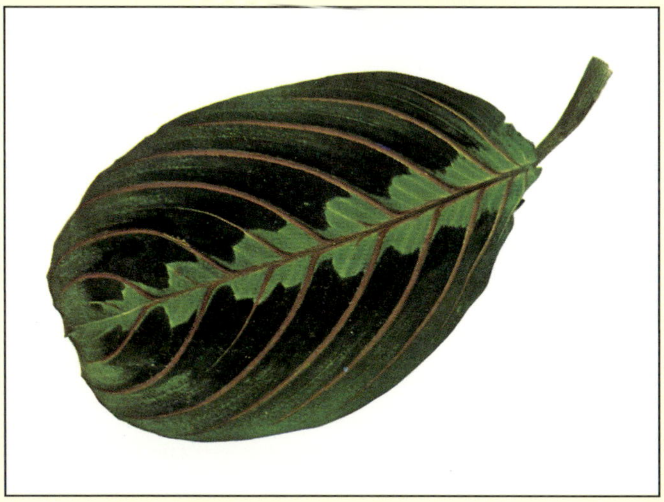

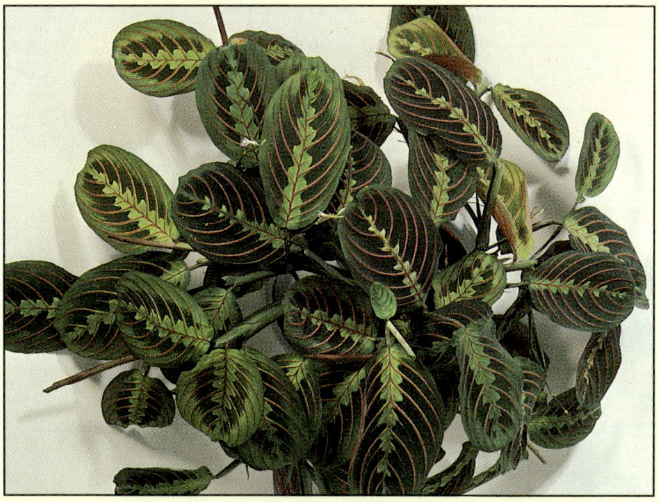

Medinilla

Family name: **Melastomaceae**

Common name:
Rose Grape

Care Tricky	**Height** 4ft (1.2m)	**Flower** Summer
Light Sunny	**Spread** 4ft (1.2m)	**Humidity** Mist spray regularly
Price Expensive	**Shape** Bushy	**Availability** Specialist nurseries

Temp. Min 60°F (15°C) Ideal 75°F (24°C) Max 80°F (27°C)

This large and diverse group contains some of the most beautiful tropical plants in cultivation, with truly outstanding flowers. Probably the finest species of all, and the one best suited to growing indoors is the aptly-named *Medinilla magnifica, right,* which has lovely weeping flower heads, up to 1½ft (45cm) long, made up of large clusters of rose pink and purple flowers, with tiers of pinkish bracts. This really handsome evergreen has thick woody stems, carrying large leathery leaves and reaches a height of about 4ft (1.2m).

Medinillas present something of a challenge — conditions must be just right for them to flourish. But if you are lucky enough to have a heated sun room or conservatory, you could be rewarded with a splendid specimen which will take pride of place among your houseplants.

Spring and summer care

Medinilla is a fairly slow-growing plant so pot on into John Innes No 3, in February every other year, until a final pot size of 8-10in (20-25cm) is reached. In years when you aren't potting on, topdress by replacing the top 1-2in (2.5-5cm) of compost. Make sure containers are well crocked when potting.

This plant needs warmth all year round; summer temperatures should not fall below 70°F (21°C) and 75-80°F (24-27°C) is certainly beneficial. A bright, sunny location is very important.

Water fairly freely so the compost is thoroughly moist, then let the top ½in (1.5cm) of soil dry out before watering again. Add a liquid fertiliser to the water every two weeks as soon as the flower buds start to open, around April, then continue feeding until September. To maintain a humid atmosphere, stand your pot on a tray of moist pebbles or mist spray regularly — spray the plant from above to avoid wetting the flowers.

Prune your plant after the last flowers have faded. Using a pair of sharp secateurs cut long branches back by as much as half.

Autumn and winter care

For your plant to get through the winter, quite high temperatures are essential: around 70°F (21°C) is ideal and never less than 60°F (15°C). Give it the sunniest position possible and enough water to keep the compost just moist, and continue mist spraying regularly to keep the air humid.

Propagation

This is best done in early spring, with cuttings of tips of shoots about 3in (8cm) long, with two pairs of leaves attached. Treat the cut ends with a rooting hormone and set them in a mixture of two parts peat and one part sharp sand; keep moist in a propagator in a lightly-shaded spot at a temperature of 85°F (30°C). The cuttings need a humid atmosphere so only open the vents of your propagator slightly.

Plants should root in three to four weeks; leave them to develop for a further four weeks or so — there should be other signs of activity, such as leaf buds starting to develop — then move the cuttings into individual 3-4in (8-10cm) pots of John Innes No 3 and treat as established plants.

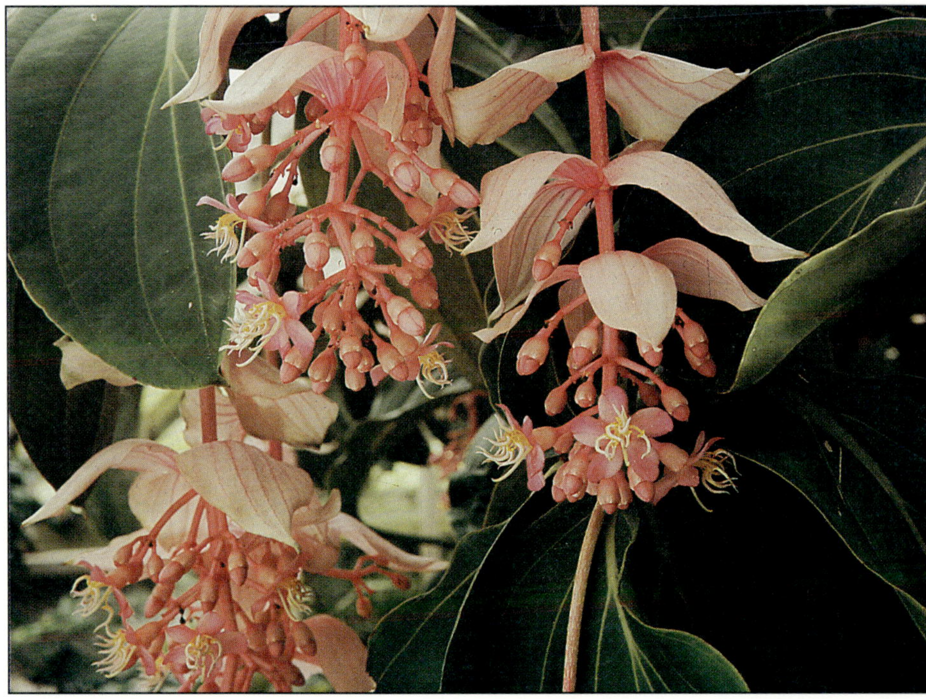

A challenging plant to grow — but the winning prize is worth all the effort!

Species

Medinilla magnifica, *above*, sometimes known as Rose Grape, is the only species commonly grown indoors. This handsome evergreen shrub comes from Java and the Philippines, where it reaches a height of 7-8ft (2.1-2.4m) though it rarely exceeds 4ft (1.2m) as a houseplant. Thick, woody stems carry heavily-veined, leathery, oval-shaped leaves, with a creamy-white midrib, up to 12in (30cm) long. From late spring until August, long, drooping flower stems carry tiers of pinkish bracts and large clusters of pink and purple flowers, each one about ½in (1.5cm) long.

M.waterhousei is something of a rarity, but well worth growing if you can get hold of the seed. A semi-climber, found only in mountainous regions of Fiji, it is one of the most beautiful tropical plants. It has short but spectacular pendulous flower heads of pinkish-white flowers and rich scarlet bracts. These appear during the summer months.

M.curtisii, from Indonesia, is sometimes available; it is an evergreen shrub, quite similar to *M.magnifica*, with lovely white flowers which appear in summer.

Trouble Shooter

Foliage will wilt and plants may not flower if they are too cold, if the air is too dry or they are too shaded. Take care also not to overwater.

They are highly susceptible to attack by red spider mite, though the regular mist spraying should help as a deterrent; if they do occur, spray with a malathion-based insecticide. Scale insect and mealy-bug are also likely pests; these can be brushed away with a cotton bud or a paintbrush dipped in methylated spirit, or spray with a malathion-based insecticide if persistent. Applying a dimethoate-based systemic insecticide is a useful overall preventative; always follow the manufacturers' instructions.

Mimosa

Family name: **Leguminosae**

Common names:
Sensitive Plant/Humble Plant/ Touch-me-not

Care Straight forward	**Height** 18-20in (45-50cm)	**Flower** July-August
Light Sunny	**Spread** 12-18in (30-45cm)	**Humidity** Mist spray regularly
Price Middle range	**Shape** Bushy	**Availability** Garden centres
Temp. Min 50°F (10°C)	Ideal 70°F (21°C)	Max 80°F (27°C)

Although the Sensitive Plant is pretty and delicate-looking, with light feathery foliage and fluffy, pink flower heads, its particular fascination lies in the way it behaves when it's handled. Touch the plant, no matter how gently, and the fern-like leaves fold up tightly, curling in towards the stem, as if shrinking away from attack. Leave it alone for a short time and the leaves slowly open up again and the plant once more stands up straight.

Not to be confused with the florist's 'Mimosa' (in fact, *Acacia dealbata*), with its sweetly-scented yellow flowers — though they are related — the true Mimosas form a large group of mainly low-growing shrubs and trees. The Sensitive Plant (*M.pudica*) is the only species commonly grown as a houseplant; up to 20in (50cm) tall, with light-green, fern-like leaves, carried on many slender, rather prickly stems and branches. In July and August, clusters of fluffy, pink, ball-shaped flowers appear, each one made up of hundreds of fine filaments.

These plants are easy to grow and easy to care for. Many people treat them as annuals, bought in the spring and discarded in the winter, but with the right care they can live — and thrive — indefinitely.

Spring and summer care

Pot in the spring into John Innes No 2, moving on to a slightly larger pot when the roots fill the current pot — they will start to appear through the drainage hole — to a final size of 5in (13cm). Then topdress annually, replacing the top 1-2in (2.5-5cm) of compost.

Mimosas like warmth, and summer temperatures can comfortably rise above 70°F (21°C), though rooms should be well ventilated. Find your plant a brightly-lit position — some direct sunlight is beneficial, but try and shade it from the midday sun.

Water freely so that the compost is kept moist and add a fertiliser to the water every two weeks. Mist spray the leaves regularly to provide humidity; standing the pot on a saucer of moist pebbles is also very effective.

Autumn and winter care

Aim for winter temperatures of 55-60°F (13-16°C); keep your plant in as sunny a spot as possible and free from draughts. Water only occasionally — allow the top half of the compost to dry out before watering again — but mist spray occasionally for humidity.

Propagation

Sow seeds just under the surface of a mixture of two parts peat to one part sand. Keep moist and in a well ventilated place at a temperature of 65-70°F (18-21°C): The seeds should germinate in four to six weeks. Prick out seedlings when they're about 2in (5cm) high, after a further two months or so, into individual 3in (7cm) pots of John Innes No 2 and pot on as necessary.

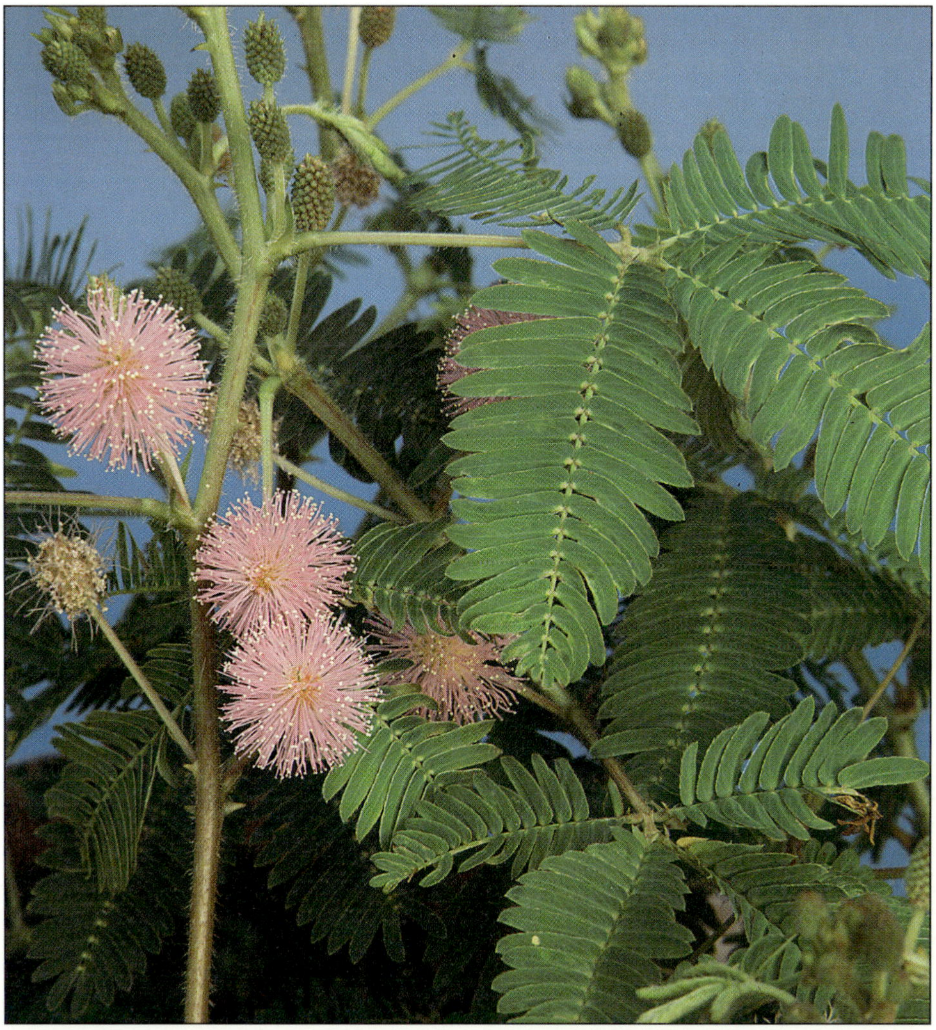

The fern-like, sensitive leaves and pink, fluffy flower heads of Mimosa.

Trouble Shooter

These plants are easy to care for and under the right conditions they will be trouble-free, but keep a sharp eye out for pests. Greenfly is one likely attacker; spray with a pyrethrum insecticide. Mealy bug may be a problem; wipe them off with a cotton bud or small paintbrush dipped in methylated spirit or spray with a malathion-based insecticide for a heavy infestation.

Species

Mimosa pudica, from South America and the West Indies, *left,* is the only one of this group commonly grown as a houseplant. It is a low-growing, shrub-like plant, rarely exceeding 18-20in (45-50cm) in height, with delicate, much-branching stems, covered in prickly spines. The stems carry light-green, feathery, fern-like leaves which fold up and recoil when touched — hence the common names of Sensitive or Humble Plant and Touch-me-not. In July and August, clusters of fluffy, pink, ball-shaped flowers appear on short stalks from the leaf axils.

M.sensitiva has similar foliage; the fronds are a little larger than those of *M.pudica,* but equally sensitive to the touch. Numerous flowers are produced during summer, in small balls of purple.

Monstera

Family name: **Araceae**

Common name:
Swiss Cheese Plant

Care Straight forward	**Height** 12ft (3-7m)	**Flower** Rare
Light Bright, indirect	**Spread** 6-7ft (1.8-2m)	**Humidity** Mist spray regularly
Price Middle range	**Shape** Climber	**Availability** Common
Temp. Min 55°F (13°C)	Ideal 70°F (21°C)	Max 80°F (27°C)

One of the most popular houseplants, *Monstera delicosa* makes a handsome and impressive addition to any room setting, and is very simple to care for. But you'll need to plan where to put it with care—in a matter of a few years, your 3ft (0.9m) houseplant in a 6in (15cm) pot may have grown into a strapping specimen some 12ft (3.7m) tall and 6-7ft (1.8-2m) across!

M.delicosa, or the Swiss Cheese Plant, is a stout-stemmed climber with long, rope-like aerial roots which are used to anchor the plant and also to take up nutrients and water. The very large, glossy, green, leathery leaves grow up to 18in (46cm) across, they are heart-shaped with deeply-cut edges and perforated with large holes suggestive of a Swiss cheese.

Monstera is a relative of the Arum Lily (*Zantedeschia aethiopica*) and bears similar blooms, consisting of a greenish-white spathe, around a cream, cone-like spadix — these are followed by greenish fruit with a pineapple flavour. However, flowers are seldom seen on houseplants.

M.delicosa borsigiana, is similar to the species, but slightly smaller and more compact, and is a better choice if space is limited.

Spring and summer care

Pot on in February or March into John Innes No 3 or a good peat-based potting compost, until a final pot size of 15-18in (38-46cm) is reached. Provide good drainage with a layer of crocks at the bottom of the pot. When the final pot size is reached, topdress every year by scraping away the top 1in (2.5cm) of compost and replacing it with fresh. When potting you'll need to stake your plant — a moss-pole provides the ideal support.

Correct watering is important: Monsteras need to be watered freely in summer, but the soil should be allowed to dry out between applications. So water thoroughly, then wait until the soil is on the dry side before watering again. Give a liquid feed every 3-4 weeks from March to September when watering. This tropical rain forest plant enjoys high temperatures and high humidity, so mist spray every few days, and every day in the hottest summer weather.

Place your plant in good light, but not in direct sunlight or the leaves may be scorched. To keep the leaves dust free, wipe them with a damp cloth, and you can spray with a leaf-shine product once a month to bring out the gloss.

As the plant grows taller the lower leaves die, so cut them off as they wither.

Autumn and winter care

Water moderately from November to March, allowing the soil to dry out slightly before re-watering. Mist spray once a week to maintain humidity — and more frequently if the air is very dry. Place your plant in good indirect light, and don't let temperatures fall below 55°F (13°C) — slightly higher is ideal.

Propagation

In early summer, remove the growing tip with leaf attached, just below the leaf joint; if the cutting has an aerial root attached, this is all to the better. Dip the cut end in a fungicidal sulphur powder and allow to dry for a few hours. Pot the cutting into John Innes No 3 or a peat-based potting compost. Enclose the cutting in a large plastic bag and root in a light position at a temperature of 75-80°F (24-27°C). When new growth appears, in four to six weeks, emerging from the leaf axil on the parent plant, remove the plastic bag and treat as a mature plant.

Cuttings can also be taken from the tips of lateral shoots, and air layering is an alternative method of propagation if your plant has become bare at the base (see page 125 for details).

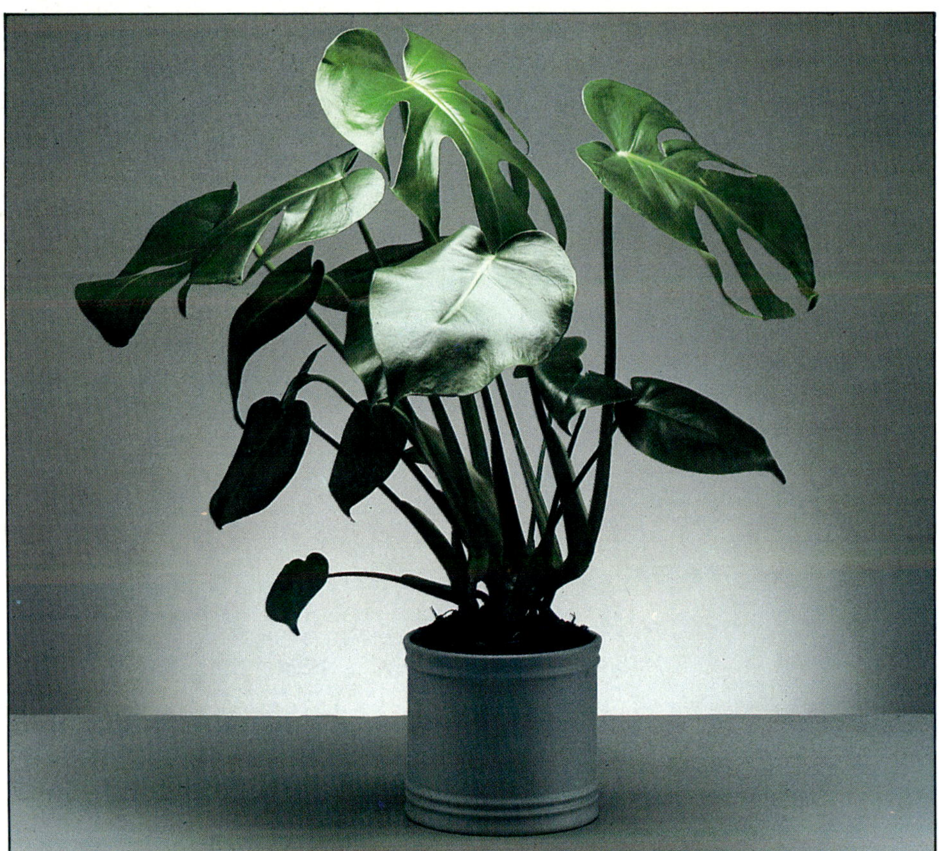

The Swiss Cheese Plant is a well-known favourite — and one of the best houseplants.

Trouble Shooter

Brown markings on leaves, especially at the edges, indicate that the plant has been kept at too low a temperature. Yellowing leaves are a result of overwatering; take care not to water the plant too frequently, especially in winter. Leaves may be scorched if your plant is placed in direct sunlight, particularly if the plant is mist sprayed in this position.

White fluffy patches on the undersides of the new leaves indicate mealy bug. These can be wiped off with a soft cloth moistened with methylated spirit. If the atmosphere is kept too dry, red spider mite may occur — so avoid this by maintaining high humidity and good air circulation.

Buying Guide

Look for a healthy-looking plant that is well supported — ideally with a moss pole. Don't worry if a very small plant has heart-shaped leaves with no holes — this is quite normal — they will develop as the plant matures.

Species

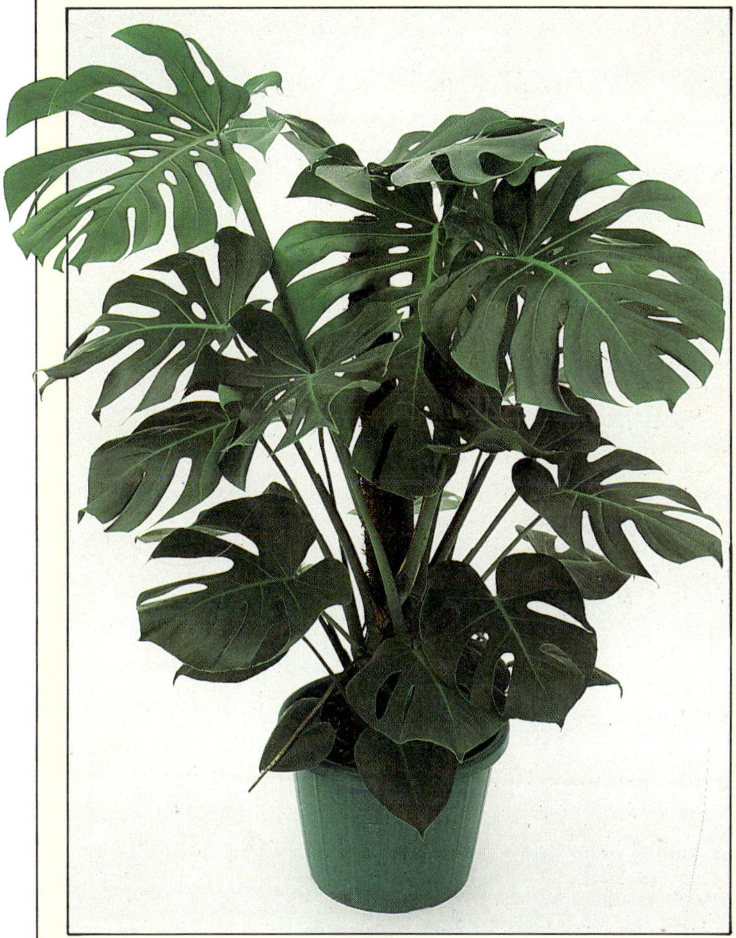

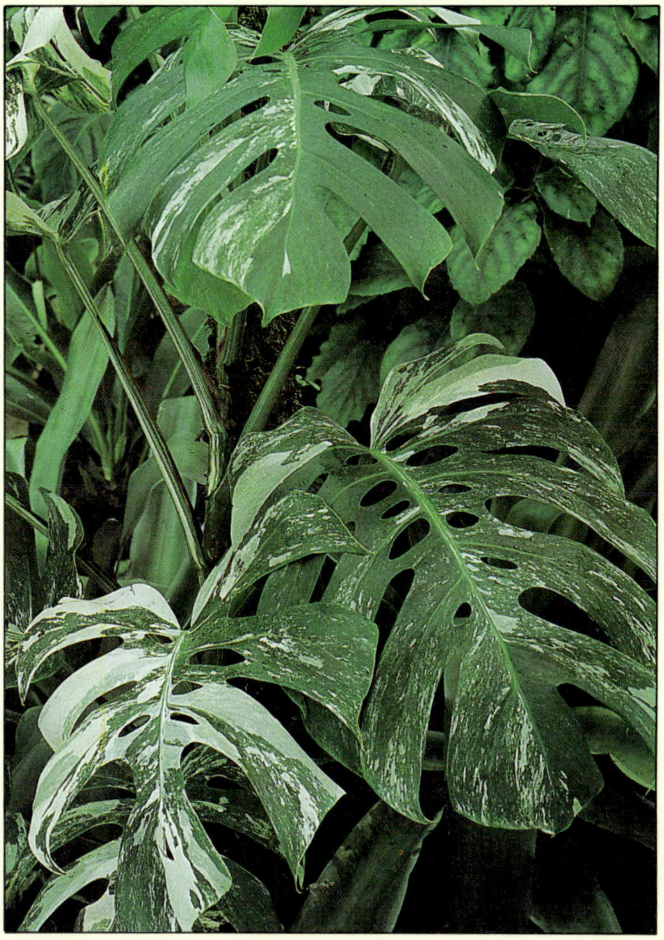

Monstera deliciosa, The Swiss Cheese Plant, from Guatamala and Southern Mexico, is a stout-stemmed climber up to 12ft (3.7m) tall and 6-7ft (1.8-2m) across. It is grown for its handsome, large,leathery, green leaves, up to 18in (46cm) across, which are deeply cut at the margins and perforated with round or oblong holes, although when young the leaves are heart-shaped with no holes or cut margins. Greenish-white flowers appear in summer followed by greenish fruits, but the plant seldom flowers when grown in the home. *M.d.borsigiana, left,* is a slightly smaller version of the species. *M.d.variegata, right,* has leaves marbled in yellow and cream — but the leaves may well revert to green.

M.pertusa, from Panama and Guyana, is another attractive climber. This is very similar to *M.deliciosa*, but with a more slender shape and soft, deep green leaves which are asymmetrical in shape.

M.pittieri, is a delightful climber from Costa Rica, with soft, thin, silvery-green leaves, pointed at the tips.

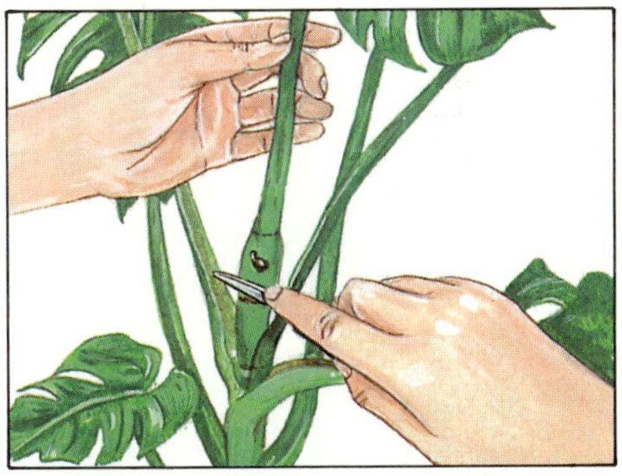

To propagate Monstera, remove the growing tip with a leaf and a tiny aerial root attached. Cut the stem just below a leaf joint, using a sharp knife.

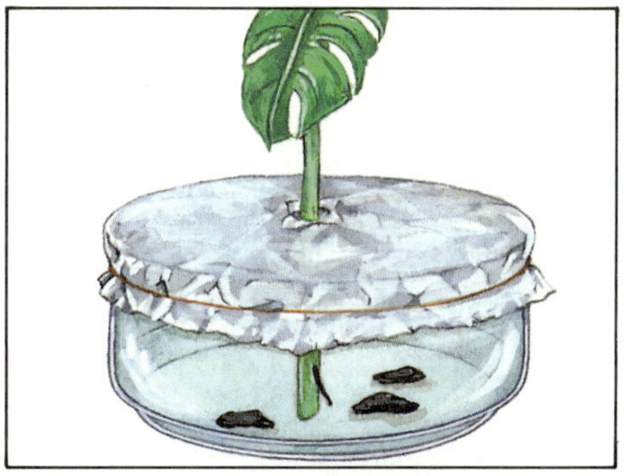

You can root the cutting by standing it in water — add some pieces of charcoal to the water and cover the container with foil or cling film.

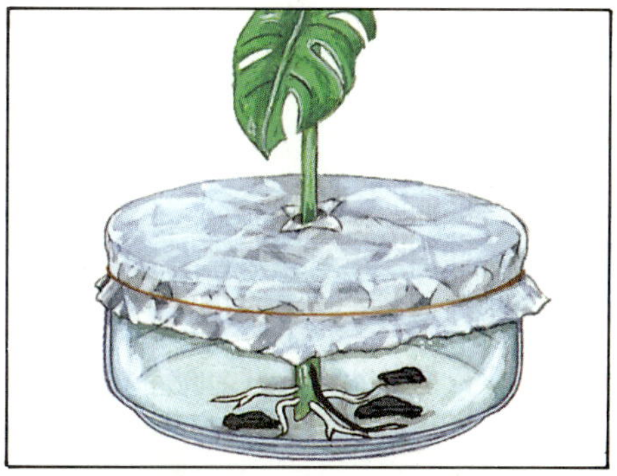

After a few weeks some roots will form at the base of the stem. Once several have appeared you can pot the cutting up, taking care not to damage the roots.

Musa

Family name: **Musaceae**

Common name: **Banana**

Care Straight forward	**Height** 6-8ft (1.8-2.4m)	**Flower** Rarely
Light Bright, indirect	**Spread** 2ft (0.6m)	**Humidity** Mist spray regularly
Price Middle range	**Shape** Palm	**Availability** Garden centres
Temp. Min 60°F (16°C)	Ideal 70°F (21°C)	Max 80°F (27°C)

As a houseplant, a Banana Plant makes not only a great talking point but also an elegant and exotic feature. *Musa acuminata,* the Dwarf Canary Banana, is the most suitable species for growing indoors. The long, leathery, but still quite delicate leaves form a loose rosette at the top of the single stem — this stem being made up of the bases of old leaves. Sadly, very few banana species will flower when grown as houseplants.

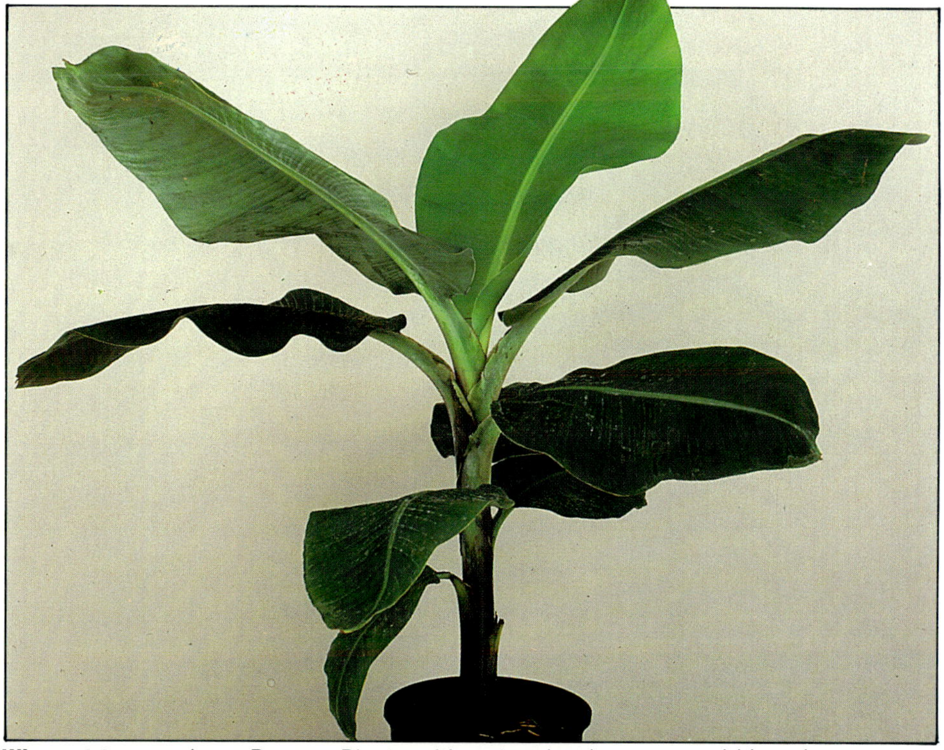

Why not try growing a Banana Plant — it's not as hard as you would imagine.

Spring and summer care

Pot on each year in spring using John Innes No 3. Once your plant has reached the height you want, just topdress it every year. Water very regularly so that the soil is always moist.

Add a few drops of a liquid fertiliser to the water every two weeks. Temperatures of between 70-75°F (21-24°C) are ideal and they can rise as high as 80°F (27°C). Keep your plant in an airy room, in bright but indirect light. Mist spray two or three times every week, in the mornings or evenings.

Autumn and winter care

In winter, the temperature must not fall below 60°F (16°F). Reduce the watering so that the soil is only just moist and add a fertiliser to the water every three weeks. Keep your plant in bright light out of direct sun. Mist spray if the temperature rises.

Propagation

M.acuminata is best propagated by removing the suckers that grow at the base of the stem. Pull these away carefully at any time of year and pot them up into pots of John Innes No 3. Maintain a temperature of 75°F (24°C) and mist spray regularly. When growth is apparent resume normal care.

Sow seeds of *M.acuminata,* as well as other Banana species in spring; soak them for three days before sowing into moist peat-based seed compost. Keep them at a temperature of 65-70°F (18-21°C) and out of bright, direct light. When the seedlings are large enough to handle, pot them up into John Innes No 3 and treat as mature plants.

Trouble Shooter

Leaves shrivel and lose colour if the compost is allowed to go dry. Too much water, especially when temperatures are low, causes root and stem rot. For overwatering, remove the pot, allow the compost to dry out, then dust the roots and stem with fungicidal sulphur powder and repot.

Cottonwool-like tufts are mealy bug; wipe infested areas with a cloth dipped in methylated spirit.

Buying Guide

Banana leaves can be rather fragile — they tear very easily — so look for a plant with undamaged leaves. A healthy plant should have plenty of firm, young growth uncurling from the tip of the stem.

Species

Musa acuminata, sometimes called *M.cavendishii nana*, the Dwarf Canary Banana, came originally from Southern China. It forms a tuft of long arching leaves and a stem made up of leaf bases. The stem may eventually reach 6-8ft (1.8-2.4m) in height. The leaves have a satiny sheen, especially when young, and are often blotched with red.

M.ventricosum, also known as *M.ensete*, from Somalia and Ethiopia is a very tall growing species — reaching as high as 20-30ft (6-9m). The variety *M.v.rubra* is much smaller, growing to about 4ft (1.2m), and has rich, reddish coloured leaves. It makes a good choice as a houseplant since it is small, easy to care for and tolerant of a wide range of conditions.

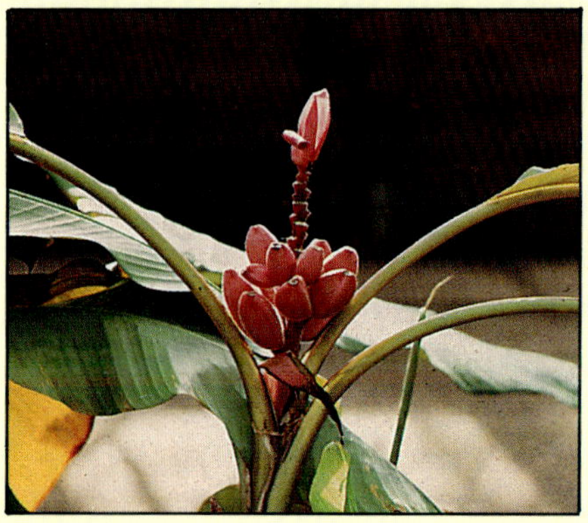

M.velutina, from Assam, *right*, is a very attractive dwarf species and one of the few that has any chance of fruiting as a houseplant. It grows to about 4ft (1.2m) and has pinkish leaf bases. After about four years flowers and fruits may be produced. The upright flower heads carry yellow flowers each surrounded by hairy red bracts. The flowers are followed by 3-4in (8-10cm) long inedible fruits. As with all species, the stem dies after fruiting.

Neoregelia

Family name: **Bromeliaceae**

Common names: **Blushing Bromeliad, Fingernail Plant**

Care Straight-forward	**Height** 1ft (0.3m)	**Flower** Summer
Light Bright	**Spread** 2ft (0.6m)	**Humidity** Mist spray regularly
Price Middle range	**Shape** Rosette	**Availability** Garden centres
Temp. Min 50°F (10°C)	Ideal 70°F (21°C)	Max 80°F (27°C)

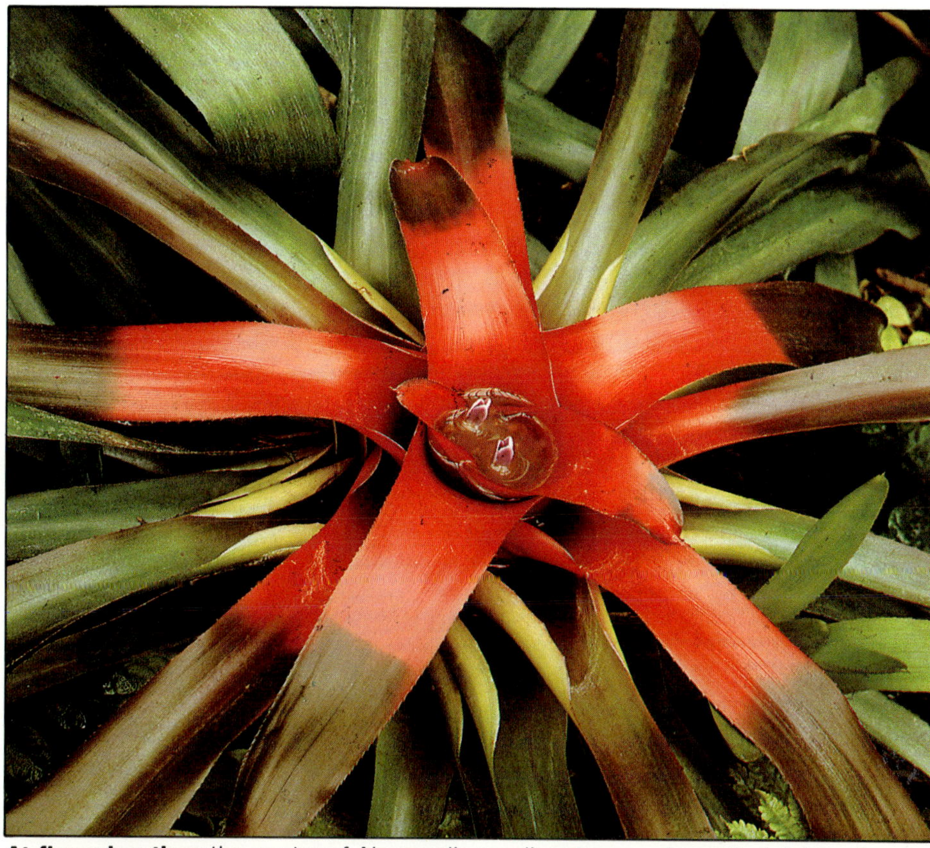

At flowering time the centre of *Neoregelia carolinae* turns a dramatic bright red.

These beautiful rosette plants, with brilliantly-coloured foliage and colourful miniature flowers, are among the most fascinating of all houseplants. One striking feature is the remarkable change in the colouring of their foliage as flowering begins; leaves take on shades of purple, pink or red at the centre or leaf tips, according to species, and may retain the colouring for several months.

Neoregelias are all native to South America, principally Brazil. They grow about 1ft (30cm) tall and up to 2ft (60cm) across, with 1ft (30cm) long leaves radiating symmetrically from a central point, arranged to form a 'cup' or 'vase' in the centre; this acts as a reservoir in their natural habitat, holding the water the plants need to survive. Flowering can take place at any time of year — though houseplants tend to be summer flowering; a tightly-packed flower head rises through an opening in the centre of the cup, with small flowers, usually blue or white, sometimes surrounded by colourful bracts.

Neoregelia carolinae is one of the most familiar, with a wide rosette of glossy green, strap-shaped leaves which turn bright red or purple at the centre when the plant is about to flower, earning it the common name of Blushing Bromeliad. It has many popular varieties, of which the favourite, and probably the most impressive of all, is 'Tricolor'; at flowering time, its cream, pink and green striped leaves blush brilliant red at the centre, and can remain that shade for many months.

Spring and summer care

Repot in May every year into a mixture of two parts peat-based compost to one part coarse sand; alternatively, extremely good results can be achieved with a mixture of three parts cactus compost to one part peat. If offsets are overcrowding the pot, either move the whole plant on to a larger container or remove the offsets and pot up individually (see 'Propagation'). Plants flower when two or three years old after which they gradually die. By this time of year any offsets which have formed will be showing brisk growth, while the parent plant will be looking rather tired. It is best then to cut the old rosette down to about 2in (5cm) above the base; any remaining leaf-bases will gradually rot away as the new growths take over.

Neoregelias will thrive at normal room temperatures — these can rise to 70-80°F (21-27°C) with no ill effect. Give them bright light, with some direct sunlight. Water the compost only moderately, but keep the cup-like centre of the rosette topped up with water; pour the water out once a month and replace it, to keep it fresh. Mist spray daily to provide a humid atmosphere and keep the foliage fresh, and add a weak liquid fertiliser (use half the recommended amount) every two or three weeks to the water for the compost, leaves and the centre of the rosette.

Autumn and winter care

Winter temperatures should be maintained at around 60°F (15°C) — they should never be allowed to fall below 50°F (10°C). Provide good light, including direct sunlight for short periods. Water must be retained in the cup at all times and replaced with fresh water every few weeks; water the compost sparingly if necessary, so that it is *just* moist — nothing more. Mist spray at least once a week to provide reasonable humidity.

Propagation

Stem offsets are easy to grow on; April or May is the best time, before the growing season begins. Remove them when they are about 4in (10cm) tall, severing the offset at the base of the stem where it joins the parent plant. Pot up and keep moist and shaded, at a temperature of 75°F (24°C). They should soon show growth, as the root system gets established, after which treat as mature plants.

Alternatively, propagate from seeds in the spring, using a mixture of three parts peat and one part coarse sand; firm the compost well and thoroughly moisten it. Sprinkle the seeds over the surface of the mixture, but don't cover them; place the container in a propagator or clear polythene bag and keep it moist and shaded, at a temperature of 75-80°F (24-27°C). When the seedlings are visible, within a few weeks, gradually expose them to more light, but maintain the temperature. About three or four months after sowing, pot the seedlings on individually into a mixture of one part peat-based compost to one part coarse sand and treat them as mature plants.

Trouble Shooter

Water and temperature are the most important factors. Leaves will twist and curl, and begin to shrivel if the plant is left too dry; this condition should be improved by soaking the soil and letting it drain, and filling the cup. The foliage will lose its lustre if winter temperatures fall too low or if there are cold draughts.

Scale insect and, especially, mealy bug may attack. These are best dealt with by wiping with a paintbrush or cotton bud dipped in methylated spirit; repeat the process a week later.

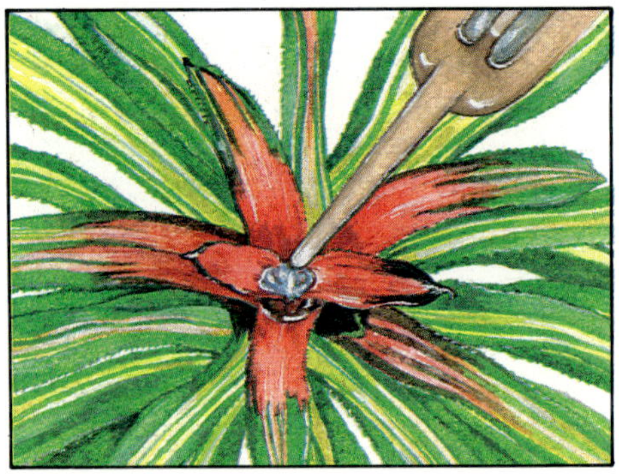

Keep the urn filled with water, even when your plant is in flower — and change the water once a month.

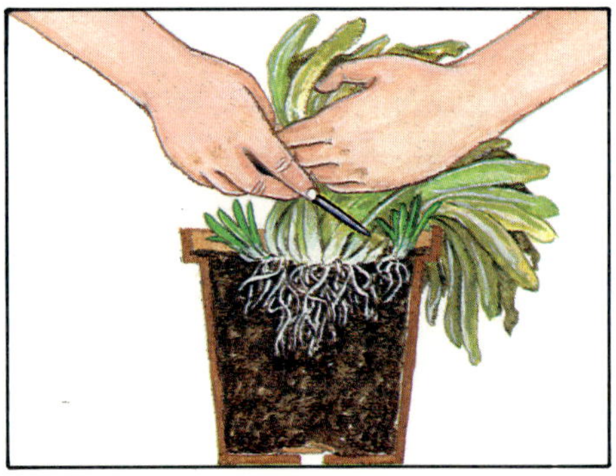

To make a large pot of rosettes, in April or May cut back the old rosette to within 2in (5cm) of its base.

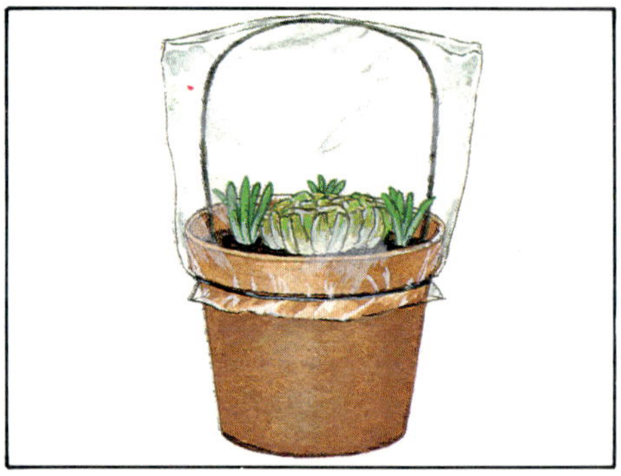

Encourage quick growth by covering the pot with polythene — use a wire hoop to stop it touching the leaves.

Species

Neoregelia carolinae has a wide rosette which is made up of numerous glossy, green, strap-shaped leaves, arranged symmetrically to form a 'cup' in the centre. When the plant is about to flower, which can occur at any time of the year, the centre of the rosette turns bright red or purple, earning it the name of Blushing Bromeliad. The leaves open out and a tightly-packed flower head rises through the centre of the cup, made up of small blue or violet flowers surrounded by glossy red bracts. The favourite variety, and the most impressive plant of all, is 'Tricolor', *right;* its glossy green leaves, with cream and rose-pink stripes, blush brilliant red at the centre at flowering time and can remain that shade for several months. As the plant matures, all of the foliage becomes suffused with pink.

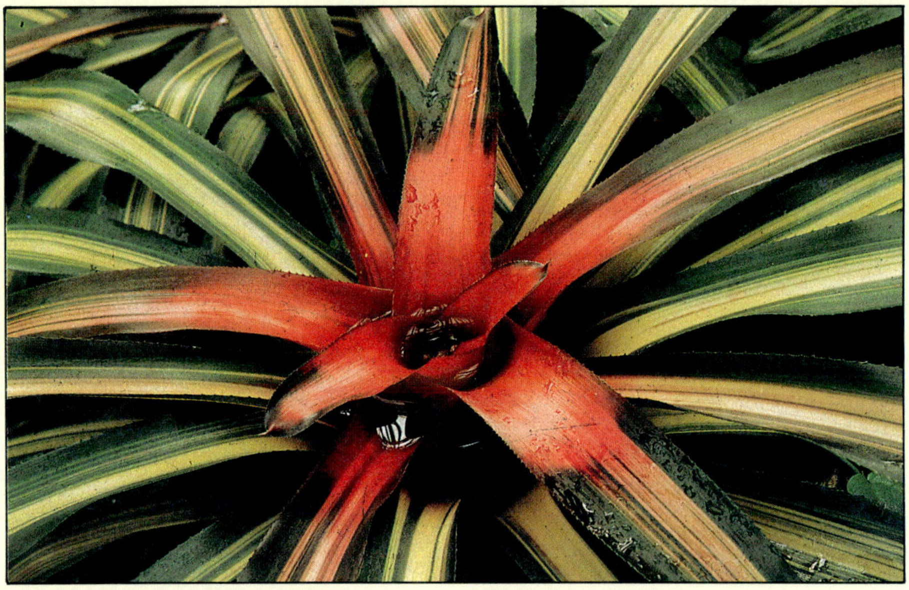

N.concentrica, *below right*, makes a flat rosette of stiff, broad leaves up to 1ft (30cm) long and 4in (10cm) wide. They are light green with purple flecks, edged with short black spines. At flowering time, the central leaves turn a pale lilac colour and a small dense head of numerous bright blue flowers appears in the cup.

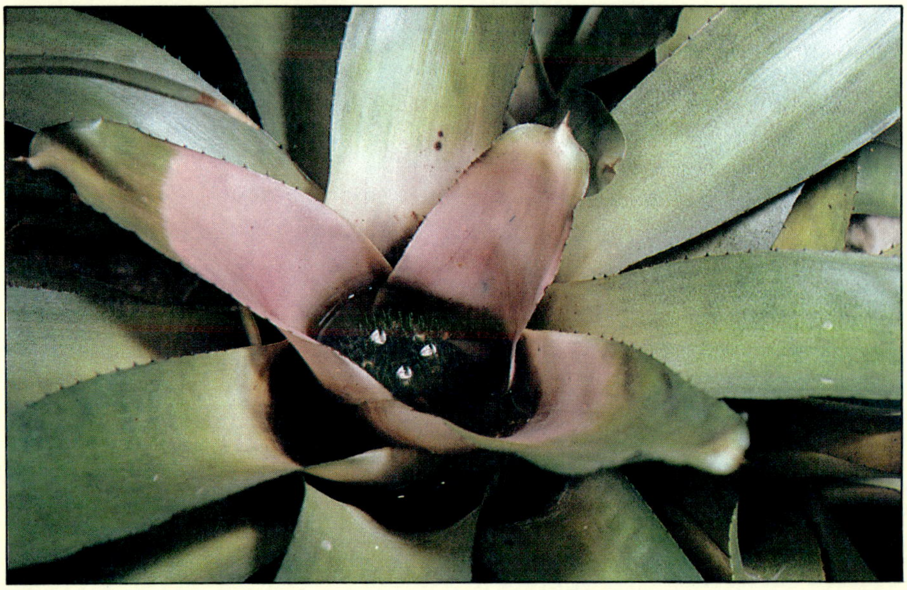

N.spectabilis has a rosette of leathery, metallic-green leaves which have white bands against a pale purple background on the underside. The leaves grow up to 15in (38cm) long and at the tip there is a 1in (2.5cm) long, bright red spot, like a painted fingernail — hence the common name of Fingernail Plant. At flowering time the heart of the plant turns purple and a dense head of small blue flowers appears, surrounded by small red bracts.

N.farinosa is sometimes called the Crimson Cup. Its widely-spreading leaves form a dense rosette; they are purplish-brown, densely covered on the underside with silvery-white scales. At flowering time, the centre leaves turn vivid red at the base, to contrast with the small purplish flowers in the centre of the cup.

Nephrolepis

Family name: **Polypodiaceae**

Common names: **Ladder Fern/ Sword Fern, Boston Fern**

Care Easy	**Height** 1-6ft (0.3-1.8m)	**Flower** None
Light Bright, indirect sun	**Spread** 1-10ft (0.3-3m)	**Humidity** Mist spray regularly
Price Middle range	**Shape** Rosette	**Availability** Common

Temp. Min 50°F (10°C) — Ideal 70°F (21°C) — Max 80°F (27°C)

If you like ferns but find them rather tricky to look after, try one from the Nephrolepis group — as well as being among the most attractive, they are one of the toughest and most versatile of all.

The most commonly available Nephrolepis ferns are varieties of *Nephrolepis exaltata* — such as *N.e.bostoniensis*, the Boston Fern. Like all the varieties, this lovely plant is made up of a clump of long, arching, slightly papery fronds with finely cut edges. The fronds vary in length from about 1-3ft (0.3-0.9m), depending on the variety. The arching, slightly translucent, bright green leaves make this fern an ideal choice for a hanging basket.

Spring and summer care

Every year in March give your plant fresh compost. Remove it from its pot, cut off any dead fronds, then knock away the loose soil. If the plant has grown too large for its container, transfer it to a new one a size larger; if the clump still seems to have plenty of room then return it to its old pot with some fresh compost. Use a peat-based potting compost for potting Nephrolepis ferns.

Normal room temperatures are perfectly adequate — though a summer temperature of about 70°F (21°C) is ideal. Always keep the atmosphere humid, particularly in high summer; mist spray regularly (ideally using rain water) or alternatively, stand your plant in a tray of moist pebbles. Water very thoroughly, making sure the soil never dries out. The best way to water a fern in a hanging basket is to dunk the whole container in a bucket of water for a few minutes every week — but don't forget to let the excess water drain away before hanging it up again. Add a liquid fertiliser to your fern's water every two to three weeks from May to September.

Although the Nephrolepis ferns are more easy-going than most, they will not thrive in full sun or deep shade for long periods — bright, indirect light is what they prefer.

Autumn and winter care

In winter temperatures of about 60°F (16°C) are ideal. At this temperature keep the compost just moist and mist spray regularly. If the temperature falls, water less often. Don't allow the temperature to fall below 50°F (10°C). Keep your plant in bright, indirect light and in an airy position, but away from cold draughts.

Propagation

In March, at potting time, you can divide your plant. Gently ease the roots apart, so that the plant pulls into two parts. Cut out any dead growth from the centre of the clump and repot the two halves separately using a peat-based potting compost. Water the divisions thoroughly and treat them as mature plants.

Some varieties produce thin, wiry stems, called stolons. These creep over the surface of the compost and root along their length, producing miniature plantlets. If they already have well-developed roots, the plantlets can be snipped away from the parent and potted up separately; if the plantlet has barely rooted, transfer it into a small pot of moist peat-based potting compost while it is still attached to its stolon — using a hair pin or small piece of wire, hooked over the stolon and pushed into the soil to anchor it. Once the plantlet begins to grow, the connecting stolon can be cut. Treat the young plantlet as a mature plant.

Ferns do not flower and fruit, instead they produce minute spores. You can grow new ferns from these, although the process requires a lot of patience and can take up to a year. Inspect the back of your plant's leaves and you'll probably find some small, brown, kidney-shaped growths — these contain the spores. Collect some of these and lay them on a piece of paper to allow them to ripen. After a day or so the spores will have been emptied out on to the paper; sow them as thinly as you can over the surface of a thoroughly moistened mixture of equal parts peat and coarse sand. Place the pot or tray in a propagator or sealed plastic bag in a lightly shaded position, and keep the temperature at about 75-85°F (24-30°C).

Once the surface of the compost becomes covered in a green mossy carpet, remove their cover but maintain the warm temperature and keep the compost moist. Pot the young ferns up individually in a peat-based potting compost when they are 3in (8cm) tall and treat them as mature plants.

Buying Guide

Since they grow quite quickly, it's a good idea to buy young, small plants; the ideal plant would be small enough to be sold in a 2in (5cm) pot. At this size it would need to be transferred to a 4in (10cm) pot within a month or so of buying and then potted on again the following spring. Look for a thick tuft of bright green foliage growing in moist compost.

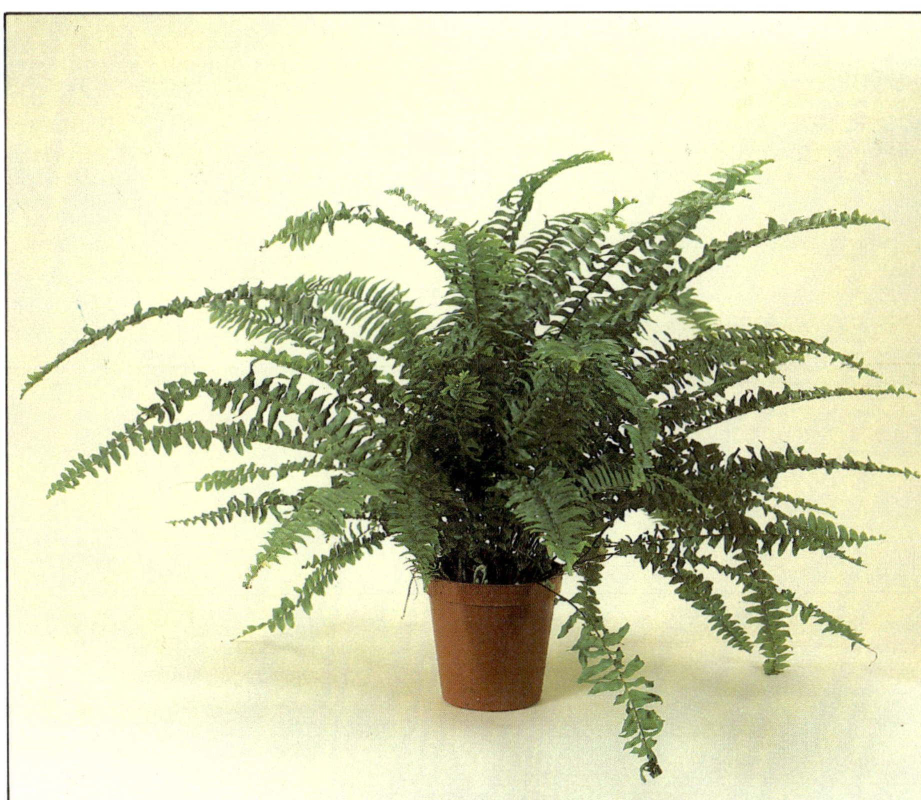

One of the varieties of the Ladder Fern — an easy-going, deservedly popular plant.

Species

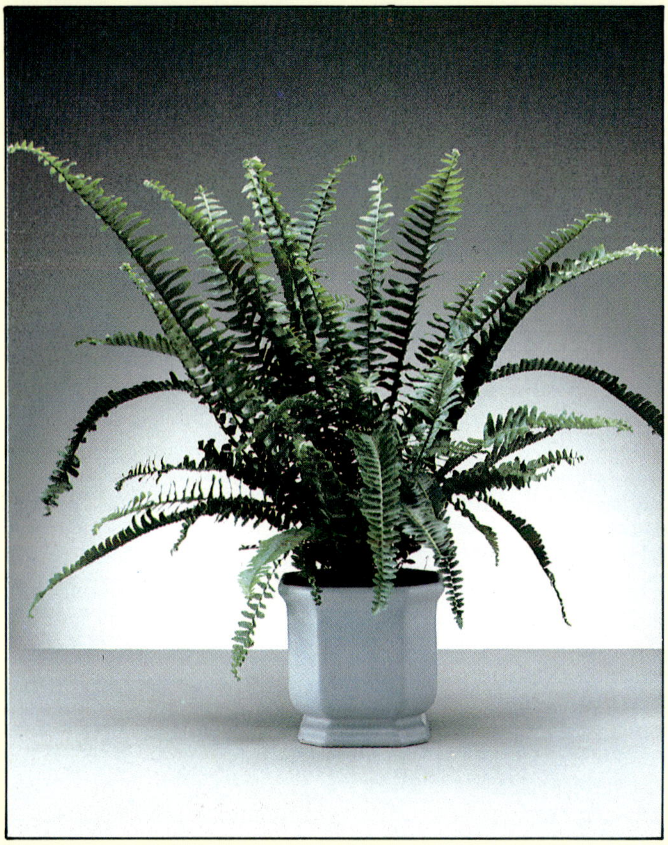

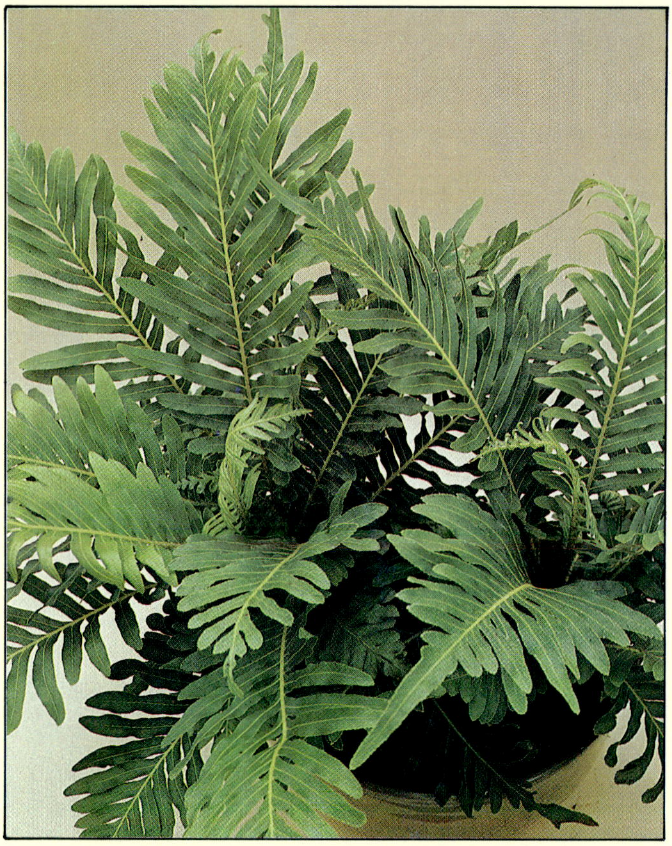

Nephrolepis exaltata, the Ladder or Sword Fern, is a tropical evergreen plant. It has rather stiff, arching fronds which can grow to 6ft (1.8m) or more, making it a magnificent and eye-catching plant — particularly suited to hanging baskets. The long fronds are paper-thin and bright green, finely cut and slightly frilled. There are numerous varieties, the most well-known one being *N.e.bostoniensis, left,* the Boston Fern, which has broader shorter fronds up to 3ft (0.9m) in length. 'Childsii' is more miniature — the fronds growing to about 1ft (0.3m) long. 'Whitmanii', sometimes called the Lace Fern, has finely cut 18in (45cm) long fronds that are more frilled than usual. 'Magnifica' has 14-15in (36-38cm) long fronds that are very frilled and lacy looking.

N.e.'Rooseveltii plumosa', right, looks rather different, although it is derived from *N.e.bostoniensis.* It has flattish, uncrinkled, arching leaves that grow to about 3ft (0.9m) in length.

N.cordifolia, sometimes called *N.tuberosa,* comes from South America. The fronds are very similar to *N.exaltata,* about 2ft (0.6m) or more in length and rather of upright growth. It has rather fleshy, tuberous roots.

N.tesselata, sometimes called *N.cordifolia.plumosa,* is a spectacular houseplant. Its arching fronds are 3ft (0.9m). The fronds are very finely cut and dark green on thin blackish stalks.

Trouble Shooter

Leaves will harden, become brittle and then turn brown without sufficient humidity and water. Cut off any brown foliage and soak your plant thoroughly. Remember never use a leaf shining product on any ferns.

Pale leaves may be due to too much bright direct sunlight. Yellowing, rather sick-looking leaves, is an indication of nutrient shortage, so feed more often. Scale insect — small wart-like bumps on the backs of leaves (not to be confused with the brown spore cases) — should be removed with a small brush dipped in methylated spirit.

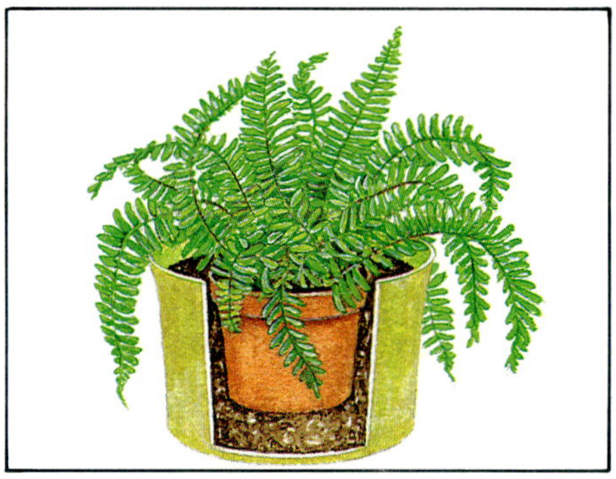

One way to provide a humid environment for your ferns is to sit your plant in its pot inside a larger container. Fill the gap between the two with moist peat — re-wet regularly.

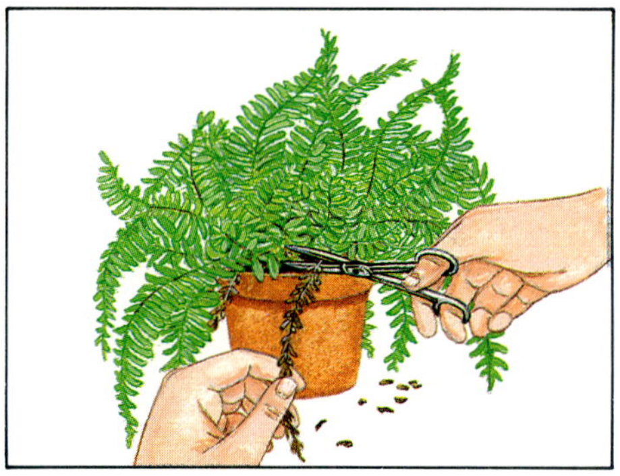

When a leaf turns brown and shrivels, snip it right back to compost level. If your plant has very many dead fronds, then it probably needs more water and humidity.

Nerium

Family name: **Apocynaceae**

Common name: **Oleander**

Care Straight-forward	**Height** 6ft (1.8m)	**Flower** Summer or early autumn
Light Sunny	**Spread** 4ft (1.2m)	**Humidity** Mist spray in hot weather
Price Middle range	**Shape** Bushy	**Availability** Garden centres

Temp. Min 45°F (7°C) Ideal 65°F (18°C) Max 80°F (27°C)

Valued for its clusters of lovely, richly-coloured flowers, with a strong, sweet fragrance, the Oleander is easily grown and makes a very colourful, large houseplant.

Of the two species of Nerium that exist, *N.oleander* is the one that is commonly found indoors. A tall, spreading bush, growing up to 6ft (1.8m) high, you'll want plenty of space to show off your Oleander to its best advantage. It has soft, woody stems and branches and long, slender, greyish-green leaves, and in summer or early autumn fragrant flowers appear in clusters towards the ends of the branches. The typical flower colour is a vivid rose-pink, but there are many varieties, in shades of red, yellow and white; most of them can be found in a very attractive, many-petalled 'double-flowered' form, each flower in its cluster looking rather like a small rose.

Remember that the wood and sap of Oleander are actually poisonous — but this is true of a number of popular indoor plants.

Spring and summer care

Repotting is best done in March, into John Innes No 2 or 3; crock well to provide good drainage. Move your plant on to a pot one size larger if the roots have completely filled the pot, up to a final pot size of 10-12in (25-30cm). After that, move on to a small tub for a very large plant, or topdress annually, replacing the top 1-2in (2.5-5cm) of compost.

A temperature of around 65°F (18°C) is ideal, but higher temperatures are not harmful. Your plant will need bright light, including direct sunlight all year round; good air circulation is beneficial.

Water freely from March, adding a liquid fertiliser to the water every two weeks from May to September. During the flowering period, remove immediately any new growths appearing at the base of the flower stems, as they will take away nourishment from the flowers.

Autumn and winter care

Oleander quickly grows straggly and needs to be pruned hard in the autumn, as soon as the last flowers have faded. Cut back the stems which have flowered by as much as half and cut back any long side shoots, to within 4in (10cm) of the base.

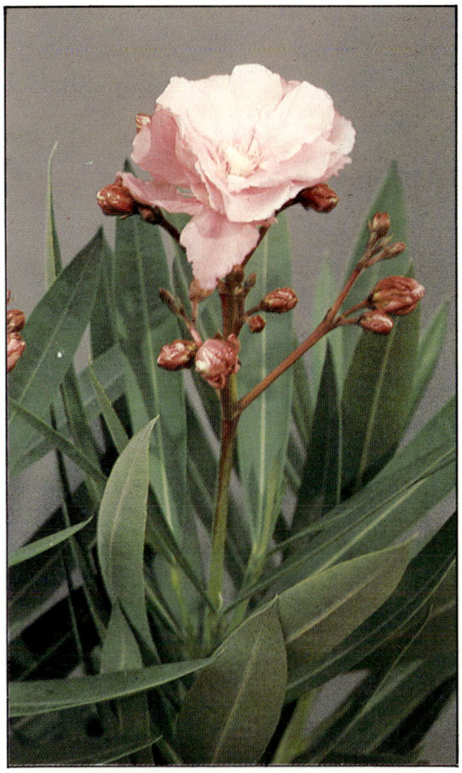

This Mediterranean shrub makes a lovely houseplant for a sunny spot.

Winter temperatures should be 45-55°F (7-13°C) and good light is still most important — the more sun the better. Water sparingly but be sure the compost is always moist.

Propagation

Take 4-6in (10-15cm) long tip cuttings, preferably in the spring. Pot them up individually into a mixture of equal parts John Innes No 2 and coarse sand. Keep the cuttings in a lightly shaded position at a steady 70°F (21°C) in a propagator or sealed polythene bag (make sure the leaves don't touch the polythene). Once the cuttings show signs of growth they can be treated as mature plants.

Cuttings can also be rooted by simply standing them in water. When roots are 1in (2.5cm) long, pot them up individually into John Innes No 2 or 3.

Species

Nerium oleander, *left*, is a tall, evergreen shrub, found mainly in the Mediterranean regions, where it can reach a height of 15-20ft (4.5-6m), though it rarely exceeds 6ft (1.8m) as a houseplant. Oleander has soft, willowy stems and branches, with slender, pointed leaves, 6-8in (15-20cm) long. When punctured, all parts of the plant exude a white latex, which is poisonous. Fragrant flowers, 1½-2in (4-5cm) across, are borne in clusters at the ends of branches, in summer or early autumn, usually in a bright rose-pink, but also in red or in white. There are many varieties. 'Variegata', *below*, is a popular form, with creamy-white striping on the leaves and flowers of pale crimson, and there are a number of double-flowered varieties such as the pure-white 'Album', 'Roseum', in a beautiful shade of pink, and 'Luteum' with creamy-yellow blooms.

N.indicum, also known as *N.odorum*, is found in the Middle East, China and Japan. It is similar in many ways to Oleander, though lower-growing, reaching about 6ft (1.8m) in height. In the wild, fragrant flowers of rose-pink or white are borne nearly all year round.

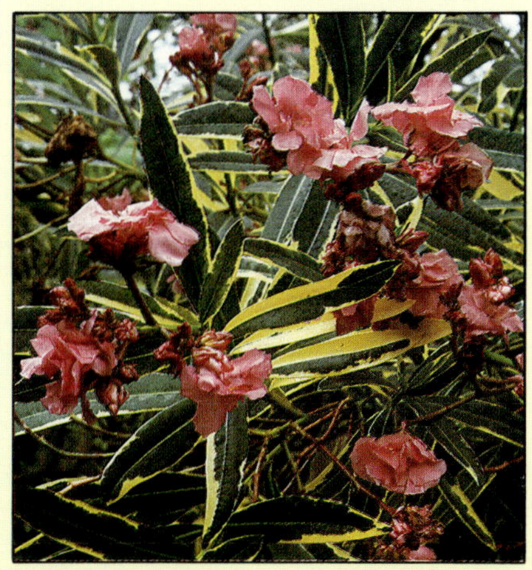

Trouble Shooter

Foliage will quickly wilt if the plant gets too dry and flower buds may fail to develop if the roots are allowed to dry out. Foliage and flowering are also affected if temperatures are too low or the light is not good enough.

Watch out for small blisters on the underside of leaves — the sign of scale insects — or the fluffy, white patches that indicate mealy bug; both pests can be removed with a cotton bud or small paintbrush dipped in methylated spirit. For a heavy infestation, spray with a malathion-based insecticide, or apply a dimethoate-based insecticide as a preventative; always follow the manufacturer's instructions.

WARNING

Every part of this plant is poisonous so it should never be placed within reach of young children or pets.

Nidularium

Family name: **Bromeliaceae**

Common name:
Bird's Nest Plant

Care Straightforward	**Height** 1ft (0.3m)	**Flower** Summer
Light Bright, indirect sun	**Spread** 18in (46cm)	**Humidity** Mist spray regularly
Price Middle range	**Shape** Rosette	**Availability** Garden centres
Temp. Min 55°F (13°C)	Ideal 75°F (24°C)	Max 80°F (27°C)

These attractive plants are yet another member of the large Bromeliad family, better known by some as the Urn Plants. Easy to look after, shade loving, and very handsome to look at, the Nidulariums deserve their place among the most popular houseplants in the family.

Nidularium billbergioides, sometimes called *N.citrina,* is one of the favourite species. Like most Bromeliads, it is made up of a rosette of arching leaves which together form a water-holding vase at the centre of the plant. This Nidularium's leafy rosette is about 18in (46cm) in diameter and each leaf is fairly glossy, sword-shaped, pointed and with short, greenish spines around the edge. The main attraction of the plant is its magnificent flower head; usually during the summer months, it rises from the central urn and grows up just above the leafy rosette. The flower stem is coated in short green bracts and topped by a flower head of brownish-red, triangular bracts with pointed tips which enclose the small white flowers; the most popular variety, *N.b.flavum, below,* has beautiful lemon-yellow bracts at its centre. Some species, such as *N.innocentii,* have reddish-coloured inner bracts around the central urn, these often becoming more richly coloured at flowering time.

Spring and summer care

Nidularium rosettes are short-lived, they flower once and then slowly die. They do produce offsets though that will flower in the next summer or the summer after, depending on how well-developed they are. Cut back the old flowered rosette in the spring, ideally April or May, to within 2in (5cm) of the base of the plant — taking care not to damage the young offsets. Repot the remaining clump of offsets into a pot one size larger, using a mixture of two parts John Innes No 2 and one part peat. Alternatively, divide the clump of offsets and pot them up individually (see 'Propagation').

Keep your plant in a shaded position, away from bright or direct light. Water freely into the central urn and keep the compost just moist. Use rainwater if possible, or boiled water, in the urn particularly, keeping it topped up to the brim. Add a liquid fertiliser or a foliar feed to the water every two to three weeks. It's wise to empty the urn about once

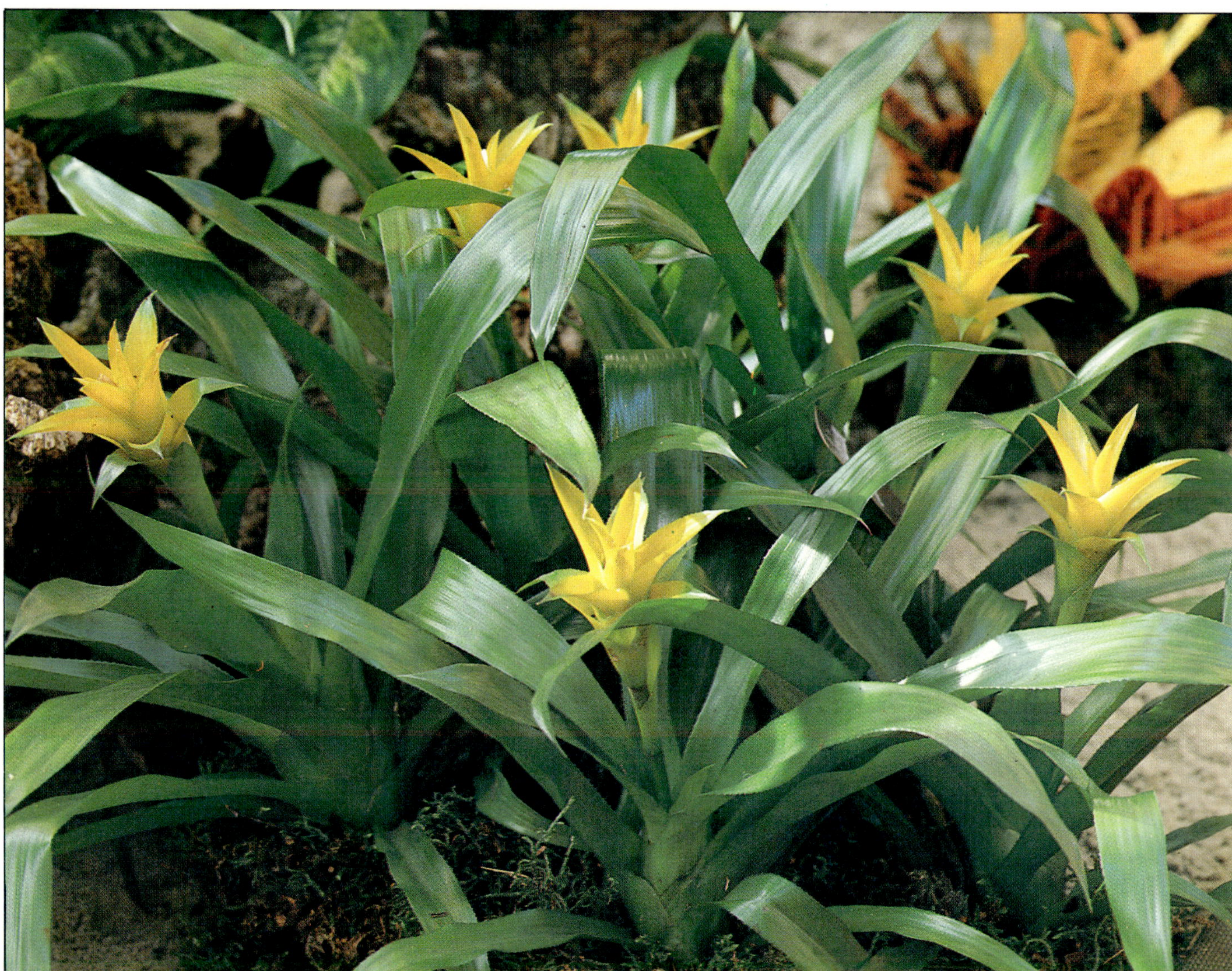

Brighten up a dull corner with the Bird's Nest Plant; the colourful bracts will last for several months.

a month and refill it with fresh water.

Normal room temperatures are perfectly satisfactory — although the ideal temperature in the growing season is about 75°F (24°C). Nidulariums like a humid atmosphere at all times so mist spray very regularly and stand your plant in a saucer of wet pebbles. Remove the flowers as soon as they've faded — this will help to maintain leaves and bracts in good condition for longer.

Autumn and winter care

Temperatures of about 60-65°F (15-18°C) are ideal in winter — they should definitely not fall lower than 55°F (13°C). Water slightly less often, making sure the cup is always kept topped up. Empty the urn every month and then refill with fresh water. Make sure the atmosphere is kept humid by mist spraying regularly every week — it's a good idea to add a little foliar feed to the water in the sprayer every so often, since this will encourage the young offsets to grow.

Keep your plant in a lightly shaded position, away from cold draughts and the fumes of gas or paraffin fires.

Propagation

Divide your plant in April or May, carefully detaching the offsets from the flowered rosette. Use a knife to cut the offsets away as close to the mother plant as possible. Pot the offsets up individually into a mixture of two parts John Innes No 2 and peat. Keep them in a warm position until growth is apparent.

Nidulariums can be grown from seed quite easily and this can give you the chance to grow some of the more unusual varieties. Fill a seed tray or flower pot with a mixture of equal parts peat and coarse sand, and moisten thoroughly. Spread the seeds thinly over the surface of the compost and put the tray or pot in a propagator or sealed polythene bag. Germinate at a temperature of 75-80°F (24-27°C) and in a shaded position. Once seeds have germinated, in three to four weeks, uncover the seedlings and maintain the temperature but give a little more light.

When they are 2in (5cm) tall, pot up the seedlings individually into their own pots, and treat them as mature plants. Pot them on as they grow out of their pots. They should flower within three years.

Trouble Shooter

Most problems are concerned with shortage of water and humidity. Leaves lose their lustre and start to shrivel prematurely. The central urn should never be allowed to dry out; dunk the whole plant in its pot in water for a few minutes and it may recover.

Low temperatures, particularly combined with overwatering, may result in the leaves at the centre of the rosette rotting at their base. Remove any rotting leaves and raise the temperature.

Scale insect and mealy bug are the only pests likely to attack; these can be wiped away with a soft cloth moistened with methylated spirit. Alternatively, spray your plant regularly with a malathion-based insecticide.

Species

N.billbergioides, the Bird's Nest Plant which is sometimes called *N.citrina*, comes from Southern Brazil. The rosette of leaves is about 18in (46cm) across and is made up of many sword-shaped leaves, slightly glossy, metallic green with short, greenish spines. The small white flowers usually appear in summer, though they can bloom at any time, at the tip of a long, thick bract-coated stem and are surrounded by pointed brownish-red bracts. *N.b.flavum, far left*, is very similar to the main species but has bright lemon-yellow bracts.

N.innocentii has many popular varieties such as the one, somewhat confusingly called *N.i.innocentii*! This is a large, showy plant with a widely spreading rosette, about 2ft (0.6m) across. The leaves are finely toothed around the edge and quite glossy — the upper surface a brownish-green and the underside a metallic purple. Usually the flower head appears in summer. It is carried on a short stem inside the central urn and consists of between six and eight red bracts which enclose a few small white flowers. The variety *N.i.lineatum* has a loose rosette of pale to deep green leaves, striped and banded with white. *N.i.striatum, below left*, is very similar but the leaves are bronzy-green striped with cream.

***N.fulgens**, below right*, sometimes called the Blushing Bromeliad, is also from Brazil. It makes a widely spreading rosette of about 12in (30cm), with green mottled leaves, sharply toothed around the edge. The flower head appears usually in summer inside the central urn. It consists of leaf-like scarlet bracts surrounding a cup containing the violet-tipped white flowers at its centre.

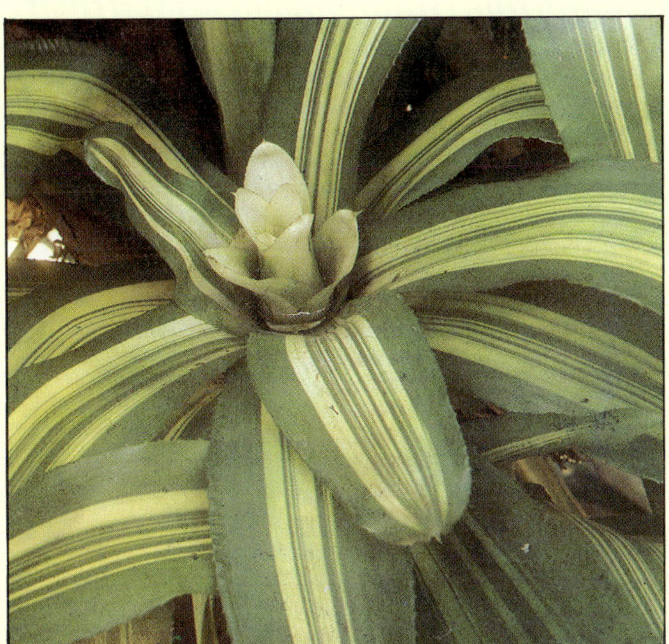

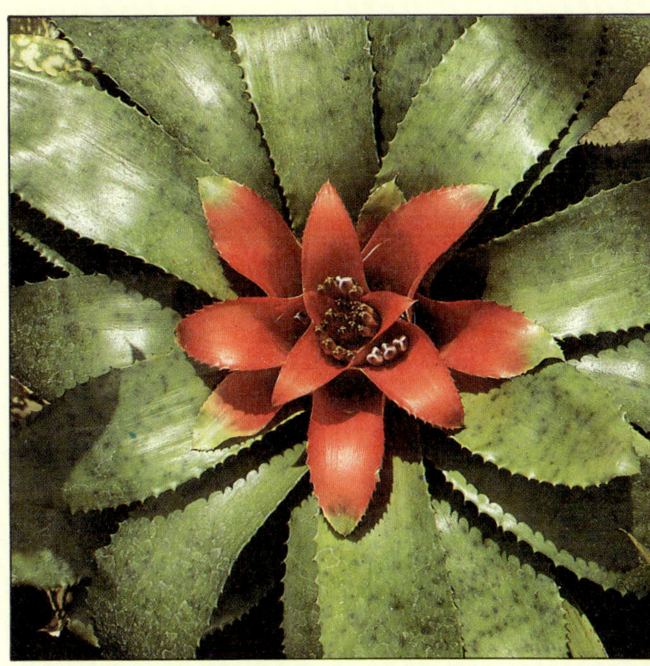

Notocactus

Family name: **Cactaceae**

Common name:
Golden Ball Cactus

Care Easy	**Height** 8-9in (20-23cm)	**Flower** Summer
Light Sunny	**Spread** 2-3in (5-8cm)	**Humidity** None
Price Cheap	**Shape** Column	**Availability** Garden centres
Temp. Min 45°F (7°C)	Ideal 70°F (21°C)	Max 80°F (27°C)

Among the easiest of cacti to grow, Notocacti are also among the very finest, with attractively coloured spines and beautiful flowers, which they bear in profusion. They are rounded or column-shaped, with numerous ribs running the length of the body, covered in bristling spines. The large colourful flowers, which are funnel- or trumpet-shaped, appear from around the crown of the plant between late spring and the end of August, often three or four at a time, each flower lasting several days.

Of South American origin, there are around 40 species, almost all of them readily available and a splendid choice for a sunny spot. *N.leninghausii, right,* is one of the tallest growing species, reaching 3ft (0.9m) in the wild, though only the most ancient specimen is likely to approach that indoors and 8-9in (20-23cm) is the usual limit. Known as the Golden Ball Cactus, it is globular at first then elongates into a column, the pale green body almost concealed by a dense covering of yellow spines. When plants are 4-5in (10-13cm) high they start to produce bright yellow, funnel-shaped flowers, each one about 2in (5cm) across.

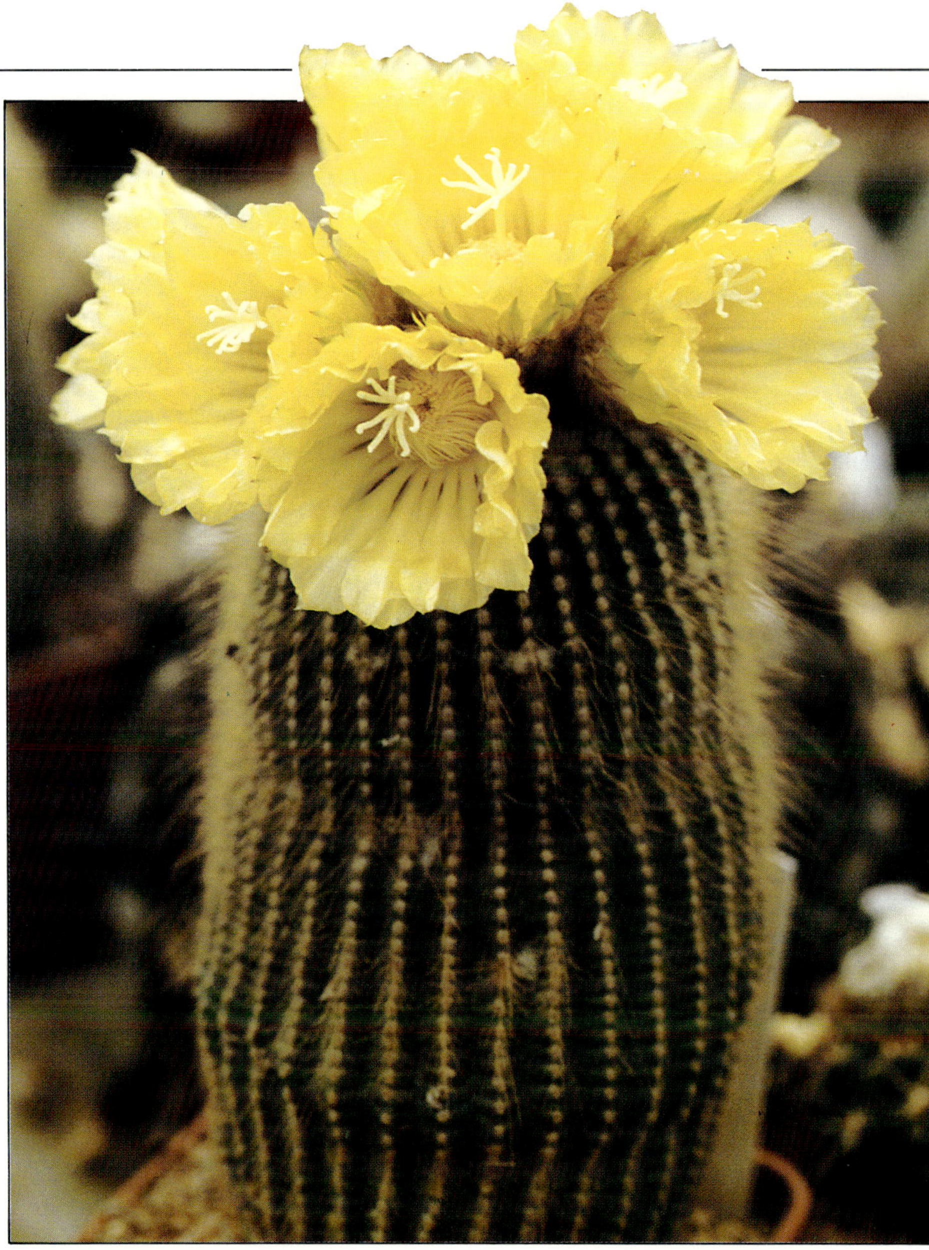

The column-shaped Golden Ball Cactus, coated with spines and crowned with flowers.

Spring and summer care

Repot in early spring, *just before* the plant starts active growth. Use a good cactus compost or a mixture of two parts John Innes No 1 to one part coarse sand. Move plants on if the roots fill the pot, to a pot one size larger only; don't 'overpot' — it will stimulate flowering if the roots of your plant are slightly pot-bound or constricted. Plants of 4in (10cm) or more should be removed from the pot every year to check the roots; if they are not being moved on, shake off as much of the old compost as possible and repot with fresh.

Normal room temperatures are suitable and they can rise as high as 75-80°F (24-27°C). Your plant should have a really bright position, with as much full sunlight as possible to keep its shape and encourage flowering.

Water freely, giving the compost a thorough soaking but leaving it almost to dry out before watering again. Add a cactus fertiliser to the water every four weeks during the growing season, from April to late September.

Autumn and winter care

Give your plant a winter rest; keep it at a cool temperature, ideally around 50°F (10°C), in the brightest possible position. At this temperature there will be no need to water at all between October and March; if it is any warmer, a *little* water may be beneficial, but only very infrequently. These plants like good air circulation, but avoid exposing them to any cold draughts.

Propagation

Although not necessarily the quickest method, propagation is best from seeds. You can expect many species to be flowering by the second year. Sow seeds in February and March. Fill your tray with a soil-based seed compost or equal parts of peat and sharp sand; soak well, then firm down and level the surface. Sprinkle the seed over the surface and cover with sharp sand, then move the tray to a shaded place, preferably in a propagator, at a temperature of 70-75°F (21-24°C); provide good ventilation — if using a propagator, open the case for an hour or two a day for the air to circulate. When the seeds germinate, within about three weeks — they will look like tiny green balls — remove the tray from the propagator and move to a brighter position, but avoid direct sunlight. The seedlings will benefit from a year's uninterrupted growth in their tray before potting up into their separate pots — during this time the temperature will have to be maintained at 65-70°F (18-21°C) throughout. Pot up individually the following spring (see 'Spring and summer care').

Alternatively, with plants that produce offsets, cut them carefully away from the parent — April or early May is the best time — and dust the cut surfaces with fungicidal sulphur powder. Leave the cuttings for a week to dry out and callus, before setting them into the normal compost; keep slightly shaded, at a temperature of 70-75°F (21-24°C) and mist spray occasionally to prevent the compost completely drying out. Offsets should be rooted within six to eight weeks — new growth will be clearly visible — after which, treat as established plants.

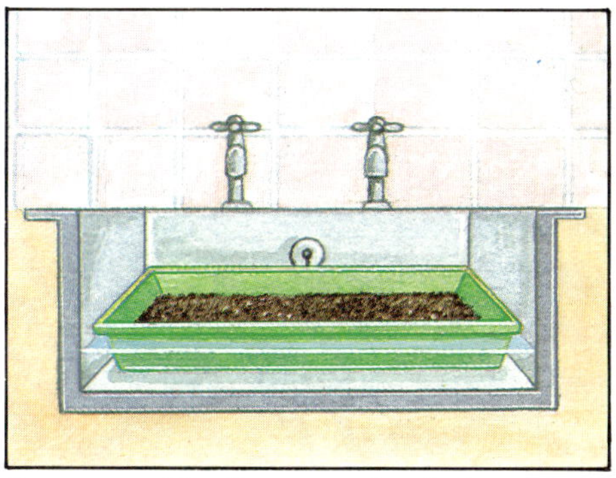

One very effective way of watering a tray of seed compost is to stand it in a sink filled with about 1in (25mm) of water. Remove the tray when the compost glistens; leave it on the draining board for a few minutes to drain the excess water.

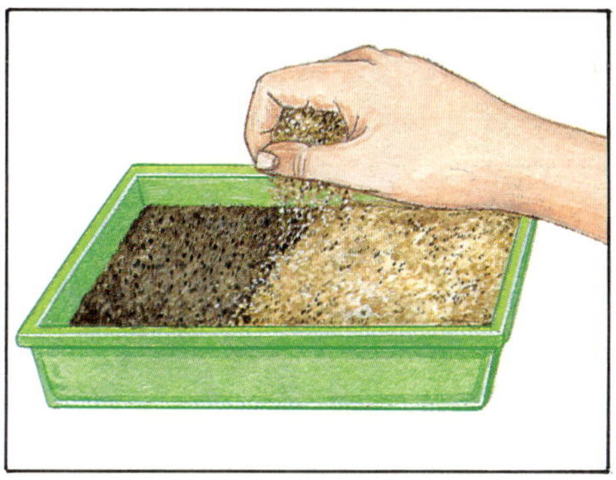

After sowing the seeds on the surface of the compost, cover them with a very thin layer of coarse sand, then place the seed tray in a propagator, in a shaded position.

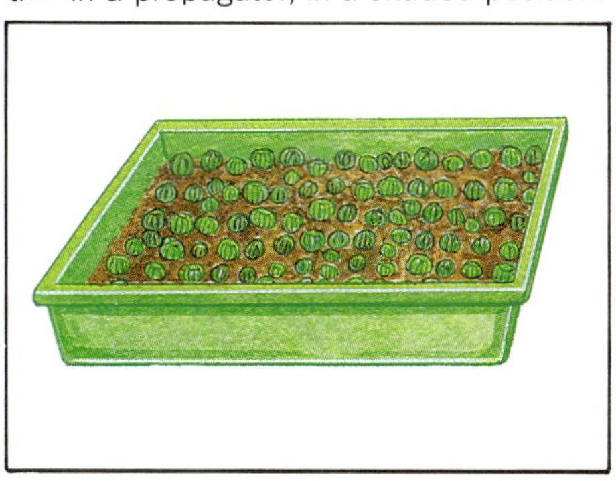

Keep the cactus seedlings uncovered, in a light, warm, draught-free position. Pot up individually when they are about ½-¾in (13-19mm) across.

Buying Guide

Before you buy, check that the cactus is securely planted in its pot. Avoid marked plants and those with soft or mushy patches on their body.

Choose a well-shaped plant — a young, rounded cushion or a straight, column shape — lop-sided plants are hard to correct and prone to toppling over and damaging themselves.

Species

Notocactus leninghausii, the Golden Ball Cactus, from southern Brazil, is one of the tallest-growing species and can reach a height of 3ft (0.9m) in the wild, though it is unlikely to exceed 8-9in (20-23cm) as a houseplant. It starts life as a globular plant and starts to elongate into a column when about three years old. The body of the plant is pale green with about 30 ribs running lengthwise under a dense covering of short, bristle-like, pale yellow spines, with three or four longer, central spines. Flowers begin to appear on or near the crown, when plants are 4-5in (10-13cm) high; the flowering period with all this group is between late spring and around the end of August. Flowers are funnel-shaped, about 2in (5cm) across, in bright yellow surrounded by greenish sepals, and several may appear at a time. This tends to remain a solitary plant for quite a time, but with maturity offsets will develop around the base.

N.scopa, *below*, from Uruguay and Brazil, is globular at first and tends to become column-shaped, growing to a height of about 7in (18cm) after 10 years. It is a beautiful pale green plant with 30-40 low ribs almost hidden by soft, white spines; the yellow flowers are about 2in (5cm) long and 2in (5cm) wide.

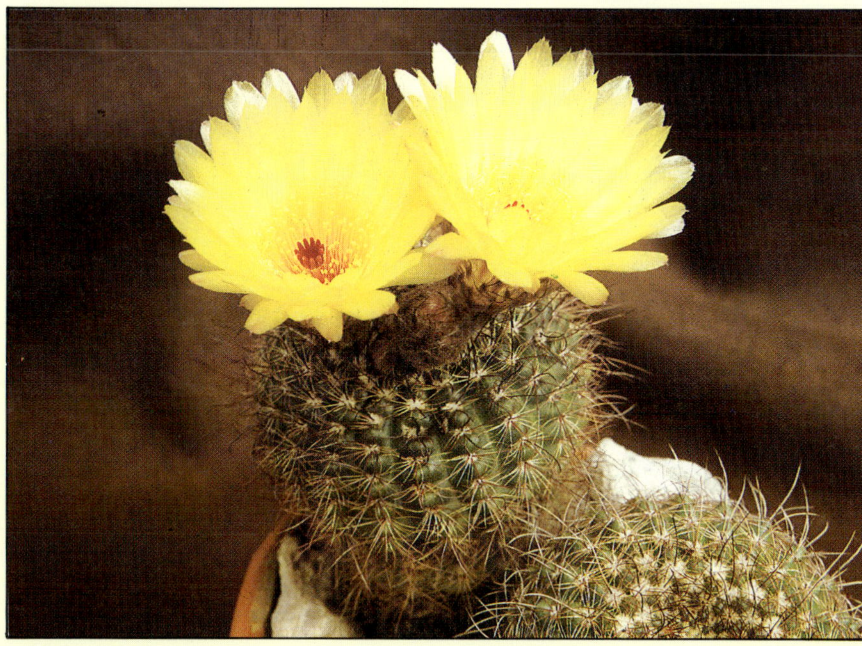

Trouble Shooter

Troubles are comparatively few and can be easily avoided. Both roots and stem will rot — totally, in time — if your plants are too cold and too wet in winter; they will take low temperatures, even below those recommended, but the compost must then be completely dry, and surroundings must be frost-free. Overwatering in summer can be equally damaging; don't give them too much, and allow the compost almost to dry out before watering again. These plants quickly use up the nutrients in the soil, so adequate feeding is important for good growth and regular flowering; too shaded a position, too, can lead to a pale and sickly growth and will discourage flowering.

The principal pest is mealy bug and, perhaps more dangerous since hidden, root mealy bug. The best plan is to apply a dimethoate-based systemic insecticide right from the beginning of the season; this acts as a deterrent as well as disposing of any pests already in evidence. Isolated fluffy white patches of mealy bug can be wiped away with a cotton bud or paintbrush dipped in methylated spirit; but if the plant begins to look really sick, take it from its pot and there's a good chance you will find both the soil and pot covered in a whitish powder, the sign of root mealy bug. Scrub the pot clean and wash the roots thoroughly to remove every trace before potting up again.

Odontoglossum

Family name: **Orchidaceae**

Common names: **Tiger Orchid, Lily-of-the-Valley Orchid**

Care Tricky	**Height** 12-18in (30-46cm)	**Flower** August-October
Light Bright	**Spread** 1ft (0.3m)	**Humidity** Mist spray regularly
Price Expensive	**Shape** Leafy clump	**Availability** Garden centres
Temp. Min 50°F (10°C)	Ideal 65°F (18°C)	Max 75°F (24°C)

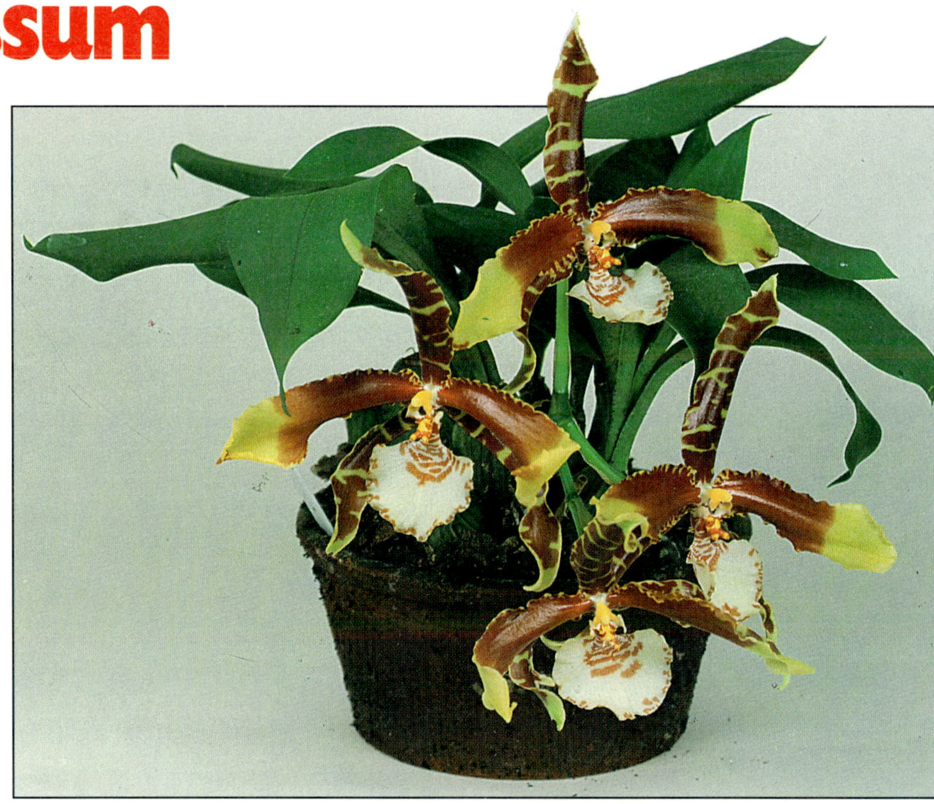

Try growing the beautiful Tiger Orchid — the flowers can last for several weeks.

Orchids have a fascination and a magic which is perhaps unmatched by any other indoor plant. But despite the mystique surrounding them — the problems, the expense, the special conditions, and so on — many orchids are well within most people's capabilities. Odontoglossums, which are among the most beautiful of this exotic family, are also among the least difficult to grow.

This is a large and free-flowering group, of around 300 species, of mainly high-altitude plants from central and south America. Most of them are epiphytes — that is, they root not on the ground, but aloft among the branches of trees or shrubs or on rocky outcrops. These plants have root and food storage systems adapted for their native environment, so when grown as houseplants their fleshy, thickened stems, called rhizomes, should lie on the surface of specially formulated compost. From these rhizomes rise fleshy, bulb-like growths, known as pseudobulbs. Two, or sometimes three, long, evergreen leaves grow from the top of each pseudobulb, while from the base grows a flower stem, up to 2½ft (75cm) in length, which may bear as many as 30 blooms. The exquisite long-lasting flowers have petals and sepals that open out flat with a lip of different colouring which is often conspicuously marked; flowering may be at any time of the year, according to species.

Odontoglossum grande, the Tiger Orchid, is one of the largest, most beautiful and easiest to grow of all; given a sunny windowsill it will thrive and it makes a first-rate choice for a beginner. The flowers normally appear from late summer into the autumn; up to 7in (18cm) across.

Spring and summer care

Repot annually in the early spring into a well-crocked container; don't overpot — it should be quite a close fit. After a few years, your plant will probably need dividing (see 'Propagation'). Proprietary epiphytic orchid composts are available but it can be worthwhile to make your own mixture: use two parts sphagnum moss peat to two parts finely-chopped osmunda fibre or bark and one part very gritty sand or perlite. Also, you can buy special terracotta pots for growing epiphytic orchids — these have holes in their sides to allow plenty of air to circulate around the roots — it's perfectly alright for the roots to grow through the holes. To plant an orchid, don't bury the pseudobulbs — make a slight mound on the surface of the compost and sit them on top. The roots, however, should be under the surface.

Your plant will do best at a temperature of 60-70°F (15-18°C). It's most important to avoid direct sunlight; bright, but filtered light is ideal, with perhaps a little more shade provided in the heat of the summer.

Water quite freely so that the compost is thoroughly moist, then allow a full half of the compost to dry out before watering again. Regular feeding is important to sustain the development of the plant and its foliage and to encourage flowering. Add a liquid fertiliser to the water every two or three weeks; ideally, a fertiliser that is high in nitrogen should be used during spring and summer, followed by a high-potash fertiliser in late summer and early autumn. Your plant requires high humidity; stand the pot on moist pebbles and mist spray regularly,

Autumn and winter care

Winter temperatures should be around 50-60°F (10-15°C). Keep your plant in a really bright spot, though not in direct sunlight; the position should be well-ventilated, but avoid cold draughts at all costs. As in the summer months, give the plant enough water to moisten the compost thoroughly, then leave it to dry out a bit before watering again; it's especially important at these temperatures never to allow the plant to stand in water.

Propagation

Divide overgrown clumps at repotting time (see facing page). At the base of the stem, are the bulb-like growths known as pseudobulbs; cut these apart in groups of two or three but leave them in the pot to allow the cut roots time to heal before disturbing them. After four to six weeks remove the divisions from the container, carefully disentangle the roots from the compost and replant them in 4in (10cm) pots of fresh potting mixture. Keep them in a semi-shaded spot and water sparingly until new growth is apparent, after four to six weeks, then treat as established plants.

Trouble Shooter

Careful control of temperature and watering is essential throughout the whole year. Foliage will wilt and flowers will suffer if temperatures are too high and the compost remains dry for too long. Conversely, overwatering, especially when temperatures are very low, will cause the roots and pseudobulbs to rot.

Mealy bug may attack the foliage; wipe away the fluffy, white patches with a cotton bud or paintbrush dipped in methylated spirit. Thrips may prove a bigger problem, damaging both the leaves and the flowers; spray with a dimethoate- or pirimiphos-methyl-based insecticide.

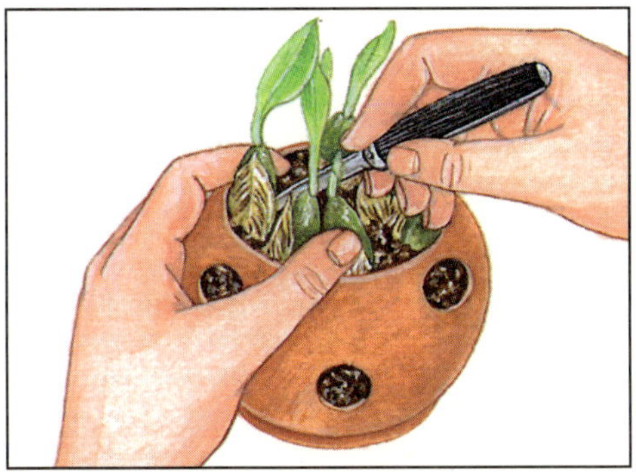

Cut overcrowded clumps into two halves — each part should have several pseudobulbs. Leave them in their pot while the cut heals over.

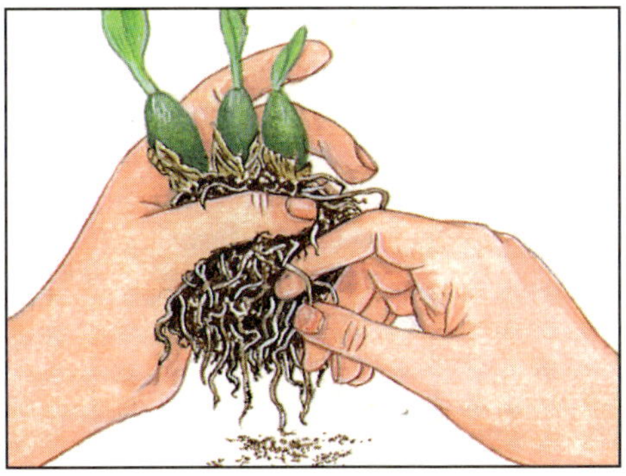

After four to six weeks, remove one of the two halves from the container and gently tease out its roots, shaking them free of potting compost.

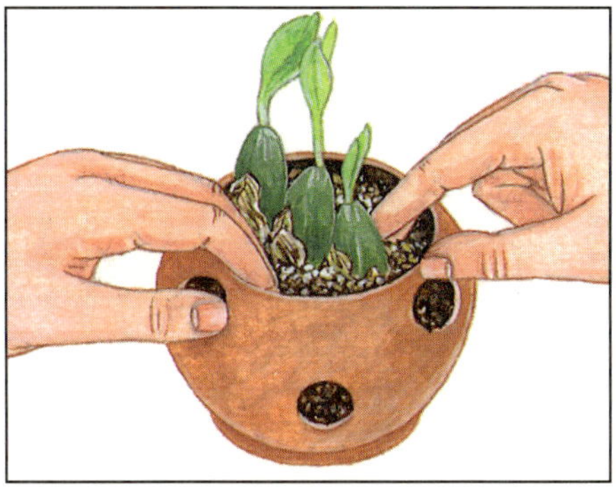

Pot it up separately; the pseudobulbs should sit on top of the compost while the feeding roots should be under the surface and well firmed in.

Species

Odontoglossum grande, the Tiger Orchid, from Guatemala, is one of the largest and most colourful of species. The large pseudobulbs carry two or three long, oval leaves; the 1ft (0.3m) long flower spike bears as many as seven flowers. Normally appearing from August to October, the flowers have bright yellow sepals and petals with cinnamon-brown markings and a short rounded lip in pale yellow or cream, with a reddish-brown base.

O.crispum, *below*, from Colombia, is the parent of many beautiful hybrids. Sturdy pseudobulbs carry two long, strap-shaped leaves. The arching flower stem is about 2ft (0.6m) long and carries numerous exquisite flowers, each 3-4in (8-10cm) across, which are white, sometimes flushed with pink, with yellow lips spotted in red. The main flowering period is in early spring, though flowers can be produced almost all year round.

O.triumphans, *below right*, another beautiful Colombian species, has large pseudobulbs with 6in (15cm) leaves. Its very long stems carry 4in (10cm) flowers of bright golden-yellow, blotched deep reddish-brown; the lip is pure white with a yellow centre at the base, turning to cinnamon brown, edged in pale yellow.

O.citrosmum is a delightfully-scented species from Mexico. Stout pseudobulbs bear a pair of leathery, strap-shaped leaves up to 1ft (0.3m) long. In the wild, the long, pendulous flower spike holds as many as 30 blooms, though five to ten is more likely for a houseplant. The flowers, which appear mainly in the spring, are about 2½in (6.5cm) across, pale pink with a lip of deep rose.

O.pulchellum, the Lily-of-the-valley Orchid, is also Mexican, with small but fragrant flowers; up to 10 of them are borne on the erect, 1ft (0.3m) tall spike, usually in the spring, in crystalline white with a yellow crest on the lip. The small pseudobulbs carry a pair of very narrow, dark green leaves, about 10-12in (25-30cm) in length.

Odontoglossom hybrids have arisen by different species cross-pollinating and then, in some cases the resulting hybrids crossing with other species or hybrids — this rather confusing situation means that the exact parentage of most of them is not known. However, within this group are some of the most beautiful orchids, such as 'Elise' which has a spike of star-like flowers in pale yellow, deepening to orange-yellow with red-brown blotches at the edges. 'Miltonia' has long-lasting flowers that are rather pansy-like in shape. They are available in many different rich colours — reds, orange, lilac just to mention a few.

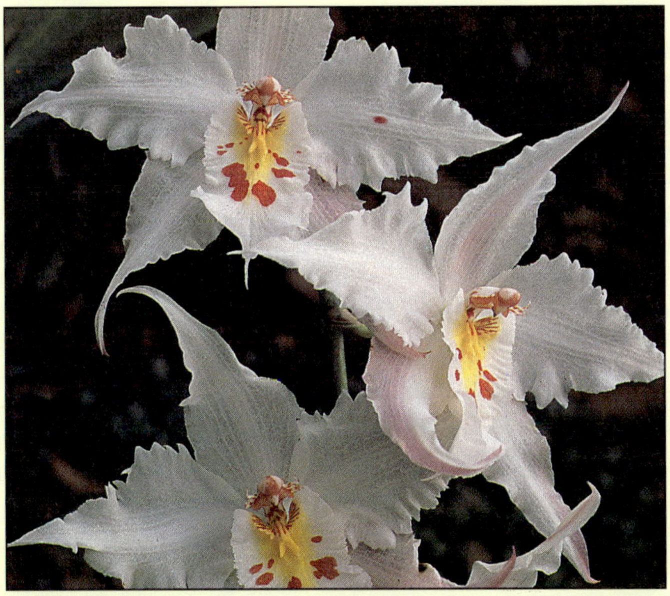

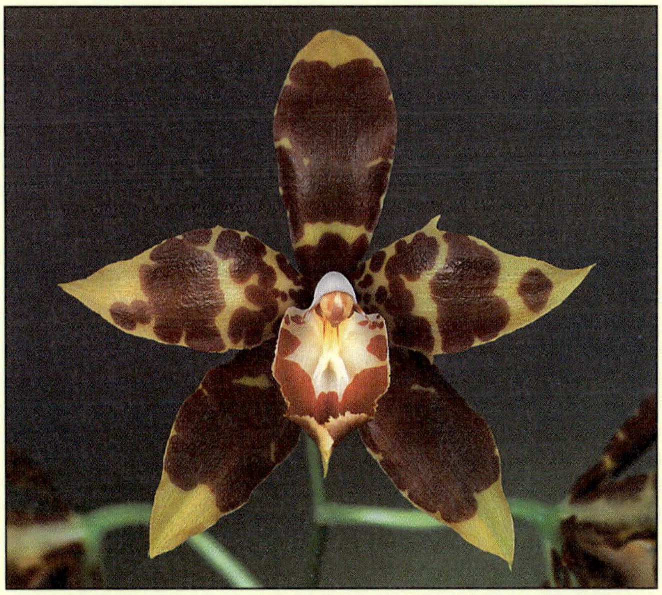

Pachystachys

Family name: **Acanthaceae**

Common name: **Lollipop Plant**

Care Straight-forward	**Height** 2ft (0.6m)	**Flower** Summer
Light Bright indirect	**Spread** 18in (45cm)	**Humidity** Mist spray regularly
Price Middle range	**Shape** Bushy	**Availability** Garden centres
Temp. Min 50°F (10°C)	Ideal 65°F (18°C)	Max 70°F (21°C)

This easy-to-grow, decorative flowering shrub, from central and South America, will bloom from late spring right through to autumn, if properly looked after.

Pachystachys lutea, below — or the Lollipop Plant — from Peru, was relatively unknown as a houseplant a few years ago. It was in fact popular in Victorian times, but for some reason, fell out of favour around the beginning of the century. Now, however, it is quite often seen on display, with its very striking, large flower heads of creamy white blooms bursting through golden yellow bracts, above dark green oval leaves. These appear thoughout the summer and the bracts retain their bright colour for eight weeks or more.

Spring and summer care

Repot in the spring every year into John Innes No 2; crock the pots well to ensure good drainage. Move plants up one size each year, to a final pot size of 6-7in (15-18cm), after which topdress, by replacing the top 1-2in (2.5-5cm) of compost with fresh. Prune to shape in the spring, for a neat plant; Pachystachys can get rather leggy and out of hand and cutting them back a bit encourages flowering, and helps show the flowers off to their best advantage.

Normal room temperatures are fine, provided they don't exceed 70°F (21°C) — a little lower is preferable — and good air circulation is important, especially at high temperatures. Keep your plant in a brightly-lit spot but definitely avoid full sunlight.

Water fairly freely to keep the compost constantly just moist but never waterlogged; add a few drops of a liquid fertiliser to the water every two weeks from April to September. Your plant should have quite a humid atmosphere; the best way to achieve this is to stand the pot on a saucer of wet pebbles and mist spray regularly.

Autumn and winter care

Aim for a winter temperature of around 55°F (13°C). It will tolerate lower temperatures, but make sure it is kept frost free; some leaves may fall but new growth will start the following spring.

Keep your plant in a very bright spot with good air circulation, but take care to avoid cold draughts. Water occasionally, just so the soil is barely moist.

Propagation

Take 4-5in (10-13cm) long stem tip cuttings in the spring; make a clean cut just below a leaf node and remove the lowest pair of leaves. Treat the cut ends with a little hormone rooting powder and insert the cutting up to the lowest leaves in a mixture of equal parts of peat and coarse sand. Enclose the cuttings in a propagator or a clear polythene bag — take care that the leaves do not touch the polythene, since this may rot them — and keep moist and shaded, at a temperature of 70°F (21°C).

When the cuttings have rooted, within about six weeks — new growth will be clearly visible — pot them on individually (see 'Spring and summer care') and treat as established plants.

Trouble Shooter

With attention to temperature, watering and humidity, your plant will be virtually problem free. Overwatering when it is too cold is the worst fault; this will certainly lead to the death of the plant, in time. Leaves will turn colour, wilt and probably fall if plants are allowed to become too dry; a good soaking should cure the problem. Lack of air circulation in summer can hinder good growth and flowering; keep your plant in a well ventilated but draught free spot.

Greenfly is a likely pest; spray with a pyrethrum-based insecticide. Red spider mite may cause problems, especially if the atmosphere is too dry; spray with a malathion-based insecticide. Applying a systemic insecticide proves an effective overall deterrent. Always follow the manufacturers' instructions when using chemicals.

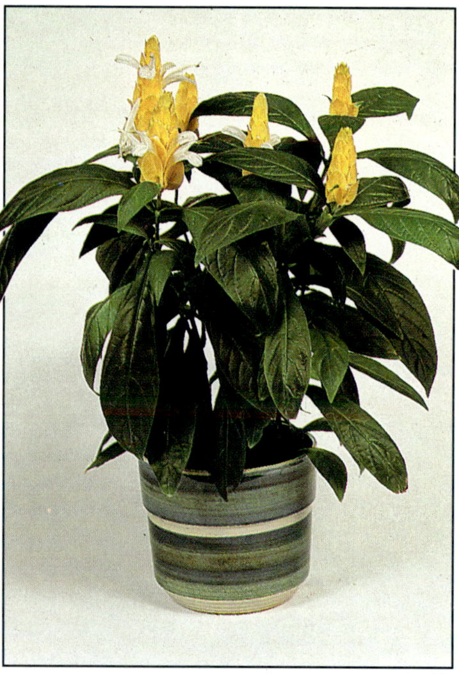

The common name comes from the shape of the bright flower buds.

Species

Pachystachys lutea, the Lollipop Plant, *left*, is a short, shrubby plant which can reach 2ft (60cm) high, but is best kept to 12-18in (30-45cm) indoors. Dark green, pointed oval leaves are carried on rather woody stems, each of which becomes tipped with 5in (13cm) long, cone-shaped flower heads, made up of golden-yellow bracts. The plant flowers continuously throughout the summer, with creamy-white 2in (5cm) blooms appearing in succession from the bottom of the spike, pushing their way between the bracts. The bracts will retain their colour for eight weeks or more.

P.coccinea, *right*, is a taller growing plant, often reaching 3-5ft (0.9-1.5m), although careful pruning provides a very compact, free-flowering houseplant. Leaves are dark green and leathery, up to 8in (20cm) long; the woody stems and branches bear large heads of crimson flowers in summer. This plant looks similar and is closely related to some Jacobinia species.

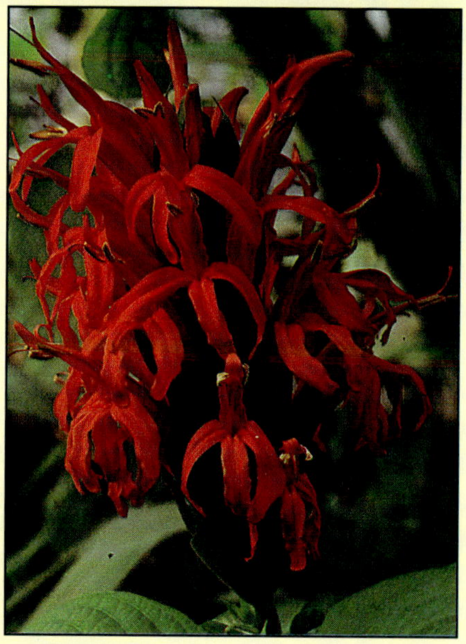

Pandanus

Family name: **Pandanaceae**

Common name:
Screw Pine

Care Easy	**Height** 3ft (0.9m)	**Flower** Insignificant
Light Bright indirect	**Spread** 3ft (0.9m)	**Humidity** Mist spray regularly
Price Middle range	**Shape** Palm-like	**Availability** Garden centres
Temp. Min 60°F (16°C)	Ideal 70°F (21°C)	Max 85°F (29°C)

This very large group of evergreen shrubs is characterised by slender, elongated leaves, which are usually finely serrated along their edge. They are tough and tolerant of a range of conditions and, given care, they will last for many years.

The attraction of the Screw Pine lies in its ornamental foliage. The shiny, leathery leaves, growing in a tuft at the top of a woody stem, are sword-shaped and gracefully arched. They grow up to 3ft (0.9m) long, in a spiral arrangement which gives the plant its popular name. The colour of the leaves varies with different species — they can be dark, glossy green, or paler green edged or striped with white.

The Screw Pine is a slow grower, but in time it will develop into a beautiful palm-like plant several feet high. It's best to grow it on its own, as a specimen plant, so that its spreading shape and lovely leaves are shown to best advantage.

Spring and summer care

Repotting needs to be done every two or three years, when the roots begin to push the plant out of its pot. Use John Innes No 2 and repot in March; wear thick gloves to protect your hands from the serrated leaves.

Place in bright, indirect light. Summer temperatures can rise as high as 80-85°F (27-30°C). Water freely, adding a liquid fertiliser to the water every three to four weeks. Mist spray from above during the hottest months, but never in full sun because the leaves will scorch. It's a good idea to stand the pot on a saucer of pebbles.

Autumn and winter care

Pandanus needs a pretty warm temperature during the winter — don't let it drop below 60°F (16°C) from October to March. Give the best light possible, preferably full sun. Water occasionally, just to keep the soil from drying out, and never subject your plant to cold draughts.

Propagation

Propagation, which should be carried out between February and April, is by detaching the suckers that grow around the base of the plant. Pot them separately using John Innes No 1 in 4in (10cm) pots. Keep them shaded at a temperature of 75°F (24°C) until they are well rooted and there are signs of new growth, then treat them as mature plants.

Species

Pandanus veitchii, from Indonesia, is the typical Screw Pine. It will grow up to 3ft (0.9m) high, its widely spreading foliage arising from a central, woody stem. The slightly serrated leaves are about 3in (8cm) wide at the base, 2ft (0.6m) long and pointed. Bright glossy green, they have creamy-white lines running from tip to base. Mature plants develop aerial roots which thrust themselves down into the soil, and also insignificant flowers. If you have a male and a female flowering plant, you'll be able to grow the fruit — it is large and attractive, but not edible.

P.baptistii, the Blue Screw Pine, is from New Guinea. It is most beautiful, with stiff, spirally arranged leaves, gently arching and narrowing to points. It can eventually reach 6ft (1.8m) in height. The foliage is bluish-green, with several brilliant yellow stripes down the centre — sometimes these are so broad that the entire leaf is yellow. Unlike *P.veitchii*, the leaves have no serrations.

You can also grow Pandanus from seed. Sow the seeds in John Innes No 1, and keep them at a temperature of 80-85°F (27-30°C), slightly shaded, and preferably in a propagator. The seeds will germinate in six to eight weeks. When they are large enough to handle, pot up the seedlings separately as above, potting them on when necessary.

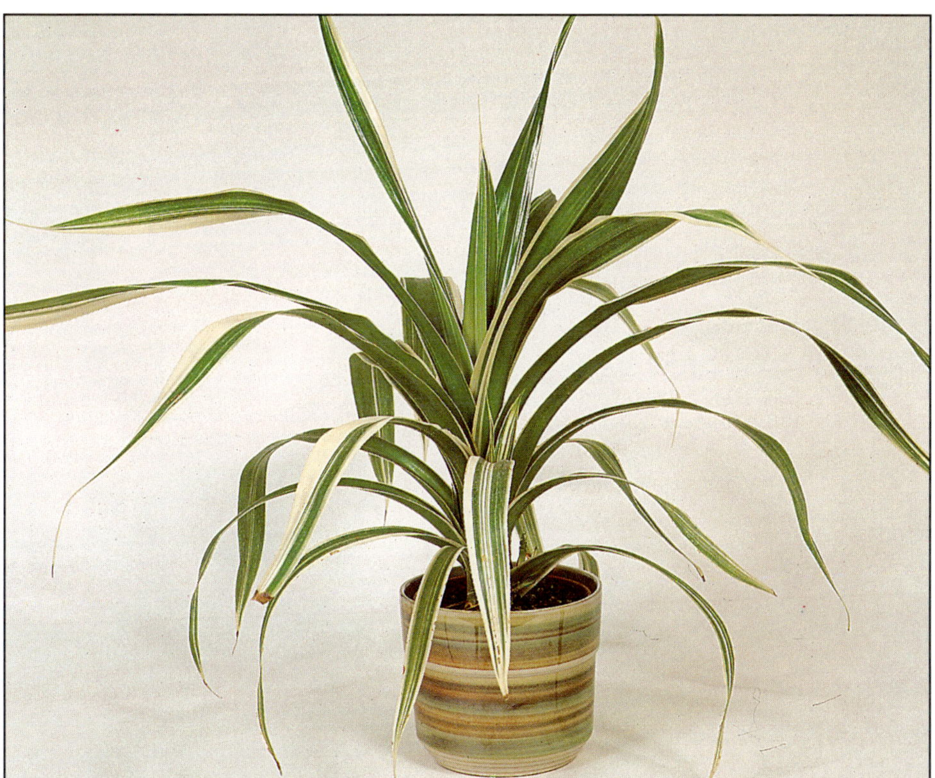

The easy-going *Pandanus veitchii* can make a dramatic and eye-catching feature.

Trouble Shooter

Leaves will shrivel and fall in winter if the plant is left standing in water in a cold temperature or draught. Underwatering is also dangerous, especially in summer; make sure you mist spray regularly. If leaves lose their lustre, there's probably too much shade; move your plant to a bright, sunny position.

Scale insects are likely attackers; wipe them off with a cloth dipped in methylated spirit and use the same treatment to get rid of mealy bug. Spray with a systemic insecticide as a preventative measure during spring and summer.

Buying Guide

There are many species other than the two named here, but unfortunately they are not available as plants, although certain specialist seed merchants do offer seeds.

Pelargonium

Family name: **Geraniaceae**

Common name: **Geranium**

Care Easy	**Height** 1-2ft (0.3-0.6m)	**Flower** Summer
Light Sunny	**Spread** 1ft (0.3m)	**Humidity** None
Price Middle range	**Shape** Bushy	**Availability** Common

Temp. Min 50°F (10°C) · Ideal 70°F (21°C) · Max 80°F (27°C)

Pelargoniums are among the most popular of all plants — they are prized for their abundant, highly colourful flowers or their attractive, sometimes scented, foliage. Rather confusingly, although they are popularly known as Geraniums, strictly speaking they should be called Pelargoniums — the true Geraniums are a separate group of hardy, herbaceous perennials.

There are over 250 species of Pelargonium. They come originally from an area spreading from South Africa to the Mediterranean, Australia and western Asia. The houseplants fall into four main groups. Zonal Pelargoniums (*Pelargonium hortorum*) are the popular and most widely grown; their common name describes the 'zonal' horseshoe-shaped marking over the leaf. In their long flowering season — with care it can last almost all year round — they produce large, round-headed clusters of flowers in white or every shade of red and pink; foliage colouring and markings also vary greatly.

Regal Pelargoniums (*P.domesticum*) have spectacular flowers, which are larger and more impressive than Zonal Pelargoniums, but the flowering period is much shorter and they are less easy to grow. The Ivy-leaved Pelargoniums (*P.peltatum*) are low-growing, trailing plants and perfect for hanging baskets. Finally, there are the scented-leaved Pelargoniums, a number of species and hybrids that are grown more for their attractive foliage than their small flowers; the leaves give off strong pleasant scents — especially when crushed.

Spring and summer care

Repot in the spring into a well-crocked container of John Innes No 1 or 2; for Ivy-leaved varieties, excellent results can be achieved with a cactus compost. Don't overpot — all Pelargoniums flourish in relatively small pots. Pot on younger plants annually — or sooner if many roots are appearing through drainage holes — using a pot one size larger, up to a final pot size of 5in (13cm). Pinch out the growing tips of young Pelargoniums to encourage a bushy plant.

Older plants should be pruned and repotted every spring (see below opposite), with the exception of Regal Pelargoniums, which

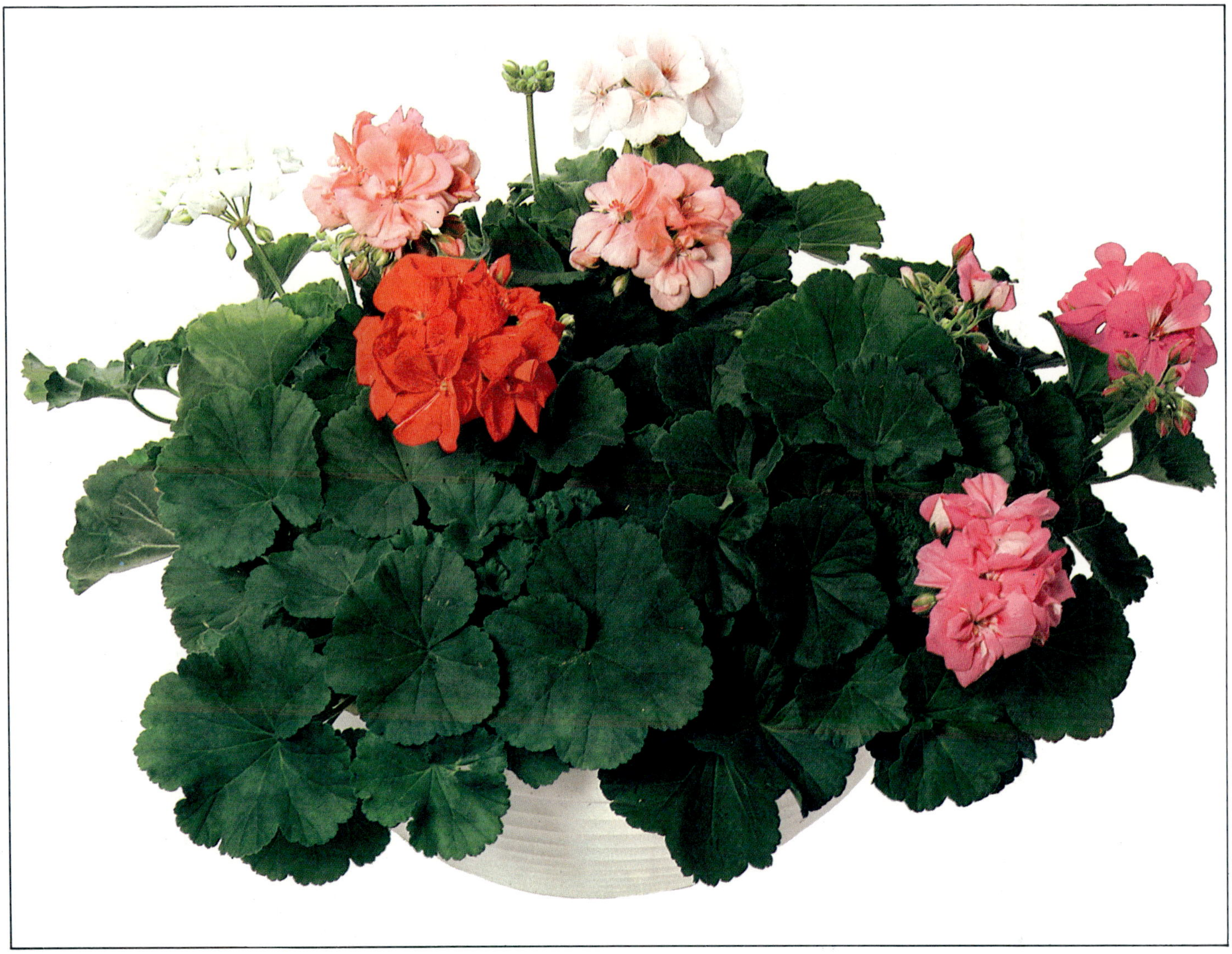

Geraniums are one of the most popular pot plants. A mixed bowl of different coloured zonal varieties makes an attractive decoration.

should be done in the late summer or early autumn. Cut back the top growth by half to encourage new shoots. Remove the plant from the pot and clean off all the loose, old compost, trim any long, thick roots, then repot the plant in fresh compost.

Throughout the year, remove any dead flower heads, cutting the stems back to the next pair of leaves, and also remove faded or discoloured leaves.

Normal room temperatures are suitable, and they can rise to 70-75°F (21-24°C) or slightly higher. Give your plants the brightest possible position — they all enjoy sunshine — and keep them well ventilated, though out of draughts.

Water freely to moisten the compost thoroughly, but allow the surface to dry out before watering again; add a liquid fertiliser every two weeks from April to September. Regal varieties again require slightly different treatment; when their flowering period is over, in midsummer, they should be rested for about six weeks with only enough water to keep the compost from drying out completely and no fertiliser, then gradually brought back to normal care.

Autumn and winter care

Winter temperatures should be between 50-60°F (10-16°C). Give the plants plenty of light, with as much direct sunlight as possible, and a dry and airy, but definitely draught-free, atmosphere.

Water only very occasionally — just enough to prevent the compost from drying out completely.

Carry on dead-heading flowers and removing discoloured leaves, as necessary.

Propagation

In summer, take 3-4in (8-10cm) stem tip cuttings from just below a leaf node. Remove any flowers or buds and the lowest leaves, dip the cut ends in rooting hormone, then insert the cuttings up to the lowest leaves in a mixture of equal parts of peat and coarse sand. Keep the mixture just moist and slightly shaded and root at a temperature of 60-65°F (16-18°C). In about six weeks, when rooting is well-established and new growth is clearly visible, pot up individually into the recommended compost and then treat the cuttings as established plants (see 'Spring and summer care').

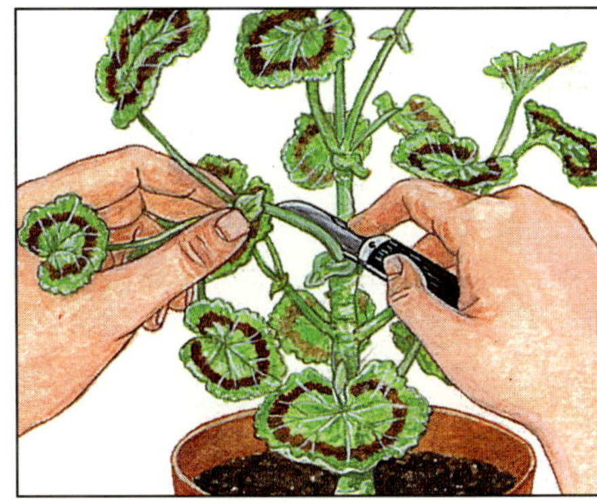

Use a sharp knife to take 3-4in (8-10cm) cuttings from healthy side shoots during the summer.

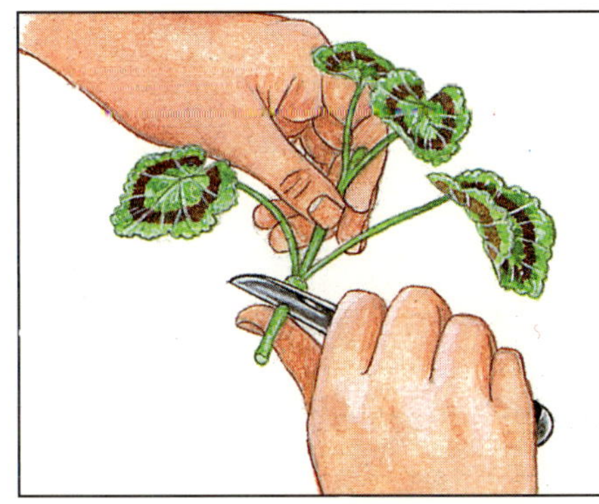

Trim the cutting to just below a pair of leaves. Treat the cut surface with a little rooting hormone.

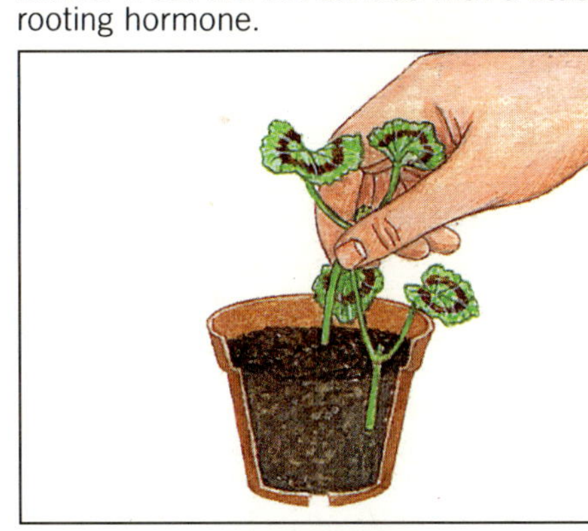

Remove the lowest pair of leaves then set the cutting into compost up to the next pair.

Trouble Shooter

Leaves will discolour and stems may turn yellowish if plants are allowed to remain in a shaded position for too long; very good light is necessary at all times of year. Overwatering is likely to cause root rot and the base of the stem will begin to turn black — if temperatures are too low the risk is increased; in this event, plants are best destroyed as this might be the forerunner of a fungus problem called blackleg. Whitefly, *right*, and mealy bug are both likely pests; wipe away the fluffy patches with a paintbrush or cotton bud dipped in methylated spirit. Get rid of whitefly and mealy bug by spraying with a malathion-based insecticide. Alternatively, apply a systemic insecticide at regular intervals as a very effective deterrent against a number of different pests.

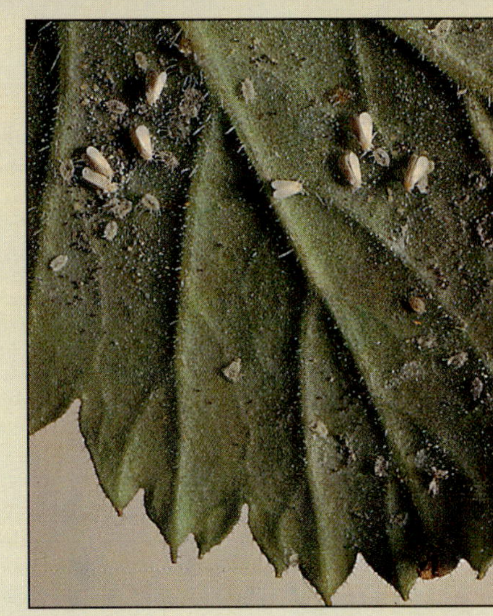

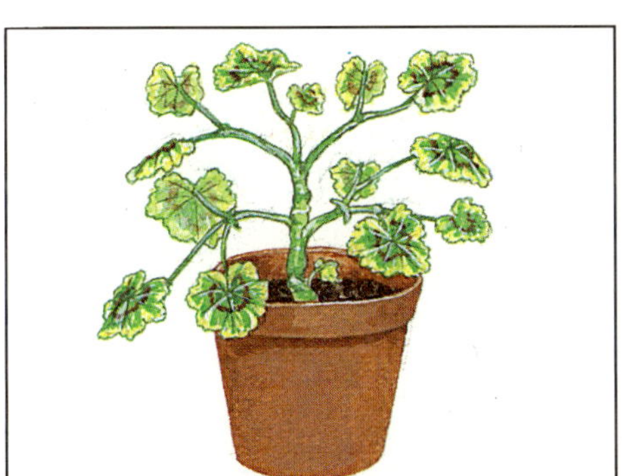

Prune according to the shape you want. For a standard, stake your plant and remove side shoots as they appear.

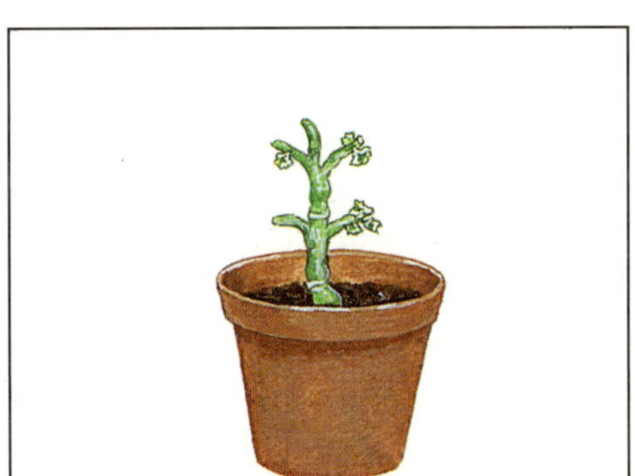

If you want a tall, spreading bush, cut back one third to a half of the last year's growth.

Buying Guide

Always buy bushy plants with plenty of young growth. Check carefully for pests and diseases and discoloration of stems or leaves, also avoid buying plants with wilting leaves — especially the lower ones.

It's a good idea to buy plants that are just coming into flower — look for plenty of buds and make sure they really are the colour you want.

Pelargoniums are tender plants so don't buy them in frosty weather.

Species

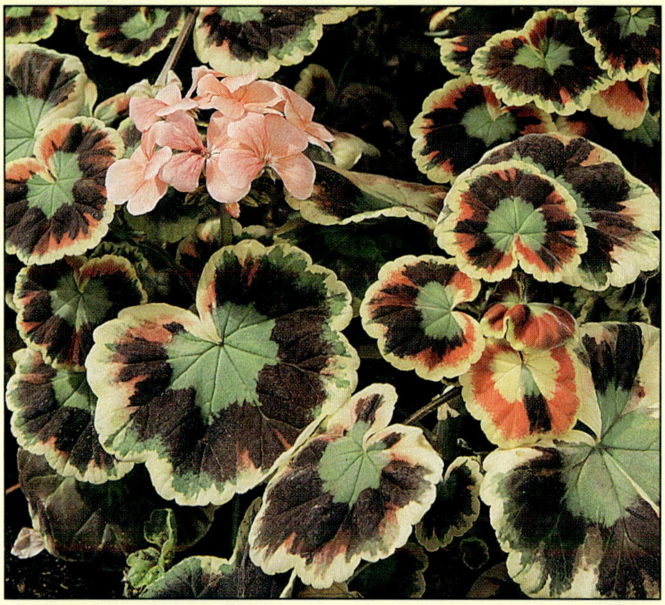

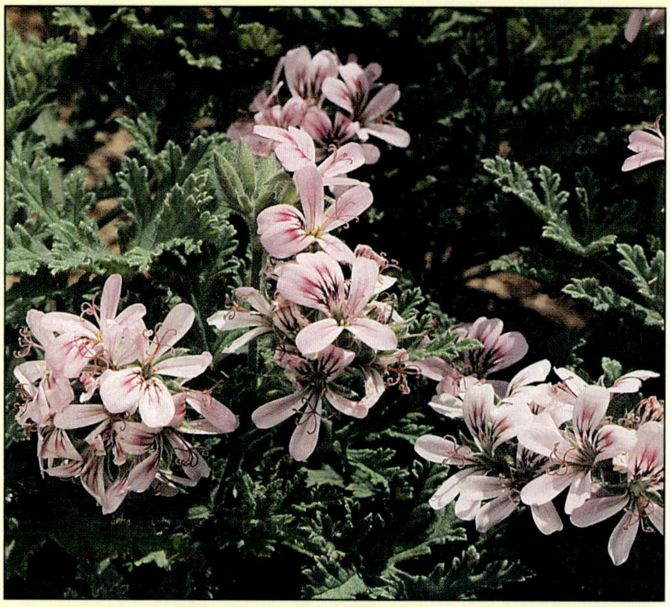

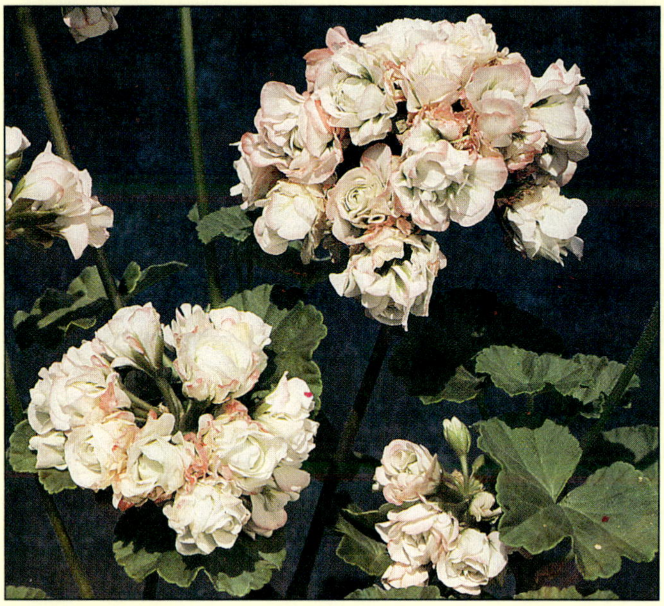

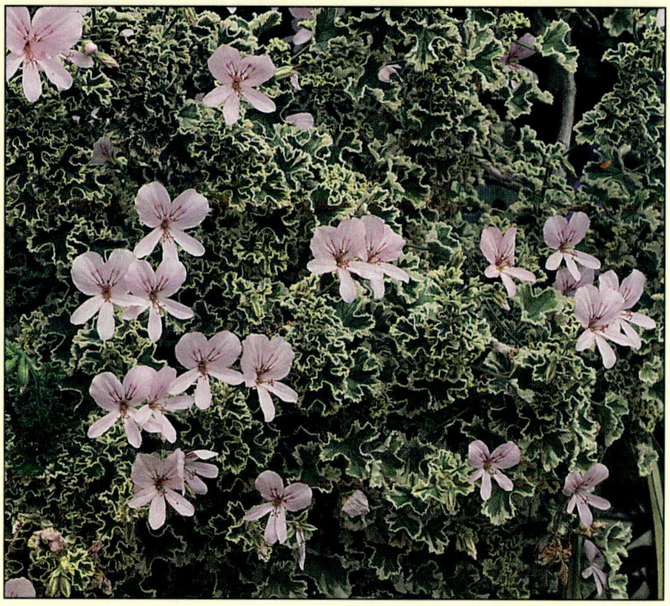

Pelargonium hortorum hybrids — the Zonal or Bedding Pelargoniums, as they are known — are the most widely grown Pelargoniums, by far. These thick-stemmed, bushy plants usually grow to 1-2ft (0.3-0.6m), though some varieties reach 4ft (1.2m) in height. The rounded, slightly crinkled leaves are 3-5in (8-13cm) wide, and usually mid-green with a horse-shoe marking or 'zone' around them, in a contrasting colour — hence the common name; some varieties have multi-coloured leaves with the horseshoe marking picked out in bands of red, orange or cream, and on other varieties the zoning is barely visible. These plants have a long flowering season — with care they can flower nearly all year round. Flowers are around 1½in (4cm) wide, coloured white or shades of red and pink, and are borne on 9in (23cm) stalks, in large, round-headed clusters.

The countless varieties include 'Mrs Henry Cox', *top left*, which has salmon-pink flowers and very impressive leaves of greyish-green with red and yellow bands. 'Happy Thought' is a variety that has been available for many years with red flowers and leaves of bright green with a creamy-yellow centre. 'Appleblossom Rosebud', *bottom left*, is an unusual and deservedly popular variety, with lovely white flowers edged in pink looking just like clusters of tiny rose buds.

P.crispum, *bottom right*, is one of the Scented-leaved Pelargoniums, which are grown for their foliage rather than their small flowers. This is a freely-branching, rather woody plant, growing to about 2ft (0.6m) with slender stems bearing rounded, three-lobed leaves; its common name of Lemon-scented Geranium describes the strong aroma which the leaves give off when gently crushed. Pale purple flowers, about 1in (2.5cm) wide, appear two or three together on short stalks, from May to October. Other popular scented-leaved species include *P.graveolens*, *top right*, with rose-scented leaves, and *P.tomentosum*, with velvety green leaves and a scent of mint.

Species

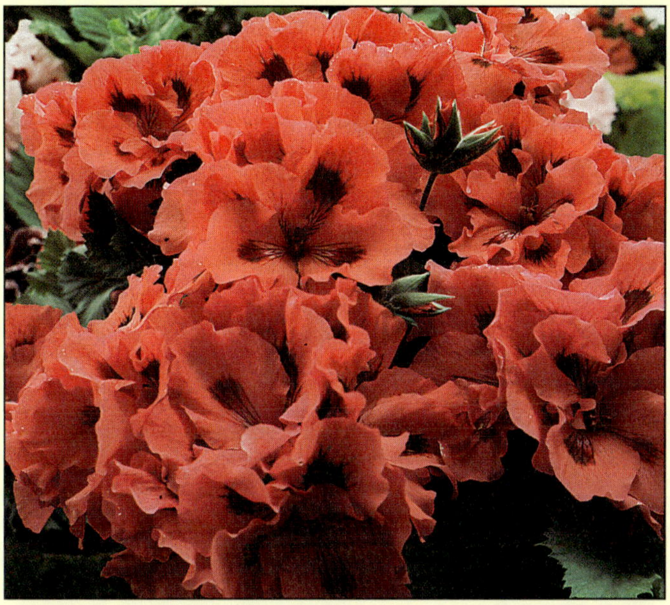

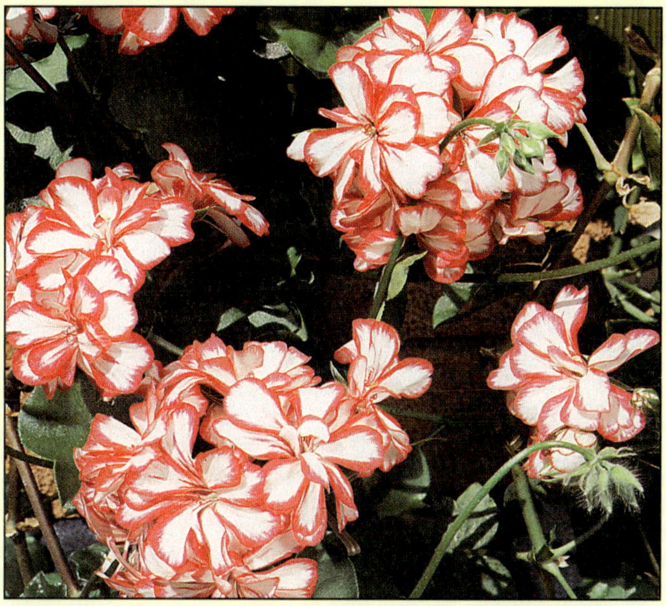

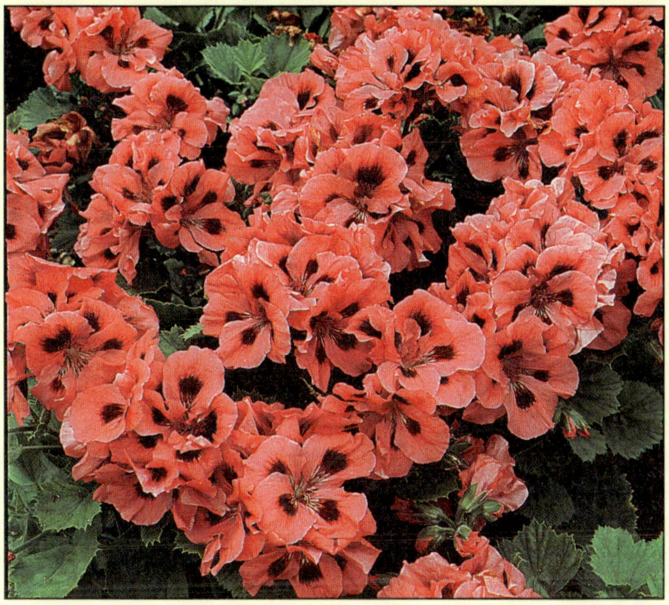

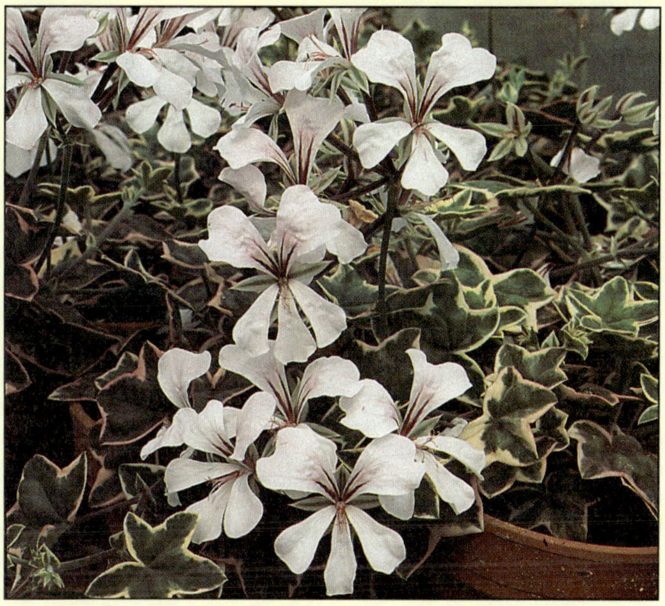

P.domesticum hybrids, commonly known as Regal Pelargoniums, have spectacular flowers, which are larger and more impressive than those of *P.hortorum*, but the flowering season is shorter, from early spring to midsummer, and they are less easy to grow. These plants normally reach 1-2ft (0.3-0.6m) in height. The leaves are plain green and rounded, about 3in (8cm) across, quite rough-textured, with a serrated edge. The funnel-shaped flowers are large and showy, about 2-2½in (5-7cm) across; petals are usually frilled and coloured in pink or cream with splashes or lines in darker shades such as deep red or purple. Flowers appear at or around the tips of stems and young branches, in groups of up to ten. Among the most attractive and widely available varieties are 'Grand Slam', *top left*, which has brilliant crimson flowers with purple on the upper petals; and the popular 'Lavender Grand Slam', with flowers of shaded lavender and deep purple blotches. 'Carisbrooke' has clusters of rose-pink blooms, while 'G. Fischer', *bottom left*, has very appealing flowers of pink with deep brown markings.

P.peltatum, the Ivy-leaved or Trailing Pelargonium, is a low-growing species which is an ideal plant for growing in a hanging basket. The bright-green, fleshy leaves are about 3in (8cm) across and five-lobed — like a rounded ivy; star-shaped flowers, up to 1½in (4cm) across are formed in small clusters on long, slender stalks, appearing in profusion during spring and less frequently through the summer and autumn. Many hybrids are available, with flowers in a range of shades from deep purple to pink: 'Rouletti', *top right*, has pink-tinged flowers, those of 'Mexican Beauty' are deep red with intense reddish-purple markings, while 'Apricot Queen' has blooms of salmon-pink which turn very pale before they die. Though mainly grown for their flowers, there are some varieties with particularly decorative foliage, such as 'L'Elegante', *bottom right*, with leaves in green, yellow and white.

Pellaea

Family name: **Polypodiaceae**

Common name: **Button Fern**

Care Straight-forward	**Height** 10in (25cm)	**Flower** None
Light Indirect	**Spread** 10in (25cm)	**Humidity** Mist spray regularly
Price Cheap	**Shape** Leafy clump	**Availability** Common

Temp. Min 50°F (10°C) Ideal 65°F (18°C) Max 80°F (27°C)

These small foliage plants can be found growing wild in many parts of the world; in Africa and New Zealand, in North and South America. *Pellaea rotundifolia*, from New Zealand, is the most popular houseplant species. Superficially, it doesn't look like a typical fern; the dark green, waxy leaflets are almost round and slightly serrated about the edge. Like many ferns, though, the fronds uncurl to form a leafy, arching rosette — making it an excellent plant for a small hanging basket, wall pot or pedestal. Pellaeas are quite straightforward to look after as long as you pay attention to their water and light requirements.

Spring and summer care

In March every year, gently slide your Pellaea out of its pot to check the roots. If it has completely filled the pot then it's time to transfer the plant to a pot one size larger; use a peat-based potting compost with plenty of drainage at the bottom of the pot. If you want to grow your fern in a hanging basket, line the inside of the container with a thick layer of sphagnum moss (you can buy this in bags from most garden centres). Fill the lined basket with a peat-based potting compost, remove your fern from its pot and plant it firmly in the compost. Don't be tempted to line your hanging basket with polythene — this won't allow sufficient water drainage for Pellaeas.

Normal room temperatures are fine. If they rise over 70°F (21°C) you'll need to mist spray your plant regularly — preferably with tepid water; the warmer the temperature, the more often you'll need to spray.

Water your plant freely so that the compost is always moist; it is vital never to let the compost dry out completely — but don't let it stand in a saucer of water for days on end either. Add a few drops of liquid fertiliser to the water every two weeks between May and September.

Pellaea likes bright light but not direct sun, since its leaves are easily scorched — so keep your plant in bright indirect light.

Autumn and winter care

Pellaeas continue to grow during the winter months, rather than having a rest period like some other plants; reduce the temperature slightly, to about 55-60°F (13-16°C), keep your plant only just moist, stop mist spraying and don't use fertiliser from September until the following May.

Propagation

Divide your Pellaea when it has become larger than you'd like in March, gently separate your plant into two halves, cutting through the fleshy rhizomes if necessary. Pot the two halves into separate pots and treat them as established plants. Alternatively, if your plant is very overgrown you can divide it into several small plants. Cut the rhizomes into small sections — each one with its own frond and root system. Pot up each section individually into peat-based compost and treat them as mature plants.

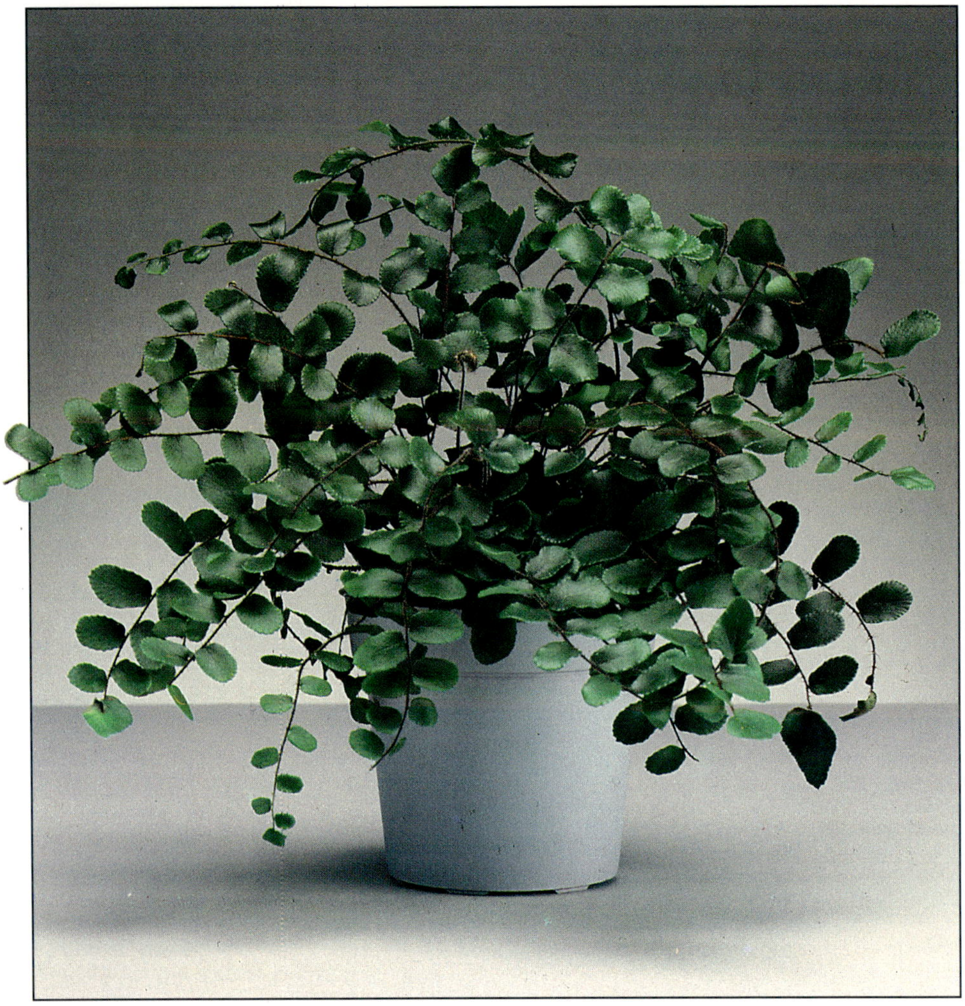

The Button Fern with its round, leathery leaves, looks unlike a typical fern.

Species

***Pellaea rotundifolia*,** the Button Fern, from New Zealand, forms a clump of 12in (0.3m) long, arching fronds. These carry small, dark green, paired, slightly serrated leaflets, which are arranged alternately along either side of their stems.

***P.viridis*,** sometimes called *P.hastata*, is from the West Indies. With its feathery, lobed fronds, it looks much more fern-like than *P.rotundifolia*. The fronds are dark green and grow to about 18in (45cm) in length and have black, shining stalks. The variety *P.v.macrophylla*, sometimes called *P.adiantoides*, has larger fronds, up to 2ft (0.6m) long, and fewer leaflets — and should not be confused with the popular Holly Fern, *Cyrtomium falcatum*, which looks rather similar.

Trouble Shooter

Stems and foliage quickly dehydrate and fall if the compost is kept too dry, there is insufficient humidity or the temperature is too cold. Raise the temperature and give your plant a good soaking. Take care though not to overwater since this can be just as damaging.

Scale insect and mealy bug are the main pests — these can both be wiped away with a cloth dipped in methylated spirit.

Peperomia

Family name: **Piperaceae**

Common names: **Desert Privet, Baby Rubber Plant**

Care Straight-forward	**Height** 1ft (0.3m)	**Flower** Rarely
Light Bright indirect	**Spread** 9in (23cm)	**Humidity** Mist spray regularly
Price Middle range	**Shape** Bushy	**Availability** Common

Temp. Min 55°F (13°C) Ideal 70°F (21°C) Max 75°F (24°C)

These fascinating, small plants are grown mainly for their interesting and attractive foliage; compact, slow-growing and easy to care for, they make very successful houseplants. The group contains hundreds of different species, mainly central and South American in origin, and over a dozen of them are commonly grown indoors. Though the appearance and habit of different species may vary considerably, their odd-shaped flowers are always recognisable — long, thin flower spikes, usually likened to upright rat-tails; however off-putting they might sound, the flowers in fact add greatly to the plant's attraction.

The Desert Privet (*Peperomia magnoliaefolia*), is one of the most popular species. It makes a sturdy, bushy plant, growing upright to a height of 1ft (0.3m) then arching over and trailing slightly. It is most commonly found in its variegated forms, *right*.

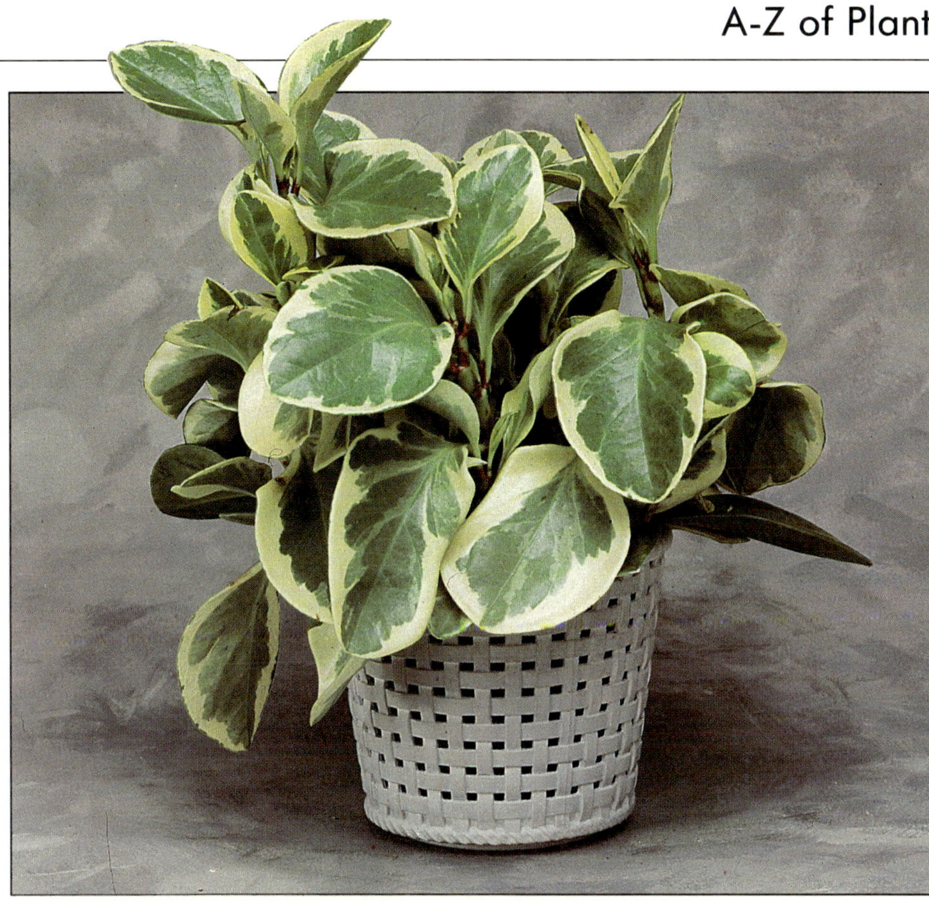

The Desert Privet is a very attractive, small foliage plant.

Spring and summer care

Pot in March or April in a peat-based compost or John Innes No 1 with some peat added; add plenty of crocks to ensure good drainage. Move young plants on to a pot one size larger, when necessary, to a final pot size of 4-5in (10-13cm), after which topdress annually, replacing the top 1in (2.5cm) with fresh compost.

Normal room temperatures are fine, up to about 75°F (24°C). Give them quite a brightly-lit spot, but avoid direct sunlight, especially during the hottest months; it's worth noting that Peperomias do well in fluorescent light.

Overwatering is the easiest way of killing these plants, so water with care and always allow the compost to dry out to some extent before watering again. Add a weak liquid fertiliser to the water (use half the recommended amount) every three weeks, from May to September. They like a humid atmosphere, so stand the pot on moist pebbles and mist spray the leaves regularly, every day if possible, particularly in hot weather.

Autumn and winter care

Aim for a winter temperature of around 60°F (16°C) and never less than 55°F (13°C). Keep your plant in a bright position, but continue to avoid full sun. Peperomias abhor dry air conditions so carry on mist spraying regularly to maintain a degree of humidity, and avoid any cold draughts. Water very sparingly, however — just enough to prevent the compost drying out completely.

Propagation

Take 2-3in (5-8cm) leaf or stem tip cuttings in spring or early summer, snipping stem tips with one or two leaves attached. Treat cut ends with a rooting hormone and insert into a mixture of equal parts of peat and sand. Keep moist and shaded, at a temperature of 65-70°F (18-21°C). Rooting should be established, with new growth clearly visible, within about six weeks, then pot cuttings up individually and treat as mature plants.

Trouble Shooter

Overwatering, especially in the colder months, leads to leaf drop and root rot. Leaves will lose much of their colour if plants are left in too shaded a position — while direct sunlight will encourage foliage to wilt and shrivel.

Mealy bug may appear; wipe away the fluffy white patches with a cotton bud or small paintbrush dipped in methylated spirit. Red spider mite may attack if plants are left in too dry an atmosphere; spray them with a malathion-based insecticide.

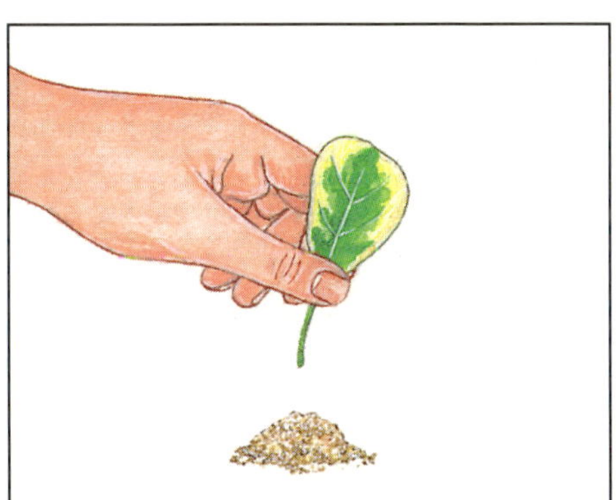

To take leaf cuttings of Peperomia, remove a healthy leaf and dip it into a little rooting hormone.

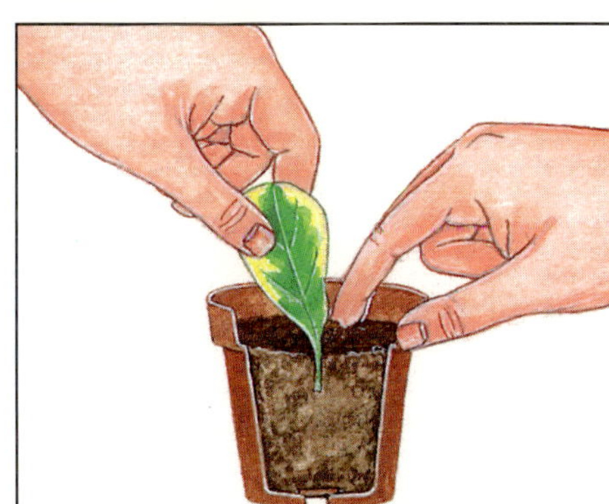

Insert the leaf into a pot of peat-based compost, or John Innes No 1, firming it well in.

Species

Peperomia magnoliaefolia, the Desert Privet from the West Indies, is the best known species. It makes a sturdy, bushy plant which generally grows to a height of about 1ft (0.3m) and then becomes a more trailing shape. Large, attractive, fleshy leaves, looking rather like privet leaves, grow from thick, fleshy stems and there are minute flowers covering a slender, pencil-like spike, but these are seldom seen on houseplants. The true species has plain, smooth leaves in a bright glossy green. There are two variegated forms, which are more popular. 'Variegata', *bottom left*, has leaves which are almost entirely cream when young, the cream variegation becoming light green in the centre as the plant matures; its stems are red at first and turn green with red spots as they age. 'Green Gold' has larger leaves with a cream border.

P.caperata is a compact, bushy plant from Brazil. It grows up to 10in (25cm) high, with attractive, deeply-ridged, rather crinkled-looking, heart-shaped leaves, up to 1½in (4cm) long. They are a deep glistening green, which together with the ridging accounts for its common name of Emerald Ripple. The leaf stalks are red or pink. White flower spikes, up to 5-6in (13-15cm) high, are produced between April and December.

P.griseoargentea, *left top*, (also known as *P.hederaefolia*), the Ivy-leaf Peperomia, is also from Brazil. The foliage looks as if it has been quilted and has a rather metallic, grey-green colouring, with a silvery shimmer — hence its other common name of Silver Ripple. During summer the attractive greenish-white flower spikes with reddish stems appear.

P.obtusifolia, from Venezuela, has long been popular. Sometimes known as the Baby Rubber Plant, it is one of the most robust and easily-cared-for species. This plant is very branching and reaches a maximum height of about 1ft (0.3m), with large, fleshy, oval-shaped, slightly concave leaves in a deep purplish green, with purple edges and paler green underneath. Numerous white flower spikes, no more than 2in (5cm) long, appear mainly from June to September.

P.sandersii, *below right*, is another Brazilian plant, reaching a height and spread of 6-9in (15-23cm) and regarded as one of the most attractive of all the species. The foliage is highly decorative, with smooth, thick, broad, oval-shaped leaves, which are a waxy bluish-green with silver bands radiating outwards from a central point; the shape and colouring lead to the name Watermelon Peperomia. Leaf stalks are red and the 3-4in (8-10cm) flower spikes, which appear throughout summer, are whitish in colour.

P.scandens from Peru, the brightly-coloured Cupid Peperomia, is of quite different habit, being a trailing or climbing plant, which can grow 4-5ft (1.2-1.5m) long. It has heart-shaped, shiny, 2in (5cm) long leaves that are delicately pointed and borne on reddish stems; in the species these are a plain glossy green, but the plant is most often found in its variegated form, the leaves almost completely cream in colour when young, then becoming pale green with a cream margin as the plant matures. Flowers do not usually occur in cultivation.

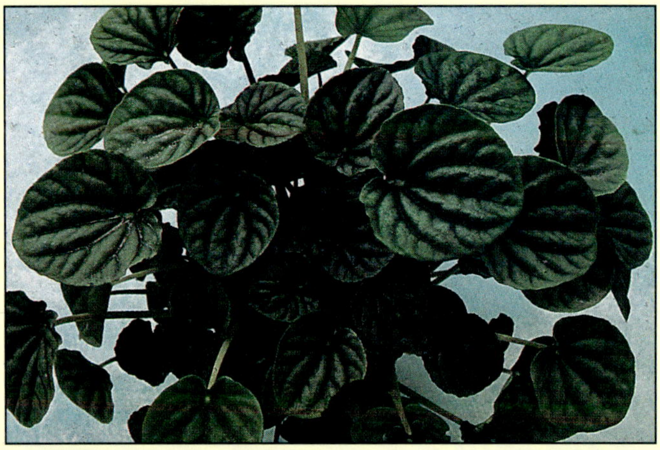

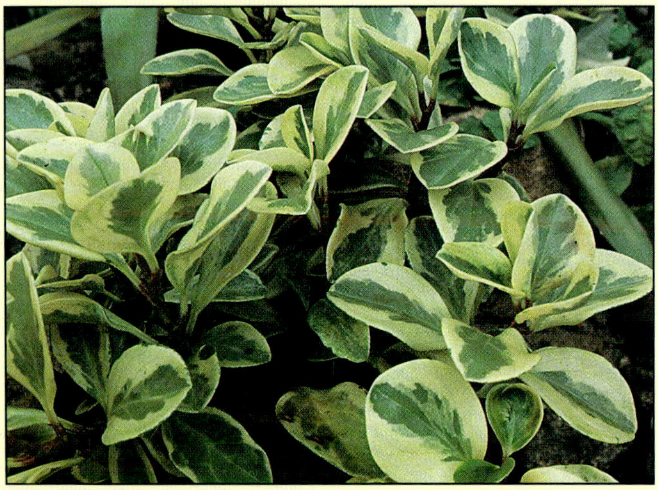

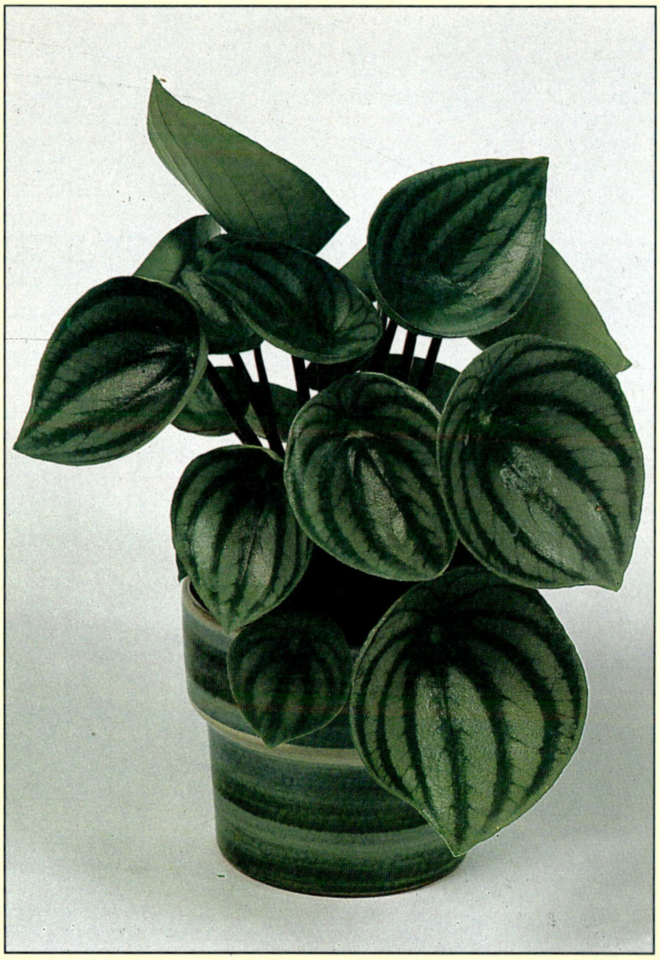

Philodendron

Family name: **Araceae**

Common names: **Sweetheart Plant/Heartleaf, Black Gold**

Care Easy	**Height** 6ft (1.8m)	**Flower** Rarely
Light Bright indirect	**Spread** 1ft (0.3m)	**Humidity** Mist spray regularly
Price Middle range	**Shape** Climber	**Availability** Common
Temp. Min 55°F (13°C)	Ideal 65°F (18°C)	Max 75°F (24°C)

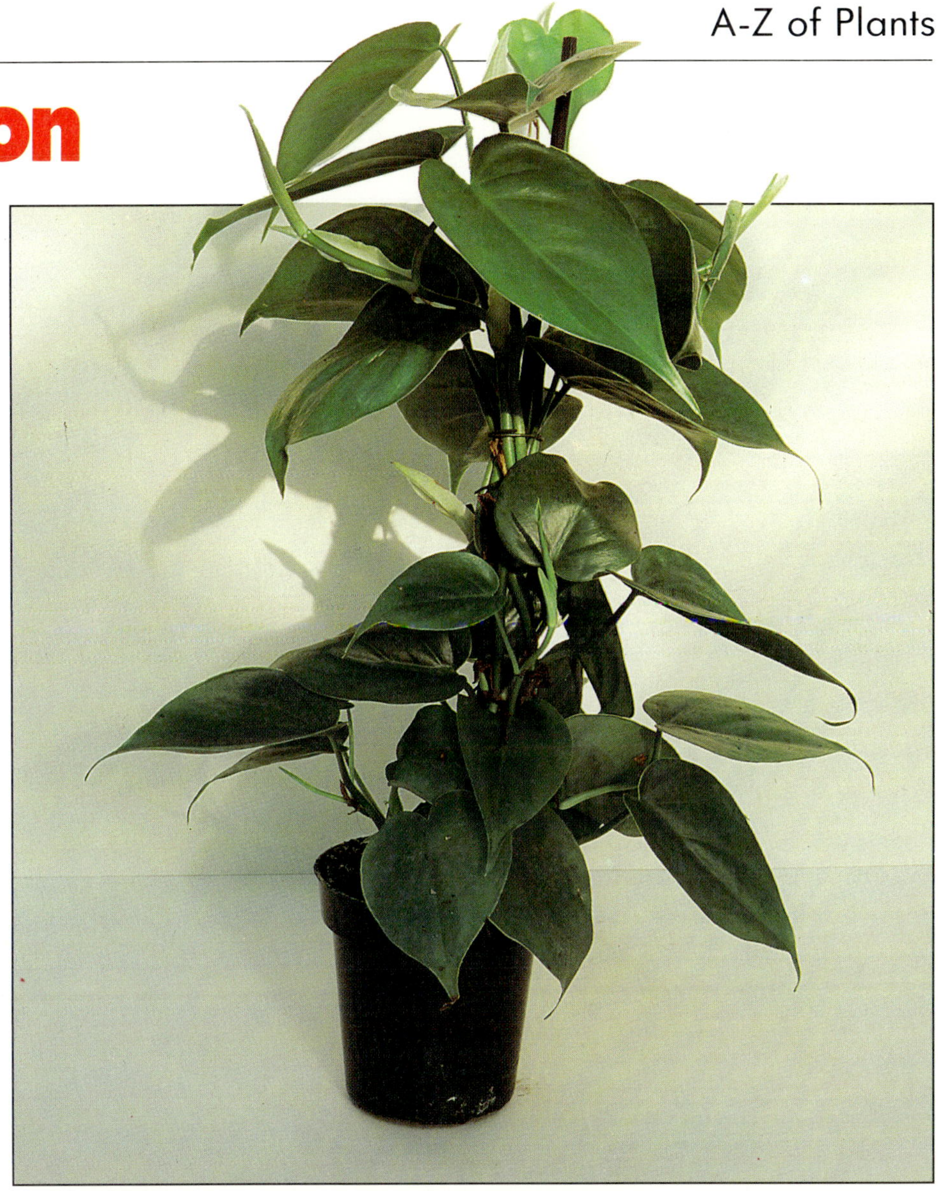

The Sweetheart Plant is one of the most easy-going and attractive foliage plants.

These beautiful evergreen foliage plants form a large and striking group, ranging from quite squat shrubs to small trees and many of them are vigorous climbers, freely producing aerial roots. With a few exceptions Philodendrons make splendid, easily-grown houseplants. In their natural environment, mostly the forests of central and South America, they often reach a considerable size; with suitable support they will comfortably grow to a height of 6ft (1.8cm) indoors. Flowers are in the form of a spathe, or large bract, surrounding a central spadix, or flower spike, of equal length, but they are very rarely produced indoors and are anyway insignificant in comparison to the impressive foliage.

The Sweetheart Plant (*Philodendron scandens*), also known as the Heartleaf Philodendron, is the most popular species and the easiest to look after. In fact, it is one of the easiest of all houseplants to grow, withstanding neglect and poor conditions and tolerant of gas and paraffin fumes. It is a climbing plant with long slender stems carrying small, glossy, heart-shaped leaves, tapering to long pointed tips. It can be grown either as a climber or trailer: trained up a moss-covered pole or a stake it makes a densely-leaved, spectacular plant; it looks equally appealing with its long stems trailing over the rim of a hanging basket.

Spring and summer care

Your plant will thrive in a free-draining mixture of peat and sand. Use a proprietary peat-based compost with some added coarse sand, though John Innes No 2 also gives good results; or make up your own mixture with equal parts of loam, peat and coarse sand to half a part of thoroughly decomposed leaf mould. Repot plants in the spring, only when the plants have very obviously grown too big and top-heavy for their pot. Move them on to a container one size larger, to a final pot size of 10-12in (25-30cm) or a small tub for a very large plant; after that, topdress your plant annually, replacing the top 2in (5cm) with fresh compost.

Climbing Philodendrons will need firm support for the stems; a moss-covered pole is particularly effective as this provides a surface for aerial roots to cling to and obtain extra nourishment and moisture. Otherwise push any aerial roots back into the compost to provide moisture for the upper leaves. Pinch out the growing tips of *P.scandens* regularly for bushy growth; no other pruning is necessary.

Normal room temperatures are suitable and they can rise to 70-75°F (21-24°C) with no ill effect. Grow plants in bright but filtered light — certainly never in direct sunlight. From April to October, water thoroughly and regularly, so that the compost is kept moist, but avoid leaving the pot standing in water and add a liquid fertiliser to the water every two weeks. It's important to provide a humid atmosphere, particularly in the hottest weather; stand pots on a tray of moist pebbles and mist spray regularly, using tepid water.

Autumn and winter care

To be totally successful, maintain winter temperatures of 60-65°F (16-18°C) — and never let temperatures drop below 55°F (13°C). Keep your plants in the brightest position possible without it being in direct sunlight. More shaded positions are only advisable in summer; plants will tolerate poor light but it can affect the growth and colouring of the foliage.

Water moderately to keep the compost just moist; it should never be allowed to dry out completely, but take care not to water to excess. An occasional mist-spraying is beneficial, especially with climbing plants — for the benefit of the moss on the moss pole as well as the Philodendron.

Propagation

Take stem cuttings in April, ideally, though any time in late spring or early summer is fine. Cut just below the leaf node and treat the cut ends with sulphur powder or a rooting hormone. Insert the cuttings in the normal compost with a little extra sand added, keep them just moist and slightly shaded, at a temperature of 75°F (24°C), preferably in a propagator or enclosed in a clear polythene bag. When there are signs of renewed growth; remove the cuttings from the propagator or polythene bag and leave for a further two weeks, at the same temperature, then pot the cuttings up individually and treat as mature plants (see 'Spring and summer care').

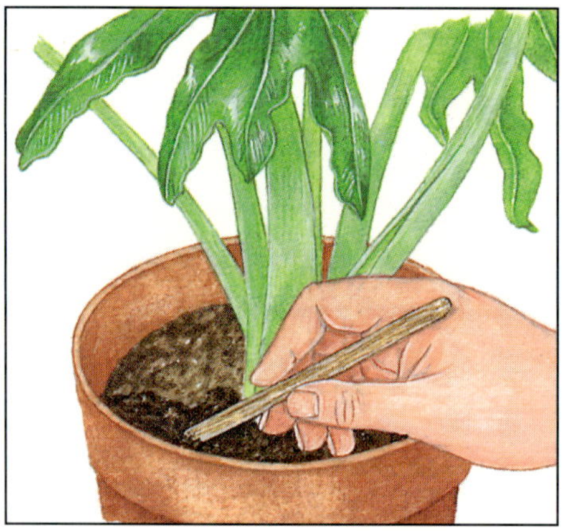

In the spring, topdress large plants by carefully removing the top 2in (5cm) of potting compost.

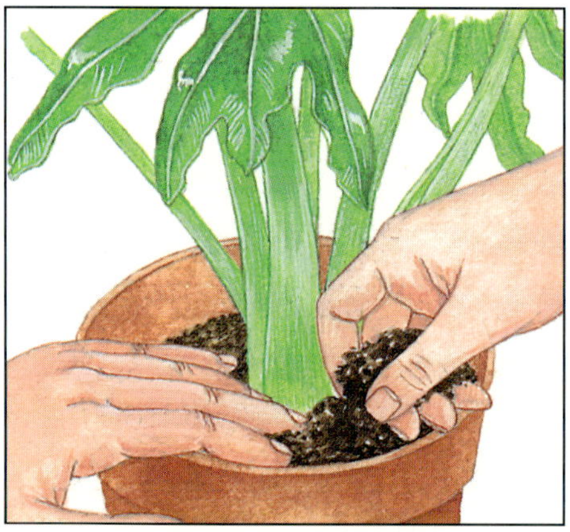

Top up with fresh compost, gently firming it down around the plant — make sure the final level covers the roots.

Trouble Shooter

Leaves will wilt if compost is allowed to become too dry, especially in summer, and if left too long, plants may not recover; a good soaking may prove sufficient to restore the plant to health. Conversely, leaf discolouration and, eventually, root rot will result from overwatering; leave the plant to dry out, perhaps at a higher temperature to encourage its recovery.

Low temperatures can often be damaging; plants can become 'chilled' with tired-looking, wilted and yellow tinged leaves, if winter temperatures fall below 55°F (13°C) and anything below 45°F (7°C) will almost certainly result in the death of the plant. Maintain a humid atmosphere but always avoid mist spraying in the hottest part of the day as this can cause leaves to scorch.

Mealy bug is one of the very few pests to attack Philodendron; wipe away the fluffy white patches with a soft cloth or brush dipped in methylated spirit.

Species

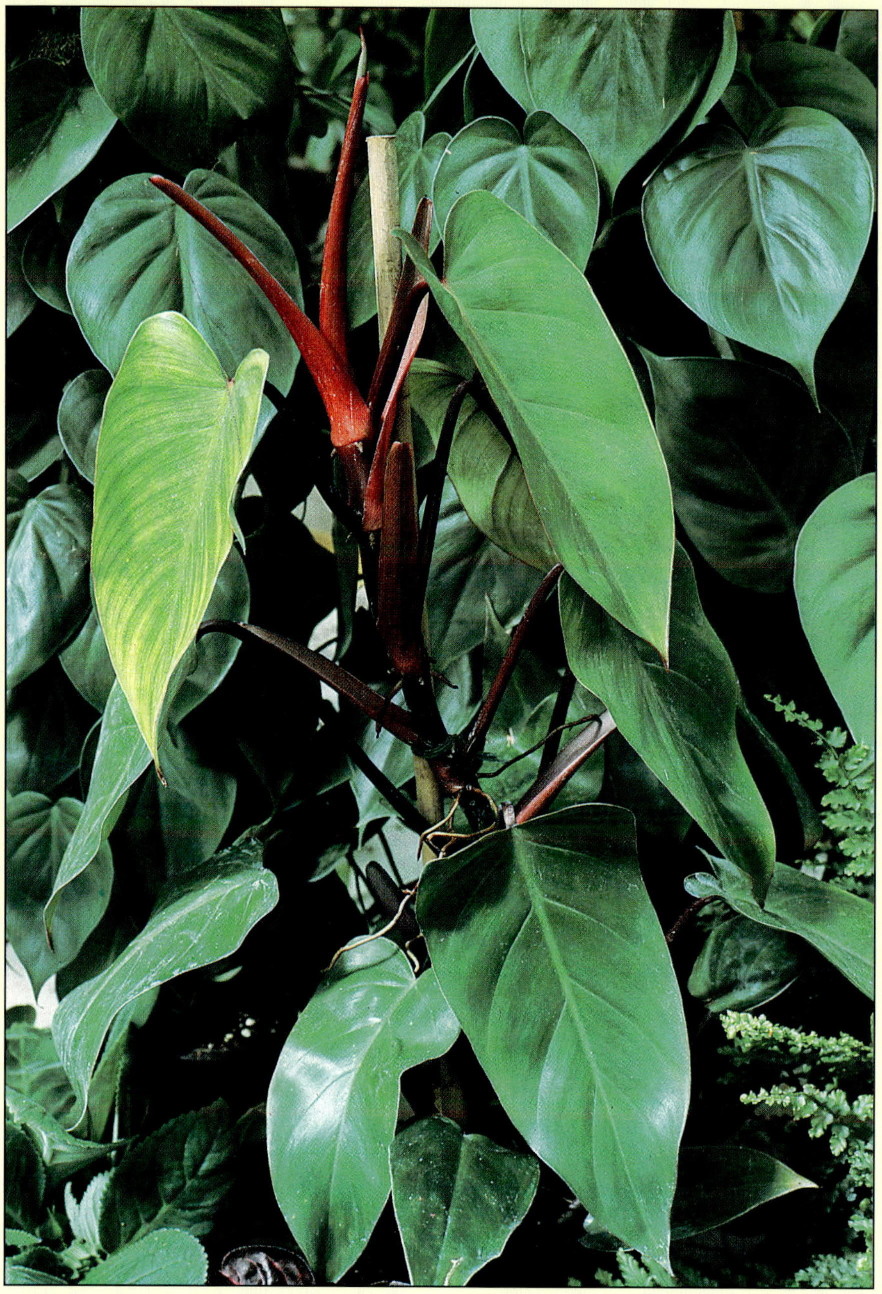

Philodendron scandens, the Sweetheart Plant or Heartleaf Philodendron, from Panama, is undoubtedly the most popular species as well as being the easiest to look after. With its long slender stems trained up a stake or moss-covered pole, this climbing plant can reach 6ft (1.8m) in height; it can also be grown as a trailing plant in a hanging basket. The leaves are heart-shaped, 4in (10cm) long by 3in (8cm) wide and tapering to long, slender points; new leaves have a bronze tint and are almost transparent, becoming deep green with maturity.

P.hastatum, *above*, is another Brazilian species, sometimes known as Elephant's Ear. It is a quite vigorous climber which can grow to 5ft (1.5m) in height. It has very glossy, thick, mid-green leaves, up to 7in (18cm) in length and shaped like a spear head, which are borne on broad, fleshy leafstalks. There is an appealing variegated form, its leaves beautifully marked in yellow and cream.

P.wendlandii, from Costa Rica, sometimes known as the Bird's Nest Philodendron, is a particularly fine, non-climbing

Species

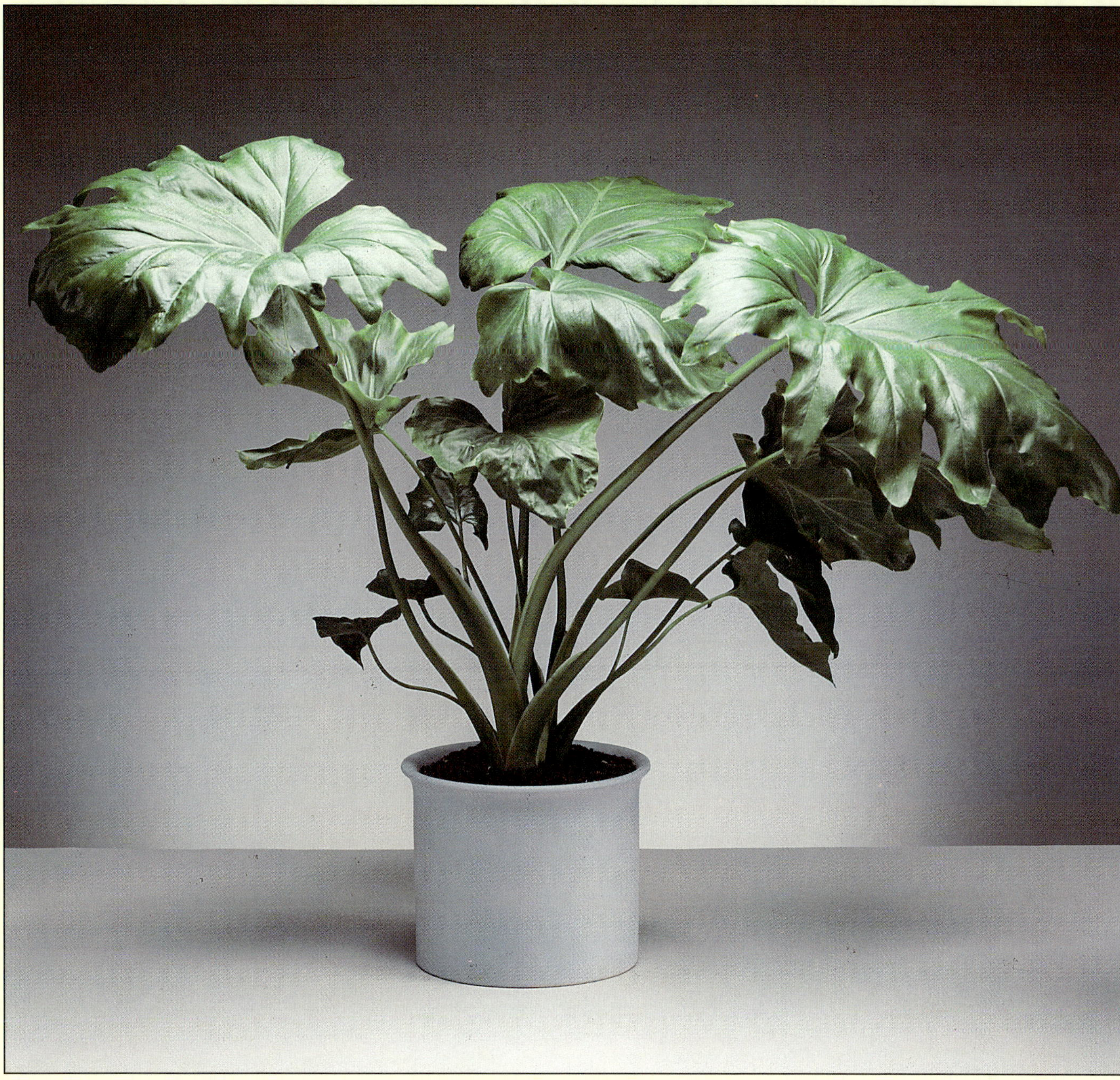

plant. It forms a bushy rosette, rather like an inverted shuttlecock, of glossy green, oval leaves about 1ft (0.3m) long, with a pronounced thick midrib, borne on 6in (15cm) leafstalks.

P.bipinnatifidum, *above*, from Brazil, sometimes called the Tree Philodendron, is a well known non-climbing species and a very good choice as a houseplant, tolerating conditions that are far from perfect. It can grow 4ft (1.2m) tall in a pot, with its very large, handsome leaves arranged in a loose rosette, radiating from a central growing point. They are dark green, sturdy and roughly arrow-shaped, up to 2ft (0.6m) long by 18in (45cm) wide, borne on 12-15in (30-38cm) leafstalks. On young plants the leaves are more heart-shaped with slight indenting of the edges; as the plant matures these indentations develop into very deep incisions, almost to the midrib, so that the leaves appear to be divided into separate leaflets.

P.selloum is also Brazilian and similar in many respects to *P.bipinnatifidum* — when young, it can be quite difficult to distinguish between them. As the plant develops it forms a trunk-like stem from which rises a rosette of leaves, 12-18in (30-45cm) long by 12in (30cm) wide, on arching leafstalks. Its leaves are deeply incised and the edges of the segments become ruffled, producing a charming, lacy effect — hence its common name of Lacy Tree Philodendron. These plants are noted for living to a great age.

P.erubescens is another very beautiful plant from Colombia, and rather easier to grow than *P.andreanum*. A fairly vigorous

Species

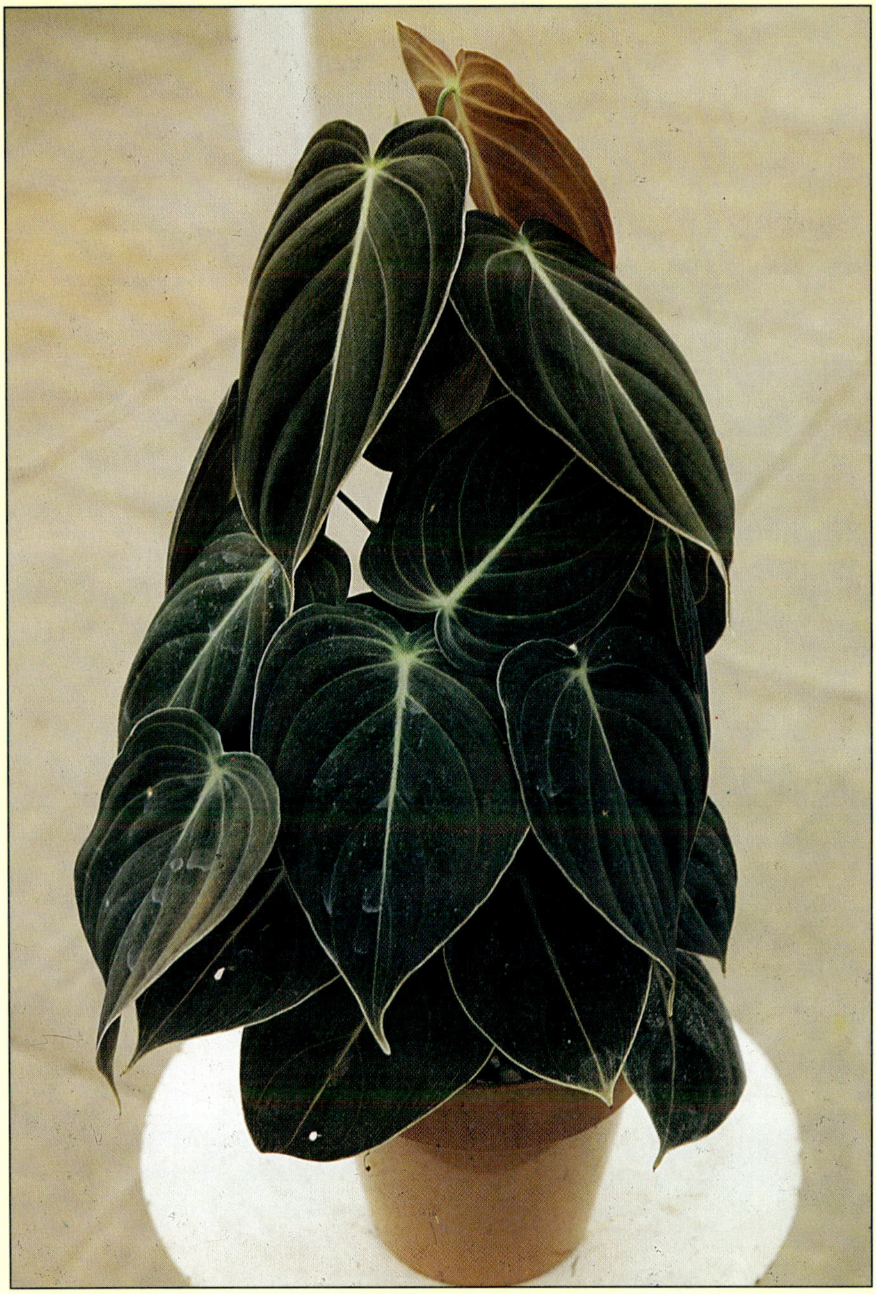

climber, it will reach a height of 6ft (1.8m) if well supported. Leaves are rather arrow-shaped, growing to 1ft (0.3m) by 7in (18cm) on 1ft (0.3m) leafstalks. New leaves are rose-pink becoming a dark glossy green with a coppery tinge, in maturity; stems and leafstalks are purple. 'Burgundy' leaves are a delightful, bright, coppery-red for the first few weeks, gradually turning olive green with deep burgundy undersides.

***P. andreanum**, above,* (often called *P. melanochryson*) is a very beautiful climber from Colombia, known as Black Gold. It needs a little more attention than other species but can produce superb results. Relatively slow-growing, it can climb to a height of 6ft (1.8m) and should be trained to a moss-pole for best effect. Heart-shaped on young plants, the leaves elongate with maturity to a spear shape, up to 24in (60cm) long and 9in (23cm) wide, hanging down from 18in (45cm) long leafstalks. With a rich, velvety texture, they are dark green in colour with prominent pale green veins and purple undersides, giving the foliage a coppery sheen.

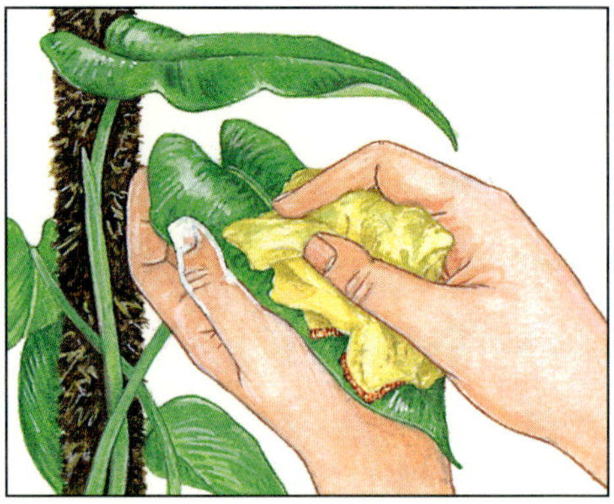

Keep glossy-leaved Philodendrons in good condition by regularly cleaning their leaves — wipe them over with a damp cloth.

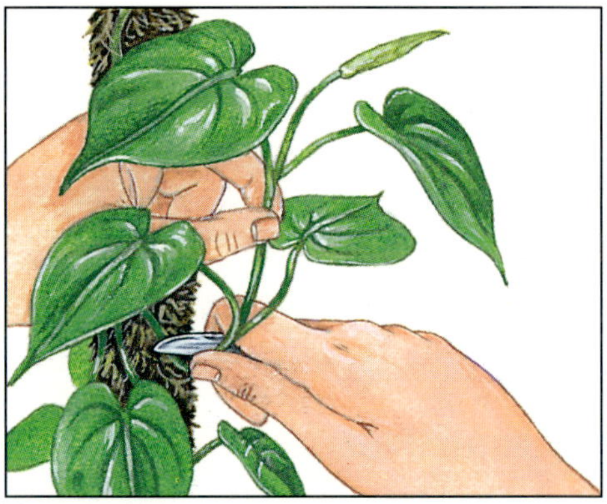

To propagate a Sweetheart Plant, snip off a stem tip with two pairs of leaves. Use a sharp knife.

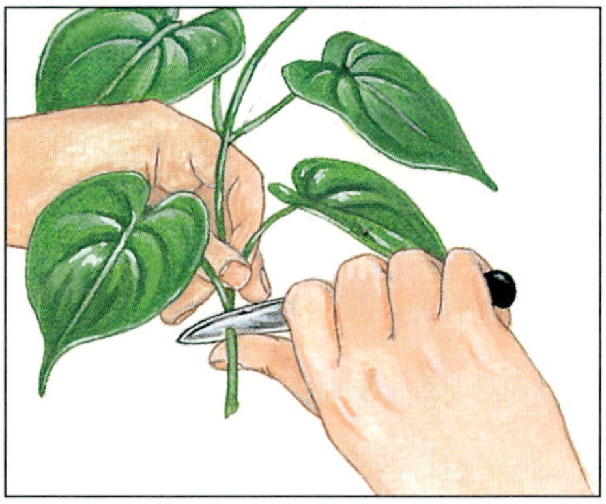

Trim the cutting to just below the lowest pair of leaves — then remove these leaves to leave one pair.

Buying guide

Avoid buying plants that have been marketed in very cold weather; low temperatures, especially chilling winds, are often fatal to Philodendrons and yet the first symptoms of chilling may not show for several days.

Look for a plant with healthy-looking foliage, although remember that the young growth is often much paler than the more mature leaves.

Phoenix

Family name: **Palmae**

Common names: **Canary Palm, Date Palm**

Care Easy	**Height** 6ft (1.8m)	**Flower** Rarely
Light Indirect	**Spread** 5ft (1.5m)	**Humidity** Mist spray occasionally
Price Middle range	**Shape** Palm	**Availability** Garden centre
Temp. Min 50°F (10°C)	Ideal 65°F (18°C)	Max 70°F (21°C)

These elegant palms, with graceful, arching fronds, are not difficult to grow and make a most striking choice for a large room. Like most palms, Phoenix will eventually mature into full-size, long-trunked trees, some of them growing very tall indeed. However, since they are very slow-growing plants, it will be many years before they become too big for most rooms.

The most popular houseplant is the Canary Palm (*Phoenix canariensis*) which has slender, dark green fronds radiating from a central stem. In a small tub it can grow 6ft (1.8m) tall with leaves up to 3ft (0.9m) long. Other species include the Date Palm (*P.dactylifera*) which is important commercially for its fruit, and plants can quite easily be raised from a single date stone. For a smaller specimen try the Miniature Date Palm (*P.roebelinii*). Since Phoenix palms don't usually bear flowers and fruit until they are quite old, however, you are unlikely to produce any dates indoors.

Spring and summer care

Repot your plant into John Innes No 3, in March or early April — no later — every two or three years; move the plant on to a pot 2in (5cm) larger to a maximum convenient size — a 10-12in (25-30cm) pot is ample for a 4ft (1.2m) plant, after which a small tub should be used. When the final container size is reached, topdress annually, removing the top 1-2in (2.5-5cm) of compost and replacing it with fresh potting compost.

P.roebelinii is a clump forming plant, which can develop suckers from the base and should be restricted to a single stem by cutting out any suckers as they appear, unless they are wanted for propagation.

Normal room temperatures are fine, up to a maximum of about 70°F (21°C); these plants can take higher temperatures, but, in that case, would be better off placed outdoors. Certainly, they like an airy atmosphere and the warmer it is the more important good ventilation becomes. They will do best in fil-

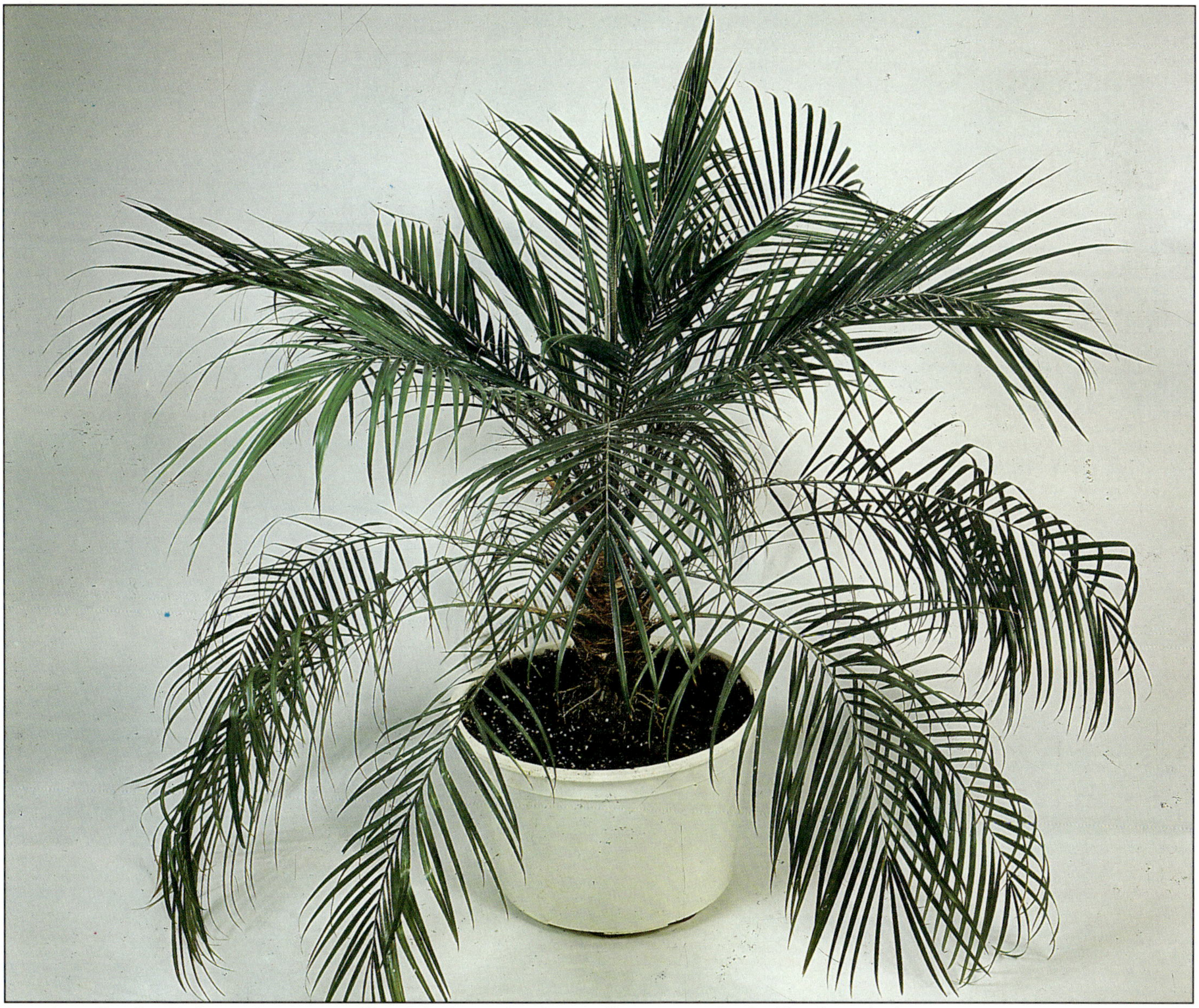

A mature Canary Palm makes a magnificent feature, standing on its own or mixed with other plants.

tered light; young plants in particular may easily scorch if left in direct sunlight.

Water the plant moderately at the beginning of the season, gradually increasing the amount until May; from May to September water freely, as much as is necessary to keep the compost thoroughly moist (though never allow the pot to stand in water) and add a liquid fertiliser to the water every two or three weeks. Mist spray the leaves occasionally, but only in the early morning or evening — never in the heat of the day; adding a foliar feed to the spray every two to three weeks can be beneficial. Never use a leaf shining product on a member of the palm family as you will damage the leaves. Instead, wipe them occasionally with a soft cloth.

Autumn and winter care

Winter temperatures are best at 50-55°F (10-13°C); good ventilation is still important, but avoid cold draughts. Keep plants in a brightly-lit position but continue to avoid direct sunlight. Water sparingly, just enough to keep the compost from drying out completely; if temperatures are a little higher you may need to increase the water slightly, but the compost should still be barely moist.

Propagation

Phoenix palms are not especially difficult to raise from seed, but it is a slow process. Some indoor gardeners plant fresh date stones; these germinate quite easily, but produce little more than a single thick, grass-like leaf for the first three or four years of life. Most other species are even more slow-growing, but perfectly good specimens can eventually be produced from seed.

Between March and May set the seeds 1-1½in (2.5-4cm) deep in John Innes No 3, mixed three to one with sharp sand; keep the mixture moist and at a temperature of 70-75°F (21-24°C), ideally in a propagator. They may take some time to germinate, though usually not more than two months. Try not to disturb them for a further six to eight months when they will be big enough to pot up individually into ordinary compost and treat as established plants (see 'Spring and summer care'). Soaking the seeds in cold water for a day or two and cracking the date stone before planting can help speed up germination considerably.

Where plants such as *P.roebelinii* produce suckers at the base of the parent plant, these can be removed in the spring and potted up individually into the usual compost (see below). Place them in filtered light, ideally in a propagator, and keep the compost just moist at a temperature of 70°F (21°C), until new growth indicates that rooting is established, then treat as mature plants.

Species

Phoenix canariensis, the Canary Palm, is the hardiest and most popular species. In its Canary Island habitat it will grow over 40ft (12m) tall, its leaves arching outwards and downwards, reaching a length of 10ft (3m) or more. Even as a houseplant it can reach a considerable size, but it is very slow-growing and can take many years to reach its full height. In a small tub it can grow 6ft (1.8m) tall with leaves up to 3ft (0.9m) long. The dark green fronds radiate from the central stem, with numerous stiff, rather spiky leaflets. The flowers and fruit of Phoenix palms are unlikely to be produced until the plant is quite old, so they are rarely seen indoors.

P.dactylifera is the Date Palm, originally a native of the Middle East and now spread widely around the Mediterranean. It is a valuable and important tree, with almost every part being used to provide fruit, wine, thatching, mats, and so on. It grows quite a lot bigger and more swiftly than the Canary Palm; in habitat it can reach a height of 100ft (30m) or more, and as a houseplant it will certainly outgrow most rooms within about 15 years. It is an elegant plant with blue-green fronds of stiff, rather prickly leaflets, arching out from a slender green stem.

P.roebelinii, *below*, the Miniature Date Palm, from India is probably the smallest species, barely reaching 10ft (3m) high in the wild and rarely exceeding 4ft (1.2m) indoors. It has fine, dark green leaflets on arching fronds, up to 2ft (0.6m) long.

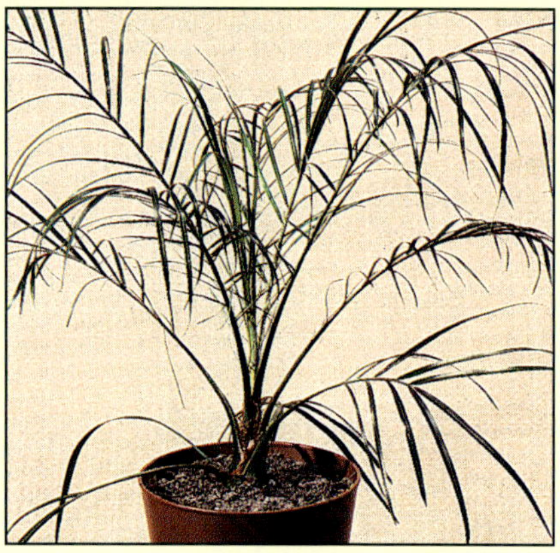

Trouble Shooter

Foliage will begin to discolour, wilt and probably fall if conditions are too dry — whether humidity is too low or the plant has been left unwatered for too long. Young plants in particular may not be tolerant of bright sunlight and too much exposure, especially in hot weather, can lead to scorching and leaf colour fading.

Scale insect may attack, with wart-like spots appearing on leaves and stems; mealy bug is another possible pest. Both of these are best dealt with by wiping with a cotton bud or small paintbrush dipped in methylated spirit, since some insecticides can damage the foliage.

Buying Guide

The ideal size plant to buy is between 1½-2ft (0.5-0.6m) — a well-established plant with plenty of growth to make before it outgrows your rooms.

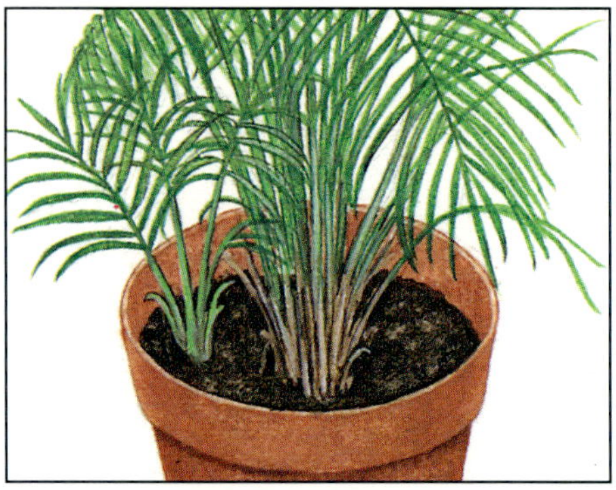

To propagate *P.roebelinii*, use the suckers that are produced around the base of the mature plant.

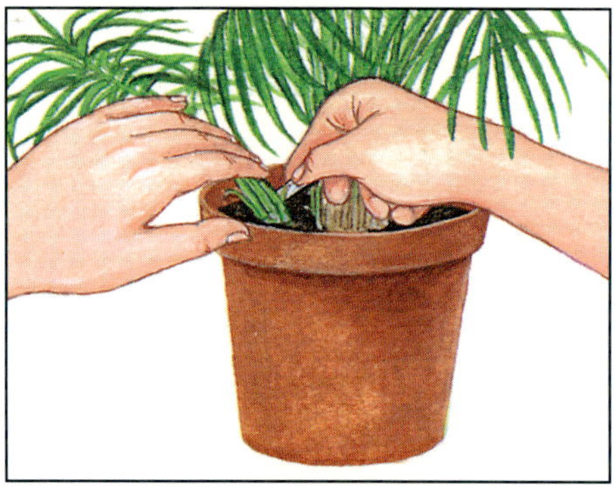

While the plant is still in its pot, cut the suckers away from the parent using a sharp knife.

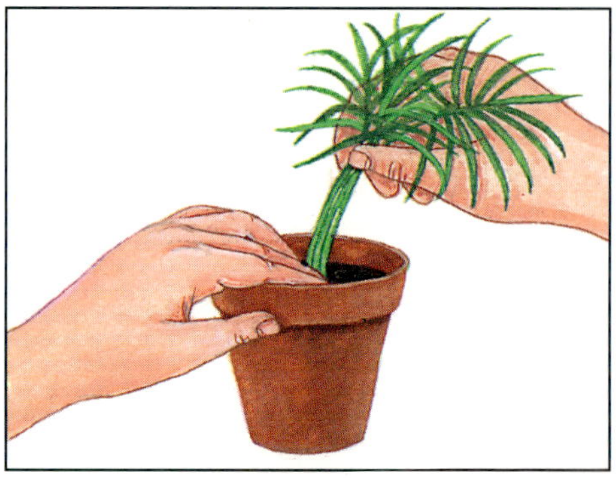

Pot it up into a container filled with John Innes No 3, and maintain a temperature of 70°F (21°C).

Pilea

Family name: **Urticaceae**

Common names: **Aluminium Plant, Artillary Plant**

Care Straight-forward	**Height** 1ft (0.3m)	**Flower** Insignificant
Light Indirect	**Spread** 1ft (0.3m)	**Humidity** Regular mist spray
Price Cheap	**Shape** Bushy	**Availability** Garden centres
Temp. Min 50°F (10°C)	Ideal 70°F (21°C)	Max 75°F (24°C)

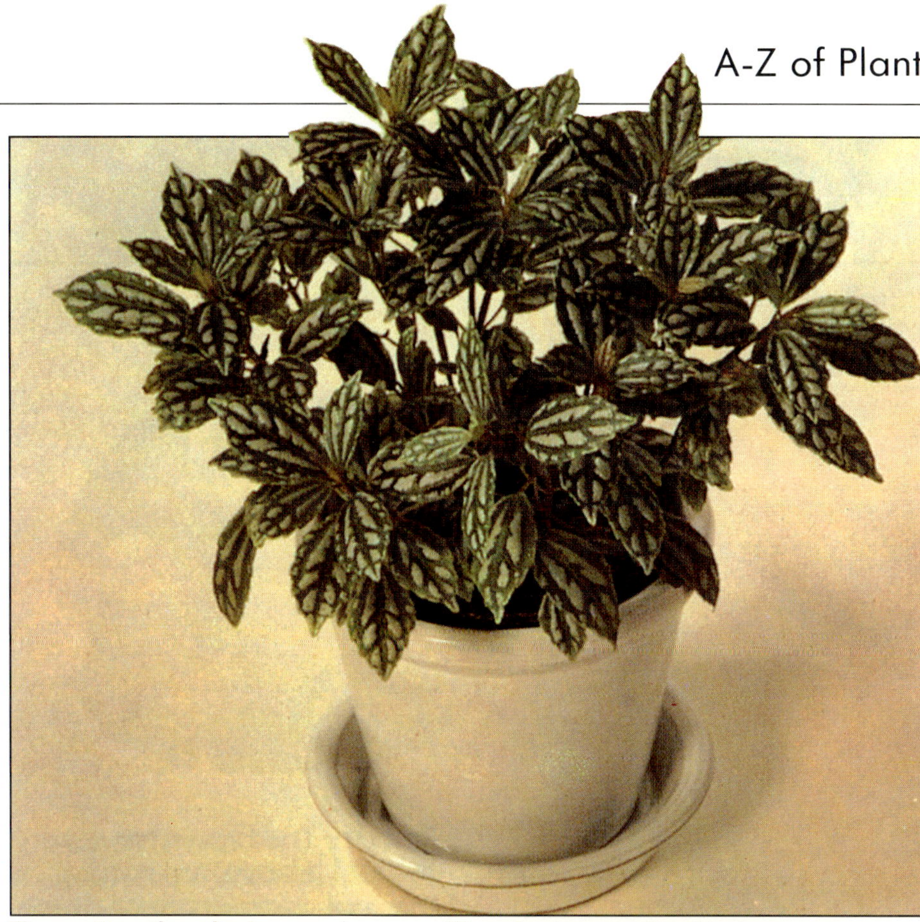

These attractive plants come in many different colours and leaf textures.

Only a few species of these evergreen perennials have been developed as houseplants. They belong to the same family as Stinging Nettles and Hop Plants — but Pileas originate from tropical Asia and America. The easiest to grow and the most popular species is *Pilea cadierei, right,* the Aluminium Plant — so called because of the attractive, white, slightly metallic-looking markings on its leaves. It makes quite a compact bushy, little foliage plant; attractive, quick-growing and quite shade tolerant, it makes a useful gap-filler at the base of taller plants.

Spring and summer care

Repot in March or April every year — into a pot one size larger if your plant has outgrown its container. Use John Innes No 2 for potting. To keep your plant compact and bushy, cut back its stems by as much as half at potting time and pinch out the tips of new shoots as they develop during the season.

Normal room temperatures are fine — and they can rise to 75°F (24°F) without harm. Pilea likes indirect light and you should protect your plant from bright sunlight at all times. Water freely, so that the compost is always moist, but not sodden. Add a liquid fertiliser to the compost every two to three weeks until October. Your plant will benefit from regular mist spraying — ideally first thing in the morning.

Autumn and winter care

Provide a temperature of about 55-65°F (13-18°C) during the colder months. — but don't worry if the temperature goes a bit lower for short spells. Reduce the watering so that the compost is kept slightly dry and stop adding fertiliser to the water. Continue to mist spray regularly and keep in good light (but still no direct sun), in an airy position but away from cold draughts.

Propagation

Taking cuttings of Pilea is very easy — in fact, many people replace their plants every year with young rooted cuttings, since older plants tend to lose their lower leaves, giving them a rather leggy appearance. Snip 3-4in (8-10cm) from stem tips in the spring (you can use your prunings). Trim each cutting to just below a pair of leaves, then remove these leaves. Insert the cuttings up to the next pair of leaves in a mixture of equal parts peat and sand, enclose them in a clear plastic bag or propagator, and maintain a temperature of 65-70°F (18-21°C) placing the cuttings in a shaded position.

Once growth is apparent (usually in about 3-4 weeks) remove the cuttings from the propagator or bag, and pot them up individually into John Innes No 2 and treat them as mature plants.

Trouble Shooter

Wilting is caused by either underwatering or overwatering. Pale, spindly growth is a sign of light shortage. Brush mealy bug away with a small brush dipped in methylated spirit. If greenfly appear, then spray with a pyrethrum-based insecticide.

Species

Pilea cadierei, the Aluminium Plant, comes originally from Vietnam. It has leaves with a slightly quilted appearance, patterned with silvery markings. The plant makes a rambling 1ft (0.3m) bush, unless it is kept well trimmed. The variety *P.c.minima* is a miniature version of the species. The flowers are small and insignificant.

P.microphylla, the Artillary Plant (also sometimes known as *P.muscosa*), comes from the West Indies and looks rather different from the other houseplant species. A small bush of 6-9in (15-23cm), it has feathery, plain green foliage and fleshy stems. When touched, the small clusters of summer flowers release their pollen in a tiny cloud rather like a puff of smoke — hence their common name.

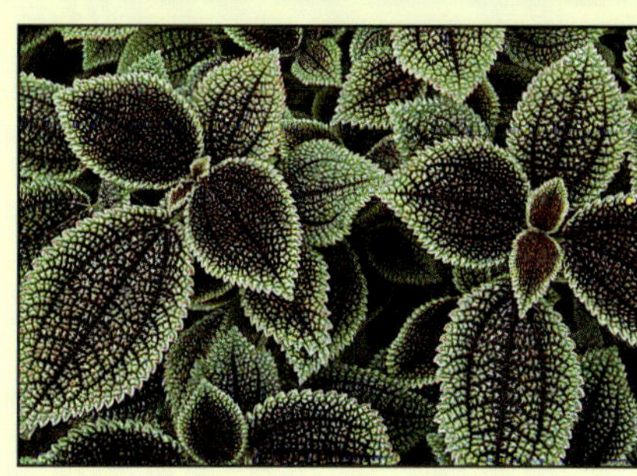

P.mollis, from central America, has quilted, bright green leaves with paler green veins, and is covered with minute white hairs. 'Moon Valley', *above*, is a very attractive variety whose leaves are overlaid with brown and yellow shades. The flowers are small and insignificant.

Platycerium

Family name: **Polypodiaceae**

Common name: **Stag Horn Fern**

Care Straight-forward	**Height** 2ft (0.6m)	**Flower** None
Light Shaded	**Spread** 4-5ft (1.2-1.5m)	**Humidity** Mist spray regularly
Price Middle range	**Shape** Leafy clump	**Availability** Garden centres
Temp. Min 60°F (16°C)	Ideal 70°F (21°C)	Max 80°F (27°C)

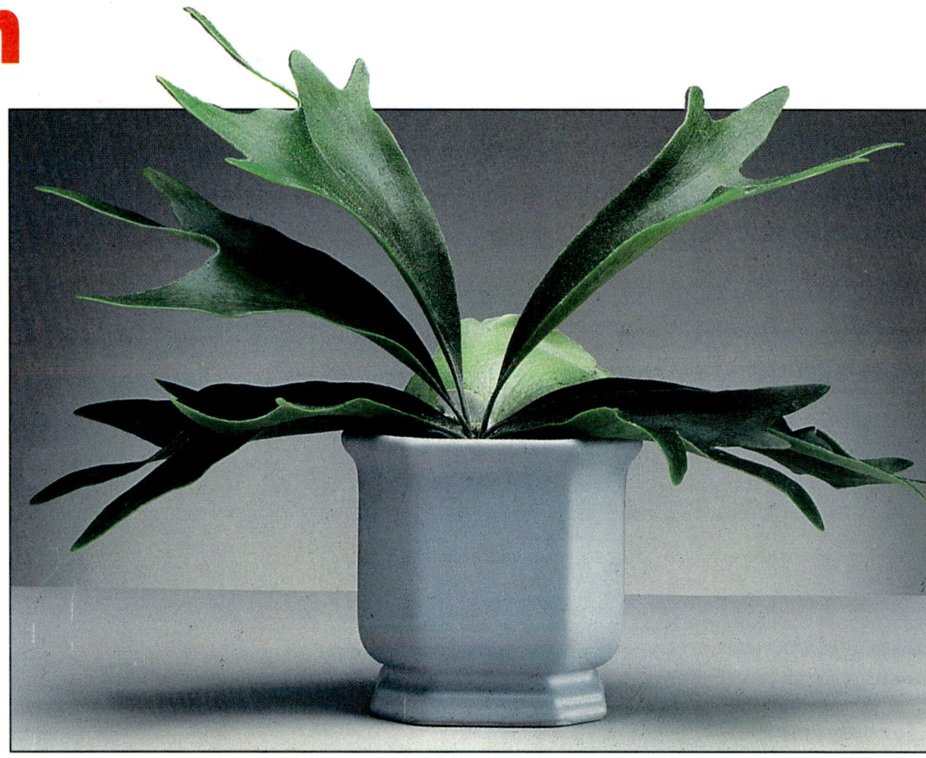

The unusual antler-like fronds of the Stag Horn Fern.

The members of this small group of ferns are among the finest, and most extraordinary, of their whole family. They come from many different tropical countries, including Africa, Asia and Australia; one species comes from South America. Their generic name 'Platycerium' comes from the Greek words for 'broad' and 'horn'. The species best known as a houseplant is *Platycerium bifurcatum* — and its common name, Stag Horn Fern, is self-explanatory when you look at the unusual broad, flat and forked leaves that do look just like antlers. These ferns are all epiphytes; that is, they live not on the soil but up on the branches of trees, drawing their moisture and nourishment from the air.

They have two quite different types of frond. They anchor themselves by means of a single, flat frond which wraps itself round a branch. This frond also traps water and dissolved nutrients from the host tree, to provide the fern's nourishment. This base frond is sterile: it does not produce any spores, but from its centre grow two or three large, flat, leathery fronds which have the deep lobes that give the plant its distinctive appearance. These are the fertile fronds, which produce spores in dense clusters on their undersides, towards the tips of the lobes. The surface of the fronds is covered in minute whitish hairs, giving them an attractive silvery-grey, slightly felt-like frosting over their surface. When they are kept as houseplants, although they will grow in a pot Platyceriums are best grown on a piece of bark, or tree branch — this can look very effective, rather like a hanging basket.

Spring and summer care

If you buy a young plant, it may be growing in a pot. Take the plant carefully from its container, and wrap the roots in fresh sphagnum moss. Then tie this securely to a piece of bark. Strips about 2in (5cm) wide cut from old nylon stockings or tights, which narrow when they are stretched, make excellent tape which will not rot. Alternatively, you could use strong cotton thread. After a short time, the base frond will gradually encircle the bark, holding the fern securely in place and concealing the tape completely.

Hang your Platycerium in a shaded area — it will tolerate full sunlight, but won't really enjoy it. Aim for a temperature of 70-75°F (21-24°C), and a well-ventilated, airy position.

The best way to water a plant growing in this way is to take the whole thing down from its position once a week and soak it in water for about 15 minutes. Let it drain thoroughly before hanging it up again. In very hot weather you should water it more often. Keep up the humidity by mist spraying regularly, every day in hot weather. Add liquid fertiliser to the water every four to six weeks during the growing season.

Autumn and winter care

Don't let the temperature drop below 60°F (16°C) and preferably keep the plant in a semi-shaded position. It can manage in bright light, provided it is not direct. Water it once a week, but let it soak up water only for a few minutes before you drain it.

Propagation

Propagate from offsets, which grow from the sterile frond at the side of the main plant. Remove these and pot them up into a mixture of equal parts peat and sphagnum moss, then treat them as new plants. Propagation from the spores of Platycerium is not practicable in the home.

Buying Guide

The only species commonly offered for sale is *P.bifurcatum* — it's the easiest to grow, too. If you want to try other species or varieties you should contact a specialist fern nursery.

Species

Platycerium bifurcatum (sometimes known as *P.alcicorne*), the Stag Horn Fern, is the best known of the family, and the easiest to care for. It comes from Australia and New Caledonia in the Pacific Ocean. It has fertile fronds up to 3ft (0.9m) long, with two to three lobes, leathery and greyish-green in colour, and covered with minute whitish hairs. They emerge from a single pale green sterile frond, which gradually turns brown and is replaced by a new one growing from its centre.

P.grande, the Elk Horn Fern, is bigger than *P.bifurcatum*, with a much showier, paler green sterile frond which can grow up to 4ft (1.2m) across — it turns upwards and divides at the ends, making it look rather like the fertile fronds of other species.

Trouble Shooter

Underwatering results in limp or falling fronds; water and spray your plant regularly. Check also that temperatures are not too cold.

The most likely pests to attack are scale insects; wipe them gently from the undersides of the fronds with a soft cloth dipped in methylated spirit. Take care not to remove or damage the white frosting on the fertile fronds.

Plectranthus

Family name: **Labiatae**

Common name: **Swedish Ivy, Candle Plant**

Care Easy	**Height** 1½-2ft (0.5-0.6m)	**Flower** Summer
Light Bright	**Spread** 5-6in (13-15cm)	**Humidity** Regular mist spray
Price Middle range	**Shape** Trailing	**Availability** Garden centres
Temp. Min 65°F (18°C)	Ideal 55°F (13°C)	Max 75°F (24°C)

The 250 evergreen species that make up this group range from low-growing, creeping plants to tall shrubs, 5ft (1.5m) high or more, with woody stems and branches. But it is the trailing types that are best known as houseplants, under the general name of Swedish Ivy — although they are in fact mainly African in origin. Quick growing and easy to care for, with very attractive foliage, they deserve to be more popular.

The most popular plant is *Plectranthus oertendahlii*, a low-growing, trailing species. It is a particularly good subject for a hanging basket, with its outstanding, colourful foliage, trailing down as much as 1½-2ft (45-60cm). As an added bonus, it produces small, pinkish-white flowers throughout the summer; in most other species the flowers are insignificant and not especially attractive.

Spring and summer care

Pot on only when your plant is bursting out of its pot. Pot your plant in April or May using John Innes No 2, with plenty of crocks under the compost. If hanging baskets are used, line them with about 1in (2.5cm) of sphagnum moss — never use a plastic liner or anything else which is likely to hold excess water and cause roots to rot. Trim plants to shape, if required, in spring and pinch out growing tips occasionally to keep the plant bushy.

These plants do best in quite warm rooms and will thrive at a temperature of 65-70°F (18-21°C). Give them a very bright but slightly shaded position — too much direct sunlight can damage the foliage.

Water freely from April through September to keep the compost thoroughly moist, and add a liquid fertiliser to the water once a week. Actively growing, trailing Plectranthus need very regular watering — as often as once a day — especially if they are in a hanging basket in a well-lit window; the moss lining should be kept moist the whole year round. Mist spray regularly with tepid water — at least twice a week, and more frequently if temperatures get higher.

Autumn and winter care

Winter temperatures should be fairly cool, around 55-58°F (13-15°C). Your plant should have a very bright position, though continue to avoid full sunlight, and keep it away from any cold draughts, which can cause leaves to wilt. Water sparingly, giving just enough to prevent the compost from drying out.

Propagation

These plants are easily propagated from cuttings. Take 3-4in (8-10cm) tip shoots, preferably in March or April, cutting below a leaf node and removing the lowest leaves; treat the cut ends with a rooting hormone and insert them into the usual compost. Water them moderately, keeping the compost just moist, and in bright indirect light, at a temperature of 60-65°F (16-18°C). Cuttings will root readily; once rooting is established (indicated by new growth) pot them individually in 3in (8cm) pots or place three or four cuttings together in a hanging basket, and treat as mature plants.

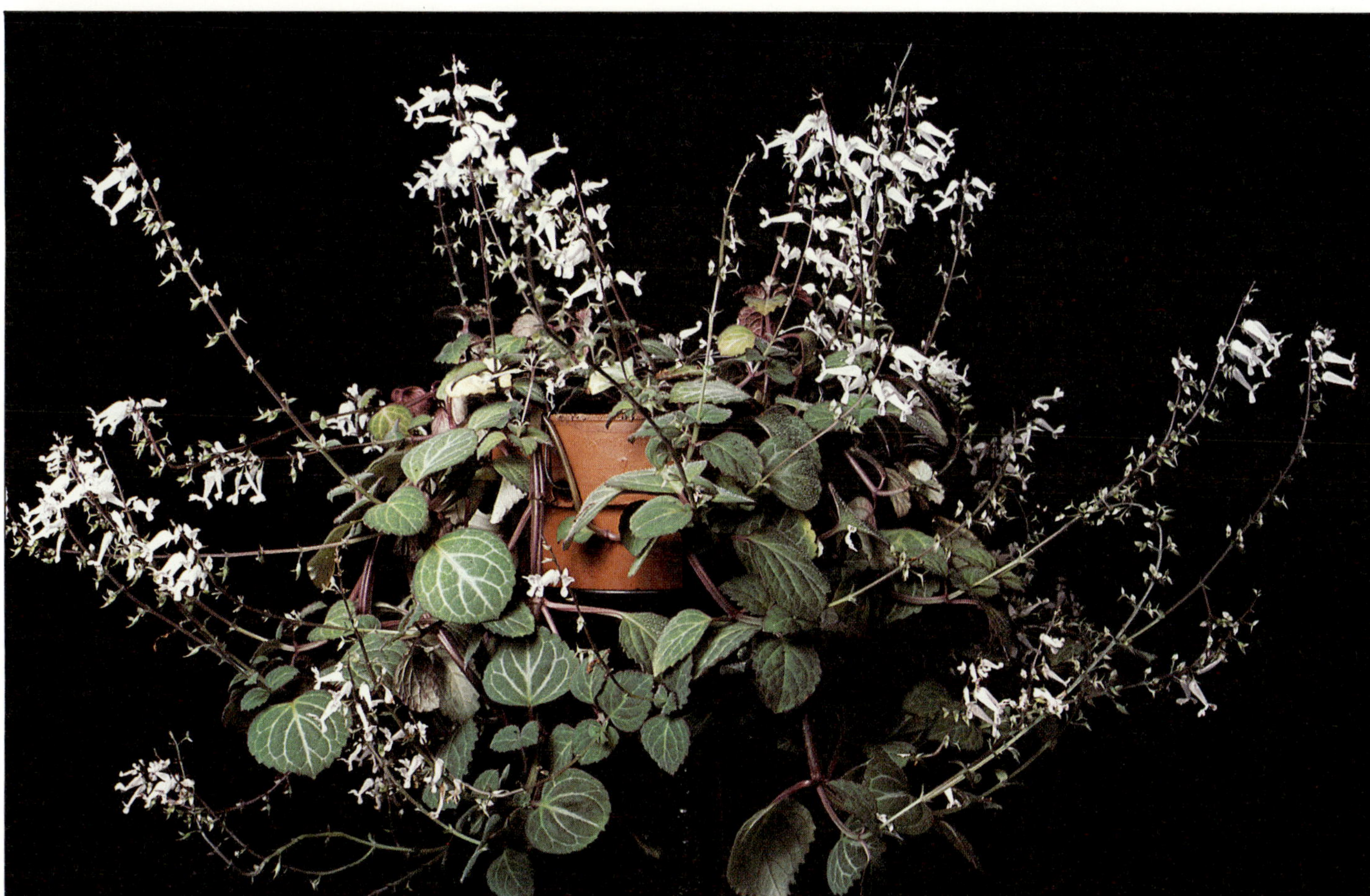

The trailing shape and pretty white flowers make the Swedish Ivy a very attractive hanging basket plant.

Trouble Shooter

Leaves will wilt and shrivel if the compost is allowed to dry out for more than a short time; a good soaking may help the plant to recover, but if it has been left too long, the chances are not good. Conversely, excessive watering can soon lead to trouble; root rot is the most likely result and a blackening of the stems which might be a forerunner of a fungus attack. If this should occur, remove any good stems and try to root them as cuttings and then destroy the infected plant. White patches of mildew may form if plants are kept in too shady a spot during winter, especially if it is at all damp and too warm; if you spot any sign, remove all affected leaves and apply a fungicide.

Pests are few, though white fly may be a problem, in which case spray with a pyrethrum-based insecticide; two or three applications may be necessary, over a period of a fortnight, to completely eliminate them. Greenfly is less likely, but if there is an infestation a pyrethrum-based insecticide should take care of it.

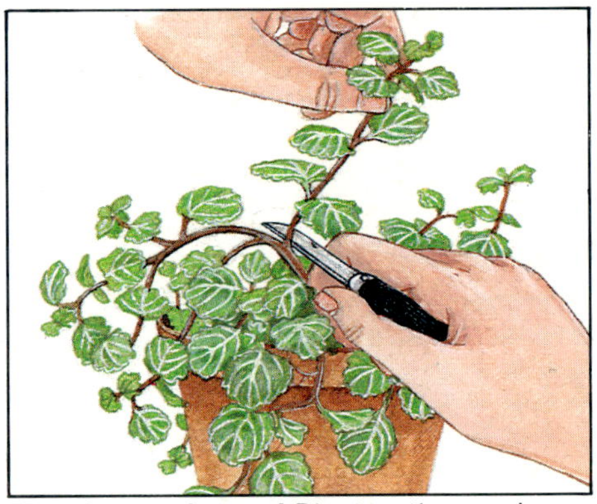

To take cuttings of Plectranthus, snip 3-4in (8-10cm) from a stem tip and remove the lowest pair of leaves.

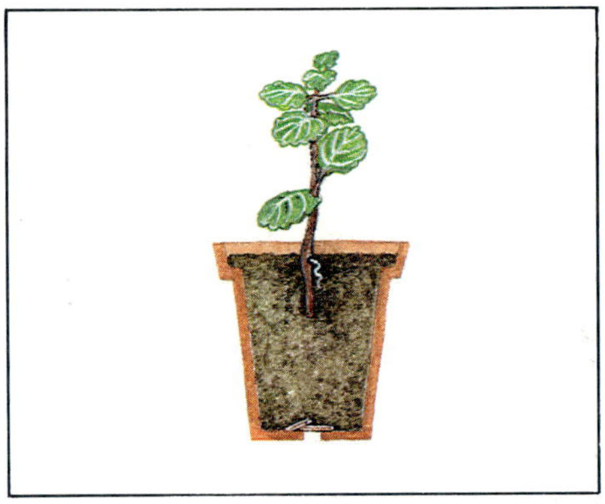

Treat the cutting with rooting powder and insert it into potting compost so that the leaf scars are just at ground level — roots will develop from this point.

Species

Plectranthus oertendahlii is the most widely grown species and the one most often referred to as Swedish Ivy, though the name can be applied to all the trailing types; South African in origin, its common name reflects its immense popularity as a houseplant in Scandinavia. This creeping plant has purple stems and very attractive, almost circular, 1in (2.5cm) diameter leaves, which are green with pronounced silvery-white veins; in maturity, the underside of the leaves goes a rosy-purple. From June to October, upright bunches of tubular, pinkish-white flowers are freely produced. It is particularly well-suited to a hanging basket and can trail down by as much as 1½-2ft (45-60cm).

P.australis, as the name suggests, is of Australian origin. Unlike most of the popular species, this is an erect, quite bushy plant, which can reach a height of about 3ft (0.9m). It has waxy, dark green leaves which are 1½in (4cm) long and pointed oval in shape.

P.saccatus from South Africa is an interesting species. It is a semi-creeper with small, pale green leaves which quickly form a densely spreading cover; in summer, it produces a mass of attractive, bluish-purple flowers.

P.coleoides, *below*, known as the Candle Plant, comes from India. It grows erect at first, to a height of about 1ft (0.3m), but then the stems begin to trail. It is usually grown in the variegated form 'Marginatus' which has hairy, heart-shaped, 2-2½in (5-7cm) leaves, in a pale green with a wide creamy white border. As with most species of Plectranthus, other than *P.oertendahlii*, the flowers are not significant or especially attractive, and they can be removed as they start to develop.

P.nummularius is another Australian species, but a trailer. It has almost circular, waxy green leaves up to 2½in (7cm) across, with purplish veining and greyish-green undersides.

P.behrii, from South Africa, is an unusual tall-growing species which makes a splendid houseplant. It grows very erect, to a height of about 3ft (0.9m), with long, colourful spikes of pink-spurred flowers. The broad, quilted leaves are a bronzy-green, with prominent red veins.

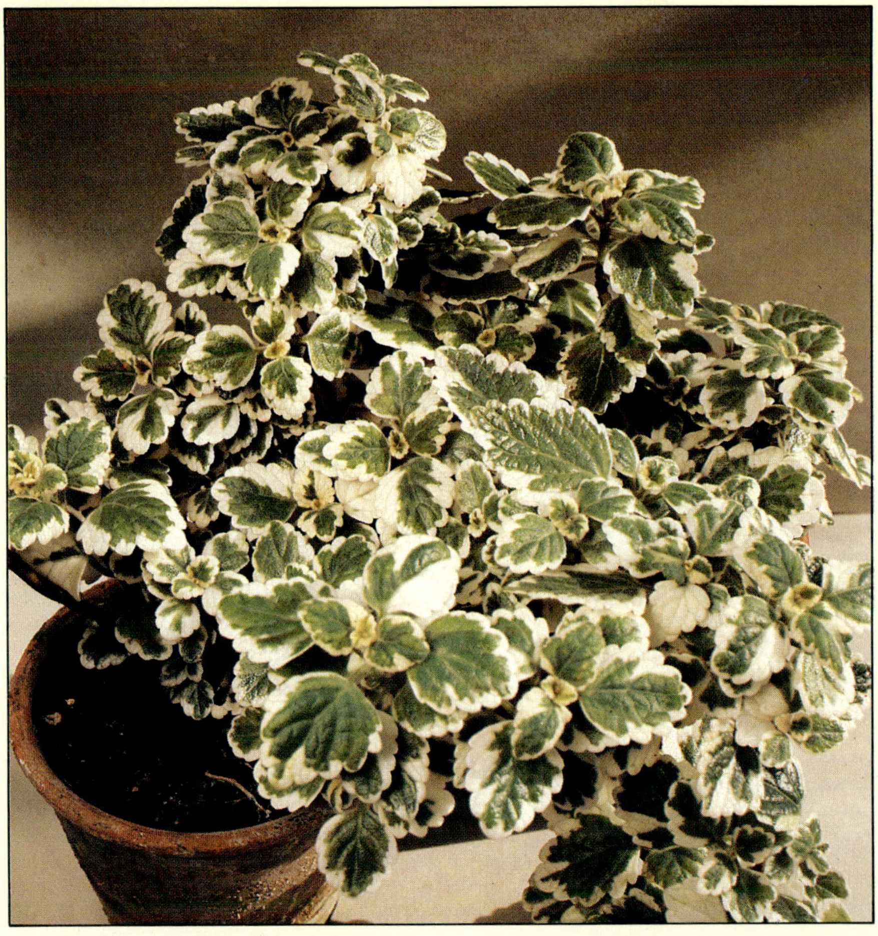

Primula

Family name: **Primulaceae**

Common names:
Primrose, Polyanthus

Care Easy	**Height** 1ft (0.3m)	**Flower** December-April
Light Bright Indirect	**Spread** 6in (15cm)	**Humidity** Mist spray
Price Cheap	**Shape** Rosette	**Availability** Common
Temp. Min 45°F (7°C)	Ideal 55°F (13°C)	Max 65°F (18°C)

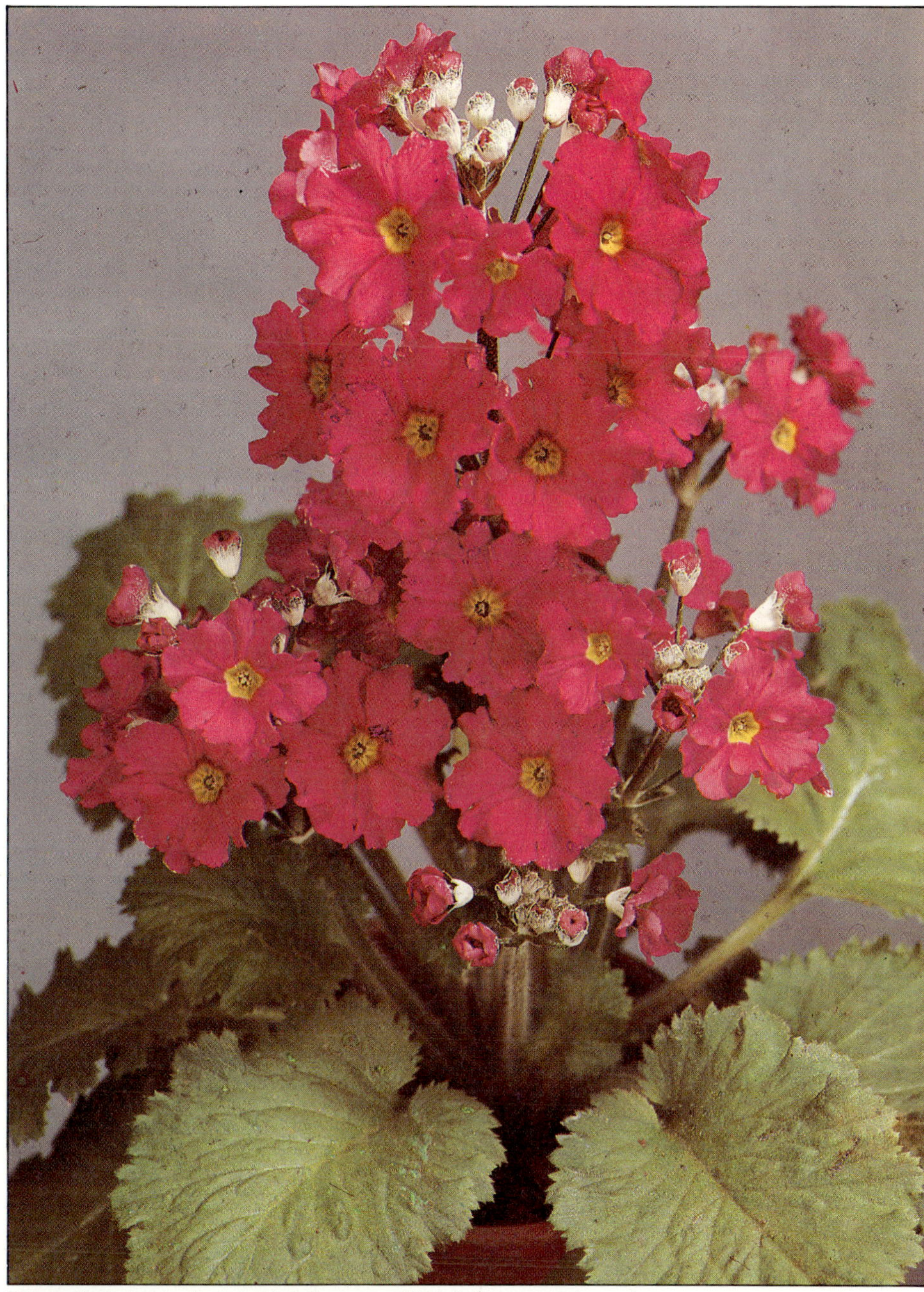

These bright and cheerful flowers will last for several weeks.

Some of the most popular and delightful of all plants grown indoors are to be found in this group. Producing large numbers of brightly coloured, often fragrant, flowers in winter and spring, they can be relied upon to brighten up any windowsill in the duller months of the year. This large, widely-distributed group has engaged the attention of botanists for many years, who have divided it into as many as 30 different sections. Some of these are best grown as garden plants, but many outdoor species make excellent, if temporary, houseplants; if they are moved to a garden after flowering, they may continue to flower and multiply every year.

The Fairy Primrose (*P.malacoides*), *right*, is one of the best known of the tender, indoor species, with tiers of fragrant, star-like flowers in shades of pale purple through red to white, carried on long slender stems. Equally popular are the Poison Primrose (*P.obconica*) — so called because its leaves can bring sensitive skins out in a rash — and the Chinese Primrose (*P.sinensis*), which has flowers of pink or purple with a deep yellow eye.

The main flowering period of the indoor types is around mid-winter and early spring, though some of them continue sporadically throughout the summer. Although perennial, they are often treated as annuals, to be enjoyed while flowering then thrown away, but these species can be kept and carried over to flower again, season after season.

Spring and summer care

The flowering season will be coming to an end by late spring (though the Poison Primrose, *P.obconica*, will continue flowering sporadically). Keep plants cool throughout the summer, with temperatures of 50-60°F (10-16°C), and lightly shaded, in a bright position but definitely protected from full sunlight. An airy atmosphere is important — keep them as well-ventilated as possible. Water your plants regularly, so that the compost is always moist.

Potting and repotting are best done in late summer just before the active growing season begins. Using John Innes No 3, repot plants every other year, moving them on to a container one size larger as clumps form, up to a maximum pot size of 6in (15cm); if plants outgrow this size, it is better to divide the clump and pot up the segments separately. Take care not to disturb the root ball when repotting; insert it into the larger pot and add extra compost. In the years that plants are not repotted they should be topdressed, by replacing the top 1in (2.5cm) of soil with fresh compost. Gently remove any dead or yellowing leaves and gradually increase the watering to bring your plants back into active growth.

Autumn and winter care

Temperatures should still be kept fairly low, around 50-55°F (10-13°C), and they can comfortably fall to 45°F (7°C) without any ill effect; 60°F (16°C) is really the maximum recommended temperature — anything over that will certainly shorten the life of the flowers. These plants need good light to thrive and it's important to provide a really bright position — particularly since daylight hours are so much shorter — but continue to protect them from direct sunlight. Equally important is good air circulation — a stuffy atmosphere will harm both flowers and foliage — so keep them very well-ventilated, but avoid cold draughts.

Primulas are quite thirsty plants, especially when flowering, so water regularly — as often as necessary to keep the compost moist at all times — but never allow the pot to become waterlogged. Add a liquid fertiliser to the water every two weeks, starting in the autumn when buds first appear. A fairly humid atmosphere is beneficial, so stand pots on moist pebbles and mist spray two or

Trouble Shooter

Excess watering can encourage disease, probably in the form of botrytis, *below*, seen as a greyish, fluffy mould on flowers and foliage. This should be dealt with immediately the symptoms are noticed. If it has got too great a hold, the plant is best destroyed. Otherwise, cut away and destroy all the affected parts and treat the plant with a benomyl-based fungicide. Poor air circulation is often a contributing factor, so make sure the plant is in a well-ventilated position.

Too high temperatures will shorten the flowering period — as will failure to remove dead flowers; temperatures should not rise above 60°F (16°C). Air that is hot and dry can also cause foliage to turn yellow.

Greenfly is a frequent problem, causing a stickiness and sooting of both leaves and flowers, distorting new growth and spoiling the whole appearance of the plant; spray them with a pyrethrum-based insecticide or apply a systemic insecticide as a deterrent, according to the manufacturer's instructions. If conditions are too dry, it will encourage red spider mite; treat them with a malathion-based insecticide.

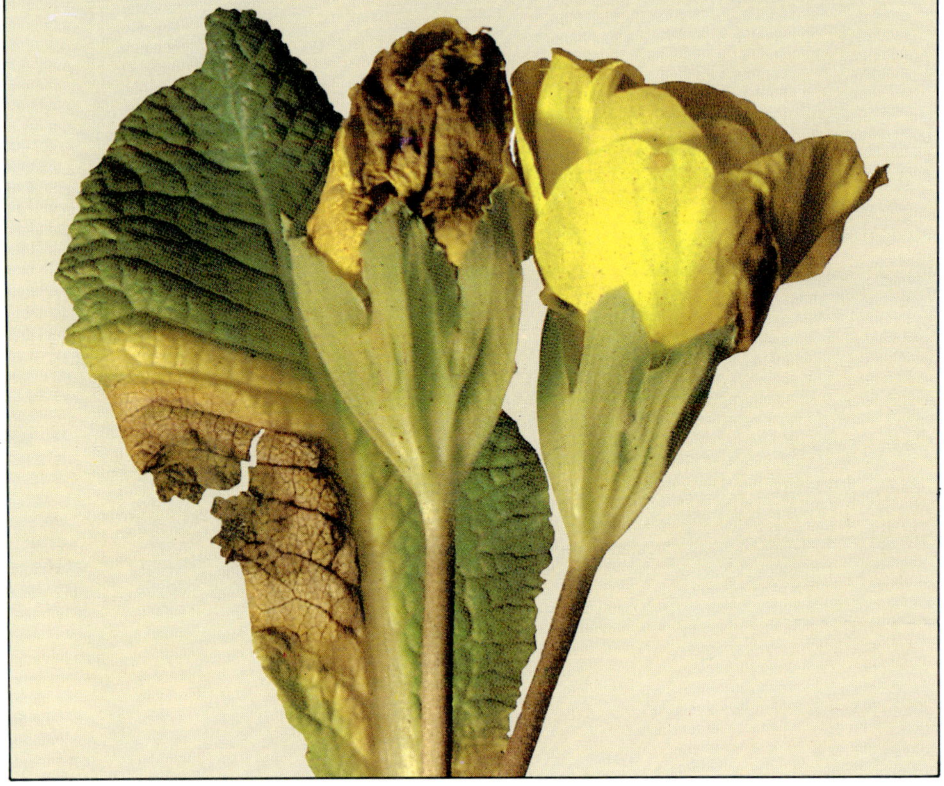

three times a week; take care when spraying always to avoid the flowers. Pull away any dead and yellowed leaves and pick off fading flowers, to prolong the flowering period.

Propagation

All Primulas can be propagated from seed, though there is no guarantee of hybrids reproducing exactly — there may well be some variation in colouring and so on. The times for sowing vary from species to species: *P.vulgaris* is best sown in February or March, *P.obconica* and *P.sinensis* from March to May and *P.malacoides* from May to July. With any other species, the best idea is to follow the sowing time recommended on the seed packet.

Sow the seeds in a pot or pan of John Innes No 3 with some coarse sand added (see *right*); firm down and thoroughly moisten the mixture, sow the seeds on to the surface, then barely cover them with a sprinkling of compost. Place the container in a propagator or a clear polythene bag and keep it in a shaded position, at a temperature of about 60°F (16°C). As soon as the seeds have germinated, within about two weeks, move them to a lighter position, but out of direct sunlight; when seedlings are large enough to handle, pot them up individually into a similar compost mixture. Make sure they are in a well-ventilated spot, kept moist, shaded and at an even temperature. Finally, when they have obviously grown too big for their container, pot them up into the normal compost and start feeding with a weak liquid fertiliser (using one quarter of the amount recommended on the bottle) until the first buds show, after which you should treat them as established plants.

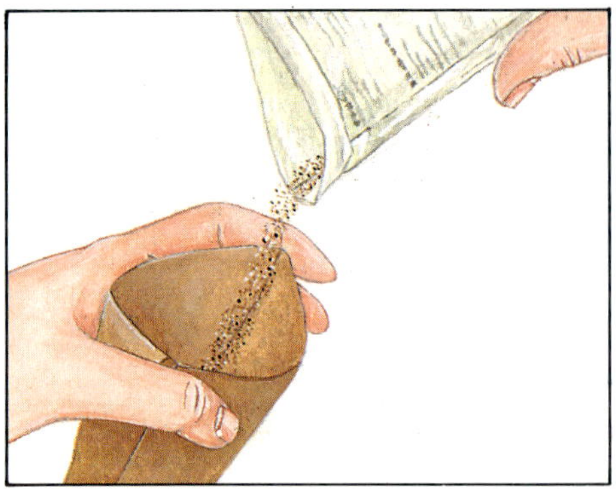

To help sow seeds evenly and thinly, empty the seed packet into an envelope of fine, dry sand.

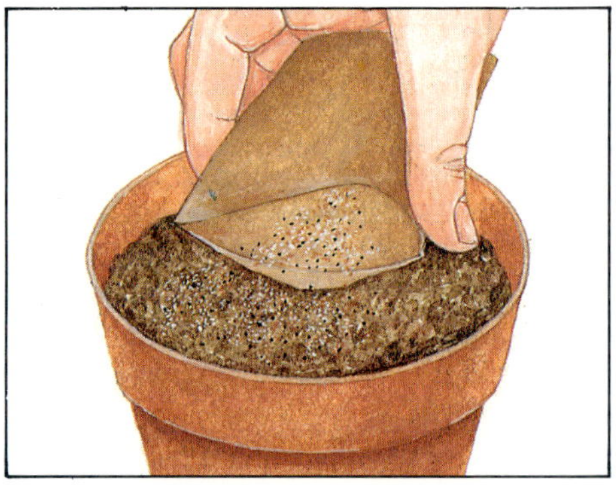

Sprinkle the sand and seed mixture over the surface of a pot containing three parts of John Innes No 3 mixed with one part of coarse sand.

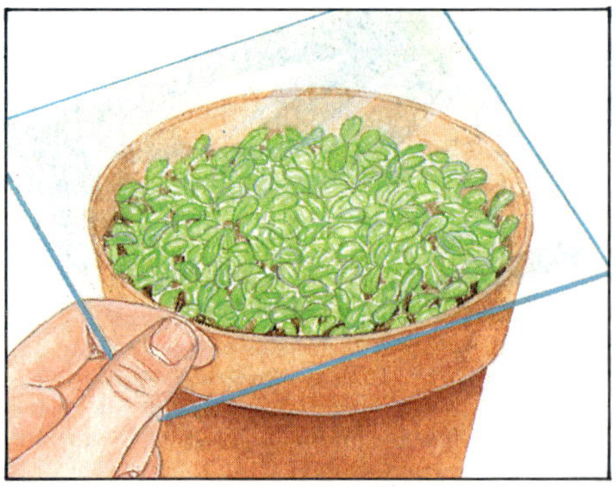

Cover the container with a piece of glass until the seedlings have germinated and place in the shade.

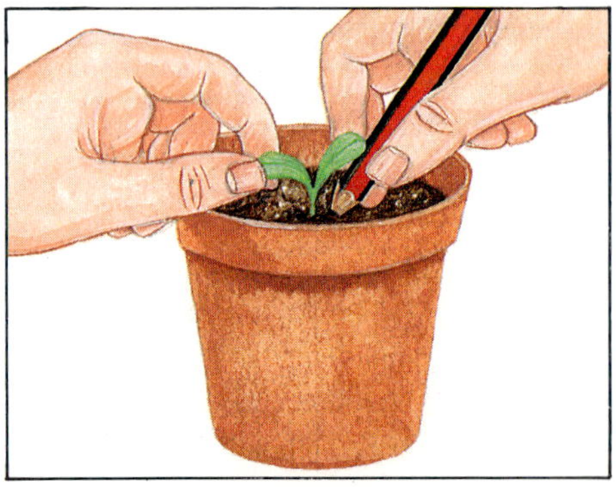

Once the seedlings are large enough to handle easily, pot them up singly.

Species

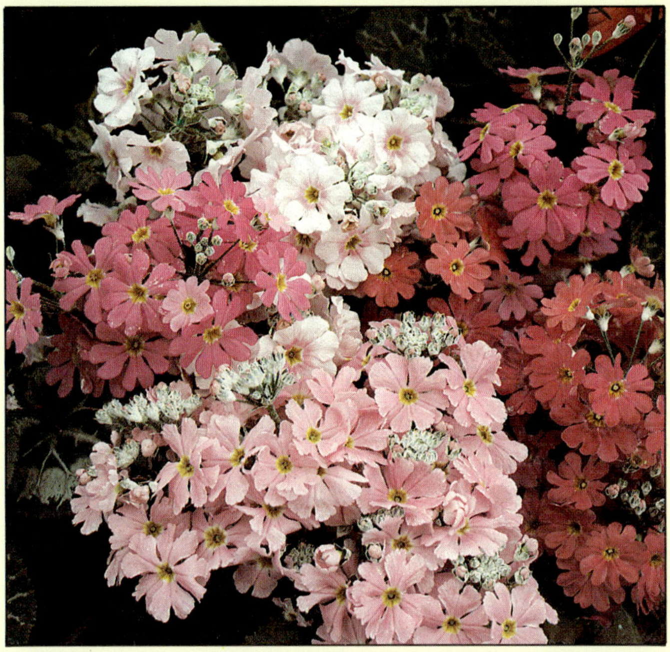

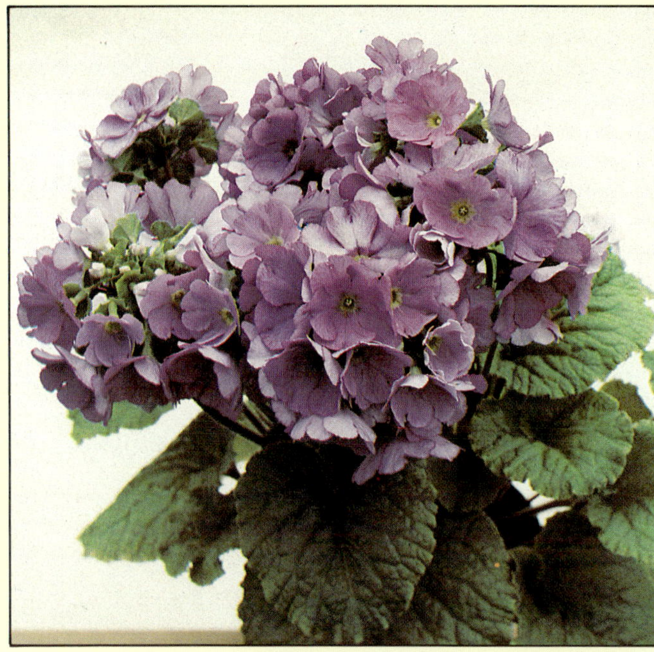

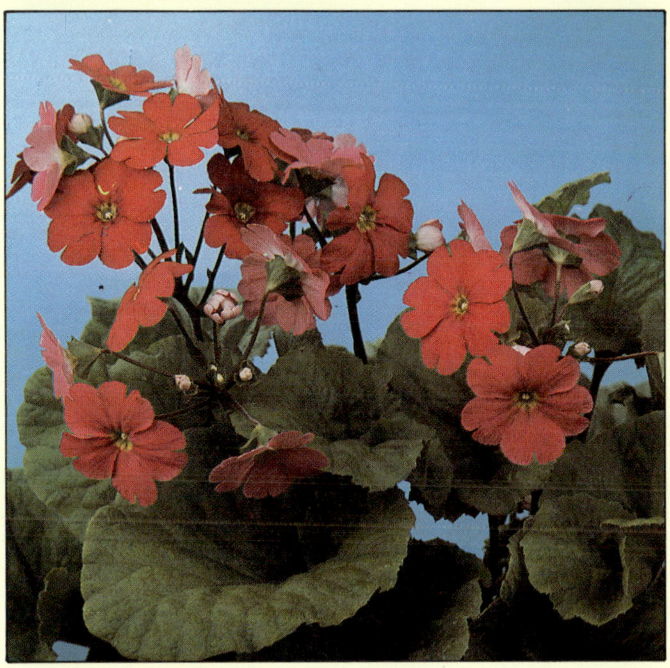

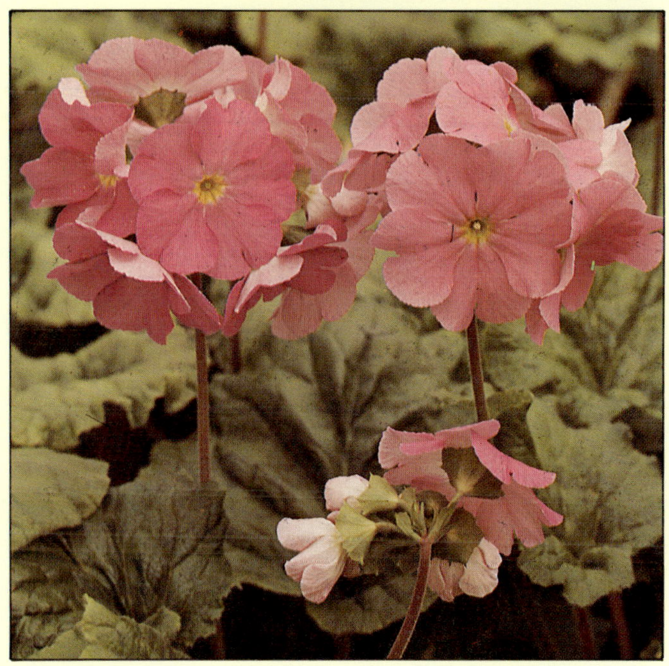

Primula malacoides, *top left*, the Fairy Primrose, from China, is a charming indoor species, up to 1ft (0.3m) tall, with pale green, hairy, slightly toothed leaves. Flowers appear between mid-winter and April, arranged in tiers on long, slender stalks. They are small and fragrant, in purple, pink, lilac, white or shades of red.

P.obconica is also from China and one of the finest Primulas. It forms a neat rosette of rounded leaves, 3-4in (8-10cm) long. The leaves are slightly hairy and can cause a painful rash on sensitive skins — hence the common name of Poison Primrose. Large, fragrant, long-lasting flowers in many shades, *top right, bottom right and bottom left*, appear in clusters on 1ft (0.3m) stalks; the main flowering season is December to May, though flowers may be produced sporadically throughout the summer.

P.sinensis takes the title Chinese Primrose. It is a remarkably pleasing plant which grows to about 10in (25cm) high, with long, hairy, lobed leaves. Flowers are carried on long stems in clusters, mostly in shades of pink or purple with a deep yellow eye; the main flowering season is from December to March. There is a number of popular varieties available, marked by their delicate, frilly-edged petals.

P.x kewensis, *overleaf top left*, is a hybrid of uncertain parentage, that was produced accidentally several years ago at the Royal Botanic Gardens at Kew. It

Species

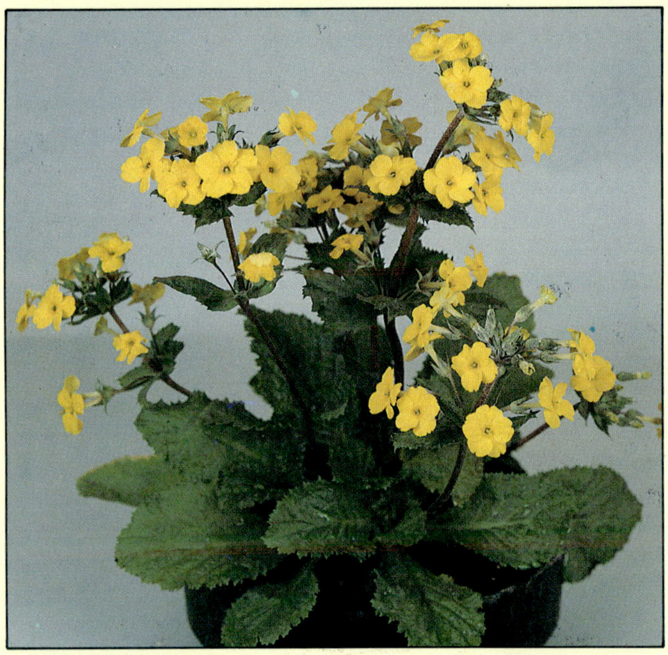

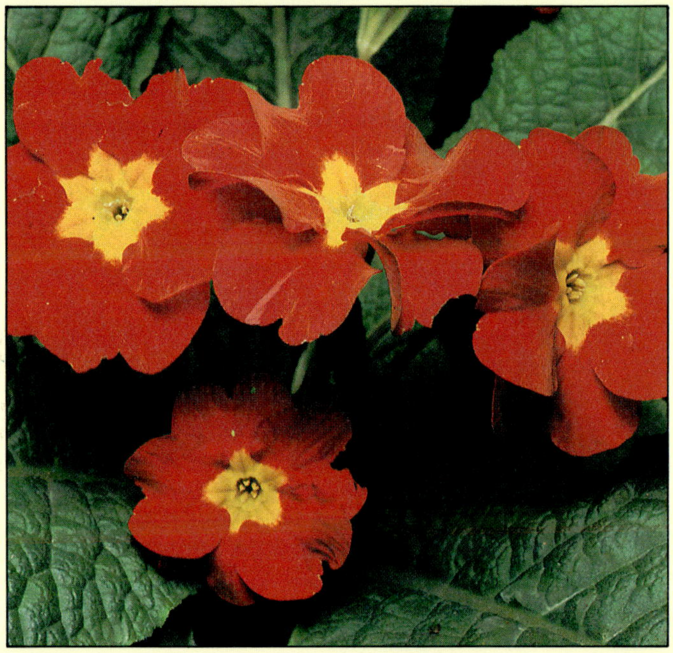

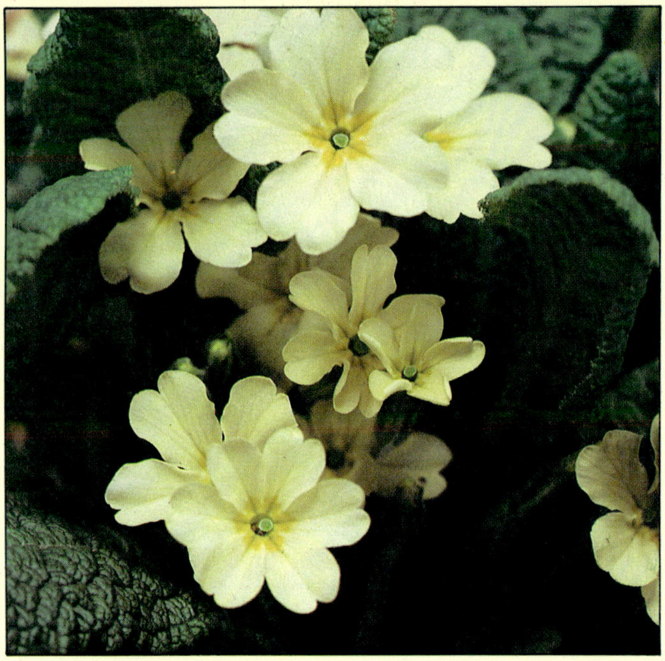

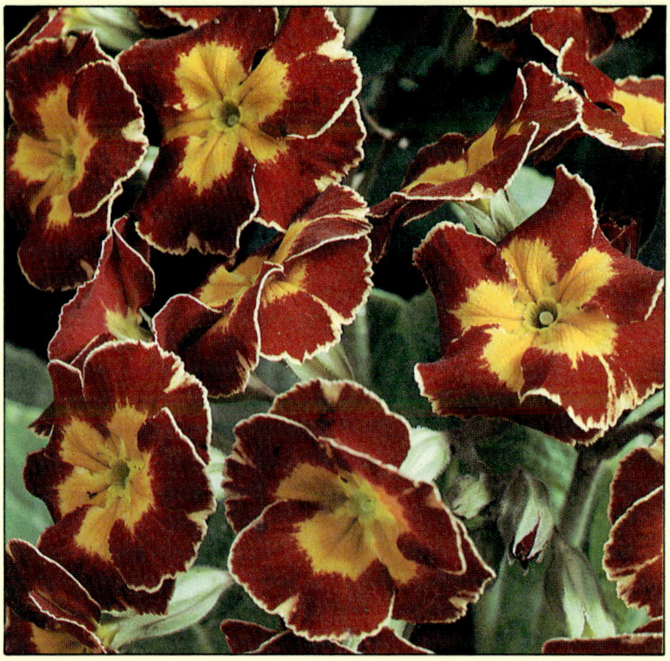

grows to a height of about 1ft (0.3m) and is the only yellow-flowered indoor species. The long-lasting flowers are borne on 10-12in (25-30cm) stalks from December to April, appearing successively in whorls, brilliantly yellow and sweetly scented. The long, light green leaves have toothed, wavy edges and are covered with a fine white powder.

P.vulgaris (also known as *P.acaulis*), *bottom left*, is the familiar Common Primrose. Of British origin, it is an outdoor species which makes an excellent, if temporary, houseplant, that should be moved to a garden after flowering. This low-growing plant grows to about 6in (15cm) and forms a neat rosette of 4-6in (10-15cm) long, bright green leaves; clustered in the centre of the rosette on very short stalks are large, showy, yellow flowers, with deep yellow centres. These appear in March and April — though some forms can flower in mid-winter. This species has been extensively hybridised, *top right*, to produce many beautiful pot plants.

P.polyantha, *bottom right*, the popular garden hybrids Polyanthus, are thought to be derived from *P.vulgaris*; they are also called *P.v.elatior*, but it is their common name that is most often used. Although Polyanthus are mainly grown outdoors, as with *P.vulgaris*, they are fine houseplants. They have bright, often two-coloured flowers, carried in large clusters on strong, 1ft (0.3m) long stems, well above the leaves. If placed in the garden after flowering, they may continue to flower and multiply year after year.

Pteris

Family name: **Polypodiaceae**

Common name: **Ribbon Fern**

Care Easy	**Height** 18in (46cm)	**Flower** None
Light Shaded	**Spread** 1ft (0.3m)	**Humidity** Mist spray regularly
Price Cheap	**Shape** Bushy	**Availability** Garden centres
Temp. Min 50°F (10°C)	Ideal 65°F (18°C)	Max 75°F (24°C)

These popular, small ferns are native to many parts of the world, from tropical rain forests to temperate European woodlands. The best known species is *Pteris cretica, right*, the Ribbon Fern, which is found growing wild in Italy and many parts of Asia and Africa. Plants within this species are very variable — so there are many distinct forms, hybrids and varieties, with different foliage — varying in size, shape and colouring.

Spring and summer care

These ferns like to be slightly pot-bound and resent being disturbed, so only pot on your plant when it is really bursting out of its pot; do this in the spring, using a peat-based potting compost.

Always keep the compost moist — your Ribbon Fern will quickly shrivel and die if it's left dry for more than a day or so. During hot weather, the compost will dry out more quickly, so you may have to water three or four times a week. These are lime-hating plants, so use rainwater, or cooled boiled water with a few drops of vinegar added if you live in a hard water area. Add a liquid fertiliser to the water every three weeks — use only half the dose recommended by the manufacturer. Like most ferns, Ribbon Ferns like a humid atmosphere, so mist spray regularly — standing your plant in a saucer of moist pebbles will also help maintain a humid atmosphere.

Your plant will thrive in a shaded position — never in direct sun, or even bright, indirect light. The ideal temperature is between 60-65°F (16-18°C) — any warmer and high humidity becomes increasingly important.

Autumn and winter care

Do not allow temperatures to fall below 50°F (10°C) between October and March. Maintain humidity by regular mist spraying and keep the plant in a shaded position.

Continue to ensure that the compost is kept moist at all times. Add the same weak solution of liquid fertiliser as was added during the warmer months, but use it less often — about every four to six weeks.

Propagation

The simplest method of propagation is to divide your plant. In March or April, gently, prise the plant apart and then pot up the divisions immediately into separate pots of peat-based potting compost and water both plants very thoroughly.

These ferns produce spores very readily. If you inspect the compost around your plant you may see some young fern plants. You can simply pot these up into 2in (5cm) pots of peat-based potting compost and treat them as mature plants, potting them on as they fill their pots.

Alternatively, if there are no young ferns that have grown up naturally then you can raise them yourself — although it can take a year to grow a plant that bears any resemblance to your fern. On the back of some of the fronds you'll find the brown spore cases; remove a few of these and spread them out on a sheet of paper to allow them to dry out for a few days. Spread the spores over the surface of a pot of thoroughly moistened compost — three parts peat-based potting compost to one part coarse sand. Place the container in a propagator, or sealed clear plastic bag, and maintain a temperature of between 75-80°F (24-27°C), in a shaded position. The surface of the compost will turn green as the first stage of the fern's life cycle proceeds; keep the compost moist and the atmosphere humid. After several weeks, recognisable fern plants will begin to develop. When they are about 2in (5cm) tall, prick out a small clump into 2in (5cm) pots of peat-based compost and treat them as adult plants, moving them into larger containers as their roots fill out the pots.

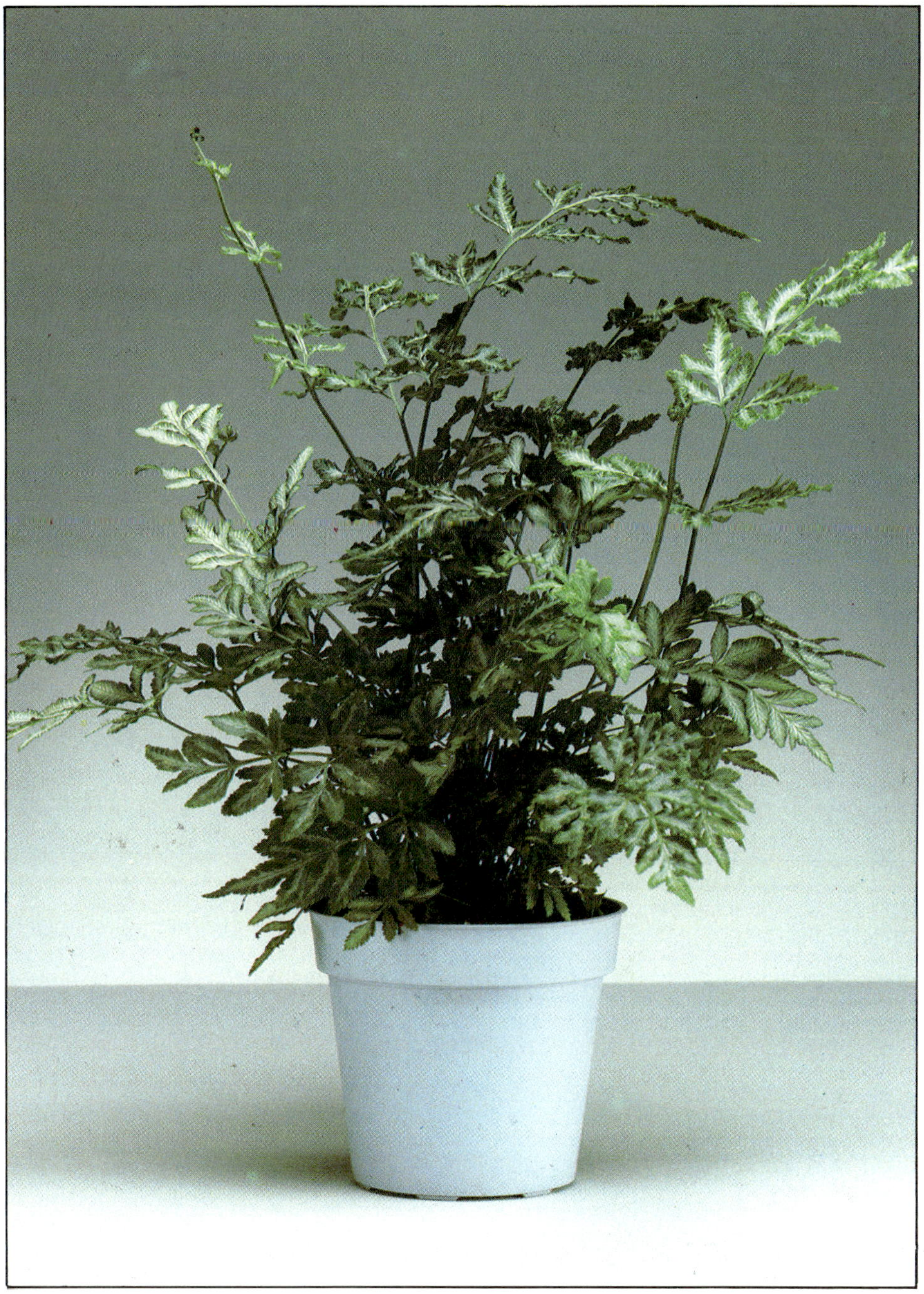

This attractive, small bush is easier to grow than many other ferns.

Species

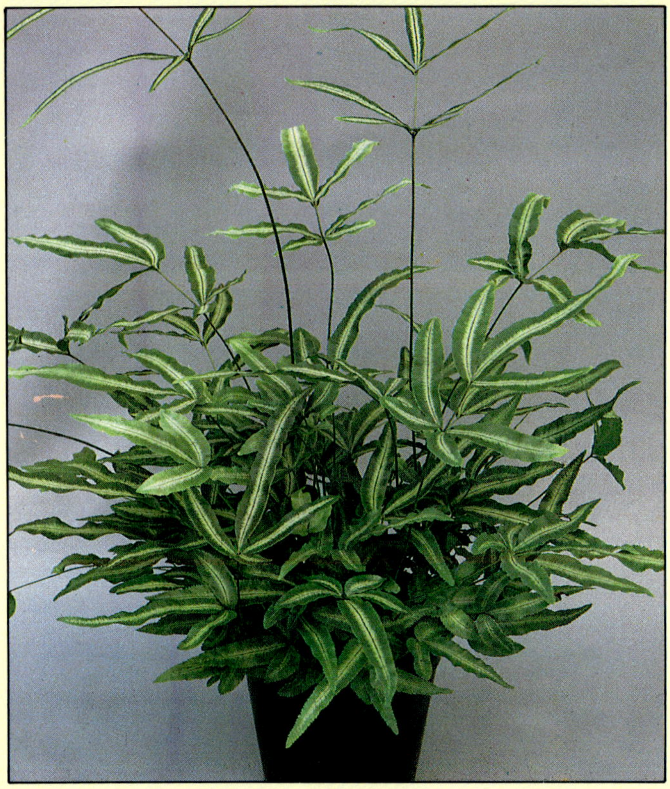

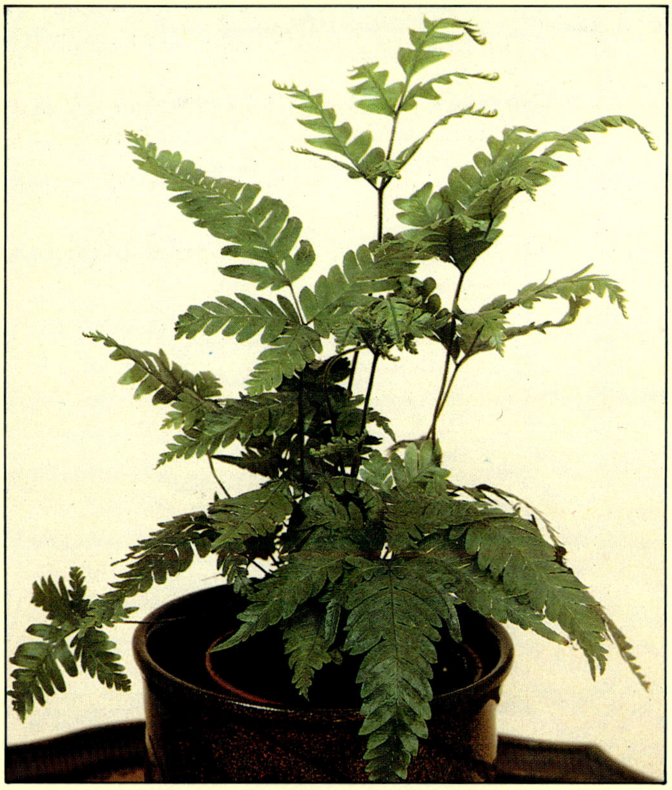

Pteris cretica, the Ribbon Fern, comes from Italy, parts of Asia and Africa. It grows to about 18in (45cm) tall with arching, brown-stalked, feathery fronds, each subdivided into several flattish, often toothed leaflets in mid-green and sometimes paler around the midrib. *P.c.albolineata, above left,* is slightly smaller than the species and has white or cream-coloured markings at the midrib of each leaflet. *P.c.ouvrardii* is a taller variety — the wiry brown stalks bear deep green fronds, about 1ft (0.3m) long with tough, narrow, paper-thin leaflets. It is native to several of the Mediterranean islands, principally Corsica — although it has found its way to other islands, like Crete. It is this naturally occurring variety that has very often been used as one of the parents of the many cultivated forms.

P.tremula, *above right,* the Australian Trembling Fern, comes from Australia and New Zealand. It has slim, arching, rather brittle but feathery fronds which grow up to about 2-3ft (0.6-0.9m) in length. Each frond carries three of four pairs of divided leaflets.

P.multifida from China is smaller and more delicate than *P.cretica*, with slender, graceful fronds, up to 18in (45cm) long, with evenly spaced, flat, narrow leaflets — giving the plant a bushy appearance. There are some forms of this species with frilled leaflets with crested tips, giving them a lacy appearance.

P.ensiformis from Australia and many parts of Asia also has a more delicate appearance than *P.cretica.* It has two different types of fronds: the fertile ones (they develop spores on their underside) are slim, about 18-20in (45-50cm) long and quite upright with deep green leaflets with wavy edges; the sterile fronds are smaller and wider-spreading with single or multiple leaflets.

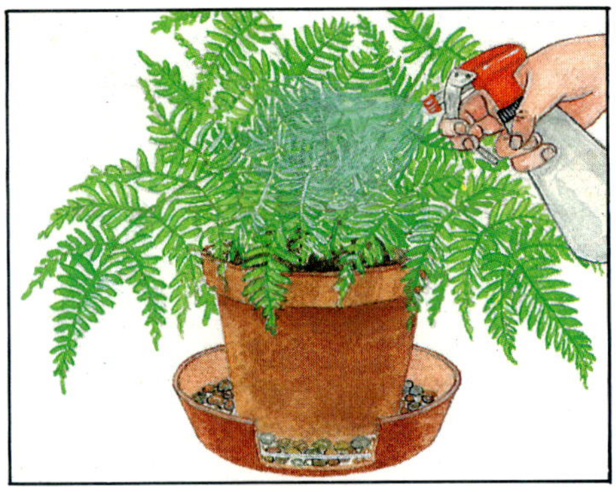

These ferns thrive in high humidity, especially during the hot weather. So stand your plant in a saucer of moist pebbles and mist spray regularly.

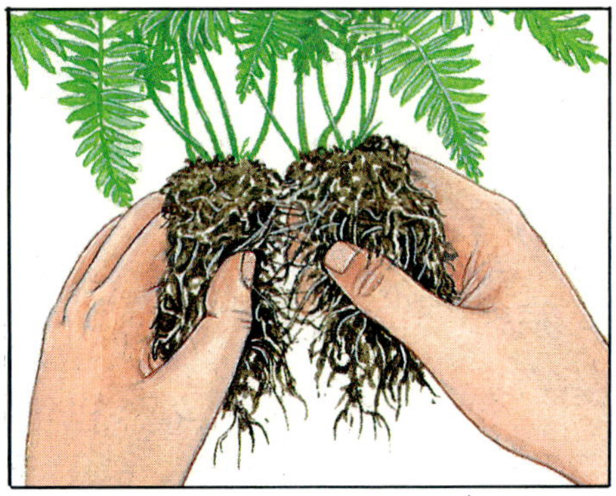

To divide overgrown ferns, gently ease the rootball apart, pot up the divisions separately into a peat-based compost and water in well.

Trouble Shooter

The fronds of an underwatered plant will quickly wilt, turn papery and fall. Dunk it in water for a few minutes — if the foliage does not recover within a few days, just snip the damaged fronds off and new ones will soon emerge. Bright light or using a leaf shining product will also shrivel the foliage.

Wipe scale insect away with a brush dipped in methylated spirit. *Never* use a malathion-based insecticide on these plants.

Rebutia

Family name: **Cactaceae**

Common name:
Mexican Sunball

Care Easy	**Height** 2-2½in (50-65mm)	**Flower** Spring and summer
Light Sunny	**Spread** 2-2½in (50-65mm)	**Humidity** None
Price Cheap	**Shape** Globe	**Availability** Garden centres
Temp. Min 50°F (10°C)	Ideal 70°F (21°C)	Max 80°F (27°C)

This is one of the best of all flowering cacti. It is easy to grow, begins to flower when very young, and flowers very freely in spring and summer. Blooms are brightly coloured and very showy, sometimes virtually encircling the entire stem, which can be either cylindrical or globe-shaped and is covered with small symmetrical growths called tubercles, each with a tiny cushion-like areole at its tip. Offsets develop very easily around the base, which adds interest to the shape of the plant and also makes it very easy to propagate.

There are many different varieties to choose from, with flowers ranging from white, through yellow, orange and pink to bright red. These truly lovely flowering cacti will never let you down — unless you just neglect them entirely! If you care for them properly, you'll certainly get good results.

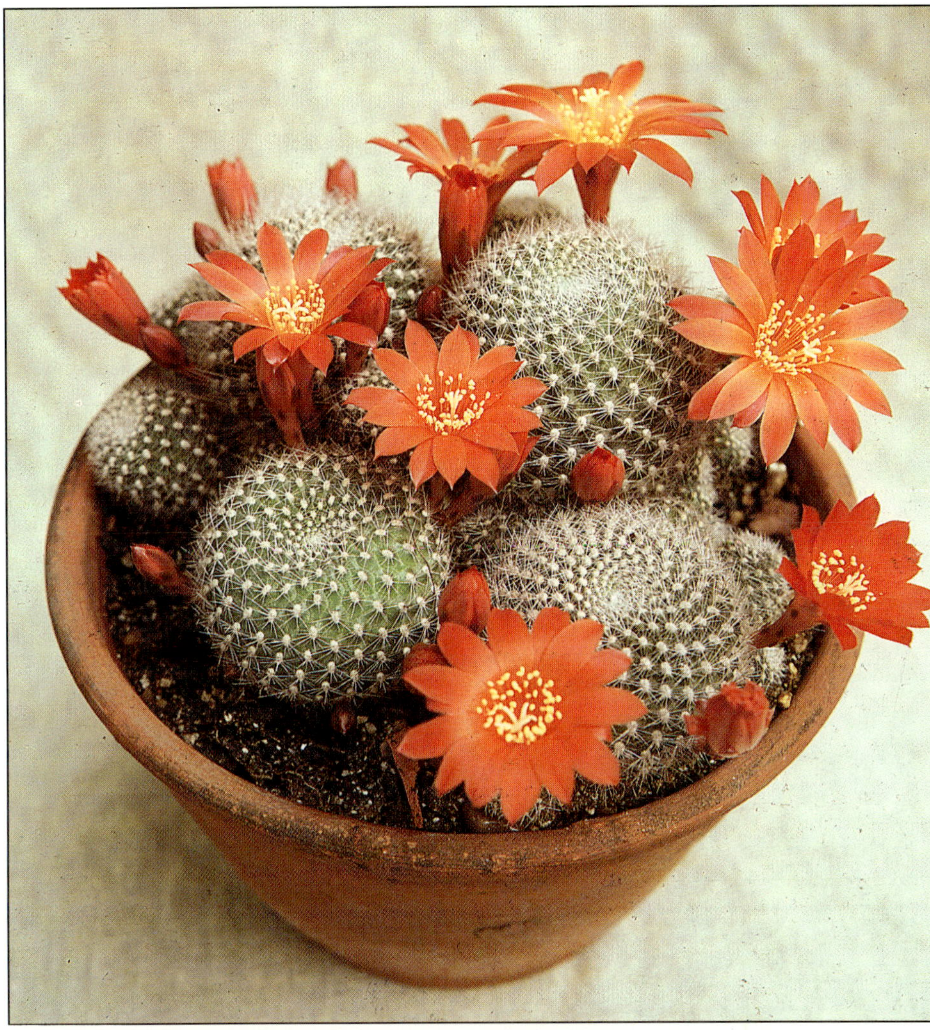

One of the most popular is *Rebutia minuscula,* the Mexican Sunball.

Spring and summer care

In early spring remove the cactus from its pot. If it is full of roots, or if the stem has begun to press against the sides of the pot, it's time to pot the plant on. Choose a container one size larger and use a good proprietary cactus compost, or a mixture of two parts John Innes No 1 and one part coarse sand.

Normal room temperatures during spring and summer are suitable for Rebutias — 65-70°F (18-21°C). Give them good light at all times, but shade them from really hot sun. They like a dry atmosphere with plenty of fresh air. Do not water until the soil is virtually dry, then water generously, and wait again until the compost has almost dried out. Feed regularly, ideally with a special cactus fertiliser, to encourage flowering. Start to reduce watering about October.

Autumn and winter care

Temperatures are best kept at a minimum of 50-55°F (10-13°C) — if you can manage 60°F (16°C), so much the better. Withhold water from November to March, but check occasionally and give a few drops so that the compost does not dry out completely. Begin gentle watering when the flower buds appear, increasing it gradually as the weather gets warmer. Keep the plant out of draughts, in as bright a position as possible — light becomes especially important after March, when the flowers begin to develop.

Propagation

You can propagate Rebutias by seeds or by offsets; offsets will always run true to type, but often with seeds you can't be sure what you're getting until the plant has grown.

In February or March, sprinkle seeds over the surface of thoroughly moistened cactus compost and cover them lightly with coarse sand. Put them in a propagator or a sealed clear polythene bag, keep them at 70-80°F (21-27°C), and well shaded. When the seeds have germinated, remove the seedlings from the propagator or bag, and put them in a lighter position, at about 60-65°F (16-18°C). Prick them out separately when the little cacti are 1in (2.5cm) or so high, which may take several months.

A quicker way to propagate them is by the offsets which grow in clusters around the base of the plant. Remove offsets carefully with a sharp knife, dip the cut ends in sulphur powder and leave them for several days to callus over. When they are quite dry, set them on slightly moist cactus compost, and keep them at a temperature of 60-65°F (16-18°C) in a good light. They will soon root and may then be treated as mature plants.

Buying Guide

When buying Rebutias, look for plants without blemishes and with several young offsets around the larger, parent plant. In the summer months plants should have several flower buds.

Trouble Shooter

Mushy or soft stems are a sign of overwatering. Leave the plant to dry out and remove any damaged parts with a sharp knife. Rotting might also be caused by too low a temperature in winter; make sure the plant is not too cold or left in a draught.

The most likely pest is mealy bug; wipe away the white fluffy insects and their eggs with a brush dipped in methylated spirit, or spray with a malathion-based insecticide.

Species

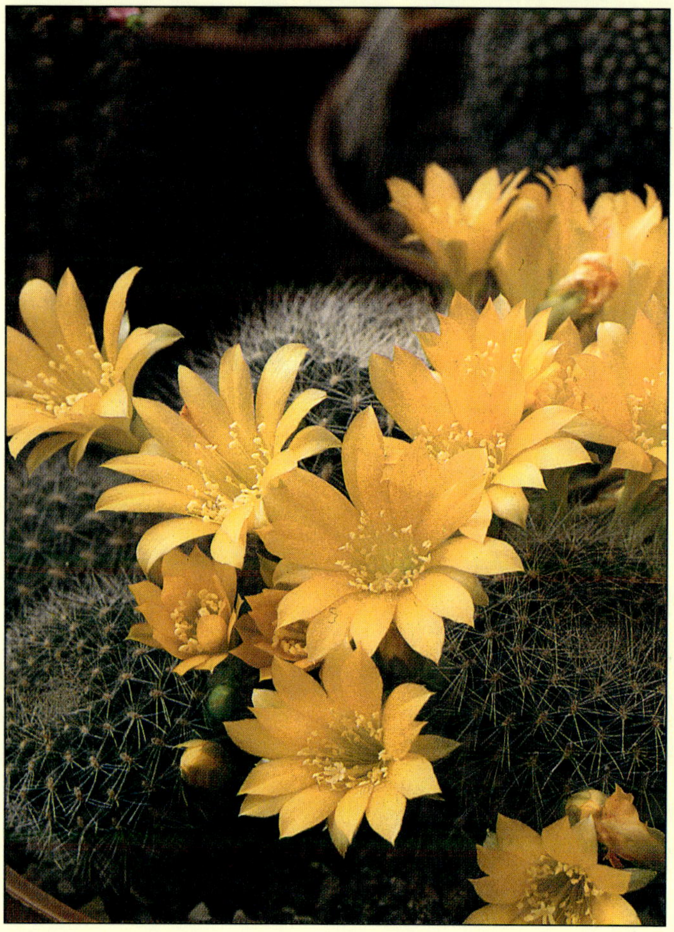

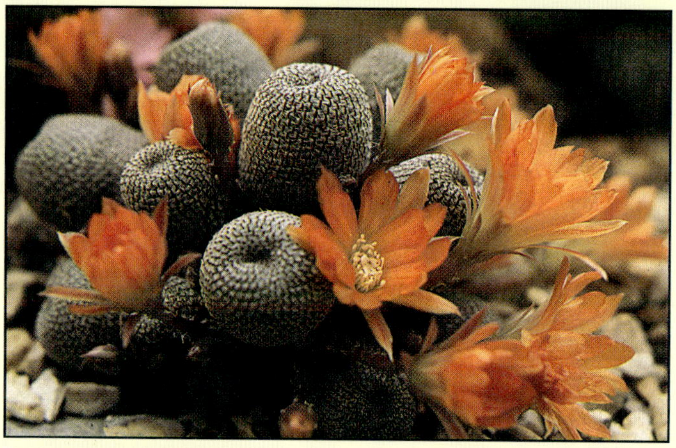

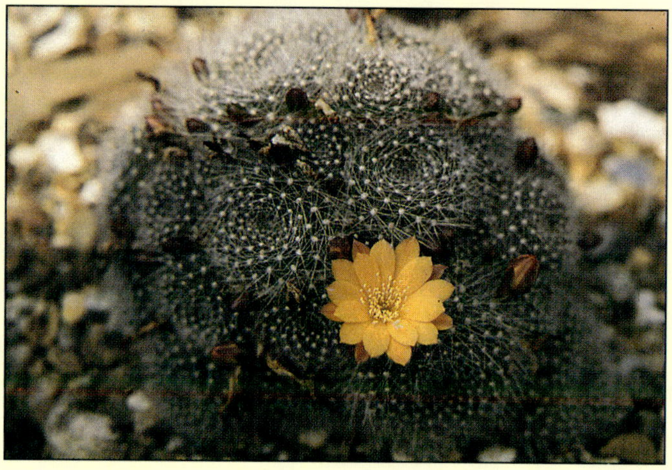

Rebutia minuscula is the commonest Rebutia. Although it is often known as the Mexican Sunball it comes from north-west Argentina, and has a pale green, globe-shaped stem 2-2½in (5-6.5cm) across, covered with minute whitish or yellowish spines. Rich red flowers appear around the base of the stem in spring and right through the summer — they are about 1in (2.5cm) across. An extremely fast-growing and very tolerant plant.

R.heliosa, *top right*, grows to only about 1in (2.5cm) tall. The indented, globular stems are covered in brown areoles with white spines. Vivid, orange flowers appear from spring until the autumn.

R.senilis, comes from the mountain regions of Argentina. Its stems are about 3in (8cm) across and covered with white, bristly spines. The funnel-shaped carmine red flowers have white throats, and are up to 1½in (4cm) long. Among the best-known varieties are *R.s.kesselringiana, above left,* with brilliant golden yellow flowers and *R.s.lilacino-rosea* with flowers of delicate lilac-pink.

R.marsoneri, from Argentina, *above right,* sometimes remains solitary, without forming clusters of stems. The flowers are funnel-shaped, up to 1½in (4cm) long and are either vivid orange or yellow.

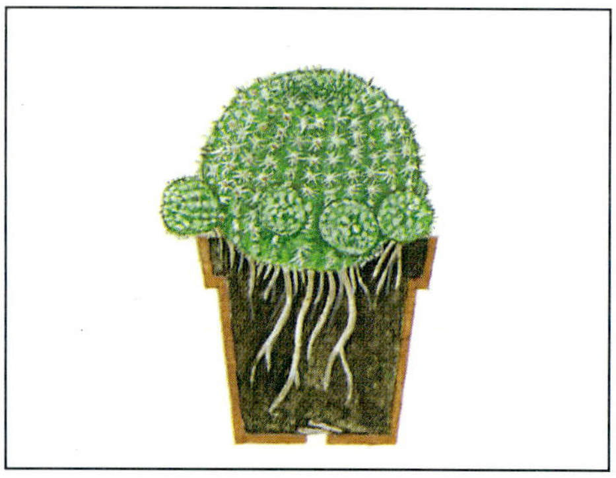

To propagate the Mexican Sunball you can remove the offsets when they are about 1in (2.5cm) across.

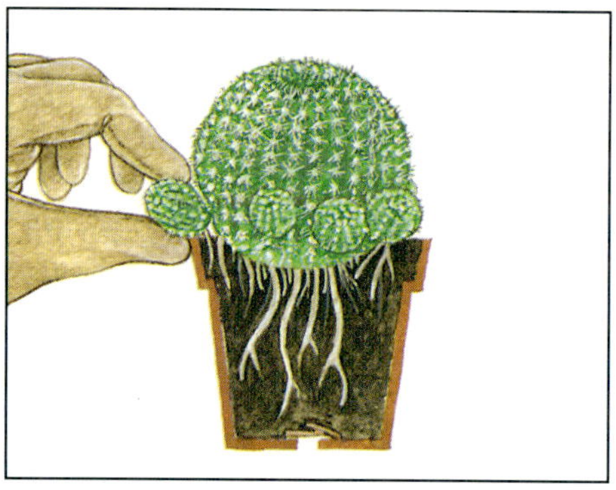

Wearing gloves, gently prise the offset away from the parent — it may just pull away.

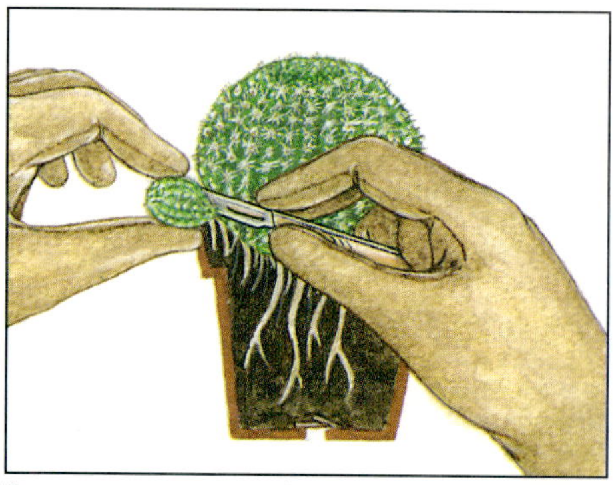

If necessary, sever the joint between the offset and the parent using a sharp knife, and pot up individually.

Rhipsalidopsis

Family name: **Cactaceae**

Common name:
Easter Cactus

Care Easy	**Height** 1ft (30cm)	**Flower** Spring
Light Bright indirect	**Spread** 1ft (30cm)	**Humidity** None
Price Cheap	**Shape** Bushy	**Availability** Garden centres
Temp. Min 55°F (13°C)	Ideal 60°F (16°C)	Max 70°F (21°C)

These attractive forest cacti come from the jungles of tropical South America. They are epiphytes — growing high up in the branches of trees rather than on the ground. Their arching branches, tipped by colourful flowers, make these plants an excellent choice for a hanging basket to brighten up those often bleak days of early spring.

Rhipsalidopsis gaertneri, below, the Easter Cactus, from southern Brazil, is probably the most popular of the two species available as houseplants. Both species have unusual fleshy stems, made up of strings of flattened and sometimes angled or prominently ridged segments. The Easter Cactus has more or less oval, flat segments, shaped rather like leaves, about 1½-2in (3.8-5cm) long and slightly notched around the edge. Its vivid, scarlet flowers are borne profusely — mostly at the stem tips.

Spring and summer care

After flowering, reduce the amount of water you give your plant for two or three weeks — adding no fertiliser and only enough water to prevent the compost drying out completely.

After this rest period, in the early summer repot your plant. Remove it from its pot, shake off the excess compost and replace it with fresh; use a proprietary cactus compost or make up your own with three parts peat-based compost to one part coarse sand. If your plant has filled its pot then repot it into a container one size larger. If you're going to put your Rhipsalidopsis in a hanging basket, then line the container with sphagnum moss; for a large display, plant several plants together — three plants to a 10in (25cm) basket will make a very attractive feature.

Keep your plant away from direct sun, in bright, indirect light. If temperatures rise above 65°F (18°C), your plant is best kept outside in a shaded position — but do remember to bring it inside again, at the beginning of September, before the weather starts to get colder. Water regularly, always keeping the compost moist but not waterlogged. Add a weak liquid fertiliser to the water every four weeks — using half the dose recommended by the manufacturers. If you keep your plant indoors, mist spray regularly, especially during very hot weather.

Autumn and winter care

Keep your plant in bright light but away from direct sun at all times. Water occasionally, so as to keep the compost just moist. Add a liquid fertiliser to the water every two weeks, using half the strength recommended by the manufacturer. Increase the watering in the late winter as the young flower buds appear. The ideal temperature during the colder months is between 55-60°F (13-16°C).

Propagation

In December or January sprinkle the seeds thinly over the surface of a pot of moistened cactus compost and put the pot into a propagator or sealed polythene bag. Keep the seeds shaded and at a temperature of 70°C (21°C). Once the seedlings are visible uncover them and put them into brighter, indirect light. When they're large enough to handle pot them up individually and treat them as mature plants.

Taking cuttings is also very easy. After the rest period, remove joined pairs of stem segments, ideally already with tiny roots, but if not, leave them to dry off for two or three days and then insert them into the usual potting compost, so that the stems stand upright and only the very bottom of the stem is beneath the surface. They can be treated as a mature plant immediately.

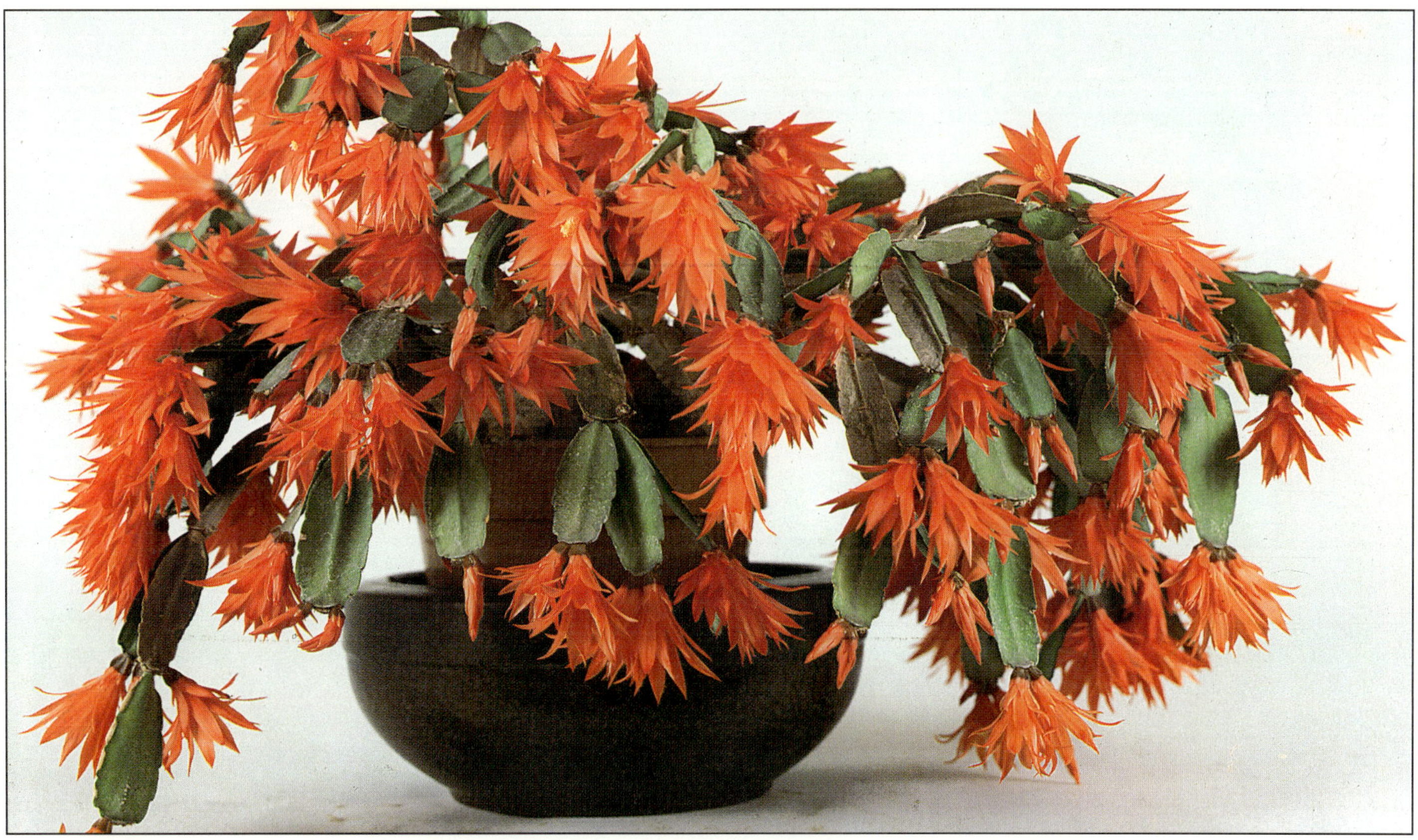

The Easter Cactus makes a colourful spring display in a pot or hanging basket.

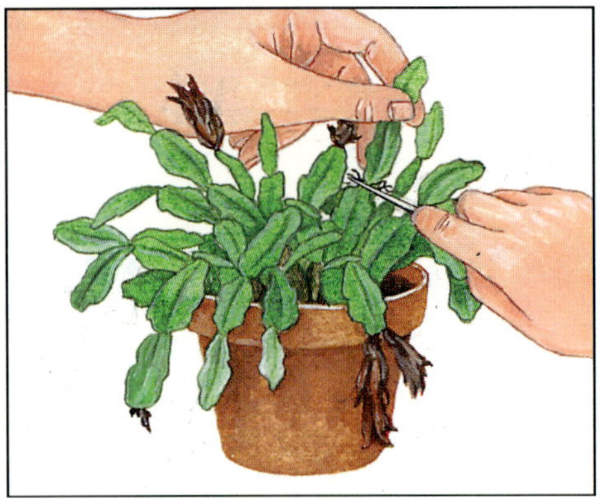

Take cuttings of Rhipsalidopsis in early summer; cut the stem at the joint between two segments, including any roots that may be present.

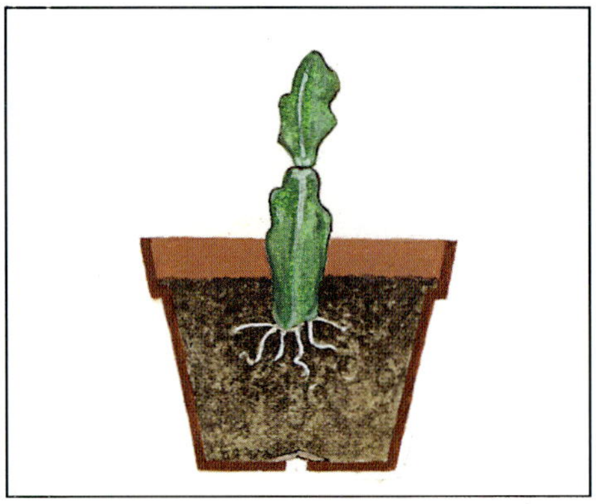

If the cutting already has roots, then insert it straight away into potting compost. If there are no roots, then allow the cutting to dry off first.

Trouble Shooter

Mealy bug and root mealy bug are the main pests; apply a malathion-based insecticide, or wipe off the fluffy patches with a brush dipped in methylated spirit; for root mealy bug wash roots clean of potting compost, soak the roots for an hour or two in a weak solution of a systemic insecticide, then repot in a fresh mixture. Sciarid or mushroom fly can attack Rhipsalidopsis. Inspect the compost for small white grubs and tiny eggs. If you see any kill them with a systemic insecticide watered on to the compost.

Species

Rhipsalidopsis gaertneri, often known as *Schlumbergera gaertneri*, the Easter Cactus, comes from southern Brazil. It has arching, leafless stems growing to about 1ft (0.3m) long and made up of chains of fleshy, oval segments, each about 1½-2in (3.8-5cm) in length. The segments are slightly notched and from each areole (the small cushion-like growths characteristic of all cacti) grow a few soft bristles. The flowers are bright red and produced prolifically for several weeks in the early spring.

***Rhipsalidopsis* hybrids** have been bred artificially by crossing *R.gaertneri* and *R.rosea*. 'Graeseri' has rosy-red flowers and is similar in size and shape to *R. rosea*; 'Elektra' has brilliant reddish-purple flowers; 'Rosea' has flowers in a pinkish orange with a rose-red centre.

R.rosea (sometimes called *Rhipsalis rosea*), *below*, is from the rain forests of Parana in southern Brazil. Its stems are made up of segments similar to *R.gaertneri* but smaller — about 1in (2.5cm) long, flat and tinged with red. In May and June flowers, 2in (5cm) across, are borne in abundance on the pendulous stems; they are slightly scented, rose-pink and carried at the tips of the branches.

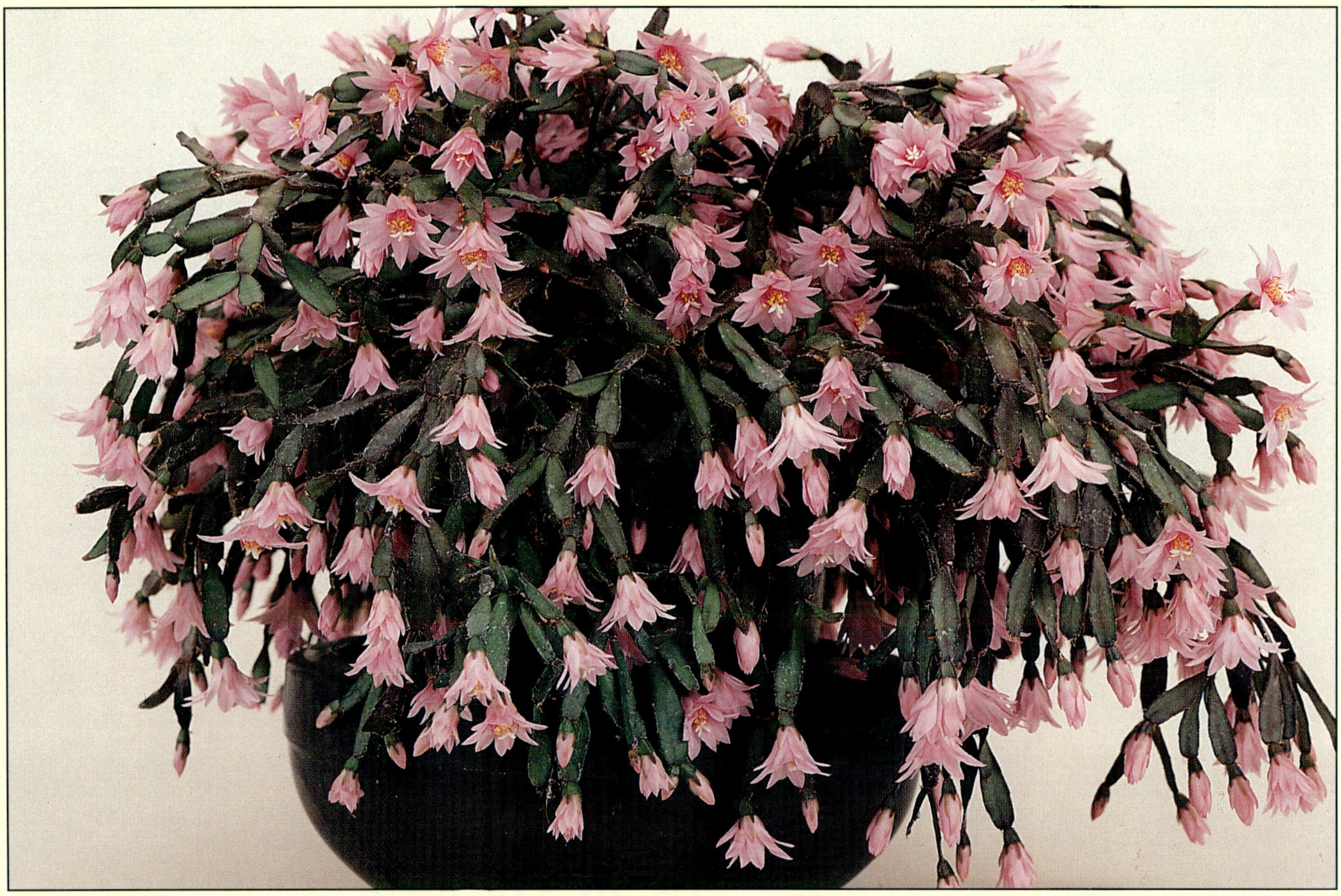

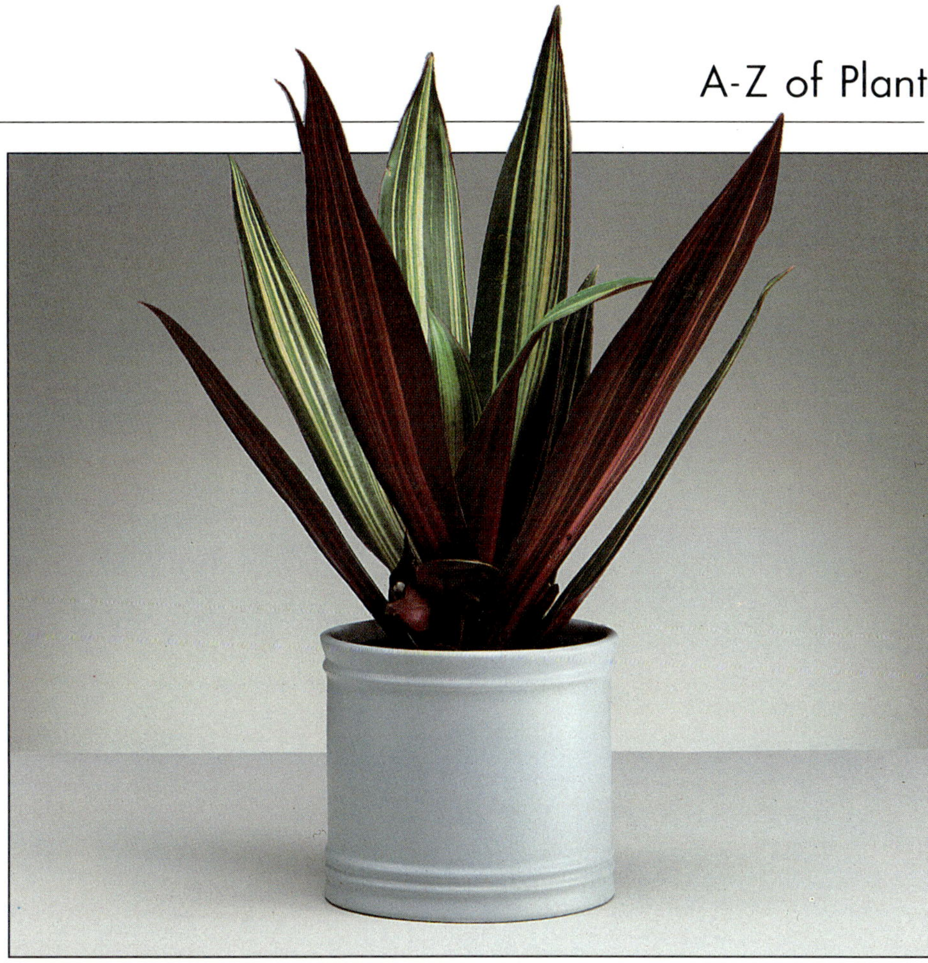

Rhoeo spathacea 'Vitata' is a fine variegated variety.

Rhoeo

Family name: **Commelinaceae**

Common names: **Moses in the Cradle/Boat Lily**

Care Easy	**Height** 12-16in (30-40cm)	**Flower** Any time
Light Shaded	**Spread** 10-12in (25-30cm)	**Humidity** Mist spray regularly
Price Middle range	**Shape** Rosette	**Availability** Garden centres
Temp. Min 55°F (13°C)	Ideal 70°F (21°C)	Max 75°F (24°C)

These striking, evergreen plants from central America and the West Indies are grown for their outstanding foliage, though their common names in fact refer to their flowers, which are small and white and 'cradled' in purple, boat-shaped bracts.

There is only one species in this group, *Rhoeo spathacea*, which has been a popular greenhouse and houseplant for very many years. It grows about 12-16in (30-40cm) tall, with a rosette of mostly upright leaves which are a metallic dark green on the upper surface and a rich purple beneath. There are also some beautifully variegated varieties, which have bright yellow stripes running the length of the leaf.

Spring and summer care

Repot every year in the spring, using John Innes No 2, up to a final pot size of 5-6in (13-15cm), after which topdress your plant annually replacing the top 1-2in (2.5-5cm) with fresh compost.

Try to maintain a temperature of 70°F (21°C) — certainly not less than 60°F (16°C) — and keep your plant moderately shaded, always protected from full sun. This plant cannot tolerate dry air, so stand the pot on moist pebbles and mist spray regularly.

Water freely, so that the compost is always moist, and add a weak liquid fertiliser to the water — using half the recommended amount — every two weeks between late April and September.

Autumn and winter care

This plant requires winter warmth, and temperatures should be kept at around 55-60°F (13-16°C). Always avoid direct sun, though don't shade your plant too densely, and provide good air circulation but keep your plant out of draughts.

Water moderately, giving only enough to keep the compost barely moist, but never allow the soil to dry out. Mist spray occasionally with tepid water on the brightest days, to maintain a degree of humidity.

Propagation

Propagation is easy using cuttings of side shoots, which are produced around the base of the plant. Take 3-4in (8-10cm) cuttings at any time in the summer, treat the cut ends with rooting hormone and set them in a mixture of three parts John Innes No 2 and one part coarse sand.

Moisten the mixture thoroughly, then place the container in a propagator or a clear polythene bag and keep in a shaded spot at a temperature of 70°F (21°C). Rooting will only take two weeks or so, and the appearance of new growth will indicate when this has taken place. Pot the rooted cuttings up individually into 3-4in (8-10cm) pots of John Innes No 1 compost and treat them as mature plants.

Trouble Shooter

Leaves will wilt and shrivel if the temperature is too low, especially if the plant is exposed to draughts. Leaves very easily scorch and brown under full sunlight, so your plant should always be moderately shaded. Water and humidity are important; both too wet and too dry conditions can damage the roots and the foliage The compost should always be moist but not sodden.

Greenfly is one of the few likely pests; spray them with a pyrethrum-based insecticide. Mealy bug may also appear; wipe away the fluffy white patches with methylated spirit on a soft cloth or brush.

Species

Rhoeo spathacea (also known as *R.discolor*), commonly called Moses in the Cradle or the Boat Lily, grows to 12-16in (30-40cm) as a houseplant, forming a rosette of upright, strap-shaped leaves, up to 1ft (0.3m) long; the leaves are a glossy, metallic dark green on the upper surface and rich purple underneath. As the plant ages, the rosette extends into a short stem and side shoots frequently appear from near the base. At the leaf bases grow small white flowers 'cradled' within purple, boat-shaped bracts — hence the common names. These can appear at any time. The flowers are short-lived, but the bracts remain decorative for months. There is a beautiful, variegated-leaved variety, 'Vittata', *above and below*.

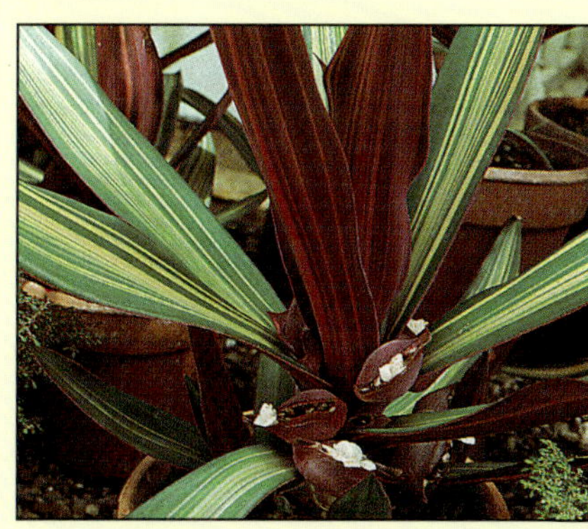

Saintpaulia

Family name: **Gesneriaceae**

Common name: **African Violet**

Care Straightforward	**Height** 3-4in (8-10cm)	**Flower** Any time
Light Bright indirect	**Spread** 6-9in (15-23cm)	**Humidity** High
Price Cheap	**Shape** Rosette	**Availability** Common
Temp. Min 55°F (13°C)	Ideal 70°F (21°C)	Max 75°F (24°C)

African Violets are arguably the most popular of all houseplants. Their compactness, their brilliant colouring and, above all, their ability to produce abundant, colourful flowers at almost any time of year, have combined to make them a world-wide favourite. The group consists of around a dozen evergreen, perennial species, of central African origin; only a few of these are of interest to the average houseplant enthusiast, who is likely to prefer one of the many striking modern varieties and hybrids. These flowers come in every shade of blue plus whites, pinks, reds and bicolours, in single and double forms, star-shaped, fringed, frilly-edged or crested.

The most important species, and the one responsible for most of the numerous hybrids and varieties to be found nowadays, is *Saintpaulia ionantha, below.* Plants of the true species have beautiful, violet-blue, single flowers with contrasting bright yellow eyes, appearing throughout the year but most freely from June to October. Though the flowers are of course the main attraction, the deep green, velvety, heart-shaped leaves are also very appealing.

When they were first introduced as houseplants in the 1920s, African Violets were notoriously difficult to grow. Since then, however, commercial growers have developed much tougher, freer-flowering strains, and under the right conditions — essentially, good light, steady warmth and reasonable moisture — plants should continue to grow and thrive, producing flowers throughout the year.

Spring and summer care

African Violets do best when slightly potbound; using a lime-free peat-based compost, pot plants on in the spring into slightly larger containers only when the roots completely fill the current one, up to a final pot size of 5-6in (13-15cm). After that, repot established plants in April every other year. Large trailing types are best grown in hanging baskets so that their stems have plenty of room to hang down. Throughout the year, remove dead flowers and damaged leaves immediately, taking care to remove the whole of the leaf stalk; if any of the stub remains it may rot.

Your plant will flourish at a steady temperature between 65-75°F (18-24°C) — it's important to avoid any sudden fluctuations. Keep it draught-free, in very bright light but out of direct sunlight which can scorch both leaves and flowers. African Violets do very well in artificial light; to grow them entirely by artificial light, place plants 1ft (0.3m) below two 40-watt fluorescent tubes for about 12 hours a day.

African Violets are easily damaged by overwatering. Moisten the compost thoroughly, then wait until the surface is dry before watering again. Keep water off the foliage to avoid the leaves becoming marked.

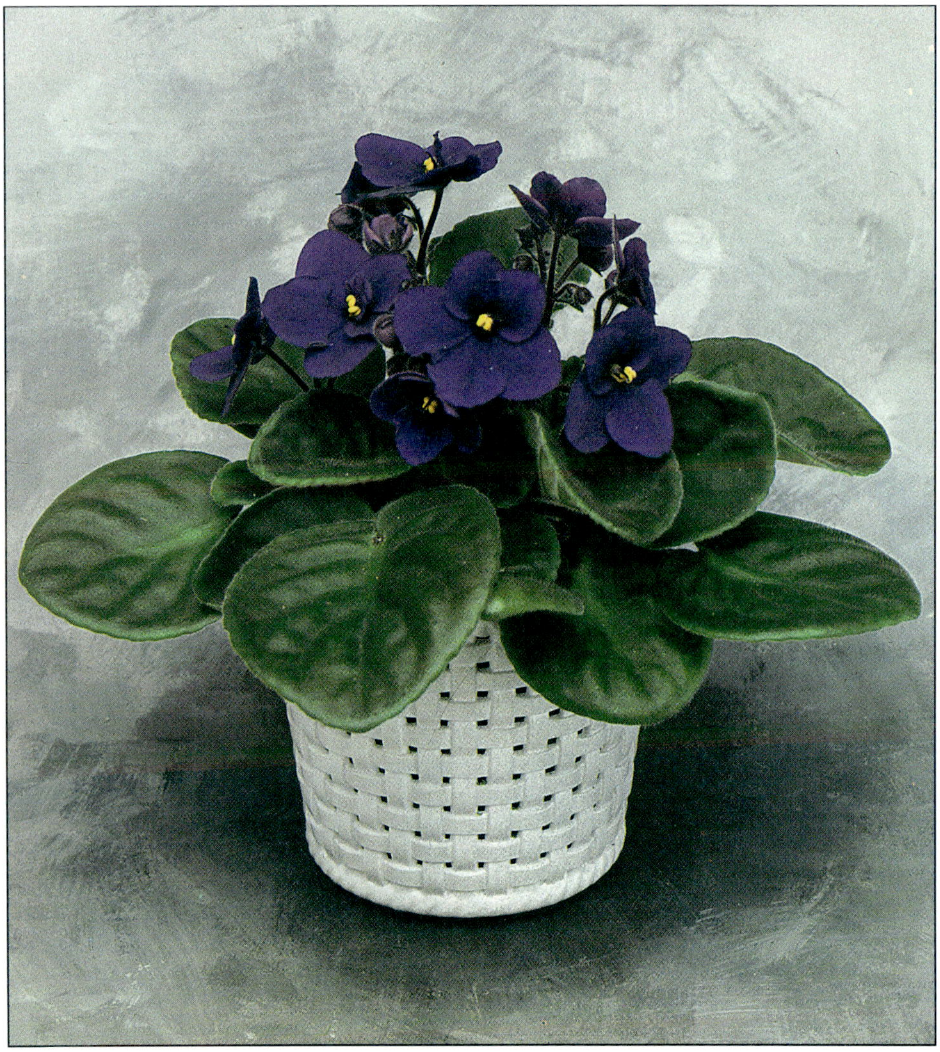

The African Violet is one of the most popular of all houseplants.

Buying Guide

If possible, choose a plant sold in a protective cardboard collar — it's much less likely to have been damaged in transit from the nursery.

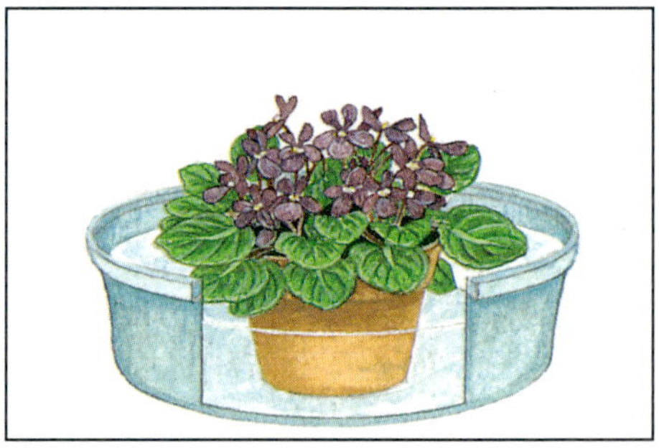

Water an African Violet by standing it in a bowl of water for a few minutes; don't wet the leaves though, or they may rot.

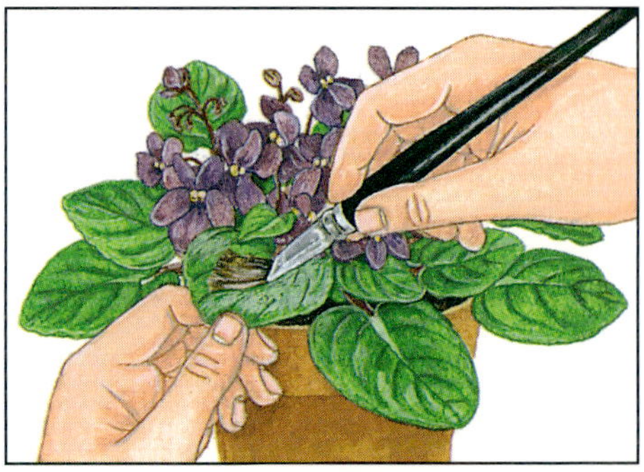

Don't wipe dusty leaves with a damp cloth; instead use a small, dry paint brush to remove any dirt.

The best method of watering is from below; stand the container in a shallow bowl of water until the compost is thoroughly soaked, then allow it to drain before returning it to its position.

Regular feeding is most important, especially if flowers are to be seen throughout most of the year. African Violets are quite greedy plants for their size and they will soon use up the nutrients contained in the compost, so add a liquid fertiliser to the water every three weeks. High humidity is essential, but since mist spraying can damage the foliage, the best way of achieving this is to stand pots on trays of moist pebbles — but not actually in water.

Autumn and winter care

Winter temperatures should not fall below 55°F (13°C) at any time and 60-65°F (16-18°C) is better. Otherwise, conditions should be much the same as those recommended for spring and summer. Keep your plant brightly-lit but out of direct sunlight. Water only when it is dry, then soak well by standing the plant pot in a bowl of water until the surface of the compost is moist, then draining thoroughly; leave the surface of the compost to dry out again before repeating the process. Continue to feed every three or four weeks and maintain a degree of humidity.

Propagation

The easiest method of propagating African Violets is from leaf cuttings. Remove a complete leaf with its stalk in April or May, trim the stalk down to a length of about 1-1½in (2.5-4cm) and insert it into moistened peat-based compost, with the blade just at soil level. Keep lightly shaded, in a propagator or clear polythene bag, at a temperature of 65-70°F (18-21°C). After about six weeks new plantlets will begin to emerge from the base of the leafstalks; over the next four weeks gradually uncover the plantlets for increasingly longer periods, give just enough water to prevent the compost from drying out and, once a week, add a little liquid fertiliser — about one-eighth of the recommended amount. Then carefully pot the plantlets up singly and treat as mature plants. An alternative, if less reliable method, of rooting is to stand the cutting in a glass of water — the bottom of the leaf should just touch the water; keep it warm and lightly shaded. When plantlets begin to appear after two to three weeks and roots visibly form, they can be potted.

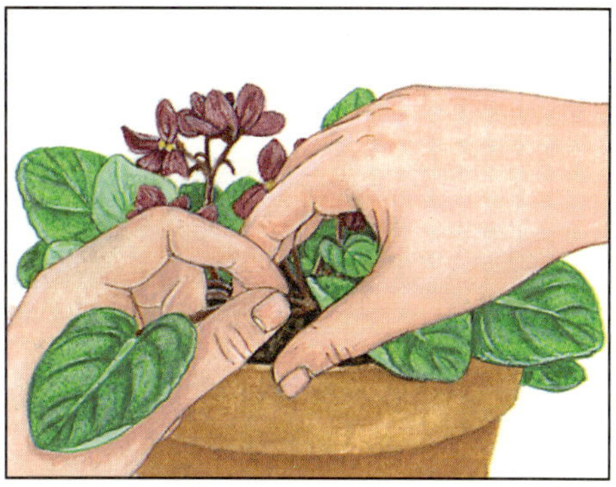

To take leaf cuttings of an African Violet remove a leaf and trim its stem to 1-1½in (2.5-4cm).

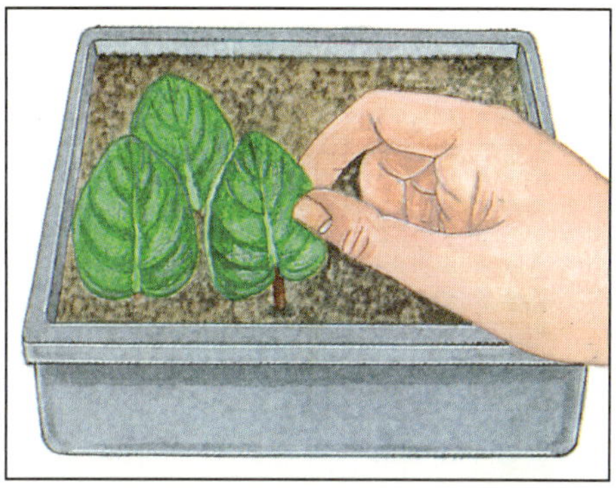

With a pencil, make a small hole in a tray of potting compost, then insert the cutting up to the base of its leaf blade.

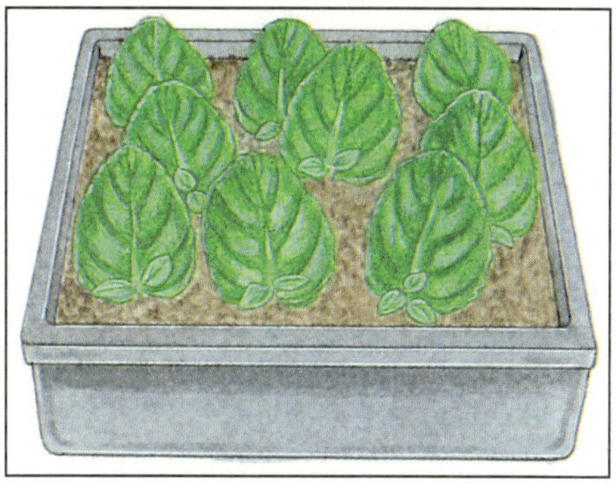

When new plantlets have developed harden them off gradually and make sure their compost never dries out.

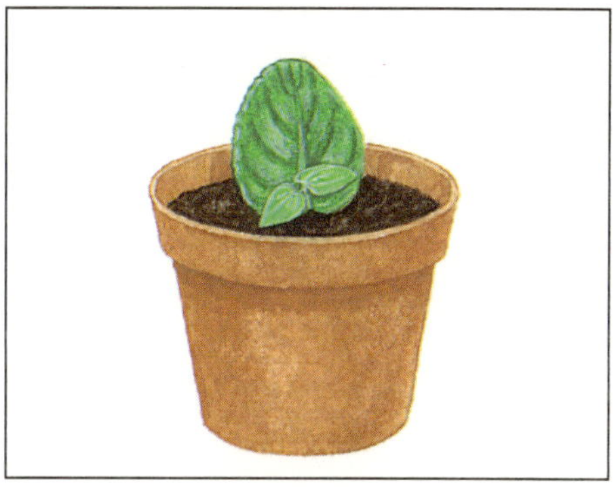

After a week or so, pot up the rooted plantlets and keep them out of bright light for a few days.

Trouble Shooter

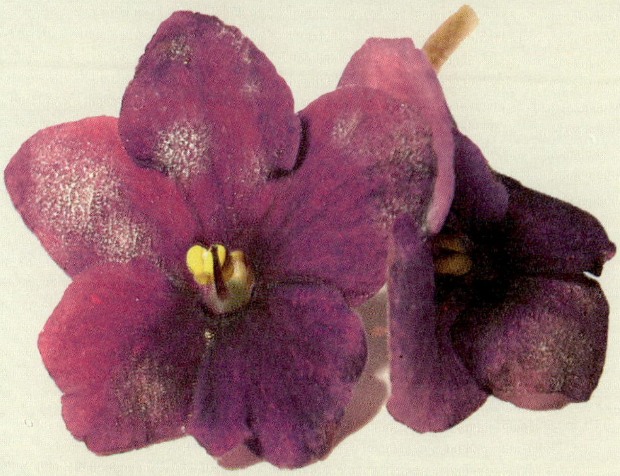

Despite a reputation for being difficult, African Violets should not present problems as long as their basic needs are considered. Direct sun will discolour the leaves; straw-coloured patches will appear and the edges may turn yellow. Leaves may shrivel or wilt and turn yellow if conditions are too dry for too long — either low humidity or insufficient watering. Too much water, however, can easily lead to the complete collapse of the plant from fungus diseases such as mildew (*above*). Water from below to avoid wetting the foliage; leave the pot to drain before returning it to its position, and allow at least the top ½in (1cm) of the compost to dry out before watering again.

If flowers are not being produced in profusion — or at all — the most likely explanation is insufficient feeding; repot your plant in fresh compost and maintain regular feeding. Poor flowering could also be due to insufficient light, especially in winter.

African Violets are susceptible to attack from greenfly, mealy bug and cyclamen mite. Care must be taken over the choice of pesticide, since the plants react badly to some common insecticides; also, sprays should be avoided as they may damage the foliage. Phostrogen Plant Pins, which are inserted directly into the compost, are recommended; if these are unavailable, check the label on other products to see if they are suitable.

Species

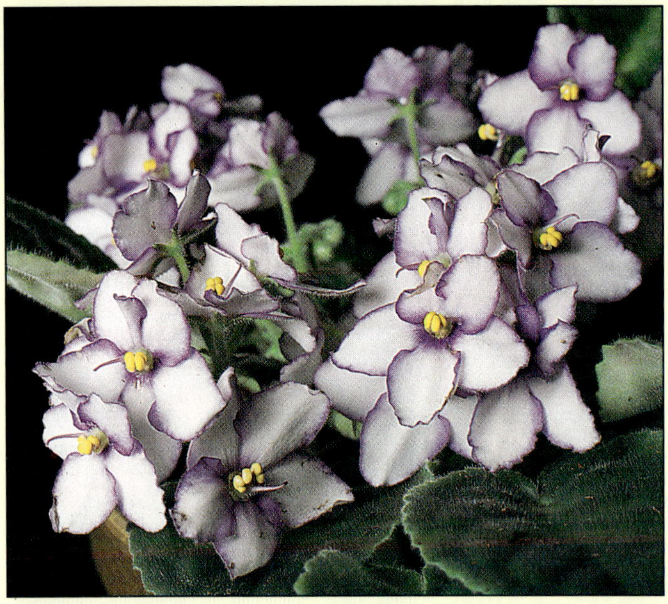

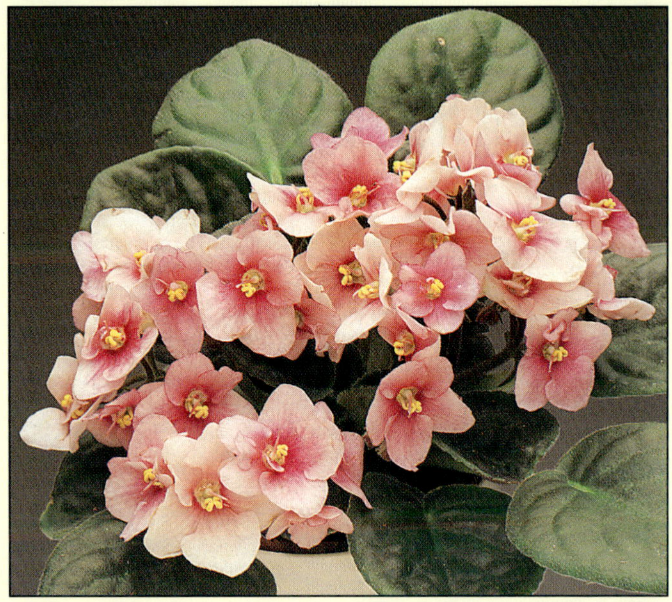

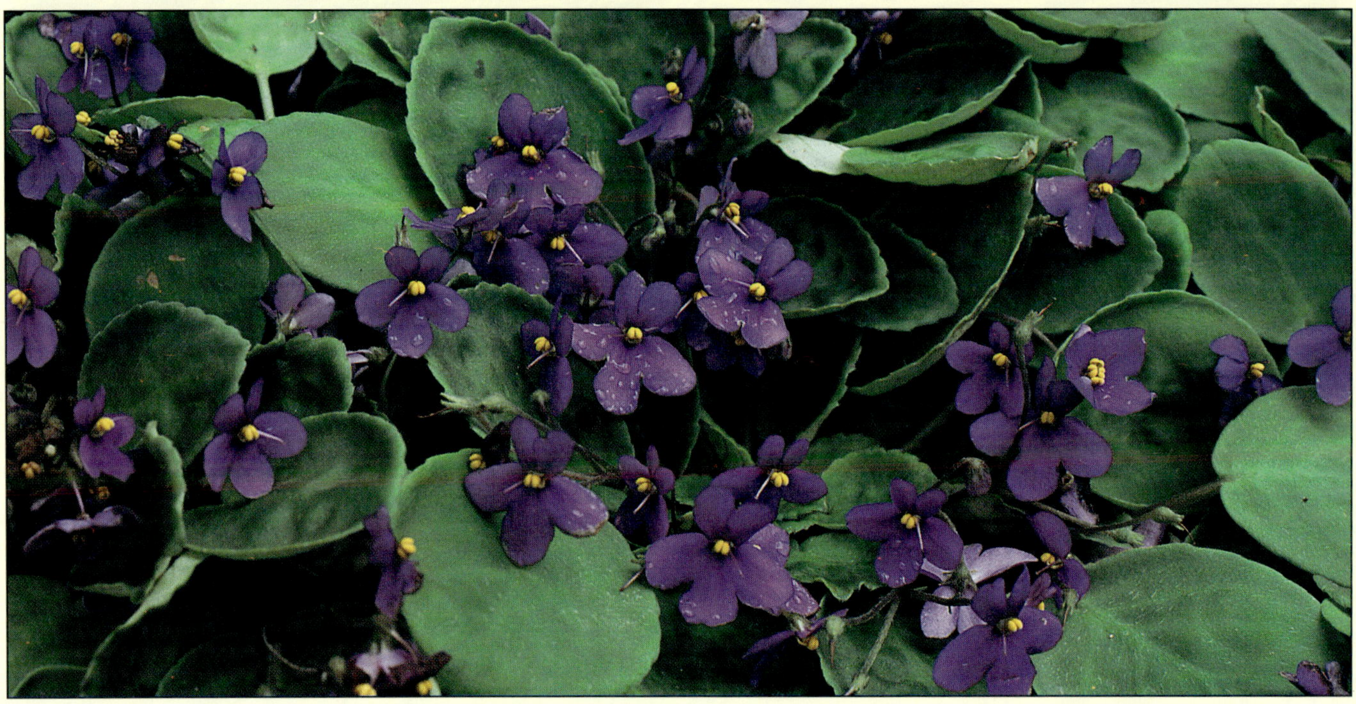

Saintpaulia ionantha is the best known species and a parent of many of the countless varieties and hybrids to be found (see below). Standing 3-4in (8-10cm) high, with a spread of 6-9in (15-23cm), it forms a rosette of slightly fleshy, heart-shaped leaves up to 3in (8cm) long on 2½in (7cm) long stalks; velvety in texture, the leaves are deep green and sometimes have a reddish tinge to the undersides. Flowers can appear almost all year round, but especially between June and October, in groups of between two and eight, on stalks up to 5in (13cm) long; measuring about 1in (2.5cm) across, the flowers, which are made up of a single layer of petals, are violet-blue with tiny pollen sacs at the centre giving a conspicuous golden-yellow eye.

S.confusa, *above*, also known as *S.diplotricha*, is another important species which has been involved in the breeding of many popular hybrids. It has downy, light-green leaves which are nearly round and toothed along the margins, 1½in (4cm) long, on 3in (8cm) long stalks. The 4in (10cm) long flower stalks carry up to four pale violet flowers, each about 1in (2.5cm) in diameter.

S.grotei is a creeping, trailing species and an ancestor of many of the trailing African Violet forms. It is a good choice for a hanging basket, with creeping, branching stems growing up to 8in (20cm) in length. Leafstalks up to 10in (25cm) long bear nearly round, 3in (8cm) long, bright green leaves with saw-toothed edges and

Species

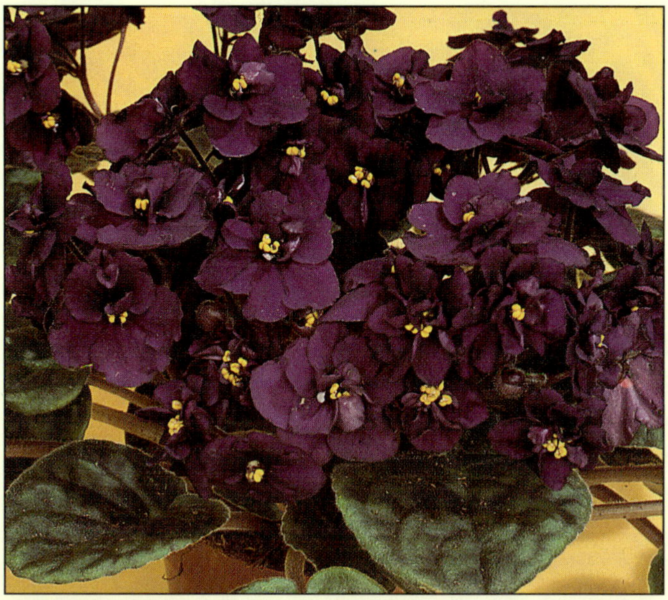
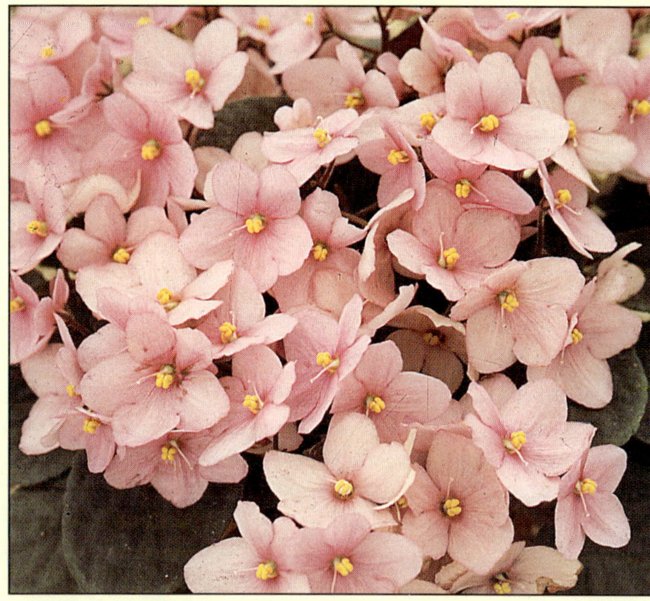
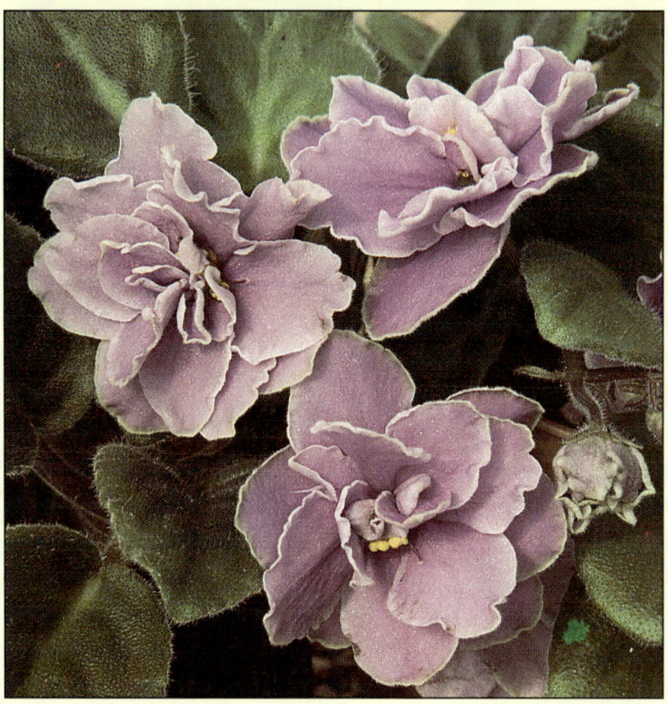
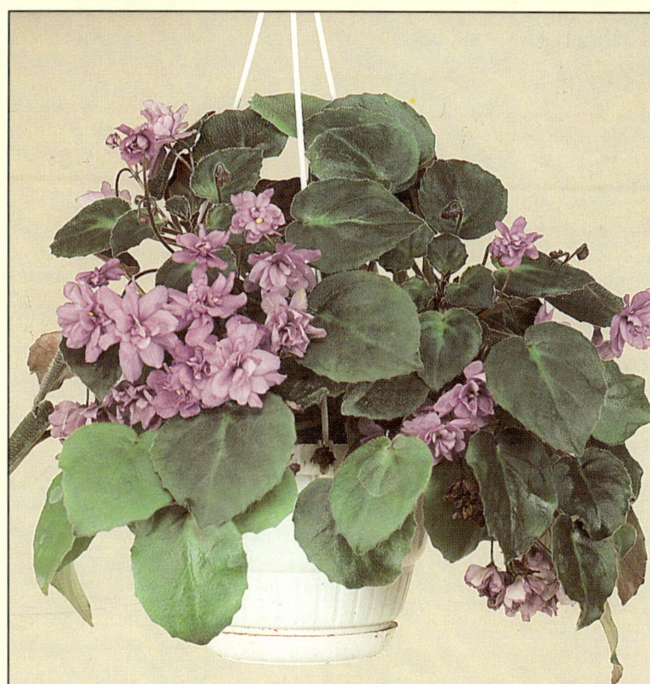

covered in short, velvety hairs; the small flowers, clustering on stalks up to 5in (13cm) in length, are a mauvish-blue shaded to a deep violet at the margins.

Saintpaulia hybrids come in many shapes and sizes. Attempts have been made to categorise the types into 'strains'. One of the most popular is the 'Ballet' group; these hybrids are especially easy to grow. They form rosettes up to about 1ft (0.3m) across, with deep green, oval leaves and flowers with ruffled lobes. 'Ballet Eva', *above left*, has semi-double flowers in an attractive shade of blue, while 'Ballet Anna' has single flowers with frilled margins, in salmon-pink and magenta. The 'Rhapsodie' series, *top left*, is equally popular and, like 'Ballet', very easy to grow, reaching up to about 1ft (0.3m) across, with dark green, roundish leaves and five-lobed or many-lobed flowers, in pink, blue or purple. A popular, but unclassified, hybrid is 'Laura', *opposite, top right.*

In recent years many charming, miniature varieties have captured the imagination of houseplant growers. Sometimes known as the 'Fairy' series, *top right,* they cover the same wide range of flower shapes and colours but the foliage and flowers are much smaller than the usual African Violets. 'Little Delight', *opposite, top left,* for example, forms a miniature rosette, under 6in (15cm) across; the many-petalled flowers are white with purple edges. 'Jet Trail', *above right*, is a good example of a miniature trailer, with clusters of dark lavender, double star-shaped flowers.

Sansevieria

Family name: **Dracaenaceae**

Common name:
Mother-in-law's Tongue

Care Easy	**Height** 1-4ft (0.3-1.2m)	**Flower** Spring and summer
Light Sunny	**Spread** 9-12in (23-30cm)	**Humidity** None
Price Middle range	**Shape** Upright	**Availability** Garden centres
Temp. Min 50°F (10°C)	Ideal 70°F (21°C)	Max 85°F (29°C)

This very accommodating and easy plant is universally popular: with its decorative banded and variegated leaves, and the ease with which it can be propagated, it certainly deserves its high reputation. The whole group of plants in fact contains considerable variation, and its wide range of common names bears this out: Good Luck Plant, Devil's Tongue, Bowstring Hemp, and of course Mother-in-law's Tongue, to name just a few.

All of them come from Africa and Asia. For many years there was doubt as to whether they belonged to the Lily family or the Agave family. This conflict is now resolved, and the answer is neither — they have been categorised with the Dracaena group.

Sansevierias come in two main types: tall with erect, sword-shaped leaves, and low-growing, rosette-shaped ones. The leaves of both types, slightly thickened and attractively patterned, arise directly from a thick rhizome that runs just below the surface of the compost. Take care never to damage the points of the leaves, because leaves with broken tips stop growing.

Flowers appear on many varieties from mid to late summer — they aren't very glamorous and don't last very long, but the bracts from which they grow are attractive, last for several weeks, and the flowers are sometimes followed by colourful fruits.

The best known of the tall plants is *Sansevieria trifasciata, above right,* known as Mother-in-law's Tongue. It has thick, sword-shaped leaves, which are usually green with lighter cross bands, and bears greenish-white flowers on bracts. The variety *S.t.laurentii* has deep golden-yellow margins along the leaves' entire length. *S.t.hahnii* is the commonest of the compact Sansevierias and forms a rosette of spirally arranged, pointed oval, deep green leaves with lighter cross-banding. All of these plants accept a wide range of light conditions, and can also withstand periods of drought.

Spring and summer care

If the plant has outgrown its pot, you should pot it on to one size larger container in March or April, using John Innes No 2 or 3 compost.

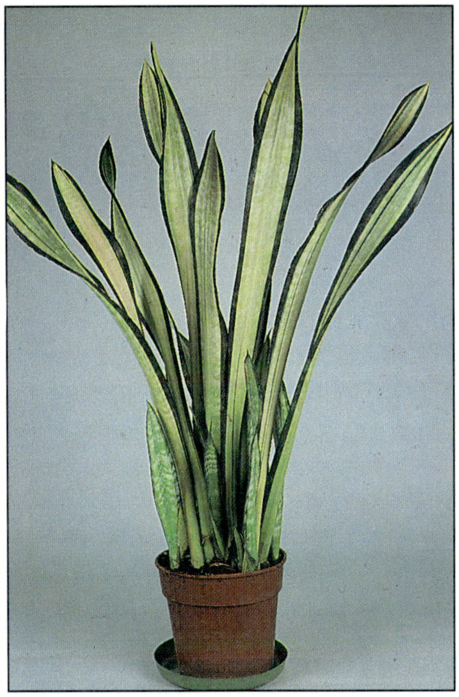

One of the toughest houseplants.

Make certain that the pot is well crocked to provide good drainage. In years when you don't pot the plant on, you should topdress by removing the first 2in (5cm) or so of soil and replacing it with fresh.

Temperatures in summer can rise to 70-75°F (21-24°C), and a really bright position is best, even full sun. Very few species will be happy in shade even for a short time.

Sansevierias should be treated like succulents when it comes to watering. Leave them until the compost is just about dry, and then water them thoroughly — this will probably be about every two weeks, but more often in really hot weather. Never overwater them, since the rhizome in the compost is easily susceptible to rot. Add liquid fertiliser to the water every three to four weeks.

Autumn and winter care

Temperatures between October and March should be kept at 55-65°F (13-18°C). Keep your plant in the brightest position possible. Very little watering is necessary at this time, perhaps about once a month when the weather is at its brightest. No humidity is necessary, so do not mist spray, but make sure you keep your plant out of draughts.

Propagation

Sansevierias may be propagated in various ways, all of them easy and rewarding.

When tall plants are at least 6in (15cm) high, and rosette plants 2in (5cm) high, they can very easily be propagated by division — this is especially useful if the plant is getting overcrowded. Divide in spring, before new growth has started. Knock the plant from its pot, and tease the potting compost out carefully from the roots.

For tall plants with sword-shaped leaves, cut the rhizome with a sharp knife into two or three divisions (depending on its size), taking some leaves and some roots into each. For rosette-shaped plants, you also cut the rhizome, taking into each section one of the developing rosettes that have begun to grow along the stolons that branch out from the main rhizome. Dust the cuts with sulphur powder, insert the sections into the usual potting compost (see 'Spring and summer care'), and keep at 70°F (21°C) until they are well established. Plants propagated by division will always grow to look identical to the parent plant in colour and patterning.

Leaf cuttings (see *below*) are taken in the summer, when the plant is growing sturdily. Remove a leaf with a sharp knife and slice it across into 2in (5cm) sections, laying them out so that you'll remember which end is the top and which the bottom. Allow the cuts to callus over for a week or so, and then plant the sections, the right way up, in moist compost — you can plant two or three together in a 3in (7cm) pot. Keep them at 70°F (21°C), and they'll soon put out roots. With most species, leaf cuttings will reproduce the parent plant, except for the variegated *Sansevieria trifasciata* — in this case the patterns will not come through and the resulting plant would be plain green. It is therefore best to reproduce this type by division.

If you want to grow a rare species, you can sow seed. In February or March scatter the seeds on a mixture of three parts compost and one part coarse sand, just slightly moistened. Keep them at 75-80°F (24-27°C), preferably in a propagator or a sealed clear polythene bag. When seedlings are large enough to be easily handled, uncover them and pot them up individually.

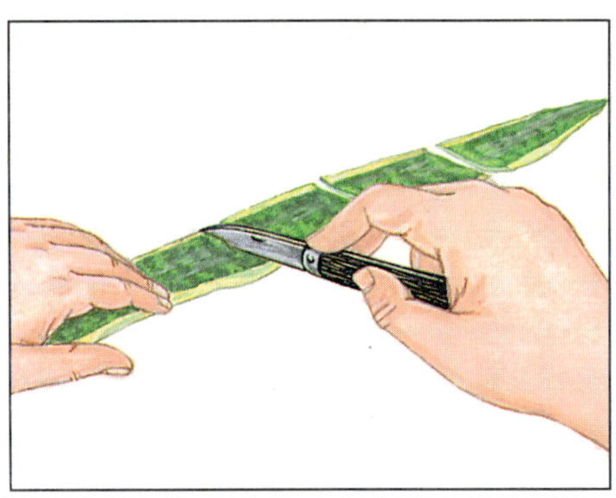

To take leaf cuttings of Mother-in-law's Tongue, cut 2in (5cm) lengths from a leaf, and allow them to callus over.

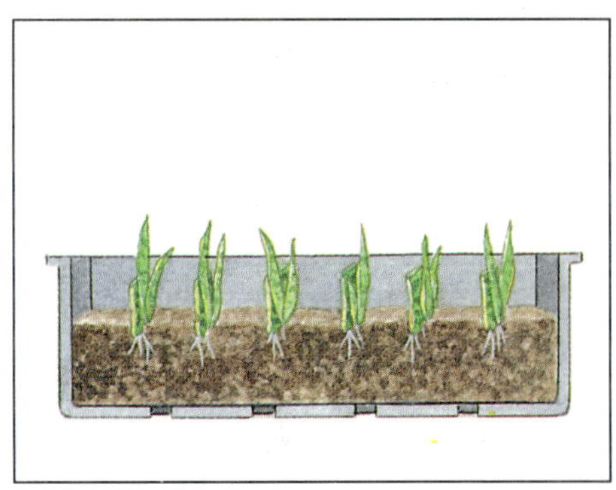

Insert the lower half of each leaf section into potting compost and new plantlets will grow from the cut surfaces.

Species

Sansevieria trifasciata, Mother-in-law's Tongue, comes from Transvaal and Natal. Its green leaves are slightly concave on the upper surface and attractively mottled and banded in greyish-white, with a wide, deep green margin along the edges. It bears clusters of small, greenish-white flowers in spring and summer on tall, erect bracts.

S.t.laurentii, below right, is one of the most popular types, with markings similar to the species but with golden yellow margins. The leaves of both of these plants can grow up to 4ft (1.2m) tall, though they are more likely to be 12-18in (30-45cm) on most houseplants.

S.t.hahnii, below, Bird's Nest Sansevieria, is very different in appearance: it grows small and compact, its leaves spirally arranged to make a rosette. The leaves are about 6in (15cm) long, deep green with lighter cross-banding. It has several varieties, including 'Golden Hahnii', with golden yellow margins, and 'Silver Hahnii', cross-banded and mottled in green and whitish-silver.

S.cylindrica is a tall species primarily from Kenya and its neighbouring countries in east Africa. It has thick, rigid, deep green leaves almost completely cylindrical in shape; they are about 1in (2.5cm) thick and up to 3ft (0.9m) long, with just a narrow furrow down the middle from tip to base. It bears pinkish flowers in spring and summer.

S.grandis is more unusual — it is epiphytic, living in the branches of trees instead of on the ground. A loose rosette shape, it comes from the coast of Somalia, and has green oval leaves, 4-6in (10-15cm) wide and 8-10in (20-25cm) long, cross-banded in darker green with the margins edged in red. Because it is epiphytic, its stolons, bearing developing rosettes, trail down from the base of the main rosette, making it a very attractive plant for growing in a hanging basket.

S.scabrifolia, from Mozambique and Zimbabwe, is much smaller, with greyish-green, narrow-leaved rosettes in clusters, only 6in (15cm) or so tall. It is one of the few species able to withstand shade.

S.liberica comes from west Africa, with leaves up to 2ft (0.6m) tall — stiff, erect and sword-shaped. They are banded with wide white or greenish-white lines and the margins are edged with red. A tall flower spike bears a dense cluster of white flowers in spring and summer.

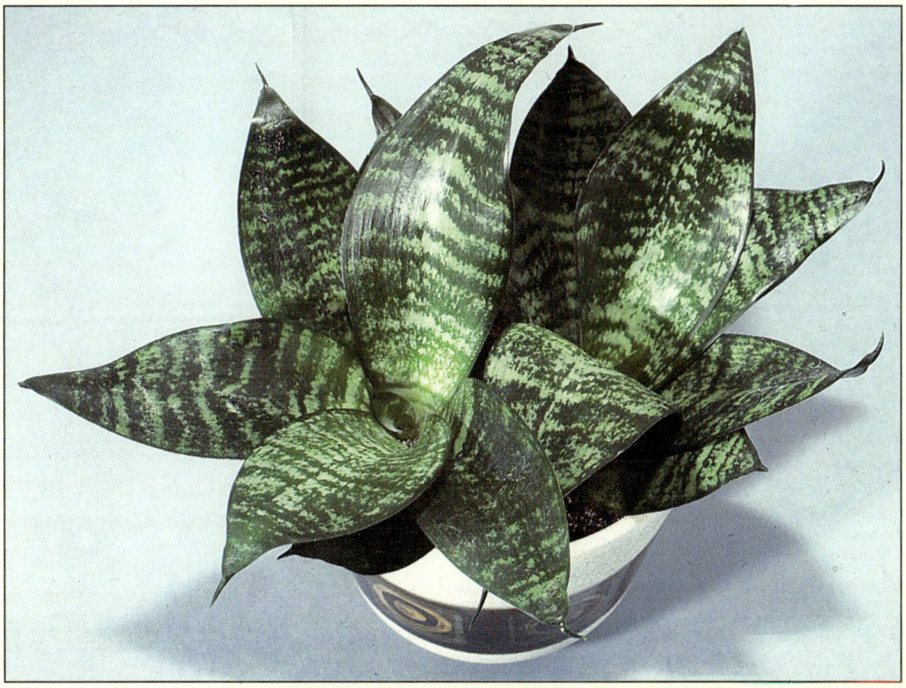

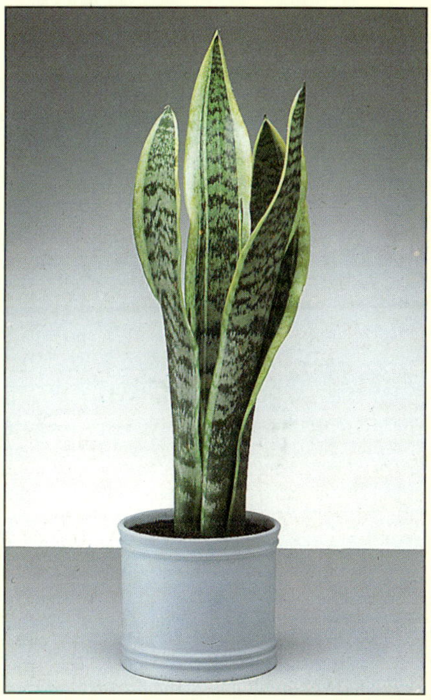

Trouble Shooter

If leaves start to rot at the base and brownish marks appear on them, especially in cold weather, this is a sign of root rot, caused by overwatering. Remove the plant from the pot, cut away any parts of the rhizome that have rotted and let it dry off for at least a week. Remove any damaged leaves also with a sharp knife, dust fungicidal sulphur on the cuts, and replant. Remember, in future, only to water when the compost is dry.

If variegated plants start to lose their patterning and become green, move them to a brighter position. Sansevierias need good light to keep their attractive variegations.

White fluffy patches on the leaves are mealy bugs and pale, brownish warts are a sign of infestation by scale insect; wipe both away with a soft cloth or brush dipped in methylated spirit, or spray every three weeks with a malathion-based insecticide.

Buying Guide

Before buying, check that the leaf bases are completely sound and show no sign of rotting — an indication that the plant is or has at some time been overwatered. Look also for damage at the edges and tips of the leaves; tall plants, especially if they're growing in lightweight pots, tend to be top-heavy so can easily be toppled over — so if you find a perfect plant in a plastic pot it's a wise precaution to repot it in a clay pot when you get it home.

Saxifraga

Family name: **Saxifragaceae**

Common names: **Saxifrage, Mother of Thousands, Strawberry Geranium**

Care Easy	**Height** 9in (23cm)	**Flower** Summer
Light Bright	**Spread** 6in (15cm)	**Humidity** Mist spray in hot weather
Price Cheap	**Shape** Rosette	**Availability** Common
Temp. Min 45°F (7°C)	Ideal 65°F (18°C)	Max 80°F (27°C)

This is a very large, popular group of attractive little plants, most commonly associated with out-of-door rockeries. There are about 350 different species in all, many of which are widespread in parts of Europe and Asia and, to a lesser extent, in North America.

There is only one species, however, which is suitable for use as a houseplant. This is *Saxifraga stolonifera* (formerly known as *S. sarmentosa*), *above right*, which bears the apt common name of Mother of Thousands because it produces so many offspring.

It has loose rosettes of tough, broad-bladed leaves, shaped and marked very much like many Geraniums, which explains its other common name, the Strawberry Geranium. The leaves are deep green, almost circular and up to 4in (10cm) across, with lobed margins, silvery veining and marbling, and light reddish-purple undersides. Its main attraction is that it produces attractive long trailing shoots which resemble strawberry runners and bear miniature plants at their tips. These runners, which can be as long as 3ft (0.9m), should be allowed to hang freely, so this plant is best grown in a hanging basket or wall display. A profusion of graceful flower spikes, up to 18in (45cm) long, is produced in summer. They carry loose clusters of tiny, star-shaped flowers that are pink or white with a yellow centre.

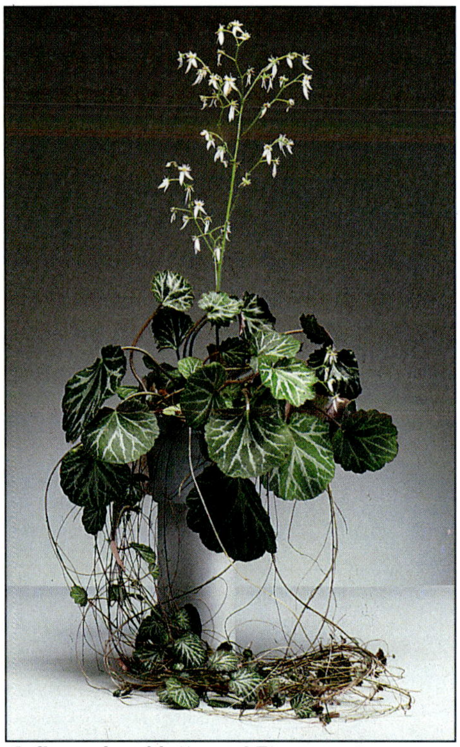

A flowering Mother of Thousands.

Spring and summer care

Repot in March, using John Innes No 2 compost in a well crocked pot, and move into a pot one size larger as and when required. If your Saxifrage is in a hanging basket, line the basket with a thick layer of sphagnum moss, then fill in with compost. Good drainage is essential, whether in a pot or basket.

Water freely so that the compost is always kept moist — in the warmest months this may mean as many as two or three times a week — while occasional overhead spraying will keep the foliage looking fresh. Add a weak liquid fertiliser to the water once every four to six weeks. Summer temperatures of 60-65°F (16-18°C) are satisfactory, but if indoor temperatures rise above this you need to increase the level of humidity by mist spraying or standing pots on trays of dampened pebbles, or suspending dishes of water under hanging baskets. Never allow plants to remain in hot, full sun for any length of time, but do not put in dense shade either. A little direct sunlight — say, an hour or two of early morning sun every day, or a little longer for the variegated *S.s.* 'Tricolor' — helps Saxifrages to keep their colouring.

Autumn and winter care

The temperature can fall as low as 45°F (7°C), but make sure that your plant remains frost-free. Keep in filtered light away from direct, bright sunlight. Water occasionally — always allowing the soil to dry out before watering again — and do not attempt to keep the compost moist all the time. Ensure good air circulation at all times.

Trouble Shooter

Troubles will definitely occur if plants are allowed to stay dry for any length of time, which will cause leaves to shrivel. Too high a temperature in winter can also prove a problem, particularly if the plants are also kept on the dry side.

Greenfly is the most likely pest, and should be dealt with as soon as signs appear or the leaves will become sticky and may eventually look sooty. Use a pyrethrum-based or systemic insecticide, and follow the manufacturer's instructions.

Buying Guide

It is perfectly normal for Mother of Thousands to have no 'babies' when you buy them — or they may have just one or two developing red runners. Plantlets will quickly form if you care for your plant correctly.

Propagation

This is best done in March or April by removing small offsets from the runners and potting them up individually in 2-3in (5-8cm) pots containing equal parts of peat and sand. These will take a few weeks to root in a lightly shaded position in a warm room and should be watered just enough to make the rooting mixture barely moist. Once they have rooted, they can be moved into larger pots of John Innes No 2 and treated as mature plants.

An alternative method of propagation is to leave young plantlets attached to the parent plant and to peg them down in nearby pots. Cut the stems when they have rooted and there are signs of fresh growth, then treat them as established plants.

Species

Saxifraga stolonifera, commonly known as Mother of Thousands or Strawberry Geranium, is a stemless plant of Asian origin that grows to no more than about 9in (23cm) tall. Its outstanding feature is the production of long, slender red runners which bear miniature plantlets at their tips, and it is best grown in a hanging basket where these can hang freely. *S.s.* 'Tricolor', *right*, is a more colourful variety, which is generally smaller and more compact, and has rich variegations of white, pink and green with red edges as long as it is kept in good light. Unfortunately, however, it is less vigorous, in terms of both rate of growth and plantlet production, and it is also more tender.

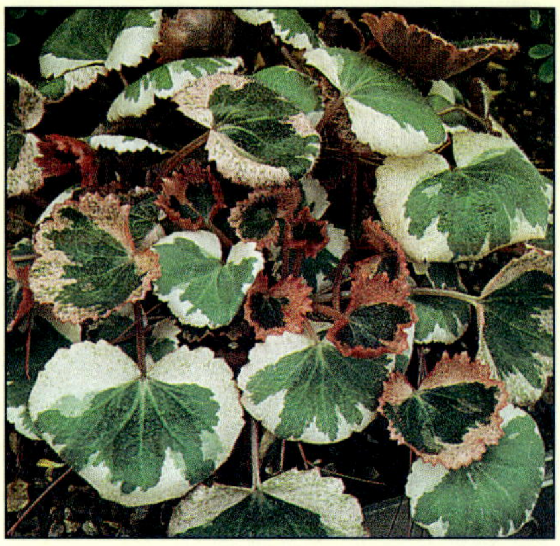

Schefflera

Family name: **Araliaceae**

Common name:
Umbrella Tree

Care Easy	**Height** 6-8ft (1.8-2.4m)	**Flower** Rare
Light Bright indirect	**Spread** 4ft (1.2m)	**Humidity** Mist spray in hot weather
Price Middle range	**Shape** Spreading bush	**Availability** Garden centres
Temp. Min 50°F (10°C)	Ideal 65°F (18°C)	Max 80°F (27°C)

This very handsome, somewhat palm-like plant is easy to grow, and its elegant, long-stemmed leaves will make an attractive adornment for any room. *Schefflera actinophylla, below,* is called the Umbrella Tree because of the way its leaves grow. Each leaf is subdivided into several leaflets, which fall downwards from the tip of an erect stem, giving the appearance of an open umbrella. It is similar to, but much bigger than, its close cousin Heptapleurum, whose more delicate appearance is reflected in the common name of Parasol Plant (see page 287).

In its natural habitat in Australasia and Indonesia, the Umbrella Tree can grow to quite a sizeable tree — even in cultivation it can reach 6ft (1.8m), if its roots are not constrained. It is a good choice for a position with no direct light, and doesn't mind a cool temperature. Looked after with care, it can make a really outstanding houseplant.

Spring and summer care

Pot on young Scheffleras every year in early spring, using John Innes No 2 compost and one size larger pot each time, to a final pot size of about 6-8in (15-20cm). After that they'll only need topdressing every two years by replacing the top 2in (5cm) or so of soil with fresh. If you want to encourage your plant to grow really tall — and you have a sufficiently high ceiling — continue to pot it on every two years into one size larger container each time.

Summer temperatures can rise to 70°F (21°C) or even a little higher. Keep your plant in bright light but out of direct sun. Water freely — in hot weather as much as two to three times a week — adding a weak solution of liquid fertiliser to the water every two to three weeks from April to October. Mist spray regularly during hot weather to increase humidity, preferably in the early morning or after sunset. If the leaves get dusty, wipe them gently with a damp sponge.

Autumn and winter care

Try to keep temperatures around 55°F (13°C). Aim for a really bright position, but avoid full sun. Equally, don't put your Schefflera in full shade — remember, it's naturally a forest plant, and is used to fairly bright, but diffused, light. Continue watering throughout the winter, keeping the compost just moist. Mist spray from overhead occasionally — say every week or so. Provide good air circulation but avoid cold draughts.

Propagation

Propagation is best from seed, sown in early spring using a good seed compost. Keep the seeds at a temperature of 70-75°F (21-24°C), preferably in a propagator, and keep them well shaded and the compost moist. It's a good idea to remove the seedlings from the propagator for an hour or so each day to prevent stagnation of the air or the soil. When the seedlings are large enough to handle, prick them out separately into small pots, using the normal potting compost (see 'Spring and summer care') then treat them just as you would a mature plant.

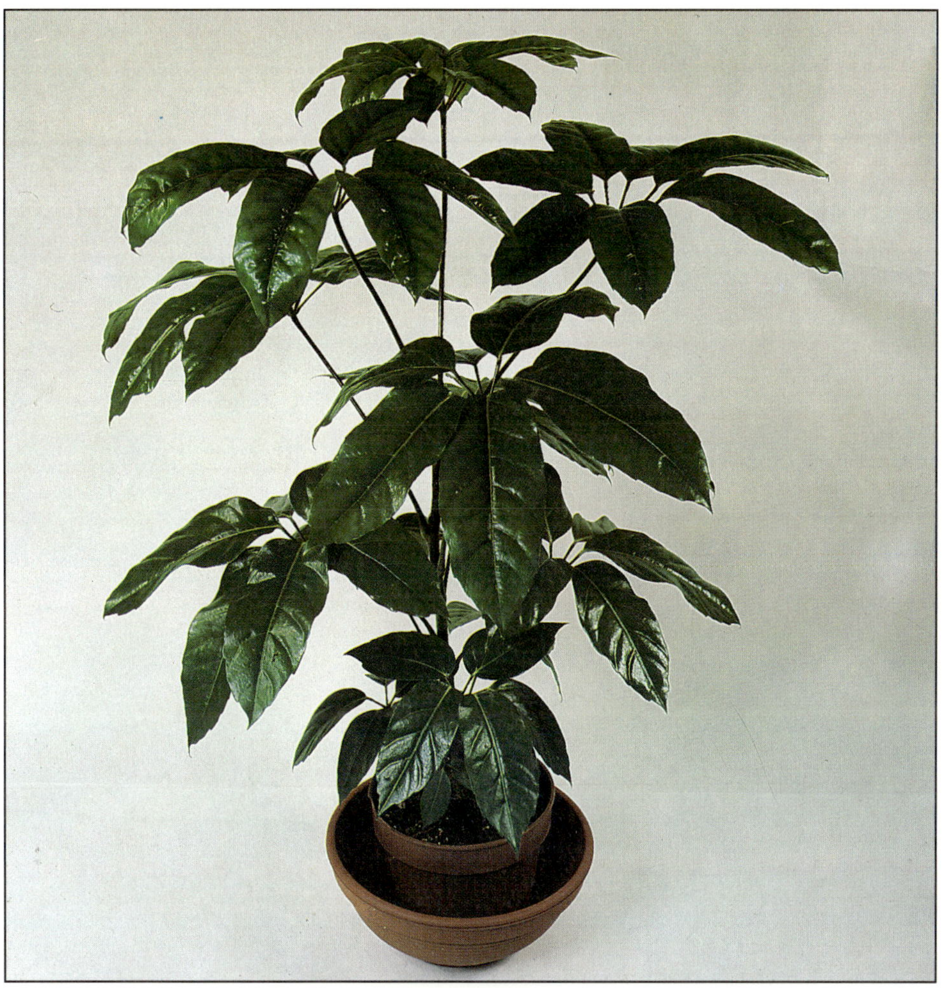

The Umbrella Tree is an excellent choice if you want a large, easy-going plant.

Species

Schefflera actinophylla (also known as *Brassaia actinophylla*), from Australasia and Indonesia, is called the Umbrella Tree due to the attractive spreading of its foliage. It is slow-growing, with a single stem and glossy, olive green leaves, divided into between three and five oval leaflets. These radiate out from a central point like the spokes of an umbrella, and grow up to 1ft (0.3m) long. Mature Scheffleras may produce a tall cluster of deep red flowers in summer, followed by purplish red fruits, but it is rare for them to flower indoors. The plant can grow up to 6ft (1.8m) or more indoors if given a large enough tub to allow for spreading roots, or it can be contained to a smaller, bushier plant if restricted to an 8in (20cm) pot.

Trouble Shooter

If the leaves wilt or droop, this will be caused by low temperatures, overwatering, underwatering or inadequate feeding. If the soil is soggy, let it dry out and restrict watering in future. If mealy bugs or scale insects attack, wipe them away with a soft brush or cloth dipped in methylated spirit. Get rid of greenfly in summer with a pyrethrum-based insecticide spray.

Schlumbergera

Family name: **Cactaceae**

Common names:
Christmas Cactus,
Claw Cactus/Crab Cactus

Care Easy	**Height** 1ft (0.3m)	**Flower** Winter
Light Light shade	**Spread** 1ft (0.3m)	**Humidity** Mist spray regularly
Price Cheap	**Shape** Arching bush	**Availability** Common
Temp. Min 55°F (13°C)	Ideal 65°F (18°C)	Max 70°F (21°C)

This group of plants has only recently become established under the now accepted name of Schlumbergera — some of the most popular members of the family were for a long time referred to as Zygocactus, a name which is now rarely used.

There are only a few species, all of which are of South American origin, mainly from the mountainous regions of southern Brazil. In their natural habitat, these are forest cacti and grow as epiphytes on trees in woodlands and jungles. As indoor plants, they have taken very kindly to pot culture and they are particularly happy in hanging baskets, where their pendant flowers, which grow at the ends of trailing stems, will completely cover the basket with a mass of bloom.

Specimens grown as houseplants are more likely to be hybrids than representatives of the true species. *Schlumbergera* 'Buckleyi' (also known as *S.* 'Bridgesi') or Christmas Cactus, is a hybrid between the free-flowering *S. truncata* and the more delicate, rarely seen *S. russelliana.* Most popular of all the hybrids, *S.* 'Buckleyi' has magenta flowers, which appear around Christmas — hence its common name.

Spring and summer care

Repot every year in spring, soon after the flowers have died. Use a lime-free compost such as a proprietary cactus compost with the addition of a little peat. Alternatively, you can make your own acid compost by mixing two parts of peat to one part of decomposed leaf mould and one part of gritty sand. Always crock the pot well or cover the base of the hanging basket with sphagnum moss before filling with compost.

Pot on into a container one size larger only when the roots have filled the current one. This will not happen very often as Schlumbergeras do not have large root systems and a specimen around 1ft (0.3m) across can survive happily in a 5-6in (13-15cm) pot.

Although these are winter-flowering plants, they grow most actively between early spring and late summer. Keep them regularly watered as often as necessary to keep the compost moist, but do not allow pots to stand in water. Since these plants do not like lime, it's wise, in a hard water area, to use boiled water with a few drops of vinegar added. Feed occasionally — say, once a month — between June and September. Summer temperatures should be around 60-65°F (16-18°C). If indoor temperatures rise above this, place the plants out of doors in a lightly shaded position — preferably on a stand to avoid any problems with slugs. Regular overhead spraying every few days — preferably with rainwater because Schlumbergeras dislike hard water — will ensure the right degree of atmospheric humidity.

Autumn and winter care

Remember to bring your plant back indoors before the onset of the cold weather and keep it at around 55-60°C (13-16°C). Although winter is the main flowering season, it is not necessary to provide particularly high temperatures, but they should not fall below 55°F (13°C). For good flowering, put your plant in bright light but not in direct sun.

Water carefully so as to keep the compost just moist — never sodden but conversely never completely dry — until flowering ceases in late winter. Then water only moderately and allow the surface of the compost to dry out a little between each watering. Liquid fertiliser is recommended at two-weekly intervals, from late September on — when buds first appear — until flowering is finished early in the new year.

Trouble Shooter

If plants are allowed to dry out for any length of time, the stem segments will begin to wither, but overwatering is equally dangerous so the soil must be kept just moist and no more. Too low temperatures and draughts will weaken the stems.

Mealy bug is the mosty likely pest; look for small fluffy patches on the stems. They can be controlled by dabbing with a soft brush dipped in methylated spirit or by applying a malathion-based systemic insecticide, either in spray form or watered directly into the soil. This latter approach will help to combat any root mealy bug which may also attack.

Propagation

Take cuttings in March or April. These should consist of at least two stem segments carefully removed from the parent plant with a very sharp knife. Allow the cut to form a callus for a few days before inserting the cutting in a similar potting medium to that recommended for mature plants. Put in a shaded position at around 65-70°F (18-21°C) and continue to keep the cuttings shaded until they can be handled easily. Then they can be potted up individually and treated as mature plants.

Alternatively, you can graft Schlumbergera on to a columnar cactus to make a weeping specimen (see facing page).

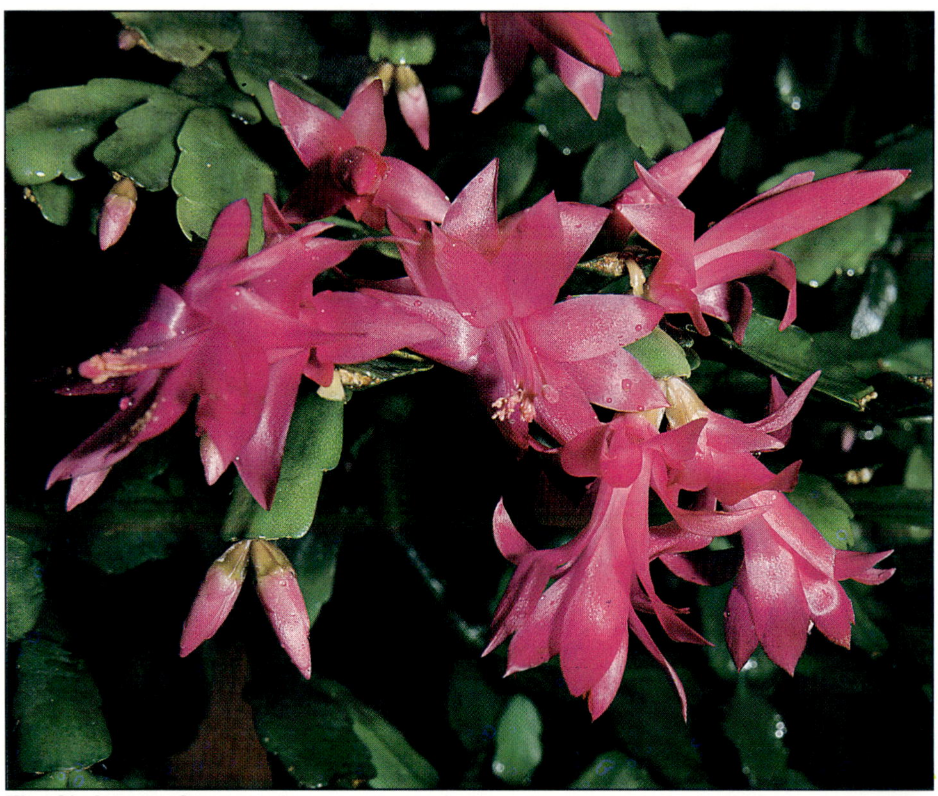

The Christmas Cactus brings a splash of colour to the depths of winter.

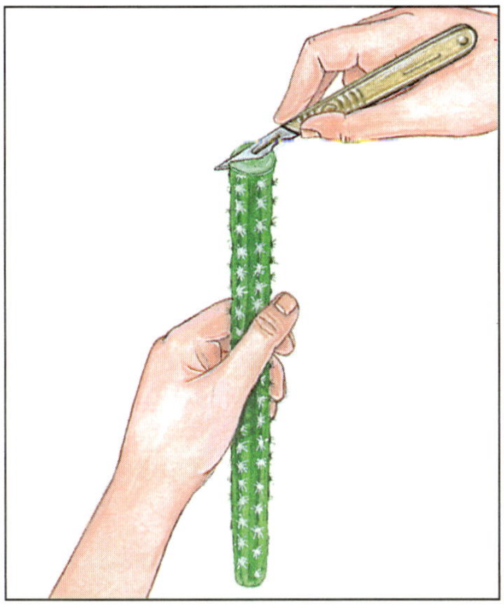

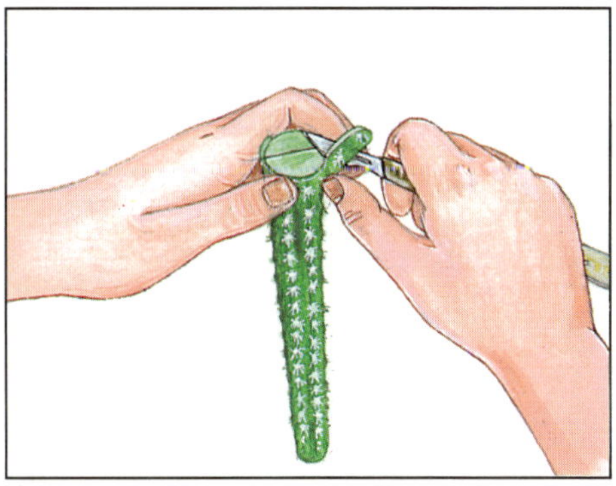

Cut the tip off a 12in (30cm) cutting of a columnar cactus such as *Selenicereus grandiflora*. Make a ½in (13mm) slit across the top of the stem (*left*). To make a neat graft between the two plants, peel the outer skin and chamfer away the flesh from around the tip of the columnar cactus (*above*).

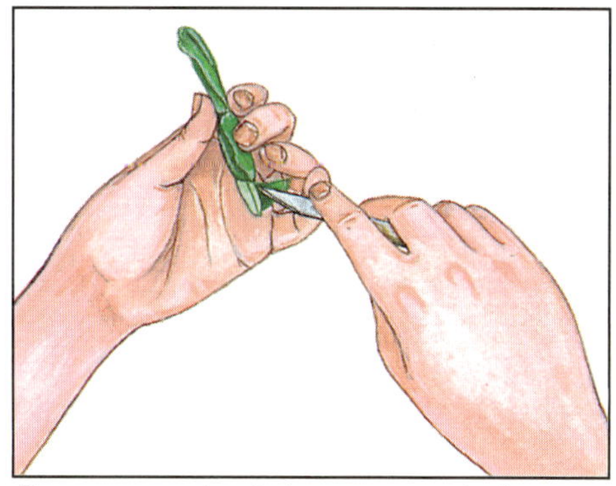

Remove a pair of stem segments from the tip of a Christmas Cactus stem. Carefully, peel the skin from the bottom ½in (13mm) of the lower of the segments.

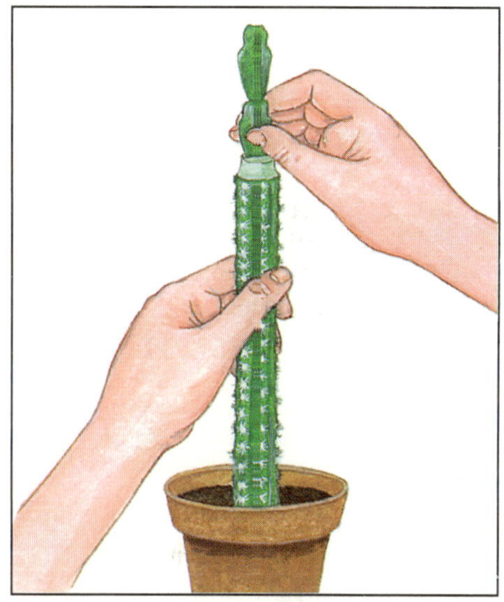

Insert the Christmas Cactus cutting into the slit at the tip of the planted Selenicereus stem — so that the flesh of both plants is in contact.

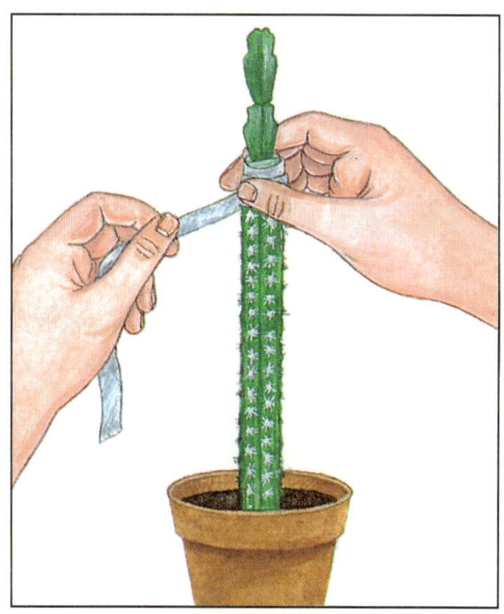

Strengthen the graft by binding the top of the planted columnar cactus with a lightweight bandage. Remove the cover in about one month.

Species

Schlumbergera truncata (also known as *Zygocactus truncatus*) is commonly called the Claw Cactus and has segmented stems with notches along the edges and prong-like projections, particularly towards the ends. A good specimen will have a height and spread of about 1ft (30cm). Flowers, varying in colour from pink to deep reddish-purple, begin to appear just before Christmas from the ends of the stems. There is also a variety of *S. truncata*, called *S. delicatus*, which has pure white flowers. *S. truncata* is a parent of most Schlumbergera hybrids (see below).

S. russelliana, *below*, is the other parent plant of the Christmas Cactus, along with *S. truncata;* it has slimmer segments without pronounced teeth. It grows to a height and spread of around 1ft (0.3m) and has deep pink flowers.

Schlumbergera hybrids come in many forms and colours. The best-known one is the popular old-fashioned Christmas Cactus, *S.* 'Buckleyi' (also known as *S.* 'Bridgesi'). The stem segments have rounded notches and rounded ends and the flowers are magenta. Two white hybrids, which have been produced by the German and American plant breeders respectively, are *S.* 'Wintermarchen' and *S.* 'White Christmas'. Danish plantsmen have developed the best yellow form to date, *S.* 'Golden Charm'. In Belgium and Holland, *S.* 'Westland' has proved very popular with its orange and red flowers.

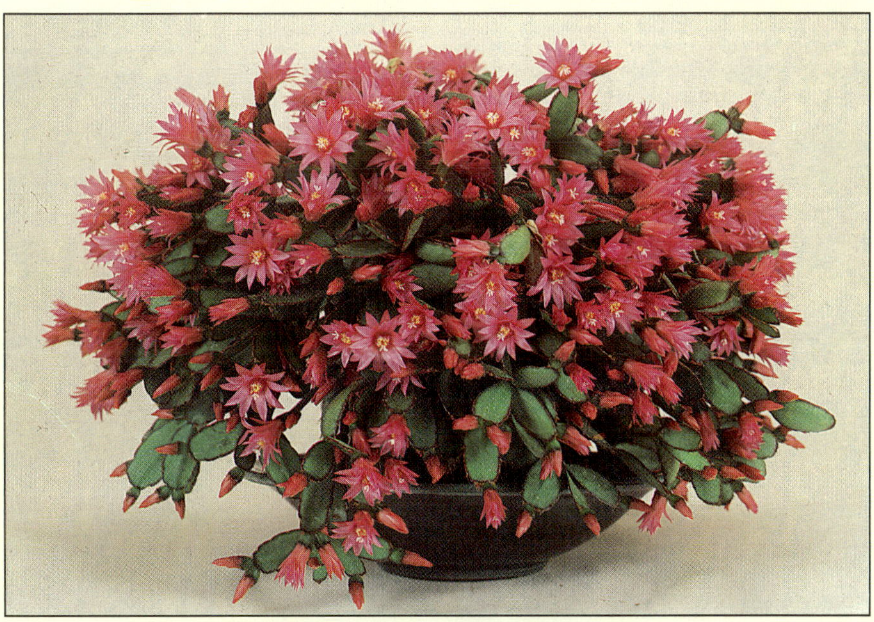

Scindapsus

Family name: **Araceae**

Common name: **Devil's Ivy**

Care Easy	**Height** 4-5ft (1.2-1.5m)	**Flower** Rare
Light Bright, indirect	**Spread** 1ft (0.3m)	**Humidity** Mist spray regularly
Price Middle range	**Shape** Climber	**Availability** Common
Temp. Min 55°F (13°C)	Ideal 70°F (21°C)	Max 80°F (27°C)

This genus has about 25 species and varieties, and they are all climbing plants, mostly with decorative foliage that resembles a little the leaves of the common ivy. They are closely related to the Philodendron or Sweetheart Plant, which is in the same family — and several varieties of Scindapsus do look very like it. A few species were once classified with the Pothos genus, and may still be offered for sale under that name.

Scindapsus has leathery, dark green leaves, heart-shaped and usually shiny. Most varieties have attractive markings, many in silvery-white, but the commonest and one of the most attractive is *Scindapsus aureus, right,* the leaves of which are splashed with golden yellow variegations.

The flowers of Scindapsus are insignificant, appearing in late summer. It is actually quite hard to get the plant to flower indoors, though you might be able to if the conditions are just right.

In the wild, Scindapsus climbs up tree trunks, anchored by aerial roots to the bark. Indoors, it can grow up to 4ft (1.2m) tall, but you must provide a support from a very young age. Canes or a trellis will do, but a moss pole is by far the best support, because the plant's roots can grow right into the moss. Alternatively, you can allow the plant to trail from a hanging basket.

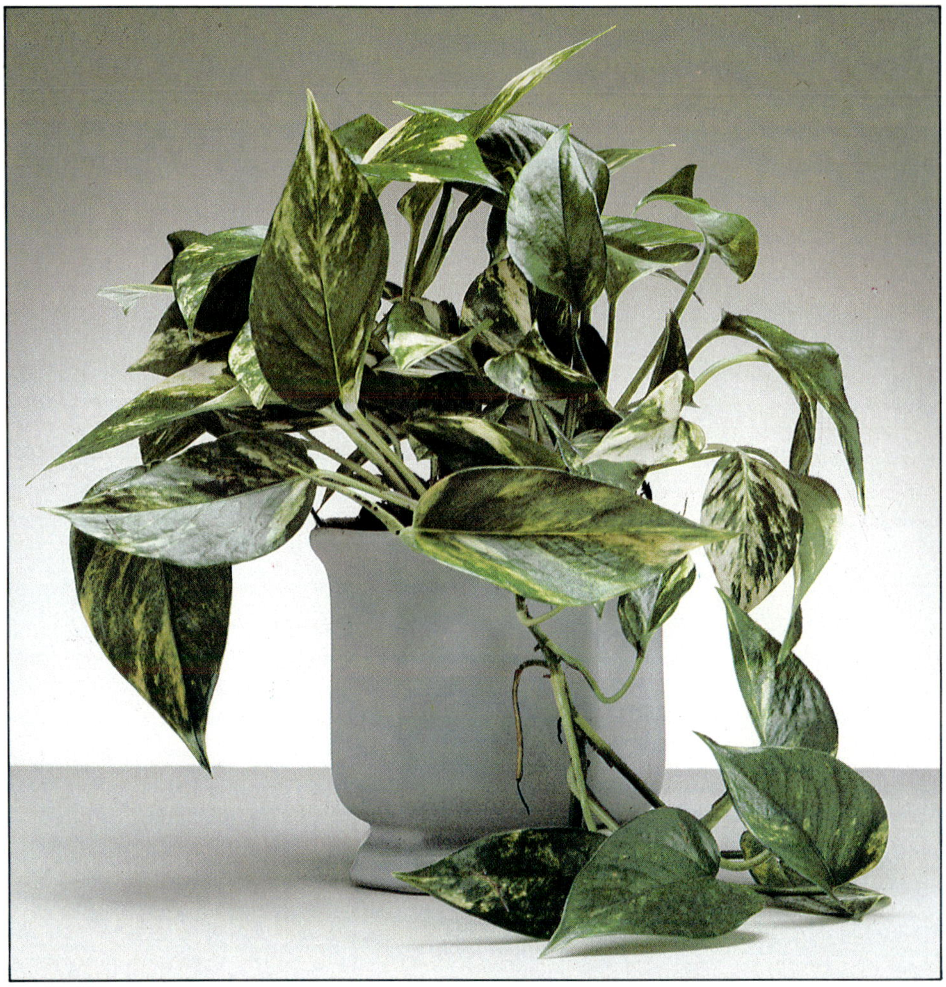

Devil's Ivy makes an easy-going and attractive climbing houseplant.

Spring and summer care

Repot the plant every year in March or April until it has reached an 8in (20cm) pot; after that, topdress by replacing the top 2in (5cm) of soil with fresh. Use an acid compost, such as two parts peat-based compost to one part coarse sand, or mix your own, using equal parts of leaf-mould, peat and coarse sand. Crock the container well to provide good drainage. If you intend the plant to climb rather than trail, arrange the moss pole or stake in the soil when you repot (see pages 88-89).

Temperatures in summer may rise to 70-80°F (21-27°C). Provide bright light to maintain the variegation in the leaves, but never put your plant in direct sunlight. Water very freely, but always leave the soil until it is virtually dry before watering again thoroughly. You will need to do this as often as two to three times a week in really hot weather.

Add liquid fertiliser every four to five weeks, but use only half the recommended amount. Mist spray from overhead two to three times a week with tepid water, always in the early morning or the evening — water drops on the leaves during the day will cause scorching. Pinch out the growing tips of the new leaves regularly to encourage compact, bushy growth.

Autumn and winter care

Temperatures in winter should be kept at 55-65°F (13-18°C), and the best position is in bright, filtered light. Water on the same principle as in summer, leaving the soil virtually to dry out between waterings. Continue to feed regularly with a weak solution of liquid fertiliser every four to five weeks, as in summer, to keep the leaves growing healthily. Mist spray from overhead occasionally to improve humidity and to keep the leaves free from dust. Keep your Scindapsus away from cold draughts at all times.

Propagation

Make new plants from stem cuttings in March or April. Take cuttings 6-8in (15-20cm) long from the stem tips, dip the bottom end in hormone rooting powder and insert it in the normal compost (see 'Spring and summer care'), not forgetting a moss pole or stake if you want the new plant to climb. Keep partially shaded and quite moist until new growth shows that roots have formed, which will take a week or so.

You can also divide the rootstock when you are potting on. Use a sharp knife and cut a clump of roots, with stems, off the parent plant and insert it in the usual compost.

Trouble Shooter

Brownish marks on the leaves, followed by yellowing and leaf fall, are caused either by excessive cold and draughts or by overwatering; remove any damaged leaves, move the plant to a warmer spot, and always let the soil become virtually dry before you water. If leaves start to lose their variegation and turn plain green, give the plant more light — although it will survive in shade, it will lose much of its attraction. The light should always be indirect, never full sunlight.

Red spider mite may attack if the air is too dry; spray with a malathion-based insecticide and mist spray regularly with tepid water to increase humidity.

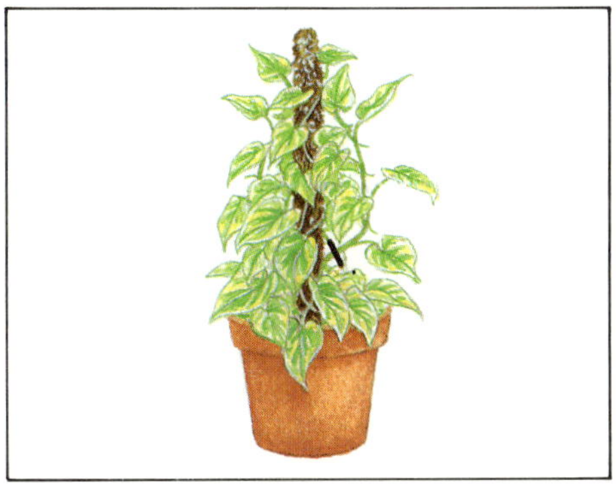

To take cuttings of Scindapsus, snip 6-8in (15-20cm) from the stem tips using a sharp knife or scalpel.

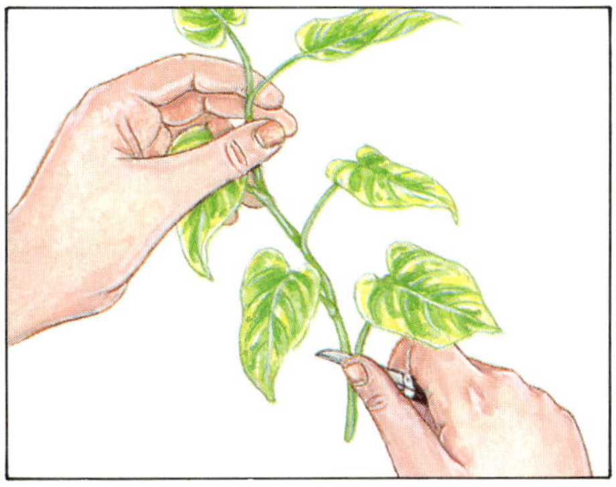

Remove the lowest leaf and trim to just below this leaf scar, then dip the cutting into rooting hormone.

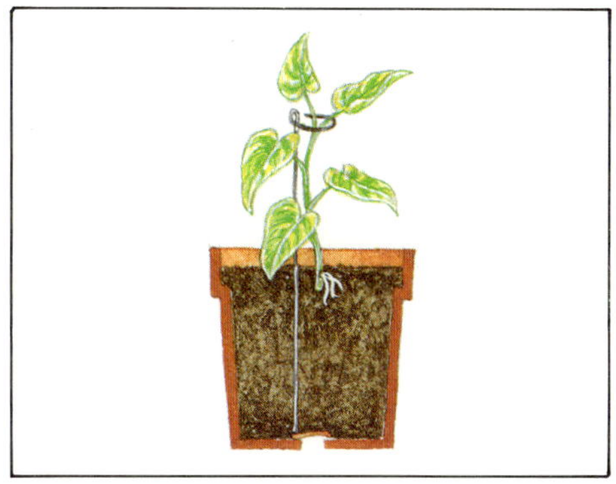

Set the cutting into compost so that the leaf scar is just below the surface; use a wire stake for support if necessary.

Species

Scindapsus aureus (*Pothos aureus*), Devil's Ivy, comes from the forests of the Solomon Islands. With glossy, oval, dark green leaves splashed with yellow, it climbs by means of fleshy, aerial roots which twine their way around tree branches. It can grow up to 20ft (6m) long in the wild, but can be contained as a houseplant to only 4-5ft (1.2-1.5m). It has an arum-like flower in the form of a boat-shaped bract surrounding a central spathe but these only rarely appear.

Some cultivars of *S.aureus* have characteristics quite distinct from the species. *S.a.* 'Marble Queen', *below right*, usually has extensive and close white marbling on the leaves, and sometimes leaves that are completely white. 'Tricolor' is more densely marbled than the species, with paler green, bright yellow and creamy white on the darker background green of the leaves. 'Wilcoxii' — easy to keep as a houseplant and long-lasting — has predominantly golden yellow variegations, with colourful stems and leaf stalks.

S.pictus, *below left* (also known as *S.argyraea* and *Pothos argyraeus*,) comes from Java and Borneo. It is a very beautiful climber with stems 6-8ft (1.8-2.4m) long indoors and reddish-brown in colour. The unusual leaves are roughly heart-shaped, matt bluish-green with pointed tips and edged and marked with silvery-white, especially when the plant is young. It flowers from a surprisingly early age, producing a small white bract on the end of a green spike.

S.siamense is a rarer species, sometimes offered by specialist nurseries. It comes from Thailand and is beautifully marked. Slender, heart-shaped leaves, pointed at the tips, are a dull green, marked in silvery-grey and paler green. Tall in its natural habitat, it is likely to grow to 3-4ft (0.9-1.2m) as a houseplant. Flowers are rarely produced indoors.

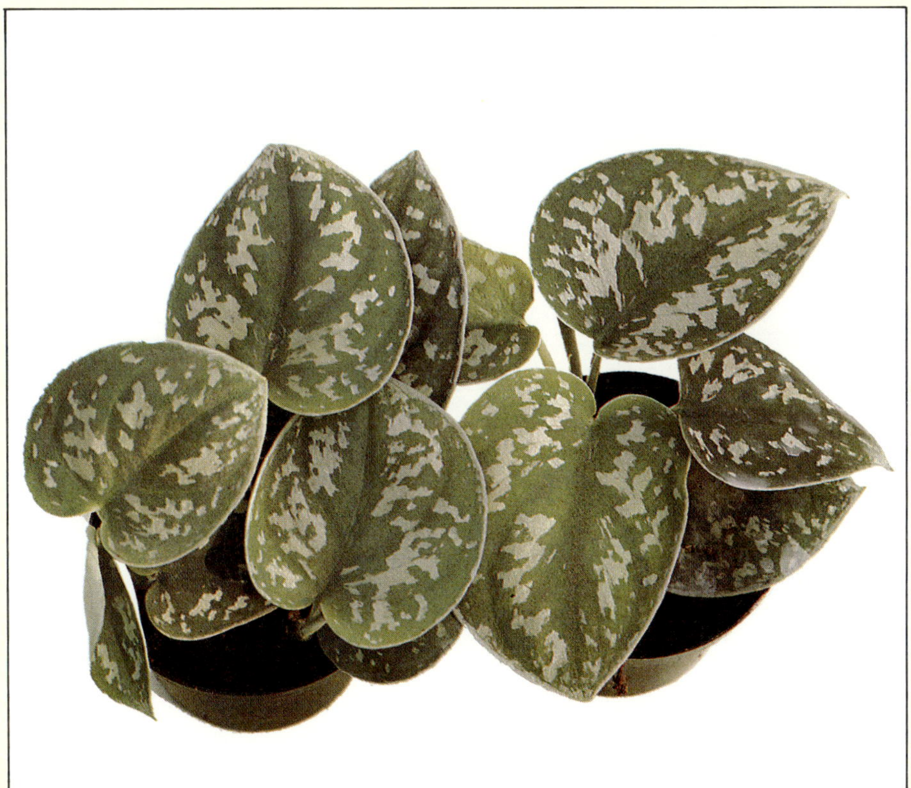

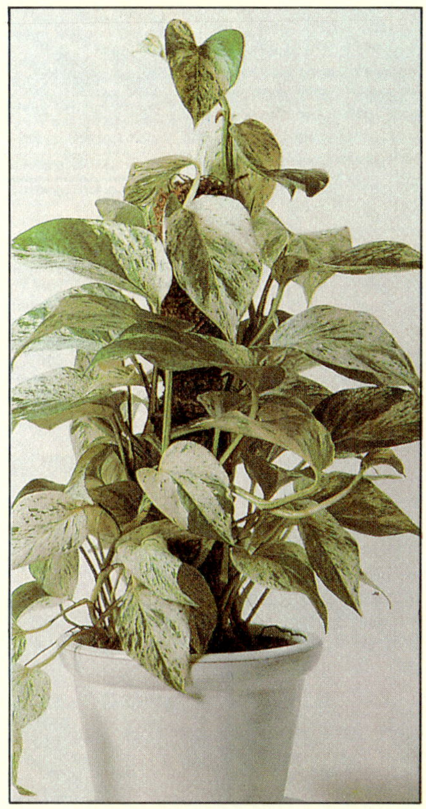

Sedum

Family name: **Crassulaceae**

Common names: **Burro's Tail/ Donkey's Tail/Beaver's Tail**

Care Easy	**Height** 2-3ft (0.6-0.9m)	**Flower** Summer
Light Bright, indirect	**Spread** 8-12in (20-30cm)	**Humidity** None
Price Cheap	**Shape** Trailing	**Availability** Garden centres
Temp. Min 50°F (10°C)	Ideal 65°F (18°C)	Max 75°F (24°C)

This large group of hardy, half-hardy and tender perennials contains several species suitable for growing as houseplants. All succulents with fleshy leaves that store water, they are mainly spreading, trailing plants, very well suited for growing in hanging baskets, but some grow in a miniature tree-like form and others make compact shrubs. The plants have many attractive features and are grown for their yellow, pink or white star-shaped flowers, as well as their overall shape and the form and colour of their leaves.

Sedums grow naturally in many different countries, but most particularly in southern Europe and Mexico. *Sedum morganianum, right*, one of the most popular and common species, has stems of up to 2-3ft (0.6-0.9m) long, covered in attractive blue-grey leaves, and looks very attractive if grown in a hanging basket. As well as the trailing species, there are stemless, rosette-shaped plants that look well on their own or among a cactus collection.

Spring and summer care

Young plants will need potting on every year up to a final pot size of about 8in (20cm). Do this in March or early April using a good proprietary brand of cactus compost, or John Innes No 2 compost with some extra coarse sand added to improve the drainage. Always crock the pot very well. If you're planting a Sedum in a hanging basket, line the basket with sphagnum moss, then add about 1in (2.5cm) of fine gravel or broken crocks.

Provide a bright position, with plenty of indirect light. Water thoroughly in the usual manner for cacti and succulents, letting the soil virtually dry out each time between waterings. Add a weak liquid fertiliser to the water every month or so.

Temperatures from April to October can go up to about 65°F (18°C). If it becomes much hotter than this, it's advisable to put your plant on a balcony or outdoors in a protected position or, failing that, make sure you give it plenty of fresh air.

Autumn and winter care

Keep the temperature at a minimum of 50°F (10°C), and give very little water — just enough to keep the compost barely moist. Give good light, even direct sun, during the winter months.

Propagation

You can propagate new Sedums easily from seeds, stem tip cuttings and leaf cuttings. Sow seeds in January to March. Use the normal compost, with a quarter part of extra coarse sand added, and moisten the mixture thoroughly. Scatter the seeds thinly over the surface — they are very fine and do not need covering, but moisten them with a light mist spray to settle them in the soil. Keep them well shaded, at 55-65°F (13-18°C). When the seedlings start to show, give more light.

Take 3-4in (8-10cm) cuttings from stem tips in the summer. Allow the cuts to callus over for a few days, then insert the cuttings in a mixture of equal parts of peat and sand and keep them at 55-60°F (13-16°C) in a shaded position until new growth shows that roots are established. Use exactly the same procedure with leaf cuttings.

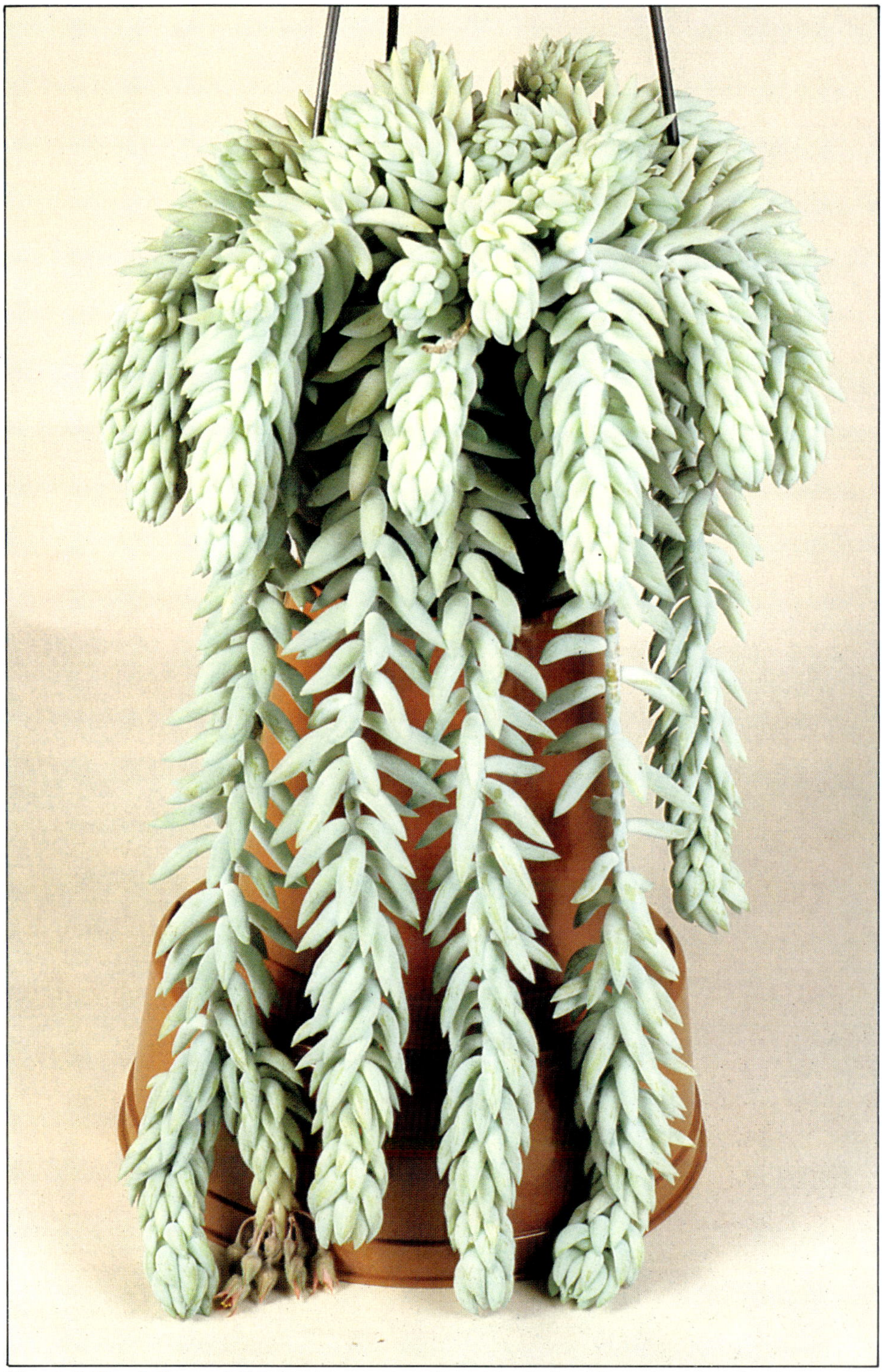

The tail-like foliage of this Sedum makes it an ideal plant for a hanging basket.

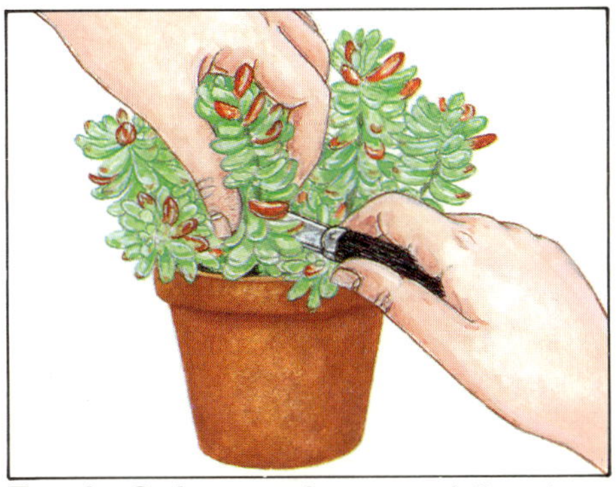

To take Sedum cuttings, carefully snip 3-4in (8-10cm) from the stem tips then remove the leaves from the bottom 1in (2.5cm) of stem.

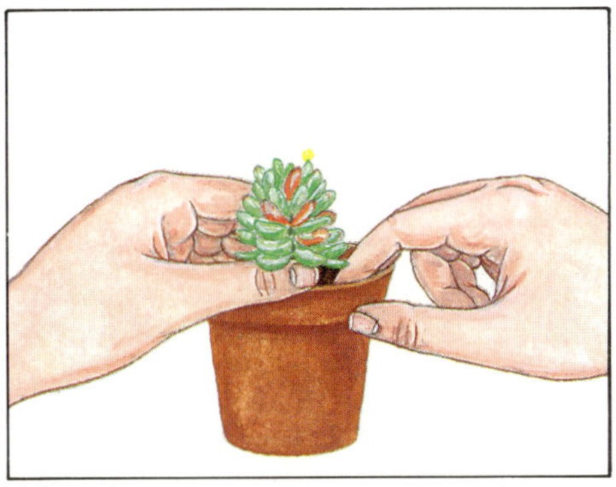

Allow the cut to callus over for a day or two, then set the cutting into a mixture of equal parts peat and sand and maintain a temperature of about 60°F (16°C).

Trouble Shooter

If leaves start to wilt and become discoloured, the fault is overwatering. Always err on the side of underwatering with succulents, which hate being too wet, especially if the weather is cold, and keep them free from frost and cold draughts. If mealy bugs attack, use a fine paintbrush dipped in methylated spirit to wipe the fluffy patches away, then rinse the leaves thoroughly in the same way with tepid water. *Never* use a malathion-based insecticide.

Species

Sedum morganianium, Burro's Tail, is presumed to have come from Mexico, but 50 years after its introduction as a houseplant its exact origin still remains uncertain. 'Burro' is the Spanish for donkey, and the 2-3ft (0.6-0.9m) long trailing stems do have the appearance of long tails. They are completely coated with thick, fleshy, pointed, overlapping, pale grey-green leaves, each ½-¾in (13-19mm) long. Clusters of pale pink or red flowers — up to 1½in (3.8cm) — are borne at the ends of the stems from June to September. It is ideal for a hanging basket.

S.sieboldii, *right*, from Japan, has beautiful spreading foliage with leaves arranged in attractive whorls that almost encircle the stems, which grow up to 9in (23cm) long. The leaves start off grey-blue, but gradually change colour to brownish-green with a hint of red at the edges. In October dense clusters, 2-3in (5-8cm) across, of flat, pink flowers appear at the ends of the stems. In mild climates this species will thrive outdoors too, though it will then lose its stems and leaves in the autumn to grow them anew in the spring. A very attractive variegated variety, *S.s.medio-variegatum*, has greyish leaves with a rich, creamy-yellow splash in the centre, and pinkish-red stems. Both the species and this variety are spreading plants and suitable for hanging baskets.

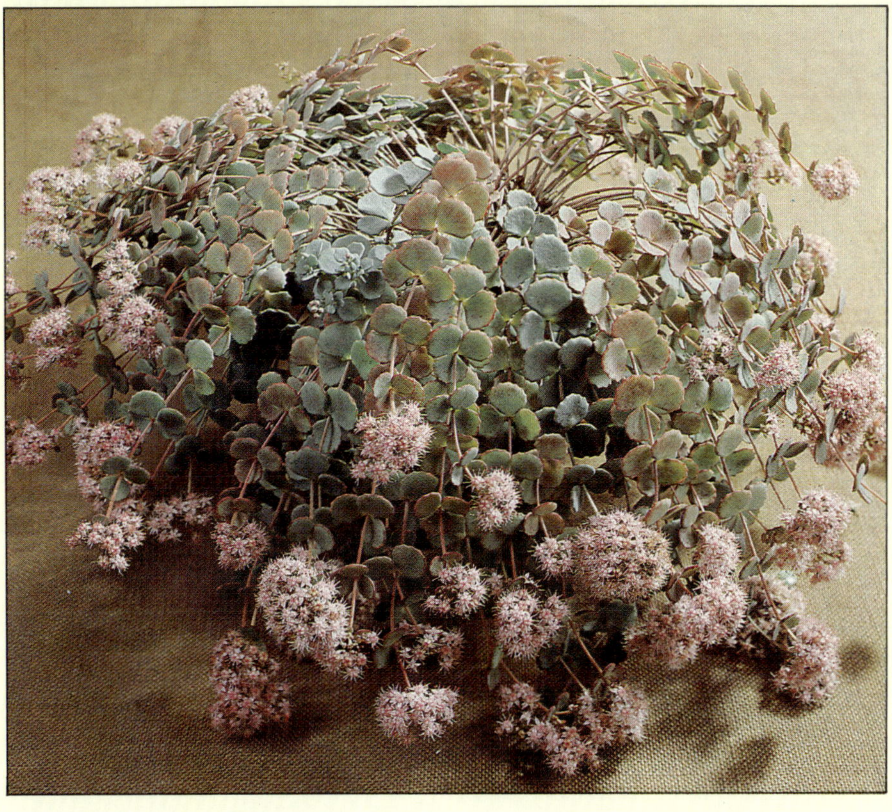

S.hintonii, from Mexico, is very delicate and pretty, though still rather rare. It has low-growing, short stems crowded with thick, rounded, pale green leaves, each barely ½in (13mm) long and less than ¼in (6mm) across, densely covered with minute white hairs. In summer it bears clusters of white flowers.

S.bellum, from Durango in central Mexico, has spreading stems, up to 1ft (0.3m) long, and small, rounded, light green leaves, about 1in (2.5cm) long and ½in (13mm) wide, covered in a powdery white bloom. Flat clusters 1-2in (2.5-5cm) wide of white flowers are borne at the ends of the stems in late winter.

S.rubrotinctum, Jelly Bean Plant, comes from Mexico. A dwarf shrub, branching from the base, it grows up to 8in (20cm) tall, with fleshy, rounded, bright green leaves about ¾in (19mm) long, which turn red in hot weather if the potting compost is kept fairly dry.

S.pachyphyllum, also called Jelly Bean Plant, comes from Mexico, but it is not known for certain whether it is a true species or a hybrid of another species. A dwarf shrub, it grows up to 10in (25cm) high, with fleshy, blue-green leaves, bright red and slightly shiny at the tips. In spring it bears clusters of yellow flowers.

S.oxypetalum grows up to 18in (45cm) in cultivation as a houseplant, though it grows taller in the wild. The stems are thick and fleshy, about 3in (8cm) across at the base, with slender, lance-shaped, green leaves 2in (5cm) long. Small red flowers, which are slightly fragrant, are borne in clusters at the tips of the branches in early summer.

Selaginella

Family name: **Selaginellaceae**

Common name:
Creeping Moss, Resurrection Plant

Care Easy	**Height** 9-12in (23-30cm)	**Flower** None
Light Shade	**Spread** 1ft (0.3m)	**Humidity** Mist spray regularly
Price Cheap	**Shape** Bushy	**Availability** Garden centres
Temp. Min 60°F (16°C)	Ideal 65°F (18°C)	Max 75°F (24°C)

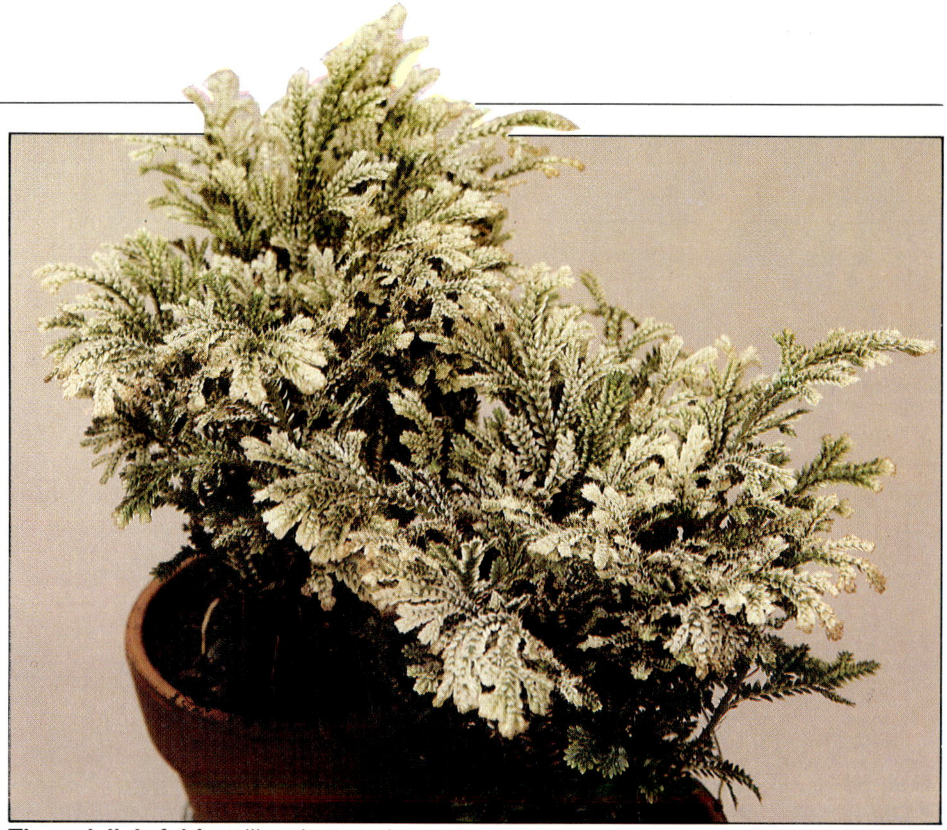

These delightful fern-like plants enjoy a shady position.

This is a large genus of decorative, non-flowering, evergreen moss-like plants. Several species can be grown indoors, ranging from low, compact hummocks to branching, fern-like plants, their stems either creeping or erect, covered in tiny leaflets.

One of the best known species is *Selaginella martensii* which has upright stems, up to 1ft (0.3m) tall, arching at the top under the mass of glistening green foliage. There is a number of attractive varieties available, including *S.m.*'Variegata', *above right*, with silvery-white and green variegated leaves.

To flourish they need conditions that are constantly moist. The one exception is the Resurrection Plant (*S.lepidophylla*), which is frequently sold rolled up in a dry ball, only to spring up fresh and green when placed in water. Selaginella do particularly well in bottle gardens or terrariums, where the humidity and moisture that they need can be guaranteed, but with care they will grow perfectly well in a pot.

Spring and summer care

Repot plants every spring in a shallow, well-drained container of lime-free, peat-based compost. Pot plants on to a larger container to a final pot size of 6-8in (15-20cm); continue to repot annually after that, into the same pot which should be cleaned and filled with fresh compost. Trim your plant back at potting time if the quick-spreading growth is threatening to get out of hand; plants can be cut back by as much as half if required.

Normal warm room temperatures are suitable throughout the year and they should be kept in a shaded position, some distance from any windows.

A moist, humid atmosphere is absolutely essential. Stand the pot on a tray of moist pebbles and mist spray at least once a day, particularly when temperatures start to climb above 70°F (21°C); be sure to use tepid water only — cold water will cause irreparable damage. Water plentifully, as often as is necessary to keep the compost thoroughly moist — though never allow the pot to stand in water. These plants hate lime so only use soft water; boil hard water first and add a little vinegar — less than a teaspoon per pint of water. They require very little feeding but it can be beneficial to add a very weak liquid fertiliser to the water every two or three weeks (use a quarter of the amount recommended by the manufacturer).

Autumn and winter care

Winter requirements are much the same as those for the rest of the year. Temperatures should be around 60-65°F (16-18°C), and can usefully be higher than that. Keep your plants shaded, draught-free and, above all, moist at all times.

Propagation

Take 2-3in (5-8cm) long stem cuttings in spring and insert them ½in (1cm) deep into the usual compost. Keep them moist and shaded, at a temperature of 65-75°F (18-24°C), ideally in a propagator or enclosed in a clear polythene bag. When new growth indicates that rooting is established, probably in about two weeks, remove from the bag or propagator and treat as mature plants.

Trouble Shooter

If you provide your plants with the constantly moist conditions that they need there should be few problems, if any. However, if you let them dry out they will just shrivel up; if the humidity is too low, the foliage will curl up and go brown. Cold and draughts are equally dangerous — and remember to mist spray with tepid rather than cold water, which can cause irreparable damage.

Fortunately, there are no pests that are likely to prove a problem.

Species

Selaginella martensii, from Mexico, is one of the best known and most robust species. Unusually for Selaginella — and unlike all the other common indoor species, which tend to have a creeping or trailing habit — this plant has stems up to 1ft (0.3m) long which are erect for most of their length, arching over towards the tips. These very slender, branching stems carry the crisp, glistening green foliage; though no more than ½in (1cm) in length, the leaves are still larger than any other common species. *S.m.*'Variegata' is one of a number of attractive varieties, with silvery-white-tipped leaves; another popular form is 'Watsoniana', which has rather paler leaves, tipped with silver.

S.kraussiana, commonly known as Creeping Moss, is an exceptionally quick-growing, creeping plant from west Africa. The thin, delicate stems root as they branch forming dense, bright green cushions of feathery leaves. Even more attractive perhaps than the species is the variety *S.k.aurea*, which has green and golden foliage.

S.lepidophylla, found in the Americas from Texas to Peru, is a small plant consisting of a rosette of green fern-like leaves, which redden as the plant matures. One of the curiosities of the plant world, in dry periods they curl up like balls of brown moss, only to unroll and display their fresh, decorative foliage as soon as the rain comes — hence the common name of Resurrection Plant.

Sempervivum

Family name: **Crassulaceae**

Common name: **Houseleek**

Care Easy	**Height** 3in (8cm)	**Flower** July
Light Sunny	**Spread** 12in (30cm)	**Winter** Frost tolerant
Price Cheap	**Shape** Rosette	**Availability** Garden centres

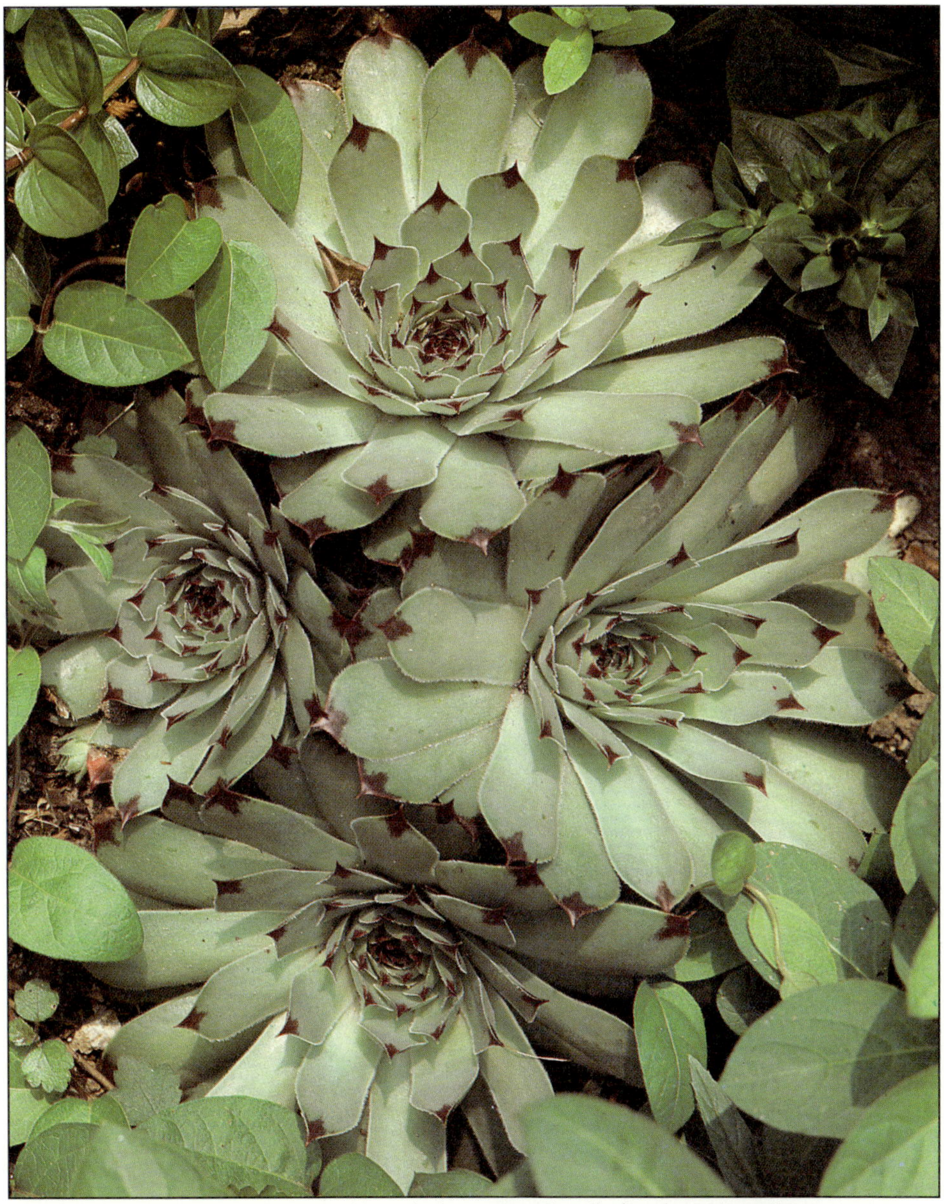

Sempervivum tectorum, Common Houseleek, creates attractively coloured rosettes.

Sempervivums are tough and decorative evergreen succulents, with neat, compact rosettes of thick, fleshy leaves. In summer they are set off by clusters of small, star-shaped flowers in shades from white to purple. The name Sempervivum – 'always alive' – refers to their hardiness and tenacity, and their ability to succeed under widely differing and often distinctly unpromising circumstances.

Certainly, they will flourish in the poorest, least nourishing soil, with scarcely any attention, and on rockeries, dry walls, narrow cracks in paving – even rooftops; they were once a common sight spreading and trailing over slated or tiled cottages – hence their common name of Houseleek. They were widely held at one time to be most effective at warding off both lightning and witchcraft – so effective that Charlemagne once ordered that every rooftop in his kingdom should be planted with them.

There are close on 50 species altogether, as well as innumerable subspecies, varieties and hybrids, originating from the mountains of Europe, western Asia and north Africa. The Common Houseleek *(Sempervivum tectorum), above right,* is a European species, found mainly in the Pyrenees and

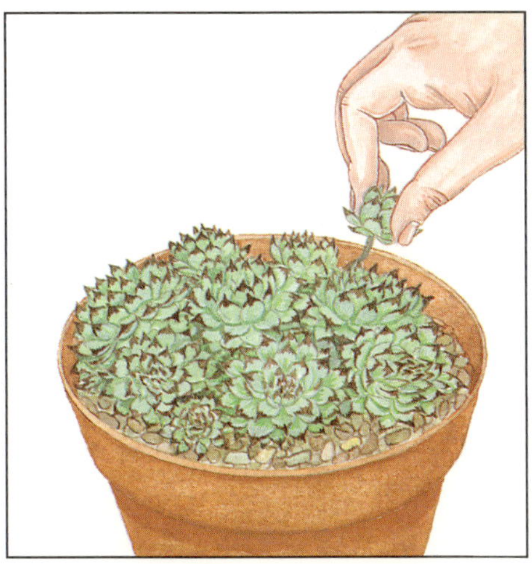

The freely produced offsets can be detached from the clustered rosettes during autumn or spring.

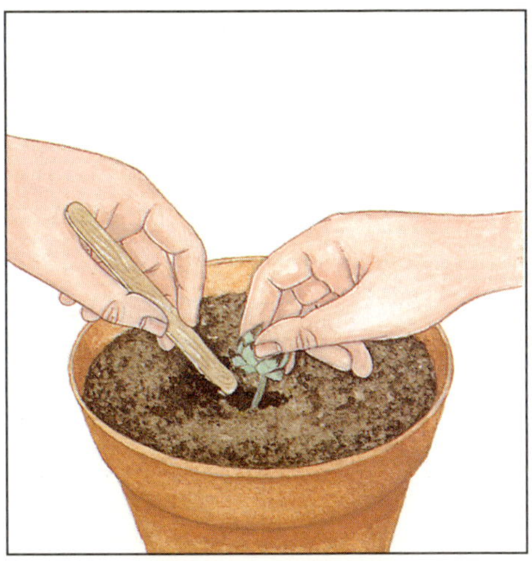

Plant them up into pots of well-drained compost, firming them well and ensuring that the small roots are spread out.

Trouble Shooter

Houseleeks are immensely easy going plants and should be virtually trouble free as long as care is taken over watering and drainage. Rosettes will open out wide, become flabby and eventually rot, if plants are overwatered and become 'wet-footed'. Similarly, too dense shade will also quickly spoil the appearance of the rosettes; always give your plants an open sunny site.

Mealy bug may be a problem, as may greenfly; the best solution is to wipe them away with a paintbrush or soft cloth dipped in methylated spirit. On no account use a malathion-based insecticide; this is extremely harmful and can detrimentally affect all members of the Crassulaceae family.

Species

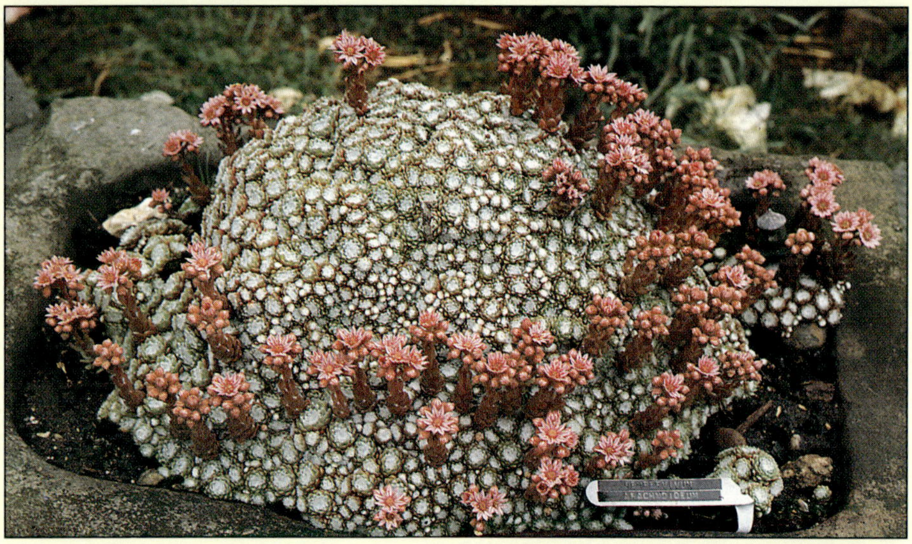

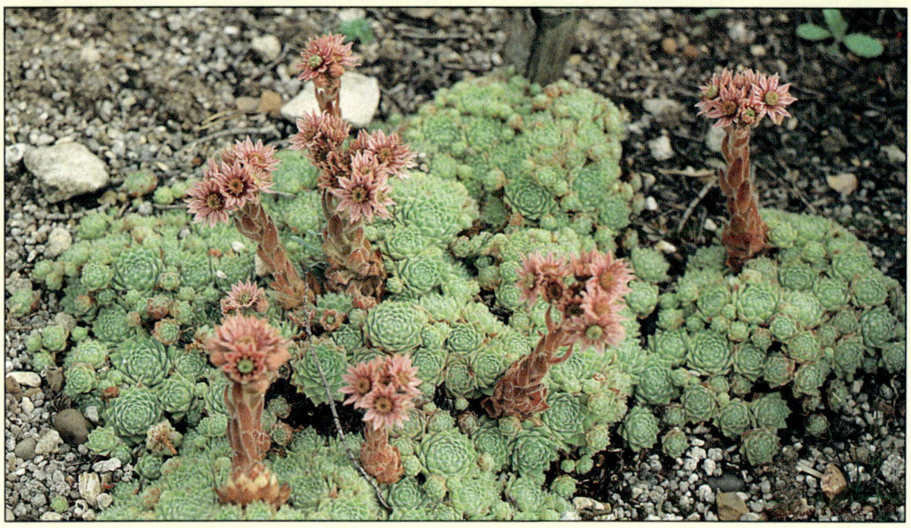

Sempervivum tectorum is the Common Houseleek, a European species widespread from the Pyrenees to the south-eastern Alps. Fleshy rosettes up to 6in (15cm) wide, very freely produce offsets, developing into a dense hummock some 3in (8cm) high and 12in (30cm) wide. The leaves are usually bright green, with purple-brown tips, and whitish underneath, but they are highly variable. Star-shaped flowers, in shades of pink or reddish-purple, are borne on erect, leafy stems sometimes 20in (50cm) tall, during midsummer – usually July.

There are numerous very appealing varieties and hybrids, including *S. t. calcareum*, a compact form with small rosettes of red-tipped, grey-green leaves, and 'Othello', which has very large rosettes in deep red.

S. arachnoideum, *top left*, also native to mountainous regions of Europe, is another very popular species, known as the Cobweb Houseleek on account of its dense coating of white hairs, woven together at the tips to form a cobweb-like mat. Set in dense, globular rosettes, about 1in (2.5cm) across, the leaves are green, sometimes flushed with red, but almost obscured by the covering of hairs. Flower stems – really, extended rosettes – up to 6in (15cm) tall bear clusters of star-like pink or rose-red flowers in June and July. As with *S. tectorum*, several attractive varieties and hybrids are available.

S. guiseppii, *bottom left*, originates from northern Spain. It has small rosettes of pale green leaves with brown tips, densely covered in down, and produces rose-red flowers on 5-6in (13-15cm) stems.

Alps. It has fleshy rosettes of bright green, red-tipped leaves which offset very freely to form a dense, compact hummock up to 1ft (0.3m) wide. Small pink or reddish flowers appear in July on tall leafy stems, rather like extended rosettes.

In addition to the species proper, there are a host of appealing varieties available, of differing sizes, with leaf colouring ranging from silvery grey to deep red or purple.

Easy to care for, long-lived and very attractive, these low-growing plants are extremely well suited to troughs and sink gardens or window-boxes, where they can trail over the sides decoratively. They are also a most interesting choice for hanging-baskets, when they can be encouraged to grow over the surface of the basket and cover the sides with their neat, spreading offset rosettes. They also grow well in barrels, eventually forming a dense mass of rosettes.

Spring and summer care

Potting is best in April; plants seldom need repotting – only if rosettes become quite congested in their container. Sempervivums do well in any soil, however poor, as long as it is well drained; try John Innes No 2 mixed with an equal amount of sharp sand to make it really porous and be sure to crock the container well. The addition of some limestone chippings can help produce a good colouring in the leaves; plants will benefit from an annual topdressing of equal parts of limestone chippings and leaf-mould.

For best results, give your plants an open sunny position. They need water but only ever in strict moderation.

Autumn and winter care

These plants require minimal attention during winter. Dead flower stems can be removed if unsightly – they will pull away easily. Houseleeks are totally hardy but continue to keep them in a good sunny location and give a very occasional watering – always very sparingly – during warmer, dry spells.

Buying Guide

When buying new plants, check that the rosettes are strong and healthy, not withered and dried up because the compost was kept too dry.

Propagation

Houseleeks are easily increased by division. Offsets are freely produced; well grown, rooted offsets can be detached and replanted in the usual compost, in autumn or spring, and treated as mature plants (see 'Spring and summer care').

Species

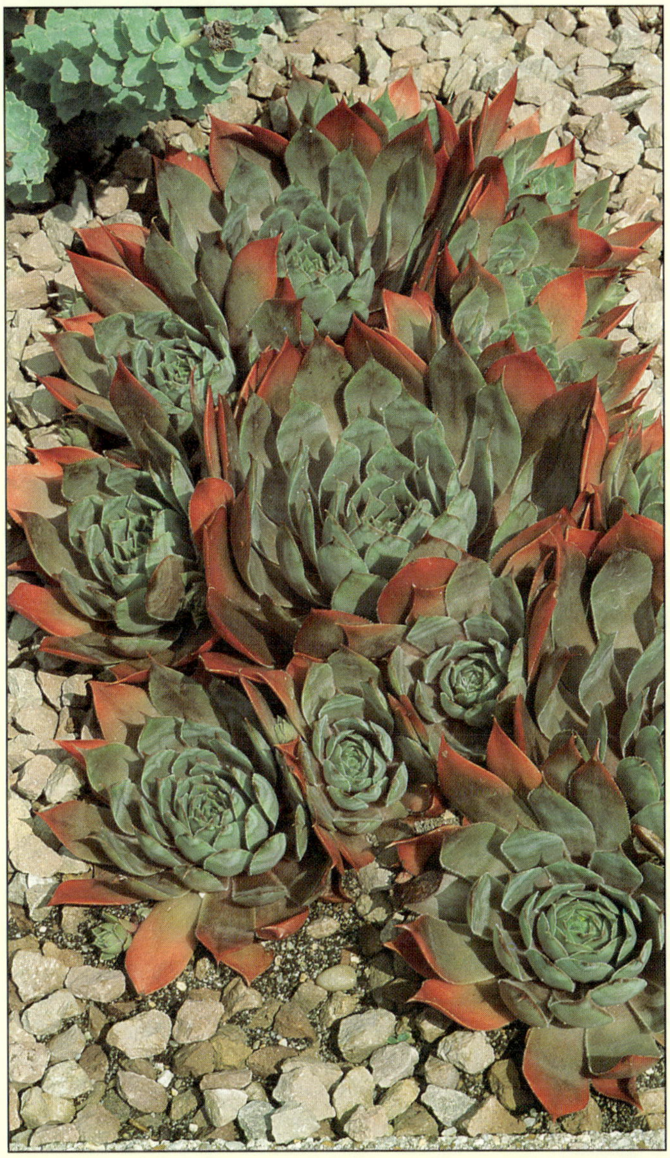
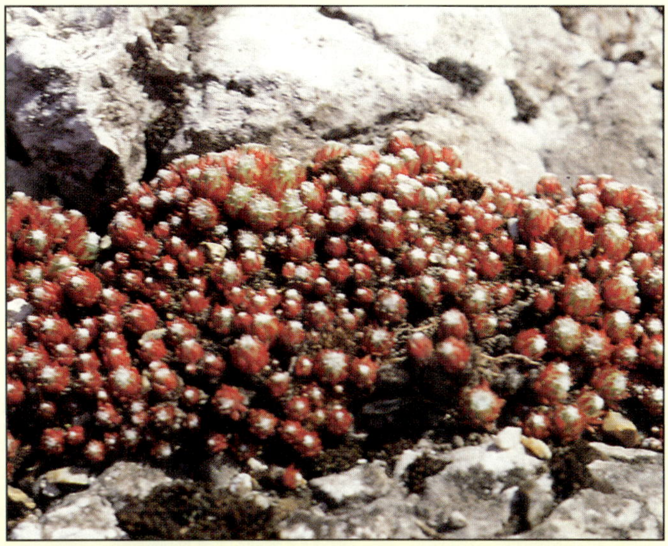
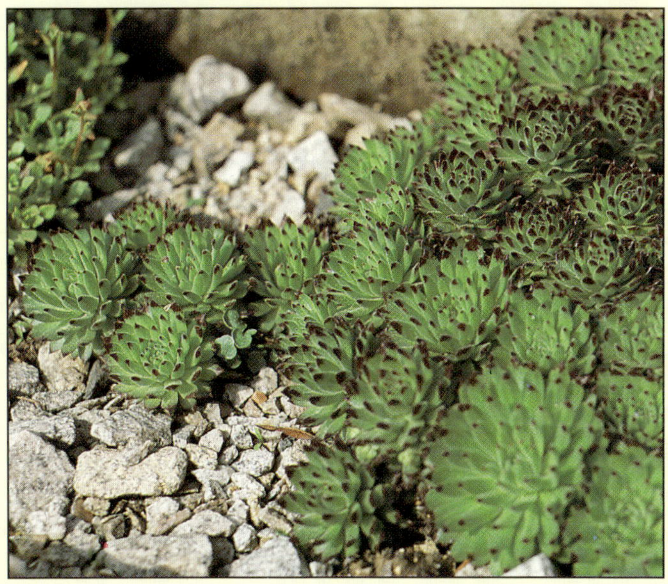

Sempervivum soboliferum (now reclassified as *Jovibarba sobolifera*), from the mountains of northern Europe, rejoices in the common name of Hen and Chicken Houseleek. It forms 2in (5cm) rosettes of bright green leaves sometimes flushed with red and produces greenish-yellow, bell-like flowers on 6-8in (15-20cm) stems in July. A peculiarity of this species is the way that new rosettes are borne on top of the parent rosette and quickly detach and root themselves to form neat hummocks.

S. grandiflorum is native to Switzerland, with a very large, rather hairy rosette of red-tipped, deep green leaves. The elongated stem bears a terminal head of large, very striking yellow flowers with purple blotches. Unfortunately, the stems and rosette are somewhat sticky with a pungent and unpleasant aroma.

S. montanum, *bottom right*, a mountain plant from the Alps, Pyrenees and Carpathians, has a neat, closed rosette, 1-2in (2.5-5cm) across, of bright green or greyish-green hairy leaves. Flowers are pale purple to violet with a distinct line down the centre of each petal, appearing from June to August on 6in (15cm) stems. There is also a large form, 'Burnatii', with 2-4in (5-10cm) rosettes in pale green; *S. m. minimum* is very similar to the species but decidedly more miniature; and *S. m. pallidum* varies only in the flower colour which is either yellow or white.

S.* x *hookeri, *top right*, is a neat, small hybrid between *S. montanum* and *S. arachnoideum*, forming small rosettes up to about 2in (5cm) high and 2½in (6cm) wide that spread to create clumps 8-12in (20-30cm) wide. The rosettes look especially attractive when caught by sun, and can be a feature of interest on a patio throughout the year.

S. marmoreum, *above left*, is also known as *S. schlehanii*. It has beautifully coloured rosettes, which grow up to about 2½in (6cm) high and 4-6in (10-15cm) wide, and can form large clumps. It is one of the most attractively coloured sempervivums. The white flowers with crimson bands grow 5-6in (13-15cm) high.

Senecio

Family name: **Compositae**

Common names: **Cineraria, Candle Plant, String-of-beads, Cape Ivy**

Care Easy	**Height** 9-24in (23-60cm)	**Flower** December-June
Light Bright, indirect	**Spread** 9-12in (23-30cm)	**Humidity** Mist spray occasionally
Price Cheap	**Shape** Bushy	**Availability** Common
Temp. Min 45°F (7°C)	Ideal 55°F (13°C)	Max 70°F (21°C)

Senecio is one of the largest of all plant genera, containing well over 2000 species of widely varying size and habit; distributed throughout most of the world, they range from common weeds such as Groundsel and Ragwort in northern Europe to the fleshy-stemmed succulents of southern Africa and include the brilliantly-flowered Cinerarias.

There have been many attempts to divide this huge genus into smaller ones and this has led to some confusion about the names of a number of species commonly grown as houseplants. These fall into three main groups. The most popular of all the indoor Senecios are the hybrids or varieties of the perennial *Senecio cruentus*, almost always referred to as Cinerarias. These compact, winter and spring-flowering plants produce masses of daisy-like flowers in a range of bright colours and are treated as annuals.

Although few of them can match Cineraria's beautiful flowers, there are many other species of Senecio that are well worth considering. These include a number of interesting and unusual succulents, some of which are frequently listed as Kleinia, and some charming, ivy-like climbing plants; they can all make excellent houseplants.

Spring and summer care

Cinerarias (*S.cruentus* and hybrids): flowers can be produced any time between December and June and ideally plants are sold as the first flower buds begin to open — any time between Christmas and May. They should continue flowering for several weeks, after which plants are usually discarded. Their requirements are the same whatever time of year they are bought: for the longest possible flowering period, keep Cinerarias at cool temperatures — 50-60°F (10-16°C) is ideal — in a good, bright location, but out of direct sunlight. Water freely, to keep plants thoroughly moist at all times, though take care not to overwater or root rot is liable to set in. Stand the pot on a tray of moist pebbles and spray around the plant occasionally, to provide a degree of humidity. Adding a liquid fertiliser to the watering every ten days or so can be beneficial, but feeding is not really necessary.

Succulent species (e.g.*S.articulatus, S.rowleyanus, S.haworthii*): repot plants in March or April, into a mixture of two parts John Innes No 1 to one part coarse sand. Move them on to a pot one size larger when the roots have filled the current pot, to a final pot size of 4-5in (10-13cm), after which it is best to propagate the plant from cuttings (see 'Propagation') and discard the parent plant. Take care not to disturb the roots, but gently shake off the old compost before repotting in fresh. If necessary trim straggly plants into shape at potting time.

Keep these plants in a very bright, sunny position, at normal room temperatures — around 65°F (18°C) is the best, and try not to go above 70°F (21°C). Give them enough water to make the compost moist throughout, then allow the surface of the compost to dry out before watering again; if they are given too much water, rotting may easily occur. Neither feeding nor mist-spraying is required.

Climbing species (e.g. *S.macroglossus, S.mikanoides)*: repot these in the spring using a mixture of three parts John Innes No 1 to one part sand. Move overcrowded plants into pots one size larger to a maximum 6-7in (15-18cm) pot; after that it is best to start new plants from cuttings since the young plants are more attractive than older ones (see 'Propagation'). Stems will need support to climb and should be trained up thin canes or to a trellis, or they can be trailed over the sides of the container to good effect. Pinch out the growing tips of your plant regularly to maintain bushiness.

The recommended conditions are much the same as for the succulent species, with normal room temperatures up to a maximun of 70°F (21°C) and bright light with some direct sun, though they will tolerate a semi-shaded position. Water fairly freely, allowing the surface of the compost to dry out before watering again, and add a liquid fertiliser to the water every three weeks or so.

Autumn and winter care

Succulent species: keep these plants in a very bright spot with as much sunlight as possible, at a temperature of about 50-60°F (10-16°C) — they can survive as low as 40°F (5°C) if necessary, but will not flourish at that level.

Take special care not to overwater during winter. Water moderately to prevent the compost from drying out completely and if temperatures should fall below about 50°F (10°C) don't water at all, unless it is very bright and there is enough sunlight to cause any excess moisture to evaporate. Probably the best method is to let the pot stand in

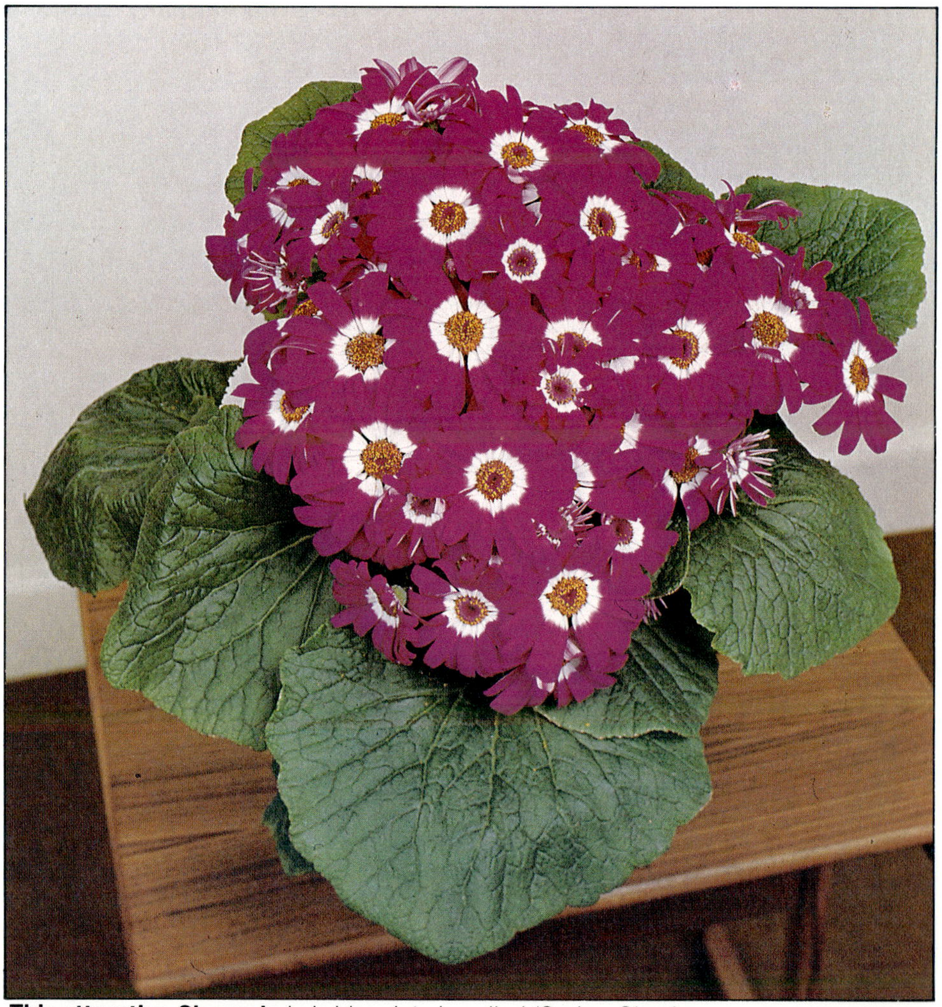

This attractive Cineraria hybrid variety is called 'Spring Glory'.

water for a few minutes so that the base roots are moistened, then leave the pot to drain before returning it to its position.

Climbing species: aim for quite cool temperatures, around 50-55°F (10-13°C) and keep plants draught-free, in the sunniest possible position. The compost should be reasonably dry throughout this period from October to March, with only enough water to keep it from drying out completely; it's worth using the same method of watering as for succulent species.

Propagation

Cinerarias: these can be propagated from seed, *below*, but it is not an easy process and young plants need to be overwintered at a temperature of about 45°F (7°C) to flower in the early spring. However, since plants are inexpensive to buy and widely available, unless you want to grow an unusual variety there is rarely any need to raise your own plants from seed.

Succulent species: new plants can easily be raised from 3-4in (8-10cm) long stem cuttings, taken in June or July. Remove the lower leaves, if any, so there is at least 1in (2.5cm) of bare stem, and leave the cut surfaces to callus for a few days before inserting them singly into 3in (7cm) pots of two parts John Innes No 1 and one part coarse sand. Don't expose the cuttings to full sun, otherwise treat them as mature plants and they will quickly root and produce top growth. Clump-forming species are simply increased by removing offsets or dividing the rootstock and potting the sections up separately. Do this either when repotting or any time during summer.

Climbing species: take 3in (8cm) stem tip cuttings in spring or early summer; cut just below a node and remove the lowest leaf, then treat the cut ends with rooting hormone and insert the cuttings into a moistened mixture of equal parts of moss peat and coarse sand. Keep warm, lightly shaded and just moist until new growth indicates that rooting is established, after about six weeks. Pot up the rooted cuttings in the usual compost and treat as mature plants; plant two or three cuttings together in a 4in (10cm) pot or use seven or eight cuttings together for a 10in (25cm) hanging basket.

Trouble Shooter

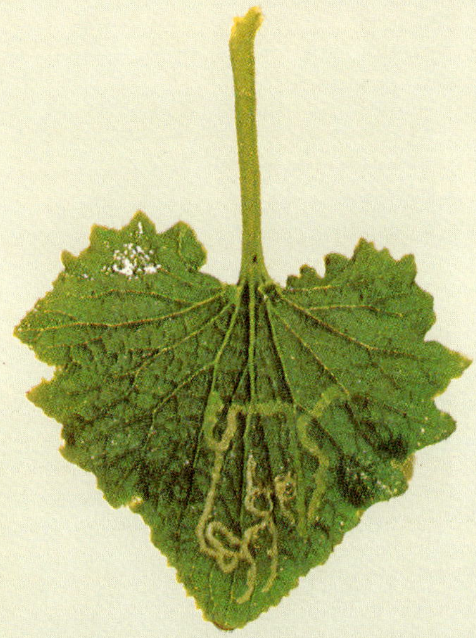

Cinerarias: yellow, wilting leaves are often due to cold draughts although wilting is also the first sign of underwatering; if the roots are allowed to dry out the plant will collapse altogether. Stand the pot in a bowl or bucket of water for half an hour to give the pot and the compost a thorough soaking; allow it to drain, then place it in a draught-free position. The plant should recover, but its life will inevitably have been shortened. As with all Senecios, too much water can be at least as harmful as too little and can lead to the plant's total collapse. One of the early symptoms of overwatering is browning at the leaf margins. Other adverse conditions that can appreciably reduce the flowering periods are too much sun and warmth — anything over 60-65°F (16-18°C) can bring flowering to a premature end — and insufficient humidity.

Cinerarias are prone to pests, and both greenfly and whitefly can be a problem. At any sign of infestation spray the plant with a malathion- or pyrethrum-based insecticide. Leaf miner may also attack, *left*; remove badly affected leaves and spray with the same insecticide. As an alternative, a systemic insecticide can be applied as an effective overall preventative; always follow the manufacturer's instructions when applying pesticides.

Succulents and other species: Although certain succulent species can be rather sensitive to less than ideal conditions, by comparison with Cinerarias other Senecios are virtually trouble free.

The essential requirement is to take care with watering; overwatering at any time is liable to set up rot in both the roots and the stems. Throughout the summer, water moderately — ideally from below, by letting the pot stand in a bowl of water for a few minutes until the surface of the compost glistens — and make sure that at least the surface of the compost is dry before watering again. Correct watering is even more important during winter, when it is far safer to err on the side of underwatering, especially when temperatures are low; the combination of cold and wet conditions is lethal. Good drainage is vital; always crock well when repotting to avoid plants getting waterlogged.

All Senecios may be infested by greenfly, which should be promptly sprayed with a pyrethrum-based insecticide. Mealy bug may also be a problem; if the attack is mild the best approach is to wipe away the fluffy white patches with a cloth or paintbrush dipped in methylated spirit. In the case of a severe infestation you may need to spray with a malathion-based insecticide.

Buying Guide

When buying a Cineraria, it's easy — especially if it's a gift — to be tempted to choose a plant in full flower; but plants in this condition will have a very limited life. Instead choose a Cineraria with plenty of flower buds at different stages of development, with only one or two open flowers so that you can check you have the variety you want. Also make sure the plant is bushy and compact with bright green foliage and that there are no aphids or other insect pests.

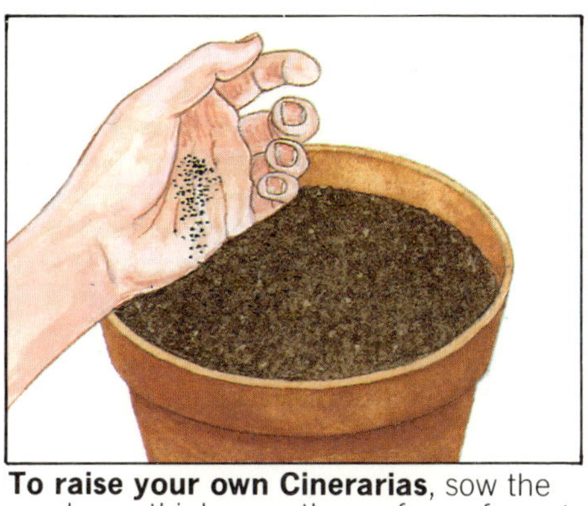

To raise your own Cinerarias, sow the seed very thinly over the surface of a pot or tray of compost.

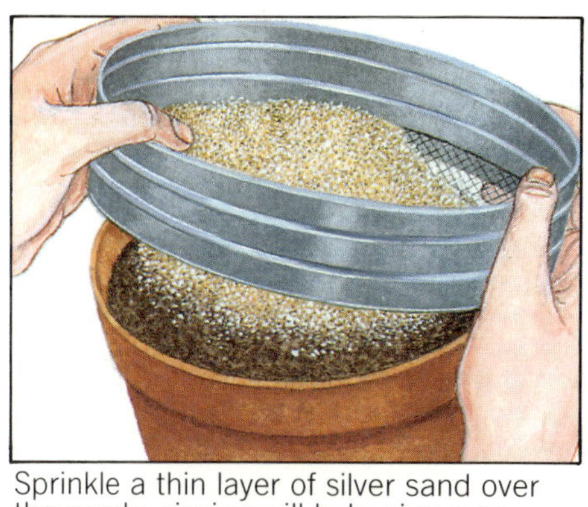

Sprinkle a thin layer of silver sand over the seeds; sieving will help give even coverage and keep out large lumps.

Species

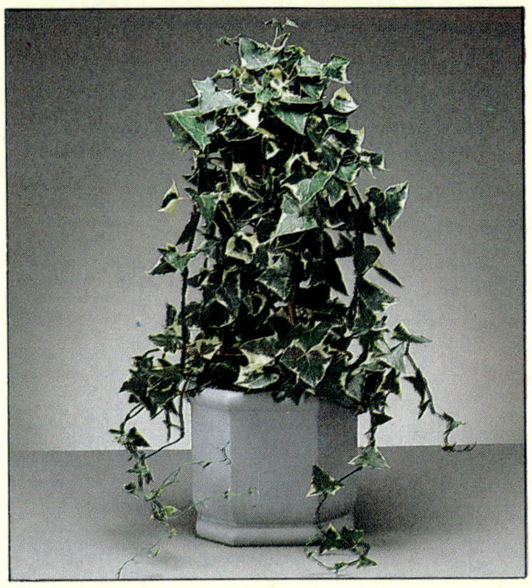

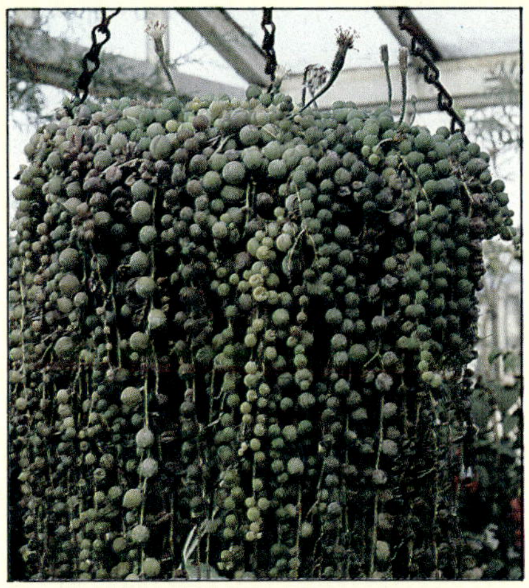

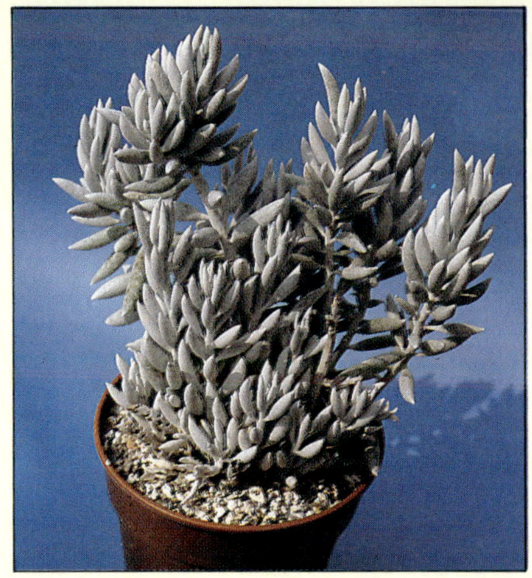

Senecio cruentus, also known as *Cineraria cruenta,* is the parent plant of the popular hybrid Cinerarias. The true species, which is less often seen, is an erect perennial plant from the Canary Islands, which grows to a height of about 2ft (0.6m), with soft, almost velvety stems and foliage; the leaves are triangular to oval in shape, between 4-8in (10-20cm) across, in deep green with reddish-tinged undersides. The daisy-like flowers are 1-3in (2.5-8cm) across, with purplish-red florets surrounding a darker central disc; they appear from December to June.

The florists' Cinerarias are hybrids and varieties of *S.cruentus* (they are often listed as *S.hybridus* or *Cineraria hybrida*). They range in height from 9-24in (23-60cm), with similar leaves to the species — heart-shaped or nearly triangular, softly hairy, deep green and with toothed edges. The daisy-like flowers are carried in a flat or dome-topped cluster, up to 9in (23cm) across, most commonly in shades of red, blue and purple, often surrounding a circle of white, with a typical daisy disc at the centre.

S.macroglossus is one of two or three popular, non-succulent, evergreen climbing plants, with twining stems that can be trained up thin canes or trail very attractively from a hanging basket. The common name of Cape Ivy reflects its marked resemblance to Common Ivy (*Hedera helix*), for which it can easily be mistaken, though the leaves are fleshier and more triangular and pointed. The difference is made obvious by the appearance of small, yellow, daisy-like flowers, though these are rarely produced indoors. *S.m.* 'Variegatum', *above left,* has slightly purple stems carrying bright green leaves that are beautifully variegated with creamy-yellow markings.

S.rowleyanus*, above centre,* known as the String-of-beads, is a succulent plant from south-west Africa, with slender, creeping stems which root freely to form a low, spreading mat. In a hanging basket, the stems will trail down 2ft (0.6m) or so, carrying a mass of small, spherical, glossy green leaves — the unusual, distinctly bead-like foliage which gives the plant its common name.

S.haworthii*, above right* (also known as *Kleinia tomentosa*), is another succulent species from South Africa, with very erect, branching stems reaching a height of 1ft (0.3m) or so. Small, fleshy, cylindrical leaves are closely packed all along the length of the stems and the whole plant is completely covered with very fine woolly white hairs.

S.articulatus (also known as *Kleinia articulata*) is a popular succulent species from South Africa, commonly known as the Candle Plant. It grows between 1-2ft (0.3-0.6m) high, with erect, fleshy, swollen stems branching profusely from the base; the stems are made up of jointed segments which are blue- or greyish-green in colour and covered with a pale grey, waxy coating. They bear small, arrow-shaped leaves with three to five deep lobes and attractive yellowish-white flowers, though these are not dependably produced indoors.

S.mikanoides is known as German Ivy though, like the Cape Ivy, it is South African in origin and another tall, evergreen climber. Again, the dark green leaves are typically ivy-shaped with five to seven pointed lobes with light green stems and stalks. Clusters of tiny, yellow, fragrant flowers are occasionally produced.

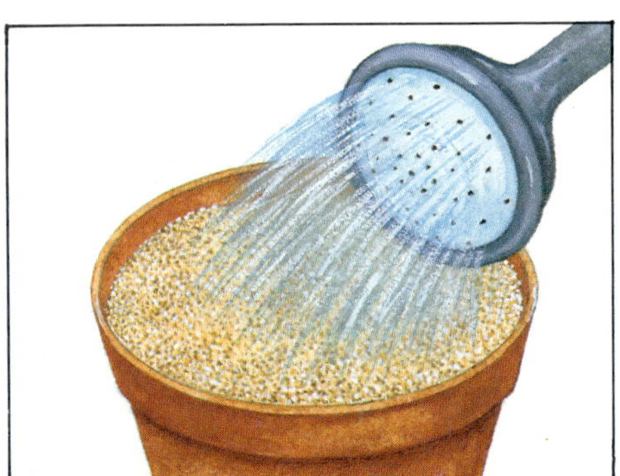

After sowing, water the pot — you can add fungicide to the water to protect seedlings from damping-off diseases.

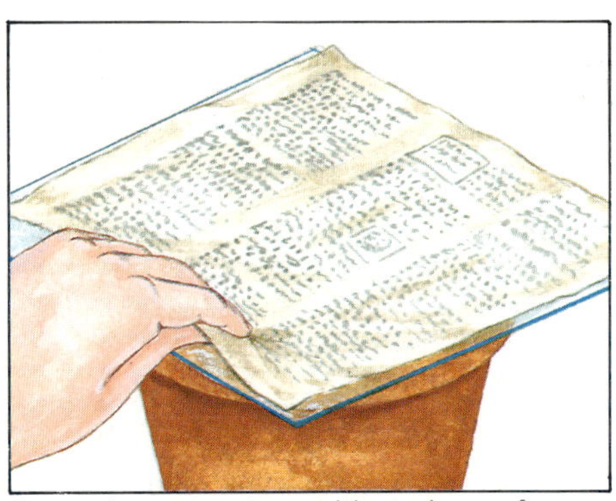

Cover the pot or tray with a piece of glass; a sheet of paper on top will shade the seeds from bright light.

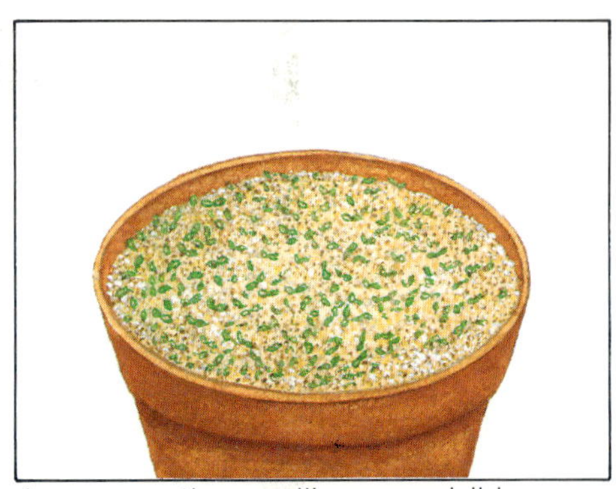

As soon as the seedlings are visible, remove the paper and the glass, but maintain the same temperature.

Setcreasea

Family name: **Commelinaceae**

Common name: **Purple Heart**

Care Easy	**Height** 9-12in (23-30cm)	**Flower** Summer
Light Bright	**Spread** 9-12in (23-30cm)	**Humidity** Mist spray regularly
Price Cheap	**Shape** Sprawling	**Availability** Garden centres
Temp. Min 45°F (7°C)	Ideal 70°F (21°C)	Max 80°F (27°C)

This attractive trailing houseplant has been known for a long time. It seems to have come originally from Mexico. It then spent many years in one of the German botanic gardens where it was ignored by botanists until its genus was recognised and redefined relatively recently, about 30 years ago.

The group is a very small one — and is closely related to the Tradescantias. *Setcreasea purpurea* has rich, purple stems and leaves — hence its common name — and is a particularly good subject for a hanging basket. Small pink flowers, *right*, are produced in summer, but these are fairly small and insignificant. Purple Heart tends to lose its rich colour with age so it is usually a good idea to take cuttings and discard old plants after a couple of years.

Spring and summer care

Setcreaseas are fast-growing and you will need to move your plant into a larger pot in March or April using John Innes No 2 compost in a well crocked container. Give the best possible light at all times. Summer temperatures can rise to 70-75°F (21-24°C). Water freely and quite frequently — say about twice weekly, though this depends on temperatures. Overhead spraying is advised to increase humidity, and this should be done in the morning before the sun is too strong. Add a weak liquid feed to the water every two weeks or so from May to September. It may be necessary to prune flowering stems, which can look straggly and spoil the appearance of the plant.

Autumn and winter care

Continue to give your Setcreasea good light — the brighter the light the better the colour of the foliage. Water occasionally to prevent the plant from going limp. Maintain a minimum temperature of 45°F (7°F).

Propagation

Take 3in (8cm) cuttings of non-flowering stems in spring, remove the lowest leaves and treat the cut end with a rooting hormone before inserting in a peat-based potting compost. Place in filtered light at about 65°F (18°C) and keep moist until rooting is established and leaf growth is apparent, then treat as a mature plant.

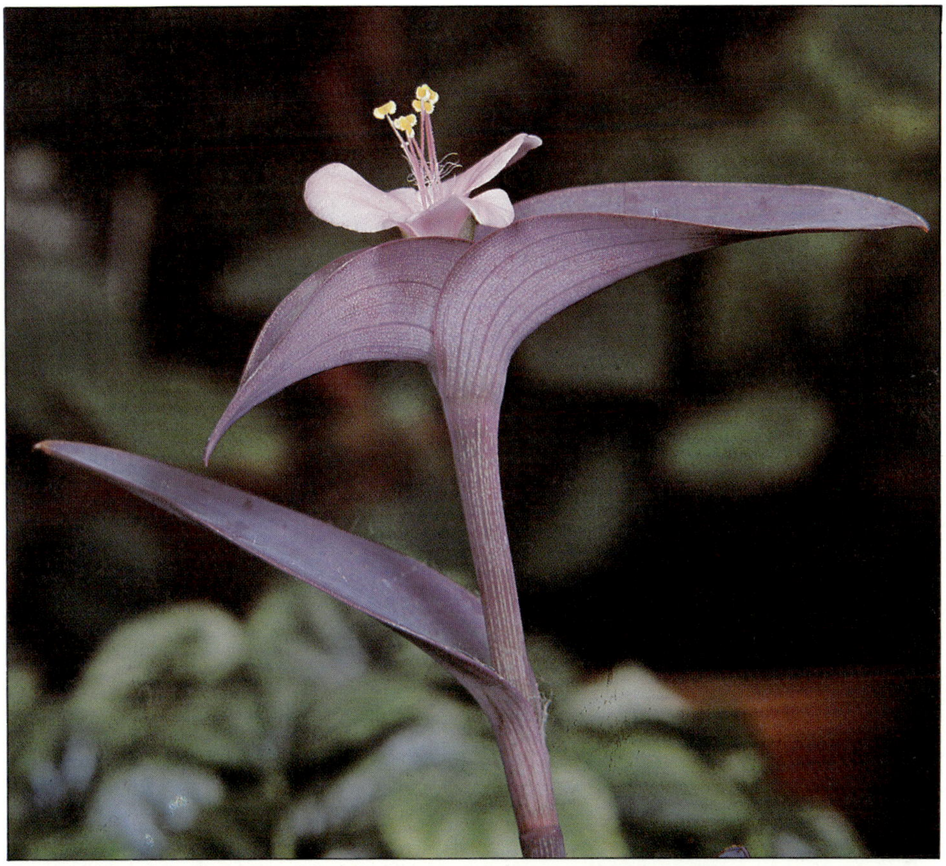

The small, pink flowers of Purple Heart appear during the summer.

Cuttings can also be rooted in water in a bright position but out of full sun. When roots have developed, pot them up carefully in peaty compost and treat as mature plants. Several newly rooted cuttings grouped together in one pot or basket often provide a more pleasing display than the one offered by the aging parent plant, so it is a good idea to renew your stock regularly.

Buying Guide

Look for a compact, bushy plant — ideally consisting of several cuttings potted together in one pot. Choose plants with well-developed, strong greyish pink or purple colouring.

Trouble Shooter

Insufficient light will spoil the colour of the leaves. Too dry compost for any length of time causes leaves to wilt and shrivel. Overhead spraying in full sun will scorch the leaves.

Greenfly is the main enemy and soon disfigures new growth. Treat with a pyrethrum-based insecticide or a systemic one.

Species

Setcreasea purpurea, *above and below*, of Mexican origin, is a sprawling plant with fleshy stems which start out erect but at about 9-12in (23-30cm) they adopt a trailing habit. The narrow, lance-shaped leaves are a greyish purple when kept in bright light, whereas shade causes the colour to fade. Small pink flowers appear in summer.

S. pallida has bright green waxy leaves, greyish-purple on the undersides, and rose-purple flowers.

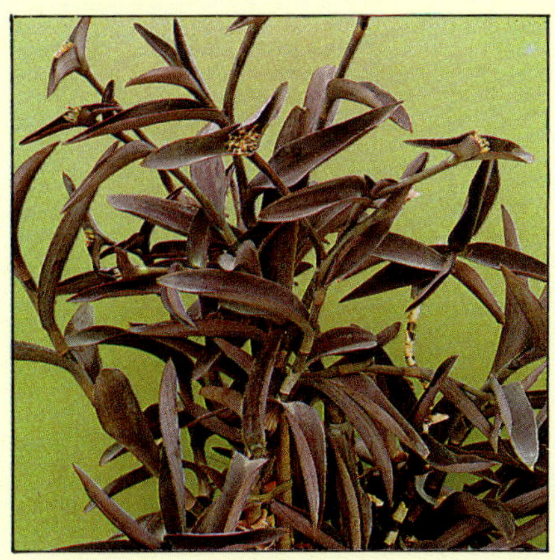

Sinningia

Family name: **Gesneriaceae**

Common name: **Gloxinia**

Care Easy	**Height** 9-10in (23-25cm)	**Flower** Summer
Light Bright, indirect	**Spread** 9-12in (23-30cm)	**Humidity** Mist spray regularly
Price Middle range	**Shape** Rosette	**Availability** Common
Temp. Min 45°F (7°C)	Ideal 70°F (21°C)	Max 75°F (24°C)

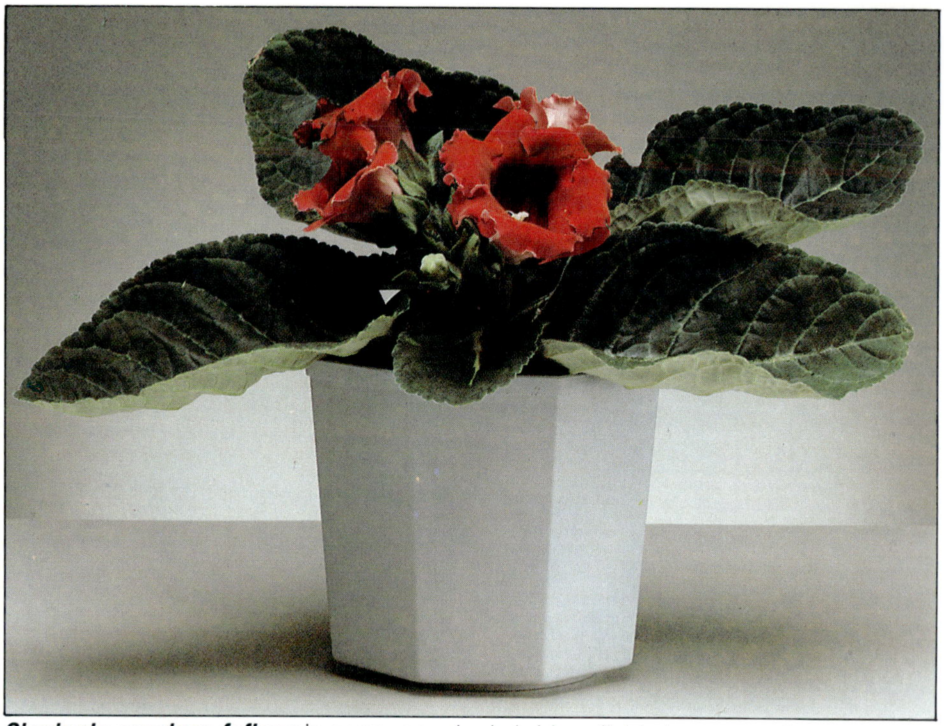

Sinningia speciosa fyfiana is a very popular hybrid available in many colours.

The most familiar plants of the genus Sinningia are commonly known as Gloxinias — not to be confused with the entirely separate genus also called Gloxinia.

Sinningia speciosa is the most popular species. It is a fairly small rosette-shaped plant with largish, hairy, deep green leaves and purple, velvety, bell-shaped flowers. It is usually bought in flower in summer and, as long as you choose a plant with plenty of unopened buds, should continue to bloom for two months or more. It is parent to innumerable hybrids in a wide range of colours.

Spring and summer care

Repot dormant tubers in early spring, using a good peat-based compost and making sure that the upper surface of each tuber is level with the surface of the compost. Then keep warm and rather dry until leaves appear, after which you should water carefully, preferably from below, and keep the compost moist at all times without wetting the leaves.

Once the buds form in summer, add liquid fertiliser to the watering every week or so until flowers begin to fade. Spray the surrounding air with tepid water in the early morning to increase the humidity, particularly in hot weather, but try to avoid wetting both flowers and leaves. Position in bright light but shaded from direct sun. A temperature of 65-70°F (18-21°C) should be maintained, rising to 75°F (24°C) in the height of summer. As flowers fade, dead head and restrict watering until tubers are dormant.

Autumn and winter care

Flowering is usually over by mid to late September, when the compost should be allowed to dry out completely. The tubers can then be removed and stored somewhere free from frost at around 45°F (7°C) until early spring. They can, of course, be left in their pots, in which case they should be kept bone dry until March, when they should be encouraged into growth again by higher temperatures and resumption of watering.

Propagation

Cut the tuber into sections, each with a growing point, and start them off in early spring. Alternatively, take leaf cuttings in summer. Carefully make several cuts through the central vein on the underside of the leaf, using a razor blade. Lay several leaves flat on a mixture of peat and sand at about 70°F (21°C) and hold down firmly with small staples. Keep constantly moist and shaded until plantlets appear from the cut areas. Another method is to sow seeds in early spring in peat-based compost with some added sand, and place in a propagator at 70°F (21°C).

Trouble Shooter

If plants are too cold while growing or exposed to frost when dormant, rot may set in and affect either tuber or foliage. Overhead spraying in full sun may scorch the foliage.

Greenfly is the main enemy and should be promptly treated either with a pyrethrum-based insecticide or a systemic.

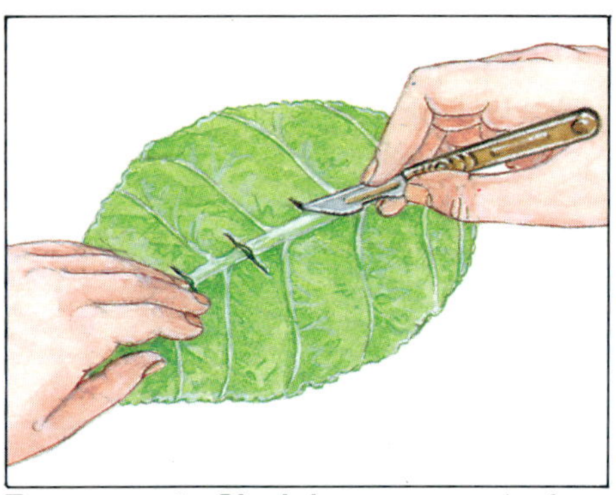

To propagate Gloxinias remove a leaf and lay it face downwards. Using a sharp knife or scalpel cut across the midrib, halfway between pairs of side veins.

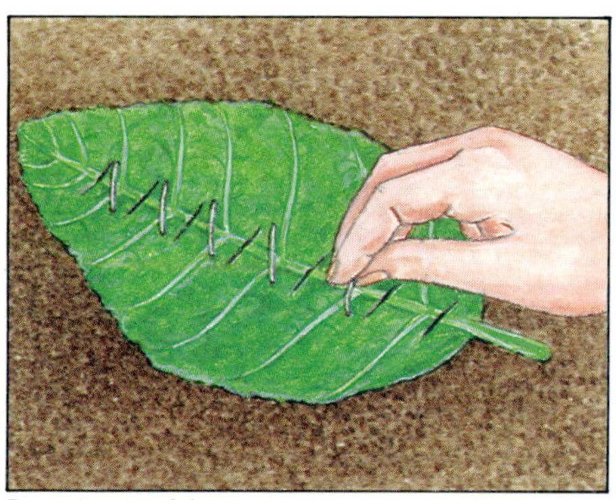

Peg the leaf face upwards on to the surface of a tray of potting compost. Hold the cuts in contact with the compost using hair pins or pieces of bent wire.

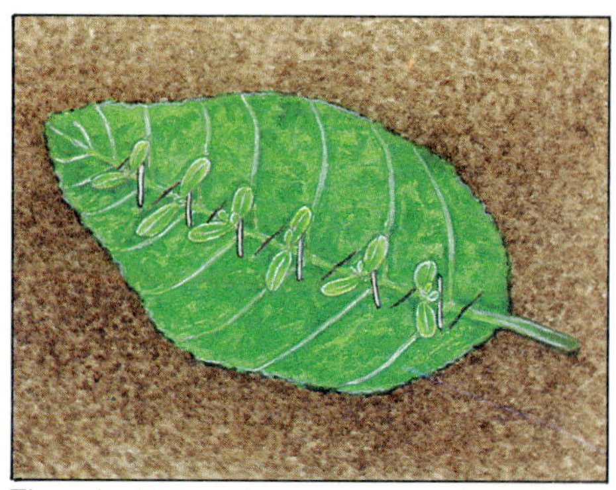

Tiny plantlets will soon emerge from the midrib. When two or three leaves have grown pull the plantlets gently away from the parent leaf and pot up individually.

Species

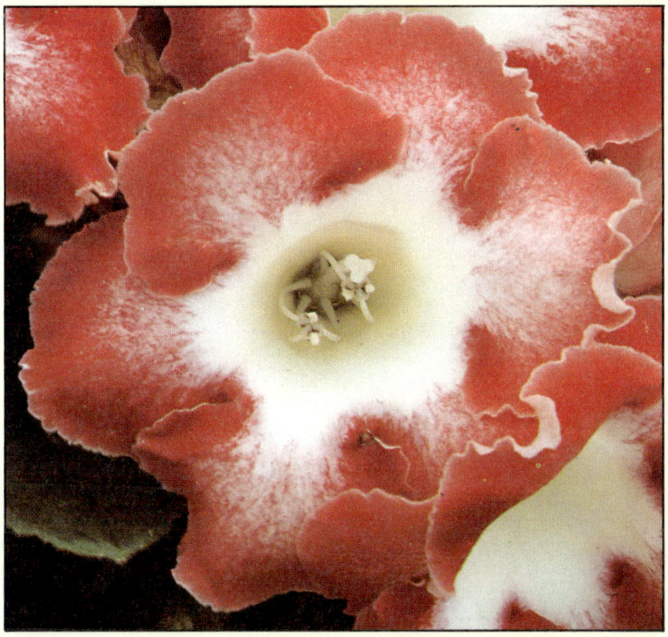

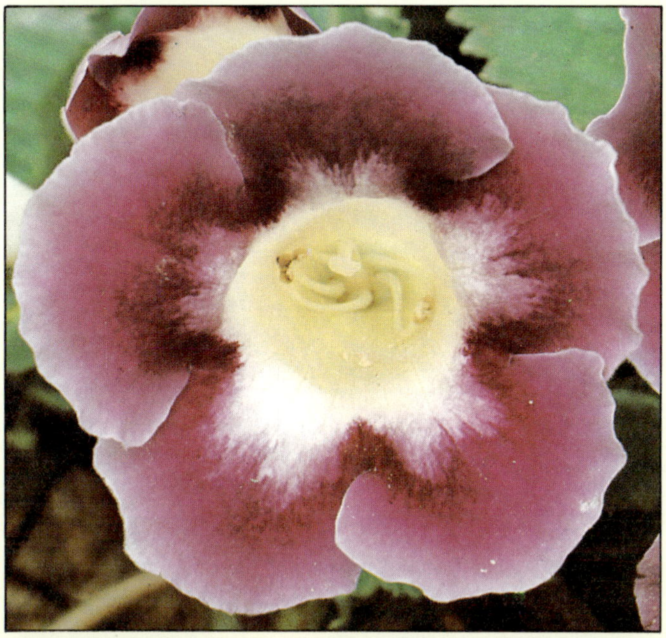

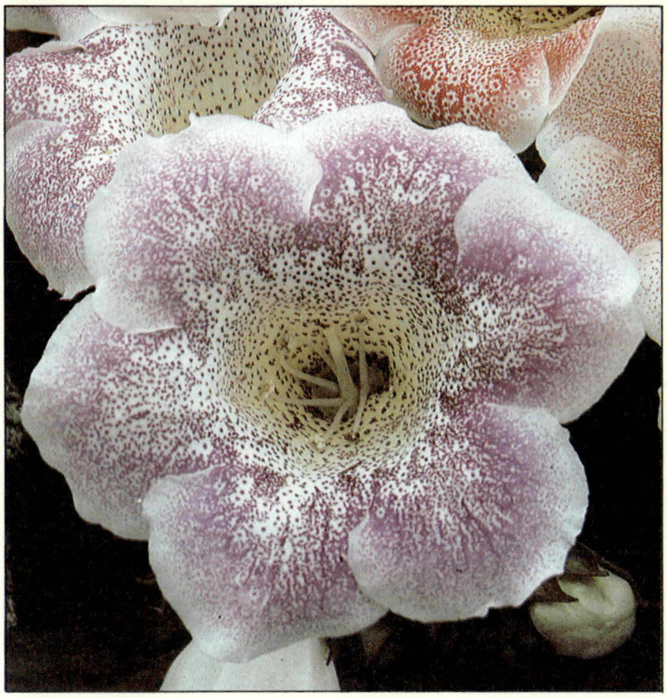

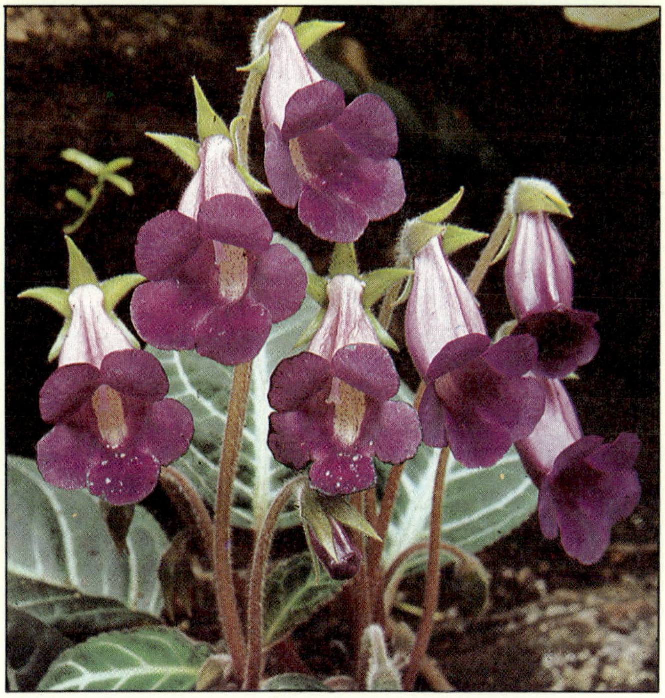

Sinningia speciosa (once known as *Gloxinia speciosa*), from Brazil, is a fairly small rosette-shaped plant which grows up to about 9-10in (23-25cm) tall, with a spread of up to 1ft (0.3m). It is almost stemless and has largish leaves, about 8in (20cm) long and 6in (15cm) across, which are deep green in colour with fine white hairs and reddish purple undersides. Violet or purple, bell-shaped, velvety flowers, about 2-4in (5-10cm) long, appear during the summer from May to August.

A large-flowered group, probably of hybrid origin, known as *S.speciosa fyfiana*, has been introduced; its flower colours include various shades of red, pink, mauve, purple and pure white, *top right, top left, above left*. Some have smooth-edged petals while others are crinkled, and some have single flowers while others are double.

S.regina, *above right*, from Brazil, grows to about 9in (23cm) and has metallic green leaves, veined in pure white and deep red on the undersides. The small, semi-pendent flowers are deep purple.

S.pusilla is the most popular miniature Sinningia species for indoor growth. It is also one parent of the miniature hybrids. It grows to only about 2in (5cm) high — so many plants would be needed to provide an eye-catching display — with a quaint little rosette of brownish-green leaves and miniature, tubular, lilac-pink flowers.

Solanum

Family name: **Solanaceae**

Common names: **Winter Cherry, Jerusalem Cherry**

Care Easy	**Height** 12-18in (30-45cm)	**Flower** Winter
Light Sunny	**Spread** 12-18in (30-45cm)	**Humidity** Mist spray daily
Price Cheap	**Shape** Bushy	**Availability** Common

Temp. Min 50°F (10°C) Ideal 65°F (18°C) Max 75°F (24°C)

The very large and varied genus Solanum contains nearly 2000 species of shrubs and climbers, ornamental plants, a number of weeds and such vegetables as the aubergine and the potato. Of this whole group there are just two which are popular houseplants. The Winter Cherry (*Solanum capsicastrum*), *right*, is the better known of the two, but the Jerusalem Cherry (*S.pseudocapsicum*) is also popular, especially in the United States, and is really quite similar.

The Winter Cherry is a bushy, evergreen, shrubby plant up to 18in (45cm) tall whose main attraction is its highly decorative, but slightly-poisonous fruit. These berries start to appear in late autumn and work their way from green through yellow and orange to an orangey-red, over the following few months. The Jerusalem Cherry is similar but somewhat taller.

This burst of winter colour makes them highly popular, especially around Christmas-time when they tend to be bought in vast quantities as presents, only to be discarded when the berries have shrivelled and fallen off. But this is an unnecessary waste, for given the right conditions they can easily be carried over to flower and fruit again the following season.

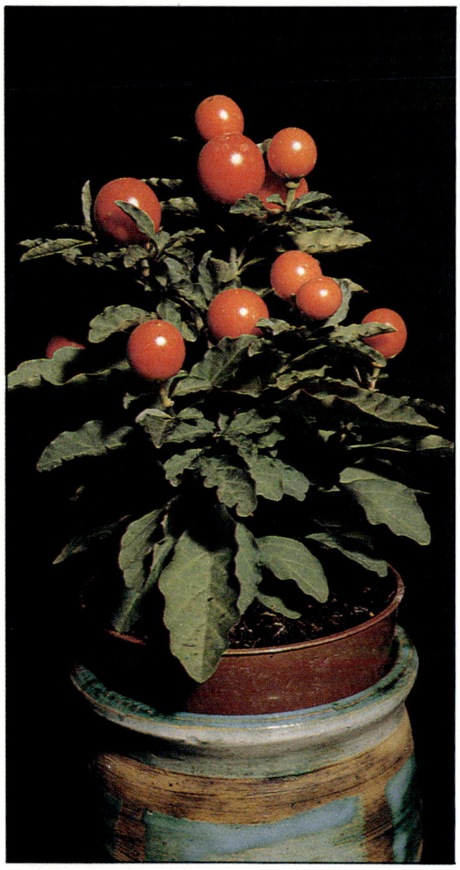

These colourful fruits will brighten up the gloomiest winter days.

Spring and summer care

Repot your plant after fruiting is over, if necessary — roots will appear on the surface of the compost or through drainage holes in the pot if the plant is overcrowded; move the plant on to a container one size larger, to a final size of 6in (15cm), using John Innes No 2 compost. Mature plants that are being kept over for a further season should be pruned back by about one-third at the same time. Pinch out the growing tips when shoots are 3in (8cm) high, to promote bushy growth.

Plants that are being carried over for a second year should ideally be stood outdoors in a sunny, sheltered position, from late spring to September. Indoors, your plant is best kept at a temperature of 60-65°F (16-18°C), in the brightest spot and with good ventilation.

Water plentifully, to keep the compost moist but not sodden; if plants are allowed to become dry, flowering will suffer as will the fruit which follows. Add a fertiliser to the water every two weeks from June onwards, and mist spray daily with tepid water to provide a humid atmosphere and encourage the fruit to set.

Autumn and winter care

Keep your plant at a temperature of 55-60°F (13-16°C), in the brightest possible position — full sun keeps the berries fresh and colourful; give good air circulation, but avoid cold draughts. Water regularly to ensure that the compost is kept moist for as long as the berries last, then decrease the watering, giving just enough water to keep the soil from drying out completely. Add a liquid fertiliser fortnightly and mist spray daily with tepid water, until the end of the fruiting season.

Propagation

Seeds sown in March will flower and fruit the same year. Sow them in the usual compost, lightly covered with a sprinkling of sharp sand; keep moist and lightly shaded, at a temperature of 60-70°F (16-21°C), enclosed in a propagator or clear polythene bag. When seeds germinate, uncover them and grow the seedlings on in a bright position, with two to three hours of direct sunlight a day. When they are around 3in (7cm) high pot them up separately into 3in (7cm) pots and treat as mature plants; pinch out the growing tips to encourage bushy growth.

Trouble Shooter

Leaves will wilt and berries fall if plants become too dry; too hot and stuffy an atmosphere is equally damaging. Take care not to overwater; leaves will turn yellowish and drop off. Plants will begin to look sickly if they are in too shady a position — Solanums need bright light and some full sun to thrive.

Greenfly may infest the young growth in early summer and whitefly may also be a problem; spray with a malathion-based insecticide. If the fine webs of Red Spider Mite appear use the same insecticide. Solanums are subject to fungus attacks on their foliage — immediately any mould is noted, remove the infected leaf and spray with a copper-based fungicide.

Species

Solanum capsicastrum, the Winter Cherry, is an extremely popular, if temporary, houseplant. A native of Brazil, this evergreen shrub grows 12-18in (30-45cm) tall, with soft, woody stems and branches bearing 3in (8cm) long, greyish-green, lance-shaped leaves. Small, star-shaped, white flowers bloom in summer and are followed in late autumn or early winter by shiny, ½in (13mm) diameter berries which last for several months, changing colour as they ripen, from green to orangey-red. The plants are generally treated as annuals, to be discarded when the berries shrivel and fall off, but they can easily be kept to flower and fruit the following season. There is also a very pretty form 'Variegatum', *right*, that has leaves edged and variegated in creamy-white.

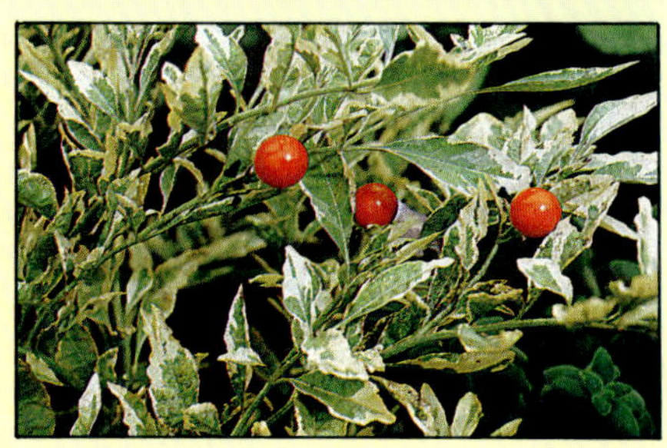

S.pseudocapsicum, the Jerusalem Cherry, is very similar to the Winter Cherry but generally more robust and therefore easier to grow. It is a taller-growing plant, which can reach a height of 2½ft (0.75m); the berries, too, are slightly larger and longer lasting.

Sparmannia

Family name: **Tiliaceae**

Common name: **African Hemp/ African Windflower/House Lime**

Care Easy	**Height** 5-6ft (1.5-1.8m)	**Flower** Early spring
Light Bright	**Spread** 3ft (0.9m)	**Humidity** Mist spray regularly
Price Middle range	**Shape** Tall bush	**Availability** Garden centres
Temp.	Min 45°F (7°C) · Ideal 65°F (18°C)	Max 75°F (24°C)

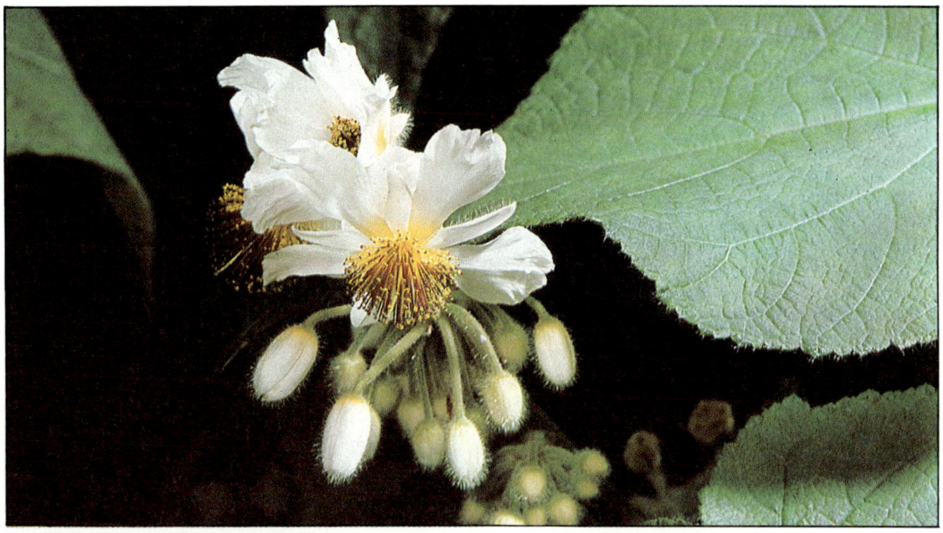

Sparmannia is a good choice if you want an easy, fast-growing plant.

Sparmannias are evergreen shrub-like plants, some of them reaching tree-like proportions, with very attractive foliage and particularly interesting flowers. There are about seven species altogether, all of them of African origin. The only one commonly found as a houseplant is *Sparmannia africana, above right,* variously known as African Hemp, House Lime or African Windflower, among other things. A vigorous grower, in its natural habitat of Cape Province it can reach a height of 18-20ft (5.4-6m), but it's hardly likely to exceed 6ft (1.8m) indoors.

The quite fragrant flowers are borne in long-stalked clusters, against a background of soft, pale green, heart-shaped leaves, with pure white petals and a mass of yellow stamens at the centre; the stamens are sensitive to the touch and open outwards if the flowers are brushed against or even if they are blown by a gentle breeze. Individual flowers are short-lived, but this is compensated for by a succession of blooms appearing over a number of weeks.

Spring and summer care

Repot every year in spring into a rich soil-based compost such as John Innes No 3. Pot plants on to larger containers as they fill their pots with roots; African Hemp is a vigorous grower so this may be necessary more than once a year, but avoid repotting in late autumn or winter. A final pot size of 10in (25cm) will be fine for a 6ft (1.8m) plant.

Pinch out the stem tips of young plants and prune back shoots and stems quite hard either at potting time or after flowering, to keep the plant in good shape; cuttings of young shoots taken in March can be used for propagation. Individual flowers are short-lived, but will remain for some weeks — remove them when they start to look unattractive and cut the stem right back when the whole cluster is finished.

Summer temperatures should be relatively cool — around 60-65°F (16-18°C) will encourage continued flowering outside the main season of May to July. These plants should always be placed in a bright position, but avoid exposing them to full sun for long periods. Keep them well-ventilated to ensure the atmosphere is not too stuffy.

Water freely, to keep the compost moist. Add a liquid fertiliser to the water every 10-14 days from spring (or earlier, if flower buds appear before that) to autumn and mist spray the foliage every few days, especially at higher temperatures; this also helps to keep the hairy leaves and stems free of dust.

Autumn and winter care

Keep winter temperatures down to about 45-50°F (7-10°C) and give your plant good light — bright, indirect light is best. Provide good air circulation but avoid cold draughts. Water only moderately, giving sufficient to prevent the compost drying out — once a week should be adequate.

Propagation

Stem cuttings will root easily, to produce flowering plants the following season. Use 4-5in (10-13cm) long tip cuttings of young stems taken during pruning, in March or April. Treat the cut ends with a rooting hormone and set them in a thoroughly-moistened mixture of equal parts of peat and sand; keep lightly shaded, and warm, at a temperature of 60-65°F (16-18°C), until new growth indicates that rooting is established. Move cuttings to 3in (7cm) pots of compost and treat as mature plants; growth is quite rapid, so one or two repottings may be needed during the first few months.

Trouble Shooter

Leaves will wilt and droop if the compost is allowed to become too dry. There will be a similar reaction, with the foliage becoming brownish and sickly looking, if they are left in too deep shade; also plants may not flower and may develop overlong leaf-stalks, giving the plant an unpleasing, straggly appearance. Conversely, avoid full sunlight, particularly when mist spraying — the leaves are sensitive and will scorch.

Mealy bug is a likely pest; if any tell-tale fluffy white patches appear, wipe them away with a cloth or paintbrush dipped in methylated spirit.

Species

Sparmannia africana, known as African Hemp or Windflower, is the only species commonly grown as a houseplant. It originates from Cape Province in southern Africa, and in habitat it can grow 18-20ft (5.4-6m) high but 5-6ft (1.5-1.8m) is the usual limit indoors. The large heart-shaped, pale green leaves are covered in fine soft hairs and serrated at the edges; they grow 6-9in (15-23cm) long, carried on leafstalks of similar length. The slightly scented flowers appear in long-stalked clusters, each group about 1½in (4cm) across, four-petalled, in pure white with a dense mass of prominent yellow stamens — often with purple tips — which are very sensitive to the touch. They are quite short-lived, fading after only a few days, but there is usually a succession of blooms opening over a period of a few weeks — and individual flowers can remain attractive for some weeks after they have faded. The main flowering period is centred on the early spring but given the right conditions they may bloom again in early summer and indeed continue to produce flowers for much of the year. A variety of *S.africana*, 'Flore Pleno', has attractive clusters of double flowers, but these are not always very readily produced; the dwarf form 'Nana', is more dependably-flowering.

Spathiphyllum

Family name: **Araceae**

Common name:
Sail Plant/Peace Lily

Care Straightforward	**Height** 1ft (0.3m)	**Flower** Late spring-early summer
Light Light shade	**Spread** 1ft (0.3m)	**Humidity** Mist spray frequently
Price Middle range	**Shape** Leafy clump	**Availability** Garden centres

Temp. Min 60°F (16°C) — Ideal 80°F (27°C) — Max 90°F (32°C)

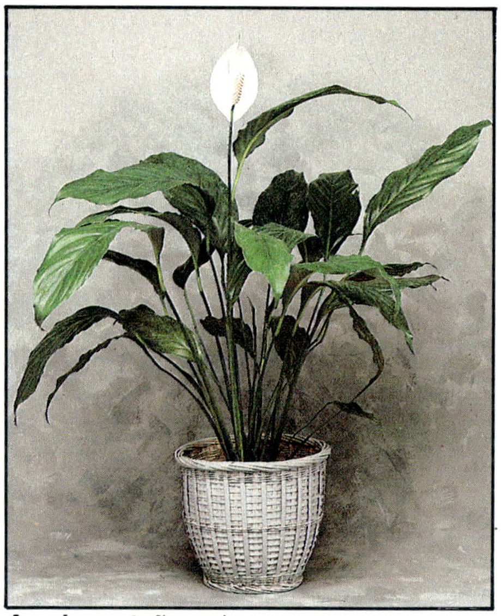

An elegant, flowering evergreen.

Spathiphyllums are very attractive, evergreen perennials, mostly of tropical American origin, which produce impressive, Arum Lily-like flowers towering over the foliage. Their glossy leaves on long, slender stalks grow from short, underground rhizomes and rise in clusters directly out of the soil.

Of the 25 or 30 species that make up this group, there are two forms in particular that have become popular houseplants. The Sail Plant, (*Spathiphyllum wallisii*) or Peace Lily, *above right*, as it is sometimes known, is the only true species commonly grown indoors. It grows about 1ft (0.3m) high and freely produces flowers from late spring into the summer. The 'flower' actually consists of a large, pure white spathe, or petal-like bract, surrounding a cream-coloured, column-like spike (called the spadix) densely packed with tiny flowers looking very much like a slender sweetcorn. The spathe gradually fades to a pale green colour and flowers remain very attractive for six weeks or more.

Spring and summer care

Repot plants every spring using a good peat-based compost with a little sand added; crock well to ensure good drainage. Move them on to a container one size larger each year, to a final pot size of 5-6in (13-15cm) — the variety 'Mauna Loa' may need to go up to 7-8in (18-20cm) — after that, you should topdress plants anually, replacing the top 1-2in (2.5-5cm) with fresh compost.

In summer, Spathiphyllum will take all the heat available; a minimum of 65-70°F (18-21°C) is recommended and 80°F (27°C) would be beneficial. A semi-shaded position is best — direct sunlight will burn the leaves.

Water your plant freely so that the compost is moist at all times and add a liquid fertiliser to the water every two or three weeks from early spring through to the autumn. A humid atmosphere is important — these plants are very sensitive to dry air; stand the pot on a tray of moist pebbles all year round and mist spray frequently — every day when temperatures are very high.

Autumn and winter care

If Spathiphyllums are to thrive they are best kept at temperatures of 60-65°F (16-18°C). Give them as brightly-lit a spot as possible, though not direct sunlight; provide good air circulation but keep the plant out of cold draughts — they don't like gas or oil fumes either. Water moderately so that the compost stays moist — it should never be allowed to dry out. Maintain a humid atmosphere and mist spray regularly.

Propagation

Divide the rootstock at potting time, gently pulling rhizomes apart — make sure each piece has at least two or three leaves attached — and pot up individually in the usual mixture. Keep moist and shaded, at a temperature of 70°F (21°C), until roots are firmly established, after which treat as mature plants.

Buying Guide

Spathiphyllums suffer badly if they are underwatered; make sure that the compost is moist before you buy.

Trouble Shooter

Foliage will begin to shrivel and wilt if a plant gets too dry — a thorough soaking should help it recover. Leaves will turn yellowish and gradually dry out if exposed to too much hot sun — always keep them shaded from direct sunlight.

Mealy bug may attack the plant; wipe away with a cloth or paintbrush dipped in methylated spirit. Greenfly is a possible pest that requires urgent attention; spray with a pyrethrum-based insecticide. If humidity is too low, red spider mite can be a problem. If you spot their fine webs spray with a malathion-based insecticide.

Species

Spathiphyllum wallisii, known as the Sail Plant or Peace Lily, is the only true species commonly grown indoors. An evergreen perennial, native to Colombia and Venezuela, it reaches a height of 1ft (0.3m) as a houseplant. It has long-stalked, glossy green leaves which grow directly out of the compost from a short, underground rhizome. The long-lasting flowers arise from the centres of leaf clusters on 8-10in (20-25cm) long stalks, appearing in late spring and into the summer. Each flower head consists of a creamy-white spadix, about 2in (5cm) long, rising from the base of an oval, 3-4in (8-10cm) long, leaf-like spathe which surrounds it. The spathe starts off as pure-white and gradually fades to pale green. 'Mauna Loa', *right*, is a popular hybrid which is very similar to *S.wallisii* but rather larger. It can grow 2ft (0.6m) tall, with 9in (23cm) long leaves on 10-12in (25-30cm) stalks. Flowers are also larger, with a 4-6in (10-15cm) spathe at the head of a 15-20in (38-50cm) stalk; they are freely produced in May and can sometimes appear intermittently throughout the year.

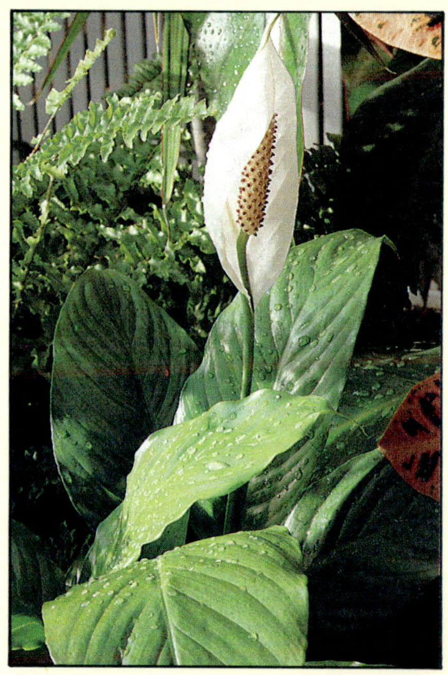

Stephanotis

Family name: **Asclepiadaceae**

Common name: **Madagascar Jasmine/Wax Flower**

Care Straightforward	**Height** 10ft (3m)	**Flower** Summer
Light Bright indirect	**Spread** 5ft (1.5m)	**Humidity** Mist spray regularly
Price Middle range	**Shape** Climber	**Availability** Garden centres
Temp. Min 50°F (10°C)	Ideal 70°F (21°C)	Max 80°F (27°C)

The exquisite climber Stephanotis is a superb choice of plant for any home, with its beautiful, waxy, white flowers that can fill a whole house with their exquisite fragrance. Madagascar Jasmine or Wax Flower, as *Stephanotis floribunda, right,* is commonly known, is the one member of this small genus generally grown indoors, and probably one of the best known of all climbing houseplants. It has fleshy, firm, evergreen leaves and bears bunches of sweetly-scented, waxy-looking, white funnel-like flowers from May to October.

This distinctive plant is a vigorous climber, twining around any available support; suitably trained, up a trellis, say, in a conservatory, it can reach a height of 10ft (3m) or more. More modestly, as a houseplant Stephanotis is usually grown with its stems laced round a wire hoop; this bunches the flowers together — making the plant look extremely prolific. Alternatively, a plant trained up a moss-covered pole can also look very attractive. However you grow it remember that Stephanotis has no tendrils to support itself, so for it to climb you will need to tie in the stems regularly.

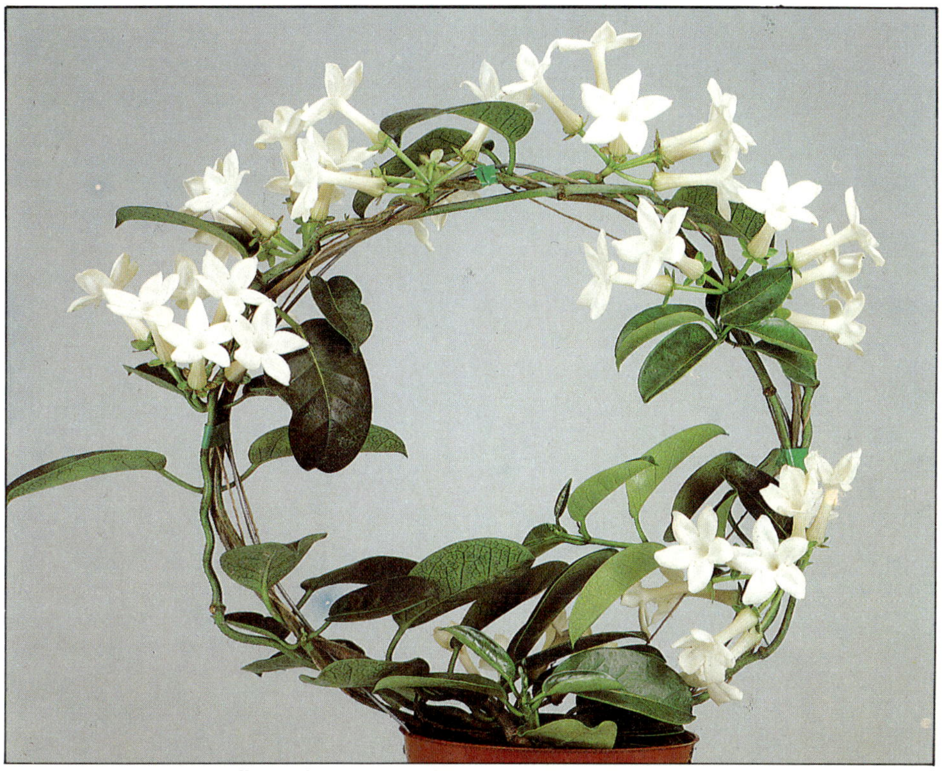

This lovely summer flowering climber has the most delicious scent.

Spring and summer care

Repot plants every year in early spring, into John Innes No 2, to a final pot size of 6in (15cm) — or 8in (20cm) for a very large plant. Thereafter topdress annually, replacing the top 1-2in (2.5-5cm) with fresh compost. Remember to provide a climbing support such as trellis, a wire hoop or moss pole at repotting time, firming the ball of your support into the compost. Use plastic covered wire twists to tie in the stems.

Keep in a well-ventilated, brightly-lit spot, though avoid direct sunshine which will damage the foliage. A temperature of around 70°F (21°C) is ideal; Stephanotis will thrive in warmer rooms, but what is important is to keep the temperature reasonably constant, as this plant hates sudden fluctuations.

Water freely, as often as necessary to keep the compost thoroughly moist, and add a liquid fertiliser to the water every three weeks or so from April to September. Stephanotis is not very lime tolerant, so if you live in an area with very hard water then it's a wise precaution to use boiled water with a few added drops of vinegar for watering your plant. Humidity is important, especially at the higher temperatures; mist spray the plant regularly, but try to avoid the flowers.

Autumn and winter care

The best time to prune is after flowering. Cut back stems that have grown too long using a pair of sharp secateurs — but don't cut them right back or you may damage the plant. The stems exude a milky sap when cut and this should be staunched by mist spraying or brushing the cut with cold water.

From October to March keep your plant at a temperature of 55-60°F (13-16°C), in a very well-lit position but not in direct sunshine. Stephanotis requires good air circulation at all times, but keep it free of any cold draughts; gas or oil fumes are also damaging. Water regularly but sparingly so as to keep the compost just moist, but don't overwater.

Propagation

Take 3-4in (8-10cm) long tip cuttings in the spring or early summer from non-flowering lateral shoots — cut just below the node and remove the lowest leaves. Dip the cuttings in water to staunch the latex, then treat the cut ends with a rooting hormone and insert them into a mixture of three parts John Innes No 2 and one part sharp sand. Keep the compost just moist and lightly shaded in a propagator or clear polythene bag, at a temperature of 70°F (21°C). When new growth is apparent, after about eight to ten weeks, plant the cuttings individually in 3in (7cm) pots of John Innes No 2 and treat as mature plants, supporting them with a thin cane.

Trouble Shooter

Yellowing leaves and falling flowers can be caused by sudden changes in temperature, underwatering or overwatering, or too much lime in the water or compost.

Both mealy bug and scale insect are likely to attack; you can wipe away the fluffy white patches or pale coloured scales with a brush dipped in methylated spirit. Alternatively, spray with a malathion-based insecticide or apply a systemic insecticide. Also use these insecticides if the fine brown webs of red spider mite appear.

Species

Stephanotis floribunda, the Madagascar Jasmine or Wax Flower, will grow to 20ft (6m) tall or more in its Madagascan habitat, and even in cultivation it can easily reach a height of 10ft (3m) if properly trained. The leathery, 3in (8cm) long, oval-shaped leaves are dark green with a prominent light green central rib; they are set in opposite pairs along the rather fleshy, twining stems. The heavily-scented, waxy, white flowers are funnel-shaped; they are borne in loose clusters from the leaf axils from May to October, as many as 10 blooms in a single bunch.

Strelitzia

Family name: **Musaceae**

Common names: **Bird of Paradise/Crane Flower**

Care Easy	**Height** 3-4ft (0.9-1.2m)	**Flower** Spring/early summer
Light Sunny	**Spread** 3ft (0.9m)	**Humidity** Mist spray occasionally
Price Middle range	**Shape** Leafy clump	**Availability** Garden centres
Temp. Min 55°F (13°C)	Ideal 70°F (21°C)	Max 80°F (27°C)

Strelitzias are famous for their unique and spectacular flowers, which are brilliantly coloured and shaped like the head of an exotic bird. Extremely beautiful and long-lasting, the Bird of Paradise flower is surely the most stunning of any flower grown in the home. Yet, in the light of its exotic appearance it may come as a surprise to learn that it is far from being a difficult houseplant, putting up with seemingly quite disagreeable conditions with no obvious discomfort.

Strelitzia reginae is the species which is widely grown indoors; with a fan of long, spear-shaped, metallic green leaves, it reaches a height of 3-4ft (0.9-1.2m). The remarkable, 6in (15cm) long flowers appear in spring and early summer on 3-4ft (0.9-1.2m) stalks; from a long, sheath-shaped bract, green flushed with purple, rise a succession of brilliant orange flowers, standing erect like a crest, with a vivid blue 'tongue' jutting from the centre.

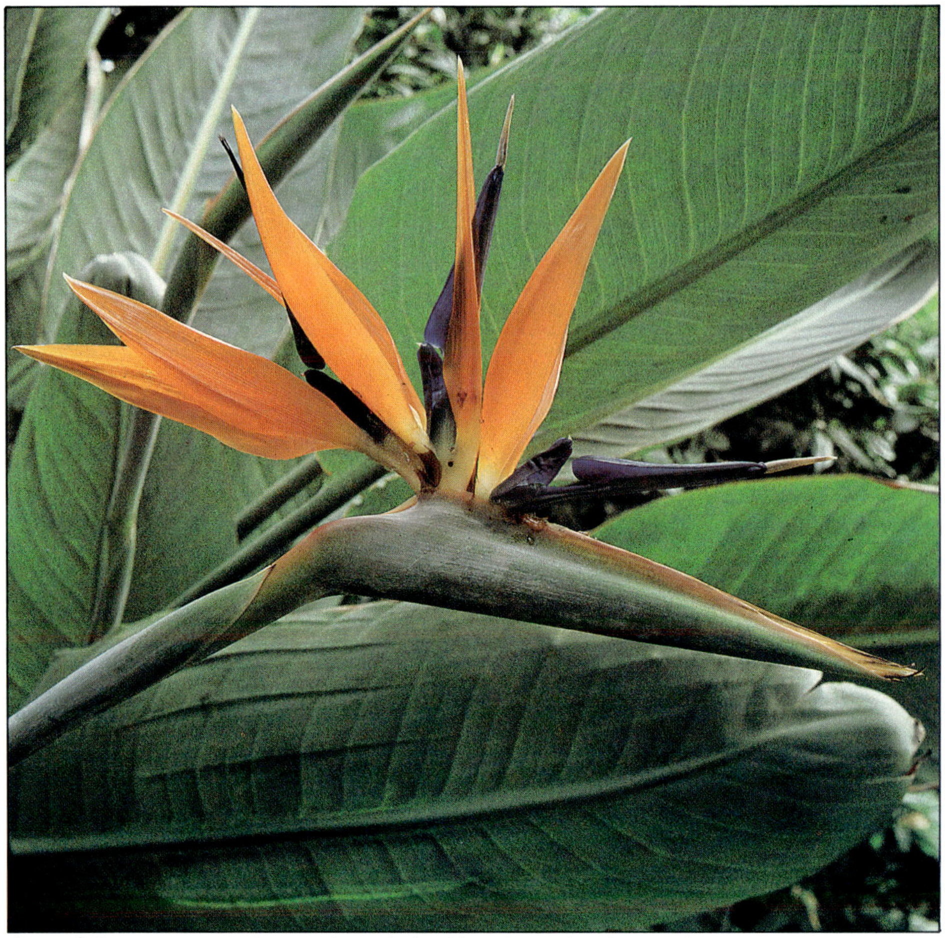

One of the most stunning and exotic looking flowering houseplants.

Spring and summer care

Repot young plants every year in early spring, into a well-crocked pot of John Innes No 2, moving them into a container one or two sizes larger to a final 10-12in (25-30cm) pot or tub. After that plants should be topdressed annually, replacing the top 1-2in (2.5-5cm) with fresh compost, but not repotted or otherwise disturbed; mature, flowering plants that are disturbed are liable to stop flowering.

Normal room temperatures of 65-70°F (18-21°C) are perfectly suitable, but Strelitzias will not flower if grown in inadequate light, so give your plant the best possible light, including full sun.

Water thoroughly, so that the compost is moist throughout the warmer months, but allow the surface to dry out before watering again. Add a liquid fertiliser to the water about every two weeks between May and September, and mist spray occasionally, taking care to avoid the flowers.

Autumn and winter care

Keep your plant at a temperature of around 55-60°F (13-16°C) during the winter, with good air circulation but out of cold draughts. Give as good light as possible — full sun will certainly be beneficial. Water sparingly — give just enough to prevent the compost from drying out completely.

Propagation

The easiest method is by division of the rootstock before flowering in the spring. Using a sharp knife, cut old, overcrowded clumps into two or gently pull away a section, with two or three leaves and some roots attached, from a mature plant. Treat any cuts with a fungicidal sulphur powder then pot the sections up individually into John Innes No 2 compost. Keep warm and just moist, in bright light but shaded from direct sunlight; roots should become established within six weeks, after which treat it as a mature plant. It should flower within about two to three years.

Species

Strelitzia reginae, the Bird of Paradise or Crane Flower, is the species most commonly grown. It grows to a height of 3-4ft (0.9-1.2m) with metallic green, spear-shaped leaves, 12-15in (30-38cm) long, on stout stems, anything from 12-30in (30-75cm) in length. Flowers appear in spring and early summer on 3-4ft (0.9-1.2m) stalks. The flower head consists of an 8in (20cm) long, boat-shaped bract, in green flushed with purple, and held nearly horizontal, from which emerges a succession of 6in (15cm) long, three-petalled flowers standing erect to give a crest-like appearance. They are orange with a blue, 6-8in (15-20cm) long projection jutting out of the centre of each flower.

Trouble Shooter

Take care not to overwater in winter — this can easily lead to rot in the roots and at the base of stems, especially at very low temperatures. Equally, don't allow the plant to get too dry in summer or foliage will begin to look unhealthy and lose its lustre.

Both scale insect and mealy bug may attack; they can be wiped away with a cloth or brush dipped in methylated spirit. Red spider mite can cause problems in summer; spray with a malathion-based insecticide. Alternatively, applying a systemic insecticide proves an effective overall deterrent; always use according to the manufacturer's instructions.

Streptocarpus

Family name: **Gesneriaceae**

Common name:
Cape Primrose

Care Straight-forward	**Height** 10-12in (25-30cm)	**Flower** Early summer
Light Bright indirect	**Spread** 8-10in (20-25cm)	**Humidity** Mist spray occasionally
Price Middle range	**Shape** Rosette	**Availability** Garden centres
Temp. Min 60°F (16°C)	Ideal 70°F (21°C)	Max 80°F (27°C)

These attractive evergreen perennials come mainly from lightly-wooded areas of southern and eastern Africa, Madagascar and parts of Asia. Of the few species commonly grown as houseplants, *Streptocarpus rexii* is one of the most popular and the one from which many hybrids have been derived. It is a small, fibrous-rooted plant with a rosette of deep green, quilted leaves, coated with fine hairs. In their native woodland they grow, rather like our primroses, massed together in clumps in damp, rich soil close to streams.

Spring and summer care

So that plants have time to settle down and put on some growth before flowering, the best time to repot is in March or early April at the latest, every year, moving plants up to a pot one size larger each time, to a final pot size of 6-8in (15-20cm); use any good peat-based compost — or use John Innes No 2 with some extra leaf-mould or peat added. To ensure continuous flowering, promptly remove faded flowers.

Throughout the year, Streptocarpus will flourish at normal warm room temperatures, around 65-70°F (18-21°), say, in summer, in a well-ventilated, but draught-free position. They want a brightly-lit spot, but must be protected from direct sunlight.

Water freely then allow the surface of the compost to dry out before watering again, and add a weak liquid fertiliser to the water every three weeks or so (use half the recommended amount). Humidity is important, particularly at high temperatures, so stand pots on trays of moist pebbles and mist spray occasionally around the plant — early morning is the best time to do this.

Autumn and winter care

Although many plants will tolerate lower temperatures, it is a good idea to maintain a minimum of 60°F (16°C). They want bright light, though they are still best kept out of full sun, with good ventilation but free from draughts and cold air. Water thoroughly — allowing the top 1in (2.5cm) of soil to dry out between waterings: mist spray around the plant occasionally to provide a little humidity on the warmest and brightest days.

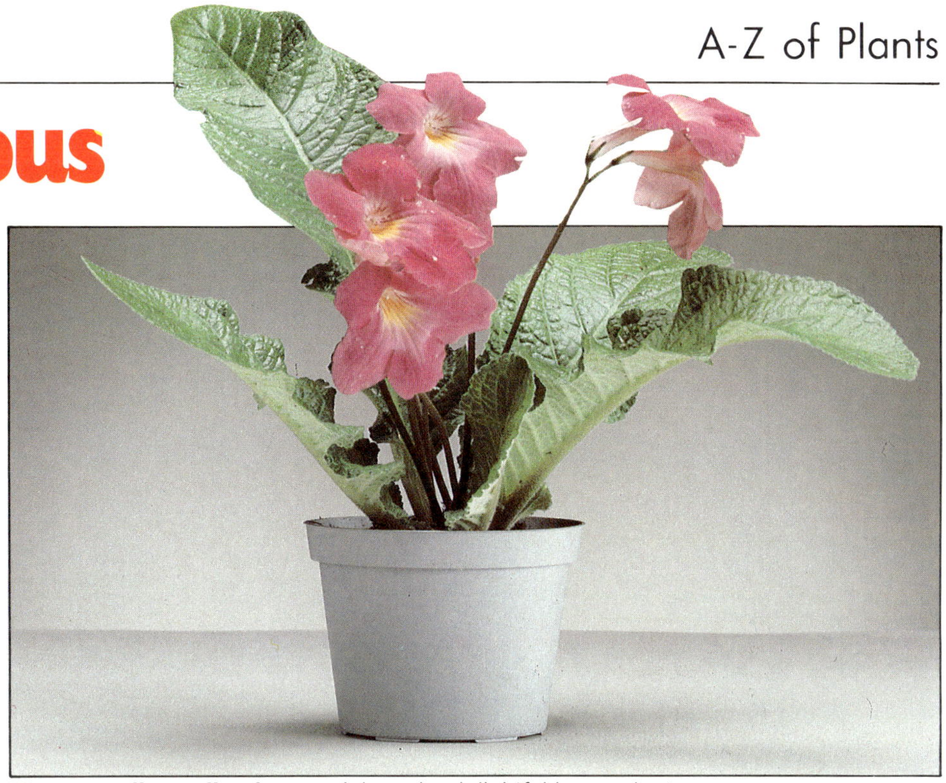

These small woodland perennials make delightful houseplants.

Propagation

Propagate from leaf cuttings in the spring or early summer. Remove a leaf and cut it widthwise into two or three sections. Insert the base of each section ½in (1cm) deep into a thoroughly moistened mixture of two parts sand to one part peat. Keep shaded and barely moist at a temperature of 65°F (18°C), enclosed in a propagating case or clear, polythene bag. Plantlets should begin to appear at the base of the sections, usually within about six weeks. When they have grown to a height of 2-3in (5-7cm), pot them up singly in 3in (7cm) pots of the usual compost and treat as mature plants — they should flower the following spring.

Trouble Shooter

High humidity without adequate air circulation can lead to a greyish mould developing on the foliage; if your plant becomes infected then cut away the affected part and spray with a fungicide. Spray greenfly with a pyrethrum-based insecticide immediately there is any sign of infestation, or the foliage will become irreparably disfigured.

Species

Streptocarpus rexii is the species from which the hybrids are mainly derived. Growing to a height of 10-12in (25-30cm), it forms a rosette of deep green, quilted, hairy leaves, which are strap shaped and 8-10in (20-25cm) in length. The main flowering period is in May and June, when 6-8in (15-20cm) tall stalks rise from near the bottom of each leaf carrying 2in (5cm) long, bluish-mauve, foxglove-like flowers.

The true species is rarely found as a houseplant, but it is the many beautiful named hybrids and varieties, sometimes listed under *S.hybrida*, that are so popular. Flowers are borne in small clusters from May to October. They come in a number of beautiful colours and colour combinations, shades of blue, purple, pink, red and white. Among the most outstanding hybrids is 'Meissen's White', *above right*, white with a yellow eye, and 'Diana', cerise with a white throat.

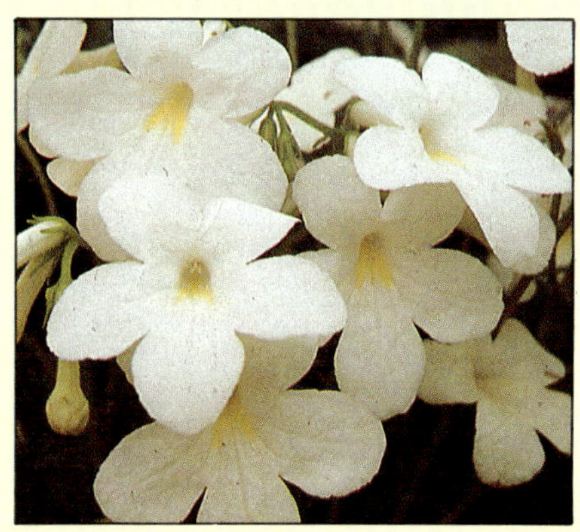

S.dunnii is another parent of many hybrids and varieties. It has a huge single leaf, which can reach 3ft (0.9m) in length, and beautiful pendulous flowers carried in summer on 1ft (0.3m) stems.

Syngonium

Family name: **Araceae**

Common names: **Arrowhead Vine/Goosefoot Plant**

Care Easy	**Height** 6ft (1.8m)	**Flower** Rare
Light Bright indirect	**Spread** 3ft (0.9m)	**Humidity** Mist spray regularly
Price Middle range	**Shape** Bushy climber	**Availability** Garden centres
Temp. Min 55°F (13°C)	Ideal 70°F (21°C)	Max 80°F (27°C)

Syngoniums are very attractive foliage plants, of a climbing or trailing habit, from central and South America. They are closely related to the large and often rather unwieldy climbers, Monstera and Philodendron, but they are a lot more easy to accommodate in smaller rooms.

These tropical, vine-like plants are easily grown, requiring much the same conditions as the climbing Philodendrons — warmth, humidity and protection from direct sunlight. The Arrowhead Vine or Goosefoot Plant (*Syngonium podophyllum*), *below*, is the one most often grown indoors. It is a very appealing species that is often bought as a small bushy plant, then soon readily climbs — or trails — to a length of 6ft (1.8m). An unusual feature which this and the other Syngoniums share with certain Philodendrons — it is, if anything, more pronounced — is the way in which the shape and colouring of the leaves often changes as the plant ages, from the tiny, arrow-shape which gives the plant its common name to the giant, many-lobed leaf, over 1ft (0.3m) in length, produced by mature plants.

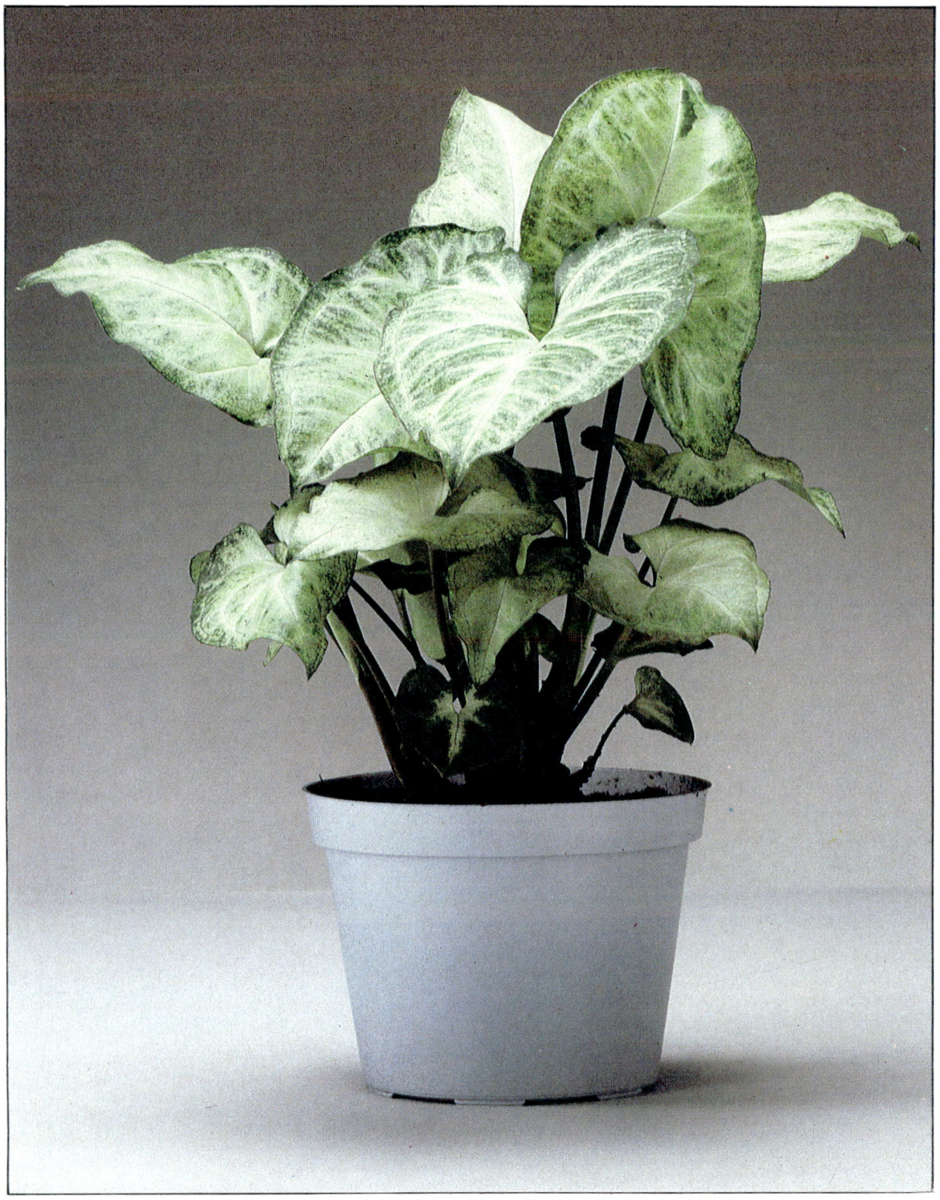

This young Syngonium will soon need support for its stems to climb up.

Spring and summer care

Repot plants every spring when active growth is about to begin, using John Innes No 2, preferably with some peat or thoroughly decomposed leaf-mould added. Pot your plant on to a container one size larger when its roots have filled the current pot, until the final pot size is reached, after which topdress every year replacing the top 1-2in (2.5-5cm) with fresh compost. Syngoniums don't need especially large containers; a maximum pot size of 5-6in (13-15cm) or 6-8in (15-20cm) for a hanging basket should be perfectly adequate. If necessary, trim back overgrown or straggly plants at potting time.

As the plant matures the stems develop a climbing habit; they can of course be allowed to trail, but for a climbing plant the stems will need support. They can be trained up thin canes, pushed into the compost, but the best choice is a moss-covered pole which provides an ideal surface for their aerial roots.

Normal warm room temperatures, up to 70°F (21°C) or a little higher, are ideal. Syngoniums can tolerate a fairly shaded position but prefer a well-lit one. They should never be allowed to stand in full sunlight — particularly the variegated types. Water freely between April and October, to keep the compost fairly moist at all times, and add a weak liquid fertiliser to the water (use half the recommended amount) every month. Mist spray regularly to provide humidity, particularly at higher temperatures.

Autumn and winter care

Winter temperatures should be maintained in the region of 60-65°F (16-18°C) — Syngoniums cannot tolerate anything lower than 55°F (13°C). Give your plant the brightest possible position, but keep it out of direct sunlight. Good ventilation is important — they don't enjoy a stuffy atmosphere — but avoid any cold draughts.

Keep plants on the dry side from November to March, but giving them only enough water to prevent the compost drying out completely; water more frequently at higher temperatures and continue to mist spray occasionally, especially on the brightest days, to provide a degree of humidity.

Propagation

Take 4-5in (10-13cm) stem cuttings any time in spring or summer. Cut just below the point where a leaf emerges, remove the lowest leaf and treat the cut end of the stem with a rooting hormone, then insert the cuttings into the normal mixture of John Innes No 2 with added leaf-mould. Keep moist and shaded, enclosed in a clear polythene bag, at a temperature of 65-70°F (18-21°C). When new growth indicates that rooting has occurred, normally within four to six weeks, uncover the cuttings; give enough water to keep the compost just moist, and after a month begin feeding with a weak liquid fertiliser. Transfer the cuttings to their growing containers — plant two or three together in a 3-4in (8-10cm) pot or five or six in a hanging basket — and treat as mature plants.

Trouble Shooter

Unless adequate warmth and humidity can be maintained all year round, plants will suffer — wilting and collapse can come with startling rapidity. Leaves will wilt and fall if plants are kept in too dry an atmosphere or are underwatered; cold air and draughts are liable to bring about the same result. Syngoniums should never be subjected to full sunlight, which will scorch the foliage. On the other hand, if variegated leaves are tending to lose their colouring, it may be due to too dense shade — move the plant to a brighter position. Take care not to overwater your plant, particularly in winter — as this can soon lead to root rot.

Syngoniums are sometimes prey to attack from mealy bug; wipe away the fluffy white patches with a soft cloth or paintbrush dipped in methylated spirit; for a heavy infestation, spray with a malathion-based insecticide. Alternatively, use a systemic insecticide as a preventative; apply according to the manufacturer's instructions. Red spider mite may also be a problem and should be eradicated by using the same insecticides; if humidity levels are sufficiently high, however, this should prove an effective deterrent.

Do not use a leaf-shiner on Syngoniums since these products will damage the foliage.

Species

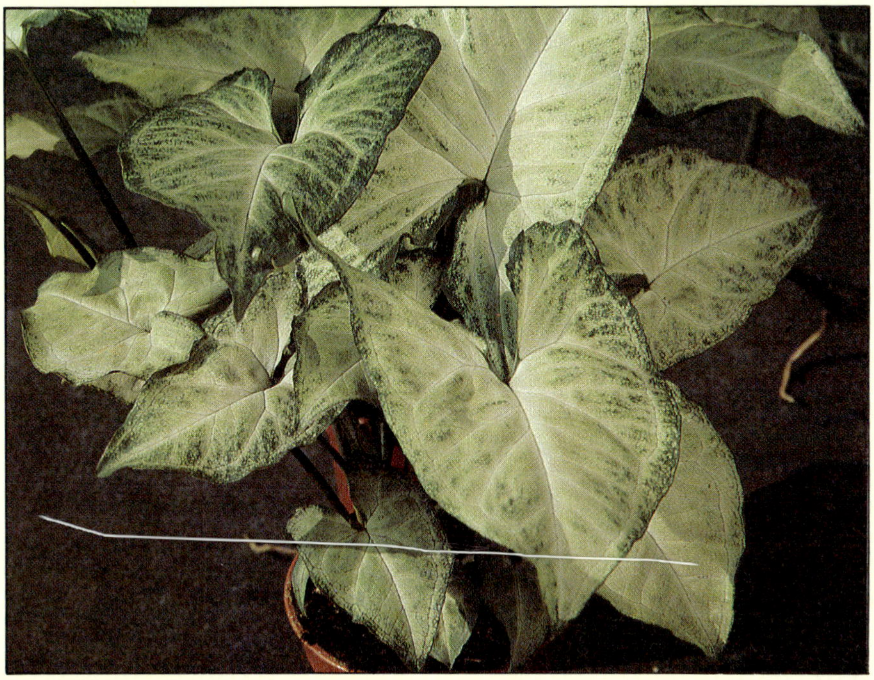

Syngonium podophyllum (formerly listed *Nephthytis liberica*), the Arrowhead Vine or Goosefoot Plant, is a very attractive, vine-like, climbing plant from Central America and the most popular species. An unusual feature, characteristic of all Syngoniums, is the marked difference in leaf-shape as the plant matures. The young leaves are usually very much arrow-shaped, bright green in colour, gradually becoming lobed as the plant gets older, the two base lobes often becoming distinctly like a pair of rabbit ears in shape. Mature plants can produce much larger leaves, which are divided into distinct segments, or leaflets, with the largest, centre leaflet up to 1ft (0.3m) in length. While the plant ages it gradually develops a climbing — or trailing — stem which hardens and thickens as it grows to an indoor height of about 6ft (1.8m). Leaf colouring may also become paler as plants age. Flowers are Arum Lily-shaped with a large spathe, but it is most unusual for them to be produced indoors.

There is also a number of appealing varieties available. One of the most desirable is 'Green Gold' which has leaves marbled with cream, golden-yellow and green; equally popular is the variety 'White Butterfly', *above*, with greenish-white leaves edged with a deeper green margin.

S.erythrophyllum is a charming, smaller growing species, also native to Central America. It's sometimes known as the Copper Syngonium, after the glossy, coppery green colouring of its foliage, generally covered with numerous pink dots. The small, arrow-shaped leaves are two-lobed at the base, developing into three deep lobes on mature foliage.

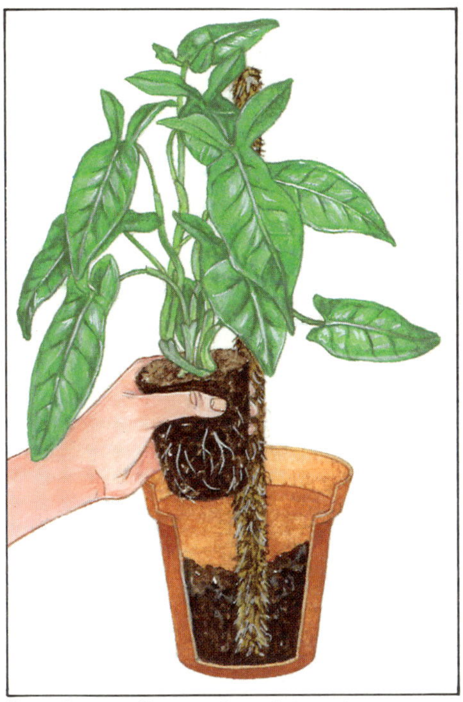

Repot your Syngonium into a larger pot if its roots are pot-bound. Position the support first, firming it into the compost.

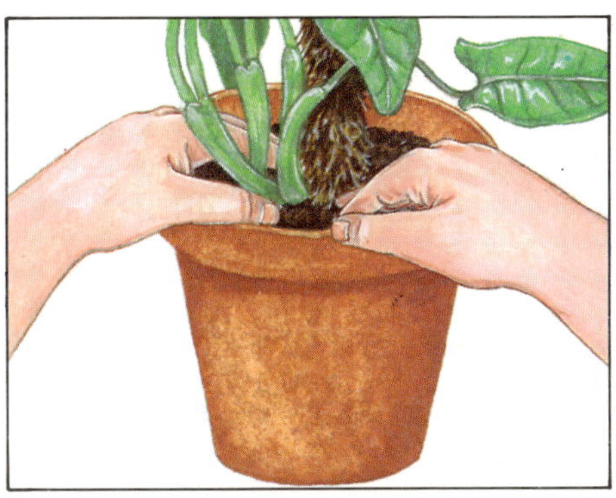

Plant your Syngonium in front of the support and top the pot up with compost, then firm down the surface.

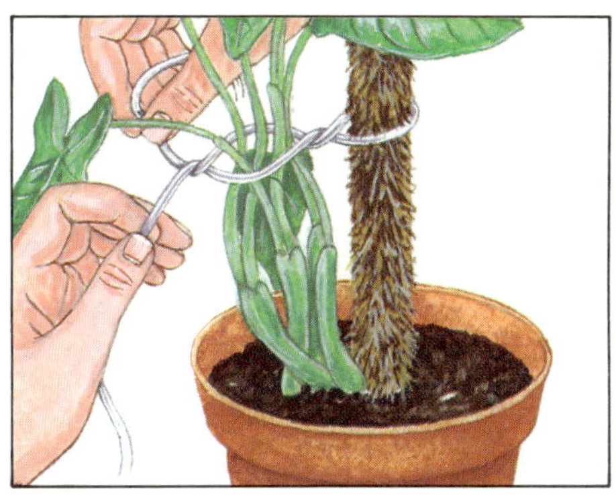

Use plastic-coated wire to tie the stems to the support — but make sure you don't crush the stems or leaf stalks.

Tillandsia

Family name: **Bromeliaceae**

Common names: **Air Plant, Spanish Moss/Old Man's Beard, Blue-flowered Torch**

Care Easy	**Height** 3-4in (8-10cm)	**Flower** Summer
Light Bright, indirect	**Spread** 2-3in (5-8cm)	**Humidity** Mist spray regularly
Price Middle range	**Shape** Rosette	**Availability** Garden centres
Temp. Min 50°F (10°C)	Ideal 70°F (21°C)	Max 80°F (27°C)

Named after the Finnish Professor Elias Tillands, this fascinating group of plants contains well over 400 different species, which vary enormously in their appearance. By far the greater number of them are epiphytes — they live in the branches of trees, gaining sustenance from the damp air, and their roots, if they have any at all, serving only to anchor them to the branches. This natural habit means that they prefer not to be grown rooted into pots of compost, but rather attached to pieces of wood or cork. This gives rise to their common name, Air Plant, since they seem literally to live on air. Certain species may be grown in pots, provided you are very careful to arrange excellent drainage.

Tillandsias come mainly from the American continent, ranging from the southern states of the USA through Mexico down to Argentina; they are also found in the West Indies. One popular, and typical, species is *Tillandsia ionantha, right,* from Central America. It is a dwarf rosette of greyish-green leaves, from the centre of which grows a deep purple, bracted flower head.

Interesting in a more unusual way is *T.usneoides*, which grows so commonly in the Americas that it is thought of as a weed. Its common names, Spanish Moss or Old Man's Beard, describe its greyish, threadlike, tangled foliage. The colour — characteristic of many Tillandsias — is an important clue to its habit: the foliage is coated with minute, greyish, furry scales which act like a sponge, absorbing moisture from the air and filtering it through to the leaf tissue. Hence a daily spray is enough to keep them thriving.

Tillandsias are sculptural and dramatic plants which are easy to care for in the home and which last for many years. The flowers are short-lived, but the colourful bracts last for many weeks. Several different ones, mounted on a piece of driftwood, or a branch set in pebbles, will make an unusual epiphyte 'tree' that looks particularly good in a modern decor.

Tillandsias can be mounted at any time of the year, except when they're in full flower. Use any quick-drying glue to stick them to cork, bark or wood or, with *T.usneoides*, simply drape it over a line of twine or rope.

Spring and summer care

Summer temperatures may rise to 75-80°F (24-27°C), but keep your plant out of direct sunlight. Mist spray regularly, as often as twice a day in really hot weather; use rainwater if possible, otherwise boiled, cooled water to reduce the risk of lime deposit on the foliage. Add a weak liquid fertiliser to the spray every 3-4 weeks, about a quarter of the recommended strength.

With rosette-shaped Tillandsias, water them, if possible, by filling the central cup, and never let it dry out. Tip the plant up and drain out any water, replacing it with fresh, at least once a month. The water from mist spraying will usually drip down and fill the cup, which is especially useful if it is too small to be filled directly, so make sure you mist spray from above.

When the weather's hot, Tillandsias benefit from being put outdoors, in the shade of a tree, but must still be mist sprayed. The exception is *T.usneoides*: if you put this outside, the birds may gather it for nest-making!

T.lindeni and *T.cyanea* can be grown in pots of very well-drained compost — an equal mixture of coarse sand and peat, or a proprietary orchid compost. Repotting is only necessary when the plant is being divided (see 'Propagation').

Tillandsias will flower in the late summer or autumn. Small flowers appear between the colourful, long-lasting bracts. Once a rosette has flowered it slowly begins to die, although it can take a year before the foliage begins to look unsightly. Then it's best to divide the plant (see 'Propagation').

Autumn and winter care

Minimum winter temperatures are 50-60°F (10-15°C), and the best position is filtered light. Don't shade the plant too densely, but don't give it direct sun either. Provide good air circulation, but keep it away from cold draughts, and never expose it to any risk of frost. Mist spray regularly every day very lightly, preferably in the early morning.

Propagation

Propagate by division in spring. With rosette-shaped plants, carefully separate the individual offsets that are growing at the base of the parent plant , taking with them a few of the roots if possible. Fix them to their new mountings and mist spray. Hang them in a shaded place and treat as mature plants.

With *T.lindeni* and *T.cyanea* grown in pots, remove offsets in the spring and set them just on the surface of the recommended compost; it is important that the roots only should be embedded in the soil in order to anchor the plant.

Divide *Tillandsia usneoides* by detaching a few stems and draping or tying clumps of foliage to a piece of cork or bark with paper-covered wire.

Trouble Shooter

Tillandsias on the whole are fairly trouble-free plants. If they look weak and leaves begin to die prematurely, they have probably been given too cold a position or left in a cold draught. Brown and brittle foliage is a sign of too much direct sun or lack of humidity; move the plant into the shade and mist spray it every day. White, fluffy patches are mealy bug; wipe them off with a brush or cloth dipped in methylated spirit. Avoid any malathion-based insecticide.

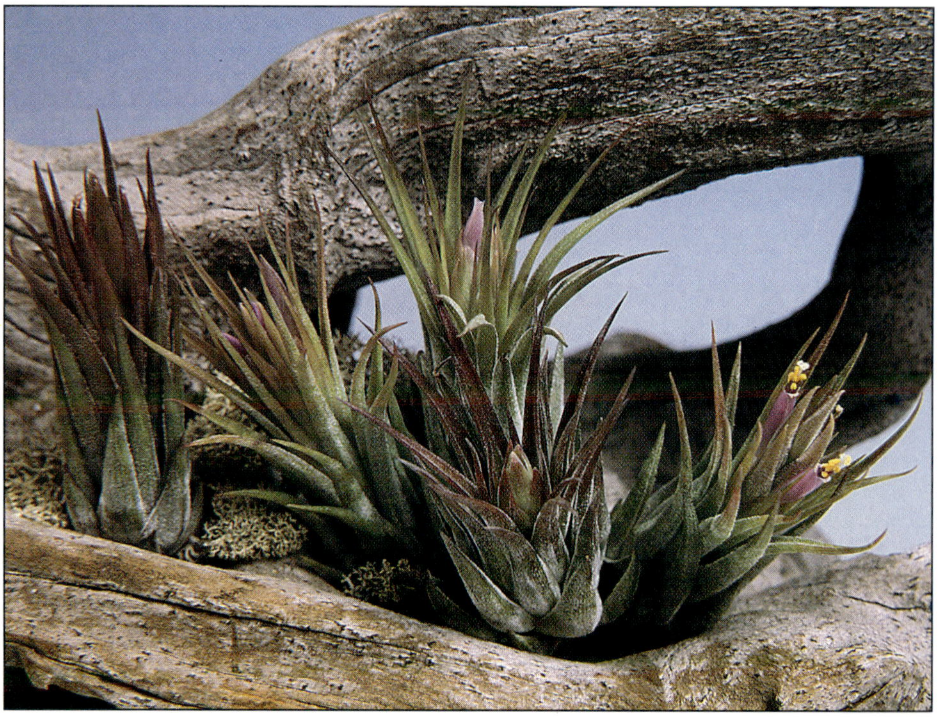

Air plants mounted on driftwood make very attractive ornaments.

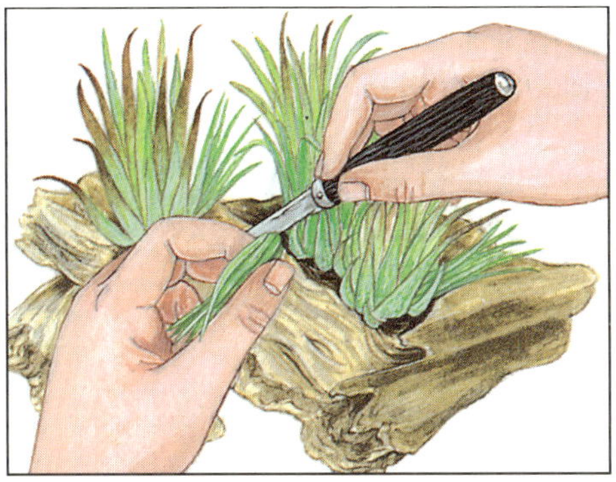

To mount Tillandsia, pull or carefully cut away offsets, ideally when they're just over half the size of the parent rosette.

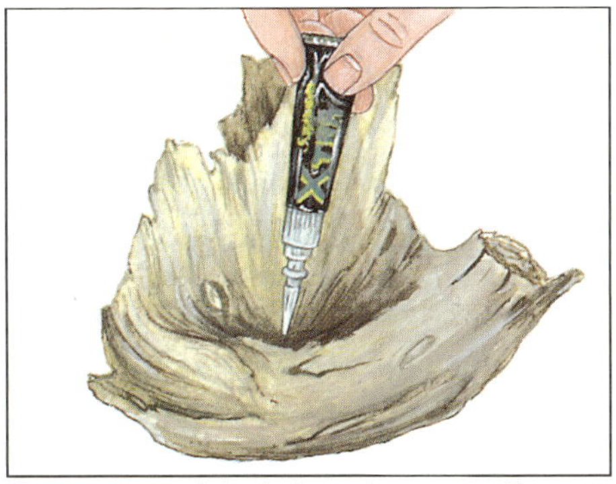

Dot some quick-drying glue on to the clean, dry surface of a piece of shell, driftwood or bark.

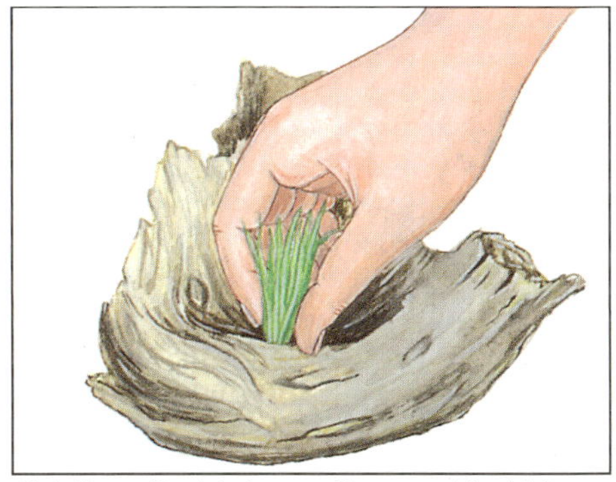

Put the offset into position and hold it until it sticks. It will soon grow roots that will anchor it to the mount.

Species

Tillandsia ionantha comes from Central America, and is often offered for sale attached to pieces of wood, coral or large shells. It is a stemless rosette, 3-4in (8-10cm) high, of numerous, overlapping, leathery, arching, sword-shaped leaves, covered in tiny scales and silvery-green in colour. Each leaf is 2-2½in (5-6cm) long, and those at the centre of the rosette flush with red before flowering. The flower is violet-purple, 2½in (6cm) long, with protruding yellow stamens, and it appears in summer on the end of a bracted flower spike.

T.usneoides, *above right,* Spanish Moss or Old Man's Beard, comes from the south eastern States of the USA. It consists of a mass of thin, tangled wiry stems covered in scaly, greyish leaves, up to 2in (5cm) long. The stems can grow several feet long. In the wild, tiny bright yellow-green flowers with three petals, ⅓in (8mm) across, appear in the leaf axils throughout the summer.

T.lindeni (also known as *T.lindeniana*), Blue-flowered Torch, comes from Peru. It is a dense rosette, with leaves 15in (38cm) long and ½in (13mm) wide. A flower stalk 1ft (0.3m) tall rises from the centre of the rosette, bearing a slender, royal blue flower with a white-spotted throat.

T.cyanea, from Guatemala, is very similar to *T.lindeni*, but with a more compact flower, violet-blue, on a stalk only 2-3in (5-8cm) tall. The leaves, however, are slightly bigger, at 16in (40cm) long and 1in (2.5cm) wide. Both this plant and *T.lindeni* may be grown in pots.

T.bulbosa, *right,* comes from the West Indies, Mexico and South America. It has a compact, bulbous base, which is formed by the closely packed bases of the leaves. These are up to 6in (15cm) long, and spread out at all angles from above the bulbous area, almost fleshy, slender and pointed. Purple flowers, tipped with white, 2-2½in (5-6cm) long, appear at the end of the bracted spike in summer.

T.argentea, Pincushion Plant, principally from Central America, is a miniature of numerous silvery-grey and very slender scaly leaves in a dense rosette, 5-6in (13-15cm) long and ½in (13mm) wide. A slender, twisting flower spike with scurfy red bracts, taller than the leaves, appears from the centre of the plant in the summer, bearing purple or reddish-purple flowers.

T.brachycaulos from southern Mexico is a colourful species, making a fast-growing plant of symmetrical rosettes each 5-6in (13-15cm) tall. Each rosette consists of stiff, curving, greenish leaves, with scaly undersides, which turn a maroon-red before flowering. A head of leafy bracts, slightly sunken in the rosette, bears purple flowers in the summer.

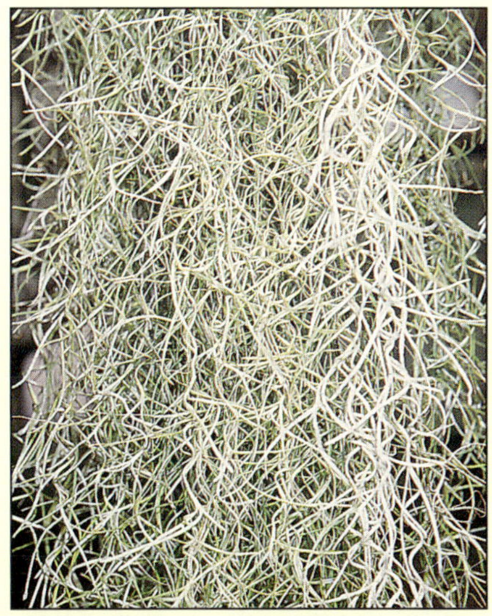

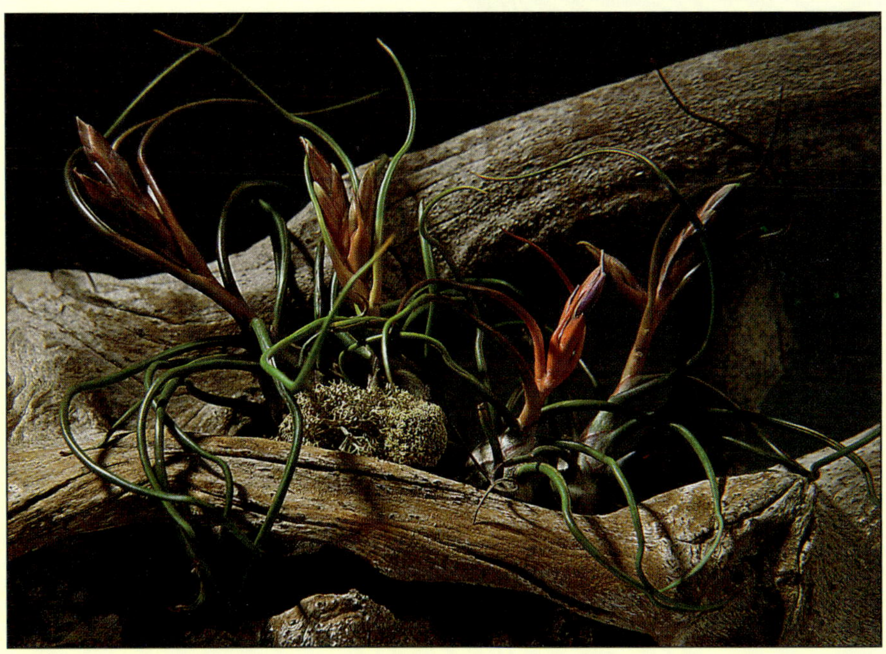

Tolmiea

Family name: **Saxifragaceae**

Common names:
Piggy-back Plant

Care Easy	**Height** 6in (15cm)	**Flower** Rare
Light Bright, indirect	**Spread** 15in (38cm)	**Humidity** Mist spray occasionally
Price Cheap	**Shape** Bushy	**Availability** Garden centres
Temp. Min 45°F (7°C)	Ideal 60°F (15°C)	Max 70°F (21°C)

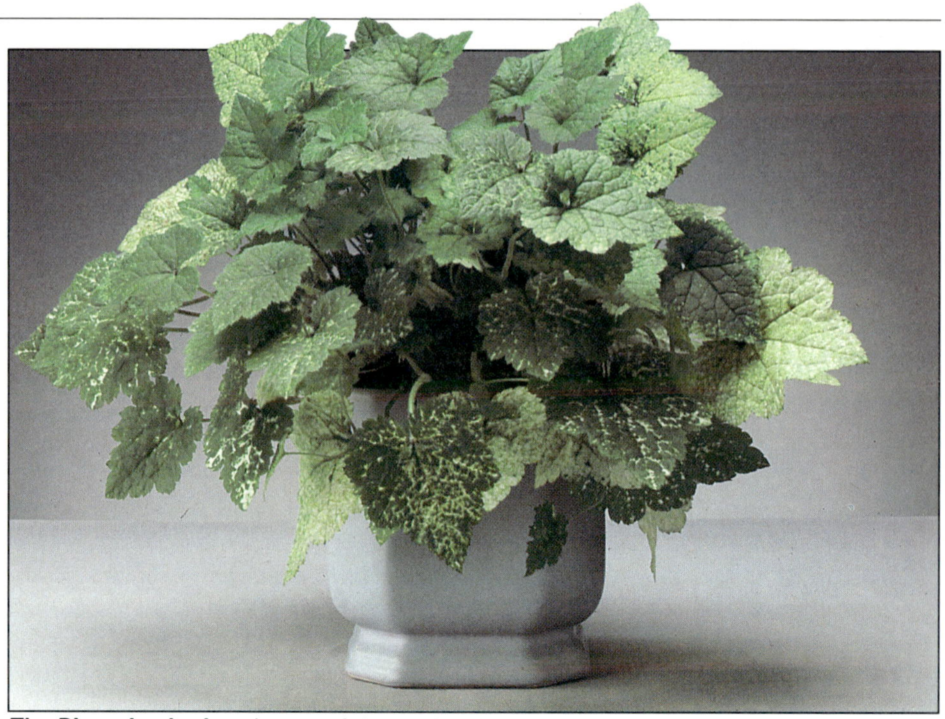

The Piggy-back plant is one of the easiest houseplants you can grow.

The Piggy-back Plant (*Tolmiea menziesi*) *right*, the only species in this genus, is an appealing, low-growing, evergreen plant, which forms a compact mound, about 6in (15cm) high, of downy, bright green, maple-like leaves. Its common name, refers to the fascinating characteristic of producing young plants from the base of mature leaves.

The plantlets grow on the surface of the leaf at the junction with the stalk; the leaf then rests on the surface of the soil and the plantlet roots down into the ground to form a new plant. As houseplants they are particularly well suited to wire mesh hanging baskets: the extra weight bearing down on the slender leafstalks makes the plants trail most attractively, while plantlets can root down to cover the whole container — sides and base included.

Apart from these attractions, Tolmieas are extremely easy to succeed with, thriving in conditions that would soon finish off many other plants — this makes them a very suitable choice for sunless, unheated rooms provided they are kept well-watered.

Spring and summer care

Repot annually in spring into John Innes No 2, moving plants on to larger containers only when their roots have filled the present ones.

Tolmieas will tolerate a wide range of temperatures but since they tend to wilt they are best kept slightly on the cool side, with summer temperatures restricted to about 70°F (21°C). If it tends to go above this, it is far better to place the plant in a shady position outside. Ideally, give them bright, filtered light out of full sun, but they will adapt perfectly well to shade. Good ventilation is important.

Water quite freely but only to keep the compost moist — don't overwater — and add a liquid fertiliser to the water every fortnight between April and September. It does no harm to mist spray occasionally, to avoid too dry an atmosphere.

Autumn and winter care

Winter presents no problems for Tolmieas. They will thrive at temperatures of 45-55°F (7-13°C), with good air circulation, though keep out draughts. While they prefer a brightly-lit spot, they will continue to do perfectly well in quite low light. Water moderately, so that the compost is kept just moist.

Propagation

Tolmieas are very easily propagated and grow quickly. Cut off leaves bearing well-developed plantlets in spring or summer, leaving about 1in (2.5cm) of stalk. Lay the leaves flat, face-up on to a moistened mixture of equal parts of peat and coarse sand. The stalk should be buried in the mixture and the plantlet-bearing part should sit on the surface. Keep barely moist, in bright light at normal temperatures, until new growth indicates that rooting has occurred, usually within two to three weeks. After that, treat as mature Tolmieas, but leave them a further five or six weeks before potting them up in the usual compost, either singly in 3in (7cm) pots or three or four together in a hanging basket. The 'mother' leaf can remain green for several months, to be removed when it eventually dries up.

Tolmieas can also be propagated by division of the whole clump or by pegging down the plantlet-bearing leaf while it is still attached to the mother plant.

Trouble Shooter

Full sun can scorch the leaves and should be avoided, while excess water retained within the compost can lead to root rot or fungus; don't overwater and make sure that pots can freely drain. But the main enemy of Tolmieas is underwatering especially in hot, dry air which can quickly cause the plant to wilt and lead to red spider mite; water regularly, don't allow temperatures to get too high and always provide good ventilation.

Fine, brownish webs indicate the presence of red spider mite; if there is an attack spray with a malathion-based insecticide. Mealy bug may also be a problem — look especially on the underside of the leaves, towards the base; wipe away the fluffy white patches with a cloth or paintbrush dipped in methylated spirit or spray with a malathion-based pesticide. If greenfly attack spray them with a pyrethrum-based insecticide; alternatively, spray at regular intervals according to the manufacturer's instructions, as a preventative measure.

Species

Tolmiea menziesii, the Piggy-back Plant, is an evergreen perennial, native to the western United States and the sole member of this genus. It forms a compact mound about 6in (15cm) high, spreading up to 15in (38cm). Covered with soft, white hair, the leaves are bright green, often speckled with yellowish green, lobed and toothed around the edges. The plantlets grow on the upper surface of mature leaves at the point where the leaf joins the stalk. Tiny, greenish-white flowers are borne in June but they are only rarely produced indoors.

Trachycarpus

Family name: **Palmae**

Common name: **Windmill Palm/ Chusan Palm**

Care Straight-forward	**Height** 5-6ft (1.5-1.8m)	**Flower** May-June
Light Sunny	**Spread** 3-5ft (0.9-1.5m)	**Winter** Frost tolerant
Price Expensive	**Shape** Palm	**Availability** Garden centres

Few plants create such a sense of tropical, sun-blessed islands as palms, but most are too tender to grow outside in the British Isles. This genus of eight evergreen palms, however, has one species that is hardy throughout most parts of the country – except the cold, wind-swept north-east. This is *Trachycarpus fortunei, above right,* the Chusan or Windmill Palm from China, Japan and parts of the Himalayas, displaying large fans up to 3ft (0.9m) wide of shiny, pleated leaves. It makes a highly distinctive feature for a patio, and is especially effective in a modern-style setting, perhaps with a white background.

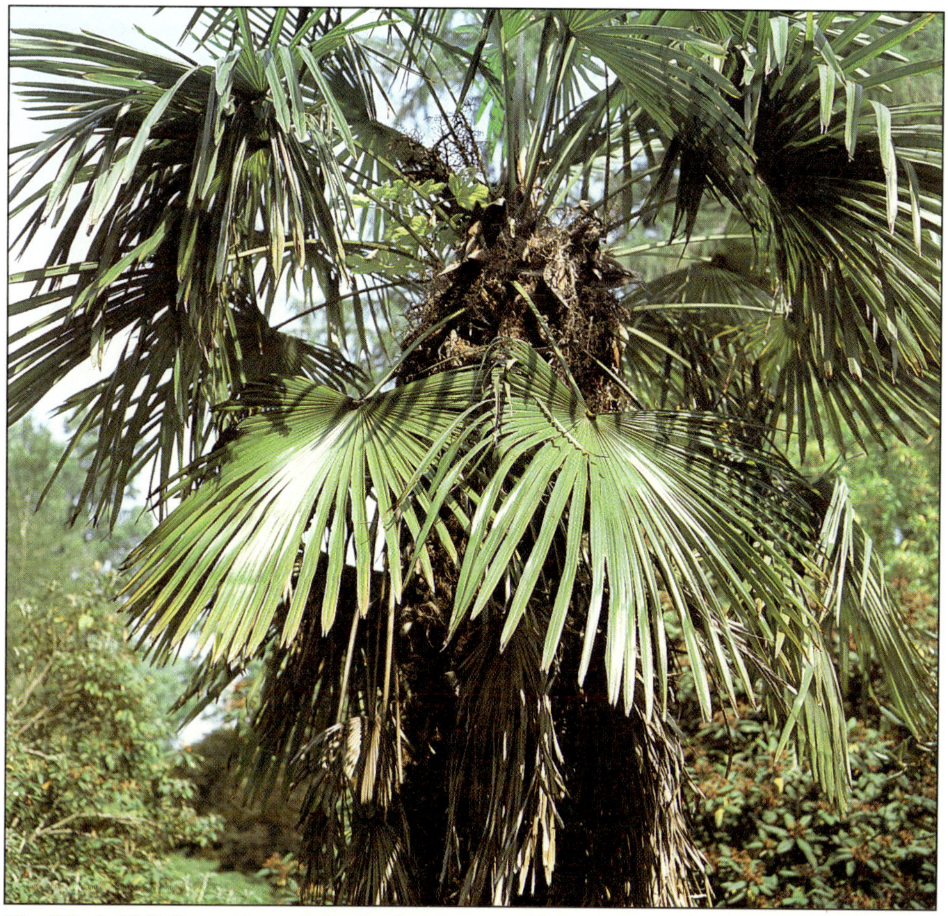

The Windmill Palm creates a distinctive feature on a patio.

Spring and summer care

Pot up your Trachycarpus in April, using John Innes No. 2 or 3 or a mixture of two parts turfy loam, one of well-decomposed leaf-mould and one of sharp sand. Drainage is important, so check that the holes in the base of the container are not blocked. Initially, if the plant is small, use a 5-8in (13-20cm) pot, in which it can usually remain for two to four years. Subsequently, as growth demands, repot into a larger container until eventually it is in an 18in (45cm) wide tub.

Place in a sunny, wind-sheltered position. During those years when not repotting, gently scrape away in spring the top 1in (2.5cm) or so of compost and replace with fresh.

Autumn and winter care

Keep your Trachycarpus in a sheltered and sunny position, keeping the compost only slightly moist. It is young plants that suffer most during cold weather, and moving them to the shelter of a south-facing wall helps their survival.

Propagation

The easiest way to increase your Trachycarpus is to remove basal suckers during April or May, potting them into small pots of the usual compost. Give them a thorough watering and place in a greenhouse at 50°F (10°C) until established – often up to eight weeks – and then reduce the temperature. During their first winter the young plants benefit from the protection of a cold frame or greenhouse. If the suckers were small they take two years before they can be safely planted into a container outside.

These palms can also be raised from seed, but this is a lengthy job – up to three years – and requires a temperature initially of 75°F (24°C) and then 50°F (10°C) for a further two years. It is better, therefore, to raise plants by suckers.

Species

Trachycarpus fortunei, the Windmill or Chusan Palm, also known as *Chamaerops excelsa,* grows 5-6ft (1.5-1.8m) high when planted in a container; in sheltered positions in gardens it often reaches 8-12ft (2.4-3.5m). The fans of mid-green, pleated leaves are borne on long stems which arise from the top of a trunk, covered with coarse hair, *right.*

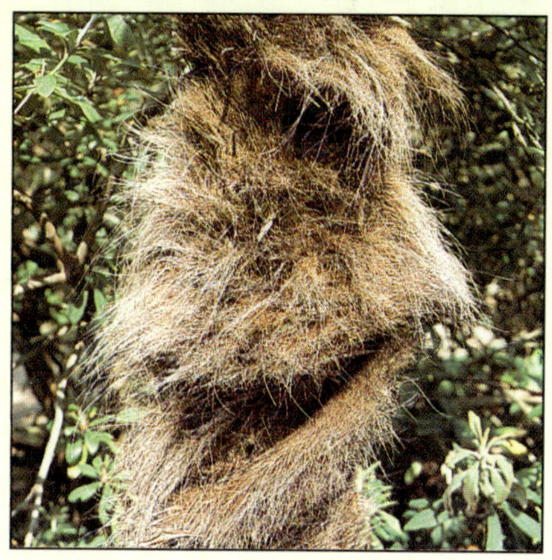

During May and June it bears dense, 1½-2ft (0.45-0.6m) long clusters of yellow flowers, occasionally followed by marble-like bluish-black berries.

T. f. nana is a recent introduction, a dwarf form with fans of foliage about 12in (30cm) wide. It is ideal for a small patio.

Trouble Shooter

Never excessively water your plant, as the roots will die – good drainage is essential. Pests are seldom a nuisance, but if seen wipe them off the leaves with a piece of cotton wool dipped in methylated spirit.

Tradescantia

Family name: **Commelinaceae**

Common names: **Wandering Jew/Wandering Sailor/Inch Plant**

Care Easy	**Trails** 1ft (0.3m)	**Flower** Spring and summer
Light Bright, indirect	**Spread** 1ft (0.3m)	**Humidity** Mist spray regularly
Price Cheap	**Shape** Trailing	**Availability** Common
Temp. Min 50°F (10°C)	Ideal 70°F (21°C)	Max 80°F (27°C)

This genus contains many delightful and familiar foliage plants, with quick-growing trailing or creeping stems densely covered in small, pointed-oval leaves; easily-grown and widely available, in a range of highly colourful forms, these are probably the most popular of all trailing plants. Named in honour of John Tradescant, gardener to Charles I and one of the most outstanding plantsmen of all time, they make excellent houseplants and are particularly well suited to growing in hanging baskets. They are also very easy to propagate and the number of specimens raised from cuttings in the home must far exceed that of shop-bought plants.

Mainly from sub-tropical south and central America, these plants have acquired many popular names, the most common ones, Wandering Jew and Inch Plant, being attributed to a number of species. One of the best known is *Tradescantia fluminensis*, a spreading, trailing plant from Brazil and Argentina. The small leaves of the species are dark- or bluish-green, with deep purple undersides, but there are many lively varieties, variegated with cream or yellow, or flushed with pink. One of the most appealing is *T.f.*'Quicksilver', *below*, an extremely fast-growing and robust variety, which has leaves profusely striped with white.

Many of the indoor species bear terminal clusters of small, three-petalled flowers in shades from white to pink. Individual flowers are generally very short-lived and insignificant by contrast to the foliage.

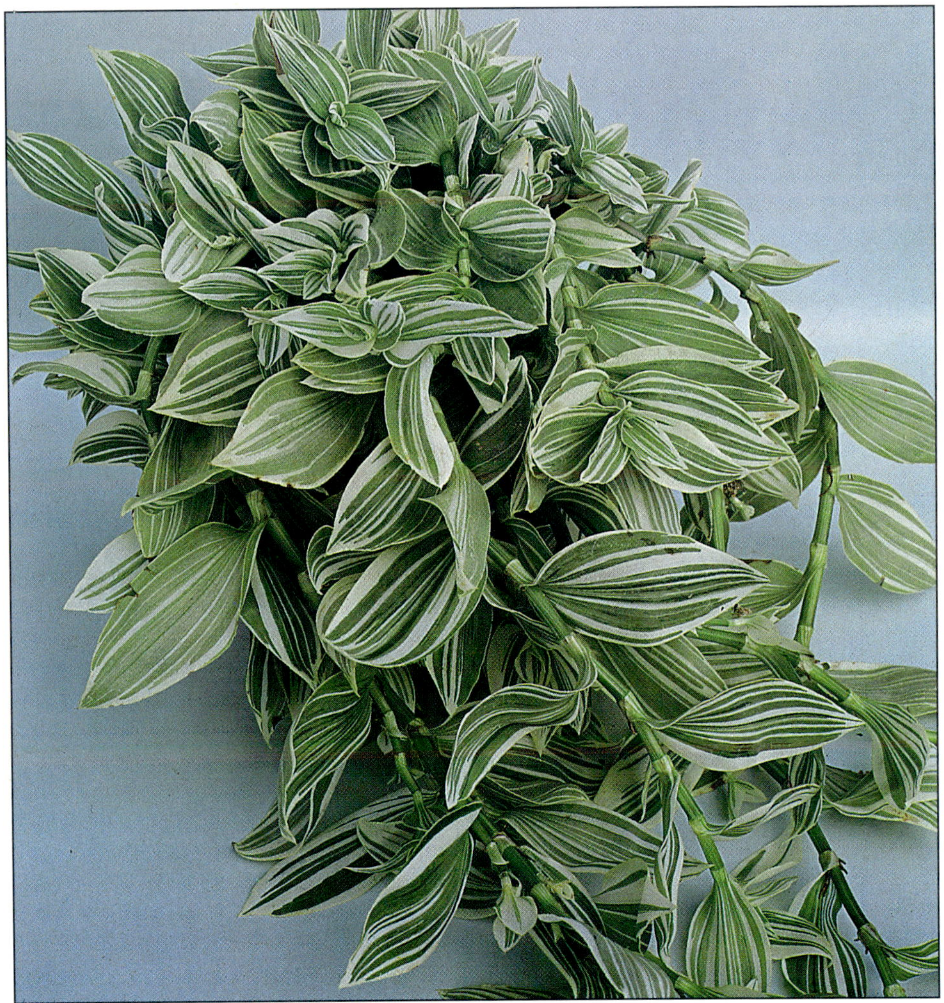

***Tradescantia fluminensis* 'Quicksilver'** — very attractive though robust.

Spring and summer care

Grow Tradescantias in 4-6in (10-15cm) pots, pans, wall pots or hanging baskets of John Innes No 2 or 3. Crock pots well to ensure good drainage and with wire mesh hanging baskets, line with a deep covering of sphagnum moss before filling in the compost; for *T.sillamontana* and *T.navicularis*, the compost should have up to one-third coarse sand added for better drainage.

Pinch out the growing tips of Tradescantias to encourage bushy growth; regularly remove any dried out or dead leaves from the base of trailing stems and remove any pure green growths on variegated forms as soon as they appear. Plants tend to deteriorate and lose their lower leaves with age and so are probably best discarded, but take cuttings first, to replace your plants.

Normal warm room temperatures are ideal and they can comfortably rise to 70-80°F (21-27°C). Bright light is essential for good colouring and normal, healthy growth, but avoid direct sunlight; good ventilation is also very beneficial.

Water freely, as often as is necessary to keep the compost thoroughly moist, with the exception of *T.sillamontana* and *T.navicularis*, which should be watered more sparingly; for all species add a weak liquid fertiliser to the water (use half the recommended amount) every two weeks between April and September. Mist spray the leaves every few days; early in the morning is the best time, but always spray out of direct sunlight or leaves may scorch.

Autumn and winter care

Winter temperatures should be in the range of 55-60°F (13-16°C) ideally, and shouldn't ever fall below 50°F (10°C). Keep plants in a really bright spot — the variegated and the succulent species, in particular, must have good light to thrive — but avoid full sun. Good air circulation is very worthwhile, but keep your plants free from draughts. Water fairly sparingly, to make the compost barely moist throughout, and allow the top half to dry out before watering again; mist spray occasionally, particularly on the brightest and warmest days.

Propagation

Tradescantias are very easily propagated from cuttings. Take 3-5in (8-13cm) long stem tip cuttings in spring or summer; cut just below a node, remove the lowest leaves and treat the cut ends with a rooting hormone. Insert them in a mixture of two parts John Innes No 2 to one part sharp sand, three or four cuttings to a 3in (7cm) pot; keep them moist and lightly shaded, ideally at a temperature of 70°F (21°C), though most will root readily at 60-65°F (16-18°C). Rooting should take place within about two weeks, as indicated by new growth, after which they can be treated as mature plants and potted on as necessary in groups into larger containers of the usual compost. Alternatively, for an easier but less reliable method, root cuttings in water as illustrated.

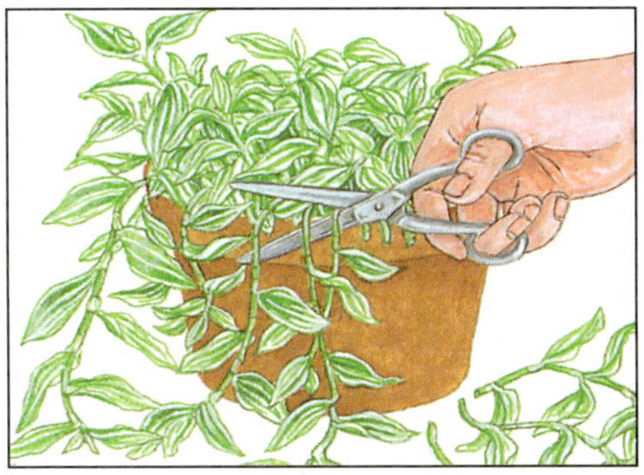

Although not always a hundred per cent successful, try taking cuttings by just giving your plant a 'haircut'.

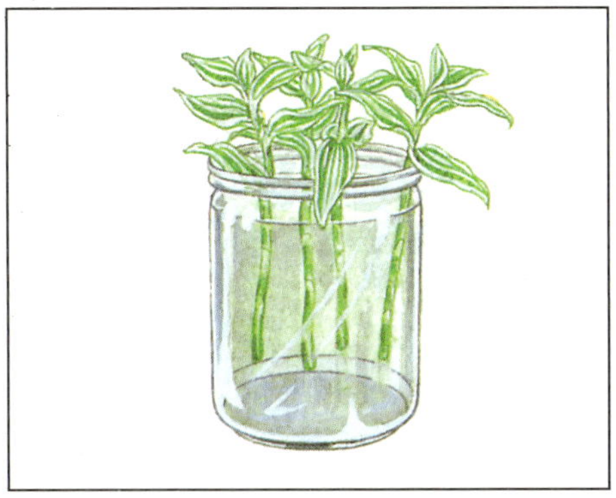

Remove lower leaves of trimmings and stand in a glass of water. Roots should appear within 10 days.

Trouble Shooter

Bright, indirect light is essential. Too shaded a position will lead to leggy stems and sickly leaves, while variegated forms will tend to lose much of their decorative colouring — and *T.sillamontana* could literally fall apart. But take care to avoid full sun, though; the foliage is prone to scorching, particularly if plants are mist sprayed in strong sunshine.

Leaves will wilt and shrivel, sometimes becoming yellow and spotted, if plants are left too dry for too long — they should be watered plentifully during the growing season. On the other hand, beware of overwatering, especially during winter — never leave pots or baskets wallowing in water. All plants will, in any case, become straggly and bare with age and should be replaced every year or two.

Mealy bug may attack your plant and should be wiped off with a paintbrush dipped in methylated spirit; or spray a more persistent infestation with a malathion-based insecticide. Greenfly can also be a problem, causing growth to become distorted unless promptly dealt with; spray with a pyrethrum-based insecticide to remove them.

Species

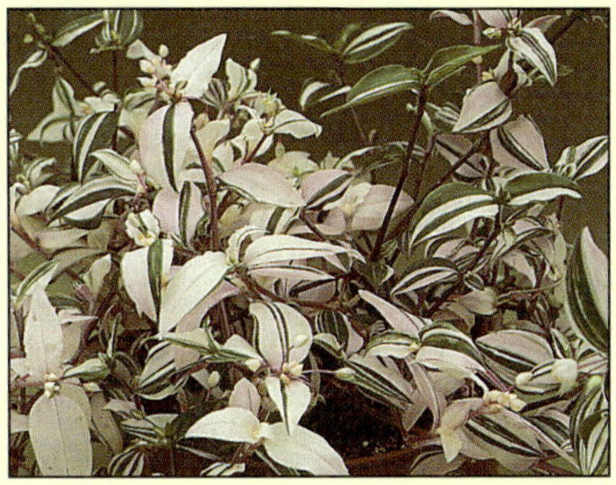

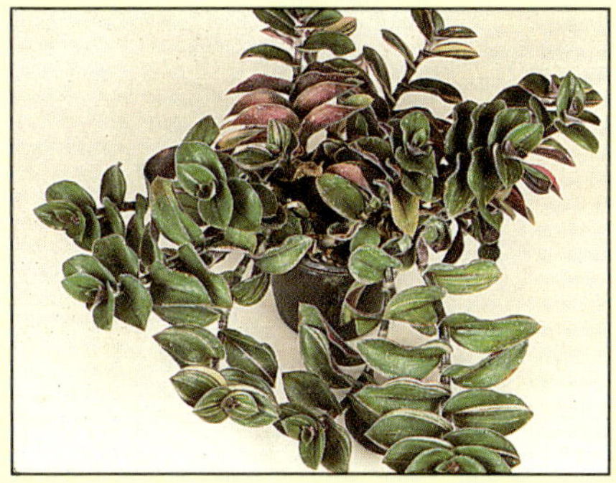

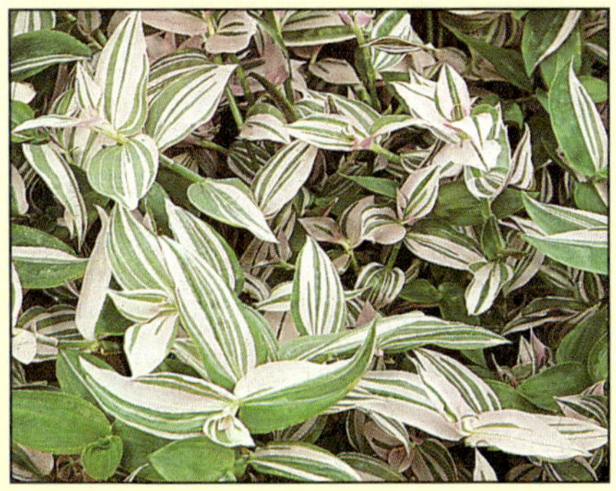

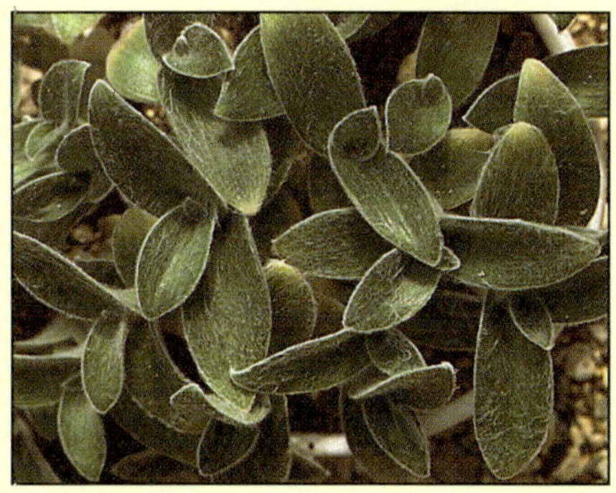

Tradescantia fluminensis, the Wandering Jew, Wandering Sailor or Inch Plant, is of Brazilian and Argentinian origin. It makes a spreading, trailing plant with fleshy, jointed stems and branches which trail to a length of 1ft (0.3m) or more. The stems, which change direction slightly at each of the prominent nodes, carry 2in (5cm) long, pointed-oval leaves, which are dark green or bluish-green, with purple undersides. Clusters of small, star-like, white flowers appear at the ends of the trailing stems in spring and summer, each of them lasting no more than a day.

There are many very popular varieties available; *T.f.variegata, bottom left*, is one of the best known, its lively foliage a bright, fresh green with irregular white and often pink-tinged stripes. 'Quicksilver' is another popular form, an extremely fast-growing and robust plant, its leaves profusely striped with silver.

T.albiflora, from central America, is a very similar species and also frequently tagged Wandering Jew. The true species has shiny, plain-green leaves, which are stemless and slightly shorter than those of *Tradescantia fluminensis*. But it is usually found as a houseplant in one of several variegated forms, such as *T.a.albovittata* with its green leaves striped and edged in white, *T.a.aurea* with leaves almost entirely yellow and *T.a.tricolor, top left*, which has shiny variegated green leaves, striped in both white and sometimes rose-pink, carried on trailing stems nearly reaching 18in (45cm) in length. Its pretty white flowers are infrequently produced indoors.

T.blossfeldiana, *top right*, sometimes called the Flowering Inch Plant, from Brazil and Argentina, has narrower leaves, some 3in (8cm) long, which are dark green above and purple beneath, covered with minute white hairs. Mature plants bear terminal clusters of ½in (1cm) long flowers from March to July, which are white tipped with rose-purple. This also has a very colourful variegated form.

T.sillamontana, *bottom right*, from the north of Mexico, is a quite different species, whose stems and branches are succulent and densely covered with minute, silvery-white hairs. The leaves have the same feature: they are 2½in (7cm) long, oval, deep green with purplish-pink undersides, and totally covered with white, woolly hairs, leading to the plant's common name of White Velvet. Unlike most other species, this is a deciduous plant, upright to a height of about 15in (38cm) then trailing. The flowers are a significant feature on this plant. They appear in summer in an attractive shade of rose-pink, making a strong contrast with the leaf colouring.

T.navicularis, sometimes known as the Chain Plant, is also of rather different habit to most common species. It is a low- and slow-growing succulent plant from Peru, with creeping stems spreading to 1ft (30cm) or more, closely packed with 1in (2.5cm) long, boat-shaped, fleshy leaves, a dullish green, the underside suffused with pale purple; the summer flowers, borne in small clusters, are a bright purplish-pink.

Vallota

Family name: **Amaryllidaceae**

Common name:
Scarborough Lily

Care Straight forward	**Height** 2ft (0.6m)	**Flower** Late summer
Light Bright	**Spread** 1-2ft (0.3-0.6m)	**Humidity** Not necessary
Price Middle range	**Shape** Leafy clump	**Availability** Garden centres
Temp. Min 50°F (10°C)	Ideal 65°F (18°C)	Max 75°F (24°C)

With handsome, evergreen leaves and brilliant scarlet-orange flowers, Vallota is an excellent houseplant and a perfect choice for a sunny windowsill. The genus consists of just the one species. *Vallota speciosa, below,* or the Scarborough Lily as it is popularly known, grows from a large, brownish bulb to reach a height of about 2ft (0.6m), with long, dark green, strap-shaped leaves. The bright scarlet, trumpet-shaped flowers generally appear in August and September, as many as 10 of them clustered together at the top of each tall upright stem.

The Scarborough Lily is an easy plant to care for: leave it undisturbed and fairly cool, feed regularly and water moderately, and it will produce several stems of long-lasting flowers each year in succession.

Spring and summer care

In April or May, pot your bulb into a 5-6in (13-15cm) pot of John Innes No 2, with the tip of the bulb just below the surface; be sure to pack the compost down firmly around the bulb. Repotting is only necessary every three or four years, in the spring, when the bulb becomes overcrowded with offsets; topdress in years when not repotting, replacing the top 1-2in (2.5-5cm) with fresh compost.

Normal room temperatures are fine for Vallotas and, if anything, should be on the cool side — ideally up to about 65°F (18°C). Your plant will need a good bright position with some direct sunshine to flower.

Water moderately from March to June, giving enough to keep the compost just moist. Plants should be kept a little drier from July to September — allow the top half of the compost to dry out between waterings. Add a liquid fertiliser to the water every two to three weeks between March and September.

Flowers appear in August and September; remove each individual flower as it dies, and cut the whole stem right off when it becomes yellow and limp.

Autumn and winter care

These are evergreen plants and if watering is continued the leaves will survive through the winter. Your plant should be kept cool in winter, at a temperature of 50-55°F (10-13°C), in a bright, sunny position. Water fairly sparingly and avoid waterlogging the compost, but don't let the compost dry out completely.

Alternatively, although they are evergreen, they can be dried off in winter, thus losing their leaves; they should be stored away in a dry place, protected from frost, then brought into growth again in March.

Propagation

During the growing season plants regularly produce offsets in the form of small, side bulbs; propagate by removing the offsets in spring, at repotting time. Pot bulbs up individually in John Innes No 2 and treat as mature plants. Use 5-6in (13-15cm) pots for bulbs of flowering size — about 2-3in (5-7cm) in diameter; for the small offsets which will grow to flowering size in one to three years, use 3in (7cm) pots and move them to bigger containers annually as they grow.

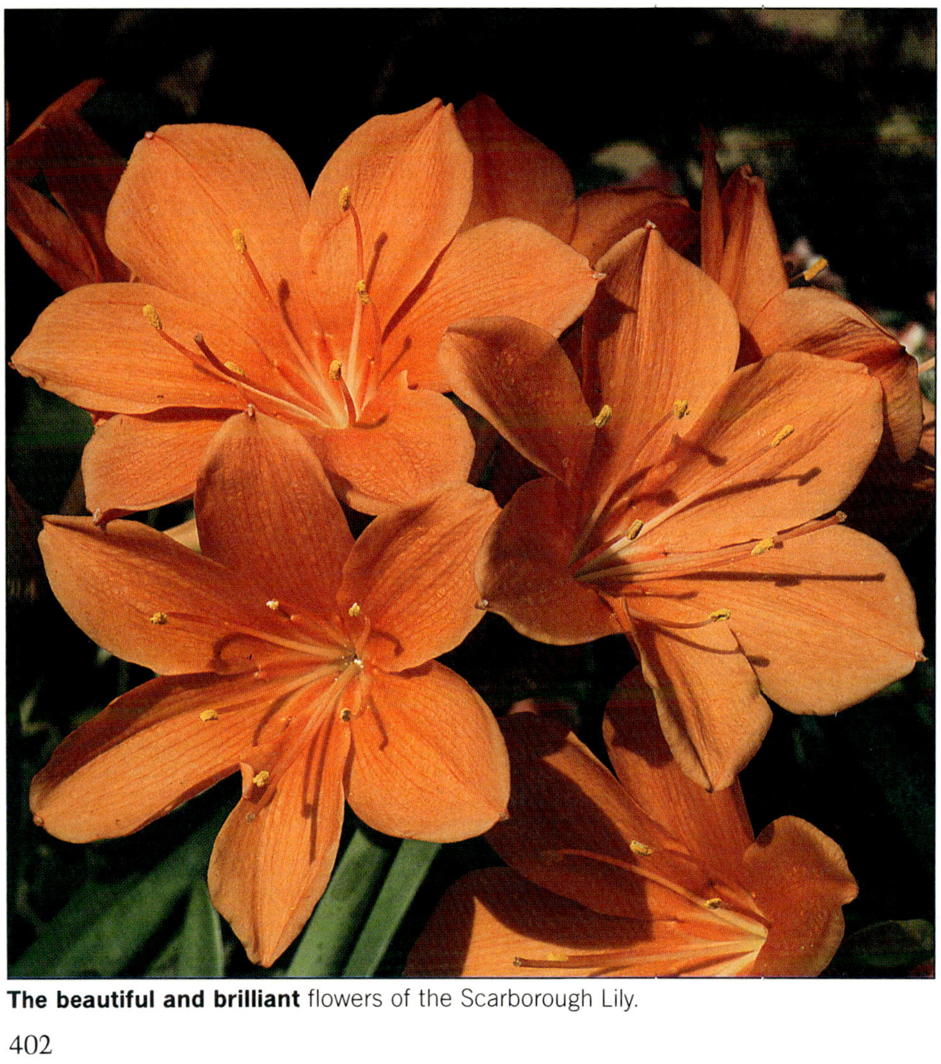

The beautiful and brilliant flowers of the Scarborough Lily.

Species

Vallota speciosa (also called *V.purpurea*), the Scarborough Lily, is the only member of this genus. A bulbous, evergreen, flowering plant, native to South Africa, it grows to a height of about 2ft (0.6m), with fleshy, erect, strap-shaped leaves which are dark green in colour and often tinged with a bronzy red at the base. Flowers are produced in late summer in clusters at the top of 2ft (0.6m) stems; they are 3-4in (8-10cm) long and funnel-shaped, in bright scarlet. There is also a white-flowered form available, *V.s.alba*, and *V.s.delicata*, with flowers in a pale salmon pink.

Trouble Shooter

Mealy bug can infest the base of the leaves; the fluffy white patches should be wiped away with a cloth or paintbrush dipped in methylated spirit.

Buying Guide

Order your Scarborough Lily bulbs from a specialist bulb nursery — they will have a much bigger range of varieties for you to choose from.

Veltheimia

Family name: **Liliaceae**

Common name: **Forest Lily**

Care Straight-forward	**Height** 12-18in (30-45cm)	**Flower** Winter
Light Sunny	**Spread** 1½-2ft (0.5-0.6m)	**Humidity** Not necessary
Price Middle range	**Shape** Leafy clump	**Availability** Specialist nurseries
Temp. Min 40°F (5°C)	Ideal 55°F (13°C)	Max 65°F (18°C)

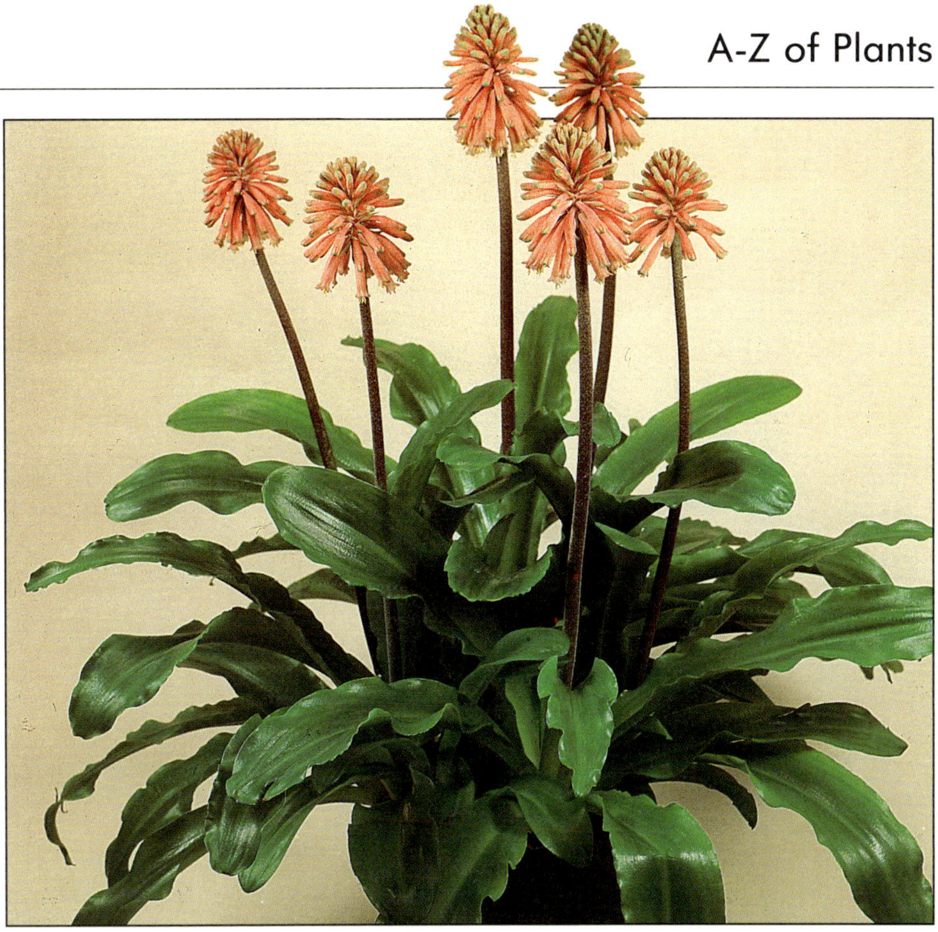

These splendid flowers appear in winter.

There are just two true species in this genus of beautiful bulbs, which come from South Africa, but several botanical names are associated with them and must be considered synonymous. *Veltheimia capensis, right,* is the commoner of the two species, but they both have very attractive leaves with crinkly edges, and unusual flowers, massed at the tips of tall, spotted stems. Each pendant flower is tubular in shape, appears late in the winter and lasts for at least a month or more.

Veltheimia needs warm temperatures in the summer when it is dormant, and must be kept fairly cool in the winter when it is growing, and needs bright sunshine. If you can provide these conditions, it is quite an easy plant to care for, and makes an ideal plant to brighten up the winter months.

Spring and summer care

During spring and summer Veltheimias are dormant. When they have finished flowering, withhold water completely and let the plant dry out — watering during the dormant period will cause bulb rot and the plant will die. When the flower stalk and the leaves have turned yellow and withered, in late February to early March, remove them.

Keep temperatures up to 55°F (13°C) to help the bulbs dry out completely in February and March. Then for the rest of the summer period, normal room temperatures will do. They should be given a bright, sunny position, with three to four hours of direct sunlight a day.

Autumn and winter care

If you get a young Veltheimia in a small pot, pot it on in early autumn to a final pot size of 5in (13cm). Set it on John Innes No 1 compost, or John Innes No 2 with extra coarse sand, leaving half the bulb exposed. Open soil and good drainage are essential, so crock the pot well. In later years, topdress by replacing the first 2in (5cm) of soil with fresh; adding a light sprinkling of some slow-acting fertiliser, such as bonemeal, can be beneficial. There is no need to pot on any further unless you are dividing the clump (see 'Propagation' below).

At the beginning of autumn moisten the sand slightly to encourage the bulb into growth. When new growth is evident, increase watering so that the compost is fairly moist at all times. But always underwater rather than overwater, and let the top ½in (13mm) or so of the compost dry out between waterings. When plants are in full growth and flower stems appear, in about November, give a liquid fertiliser every four weeks or so until March.

Temperatures throughout the winter should be 50-55°F (10-13°C) — higher than this and the plant will not thrive —and never lower than 40°F (5°C). A bright, sunny position, with a few hours of direct sunlight every day, and good ventilation are both essential at this time of year.

Propagation

Propagation is by division of clumps of bulbs every three to four years when the pot is crowded with offset bulbs. In late summer or early autumn, detach offsets that have at least one pair of leaves. Pot them individually in 3in (7cm) pots in the normal compost (see 'Autumn and winter care'). They should begin to flower after two to three years, and should by then be potted in 5in (13cm) pots.

At the same time as you detach the offsets, repot the main bulb in new compost, leaving it in a 5in (13cm) pot.

Trouble Shooter

Wilting leaves and no proper development of the flower spike are signs that the proper conditions are not being met — if they are, Veltheimias are very easy to care for and trouble-free. The main requirements are the correct temperatures and full, direct sunlight. *V.capensis* is more tolerant of house conditions than *V.glauca*. No insect pests are likely.

Species

Veltheimia capensis (also known as *V.viridifolia*), Forest Lily, is from Cape Province in South Africa. Its leaves are thick and broadly sword-shaped, bright green and shiny with very crinkly edges, up to 15in (38cm) long and 4in (10cm) wide. Flowers appear between November and March on a purplish stem 12-18in (30-45cm) tall with yellow or reddish spots along its length. The flowers, up to 60 in the cluster, can be pinkish-red or yellowish-green, with tubular, nodding blooms that last for several weeks.

V.glauca (also known as *V.deasii*) comes from the western Cape. It has dusty green or greyish-green leaves, leathery in texture and with wavy margins, 6-8in (15-20cm) in length. They grow almost in a rosette shape from the base of the plant. Flowers are similar to *V.capensis*, on a stalk about 15in (38cm) tall, but whitish in colour and spotted with pink.

Vinca

Family name: **Apocynaceae**

Common name:
Madagascar Periwinkle

Care Easy	**Height** 12-15in (30-38cm)	**Flower** Spring and summer
Light Sunny	**Spread** 1ft (0.3m)	**Humidity** Not necessary
Price Cheap	**Shape** Bushy	**Availability** Common
Temp. Min 60°F (16°C)	Ideal 70°F (21°C)	Max 85°F (29°C)

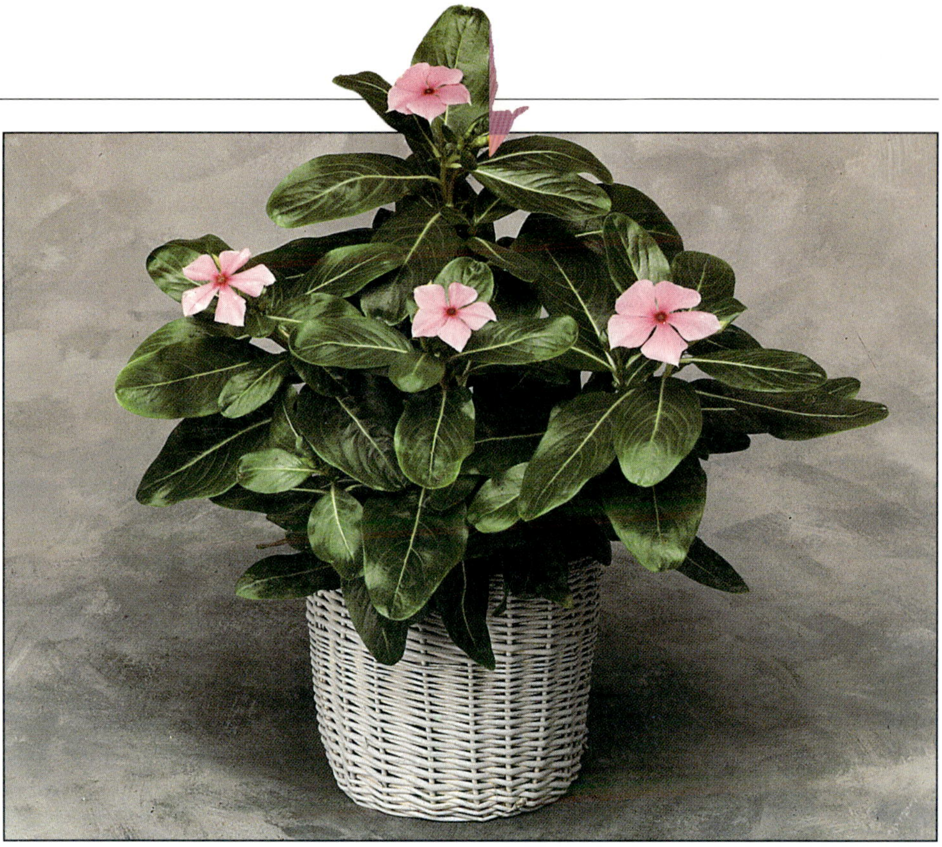

The Madagascar Periwinkle is a really delightful little plant.

The Periwinkles are a small group of charming plants, hardy or tender, mostly evergreen shrubs and herbaceous perennials, with pleasing foliage and colourful flowers. Of the six or seven species that make up this genus, only one is commonly grown as a houseplant — and that one has officially now been transferred to an entirely different genus, Catharanthus! However, it is as *Vinca rosea, above right*, that the Madagascar Periwinkle is still best known.

It is a compact, bushy, evergreen perennial plant (usually grown as an annual), which can reach a height of 12in (30cm) or more in a pot. But it's also well suited to growing in a hanging basket and seems equally happy with its stems spreading over the edge of the container. The very attractive flowers have spreading rose-pink petals with a purple centre. They appear from March, and under the right conditions they can be produced non-stop for weeks on end, the colourful display continuing well into the autumn.

Spring and summer care

Repot plants between January and March of each year in John Innes No 2. Move plants on to larger pots when they fill their current containers, to a final pot size of 5-6in (13-15cm) or grow a group in a hanging basket. Whatever container is used, make sure it drains well.

For a bushy, upright plant, prune the stems back to within 3-4in (8-10cm) of the base; use the cuttings for propagation. Otherwise, in a hanging basket, nip out the growing tips, but not too drastically or your plant may lose its spreading shape. Growth is usually quite rapid, so occasional pruning may prove necessary at times during the summer.

Your plant wants full sun and real warmth to thrive. Aim for summer temperatures of 70°F (21°C) or more — they'll happily tolerate temperatures up to as much as 85°F (29°C). Keep the plant in a really sunny position, but try to keep it well ventilated.

Water freely from April to October — though take care to avoid 'wet feet'; pots should never be left to stand in water. It is certainly a thirsty plant and should not be allowed to get too dry during this period. Feeding is also important — add a liquid fertiliser to the water every two weeks throughout the spring until the autumn.

If you have a suitable spot, your plant will flourish in a sunny, sheltered position outdoors in the summer; given regular watering, it can produce flowers continuously for weeks on end. Bring your plant back inside before the frosts set in and it should continue flowering well into the autumn.

Autumn and winter care

To ensure continuous growth and a long flowering season, keep your plant in as bright and sunny a position as possible and make sure that temperatures from October to March don't fall below 60-65°F (16-18°C). Water occasionally, but only enough to prevent the compost from drying out completely. Many people grow these plants as annuals — replacing them each year with a new plant. This is unnecessary if you can easily maintain the winter temperatures.

Propagation

Take 3-4in (8-10cm) long cuttings of young shoots, in March. Remove the lowest leaves, treat the cut ends with a rooting hormone and insert them into a moistened mixture of two parts John Innes No 2 and one part coarse sand. Keep moist and lightly shaded — ideally in a propagator, or enclosed in a clear polythene bag — at a temperature of 75°F (24°C).

When new growth indicates that rooting is established, uncover the cuttings and provide them with more light, maintaining the temperature but gradually hardening them off. Transfer the rooted cuttings to 3-3½in (8-9cm) pots of John Innes No 2, or plant three or four together in a hanging basket; pinch out the growing tips once or twice for bushy growth, and treat as mature plants.

Species

Vinca rosea (now often classified as *Catharanthus rosea*), the Madagascar Periwinkle, is a bushy, glossy-leaved evergreen, which can grow to a height of 12-15in (30-38cm). The flowers have a rose-purple centre and five spreading, rose-pink petals, opening out flat, and 1-1½in (2.5-4cm) across; they appear from April to October. Varieties include 'Little Pinkie', a compact form growing 9in (23cm) high, with rose-pink flowers, and 'Little Bright Eye', which has pure white flowers with deep rose-pink centres.

Trouble Shooter

Foliage will wither and flowering be affected if plants are left too dry, but take care to avoid overwatering, which could lead to root rot. If flowers are not readily forthcoming it may be due to lack of fertiliser; feed regularly, particularly in summer. Flowers will not be produced if plants are in too shaded a position — give them the sunniest possible spot.

Pests are not likely to be a problem. If mealy bug attacks, wipe away the fluffy white patches with a soft cloth or paintbrush dipped in methylated spirit, or spray the plant with a malathion-based insecticide. In the event of scale insect, and possibly red spider mite, use the same insecticide.

Vriesea

Family name: **Bromeliaceae**

Common name:
Flaming Sword

Care Straight-forward	**Height** 1/-2ft (0.5-0.6m)	**Flower** Late summer
Light Bright, mostly indirect	**Spread** 1/ ft (0.5m)	**Humidity** Mist spray regularly
Price Middle range	**Shape** Rosette	**Availability** Garden centres
Temp. Min 55°F (13°C)	Ideal 75°F (24°C)	Max 80°F (27°C)

Vrieseas are a group of houseplants named 150 years ago in honour of a Professor of Botany at Amsterdam University, W. H. de Vries. The group is large, having about 200 species, and in addition numerous cultivars have become very popular as houseplants. They deserve their renown, being extremely dramatic and beautiful plants, with strongly cross-banded leaves arranged in a rosette and a breathtaking flower spike, which appears once the plant is two or three years old and lasts four to five months.

Vrieseas come from central and South America, mainly Brazil, and are also found in the West Indies. The commonest plant in the group is *Vriesea splendens, above right*, with a rosette of bluish-green leaves banded with deep purple and a dramatic spike, bearing scarlet bracts and small yellow flowers which come out at night. The flower spikes can appear at any time of year.

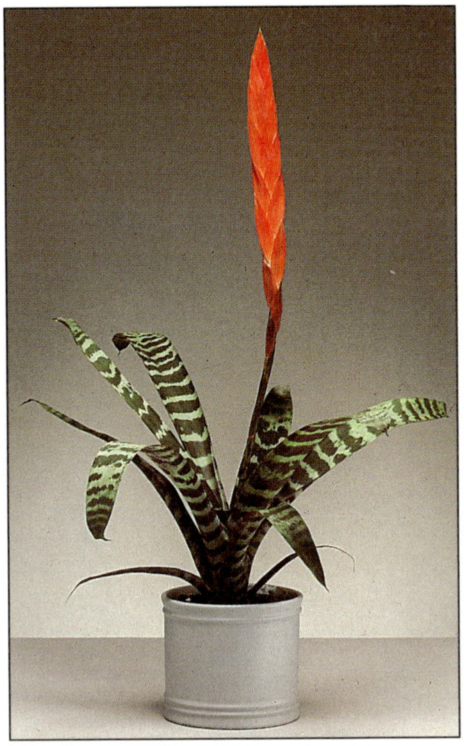

The flower spike of this splendid Bromeliad is covered with brilliant red bracts which last for several months.

Spring and summer care

Vriesea rosettes die after flowering, and offsets take over around the base and produce new flowers. These offsets can either be potted up separately (see 'Propagation') or potted on and left for two or three years to form a large, multiple rosette plant. For potting use a lime-free peat-based compost mixed with a quarter part coarse sand. The dying rosettes should be cut down to within 1-2in (2.5-5cm) of their base at any time of year, as they begin to look unsightly.

Temperatures may rise to 75-80°F (24-27°C), with a few hours of direct sunlight every day in the morning or evening, and a position of filtered light the rest of the time. Water freely, ensuring that the central cup at the heart of the rosette is always full and the compost is kept moist. Empty and refill the cup every month to keep the water fresh. Vrieseas don't like lime, so if you live in a hard water area, water your plants with boiled water or add a few drops of vinegar to your tap water. Use a liquid fertiliser at half strength every 3-4 weeks — and water this into the rosette. To keep up the humidity, place the pot on a tray of damp pebbles or mist spray regularly from overhead using tepid lime-free water.

Autumn and winter care

When the flower spike has dried out (this can take four or five months), remove it at the base with a pair of sharp scissors or secateurs. Don't let the temperature drop below 55°F (13°C), and give a position of indirect light. Water regularly to keep the compost moist. Give good air circulation but keep out of draughts, and mist spray occasionally.

Propagation

In March or April remove established offsets of at least 5in (13cm) tall. Cut them from the parent plant with a sharp knife, if possible taking roots with each one. Pot the offsets up individually into 3in (7cm) pots, using the recommended lime-free compost (see 'Spring and summer care') with ample crocks to provide free drainage. Keep the offsets moist and well-shaded, at 75-80°F (24-27°C), in a propagator or enclosed in a sealed clear polythene bag. Place in bright filtered light until roots are established, in four to six weeks, then treat as mature plants. Move on the following year to 5in (13cm) pots.

Trouble Shooter

If leaves begin to discolour and look sickly, before the rosette has flowered, increase watering — the cup should never be allowed to dry out. Cold can have the same effect — make sure your Vriesea is warm enough. Never leave the plant standing in water or it will rot.

If mealy bug attacks, wipe off the fluffy patches with a brush or cloth dipped in methylated spirit. Don't use insecticides containing malathion, as it will get into the cup and could damage the foliage. Red spider mite may be a problem if the plant has been allowed to get too dry; don't use an insecticide spray but scrape the pests and the webs off with a fingernail or a dry brush. If you can't manage this, then cut the affected parts of the leaves off completely. Increase the humidity by mist-spraying.

Species

Vriesea splendens, Flaming Sword, comes from Venezuela. It grows up to 18in (45cm) tall, with bluish-green leaves, greyish on the undersides, cross-banded with broad stripes of dark purple. Leaves are 1½-2in (4-5cm) wide and there are about 20 to a rosette. The flowering stem is up to 2ft (0.6m) tall, with a 12in (30cm) long, sword-shaped section at the top, covered with neat, overlapping, brilliant red bracts. Bright yellow flowers, 1½-2in (4-5cm) long, emerge successively from between the bracts, usually in late summer — though they can appear at any time from spring until the autumn.

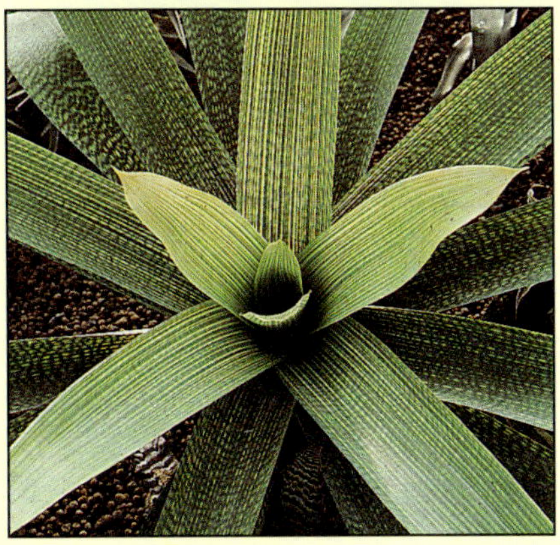

V.fenestralis, *right*, comes from Brazil. Its large rosette is formed of about 20 shiny, yellowish-green leaves, 18in (45cm) long and 2in (5cm) wide, marked all over with numerous, darker green, veins, and spotted with red or purplish-red on the underside. The flower spike, appearing any time in spring, autumn or summer, is about 18in (45cm) high and bears up to 20 shiny green bracts spotted with deep purple, and 2½in (6cm) long tubular flowers of a rich sulphur-yellow.

Yucca

Family name: **Agavaceae**

Common names: **Spineless Yucca, Spanish Bayonet**

Care Easy	**Height** 6ft (1.8m)	**Flower** Rare
Light Sunny	**Spread** 2ft (0.6m)	**Humidity** Mist spray in hot weather
Price Middle range	**Shape** Leafy clump or tree-like	**Availability** Common
Temp. Min 45°F (7°C)	Ideal 70°F (21°C)	Max 80°F (27°C)

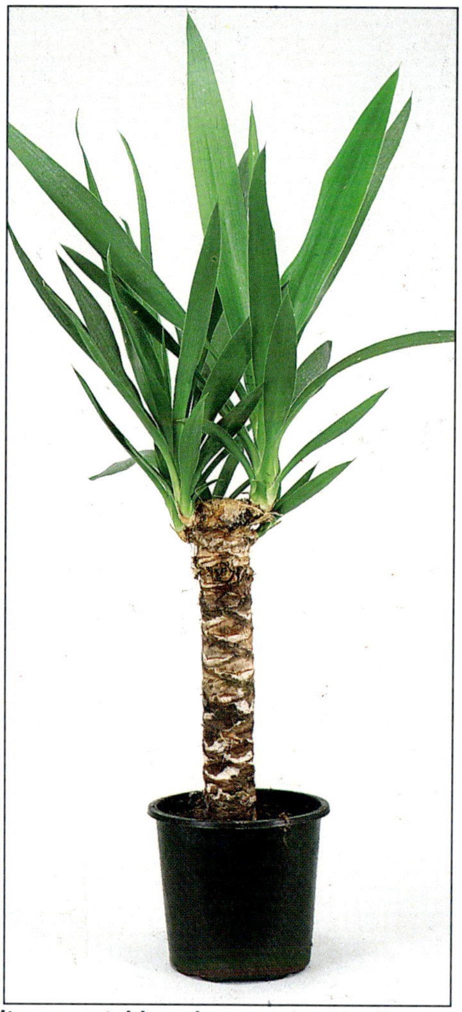

Its eye-catching shape makes the Yucca a very popular plant.

Trouble Shooter

If many of the lower leaves begin to lose their colour, your Yucca isn't getting enough light, and unless you do something about it, the colour loss will spread to the rest of the roliage. Cut off the discoloured, yellow leaves and move the plant into a better position. A wilting, unhappy looking plant could be suffering from overwatering. Take steps to correct this or it may prove fatal.

Furry grey mould on the leaves means botrytis; remove the affected parts and spray with a fungicide. White, fluffy patches are a sign of mealy bug, while brown, scaly creatures under the leaves and on the stems are scale insects. Either way, wipe them away with a soft cloth or cotton bud dipped in methylated spirit, or spray with a malathion-based pesticide.

Buying Guide

When buying a Yucca as a leafy side rosette at the top of a thick stem, choose the size of stem that you want since it won't grow any taller — only the rosette grows not the woody trunk.

Many of the most attractive species are hard to find. Buy them from a nursery specialising in succulent plants or contact a specialist seedsman.

With its characteristic thick, rough and woody stem, topped with a crown (or crowns) of sword-shaped leaves, the Yucca is one of the most instantly recognisable of houseplants. Capable of growing up to 40ft (12m) or more in the wilds of Central America and the West Indies, many of the 40 or so species would present problems as houseplants if grown to maturity! Fortunately, young plants of certain species can be kept inside where they will grow very slowly.

During the last 10 to 15 years the Spineless Yucca (*Yucca elephantipes*), *right*, has become a great favourite with houseplant enthusiasts, mainly because it's easy to care for as well as being an eye-catching shape. It is found in one of two forms. It can be grown — as it does in its natural habibat — as a plume of foliage emerging straight from the soil, its stem gradually lengthening and eventually becoming woody as the lower leaves drop. But it's more commonly available as a tree-like plant with two or three leafy side shoots at the top of a length of woody stem.

In their native habitat, Yuccas produce huge creamy-white flowering stems but these very rarely appear on plants which are grown indoors.

Spring and summer care

Pot on your Yucca in the spring every year. The main reason for regular potting on to a larger pot is not because your plant's roots need more room (although they do enjoy having plenty of space) but because the plant will become top-heavy and therefore unstable in its pot. Once you've reached the maximum manageable pot size, simply topdress the plant each year by replacing the top 2in (5cm) of compost. Use John Innes No 2 for potting and topdressing.

Water freely between April and October, and during this period of active growth add a liquid fertiliser to the water every four weeks. Don't let the plants stand in water, though. Give them the best possible light at all times, the more sun the better, since they need at least three hours of direct sunlight a day to make good growth.

In the summer, it's a good idea to stand them outside during the warmest months, but be sure to harden them off carefully if you do. This will encourage more mature plants to flower in mid-summer. However, there's no guarantee that they will produce their tall columns of bell-shaped white or violet-tinged flowers.

Yuccas tolerate a wide temperature range — up to 75°F (24°C), and higher if there's plenty of fresh air — and they'll benefit from mist spraying first thing in the morning before the sun gets on them, during the warmest weather.

Autumn and winter care

Winter temperatures as low as 45°F (7°C) won't bother the Yucca, though it prefers a lower temperature limit of 50°F (10°C).

Accustomed to withstanding long periods of drought in its native habitat, it will enjoy a winter rest when watering should be kept to a minimum. From November to March, stop feeding and give plants only enough water to keep the compost from drying out.

Propagation

In February or March, sow seeds, ¼in (6mm) deep, in a mixture of two parts of the usual potting compost and one part gritty sand. Make sure the compost is nice and moist. Place the container inside a propagator and keep it in the shade, at a temperature of 70°F (21°C), until the seeds germinate then move it into the light.

Within three months, once the seedlings are 2-3in (5-8cm) tall, transplant them individually, into a small, crocked 5in (13cm) pot filled with the usual potting compost. The plant can now be cared for in the usual way.

If your plant has become overgrown and unshapely then propagate it from stem sections in the spring or summer — bear in mind though that this procedure destroys your original plant. Remove the old plant from its pot and lay the woody stem on a flat, stable surface, and saw it into lengths of any size, but a minimum of 4in (10cm) long.

Dip the cut sections into a hormone rooting powder and put them into a seed tray or propagator containing a mixture of half coarse sand and half peat-based potting compost. Push the sections down until they can stand upright in the compost — but make sure they don't actually touch the bottom of the tray. Cover with clear polythene or a plastic dome, and keep it away from direct sunlight at a temperature of 75-80°F (24-27°C). Make sure the compost stays moist.

After about three weeks, remove the cover from the propagator. Once rooting is established, and young shoots have developed,

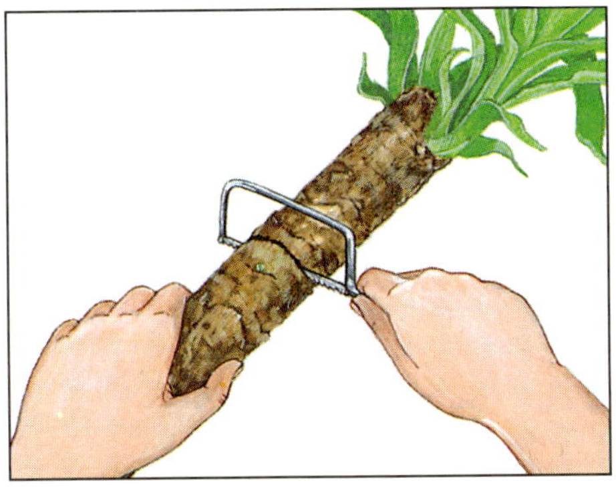

For several small Yuccas, rather than a single large one, saw your plant into lengths, each a minimum of 4in (10cm) long and with at least one bud.

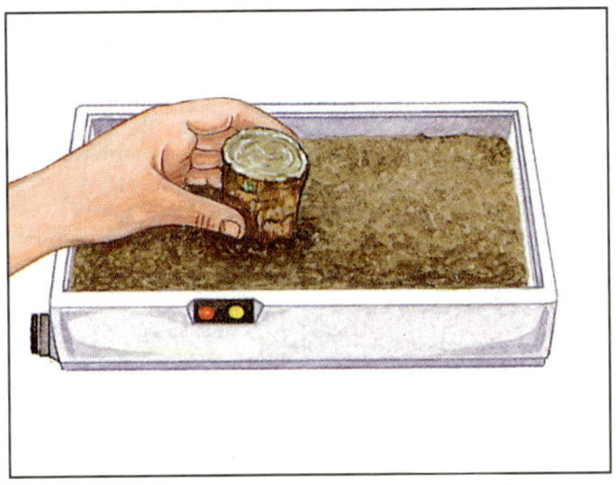

Dip the cut surface into a saucer of hormone rooting powder and set each cut section into potting compost — deep enough for it to stand upright.

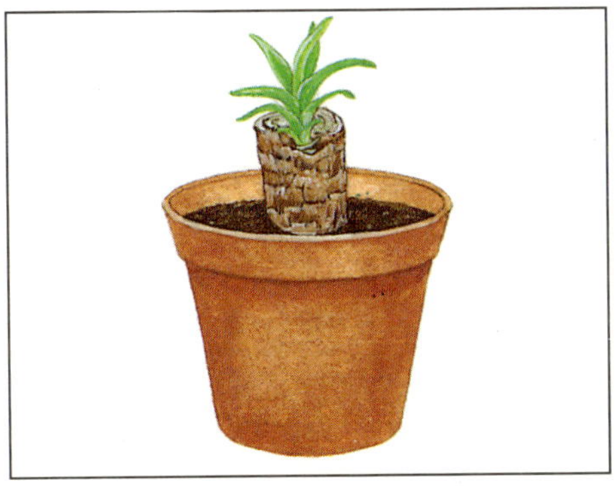

When growth is well established, pot the sections up individually or in closely spaced groups of two or three.

repot each new plant into individual pots or in groups of two or three to a pot, filled with the normal potting mixture. You can then treat them as established plants.

Some species can be propagated, in early spring, from the suckers which sometimes appear at the base of the plant. Choose one that has at least four leaves, about 6in (15cm) long, and sever it with a sharp blade. Insert the cutting into a moistened mixture of half potting compost, half coarse sand. Put it into a propagator, in a shady spot at a temperature of 75°F (24°C). Check that the compost stays moist. Once the cutting starts into growth, in six to eight weeks, remove from the propagator and treat it in the usual way.

Species

Yucca elephantipes, the Spineless Yucca, from Mexico and Guatemala, has bright, glossy green, pointed leaves arranged in a rosette shape, either grouped at the top of a woody stem or growing as a single rosette rising straight from the soil. These leaves are quite stiff and upright when they're young, but as they mature they arch over and eventually fall — thereby increasing the length of the stem. It's sometimes called the Palm Lily because the leaves tend to appear only at the top of the stem — just like a palm tree. In the wild, it can reach 40ft (12m), and branches frequently, but as a houseplant it usually stops at 3-6ft (0.9-1.8m). Any flowers will appear in late summer carried in scented, ivory-white spires.

Y.aloifolia, *below*, the Spanish Bayonet or Dagger Plant, earns its common name from the ferociously serrated edges of its thick-fleshed, deep green leaves which are arranged in a rosette shape at the top of its stem. Its trunk can grow up to 3-4ft long (0.9-1.2m) and offset rosettes may develop at the base. Widespread around the southern parts of the USA, Mexico and the West Indies, this species has a number of interesting forms worth looking out for. *Y.a.marginata*, for instance, is enhanced by the creamy-white margins which fringe its rich green leaves, and has the advantage of being one of the slower growers. Whichever you choose, make sure you position it where the leaves can do no harm! Flower heads, if they develop, come in summer on tall spires made up of quite dense clusters of yellowish-white blooms sometimes with a tinge of purple.

Y. texanum, is one of the choicest of species. But since it's nearly extinct in its native habitat of the southern USA, and scarcely available in cultivation, it's rarely encountered in Britain — and is therefore very expensive. Its slender, bluish-grey leaves, forming an elegant rosette, are about 2ft (0.6m) long, and adorned with long, coarse, white hairs. Creamy white flowers appear in midsummer, but not on houseplants.

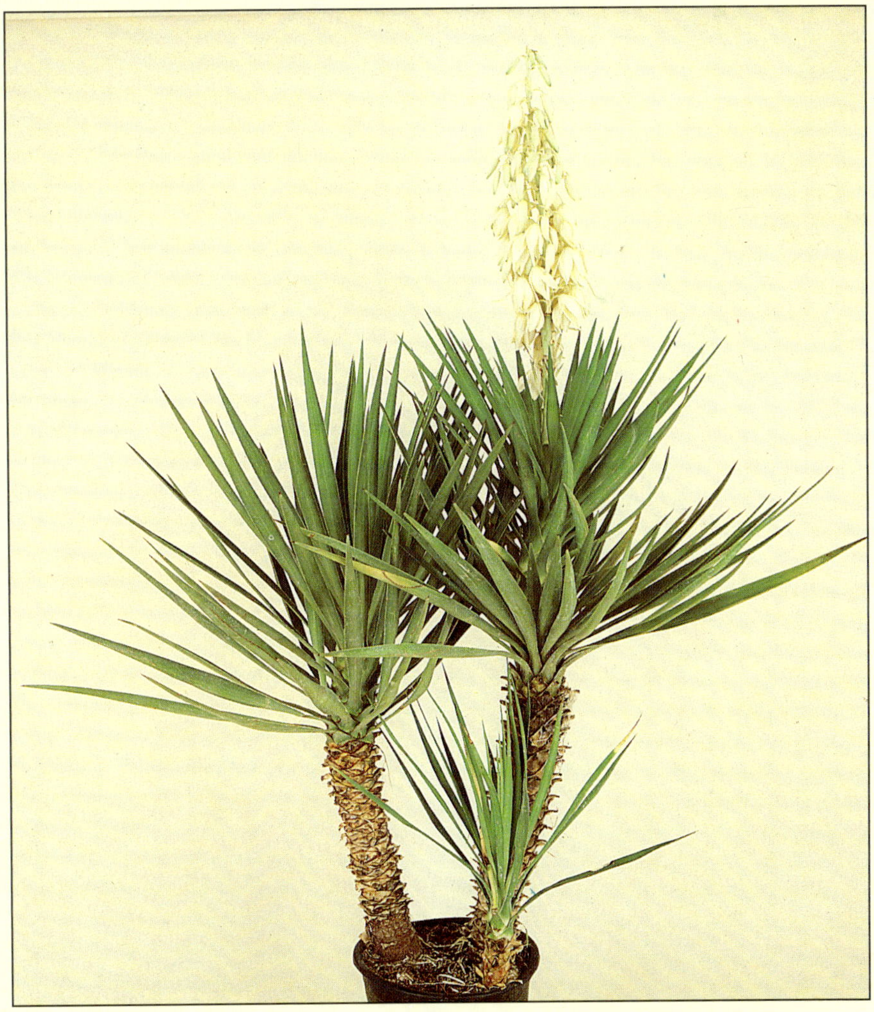

Zantedeschia

Family name: **Araceae**

Common names: **Arum Lily, Calla Lily**

Care Tricky	**Height** 3ft (0.9m)	**Flower** Late winter/ early spring
Light Bright, indirect	**Spread** 3ft (0.9m)	**Humidity** Mist spray occasionally
Price Middle range	**Shape** Leafy clump	**Availability** Specialist nurseries
Temp. Min 40°F (4°C)	Ideal 55°F (13°C)	Max 70°F (21°C)

These stunning South African plants have been well-known and deservedly popular for nearly 200 years, and since then the plant breeders have been working to develop even more handsome and trouble-free hybrids and varieties. Their natural habitat is sub-tropical swamp land which becomes parched during the dry season — and during this time the plants shrivel above ground and lose their leaves. When grown as house-plants Zantedeschias need a similar, dry dormant period — usually during summer or autumn/winter depending on flowering time — and to be started into growth again a few months later.

Zantedeschia aethiopica, below, is the classic Arum Lily; a very elegant, deciduous plant with large, arrow-shaped leaves carried on thick, fleshy stalks and above the leaves in spring (much earlier than other species) the beautiful, long-lasting flowers appear — each made up of a central, erect spike of tiny, tightly packed flowers and surrounded by a large velvety-white spathe. The varieties look similar to the species but have yellow, orange or even, like the variety *Z.a.*'Green Goddess', green-tinged flowers.

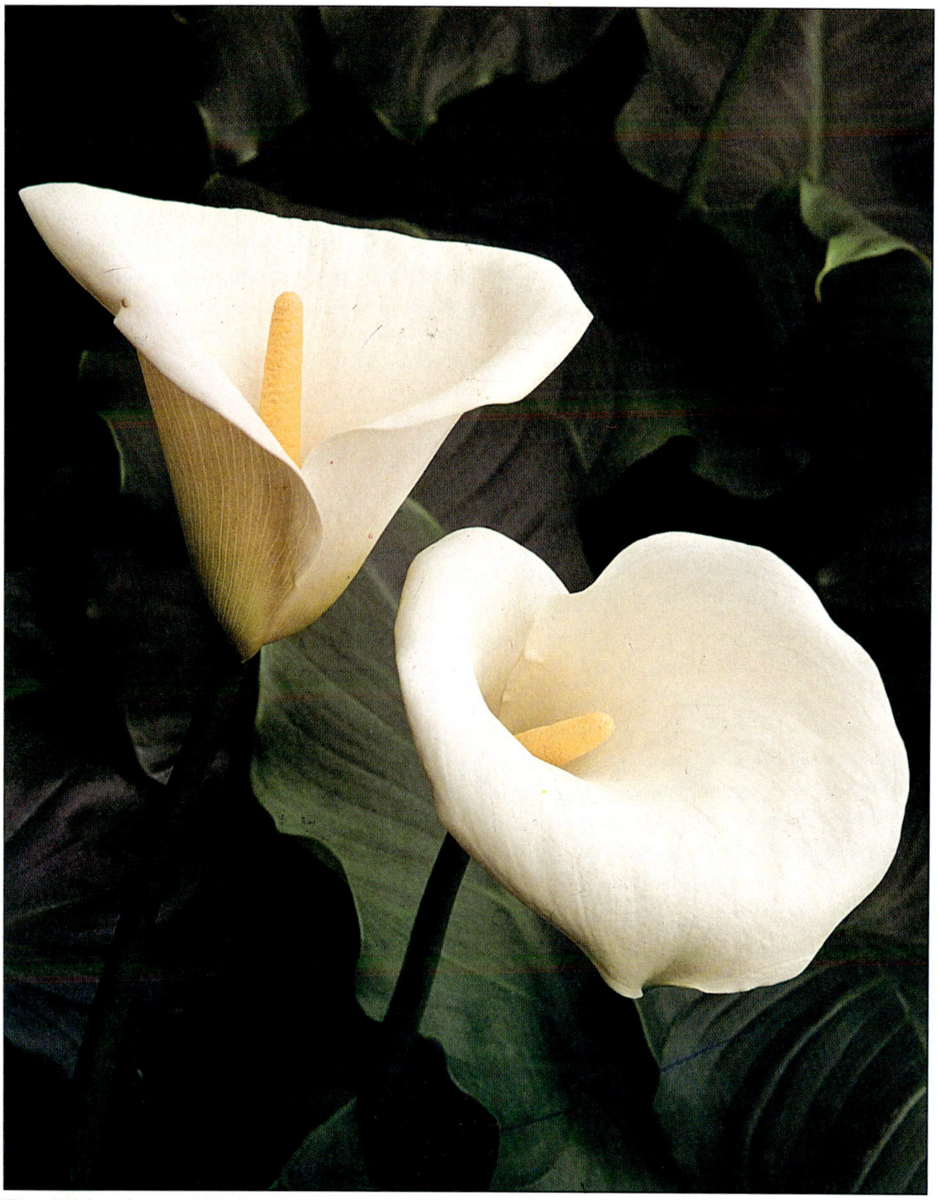

The White Arum Lily is a handsome plant with stunning flowers.

Spring and summer care

Repot *Z.aethiopica* in late August or September, other species in February, using John Innes No 2, ideally with a little added peat; plant the rhizome about 2in (5cm) below the surface of the compost. A 6-8in (15-20cm) pot will accommodate a single flowering plant, but larger clumps will need to be moved on into bigger pots. When the maximum convenient pot or tub size is reached, they should be divided up (see 'Propagation').

Z.aethiopica is best kept at around 55-60°F (13-16°C) from late February to May, by which time flowering will have finished and the leaves will be dying; after this it should be kept fairly cool, ideally at a temperature of about 50°F (10°C). Other species will do best at a temperature of 65-70°F (18-21°C) from late March to October; higher temperatures than this may shorten the flowering period and cause leaves to wither prematurely. All Zantedeschias require bright light, but are best protected from direct sunshine.

Water all species moderately as growth begins to appear, gradually increasing the amount until plants are in full leaf. Thereafter water freely, as often as needed to keep the compost thoroughly moist. As flowers fade and the foliage starts to yellow, gradually

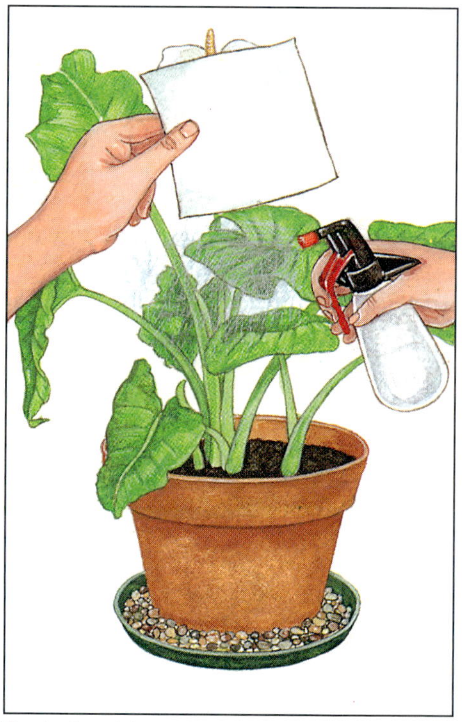

Zantedeschia enjoy a humid atmosphere; mist spray regularly, but prevent the flowers from getting wet.

Buying Guide

These plants are now being offered for sale more frequently — especially as the new hybrids become increasingly available. These hybrids are far less fussy than the true species and make splendid flowering houseplants, so look out for them at your local shops or garden centre.

reduce the watering to a minimum, and keep the compost barely moist.

Add a liquid fertiliser to the water every two weeks from the time when flower buds appear until the end of the flowering period, and mist spray the foliage occasionally to provide a degree of humidity.

Autumn and winter care

Provide your plants with bright but filtered light at a temperature of around 55°F (13°C), except for *Z.aethiopica*, which is best at around 50°F (10°C) and will survive at a temperature of 40°F (5°C). As growth becomes apparent, towards the end of winter, this should be increased to about 60°F (16°C). With *Z.aethiopica*, keep the compost just moist, and gradually increase watering as growth develops, then water freely. When flower spikes start to appear in late winter, start adding a weak liquid fertiliser to the water every week or so, using half the recommended amount. The other species flower later — in late spring or summer — and should be left barely moist from October to February, then watering should be gradually increased, to bring them into new growth.

Propagation

Zantedeschias are easily propagated by detaching offsets of the rhizome at repotting time. Cut the offsets away from the old rhizome using a scalpel or sharp knife, treat any cut surface with fungicidal sulphur powder and leave the offsets to dry off for a day or two. Plant the offsets individually into 3-4in (8-10cm) pots of the usual compost until they are large enough to pot on; otherwise, they should be treated in the same way as the larger rhizomes, although they may not flower in the first season.

Trouble Shooter

If plants are allowed to get too cold during their rest period — especially if affected by frost — they are unlikely to recover. Plants may rot if they are too wet during their dormant period; they should be kept barely moist from the time they lose their foliage until they are brought back into growth the following season. Conversely, too dry compost once growth commences will retard progress; leaves will discolour and the general appearance of the plant will be spoilt. Foliage will be scorched if plants are exposed to too much sun; they must always have a semi-shaded position.

Mealy bug is a possible pest; remove with a soft cloth or paintbrush dipped in methylated spirit. Red spider mite will only be a problem if plants are kept in too dry an atmosphere; spray with a malathion-based insecticide and increase the level of humidity around the plant.

Species

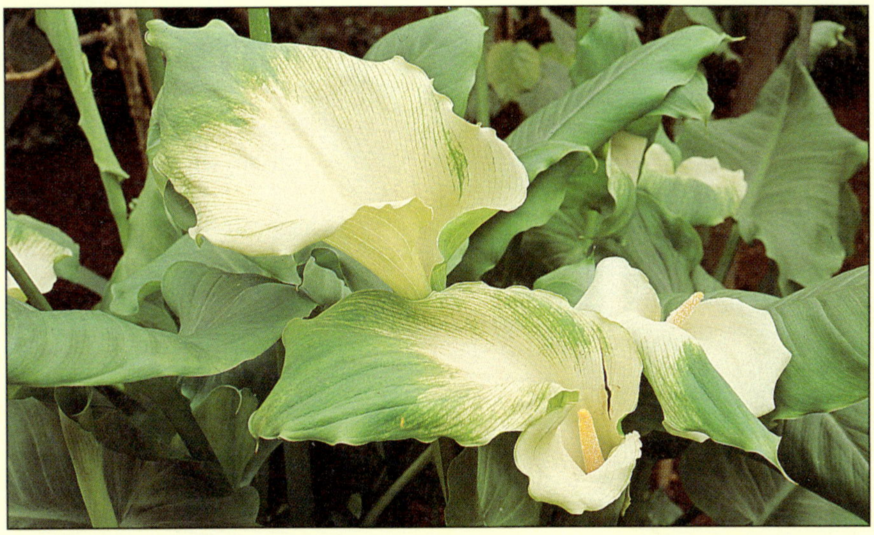

Zantedeschia aethiopica, also known as the White Arum Lily or White Calla Lily, is the most popular species. It grows to a height of about 3ft (0.9m), with deep green, arrow-shaped leaves, 18in (45cm) long by 10in (25cm) wide, on long, thick, fleshy stalks. Flower stalks can appear at any time from late winter to early spring, bearing a creamy-white, open spathe, 6-8in (15-20cm) long, enclosing a conspicuous, golden-yellow spadix. Attractive varieties include *Z.a.childsiana*, which is more compact than the true species and very free-flowering; 'Green Goddess', *above*, is an unusual form, with a white spathe marbled with light green.

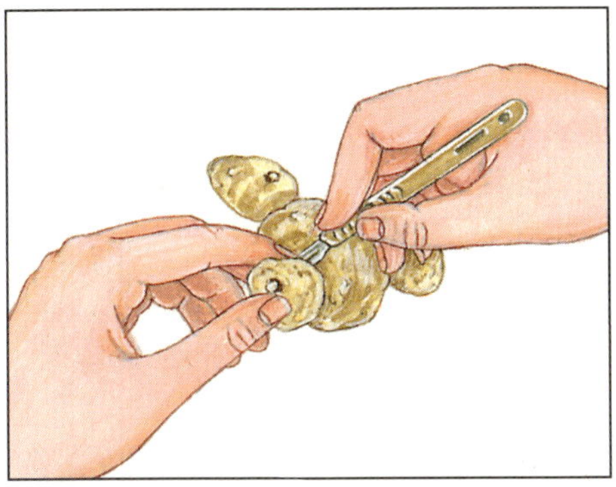

Use a scalpel to sever offsets from the parent rhizome — making sure each has at least one bud.

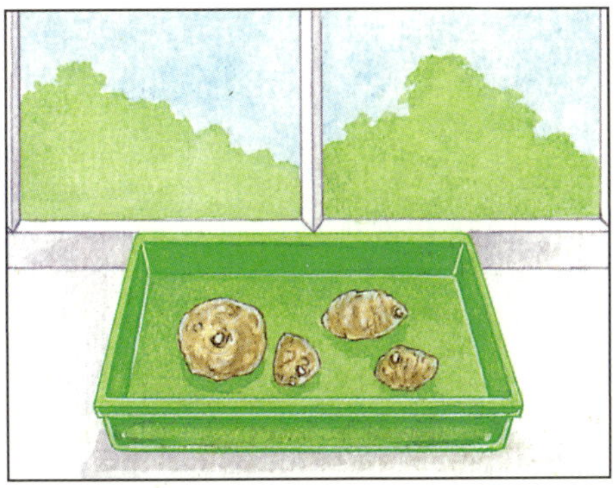

Dust the cut surfaces with sulphur powder and leave the offsets to dry off for one or two days.

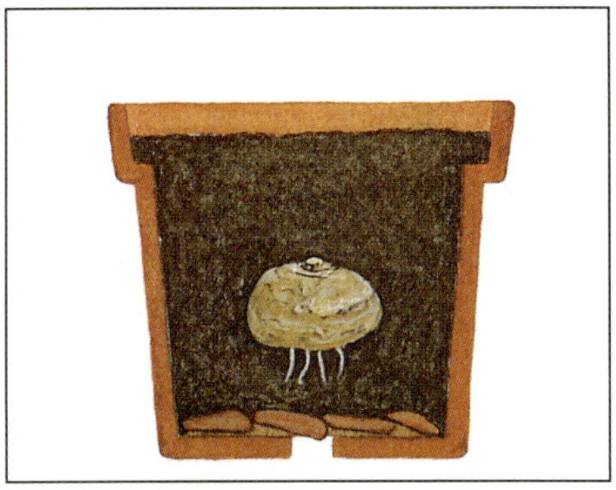

Plant each offset individually, 2-3in (5-8cm) deep, in John Innes No 2 with a little added peat.

Species

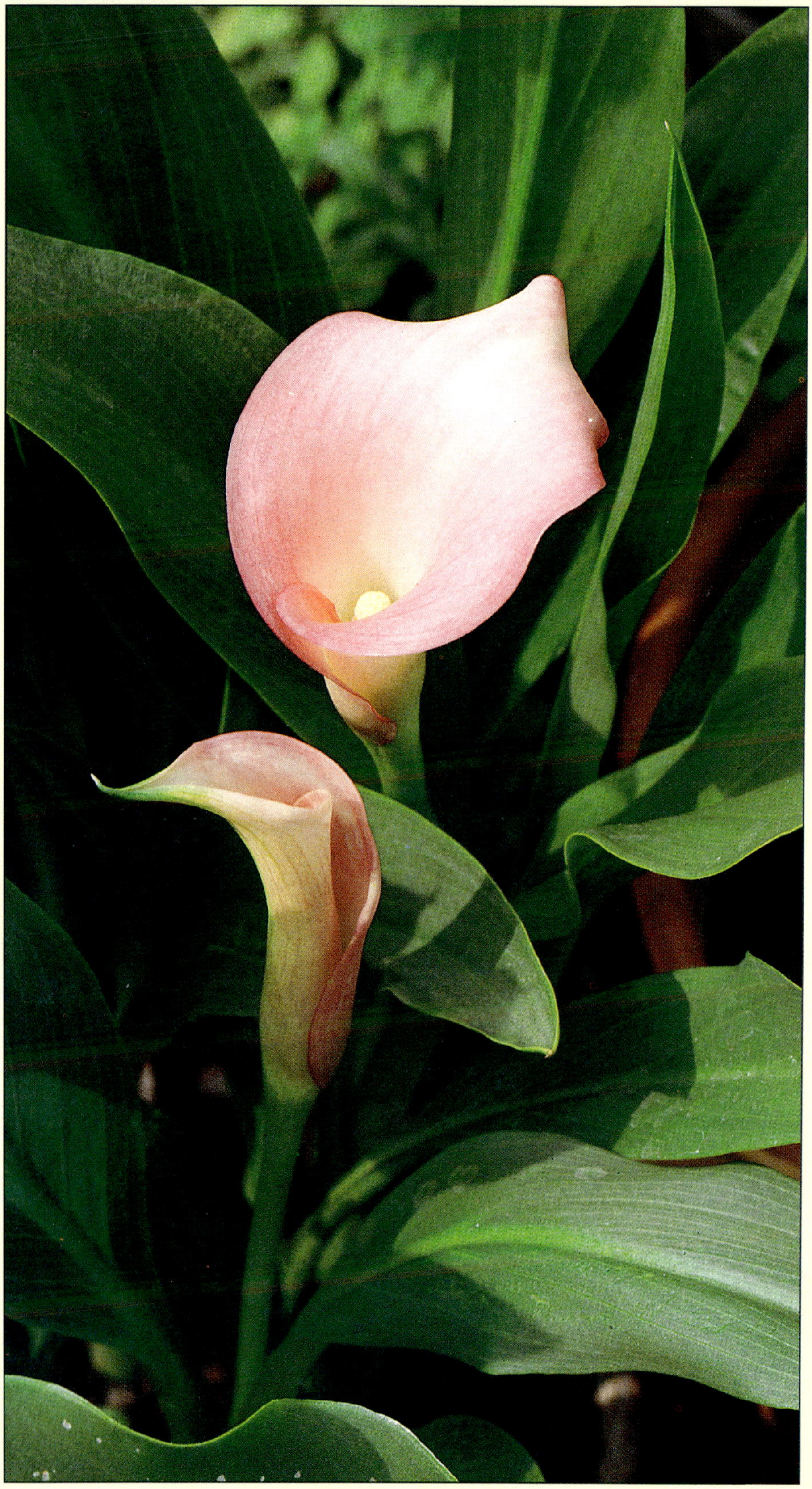

Z.elliottiana is sometimes called the Golden Calla, after the brilliant flowers. Showy, 4in (10cm) long, golden-yellow spathes, around a yellow spadix, appear in May and June. The plant grows to a height of 2-3 ft (0.6-0.9m), with elongated, heart-shaped leaves, up to 10in (25cm) long, on 2ft (0.6m) stalks, which are dark green with silvery spots.

Z.rehmannii, *left*, known as the Pink Arum or Calla, grows up to 2ft (0.6m) tall, with 10-12in (25-30cm) long, narrow, arrow-shaped leaves, tapering almost to a point at each end; they are mid-green in colour and often spotted with silvery-white flecks. Flowers are borne mainly from April to June; they consist of 4-5in (10-13cm) long, open, trumpet-shaped spathes, ranging from pale pink to wine-red in colour, surrounding a central, upright, creamy white spadix.

Z.albomaculata grows into a 2-3ft (0.6-0.9m) tuft of narrowly triangular leaves, up to 18in (45cm) long, which are bright green with translucent, silvery-white markings. In summer the flowers are trumpet-shaped, with a 4-5in (10-13cm) long, tube-like spathe, varying from white to creamy yellow, with a reddish-purple throat, around a white spadix.

New hybrids: recent research in New Zealand has led to the introduction of new colour forms, with a neat, compact growth, 12-18in (30-45cm) tall, making excellent houseplants. The flowers come in a wide range of colours: from red, pink, orange and yellow, to maroon or purple, *below, top and bottom.*

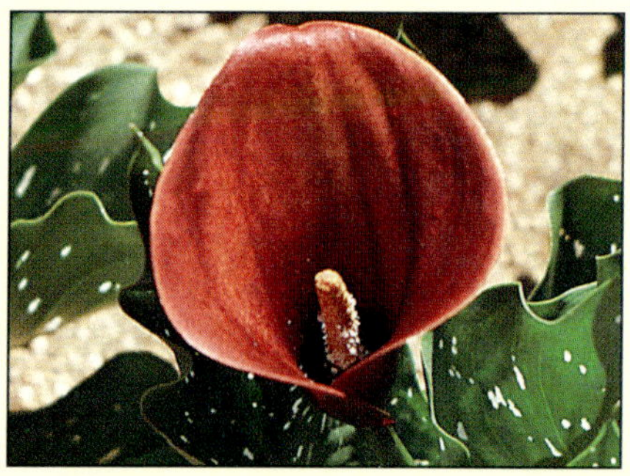

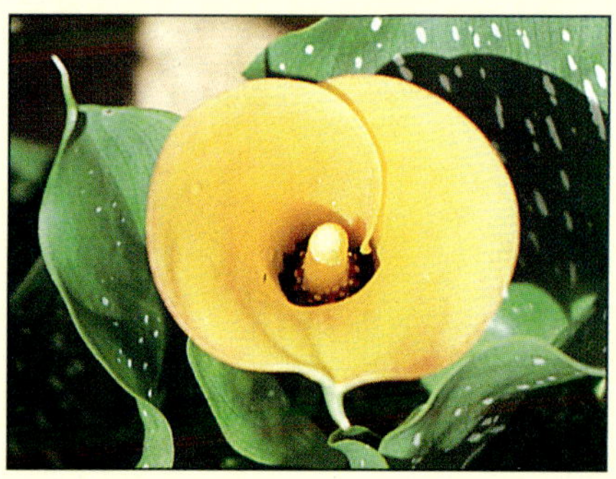

Zebrina

Family name: **Commelinaceae**

Common names: **Wandering Jew/Wandering Sailor/ Inch Plant**

Care Easy	**Height** 1ft (30cm)	**Flower** Spring and summer
Light Bright	**Spread** 9-12in (23-30cm)	**Humidity** Not required
Price Cheap	**Shape** Trailing	**Availability** Common
Temp. Min 45°F (7°C)	Ideal 70°F (21°C)	Max 80°F (27°C)

This popular group of fleshy, trailing evergreen plants is closely related to the Tradescantias — in fact, many botanists believe that the two groups should be merged together because they are so similar.

A quick-growing, easy plant with trailing stems and colourful leaves, Zebrina is an excellent choice for a hanging basket or to train up a small trellis. *Zebrina pendula*, the most popular species, has pointed-oval, slightly glistening leaves, striped in green and silver — though its varieties come in a wide range of colours, such as bronze, pink, purple or cream. Its fleshy stems are rather weak and floppy, and will creep or trail over the surface of the container.

Spring and summer care

Repot your Zebrina every spring, into a pot one size larger if the roots have filled the container; for a good bushy effect, plant several cuttings together — as many as 12 or 15 in a single hanging basket. Use John Innes No 2 for potting and make sure you put plenty of drainage material under the compost. If you don't want to encourage your plant to grow bigger then topdress by replacing the top 1-2in (2.5-5cm) of compost. As old leaves tend to shrivel and drop, leaving the stems bare, instead of potting or top-dressing it may be better to raise new plants every year from cuttings (see 'Propagation'); Zebrina is so quick-growing that you'll find plants will soon put on a fine display.

Straggly stems, or stems with plain green leaves, should be pruned back at any time; keep trailing stems trimmed to a maximum length of 1ft (0.3m) or so, or they will start to become bare and leafless. Regular pinching out of stem tips will also help keep your plant thick and bushy. If your plant is climbing up a trellis, you'll need to tie in the stems with plastic covered wire twists to provide adequate support.

Zebrinas grow best when they're kept slightly dry so water your plant regularly but allow the top 1in (2.5cm) of compost to dry out before watering again. Add a liquid fertiliser to the water every two weeks.

Normal room temperatures suit Zebrinas well and, although they can tolerate quite shaded conditions, bright light will help maintain good leaf colour, but keep shaded from direct sun. In warm weather your plant will benefit from being outside in the fresh air — but put it in a shaded position.

Autumn and winter care

These plants can put up with quite low temperatures but not below 45°F (7°C) and always keep them sheltered from cold draughts. Stop feeding and reduce the watering, but don't let the compost become bone dry.

Propagation

Zebrina stems root very easily and if your friends have varieties that are different from yours, it's a good idea to take cuttings from their plants, perhaps to make up a mixed pot or basket of complementary leaf patterns and colours. Anytime from March to September, snip off 3-5in (8-13cm) lengths of stem. Trim the cuttings to just below a leaf node and remove the leaves from the bottom 1in (2.5cm) of stem. Set the cuttings, up to their lowest leaves, in a pot or tray of well-drained compost, such as a mixture of equal parts of John Innes No 2 and coarse sand.

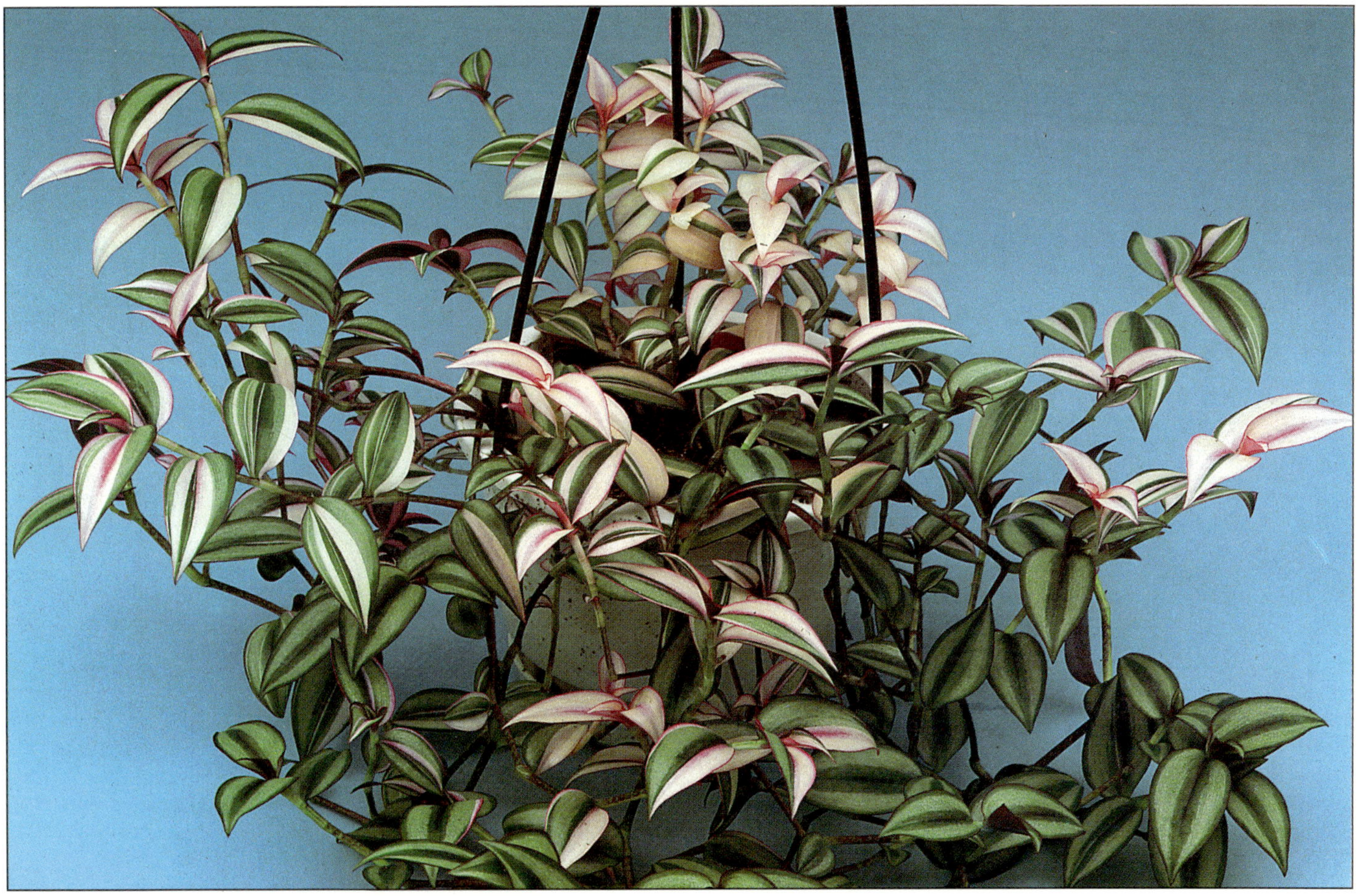

Some of the young leaves of this attractive variety of *Zebrina pendula* are tinged and striped with pink.

Keep the cuttings in indirect light and a temperature of about 70°F (21°C). Once new leaves begin to form pot up the cuttings in John Innes No 2 — spacing them about 2in (5cm) apart. If you're planting up a wire hanging basket, line it with sphagnum moss before adding the compost. Pinch out growing tips of the rooted cuttings at regular intervals and treat them as mature plants.

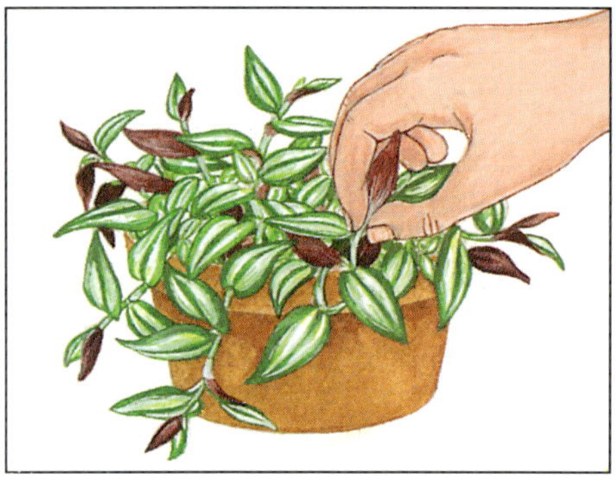

To encourage your plant to produce lots of leafy, trailing stems pinch out the growing tips regularly.

Trouble Shooter

While these plants can survive a lot of neglect, they will quickly become straggly and lose their colour if they are grown in too shaded a position; remove any plain green shoots as they appear and cut back straggly stems, or if the plant is old take cuttings and throw it away. Zebrinas rarely suffer from insect pests or fungus diseases.

Buying Guide

Choose plants made up of several young cuttings; look for good, strong leaf colouring and well-clothed stems without shrivelled foliage.

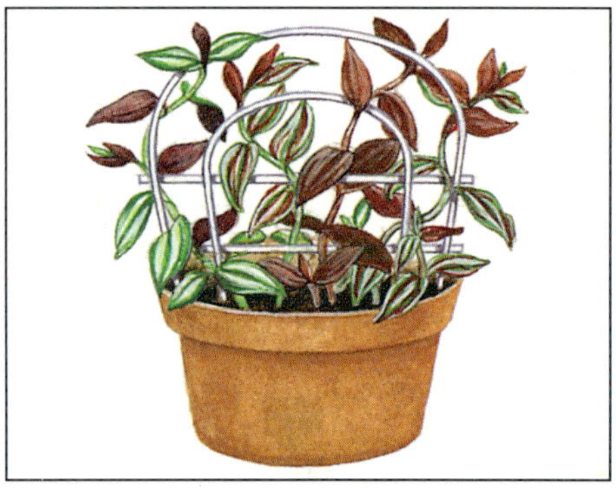

Cuttings of different varieties potted together can look very attractive — either trailing downwards from a hanging basket, or climbing up a small trellis.

Species

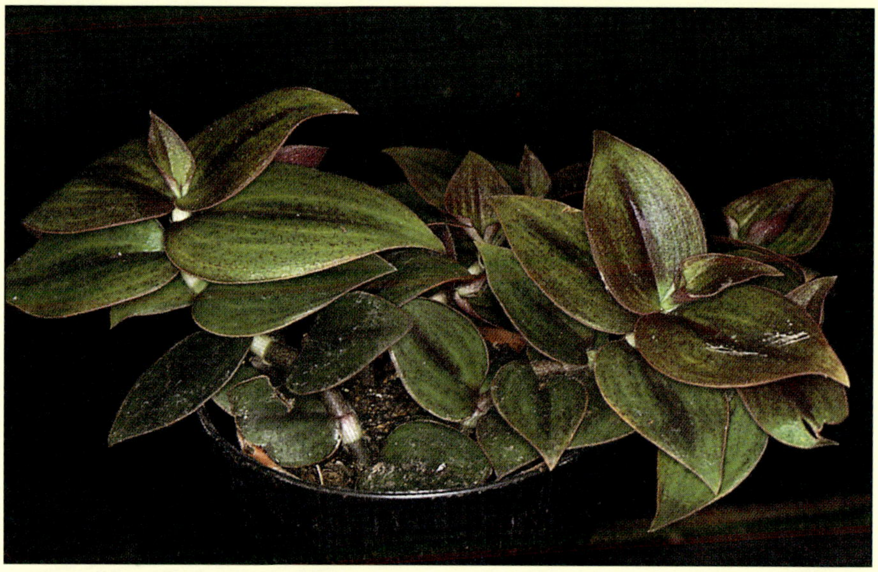

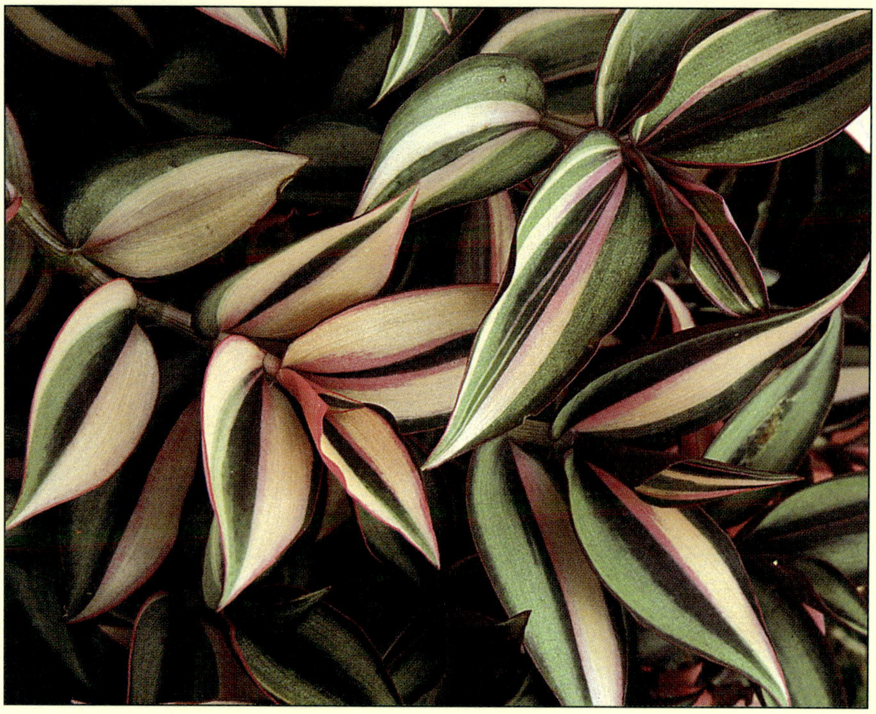

Zebrina pendula, sometimes called *Tradescantia zebrina*, comes from Mexico. It has fleshy, creeping stems that will trail attractively, to a length of about 1ft (30cm), over the sides of a container, making it an ideal subject for a hanging basket. The leaves are 1-2in (2.5-5cm) long, pointed-oval and slightly fleshy, widely striped in dark green or purple and glistening silver and purple on the underside. Clusters of small, dark pink flowers appear in summer. There are many varieties with different leaf-colouring.

Z.p.quadricolor, bottom, has purple-tinged green leaves banded with creamy-white, often with pinkish stripes edged in rich purple, and the undersurface in dark purple. Reddish-purple flowers are carried in clusters in spring and summer.

Z.purpusii, *top,* is also from Mexico and very similar to *Z.pendula*. It is a vigorous trailing and creeping plant with fleshy 10-12in (25-30cm) stems. The slightly succulent leaves are greenish with very faint purplish-brown stripes, and vivid purple on the undersurface. Bright purple flowers are borne in late summer.

INDEX

Entries in **bold** refer to articles in the A-Z section.

Picture credits

A-Z Botanical Collection:157(tr,bl), 158(t), 161(cr), 162(b), 168(cr), 169(t), 170(bl), 185, 189(tl,bl), 198(cr,bl), 199(cr).
A-Z Collection: 119, 201(r), 204, 223(cl), 225(cl), 226(cl), 227(br), 230, 232(tr), 234(tl), 241(c), 244(bl,br), 269(cl), 271(tr), 272(tl,tr), 286(b), 305(bl), 306, 309, 311(tl), 315(l), 322(t), 324(b), 343, 348, 355(bl), 369(cl), 385(tr), 388(t), 389, 390(br), 407.
Bernard Alfieri: 56, 57, 197(t), 279(tr), 281(b), 284(tr), 296(b), 297, 298(br), 302, 322(b), 327(t), 358(tl), 375(bl), 387(tr), 388(br), 412(tr).
Autogrow Products Ltd:128.
Gillian Beckett: 219, 225(cr), 284(bl).
Ken Beckett: 58 (tr), 330.
Michael Boys: 64.
Michael Boys Syndication: 44, 45, 46.
Pat Brindley: 75(bottom box bl), 146(br), 168(cl), 169(cr), 174(b), 194(r), 197(b), 203(tr), 205, 206(bl), 214(cl), 250(tr), 254(tr), 255(tr), 265(tr), 273(bl), 274(tr), 285(l), 288(b), 289(b), 295, 298(tr,bl), 305(c), 307(tr,bl), 308(t), 318, 319, 321(l), 326(tr), 329(br), 338, 339(tr,bl,br), 342(bl), 352, 355(tr), 363(br), 367(tl,cl), 370(br), 378, 383, 384(tc), 385(br), 387(tl,bl), 395, 400, 401(tc), 402, 409, 412(cr).
Richard Bryant: 47.
Clive Corless: 23(cr), 25(b), 37.
Eric Crichton: 40, 49, 75(top box bl), 144(br), 161(t), 239(l), 277(br), 298(tl), 321(r), 333(br), 342(br), 356(tr).
George Crouter:105(bl).
EWA: 9, 19, 20, 21, 25(t).
Vaughan Fleming: 99(cl), 315(r).
Flower Council of Holland: 66.
John Glover: 55, 58(cr).
Ian Howes:87, 88, 114, 148, 149, 151, 154(tr).
Clive Innes:177(t).
Peter McHoy: 207, 380(b), 381(tr,cr).
Bill McLaughlin: 23(tl,tr), 24, 26(tr), 30.
Maison de Marie Claire: 105(tr).
Tania Midgley: 214(t).
Quintet: 63, 159(tr), 168(b), 173(br), 181(r), 184(l,r), 187, 188(tl), 189(tr,cr,br), 190(b), 191(b), 196(b).
Jo Reid & John Peck: 17.
David Ridge: 51, 72, 83, 85, 100, 103, 104, 132, 136.
David Ridge/Quintet: 36.
Daan Smit: 152, 223(c), 226(br), 229(b), 231(tr), 232(bl), 235(bc), 241(t,b), 248(tr), 257(br), 262(tl,tr), 274(tl), 279(cr), 280(br), 299(t), 300(bl), 301(b), 303(t), 307(br), 311(tr), 313, 314(t), 333(bl), 351, 366(tl,c).
Harry Smith: 32(bl), 33(bl), 38(c), 39(t), 41, 42, 43, 48, 50(b), 55, 75(top box br, bottom box tr), 86, 116(r), 129, 130, 138, 139, 141, 146(tr), 147(c), 153(bl), 202(cr), 203(cr), 213, 234(tr), 235(t,bl), 237(t,c), 239(r), 242(b), 243(tr), 250(tl), 253(bl), 255(tl), 256(tr), 258(br), 259(br), 263(tr,br), 264(bl,br), 270(tr), 271(br), 272(cl), 275(t,br), 276, 281(t), 284(tl,br), 285(tc), 288(t), 289(t), 292(c,cr), 293, 296(t), 299(b), 300(cr), 301(t), 304, 305(br), 307(tl), 308(b), 310, 311(br), 312(t,b), 314(b), 316, 323, 324(t), 325, 327(cr), 329(bl), 331, 332, 334(bl,br), 335, 339(tl), 342(cl), 346, 347, 353, 355(tl,br), 356(tl), 358(tr), 359, 361, 362, 367(tr,cr), 368, 371, 372, 373, 376, 377, 382, 387(br), 391, 393(br), 397(cr), 401(tr,bc), 403, 405(br), 406, 408.
Harry Smith Horticultural: 157(tl), 163(b), 172(b), 198(tr).
David Squire: 399.
Peter Stiles: 75 (top box tr, centre box tl,br, bottom box tl), 133(tl), 140, 142, 143, 144(bc), 145, 147(br), 159(br), 166(b), 170(br), 179(b), 209, 211, 229(t), 282(t,b), 360(tr,cr), 384(tr), 396, 397(br), 401(br).
Jessica Strang: 50(t), 54(r).
Thorn EMI Lighting: 54(l).
Pamela Toler/Impact:356(bl,br).
Michael Warren: 33(tr), 39(b), 58(l), 71(br), 75(top box tl, centre box bl), 106, 112, 157(t,c), 158(c,br), 159(tc), 163(c), 164(c), 165(cr), 168(tr), 171(bl), 173(tr), 175, 176, 177(b), 179(t), 181(l), 182, 183, 188(b), 191(t), 192(b), 193, 194(l), 195, 196(t), 199(t,bc,br), 206(cr), 217(b), 220, 220-221(t), 221(tr,b), 228(b), 231(c), 233, 237(b), 246(bl), 248(tc), 257(tl), 287(t), 294(t), 311(bl), 328, 344, 360(tl), 379, 380(t), 381(l), 410, 411.
D. Wildridge: 15, 144(t), 154(tc), 243(br), 274(br), 294(b), 303(b), 349(br), 392.

Artwork credits

J. Pickering: 71.
QED: 73.